THE AMERICAN SPIRIT

United States History as Seen by Contemporaries

THE
AMERICAN SPIRIT

UNITED STATES HISTORY
AS SEEN BY CONTEMPORARIES

Second Edition

Selected and *Edited* with
Introductions and *Commentary* by
THOMAS A. BAILEY
Byrne Professor of American History
Stanford University

D. C. HEATH AND COMPANY
A DIVISION OF
RAYTHEON EDUCATION COMPANY
LEXINGTON, MASSACHUSETTS

Cover Designer: Homer Hill

LIBRARY OF CONGRESS CATALOG CARD NUMBER:

68–15317

PRINTED IN THE UNITED STATES OF AMERICA

PRINTED NOVEMBER 1968

Foreword

The American Spirit attempts to recapture the spirit and reveal the meaning of American history by focusing the spotlight on personalities. These include the great and the near-great who shaped events, and the not-so-great and obscure whose lives were touched by them. I have therefore ferreted out clearly written and pungently phrased items that combine intrinsic human interest with significant observations or conclusions.

The men and women who made American history were not ghostly skeletons rattling around in a vacuum. To reclothe them with flesh and blood, to restage the color and drama, to revive the clash and controversy I have sifted countless personal letters, diaries, autobiographies, editorials, propaganda leaflets, public debates, and interviews. These are the documents behind the official documents. Virtually all of them are in the words of contemporaries, and many of them are here republished for the first time. They are supplemented by scores of illustrations, most of them cartoons—"pictorial editorials."

The general approach is designed to stimulate thoughtful analysis rather than memory work. My primary objectives are to implant meaningful ideas, attitudes, and viewpoints; to cultivate an open mind, a balanced judgment, and an appreciation of the problems and prejudices of others. I consequently devote much attention to the unpopular or unsuccessful side of controversial issues, to the grievances of minorities, and to the criticisms of foreigners. A number of these selections will incidentally introduce the reader to the techniques of historical criticism.

I have designed *The American Spirit* to be a chapter-by-chapter companion piece to my *The American Pageant,* but the orthodox chronological framework will facilitate its use with other basic survey textbooks. It can stand on its own feet. Continuity is provided by the Prologues, the prefatory notes, the inserted explanations, and the italicized postscripts. Cohesion is provided by grouping the individual selections under heads and subheads. Guidance is provided by the pre-questions in the introductions, by the end-chapter Thought Provokers and bibliographies, and by the twenty-two specially drawn maps.

The archaic language of bygone days, though quaint, can often be difficult or misleading. I have therefore undertaken, in accord with accepted practice, to modernize obsolete spelling, italicizing, punctuation, and capitalization. I have also broken up overlong paragraphs. The original meaning remains unaffected.

THOMAS A. BAILEY

Stanford University

Preface to the Second Edition

The chief feature of this second edition is the addition of three new chapters. I have eliminated most of the original last chapter because some of the topics there treated are now more fully developed in the new material. The Vietnam involvement, which concerned both Presidents Kennedy and Johnson, is of such significance that I have treated it in a separate and concluding chapter.

I have updated the end-chapter bibliographies throughout under the rubric "Recent" and have indicated the titles in paperback. I have retained the original bibliographical structure so that the reader may tell at a glance what new titles have appeared.

As before, *The American Spirit* is available in a one-volume hardback edition or in a two-volume paperbound edition, with the chapter on Reconstruction appearing in both volumes.

I am especially indebted to my colleague, Dr. Claude A. Buss, an expert on Vietnam and a frequent visitor to that troubled land, for a critical reading of the last chapter. Additionally, Mr. George D. Bullock and Mrs. Elaine D. Atkins rendered indispensable service throughout as research assistants.

Stanford University   THOMAS A. BAILEY

ACKNOWLEDGMENTS

For assistance rendered or favors conferred, I wish to express my grateful appreciation

To the authors of numerous monographs and the compilers of countless collections, who put me on the trail of nuggets that might have been overlooked.

To the publishers, individual authors, and others, who graciously granted permission to reproduce needed materials. Specific acknowledgment appears in the footnotes.

To Professor Claude A. Buss of Stanford University, Professor Gerald D. Nash of the University of New Mexico, Professor Daniel M. Smith of the University of Colorado, all of whom read individual chapters; and to Professor Russell E. Miller of Tufts College, who read the entire manuscript.

To Professor Don E. Fehrenbacher and Professor Otis A. Pease, colleagues in the History Department of Stanford University, who not only criticized the prospectus and the pilot chapters but read critically the entire book in galley proof.

To eighteen Stanford University students, who, as willing guinea pigs on a special project, read the manuscript chapters and provided critical student reactions. They are: Marjorie A. Beyer, Nancy Boland, Julie O. Bramkamp, Michael K. Copass, Jr., Mildred E. S. Corcoran, Glenda J. Fulton, Franklin E. Hatfield, II, Larry N. Horton, Ann Hulsing, Robert W. Lemmon, Robert W. McGuffin, John E. Miller, Gail S. Novak, Robert F. Oaks, Joan E. Pettefer, Kent W. Smith, Kenneth R. Veronda, Sylvia L. Wiest.

To the Library of Congress, the New York Public Library, the Harvard University Library, the Boston Public Library, and the staffs of the Stanford University Libraries (including the Hoover Institution), all of which extended numerous courtesies, including the providing of much microfilmed or photostated material.

To Miss M. Theressa Gay and Mrs. Marjory W. Smith for typing, checking, and collating; to Miss Ruth E. Johnson for typing; and to Mrs. Celeste C. McKee for typing parts of the manuscript and expertly handling the voluminous correspondence in connection with permissions and other matters.

To Mr. Russell H. Lenz, Chief Cartographer of the *Christian Science Monitor,* who drew the maps for *The American Pageant* and who continued the same high standards in preparing the maps for *The American Spirit.*

To the eminently cooperative staff of D. C. Heath and Company, and particularly to Dr. Marie L. Edel, whose superlative editorial collaboration, far above and beyond the call of duty, left few pages unimproved.

Contents

Maps

THE AMERICAN SPIRIT

United States History as Seen by Contemporaries

Chapter 1

England's Southern Mainland Colonies

. . . May it not then be lawful now to attempt the possession of such lands as are void of Christian inhabitants, for Christ's sake?

WILLIAM STRACHEY, *c.* 1620

PROLOGUE: After Columbus stumbled upon the American barrier in 1492, Spanish explorers sought desperately for a through passage to the wealth of the Indies. They finally had to settle for the treasure chests of the red Indians. The spectacular success of the Spanish conquerors excited the cupidity and rivalry of Englishmen, and partly inspired Sir Humphrey Gilbert's ill-fated colony in Newfoundland in 1583 and Sir Walter Raleigh's luckless venture on Roanoke Island, off the North Carolina coast, in the 1580's. But England was not prepared for ambitious colonial ventures until the defeat of the Spanish Armada in 1588 and the perfection of the joint-stock company—a device which enabled "adventurers" to pool their capital. Virginia, which got off to a shaky start in 1607, was finally saved by tobacco. Maryland, launched in 1634 by Lord Baltimore as a Catholic haven, profited from Virginia's experience and assistance. The Carolinas, formally begun in 1670 to provide semi-tropical products like olive oil, only partially justified the hopes of their promoters. Finally, Georgia was founded in 1733 for both humanitarian and defensive purposes.

A. NEW WORLDS FOR THE TAKING

1. John Cabot Voyages for England (1497)

John Cabot was a Genoese (like Columbus) who became a naturalized Venetian and then took up residence at the port of Bristol, England. Inspired by the Columbian discovery and commissioned by Henry VII, he sailed into the stormy North Atlantic in 1497 with a single ship and eighteen men. Seeking the territory of the Grand Khan of China, he landed on or somewhere near Newfoundland, Labrador, or Cape Breton Island. A proud fellow Venetian dwelling in London wrote to his brothers in Venice describing the excitement. Note what this account foreshadows about the future of English colonizing, especially the quality of the participants.

The Venetian, our countryman, who went with a ship from Bristol in quest of new islands, is returned, and says that 700 leagues hence he discovered land, the territory of the Grand Cham [Khan]. He coasted for 300 leagues and landed; saw no human beings, but he has brought hither to the King certain snares which had been set to catch game, and a needle for making nets. He also found some felled trees, wherefore he supposed there were inhabitants, and returned to his ship in alarm.

1. Rawdon Brown, ed., *Calendar of State Papers . . . Venice . . .* (1864), I, 262.

He was three months on the voyage, and on his return he saw two islands to starboard, but would not land, time being precious, as he was short of provisions. He says that the tides are slack and do not flow as they do here. The King of England is much pleased with this intelligence.

The King has promised that in the spring our countryman shall have ten ships, armed to his order, and at his request has conceded him all the prisoners, except such as are confined for high treason, to man his fleet. The King has also given him money wherewith to amuse himself till then, and he is now at Bristol with his wife, who is also Venetian, and with his sons. His name is Zuan Cabot, and he is styled the Great Admiral. Vast honor is paid him; he dresses in silk. And these English run after him like mad people, so that he can enlist as many of them as he pleases, and a number of our own rogues besides.

2. Hakluyt Calls for an Empire (1582)

Richard Hakluyt, a remarkable clergyman-scholar-geographer who lies buried in Westminster Abbey, deserves high rank among the indirect founding fathers of the United States. His published collections of documents relating to early English explorations must be regarded as among the "great books" of American history for their stimulation of interest in New World colonization. (Hakluyt even gambled some of his own small fortune in the company that planted Virginia.) Passionately concerned about England's "sluggish security," he argued as follows in the dedicatory letter of his first published work (1582). It was addressed to Sir Philip Sidney— scholar, diplomat, author, poet, soldier, and knightly luminary of Queen Elizabeth's court. Evaluate Hakluyt's various arguments for settling the Atlantic Coast north of Florida and note which ones probably appealed most strongly (a) to Sidney's patriotism and (b) to his religious faith.

I marvel not a little, right worshipful, that since the first discovery of America (which is now full four score and ten years), after so great conquests and plantings of the Spaniards and Portuguese there, that we of England could never have the grace to set fast footing in such fertile and temperate places as are left as yet unpossessed of them. But . . . I conceive great hope that the time approacheth and now is that we of England may share and part stakes [divide the prize] (if we will ourselves) both with the Spaniard and the Portuguese in part of America and other regions as yet undiscovered.

And surely if there were in us that desire to advance the honor of our country which ought to be in every good man, we would not all this while have forslown [neglected] the possessing of those lands which of equity and right appertain unto us, as by the discourses that follow shall appear most plainly.

Yea, if we would behold with the eye of pity how all our prisons are pestered and filled with able men to serve their country, which for small robberies are daily hanged up in great numbers, . . . we would hasten . . .

2. Richard Hakluyt, *Divers Voyages Touching the Discovery of America and the Islands Adjacent,* ed. J. W. Jones (1850), pp. 8–18.

the deducting [conveying] of some colonies of our superfluous people into those temperate and fertile parts of America, which, being within six weeks' sailing of England, are yet unpossessed by any Christians, and seem to offer themselves unto us, stretching nearer unto Her Majesty's dominions than to any other part of Europe. . . .

It chanced very lately that upon occasion I had great conference in matters of cosmography with an excellent learned man of Portugal, most privy to all the discoveries of his nation, who wondered that those blessed countries from the point of Florida northward were all this while unplanted by Christians, protesting with great affection and zeal that if he were now as young as I (for at this present he is three score years of age) he would sell all he had, being a man of no small wealth and honor, to furnish a convenient number of ships to sea for the inhabiting of those countries and reducing those gentile [heathen] people to Christianity. . . .

If this man's desire might be executed, we might not only for the present time take possession of that good land, but also, in short space, by God's grace find out that short and easy passage by the Northwest which we have hitherto so long desired. . . .

Certes [certainly], if hitherto in our own discoveries we had not been led with a preposterous desire of seeking rather gain than God's glory, I assure myself that our labors had taken far better effect. But we forgot that godliness is great riches, and that if we first seek the kingdom of God, all other things will be given unto us. . . .

I trust that now, being taught by their manifold losses, our men will take a more godly course and use some part of their goods to his [God's] glory. If not, he will turn even their covetousness to serve him, as he hath done the pride and avarice of the Spaniards and Portuguese, who, pretending in glorious words that they made their discoveries chiefly to convert infidels to our most holy faith (as they say), in deed and truth sought not them, but their goods and riches. . . .

Here I cease, craving pardon for my overboldness, trusting also that Your Worship will continue and increase your accustomed favor toward these godly and honorable discoveries.

3. Peckham Preaches Christ and Calico (1583)

Richard Hakluyt's most famous work was a three-volume collection of documents entitled *Principal Navigations, Voyages, Traffiques and Discoveries of the English Nation* (1598–1600). The 19th-Century historian J. A. Froude praised it as "the prose epic of the English nation." Included among the materials was an eloquent appeal for further colonization earlier written by Sir George Peckham, the chief investor in Sir Humphrey Gilbert's ill-starred Newfoundland scheme (1583). Peckham argued that colonizing would promote the New World fishing industry, bolster the English navy and merchant marine, and bring to England such wealth as Spain and Portugal had extracted from their colonies. In the following excerpt from Peckham's

3. Edmund Goldsmid, ed., *The Voyages of the English Nation to America Collected by Richard Hakluyt* (1889), II, 17–18, 23–25.

lengthy discourse, note what new points he makes, and decide which of his arguments regarding the Indians seem valid and which mere excuses for greed.

Moreover, it is well known that all savages . . . so soon as they shall begin but a little to taste of civility [civilized behavior] will take marvelous delight in any garment, be it never so simple—as a shirt; a blue, yellow, red, or green cotton cassock; a cap, or such like—and will take incredible pains for such a trifle.

For I myself have heard this report made sundry times by divers of our countrymen who have dwelt in the southerly parts of the West Indies . . . that the people in those parts are easily reduced to civility, both in manners and garments. Which being so, what vent [market] for our English clothes will thereby ensue, and how great benefit to . . . artificers, . . . I do leave to the judgment of such as are discreet.

And unquestionably hereby it will also come to pass that all such [English] towns and villages as both have been and now are utterly decayed and ruinated . . . shall by this means be restored to their pristinate [original] wealth and estate. All which does likewise tend to the enlargement of our navy, and maintenance of our navigation. . . .

Now to the end it may appear that this voyage is not undertaken altogether for the peculiar commodity [advantage] of ourselves and our country (as generally other trades and journeys be), it shall fall out in proof that the savages shall hereby have just cause to bless the hour when this enterprise was undertaken.

First and chiefly, in respect of the most happy and gladsome tidings of the most glorious Gospel of our Saviour Jesus Christ, whereby they may be brought from falsehood to truth, from darkness to light, from the highway of death to the path of life, from superstitious idolatry to sincere Christianity, from the Devil to Christ, from hell to heaven. And if in respect of all the commodities they can yield us . . . they should but receive this only benefit of Christianity, they were more than fully recompensed. . . .

These heavenly tidings which those laborers our countrymen (as messengers of God's great goodness and mercy) will voluntarily present unto them do far exceed their earthly riches. Moreover, if the other inferior worldly and temporal things which they shall receive from us be weighed in equal balance, I assure myself that . . . the benefits which they then receive shall far surmount those which they shall depart [impart] withal unto us.

And admit that they had (as they have not) the knowledge to put their land to some use; yet being brought from brutish ignorance to civility and knowledge, and made to understand how the tenth part of their land may be so manured and employed as it may yield more commodities to the necessary use of man's life than the whole now doeth, what just cause of complaint may they have? And in my private opinion, I do verily think that God did create land to the end that it should by culture and husbandry yield things necessary for man's life.

But this is not all the benefit which they shall receive by the Christians. For, over and beside the knowledge how to till and dress their grounds, they shall be reduced from unseemly customs to honest manners, from disordered riotous routs and companies to a well-governed commonwealth, and withal shall be taught mechanical occupations, arts, and liberal sciences. And . . . they shall be defended from the cruelty of their tyrannical and blood-sucking neighbors, the cannibals, whereby infinite numbers of their lives shall be preserved. And lastly, by this means many of their poor innocent children shall be preserved from the bloody knife of the sacrificer, a most horrible and detestable custom in the sight of God and man, and now and ever heretofore used amongst them.

B. PRECARIOUS BEGINNINGS IN VIRGINIA

1. John Smith Reports Hardships (1608)

Captain John Smith, his twenty-six years already crowded with incredible adventures, played a significant role in organizing the historic expedition to Virginia in 1607. Never a good "team man," he was constantly at odds with his associates (he arrived in irons for alleged mutiny). His great contribution was in exploring the countryside and in securing food from the Indians for the starving colonists. The first account of his experiences, published in 1608, failed to mention how the Indian maiden Pocahontas had dramatically saved his life. In 1624, some sixteen years after the event, he belatedly published the Pocahontas tale. Suspicions were aroused, but recent scholarship has tended to rehabilitate his reputation for truthfulness. From this passage in Smith's first account, determine what the most serious difficulties at Jamestown were, and what saved the colony at this stage.

Captain Newport, having set things in order, set sail for England the twenty-second of June [1607], leaving provision for thirteen or fourteen weeks.

The day before the ship's departure, the King of Pamaunke sent the Indian that had met us before in our discovery to assure us peace; our fort being then palisaded round, and all our men in good health and comfort, albeit . . . it did not so long continue. For the President [Wingfield] and Captain Gosnold, with the rest of the Council, . . . [were] for the most part discontented with one another, insomuch that things were neither carried with that discretion nor any business effected in such good sort as wisdom would, nor our own good and safety required. . . . Through which disorder God (being angry with us) plagued us with such famine and sickness that the living were scarce able to bury the dead; our want of sufficient and good victuals, with continual watching, four or five each night at three bulwarks [fortifications], being the chief cause. Only of sturgeon we had great store, whereupon our men would so greedily surfeit as it cost many their lives: the sack [wine], aquavitae [liquor], and other preservatives for

1. Edward Arber, ed., *Travels and Works of Captain John Smith* (1910), I, 8–9 (*A True Relation* . . . [1608]).

C: Smith takes the King of Paſpahegh priſoner. Aᵒ 1609.

our health being kept only in the President's hands, for his own diet and his few associates.

Shortly after, Captain Gosnold fell sick, and within three weeks died; Captain Ratcliffe being then also very sick and weak, and myself having also tasted of the extremity thereof, but by God's assistance being well recovered. . . . Shortly after, it pleased God (in our extremity) to move the Indians to bring us corn, ere it was half ripe, to refresh us, when we rather expected when they would destroy us.

About the tenth of September there was about 46 of our men dead [out of 105], at which time Captain Wingfield having ordered the affairs in such sort that he was generally hated of all, in which respect with one consent he was deposed from his presidency, and Captain Ratcliffe according to his course was elected.

Our provision being now within twenty days spent, the Indians brought us great store both of corn and bread ready made; and also there came such abundance of fowls into the rivers as greatly refreshed our weak estates, whereupon many of our weak men were presently able to go abroad [out of doors].

As yet we had no houses to cover us, our tents were rotten, and our cabins worse than nought; our best commodity was iron, which we made into little chisels.

The President's and Captain Martin's sickness constrained me to be cape [chief] merchant, and yet to spare no pains in making houses for the company; who, notwithstanding our misery, little ceased their malice, grudging, and muttering.

2. The Starving Time (1609)

Captain John Smith—adventurer, colonizer, explorer, author, and mapmaker—now becomes an historian, and as such ranks as America's first. Writing from the vantage point of England some fifteen years later, and of events that he did not personally witness, he tells a tale that had come to him at second hand. Note the indications of modesty or lack of it. Account for the difficulties, and ascertain what pulled the settlers through.

The day before Captain Smith returned for England with the ships [October 4, 1609], Captain Davis arrived in a small pinnace, with some sixteen proper men more. . . . For the savages [Indians] no sooner understood Smith was gone but they all revolted, and did spoil and murder all they encountered. . . .

Now we all found the loss of Captain Smith; yea, his greatest maligners could now curse his loss. As for corn provision and contribution from the savages, we [now] had nothing but mortal wounds, with clubs and arrows. As for our hogs, hens, goats, sheep, horses, and what lived, our commanders, officers, and savages daily consumed them. Some small proportions sometimes we tasted, till all was devoured; then swords, arms, [fowling] pieces, or anything we traded with the savages, whose cruel fingers were so often imbrued in our blood that what by their cruelty, our Governor's indiscretion, and the loss of our ships, of five hundred [persons] within six months after Captain Smith's departure there remained not past sixty men, women, and children, most miserable and poor creatures. And those were preserved for the most part by roots, herbs, acorns, walnuts, berries, now and then a little fish. They that had starch [courage] in these extremities made no small use of it; yea, [they ate] even the very skins of our horses.

Nay, so great was our famine that a savage we slew and buried, the poorer sort took him up again and ate him; and so did divers one another boiled and stewed, with roots and herbs. And one amongst the rest did kill his wife, powdered [salted] her, and had eaten part of her before it was known, for which he was executed, as he well deserved. Now whether she was better roasted, boiled, or carbonadoed [broiled], I know not; but of such a dish as powdered wife I never heard of.

This was the time which still to this day [1624] we called the starving time. It were too vile to say, and scarce to be believed, what we endured. But the occasion was our own, for want of providence, industry, and government, and not the barrenness and defect of the country, as is generally supposed. For till then in three years . . . we had never from England provisions sufficient for six months, though it seemed by the bills of loading

2. *Ibid.,* II, 497–99 *(The General History of Virginia . . . [1624]).*

sufficient was sent us, such a glutton is the sea, and such good fellows the mariners. We as little tasted of the great proportion sent us, as they of our want and miseries. Yet notwithstanding they ever overswayed and ruled the business, though we endured all that is said, and chiefly lived on what this good country naturally afforded, yet had we been even in Paradise itself with these governors, it would not have been much better with us. Yet there were amongst us who, had they had the government as Captain Smith appointed but . . . could not maintain it, would surely have kept us from those extremities of miseries.

3. The Great Indian Massacre (1622)

At the outset the Indians attacked the Virginia colonists with arrows, and relations between the two races continued uneasy for many years after 1607. As if deaths from famine, exposure, improper food, and malarial fever were not enough, the colonists lost perhaps one-fourth of their number in the great massacre of 1622. Among other grievances, the Indians resented the clearing of their forests and the seizure of their cornfields by the whites. Edward Waterhouse, a prominent Virginian official, sent home this first-hand report. Note what it reveals as to how the colony subsisted, how earnest the Christianizing efforts of the colonists were, and how the great massacre could be used to the advantage of the Virginians.

And such was the conceit of firm peace and amity [with the Indians] as that there was seldom or never a sword worn and a [fowling] piece seldomer, except for a deer or fowl. By which assurance of security the plantations of particular adventurers and planters were placed scatteringly and stragglingly as a choice vein of rich ground invited them, and the farther from neighbors held the better. The houses generally sat open to the savages, who were always friendly entertained at the tables of the English, and commonly lodged in their bed-chambers . . . [thus] seeming to open a fair gate for their conversion to Christianity. . . .

Yea, such was the treacherous dissimulation of that people who then had contrived our destruction, that even two days before the massacre, some of our men were guided through the woods by them in safety. . . . Yea, they borrowed our own boats to convey themselves across the river (on the banks of both sides whereof all our plantations were) to consult of the devilish murder that ensued, and of our utter extirpation, which God of his mercy (by the means of some of themselves converted to Christianity) prevented. . . .

On the Friday morning (the fatal day) the 22nd of March [1622], as also in the evening, as in other days before, they came unarmed into our houses, without bows or arrows, or other weapons, with deer, turkeys, fish, furs, and other provisions to sell and truck with us for glass, beads, and other trifles; yea, in some places, sat down at breakfast with our people at their tables, whom immediately with their own tools and weapons, either laid down, or standing in their houses, they basely and barbarously

3. Susan M. Kingsbury, ed., *The Records of the Virginia Company of London* (1933), III, 550–51, 556–57.

murdered, not sparing either age or sex, man, woman, or child; so sudden in their cruel execution that few or none discerned the weapon or blow that brought them to destruction. In which manner they also slew many of our people then at their several works and husbandries in the fields, and without [outside] their houses, some in planting corn and tobacco, some in gardening, some in making brick, building, sawing, and other kinds of husbandry—they well knowing in what places and quarters each of our men were, in regard of their daily familiarity and resort to us for trading and other negotiations, which the more willingly was by us continued and cherished for the desire we had of effecting that great masterpiece of works, their conversion.

And by this means, that fatal Friday morning, there fell under the bloody and barbarous hands of that perfidious and inhumane people, contrary to all laws of God and man, and nature and nations, 347 men, women, and children, most by their own weapons. And not being content with taking away life alone, they fell after again upon the dead, making, as well as they could, a fresh murder, defacing, dragging, and mangling the dead carcasses into many pieces, and carrying away some parts in derision, with base and brutish triumph. . . .

Our hands, which before were tied with gentleness and fair usage, are now set at liberty by the treacherous violence of the savages . . . so that we, who hitherto have had possession of no more ground than their waste and our purchase at a valuable consideration to their own contentment gained, may now by right of war, and law of nations, invade the country, and destroy them who sought to destroy us; whereby we shall enjoy their cultivated places. . . . Now their cleared grounds in all their villages (which are situate in the fruitfulest places of the land) shall be inhabited by us, whereas heretofore the grubbing of woods was the greatest labor.

C. RELIGIOUS STRIFE IN MARYLAND

1. The Intolerant Act of Toleration (1649)

Lord Baltimore, who had founded Maryland as a refuge for Catholics in 1634, pursued a policy of religious toleration from the outset. But the influx of hostile Protestants, combined with the success of the Puritans under Cromwell in the English Civil War, prompted him to protect his Catholic co-religionists. He appointed a Protestant governor, and urged the Maryland Assembly to pass "An Act Concerning Religion," which he had drafted back home in England. Protestants joined with Catholics in passing it. Note the specific protection for Catholics, and what would have happened to all Jews and atheists if the law had been strictly enforced.

Forasmuch as, in a well-governed and Christian commonwealth, matters concerning religion and the honor of God ought in the first place to be taken into serious consideration and endeavored to be settled, be it therefore ordered and enacted by the Right Honorable Cecilius Lord Baron of

1. W. H. Browne, ed., *Archives of Maryland* (1883), I, 244–46.

Baltimore, absolute Lord and Proprietary of this Province, with the advice and consent of this General Assembly:

That whatsoever person or persons within this Province . . . shall from henceforth blaspheme God, that is, curse him; or deny our Saviour Jesus Christ to be the son of God; or shall deny the Holy Trinity, the Father, Son, and Holy Ghost; or [shall deny] the Godhead of any of the said three Persons of the Trinity, or the unity of the Godhead; or shall use or utter any reproachful speeches, words, or language concerning the said Holy Trinity, or any of the said three Persons thereof, shall be punished with death and confiscation or forfeiture of all his or her lands and goods to the Lord Proprietary and his heirs.

And be it also enacted . . . that whatsoever person or persons shall from henceforth use or utter any reproachful words or speeches concerning the Blessed Virgin Mary, the Mother of our Saviour, or the Holy Apostles or Evangelists, or any of them, shall in such case for the first offense forfeit . . . the sum of five pounds sterling. . . . But in case such offender or offenders shall not then have goods or chattels sufficient for the satisfying of such forfeiture . . . then such offender or offenders shall be publicly whipped and be imprisoned during the pleasure of the Lord Proprietary. . . .

[Harsher penalties are here prescribed for second and third offenses.]

And be it also further enacted . . . that whatsoever person or persons shall from henceforth . . . in a reproachful manner or way declare, call, or denominate any person or persons . . . an heretic, schismatic, idolater, Puritan, Independent, Presbyterian, popish priest, Jesuit, Jesuited papist, Lutheran, Calvinist, Anabaptist, Brownist, Antinomian, Barrowist, Roundhead, Separatist, or any other name or term in a reproachful manner relating to matter of religion, shall for every such offense forfeit and lose the sum of ten shillings . . . the one half thereof to be forfeited and paid unto the person and persons of whom such reproachful words are or shall be spoken or uttered. . . .

[Harsher penalties are here prescribed for those unable to pay the fine.]

Be it therefore also . . . enacted . . . that no person or persons whatsoever within this Province . . . professing to believe in Jesus Christ, shall from henceforth be in any ways troubled, molested, or discountenanced for . . . his or her religion nor in the free exercise thereof . . . nor any way compelled to the belief or exercise of any other religion against his or her consent, so as they be not unfaithful to the Lord Proprietary, or [do not] molest or conspire against the civil government established, or to be established, in this Province, under him or his heirs.

And that all and every person and persons that shall presume contrary to this act . . . to wrong, disturb, trouble, or molest any person whatsoever . . . professing to believe in Jesus Christ for or in respect of his or her religion or the free exercise thereof . . . shall be compelled to pay treble damages to the party so wronged or molested, and for every such offense shall also forfeit twenty shillings sterling in money or the value thereof, half thereof for the use of the Lord Proprietary and his heirs . . . and the other half for the use of the party so wronged or molested . . . or if the party so offending . . . shall refuse or be unable to recompense the party so wronged, or to satisfy such fine or forfeiture, then such offender shall be severely punished by public whipping and imprisonment during the pleasure of the Lord Proprietary. . . .

2. Persecutions of the Catholics (1656)

Lord Baltimore's beautiful dream soon turned into a nightmare. In 1654, after five years of so-called toleration, the aggressive Protestant majority in Maryland passed a law which specifically "restrained" Roman Catholics from worshiping according to their faith. Civil war broke out, with the Puritans, aided by Virginians, vanquishing the Catholics in a pitched battle in which some fifty men were killed or wounded. The subsequent persecutions of the Jesuit fathers, resembling anti-Catholic cruelties already familiar in England, are graphically portrayed in the *Annual Letter* for 1656. Note the various manifestations of the religious intolerance of the age, and form appropriate conclusions.

In Maryland, during the year last past, our [Catholic] people have escaped grievous dangers, and have had to contend with great difficulties and straits, and have suffered many unpleasant things, as well from enemies as [from] our own people.

The English who inhabit Virginia had made an attack on the colonists, themselves Englishmen too; and safety being guaranteed on certain conditions, received indeed the governor of Maryland, with many others in surrender. But the conditions being treacherously violated, four of the captives, and three of them Catholics, were pierced with leaden balls. Rushing into our houses, they demanded for death the impostors, as they called them, intending inevitable slaughter to those who should be caught. But the Fathers, by the protection of God, unknown to them, were carried from before their faces [*i.e.*, saved]; their books, furniture, and whatever was in the house, fell a prey to the robbers. With almost the entire loss of their property, private and domestic, together with great peril of life, they were secretly carried into Virginia; and in the greatest want of necessaries, scarcely, and with difficulty, do they sustain life. They live in a mean hut, low and depressed, not much unlike a cistern, or even a tomb, in which that great defender of the faith, St. Athanasius, lay concealed for many years.

To their other miseries this inconvenience was added, that whatever comfort or aid this year, under name of stipend, from pious men in England, was destined for them, had been lost, the ship being intercepted in which it was carried. But nothing affects them more than that there is not a supply of wine which is sufficient to perform the sacred mysteries of the altar.

2. Peter Force, *Tracts* . . . (1846), IV, no. 12, pp. 43–44.

They have no servant, either for domestic use, or for directing their way through unknown and suspected places, or even to row and steer the boat, if at any time there is need. Often, over spacious and vast rivers, one of them, alone and unaccompanied, passes and repasses long distances, with no other pilot directing his course than Divine Providence. By and by the enemy may be gone and they may return to Maryland; the things which they have already suffered from their people, and the disadvantages which still threaten, are not much more tolerable.

3. Increasing Protestant Fears (1679)

The persecution of Catholics in Maryland gradually subsided. Two Protestant missionaries from Holland traveled through the Maryland-Virginia area late in 1679, and were distressed to report as follows. One should note that Protestant (Anglican) clergymen in this region were not of the highest quality: a scandalously large number of them took to drinking, horse racing, and gambling at cards. Form conclusions as to why there were so few able ministers, and why the Catholics were particularly suspect.

The lives of the planters in Maryland and Virginia are very Godless and profane. They listen neither to God nor his commandments, and have neither church nor cloister. Sometimes there is someone who is called a minister, who does not, as elsewhere, serve in one place—for in all Virginia and Maryland there is not a city or a village—but travels for profit, and for that purpose visits the plantations through the country, and there addresses the people. But I know of no public assemblages being held in these places; you hear often that these ministers are worse than anybody else, yea, are an abomination. . . .

It remains to be mentioned that those persons who profess the Roman Catholic religion have great, indeed all, freedom in Maryland, because the governor makes profession of that faith, and consequently there are priests and other ecclesiastics who travel and disperse themselves everywhere, and neglect nothing which serves for their profit and purpose. The priests of [French] Canada take care of this region, and hold correspondence with those here, as is supposed, as well as with those who reside among the Indians. It is said there is not an Indian fort between Canada and Maryland where there is not a Jesuit who teaches and advises the Indians, who begin to listen to them too much; so much so that some people in Virginia and Maryland, as well as in New Netherland [New York], have been apprehensive lest there might be an outbreak, hearing what has happened in Europe, as well as among their neighbors at Boston; but they hope the result of the troubles there will determine many things elsewhere. The Lord grant a happy issue there and here, as well as in other parts of the world, for the help of his own elect, and the glory of his name.

3. Jasper Dankers and Peter Sluyter, *Journal of a Voyage to New York and a Tour in Several of the American Colonies in 1679–1680*, in Long Island Historical Society, *Memoirs* (1867), I, 218, 220–21.

D. THE GROWING PAINS OF VIRGINIA

1. Governor Berkeley Reports (1671)

Sir William Berkeley, a polished Oxford graduate, courtier, and playwright, was appointed governor of Virginia in 1642, when only thirty-six years of age. Conciliatory, energetic, and courageous, he served well in his early years, both as administrator and as military leader. He cultivated flax, cotton, rice, and silk on his own lands, and in one year sent a gift of 300 pounds of silk to the King. In response to specific questions from London, he prepared the able report from which the following extract is taken. Note the economic and social handicaps from which Virginia suffered, and determine which one was the most burdensome; also what is significantly revealed of Berkeley's character and outlook.

12. What commodities are there of the production, growth, and manufacture of your plantation [colony]; and particularly, what materials are there already growing, or may be produced for shipping in the same?

Answer. Commodities of the growth of our country we never had any but tobacco, which in this yet is considerable, that it yields His Majesty a great revenue. But of late we have begun to make silk, and so many mulberry trees are planted, and planting, that if we had skillful men from Naples or Sicily to teach us the art of making it perfectly, in less than half an age [generation] we should make as much silk in an year as England did yearly expend three score years since. But now we hear it is grown to a greater excess, and more common and vulgar usage. Now, for shipping, we have admirable masts and very good oaks; but for iron ore I dare not say there is sufficient to keep one iron mill going for seven years. . . .

15. What number of planters, servants, and slaves; and how many parishes are there in your plantation?

Answer. We suppose, and I am very sure we do not much miscount, that there is in Virginia above forty thousand persons, men, women, and children, and of which there are two thousand black slaves, six thousand Christian servants [indentured] for a short time. The rest are born in the country or have come in to settle and seat, in bettering their condition in a growing country.

16. What number of English, Scots, or Irish have for these seven years last past come yearly to plant and inhabit within your government; as also what blacks or slaves have been brought in within the said time?

Answer. Yearly, we suppose there comes in, of servants, about fifteen hundred, of which most are English, few Scotch, and fewer Irish, and not above two or three ships of Negroes in seven years.

17. What number of people have yearly died, within your plantation and government, for these seven years last past, both whites and blacks?

Answer. All new plantations are, for an age or two, unhealthy, till they are thoroughly cleared of wood. But unless we had a particular register office for the denoting of all that died, I cannot give a particular answer to this query. Only this I can say, that there is not often unseasoned hands

1. W. W. Hening, *The Statutes at Large . . . of Virginia . . .* (1823), II, 514–17.

(as we term them) that die now, whereas heretofore not one of five escaped the first year. . . .

23. What course is taken about the instructing of the people, within your government, in the Christian religion; and what provision is there made for the paying of your ministry?

Answer. The same course that is taken in England out of towns: every man, according to his ability, instructing his children. We have forty-eight parishes, and our ministers are well paid, and by my consent should be better if they would pray oftener and preach less. But of all other commodities, so of this, the worst are sent us, and we had few that we could boast of, since the persecution in Cromwell's tyranny drove divers worthy men hither. But, I thank God, there are no free schools nor printing, and I hope we shall not have these hundred years. For learning has brought disobedience, and heresy, and sects into the world, and printing has divulged them, and libels against the best government. God keep us from both!

2. The Baconite Grievances (1677)

Berkeley may have been a good governor in his younger days, but with the passing years he became more arrogant and ill-tempered, more inclined to favor the tidewater aristocrats at the expense of the back-country settlers. His unwillingness to protect the tobacco planters on the frontier against Indian butcheries gave rise to ugly rumors of graft, and helped spark a rebellion which was led by his wife's kinsman, the well-born Nathaniel Bacon. After the uprising had collapsed, a royal commission sent out from England prepared the following report, which was not friendly to Berkeley. Analyze the governor's alleged shortcomings, and determine whether they justified Bacon's defiance of his authority.

The unsatisfied people, finding themselves still liable to the Indian cruelties, and the cries of their wives and children growing grievous and intolerable to them, gave out in speeches that they were resolved to plant tobacco rather than pay the tax for maintaining of forts; and that the erecting of them was a great grievance, juggle, and cheat, and of no more use or service to them than another plantation with men at it; and that it was merely a design of the [tidewater] grandees to engross [monopolize] all their tobacco into their own hands.

Thus the sense of this oppression and the dread of a common approaching calamity made the giddy-headed multitude mad, and precipitated them upon that rash overture of running out upon the Indians themselves, at their own voluntary charge and hazard of their lives and fortunes. Only they first by petition humbly craved leave or commission to be led by any commander or commanders as the Governor should please to appoint over them to be their chieftain or general. But instead of granting this petition, the Governor by proclamation, under great penalty, forbade the like petitioning for the future.*

2. *The Virginia Magazine of History and Biography,* IV (1896), 121–22.
* The Governor feared that the settlers would attack, as they did, both friendly and unfriendly tribes.

This made the people jealous that the Governor for the lucre of the beaver and otter trade, etc., with the Indians, rather sought to protect the Indians than them, since after public proclamation prohibiting all trade with the Indians (they complain), he privately gave commission to some of his friends to truck with them, and that those persons furnished the Indians with powder, shot, etc., so that they were better provided than His Majesty's subjects.

The people of Charles City County (near Merchants Hope) being devised [denied] a commission by the Governor, although he was truly informed . . . of several formidable bodies of Indians coming down on the heads of James River within fifty or sixty miles of the English plantations . . . , they begin to beat up drums for volunteers to go out against the Indians, and so continued sundry days drawing into arms, the magistrates being either so remiss or of the same faction that they suffered this disaster without contradiction or endeavoring to prevent so dangerous a beginning and going on.

The rout [mob] being got together now wanted nor waited for nothing but one to head and lead them out on their design. It so happened that one Nathaniel Bacon, Jr., a person whose lost and desperate fortunes had thrown him into that remote part of the world about fourteen months before . . . , framed him fit for such a purpose. . . .

3. The Governor Upholds the Law (1676)

The youthful Bacon, putting himself at the head of about a thousand men, chastised both the Indians and Berkeley's forces. He died mysteriously in the arms of victory, and his rebellion ended. The ferocity with which Berkeley executed Bacon's followers (more than twenty all told) shocked Charles II, who allegedly remarked, "That old fool has killed more people in that naked country than I have done for the murder of my father." Before the rebellion collapsed, Berkeley pleaded his own case with the people of Virginia as follows. Ascertain the strongest argument in defense of his position and comment critically on it.

But for all this, perhaps I have erred in things I know not of. If I have, I am so conscious of human frailty and my own defects that I will not only acknowledge them, but repent of and amend them, and not, like the rebel Bacon, persist in an error only because I have committed it. . . .

And now I will state the question betwixt me as a governor and Mr. Bacon, and say that if any enemies should invade England, any counselor, justice of peace, or other inferior officer might raise what forces they could to protect His Majesty's subjects. But I say again, if, after the King's knowledge of this invasion, any the greatest peer of England should raise forces against the King's prohibition, this would be now, and ever was in all ages and nations, accounted treason. . . .

Now, my friends, I have lived thirty-four years amongst you, as uncorrupt and diligent as ever governor was. Bacon is a man of two years among

3. Massachusetts Historical Society, *Collections,* Fourth Series (1871), IX, 179–81.

you; his person and qualities unknown to most of you, and to all men else, by any virtuous action that ever I heard of. And that very action [against the Indians] which he boasts of was sickly and foolishly and, as I am informed, treacherously carried to the dishonor of the English nation. Yet in it he lost more men than I did in three years' war; and by the grace of God will put myself to the same dangers and troubles again when I have brought Bacon to acknowledge the laws are above him, and I doubt not but by God's assistance to have better success than Bacon hath had. The reasons of my hopes are, that I will take counsel of wiser men than myself; but Mr. Bacon hath none about him but the lowest of the people.

Yet I must further enlarge that I cannot, without your help, do anything in this but die in defense of my King, his laws and subjects, which I will cheerfully do, though alone I do it. And considering my poor fortunes, I cannot leave my poor wife and friends a better legacy than by dying for my King and you: for his sacred Majesty will easily distinguish between Mr. Bacon's actions and mine; and kings have long arms, either to reward or punish.

Now after all this, if Mr. Bacon can show one precedent or example where such acting in any nation whatever was approved of, I will mediate with the King and you for a pardon and excuse for him. But I can show him an hundred examples where brave and great men have been put to death for gaining victories against the command of their superiors.

Lastly, my most assured friends, I would have preserved those Indians that I knew were hourly at our mercy to have been our spies and intelligence, to find out our bloody enemies. But as soon as I had the least intelligence that they also were treacherous enemies, I gave out commissions to destroy them all, as the commissions themselves will speak it.

To conclude, I have done what was possible both to friend and enemy; have granted Mr. Bacon three pardons, which he hath scornfully rejected, supposing himself stronger to subvert than I and you to maintain the laws, by which only, and God's assisting grace and mercy, all men must hope for peace and safety.

4. Negro Slavery Is Justified (1757)

Following Bacon's ill-starred rebellion, tobacco culture continued to flourish. The Virginians had early learned that the path to wealth and leisure involved the use of Negro slaves. Even ministers of the gospel parroted the arguments in behalf of slavery, as is evident in this brutally frank letter by the Reverend Peter Fontaine, of Westover, Virginia, to his brother Moses. Decide whether the attempt to shift the blame onto the British is convincing, and whether there was a valid economic basis for slavery.

As to your second query, if enslaving our fellow creatures be a practice agreeable to Christianity, it is answered in a great measure in many

4. Ann Maury, ed., *Memoirs of a Huguenot Family* (1853), pp. 351–52.

treatises at home, to which I refer you. I shall only mention something of our present state here.

Like Adam, we are all apt to shift off the blame from ourselves and lay it upon others, how justly in our case you may judge. The Negroes are enslaved [in Africa] by the Negroes themselves before they are purchased by the masters of the ships who bring them here. It is, to be sure, at our choice whether we buy them or not; so this then is our crime, folly, or whatever you will please to call it. But our Assembly, foreseeing the ill consequences of importing such numbers amongst us, hath often attempted to lay a duty upon them which would amount to a prohibition, such as ten or twenty pounds a head. But no governor dare pass such a law, having instructions to the contrary from the Board of Trade at home. By this means they are forced upon us, whether we will or will not. This plainly shows the African Company has the advantage of the colonies, and may do as it pleases with the [London] ministry.

Indeed, since we have been exhausted of our little stock of cash by the [French and Indian] war, the importation has stopped; our poverty then is our best security. There is no more picking for their [slave traders'] ravenous jaws upon bare bones, but should we begin to thrive, they will be at the same again. . . .

This is our part of the grievance, but to live in Virginia without slaves is morally impossible. Before our troubles, you could not hire a servant or slave for love or money, so that unless robust enough to cut wood, to go to mill, to work at the hoe, etc., you must starve, or board in some family where they both fleece and half starve you. There is no set price upon corn, wheat, and provisions, so they take advantage of the necessities of strangers, who are thus obliged to purchase some slaves and land. This, of course, draws us all into the original sin and the curse of the country of purchasing slaves, and this is the reason we have no merchants, traders, or artificers of any sort but what become planters in a short time.

A common laborer, white or black, if you can be so much favored as to hire one, is a shilling sterling or fifteen pence currency per day; a bungling carpenter two shillings or two shillings and sixpence per day; besides diet and lodging. That is, for a lazy fellow to get wood and water, £19.16.3 current per annum; add to this seven or eight pounds more and you have a slave for life.

E. PROBLEMS OF THE SOUTHERN COLONIES

1. Byrd Visits Carolina's Lubberland (1728)

Wealthy, cultivated, and socially charming, William Byrd II, whose portrait reveals elegant finery and a rather haughty demeanor, was a leading Virginia planter and official. Born on the frontier but well educated in England, he finally acquired

1. William Byrd, "History of the Dividing Line," in *The Writings of Colonel William Byrd* ed. J. S. Bassett (1901), pp. 47, 75–76, 79–81, 87.

179,000 acres of land, a palatial home, and perhaps the largest private library in the colonies. His secret diary, kept in a shorthand that was not deciphered until recent years, reveals scandalously intimate details of his private life. More than once, like other land-poor aristocrats, he was forced to sell land and slaves to satisfy his creditors. Appointed one of the commissioners to run a surveyor's line between Virginia and North Carolina, he formed a low estimate of the swine-eating Carolinians. Making due allowance for his personal fastidiousness, form conclusions as to the character of these people and their government, and what it portended for the future.

Nor were these worthy borderers content to shelter runaway slaves, but debtors and criminals have often met with the like indulgence. But if the government of North Carolina has encouraged this unneighborly policy in order to increase their people, it is no more than what ancient Rome did before them, which was made a city of refuge for all debtors and fugitives. . . .

Surely there is no place in the world where the inhabitants live with less labor than in North Carolina. It approaches nearer to the description of Lubberland* than any other, by the great felicity of the climate, the easiness of raising provisions, and the slothfulness of the people.

Indian corn is of so great increase that a little pains will subsist a very large family with bread, and then they may have meat without any pains at all by the help of the low grounds and the great variety of mast [nuts] that grows on the highland.

The men, for their parts, just like the Indians, impose all the work upon the poor women. They make their wives rise out of their beds early in the morning, at the same time that they lie and snore, till the sun has run one-third of his course, and dispersed all the unwholesome damps. Then, after stretching and yawning for half an hour, they light their pipes and, under the protection of a cloud of smoke, venture out into the open air; though, if it happens to be never so little cold, they quickly return shivering into the chimney corner. When the weather is mild, they stand leaning with both their arms upon the cornfield fence, and gravely consider whether they had best go and take a small heat at the hoe, but generally find reasons to put it off till another time. . . .

This town [Edenton, N.C.] is situate on the north side of Albemarle Sound. . . . Justice herself is but indifferently lodged, the court house having much the air of a common tobacco house. I believe this is the only metropolis in the Christian or Mohammedan world where there is neither church, chapel, mosque, synagogue, or any other place of public worship of any sect or religion whatsoever.

What little devotion there may happen to be is much more private than their vices. The people seem easy without a minister, as long as they are exempted from paying him. Sometimes the Society for Propagating the Gospel has had the charity to send over missionaries to this country. But, unfortunately, the priest has been too lewd for the people or, which oftener

---

* An imaginary land of plenty and idleness, where, as the English proverb has it, "the pigs run about ready-roasted and cry, 'Come, eat me !' "

happens, they too lewd for the priest. For these reasons these reverend
gentlemen have always left their flocks as arrant heathen as they found
them. Thus much, however, may be said for the inhabitants of Edenton, that
not a soul has the least taint of hypocrisy or superstition, acting very frankly
and aboveboard in all their excessès.

Provisions here are extremely cheap and extremely good, so that people
may live plentifully at a trifling expense. Nothing is dear but law, physic,
and strong drink, which are all bad in their kind, and the last they get with
so much difficulty that they are never guilty of the sin of suffering it to sour
upon their hands. . . .

They are rarely guilty of flattering or making any court to their governors,
but treat them with all the excesses of freedom and familiarity. They are of
opinion their rulers would be apt to grow insolent if they grew rich, and for
that reason take care to keep them poorer, and more dependent, if possible,
than the saints in New England used to do their governors. . . .

The [surveyor's] line cut William Spight's plantation in two, leaving little
more than his dwelling house and orchard in Virginia. Sundry other plantations were split in the same unlucky manner, which made the owners accountable to both governments. Wherever we passed, we constantly found
the borderers laid it to heart if their land was taken into Virginia. They
chose much rather to belong to Carolina, where they pay no tribute, either
to God or to Caesar.

Another reason was that the government there is so loose, and the laws so
feebly executed, that, like those in the neighborhood of Sidon formerly,
everyone does just what seems good in his own eyes. If the governor's hands
have been weak in that province under the authority of the lord proprietors,
much weaker then were the hands of the magistrate, who, though he might
have had virtue enough to endeavor to punish offenders, which very rarely
happened, yet that virtue had been quite impotent, for want of ability to
put it in execution.

Besides, there might have been some danger, perhaps, in venturing to be
so rigorous for fear of undergoing the fate of an honest justice in Corotuck
precinct. This bold magistrate, it seems, taking upon him to order a fellow
to the stocks for being disorderly in his drink, was, for his intemperate zeal,
carried thither himself, and narrowly escaped being whipped by the rabble
into the bargain.

2. Georgia's Founders Appeal for Support (1733)

James Oglethorpe—distinguished idealist, reformer, legislator, soldier, colonizer,
imperialist—was aroused against debtors' prisons when one of his friends died after
being thrust into jail with smallpox victims. He headed a Parliamentary investigation
which found jailers who were corrupt, arbitrary, and sadistic, who applied thumb-
screws and strangled prisoners until blood flowed from noses, ears, and eyes. Moved
to find an asylum for the poor of England, Oglethorpe became the leading spirit

2. Peter Force, *Tracts* . . . (1836), I, no. 2, pp. 5–7.

among the twenty trustees who founded Georgia in 1733. The following appeal, issued in London by the promoters, reveals both humanitarian and materialistic motives. Decide which type seems to dominate, and form relevant conclusions.

The Trustees intend to relieve such unfortunate persons as cannot subsist here, and establish them in an orderly manner, so as to form a well-regulated town. As far as their fund goes, they will defray the charge of their passage to Georgia; give them necessaries, cattle, land, and subsistence till such time as they can build their houses and clear some of their land. . . .

By such a colony many families who would otherwise starve will be provided for, and made masters of houses and lands. The people in Great Britain, to whom these necessitous families were a burden, will be relieved. Numbers of manufacturers will be here employed for supplying them with clothes, working tools, and other necessaries. And by giving refuge to the distressed Salzburgers [Austrians], and other persecuted Protestants, the power of Britain, as a reward for its hospitality, will be increased by the addition of so many religious and industrious subjects.

CATHOLIC BOOK-BURNERS PERSECUTE
PROTESTANT SALZBURGERS

Some Salzburgers came to Georgia. From a book published at Frankfurt am Main, 1732.

The colony of Georgia lying about the same latitude with part of China, Persia, Palestine, and the Madeiras, it is highly probable that when hereafter it shall be well peopled and rightly cultivated, England may be supplied from thence with raw silk, wine, oil, dyes, drugs, and many other materials for manufactures which she is obliged to purchase from southern countries. As towns are established and grow populous along the rivers Savannah and Altamaha, they will make such a barrier as will render the southern frontier of the British colonies on the continent of America safe from Indian and other enemies.

All human affairs are so subject to chance that there is no answering for events. Yet from reason and the nature of things it may be concluded that the riches and also the number of the inhabitants in Great Britain will be increased, by importing, at a cheap rate from the new colony, the materials requisite for carrying on in Britain several manufactures. . . .

Christianity will be extended by the execution of this design, since the good discipline established by the society will reform the manners of those miserable objects [debtors] who shall be by them subsisted. And the example of a whole colony, who shall behave in a just, moral, and religious manner, will contribute greatly towards the conversion of the Indians. . . .

The Trustees in their general meetings will consider of the most prudent methods for effectually establishing a regular colony; and that it may be done is demonstrable. Under what difficulties was Virginia planted? The coast and climate then unknown; the Indians numerous, and at enmity with the first planters, who were forced to fetch all provisions from England. Yet it is grown a mighty province, and the revenue receives £100,000 for duties upon the goods that they send yearly home. Within this fifty years Pennsylvania was as much a forest as Georgia is now; and in these few years, by the wise economy of William Penn and those who assisted him, it now gives food to 80,000 inhabitants, and can boast of as fine a city as most in Europe.

This new colony is more likely to succeed than either of the former were, since Carolina abounds with provisions, the climate is known, and there are men to instruct in the seasons and nature of cultivating the soil. There are but few Indian families within four hundred miles; and those in perfect amity with the English.

THOUGHT PROVOKERS

1. If a large area in Africa were suddenly to become open for colonization, what arguments that were used for colonization in the 16th and 17th Centuries would still be valid?

2. Why was colonization in the New World more difficult in the 17th Century than similar enterprises would be today? Was the concern for Christianizing the Indians sincere? Does this zeal for missionary work seem to foreshadow the White Man's Burden of latter-day imperialism?

3. In what respects would the Maryland Act of Toleration be regarded as intoleration today?

4. Were the Baconites justified in rebelling? Recent scholarship has claimed that it is farfetched to regard Bacon's rebellion as the "opening gun" of the American War of Independence. Comment critically in the light of the documents herein presented.

5. What does one find in the character of the people of Virginia and North Carolina, as well as in the nature of their laws, that foreshadows the coming of the American Revolution in 1775–1776? Taking the Southern mainland colonies as a group, what motives seem to have predominated in their founding?

FURTHER EXPLORATION

General: C. M. Andrews, *The Colonial Period of American History* (4 vols., 1934–1938). **New Worlds:** Wallace Notestein, *The English People on the Eve of Colonization, 1603–1630* (1954); A. L. Rowse, *The Elizabethans and America* (1959). **Early Virginia:** Bradford Smith, *Captain John Smith* (1953); R. L. Morton, *Colonial Virginia* (2 vols., 1960). **Maryland:** W. H. Browne, *Maryland: The History of a Palatinate* (1912); T. O. Hanley, *Their Rights and Liberties* (1959). **Later Virginia:** T. J. Wertenbaker, *Torchbearer of the Revolution* (1940) [anti-Berkeley]; W. E. Washburn, *The Governor and the Rebel* (1957) [pro-Berkeley]. **Southern Colonies:** W. F. Craven, *The Southern Colonies in the Seventeenth Century* (1949); A. A. Ettinger, *James Edward Oglethorpe* (1936). **Recent:** P. L. Barbour, *The Three Worlds of Captain John Smith* (1964); R. T. Reese, *Colonial Georgia* (1963).

Chapter *2*

The New England and Middle Colonies

To Banbury [England] came I, O profane one!
Where I saw a Puritan once
Hanging of his cat on Monday,
For killing of a mouse on Sunday.

RICHARD BRATHWAITE, 1638

PROLOGUE: The English authorities, angered by the efforts of Puritans further to de-Catholicize the established Church of England, launched persecutions that led to the founding of Plymouth in 1620 and the Massachusetts Bay Colony in 1628. The Bay Colony early fell under the leadership of Puritan (Congregational) clergymen. Although the victims of intolerance in England, they understandably sought to enforce conformity by the persecution of Quakers and the banishment of dissenters like Anne Hutchinson and Roger Williams. Partly as a result of the uncongenial atmosphere in Massachusetts Bay, settlements in Connecticut and Rhode Island sprang into existence. These offshoot colonies, as well as the older ones, developed the pure-democracy town meeting and other significant institutions. A more hospitable atmosphere in the Quaker colonies, notably Penn's Pennsylvania, attracted heavy immigration, largely German. The Dutch in New Netherland, after a precarious existence from 1624 to 1664, were finally absorbed by the English, who renamed the colony New York.

A. THE PLANTING OF PLYMOUTH

1. The Pilgrims Leave Holland (1620)

William Bradford, then a youth of nineteen, was one of the small group of Puritan Separatists who in 1609 fled from England to Holland in search of religious freedom. But the new home proved to be unsatisfactory. The Pilgrims complained of theological controversy, unremitting toil, grinding poverty, and the unhealthy condition of their children, who were becoming Dutchified and developing "licentious" habits. It seemed better to make a new start in the New World, where they could all live and die as Englishmen while advancing the "gospel of the Kingdom of Christ." Bradford became not only the kingpin leader of Plymouth but also its distinguished historian, as his classic *History of Plymouth Plantation* attests. In his account of the decision to leave Holland, note whether the Pilgrims were fully aware of their perils, and what light his analysis casts on their character. As the selection opens, Bradford has just reported that the Pilgrims first discussed the perils of the long sea voyage, the dangers of famine and nakedness, and the diseases that might come from the "change of air, diet, and drinking water."

And also those which should escape or overcome these difficulties should yet be in continual danger of the savage people, who are cruel, barbarous,

1. William Bradford, *Of Plymouth Plantation, 1620–1647*, ed. S. E. Morison (1952), pp. 26–27. By permission of Alfred A. Knopf, Inc.

24

and most treacherous, being most furious in their rage, and merciless where they overcome; not being content only to kill and take away life, but delight to torment men in the most bloody manner that may be; flaying some alive with the shells of fishes, cutting off the members and joints of others by piecemeal and broiling on the coals, eat the collops [slices] of their flesh in their sight whilst they live, with other cruelties horrible to be related.

And surely it could not be thought but the very hearing of these things could not but move the very bowels of men to grate within them and make the weak to quake and tremble.

It was further objected that it would require greater sums of money to furnish such a voyage, and to fit them with necessaries, than their consumed estates would amount to; and yet they must as well look to be seconded with supplies as presently to be transported. Also many precedents of ill success and lamentable miseries befallen others in the like designs were easy to be found, and not forgotten to be alleged; besides their own experience, in their former troubles and hardships in their removal into Holland, and how hard a thing it was for them to live in that strange place, though it was a neighbor country and a civil and rich commonwealth.

It was answered that all great and honorable actions are accompanied with great difficulties, and must be both enterprised and overcome with answerable courages. It was granted the dangers were great, but not desperate. The difficulties were many, but not invincible. For though there were many of them likely, yet they were not certain. It might be sundry of the things feared might never befall; others by provident care and the use of good means might in a great measure be prevented. And all of them, through the help of God, . . . might either be borne or overcome.

True it was that such attempts were not to be made and undertaken without good ground and reason, not rashly or lightly, as many have done for curiosity or hope of gain, etc. But their condition was not ordinary, their ends were good and honorable, their calling lawful and urgent; and therefore they might expect the blessing of God in their proceeding. Yea, though they should lose their lives in this action, yet might they have comfort in the same and their endeavors would be honorable.

They lived here [in Holland] but as men in exile and in a poor condition, and as great miseries might possibly befall them in this place. For the twelve years of truce were now out,* and there was nothing but beating of drums and preparing for war, the events whereof are always uncertain. The Spaniard might prove as cruel as the savages of America, and the famine and pestilence as sore here as there, and their liberty less to look out for remedy.

After many other particular things answered and alleged on both sides, it was fully concluded by the major part to put this design in execution and to prosecute it by the best means they could.

---

* The twelve years' truce in Holland's bitter war of independence against Spain had been negotiated in 1609.

2. Framing the Mayflower Compact (1620)

Leaving Plymouth (England) in the overburdened *Mayflower,* the plucky band of Pilgrims crossed the Atlantic. After severe storms and much seasickness, they sighted the Cape Cod coast of Massachusetts, far to the north of the site to which they had been granted patent privileges by the Virginia Company. The absence of valid rights in the Plymouth area, so William Bradford recorded, caused "some of the strangers amongst them" to utter "discontented and mutinous speeches" to the effect that when they "came ashore they would use their own liberty; for none had the power to command them, the patent they had being for Virginia, and not for New England. . . ." In an effort to hold the tiny band together, the leaders persuaded forty-one male passengers to sign a solemn pledge known as the Mayflower Compact. A constitution is "a document defining and limiting the functions of government." Ascertain whether the Compact was, as often claimed, the first American constitution or merely a germ of democracy.

In the name of God, amen. We whose names are underwritten, the loyal subjects of our dread sovereign lord, King James, by the grace of God, of Great Britain, France, and Ireland King, Defender of the Faith, etc., having undertaken, for the glory of God, and advancement of the Christian faith, and honor of our King and country, a voyage to plant the first colony in the northern parts of Virginia, do by these presents solemnly and mutually, in the presence of God and one another, covenant and combine ourselves together into a civil body politic, for our better ordering and preservation and furtherance of the ends aforesaid; and by virtue hereof to enact, constitute, and frame such just and equal laws, ordinances, acts, constitutions, and offices, from time to time, as shall be thought most meet and convenient for the general good of the colony, unto which we promise all due submission and obedience. In witness whereof we have hereunto subscribed our names at Cape Cod the eleventh of November, in the reign of our sovereign lord, King James, of England, France, and Ireland, the eighteenth, and of Scotland, the fifty-fourth. Anno Domini 1620.

3. Abandoning Communism at Plymouth (1623)

Some wag has said that the Pilgrims first fell on their knees, and then on the aborigines. The truth is that a plague—probably smallpox, possibly measles—had virtually exterminated the Indians near Plymouth, and the Pilgrims got along reasonably well with the survivors. The red men taught the whites how to grow Indian corn, which did much to rescue the ragged, starving, disease-decimated newcomers. The story of the first Thanksgiving (1621) is well known, but less well known is the fact that the abundant harvest of 1623 would not have been possible if the Pilgrims had not abandoned communism. For seven years there was to have been no private ownership of land, and everyone was to have been fed and clothed from the common stock. William Bradford, the historian and oft-elected governor of the colony, here tells what happened when each family was given its own parcel of land. Discover why basically the individual-ownership scheme succeeded.

2. B. P. Poore, ed., *The Federal and State Constitutions* (2nd ed., 1878), Pt. I, p. 931.
3. William Bradford. *Of Plymouth Plantation, 1620–1647,* ed. S. E. Morison (1952), pp. 120–21. By permission of Alfred A. Knopf, Inc.

This had very good success, for it made all hands very industrious, so as much more corn was planted than otherwise would have been by any means the Governor or any other could use, and saved him a great deal of trouble, and gave far better content. The women now went willingly into the field and took their little ones with them to set corn, which before would allege weakness and inability, whom to have compelled would have been thought great tyranny and oppression.

The experience that was had in this common course and condition, tried sundry years and that amongst godly and sober men, may well evince the vanity of that conceit of Plato's and other ancients, applauded by some of later times, that the taking away of property and bringing in community [communism] into a commonwealth would make them happy and flourishing, as if they were wiser than God. For this community (so far as it was) was found to breed much confusion and discontent and retard much employment that would have been to their benefit and comfort. For the young men that were most able and fit for labor and service did repine that they should spend their time and strength to work for other men's wives and children, without any recompense. The strong, or man of parts, had no more in division of victuals and clothes than he that was weak and not able to do a quarter the other could; this was thought injustice. The aged and graver men to be ranked and equalized in labors and victuals, clothes, etc., with the meaner and younger sort, thought it some indignity and disrespect unto them. And for men's wives to be commanded to do service for other men, as dressing their meat, washing their clothes, etc., they deemed it a kind of slavery, neither could many husbands well brook it.

B. CONFORMITY IN THE BAY COLONY

1. Anne Hutchinson Is Banished (1637)

The powerful Massachusetts Bay Colony soon became a Bible Commonwealth, centered at Boston, and the clergymen who dominated it could not permit heretics to undermine their authority. Mistress Anne Hutchinson, who bore her husband fourteen children, was a kindly woman of nimble wit and even more nimble tongue. Gathering at her home a select group, she would review and even reinterpret the ministers' sermons in the light of her own brand of Calvinism. Haled before the General Court, she was subjected to a rigid cross-examination. The case against her seemed to be breaking down when her voluble tongue revealed that she was in direct communication with God—a heresy that the religious leaders could not tolerate. From this record of the Court, form relevant conclusions as to the Puritan way of thinking, and as to the justice or injustice of these proceedings.

[ANNE HUTCHINSON.] Therefore take heed what ye go about to do unto me. You have power over my body, but the Lord Jesus hath power over my body and soul; neither can you do me any harm, for I am in the hands

1. C. F. Adams, *Three Episodes of Massachusetts History* (1892), I, 501–02, 507–08.

of the eternal Jehovah, my Saviour. I am at his appointment, for the bounds of my habitation are cast in Heaven, and no further do I esteem of any mortal man than creatures in his hand. I fear none but the great Jehovah, which hath foretold me of these things, and I do verily believe that he will deliver me out of your hands. Therefore take heed how you proceed against me; for I know that for this you go about to do to me, God will ruin you and your posterity, and this whole state.

MR. NOWELL. How do you know that it was God that did reveal these things to you, and not Satan?

MRS. HUTCHINSON. How did Abraham know that it was God that bid him offer [sacrifice] his son, being a breach of the sixth commandment?

DEPUTY-GOVERNOR DUDLEY. By an immediate voice.

MRS. HUTCHINSON. So to me by an immediate revelation.

DEPUTY-GOVERNOR. How! an immediate revelation?

MRS. HUTCHINSON. By the voice of his own spirit to my soul.

GOVERNOR WINTHROP. Daniel was delivered by miracle; do you think to be delivered so too?

MRS. HUTCHINSON. I do here speak it before the Court. I look that the Lord should deliver me by his providence. . . .

GOVERNOR WINTHROP. The Court hath already declared themselves satisfied concerning the things you hear, and concerning the troublesomeness of her spirit, and the danger of her course amongst us, which is not to be suffered. Therefore, if it be the mind of the Court that Mrs. Hutchinson, for these things that appear before us, is unfit for our society, and if it be the mind of the Court that she shall be banished out of our liberties, and imprisoned till she be sent away, let them hold up their hands.

All but three held up their hands.

[GOVERNOR WINTHROP.] Those that are contrary minded, hold up yours.

Mr. Coddington and Mr. Colburn only.

MR. JENNISON. I cannot hold up my hand one way or the other, and I shall give my reason if the Court require it.

GOVERNOR WINTHROP. Mrs. Hutchinson, you hear the sentence of the Court. It is that you are banished from out our jurisdiction as being a woman not fit for our society. And you are to be imprisoned till the Court send you away.

MRS. HUTCHINSON. I desire to know wherefore I am banished.

GOVERNOR WINTHROP. Say no more. The Court knows wherefore, and is satisfied.

2. Winthrop's Concept of Liberty (1645)

Governor John Winthrop, who pronounced Anne Hutchinson's banishment, was the most distinguished lay leader in the Massachusetts Bay Colony. Cambridge-educated and trained in the law, he was modest, tender, self-sacrificing, and deeply religious. After a furious quarrel had broken out at Hingham over the election of a militia leader, he caused certain of the agitators to be arrested. His foes brought

2. John Winthrop, *The History of New England* (1853), II, 281–82.

impeachment charges against him, but they instead were fined. After his acquittal, Winthrop delivered this famous speech to the court. It illustrates the close tie-in between the aristocratic lay leaders of the Bay Colony and the leading clergymen. Would the kind of liberty that Winthrop describes be regarded as liberty today?

There is a twofold liberty: natural (I mean as our nature is now corrupt) and civil or federal. The first is common to man with beasts and other creatures. By this, man, as he stands in relation to man simply, hath liberty to do what he lists. It is a liberty to evil as well as to good. This liberty is incompatible and inconsistent with authority, and cannot endure the least restraint of the most just authority. The exercise and maintaining of this liberty makes men grow more evil, and in time to be worse than brute beasts. . . .

The other kind of liberty I call civil or federal. It may also be termed moral, in reference to the covenant between God and man in the moral law, and the politic covenants and constitutions amongst men themselves. . . . Whatsoever crosseth this, is not authority, but a distemper thereof. This liberty is maintained and exercised in a way of subjection to authority. It is of the same kind of liberty wherewith Christ hath made us free.

The woman's own choice makes such a man her husband; yet being so chosen, he is her lord, and she is to be subject to him, yet in a way of liberty, not of bondage. And a true wife accounts her subjection her honor and freedom, and would not think her condition safe and free, but in her subjection to her husband's authority.

Such is the liberty of the church under the authority of Christ, her king and husband. His yoke is so easy and sweet to her as a bride's ornaments; and if through frowardness or wantonness, etc., she shake it off at any time, she is at no rest in her spirit until she take it up again. And whether her lord smiles upon her, and embraceth her in his arms, or whether he frowns, or rebukes, or smites her, she apprehends the sweetness of his love in all, and is refreshed, supported, and instructed by every such dispensation of his authority over her. On the other side, ye know who they are that complain of this yoke and say, let us break their bands, etc., we will not have this man to rule over us.

Even so, brethren, it will be between you and your magistrates. If you stand for your natural corrupt liberties, and will do what is good in your own eyes, you will not endure the least weight of authority, but will murmur, and oppose, and be always striving to shake off that yoke. But if you will be satisfied to enjoy such civil and lawful liberties, such as Christ allows you, then will you quietly and cheerfully submit unto that authority which is set over you, in all the administrations of it, for your good. Wherein if we [magistrates] fail at any time, we hope we shall be willing (by God's assistance) to hearken to good advice from any of you, or in any other way of God. So shall your liberties be preserved, in upholding the honor and power of authority amongst you.

3. Puritan Mistreatment of Quakers (1660)

The peace-loving Quakers, who opposed a paid clergy and a tax-supported Church, likewise felt the restraining hand of Massachusetts authority. The Reverend Increase Mather wrote in 1684 that they were "under the strong delusion of Satan." Their stubborn devotion and courage under punishment were so exasperating as to provoke increasingly severe measures. Edward Burrough, one of their co-religionists in England, presented the following appeal on their behalf to the King, who thereupon sent orders to Massachusetts to end the persecutions. It should be noted, however, that the Quakers gloried in being fanatically persistent, and that about five hundred died in England of harsh usage. From this document determine the chief offenses of the Quakers, and the most serious injustices, aside from physical abuse, that they suffered.

2. Twelve strangers in that country [Massachusetts], but free-born of this [English] nation, received twenty-three whippings, the most of them being with a whip of three cords, with knots at the ends, and laid on with as much strength as they could be by the arm of their executioner, the stripes amounting to three hundred and seventy. . . .

3. Eighteen inhabitants of the country, being free-born English, received twenty-three whippings, the stripes amounting to two hundred and fifty.

4. Sixty-four imprisonments of the Lord's people, for their obedience to his will, amounting to five hundred and nineteen weeks, much of it being very cold weather, and the inhabitants kept in prison in harvest time. . . .

5. Two beaten with pitched ropes, the blows amounting to an hundred thirty-nine. . . .

6. Also, an innocent man, an inhabitant of Boston, they banished from his wife and children, and put to seek a habitation in the winter. And in case he returned again, he was to be kept prisoner during his life; and for returning again, he was put in prison, and hath been now a prisoner above a year.

7. Twenty-five banishments, upon the penalties of being whipped, or having their ears cut; or branded in the hand, if they returned.

8. Fines laid upon the inhabitants for meeting together, and edifying one another, as the saints ever did; and for refusing to swear [take oaths], it being contrary to Christ's command, amounting to about a thousand pound. . . .

9. Five kept fifteen days (in all) without food, and fifty-eight days shut up close by the jailor. . . .

10. One laid neck and heels in irons for sixteen hours.

11. One very deeply burnt in the right hand with the letter H [for *heretic*], after he had been whipped with above thirty stripes.

12. One chained the most part of twenty days to a log of wood in an open prison in the winter-time.

13. Five appeals to England, denied at Boston.

14. Three had their right ears cut by the hangman in the prison, the door being barred, and not a friend suffered to be present while it was doing, though some much desired it. . . .

3. [Edward Burrough]. *A Declaration of the Sad and Great Persecution and Martyrdom of the People of God, Called Quakers, in New England . . .* ([1660]), pp. 17–19.

15. One of the inhabitants of Salem, who since is banished upon pain of death, had one half of his house and land seized on while he was in prison, a month before he knew of it.

16. At a General Court in Boston, they made an order, that those who had not wherewithal to answer the fines that were laid upon them (for their consciences) should be sold for bond-men and bond-women to Barbados, Virginia, or any of the English plantations. . . .

17. Eighteen of the people of God were at several times banished upon pain of death. . . .

18. Also three of the servants of the Lord they put to death [hanged], all of them for obedience to the truth, in the testimony of it against the wicked rulers and laws at Boston.

QUAKERS ABUSED IN ENGLAND
New England persecutions were on a smaller scale. S. Seyer, *Memoirs Historical and Topographical of Bristol*, 1823, Vol. II.

19. And since they have banished four more, upon pain of death. . . .

These things, O King, from time to time have we patiently suffered, and not for the transgression of any just or righteous law, either pertaining to the worship of God or the civil government of England, but simply and barely for our consciences to God. . . .

C. THE RULE OF BIBLICAL LAW

1. The Blue Laws of Connecticut (1672)

Blue laws—or statutes of extreme rigor—were to be found both in Europe and in all of the American colonies. They obviously could not be enforced with literal severity, and they generally fell into disuse after the Revolution. Those of Connecticut received unpleasant notoriety in the Reverend Samuel Peters' *General History of Connecticut* (1781), which fabricated such decrees as "No woman shall kiss her child on the Sabbath or fasting-day." But the valid laws of Connecticut, some of which are here reproduced with Biblical chapter and verse, were harsh enough. Locate the offenses that today would not be regarded as criminal; the statutes that reinforced the Ten Commandments.

1. If any man or woman, after legal conviction, shall have or worship any other God but the Lord God, he shall be put to death. (Deuteronomy 13.6. Exodus 22.20.)

2. If any person within this colony shall blaspheme the name of God, the Father, Son, or Holy Ghost, with direct, express, presumptuous, or

1. George Brinley, ed., *The Laws of Connecticut* (1865), pp. 9–10.

high-handed blasphemy, or shall curse in the like manner, he shall be put to death. (Leviticus 24.15, 16.)

3. If any man or woman be a witch, that is, has or consults with a familiar spirit, they shall be put to death. (Exodus 22.18. Leviticus 20.27. Deuteronomy 18.10, 11.)

4. If any person shall commit any willful murder, committed upon malice, hatred, or cruelty, not in a man's just and necessary defense, nor by casualty [accident] against his will, he shall be put to death. (Exodus 21.12, 13, 14. Numbers 35.30, 31.)

5. If any person shall slay another through guile, either by poisoning or other such devilish practices, he shall be put to death. (Exodus 21.14.). . .

10. If any man steals a man or mankind and sells him, or if he be found in his hand, he shall be put to death. (Exodus 21.16.)

11. If any person rise up by false witness wittingly and of purpose to take away any man's life, he or she shall be put to death. (Deuteronomy 19.16, 18, 19.). . .

14. If any child or children above sixteen years old, and of sufficient understanding, shall curse or smite their natural father or mother, he or they shall be put to death, unless it can be sufficiently testified that the parents have been very unchristianly negligent in the education of such children, or so provoked them by extreme and cruel correction that they have been forced thereunto to preserve themselves from death or maiming. (Exodus 21.17. Leviticus 20.9. Exodus 21.15.)

15. If any man have a stubborn or rebellious son, of sufficient under-standing and years, viz. sixteen years of age, which will not obey the voice of his father, or the voice of his mother, and that when they have chastened him, he will not harken unto them; then may his father or mother, being his natural parents, lay hold on him, and bring him to the magistrates assembled in court, and testify unto them that their son is stubborn and rebellious, and will not obey their voice and chastisement, but lives in sundry notorious crimes, such a son shall be put to death. (Deuteronomy 21.20, 21.). . .

2. The Salem Witchcraft Hysteria (1692)

Thousands of suspected witches were hanged or burned in Europe in the 16th and 17th Centuries, and belief in witches was common in the American colonies. In fact, the Bible decreed, "Thou shalt not suffer a witch to live" (Exodus 22:18). Hysteria swept Salem Village, Massachusetts, in 1692 after some children, presumably feigning fits, brought witchcraft charges against certain persons whom they disliked. Before the special court had adjourned, nineteen persons and two dogs had been hanged, one man had been pressed to death in an attempt to elicit from him an answer to the indictment, and one hundred and fifty victims were in prison awaiting trial. Note which aspects of the following testimony seem least credible, and judge whether any of it would be accepted in courts today.

2. G. L. Burr, ed., *Narratives of the Witchcraft Cases, 1648–1706* (1914), pp. 241–42, 244. By permission of Barnes and Noble, Inc.

Martha Carrier was indicted for the bewitching of certain persons, according to the form usual in such cases pleading not guilty to her indictment. There were first brought in a considerable number of the bewitched persons, who not only made the court sensible to an horrid witchcraft committed upon them, but also deposed that it was Martha Carrier, or her shape, that grievously tormented them by biting, pricking, pinching, and choking of them. It was further deposed that while this Carrier was on her examination before the magistrates, the poor people were so tortured that every one expected their death upon the very spot, but that upon the binding [arrest] of Carrier they were eased. . . .

Before the trial of this prisoner, several of her own children had frankly and fully confessed, not only that they were witches themselves, but that this, their mother, had made them so. This confession they made with great shows of repentance, and with much demonstration of truth. They related place, time, occasion; they gave an account of journeys, meetings, and mischiefs by them performed, and were very credible in what they said. . . .

WITCHES HANGED IN ENGLAND

New England hangings were on a smaller scale. Ralph Gardner, *England's Grievance Discovered in Relation to the Coal Trade*, 1655.

Benjamin Abbot gave in his testimony that . . . this Carrier was very angry with him upon laying out some land near her husband's. Her expressions in this anger were that she "would stick as close to Abbot as the bark stuck to the tree; and that he should repent of it afore seven years came to an end, so as Doctor Prescot should never cure him." . . . Presently after this he was taken with a swelling in his foot, and then with a pain in his side, and exceedingly tormented. It bred into a sore, which was lanced by Doctor Prescot, and several gallons of corruption [pus] ran out of it. For six weeks it continued very bad, and then another sore bred in his groin, which was also lanced by Doctor Prescot. Another sore then bred in his groin, which was likewise cut, and put him to very great misery. He was brought unto death's door, and so remained until Carrier was taken and carried away by the constable, from which very day he began to mend and so grew better every day, and is well ever since.

Sarah Abbot also, his wife, testified that her husband was not only all this while afflicted in his body, but also that strange, extraordinary, and unaccountable calamities befell his cattle, their death being such as they could guess at no natural reason for. . . .

One Foster, who confessed her own share in the witchcraft for which the prisoner stood indicted, affirmed that she had seen the prisoner at some of their witch meetings, and that it was this Carrier who persuaded her to be a witch. She confessed that the devil carried them on a pole to a witch meeting; but the pole broke, and she hanging about Carrier's neck, they both fell down, and she then received an hurt by the fall whereof she was not at this very time recovered.

3. A Defense of Buying Indian Land (1722)

The Reverend Solomon Stoddard, for fifty-six years pastor of the Congregational church in Northampton, was easily the most influential figure of his day in western Massachusetts. Tall, dignified, and domineering, he was dubbed by his critics "the Pope." He advocated the frequent preaching of hell-fire as a restraint against sin, and he bitterly opposed long hair and wigs for men, extravagance in dress, and intemperance in drink. The following is a part of a tract that he published in 1722 entitled *An Answer to Some Cases of Conscience Respecting the Country*. Determine which of his arguments is the most convincing, and whether the land really "belonged" to the Indians in the first place.

Question VIII. Did we any wrong to the Indians in buying their land at a small price?

Answer. 1. There was some part of the land that was not purchased, neither was there need that it should; it was *vacuum domicilium* [a vacant dwelling place]; and so might be possessed by virtue of God's grant to mankind, Genesis 1.28: "And God blessed them, and God said unto them, Be fruitful and multiply and replenish the earth, and subdue it; and have dominion over the fish of the sea, and over the fowl of the air, and over every living thing that moveth upon the earth." The Indians made no use of it but for hunting. By God's first grant men were to subdue the earth. When Abraham came into the land of Canaan, he made use of vacant land as he pleased; so did Isaac and Jacob.

2. The Indians were well contented that we should sit down by them. And it would have been for great advantage, both for this world and the other, if they had been wise enough to make use of their opportunities. It has been common with many people, in planting this world since the Flood, to admit neighbors, to sit down by them.

3. Though we gave but a small price for what we bought, we gave them

3. Solomon Stoddard, *An Answer to Some Cases of Conscience Respecting the Country* (1722; reprinted 1917), pp. 14–15.

their demands. We came to their market, and gave them their price. And, indeed, it was worth but little; and had it continued in their hands, it would have been of little value. It is our dwelling on it, and our improvements, that have made it to be of worth.

D. A DEVELOPING PEOPLE

1. Roger Williams Defines Liberty (1655)

Two years before Mrs. Hutchinson suffered banishment, a similar fate befell **Roger Williams**, a troublesome thirty-two-year-old clergyman whose ultra-liberal ideals offended the Massachusetts leaders. To them his advocacy of a separation of church and state was intolerable. Fleeing to Providence, Rhode Island, he set up a beacon light of religious toleration in a darkly intolerant world. But an excess of freedom begot serious disorders, and Williams, then absent, wrote to the colony this famous letter. Form conclusions as to the soundness of his ship analogy.

That ever I should speak or write a tittle that tends to such an infinite liberty of conscience, is a mistake, and [one] which I have ever disclaimed and abhorred. To prevent such mistakes, I shall at present only propose this case:

There goes many a ship to sea, with many hundred souls in one ship, whose weal or woe is common, and is a true picture of a commonwealth, or a human combination or society. It has fallen out sometimes that both Papists and Protestants, Jews and Turks, may be embarked in one ship; upon which supposal I affirm that all the liberty of conscience that ever I pleaded for turns upon these two hinges—that none of the Papists, Protestants, Jews, or Turks be forced to come to the ship's prayers or worship, nor compelled from their own particular prayers or worship, if they practice any.

I further add that I never denied that, notwithstanding this liberty, the commander of this ship ought to command the ship's course, yea, and also command that justice, peace, and sobriety be kept and practiced both among the seamen and all the passengers. If any of the seamen refuse to perform their services or passengers to pay their freight; if any refuse to help, in person or purse, towards the common charges or defense; if any refuse to obey the common laws and order of the ship concerning their common peace or preservation; if any shall mutiny and rise up against their commanders and officers; if any should preach or write that there ought to be no commanders or officers, because all are equal in Christ, therefore no masters nor officers, no laws nor orders, nor corrections nor punishments —I say I never denied but in such cases, whatever is pretended, the commander or commanders may judge, resist, compel, and punish such transgressors, according to their deserts and merits.

This, if seriously and honestly minded, may, if it so please the Father of lights, let in some light to such as willingly shut not their eyes.

I remain studious of your common peace and liberty.

1. Narragansett Club, Providence, *Publications: Letters of Roger Williams, 1632–1682*, First Series (1874), VI, 278–79.

2. A Clergyman Visits New England (1760)

The New England Puritan has been traditionally pictured as an abstemious, sour-faced, hypocritical, bigoted, beauty-hating, nosy killjoy. Recent defenders have portrayed him as a jolly good fellow, with Priscilla sitting on his left knee and a tankard of ale upraised in his right hand. The truth lies between these extremes, for the Puritans were human beings. They saw nothing wrong in drinking alcohol in moderation; their interest in sex is attested by large families and a surprising number of illegitimate births; they engaged in much merriment; they evidently enjoyed their religion; they loved bright colors; and they had a well-developed artistic sense. Moreover, the austerity of pioneer life softened as generations passed. The Reverend Andrew Burnaby, M.A., a visiting Church of England clergyman, has left us this revealing picture of the Massachusetts Bay Colony in 1760. Detect the most striking evidences of a changed atmosphere.

The established religion here, as in all the other provinces of New England, is that of the Congregationalists—a religion different in some trifling articles, though none very material, from the Presbyterian. There are, besides these, however, great numbers of people of different persuasions, particularly of the religion of the Church of England, which seems to gain ground, and to become more fashionable every day. A church has been lately erected at Cambridge, within sight of the College, which has greatly alarmed the Congregationalists, who consider it as the most fatal stroke that could possibly have been leveled at their religion. The building is elegant, and the minister of it (the Reverend Mr. Apthorpe) is a very amiable young man, of shining parts [abilities], great learning, and pure and engaging manners.

Arts and sciences seem to have made a greater progress here than in any other part of America. Harvard College has been founded above a hundred years; and although it is not upon a perfect plan, yet it has produced a very good effect. The arts are undeniably forwarder in Massachusetts Bay than either in Pennsylvania or New York. The public buildings are more elegant; and there is a more general turn for music, painting, and the belles-lettres.

The character of the inhabitants of this province is much improved, in comparison of what it was; but Puritanism and a spirit of persecution is not yet totally extinguished. The gentry of both sexes are hospitable and good-natured; there is an air of civility in their behavior, but it is constrained by formality and preciseness. Even the women, though easiness of carriage is peculiarly characteristic of their nature, appear here with more stiffness and reserve than in the other colonies. They are formed with symmetry, are handsome, and have fair and delicate complexions; but are said universally, and even proverbially, to have very indifferent teeth.

The lower class of the people are more in the extreme of this character; and, which is constantly mentioned as singularly peculiar to them, are impertinently curious and inquisitive. I was told of a gentleman of Philadelphia who, in traveling through the provinces of New England, having

2. Andrew Burnaby, *Travels through the Middle Settlements of North-America in the Years 1759 and 1760* (1960 reprint), pp. 100–02.

met with many impertinencies from this extraordinary turn of character, at length fell upon an expedient almost as extraordinary, to get rid of them. He had observed, when he went into an ordinary [tavern], that every individual of the family had a question or two to propose to him, relative to his history; and that, till each was satisfied, and they had conferred and compared together their information, there was no possibility of procuring any refreshment. He, therefore, the moment he went into any of these places, inquired for the master, the mistress, the sons, the daughters, the men-servants and the maid-servants; and having assembled them all together, he began in this manner. "Worthy people, I am B. F. of Philadelphia, by trade a ———, and a bachelor; I have some relations at Boston, to whom I am going to make a visit; my stay will be short, and I shall then return and follow my business, as a prudent man ought to do. This is all I know of myself, and all I can possibly inform you of; I beg therefore that you will have pity upon me and my horse, and give us both some refreshment."

3. John Adams Confesses His Prejudice (1775)

Many of the early Puritan leaders regarded themselves as the chosen people of God. Some of their descendants came to believe, with Dr. Oliver Wendell Holmes, that Boston was the "hub of the solar system." John Adams, a leader of the American Revolution and second President of the United States, reflects something of this attitude in a letter to his wife. Decide whether he is unduly provincial and what his strongest argument seems to be.

There is in the human breast a social affection which extends to our whole species, faintly indeed, but in some degree. The nation, kingdom, or community to which we belong is embraced by it more vigorously. It is stronger still towards the province to which we belong, and in which we had our birth. It is stronger and stronger as we descend to the county, town, parish, neighborhood, and family which we call our own. And here we find it often so powerful as to become partial, to blind our eyes, to darken our understandings, and pervert our wills.

It is to this infirmity in my own heart that I must perhaps attribute that local attachment, that partial fondness, that overweening prejudice in favor of New England, which I feel very often, and which, I fear, sometimes leads me to expose myself to just ridicule.

New England has, in many respects, the advantage of every other colony in America, and, indeed, of every other part of the world that I know anything of.

1. The people are purer English blood; less mixed with Scotch, Irish, Dutch, French, Danish, Swedish, etc., than any other; and descended from Englishmen, too, who left Europe in purer times than the present, and less tainted with corruption than those they left behind them.

2. The institutions in New England for the support of religion, morals,

3. C. F. Adams, ed., *Familiar Letters of John Adams and His Wife* (1876), pp. 120–21.

and decency exceed any other; obliging every parish to have a minister, and every person to go to meeting, etc.

3. The public institutions in New England for the education of youth, supporting colleges at the public expense, and obliging towns to maintain grammar schools, are not equaled, and never were, in any part of the world.

4. The division of our territory, that is, our counties, into townships; empowering towns to assemble [in town meeting], choose officers, make laws, mend roads, and twenty other things, gives every man an opportunity of showing and improving that education which he received at college or at school, and makes knowledge and dexterity at public business common.

5. Our law for the distribution of intestate estates [not bequeathed by will] occasions a frequent division of landed property, and prevents monopolies of land.

E. FOUNDING THE MIDDLE COLONIES

1. Irving Pillories Stuyvesant (1809)

Henry Hudson's famous voyage in 1609 laid the foundations for the formal establishment of New Netherland (New York) in 1624. Hotheaded Peter Stuyvesant, who had lost a leg in the service of the Dutch West India Company, became governor in 1647, following several inept predecessors. Washington Irving's classic *Knickerbocker's History of New York* (1809) is a biting satire that contains much truth. Find the aspect of Stuyvesant's character that emerges most clearly, and what it presaged for the development of a democratic tradition.

He was, in fact, the very reverse of his predecessors, being neither tranquil and inert, like Walter the Doubter [Wouter van Twiller], nor restless and fidgeting, like William the Testy [Willem Kiefft]; but a man, or rather a governor, of such uncommon activity and decision of mind that he never sought or accepted the advice of others; depending confidently upon his single head, as did the heroes of yore upon their single arms, to work his way through all difficulties and dangers. To tell the simple truth, he wanted no other requisite for a perfect statesman than to think always right, for no one can deny that he always acted as he thought. And if he wanted in correctness, he made up for it in perseverance. An excellent quality! since it is surely more dignified for a ruler to be persevering and consistent in error than wavering and contradictory in endeavoring to do what is right.

This much is certain—and it is a maxim worthy the attention of all legislators, both great and small, who stand shaking in the wind, without knowing which way to steer—a ruler who acts according to his own will is sure of pleasing himself, while he who seeks to satisfy the wishes and whims of others runs a great risk of pleasing nobody. The clock that stands still, and points steadfastly in one direction, is certain of being right twice

1. Washington Irving, *Knickerbocker's History of New York* (1897 reprint), pp. 202–03.

in the four-and-twenty hours—while others may keep going continually, and continually be going wrong.

Nor did this magnanimous virtue escape the discernment of the good people of Nieuw Nederlandts. On the contrary, so high an opinion had they of the independent mind and vigorous intellect of their new governor that they universally called him *Hardkoppig Piet,* or Peter the Headstrong— a great compliment to his understanding!

If from all that I have said thou dost not gather, worthy reader, that Peter Stuyvesant was a tough, sturdy, valiant, weather-beaten, mettlesome, obstinate, leathern-sided, lion-hearted, generous-spirited old governor, either I have written to but little purpose or thou art very dull at drawing conclusions.

2. The Misrule of "Peter the Headstrong" (1650)

Stuyvesant announced at the outset that he would be "as a father over his children." He proved to be covetous, dictatorial, and tyrannical. But he did attempt to curb drunkenness and knife-wielding in the streets, and ultimately instituted some overdue reforms. After three years of his misrule, eleven prominent members of the colony protested as follows over the head of the Dutch West India Company to the "High Mightinesses" of the Dutch government in Holland. Form conclusions as to the progress of democracy in the colony at this stage, and note to what extent this document supports Washington Irving's satire.

The fort under which we shelter ourselves, and from which as it seems all authority proceeds, lies like a mole-heap or a tottering wall, on which there is not one gun carriage or one piece of cannon in a suitable frame or on a good platform. . . .

His [Stuyvesant's] first arrival . . . was like a peacock, with great state and pomp. The declaration of His Honor that he wished to stay here only three years, with other haughty expressions, caused some to think that he would not be a father. The appellation of Lord General, and similar titles, were never before known here. Almost every day he caused proclamations of various import to be published, which were for the most part never observed, and have long since been a dead letter, except the wine excise, as that yielded a profit. . . .

At one time, after leaving the house of the minister, where the consistory had been sitting and had risen, it happened that Arnoldus Van Herdenbergh related the proceedings relative to the estate of Zeger Teunisz, and how he himself, as curator, had appealed from the sentence. Whereupon the Director [Stuyvesant], who had been sitting there with them as an elder, interrupted him and replied, "It may during my administration be contemplated to appeal, but if any one should do it, I will make him a foot shorter, and send the pieces to Holland, and let him appeal in that way." . . .

In our opinion this country will never flourish under the government of

2. *The Representation of New Netherland* (16⁻0), in New York Historical Society, *Collections,* Second Series (1849), II, 298, 308, 309, 319.

the Honorable [West India] Company, but will pass away and come to an end of itself, unless the Honorable Company be reformed. And therefore it would be more profitable for them, and better for the country, that they should be rid thereof, and their effects transported hence.

To speak specifically. Care ought to be taken of the public property, as well ecclesiastical as civil, which, in beginnings, can be illy dispensed with. It is doubtful whether divine worship will have to cease altogether in consequence of the departure of the minister and the inability of the Company.

There should be a public school, provided with at least two good masters, so that first of all in so wild a country, where there are many loose people, the youth be well taught and brought up, not only in reading and writing, but also in the knowledge and fear of the Lord. As it is now, the school is kept very irregularly, one and another keeping it according to his pleasure and as long as he thinks proper. There ought also to be an almshouse, and an orphan asylum, and other similar institutions. The minister who now goes home can give a much fuller explanation thereof. The country must also be provided with godly, honorable, and intelligent rulers who are not very indigent, or, indeed, are not too covetous. . . .

[*In 1664, fourteen years after this remonstrance, an English fleet, without firing a shot, forced a fuming Stuyvesant to surrender his flimsily fortified colony.*]

3. Penn Turns Philosopher (1682)

William Penn, best known as the persecuted Quaker who founded Pennsylvania and dealt fairly with the Indians, deserves to be remembered as a political theorist. He gave much thought to the government of his colony, and the liberal path that he followed is foreshadowed in this famous essay. Observe why the character of the people is more important than the character of their government.

For particular frames and models [of government] it will become me to say little. . . . My reasons are: First, that the age is too nice and difficult for it, there being nothing the wits of men are more busy and divided upon. . . .

Secondly, I do not find a model in the world that time, place, and some singular emergencies have not necessarily altered; nor is it easy to frame a civil government that shall serve all places alike.

Thirdly, I know what is said by the several admirers of monarchy, aristocracy, and democracy, which are the rule of one, a few, and many, and are the three common ideas of government when men discourse on that subject. But I choose to solve the controversy with this small distinction, and it belongs to all three: any government is free to the people under it (whatever be the frame) where the laws rule, and the people are a party to those laws; and more than this is tyranny, oligarchy, and confusion.

3. *Minutes of the Provincial Council of Pennsylvania* . . . (1852), I, 30–31.

But lastly, when all is said, there is hardly one frame of government in the world so ill designed by its first founders that in good hands would not do well enough. . . . Governments, like clocks, go from the motions men give them, and as governments are made and moved by men, so by them they are ruined too. Wherefore governments rather depend upon men than men upon governments. Let men be good, and the government cannot be bad; if it be ill, they will cure it. But if men be bad, let the government be never so good, they will endeavor to warp and spoil to their turn.

4. Early Settlers in Pennsylvania (1682)

Richard Townsend, a Quaker who had come from England with William Penn in the ship *Welcome*, remembered through the haze of the years the founding of the colony. He set down his recollections about 1727, when eighty-three years of age. Note what peculiar advantages this colony had that the others had not enjoyed; also other distinctive features.

At our arrival [in Pennsylvania] we found it a wilderness. The chief inhabitants were Indians, and some Swedes, who received us in a friendly manner. And though there was a great number of us, the good hand of Providence was seen in a particular manner, in that provisions were found for us, by the Swedes and Indians, at very reasonable rates, as well as brought from divers other parts that were inhabited before.

Our first concern was to keep up and maintain our religious worship; and, in order thereunto, we had several meetings in the houses of the inhabitants; and one boarded meeting-house was set up, where the city was to be, near Delaware. And, as we had nothing but love and good will in our hearts, one to another, we had very comfortable meetings from time to time; and after our meeting was over, we assisted each other in building little houses, for our shelter.

After some time I set up a mill, on Chester creek, which I brought ready framed from London; which served for grinding of corn and sawing of boards, and was of great use to us. Besides, I with Joshua Tittery made a net and caught great quantities of fish, which supplied ourselves and many others; so that, notwithstanding it was thought near three thousand persons came in the first year, we were so providentially provided for that we could buy a deer for about two shillings, and a large turkey for about one shilling, and Indian corn for about two shillings and sixpence per bushel.

And, as our worthy Proprietor [Penn] treated the Indians with extraordinary humanity, they became very civil and loving to us, and brought in abundance of venison. As in other countries the Indians were exasperated by hard treatment, which hath been the foundation of much bloodshed, so the contrary treatment here hath produced their love and affection.

About a year after our arrival, there came in about twenty families from high and low Germany, of religious, good people; who settled about six

4. Robert Proud, *The History of Pennsylvania* ... (1797). I, 229–31.

miles from Philadelphia, and called the place Germantown. The country continually increasing, people began to spread themselves further back. . . .

About the time in which Germantown was laid out, I settled upon my tract of land, which I had purchased of the Proprietor in England, about a mile from thence; where I set up a house and a corn mill, which was very useful to the country for several miles round. But there not being plenty of horses, people generally brought their corn on their backs many miles. . . .

As people began to spread and improve their lands, the country became more fruitful; so that those who came after us were plentifully supplied; and with what we abounded we began a small trade abroad. And as Philadelphia increased, vessels were built, and many employed. Both country and trade have been wonderfully increasing to this day; so that, from a wilderness, the Lord, by his good hand of Providence, hath made it a fruitful field. . . .

THOUGHT PROVOKERS

1. In regard to the Plymouth Pilgrims, what support does one find for this statement: "The cowards never started; the weak died on the way"? An English writer claims that the brave ones were those who stayed at home and fought the authorities for religious freedom instead of fleeing from them. Comment.

2. How can one justify the so-called intolerance of the Puritans, especially since they were the victims of intolerance at home? What light does this statement of Pope Leo XIII in 1885 throw on the problem: "The equal toleration of all religions . . . is the same thing as atheism"? A recent writer claims that the Quakers developed a martyrdom complex and actually enjoyed tortures. Comment.

3. It has been said that the Puritans were misguided in following Biblical law, which did not fit conditions of the 17th Century. Comment. Among the Bantu natives of South Africa there is this proverb: "At first we had the land and the white man had the Bible. Now we have the Bible and the white man has the land." Comment with reference to North America.

4. What is the essential difference between liberty and license? Account for the decline of austerity in New England by 1760.

5. In which of the colonies from Pennsylvania to Massachusetts would you have preferred to be a settler? Explain fully why.

FURTHER EXPLORATION

General: C. M. Andrews, *The Colonial Period of American History* (4 vols., 1934–1938). **Plymouth:** Arthur Lord, *Plymouth and the Pilgrims* (1920). **Bay Colony:** S. E. Morison, *Builders of the Bay Colony* (1930); T. J. Wertenbaker, *The Puritan Oligarchy* (1947); S. E. Morison, *The Puritan Pronaos* (1936). **Biblical Law:** L. B. Wright, *The Cultural Life of the American Colonies, 1607–1763* (1957). Perry Miller, *The New England Mind* (1939); M. L. Starkey, *The Devil in Massachusetts* (1949). **Developing People:** S. H. Brockunier, *The Irrepressible Democrat: Roger Williams* (1940). **Middle Colonies:** T. J. Wertenbaker, *The Founding of American Civilization: The Middle Colonies* (1938). **Recent:** E. B. Bronner, *William Penn's "Holy Experiment"* (1962).

Chapter *3*

The Clash between France and England

*The most momentous and far-reaching question ever brought to issue
on this continent was: Shall France remain here or shall she not?*

FRANCIS PARKMAN, 1884

PROLOGUE: French exploration of North America penetrated deeply into
Canada and the Mississippi Valley. At first there was elbow room for both the
French and the English, but wars that were ignited in Europe spread to the New
World and involved the colonials of both nations in a series of bloody clashes:
King William's War (1689–1697), Queen Anne's War (1702–1713), King
George's War (1744–1748), and the French and Indian War (1754–1763).
Continuing rivalry between the English colonists and the French traders gradu-
ally became intense, and the showdown came in 1754 in the wilds of the Ohio
Valley, where young George Washington's tiny army of Virginians was forced
to surrender. The French and Indian War (called the Seven Years' War in
Europe), thus begun inauspiciously for the British, continued disastrously for
them. In 1755 General Braddock's army was almost wiped out near what is now
Pittsburgh. At length a new Prime Minister, William Pitt, infused life into the
flagging cause. In 1759 Quebec fell to the heroic Wolfe, and the next year
Montreal capitulated. By the Treaty of 1763 France was completely and permanently ejected from the mainland of North America.

A. THE DEVELOPMENT OF NEW FRANCE

1. Father Jogues Endures Tortures (1642)

The Catholic (Jesuit) missionaries in French Canada, among other activities,
established a mission among the 2000 or so pestilence-ridden Huron Indians of the
Lake Huron area. Father Isaac Jogues, returning from Quebec to this spiritual vine-
yard with two French associates and a small band of Huron Indians, was captured
in 1642 by a hostile Mohawk (Iroquois) raiding party. He here relates his harrowing
experiences to his superiors. Consider how deeply his conversion of the savages penetrated, and how this timid, tender, and scholarly man could endure such hardships.
Father Jogues has just been captured and one of his French associates (Couture) is
being tortured as this part of the narrative begins.

When I beheld him [Couture] thus bound and naked, I could not contain
myself, but, leaving my keepers, rushed through the midst of the savages
who had brought him; embraced him most tenderly; exhorted him to offer
all this to God for himself, and those at whose hands he suffered. They at
first looked on in wonder at my proceeding; then, as if recollecting themselves, and gathering all their rage, they fell upon me, and with their fists,

---

1. New York Historical Society, *Collections*, Second Series (1857), III, pt. 1, pp. 177–204,
passim.

thongs, and clubs beat me till I fell senseless. Two of them then dragged
me back to where I had been before; and scarcely had I begun to breathe
when some others, attacking me, tore out, by biting, almost all my nails,
and crunched my two forefingers with their teeth, giving me intense pain.
The same was done to René Goupil. . . .

MUTILATED FATHER JOGUES

Jesuit Relations, 1898, vol. XXIII.

We were twenty-two; three had
been killed. By the favor of God our
sufferings on that march, which lasted
thirteen days, were indeed great:
hunger and heat and menaces, the
savage fury of the Indians, the intense
pain of our untended and now putre-
fying wounds, which actually swarmed
with worms. No trial, however, came
harder upon me than to see them
[the Iroquois] five or six days after
approach us, jaded with the march,
and, in cold blood, with minds in no
wise excited by passion, pluck out
our hair and beard and drive their
[finger]nails, which are always very
sharp, deep into parts most tender
and sensitive to the slighest impression.

But this was outward; my internal sufferings affected me still more when
I beheld that funeral procession of doomed [Indian] Christians pass before
my eyes, among them five old converts, the main pillars of the infant
Huron Church. Indeed I ingenuously admit that I was again and again
unable to withhold my tears, mourning over their lot and that of my other
companions, and full of anxious solicitude for the future. For I beheld the
way to the Christian faith closed by these Iroquois on the Hurons and
countless other nations, unless they were checked by some seasonable dispensation of Divine Providence. . . .

At last, on the eve of the Assumption of the Blessed Virgin, we reached
the first village of the Iroquois. I thank our Lord Jesus Christ that on the
day when the whole Christian world exults in the glory of his Mother's
Assumption into heaven, he called us to some small share and fellowship
of his sufferings and cross. Indeed we had, during the journey, always
foreseen that it would be a sad and bitter day for us. It would have been
easy for René and me to escape that day and the flames, for, being often
unbound and at a distance from our guards, we might, in the darkness of
night, have struck off from the road, and even though we should never
reach our countrymen, we would at least meet a less cruel death in the
woods. He constantly refused to do this, and I was resolved to suffer all
that could befall me, rather than forsake in death Frenchmen and Christian
Hurons, depriving them of the consolation which a priest can afford. . . .

[Father Jogues endured further tortures, including the cutting off of one thumb, but even so he managed quietly to baptize several Indian children, "two with raindrops gathered from the leaves of a stalk of Indian corn given us to chew . . . ." He witnessed the brutal tomahawking of his French colleague René Goupil, and was made a slave by his captors.]

Mindful of the character imposed upon me by God, I began with modesty to discourse with them [Iroquois] of the adoration of one only God; of the observance of his commandments; of heaven, hell, and the other mysteries of our faith, as fully as I was able. At first, indeed, they listened; but when they saw me constantly recur to these things, and especially when the chase did not meet with the desired success, then they declared that I was a demon who caused them to take so little game. . . .

How often on the stately trees of the forest did I carve the most sacred name of Jesus, that, seeing it, the demons might fly, who tremble when they hear it! How often, too, did I not strip off the bark, to form the most holy cross of the Lord, that the foe might fly before it. . . .

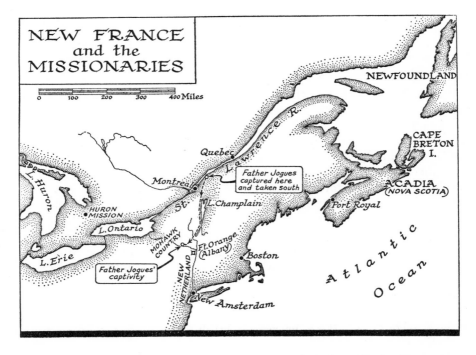

Although I could in all probability escape either through the Europeans or the Indian nations around us did I wish to fly, yet on this cross to which our Lord has nailed me, beside himself, am I resolved by his grace to live and die. For who in my absence would console the French captives? who absolve the penitent? who remind the christened Huron of his duty? who instruct the prisoners constantly brought in? who baptize them dying, encourage them in their torments? who cleanse the infants in the saving

waters? who provide for the salvation of the dying adult, the instruction
of those in health? . . .

[*After a year of slavery in central New York, Father Jogues escaped to the
Dutch in New Netherland, and then sailed to France, where he was greeted as
one raised from the dead. The Queen summoned him to an audience, and the
Pope, as a special dispensation, granted him permission to celebrate mass with
mutilated hands. Eager to continue his work of conversion among the unregen-
erate Mohawks, he returned in 1646. He was promptly tortured, then toma-
hawked. In 1930 Pope Pius XI canonized him.*]

2. A Swede Depicts the Indian Trade (1749)

Peter Kalm, a noted Swedish botanist then in his early thirties, was sent on a
scientific expedition to America in 1748–1751. His primary purpose was to discover
seeds and plants that could profitably be adapted to the rigorous climate of Sweden.
Alert, open-minded, and energetic, he recorded in his journal a gold mine of information, ranging in subject from the vocal cords of bullfrogs to the shortness of women's
skirts in Canada. He found in Benjamin Franklin a kindred scientific spirit, and
while in New Jersey he not only occupied the pulpit of a deceased Swedish pastor
but married his widow as well. In Kalm's account of the fur trade in Canada, note
the most surprising aspects of the Indian's sense of values, the most significant impact
of the white man on Indian culture, and the effects of international rivalry on the
red man.

Indian Trade. The French in Canada carry on a great trade with the
Indians; and though it was formerly the only trade of this extensive country,
its inhabitants were considerably enriched by it. At present they have,
besides the Indian goods, several other articles which are exported. The
Indians in this neighborhood [Montreal], who go hunting in winter like
the other Indian nations, commonly bring their furs and skins to sell in the
neighboring French towns; however, this is not sufficient. The red men
who live at a greater distance never come to Canada at all; and lest they
should bring their goods to the English, or the English go to them, the
French are obliged to undertake journeys and purchase the Indian goods
in the country of the natives. This trade is carried on chiefly at Montreal,
and a great number of young and old men every year undertake long and
troublesome voyages for that purpose, carrying with them such goods as
they know the Indians like and want. It is not necessary to take money on
such a journey, as the Indians do not value it; and indeed I think the
French who go on these journeys scarcely ever take a sol or penny
with them.

Goods Sold to the Natives. I will now enumerate the chief goods which
the French carry with them for this trade, and which have a good sale
among the Indians:

1. *Muskets, powder, shot, and balls.* The Europeans have taught the
Indians in their neighborhood the use of firearms, and so they have laid

2. A. B. Benson, ed., *The America of 1750; Peter Kalm's Travels in North America* (1937),
II, 518–22. By permission of the editor-translator.

aside their bows and arrows, which were formerly their only arms, and use muskets. If the Europeans should now refuse to supply the natives with muskets, they would starve to death, as almost all their food consists of the flesh of the animals which they hunt; or they would be irritated to such a degree as to attack the colonists. The savages have hitherto never tried to make muskets or similar firearms, and their great indolence does not even allow them to mend those muskets which they have. They leave this entirely to the settlers.

When the Europeans came into North America, they were very careful not to give the Indians any firearms. But in the wars between the French and English, each party gave their Indian allies firearms in order to weaken the force of the enemy. The French lay the blame upon the Dutch settlers in Albany, saying that the latter began in 1642 to give their Indians firearms, and taught the use of them in order to weaken the French. The inhabitants of Albany, on the contrary, assert that the French first introduced this custom, as they would have been too weak to resist the combined force of the Dutch and English in the colonies. Be this as it may, it is certain that the Indians buy muskets from the white men, and know at present better how to make use of them than some of their teachers. It is likewise certain that the colonists gain considerably by their trade in muskets and ammunition.

2. a. *Pieces of white cloth,* or of a coarse uncut material. The Indians constantly wear such cloth, wrapping it round their bodies. Sometimes they hang it over their shoulders; in warm weather they fasten the pieces round the middle; and in cold weather they put them over the head. Both their men and women wear these pieces of cloth, which have commonly several blue or red stripes on the edge.

b. *Blue or red cloth.* Of this the Indian women make their skirts, which reach only to their knees. They generally choose the blue color.

c. *Shirts and shifts of linen.* As soon as an Indian, either man or woman, has put on a shirt, he (or she) never washes it or strips it off till it is entirely worn out.

d. *Pieces of cloth,* which they wrap round their legs instead of stockings, like the Russians.

3. *Hatchets, knives, scissors, needles, and flint.* These articles are now common among the Indians. They all get these tools from the Europeans, and consider the hatchets and knives much better than those which they formerly made of stone and bone. The stone hatchets of the ancient Indians are very rare in Canada.

4. *Kettles of copper or brass,* sometimes tinned on the inside. In these the Indians now boil all their meat, and they produce a very large demand for this ware. They formerly made use of earthen or wooden pots, into which they poured water, or whatever else they wanted to boil, and threw in red hot stones to make it boil. They do not want iron boilers because they cannot be easily carried on their continual journeys, and would not bear such falls and knocks as their kettles are subject to.

5. *Earrings* of different sizes, commonly of brass, and sometimes of tin. They are worn by both men and women, though the use of them is not general.

6. *Cinnabar.* With this they paint their face, shirt, and several parts of the body. They formerly made use of a reddish earth, which is to be found in the country; but, as the Europeans brought them vermilion, they thought nothing was comparable to it in color. Many persons told me that they had heard their fathers mention that the first Frenchmen who came over here got a heap of furs for three times as much cinnabar as would lie on the tip of a knife.

7. *Verdigris,* to paint their faces green. For the black color they make use of the soot off the bottom of their kettles, and daub the whole face with it.

CANADIAN DRESSED FOR WINTER WARFARE

B. de la Potherie, *Histoire de l'Amérique Septentrionale,* 1722, Vol. I. Boston Public Library.

8. *Looking glasses.* The Indians like these very much and use them chiefly when they wish to paint themselves. The men constantly carry their looking glasses with them on all their journeys; but the women do not. The men, upon the whole, are more fond of dressing than the women.

9. *Burning glasses.* These are excellent utensils in the opinion of the Indians because they serve to light the pipe without any trouble, which pleases an indolent Indian very much.

10. *Tobacco* is bought by the northern Indians, in whose country it will not grow. The southern Indians always plant as much of it as they want for their own consumption. Tobacco has a great sale among the northern Indians, and it has been observed that the further they live to the northward, the more tobacco they smoke.

11. *Wampum,* or as it is here called, *porcelain.* It is made of a particular kind of shell and turned into little short cylindrical beads, and serves the Indians for money and ornament.

12. *Glass beads,* of a small size, white or other colors. The Indian women know how to fasten them in their ribbons, bags, and clothes.

13. *Brass and steel wire,* for several kinds of work.

14. *Brandy,* which the Indians value above all other goods that can be brought them; nor have they anything, though ever so dear to them, which they would not give away for this liquor. But on account of the many irregularities which are caused by the use of brandy, the sale of it has been prohibited under severe penalties; however, they do not always pay implicit obedience to this order.

These are the chief goods which the French carry to the Indians and they do a good business among them. . . .

It is inconceivable what hardships the people in Canada must undergo on their hunting journeys. Sometimes they must carry their goods a great way by land. Frequently they are abused by the Indians, and sometimes they are killed by them. They often suffer hunger, thirst, heat, and cold, and are bitten by gnats, and exposed to the bites of poisonous snakes and other dangerous animals and insects. These destroy a great part of the youth in Canada, and prevent the people from growing old. By this means, however, they become such brave soldiers, and so inured to fatigue, that none of them fears danger or hardships. Many of them settle among the Indians far from Canada, marry Indian women, and never come back again.

B. PROBLEMS OF COLONIAL DEFENSE

1. Dutch Disloyalty in New York (1749)

The Swedish botanist Peter Kalm, still seeking seeds and plants for his homeland, left Pennsylvania and New Jersey for upper New York in 1749. There he picked up some ugly reports about the Dutch settlers in that area. Observe the light they shed on colonial unity during the French wars and the prospects of forming a firm union of the colonies in the future.

The behavior of the [Dutch] inhabitants of Albany during . . . [King George's War] has, among several other causes, contributed to make them the object of hatred in all the British colonies, but more especially in New England. For at the beginning of that war, when the Indians of both parties had received orders to commence hostilities, the French engaged theirs to attack the inhabitants of New England, which they faithfully executed, killing everybody they met with, and carrying off whatever they found. During this time the people of Albany remained neutral, and carried on a great trade with the very Indians who murdered the inhabitants of New England.

Articles such as silver spoons, bowls, cups, etc., of which the Indians robbed the houses in New England, were carried to Albany for sale. The people of that town bought up these silver vessels, though the names of the owners were engraved on many of them, and encouraged the Indians to get more of them, promising to pay them well, and whatever they would demand. This was afterwards interpreted by the inhabitants of New Eng-

1. *Ibid.,* I, 345–46.

land to mean that the colonists of Albany encouraged the Indians to kill more of the New England people, who were in a manner their brothers, and who were subjects of the same crown. Upon the first news of this behavior, which the Indians themselves spread in New England, the inhabitants of the latter province were greatly incensed, and threatened that the first step they would take in another war would be to burn Albany and the adjacent parts.

In the present [recent] war it will sufficiently appear how backward the other British provinces in America are in assisting Albany, and the neighboring places, in case of an attack from the French or Indians. The hatred which the English bear against the people at Albany is very great, but that of the Albanians against the English is carried to a ten times higher degree. This hatred has subsisted ever since the time when the English conquered this section [from Holland], and is not yet extinguished, though they could never have gotten larger advantages under the Dutch government than they have obtained under that of the English. For, in a manner, their privileges are greater than those of Englishmen themselves.

2. The Influence of the French Menace (1748)

While still in New York, Peter Kalm recorded certain observations on the effects of the French menace in Canada on the English colonials. Account for colonial dissatisfaction and the view that the British government did not really want to dispossess the French.

The French in Canada, who are but an unimportant body in comparison with the English in America, have by this position of affairs been able to obtain great advantages in times of war. For if we judge from the number and power of the English, it would seem very easy for them to get the better of the French in America. It is, however, of great advantage to the crown of England that the North American colonies are near a country under the government of the French, like Canada. There is reason to believe that the King never was earnest in his attempts to expel the French from their possessions there; though it might have been done with little difficulty. For the English colonies in this part of the world have increased so much in their number of inhabitants, and in their riches, that they almost vie with Old England.

Now in order to keep up the authority and trade of their mother country, and to answer several other purposes, they are forbidden to establish new manufactures, which would turn to the disadvantage of the British commerce. They are not allowed to dig for any gold or silver, unless they send it to England immediately. They have not the liberty of trading with any parts that do not belong to the British dominion, excepting a few places. Nor are foreigners allowed to trade with the English colonies of North America.

These and some other restrictions occasion the inhabitants of the English

2. *Ibid.,* I, 139–40.

colonies to grow less tender for their mother country. This coldness is kept up by the many foreigners, such as Germans, Dutch, and French, who live among the English and have no particular attachment to Old England. Add to this also that many people can never be contented with their possessions, though they be ever so large. They will always be desirous of getting more, and of enjoying the pleasure which arises from a change. Their extraordinary liberty and their luxury often lead them to unrestricted acts of selfish and arbitrary nature.

I have been told by Englishmen, and not only by such as were born in America but also by those who came from Europe, that the English colonies in North America, in the space of thirty or fifty years, would be able to form a state by themselves entirely independent of Old England. But as the whole country which lies along the seashore is unguarded, and on the land side is harassed by the French, these dangerous neighbors in times of war are sufficient to prevent the connection of the colonies with their mother country from being quite broken off. The English government has therefore sufficient reason to consider means of keeping the colonies in due submission.

C. THE FRENCH AND INDIAN WAR

1. Franklin Characterizes General Braddock (1755)

Once the French and Indian War had begun, the British aimed their main thrust of 1755 at Fort Duquesne, on the present site of Pittsburgh. Their commander was General Edward Braddock, a sixty-two-year-old veteran of European battlefields. Transportation over uncut roads from Virginia was but one of the many difficulties facing the invaders, and Benjamin Franklin won laurels by rounding up 150 wagons. Within about ten miles of Fort Duquesne, Braddock's vanguard of some 1200 officers and men encountered an advancing force of about 250 French and 600 Indians. Both sides were surprised, but the French, at first driven back, rallied and attacked the flanks of the crowded Redcoats from nearby ravines. In Franklin's account, written some sixteen years after the event, determine who or what was responsible for the disaster.

This general [Braddock] was, I think, a brave man, and might probably have made a figure as a good officer in some European war. But he had too much self-confidence, too high an opinion of the validity of regular troops, and too mean a one of both Americans and Indians. George Croghan, our Indian interpreter, joined him on his march with one hundred of those people, who might have been of great use to his army as guides, scouts, etc., if he had treated them kindly. But he slighted and neglected them, and they gradually left him.

In conversation with him one day, he was giving me some account of his intended progress. "After taking Fort Duquesne," says he, "I am to proceed to [Fort] Niagara; and, having taken that, to [Fort] Frontenac, if the season will allow time; and I suppose it will, for Duquesne can hardly detain me

1. John Bigelow, ed., *Autobiography of Benjamin Franklin* (1868), pp. 309–13.

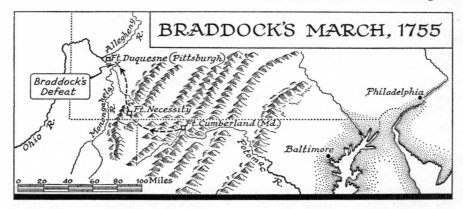

BRADDOCK'S MARCH, 1755

above three or four days; and then I see nothing that can obstruct my march to Niagara."

Having before revolved in my mind the long line his army must make in their march by a very narrow road, to be cut for them through the woods and bushes, and also what I had read of a former defeat of 1500 French who invaded the Iroquois country, I had conceived some doubts and some fears for the event of the campaign. But I ventured only to say, "To be sure, sir, if you arrive well before Duquesne, with these fine troops, so well provided with artillery, that place, not yet completely fortified, and as we hear with no very strong garrison, can probably make but a short resistance. The only danger I apprehend of obstruction to your march is from ambuscades of Indians, who, by constant practice, are dexterous in laying and executing them; and the slender line, near four miles long, which your army must make, may expose it to be attacked by surprise in its flanks, and to be cut like a thread into several pieces, which, from their distance, cannot come up in time to support each other."

He smiled at my ignorance, and replied, "These savages may, indeed, be a formidable enemy to your raw American militia, but upon the King's regular and disciplined troops, sir, it is impossible they should make any impression." I was conscious of an impropriety in my disputing with a military man in matters of his profession, and said no more.

The enemy, however, did not take the advantage of his army which I apprehended its long line of march exposed it to, but let it advance without interruption till within nine miles of the place; and then, when more in a body (for it had just passed a river, where the front had halted till all were come over), and in a more open part of the woods than any it had passed, attacked its advanced guard by a heavy fire from behind trees and bushes, which was the first intelligence the General had of an enemy's being near him. This guard being disordered, the General hurried the troops up to their assistance, which was done in great confusion, through wagons, baggage, and cattle; and presently the fire came upon their flank. The officers, being on horseback, were more easily distinguished, picked out as marks, and fell very fast; and the soldiers were crowded together in a huddle, having or hearing no orders, and standing to be shot at till two-thirds of them were killed; and then, being seized with a panic, the whole fled with precipitation.

The wagoners took each a horse out of his team and scampered. Their example was immediately followed by others; so that all the wagons, provisions, artillery, and stores were left to the enemy. The General, being wounded, was brought off with difficulty; his secretary, Mr. Shirley, was killed by his side; and out of 86 officers, 63 were killed or wounded, and 714 men killed out of 1100. . . .

Captain Orme, who was one of the General's aides-de-camp, and, being grievously wounded, was brought off with him and continued with him to his death, which happened in a few days, told me that he was totally silent all the first day, and at night only said, "Who would have thought it?" That he was silent again the following day, saying only at last, "We shall better know how to deal with them another time"; and died in a few minutes after.

2. Washington Reassures His Mother (1755)

George Washington, then only twenty-three, served as an aide-de-camp to General Braddock, who formed a strong attachment for him. The efforts of the young Virginian, who miraculously survived the disaster, were heroic. Dr. Stanley Pargellis concluded in 1936 that the British troops sustained a murderous fire from an unseen foe for two hours before breaking, and that they were led into a hopeless situation because their officers, including Braddock, ignored elementary precautions outlined by the European military manuals. In the light of this recent scholarship decide whether Washington, in the following letter to his mother (written on July 18, nine days after the battle), is fair in all his criticisms.

Honored Madam: As I doubt not but you have heard of our defeat, and perhaps have it represented in a worse light (if possible) than it deserves, I have taken this earliest opportunity to give you some account of the engagement, as it happened within seven miles of the French fort, on Wednesday the 9th instant.

We marched on to that place without any considerable loss, having only now and then a straggler picked up by the French scouting Indians. When we came here, we were attacked by a body of French and Indians whose number (I am certain) did not exceed 300 men; ours consisted of about 1300 well-armed troops, chiefly of the English soldiers, who were struck with such a panic that they behaved with more cowardice than it is possible to conceive. The officers behaved gallantly in order to encourage their men, for which they suffered greatly; there being near 60 killed and wounded; a large proportion out of the number we had!

The Virginia troops showed a good deal of bravery, and were near all killed; for I believe out of three companies that were there, there is scarce

2. J. C. Fitzpatrick, ed., *The Writings of George Washington* (1931), I, 150–52. See also Stanley Pargellis, "Braddock's Defeat," *American Historical Review*, XLI (1936), 253–69.

30 men left alive. Capt. Peyrouny and all his officers down to a corporal was killed. Capt. Polson shared near as hard a fate; for only one of his was left. In short, the dastardly behavior of those they call regulars exposed all others that were inclined to do their duty to almost certain death. And at last, in despite of all the efforts of the officers to the contrary, they broke and run as sheep pursued by dogs; and it was impossible to rally them.

The General was wounded, of which he died three days after. Sir Peter Halkett was killed in the field, where died many other brave officers. I luckily escaped without a wound, though I had four bullets through my coat, and two horses shot under me. Captains Orme and Morris, two of the General's aides-de-camp, were wounded early in the engagement, which rendered the duty hard upon me, as I was the only person then left to distribute the General's orders, which I was scarcely able to do, as I was not half recovered from a violent illness that confined me to my bed and a wagon for above ten days. I am still in a weak and feeble condition, which induces me to halt here [Fort Cumberland] two or three days in hopes of recovering a little strength, to enable me to proceed homewards; from whence I fear I shall not be able to stir till towards September. . . .

3. A Frenchman Reports Braddock's Defeat (1755)

An anonymous Frenchman, presumably stationed at Fort Duquesne, sent the fol lowing report of the battle home to Paris. Note in what important respects it differs from the Franklin and Washington accounts just given. Where the three versions conflict, determine which one is to be accorded the most credence and why. Observe what light this report casts on the legend that Braddock was ambushed.

M. de Contrecoeur, captain of infantry, Commandant of Fort Duquesne, on the Ohio, having been informed that the English were taking up arms in Virginia for the purpose of coming to attack him, was advised, shortly afterwards, that they were on the march. He dispatched scouts, who reported to him faithfully their progress. On the 7th instant he was advised that their army, consisting of 3000 regulars from Old England, were within six leagues [eighteen miles] of this fort.

That officer employed the next day in making his arrangements; and on the 9th detached M. de Beaujeu, seconded by Messrs. Dumas and de Lignery, all three captains, together with 4 lieutenants, 6 ensigns, 20 cadets, 100 soldiers, 100 Canadians, and 600 Indians, with orders to lie in ambush at a favorable spot, which he had reconnoitred the previous evening. The detachment, before it could reach its place of destination, found itself in presence of the enemy within three leagues of that fort.

M. de Beaujeu, finding his ambush had failed, decided on an attack. This he made with so much vigor as to astonish the enemy, who were waiting for us in the best possible order; but their artillery, loaded with grape[shot] . . . , having opened its fire, our men gave way in turn. The

3. E. B. O'Callaghan, ed., *Documents Relative to the Colonial History of the State of New York* (1858), X, 303–04.

Indians, also frightened by the report of the cannon, rather than by any damage it could inflict, began to yield, when M. de Beaujeu was killed.

M. Dumas began to encourage his detachment. He ordered the officers in command of the Indians to spread themselves along the wings so as to take the enemy in flank, whilst he, M. de Lignery, and the other officers who led the French, were attacking them in front. This order was executed so promptly that the enemy, who were already shouting their "Long live the King," thought now only of defending themselves.

The fight was obstinate on both sides and success long doubtful; but the enemy at last gave way. Efforts were made, in vain, to introduce some sort of order in their retreat. The whoop of the Indians, which echoed through the forest, struck terror into the hearts of the entire enemy. The rout was complete. We remained in possession of the field with six brass twelves and sixes [cannon], four howitz-carriages of fifty, eleven small royal grenade mortars, all their ammunition, and, generally, their entire baggage.

Some deserters, who have come in since, have told us that we had been engaged with only 2000 men, the remainder of the army being four leagues further off. These same deserters have informed us that the enemy were retreating to Virginia, and some scouts, sent as far as the height of land, have confirmed this by reporting that the thousand men who were not engaged had been equally panic-stricken, and abandoned both provisions and ammunition on the way. On this intelligence, a detachment was dispatched after them, which destroyed and burnt everything that could be found.

The enemy have left more than 1000 men on the field of battle. They have lost a great portion of the artillery and ammunition, provisions, as also their general, whose name was Mr. Braddock, and almost all their officers. We have had 3 officers killed; 2 officers and 2 cadets wounded. Such a victory, so entirely unexpected, seeing the inequality of the forces, is the fruit of M. Dumas' experience, and of the activity and valor of the officers under his command.

4. Parkman Analyzes the Conflict (1884)

Francis Parkman (1823–1893), the partially blind and nervously afflicted Boston historian, produced the classic multi-volume epic of the struggle between England and France for supremacy in North America. Determined to absorb local color, he ranged widely in canoe and on foot over the region about which he wrote. Although best known for his descriptive powers, his analytical talents are brilliantly revealed in these observations following his account of the surrender of Montreal, the last French stronghold, in 1760. Ascertain the main reason why the French held out as long as they did, and why the English seemed inept.

Half the continent had changed hands at the scratch of a pen. Governor Bernard, of Massachusetts, proclaimed a day of thanksgiving for the great

4. Francis Parkman, *Montcalm and Wolfe* (1884; 1899 reprint), II, 391–96, *passim*.

event, and the Boston newspapers recount how the occasion was celebrated with a parade of the cadets and other volunteer corps, a grand dinner in Faneuil Hall, music, bonfires, illuminations, firing of cannon, and, above all, by sermons in every church of the province; for the heart of early New England always found voice through her pulpits. . . .

On the American continent the war was ended, and the British colonists breathed for a space, as they drifted unwittingly towards a deadlier strife. They had learned hard and useful lessons. Their mutual jealousies and disputes, the quarrels of their governors and assemblies, the want of any general military organization, and the absence, in most of them, of military habits, joined to narrow views of their own interest, had unfitted them to the last degree for carrying on offensive war. Nor were the British troops sent for their support remarkable in the beginning for good discipline or efficient command.

When hostilities broke out, the army of Great Britain was so small as to be hardly worth the name. A new one had to be created; and thus the inexperienced [Governor] Shirley [of Massachusetts] and the incompetent [Earl of] Loudon, with the futile [Prime Minister] Newcastle behind them, had, besides their own incapacity, the disadvantage of raw troops and half-formed officers; while against them stood an enemy who, though weak in numbers, was strong in a centralized military organization, skillful leaders armed with untrammeled and absolute authority, practiced soldiers, and a population not only brave, but in good part inured to war.

The nature of the country was another cause that helped to protract the contest. "Geography," says Von Moltke, "is three-fourths of military science"; and never was the truth of his words more fully exemplified. Canada was fortified with vast outworks of defense in the savage forests, marshes, and mountains that encompassed her, where the thoroughfares were streams choked with fallen trees and obstructed by cataracts. Never was the problem of moving troops, encumbered with baggage and artillery, a more difficult one. The question was less how to fight the enemy than how to get at him. If a few practicable roads had crossed this broad tract of wilderness, the war would have been shortened and its character changed.

From these and other reasons, the numerical superiority of the English was to some extent made unavailing. This superiority, though exaggerated by French writers, was nevertheless immense, if estimated by the number of men called to arms. But only a part of these could be employed in offensive operations. The rest garrisoned forts and blockhouses and guarded the far reach of frontier from Nova Scotia to South Carolina, where a wily enemy, silent and secret as fate, choosing their own time and place of attack, and striking unawares at every unguarded spot, compelled thousands of men, scattered at countless points of defense, to keep unceasing watch against a few hundred savage marauders. Full half the levies of the colonies, and many of the regulars, were used in service of this kind.

In actual encounters the advantage of numbers was often with the French, through the comparative ease with which they could concentrate their forces at a given point. Of the ten considerable sieges or battles of the war, five, besides the great bush-fight in which the Indians defeated Braddock, were victories for France; and in four of these—Oswego, Fort William Henry, Montmorenci, and Ste.-Foy—the odds were greatly on her side.

Yet in this most picturesque and dramatic of American wars, there is nothing more noteworthy than the skill with which the French and Canadian leaders used their advantages; the indomitable spirit with which, slighted and abandoned as they were, they grappled with prodigious difficulties; and the courage with which they were seconded by regulars and militia alike. In spite of occasional lapses, the defense of Canada deserves a tribute of admiration.

THE COLONIAL BIRD READY TO FLY FROM ITS CAGE
Engraving by Paul Revere, Boston *Gazette*, 1770. American Antiquarian Society.

D. A NEW RESTLESSNESS

1. Burnaby Scoffs at Colonial Unity (1760)

Andrew Burnaby, the broad-minded Church of England clergyman who traveled extensively in the colonies during the closing months of the French and Indian War, recorded many penetrating observations. But he scoffed at the idea that the Americans would one day form a mighty nation or even come together in a voluntary union. Locate those of his arguments that were most farfetched; those that were borne out when the colonies did attempt to form one nation.

An idea, strange as it is visionary, has entered into the minds of the generality of mankind, that empire is traveling westward; and everyone is looking forward with eager and impatient expectation to that destined moment when America is to give law to the rest of the world. But if ever an idea was illusory and fallacious, I will venture to predict that this will be so.

1. Andrew Burnaby, *Travels through the Middle Settlements in North-America in the Years 1759 and 1760* (1960 reprint), pp. 110–14.

America is formed for happiness, but not for empire. In a course of 1200 miles I did not see a single object that solicited charity. But I saw insuperable causes of weakness, which will necessarily prevent its being a potent state. . . .

The Southern colonies have so many inherent causes of weakness that they never can possess any real strength. The climate operates very powerfully upon them, and renders them indolent, inactive, and unenterprising; this is visible in every line of their character. I myself have been a spectator —and it is not an uncommon sight—of a man in the vigor of life, lying upon a couch, and a female slave standing over him, wafting off the flies, and fanning him, while he took his repose. . . .

The mode of cultivation by slavery is another insurmountable cause of weakness. The number of Negroes in the Southern colonies is upon the whole nearly equal, if not superior, to that of the white men; and they propagate and increase even faster. Their condition is truly pitiable: their labor excessively hard, their diet poor and scanty, their treatment cruel and oppressive; they cannot therefore but be a subject of terror to those who so unhumanly tyrannize over them.

The Indians near the frontiers are a still farther formidable cause of subjection. The southern Indians are numerous, and are governed by a sounder policy than formerly; experience has taught them wisdom. They never make war with the colonists without carrying terror and devastation along with them. They sometimes break up entire counties together. Such is the state of the Southern colonies.

The Northern colonies are of stronger stamina, but they have other difficulties and disadvantages to struggle with, not less arduous, or more easy to be surmounted, than what have been already mentioned. . . . They are composed of people of different nations, different manners, different religions, and different languages. They have a mutual jealousy of each other, fomented by considerations of interest, power, and ascendancy. Religious zeal, too, like a smothered fire, is secretly burning in the hearts of the different sectaries that inhabit them, and were it not restrained by laws and superior authority, would soon burst out into a flame of universal persecution. Even the peaceable Quakers struggle hard for pre-eminence, and evince in a very striking manner that the passions of mankind are much stronger than any principles of religion. . . .

Indeed, it appears to me a very doubtful point, even supposing all the colonies of America to be united under one head, whether it would be possible to keep in due order and government so wide and extended an empire, the difficulties of communication, of intercourse, of correspondence, and all other circumstances considered.

A voluntary association or coalition, at least a permanent one, is almost as difficult to be supposed: for fire and water are not more heterogeneous than the different colonies in North America. Nothing can exceed the jealousy and emulation which they possess in regard to each other. The inhabitants of Pennsylvania and New York have an inexhaustible source of animosity in their jealousy for the trade of the Jerseys. Massachusetts Bay and Rhode Island are not less interested in that of Connecticut. The West Indies are a common subject of emulation to them all. Even the limits and boundaries of each colony are a constant source of litigation.

In short, such is the difference of character, of manners, of religion, of interest, of the different colonies, that I think, if I am not wholly ignorant of the human mind, were they left to themselves there would soon be a civil war from one end of the continent to the other, while the Indians and Negroes would, with better reason, impatiently watch the opportunity of exterminating them all together.

2. Otis Denounces Search Warrants (1761)

During the French and Indian War, the American merchant-smugglers kept up a lucrative illicit trade with the French and Spanish West Indies. They argued that they could not pay wartime taxes if they could not make profits out of their friends, the enemy. Angered by such disloyalty, the royal authorities in Massachusetts undertook to revive the hated writs of assistance. Ordinary search warrants describe the specific premises to be searched; writs of assistance were general search warrants that authorized indiscriminate search of ships and dwellings for illicit goods. Colonial participation in the recent war against the French had inspired a spirit of resistance, and John Adams, later President of the United States, remembered in his old age the following dramatic episode. Note why the colonials were alarmed and what were Adams' most obvious exaggerations.

When the British ministry received from General Amherst his despatches announcing his conquest of Montreal, and the consequent annihilation of the French government in America, in 1759,* they immediately conceived the design and took the resolution of conquering the English colonies, and subjecting them to the unlimited authority of Parliament. With this view and intention, they sent orders and instructions to the collector of the customs in Boston, Mr. Charles Paxton, to apply to the civil authority for writs of assistance, to enable the custom-house officers, tidewaiters, land-waiters, and all, to command all sheriffs and constables, etc., to attend and aid them in breaking open houses, stores, shops, cellars, ships, bales, trunks, chests, casks, packages of all sorts, to search for goods, wares, and merchandises which had been imported against the prohibitions or without paying the taxes imposed by certain acts of Parliament, called "The Acts of Trade." . . .

An alarm was spread far and wide. Merchants of Salem and Boston applied to [lawyers] Mr. Pratt, who refused, and to Mr. Otis and Mr. Thacher, who accepted, to defend them against this terrible menacing monster, the writ of assistance. Great fees were offered, but Otis, and I believe Thacher, would accept of none. "In such a cause," said Otis, "I despise all fees."

2. C. F. Adams, ed., *The Works of John Adams* (1856), X, 246–48.
* Actually 1760.

I have given you a sketch of the stage and the scenery, and the brief of the cause; or, if you like the phrase better, the tragedy, comedy, or farce.

Now for the actors and performers. Mr. Gridley argued [for the government] with his characteristic learning, ingenuity, and dignity, and said everything that could be said in favor of Cockle's [deputy collector at Salem] petition, all depending, however, on the "If the Parliament of Great Britain is the sovereign legislature of all the British empire."

Mr. Thacher followed him on the other side, and argued with the softness of manners, the ingenuity, and the cool reasoning which were remarkable in his amiable character.

But Otis was a flame of fire! With a promptitude of classical allusions, a depth of research, a rapid summary of historical events and dates, a profusion of legal authorities, a prophetic glance of his eye into futurity, and a torrent of impetuous eloquence he hurried away everything before him. American independence was then and there born; the seeds of patriots and heroes were then and there sown. . . .

Every man of a crowded audience appeared to me to go away, as I did, ready to take arms against writs of assistance. Then and there was the first scene of the first act of opposition to the arbitrary claims of Great Britain. Then and there the child Independence was born. In fifteen years, namely in 1776, he grew up to manhood and declared himself free. . . .

Mr. Otis' popularity was without bounds. In May, 1761, he was elected into the House of Representatives by an almost unanimous vote. On the week of his election, I happened to be at Worcester attending a Court of Common Pleas, of which Brigadier Ruggles was Chief Justice, when the news arrived from Boston of Mr. Otis' election. You can have no idea of the consternation among the government people. Chief Justice Ruggles, at dinner at Colonel Chandler's on that day, said, "Out of this election will arise a d——d faction, which will shake this province to its foundation."

THOUGHT PROVOKERS

1. It has been said that the true martyr does not feel pain, as other men do, but actually takes pleasure in suffering for his cause. Comment in the light of the Jesuit experience in Canada. Explain why there was prolonged conflict in New France between the missionaries and the fur traders. Did the white man "rob" the Indians when he exchanged a string of beads for valuable furs?

2. Did the British err in depriving France of Canada in 1763? How would the history of the English colonies have been changed in the 18th and 19th Centuries if the French had been allowed to remain?

3. Compare and contrast the advantages and disadvantages of the French and the English in their intercolonial wars in America. Assess the effects of these wars on colonial attitudes.

4. The seeds of American nationalism were sown during the colonial period. In parallel columns list those forces and factors that made for a spirit of unity or nationality and those that militated against it. Then form conclusions as to which forces predominated and what they foreshadowed.

FURTHER EXPLORATION

General: The classic works of Francis Parkman are abridged in S. E. Morison, ed., *The Parkman Reader* (1955). **New France:** G. M. Wrong, *The Rise and Fall of New France* (2 vols., 1929); and Francis Parkman's volumes: *Pioneers of France in the New World* (2 vols., 1865); *The Jesuits in North America* (2 vols., 1867); *The Old Regime in Canada* (1874). **Colonial Defense:** Francis Parkman, *Count Frontenac and New France under Louis XIV* (2 vols., 1877) and *A Half Century of Conflict* (2 vols., 1892). **French and Indian War:** Francis Parkman, *Montcalm and Wolfe* (2 vols., 1884); L. H. Gipson, *The British Empire before the American Revolution: The Years of Defeat, 1754–1757* (vol. VI, 1946); Lee McCardell, *Ill-Starred General* [Braddock] (1958); D. S. Freeman, *George Washington* (1948), vol. II. **Disunity:** L. H. Gipson, *The British Empire before the American Revolution: The Triumphant Empire* (vol. IX, 1956).

Recent: C. L. Ver Steeg, *The Formative Years, 1607–1763* (1964); P. C. Phillips, *The Fur Trade* (2 vols., 1961); H. H. Peckham, *The Colonial Wars, 1689–1762* (1964) [paperback]; Bernhard Knollenberg, *George Washington: The Virginia Period, 1732–1775* (1964).

Chapter 4

Life in the Colonies

Driven from every other corner of the earth, freedom of thought and the right of private judgment in matters of conscience direct their course to this happy country as their last asylum.

SAMUEL ADAMS, 1776

PROLOGUE: The population of the English colonies increased amazingly, owing largely to the fertility of a pioneer people. Immigrants were pouring in from the British Isles and Europe, and although the English language remained predominant, the now-famed melting pot was beginning to bubble. Thousands of the newcomers were indentured servants, who, on serving out their terms, often received a plot of land. As the population spread, the austerity of the old time worship weakened, though given a temporary revival by the Great Awakening of the 1730's. The rational thought inspired by the European Enlightenment found a ready disciple in Benjamin Franklin, whose sly pokes at religion no doubt helped undermine the dominance of the clergy. A ruling class of sorts existed in all the colonies, although the governing clique in New York received a sharp jolt in the famed Zenger libel case. The ease with which the individual colonial could rise from one social rung to another, quite in contrast with Old World rigidity, suggested that a near-classless society was emerging.

A. THE COLONIAL MELTING POT

1. Franklin Analyzes the Population (1751)

The baby boom in the English colonies was an object of wonderment. Peter Kalm recorded that Mrs. Maria Hazard, who died in her hundredth year, left five hundred children, grandchildren, great-grandchildren, and great-great-grandchildren. Benjamin Franklin, the incredibly versatile printer, businessman, philosopher, scientist, and diplomat, made the following observations in 1751. Explain why families were so large, why labor was not cheap, and why slave labor was uneconomical.

Land being thus plenty in America, and so cheap as that a laboring man that understands husbandry can, in a short time, save money enough to purchase a piece of new land sufficient for a plantation, whereon he may subsist a family, such are not afraid to marry. For, if they even look far enough forward to consider how their children, when grown up, are to be provided for, they see that more land is to be had at rates equally easy, all circumstances considered.

Hence marriages in America are more general, and more generally early, than in Europe. And if it is reckoned there that there is but one marriage per annum among one hundred persons, perhaps we may here reckon two;

1. Jared Sparks, ed., *The Works of Benjamin Franklin* (1840), II, 313–15.

and if in Europe they have but four births to a marriage (many of their marriages being late), we may here reckon eight, of which, if one half grow up, and our marriages are made, reckoning one with another, at twenty years of age, our people must at least be doubled every twenty years.

But notwithstanding this increase, so vast is the territory of North America that it will require many ages to settle it fully. And till it is fully settled, labor will never be cheap here, where no man continues long a laborer for others, but gets a plantation of his own; no man continues long a journeyman to a trade, but goes among those new settlers, and sets up for himself, etc. Hence labor is no cheaper now in Pennsylvania than it was thirty years ago, though so many thousand laboring people have been imported.

The danger therefore of these colonies interfering with their mother country in trades that depend on labor, manufactures, etc., is too remote to require the attention of Great Britain. . . .

It is an ill-grounded opinion that, by the labor of slaves, America may possibly vie in cheapness of manufactures with Britain. The labor of slaves can never be so cheap here as the labor of workingmen is in Britain. Any one may compute it. Interest of money is in the colonies from 6 to 10 percent. Slaves, one with another, cost thirty pounds sterling per head. Reckon then the interest of the first purchase of a slave, the insurance or risk on his life, his clothing and diet, expenses in his sickness and loss of time, loss by his neglect of business (neglect is natural to the man who is not to be benefited by his own care or diligence), expense of a driver to keep him at work, and his pilfering from time to time, almost every slave being by nature a thief, and compare the whole amount with the wages of a manufacturer of iron or wool in England, you will see that labor is much cheaper there than it ever can be by Negroes here.

Why then will Americans purchase slaves? Because slaves may be kept as long as a man pleases, or has occasion for their labor; while hired men are continually leaving their masters (often in the midst of his business) and setting up for themselves.

2. Mittelberger Voyages to Pennsylvania (c. 1750)

In the 18th Century tens of thousands of Germans, largely from the war-ravaged Rhineland, came to Pennsylvania for economic and social betterment. Often they were lured to the dock by the glib misrepresentations of "soul-traffickers," who received a commission for each victim enticed. Floating down the Rhine past thirty-six customhouses, the immigrants were fleeced at every turn by greedy officials and delayed by as much as six weeks. Then came delays up to six weeks in Holland and six more weeks in England, while scanty savings melted away. Many immigrants were exhausted before the beginning of the real ordeal—the seven- to twelve-week voyage. It is here described by a German pastor, Gottlieb Mittelberger, who crossed the Atlantic about 1750 to investigate conditions and to alert the people back home to

2. Gottlieb Mittelberger, *Journey to Pennsylvania in the Year 1750* . . . (1898), pp. 20–29.

their peril. His description of "the sale of human beings" at the end of the voyage (like his description of the voyage itself), though overdrawn, is basically sound. Yet he fails to observe that this system, which forced many immigrants into indentured servitude to pay for their passage, enabled tens of thousands of hard-working immigrants to get a start in America. Note why sickness and death on the voyage were common, in what respects indentured servitude was similar to Negro slavery, and in what important respect it was dissimilar.

During the voyage there is on board these ships terrible misery, stench, fumes, horror, vomiting, many kinds of sea-sickness, fever, dysentery, headache, heat, constipation, boils, scurvy, cancer, mouth-rot, and the like, all of which come from old and sharply salted food and meat, also from very bad and foul water, so that many die miserably.

Add to this, want of provisions, hunger, thirst, frost, heat, dampness, anxiety, want, afflictions, and lamentations, together with other trouble, as for example, the lice abound so frightfully, especially on sick people, that they can be scraped off the body. The misery reaches the climax when a gale rages for two or three nights and days, so that every one believes that the ship will go to the bottom with all human beings on board. In such a visitation the people cry and pray most piteously. . . .

Among the healthy, impatience sometimes grows so great and cruel that one curses the other, or himself and the day of his birth, and sometimes come near killing each other. Misery and malice join each other, so that they cheat and rob one another. One always reproaches the other with having persuaded him to undertake the journey. Frequently children cry out against their parents, husbands against their wives and wives against their husbands, brothers and sisters, friends and acquaintances against each other. But most against the soul-traffickers.

Many sigh and cry: "Oh, that I were at home again, and if I had to lie in my pig-sty!" Or they say: "O God, if I only had a piece of good bread, or a good fresh drop of water!" Many people whimper, sigh, and cry piteously for their homes; most of them get homesick. Many hundred people necessarily die and perish in such misery, and must be cast into the sea, which drives their relatives, or those who persuaded them to undertake the journey, to such despair that it is almost impossible to pacify and console them. . . .

No one can have an idea of the sufferings which women in confinement have to bear with their innocent children on board these ships. Few of this class escape with their lives; many a mother is cast into the water with her child as soon as she is dead. One day, just as we had a heavy gale, a woman in our ship, who was to give birth and could not give birth under the circumstances, was pushed through a loophole [porthole] in the ship and dropped into the sea, because she was far in the rear of the ship and could not be brought forward.

Children from 1 to 7 years rarely survive the voyage; and many a time parents are compelled to see their children miserably suffer and die from hunger, thirst, and sickness, and then to see them cast into the water. I witnessed such misery in no less than thirty-two children in our ship, all of whom were thrown into the sea. The parents grieve all the more since their children find no resting-place in the earth, but are devoured by the monsters of the sea. It is a notable fact that children who have not yet had the measles or smallpox generally get them on board the ship, and mostly die of them.

Often a father is separated by death from his wife and children, or mothers from their little children, or even both parents from their children; and sometimes whole families die in quick succession; so that often many dead persons lie in the berths beside the living ones, especially when contagious diseases have broken out on board the ship. . . .

[*Pastor Mittelberger, after describing accidental falls that resulted in cripples or men lost overboard, turns to less serious inconveniences.*]

That most of the people get sick is not surprising, because, in addition to all other trials and hardships, warm food is served only three times a week, the rations being very poor and very little. Such meals can hardly be eaten, on account of being so unclean. The water which is served out on the ship is often very black, thick, and full of worms, so that one cannot drink it without loathing, even with the greatest thirst. O surely, one would often give much money at sea for a piece of good bread, or a drink of good water, not to say a drink of good wine, if it were only to be had. I myself experienced that difficulty, I am sorry to say. Towards the end we were compelled to eat the ship's biscuit which had been spoiled long ago, though in a whole biscuit there was scarcely a piece the size of a dollar that had not been full of red worms and spiders' nests. Great hunger and thirst force us to eat and drink everything; but many a one does so at the risk of his life. . . .

At length, when, after a long and tedious voyage, the ships come in sight of land, so that the promontories can be seen, which the people were so eager and anxious to see, all creep from below on deck to see the land from afar, and they weep for joy, and pray and sing, thanking and praising God. The sight of the land makes the people on board the ship, especially the sick and the half dead, alive again, so that their hearts leap within them. They shout and rejoice, and are content to bear their misery in patience, in the hope that they may soon reach the land in safety.

But alas! When the ships have landed at Philadelphia after their long voyage, no one is permitted to leave them, except those who pay for their passage or can give good security. The others, who cannot pay, must remain on board the ships till they are purchased, and are released from the ships by their purchasers. The sick always fare the worst, for the healthy are naturally preferred and purchased first. And so the sick and wretched must often remain on board in front of the city for two or three weeks, and frequently die; whereas many a one, if he could pay his debt and were permitted to leave the ship immediately, might recover and remain alive. . . .

The sale of human beings in the market on board the ship is carried on thus: every day Englishmen, Dutchmen, and High-German people come from the city of Philadelphia and other places, in part from a great distance, say 20, 30, or 40 hours away, and go on board the newly arrived ship that has brought and offers for sale passengers from Europe, and select among the healthy persons such as they deem suitable for their business, and bargain with them how long they will serve for their passage-money, which most of them are still in debt for. When they have come to an agreement, it happens that adult persons bind themselves in writing to serve 3, 4, 5, or 6 years for the amount due by them, according to their age and strength. But very young people, from 10 to 15 years, must serve till they are 21 years old.

Many parents must sell and trade away their children like so many head of cattle; for if their children take the debt upon themselves, the parents can leave the ship free and unrestrained. But as the parents often do not know where and to what people their children are going, it often happens that such parents and children, after leaving the ship, do not see each other again for many years, perhaps no more in all their lives.

When people arrive who cannot make themselves free, but have children under 5 years, the parents cannot free themselves by them; for such children must be given to somebody without compensation to be brought up, and they must serve for their bringing up till they are 21 years old. Children from 5 to 10 years, who pay half price for their passage, viz. 30 florins, must likewise serve for it till they are 21 years of age. They cannot, therefore, redeem their parents by taking the debt of the latter upon themselves. But children above 10 years can take part of their parents' debt upon themselves.

A woman must stand for her husband if he arrives sick, and in like manner a man for his sick wife, and take the debt upon herself or himself, and thus serve 5 to 6 years, not alone for his or her own debt, but also for that of the sick husband or wife. But if both are sick, such persons are sent from the ship to the sick-house, but not until it appears probable that they will find no purchasers. As soon as they are well again they must serve for their passage, or pay if they have means.

It often happens that whole families—husband, wife, and children—are separated by being sold to different purchasers, especially when they have not paid any part of their passage-money.

When a husband or wife has died at sea when the ship has made more than half of her trip, the survivor must pay or serve not only for himself or herself, but also for the deceased. . . .

If some one in this country runs away from his master, who has treated him harshly, he cannot get far. Good provision has been made for such cases, so that a runaway is soon recovered. He who detains or returns a deserter receives a good reward.

If such a runaway has been away from his master one day, he must serve for it as a punishment a week, for a week a month, and for a month half a year. But if the master will not keep the runaway after he has got him back, he may sell him for so many years as he would have to serve him yet.

3. Crèvecoeur Discovers a New Man (*c.* 1770)

Michel-Guillaume Jean de Crèvecoeur, a young Frenchman of noble family, served with the French army in Canada from 1758 to 1759. Finally reaching the English colonies in 1759, he traveled widely, married an American woman, and settled down to an idyllic existence on his New York estate, "Pine Hill." A born farmer, he introduced into America a number of plants, including alfalfa. Probably during the decade before 1775, he wrote in English the classic series of essays known as *Letters from an American Farmer* (published in 1782). This glowing account was blamed for luring some 500 French families to the wilds of the Ohio Country, where they perished. Observe what the author of the *Letters* reveals regarding the racial composition of the colonies and what he regards as the most important factors in creating the new man.

. . . Whence came all these people?

They are a mixture of English, Scotch, Irish, French, Dutch, Germans, and Swedes. From this promiscuous breed, that race now called Americans have arisen. The Eastern [New England] provinces must indeed be excepted, as being the unmixed descendants of Englishmen. I have heard many wish that they had been more intermixed also. For my part, I am no wisher, and think it much better as it has happened. They exhibit a most conspicuous figure in this great and variegated picture; they too enter for a great share in the pleasing perspective displayed in these thirteen provinces. I know it is fashionable to reflect on them, but I respect them for what they have done; for the accuracy and wisdom with which they have settled their territory; for the decency of their manners; for their early love of letters; their ancient college, the first in this hemisphere;* for their industry, which to me, who am but a farmer, is the criterion of everything. There never was a people, situated as they are, who with so ungrateful a soil have done more in so short a time. . . .

In this great American asylum, the poor of Europe have by some means met together, and in consequence of various causes; to what purpose should they ask one another what countrymen they are? Alas, two-thirds of them had no country. Can a wretch who wanders about, who works and starves, whose life is a continual scene of sore affliction or pinching penury—can that man call England or any other kingdom his country? A country that had no bread for him, whose fields procured him no harvest, who met with nothing but the frowns of the rich, the severity of the laws, with jails and

3. M. G. J. de Crèvecoeur, *Letters from an American Farmer* (1904 reprint), pp. 51–56.
* The Spanish universities in Mexico City and Lima (Peru) antedated Harvard by eighty-five years.

punishments; who owned not a single foot of the extensive surface of this planet? No! urged by a variety of motives, here they came. Everything has tended to regenerate them: new laws, a new mode of living, a new social system. Here they are become men. In Europe they were as so many useless plants, wanting vegetative mould, and refreshing showers; they withered, and were mowed down by want, hunger, and war. But now by the power of transplantation, like all other plants, they have taken root and flourished! Formerly they were not numbered in any civil lists of their country, except in those of the poor. Here they rank as citizens.

By what invisible power has this surprising metamorphosis been performed? By that of the laws and that of their industry. The laws, the indulgent laws, protect them as they arrive, stamping on them the symbol of adoption. They receive ample rewards for their labors; these accumulated rewards procure them lands; those lands confer on them the title of freemen, and to that title every benefit is affixed which men can possibly require. . . .

What then is the American, this new man? He is either an European, or the descendant of an European; hence that strange mixture of blood, which you will find in no other country. I could point out to you a family whose grandfather was an Englishman, whose wife was Dutch, whose son married a French woman, and whose present four sons have now four wives of different nations.

He is an American who, leaving behind him all his ancient prejudices and manners, receives new ones from the new mode of life he has embraced, the new government he obeys, and the new rank he holds. He becomes an American by being received in the broad lap of our great *alma mater*. Here individuals of all nations are melted into a new race of men whose labors and posterity will one day cause great changes in the world. Americans are the western pilgrims, who are carrying along with them the great mass of arts, sciences, vigor, and industry which began long since in the East. They will finish the great circle. . . .

The American ought therefore to love this country much better than that wherein either he or his forefathers were born. Here the rewards of his industry follow with equal steps the progress of his labor; his labor is founded on the basis of nature, *self-interest;* can it want a stronger allurement? Wives and children, who before in vain demanded of him a morsel of bread, now, fat and frolicsome, gladly help their father to clear those fields whence exuberant crops are to arise to feed and to clothe them all; without any part being claimed, either by a despotic prince, a rich abbot, or a mighty lord. Here religion demands but little of him: a small voluntary salary to the minister, and gratitude to God. Can he refuse these?

The American is a new man, who acts upon new principles; he must therefore entertain new ideas, and form new opinions. From involuntary idleness, servile dependence, penury, and useless labor, he has passed to toils of a very different nature, rewarded by ample subsistence.

This is an American.

B. THE FOUNDATIONS OF EDUCATION

1. Satan Inspires a School System (1647)

The pious Puritans of Massachusetts Bay, deeply concerned about the education of their children, enacted a law in 1642 designed to encourage the teaching of reading in the home. But they did not establish schools or direct the hiring of schoolmasters. The next step was the epochal Massachusetts School Law of 1647, perhaps the most important single foundation stone of public education in America. It made provision for school systems at both the elementary and the secondary (grammar) levels. Note why the authors of the law, the text of which follows, regarded education as important, and in what sense they established compulsory education.

It being one chief project of the old deluder, Satan, to keep men from the knowledge of the Scriptures, as in former times by keeping them in an unknown tongue, so in these latter times by persuading from the use of tongues, that so at least the true sense and meaning of the original might be clouded by false glosses of saints-seeming deceivers; that learning may not be buried in the grave of our fathers in the church and commonwealth, the Lord assisting our endeavors—

It is therefore ordered that every township in this jurisdiction, after the Lord hath increased them to the number of 50 householders, shall then forthwith appoint one within their town to teach all such children as shall resort to him to write and read, whose wages shall be paid either by the parents or masters of such children, or by the inhabitants in general, by way of supply, as the major part of those that order the prudentials of the town shall appoint; provided, those that send their children be not oppressed by paying much more than they can have them taught for in other towns.

And it is further ordered that where any town shall increase to the number of 100 families or householders, they shall set up a [Latin] grammar school, the master thereof being able to instruct youth so far as they may be fitted for the university; provided, that if any town neglect the performance hereof above one year, that every such town shall pay five pounds to the next [nearest] school till they shall perform this order.

THE BURNING OF JOHN ROGERS (1555)

This Protestant clergyman was the first martyr in the reign of Catholic Queen Mary ("Bloody Mary"). In the words of the *New England Primer*, "His Wife, with nine fmall Children, and one at her Breaft, following him to the Stake, with which forrowful fight he was not in the leaft daunted, but with wonderful Patience died couragioufly for the Gofpel of Jefus Chrift." An illustration in the *New England Primer*.

1. N. B. Shurtleff, ed., *Records of the Governor and Company of the Massachusetts Bay in New England* (1853), II, 203.

2. John Harvard's Legacy (1643)

The devout Puritans actually established an institution for higher learning before they provided for an elementary school system. Founded in 1636, it is the oldest corporation in the United States today—and one of the wealthiest. It honors the name of John Harvard, a butcher's son who had graduated from Cambridge University —"a scholar and pious"—and who left a modest monetary bequest to the college when he died of tuberculosis in 1638. He also contributed his library of four hundred volumes, which ran heavily to the classics, theology, and general literature. Seldom has anyone received so much fame from so little. An anonymous pamphlet, published in 1643, described the founding as follows. Ascertain why the college was established; and form conclusions as to the nature of the training given the students.

After God had carried us safe to New England, and we had builded our houses, provided necessaries for our livelihood, reared convenient places for God's worship, and settled the civil government, one of the next things we longed for and looked after was to advance learning and perpetuate it to posterity; dreading to leave an illiterate ministry to the churches when our present ministers shall lie in the dust.

And as we were thinking and consulting how to effect this great work, it pleased God to stir up the heart of one Mr. Harvard (a godly gentleman, and a lover of learning, there living amongst us) to give one half of his estate (it being in all about £1700) towards the erecting of a college, and all his library. After him another gave £300; others after them cast in more, and the public hand of the state added the rest. The college was, by common consent, appointed to be at Cambridge, a place very pleasant and accommodate, and is called (according to the name of the first founder) Harvard College.

The edifice is very fair and comely within and without, having in it a spacious hall, where they daily meet at commons, lectures, exercises; and a large library with some books to it, the gifts of divers of our friends; their chambers and studies also fitted for and possessed by the students, and all other rooms of office necessary and convenient, with all needful offices thereto belonging. And by the side of the college a fair grammar [secondary] school, for the training up of young scholars and fitting them for academical learning, that still, as they are judged ripe, they may be received into the college of [from] this school. . . .

Over the college is Master Dunster placed, as president, a learned, conscionable, and industrious man, who hath so trained up his pupils in the tongues and arts, and so seasoned them with the principles of divinity and Christianity, that we have to our great comfort, and, in truth, beyond our hopes, beheld their progress in learning and godliness also. The former of these hath appeared in their public declamations in Latin and Greek, and disputations logical and philosophical. . . . The latter hath been manifested in sundry of them by the savory breathings of their spirits in their godly conversation. . . .

2. *New England's First Fruits* (1865 reprint), pp. 23–25.

C. RELIGIOUS CROSS CURRENTS

1. Whitefield Fascinates Franklin (1739)

The frenzied religious revival that swept the colonies in the 1730's, known as the Great Awakening, featured George Whitefield as one of the Awakeners. Although he was only twenty-five years old when Benjamin Franklin heard him in Philadelphia during the second of his seven trips to America, he had already preached with such emotional power in England that crowds would assemble at his church door before daybreak. When orthodox clergymen denied him their pulpits, he would speak in the open air, at times to crowds of 20,000 persons. Franklin, then thirty-six years of age and a hardheaded Philadelphia businessman, was of a skeptical turn of mind. From his famed autobiography, written many years later, form conclusions as to Franklin's character, and as to the presence of a liberal or illiberal atmosphere in Philadelphia.

In 1739 arrived among us from Ireland the Reverend Mr. Whitefield, who had made himself remarkable there as an itinerant preacher. He was at first permitted to preach in some of our churches; but the clergy, taking a dislike to him, soon refused him their pulpits, and he was obliged to preach in the fields. The multitudes of all sects and denominations that attended his sermons were enormous, and it was matter of speculation to me, who was one of the number, to observe the extraordinary influence of his oratory on his hearers, and how much they admired and respected him, notwithstanding his common abuse of them, by assuring them they were naturally *half beasts and half devils.* It was wonderful to see the change soon made in the manners of our inhabitants. From being thoughtless or indifferent about religion, it seemed as if all the world were growing religious, so that one could not walk through the town in an evening without hearing psalms sung in different families of every street.

And it being found inconvenient to assemble in the open air, subject to its inclemencies, the building of a house to meet in was no sooner proposed, and persons appointed to receive contributions, but sufficient sums were soon received to procure the ground and erect the building, which was one hundred feet long and seventy broad, about the size of Westminster Hall; and the work was carried on with such spirit as to be finished in a much shorter time than could have been expected. Both house and ground were vested in trustees, expressly for the use of any preacher of any religious persuasion who might desire to say something to the people at Philadelphia; the design in building not being to accommodate any particular sect, but the inhabitants in general; so that even if the Mufti of Constantinople were to send a missionary to preach Mohammedanism to us, he would find a pulpit at his service.

Mr. Whitefield, in leaving us, went preaching all the way through the colonies to Georgia. The settlement of that province had lately been begun, but, instead of being made with hardy, industrious husbandmen, accustomed to labor, the only people fit for such an enterprise, it was with families of broken shopkeepers and other insolvent debtors, many of in-

1. John Bigelow, ed., *Autobiography of Benjamin Franklin* (1868), pp. 251–55.

dolent and idle habits, taken out of the jails, who, being set down in the woods, unqualified for clearing land, and unable to endure the hardships of a new settlement, perished in numbers, leaving many helpless children unprovided for. The sight of their miserable situation inspired the benevolent heart of Mr. Whitefield with the idea of building an Orphan House there, in which they might be supported and educated. Returning northward, he preached up this charity, and made large collections, for his eloquence had a wonderful power over the hearts and purses of his hearers, of which I myself was an instance.

I did not disapprove of the design, but, as Georgia was then destitute of materials and workmen, and it was proposed to send them from Philadelphia at a great expense, I thought it would have been better to have built the house there, and brought the children to it. This I advised; but he was resolute in his first project, rejected my counsel, and I therefore refused to contribute.

I happened soon after to attend one of his sermons, in the course of which I perceived he intended to finish with a collection, and I silently resolved he should get nothing from me. I had in my pocket a handful of copper money, three or four silver dollars, and five pistoles in gold. As he proceeded I began to soften, and concluded to give the coppers. Another stroke of his oratory made me ashamed of that, and determined me to give the silver; and he finished so admirably that I emptied my pocket wholly into the collector's dish, gold and all.

At this sermon there was also one of our club who, being of my sentiments respecting the building in Georgia, and suspecting a collection might be intended, had, by precaution, emptied his pockets before he came from home. Towards the conclusion of the discourse, however, he felt a strong desire to give, and applied to a [Quaker] neighbor, who stood near him, to borrow some money for the purpose. The application was unfortunately to perhaps the only man in the company who had the firm-

T H E

TESTIMONY

Of the

Prefident, *Profeffors*, *Tutors* and *Hebrew Inftructor* of HARVARD COLLEGE in *Cambridge*,

Againft the Reverend

Mr. *George Whitefield*,

And his Conduct.

B O S T O N, N. E.

Printed and fold By *T. Fleet*, at the *Heart* and *Crown* in Cornhill. 1744.

OPPOSITION TO WHITEFIELD

ness not to be affected by the preacher. His answer was, "At any other time, Friend Hopkinson, I would lend to thee freely; but not now, for thee seems to be out of thy right senses."

2. Edwards Paints the Horrors of Hell (1741)

Paired with George Whitefield as a Great Awakener was Jonathan Edwards, a New England Congregational minister. Tall, slender, and delicate, he had a weak voice but a powerful mind. He still ranks as the greatest Protestant theologian yet produced in America, and his books have sold internationally. His command of the English language was exceptional, and his vision of hell, peopled with pre-damned infants and others, was horrifying. As he preached hell-fire to his Enfield, Connecticut, congregation, there was a great moaning and crying, "What shall I do to be saved? Oh, I am going to hell!" Men and women groveled on the floor or lay inert on the benches. After reading this excerpt from Edwards' famous sermon "Sinners in the Hands of an Angry God," form some judgment as to how effective this type of appeal would be today, and as to whether one can be scared into reformation by such horrors.

The God that holds you over the pit of hell, much as one holds a spider or some loathsome insect over the fire, abhors you, and is dreadfully provoked. His wrath towards you burns like fire; he looks upon you as worthy of nothing else but to be cast into the fire. He is of purer eyes than to bear you in his sight; you are ten thousand times as abominable in his eyes as the most hateful, venomous serpent is in ours.

You have offended him infinitely more than ever a stubborn rebel did his prince, and yet it is nothing but his hand that holds you from falling into the fire every moment. It is to be ascribed to nothing else that you did not go to hell the last night; that you were suffered to awake again in this world, after you closed your eyes to sleep. And there is no other reason to be given why you have not dropped into hell since you arose in the morning, but that God's hand has held you up. There is no other reason to be given why you have not gone to hell since you have sat here in the house of God provoking his pure eye by your sinful, wicked manner of attending his solemn worship. Yea, there is nothing else that is to be given as a reason why you do not this very moment drop down into hell.

O sinner! consider the fearful danger you are in! It is a great furnace of wrath, a wide and bottomless pit, full of the fire of wrath that you are held over in the hand of that God whose wrath is provoked and incensed as much against you as against many of the damned in hell. You hang by a slender thread, with the flames of Divine wrath flashing about it, and ready every moment to singe it and burn it asunder. . . .

It would be dreadful to suffer this fierceness and wrath of Almighty God one moment; but you must suffer it to all eternity. There will be no end to this exquisite, horrible misery. When you look forward, you shall see along forever a boundless duration before you, which will swallow up your thoughts, and amaze your soul. And you will absolutely despair of

2. Jonathan Edwards, *Works* (1840), II, 10–11.

ever having any deliverance, any end, any mitigation, any rest at all. You will know certainly that you must wear out long ages, millions of millions of ages in wrestling and conflicting with this Almighty, merciless vengeance. And then when you have so done, when so many ages have actually been spent by you in this manner, you will know that all is but a point [dot] to what remains. So that your punishment will indeed be infinite.

Oh! who can express what the state of a soul in such circumstances is! All that we can possibly say about it gives but a very feeble, faint representation of it. It is inexpressible and inconceivable: for "who knows the power of God's anger"!

How dreadful is the state of those that are daily and hourly in danger of this great wrath and infinite misery! But this is the dismal case of every soul in this congregation that has not been born again, however moral and strict, sober and religious, they may otherwise be. Oh! that you would consider it, whether you be young or old!

There is reason to think that there are many in this congregation, now hearing this discourse, that will actually be the subjects of this very misery to all eternity. We know not who they are, or in what seats they sit, or what thoughts they now have. It may be they are now at ease, and hear all these things without much disturbance, and are now flattering themselves that they are not the persons, promising themselves that they shall escape.

If we knew that there was one person, and but one, in the whole congregation, that was to be the subject of this misery, what an awful thing it would be to think of! If we knew who it was, what an awful sight would it be to see such a person! How might all the rest of the congregation lift up a lamentable and bitter cry over him!

But, alas! instead of one, how many is it likely will remember this discourse in hell! And it would be a wonder, if some that are now present should not be in hell in a very short time, before this year is out. And it would be no wonder if some persons that now sit here in some seats of this meeting-house, in health, and quiet and secure, should be there before tomorrow morning!

3. Poor Richard's Earthy Religion (1732–1758)

Benjamin Franklin, America's most famous printer, launched his *Poor Richard's Almanack* in Philadelphia in 1732. Although there were seven competing almanacs then being issued in the same city, within a year his brain child became the most popular book in the colonies, except the Bible. Sales ultimately reached 10,000 copies annually. In addition to the usual information about the weather, tides, and self-medication, Franklin reproduced wise sayings which he liberally borrowed from the wits of other ages, adding a generous dash of his own homespun philosophy. Assuming that the following selections from the *Almanack* represent Franklin's views, determine whether he was truly religious and how he was probably regarded by contemporary clergymen.

3. See *Poor Richard's Almanack*, ed. B. E. Smith (1898).

How many observe Christ's birthday; how few his precepts! O! 'tis easier to keep holidays than commandments.

Serving God is doing good to man, but praying is thought an easier service, and therefore more generally chosen.

When knaves fall out, honest men get their goods; when priests dispute, we come at the truth.

Many a long dispute among divines [clergymen] may be thus abridged: It is so; It is not so; It is so; It is not so.

Different sects, like different clocks, may be all near the matter though they don't quite agree.

Many have quarreled about religion that never practiced it.

A good example is the best sermon.

Christianity commands us to pass by injuries; policy, to let them pass by us.

Fear God, and your enemies will fear you.

Think of three things: whence you came, where you are going, and to whom you must account.

Fear not death; for the sooner we die, the longer shall we be immortal.

Work as if you were to live a hundred years; pray as if you were to die tomorrow.

Danger is sauce for prayers.

If your riches are yours, why don't you take them with you to t'other world?

D. COLONIAL MORALITY

1. Franklin on Women and Ethics (1732–1758)

On the subject of women, Franklin was something of an authority. Of an extremely ardent nature, he confesses in his *Autobiography* how, as a young man, he entered into low intrigues with fallen women, but fortunately escaped disease. He fathered at least one illegitimate child, and probably more. He ultimately married a respectable if uninspiring Philadelphia housewife, and thus contrived to keep his passions in check. Two of his most famous writings are "The Speech of Polly Baker," in which the fictitious Miss Baker, haled before a Connecticut court for having given birth to her fifth child out of wedlock, pleads for a husband; and "Advice to a Young Man," in which Franklin shrewdly urges his correspondent, if he must take a mistress rather than a wife, to take an old one. Ascertain from these passages from *Poor Richard's Almanack* how much of this advice given in the 18th Century seems applicable to the 20th.

Neither a fortress nor a maidenhead will hold out long after they begin to parley.

Let thy maidservant be faithful, strong, and homely.

1. "The Speech of Polly Baker" and "Advice to a Young Man" may be found in Carl Van Doren, ed., *Benjamin Franklin: The Autobiography with Sayings of Poor Richard, Hoaxes, Bagatelles, Essays, and Letters* (1940).

Old boys have their playthings as well as young ones; the difference is only in the price.

Keep your eyes wide open before marriage, half shut afterwards.

Where there's marriage without love, there will be love without marriage.

Virtue may not always make a face handsome, but vice will certain make it ugly.

Drink does not drown care, but waters it and makes it grow faster.

Many a man thinks he is buying pleasure, when he is really selling himself a slave to it.

'Tis easier to suppress the first desire than to satisfy all that follow it.

What maintains one vice would bring up two children.

Search others for their virtues, thyself for thy vices.

Love your enemies, for they tell you your faults.

Doing an injury puts you below your enemy; revenging one makes you but even with him; forgiving it sets you above him.

2. Bundling in New England (*c.* 1776)

Bundling was normally a form of courtship, common in all the colonies from Pennsylvania north, in which the couples lay on or in a bed with their clothes on, often with an upright center board between them. Visiting strangers might be similarly bedded down with the farmer's daughter. Originating in Europe, the practice was most common among the poorer classes, and reflected a shortage of beds, space, privacy, candles, and firewood. Bundling was not always innocent, and New England clergymen like Jonathan Edwards lashed out against it. Here the Reverend Samuel Peters, writing in 1781 of Connecticut, offers some views on the practice. Form a critical judgment as to the moral standards and safeguards in New England at this time.

Notwithstanding the modesty of the females is such that it would be accounted the greatest rudeness for a gentleman to speak before a lady of a garter, knee, or leg, yet it is thought but a piece of civility to ask her to bundle; a custom as old as the first settlement in 1634 [1635]. It is certainly innocent, virtuous, and prudent, or the Puritans would not have permitted it to prevail among their offspring, for whom in general they would suffer crucifixion.

Children brought up with the chastest ideas, with so much religion as to believe that the omniscient God sees them in the dark, and that angels guard them when absent from their parents, will not, nay, cannot, act a wicked thing. People who are influenced more by lust than a serious faith in God, who is too pure to behold iniquity with approbation, ought never to bundle. If any man, thus a stranger to the love of virtue, of God, and the Christian religion, should bundle with a young lady in New England, and behave himself unseemly towards her, he must first melt her into passion, and expel heaven, death, and hell from her mind, or he will undergo the chastisement of Negroes turned mad. If he escapes with life, it will be owing to the parents flying from their bed to protect him. . . .

2. Samuel Peters, *General History of Connecticut* (1877), pp. 224–27.

I am no advocate for temptation; yet must say that bundling has pre-vailed 160 years in New England, and, I verily believe, with ten times more chastity than sitting on a sofa. . . . About the year 1756, Boston, Salem, Newport, and New York, resolving to be more polite than their ancestors, forbade their daughters bundling on the bed with any young man whatever, and introduced a sofa to render courtship more palatable and Turkish. Whatever it was owing to, whether to the sofa, or any uncommon excess of the *feu d'esprit* [passion], there went abroad a report that this *raffinage* [refinement] produced more natural consequences than all the bundling among the boors. . . .

In 1776, a clergyman from one of the polite towns went into the country, and preached against the unchristian custom of young men and maidens lying together on a bed. He was no sooner out of the church than attacked by a shoal of good old women with "Sir, do you think we and our daughters are naughty, because we allow of bundling?"

"You lead yourselves into temptation by it."

They all replied at once, "Sir, have you been told thus, or has experience taught it you?"

The Levite began to lift up his eyes, and to consider of his situation, and bowing, said, "I have been told so."

The ladies, *una voce* [with one voice], bawled out, "Your informants, sir, we conclude, are those city ladies who prefer a sofa to a bed. We advise you to alter your sermon by substituting the word 'sofa' for 'bundling,' and on your return home preach it to them, for experience has told us that city folks send more children into the country without fathers or mothers to own them than are born among us. Therefore, you see, a sofa is more dangerous than a bed."

The poor priest, seemingly convinced of his blunder, . . . confessed his error, begged pardon, and promised never more to preach against bundling, or to think amiss of the custom. The ladies generously forgave him, and went away.

It may seem very strange to find this custom of bundling in bed attended with so much innocence in New England, while in Europe it is thought not safe or scarcely decent to permit a young man and maid to be together in private anywhere. But in this quarter of the old world the viciousness of the one, and the simplicity of the other, are the result merely of education and habit.

E. THE SHOOTS OF DEMOCRACY

1. The Epochal Zenger Trial (1735)

William Cosby, a hotheadedly incompetent New York governor, peremptorily removed the Chief Justice of the colony and substituted a stooge, young James Delancey. New Yorkers of the "popular party" decided to strike back by supporting the New York *Weekly Journal*, edited by John Peter Zenger, a struggling printer who had earlier come from Germany as an indentured servant. His attacks on Gover-

1 J. P. Zenger, *Zenger's Own Story* (1736; reprint 1954), pp. 20–41, *passim*.

nor Cosby brought on a famous trial for seditious libel. The outlook seemed dark after
Zenger's two attorneys were summarily disbarred. But at the critical moment Andrew
Hamilton, an aging but eminent Philadelphia lawyer, put in a surprise appearance as
defense counsel. At the outset he seemingly gave away his case when he admitted
that Zenger had published the alleged libels, but he contended that since they were
true, they were not libelous. The accepted law was that a libel was a libel, regardless
of its truth. Here Zenger describes his defense by Hamilton and the outcome of the
trial. Comment critically on the propositions that the suppression of evidence is the
strongest kind of evidence; that oppression creates grounds for new oppression; and
that the jurors, in their own long-range interests, were bound to vote "Not guilty."

MR. ATTORNEY. . . . The case before the court is whether Mr. Zenger is
guilty of libeling His Excellency the Governor of New York, and indeed
the whole administration of the government. Mr. Hamilton has confessed
the printing and publishing, and I think nothing is plainer than that the
words in the information [indictment] are scandalous, and tend to sedition,
and to disquiet the minds of the people of this province. And if such papers
are not libels, I think it may be said there can be no such thing as a libel.

MR. HAMILTON. May it please Your Honor, I cannot agree with Mr.
Attorney. For though I freely acknowledge that there are such things as
libels, yet I must insist, at the same time, that what my client is charged
with is not a libel. And I observed just now that Mr. Attorney, in defining
a libel, made use of the words "scandalous, seditious, and tend to disquiet
the people." But (whether with design or not I will not say) he omitted
the word "false."

MR. ATTORNEY. I think I did not omit the word "false." But it has been
said already that it may be a libel, notwithstanding it may be true.

MR. HAMILTON. In this I must still differ with Mr. Attorney; for I depend
upon it, we are to be tried upon this information now before the court and
jury, and to which we have pleaded not guilty, and by it we are charged
with printing and publishing a certain false, malicious, seditious, and
scandalous libel. This word "false" must have some meaning, or else how
came it there? . . .

MR. CHIEF JUSTICE [DELANCEY]. You cannot be admitted, Mr. Hamilton,
to give the truth of a libel in evidence. A libel is not to be justified; for it
is nevertheless a libel that it is true [*i.e.,* the fact that it is true makes it
none the less a libel].

MR. HAMILTON. I am sorry the court has so soon resolved upon that
piece of law; I expected first to have been heard to the point. I have not
in all my reading met with an authority that says we cannot be admitted
to give the truth in evidence, upon an information for a libel.

MR. CHIEF JUSTICE. The law is clear, that you cannot justify a libel. . . .

MR. HAMILTON. I thank Your Honor. Then, gentlemen of the jury, it is
to you we must now appeal, for witnesses, to the truth of the facts we have
offered, and are denied the liberty to prove. And let it not seem strange
that I apply myself to you in this manner. I am warranted so to do both
by law and reason.

The law supposes you to be summoned out of the neighborhood where the fact [crime] is alleged to be committed; and the reason of your being taken out of the neighborhood is because you are supposed to have the best knowledge of the fact that is to be tried. And were you to find a verdict

Numb. LV.

THE

New-York Weekly JOURNAL.

Containing the frefheft Advices, Foreign, and Domeftick.

MUNDAY November 25th, 1734.

To all my Subfcribers and Benefactors who take my weekly Journall.

Gentlemen, Ladies and Others;

AS you laft week were Difappointed of my Journall, I think it Incumbent upon me, to publifh my Apoligy which is this. On the Lords Day, the Seventeenth of this Inftant, I was Arrefted, taken and Imprifoned in the common Goal of this Citty, by Virtue of a Warrant from the *Governour*, and the Honorable *Francifs Harrifon*, Efq; and others in Councill of which (God willing) yo'l have a Coppy, whereupon I was put under fuch Reftraint that I had not the Liberty of Pen, Ink, or Paper, or to fee, or fpeak with People, till upon my Complaint to the Honourable the Chief Juftice, at my appearing before him upon my *Habias Corpus* on the *Wednefday* following. Who difcountenanced that Proceeding, and therefore I have had fince that Time, the Liberty of Speaking through the Hole of the Door, to my Wife and Servants by which I doubt not yo'l think me fufficiently Excufed for not fending my laft weeks *Journall*, and I hope for the future by the Liberty of Speaking to my Servants thro' the Hole of the Door of the Prifon, to enfertain you with my weekly *Journal* as formerly.   *And am your obliged Humble Servant,*
      J. *Peter Zenger.*

Mr. *Zenger*;

AS the Liberty of the Prefs is juftly efteemed and univerfally acknowledged by Englifhmen, to be the grand Paladium of all their Liberties, which Liberty of the Prefs, I have rejoyced to fee well defended in Sundry of your Papers, and particularly by your No. 2. 3. 10. 11. 15. 16. 17. 18. 24. & 54. and by an annonimous Authors Obfervations on the chief Juftices Charge of *January* laft; now, for as much as it may not only be of prefent Ufe, but of future Advantage, that fuch Matters of Fact, that concern the Liberty of the Prefs, may be faithfully recorded and tranfmitted to Pofterity. therefore I have fent you a Detail of fuch particulars that concern the Liberty of the Prefs within this Colony, and becaufe I would not have you or my felf charged with the Publication of a Libel, I fhall confine my felf to a plain Narration of Facts without any comments.

On Tuefday *the* 15th *of* Octo. 1734. *The fupream Court of* New-York, *began, when the Honourable* James De Lancey, Efq; *Cheif Juftie charged the Grand Jury. The Conclufion of which Charge was as follows.*

Gentlemen, I fhall conclude with reading a Paragraph or two out of the fame Book, † concerning Libels; they are arrived to that height, that they call

ZENGER CONTINUES PUBLICATION FROM PRISON
New-York Historical Society.

against my client, you must take upon you to say the papers referred to in the information, and which we acknowledge we printed and published, are false, scandalous, and seditious. But of this I can have no apprehension. You are citizens of New York; you are really what the law supposes you to be, honest and lawful men. And, according to my brief, the facts which we offer to prove were not committed in a corner; they are notoriously known to be true; and therefore in your justice lies our safety. And as we are denied the liberty of giving evidence to prove the truth of what we have published, I will beg leave to lay it down, as a standing rule in such cases, that the suppressing of evidence ought always to be taken for the strongest evidence; and I hope it will have that weight with you. . . .

I hope to be pardoned, sir, for my zeal upon this occasion. It is an old and wise caution that when our neighbor's house is on fire, we ought to take care of our own. For though, blessed be God, I live in a government [Pennsylvania] where liberty is well understood, and freely enjoyed, yet experience has shown us all (I'm sure it has to me) that a bad precedent in one government is soon set up for an authority in another. And therefore I cannot but think it mine, and every honest man's duty, that (while we pay all due obedience to men in authority) we ought at the same time to be upon our guard against power, wherever we apprehend that it may affect ourselves or our fellow subjects.

I am truly very unequal to such an undertaking on many accounts. And you see I labor under the weight of many years, and am borne down with great infirmities of body. Yet old and weak as I am, I should think it my duty, if required, to go to the utmost part of the land, where my service could be of any use, in assisting to quench the flame of prosecutions upon informations, set on foot by the government, to deprive a people of the right of remonstrating (and complaining too) of the arbitrary attempts of men in power. Men who injure and oppress the people under their administration provoke them to cry out and complain; and then make that very complaint the foundation for new oppressions and prosecutions. I wish I could say there were no instances of this kind.

But to conclude. The question before the court and you, gentlemen of the jury, is not of small nor private concern. It is not the cause of a poor printer, nor of New York alone, which you are now trying. No! It may, in its consequence, affect every freeman that lives under a British government on the main[land] of America. It is the best cause. It is the cause of liberty. And I make no doubt but your upright conduct, this day, will not only entitle you to the love and esteem of your fellow citizens; but every man who prefers freedom to a life of slavery will bless and honor you, as men who have baffled the attempt of tyranny, and, by an impartial and uncorrupt verdict, have laid a noble foundation for securing to ourselves, our posterity, and our neighbors, that to which nature and the laws of our country have given us a right—the liberty both of exposing and opposing arbitrary power (in these parts of the world, at least) by speaking and writing truth. . . .

The jury withdrew, and in a small time returned, and being asked by the clerk whether they were agreed of their verdict, and whether John Peter Zenger was guilty of printing and publishing the libels in the information mentioned, they answered by Thomas Hunt, their foreman, "Not guilty."

Upon which there were three huzzas in the hall, which was crowded with people, and the next day I was discharged from my imprisonment.

[*The jurors, who might have suffered fines and imprisonment, were guilty of "bad law," for at that time they had no legal alternative to finding Zenger guilty. But the trial, which was widely publicized at home and abroad, provided a setback for judicial tyranny, a partial triumph for freedom of the press, a gain for the privilege of criticizing public officials, and a boost to the ideal of liberty generally. Andrew Hamilton, in truth, was contending for the law as it should be and ultimately became. But not for many years did the two principles for which he argued become accepted practice in England and America: (1) the admissibility of evidence as to the truth of an alleged libel, and (2) the right of the jury to judge the libelous nature of the alleged libel.*]

2. Crèvecoeur Finds a Perfect Society (*c.* 1770)

Crèvecoeur, the happy Frenchman dwelling on a New York farm before the Revolution (see earlier, p. 67), wrote in glowing terms of the almost classless society developing in the colonies. Note the important respects in which his analysis is sound; unsound. Reconcile his statements with the existence of slavery and indentured servitude; a planter aristocracy; a tax-supported church; and the widespread flouting of the Navigation Laws.

He [the English traveler to America] is arrived on a new continent; a modern society offers itself to his contemplation, different from what he had hitherto seen. It is not composed, as in Europe, of great lords who possess everything, and of a herd of people who have nothing. Here are no aristocratical families, no courts, no kings, no bishops, no ecclesiastical dominion, no invisible power giving to a few a very visible one; no great manufacturers employing thousands, no great refinements of luxury. The rich and the poor are not so far removed from each other as they are in Europe.

Some few towns excepted, we are all tillers of the earth, from Nova Scotia to West Florida. We are a people of cultivators, scattered over an immense territory, communicating with each other by means of good roads and navigable rivers, united by the silken bands of mild government, all respecting the laws, without dreading their power, because they are equitable. We are all animated with the spirit of an industry which is unfettered and unrestrained, because each person works for himself.

If he [the English visitor] travels through our rural districts, he views not the hostile castle and the haughty mansion, contrasted with the clay-built hut and miserable cabin, where cattle and men help to keep each other warm, and dwell in meanness, smoke, and indigence. A pleasing uniformity of decent competence appears throughout our habitations. The meanest of our log-houses is a dry and comfortable habitation. Lawyer or merchant are the fairest titles our towns afford; that of a farmer is the

2. M. G. J. de Crèvecoeur, *Letters from an American Farmer* (1904 reprint), pp. 49–50.

only appellation of the rural inhabitants of our country. It must take some time ere he can reconcile himself to our dictionary, which is but short in words of dignity and names of honor.

There, on a Sunday, he sees a congregation of respectable farmers and their wives, all clad in neat homespun, well mounted, or riding in their own humble wagons. There is not among them an esquire, saving the unlettered magistrate. There he sees a parson as simple as his flock, a farmer who does not riot on the labor of others. We have no princes, for whom we toil, starve, and bleed: we are the most perfect society now existing in the world. Here man is free as he ought to be; nor is this pleasing equality so transitory as many others are.

THOUGHT PROVOKERS

1. Compare and contrast social conditions in the New World with those in the Old, and explain why the New World had certain advantages. Did the indentured servants pay too high a price for their shift to America? What connection can be found between the long ocean voyage of the immigrants and the rise of a spirit of independence?

2. Why did education spread most rapidly in New England? The Massachusetts law of 1647 established certain principles regarding the obligation of the parent, the role of the state, and the raising of money, all of which may be found in our school systems today. What are they?

3. Compare and contrast religion in colonial times with religion today. Did the threat of hell-fire promote better morals? Reconcile the wrathful Old Testament God of Jonathan Edwards with the New Testament concept "God is love." Account for the popularity of Franklin's wit and wisdom. Would his *Almanack* have done as well in England?

4. Did Franklin's pithy sayings promote morality? Explain how the strict Puritans could tolerate the practice of bundling.

5. How can one reconcile the case of Zenger with the classless society described by Crèvecoeur? Can the truth be libel today?

FURTHER EXPLORATION

General: Max Savelle, *Seeds of Liberty* (1948); J. T. Adams, *Provincial Society, 1690–1763* (1927). **Melting Pot:** L. B. Wright, *The Cultural Life of the American Colonies* (1957); A. E. Smith, *Colonists in Bondage* (1947); M. W. Jernegan, *Laboring and Dependent Classes in Colonial America* (1931). **Education:** G. H. Martin, *The Evolution of the Massachusetts Public School System* (1894); E. P. Cubberley, *Public Education in the United States* (1934). **Religion:** Perry Miller, *Jonathan Edwards* (1949); A. D. Belden, *George Whitefield, the Awakener* (1930); E. S. Gaustad, *The Great Awakening in New England* (1957). **Morality:** Carl Van Doren, *Benjamin Franklin* (1938); H. R. Stiles, *Bundling* (1934). **Shoots of Democracy:** Vincent Buranelli, *The Trial of Peter Zenger* (1957); L. W. Levy, *Legacy of Suppression* (1960).

Recent: H. M. Jones, *O Strange New World: American Culture, The Formative Years* (1964); J. R. Alden, *Pioneer America* (1966); J. G. Leyburn, *The Scotch-Irish: A Social History* (1962); J. T. Ellis, *Catholics in Colonial America* (1965); R. E. and B. K. Brown, *Virginia, 1705–1786: Democracy or Aristocracy?* (1964); Carl Bridenbaugh, *Mitre and Sceptre* (1962).

Chapter 5

The Eve of Rebellion

We cannot be happy without being free; we cannot be free without being secure in our property; we cannot be secure in our property if, without our consent, others may, as by right, take it away; taxes imposed on us by Parliament do thus take it away.

JOHN DICKINSON, 1767

PROLOGUE: The British Empire was erected on the then popular mercantilist philosophy (mercantile theory)—that is, colonies exist for the benefit of the Mother Country. British regulations imposed burdens and conferred benefits, but on balance the advantages to the colonials probably outweighed the disadvantages. After the Seven Years' War had saddled Britain with a staggering debt, the Ministry decided to tax the colonies for a portion of their defense upkeep. The result was the Stamp Act of 1765, which stirred up such a furor that Parliament was forced to repeal it the next year. A renewed attempt at taxation in 1773 goaded the colonials into destroying a number of tea cargoes, notably at Boston. Parliament retaliated by passing legislation which was directed at Massachusetts and which, among other restrictions, closed the port of Boston. The other colonies rallied to the defense of their beleaguered sister; tensions increased; and the first formal shooting erupted at Lexington in 1775.

A. THE BURDEN OF MERCANTILISM

1. Virginia Resents Restrictions (1671)

The foundation stones of British mercantilism in America were the Navigation Acts of 1651 and 1660. All commerce with the colonies had to be carried on in English-built and English-owned ships (a blow at Dutch competitors), and certain "enumerated articles," such as sugar, tobacco, and indigo, could be exported only to England. To the English mainland colonies, tobacco was by far the most important "enumerated" product, and Virginia was especially hard hit. The Virginians, to be sure, were guaranteed a monopoly of the English market, but they were denied the profits of direct sales to Spanish and other European customers. As early as 1671 the testy Governor Berkeley of Virginia (see p. 15) lodged the following bitter protest with the London officials in response to specific questions from them. Note how these restrictions hampered the development of Virginia.

What obstructions do you find to the improvement of the trade and navigation of the plantations within your government?

Answer. Mighty and destructive, by that severe act of Parliament which excludes us the having any commerce with any nation in Europe but our own, so that we cannot add to our plantation any commodity that grows out of it, as olive trees, cotton, or vines. Besides this, we cannot procure

---

1. W. W. Hening, *The Statutes at Large . . . of Virginia . . .* (1823), II, 515–16.

any skillful men for one now hopeful commodity, silk; for it is not lawful for us to carry a pipe stave, or a barrel of corn, to any place in Europe out of the King's dominions. If this were for His Majesty's service or the good of his subjects, we should not repine, whatever our sufferings are for it; but on my soul, it is the contrary for both. And this is the cause why no small or great vessels are built here; for we are most obedient to all laws, whilst the New England men break through, and men trade to any place that their interest lead them.

What advantages or improvement do you observe that may be gained to your trade or navigation?

Answer. None, unless we had liberty to transport our pipe staves, timber, and corn to other places besides the King's dominions.

2. Adam Smith's Balance Sheet (1776)

The Navigation Laws, as perfected in the 18th Century, bore most harshly on the Southern colonies, with their staple enumerated products. To strengthen the Royal Navy, the London government paid bounties for the production of pitch, tar, rosin, turpentine, hemp, masts, yards, and bowsprits, but the Northern colonies came off with a lion's share of the bounty payments. The whole system was reviewed in 1776, the year the colonies declared independence, by the Scottish philosopher-economist Adam Smith in his monumental *Wealth of Nations.* As a declaration of independence from current mercantilistic restrictions, it ranks as one of the great books of all time. Smith, who has been dubbed "the Father of Modern Economics," was a liberal-minded exponent of the greatest good to the greatest number. In the passage here reproduced from his *Wealth of Nations*, decide what British restrictions were most galling, and why they were not so intolerable as one might have expected.

The most perfect freedom of trade is permitted between the British colonies of America and the West Indies, both in the enumerated and in the non-enumerated commodities. Those colonies are now become so populous and thriving that each of them finds in some of the others a great and extensive market for every part of its produce. All of them taken together, they make a great internal market for the produce of one another.

The liberality of England, however, towards the trade of her colonies has been confined chiefly to what concerns the market for their produce, either in its rude state or in what may be called the very first stage of manufacture. The more advanced or more refined manufactures, even of the colony produce, the merchants and manufacturers of Great Britain choose to reserve to themselves, and have prevailed upon the legislature [Parliament] to prevent their establishment in the colonies, sometimes by high duties, and sometimes by absolute prohibitions. . . .

While Great Britain encourages in America the manufactures of pig and bar iron, by exempting them from duties to which the like commodities are subject when imported from any other country, she imposes an absolute prohibition upon the erection of steel furnaces and slit-mills in any of her American plantations. She will not suffer her colonists to work in those

2. Adam Smith, *An Inquiry into the Nature and Causes of the Wealth of Nations* (1904), II, 82–84.

THE COLONIES REDUCED

A famous cartoon "invented" by Benjamin Franklin and published in the *Political Register*, London, 1768. It foresaw that Britain's policies would cause her to become dismembered, much as the famous Roman general Belisarius was ultimately defeated and allegedly reduced to blind beggary. "Give a penny to Belisarius" is the Latin inscription. Boston Public Library.

more refined manufactures, even for their own consumption; but insists upon their purchasing of her merchants and manufacturers all goods of this kind which they have occasion for.

She prohibits the exportation from one province to another by water, and even the carriage by land upon horseback or in a cart, of hats, of wools and woolen goods, of the produce of America—a regulation which effectually prevents the establishment of any manufacture of such commodities for distant sale, and confines the industry of her colonists in this way to such coarse and household manufactures as a private family commonly makes for its own use, or for that of some of its neighbors in the same province.

To prohibit a great people, however, from making all that they can of every part of their own produce, or from employing their stock and industry in the way that they judge most advantageous to themselves, is a manifest violation of the most sacred rights of mankind.

Unjust, however, as such prohibitions may be, they have not hitherto been very hurtful to the colonies. Land is still so cheap and, consequently, labor so dear among them that they can import from the Mother Country almost all the more refined or more advanced manufactures cheaper than they could make them for themselves. Though [even if] they had not, therefore, been prohibited from establishing such manufactures, yet in their present state of improvement a regard to their own interest would probably have prevented them from doing so. In their present state of improvement those prohibitions, perhaps, without cramping their industry, or restraining it from any employment to which it would have gone of its own accord, are only impertinent badges of slavery imposed upon them, without any sufficient reason, by the groundless jealousy of the merchants and manufacturers of the Mother Country. In a more advanced state they might be really oppressive and insupportable.

B. THE TEMPEST OVER TAXATION

1. Franklin Testifies against the Stamp Act (1766)

The British Parliament undertook in 1765 to levy a direct (internal) stamp tax on the American colonies to defray one-third of the expenses of keeping a military force there. The colonials had long paid taxes voted by their own assemblies, as well as customs duties (external taxes) passed by Parliament primarily to regulate trade. But they objected heatedly to paying direct or internal taxes voted by a Parliament in which they were not specifically represented. Benjamin Franklin, then in London as a prominent colonial agent, testified as follows before a committee of the House of Commons. He made a brilliant showing with his incisive answers, especially since he had "planted" a number of questions in advance among his friends on the committee. Form conclusions as to the ability of the Americans to bear additional taxes, and as to the defenses available to them against the odious stamp tax.

Q. What is your name, and place of abode?

A. Franklin, of Philadelphia.

Q. Do the Americans pay any considerable taxes among themselves?

A. Certainly many, and very heavy taxes.

Q. What are the present taxes in Pennsylvania, laid by the laws of the colony?

A. There are taxes on all estates, real and personal; a poll tax; a tax on all offices, professions, trades, and businesses, according to their profits; an excise on all wine, rum, and other spirit; and a duty of ten pounds per head on all Negroes imported, with some other duties.

Q. For what purposes are those taxes laid?

A. For the support of the civil and military establishments of the country, and to discharge the heavy debt contracted in the last [Seven Years'] war. . . .

Q. Are not all the people very able to pay those taxes?

A. No. The frontier counties, all along the continent, having been frequently ravaged by the enemy and greatly impoverished, are able to pay very little tax. . . .

Q. Are not the colonies, from their circumstances, very able to pay the stamp duty?

A. In my opinion there is not gold and silver enough in the colonies to pay the stamp duty for one year.

1. *The Parliamentary History of England* . . . (1813), XVI, 138–59, *passim.*

Q. Don't you know that the money arising from the stamps was all to be laid out in America?

A. I know it is appropriated by the act to the American service; but it will be spent in the conquered colonies, where the soldiers are, not in the colonies that pay it. . . .

Q. Do you think it right that America should be protected by this country and pay no part of the expense?

A. That is not the case. The colonies raised, clothed, and paid, during the last war, near 25,000 men, and spent many millions.

Q. Were you not reimbursed by Parliament?

A. We were only reimbursed what, in your opinion, we had advanced beyond our proportion, or beyond what might reasonably be expected from us; and it was a very small part of what we spent. Pennsylvania, in particular, disbursed about 500,000 pounds, and the reimbursements, in the whole, did not exceed 60,000 pounds. . . .

Q. Do not you think the people of America would submit to pay the stamp duty, if it was moderated?

A. No, never, unless compelled by force of arms. . . .

Q. What was the temper of America towards Great Britain before the year 1763?

A. The best in the world. They sub-

HANGING JOHN HUSKE IN EFFIGY

A Paul Revere engraving showing the fate in America of an alleged supporter of the Stamp Act. American Antiquarian Society.

mitted willingly to the government of the Crown, and paid, in all their courts, obedience to acts of Parliament. . . .

Q. What is your opinion of a future tax, imposed on the same principle with that of the Stamp Act? How would the Americans receive it?

A. Just as they do this. They would not pay it.

Q. Have not you heard of the resolutions of this House, and of the House of Lords, asserting the right of Parliament relating to America, including a power to tax the people there?

A. Yes, I have heard of such resolutions.

Q. What will be the opinion of the Americans on those resolutions?

A. They will think them unconstitutional and unjust.

Q. Was it an opinion in America before 1763 that the Parliament had no right to lay taxes and duties there?

A. I never heard any objection to the right of laying duties to regulate commerce; but a right to lay internal taxes was never supposed to be in Parliament, as we are not represented there. . . .

Q. Did the Americans ever dispute the controlling power of Parliament to regulate the commerce?

A. No.

Q. Can anything less than a military force carry the Stamp Act into execution?

A. I do not see how a military force can be applied to that purpose.

Q. Why may it not?

A. Suppose a military force sent into America; they will find nobody in arms; what are they then to do? They cannot force a man to take stamps who chooses to do without them. They will not find a rebellion; they may indeed make one.

Q. If the act is not repealed, what do you think will be the consequences?

A. A total loss of the respect and affection the people of America bear to this country, and of all the commerce that depends on that respect and affection.

Q. How can the commerce be affected?

A. You will find that, if the act is not repealed, they will take very little of your manufactures in a short time.

Q. Is it in their power to do without them?

A. I think they may very well do without them.

Q. Is it their interest not to take them?

A. The goods they take from Britain are either necessaries, mere conveniences, or superfluities. The first, as cloth, etc., with a little industry they can make at home; the second they can do without till they are able to provide them among themselves; and the last, which are much the greatest part, they will strike off immediately. They are mere articles of fashion, purchased and consumed because the fashion in a respected country; but will now be detested and rejected. The people have already struck off, by general agreement, the use of all goods fashionable in mournings. . . .

Q. If the Stamp Act should be repealed, would it induce the assemblies of America to acknowledge the right of Parliament to tax them, and would they erase their resolutions [against the Stamp Act]?

A. No, never.

Q. Is there no means of obliging them to erase those resolutions?

A. None that I know of; they will never do it, unless compelled by force of arms.

Q. Is there a power on earth that can force them to erase them?

A. No power, how great soever, can force men to change their opinions. . . .

Q. What used to be the pride of the Americans?

A. To indulge in the fashions and manufactures of Great Britain.

Q. What is now their pride?

A. To wear their old clothes over again, till they can make new ones.

2. Philadelphia Threatens Tea Men (1773)

Parliament, faced with rebellion and a crippling commercial boycott, repealed the Stamp Act in 1766. The next year the Ministry devised a light indirect tax on tea which, being external, presumably met the colonial objections to a direct tax. Opposition to the new levy was fading when, in 1773, the London officials granted a monopoly of the tea business in America to the powerful and hated British East India Company. These arrangements would make the tea, even with the three-penny tax included, cheaper than ever. The colonials, resenting this transparent attempt to trick them into paying the tax, staged several famous tea parties. Those in Boston and at New York involved throwing the tea overboard; the affair at Annapolis resulted in the burning of both vessel and cargo. At Portsmouth and Philadelphia the tea ships were turned away. Of the reasons here given by the Philadelphians for action, determine which was the strongest, and whether it was strong enough to warrant the measures threatened.

TO CAPT. AYRES

Of the Ship *Polly*, on a Voyage
from London to Philadelphia

Sir: We are informed that you have imprudently taken charge of a quantity of tea which has been sent out by the [East] India Company, under the auspices of the Ministry, as a trial of American virtue and resolution.

Now, as your cargo, on your arrival here, will most assuredly bring you into hot water, and as you are perhaps a stranger to these parts, we have concluded to advise you of the present situation of affairs in Philadelphia, that, taking time by the forelock, you may stop short in your dangerous errand, secure your ship against the rafts of combustible matter which may be set on fire and turned loose against her; and more than all this, that you may preserve your own person from the pitch and feathers that are prepared for you.

In the first place, we must tell you that the Pennsylvanians are, to a man, passionately fond of freedom, the birthright of Americans, and at all events are determined to enjoy it.

That they sincerely believe no power on the face of the earth has a right to tax them without their consent.

That, in their opinion, the tea in your custody is designed by the Ministry to enforce such a tax, which they will undoubtedly oppose, and in so doing, give you every possible obstruction.

2. *Pennsylvania Magazine of History and Biography*, XV (1891), 391.

We are nominated to a very disagreeable, but necessary, service: to our care are committed all offenders against the rights of America; and hapless is he whose evil destiny has doomed him to suffer at our hands.

You are sent out on a diabolical service; and if you are so foolish and obstinate as to complete your voyage by bringing your ship to anchor in this port, you may run such a gauntlet as will induce you in your last moments most heartily to curse those who have made you the dupe of their avarice and ambition.

What think you, Captain, of a halter around your neck—ten gallons of liquid tar decanted on your pate—with the feathers of a dozen wild geese laid over that to enliven your appearance?

Only think seriously of this—and fly to the place from whence you came— fly without hesitation—without the formality of a protest—and above all, Captain Ayres, let us advise you to fly without the wild geese feathers.

Your friends to serve,

THE COMMITTEE OF TARRING AND FEATHERING

3. Connecticut Decries the Boston Port Act (1774)

The Boston Tea Party, which involved the destruction of three cargoes of tea by colonials thinly disguised as Indians, provoked an angry response in Parliament. Even so good a friend of America as Colonel Barré so far forgot his grammar as to burst out, "Boston ought to be punished; *she* is your eldest son!" Parliament speedily passed a series of punitive measures ("Intolerable Acts"), notable among them being the act closing the port of Boston until the tea was paid for. The other colonies, deeply resentful, responded with assurances of support. Virginia raised food and money; Philadelphia contributed one thousand barrels of flour. Various groups passed resolutions of protest, including the citizens of Farmington, Connecticut. Ascertain to what extent their statement blames the King; to what extent, if any, it reflects a desire for independence.

Early in the morning was found the following handbill, posted up in various parts of the town, viz.:

> To pass through the fire at six o'clock this
> evening, in honor to the immortal goddess of
> Liberty, the late infamous Act of the British
> Parliament for farther distressing the Amer-
> ican Colonies. The place of execution will be
> the public parade, where all Sons of Liberty
> are desired to attend.

Accordingly, a very numerous and respectable body were assembled of near one thousand people, when a huge pole, just forty-five feet high, was erected, and consecrated to the shrine of liberty; after which the Act of Parliament for blocking up the Boston harbor was read aloud, sentenced to the flames, and executed by the hands of the common hangman. Then the following resolves were passed, *nem. con.* [unanimously]:

3. Peter Force, ed., *American Archives*, Fourth Series (1837), I, 336.

1st. That it is the greatest dignity, interest, and happiness of every American to be united with our parent state while our liberties are duly secured, maintained, and supported by our rightful sovereign, whose person we greatly revere; whose government, while duly administered, we are ready with our lives and properties to support.

2nd. That the present Ministry, being instigated by the Devil, and led on by their wicked and corrupt hearts, have a design to take away our liberties and properties, and to enslave us forever.

3rd. That the late Act, which their malice hath caused to be passed in Parliament, for blocking up the port of Boston, is unjust, illegal, and oppressive; and that we, and every American, are sharers in the insults offered to the town of Boston.

4th. That those pimps and parasites who dared to advise their master [George III] to such detestable measures be held in utter abhorrence by us and every American, and their names loaded with the curses of all succeeding generations.

5th. That we scorn the chains of slavery; we despise every attempt to rivet them upon us; we are the sons of freedom, and resolved that, till time shall be no more, that godlike virtue shall blazon our hemisphere.

C. BRITAIN AT THE CROSSROADS

1. Dean Tucker Advises a Divorce (1774)

Josiah Tucker (Dean of Gloucester), a British clergyman-economist, was a born controversialist who for fifty years penned numerous pamphlets on varied subjects. A man of prodigious energy, he had, as a student at Oxford, regularly walked the 150 miles between the university and his native Wales. Regarding England as underpopulated, he doubted the utility of colonies and criticized many aspects of mercantilism. After critical difficulties over taxation again developed with America in 1774, he examined, in a pamphlet, four possible courses: (1) let affairs drift; (2) persuade the colonies to accept representation in Parliament; (3) crush the colonies with arms; (4) separate peacefully from the colonies, with an offer of protection against foreign foes. In the following passage he develops the theme that the British Empire would actually be strengthened by the expulsion of its most valuable part. In the light of subsequent history, was he more right than wrong?

The first and capital supposed [dis]advantage is that if we separate from the colonies, we shall lose their trade. But why so? And how does this appear? The colonies, we know by experience, will trade with any people, even with their bitterest enemies, during the hottest of a war, and a war [French and Indian War] undertaken at their own earnest request, and for their own sakes—the colonies, I say, will trade even with them, provided they shall find it their interest so to do. Why then should any man suppose that the same self-interest will not induce them to trade with us? . . .

The second objection against giving up the colonies is that such a

1. R. L. Schuyler, ed., *Josiah Tucker* (1931), pp. 359–66, *passim.* By permission of the Columbia University Press.

measure would greatly decrease our shipping and navigation, and consequently diminish the breed of sailors. But this objection has been fully
obviated already. For if we shall not lose our trade, at least in any important
degree, even with the northern colonies (and most probably we shall
increase it with other countries), then it follows that neither the quantity
of shipping nor the breed of sailors can suffer any considerable diminution;
so that this supposition is merely a panic, and has no foundation. Not to
mention that in proportion as the Americans shall be obliged to exert themselves to defend their own coasts in case of war, in the same proportion
shall Great Britain be exonerated from that burden, and shall have more
ships and men at command to protect her own channel trade, and for
other services.

The third objection is that if we were to give up these colonies, the
French would take immediate possession of them. Now this objection is
entirely built on . . . very wild, very extravagant, and absurd supposi-
tions. . . .

The manifold advantages attendant on such a scheme:

And first, a disjunction from the northern colonies would effectually put
a stop to our present emigrations. . . .

Secondly. Another great advantage to be derived from a separation is
that we shall then save between £300,000 and £400,000 a year, by being
discharged from the payment of any civil or military establishment belonging to the colonies; for which generous benefaction we receive at present
no other return than invectives and reproaches.

Thirdly. The ceasing of the payment of bounties on certain colony productions will be another great saving, perhaps not less than £200,000 a
year. And it is very remarkable that the goods imported from the colonies,
in consequence of these bounties, could not have been imported into any
other part of Europe, were there a liberty to do it, because the freight and
first cost would have amounted to more than they could be sold for. So that,
in fact, we give premiums to the colonies for selling goods to us which
would not have been sold at all anywhere else. . . .

Fourthly. When we are no longer connected with the colonies by the
imaginary tie of an identity of government, then our merchant-exporters
and manufacturers will have a better chance of having their debts paid
than they have at present. For as matters now stand, the colonists choose
to carry their ready cash to other nations, while they are contracting debts
with their mother country, with whom they think they can take greater
liberties. . . .

Fifthly. After a separation from the colonies, our influence over them
will be much greater than ever it was since they began to feel their own
weight and importance. For at present we are looked upon in no better a
light than that of robbers and usurpers; whereas we shall then be considered
as their protectors, mediators, benefactors. The moment a separation takes
effect, intestine quarrels will begin. For it is well known that the seeds of
discord and dissension between province and province are now ready to

shoot forth; and they are only kept down by the present combination of all the colonies against us, whom they unhappily fancy to be their common enemy. When, therefore, this object of their hatred shall be removed by a declaration on our parts that, so far from usurping all authority, we, from henceforward, will assume none at all against their own consent, the weaker provinces will entreat our protection against the stronger, and the less cautious against the more crafty and designing. So that, in short, in proportion as their factious, republican spirit shall intrigue and cabal, shall split into parties, divide, and subdivide—in the same proportion shall we be called in to become their general umpires and referees.

2. Adam Smith Criticizes Empire (1776)

Like Dean Tucker and British officialdom, Adam Smith was concerned about the expense of mercantilism. When serious friction developed with America, he advocated colonial membership in Parliament, with representation based on taxes paid. If the American tax revenues should ultimately exceed those of England, as was not unlikely, the capital of the Empire might be moved from London to the New World. Such views were not popular in the Mother Country. Evaluate the alternatives that Smith here presents in the concluding passage of his *Wealth of Nations*. Judge whether he regards the colonies as more a burden than an asset, and why.

The expense of the peace establishment of the colonies . . . , though very great, is insignificant in comparison with what the defense of the colonies has cost us in time of war. The last war [Seven Years' War], which was undertaken altogether on account of the colonies, cost Great Britain, it has already been observed, upwards of ninety millions [of pounds]. The Spanish war of 1739 [War of Jenkins' Ear] was principally undertaken on their account; in which, and in the French war [King George's] that was the consequence of it, Great Britain spent upwards of forty millions, a great part of which ought justly to be charged to the colonies.

In those two wars the colonies cost Great Britain much more than double the sum which the national debt amounted to before the commencement of the first of them. Had it not been for those wars, that debt might, and probably would, by this time, have been completely paid. And had it not been for the colonies, the former of those wars might not, and the latter certainly would not, have been undertaken. It was because the colonies were supposed to be provinces of the British empire that this expense was laid out upon them.

But the countries which contribute neither revenue nor military force towards the support of the empire cannot be considered as provinces. They may perhaps be considered as appendages, as a sort of splendid and showy equipage of the empire. But if the empire can no longer support the expense of keeping up this equipage, it ought certainly to lay it down. And if it cannot raise its revenue in proportion to its expense, it ought, at least,

2. Adam Smith, *An Inquiry into the Nature and Causes of the Wealth of Nations* (1904), II, 432.

to accommodate its expense to its revenue. If the colonies, notwithstanding their refusal to submit to British taxes, are still to be considered as provinces of the British empire, their defense in some future war may cost Great Britain as great an expense as it ever has done in any former war.

The rulers of Great Britain have, for more than a century past, amused the people with the imagination that they possessed a great empire on the west side of the Atlantic. This empire, however, has hitherto existed in imagination only. It has hitherto been, not an empire, but the project of an empire; not a gold mine, but the project of a gold mine—a project which has cost, which continues to cost, and which, if pursued in the same way as it has been hitherto, is likely to cost, immense expense, without being likely to bring any profit. For the effects of the monopoly of the colony trade, it has been shown, are, to the great body of the people, mere loss instead of profit.

It is surely now time that our rulers should realize this golden dream, in which they have been indulging themselves, perhaps, as well as the people; or that they should awake from it themselves, and endeavor to awaken the people. If the project cannot be completed, it ought to be given up. If any of the provinces of the British empire cannot be made to contribute toward the support of the whole empire, it is surely time that Great Britain should free herself from the expense of defending those provinces in time of war, and of supporting any part of their civil or military establishments in time of peace, and endeavor to accommodate her future views and designs to the real mediocrity [moderateness] of her circumstances.

3. Samuel Johnson Urges the Iron Fist (1775)

The conservative Samuel Johnson, famed for his English dictionary, was no friend of Americans, who, he wrote, "multiplied with the fecundity of their own rattlesnakes." In 1762 he accepted a pension of £300 annually from the Crown; in 1775 he repaid his royal master by publishing a pamphlet, "Taxation No Tyranny," in which he proved himself to be a political babe in the woods. He privately admitted that his manuscript was revised and shortened by the royal officials. Note which one of his proposals would be most likely to arouse the American frontier; which one the South; and which one would be most likely to stir up renewed rebellion generally. Locate the one proposal that has real merit and the one that is the most fantastic.

The Dean of Gloucester has proposed, and seems to propose it seriously, that we should, at once, release our claims, declare them [the Americans] masters of themselves, and whistle them down the wind. His opinion is that our gain from them will be the same, and our expense less. What they can have most cheaply from Britain, they will still buy; what they can sell to us at the highest price, they will still sell.

It is, however, a little hard that, having so lately fought and conquered for their safety, we should govern them no longer. By letting them loose

3. *The Works of Samuel Johnson* (1825), VI, 259–62.

before the [Seven Years'] war, how many millions might have been saved? One wild proposal is best answered by another. Let us restore to the French what we have taken from them. We shall see our colonists at our feet, when they have an enemy so near them [Canada]. Let us give the Indians arms, and teach them discipline, and encourage them, now and then, to plunder a plantation. Security and leisure are the parents of sedition.

While these different opinions are agitated, it seems to be determined by the legislature that force shall be tried. Men of the pen have seldom any great skill in conquering kingdoms, but they have strong inclination to give advice. I cannot forbear to wish that this commotion may end without bloodshed, and that the rebels may be subdued by terror rather than by violence; and, therefore, recommend such a force as may take away not only the power but the hope of resistance, and, by conquering without a battle, save many from the sword.

If their obstinacy continues, without actual hostilities, it may, perhaps, be mollified by turning out the soldiers to free quarters, forbidding any personal cruelty or hurt. It has been proposed that the slaves should be set free, an act which, surely, the [American] lovers of liberty cannot but commend. If they are furnished with firearms for defense, and utensils for husbandry, and settled in some simple form of government within the country, they may be more grateful and honest than their masters. . . .

Since the Americans have made it necessary to subdue them, may they be subdued with the least injury possible to their persons and their possessions! When they are reduced to obedience, may that obedience be secured by stricter laws and stronger obligations!

Nothing can be more noxious to society than that erroneous clemency which, when a rebellion is suppressed, exacts no forfeiture and establishes no securities, but leaves the rebels in their former state. Who would not try the experiment which promises advantage without expense? If rebels once obtain a victory, their wishes are accomplished. If they are defeated, they suffer little, perhaps less than their conquerors. However often they play the game, the chance is always in their favor. In the meantime they are growing rich by victualing the troops we have sent against them, and, perhaps, gain more by the residence of the army than they lose by the obstruction of their port [Boston].

Their charters, being now, I suppose, legally forfeited, may be modeled as shall appear most commodious to the Mother Country. Thus the privileges [of self-government] which are found, by experience, liable to misuse will be taken away, and those who now bellow as patriots, bluster as soldiers, and domineer as legislators will sink into sober merchants and silent planters, peaceably diligent and securely rich. . . .

We are told that the subjection of Americans may tend to the diminution of our own liberties—an event which none but very perspicacious politicians are able to foresee. If slavery be thus fatally contagious, how is it that we hear the loudest yelps for liberty among the [American] drivers of Negroes?

D. LOYALISTS VERSUS PATRIOTS

1. Daniel Leonard Deplores Rebellion (1775)

Daniel Leonard, of an aristocratic Massachusetts family, was the cleverest Tory pamphleteer in America. His writings, declared his pen adversary John Adams, "shone like the moon among the lesser stars." Forced to flee from Boston when the British troops withdrew in 1776, he subsequently became Chief Justice of Bermuda and dean of the English bar. He is best known in America for a series of seventeen newspaper articles, published in 1774–1775 over the signature "Massachusettensis." He warned his readers that rebellion was "the most atrocious offense," and that it would open the doors to anarchy. Legal punishment for the rebel was that he be dragged to the gallows; "that he be hanged by the neck, and then cut down alive; that his entrails be taken out and burned while he is yet alive; that his head be cut off; that his body be divided into four parts; that his head and quarters be at the king's disposal." As the clash neared between the American patriots (Whigs) and the British troops in Massachusetts, Leonard issued this final appeal to his countrymen two weeks before the bloodshed at Lexington. Evaluate his most convincing and his least convincing arguments in support of the view that the colonials could not win.

Do you expect to conquer in war? War is no longer a simple, but an intricate science, not to be learned from books or two or three campaigns, but from long experience. You need not be told that His Majesty's generals, Gage and Haldimand, are possessed of every talent requisite to great commanders, matured by long experience in many parts of the world, and stand high in military fame; that many of the officers have been bred to arms from their infancy, and a large proportion of the army now here have already reaped immortal honors in the iron harvest of the field.

Alas! My friends, you have nothing to oppose to this force but a militia unused to service, impatient of command, and destitute of resources. Can your officers depend upon the privates, or the privates upon the officers? Your war can be but little more than mere tumultuary rage. And besides, there is an awful disparity between troops that fight the battles of their sovereign and those that follow the standard of rebellion.

These reflections may arrest you in an hour that you think not of, and come too late to serve you. Nothing short of a miracle could gain you one battle; but could you destroy all the British troops that are now here, and burn the men-of-war that command our coast, it would be but the beginning of sorrow. And yet without a decisive battle, one campaign would ruin you. This province [Massachusetts] does not produce its necessary provision when the husbandman can pursue his calling without molestation. What then must be your condition when the demand shall be increased and the resource in a manner cut off? Figure to yourselves what must be your distress should your wives and children be driven from such places as the King's troops shall occupy, into the interior parts of the province, and they, as well as you, be destitute of support.

I take no pleasure in painting these scenes of distress. The Whigs [rebels] affect to divert you from them by ridicule; but should war com-

1. Daniel Leonard, *Massachusettensis* (1810), pp. 187–88.

mence, you can expect nothing but its severities. Might I hazard an opinion, but few of your leaders ever intended to engage in hostilities, but they may have rendered inevitable what they intended for intimidation. Those that unsheathe the sword of rebellion may throw away the scabbard; they cannot be treated with while in arms; and if they lay them down, they are in no other predicament than conquered rebels. The conquered in other wars do not forfeit the rights of men, nor all the rights of citizens. Even their bravery is rewarded by a generous victor. Far different is the case of a routed rebel host.

My dear countrymen, you have before you, at your election, peace or war, happiness or misery. May the God of our forefathers direct you in the way that leads to peace and happiness, before your feet stumble on the dark mountains, before the evil days come, wherein you shall say, we have no pleasure in them.

2. Patrick Henry Demands Boldness (1775)

Daniel Leonard's well-justified lack of confidence in the ill-trained colonial militia was more than shared by the Earl of Sandwich. In the House of Lords he scorned the colonials as "raw, undisciplined, cowardly men," and hoped that they would assemble 200,000 "brave fellows" rather than 50,000, for they would thus starve themselves out and then run at the first "sound of cannon." But the great William Pitt (now Lord Chatham), also speaking in Parliament, warned against "an impious war with a people contending in the great cause of public liberty." "All attempts to enforce servitude upon such men must be vain, must be futile." A few weeks later Patrick Henry, the flaming young lawyer-orator, urging warlike preparations before the Virginia Assembly, spelled out the reasons for action in his famous speech ending with the immortal words, "Give me liberty or give me death!" Analyze his several arguments and determine which is the strongest.

They tell us, sir, that we are weak; unable to cope with so formidable an adversary. But when shall we be stronger? Will it be the next week, or the next year? Will it be when we are totally disarmed, and when a British guard shall be stationed in every house? Shall we gather strength by irresolution and inaction? Shall we acquire the means of effectual resistance by lying supinely on our backs and hugging the delusive phantom of hope, until our enemies shall have bound us hand and foot?

Sir, we are not weak if we make a proper use of those means which the God of nature hath placed in our power. Three millions of people armed in the holy cause of liberty, and in such a country as that which we possess, are invincible by any force which our enemy can send against us. Besides, sir, we shall not fight our battles alone. There is a just God who presides over the destinies of nations and who will raise up friends to fight our battles for us. The battle, sir, is not to the strong alone; it is to the vigilant, the active, the brave.

Besides, sir, we have no election. If we were base enough to desire it, it is now too late to retire from the contest. There is no retreat but in

2. C. M. Depew, ed., *The Library of Oratory* (1902), III, 30–31.

submission and slavery! Our chains are forged! Their clanking may be heard on the plains of Boston! The war is inevitable—and let it come! I repeat, sir, let it come!

3. New Yorkers Abuse Tories (1775)

In 1773 James Rivington, a former London bookseller who had emigrated to New York after losing his fortune in race-track gambling, launched one of the best colonial newspapers. Named *Rivington's New York Gazetteer*, its columns at first were open to both sides in the increasingly bitter war of words between Loyalists (Tories) and Patriots (Whigs). American Patriots (Sons of Liberty), resenting additional criticisms about to be published, wrecked Rivington's plant in November, 1775. The pro-Loyalist publisher then fled to England. Ascertain why the Patriots should have objected to accounts like the following published by Rivington.

This afternoon, at New York, as William Cunningham and John Hill were coming from the North River, they stopped near the liberty pole to see a boxing match, but had not stood long when Cunningham was struck at by Smith Richards, James Vandyke, and several others; called Tory; and used in a most cruel manner by a mob of above two hundred men. Mr. Hill, coming up to his assistance, was beaten and abused most barbarously, though neither of them gave the least offense, except being on the King's side of the question at the meeting this morning.

The leaders of this mob brought Cunningham under the liberty pole, and told him to go down on his knees and damn his Popish King George, and they would then set him free. But, on the contrary, he exclaimed, "God bless King George!" They then dragged him through the green, tore the clothes off his back, and robbed him of his watch. They also insisted on Hill's damning the King, but he, refusing, was used in the same manner, and were it not for some of the peace officers, viz., Captain Welsh, John Taylor, William Dey, and Joseph Wilson, together with ———— Goldstream, who rescued them from the violence of this banditti and brought them to the jail for the security of their persons from further injuries, they would inevitably have been murdered.

E. THE CLASH OF ARMS

1. Conflicting Versions of the Outbreak (1775)

British troops from Boston, seeking secret military stores and presumably rebel leaders, clashed with the colonials at Lexington and then Concord, on April 19, 1775, in the first bloodshed of the American Revolution. Among the numerous conflicting accounts that exist, these two excerpts, representing an American version and an official British version, are noteworthy. To this day scholars have not proved who

3. *Rivington's Gazetteer*, March 9, 1775, in Frank Moore, *Diary of the American Revolution* (1860), I, 36–37. For a variant Whig account of the episode, see *ibid.*, I, 45–48.
1. The American version is from the Salem (Mass.) *Gazette* of April 25, 1775; the British, from the London *Gazette* of June 10, 1775. Reprinted in Peter Force, ed., *American Archives*, Fourth Series (1839), II, 391–92, 945–46. For numerous other versions, see A. C. McLaughlin *et al., Source Problems in United States History* (1918), pp. 3–53.

fired the first shot. Decide what undisputed and what probable facts emerge from these accounts, and draw conclusions as to the task of the historian in extracting truth from contemporary testimony.

AMERICAN VERSION

At Lexington . . . a company of militia . . . mustered near the meeting house. The [British] troops came in sight of them just before sunrise; and running within a few rods of them, the Commanding Officer [Pitcairn] accosted the militia in words to this effect: "Disperse, you rebels—damn you, throw down your arms and disperse"; upon which the troops huzzaed, and immediately one or two officers discharged their pistols, which were instantaneously followed by the firing of four or five of the soldiers, and then there seemed to be a general discharge from the whole body. Eight of our men were killed and nine wounded. . . .

In Lexington [the British] . . . also set fire to several other houses. . . . They pillaged almost every house they passed. . . . But the savage barbarity exercised upon the bodies of our unfortunate brethren who fell is almost incredible. Not contented with shooting down the unarmed, aged, and infirm, they disregarded the cries of the wounded, killing them without mercy, and mangling their bodies in the most shocking manner.

BRITISH VERSION

. . . Six companies of [British] light infantry . . . at Lexington found a body of the country people under arms, on a green close to the road. And upon the King's troops marching up to them, in order to inquire the reason of their being so assembled, they went off in great confusion. And several guns were fired upon the King's troops from behind a stone wall, and also from the meeting-house and other houses, by which one man was wounded, and Major Pitcairn's horse shot in two places. In consequence of this attack by the rebels, the troops returned the fire and killed several of them. . . .

On the return of the troops from Concord, they [the rebels] . . . began to fire upon them from behind stone walls and houses, and kept up in that manner a scattering fire during the whole of their march of fifteen miles, by which means several were killed and wounded. And such was the cruelty and barbarity of the rebels that they scalped and cut off the ears of some of the wounded men who fell into their hands.

2. Franklin Embittered by Bloodshed (1775)

News of Lexington and Concord, embellished by atrocity stories that were either exaggerated or wholly fabricated, elicited the following reaction from the well-balanced and benign Franklin. He had recently returned to Philadelphia from England. He wrote, but apparently did not send, the following letter.

Mr. Strahan, You are a member of Parliament, and one of that majority which has doomed my country to destruction. You have begun to burn our towns and murder our people. Look upon your hands! They are stained with the blood of your relations! You and I were long friends; you are now my enemy, and I am

Yours,

B. Franklin

2. To William Strahan, July 5, 1775, in A. E. Smyth, ed., *The Writings of Benjamin Franklin* (1906), VI, 407.

3. Why an Old Soldier Fought

Many years after the bloodshed at Lexington, Mellen Chamberlain, a prominent Massachusetts lawyer-politician-historian-librarian, published the following account of an interview with a veteran participant. Note its most striking feature, and form a critical judgment as to the value of this kind of testimony.

When the action at Lexington, on the morning of the 19th [of April], was known at Danvers, the minute men there, under the lead of Captain Gideon Foster, made that memorable march—or run, rather—of sixteen miles in four hours, and struck Percy's flying column at West Cambridge. Brave but incautious in flanking the Redcoats, they were flanked themselves and badly pinched, leaving seven dead, two wounded, and one missing. Among those who escaped was Levi Preston, afterwards known as Captain Levi Preston.

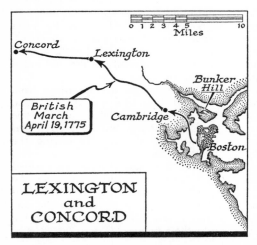

When I was about twenty-one and Captain Preston about ninety-one, I "interviewed" him as to what he did and thought sixty-seven years before, on April 19, 1775. And now, fifty-two years later, I make my report—a little belated perhaps, but not too late, I trust, for the morning papers!

At that time, of course, I knew all about the American Revolution—far more than I do now! And if I now know anything truly, it is chiefly owing to what I have since forgotten of the histories of that event then popular.

With an assurance passing even that of the modern interviewer—if that were possible—I began: "Captain Preston, why did you go to the Concord fight, the 19th of April, 1775?"

The old man, bowed beneath the weight of years, raised himself upright, and turning to me said: "Why did I go?"

"Yes," I replied; "my histories tell me that you men of the Revolution took up arms against 'intolerable oppressions.' What were they?"

"Oppressions? I didn't feel them."

"What, were you not oppressed by the Stamp Act?"

"I never saw one of those stamps, and always understood that Governor Bernard [of Massachusetts] put them all in Castle William [Boston]. I am certain I never paid a penny for one of them."

3. Mellen Chamberlain, *John Adams, the Statesman of the American Revolution* (1898), pp. 248–49.

"Well, what then about the tea-tax?"

"Tea-tax! I never drank a drop of the stuff; the boys threw it all overboard."

"Then I suppose you had been reading Harrington or Sidney and Locke about the eternal principles of liberty."

"Never heard of 'em. We read only the Bible, the Catechism, Watts' Psalms and Hymns, and the Almanack."

"Well, then, what was the matter? and what did you mean in going to the fight?"

"Young man, what we meant in going for those Redcoats was this: we always had governed ourselves, and we always meant to. They didn't mean we should."

THOUGHT PROVOKERS

1. It has been said that the American colonists attempted to reverse the maxim and have it read, "Mother countries exist for the benefit of their colonies." Comment on the reasonableness of such a position. It has been said that we ought to understand 17th Century mercantilism because so much of it persists today. Explain.

2. Is it justifiable for the people to take mob action against lawful measures that they deem harmful or illegal? Comment critically on the following propositions in the light of the American Revolution: (a) He who strikes a king must strike to kill. (b) Rebellion is a great crime—unless it succeeds.

3. Following the Boston Tea Party, what possible courses were open to England, and which one would have been most likely to keep the colonies in the Empire?

4. If you had been a wealthy citizen in Massachusetts in 1776, would you have remained loyal to the King? Explain.

5. Why did each side blame the other for the first shot at Lexington? Is it probable that there were atrocities on both sides? Are the people who fight in a war the best judges of its causes and significance?

FURTHER EXPLORATION

General: L. H. Gipson, *The Coming of the Revolution* (1954); J. C. Miller, *Origins of the American Revolution* (1943). **Mercantilism:** L. A. Harper, *The English Navigation Laws* (1939). **Taxation:** E. S. and H. M. Morgan, *The Stamp Act Crisis* (1953); A. M. Schlesinger, *Prelude to Independence* (1958). **Britain at the Crossroads:** Dora M. Clark, *British Opinion and the American Revolution* (1930). **Loyalists:** C. H. Van Tyne, *The Loyalists in the American Revolution* (1902); W. N. Nelson, *The American Tory* (1961). **The Clash:** C. H. Van Tyne, *The Causes of the War of Independence* (1922); J. R. Alden, *The American Revolution, 1775–1783* (1954).

Recent: L. H. Gipson, *The British Empire before the American Revolution* (XI, XII, 1965); Bernhard Knollenberg, *Origin of the American Revolution, 1759–1766* (1960) [paperback]; Bernard Bailyn, *The Ideological Origins of the American Revolution* (1967); J. T. Main, *The Social Structure of Revolutionary America* (1965); John W. Shy, *Toward Lexington: The Role of the British Army in the Coming of the American Revolution* (1965); B. W. Labaree, *The Boston Tea Party* (1964); J. M. Sosin, *Agents and Merchants: British Colonial Policy and the Origins of the American Revolution, 1763–1775* (1965).

Chapter 6

The First American Civil War

And if ever there was a just war since the world began, it is this in which America is now engaged. . . . We fight not to enslave, but to set a country free, and to make room upon the earth for honest men to live in.

THOMAS PAINE, *The Crisis, 1776*

PROLOGUE: Following the bloodshed at Lexington, the colonials raised a nondescript army and put George Washington in command. The undisciplined and unreliable amateur soldiers exasperated their leader, and not until later in the war was a nucleus of several thousand trained veterans whipped into line. Meanwhile the colonials, goaded by harsh British acts, finally declared their independence in 1776. They kept their flickering cause alive with secret French aid until 1778, when France formed an alliance with them following the decisive American victory over General Burgoyne at Saratoga in 1777. Spain and Holland ultimately entered the general conflict against the British. With much of the rest of Europe unfriendly, Britain found that the war had become too big to handle. Following a crushing defeat by a joint Franco-American force at Yorktown in 1781, the British decided to cut their losses and come to terms with their rebellious subjects. The final treaty was signed in 1783.

A. GENERAL WASHINGTON IN COMMAND

1. Washington Scorns Independence (1775)

Jonathan Boucher, a prominent Virginia clergyman who had married money, was so outspoken a Loyalist and an Anglican as to be ultimately burned in effigy by Patriots. He had tutored George Washington's stepson, and was on terms of dinner-table friendship with the future General. At the time of which he writes, the colonials were fighting near Boston for a redress of grievances, not for independence, and the newly appointed George Washington was about to join them as their commander. Note what is revealed of Washington's character and the Patriot aims by the following incident, as related by Boucher.

I happened to be going across the Potomac to Alexandria [Virginia] with my wife and some other of our friends, exactly at the time that General Washington was crossing it on his way to the northward, whither he was going to take command of the Continental Army. There had been a great meeting of people, and great doings in Alexandria on the occasion; and everybody seemed to be on fire, either with rum, or patriotism, or both.

Some patriots in our boat huzzaed, and gave three cheers to the General as he passed us; whilst Mr. Addison and myself contented ourselves with

1. Jonathan Bouchier, ed., *Reminiscences of an American Loyalist* (1925), p. 109. By permission of Houghton Mifflin Company.

102

pulling off our hats. The General (then only Colonel) Washington beckoned us to stop, as we did, just, as he said, to shake us by the hand. His behavior to me was now, as it had always been, polite and respectful, and I shall forever remember what passed in the few disturbed moments of conversation we then had.

From his going on the errand he was, I foresaw and apprised him of much that has since happened; in particular that there would certainly then be a civil war, and that the Americans would soon declare for independency. With more earnestness than was usual with his great reserve, he scouted my apprehensions, adding (and I believe with perfect sincerity) that if ever I heard of his joining in any such measures, I had his leave to set him down for everything wicked.

2. Anti-Catholicism in the Army (1775)

After Washington assumed command of the Patriot army near Boston, in July, 1775, other American forces unsuccessfully invaded Canada from two quarters, seeking to wrest from the British the so-called Fourteenth Colony. Guy Fawkes Day came on November 5, when the thrust toward Montreal had met with initial success. Fawkes had been the trigger-man of the notorious Gunpowder Plot of 1605, designed to blow up the King and both Houses of Parliament as revenge for anti-Catholic laws. He was foiled at the last moment, and American Protestants commonly observed Guy Fawkes Day in a fashion that elicited the following order from General Washington. Ascertain what light it throws on the failure of the Catholic French Canadians to rise en masse to greet their so-called American deliverers.

As the Commander-in-Chief has been apprised of a design formed for the observance of that ridiculous and childish custom of burning the effigy of the Pope, he cannot help expressing his surprise that there should be officers and soldiers in this army so void of common sense as not to see the impropriety of such a step at this juncture—at a time when we are soliciting, and have really obtained, the friendship and alliance of the people of Canada, whom we ought to consider as brethren embarked in the same cause: the defense of the general liberty of America.

At such a juncture, and in such circumstances, to be insulting their religion is so monstrous as not to be suffered or excused. Indeed, instead of offering the most remote insult, it is our duty to address public thanks to these our brethren, as to them we are so much indebted for every late happy success over the common enemy in Canada.

3. Washington's Deep Discouragements (1775–1776)

General Washington's homespun army of plowmen and artisans, gathered around Boston, was an ill-disciplined force. It may not have frightened the British, but it certainly worried its commander. Washington's complaints, as herewith recorded in letters and repeated endlessly, are most revealing. Observe who and what were responsible for his chief difficulties; and how these criticisms change the traditional concept of both Washington and the army at this early stage of the war.

2. J. C. Fitzpatrick, ed., *The Writings of George Washington* (1931), IV, 65.
3. *Ibid.*, III, 512; IV, 124–25, 243.

[September 21, 1775, to the President of Congress] It gives me great pain to be obliged to solicit the attention of the honorable Congress to the state of this army. . . . But my situation is inexpressibly distressing, to see the winter fast approaching upon a naked army, the time of their service within a few weeks of expiring, and no provision yet made for such important events. Added to this, the military chest is totally exhausted; the paymaster has not a single dollar in hand; the commissary-general assures me he has strained his credit to the utmost for the subsistence of the army. The quartermaster-general is precisely in the same situation; and the greater part of the army are in a state not far from mutiny, upon the deduction from their stated allowance. I know not to whom I am to impute this failure; but I am of opinion, if the evil is not immediately remedied, and more punctually observed in future, the army must absolutely break up.

[November 28, 1775, to Joseph Reed] What an astonishing thing it is that those who are employed to sign the Continental bills should not be able, or inclined, to do it as fast as they are wanted. They will prove the destruction of the army, if they are not more attentive and diligent. Such a dearth of public spirit and want of virtue, such stock-jobbing and fertility in all the low arts to obtain advantages of one kind or another, in this great change of military arrangement, I never saw before, and pray God I may never be witness to again. What will be the ultimate end of these manoeuvres is beyond my scan. I tremble at the prospect.

We have been till this time enlisting about three thousand five hundred men. To engage these I have been obliged to allow furloughs as far as fifty men a regiment, and the officers, I am persuaded, indulge as many more. The Connecticut troops will not be prevailed upon to stay longer than their term (saving those who have enlisted for the next campaign, and mostly on furlough), and such a dirty, mercenary spirit pervades the whole that I should not be at all surprised at any disaster that may happen.

In short, after the last of this month our lines will be so weakened that the minute men and militia must be called in for their defense. These, being under no kind of government themselves, will destroy the little subordination I have been laboring to establish, and run me into one evil whilst I am endeavoring to avoid another. But the lesser must be chosen. Could I have foreseen what I have, and am likely to experience, no consideration upon earth should have induced me to accept this command. . . .

[January 14, 1776, to Joseph Reed] . . . I have often thought how much happier I should have been if, instead of accepting of a command under such circumstances, I had taken my musket on my shoulder and entered the ranks; or, if I could have justified the measure to posterity and my own conscience, had retired to the back country, and lived in a wigwam. If I shall be able to rise superior to these and many other difficulties which might be enumerated, I shall most religiously believe that the finger of

Providence is in it, to blind the eyes of our enemies. For surely, if we get well through this month, it must be for want of their knowing the disadvantages we labor under.

4. The Unreliable Militia (1776)

Washington's makeshift army, after finally forcing the British out of Boston in March, 1776, was badly defeated later in the year while defending New York City. On one occasion Washington tried to beat the fleeing militia into line with the flat of his sword. From the discouraging letter that he wrote several weeks later to the President of Congress, determine why he regarded the militiamen as poor fighters, poor soldiers, and prone to desertion.

To place any dependence upon militia is assuredly resting upon a broken staff. Men just dragged from the tender scenes of domestic life, unaccustomed to the din of arms, totally unacquainted with every kind of military skill, which (being followed by want of confidence in themselves when opposed to troops regularly trained, disciplined, and appointed, superior in knowledge and superior in arms) makes them timid and ready to fly from their own shadows.

Besides, the sudden change in their manner of living (particularly in the lodging) brings on sickness in many, impatience in all, and such an unconquerable desire of returning to their respective homes that it not only produces shameful and scandalous desertions among themselves, but infuses the like spirit in others.

Again, men accustomed to unbounded freedom and no control cannot brook the restraint which is indispensably necessary to the good order and government of an army, without which licentiousness and every kind of disorder triumphantly reign. . . .

The jealousies [suspicions] of a standing army, and the evils to be apprehended from one, are remote, and, in my judgment, situated and circumstanced as we are, not at all to be dreaded. But the consequence of wanting [lacking] one, according to my ideas formed from the present view of things, is certain and inevitable ruin. For, if I was called upon to declare upon oath whether the militia have been most serviceable or hurtful upon the whole, I should subscribe to the latter.

B. THE FORMAL BREAK WITH BRITAIN

1. Paine Talks Common Sense (1776)

Despite the shooting at Lexington, Concord, and Bunker Hill; despite the British burning of Falmouth (Maine) and Norfolk (Virginia); despite the King's hiring of German (Hessian) mercenaries, the American colonials professed to be fighting merely for reconciliation. But killing Redcoats with one hand and waving the olive branch with the other seemed ridiculous to Thomas Paine, a thirty-nine-year-old agitator from

4. *Ibid.*, VI, 110–12 (Sept. 24, 1776).
1. Thomas Paine, *Common Sense* (1894), pp. 84–101, *passim.*

England who had arrived in Philadelphia about a year earlier. Of humble birth, impoverished, largely self-educated, and early apprenticed to a corset maker, he was a born rebel who had failed at various undertakings. But he rocketed to fame with a 47-page pamphlet, published in January, 1776, under the title *Common Sense*. Selling the incredible total of 120,000 copies in three months, it sharply accelerated the drift toward independence. Paine urged an immediate break, not only to secure foreign assistance but to fulfill America's moral mandate from the world. Assess critically his views on mercantilism, isolationism, and reconciliation, and determine whether his argument is more impassioned than reasonable.

In the following pages I offer nothing more than simple facts, plain arguments, and common sense: . . .

I have heard it asserted by some that, as America has flourished under her former connection with Great Britain, the same connection is necessary towards her future happiness, and will always have the same effect. Nothing can be more fallacious than this kind of argument. We may as well assert that, because a child has thrived upon milk, it is never to have meat, or that the first twenty years of our lives is to become a precedent for the next twenty. But even this is admitting more than is true. For I answer roundly that America would have flourished as much, and probably much more, had no European power taken any notice of her. The commerce by which she hath enriched herself are the necessaries of life, and will always have a market while eating is the custom of Europe.

But she [England] has protected us, say some. That she hath engrossed [monopolized] us is true, and defended the continent at our expense, as well as her own, is admitted; and she would have defended Turkey from the same motive, viz. for the sake of trade and dominion. . . .

But Britain is the parent country, say some. Then the more shame upon her conduct. Even brutes do not devour their young, nor savages make war upon their families; wherefore the assertion, if true, turns to her reproach. But it happens not to be true, or only partly so. . . . Europe, and not England, is the parent country of America. This new world hath been the asylum for the persecuted lovers of civil and religious liberty from every part of Europe. Hither have they fled, not from the tender embraces of the mother, but from the cruelty of the monster; and it is so far true of England that the same tyranny which drove the first emigrants from home pursues their descendants still. . . .

. . . Any submission to, or dependence on, Great Britain tends directly to involve this continent in European wars and quarrels, and set us at variance with nations who would otherwise seek our friendship, and against whom we have neither anger nor complaint. As Europe is our market for trade, we ought to form no partial [preferential] connection with any part of it. It is the true interest of America to steer clear of European contentions, which she never can do while, by her dependence on Britain, she is made the makeweight in the scale of British politics. . . .

Everything that is right or reasonable pleads for separation. The blood of the slain, the weeping voice of nature, cries, 'TIS TIME TO PART. Even the

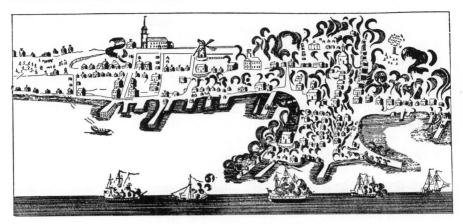

THE BURNING OF FALMOUTH

This town (Portland, Me.) was destroyed by the British, October 18, 1775. Houghton Library, Harvard University.

distance at which the Almighty hath placed England and America is a strong and natural proof that the authority of the one over the other was never the design of Heaven. . . .

But if you say, you can still pass the violations over, then I ask, Hath your house been burnt? Hath your property been destroyed before your face? Are your wife and children destitute of a bed to lie on, or bread to live on? Have you lost a parent or a child by their hands, and yourself the ruined and wretched survivor? If you have not, then are you not a judge of those who have. But if you have, and can still shake hands with the murderers, then are you unworthy the name of husband, father, friend, or lover; and whatever may be your rank or title in life, you have the heart of a coward, and the spirit of a sycophant. . . .

Every quiet method for peace hath been ineffectual. Our prayers have been rejected with disdain. . . . Wherefore, since nothing but blows will do, for God's sake let us come to a final separation. . . .

Small islands, not capable of protecting themselves, are the proper objects for government to take under their care. But there is something absurd in supposing a continent to be perpetually governed by an island. In no instance hath nature made the satellite larger than its primary planet; and as England and America, with respect to each other, reverse the common order of nature, it is evident that they belong to different systems. England to Europe: America to itself. . . .

No man was a warmer wisher for a reconciliation than myself before the fatal nineteenth of April, 1775 [Lexington]. But the moment the event of that day was made known, I rejected the hardened, sullen-tempered Pharaoh of England [George III] for ever; and disdain the wretch that, with the pretended title of FATHER OF HIS PEOPLE, can unfeelingly hear of their slaughter, and composedly sleep with their blood upon his soul. . . .

And in order to show that reconciliation now is a dangerous doctrine, I affirm that it would be policy in the King at this time to repeal the acts, for the sake of reinstating himself in the government of the provinces; in order that HE MAY ACCOMPLISH BY CRAFT AND SUBTLETY IN THE LONG RUN WHAT HE CANNOT DO BY FORCE AND VIOLENCE IN THE SHORT ONE. Reconciliation and ruin are nearly related. . . .

You that tell us of harmony and reconciliation, can you restore to us the time that is past? Can you give to prostitution its former innocence? Neither can you reconcile Britain and America. . . . There are injuries which nature cannot forgive; she would cease to be nature if she did. As well can the lover forgive the ravisher of his mistress as the continent forgive the murders of Britain. The Almighty hath implanted in us these unextinguishable feelings for good and wise purposes. . . . They distinguish us from the herd of common animals. . . .

O! you that love mankind! You that dare oppose not only the tyranny but the tyrant, stand forth! Every spot of the old world is overrun with oppression. Freedom hath been hunted round the globe. Asia and Africa have long expelled her. Europe regards her like a stranger, and England hath given her warning to depart. O! receive the fugitive, and prepare in time an asylum for mankind.

2. Lee's Resolution of Independence (1776)

Richard Henry Lee of Virginia, one of the earliest advocates of a complete break, proposed the following three resolutions in the Continental Congress at Philadelphia on June 7, 1776. After a spirited debate, the first one was approved on July 2 by the representatives of twelve states. This was in fact the "declaration," or declaring, of independence; and John Adams wrote his wife that the day would thereafter be observed by future generations as the great anniversary festival, with fireworks and other manifestations of joy. But he miscalculated by two days. Ascertain why the resolution for independence should have been grouped with the two others.

Resolved, That these United Colonies are, and of right ought to be, free and independent States; that they are absolved from all allegiance to the British Crown; and that all political connection between them and the State of Great Britain is, and ought to be, totally dissolved.

That it is expedient forthwith to take the most effectual measures for forming foreign alliances.

That a plan of confederation be prepared and transmitted to the respective Colonies for their consideration and approbation.

3. Jefferson's Declaration of Independence (1776)

Lee's immortal resolution of independence, passed on July 2, formally cut all ties with Britain. But so momentous a step could not be taken without a convincing explanation, partly in the hope of eliciting foreign sympathy and military aid. The Continental Congress had appointed a committee to prepare such an appeal, and the tall, sandy-haired Thomas Jefferson, then only thirty-three years old, was named

2. W. C. Ford, ed., *Journals of the Continental Congress* (1906), V, 425.
3. *Ibid.*, V, 510–15.

chief draftsman. The Declaration (Explanation) of Independence, formally adopted on July 4, 1776, contained little new. It embodied the doctrine of natural rights and John Locke's ancient "compact theory" of government, as well as a formidable and partisan list of grievances, as though from a prosecuting attorney. But the language of the Declaration was so incisive and eloquent that this subversive document—designed primarily to subvert British rule—was magnificently successful. Note what persons or groups of persons are blamed, and which one is blamed the most. Try to connect specific grievances with each complaint. Find, if possible, any hint that the colonials were partly at fault.

[I]

When, in the course of human events, it becomes necessary for one people to dissolve the political bands which have connected them with another, and to assume, among the powers of the earth, the separate and equal station to which the laws of nature and of nature's God entitle them, a decent respect to the opinions of mankind requires that they should declare the causes which impel them to the separation.

We hold these truths to be self-evident: that all men are created equal; that they are endowed by their Creator with certain unalienable rights; that among these are life, liberty, and the pursuit of happiness. That to secure these rights, governments are instituted among men, deriving their just powers from the consent of the governed. That, whenever any form of government becomes destructive of these ends, it is the right of the people to alter or to abolish it, and to institute new government, laying its foundation on such principles, and organizing its powers in such form, as to them shall seem most likely to effect their safety and happiness.

Prudence, indeed, will dictate that governments long established should not be changed for light and transient causes; and accordingly all experience hath shown that mankind are more disposed to suffer, while evils are sufferable, than to right themselves by abolishing the forms to which they are accustomed. But when a long train of abuses and usurpations, pursuing invariably the same object, evinces a design to reduce them under absolute despotism, it is their right, it is their duty, to throw off such government, and to provide new guards for their future security. Such has been the patient sufferance of these colonies; and such is now the necessity which constrains them to alter their former systems of government.

[II]

The history of the present King of Great Britain is a history of repeated injuries and usurpations, all having in direct object the establishment of an absolute tyranny over these states. To prove this, let facts be submitted to a candid world.

He has refused his assent to laws the most wholesome and necessary for the public good.

He has forbidden his governors to pass laws of immediate and pressing importance, unless suspended in their operation till his assent should be obtained; and when so suspended, he has utterly neglected to attend to them.

He has refused to pass other laws for the accommodation of large districts of people, unless those people would relinquish the right of representation in the legislature, a right inestimable to them and formidable to tyrants only.

He has called together legislative bodies at places unusual, uncomfortable, and distant from the depository of their public records, for the sole purpose of fatiguing them into compliance with his measures.

He has dissolved representative houses repeatedly for opposing, with manly firmness, his invasions on the rights of the people.

He has refused for a long time, after such dissolutions, to cause others to be elected; whereby the legislative powers, incapable of annihilation, have returned to the people at large for their exercise; the state remaining, in the mean time, exposed to all the dangers of invasion from without and convulsions within.

He has endeavored to prevent the population [populating] of these states; for that purpose obstructing the laws for naturalization of foreigners, refusing to pass others to encourage their migration hither, and raising the conditions of new appropriations of lands.

He has obstructed the administration of justice by refusing his assent to laws for establishing judiciary powers.

He has made judges dependent on his will alone for the tenure of their offices and the amount and payment of their salaries.

He has erected a multitude of new offices, and sent hither swarms of officers to harass our people and eat out their substance.

He has kept among us, in times of peace, standing armies without the consent of our legislatures.

He has affected to render the military independent of and superior to the civil power.

[III]

He has combined with others to subject us to a jurisdiction [by Parliament] foreign to our constitution, and unacknowledged by our laws; giving his assent to their acts of pretended legislation:

For quartering large bodies of armed troops among us;

For protecting them, by a mock trial, from punishment for any murders which they should commit on the inhabitants of these states;

For cutting off our trade with all parts of the world;

For imposing taxes on us without our consent;

For depriving us, in many cases, of the benefits of trial by jury;

For transporting us beyond seas to be tried for pretended offenses;

For abolishing the free system of English laws in a neighboring province [Quebec], establishing therein an arbitrary government, and enlarging its boundaries so as to render it at once an example and fit instrument for introducing the same absolute rule into these colonies [a reference to the Quebec Act of 1774];

THE ALLIES

George III eats his American subjects in company with his cannibalistic Indian allies. British satire, 1780. Boston Public Library.

For taking away our charters, abolishing our most valuable laws, and altering fundamentally the forms of our governments;

For suspending our own legislatures and declaring themselves invested with power to legislate for us in all cases whatsoever.

[IV]

He has abdicated government here by declaring us out of his protection and waging war against us.

He has plundered our seas, ravaged our coasts, burnt our towns, and destroyed the lives of our people.

He is at this time transporting large armies of foreign mercenaries to complete the works of death, desolation, and tyranny already begun with circumstances of cruelty and perfidy scarcely paralleled in the most barbarous ages, and totally unworthy the head of a civilized nation.

He has constrained our fellow citizens, taken captive on the high seas, to bear arms against their country, to become the executioners of their friends and brethren, or to fall themselves by their hands.

He has excited domestic insurrections amongst us, and has endeavored to bring on the inhabitants of our frontiers the merciless Indian savages, whose known rule of warfare is an undistinguished destruction of all ages, sexes, and conditions.

In every stage of these oppressions we have petitioned for redress in the most humble terms; our repeated petitions have been answered only by repeated injury. A prince whose character is thus marked by every act which may define a tyrant is unfit to be the ruler of a free people.

[v]

Nor have we been wanting in attention to our British brethren. We have warned them from time to time of attempts by their legislature to extend an unwarrantable jurisdiction over us. We have reminded them of the circumstances of our emigration and settlement here. We have appealed to their native justice and magnanimity, and we have conjured them, by the ties of our common kindred, to disavow these usurpations, which would inevitably interrupt our connections and correspondence. They too have been deaf to the voice of justice and of consanguinity. We must, therefore, acquiesce in the necessity which denounces [announces] our separation, and hold them, as we hold the rest of mankind, enemies in war, in peace friends.

[vi]

We, therefore, the representatives of the United States of America, in General Congress assembled, appealing to the Supreme Judge of the world for the rectitude of our intentions, do, in the name and by the authority of the good people of these colonies, solemnly publish and declare, That these United Colonies are, and of right ought to be, FREE AND INDEPENDENT STATES; that they are absolved from all allegiance to the British Crown, and that all political connection between them and the state of Great Britain is, and ought to be, totally dissolved; and that as free and independent states they have full power to levy war, conclude peace, contract alliances, establish commerce, and to do all other acts and things which independent states may of right do. And for the support of this Declaration, with a firm reliance on the protection of Divine Providence, we mutually pledge to each other our lives, our fortunes, and our sacred honor.

4. The Abortive Slave-Trade Indictment (1776)

Farseeing colonials had repeatedly attempted in their local assemblies to restrict or stop the odious African slave trade. But the London government, responding to the anguished cries of the British (and New England) slave traders, had killed all such laws with the royal veto—five times in the case of Virginia alone. Jefferson added this grievance to the original indictment, but Congress threw it out, largely because of opposition from those parts of the South heavily dependent on the slave trade. Would this clause have added to the effectiveness of the Declaration of Independence, especially in view of the hypocrisy involved?

He [George III] has waged cruel war against human nature itself, violating its most sacred rights of life and liberty in the persons of a distant people who never offended him, captivating and carrying them into slavery in another hemisphere, or to incur miserable death in their transportation thither. This piratical warfare, the opprobrium of infidel powers, is the warfare of the Christian King of Great Britain. Determined to keep open a market where MEN should be bought and sold, he has prostituted his negative [royal veto] for suppressing every legislative attempt to prohibit

4. J. H. Hazelton, *The Declaration of Independence* (1906), p. 144.

or to restrain this execrable commerce. And that this assemblage of horrors might want no fact of distinguished dye [might lack no flagrant crime], he is now exciting those very people to rise in arms among us, and to purchase that liberty of which he has deprived them by murdering the people upon whom he also obtruded them: thus paying off former crimes committed against the liberties of one people with crimes which he urges them to commit against the lives of another.

C. VOICES OF DISSENT

1. Lord Chatham Assails the War (1777)

Partisan clamor in England between the ruling Tories and the out-of-office Whigs aided the Patriot cause in America. Many English Whigs, partly to embarrass the Tory government, proclaimed that the Americans were merely fighting for English liberties. After the bloodshed at Lexington and Concord, some English Whigs wore mourning out of respect for the colonials who had died. William Pitt, the great organizer of victory in the Seven Years' War, had become a peer (Lord Chatham) in 1766. Suffering acutely from gout and other afflictions, he pulled himself together for the following superlative oratorical effort six months before his death at the age of sixty-nine. The shocking news of General Burgoyne's surrender at Saratoga had not yet reached England. Decide whether Pitt's speech was treasonable, whether he favored independence, and whether he was justified in criticizing Britain's military policies.

My lords, this ruinous and ignominious situation, where we cannot act with success, nor suffer with honor, calls upon us to remonstrate in the strongest and loudest language of truth, to rescue the ear of majesty from the delusions which surround it.

The desperate state of our arms abroad is in part known: no man thinks more highly of them than I do. I love and honor the English troops. I know their virtues and their valor. I know they can achieve anything except impossibilities; and I know that the conquest of English America is an impossibility.

You cannot, I venture to say it, you cannot conquer America. Your armies in the last [Seven Years'] war effected everything that could be effected; and what was it? It cost a numerous army, under the command of a most able general [Amherst], now a noble lord in this house, a long and laborious campaign, to expel five thousand Frenchmen from French America. My lords, you cannot conquer America. What is your present situation there? We do not know the worst; but we know that in three campaigns we have done nothing and suffered much. . . .

As to conquest, therefore, my lords, I repeat, it is impossible. You may swell every expense and every effort still more extravagantly; pile and accumulate every assistance you can buy or borrow; traffic and barter with every little pitiful German prince that sells and sends his subjects to the shambles of a foreign prince. Your efforts are forever vain and impotent;

1. D. J. Brewer, ed., *World's Best Orations* (1899), III, 1069–73.

The Generals in America doing nothing, or worse than nothing.

British satire on the sloth and ineptitude of General Burgoyne, who is indifferently surrendering his army at Saratoga. Boston Public Library.

doubly so from this mercenary aid on which you rely. For it irritates, to an incurable resentment, the minds of your enemies—to overrun them with the mercenary sons of rapine and plunder; devoting them and their possessions to the rapacity of hireling cruelty! If I were an American, as I am an Englishman, while a foreign troop was landed in my country, I never would lay down my arms—never—never—never!

Your own army is infected with the contagion of these illiberal allies. The spirit of plunder and of rapine is gone forth among them. . . . I know from authentic information, and the most experienced officers, that our discipline is deeply wounded. Whilst this is notoriously our sinking situation, America grows and flourishes; whilst our strength and discipline are lowered, hers are rising and improving.

But, my lords, who is the man that, in addition to these disgraces and mischiefs of our army, has dared to authorize and associate to our arms the tomahawk and scalping knife of the savage? To call into civilized alliance the wild and inhuman savage of the woods; to delegate to the merciless Indian the defense of disputed rights; and to wage the horrors of his barbarous war against our brethren? My lords, these enormities cry aloud for redress and punishment. Unless thoroughly done away, it will be a stain on the national character. It is a violation of the constitution. I believe it is against law. It is not the least of our national misfortunes that the strength and character of our army are thus impaired. Infected with the mercenary spirit of robbery and rapine, familiarized to the horrid scenes of savage cruelty, it can no longer boast of the noble and generous principles which dignify a soldier. . . .

My lords, no man wishes for the due dependence of America on this country more than I do. To preserve it, and not confirm that state of independence into which your measures hitherto have driven them, is the object which we ought to unite in attaining. The Americans, contending for their rights against arbitrary exactions, I love and admire. It is the struggle of free and virtuous patriots. But contending for independency and total disconnection from England, as an Englishman, I cannot wish them success. For, in a due constitutional dependency, including the ancient supremacy of this country in regulating their commerce and navigation, consists the mutual happiness and prosperity both of England and America. She derived assistance and protection from us; and we reaped from her the most important advantages. She was, indeed, the fountain of our wealth, the nerve of our strength, the nursery and basis of our naval power.

It is our duty, therefore, my lords, if we wish to save our country, most seriously to endeavor the recovery of these most beneficial subjects. And in this perilous crisis, perhaps the present moment may be the only one in which we can hope for success. For in their negotiations with France they have, or think they have, reason to complain: though it be notorious that they have received from that power important supplies and assistance of various kinds, yet it is certain they expected it in a more decisive and immediate degree. America is in ill humor with France on some points that have not entirely answered her expectations. Let us wisely take advantage of every possible moment of reconciliation. . . .

You cannot conciliate America by your present measures. You cannot subdue her by your present, or by any, measures. What, then, can you do? You cannot conquer; you cannot gain; but you can address. . . . In a just and necessary war, to maintain the rights or honor of my country, I would strip the shirt from my back to support it. But in such a war as this, unjust in its principle, impracticable in its means, and ruinous in its consequences, I would not contribute a single effort, nor a single shilling.

2. Tories Fear French Catholics (1779)

The French, thirsting for revenge after the Seven Years' War, were eager to break up Britain's empire. After the hope-inspiring American victory at Saratoga, they concluded a treaty of alliance with the rebels in 1778. But France had been the traditional enemy of the colonials in four bitter wars, and besides was a Catholic monarchy. American Loyalists attempted to weaken the alliance by arousing anti-Catholic fears, notably in this fictitious diary prophesying horrible events ten years distant. It appeared in *Rivington's Royal Gazette* ("Rivington's Lying Gazette"). Rivington (see p. 98) had fled New York in 1776, but had returned in 1777 to publish his new Loyalist journal under the protection of British bayonets. Ascertain in the following satire what were the most fundamental of the liberties allegedly lost, and determine what would be most alarming to Protestant Patriots.

Boston, November 10, 1789.—His Excellency Count Tyran has this day published, by authority from His [French] Majesty, a proclamation for the suppression of heresy and establishment of the Inquisition in this town, which has already begun its functions in many other places of the continent under His Majesty's dominion.

2. *Rivington's Royal Gazette*, March 17, 1779, quoted in Frank Moore, *Diary of the American Revolution* (1859), II, 148–50.

The use of the Bible in the vulgar tongue [English vernacular] is strictly prohibited, on pain of being punished by discretion of the Inquisition.

November 11.—The Catholic religion is not only outwardly professed, but has made the utmost progress among all ranks of people here, owing in a great measure to the unwearied labors of the Dominican and Franciscan friars, who omit no opportunity of scattering the seeds of religion, and converting the wives and daughters of heretics. We hear that the building formerly called the Old South Meeting is fitting up for a cathedral, and that several other old meeting-houses are soon to be repaired for convents. . . .

Philadelphia, November 16.—On Tuesday last arrived here the *St. Esprit*, from Bordeaux, with a most valuable cargo of rosaries, mass books, and indulgences, which have been long expected. . . .

. . . Father Le Cruel, president of the Inquisition in this city, out of a tender regard for the salvation of mankind, has thought proper that an example should be made of an old fellow of the age of ninety, convicted of Quakerism, and of reading the Bible, a copy of which, in the English language, was found in his possession. He was hardened and obstinate beyond measure, and could not be prevailed on to retract his errors. . . .

November 21.—Obadiah Standfast, the Quaker, was this day burnt, pursuant to his sentence. . . .

November 23.—His Majesty has directed his viceroy to send five hundred sons of the principal inhabitants of America to be educated in France, where the utmost care will be taken to imbue them with a just regard for the Catholic faith and a due sense of subordination to government. . . .

Such is the glorious specimen of happiness to be enjoyed by America, in case the interposition of France shall enable her to shake off her dependence on Great Britain.

D. A CIVIL WAR WITHIN A CIVIL WAR

1. Pistols on the Pulpit (1775)

Jonathan Boucher, the slaveowning Anglican clergyman who knew Washington (see p. 102), was so disdainfully Loyalist that he provoked violence. Once he felled with one punch a blacksmith armed with a stick and gun. Boucher was finally forced to abandon his valuable plantation property in Maryland and sail for England in September, 1775, nine months before independence was declared. From his later reminiscences decide whether he was a good Christian, and whether he did the Loyalist cause more harm than good.

. . . In the usual and regular course of preaching, I happened one Sunday to recommend peaceableness; on which a Mr. Lee and sundry others, supposing my sermon to be what they called a stroke at the times, rose up and left the church. This was a signal to the people to consider every

1. Jonathan Bouchier, ed., *Reminiscences of an American Loyalist* (1925), p. 113. By permission of Houghton Mifflin Company.

sermon of mine as hostile to the views and interests of America; and accordingly I never after went into a pulpit without something very disagreeable happening. I received sundry messages and letters threatening me with the most fatal consequences if I did not (not desist from preaching at all, but) preach what should be agreeable to the friends of America.

All the answer I gave to these threats was in my sermons, in which I uniformly and resolutely declared that I never could suffer any merely human authority to intimidate me from performing what in my conscience I believed and knew to be my duty to God and his Church. And for more than six months I preached, when I did preach, with a pair of loaded pistols lying on the cushion; having given notice that if any man, or body of men, could possibly be so lost to all sense of decency and propriety as to attempt really to do what had been long threatened, that is, to drag me out of my own pulpit, I should think myself justified before God and man in repelling violence by violence.

2. Vengeance on the Tories (1779)

The Loyalists, remaining true to their King, fought back against their Patriot neighbors with all the weapons at their command, including murderous Indian allies. This was a civil war; and civil wars are inevitably bitter. Even the judicious Washington called the Loyalists "pests of society," many of whom, he thought, ought to commit suicide or be hanged. All told, about 80,000 of these unfortunates were expelled, some of whom later received partial compensation for their losses from the London government. The following outcry by "A Whig" summarizes the chief Patriot grievances, many of which were soundly based. Consider the chief economic complaints and particularly those practices that would hinder reconciliation between the Patriots and Loyalists after the war.

Among the many errors America has been guilty of during her contest with Great Britain, few have been greater, or attended with more fatal consequences to these States, than her lenity to the Tories. . . . We are all crying out against the depreciation of our money, and entering into measures to restore it to its value; while the Tories, who are one principal cause of the depreciation, are taken no notice of, but suffered to live quietly among us.

We can no longer be silent on this subject, and see the independence of the country, after standing every shock from without, endangered by internal enemies. Rouse, America! your danger is great—great from a quarter where you least expect it. The Tories, the Tories will yet be the ruin of you! 'Tis high time they were separated from among you. They are now busy engaged in undermining your liberties. They have a thousand ways of doing it, and they make use of them all.

Who were the occasion of this war? The Tories! Who persuaded the tyrant of Britain to prosecute it in a manner before unknown to civilized nations, and shocking even to barbarians? The Tories! Who prevailed on

2. *Pennsylvania Packet,* Aug. 5, 1779, in Frank Moore, *Diary of the American Revolution* (1859), II, 166–68.

the savages of the wilderness to join the standard of the enemy? The Tories! Who have assisted the Indians in taking the scalp from the aged matron, the blooming fair one, the helpless infant, and the dying hero? The Tories! Who advised and who assisted in burning your towns, ravaging your country, and violating the chastity of your women? The Tories! Who are the occasion that thousands of you now mourn the loss of your dearest connections? The Tories! Who have always counteracted the endeavors of Congress to secure the liberties of this country? The Tories!

Who refused their money when as good as specie, though stamped with the image of his most sacred Majesty? The Tories! Who continue to refuse it? The Tories! Who do all in their power to depreciate it? The Tories! Who propagate lies among us to discourage the Whigs? The Tories! Who corrupt the minds of the good people of these States by every species of insidious counsel? The Tories! Who hold a traitorous correspondence with the enemy? The Tories! Who daily send them intelligence? The Tories! Who take the oaths of allegiance to the States one day, and break them the next? The Tories! Who prevent your battalions from being filled? The Tories! Who dissuade men from entering the army? The Tories! Who persuade those who have enlisted to desert? The Tories! Who harbor those who do desert? The Tories! In short, who wish to see us conquered, to see us slaves, to see us hewers of wood and drawers of water? The Tories! . . .

Awake, Americans, to a sense of your danger. No time to be lost. Instantly banish every Tory from among you. Let America be sacred alone to freemen.

Drive far from you every baneful wretch who wishes to see you fettered with the chains of tyranny. Send them where they may enjoy their beloved slavery to perfection—send them to the island of Britain; there let them drink the cup of slavery and eat the bread of bitterness all the days of their existence—there let them drag out a painful life, despised and accursed by those very men whose cause they have had the wickedness to espouse. Never let them return to this happy land—never let them taste the sweets of that independence which they strove to prevent. Banishment, perpetual banishment, should be their lot.

3. The Hanging of a Loyalist (*c.* 1778)

The untroubled existence of the French émigré Crèvecoeur (see above, pp. 67, 81) ended with the Revolution. His aristocratic breeding caused him to recoil from the excesses of the Patriots, who forced him off his New York farm to the British sanctuary of New York City. Impoverished, he finally fled to France in 1780. Returning after the war, he learned that his home was in ashes, his wife was dead, and his two children had disappeared during an Indian raid. He ultimately found his offspring, and served for a number of years as French consul in New York City. In the following sketch he describes an incident that presumably occurred following a Tory-Indian raid on the Pennsylvania frontier. A Loyalist by the name of Joseph Wilson, accused

3. M. G. J. de Crèvecoeur, *Sketches of Eighteenth Century America* (1925 reprint), pp. 183–85. By permission of Yale University Press.

of having sheltered three of the Tory attackers, is being hung by his toes and thumbs to extort a confession. Note the light that this episode casts on the nature of frontier warfare, and on the difficulties of remaining mildly Loyalist or even neutral. Could this man Wilson be regarded as a genuine Loyalist?

Whilst in this painful suspension he [Wilson] attested his innocence with all the energy he was master of. By this time his wife, who had been informed of the tragical scene, came from her house, with tears gushing in streams, and with a countenance of terror. In the most supplicating posture she implored their mercy, but they rejected her request. They accused her of having participated also in her husband's abominable crime. She repeated her entreaties, and at last prevailed on them to relieve her husband. They took him down after a suspension of six minutes, which will appear a long interval to whoever considers it anatomically.

The bitter cries of the poor woman, the solemn asseverations of her husband, seemed for a few moments to lull the violence of their rage, as in a violent gale of wind nature admits of some kind intermission which enables the seaman to bring his vessel to. But all of a sudden one of the company arose, more vindictive than the rest. He painted to them their conflagrated houses and barns, the murder of their relations and friends. The sudden recollection of these dreadful images wrought them up to a pitch of fury fiercer than before. Conscious as they were that he was the person who had harbored the destroyers of their country, they resolved finally to hang him by the neck.

Hard was this poor man's fate. He had been already suspended in a most excruciating situation for not having confessed what was required of him. Had he confessed the crime laid to his charge, he must have been hung according to the principle of self-preservation which filled the breasts of these people. What was he then to do? Behold here innocence pregnant with as much danger as guilt itself, a situation which is very common and is characteristic of these times. You may be punished tomorrow for thoughts and sentiments for which you were highly commended the preceding day, and alternately.

On hearing of his doom, he flung himself at the feet of the first man. He solemnly appealed to God, the searcher of hearts, for the truth of his assertions. He frankly owned that he was attached to the King's cause from ancient respect and by the force of custom; that he had no idea of any other government, but that at the same time he had never forcibly opposed the measures of the country; that his opinions had never gone beyond his house; that in peace and silence he had submitted to the will of heaven without ever intending to take part with either side; that he detested from the bottom of his heart this mode of war which desolated and ruined so many harmless and passive inhabitants who had committed no other crime than that of living on the frontiers. He earnestly begged and entreated them that they would give him an opportunity of proving his innocence: "Will none of you hear me with patience? I am no stranger, no unknown person; you well know that I am a home-staying man, laborious and peaceable. Would you destroy me on a hearsay? For the sake of that God which knows and sees and judges all men, permit me to have a judicial hearing."

The passive character of this man, though otherwise perfectly inoffensive, had long before been the cause of his having been suspected. Their hearts were hardened and their minds prepossessed; they refused his request and justified the sentence of death they had passed. They, however, promised him his life if he would confess who were those traitors that came to his house, and who guided them through the woods to ————. With a louder voice than usual, the poor culprit denied his having the least knowledge whatever of these persons, but, seeing that it was all in vain, he peaceably submitted to his fate, and gave himself up to those who were preparing the fatal cord. It was soon tied round the limb of a tree to which they hanged him.

[*Some of the executioners, Crèvecoeur relates, experienced a change of heart, and cut Wilson down in time to revive him with water. He was subsequently given an impartial trial and acquitted.*]

THOUGHT PROVOKERS

1. Why were many Patriot soldiers who had volunteered to defend their liberties so untrustworthy and even cowardly?
2. Paine's *Common Sense* and the Declaration of Independence have both been referred to as the most potent propaganda documents in American history. Comment. Prepare a British rejoinder to the Declaration of Independence. The Declaration was designed primarily to achieve American independence, but it was much more than that. Assess its worldwide, long-range significance.
3. It has been said that the Whigs in England and the Tories (Loyalists) in America were both traitors to a cause. Explain. Seneca wrote, "Loyalty is the holiest good in the human breast." If this is true, why were the American Loyalists regarded as despicable creatures?
4. The War of Independence has been called a civil war within a civil war. Comment. Were the Patriots justified in abusing the Loyalists and expelling them? Argue both sides and come to a conclusion.

FURTHER EXPLORATION

General: J. R. Alden, *The American Revolution* (1954); J. C. Miller, *Triumph of Freedom* (1948). **Washington:** D. S. Freeman, *George Washington* (6 vols., 1948–1954), vols. III, IV, V; C. P. Nettels, *George Washington and American Independence* (1951). **Formal Break:** C. L. Becker, *The Declaration of Independence* (1922); Edward Dumbauld, *The Declaration of Independence and What It Means Today* (1950); R. G. Adams, *The Political Ideas of the American Revolution* (1922). **Dissent:** D. M. Clark, *British Opinion and the American Revolution* (1930); C. H. Van Tyne, *The Loyalists in the American Revolution* (1902). **Civil War:** Lewis Einstein, *Divided Loyalties* (1933); W. N. Nelson, *The American Tory* (1961).

Recent: P. H. Smith, *Loyalists and Redcoats* (1964); David Hawke, *A Transaction of Free Men* [Declaration of Independence] (1964); Carl Berger, *Broadsides and Bayonets* (1961); Forrest McDonald, *The Formation of the American Republic, 1776–1790* (1965) [paperback].

Chapter 7

The Struggle for the Constitution

Should the states reject this excellent Constitution, the probability is that an opportunity will never again offer to make another in peace—the next will be drawn in blood.

GEORGE WASHINGTON, ON SIGNING THE CONSTITUTION, 1787

PROLOGUE: The nation's first written constitution—the Articles of Confederation (in force 1781–1789)—provided a toothless central government. Disorders inevitably erupted, notably in Massachusetts, but they were exaggerated by the wealthier groups (the federalists) in the hope of substituting a potent federal government. Such pressures eventually bore fruit in the new Constitution framed in Philadelphia during the humid summer of 1787. A century and a quarter later, Dr. Charles A. Beard advanced the sensational thesis that the propertied men foisted the Constitution upon the less privileged classes. He underscored the fact that many of the fifty-five framers owned depreciated government securities that would rise in value with the establishment of a powerful central regime. But recent scholarship has indicated that economic motivation has been greatly overstressed and widely misinterpreted.* The crucial struggle was between the big states, which had reluctantly accepted an equal vote in the Senate, and the small states, which rather promptly approved the Constitution. Several of the stronger and more self-sufficing commonwealths, notably Virginia and New York, were among the last to ratify.

A. REACTIONS TO SHAYS' REBELLION

1. Washington Expresses Alarm (1786)

The retired war hero Washington, struggling to repair his damaged fortunes at Mount Vernon, was alarmed by the inability of the Congress under the Articles of Confederation to collect taxes and regulate interstate commerce. The states, racked by the depression of 1784–1788, seemed to be going their thirteen separate ways. The worthy farmers of western Massachusetts were especially hard hit, burdened as they were with inequitable and delinquent taxes, mortgage foreclosures, and the prospect of imprisonment for debt. Hundreds of them, under the Revolutionary Captain Daniel Shays, formed armed mobs in an effort to close the courts and to force the issuance of paper money. "Good God!" burst out Washington on hearing of these disorders; "who, besides a Tory, could have foreseen, or a Briton have predicted them?" He wrote despairingly as follows to John Jay, the prominent New York statesman and diplomat. Ascertain what single fear seems to disturb Washington most, and why.

---

* Charles A. Beard, *An Economic Interpretation of the Constitution of the United States* (1913); Robert E. Brown, *Charles Beard and the Constitution* (1956); Forrest McDonald, *We the People: The Economic Origins of the Constitution* (1958).
1. J. C. Fitzpatrick, ed., *Writings of George Washington* (1938), XXVIII, 502–03 (Aug. 1, 1786).

Your sentiments, that our affairs are drawing rapidly to a crisis, accord with my own. What the event will be is also beyond the reach of my foresight. We have errors to correct; we have probably had too good an opinion of human nature in forming our Confederation. Experience has taught us that men will not adopt, and carry into execution, measures the best calculated for their own good, without the intervention of coercive power. I do not conceive we can exist long as a nation without lodging, somewhere, a power which will pervade the whole Union in as energetic a manner as the authority of the state governments extends over the several states.

To be fearful of investing Congress, constituted as that body is, with ample authorities for national purposes, appears to me the very climax of popular absurdity and madness. Could Congress exert them for the detriment of the people without injuring themselves in an equal or greater proportion? Are not their interests inseparably connected with those of their constituents? By the rotation of appointments [annual elections], must they not mingle frequently with the mass of citizens? . . .

What then is to be done? Things cannot go on in the same train forever. It is much to be feared, as you observe, that the better kind of people, being disgusted with these circumstances, will have their minds prepared for any revolution whatever. We are apt to run from one extreme to another. To anticipate and prevent disastrous contingencies would be the part of wisdom and patriotism.

What astonishing changes a few years are capable of producing! I am told that even respectable characters speak of a monarchical form of government without horror. From thinking proceeds speaking; thence to acting is often but a single step. But how irrevocable and tremendous! What a triumph for our enemies to verify their predictions! What a triumph for the advocates of despotism to find that we are incapable of governing ourselves, and that systems founded on the basis of equal liberty are merely ideal and fallacious. Would to God that wise measures may be taken in time to avert the consequences we have but too much reason to apprehend.

2. Abigail Adams Detests the Mob (1787)

The sprightly Abigail Adams, whose courtship by the young lawyer John Adams had not met with parental enthusiasm, never attended school because, as she says, "I was always sick." But she developed into a notable letter writer, largely because her husband was absent so long on affairs of state. She joined him when he took up his post as the first American minister in London, and George III went so far as to kiss her on the cheek at the presentation. Her appraisal of Shays' Rebellion, obviously based on information provided by upper-class sources, appears in the following letter to Thomas Jefferson, then across the Channel in Paris. Note in what respects she betrays the bias of the ruling class of Massachusetts.

With regard to the tumults in my native state which you inquire about, I wish I could say that report had exaggerated them. It is too true, sir, that

2. J. P. Boyd, ed., *The Papers of Thomas Jefferson* (1955), XI, 86–87 (Jan. 29, 1787). By permission of the Princeton University Press.

they have been carried to so alarming a height as to stop the courts of justice in several counties. Ignorant, restless desperados, without conscience or principles, have led a deluded multitude to follow their standard, under pretense of grievances which have no existence but in their imaginations. Some of them were crying out for a paper currency, some for an equal distribution of property. Some were for annihilating all debts, others complaining that the Senate was a useless branch of government, that the court of common pleas was unnecessary, and that the sitting of the General Court in Boston was a grievance.

By this list you will see the materials which compose this rebellion, and the necessity there is of the wisest and most vigorous measures to quell and suppress it. Instead of that laudable spirit which you approve, which makes a people watchful over their liberties and alert in the defense of them, these mobbish insurgents are for sapping the foundation, and destroying the whole fabric at once.

But as these people make only a small part of the state, when compared to the more sensible and judicious, and although they create a just alarm and give much trouble and uneasiness, I cannot help flattering myself that they will prove salutary to the state at large, by leading to an investigation of the causes which have produced these commotions. Luxury and extravagance, both in furniture and dress, had pervaded all orders of our countrymen and women, and was hastening fast to sap their independence by involving every class of citizens in distress, and accumulating debts upon them which they were unable to discharge. Vanity was becoming a more powerful principle than patriotism. The lower order of the community were pressed for taxes, and though possessed of landed property they were unable to answer the demand, whilst those who possessed money were fearful of lending, lest the mad cry of the mob should force the legislature upon a measure [paper money] very different from the touch of Midas.

[*Early in February, 1787, only a few days after Abigail Adams wrote this letter, a small army raised by the conservatives of eastern Massachusetts routed the Shaysites.*]

3. Jefferson Favors Rebellion (1787)

Thomas Jefferson was the successor to Dr. Benjamin Franklin as American minister to France, 1785 to 1789. ("I do not replace him, sir; I am only his successor," he remarked with both wit and modesty.) As an ultra-liberal and a specialist in revolution, this author of the Declaration of Independence wrote as follows about the Shays' Rebellion to his Virginia neighbor, James Madison. The complete crushing of the uprising had not yet occurred. Observe what Jefferson regards as the most important cause of the disturbance (in contrast to Abigail Adams), and what is most extreme about his judgment.

. . . I am impatient to learn your sentiments on the late troubles in the Eastern [New England] states. So far as I have yet seen, they do not

3. P. L. Ford, ed., *Writings of Thomas Jefferson* (1894), IV, 361–63.

appear to threaten serious consequences. Those states have suffered by the stoppage of the channels of their commerce, which have not yet found other issues. This must render money scarce, and make the people uneasy. This uneasiness has produced acts absolutely unjustifiable; but I hope they will provoke no severities from their governments. A consciousness of those in power that their administration of the public affairs has been honest may perhaps produce too great a degree of indignation; and those characters wherein fear predominates over hope may apprehend too much from these instances of irregularity. They may conclude too hastily that nature has formed man insusceptible of any other government but that of force, a conclusion not founded in truth, nor experience. . . .

Even this evil is productive of good. It prevents the degeneracy of government, and nourishes a general attention to the public affairs. I hold it that a little rebellion now and then is a good thing, and as necessary in the political world as storms in the physical. Unsuccessful rebellions indeed generally establish the encroachments on the rights of the people which have produced them. An observation of this truth should render honest republican governors so mild in their punishment of rebellions as not to discourage them too much. It is a medicine necessary for the sound health of government.

B. CLASHES IN THE PHILADELPHIA CONVENTION

1. The Debate on Representation in Congress (1787)

After Shays' Rebellion collapsed, pressures for a stronger central government mounted. Finally, in the summer of 1787, delegates from twelve states met in Philadelphia to strengthen the Articles of Confederation—actually to frame a new constitution. The most complete record of the debates was kept by James Madison of Virginia, the youthful "Father of the Constitution," a portion of whose notes follows. The reader must be warned that two of the speakers, Elbridge Gerry of Massachusetts and George Mason of Virginia, not only refused to sign the Constitution but fought its adoption. From these interchanges ascertain whether the Framing Fathers were really democratic. Locate the most impressive arguments against popular election of Representatives and the most impressive for it, and determine which side was right.

Resolution 4, first clause: "that the members of the first branch [House of Representatives] of the national legislature ought to be elected by the people of the several states" (being taken up),

Mr. SHERMAN [of Conn.] opposed the election by the people, insisting that it ought to be by the state legislatures. The people, he said, immediately should have as little to do as may be about the government. They want [lack] information and are constantly liable to be misled.

Mr. GERRY [of Mass.]. The evils we experience flow from the excess of democracy. The people do not want virtue, but are the dupes of pretended patriots. In Massachusetts, it has been fully confirmed by experience that

1. Max Farrand, ed., *The Records of the Federal Convention of 1787* (1911), I, 48–50 (May 31, 1787). By permission of the Yale University Press.

they are daily misled into the most baneful measures and opinions by the false reports circulated by designing men, and which no one on the spot can refute. . . . He had, he said, been too republican heretofore: he was still, however, republican, but had been taught by experience the danger of the leveling spirit.

Mr. MASON [of Va.] argued strongly for an election of the larger branch by the people. It was to be the grand depository of the democratic principle of the government. It was, so to speak, to be our House of Commons. It ought to know and sympathize with every part of the community, and ought therefore to be taken not only from different parts of the whole republic, but also from different districts of the larger members of it, which had in several instances, particularly in Virginia, different interests and views arising from difference of produce, of habits, etc., etc.

He admitted that we had been too democratic but was afraid we should incautiously run into the opposite extreme. We ought to attend to the rights of every class of the people. . . .

Mr. WILSON [of Pa.] contended strenuously for drawing the most numerous branch of the legislature immediately from the people. He was for raising the federal pyramid to a considerable altitude, and for that reason wished to give it as broad a basis as possible. No government could long subsist without the confidence of the people. In a republican government this confidence was peculiarly essential. He also thought it wrong to increase the weight of the state legislatures by making them the electors of the national legislature. All interference between the general and local governments should be obviated as much as possible. On examination it would be found that the opposition of states to federal measures had proceeded much more from the officers of the states than from the people at large.

Mr. MADISON [of Va.] considered the popular election of one branch of the national legislature as essential to every plan of free government. . . . He thought, too, that the great fabric to be raised would be more stable and durable if it should rest on the solid foundation of the people themselves than if it should stand merely on the pillars of the legislatures. . . .

On the question for an election of the first branch of the national legislature by the people: Massachusetts, aye; Connecticut, divided; New York, aye; New Jersey, no; Pennsylvania, aye; Delaware, divided; Virginia, aye; North Carolina, aye; South Carolina, no; Georgia, aye. (Ayes—6; noes—2; divided—2.)

2. The Argument over Slave Importations (1787)

The issue of slavery provoked spirited debate at Philadelphia. Should the Negro slave count as a whole man or no man in the apportioning of representation in Congress? The compromise: he would count as three-fifths of a man. Should the further importation of slaves be shut off or allowed to continue forever? The compromise: Congress could not touch slave importations for twenty years (a con-

2. *Ibid.*, II, 364–65, 369–72. By permission of the Yale University Press.

cession to the South), while Congress by a simple majority rather than by a two-thirds vote could pass laws to control shipping (a concession to the commercial North). As this portion of the debate opens, as recorded by James Madison, delegate Luther Martin of Maryland, a man of well-known liberal tendencies, is endeavoring to amend the draft before the convention, which stipulated that slave importation was not to be prohibited or taxed. List the arguments for non-importation and those for continued importation, and determine which side, in the light of existing circumstances, had the better of the debate. Form some judgment as to the prophetic insight of the Founding Fathers, and as to what would have happened if the convention had voted to stop all slave importations at once.

[August 21.] Mr. L. MARTIN [of Md.] proposed to vary article 7, sect. 4 so as to allow a prohibition or tax on the importation of slaves. First, as five slaves are to be counted as three freemen in the apportionment of representatives, such a clause would leave an encouragement to this traffic. Second, slaves [through danger of insurrection] weakened one part of the Union, which the other parts were bound to protect; the privilege of importing them was therefore unreasonable. Third, it was inconsistent with the principles of the Revolution, and dishonorable to the American character, to have such a feature in the Constitution.

Mr. RUTLEDGE [of S. C.] did not see how the importation of slaves could be encouraged by this section [as now phrased]. He was not apprehensive of insurrections, and would readily exempt the other states from the obligation to protect the Southern against them. Religion and humanity had nothing to do with this question. Interest alone is the governing principle with nations. The true question at present is whether the Southern states shall or shall not be parties to the Union. If the Northern states consult their interest, they will not oppose the increase of slaves, which will increase the commodities of which they will become the carriers.

Mr. ELLSWORTH [of Conn.] was for leaving the clause as it stands. Let every state import what it pleases. The morality or wisdom of slavery are considerations belonging to the states themselves. What enriches a part enriches the whole, and the states are the best judges of their particular interest. The old Confederation had not meddled with this point; and he did not see any greater necessity for bringing it within the policy of the new one.

Mr. [Charles] PINCKNEY [of S. C.]. South Carolina can never receive the plan if it prohibits the slave trade. In every proposed extension of the powers of Congress, that state has expressly and watchfully excepted that of meddling with the importation of Negroes. If the states be all left at liberty on this subject, South Carolina may perhaps, by degrees, do of herself what is wished, as Virginia and Maryland already have done. . . .

Mr. SHERMAN [of Conn.] was for leaving the clause as it stands. He disapproved of the slave trade; yet, as the states were now possessed of the right to import slaves, as the public good did not require it to be taken from them, and as it was expedient to have as few objections as possible to the proposed scheme of government, he thought it best to leave the matter as we find it. He observed that the abolition of slavery seemed to be going on in the United States, and that the good sense of the several states would probably by degrees complete it. . . .

Col. MASON [of Va.]. This infernal traffic originated in the avarice of British merchants. The British government constantly checked the attempts of Virginia to put a stop to it. The present question concerns not the importing states alone, but the whole Union. . . . Maryland and Virginia, he said, had already prohibited the importation of slaves expressly. North Carolina had done the same in substance. All this would be in vain if South Carolina and Georgia be at liberty to import. The Western people are already calling out for slaves for their new lands, and will fill that country with slaves, if they can be got through South Carolina and Georgia. Slavery discourages arts and manufactures. The poor despise labor when performed by slaves. They prevent the immigration of whites, who really enrich and strengthen a country. They produce the most pernicious effect on manners. Every master of slaves is born a petty tyrant. They bring the judgment of Heaven on a country. As nations cannot be rewarded or pun-

ished in the next world, they must be in this. By an inevitable chain of causes and effects, Providence punishes national sins by national calamities. He lamented that some of our Eastern [New England] brethren had, from a lust of gain, embarked in this nefarious traffic. . . . He held it essential, in every point of view, that the general government should have power to prevent the increase of slavery.

Mr. ELLSWORTH [of Conn.], as he had never owned a slave, could not judge of the effects of slavery on character. He said, however, that if it was to be considered in a moral light, we ought to go further, and free those already in the country. As slaves also multiply so fast in Virginia

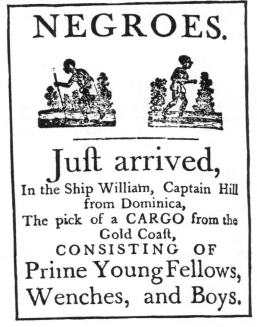

CHARLESTON SLAVE ADVERTISEMENT
State Gazette of South Carolina, 1787.

and Maryland that it is cheaper to raise than import them, whilst in the sickly rice swamps foreign supplies are necessary, if we go no further than is urged, we shall be unjust towards South Carolina and Georgia. Let us not intermeddle. As population increases, poor laborers will be so plenty as to render slaves useless. Slavery, in time, will not be a speck in our country. . . .

Gen. [Charles C.] PINCKNEY [of S. C.] declared it to be his firm opinion that if himself and all his colleagues were to sign the Constitution, and use their personal influence, it would be of no avail towards obtaining the assent of their constituents [to a slave-trade prohibition]. South Carolina and Georgia cannot do without slaves. As to Virginia, she will gain by stopping the importations. Her slaves will rise in value, and she has more than she wants. It would be unequal to require South Carolina and Georgia to confederate on such unequal terms. . . . He contended that the importation of slaves would be for the interest of the whole Union. The more slaves, the more produce to employ the carrying trade; the more consumption also; and the more of this, the more of revenue for the common treasury. He admitted it to be reasonable that slaves should be dutied like other imports; but should consider a rejection of the clause as an exclusion of South Carolina from the Union.

[*The final compromise, as written into the Constitution, permitted Congress to levy a maximum duty of $10 a head on each slave imported. In 1808, the earliest date permitted by the framers, Congress ended all legal importation of slaves.*]

C. FIRST REACTIONS TO THE CONSTITUTION

1. A Philadelphia Editor Is Expectant (1787)

A curious public had little inkling of what was going on in the Philadelphia convention. The delegates, who were sworn to secrecy, deliberated behind closed doors guarded by soldiers. But the general expectation was that a stronger government would emerge, designed to subdue disorders and bring the headstrong states to heel. The following Philadelphia editorial fairly glows with optimism. Ascertain which one of the anticipated arguments against the Constitution seems most formidable, and why the Shaysites could be compared to the Tories.

The year 1776 is celebrated (says a correspondent) for a revolution in favor of Liberty. The year 1787, it is expected, will be celebrated with equal joy for a revolution in favor of Government. The impatience with which all classes of people (a few officers of government only excepted) wait to receive the new federal constitution can only be equaled by their zealous determination to support it.

Every state (adds our correspondent) has its Shays, who either with their pens—or tongues—or offices—are endeavoring to effect what Shays attempted in vain with his sword. In one of the states, this demagogue tries to persuade the people that it is dangerous to increase the powers of Congress. In another, he denies the authority of the Convention to redress our national grievances. In a third, he whispers distrust, saying the states will not adopt the new frame of government. In a fourth, he says the state constitutions,

1. *Pennsylvania Gazette*, Sept. 5, 1787.

and the officers who act under them, are of divine right, and can be altered by no human power—and of course considers all attempts to restore order and government in the United States as a "laughable" thing. In the fifth, he opposes a general confederacy, and urges the division of the states into three smaller confederacies, that he may the more easily place himself at the head of one of them.

The spirit and wickedness of Shays is in each of these principles and measures. Let Americans be wise. Toryism and Shaysism are nearly allied. They both lead to slavery, poverty, and misery.

We hear that the Convention propose to adjourn next week, after laying America under such obligations to them for their long, painful, and disinterested labors to establish her liberty upon a permanent basis as no time will ever cancel.

AN ALLEGORICAL SALUTE TO THE STATES
UNDER THE CONSTITUTION

Frontispiece of the *Columbian Magazine*, 1788. William L. Clements Library, University of Michigan.

2. Hamilton Scans the Future (1787)

Alexander Hamilton of New York, though only thirty-two, was probably the most brilliant and eloquent member of the Philadelphia assemblage. But his great contribution was in engineering the call for the convention and in campaigning for the Constitution. At Philadelphia, he was outvoted by his two anti-federalist colleagues from New York, and his own federalist and centralist views were too extreme for the other delegates. His superlative five-hour oratorical effort championed a plan which, among other things, would have had the President and the Senators holding office during good behavior, and the state governors appointed by the federal government. The scheme received one vote—his own. In reading the following memorandum by Hamilton, evidently prepared shortly after the Constitution was drafted, determine why the rich would be favorable to the new instrument; why the poor and the states'-righters would be unfavorable.

The new Constitution has in favor of its success these circumstances: A very great weight of influence of the persons who framed it, particularly

2. H. C. Lodge, ed., *The Works of Alexander Hamilton* (1904), I, 420–23.

in the universal popularity of General Washington. The good will of the commercial interest throughout the states, which will give all its efforts to the establishment of a government capable of regulating, protecting, and extending the commerce of the Union. The good will of most men of property in the several states, who wish a government of the Union able to protect them against domestic violence and the depredations which the democratic spirit is apt to make on property, and who are besides anxious for the respectability of the nation. The hopes of the creditors of the United States, that a general government, possessing the means of doing it, will pay the debt of the Union. A strong belief in the people at large of the insufficiency of the present Confederation to preserve the existence of the Union, and of the necessity of the Union to their safety and prosperity. Of course, a strong desire of a change, and a predisposition to receive well the propositions of the convention.

Against its success is to be put: The dissent of two or three important men in the convention, who will think their characters pledged to defeat the plan. The influence of many *inconsiderable* men in possession of considerable offices under the state governments, who will fear a diminution of their consequence, power, and emolument by the establishment of the general government, and who can hope for nothing there. The influence of some *considerable* men in office, possessed of talents and popularity, who, partly from the same motives, and partly from a desire of *playing a part* in a convulsion for their own aggrandizement, will oppose the quiet adoption of the new government. (Some considerable men out of office, from motives of ambition, may be disposed to act the same part.)

Add to these causes: The disinclination of the people to taxes, and of course to a strong government. The opposition of all men much in debt, who will not wish to see a government established, one object of which is to restrain the means of cheating creditors. The democratical jealousy of the people, which may be alarmed at the appearance of institutions that may seem calculated to place the power of the community in few hands, and to raise a few individuals to stations of great pre-eminence. And the influence of some foreign powers, who, from different motives, will not wish to see an energetic government established throughout the states.

In this view of the subject, it is difficult to form any judgment whether the plan will be adopted or rejected. It must be essentially matter of conjecture. The present appearances and all other circumstances considered, the probability seems to be on the side of its adoption. But the causes operating against its adoption are powerful, and there will be nothing astonishing in the contrary.

If it do not finally obtain, it is probable the discussion of the question will beget such struggles, animosities, and heats in the community that this circumstance, conspiring with the *real necessity* of an essential change in our present situation, will produce civil war. . . .

A reunion with Great Britain, from universal disgust at a state of commotion, is not impossible, though not much to be feared. The most plausible shape of such a business would be the establishment of a son of the present monarch [George III] in the supreme government of this country, with a family compact.

If the government be adopted, it is probable General Washington will be the President of the United States. This will ensure a wise choice of men to administer the government, and a good administration. A good administration will conciliate the confidence and affection of the people, and perhaps enable the government to acquire more consistency than the proposed Constitution seems to promise for so great a country. . . .

3. Mason Is Critical (1787)

George Mason, a wealthy Virginia planter owning 5000 acres, had played a leading role in the Revolutionary movement. A self-taught constitutional lawyer of high repute, a dedicated advocate of states' rights, and an undying foe of Negro slavery, he was one of the five most frequent speakers at the Philadelphia convention. Shocked by the whittling down of states' rights, he finally refused to sign the Constitution and fought it bitterly in Virginia. His chief grievance was the compromise by which the South conceded a simple majority vote in Congress on navigation laws in return for twenty more years of African slave trade, of which he disapproved anyhow. He set forth his objections in the following influential pamphlet. Note which of his criticisms related to states' rights; which to the rights of the South; and which seem overdrawn or absurd in the light of subsequent events.

There is no Declaration [Bill] of Rights, and the laws of the general government being paramount to the laws and constitution of the several states, the declarations of rights in the separate states are no security. . . .

The Judiciary of the United States is so constructed and extended as to absorb and destroy the judiciaries of the several states; thereby rendering law as tedious, intricate, and expensive, and justice as unattainable, by a great part of the community, as in England, and enabling the rich to oppress and ruin the poor.

The President of the United States has no Constitutional Council, a thing unknown in any safe and regular government. He will therefore be unsupported by proper information and advice, and will generally be directed by minions and favorites; or he will become a tool to the Senate— or a council of state will grow out of the principal officers of the great departments; the worst and most dangerous of all ingredients for such a council in a free country. From this fatal defect has arisen the improper power of the Senate in the appointment of public officers, and the alarming dependence and connection between that branch of the legislature and the Supreme Executive.

Hence also sprung that unnecessary officer, the Vice-President, who, for want of other employment, is made president of the Senate, thereby dangerously blending the executive and legislative powers, besides always

3. Kate M. Rowland, *The Life of George Mason* (1892), II, 387–90.

giving to some one of the states an unnecessary and unjust pre-eminence over the others. . . .

By declaring all treaties supreme laws of the land, the Executive and the Senate have, in many cases, an exclusive power of legislation; which might have been avoided by proper distinctions with respect to treaties, and requiring the assent of the House of Representatives, where it could be done with safety.

By requiring only a majority [of Congress] to make all commercial and navigation laws, the five Southern states, whose produce and circumstances are totally different from that of the eight Northern and Eastern states, may be ruined. For such rigid and premature regulations may be made as will enable the merchants of the Northern and Eastern states not only to demand an exorbitant freight, but to monopolize the purchase of the commodities at their own price, for many years, to the great injury of the landed interest and impoverishment of the people. And the danger is the greater as the gain on one side will be in proportion to the loss on the other. Whereas requiring two-thirds of the members present in both Houses would have produced mutual moderation, promoted the general interest, and removed an insuperable objection to the adoption of this government.

Under their own construction of the general clause [Art. I, Sec. VIII, para. 18], at the end of the enumerated powers, the Congress may grant monopolies in trade and commerce, constitute new crimes, inflict unusual and severe punishments, and extend their powers as far as they shall think proper; so that the state legislatures have no security for the powers now presumed to remain to them, or the people for their rights.

There is no declaration of any kind for preserving the liberty of the press, or the trial by jury in civil causes [cases]; nor against the danger of standing armies in time of peace. . . .

This government will set out a moderate aristocracy; it is at present impossible to foresee whether it will, in its operation, produce a monarchy or a corrupt, tyrannical aristocracy. It will most probably vibrate some years between the two, and then terminate in the one or the other.

4. Jefferson Is Unenthusiastic (1787)

Thomas Jefferson, the American minister in Paris, learned of the Philadelphia convention with some misgivings. While recognizing the need for a stronger central government, especially in foreign affairs, he regarded the Confederation as a "wonderfully perfect instrument," considering the times. A comparison of the United States government with the governments of Continental Europe, he declared, "is like a comparison of heaven and hell. England, like the earth, may be allowed to take the intermediate station." He evidently believed that some judicious patchwork would provide the needed bolstering. Upon receiving a copy of the new Constitution he was troubled by some of its features, particularly by the absence of a Bill of Rights. Note why, in the following letter to William Smith, he belittled reports of anarchy; why he condoned periodic rebellions; and why he would probably have favored the 22nd Amendment (anti-third term).

4. P. L. Ford, ed., *The Writings of Thomas Jefferson* (1894), IV, 466–67 (Nov. 13, 1787).

I do not know whether it is to yourself or Mr. [John] Adams I am to give my thanks for the copy of the new Constitution. . . . There are very good articles in it; and very bad. I do not know which preponderate. What we have lately read in the history of Holland . . . would have sufficed to set me against a chief magistrate eligible for a long duration, if I had ever been disposed towards one. And what we have always read of the elections of Polish kings should have forever excluded the idea of one continuable for life.

Wonderful is the effect of impudent and persevering lying. The British ministry have so long hired their gazetteers to repeat, and model into every form, lies about our being in anarchy, that the world has at length believed them, the English nation has believed them, the ministers themselves have come to believe them, and what is more wonderful, we have believed them ourselves.

Yet where does this anarchy exist? Where did it ever exist, except in the single instance of [Shays' Rebellion in] Massachusetts? And can history produce an instance of rebellion so honorably conducted? I say nothing of its motives. They were founded in ignorance, not wickedness.

God forbid we should ever be twenty years without such a rebellion. The people cannot be all, and always, well informed. The part which is wrong will be discontented, in proportion to the importance of the facts they misconceive. If they remain quiet under such misconceptions, it is a lethargy, the forerunner of death to the public liberty.

We have had thirteen states independent for eleven years. There has been one rebellion. That comes to one rebellion in a century and a half for each state. What country before ever existed a century and a half without a rebellion? And what country can preserve its liberties if its rulers are not warned from time to time that their people preserve the spirit of resistance? Let them take arms. The remedy is to set them right as to facts, pardon, and pacify them.

What signify a few lives lost in a century or two? The tree of liberty must be refreshed from time to time with the blood of patriots and tyrants. It is its natural manure. Our convention has been too much impressed by the insurrection of Massachusetts; and on the spur of the moment they are setting up a kite [hawk] to keep the henyard in order.

I hope in God this article [perpetual re-eligibility of the President] will be rectified before the Constitution is accepted.

D. THE RATIFICATION DEBATE IN MASSACHUSETTS

1. A Delegate Fears for the Little People (1788)

When the crucial Massachusetts ratifying convention met, it at first mustered a majority against the Constitution. As Hamilton had predicted, the propertied and commercial elements favored it; the debtors (including many Shaysites), small farmers, and states'-rights people generally fought it. The following outburst by Amos Single-

1. Jonathan Elliot, *The Debates on the Federal Constitution* (1836), II, 101–02.

tary, one of the small-fry group, who had never attended school, is typical of much of the debate in the state conventions. Decide whether he feared taxation without representation or merely taxation, and to what extent he anticipates the thesis of Dr. Charles A. Beard regarding the self-seeking economic motives of the propertied Founding Fathers.

We contended with Great Britain—some said for a three-penny duty on tea; but it was not that. It was because they claimed a right to tax us and bind us in all cases whatever. And does not this Constitution do the same? Does it not take away all we have—all our property? Does it not lay *all* taxes, duties, imposts, and excises? And what more have we to give?

They tell us Congress won't lay dry [direct] taxes upon us, but collect all the money they want by impost [import duties]. I say, there has always been a difficulty about impost. . . . They won't be able to raise money enough by impost, and then they will lay it on the land and take all we have got.

These lawyers, and men of learning, and moneyed men, that talk so finely and gloss over matters so smoothly, to make us poor illiterate people swallow down the pill, expect to get into Congress themselves. They expect to be the managers of this Constitution, and get all the power and all the money into their own hands. And then they will swallow up all us little folks, like the great Leviathan, Mr. President; yes, just as the whale swallowed up Jonah. This is what I am afraid of. . . .

2. A Storekeeper Blasts Standing Armies (1788)

Samuel Nasson, a saddler and then a storekeeper, expressed a common fear in the Massachusetts ratifying convention. Ascertain why this unmoneyed Massachusetts man should have been so deeply concerned about an army, and whether his fears had any real basis.

The eighth section, Mr. President, provides that Congress shall have power to lay and collect taxes, duties, imposts, excise, etc. We may, sir, be poor; we may not be able to pay these taxes, etc. We must have a little meal, and a little meat, whereon to live, and save a little for a rainy day. But what follows? Let us see. To raise and support armies. Here, sir, comes the key to unlock this cabinet; here is the means by which you will be made to pay taxes! But will ye, my countrymen, submit to this?

Suffer me, sir, to say a few words on the fatal effects of standing armies, that bane of republican governments. A standing army! Was it not with this that Caesar passed the Rubicon, and laid prostrate the liberties of his country? By this have seven eighths of the once free nations of the globe been brought into bondage! Time would fail me, were I to attempt to recapitulate the havoc made in the world by standing armies. . . .

Sir, had I a voice like Jove, I would proclaim it throughout the world; and had I an arm like Jove, I would hurl from the globe those villains that

2. *Ibid.*, II, 136–37.

would dare attempt to establish in our country a standing army. I wish, sir, that the gentlemen of Boston would bring to their minds the fatal evening of the 5th of March, 1770, when by standing troops they lost five of their fellow townsmen [in the Boston Massacre]. I will ask them, What price can atone for their lives? What money can make satisfaction for the loss? . . .

What occasion have we for standing armies? We fear no foe. If one should come upon us, we have a militia, which is our bulwark. . . . Therefore, sir, I am utterly opposed to a standing army in time of peace. . . .

3. A Farmer Favors the Constitution (1788)

The Massachusetts convention finally ratified the Constitution by the narrow margin of 187 to 168 votes. But the majority did not fall into line until Samuel Adams, an experienced subverter of strong governments, had reluctantly thrown his weight behind the document, and not until the members agreed to recommend nine fear-quieting amendments (Bill of Rights). Not all farmers opposed ratification, as this earthy convention speech of Jonathan Smith attests. Determine how convincingly he makes his points that mob rule is tyranny, that anarchy begets despotism, and that the moneyed class was not thinking solely of its narrowly selfish interests.

Mr. President, I am a plain man, and get my living by the plough. I am not used to speak in public, but I beg your leave to say a few words to my brother plough-joggers in this house.

I have lived in a part of the country where I have known the worth of good government by the want of it. There was a black cloud [Shays' Rebellion] that rose in the east last winter, and spread over the west. . . . It brought on a state of anarchy and that led to tyranny. I say, it brought anarchy. People that used to live peaceably, and were before good neighbors, got distracted, and took up arms against government. . . . People, I say, took up arms, and then, if you went to speak to them, you had the musket of death presented to your breast. They would rob you of your property, threaten to burn your houses; oblige you to be on your guard night and day. Alarms spread from town to town; families were broken up; the tender mother would cry, O my son is among them! . . .

Our distress was so great that we should have been glad to snatch at anything that looked like a government. Had any person that was able to protect us come and set up his standard, we should all have flocked to it, even if it had been a monarch, and that monarch might have proved a tyrant. So that you see that anarchy leads to tyranny; and better have one tyrant than so many at once.

Now, Mr. President, when I saw this Constitution, I found that it was a cure for these disorders. It was just such a thing as we wanted. I got a copy of it and read it over and over. I had been a member of the convention to form our own state constitution, and had learnt something of the checks and balances of power; and I found them all here. I did not go to any lawyer, to ask his opinion—we have no lawyer in our town, and do well

3. *Ibid.,* II, 102–04.

enough without. I formed my own opinion, and was pleased with this Constitution. . . .

But I don't think the worse of the Constitution because lawyers, and men of learning, and moneyed men are fond of it. I don't suspect that they want to get into Congress and abuse their power. I am not of such a jealous make. They that are honest men themselves are not apt to suspect other people. . . .

B O S T O N, October 20.

On Wednefday laft, the Hon. General Court met at the State Houfe in this town—and on Thurfday his Excellency communicated the new Conftitution to them, which with his Excellency's fpeech, was committed to a large and refpeƈable Committee of both branches.

From the very handfome manner in which our worthy Governour fpeaks of the new Conftitution —and from the obfervations of feveral refpeƈable gentlemen of the Legiflature, yefterday on it, we anticipate an early day being fixed on by the General Court for the meeting of our Convention—that this State may have the great honour and fingular happinefs of being the firft to adopt a fyftem, fecond to none in the world.

The refpeƈable town of Derby, in Conneƈicut has unanimoufly voted to inftruƈ their deputies to ufe their endeavours that their convention **may** be immediately called.

FIRST REACTIONS TO THE CONSTITUTION
REPORTED IN NEW YORK

A dispatch from *The Independent Journal and General Advertiser*, October 27, 1787. This pro-Constitution paper later published *The Federalist* serially. New-York Historical Society.

Brother farmers, let us suppose a case, now. Suppose you had a farm of 50 acres, and your title was disputed, and there was a farm of 5000 acres joined to you that belonged to a man of learning, and his title was involved in the same difficulty. Would you not be glad to have him for your friend, rather than to stand alone in the dispute?

Well, the case is the same— these lawyers, these moneyed men, these men of learning, are all embarked in the same cause with us, and we must all swim or sink together. And shall we throw the Constitution overboard because it does not please us alike? Suppose two or three of you had been at the pains to break up a piece of rough land, and sow it with wheat— would you let it lie waste because you could not agree what sort of a fence to make? Would it not be better to put up a fence that did not please everyone's fancy, rather than not fence it at all, or keep disputing about it until the wild beasts came in and devoured it?

Some gentlemen say, don't be in a hurry; take time to consider; and don't take a leap in the dark. I say, take things in time—gather fruit when it is ripe. There is a time to sow, and a time to reap. We sowed our seed when we sent men to the federal convention. Now is the harvest; now is the time to reap the fruit of our labor. And if we won't do it now, I am afraid we never shall have another opportunity.

[*The common talk of calling another convention to do a better job was folly. It was either this constitution or failure.*]

E. THE RATIFICATION DEBATE IN NEW YORK

1. An Anti-Federalist Demands Deliberation (1787)

Last-ditch opposition to the Constitution formed in New York under the states'-rights banner of the redoubtable George Clinton, the first governor and so-called "Father of New York State." The strategic location of New York City, he saw clearly, promised commercial ascendancy, and he did not welcome the restraints of a powerful federal government. His views were evidently shared by this anonymous contributor to a New York newspaper. Locate the strongest arguments against a hasty and uncritical acceptance of the Constitution, and determine how much of this reasoning is applicable to present-day political affairs. Explain why this author takes an unusually optimistic view of conditions.

I have read with a degree of attention several publications which have lately appeared in favor of the new Constitution; and as far as I am able to discern, the arguments (if they can be so termed) of most weight which are urged in its favor may be reduced to the two following:

1st. That the men who formed it were wise and experienced; that they were an illustrious band of patriots and had the happiness of their country at heart; that they were four months deliberating on the subject; and therefore it must be a perfect system.

2nd. That if the system be not received, this country will be without any government, and, of consequence, will be reduced to a state of anarchy and confusion, and involved in bloodshed and carnage; and in the end a government will be imposed upon us, not the result of reason and reflection, but of force and usurpation. . . .

With respect to the first, it will be readily perceived that it precludes all investigation of the merits of the proposed Constitution, and leads to an adoption of the plan without enquiring whether it be good or bad. For if we are to infer the perfection of this system from the characters and abilities of the men who formed it, we may as well determine to accept it without any enquiry as with. A number of persons in this as well as the other states have upon this principle determined to submit to it without even reading or knowing its contents. . . .

In answer to the second argument, I deny that we are in immediate danger of anarchy and commotions. Nothing but the passions of wicked and ambitious men will put us in the least danger on this head. Those who are anxious to precipitate a measure will always tell us that the present is the critical moment; now is the time, the crisis is arrived, and the present minute must be seized. Tyrants have always made use of this plea; and nothing in our circumstances can justify it.

The country is in profound peace, and we are not threatened by invasion from any quarter. The governments of the respective states are in the full exercise of their powers; and the lives, the liberty, and property of individuals are protected. All present exigencies are answered by them.

It is true, the regulation of trade and a competent provision for the

1. New York *Journal and Weekly Register*, Nov. 8, 1787.

payment of the interest of the public debt is wanting; but no immediate commotion will rise from these. Time may be taken for calm discussion and deliberate conclusions.

Individuals are just recovering from the losses and embarrassments sustained by the late war. Industry and frugality are taking their station and banishing from the community idleness and prodigality. Individuals are lessening their private debts, and several millions of the public debt is discharged by the sale of Western territory.

There is no reason, therefore, why we should precipitately and rashly adopt a system which is imperfect or insecure. We may securely deliberate and propose amendments and alterations. I know it is said we cannot change for the worse; but if we act the part of wise men, we shall take care that we change for the better. It will be labor lost if, after all our pains, we are in no better circumstances than we were before.

If any tumults arise, they will be justly chargeable on those artful and ambitious men who are determined to cram this government down the throats of the people before they have time deliberately to examine it.

2. Hamilton Condemns the Confederation (1787)

When the New York convention met at Poughkeepsie to vote on the Constitution, a two-thirds majority at first opposed it. Alexander Hamilton played a crucial role in the final favorable decision. Not only did he speak eloquently at Poughkeepsie and lobby skillfully behind the scenes, but he had written a series of persuasive newspaper articles over the name of "Publius." These essays, combined with a lesser number of contributions by James Madison of Virginia and John Jay of New York—eighty-five all told—were immediately published in book form as *The Federalist* and used effectively in other states. Though high-class propaganda, this treatise is still the most brilliant commentary on the basic principles underlying the Constitution.

The treaty of peace with Britain in 1783 had bound the United States to leniency toward the Loyalists and honesty toward pre-war British creditors. But the impotent central government under the Articles of Confederation was unable to force the states to honor these solemn obligations. The British, partly in retaliation, had stubbornly refused to evacuate a half-dozen American trading posts along the northern frontier. In Number 15 of *The Federalist*, Hamilton eloquently summarizes these difficulties under the Articles of Confederation. Decide whether he is more concerned with domestic than foreign affairs, and which phase of the latter disturbs him most, and why. Explain why he may have been taking an unduly pessimistic view of conditions.

We may indeed with propriety be said to have reached almost the last stage of national humiliation. There is scarcely any thing that can wound the pride or degrade the character of an independent nation which we do not experience.

Are there [treaty] engagements [with England] to the performance of which we are held by every tie respectable among men? These are the subjects of constant and unblushing violation.

Do we owe debts to foreigners [France, Holland] and to our own citizens, contracted in a time of imminent peril for the preservation of our

2. H. C. Lodge, ed., *The Federalist* (1895), pp. 84–85.

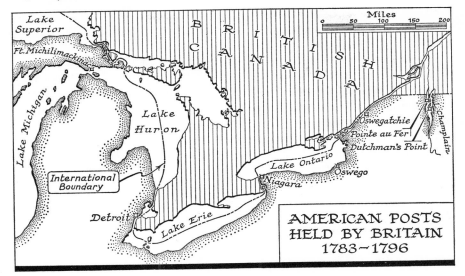

AMERICAN POSTS
HELD BY BRITAIN
1783–1796

political existence? These remain without any proper or satisfactory provision for their discharge.

Have we valuable territories and important posts in the possession of a foreign power [England] which, by express stipulations, ought long since to have been surrendered? These are still retained, to the prejudice of our interests, not less than our rights. Are we in a condition to resent or to repel the aggression? We have neither troops, nor treasury, nor [national] government. Are we even in a condition to remonstrate with dignity? The just imputations on our own faith, in respect to the same treaty, ought first to be removed.

Are we entitled by nature and compact [treaty] to a free participation in the navigation of the Mississippi? Spain excludes us from it.

Is public credit an indispensable resource in time of public danger? We seem to have abandoned its cause as desperate and irretrievable.

Is commerce of importance to national wealth? Ours is at the lowest point of declension.

Is respectability in the eyes of foreign powers a safeguard against foreign encroachments? The imbecility of our government even forbids them to treat with us. Our ambassadors abroad are the mere pageants of mimic sovereignty.

Is a violent and unnatural decrease in the value of land a symptom of national distress? The price of improved land in most parts of the country is much lower than can be accounted for by the quantity of waste land at market, and can only be fully explained by that want of private and public confidence, which are so alarmingly prevalent among all ranks, and which have a direct tendency to depreciate property of every kind.

Is private credit the friend and patron of industry? That most useful kind, which relates to borrowing and lending, is reduced within the narrowest limits, and this still more from an opinion of insecurity than from the scarcity of money.

To shorten an enumeration of particulars which can afford neither pleasure nor instruction, it may in general be demanded, what indication is there of national disorder, poverty, and insignificance that could befall a community so peculiarly blessed with natural advantages as we are, which does not form a part of the dark catalogue of our public misfortunes?

This is the melancholy situation to which we have been brought by those very maxims and councils which would now deter us from adopting the proposed Constitution. . . .

[*New York, the eleventh state to approve, finally ratified the Constitution on July 26, 1788. Its action was something of an anticlimax, for with ratification by the ninth state, New Hampshire, the necessary two-thirds had been achieved. North Carolina and Rhode Island did not approve until after the new government was launched in 1789.*]

THOUGHT PROVOKERS

1. In view of the conflicting testimony as to anarchic conditions under the Articles of Confederation, what conclusions may be safely drawn as to the true state of affairs? To what extent may Daniel Shays be regarded as one of the indirect Founding Fathers? Would Jefferson today be permitted to express publicly his views on rebellion?

2. In what sense was the Constitution a democratic document, and in what sense not? a conservative document? Interpret democracy as conceived by the Founding Fathers.

3. What groups seem to have been the strongest supporters of the Constitution? the strongest foes? Why? What probably would have happened in the short run and in the long run if the Constitution had failed of ratification?

4. What is meant by "enlightened self-interest" in public affairs? Were the Founding Fathers motivated by it rather than by "pocketbook patriotism"?

5. Was *The Federalist* really propaganda in the same sense as the Declaration of Independence and Paine's *Common Sense*? Or was it merely an instrument in a campaign of education?

FURTHER EXPLORATION

General: See books by Beard, Brown, and McDonald listed in the first footnote of this chapter. Also Merrill Jensen, *The New Nation* (1950); J. T. Main, *The Antifederalists* (1961). **Shays' Rebellion:** M. L. Starkey, *A Little Rebellion* (1955). **Convention Clashes:** Max Farrand, *The Framing of the Constitution* (1913); Carl Van Doren, *The Great Rehearsal* (1948). **First Reactions:** Broadus Mitchell, *Alexander Hamilton: Youth to Maturity 1755–1788* (1957); R. A. Rutland, *George Mason: Reluctant Statesman* (1961). **Massachusetts Debate:** S. B. Harding, *The Contest over the Ratification of the Federal Constitution in Massachusetts* (1896). **New York Debate:** C. E. Miner, *The Ratification of the Federal Constitution by the State of New York* (1921); J. C. Miller, *Alexander Hamilton* (1959). **Recent:** Clinton Rossiter, *1787: The Grand Convention* (1966); B. and L. P. Mitchell, *A Biography of the Constitution . . .* (1964).

Chapter 8

The Hamilton—Jefferson Clash

Hamilton was honest as a man, but, as a politician, believed in the necessity of either force or corruption to govern men.

THOMAS JEFFERSON, 1811

[Jefferson is] a man of profound ambition and violent passions.

ALEXANDER HAMILTON, 1792

PROLOGUE: When Washington took the presidential oath at New York, the temporary capital, he was determined to get the ship of state off on an even keel. He therefore "packed" the new offices with federalists, as the supporters of the Constitution were called. The one conspicuous exception was the Secretary of State, Thomas Jefferson. As a vigilant champion of states' rights, he was an antifederalist, or a foe of a powerful central government. One result was an inevitable clash between him and Secretary of the Treasury Hamilton, a staunch federalist, over foreign affairs and fiscal policy. From these heated differences there emerged, about 1793, two political parties: the Hamiltonian Federalists and the Jeffersonian Republicans. Jefferson naturally opposed the Hamiltonian plans for assuming the state debts, establishing the Bank of the United States, and levying an excise tax on whiskey. In his eyes, all these schemes would increase the power of the federal octopus, encroach on states' rights, promote corruption, and enrich the ruling class at the expense of the common man.

A. LAUNCHING THE NEW GOVERNMENT

1. The Senate Snubs Washington (1789)

The new Constitution empowered the President to "make treaties" with "the advice and consent of the Senate." Early in his administration Washington, accompanied by Secretary of War Knox, appeared before the then tiny group of Senators to explain an Indian treaty. The deliberations proceeded so haltingly in the President's awesome presence that Senator Maclay finally supported a motion to refer the papers to a committee. Washington was visibly annoyed. Tradition has him saying, as he left the chamber, that he would "be damned" if he ever came back again, but he did return—once. No other President has attempted to discuss treaties personally with the entire Senate. In reading the following extract from Senator Maclay's diary, one should bear in mind that the author was an ardent republican who resented Washington's aristocratic airs and who privately wished that the General "were in heaven" and not "brought forward as the constant cover to every unconstitutional and irrepublican act." Determine why this type of personal conferring with the Senators failed, and whether the precedent of non-conference thus established was a good one. As this diary entry begins, Maclay has just spoken for deferment.

1. E. S. Maclay, ed., *Journal of William Maclay* (1890), pp. 131–32.

As I sat down, the President of the United States started up in a violent fret. "This defeats every purpose of my coming here" were the first words that he said. He then went on that he had brought his Secretary of War with him to give every necessary information; that the Secretary knew all about the business; and yet he [Washington] was delayed and could not go on with the matter. He cooled, however, by degrees. Said he had no objection to putting off this matter until Monday, but declared he did not understand the matter of commitment [referral]. He might be delayed; he could not tell how long.

He rose a second time, and said he had no objection to postponement until Monday at ten o'clock. By the looks of the Senate this seemed agreed to. A pause for some time ensued. We waited for him to withdraw. He did so with a discontented air. Had it been any other man than the man whom I wish to regard as the first character in the world, I would have said, with sullen dignity.

I cannot now be mistaken. The President wishes to tread on the necks of the Senate. Commitment will bring the matter to discussion, at least in the committee, where he is not present. He wishes us to see with the eyes and hear with the ears of his Secretary [of War] only. The Secretary to advance the premises, the President to draw the conclusions, and to bear down our deliberations with his personal authority and presence. Form only will be left to us. This will not do with Americans. But let the matter work; it will soon cure itself.

August 24th, Monday.—The Senate met. The President of the United States soon took his seat, and the business began. The President wore a different aspect from what he did Saturday. He was placid and serene, and manifested a spirit of accommodation; declared his consent that his questions should be amended.

2. Hamilton versus Jefferson on Popular Rule

President Washington's aristocratic and monarchical appearance may have offended Senator Maclay, who became a follower of Thomas Jefferson, but it did not disturb Secretary of the Treasury Hamilton. The youthful financier, though born in humble circumstances, had developed a profound distrust of the common clay. In contrast, Jefferson, a Virginia planter-aristocrat, championed the forgotten man. Faith in the informed masses became the cornerstone of Jefferson's Democratic-Republican Party; distrust of the masses and the cultivation of special interests became the cornerstone of Hamilton's Federalist Party. Herewith are presented the conflicting opinions of the two great leaders over a period of years. The initial quotations from Hamilton formed a part of his five-hour speech before the Constitutional Convention in Philadelphia (see p. 129). Decide to what extent Hamilton and Jefferson were both right and wrong in the light of subsequent history, and who on balance was the more sound. Note that Jefferson particularly was prone to make exaggerated statements, and that some of these observations were written privately and during the heat of bitter partisan struggles.

2. Excerpts found for the most part in S. K. Padover, ed., *The Mind of Alexander Hamilton* (1958) ; R. B. Morris, ed., *The Basic Ideas of Alexander Hamilton* (1957) ; S. K. Padover, ed., *Thomas Jefferson on Democracy* (1939).

HAMILTON

All communities divide themselves into the few and the many. The first are the rich and well born; the other, the mass of the people. The voice of the people has been said to be the voice of God; and however generally this maxim has been quoted and believed, it is not true in fact. The people are turbulent and changing; they seldom judge or determine right. Give therefore to the first class a distinct, permanent share in the government. They will check the unsteadiness of the second; and as they cannot receive any advantage by a change, they therefore will ever maintain good government.

Can a democratic assembly, who annually [through annual elections] revolve in the mass of the people, be supposed steadily to pursue the public good? Nothing but a permanent body can check the imprudence of democracy. Their turbulent and uncontrolling disposition requires checks. (1787)

Take mankind in general, they are vicious—their passions may be operated upon. . . . Take mankind as they are, and what are they governed by? Their passions. There may be in every government a few choice spirits, who may act from more worthy motives. One great error is that we suppose mankind more honest than they are. Our prevailing passions are ambition and interest; and it will be the duty of a wise government to avail itself of those passions, in order to make them subservient to the public good. (1787)

Your people, sir, is a great beast. (According to legend, *c.* 1792)

I have an indifferent [low] opinion of the honesty of this country, and ill forebodings as to its future system. (1783)

JEFFERSON

Those who labor in the earth are the chosen people of God, if ever he had a chosen people, whose breasts he has made his peculiar deposit for substantial and genuine virtue. (1784)

Men . . . are naturally divided into two parties. Those who fear and distrust the people. . . . Those who identify themselves with the people, have confidence in them, cherish and consider them as the most honest and safe . . . depository of the public interest. (1824)

The mass of mankind has not been born with saddles on their backs, nor a favored few booted and spurred, ready to ride them legitimately, by the grace of God. (1826)

Every government degenerates when trusted to the rulers . . . alone. The people themselves are its only safe depositories. (1787)

I have such reliance on the good sense of the body of the people and the honesty of their leaders that I am not afraid of their letting things go wrong to any length in any cause. (1788)

Whenever the people are well-informed, they can be trusted with their own government; whenever things get so far wrong as to attract their notice, they may be relied on to set them to rights. (1789)

I am not among those who fear the people. They, and not the rich, are our dependence for continued freedom. (1816)

I have great confidence in the common sense of mankind in general. (1800)

I said that I was affectionately attached to the republican theory. . . . I add that I have strong hopes of the success of that theory; but, in candor, I ought also to add that I am far from being without doubts. I consider its success as yet a problem. (1792)

My most earnest wish is to see the republican element of popular control pushed to the maximum of its practicable exercise. I shall then believe that our government may be pure and perpetual. (1816)

B. FUNDING THE NATIONAL DEBT AT PAR

1. Jefferson Accuses Hamilton of Graft (1790)

President Washington's new government inherited a burdensome debt of more than $54,000,000 from its predecessor. Secretary of the Treasury Hamilton, in his famed First Report on the Public Credit (January 14, 1790), boldly recommended that the depreciated securities representing this obligation be redeemed at par by exchanging them for interest-bearing bonds. His purposes were to establish the public credit by one dramatic stroke and also to enlist solid support for the new regime. He was later savagely (and unfairly) criticized for enriching the speculators who had bought up the depreciated certificates, and for not having attempted to search out the original security holders. The truth is that a lively speculation in the depreciated securities had begun just as soon as there was any real prospect of a new Constitution. Secretary of State Jefferson put together the following version of this episode some twenty-eight years later from notes taken at the time. Ascertain in what respects Jefferson was unfair to Hamilton, and why.

. . . Hamilton's financial system had then passed. It had two objects: 1st, as a puzzle, to exclude popular understanding and inquiry; 2nd, as a machine for the corruption of the legislature. For he avowed the opinion that man could be governed by one of two motives only, force or interest. Force, he observed, in this country was out of the question; and the interests, therefore, of the members must be laid hold of, to keep the legislative in unison with the executive. And with grief and shame it must be acknowledged that his machine was not without effect; that even in this, the birth of our government, some members were found sordid enough to bend their duty to their interests, and to look after personal rather than public good.

It is well known that during the [Revolutionary] war the greatest difficulty we encountered was the want of money or means to pay our soldiers who fought, or our farmers, manufacturers, and merchants who furnished the necessary supplies of food and clothing for them. After the expedient of paper money had exhausted itself, certificates of debt were given to the individual creditors, with assurance of payment so soon as the United States should be able. But the distresses of these people often obliged them to part with these for the half, the fifth, and even a tenth of their value; and speculators had made a trade of cozening them from the holders by the most fraudulent practices, and persuasions that they would never be paid. In the bill for funding and paying these, Hamilton made no difference between the original holders and the fraudulent purchasers of this paper.

1. A. A. Lipscomb, ed., *Writings of Thomas Jefferson* (1904), I, 271–73.

Great and just repugnance arose at putting these two classes of creditors on the same footing, and great exertions were used to pay the former the full value, and to the latter the price only which they had paid, with interest. But this would have prevented the game which was to be played, and for which the minds of greedy members [of Congress] were already tutored and prepared. When the trial of strength on these several efforts had indicated the form in which the bill would finally pass, this being known within doors sooner than without, and especially, [sooner] than to those who were in distant parts of the Union, the base scramble began. Couriers and relay horses by land, and swift sailing pilot boats by sea, were flying in all directions. Active partners and agents were associated and employed in every state, town, and country neighborhood, and this paper was bought up at five shillings, and even as low as two shillings, in the pound, before the holder knew that Congress had already provided for its redemption at par.

SATIRE ON THE JEFFERSONIANS

As illiterate boors, they are here aping the radical Jacobin clubs of France. Massachusetts Historical Society.

Immense sums were thus filched from the poor and ignorant, and fortunes accumulated by those who had themselves been poor enough before. Men thus enriched by the dexterity of a leader [Hamilton] would follow of course the chief who was leading them to fortune, and become the zealous instruments of all his enterprises.

2. A Defense of Speculators (1790)

Secretary Hamilton had electrified the nation, on January 14, 1790, by his report urging the funding of the national debt at par. But not until nearly seven months later did Congress approve the scheme, and with the votes of certain members who held the depreciated securities. Note that the following anonymous letter to the press appeared two weeks *after* Hamilton's report, and long before anyone actually knew that Congress would act favorably. Observe what light it sheds on the charge that Hamilton helped cheat the original holders out of their securities. Note also what prejudices are appealed to.

2. *Pennsylvania Gazette*, Feb. 3, 1790.

The holders of such certificates are called speculators. And what then? Is not every member of the community a speculator? Is it not as just and as honorable to speculate in certificates as in houses, land, articles of merchandise, etc.? Nay, in many instances, much more so; especially when the present holders had compassion on the original holders, and bought their certificates at the market price, and at a considerable risk, while those of Toryish principles would not touch them. And I am mistaken if it be not these [Tories] that are now endeavoring to raise an outcry.

But the certificates have altered in value. Very true. And what species of property is it that has not undergone the same fate, gold itself not excepted? Did they not change value in the hands of the holders for the time being? Must not every holder of property, be it of what kind it may, abide by the change of its value? Have not houses and land fell one half in value within ten years? He that sells a house or land for five hundred pounds, for which he gave a thousand pounds but a few years ago, must he come on [demand reimbursement from] the person he bought it of, or does anyone dream that he ought to petition Congress?

If the holders of alienated certificates are to be stripped of their property, it must be on the footing of equity, or justice, or the leveling [share-the-wealth] principle. The latter of these would, I imagine, suit a great many among us; and something of it, I fear, is in fact at bottom, if those writers alluded to above would but speak out plainly.

3. A Farmer Condemns Hamilton (1790)

Injustices would result if Hamilton did not seek out the original holders of the depreciated securities; injustices would result if he did. So he (and Congress) were prepared to follow the quicker and easier path. In reading the following complaint by a farmer to the press, discover the most serious grievance of the original security holder, aside from losing his investment.

In a former paper [letter] I took notice of the injuries which the proposed funding system will do the soldiers and other original holders of certificates, by compelling them to pay taxes in order to appreciate [increase the value of] their certificates in the hands of quartermasters, speculators, and foreigners. The Secretary of the Treasury has declared in his report that these people sold their certificates from choice, and not always from necessity. This I believe is true in a very few instances. A hungry creditor, a distressed family, or perhaps, in some instances, the want of a meal's victuals, drove most of them to the brokers' offices, or compelled them to surrender up their certificates.

Two cases of this kind I shall briefly relate. A merchant in the city of Philadelphia put £10,000 into the [public] funds in 1777. In the year 1788 his British creditors called upon him for payment of some old debts. In vain he looked up to Congress to refund him the principal he loaned to them. He had their notes, but they were worth only £2,500, and at that rate only,

3. *Ibid.*

his creditors received them from him. Now, is it just that the British creditor should receive from our government £10,000, instead of the £2,500, and the person from whom they were torn by the treaty of peace be abandoned to poverty, despair, and death by his country? Perhaps that very £10,000 fed the American army on the very day that General Gates captured General Burgoyne [at Saratoga].

The other case I shall mention is of a sick soldier, who sold his certificates of £69.7.0 for £3.0.11 to a rich speculator. He went to this speculator after he recovered, and offered to redeem his certificate—but he refused to give it up. Now, can it be right that this poor soldier, every time he sips his bohea tea, or tastes a particle of sugar, should pay a tax to raise £3.0.11 to £69.7.0 in the hands of this speculator?

Thus we see public credit (that much hackneyed and prostituted phrase) must be established at the expense of national justice, gratitude, and humanity.

The whole report of the Secretary (as he so often styles himself) is so flimsy, and so full of absurdities, contradictions, and impracticabilities, that it is to be hoped it will be voted out of Congress without a dissenting voice. It would be well enough to ask this Mr. Secretary, whether his friends have bought or sold most certificates? . . .

Would it not be proper for the farmers to unite immediately, and remonstrate against all these evils? They never were in half the danger of being ruined by the British government that they now are by their own.

Had any person told them in the beginning of the war that, after paying the yearly rent of their farms for seven years to carry on this war, at the close of it their farms should not be worth more than one fourth of their original cost and value, in consequence of a funding system—is there a farmer that would have embarked in the war? No, there is not. Why then should we be deceived, duped, defrauded, and ruined by our new rulers?

Let us do justice to our brave officers and soldiers. Great Britain paid the Tories for their loyalty, although they did her cause more harm than good. Certainly the United States should not have less gratitude to her most deserving citizens than Great Britain has shown to her least deserving subjects.

C. STATE DEBTS AND THE NATIONAL BANK

1. Jefferson Duped (?) by Hamilton (1790)

The brilliant young Secretary Hamilton, in his First Report on the Public Credit, proposed to couple the national debt with an assumption of state debts amounting to $21,500,000. His argument was that the states had incurred these burdens while fighting for independence, and hence the obligation was shared by all. One of his main purposes was to weaken states' rights and strengthen the federal government by tying the states financially to the federal chariot. Those states staggering under large

1. A. A. Lipscomb, ed., *The Writings of Thomas Jefferson* (1904), I, 273–76.

unpaid debts, chiefly in New England, applauded the scheme; those in better financial shape, chiefly in the South, condemned the scheme. The resulting stalemate was
broken by a compromise allegedly engineered by Hamilton and Jefferson together.
Jefferson, who had recently come to New York after a five-year sojourn in France as
minister, here recounts the story from contemporary notes and the vantage point of
1818. Decide whether he was really as naïve as he professes to have been, and whether
he is fair in his analysis of Hamilton's motives. Assess also the significance of the early
talk of secession, and determine why Southern Congressmen should have been parties
to this logrolling operation.

This [funding] game was over, and another was on the carpet at the
moment of my arrival; and to this I was most ignorantly and innocently
made to hold the candle. This fiscal manoeuvre is well known by the name
of the Assumption.

Independently of the debts of Congress, the states had during the war
contracted separate and heavy debts; . . . and the more debt Hamilton
could rake up, the more plunder for his mercenaries. This money, whether
wisely or foolishly spent, was pretended to have been spent for general
purposes, and ought, therefore, to be paid from the general purse.

But it was objected that nobody knew what these debts were, what their
amount, or what their proofs. No matter; we will guess them to be twenty
millions. But of these twenty millions, we do not know how much should
be reimbursed to one state, or how much to another. No matter; we will
guess. And so another scramble was set on foot among the several states,
and some got much, some little, some nothing. But the main object was
obtained: the phalanx of the Treasury was reinforced by additional recruits
[bureaucrats].

This measure produced the most bitter and angry contest ever known
in Congress, before or since the Union of the states. I arrived [in New
York] in the midst of it. But a stranger to the ground, a stranger to the
actors on it, so long absent as to have lost all familiarity with the subject,
and as yet unaware of its object, I took no concern in it.

The great and trying question [of assumption], however, was lost in
the House of Representatives [31 to 29]. So high were the feuds excited by this subject that on its rejection business was suspended. Congress met and adjourned from day to day without doing anything, the
parties being too much out of temper to do business together. The Eastern
[New England] members particularly, who, with Smith from South Carolina, were the principal gamblers in these scenes, threatened a secession
and dissolution.

Hamilton was in despair. As I was going to the President's one day, I
met him in the street. He walked me backwards and forwards before the
President's door for half an hour. He painted pathetically the temper into
which the legislature had been wrought; the disgust of those who were
called the creditor states; the danger of the secession of their members,
and the separation of the states. He observed that the members of the
Administration ought to act in concert; that though this question was not

of my [State] Department, yet a common duty should make it a common concern; that the President was the center on which all administrative questions ultimately rested; and that all of us should rally around him, and support, with joint efforts, measures approved by him; and that the question having been lost by a small majority only, it was probable that an appeal from me to the judgment and discretion of some of my friends might effect a change in the vote, and the machine of government, now suspended, might be again set into motion.

I told him that I was really a stranger to the whole subject; that not having yet informed myself of the system of finances adopted, I knew not how far this was a necessary sequence; that undoubtedly, if its rejection endangered a dissolution of our Union at this incipient stage, I should deem that the most unfortunate of all consequences, to avert which all partial and temporary evils should be yielded. I proposed to him, however, to dine with me the next day, and I would invite another friend or two, bring them into conference together, and I thought it impossible that reasonable men, consulting together coolly, could fail, by some mutual sacrifices of opinion, to form a compromise which was to save the Union.

The discussion took place. I could take no part in it but an exhortatory one, because I was a stranger to the circumstances which should govern it. But it was finally agreed that, whatever importance had been attached to the rejection of this proposition, the preservation of the Union and of concord among the states was more important, and that therefore it would be better that the vote of rejection should be rescinded, to effect which some members should change their votes. But it was observed that this pill would be peculiarly bitter to the Southern states, and that some concomitant measure should be adopted, to sweeten it a little to them.

There had before been propositions to fix the [permanent] seat of government either at Philadelphia, or at Georgetown on the Potomac; and it was thought that by giving it to Philadelphia for ten years, and to Georgetown permanently afterwards, this might, as an anodyne, calm in some degree the ferment which might be excited by the other measure alone. So two of the Potomac members (White and Lee, but White with a revulsion of stomach almost convulsive) agreed to change their votes, and Hamilton undertook to carry the other point. In doing this, the influence he had established over the Eastern members, with the agency of Robert Morris with those of the Middle states, effected his side of the engagement.

And so the Assumption was passed, and twenty millions of stock divided among favored states, and thrown in as a pabulum to the stock-jobbing herd. This added to the number of votaries to the Treasury, and made its chief the master of every vote in the legislature which might give to the government the direction suited to his political views.

I know well . . . that nothing like a majority in Congress had yielded to this corruption. Far from it. But a division . . . had already taken place . . . between the parties styled republican and federal.

2. Hamilton Defends Assumption (1792)

The scheme for assuming the state debts, proposed formally by Hamilton early in 1790, was not passed by Congress until nearly seven months later, again with the votes of certain members who stood to gain personally. During this delay a brisk speculation in the depreciated state securities occurred, largely among Northern financiers. Hamilton, in this private memorandum for Washington, denies that there was anything sinister in such purchases. Locate his strongest argument, and decide who took advantage of whom. Note that much of the same argument could be used to support the funding of the national debt at par.

. . . Is a government to bend the general maxims of policy and to mold its measures according to the accidental course of private speculations? Is it to do this, or omit that, in cases of great national importance, because one set of individuals may gain, another lose, from unequal opportunities of information, from unequal degrees of resource, craft, confidence, or enterprise?

Moreover, there is much exaggeration in stating the manner of the alienation of the debt. The principal speculations in state debts, whatever may be pretended, certainly began after the promulgation of the plan for assuming by the report of the Secretary of the Treasury to the House of Representatives. The resources of individuals in this country are too limited to have admitted of much progress in purchases before the knowledge of that plan was diffused throughout the country. After that, purchasers and sellers were upon equal ground. If the purchasers speculated upon the sellers, in many instances the sellers speculated upon the purchasers. Each made his calculation of chances, and founded upon it an exchange of money for certificates. It has turned out generally that the buyer had the best of the bargain, but the seller got the value of his commodity according to his estimate of it, and probably in a great number of instances more. This shall be explained.

It happened that Mr. Madison, and some other distinguished characters of the South, started in opposition to the assumption. The high opinion entertained of them made it be taken for granted in that quarter that the opposition would be successful. The securities quickly rose, by means of purchases, beyond their former prices. It was imagined that they would soon return to their old station by a rejection of the proposition for assuming. And the certificate holders were eager to part with them at their current prices, calculating on a loss to the purchasers from their future fall. This representation is not conjectural; it is founded on information from respectable and intelligent Southern characters, and may be ascertained by inquiry.

Hence it happened that the inhabitants of the Southern states sustained a considerable loss by the opposition to the assumption from Southern gentlemen, and their too great confidence in the efficacy of that opposition.

Further, a great part of the debt which has been purchased by the

2. H. C. Lodge, ed., *The Works of Alexander Hamilton* (1904), II, 468–70 (Aug. 18, 1792).

Northern and Southern citizens has been at higher prices—in numerous instances beyond the true value. In the late delirium of speculation large sums were purchased at 25 percent above par and upward.

The Southern people, upon the whole, have not parted with their property for nothing. They parted with it voluntarily, in most cases, upon fair terms, without surprise or deception—in many cases for more than its value. 'Tis their own fault if the purchase money has not been beneficial to them; and, the presumption is, it has been so in a material degree.

3. Jefferson versus Hamilton on the Bank (1791)

There were only three banks in the entire country when Hamilton, in 1790, proposed the Bank of the United States as the keystone of his financial edifice. Modeled upon the Bank of England and located in Philadelphia, it would be capitalized at $10,000,000, one-fifth of which might be held by the federal government. As a private concern under strict government supervision, it would be useful to the Treasury in issuing notes, in safeguarding surplus tax money, and in facilitating numerous public financial transactions. Before signing such a bank bill, Washington solicited the views of his Cabinet members. The opinions of Jefferson, given below, elicited a rebuttal from Hamilton, also given below. Note that Jefferson, the strict constructionist of the Constitution, based his case on the tenth amendment in the Bill of Rights, about to be ratified. Hamilton, the loose constructionist of the Constitution, based his views on the implied powers in Article I, Section VIII, paragraph 18, which stipulates that Congress is empowered "to make all laws which shall be *necessary* and proper for carrying into execution the foregoing powers. . . ." Which of the two men seems to be on sounder ground in interpreting "necessary"?

JEFFERSON
Feb. 15, 1791

I consider the foundation of the Constitution as laid on this ground— that *all powers not delegated to the United States by the Constitution, nor prohibited by it to the states, are reserved to the states, or to the people* (12th [10th] amend.). To take a single step beyond the boundaries thus specifically drawn around the powers of Congress is to take possession of a boundless field of power, no longer susceptible of any definition.

The incorporation of a bank, and the powers assumed by this bill, have not, in my opinion, been delegated to the United States by the Constitution.

The second general phrase is "to make all laws *necessary* and proper for carrying into execution the enumerated powers." But they can all be

HAMILTON
Feb. 23, 1791

If the *end* be clearly comprehended within any of the specified powers, and if the measure have an obvious relation to that *end*, and is not forbidden by any particular provision of the Constitution, it may safely be deemed to come within the compass of the national authority.

There is also this further criterion, which may materially assist the decision: Does the proposed measure abridge a pre-existing right of any state or of any individual? If it does not, there is a strong presumption in favor of its constitutionality. . . .

. . . "Necessary" often means no more than needful, requisite, incidental, useful, or conducive to. . . . [A] restrictive interpretation of the word

3. *Ibid.*, III, 458, 452, 455, 485–86; P. L. Ford, ed., *The Writings of Thomas Jefferson* (1895), V, 285, 287.

carried into execution without a bank. A bank therefore is not *necessary*, and consequently not authorized by this phrase.

It has been much urged that a bank will give great facility or convenience in the collection of taxes. Suppose this were true; yet the Constitution allows only the means which are "necessary," not those which are merely "convenient," for effecting the enumerated powers. If such a latitude of construction be allowed to this phrase as to give any non-enumerated power, it [the latitude] will go to every one; for there is not one [power] which ingenuity may not torture into a convenience, in some instance or other, to some one of so long a list of enumerated powers. It would swallow up all the delegated powers [of the states], and reduce the whole to one power. . . .

"necessary" is also contrary to this sound maxim of construction: namely, that the powers contained in a constitution . . . ought to be construed liberally in advancement of the public good.

A hope is entertained that it has, by this time, been made to appear to the satisfaction of the President, that a bank has a natural relation to the power of collecting taxes—to that of regulating trade—to that of providing for the common defense—and that, as the bill under consideration contemplates the government in the light of a joint proprietor of the stock of the bank, it brings the case within the provision of the clause of the Constitution which immediately respects [relates to] the property of the United States. [Evidently Art. IV, Sec. III, para. 2: "The Congress shall have power to . . . make all needful rules and regulations respecting the territory or other property belonging to the United States. . . ."]

D. OVERAWING THE WHISKEY BOYS

1. Hamilton Upholds Law Enforcement (1794)

Secretary Hamilton's excise tax on whiskey hit the impoverished Pennsylvania frontiersmen especially hard. Their roads were so poor that they could profitably transport their corn and rye to market only in liquid concentrate. If sued by the government, they were forced to incur the heavy expense of traveling three hundred miles and undergoing trial before strange judges and jurors. Numerous other grievances caused the Whiskey Boys to form armed mobs which intimidated would-be taxpayers or roughly handled the federal tax collectors. Some agents were tarred, feathered, and beaten; the home of one was burned. An outraged Secretary Hamilton, prejudiced against those who "babble republicanism," set forth the following views in the press over the pen name "Tully." Find the weakness, if any, in his argument that the federal government should take drastic measures against the lawless rabble.

Let us see then what is this question. It is plainly this: Shall the majority govern or be governed? Shall the nation rule or be ruled? Shall the general will prevail, or the will of a faction? Shall there be government or no government? It is impossible to deny that this is the true and the whole question. No art, no sophistry can involve it in the least obscurity.

The Constitution *you* have ordained for yourselves and your posterity contains this express clause: "The Congress shall have power to lay and

1. H. C. Lodge, ed., *The Works of Alexander Hamilton* (1904), VI, 414–16 (Aug. 26, 1794).

collect taxes, duties, imposts, and excises, to pay the debts, and provide for the common defense and general welfare of the United States." You have, then, by a solemn and deliberate act, the most important and sacred that a nation can perform, pronounced and decreed that your representatives in Congress shall have power to lay excises. You have done nothing since to reverse or impair that decree.

Your representatives in Congress, pursuant to the commission derived from you, and with a full knowledge of the public exigencies, have laid an excise. At three succeeding sessions they have revised that act, and have as often, with a degree of unanimity not common, and after the best opportunities of knowing your sense, renewed their sanction to it. You have acquiesced in it; it has gone into general operation; and *you* have actually paid more than a million of dollars on account of it.

But the four western counties of Pennsylvania undertake to rejudge and reverse your decrees. You have said, "The Congress shall have power to lay excises." They say, "The Congress shall not have this power," or—what is equivalent—"they shall not exercise it": for a power that may not be exercised is a nullity. Your representatives have said, and four times repeated it, "An excise on distilled spirits shall be collected." They say, "It shall not be collected. We will punish, expel, and banish the officers who shall attempt the collection. We will do the same by every other person who shall dare to comply with your decree expressed in the constitutional charter, and with that of your representatives expressed in the laws. The sovereignty shall not reside with you, but with us. If you presume to dispute the point by force, we are ready to measure swords with you, and if unequal ourselves to the contest, we will call in the aid of a foreign nation [Britain]. We will league ourselves with a foreign power."

2. Jefferson Deplores Undue Force (1794)

Hamilton was accused of deliberately aggravating the Whiskey Rebellion so that he might strengthen the prestige of the new government with an overpowering show of might. At all events, he marched out to the disaffected region with an army of some 13,000 militiamen. Resistance evaporated before such a force. Jefferson was appalled that these extravagant measures should have been taken against "occasional riots," and charged that Hamilton was merely pursuing his "favorite purpose of strengthening government and increasing public debt," all under "the sanction of a name [Washington] which has done too much good not to be sufficient to cover harm also." From his luxurious home, Monticello, Jefferson wrote indignantly as follows to James Madison, his friend and neighbor. Six years later these same back-country rebels, who had incurred Hamilton's upper-class scorn, helped elect Jefferson President. Hamilton's show of sledge-hammer force no doubt helped the prestige of the national government, but in the light of Jefferson's letter ascertain how the government probably hurt itself.

The excise law is an infernal one. The first error was to admit it by the Constitution; the second, to act on that admission; the third and last will

2. P. L. Ford, *The Writings of Thomas Jefferson* (1895), VI, 518–19 (Dec. 28, 1794).

be to make it the instrument of dismembering the Union, and setting us all afloat to choose which part of it we will adhere to.

The information of our militia, returned from the westward, is uniform, that though the people there let them pass quietly, they were objects of their laughter, not of their fear; that a thousand men could have cut off their whole force in a thousand places of the Allegheny; that their detestation of the excise law is universal, and has now associated to it a detestation of the government; and that separation, which perhaps was a very distant and problematical event, is now near, and certain, and determined in the mind of every man.

I expected to have seen justification of arming one part of the society against another; of declaring a civil war the moment before the meeting of that body [Congress] which has the sole right of declaring war; of being so patient of the kicks and scoffs of our [British] enemies,[*] and rising at a feather against our friends; of adding a million to the public debt and deriding us with recommendations to pay it if we can, etc., etc.

E. THE CONTINUING JEFFERSON–HAMILTON FEUD

1. The Clash over States' Rights

Hamilton, distrusting and fearing the states, strove to build up a powerful central government at their expense. Jefferson, distrusting and fearing a potent central government, strove to safeguard states' rights at its expense. Decide which of the two men was closer to the truth in the light of subsequent history, particularly in the matter of grass-roots supervision of government.

HAMILTON	JEFFERSON
A firm Union will be of the utmost moment to the peace and liberty of the states, as a barrier against domestic faction and insurrection. (1787)	. . . I am not a friend to a very energetic government. It is always oppressive. It places the governors indeed more at their ease, at the expense of the people. (1787)
A state government will ever be the rival power of the general government. (1787)	If ever this vast country is brought under a single government, it will be one of the most extensive corruption. (1822)
As to the destruction of state governments, the great and real anxiety is to be able to preserve the national [government] from the too potent and counteracting influence of those governments. . . . As to the state governments, the prevailing bias of my judgment is that if they can be cir-	Our country is too large to have all its affairs directed by a single government. Public servants, at such a distance and from under the eye of their constituents, must, from the circumstance of distance, be unable to administer and overlook all the details necessary for the good government

---

[*] A reference to British seizures of American ships prior to Jay's Treaty.
1. See the works of Padover and Morris previously cited.

cumscribed within bounds consistent with the preservation of the national government, they will prove useful and salutary.

If the states were all of the size of Connecticut, Maryland, or New Jersey, I should decidedly regard the local governments as both safe and useful. As the thing now is, however, I acknowledge the most serious apprehensions that the government of the United States will not be able to maintain itself against their influence. I see that influence already penetrating into the national councils and preventing their direction.

Hence, a disposition on my part towards a liberal construction of the powers of the national government, and to erect every fence to guard it from depredations which is, in my opinion, consistent with constitutional propriety. As to any combination to prostrate the state governments, I disavow and deny it. (1792)

of the citizens; and the same circumstance, by rendering detection impossible to their constituents, will invite the public agents to corruption, plunder, and waste. . . .

What an augmentation of the field for jobbing, speculating, plundering, office-building, and office-hunting would be produced by an assumption of all the state powers into the hands of the general government. The true theory of our Constitution [strict construction] is surely the wisest and best —that the states are independent as to everything within themselves, and united as to everything respecting foreign nations. Let the general government be reduced to foreign concerns only, and let our affairs be disentangled from those of all other nations, except as to commerce, which the merchants will manage the better, the more they are left free to manage themselves. And our general government may be reduced to a very simple organization and a very unexpensive one: a few plain duties to be performed by a few servants. (1800)

2. The Spectrum of Disagreement

At the rear entrance of Jefferson's imposing Virginia home, Monticello, busts of Hamilton and Jefferson stood opposite each other. The Negro guide used to tell tourists that Jefferson placed them there because the two men had opposed each other in life, and they might as well stand opposite each other in death. Judge from the following quotations what they agreed on, what their most fundamental disagreements were, and whether they were fair in assessing each other.

HAMILTON

A national debt, if it is not excessive, will be to us a national blessing. (1781)

If all the public creditors receive their dues from one source . . . their interest will be the same. And having the same interests, they will unite in support of the fiscal arrangements of the government. (*c.* 1791)

Real liberty is neither found in despotism or the extremes of democracy,

JEFFERSON

. . . No man is more ardently intent to see the public debt soon and sacredly paid off than I am. This exactly marks the difference between Colonel Hamilton's views and mine, that I would wish the debt paid tomorrow; he wishes it never to be paid, but always to be a thing wherewith to corrupt and manage the legislature [Congress]. (1792)

. . . Were it left to me to decide whether we should have a govern-

2. *Ibid.*

but in moderate governments. (1787)

Beware, my dear sir, of magnifying a riot into an insurrection, by employing in the first instance an inadequate force. 'Tis better far to err on the other side. Whenever the government appears in arms, it ought to appear like a Hercules, and inspire respect by the display of strength. (1799)

I believe the British government forms the best model the world ever produced, and such has been its progress in the minds of the many that this truth gradually gains ground. (1787)

It must be by this time evident to all men of reflection . . . that it [Articles of Confederation] is a system so radically vicious and unsound as to admit not of amendment but by an entire change in its leading features and characters. (1787)

Let me observe that an Executive is less dangerous to the liberties of the people when in office during life than for seven years. (1787)

Standing armies are dangerous to liberty. (1787)

[Jefferson is] an atheist in religion and a fanatic in politics. (1800)

It was not long before I discovered he [Washington] was neither remarkable for delicacy nor good temper. . . .
The General [Washington] is a very honest man. His competitors have slender abilities, and less integrity. His popularity has often been essential to the safety of America. . . . These con-

ment without newspapers, or newspapers without a government, I should not hesitate a moment to prefer the latter. (1787)

. . . A little rebellion now and then is a good thing, and as necessary in the political world as storms in the physical. . . . It is a medicine necessary for the sound health of government. (1787)

. . . It is her [England's] government which is so corrupt, and which has destroyed the nation—it was certainly the most corrupt and unprincipled government on earth. (1810)

But with all the imperfections of our present government [Articles of Confederation], it is without comparison the best existing or that ever did exist. . . . Indeed, I think all the good of this new Constitution might have been couched in three or four new articles, to be added to the good, old, and venerable fabric. . . . (1787)

I disapproved, also, the perpetual re-eligibility of the President. (1789)

A naval force can never endanger our liberties, nor occasion bloodshed; a land force would do both. (1786)

I am a Christian, in the only sense in which he [Jesus] wished anyone to be: sincerely attached to his doctrines, in preference to all others. (1803)

His [Washington's] integrity was most pure, his justice the most inflexible I have ever known. . . . He was, indeed, in every sense of the words, a wise, a good, and a great man. His temper was naturally irritable and high toned; but reflection and resolution had obtained a firm and habitual ascendancy over it. If ever, however, siderations have influenced my past conduct respecting him, and will influence my future. (1781)

That gentleman [Jefferson] whom I once *very much esteemed*, but who does not permit me to retain that sentiment for him, is certainly a man of sublimated and paradoxical imagination, entertaining and propagating opinions inconsistent with dignified and orderly government. (1792)

it broke its bonds, he was most tremendous in his wrath. (1814)

Hamilton was indeed a singular character. Of acute understanding, disinterested, honest, and honorable in all private transactions, amiable in society, and duly valuing virtue in private life, yet so bewitched and perverted by the British example as to be under thorough conviction that corruption was essential to the government of a nation. (1818)

THOUGHT PROVOKERS

1. Which principles of Jefferson, the founder of the Democratic Party, are upheld by Democrats today and which are not? Which principles of Hamilton, the godfather of the present Republican Party, are upheld by Republicans today and which are not? Explain.

2. It has often been said that Hamilton connived at corruption in funding the national debt. Argue both sides and come to a conclusion. How could he have handled the situation so as to have softened these charges?

3. What credit can we give to the testimony of a man like Jefferson, a bitter foe of Hamilton, as revised more than a quarter of a century after the event?

4. Hamilton had written in 1783: "The rights of government are as essential to be defended as the rights of individuals. The security of the one is inseparable from that of the other." Comment in the light of his handling of the Whiskey Rebellion of 1794.

5. Has the federal government become more or less Hamiltonian during the past century and a half? Which man—Hamilton or Jefferson—would have done the greatest good for the greatest possible number?

FURTHER EXPLORATION

General: J. C. Miller, *The Federalist Era, 1789–1801* (1960); C. G. Bowers, *Jefferson and Hamilton* (1925); D. S. Freeman, *George Washington* (1954), vol. VI. **Launching:** L. D. White, *The Federalists* (1948); Joseph Charles, *The Origins of the American Party System* (1956). **Funding:** C. A. Beard, *Economic Origins of Jeffersonian Democracy* (1915). **State Debts and Bank:** J. C. Miller, *Alexander Hamilton* (1959); Dumas Malone, *Jefferson and His Times* (2 vols., 1948–1951). **Whiskey Boys:** L. D. Baldwin, *Whiskey Rebels* (1939). **Continuing Feud:** Adrienne Koch, *The Philosophy of Thomas Jefferson* (1943); M. D. Peterson, *The Jefferson Image in the American Mind* (1960).

Recent: A. T. Mason, *The States Rights Debate: Antifederalism and the Constitution* (1964); W. N. Chambers, *Political Parties in a New Nation: The American Experience, 1776–1809* (1963) [paperback]; Clinton Rossiter, *Alexander Hamilton and the Constitution* (1964); Broadus Mitchell, *Alexander Hamilton: The National Adventure, 1788–1804* (1962); C. P. Nettels, *The Emergence of a National Economy, 1775–1815* (1962); D. F. Swanson, *The Origins of Hamilton's Fiscal Policies* (1963); E. J. Ferguson, *The Power of the Purse: A History of American Public Finance, 1776–1790* (1961).

Chapter 9

Federalist Foreign Policy and Free Speech

Let me now . . . warn you in the most solemn manner against the baneful effects of the spirit of party generally.

WASHINGTON'S FAREWELL ADDRESS, 1796

PROLOGUE: The opening rumbles of the French Revolution in 1789 generated wild enthusiasm in liberty-loving America. Thomas Jefferson, then American minister in Paris, was sympathetic with the nobility-ridden masses and served as a consultant of the revolutionary leaders. But in 1791 the radicals gained the upper hand, and the King, attempting to flee, was dragged back. In 1792 the exiled nobles, supported by monarchical Prussian and Austrian armies, were repelled by the aroused revolutionists. In 1793 the French King and Queen were beheaded; Britain joined the other powers in a declaration of war on France; and the Reign of Terror, during which hundreds of nobles fell prey to the thirsty guillotine, was at its peak. The world conflict touched off by these momentous events inevitably involved the newly born United States in serious quarrels abroad with both Britain and France. At home, the ruling Federalists attempted to stifle Jeffersonian opposition with the Alien and Sedition Acts, which elicited ringing Republican protests from the legislatures of Virginia and Kentucky.

A. THE BIRTH OF A NEUTRALITY POLICY

1. The French Revolution: Conflicting Views

Hamilton and Jefferson, disagreeing on many other issues, naturally took opposite sides on the French Revolution. The philosophical Virginian, dedicated to liberty, rejoiced over the liberation of oppressed humanity. The practical-minded New Yorker, concerned about property, was profoundly shocked by the bloody excesses. On the basis of the following excerpts, decide why Hamilton rejected the parallel to the American Revolution, why Jefferson was so deeply concerned, and whether he went too far in his justification of the French Revolution.

HAMILTON

In France, he [Jefferson] saw government only on the side of its abuses. He drank freely of the French philosophy, in religion, in science, in politics. He came from France in the moment of a fermentation which he had a share in exciting, and in the passions and feelings of which he shared, both from temperament and

JEFFERSON

But it is a fact, in spite of the mildness of their governors, the [French] people are ground to powder by the vices of the form of government. Of twenty millions of people supposed to be in France, I am of opinion there are nineteen millions more wretched, more accursed in every circumstance of human exist-

1. Convenient compilations of quotations are found in S. K. Padover, ed., *The Mind of Alexander Hamilton* (1958) and *Thomas Jefferson on Democracy* (1939).

158

situation. . . . He came electrified with attachment to France, and with the project of knitting together the two countries in the closest political bands. (1792)

. . . The cause of France is compared with that of America during its late revolution. Would to heaven that the comparison were just. Would to heaven we could discern in the mirror of French affairs the same humanity, the same decorum, the same gravity, the same order, the same dignity, the same solemnity, which distinguished the cause of the American Revolution. Clouds and darkness would not then rest upon the issue as they now do. I own I do not like the comparison. (1793?)

. . . There was a time when all men in this country entertained the same favorable view of the French Revolution. At the present time, they all still unite in the wish that the troubles of France may terminate in the establishment of a free and good government; and dispassionate, well-informed men must equally unite in the doubt whether this be likely to take place under the auspices of those who now govern . . . that country. But agreeing in these two points, there is a great and serious diversity of opinion as to the real merits and probable issue of the French Revolution. (1794)

None can deny that the cause of France has been stained by excesses and extravagances for which it is not easy, if possible, to find a parallel in the history of human affairs, and from which reason and humanity recoil. . . . (1794)

ence than the most conspicuously wretched individual of the whole United States. (1785)

You will have heard, before this reaches you, of the peril into which the French Revolution is brought by the flight of their King. Such are the fruits of that form of government which heaps importance on idiots, and of which the Tories of the present day are trying to preach into our favor. I still hope the French Revolution will issue happily. I feel that the permanence of our own leans in some degree on that; and that a failure there would be a powerful argument to prove there must be a failure here. (1791)

In the struggle which was necessary, many guilty persons fell without the forms of trial, and with them some innocent. These I deplore as much as anybody, and shall deplore some of them to the day of my death. But I deplore them as I should have done had they fallen in battle. . . . But time and truth will rescue and embalm their very liberty for which they would never have hesitated to offer up their lives. The liberty of the whole earth was depending on the issue of the contest, and was ever such a prize won with so little innocent blood? (1793)

My own affections have been deeply wounded by some of the martyrs to this cause, but rather than it should have failed I would have seen half the earth desolated; were there but an Adam and an Eve left in every country, and left free, it would be better than it now is. (1793)

2. A Jeffersonian Condemns Neutrality (1793)

The treaty of alliance with France in 1778 bound the United States "forever" to help defend the French West Indies. The entrance of Britain into the War of the French Revolution in 1793 consequently threatened to involve the American people. Both Hamilton and Jefferson agreed (for once) on the wisdom of a Neutrality Proc-

2. *National Gazette* (Philadelphia), June 5, 1793.

lamation. President Washington thereupon issued a stern admonition reminding Americans of their "duty" to be "friendly and impartial" toward both Britain and France. But many Jeffersonians, including the anonymous author of the following open letter to Washington, emitted pained outcries. Discover his most serious griev- ance against the President, and the reason for it; also whether moral considerations argued for a policy of favoritism to France.

In countries where the people have little or no share in the government (as in Great Britain, for instance), it is not uncommon for the executive to act in direct opposition to the will of the nation. It is to be hoped that the practice of aping the absurd and tyrannical systems of Britain, though already carried to an alarming extent in this country, will never proceed so far as to induce our executive to try the vain experiment of officially opposing the national will. . . .

Had you, sir, before you ventured to issue a proclamation which appears to have given much uneasiness, consulted the general sentiments of your fellow citizens, you would have found them, from one extremity of the Union to the other, firmly attached to the cause of France. You would not have found them disposed to consider it as a "duty" to forget their debt of gratitude to the French nation; or to view with unconcern the magnani- mous efforts of a faithful ally to baffle the infernal projects of those despots who have confederated for the purpose of crushing her infant liberty. Neither would you have found them so far divested of the feelings of men as to treat with "impartiality," and equal "friendship," those tigers who so lately deluged our country with the blood of thousands, and the men who generously flew to her rescue and became her deliverers.

No, sir—had even no written treaty existed between France and the United States, still would the strongest ties of amity have united the people of both nations; still would the republican citizens of America have re- garded Frenchmen, contending for liberty, as their brethren; still would they have sympathized with them in their misfortunes, and have exulted in their success. . . .

It ought never to be forgotten by our magistrates that popular opinion is the basis of our government; and that when any public measure is not well understood, it would be by no means degrading to the authors of that measure, however exalted their station, to explain. Let me entreat you, sir, to deal candidly with the people; and, without loss of time, to remove their anxiety by informing them whether it is intended that the treaties with France are to be observed or not.

I am aware, sir, that some court satellites may have deceived you with respect to the sentiments of your fellow citizens. The first magistrate of a country, whether he be called a king or a president, seldom knows the real state of the nation, particularly if he be so much buoyed up by official importance as to think it beneath his dignity to mix occasionally with the people. Let me caution you, sir, to beware that you do not view the state of the public mind, at this critical moment, through a fallacious medium.

THE CONTRAST

Adaptation of an English cartoon. C. C. Coffin, *Building a Nation*, 1882.

Let not the little buzz of the aristocratic few and their contemptible minions, of speculators, Tories, and British emissaries, be mistaken for the exalted and general voice of the American people. The spirit of 1776 is again roused; and soon shall the mushroom-lordlings of the day, the enemies of American as well as French liberty, be taught that American Whigs of 1776 will not suffer French patriots of 1792 to be vilified with impunity by the common enemies of both.

3. Washington Resents His Traducers (1793)

The pro-French Jeffersonians launched venomous verbal attacks on President Washington for his policy of neutrality. Among the most savage journalistic assailants was the poet Philip Freneau, whom Secretary Jefferson employed in the Department of State at a salary of $250 a year. Secretary Hamilton privately supported an anti-Jeffersonian editor, John Fenno. Jefferson, with probable bias, later recalled the following outburst in a Cabinet meeting in the summer of 1793. Account for the bitterness of Washington's reaction.

[Secretary of War] Knox, in a foolish incoherent sort of a speech, introduced the pasquinade [satire] lately printed, called the funeral of George W[ashingto]n and James W[ilso]n, King and Judge, etc., where the President was placed on a guillotine.

The President was much inflamed; got into one of those passions where he cannot command himself; ran on much on the personal abuse which had been bestowed on him; defied any man on earth to produce one single act of his since he had been in the government which was not done on the purest motives. That he had never repented but once the having slipped the moment of resigning his office, and that was every moment since; that by God he had rather be in his grave than in his present situation; that he had rather be on his farm than to be made the emperor of the world;

3. A. A. Lipscomb, ed., *The Writings of Thomas Jefferson* (1904), I, 382 (The Anas, 1818).

and yet that they were charging him with wanting to be king. That that rascal Freneau sent him three of his papers every day, as if he thought he would become the distributor of his papers; that he could see in this nothing but an impudent design to insult him. He ended in this high tone.

B. THE CONTROVERSIAL JAY TREATY

1. Virginians Oppose Jay's Appointment (1794)

After British cruisers had suddenly seized scores of American food ships bound for the French West Indies, a crisis developed. President Washington, desperately seeking to avoid hostilities, decided to send to London a pro-British Federalist, John Jay, in a last-gasp effort to patch up peace. Pro-French Jeffersonians reacted angrily, notably in this "Address to the People of the United States" from the Democratic Society in Wythe County, Virginia. Decide whether these Jeffersonians were pro-French, pro-British, or merely partisan.

While with anxious expectation we contemplate the affairs of Europe, it will be criminal to forget our own country. A session of Congress having just passed, the first in which the people were equally represented, it is a fit time to take a retrospective view of the proceedings of government. We have watched each motion of those in power, but are sorry we cannot exclaim, "Well done, thou good and faithful servant." We have seen the nation insulted, our rights violated, our commerce ruined—and what has been the conduct of government? Under the corrupt influence of the [Hamiltonian] paper system, it has uniformly crouched to Britain; while on the contrary our allies, the French, to whom we owe our political existence, have been treated unfriendly; denied any advantages from their treaties with us; their minister abused; and those individuals among us who desired to aid their arms, prosecuted as traitors—blush, Americans, for the conduct of your government.

Citizens! Shall we Americans who have kindled the spark of liberty stand aloof and see it extinguished when burning a bright flame in France, which hath caught it from us? Do you not see, if despots prevail, you must have a despot like the rest of the nations? If all tyrants unite against free people, should not all free people unite against tyrants? Yes! Let us unite with France and stand or fall together.

We lament that a man who hath so long possessed the public confidence as the head of the Executive Department [Washington] hath possessed it, should put it to so severe a trial as he hath by a late appointment [of Jay]. The Constitution hath been trampled on, and your rights have no security. . . .

Fellow citizens!

We hope the misconduct of the Executive may have proceeded from bad advice; but we can only look to the immediate cause of the mischief. To us it seems a radical change of measures is necessary. How shall this be

1. *Independent Chronicle* (Boston), Aug. 11, 1794.

effected? Citizens! It is to be effected by a change of men. Deny the continuance of your confidence to such members of the legislative body as have an interest distinct from that of the people.

2. Hamilton Attacks Jay's Attackers (1795)

The Federalist diplomat John Jay, who held few high cards, finally signed a treaty in London in 1794 that was keenly disappointing. Although the British belatedly agreed to evacuate the half-dozen frontier trading posts on American soil and grant certain trade concessions, they gave no satisfaction regarding the impressment of American seamen, the future seizure of ships, and the alleged inciting of the Northwest Indians. But to a financially shaky America a humiliating treaty was better than a devastating war, and Federalists defended the pact with vigor. Alexander Hamilton, after being bloodily stoned from a New York platform, contributed to the newspaper press his series of potent Camillus Papers, from which the following excerpt is taken. Form pertinent conclusions as to the operation of the democratic processes then, as compared with now. Determine on what side all the "respectable" people were, and to what extent Hamilton was biased.

Before the treaty was known, attempts were made to prepossess the public mind against it. It was absurdly asserted that it was not expected by the people that Mr. Jay was to make any treaty; as if he had been sent, not to accommodate differences by negotiation and agreement, but to dictate to Great Britain the terms of an unconditional submission.

Before it was published at large, a sketch, calculated to produce false impressions, was handed out to the public, through a medium noted for hostility to the administration of the government. Emissaries flew through the country, spreading alarm and discontent; the leaders of [Jeffersonian] clubs were everywhere active to seize the passions of the people, and preoccupy their judgments against the treaty.

At Boston it was published one day, and the next a town-meeting was convened to condemn it; without ever being read, without any serious discussion, sentence was pronounced against it.

Will any man seriously believe that in so short a time an instrument of this nature could have been tolerably understood by the greater part of those who were thus induced to a condemnation of it? Can the result be considered as anything more than a sudden ebullition of popular passion, excited by the artifices of a party which had adroitly seized a favorable moment to furorize the public opinion? This spirit of precipitation, and the intemperance which accompanied it, prevented the body of the merchants and the greater part of the most considerate citizens from attending the meeting, and left those who met, wholly under the guidance of a set of men who, with two or three exceptions, have been the uniform opposers of the government.

The intelligence of this event had no sooner reached New York than the leaders of the clubs were seen haranguing in every corner of the city, to stir up our citizens into an imitation of the example of the meeting at Boston.

2. H. C. Lodge, ed., *The Works of Alexander Hamilton* (1904), V, 195–97.

An invitation to meet at the city hall quickly followed, not to consider or discuss the merits of the treaty, but to unite with the meeting at Boston to address the President against its ratification.

This was immediately succeeded by a hand-bill, full of invectives against the treaty, as absurd as they were inflammatory, and manifestly designed to induce the citizens to surrender their reason to the empire of their passions.

In vain did a respectable meeting of the merchants endeavor, by their advice, to moderate the violence of these views, and to promote a spirit favorable to a fair discussion of the treaty; in vain did a respectable majority of the citizens of every description attend for that purpose. The leaders of the clubs resisted all discussion, and their followers, by their clamors and vociferations, rendered it impracticable, notwithstanding the wish of a manifest majority of the citizens convened upon the occasion.

Can we believe that the leaders were really sincere in the objections they made to a discussion, or that the great and mixed mass of citizens then assembled had so thoroughly mastered the merits of the treaty as that they might not have been enlightened by such a discussion?

It cannot be doubted that the real motive to the opposition was the fear of a discussion; the desire of excluding light; the adherence to a plan of surprise and deception. Nor need we desire any fuller proof of the spirit of party which has stimulated the opposition to the treaty than is to be found in the circumstances of that opposition.

3. Jefferson Slanders the Federalists (1796)

With heavy heart, and facing a devil's choice, Washington threw his weighty influence behind the unpopular Jay Treaty, and the Senate reluctantly approved it. "Curse on his virtues; they have undone the country!" groaned Jefferson. Fearing that the pact with Britain would bring new woes, he wrote as follows to Philip Mazzei, the famed Italian horticulturist who had been his neighbor in Virginia. Detect which of his grievances against the Federalists seems to rankle most deeply, and what this letter reveals about the "philosophical Jefferson."

The aspect of our politics has wonderfully changed since you left us. In place of that noble love of liberty and republican government which carried us triumphantly through the war, an anglican, monarchical, and aristocratical party has sprung up, whose avowed object is to draw over us the substance, as they have already done the forms, of the British government. The main body of our citizens, however, remain true to their republican principles; the whole landed interest is Republican, and so is a great mass of talents.

Against us are the Executive, the Judiciary, two . . . branches of the legislature, all the officers of the government, all who want to be officers, all timid men who prefer the calm of despotism to the boisterous sea of liberty, British merchants and Americans trading on British capitals, spec-

3. P. L. Ford, ed., *The Writings of Thomas Jefferson* (1896), VII, 75–77.

THE PROVIDENTIAL DETECTION

The American Eagle snatches the Constitution from Jefferson, who is about to burn it (together with the works of Voltaire, Paine, and others) on the altar to French revolutionary despotism. Massachusetts Historical Society.

ulators and holders in the banks and public funds, a contrivance invented for the purposes of corruption, and for assimilating us in all things to the rotten as well as the sound parts of the British model.

It would give you a fever were I to name to you the apostates who have gone over to these heresies, men who were Samsons in the field and Solomons in the council, but who have had their heads shorn by the harlot England.

In short, we are likely to preserve the liberties we have obtained only by unremitting labors and perils. But we shall preserve them; and our mass of weight and wealth on the good side is so great as to leave no danger that force will ever be attempted against us. We have only to awake and snap the Lilliputian cords with which they have been entangling us during the first sleep which succeeded our labors.

C. THE RETIREMENT OF WASHINGTON

1. A President Bids Farewell (1796)

Weary of body and outraged by political abuse, Washington announced his decision to retire in his Farewell Address, which he simply gave as a gratuitous "scoop" to a Philadelphia newspaper. At first a non-partisan but now a Federalist, he had leaned heavily on Hamilton's collaboration in its composition. The bulk of the address deals with domestic difficulties, but the part relating to foreign affairs is best known. The document was clearly partisan. It served as the opening gun in the forthcoming presidential campaign of 1796 by indirectly defending Jay's Treaty and by directly alerting the public to flagrant French intrigue in the nation's capital. Many Jeffersonian Republicans, recognizing the attack on them, condemned the document. Note the evils that emotional attachments to foreign nations may bring; why it was to the advantage of America to remain aloof; and whether Washington would have rejected all alliances and all other foreign connections.

Observe good faith and justice toward all nations. Cultivate peace and harmony with all. Religion and morality enjoin this conduct. And can it be that good policy does not equally enjoin it? It will be worthy of a free, enlightened, and, at no distant period, a great nation to give to mankind the magnanimous and too novel example of a people always guided by an exalted justice and benevolence. . . .

In the execution of such a plan nothing is more essential than that permanent, inveterate antipathies against particular nations and passionate attachments for others should be excluded, and that, in place of them, just and amicable feelings toward all should be cultivated. The nation which indulges toward another an habitual hatred or an habitual fondness is in some degree a slave. It is a slave to its animosity or to its affection, either of which is sufficient to lead it astray from its duty and its interest. . . .

The nation prompted by ill will and resentment sometimes impels to war the government, contrary to the best calculations of policy. The government sometimes participates in the national propensity, and adopts through passion what reason would reject. . . .

So, likewise, a passionate attachment of one nation for another produces a variety of evils. Sympathy for the favorite nation, facilitating the illusion of an imaginary common interest in cases where no real common interest exists, and infusing into one the enmities of the other, betrays the former into a participation in the quarrels and wars of the latter without adequate inducement or justification. . . .

As avenues to foreign influence in innumerable ways, such attachments are particularly alarming to the truly enlightened and independent patriot. How many opportunities do they afford to tamper with domestic factions, to practice the arts of seduction, to mislead public opinion, to influence or awe the public councils! Such an attachment of a small or weak toward a great and powerful nation dooms the former to be the satellite of the latter.

1. J. D. Richardson, ed., *Messages and Papers of the Presidents* (1896), I, 221–23.

Against the insidious wiles of foreign influence (I conjure you to believe me, fellow citizens) the jealousy of a free people ought to be *constantly* awake, since history and experience prove that foreign influence is one of the most baneful foes of republican government. . . .

The great rule of conduct for us in regard to foreign nations is, in extending our commercial relations, to have with them as little *political* connection as possible. So far as we have already formed engagements [French treaty], let them be fulfilled with perfect good faith. Here let us stop.

Europe has a set of primary interests which to us have none, or a very remote, relation. Hence she must be engaged in frequent controversies, the causes of which are essentially foreign to our concerns. Hence, therefore, it must be unwise in us to implicate ourselves by artificial ties in the ordinary vicissitudes of her politics, or the ordinary combinations and collisions of her friendships or enmities.

Our detached and distant situation invites and enables us to pursue a different course. If we remain one people, under an efficient government, the period is not far off when we may defy material injury from external annoyance; when we may take such an attitude as will cause the neutrality we may at any time resolve upon to be scrupulously respected; when belligerent nations, under the impossibility of making acquisitions upon us, will not lightly hazard the giving us provocation; when we may choose peace or war, as our interest, guided by justice, shall counsel.

Why forgo the advantages of so peculiar a situation? Why quit our own to stand upon foreign ground? Why, by interweaving our destiny with that of any part of Europe, entangle our peace and prosperity in the toils of European ambition, rivalship, interest, humor, or caprice?

It is our true policy to steer clear of permanent alliances with any portion of the foreign world, so far, I mean, as we are now at liberty to do it. For let me not be understood as capable of patronizing infidelity to existing engagements. I hold the maxim no less applicable to public than to private affairs that honesty is always the best policy. I repeat, therefore, let those engagements be observed in their genuine sense. But in my opinion it is unnecessary and would be unwise to extend them.

Taking care always to keep ourselves by suitable establishments on a respectable defensive posture, we may safely trust to temporary alliances for extraordinary emergencies.

Harmony, liberal intercourse with all nations, are recommended by policy, humanity, and interest. But even our commercial policy should hold an equal and impartial hand, neither seeking nor granting exclusive favors or preference; . . . constantly keeping in view that it is folly in one nation to look for disinterested favors from another; that it must pay with a portion of its independence for whatever it may accept under that character; that by such acceptance it may place itself in the condition of having given equivalents for nominal favors, and yet of being reproached with ingratitude for not giving more. There can be no greater error than to expect or calculate upon real favors from nation to nation. It is an illusion which experience must cure, which a just pride ought to discard.

2. Editor Bache Berates Washington (1797)

Benjamin Franklin Bache, grandson of "Old Ben," was a newspaper editor notorious for his malicious attacks on the Federalists in general and on Washington in particular. He published the following tirade when the President retired, but fortunately his sentiments were not shared by the vast majority of Washington's appreciative countrymen. In retaliation, Federalist rowdies wrecked the office of the Philadelphia *Aurora* and manhandled editor Bache. In analyzing this incendiary editorial, estimate how much is anti-Federalist partisanship and how much is pure libel.

"Lord, now lettest thou thy servant depart in peace, for mine eyes have seen thy salvation," was the pious ejaculation of a man who beheld a flood of happiness rushing upon mankind [Simeon, who had just seen Jesus]. If ever there was a time that would license the reiteration of the exclamation, that time is now arrived. For the man who is the source of all the misfortunes of our country is this day reduced to a level with his fellow citizens, and is no longer possessed of power to multiply evils upon the United States.

If ever there was a period for rejoicing, this is the moment. Every heart in unison with the freedom and happiness of the people ought to beat high with exultation that the name of Washington, from this day, ceases to give a currency to political iniquity and to legalize corruption. A new era is opening upon us—a new era which promises much to the people. For public measures must now stand upon their own merits, and nefarious projects can no longer be supported by a name.

When a retrospect is taken of the Washington administration for eight years, it is a subject of the greatest astonishment that a single individual should have canceled the principles of republicanism in an enlightened people, and should have carried his designs against the public liberty so far as to have put in jeopardy its very existence. Such, however, are the facts, and with these staring us in the face, this day ought to be a jubilee in the United States.

3. Editor Cobbett Blasts Bache (1797)

Newspaper editor William Cobbett, a violent pro-Federalist, was the Federalist answer to Benjamin Franklin Bache. An English émigré so pro-British that he insolently displayed portraits of George III in his bookshop window, he was threatened with tar and feathers by the Philadelphia mob. Here he pays his editorial disrespects to his rival Bache. Note his explanation of Bache's hostility to Washington, and ascertain what aspects of this type of journalism may no longer be found, and why.

2. Philadelphia *Aurora*, March 6, 1797, in Allan Nevins, ed., *American Press Opinion* (1928), pp. 21–22. Benjamin Franklin Bache was nicknamed "Lightning Rod, Junior," an obvious reference to his inventive grandfather and to his own high-voltage journalism.
3. *Porcupine's Gazette* (Philadelphia), Nov. 15, 1797, in William Cobbett, *Porcupine's Works* . . . (1801), VII, 294–95.

This atrocious wretch (worthy descendant of old Ben) knows that all men of any understanding set him down as an abandoned liar, as a tool, and a hireling; and he is content that they should do so. He does not want to be thought anything else. . . . As this *Gazette* is honored with many readers in foreign countries, it may not be improper to give them some little account of this miscreant.

If they have read the old hypocrite Franklin's will, they must have observed that part of his library, with some other things, are left to a certain grandson; this is the very identical Market Street scoundrel. He spent several years in hunting offices under the federal government, and being constantly rejected, he at last became its most bitter foe. Hence his abuse of General Washington, whom, at the time he was soliciting a place, he panegyrized up to the third heaven.

He was born for a hireling, and therefore when he found he could not obtain employ in one quarter, he sought it in another. The first effect of his paw being greased appeared soon after [the French envoy] Genet's arrival, and he has from that time to this been as faithful to the cutthroats of Paris as ever dog was to his master.

He is an ill-looking devil. His eyes never get above your knees. He is of a sallow complexion, hollow-cheeked, dead-eyed, and has a *tout ensemble* [general effect] just like that of a fellow who has been about a week or ten days on a gibbet.

D. THE ALIEN AND SEDITION HYSTERIA

1. Pickering Upholds the Repressive Laws (1798)

Angered by Jay's pro-British treaty, the French seized scores of American ships, thereby paving the way for the undeclared naval war of 1798–1800 during the presidency of John Adams. The pro-British Federalists, riding the wave of anti-French hysteria, undertook to curb and gag the pro-French Jeffersonians by passing the Alien and Sedition laws of 1798. The Alien Act empowered the President to deport undesirable aliens (largely Irish and French refugees); the Sedition Act prescribed fines and imprisonment for false maligning of federal officials. Timothy Pickering, Secretary of State under President Adams, offered the following spirited defense of the Alien and Sedition Acts. Comment critically on his views regarding (a) inferior rights of aliens and (b) the similarity between abusing free speech and committing murder.

The Alien Law has been bitterly inveighed against as a direct attack upon our liberties, when in fact it affects only foreigners who are conspiring against us, and has no relation whatever to an American citizen. It gives authority to the First Magistrate [President] of the Union to order all such aliens as he shall judge dangerous to the peace and safety of the United States, or shall have reasonable grounds to suspect are concerned in any treasonable or secret machinations against the government thereof, to depart out of our territory.

1. C. W. Upham, *Life of Timothy Pickering* (1873), III, 475–76.

It is only necessary to ask whether, without such a power vested in some department, any government ever did, or ever can, long protect itself. The objects of this act are strangers merely, persons not adopted and naturalized—a description of men who have no lot nor interest with us, and who even manifest a disposition the most hostile to this country, while it affords them an asylum and protection. It is absurd to say that, in providing by law for their removal, the Constitution is violated. For he must be ignorant indeed who does not know that the Constitution was established for the protection and security of American citizens, and not of intriguing foreigners.

The Sedition Act has likewise been shamefully misrepresented as an attack upon the freedom of speech and of the press. But we find, on the contrary, that it prescribes a punishment only for those pests of society and disturbers of order and tranquillity "who write, print, utter, or publish any false, scandalous, and malicious writings against the government of the United States, or either house of the Congress of the United States, or the President, with intent to defame, or bring them into contempt or disrepute, or to excite against them the hatred of the good people of the United States; or to stir up sedition, or to abet the hostile designs of any foreign nation."

What honest man can justly be alarmed at such a law, or can wish unlimited permission to be given for the publication of malicious falsehoods, and with intentions the most base? They who complain of legal provisions for punishing intentional defamation and lies as bridling the liberty of speech and of the press, may, with equal propriety, complain against laws made for punishing assault and murder, as restraints upon the freedom of men's actions. Because we have the right to speak and publish our opinions, it does not necessarily follow that we may exercise it in uttering false and malicious slanders against our neighbor or our government, any more than we may under cover of freedom of action knock down the first man we meet, and exempt ourselves from punishment by pleading that we are free agents. We may indeed use our tongues, employ our pens, and carry our cudgels or our muskets whenever we please. But, at the same time, we must be accountable and punishable for making such "improper use of either as to injure others in their characters, their persons, or their property."

2. Kentuckians Denounce the Sedition Act (1798)

The Federalist Sedition Act was plainly a violation of the free-speech and free-press guarantees of the Constitution (Amendment I, Bill of Rights). But the Federalist Supreme Court was not yet declaring acts of Congress unconstitutional. Jeffersonians branded the Sedition Act the "gag law." One Federalist editor replied: "Nothing can so completely gag a Jeffersonian Democrat as to restrain him from lying. If you forbid his lying, you forbid his speaking." A score or so of Jeffersonian editors were arrested, including the unbridled Benjamin Franklin Bache, who died

2 I. Mark and E. I. Schwaab, *The Faith of Our Fathers* (1952), pp. 9–10.

before his trial. The following public protest from Woodford County, Kentucky, tells its own story. Evaluate the observation that servants should not restrain the criticisms of their masters.

Resolved, That the acts passed during the present session of Congress, respecting aliens, and for the punishment of sedition, are direct violations of the Constitution, and outrages against our most valuable rights. That to speak, write, and censure freely are privileges of which a freeman cannot divest himself, much less be abridged in them by others. That for the servants of the people to tell those who created them that they shall not, at their peril, examine into the conduct of, nor censure, those servants for the abuse of power committed to them, is tyranny more insufferable than Asiatic. That the freedom of speech, the liberty of the press, trial by jury, and self-defense are among the inseparable rights of freemen; no one of which can be abridged or taken away without sinking and debasing him into the condition of a slave.

3. The Virginia Legislature Protests (1798)

Vice-President Jefferson and James Madison (who was then in private life) both feared that the Sedition Act would terrorize the Jeffersonian Republican Party into silence and destroy it. Madison, working secretly with Jefferson, drafted the following resolutions, which were approved by the Virginia legislature. Determine whether they seem unreasonable, especially the views on the "compact theory," the First Amendment, and the proposed method of voiding the Alien and Sedition laws.

[*Resolved:*]
That this Assembly most solemnly declares a warm attachment to the union of the states, to maintain which it pledges its powers; and that, for this end, it is their duty to watch over and oppose every infraction of those principles which constitute the only basis of that union, because a faithful observance of them can alone secure its existence and the public happiness.

That this Assembly does explicitly and peremptorily declare that it views the powers of the federal government as resulting from the compact to which the states are parties, as limited by the plain sense and intention of the instrument [Constitution] constituting that compact, as no further valid than they are authorized by the grants enumerated in that compact; and that, in case of a deliberate, palpable, and dangerous exercise of other powers not granted by the said compact, the states who are parties thereto have the right, and are in duty bound, to interpose for arresting the progress of the evil, and for maintaining, within their respective limits, the authorities, rights, and liberties appertaining to them. . . .

That the General Assembly does also express its deep regret that a spirit has, in sundry instances, been manifested by the federal government to enlarge its powers by forced constructions of the constitutional charter which defines them, . . . so as to consolidate the states, by degrees, into

3. Jonathan Elliot, *The Debates . . . on the Adoption of the Federal Constitution* (1836), IV, 528–29.

one sovereignty, the obvious tendency and inevitable result of which would be to transform the present republican system of the United States into an absolute, or, at best, a mixed monarchy.

That the General Assembly does particularly protest against the palpable and alarming infractions of the Constitution in the two late cases of the "Alien and Sedition Acts," passed at the last session of Congress; the first of which exercises a power nowhere delegated to the federal government, and which, by uniting legislative and judicial powers to those of executive, subverts the general principles of free government, as well as the particular organization and positive provisions of the federal Constitution; and the other of which acts exercises, in like manner, a power not delegated by the Constitution, but, on the contrary, expressly and positively forbidden by one of the amendments thereto—a power which, more than any other, ought to produce universal alarm, because it is leveled against the right of freely examining public characters and measures, and of free communication among the people thereon, which has ever been justly deemed the only effectual guardian of every other right.

That this state having, by its convention [of 1788] which ratified the federal Constitution, expressly declared that, among other essential rights, "the liberty of conscience and the press cannot be canceled, abridged, restrained, or modified by any authority of the United States," and, from its extreme anxiety to guard these rights from every possible attack of sophistry and ambition, having, with other states, recommended an amendment for that purpose, which amendment [the First] was, in due time, annexed to the Constitution, it would mark a reproachful inconsistency and criminal degeneracy if an indifference were now shown to the most palpable violation of one of the rights thus declared and secured, and to the establishment of a precedent which may be fatal to the other.

That the good people of the commonwealth having ever felt, and continuing to feel, the most sincere affection for their brethren of the other states, the truest anxiety for establishing and perpetuating the union of all, and the most scrupulous fidelity to that Constitution, which is the pledge of mutual friendship, and the instrument of mutual happiness, the General Assembly does solemnly appeal to the like dispositions in the other states, in confidence that they will concur with this commonwealth in declaring, as it does hereby declare, that the acts aforesaid are unconstitutional, and that the necessary and proper measures will be taken by each for cooperating with this state in maintaining unimpaired the authorities, rights, and liberties reserved to the states respectively, or to the people.

4. Rhode Island Rebuffs Virginia's Plea (1799)

The appeal of Virginia to her sister states for support fell on barren ground. A half-dozen or so Northern state legislatures, with varying degrees of heat, registered dissent, particularly in the Federalist centers. Decide whether the Rhode Island resolutions,

4. *Ibid.,* IV, 533.

herewith reproduced, propose a sounder solution of the constitutional problem than those of Virginia.

1. *Resolved,* That, in the opinion of this legislature, the second section of the third article of the Constitution of the United States, in these words, to wit, "The judicial power shall extend to all cases arising under the laws of the United States," vests in the federal courts exclusively, and in the Supreme Court of the United States ultimately, the authority of deciding on the constitutionality of any act or law of the Congress of the United States.

2. *Resolved,* That for any state legislature to assume that authority would be—

1st. Blending together legislative and judicial powers;

2nd. Hazarding an interruption of the peace of the states by civil discord, in case of a diversity of opinions among the state legislatures; each state having, in that case, no resort for vindicating its own opinions but the strength of its own arm;

3rd. Submitting most important questions of law to less competent tribunals [legislatures]; and,

4th. An infraction of the Constitution of the United States, expressed in plain terms.

3. *Resolved,* That, although, for the above reasons, this legislature, in their public capacity, do not feel themselves authorized to consider and decide on the constitutionality of the Sedition and Alien laws (so called), yet they are called upon, by the exigency of this occasion, to declare that, in their private opinions, these laws are within the powers delegated to Congress, and promotive of the welfare of the United States.

4. *Resolved,* That the governor communicate these resolutions to the supreme executive of the state of Virginia, and at the same time express to him that this legislature cannot contemplate without extreme concern and regret the many evil and fatal consequences which may flow from the very unwarrantable resolutions aforesaid. . . .

[*Vice-President Jefferson, again collaborating secretly with James Madison, prepared two sets of resolutions which were adopted in 1798 and 1799 by the Kentucky legislature. Jefferson kept his authorship secret for twenty-three years, partly because it was improper for the Vice-President to be engaged in such activity, and partly because he feared Federalist prosecution for sedition. The second set of Kentucky resolutions reaffirmed the Virginia resolutions in protesting against violations of the Constitution, but went further in baldly approving nullification by the "sovereign" states as follows: "That a nullification, by those sovereignties, of all unauthorized acts done under color of that instrument [Constitution] is the rightful remedy: That this commonwealth does, under the most deliberate reconsideration, declare, that the said Alien and Sedition Laws are, in their opinion, palpable violations of the said Constitution; and . . . in momentous regulations like the present . . . it would consider a silent acquiescence as highly criminal. . . .*]

THOUGHT PROVOKERS

1. Jefferson, in defending the bloody excesses of the French Revolution, argued in effect that the end justified the means. Communists today use the same argument. Comment. In reviewing Franco-American relations during these years, assess Washington's observation that a nation which develops too great a fondness for another is in some degree its slave.

2. Henry Cabot Lodge once remarked that politics should stop at the water's edge. Comment with reference to foreign affairs in the 1790's.

3. Was Washington's Farewell Address necessary? What have been the most misunderstood parts, and why? Was it designed as a prescription for all future years? Which parts are still valid and which are not?

4. Can you justify the Alien and Sedition laws, especially in view of the excesses of editors Bache and Cobbett? Assuming that free speech ought to be curbed, who should do the curbing? Why is free speech necessary for the workings of a free government? It has been said that many a minority has become a majority because its foes were unwise enough to persecute it. Comment with reference to the Jeffersonian Republicans of 1798.

FURTHER EXPLORATION

General: J. C. Miller, *The Federalist Era, 1789–1801* (1960); J. A. Carroll and M. W. Ashworth, *First in Peace* (1957); Gilbert Chinard, *Honest John Adams* (1933); S. G. Kurtz, *The Presidency of John Adams* (1957). **Neutrality Policy:** C. M. Thomas, *American Neutrality in 1793* (1931); Alexander DeConde, *Entangling Alliance* (1958); L. M. Sears, *George Washington and the French Revolution* (1960). **Jay's Treaty:** S. F. Bemis, *Jay's Treaty* (1923). **Washington's Retirement:** V. H. Paltsits, ed., *Washington's Farewell Address* (1935). **Alien and Sedition Hysteria:** J. C. Miller, *Crisis in Freedom* (1951); J. M. Smith, *Freedom's Fetters* (1956); Adrienne Koch and Harry Ammon, "The Virginia and Kentucky Resolutions . . . ," *William and Mary Quarterly*, Third Series, V (1948), 145–76.

Recent: Page Smith, *John Adams* (2 vols., 1962); P. A. Varg, *Foreign Policies of the Founding Fathers* (1963; Dumas Malone, *Jefferson and the Ordeal of Liberty* (1962) and *Thomas Jefferson as Political Leader* (1963); D. H. Fischer, *The Revolution of American Conservatism: The Federalist Party in the Era of Jeffersonian Democracy* (1965); L. W. Levy, *Jefferson and Civil Liberties: The Darker Side* (1963).

Chapter 10

Jeffersonian Triumphs and Failures

We have a perfect horror at everything like connecting ourselves with the politics of Europe.

THOMAS JEFFERSON, 1801

PROLOGUE: Thomas Jefferson, branded by his foes a radical, defeated John Adams for the Presidency in 1800—the so-called Revolution of 1800. But the lanky Virginian, sobered by realities, proved to be no bull in a china shop. Except for a repeal of the odious excise tax and an unsuccessful assault on the Supreme Court, he left the elaborate Federalist structure virtually unshaken. The real revolution occurred in Jefferson's thinking. Anti-war and anti-navy, he was forced to use the navy to fight the Barbary pirates. Anti-British, pro-French, anti-alliance, and pacifistic, he seriously considered an alliance with Britain and war against France to keep Napoleon out of New Orleans. The two most memorable acts of his presidency—the Louisiana Purchase and the self-crucifying embargo—were both of dubious constitutionality, and could hardly be reconciled with his pre-1801 insistence on a strict or literal interpretation of the Constitution.

A. THE NEGOTIATIONS FOR LOUISIANA

1. Jefferson Alerts Livingston (1802)

Rumors of the secret treaty of 1800, under which Spain agreed to cede Louisiana to France, filled President Jefferson with apprehension. The extent of his concern is betrayed in this remarkable letter, addressed to the American minister in Paris, Robert R. Livingston, a distinguished lawyer and diplomat also known to fame as the financial backer of Robert Fulton's successful steamboat in 1807. Ascertain why Jefferson felt that French occupancy of Louisiana would force the United States to reverse its "political relations," and how that reversal would affect America's traditional foreign policies. Note why he did not actually fear France.

The cession of Louisiana . . . by Spain to France works most sorely on the United States. On the subject the Secretary of State has written to you fully. Yet I cannot forbear recurring to it personally, so deep is the impression it makes in my mind. It completely reverses all the political relations of the United States and will form a new epoch in our political course.

Of all nations of any consideration, France is the one which hitherto has offered the fewest points on which we could have any conflict of right, and the most points of a communion of interests. From these causes we have ever looked to her as our natural friend, as one with which we never could have an occasion of difference.* Her growth therefore we viewed as our own, her misfortunes ours.

1. P. L. Ford, *Writings of Thomas Jefferson* (1897), VIII, 144–46 (April 18, 1802).
* Jefferson conveniently overlooks the undeclared naval war of 1798–1800.

There is on the globe one single spot, the possessor of which is our natural and habitual enemy. It is New Orleans, through which the produce of three-eighths of our territory must pass to market, and from its fertility it will ere long yield more than half of our whole produce and contain more than half our inhabitants. France, placing herself in that door, assumes to us the attitude of defiance.

Spain might have retained it quietly for years. Her pacific dispositions, her feeble state, would induce her to increase our facilities there, so that her possession of the place would be hardly felt by us. And it would not perhaps be very long before some circumstances might arise which might make the cession of it to us the price of something of more worth to her.

Not so can it ever be in the hands of France. The impetuosity of her temper, the energy and restlessness of her character . . . render it impossible that France and the United States can continue long friends when they meet in so irritable a position. They, as well as we, must be blind if they do not see this; and we must be very improvident if we do not begin to make arrangements on that hypothesis.

The day that France takes possession of New Orleans fixes the sentence which is to restrain her forever within her low-water mark. It seals the union of two nations who in conjunction can maintain exclusive possession of the ocean. From that moment we must marry ourselves to the British fleet and nation. We must turn all our attentions to a maritime force, for which our resources place us on very high grounds; and having formed and cemented together a power which may render reinforcement of her settlements here impossible to France, make the first cannon which shall be fired in Europe the signal for tearing up any settlement she may have made, and for holding the two continents of America in sequestration for the common purposes of the united British and American nations.

This is not a state of things we seek or desire. It is one which this measure, if adopted by France, forces on us, as necessarily as any other cause, by the laws of nature, brings on its necessary effect. It is not from a fear of France that we deprecate this measure proposed by her. For however greater her force is than ours compared in the abstract, it is nothing in comparison of ours when to be exerted on our soil. But it is from a sincere love of peace, and a firm persuasion that, bound to France by the interests and the strong sympathies still existing in the minds of our citizens, and holding relative positions which ensure their continuance, we are secure of a long course of peace. Whereas the change of friends, which will be rendered necessary if France changes that position, embarks us necessarily as a belligerent power in the first war of Europe. In that case, France will have held possession of New Orleans during the interval of a peace, long or short, at the end of which it will be wrested from her. . . .

She may say she needs Louisiana for the supply of her West Indies. She does not need it in time of peace. And in war she could not depend on them because they would be so easily intercepted [by the British navy]. . . .

If France considers Louisiana, however, as indispensable for her views, she might perhaps be willing to look about for arrangements which might reconcile it to our interests. If anything could do this, it would be the ceding to us the Island of New Orleans and the Floridas. This would certainly in a great degree remove the causes of jarring and irritation between us, and perhaps for such a length of time as might produce other means of making the measure permanently conciliatory to our interests and friendships.

2. Napoleon Conceals His Motives (1803)

In 1802 the Spanish officials in New Orleans suddenly withdrew the right of deposit or storage, so essential to American down-river commerce, without naming another place, as required by the Treaty of 1795. Seeking to calm the hair-trigger Westerners by eliminating such restrictions, Jefferson dispatched James Monroe to Paris to assist Minister Livingston. The two envoys were instructed to pay up to $10,000,000 for New Orleans and as much land to the east in the Floridas as they could obtain. If France then proposed to close the Mississippi or seemed to "meditate hostilities," Monroe and Livingston were to seek an alliance with Britain. Napoleon, for purely realistic reasons, had meanwhile decided to sell all of Louisiana. He had failed disastrously in his efforts to reconquer the sugar-rich colony of Santo Domingo from the revolted Negroes, and he valued Louisiana primarily as a feeder for this colony. He was about to reopen war with the British, who could speedily capture Louisiana with their mighty fleet. If he sold the territory to the Americans for $15,000,000, he would strengthen his short-run position and build up a long-run rival of Britain in North America. His motives, as expressed to Monroe, do not square with all the facts. Ascertain what is most improbable about Napoleon's version as reported by Monroe.

. . . I [Monroe] added that it was the wish of the President that I should assure him [Napoleon] before my departure of his high respect and esteem for him personally and for the French nation, and of his earnest desire to preserve peace and friendship with it.

The First Consul [Napoleon] reciprocated the sentiment toward the President and the United States in strong terms. He said that he considered the President as a virtuous and enlightened man, who understood and pursued the interest of his country, as a friend of liberty and equality; that no one wished more than himself the preservation of a good understanding between the two republics; that he had been prompted to make the late cession to the United States not so much on account of the sum given for the territory as from views of policy; that France had been their first friend and he wished to preserve that relation between the two countries for ever. He had perceived that we entertained a jealousy of their possession of Louisiana which was likely to drive us into measures and connections [with Britain] that would prove not only hurtful to France but, as he presumed, to ourselves also. He therefore wished to remove the cause by an act which would free us from all apprehension on that head, and leave us at liberty to pursue our course according to our interest and inclination.

2. S. M. Hamilton, ed., *Writings of James Monroe* (1900), IV, 48–49.

I told him in reply that I had considered the cession of Louisiana as having been prompted by the motives which he stated, as being an act of great and enlightened policy rather than an affair of commerce, and was persuaded that our government would view it in the same light; that the cession would place us on the ground he mentioned of real independence; that we had, however, been willing to give what was deemed an equivalent for it.

He observed that there was no rivalship between us, our relation to France being chiefly commercial; but that we must be on our guard not to give the protection of our flag to the British.

3. Hamilton Backs Jefferson Lukewarmly (1803)

The loose-constructionist Alexander Hamilton, destined to die in a duel a year later, could not have been altogether displeased by Jefferson's sudden conversion from a strict construction of the Constitution to a loose construction. Then a prominent New York attorney, Hamilton prepared the following newspaper editorial in which he deplored the acquisition of the vast trans-Mississippi wilderness as unneeded and as likely in time to cause the dismemberment of the Union by diffusing the population too widely. As he develops his argument, note to what extent he favors the purchase and why he gives Jefferson little credit for it. Comment on Hamilton's vision.

At length the business of New Orleans has terminated favorably to this country. Instead of being obliged to rely any longer on the force of treaties for a place of deposit, the jurisdiction of the territory is now transferred to our hands, and in future the navigation of the Mississippi will be ours unmolested. This, it will be allowed, is an important acquisition; not, indeed, as territory, but as being essential to the peace and prosperity of our Western country, and as opening a free and valuable market to our commercial states.

This purchase has been made during the period of Mr. Jefferson's presidency, and will, doubtless, give éclat to his administration. Every man, however, possessed of the least candor and reflection will readily acknowledge that the acquisition has been solely owing to a fortuitous concurrence of unforeseen and unexpected circumstances, and not to any wise or vigorous measures on the part of the American government. . . .

As soon as we experienced from Spain a direct infraction of an important article of our treaty [of 1795], in withholding the deposit of New Orleans, it afforded us justifiable cause of war, and authorized immediate hostilities. Sound policy unquestionably demanded of us to begin with a prompt, bold, and vigorous resistance against the injustice; to seize the object at once. And having this vantage ground, should we have thought it advisable to terminate hostilities by a purchase, we might then have done it on almost our own terms. This course, however, was not adopted. . . .

On the part of France, the short interval of peace had been wasted in

3. "Hamilton on the Louisiana Purchase: A Newly Identified Editorial from the *New-York Evening Post*," *William and Mary Quarterly*, Third Series, XII (1955), 273–76, *passim*. By permission of the *William and Mary Quarterly*.

repeated and fruitless efforts to subjugate Santo Domingo; and those means which were originally destined to the colonization of Louisiana had been gradually exhausted by the unexpected difficulties of this ill-starred enterprise. To the deadly climate of Santo Domingo, and to the courage and obstinate resistance made by its black inhabitants, are we indebted for the obstacles which delayed the colonization of Louisiana till the auspicious moment when a [prospective] rupture between England and France gave a new turn to the projects of the latter, and destroyed at once all her schemes as to this favorite object of her ambition.

It was made known to Bonaparte that among the first objects of England would be the seizure of New Orleans, and that preparations were even then in a state of forwardness for that purpose. The First Consul could not doubt that, if an English fleet was sent thither, the place must fall without resistance. It was obvious, therefore, that it would be in every shape preferable that it should be placed in the possession of a neutral power. And when, besides, some millions of money, of which he was extremely in want, were offered him to part with what he could no longer hold, it affords a moral certainty that it was to an accidental state of circumstances, and not to wise plans, that this cession, at this time, has been owing. We shall venture to add that neither of the ministers through whose instrumentality it was effected will ever deny this, or even pretend that, previous to the time when a rupture was believed to be inevitable, there was the smallest chance of inducing the First Consul, with his ambitious and aggrandizing views, to commute the territory for any sum of money in their power to offer.

The real truth is, Bonaparte found himself absolutely compelled, by situation, to relinquish his darling plan of colonizing the banks of the Mississippi. And thus have the government of the United States, by the unforeseen operation of events, gained what the feebleness and pusillanimity of its miserable system of measures could never have acquired. . . .

Those disposed to magnify its [Louisiana's] value will say that this Western region is important as keeping off a troublesome neighbor, and leaving us in the quiet possession of the Mississippi. Undoubtedly this has some force, but, on the other hand, it may be said that the acquisition of New Orleans is perfectly adequate to every purpose. For whoever is in possession of that, has the uncontrolled command of the river.

Again, it may be said, and this probably is the most favorable point of view in which it can be placed, that although not valuable to the United States for settlement, it is so to Spain, and will become more so, and therefore at some distant period will form an object which we may barter with her for the Floridas, obviously of far greater value to us than all the immense, undefined region west of the river. . . .

. . . When we consider the present extent of the United States, and that not one sixteenth part of its territory is yet under occupation, the advantage of the acquisition, as it relates to actual settlement, appears too distant and remote to strike the mind of a sober politician with much force. This, there-

A STOPPAGE TO A STRIDE OVER THE GLOBE
Napoleon thwarted in global despotism by England. British Museum.

fore, can only rest in speculation for many years, if not centuries to come, and consequently will not perhaps be allowed very great weight in the account by the majority of readers.

But it may be added that, should our own citizens, more enterprising than wise, become desirous of settling this country, and emigrate thither, it must not only be attended with all the injuries of a too widely dispersed population, but by adding to the great weight of the western part of our territory, must hasten the dismemberment of a large portion of our country, or a dissolution of the government. On the whole, we think it may with candor be said that whether the possession at this time of any territory west of the river Mississippi will be advantageous, is at best extremely problematical.

B. THE APPROVAL OF THE PURCHASE

1. Jefferson Favors an Unconstitutional Act (1803)

Jefferson, in opposing Hamilton's Bank, had argued (see p. 151) that powers not conferred on the central government were reserved to the states. The Constitution

1. A. A. Lipscomb, ed., *Writings of Thomas Jefferson* (1904), X, 410–11 (Aug. 12, 1803).

did not specifically empower the President and Congress to annex foreign territory, especially territory as large as the nation itself, and incorporate its 50,000 or so multi-colored inhabitants into the Union as citizens. Jefferson hastily drafted proposals for a constitutional amendment, but since time pressed and the bargain was breath-taking, he finally pigeonholed them. (In 1828 the Supreme Court upheld the acquisition of territory under the war- and treaty-making clauses of the Constitution.) In reading Jefferson's letter to John Breckinridge, Senate leader, judge whether the guardian analogy is sound.

This treaty must, of course, be laid before both Houses, because both have important functions to exercise respecting it. They, I presume, will see their duty to their country in ratifying and paying for it, so as to secure a good which would otherwise probably be never again in their power. But I suppose they must then appeal to the nation for an additional article [amendment] to the Constitution, approving and confirming an act which the nation had not previously authorized.

The Constitution has made no provision for our holding foreign territory, still less for incorporating foreign nations into our Union. The Executive, in seizing the fugitive occurrence which so much advances the good of their country, have done an act beyond the Constitution. The Legislature, in casting behind them metaphysical subtleties, and risking themselves like faithful servants, must ratify and pay for it, and throw themselves on their country for doing for them, unauthorized, what we know they would have done for themselves had they been in a situation to do it.

It is the case of a guardian, investing the money of his ward in purchasing an important adjacent territory; and saying to him when of age, "I did this for your good. I pretend to no right to bind you: you may disavow me, and I must get out of the scrape as I can. I thought it my duty to risk myself for you."

But we shall not be disavowed by the nation, and their act of indemnity will confirm and not weaken the Constitution, by more strongly marking out its lines.

2. Representative Griswold Is Unhappy (1803)

Jefferson summoned Congress into special session because the Senate had to approve the Louisiana Purchase treaties, and the House and Senate had to vote the money. The New England Federalists fought the acquisition, largely because "the mixed race of Anglo-Hispano-Gallo-Americans" would ultimately outvote the charter-member states of the Union and, as they feared, cause its dismemberment. Representative Griswold of Connecticut, perhaps the ablest Federalist spokesman in the House, had already attained notoriety in 1798 by caning Representative Lyon, after the latter had spat in his face. Note on what terms Griswold, in the following speech, would have accepted Louisiana; and form some conclusions as to the relevance of the "compact theory," hitherto widely used by Jeffersonians.

It is, in my opinion, scarcely possible for any gentleman on this floor to advance an opinion that the President and Senate may add to the members of the Union by treaty whenever they please, or, in the words of this treaty,

2. *Annals of Congress,* 8 Cong., 1 sess., I, cols. 461–62, 463, 465.

may "incorporate in the union of the United States" a foreign nation who, from interest or ambition, may wish to become a member of our government. Such a power would be directly repugnant to the original compact between the states, and a violation of the principles on which that compact was formed.

It has been already well observed that the union of the states was formed on the principle of a co-partnership, and it would be absurd to suppose that the agents of the parties who have been appointed to execute the business of the compact, in behalf of the principals, could admit of a new partner without the consent of the parties themselves. . . .

The incorporation of a foreign nation into the Union, so far from tending to preserve the Union, is a direct inroad upon it. It destroys the perfect union contemplated between the original parties, by interposing an alien and a stranger to share the powers of government with them. . . .

A gentleman from Pennsylvania, however (Mr. Smilie), has said that it is competent for this government to obtain a new territory by conquest, and if a new territory can be obtained by conquest, he infers that it can be procured in the manner provided for by the treaty.

While I admit the premises of the gentleman from Pennsylvania, I deny his conclusion. A new territory and new subjects may undoubtedly be obtained by conquest and by purchase; but neither the conquest nor the purchase can incorporate them into the Union. They must remain in the condition of colonies, and be governed accordingly. The objection to the third article is not that the province of Louisiana could not have been purchased, but that neither this nor any other foreign nation can be incorporated into the Union by treaty or by a law. And as this country has been ceded to the United States only under the condition of an incorporation, it results that, if the condition is unconstitutional or impossible, the cession itself falls to the ground. . . .

This subject was much considered during the last session of Congress, but it will not be found . . . that any individual entertained the least wish to obtain the province of Louisiana. Our views were then confined to New Orleans and the Floridas, and, in my judgment, it would have been happy for the country if they were still confined within those limits. The vast and unmanageable extent which the accession of Louisiana will give to the United States; the consequent dispersion of our population; and the destruction of that balance which it is so important to maintain between the Eastern and the Western states, threatens, at no very distant day, the subversion of our Union.

3. Senator Breckinridge Supports the Purchase (1803)

Virginia-born Senator John Breckinridge of Kentucky, then the ablest spokesman for the West, had sponsored Jefferson's secretly prepared Kentucky resolutions of 1798–1799 in his state legislature. Alert both to Western interests and to partisan

3. *Ibid.,* cols. 60–62, 65.

politics, he urged the Louisiana Purchase in this noteworthy speech. He took sharp issue with the Federalist Senators, including Senator White of Delaware, who held that Louisiana would "be the greatest curse that could at present befall us. . . ." Breckinridge made particular note of the disagreement of the Federalists among themselves as to the extravagance of the price, the validity of the title, and the unconstitutionality of acquiring foreign territory. He then launched into his argument as follows. Determine how effectively he meets the Federalist objections, especially with reference to the problem of the Westerners.

As to the enormity of price, I would ask that gentleman [Senator White], would his mode of acquiring it [by war] through 50,000 men have cost nothing? Is he so confident of this as to be able to pronounce positively that the price is enormous? Does he make no calculation on the hazard attending this conflict? Is he sure the God of battles was enlisted on his side? Were France and Spain, under the auspices of Bonaparte, contemptible adversaries? Good as the cause was, and great as my confidence is in the courage of my countrymen, sure I am that I shall never regret, as the gentleman seems to do, that the experiment was not made. . . .

To acquire an empire of perhaps half [once again] the extent of the one we possessed, from the most powerful and warlike nation on earth, without bloodshed, without the oppression of a single individual, without in the least embarrassing the ordinary operations of your finances, and all this through the peaceful forms of negotiation, and in despite too of the opposition of a considerable portion of the community, is an achievement of which the archives of the predecessors, at least, of those now in office cannot furnish a parallel.

The same gentleman has told us, that this acquisition will, from its extent, soon prove destructive to the confederacy [Union]. . . .

So far from believing in the doctrine that a republic ought to be confined within narrow limits, I believe, on the contrary, that the more extensive its dominion the more safe and more durable it will be. In proportion to the number of hands you entrust the precious blessings of a free government to, in the same proportion do you multiply the chances for their preservation. I entertain, therefore, no fears for the confederacy on account of its extent. . . .

The gentlemen from Delaware [White] and Massachusetts [Pickering] both contend that the third article of the treaty is unconstitutional, and our consent to its ratification a nullity, because the United States cannot acquire foreign territory. . . . Cannot the Constitution be so amended (if it should be necessary) as to embrace this territory? If the authority to acquire foreign territory be not included in the treaty-making power, it remains with the people; and in that way all the doubts and difficulties of gentlemen may be completely removed; and that, too, without affording France the smallest ground of exception to the literal execution on our part of that article of the treaty. . . .

What palliation can we offer to our Western citizens for a conduct like this? Will they be content with the refined and metaphysical reasonings and constructions upon which gentlemen have bottomed their opposition today? Will it be satisfactory to them to be told that the title is good, the price low, the finances competent, and the authority, at least to purchase, constitutional; but that the country is too extensive, and that the admission of these people to all the privileges we ourselves enjoy is not permitted by the Constitution? It will not, sir.

C. THE ISSUE OF SAILORS' RIGHTS

1. A Briton (Stephen) Recommends Firmness (1805)

The titanic struggle between France and Britain flared up anew in 1803. American shipping boomed, especially in carrying coffee and sugar from the French and Spanish West Indies to blockaded France and Spain. Yankee shipowners, shorthanded, used high wages to lure hundreds of sailors from the British merchant fleet and the Royal Navy, where pay was poor and flogging frequent. Some deserters became naturalized; others purchased faked naturalization papers for as little as one dollar. Knowing of these tricks at first hand, James Stephen published in England a popular and potent pamphlet which stiffened the London government in its determination to stifle Yankee-carried traffic between Britain's enemies and the West Indies. Of the grievances mentioned by Stephen, decide which one he regards as most serious, and why.

The worst consequence, perhaps, of the independence and growing commerce of America is the seduction of our seamen. We hear continually of clamors in that country on the score of its sailors being [im]pressed at sea by our frigates. But how have these sailors become subjects of the United States? By engaging in their merchant service during the last or the present war; or at most by obtaining that formal naturalization which they are entitled to receive by law after they have sailed two years from an American port, but the fictitious testimonials of which are to be bought the moment they land in the country, and for a price contemptible even in the estimate of a common sailor.

If those who by birth, and by residence and employment, prior to 1793, were confessedly British, ought still to be regarded as His Majesty's subjects, a very considerable part of the navigators [sailors] of American ships are such at this moment; though, unfortunately, they are not easily distinguishable from genuine American seamen. . . .

The unity of language and the close affinity of manners between English and American seamen are the strong inducements with our sailors for preferring the service of that country to any other foreign employment. Or, to speak more correctly, these circumstances remove from the American service, in the minds of our sailors, those subjects of aversion which they find in other foreign ships; and which formerly counteracted, effectually, the general motives to desert from, or avoid, the naval service of their country.

What these motives are, I need not explain. They are strong, and not easy to be removed; though they might perhaps be palliated by alterations in our naval system. . . . If we cannot remove the general causes of predilection

1. James Stephen, *War in Disguise* (2nd ed., 1805), pp. 120–24.

for the American service, or the difficulty of detecting and reclaiming British seamen when engaged in it, it is, therefore, the more unwise to allow the merchants of that country, and other neutrals, to encroach on our maritime rights in time of war; because we thereby greatly, and suddenly, increase their demand for mariners in general; and enlarge their means, as well as their motives, for seducing the sailors of Great Britain. . . .

It is truly vexatious to reflect that, by this abdication of our belligerent rights, we not only give up the best means of annoying the enemy, but raise up, at the same time, a crowd of dangerous rivals for the seduction of our sailors, and put bribes into their hands for the purpose. We not only allow the trade of the hostile [French] colonies to pass safely, in derision of our impotent warfare, but to be carried on by the mariners of Great Britain. This illegitimate and noxious navigation, therefore, is nourished with the lifeblood of our navy.

2. A Briton (Hall) Urges Discretion (1804)

British cruisers, hovering off New York harbor, blockaded French ships that had sought refuge there. They also visited and searched incoming and outgoing American merchantmen, and impressed British seamen (and sometimes Americans by mistake). Basil Hall, later both a captain and a distinguished author, entered the British navy as a midshipman in 1802, when only thirteen years of age. Many years later he published these recollections of his early service on the 50-gun frigate *Leander* in American waters. Form some judgment as to his bias, and as to which was the most infuriating of the practices he describes.

. . . It seems quite clear that, while we can hold it, we will never give up the right of search, or the right of impressment. We may and ought, certainly, to exercise so disagreeable a power with such temper and discretion as not to provoke the enmity of any friendly nation.

But at the time I speak of, and on board our good old ship the *Leander*, whose name, I was grieved, but not surprised, to find, was still held in detestation three or four and twenty years afterwards at New York, I am sorry to own that we had not much of this discretion in our proceedings; or, rather, we had not enough consideration for the feelings of the people we were dealing with. . . .

To place the full annoyance of these matters in a light to be viewed fairly by English people, let us suppose that the Americans and French were to go to war, and that England for once remained neutral—an odd case, I admit, but one which might happen. Next, suppose that a couple of French frigates were chased into Liverpool, and that an American squadron stationed itself off that harbor to watch the motions of these French ships, which had claimed the protection of our neutrality, and were accordingly received into "our waters." I ask, "Would this blockade of Liverpool be agreeable to us or not?"

Even if the blockading American frigates did nothing but sail backwards

2. Basil Hall, *Fragments of Voyages and Travels*, First Series (1840), pp. 47–49.

and forwards across the harbor's mouth, or occasionally run up and anchor abreast of the town, it would not, "I guess," be very pleasant to be thus superintended. If, however, the American ships, in addition to this legitimate surveillance of their enemy, were to detain off the port, with equal legitimacy of usage, and within a league or so of the lighthouse, every British vessel coming from France, or from a French colony; and if, besides looking over the papers of these vessels to see whether all was regular, they were to open every private letter, in the hope of detecting some trace of French ownership in the cargo, what should we say? And if, out of some twenty ships arrested daily in this manner, one or two of our own were to be completely diverted from their course, from time to time, and sent off under a prize-master to New York for adjudication, I wonder how the Liverpool folks would like it? But if, in addition to this perfectly regular and usual exercise of a belligerent right on the part of the Americans, under such circumstances, we bring in that most awkward and ticklish of questions, the impressment of seamen, let us consider how much the feeling of annoyance on the part of the English neutral would be augmented.

Conceive, for instance, that the American squadron employed to blockade the French ships in Liverpool were shorthanded, but, from being in daily expectation of bringing their enemy to action, it had become an object of great consequence with them to get their ships manned. And suppose, likewise, that it were perfectly notorious to all parties that, on board every English ship arriving or sailing from the port in question, there were several American citizens, but calling themselves English, and having in their possession "protections," or certificates to that effect, sworn to in regular form, but well known to be false, and such as might be bought for 4s. 6d. any day. Things being in this situation, if the American men-of-war off the English port were then to fire at and stop every ship, and, besides overhauling her papers and cargo, were to take out any seamen, to work their own guns withal, whom they had reason, or supposed or said they had reason, to consider American citizens, or whose country they guessed, from dialect or appearance; I wish to know with what degree of patience this would be submitted to on the Exchange at Liverpool, or elsewhere in England. . . .

Suppose the blockading American ships off Liverpool, in firing a shot ahead of a vessel they wished to examine, had accidentally hit, not that vessel, but a small coaster, so far beyond her that she was not even noticed by the blockading ships. And suppose, further, this unlucky chance-shot to have killed one of the crew on board the said English ship. The vessel would, of course, proceed immediately to Liverpool with the body of their slaughtered countryman; and in fairness it may be asked, what would have been the effect of such a spectacle on the population of England . . . ?

This is not an imaginary case; for it actually occurred in 1804 [1806], when we were blockading the French frigates in New York. A consul-shot from the *Leander* hit an unfortunate sloop's mainboom; and the broken spar striking the mate, John Pierce by name, killed him instantly. The sloop sailed on to New York, where the mangled body, raised on a platform, was paraded through the streets, in order to augment the vehement indignation, already at a high pitch, against the English.

Now, let us be candid to our rivals; and ask ourselves whether the Americans would have been worthy of our friendship, or even of our hostility, had they tamely submitted to indignities which, if passed upon ourselves, would have roused not only one seaport, but the whole country, into a towering passion of nationality.

D. THE RESORT TO ECONOMIC COERCION

1. A Federalist (Key) Attacks the Embargo (1808)

With the nation militarily weak, Jefferson decided to force respect for the nation's rights by an economic boycott. In 1807 Congress passed his embargo, which prohibited shipments from leaving American shores for foreign ports, including the West Indies. Paralysis gradually gripped American shipping and agriculture, except for illicit trade. Representative Philip Barton Key, uncle of Francis Scott Key and a former Maryland Loyalist who had fought under George III, here assails the embargo. Note why, in his view, it was playing into Britain's hands, and why he regarded his proposed alternative as more effective.

But, Mr. Chairman, let us review this [embargo] law and its effects. In a commercial point of view, it has annihilated our trade. In an agricultural point of view, it has paralyzed industry. . . . Our most fertile lands are reduced to sterility, so far as it respects our surplus product. As a measure of political economics, it will drive (if continued) our seamen into foreign employ, and our fishermen to foreign sandbanks. In a financial point of view, it has dried up our revenue, and if continued will close the sales of Western lands, and the payment of installments of past sales. For unless produce can be sold, payments cannot be made. As a war measure, the embargo has not been advocated.

It remains then to consider its effects as a peace measure—a measure inducing peace. I grant, sir, that if the friends of the embargo had rightly calculated its effects—if it had brought the belligerents of Europe to a sense of justice and respect for our rights, through the weakness and dependence of their West India possessions—it would have been infinitely wise and desirable. . . . But, sir, the experience of near four months has not produced that effect. . . .

If that be the case, if such should be the result, then will the embargo, of all measures, be the most acceptable to Britain. By occluding [closing] our ports, you give to her ships the exclusive use of the ocean; and you give to her despairing West India planter the monopoly of sugar and rum and coffee to the European world. . . .

But, sir, who are we? What are we? A peaceable agricultural people, of simple and, I trust, virtuous habits, of stout hearts and willing minds, and a brave, powerful, and badly disciplined militia, unarmed, and without troops.

1. *Annals of Congress,* 10 Cong., 1 sess., II, cols. 2122–23.

O-GRAB-ME, OR, THE AMERICAN SNAPPING-TURTLE

The embargo (spelled backwards) was portrayed as a negative "turtle" or "terrapin" policy, with Jeffersonians rejoicing at the stoppage of Federalist exports to England. New-York Historical Society.

And whom are we to come in conflict with? The master of continental Europe [Napoleon] in the full career of universal domination, and the mistress of the ocean [Britain] contending for self-preservation; nations who feel power and forget right.

What man can be weak enough to suppose that a sense of justice can repress or regulate the conduct of Bonaparte? We need not resort to other nations for examples. Has he not in a manner as flagrant as flagitious, directly, openly, publicly violated and broken a solemn treaty [of 1800] entered into with us? Did he not stipulate that our property should pass free even to enemy ports, and has he not burnt our ships at sea under the most causeless pretexts?

Look to England; see her conduct to us. Do we want any further evidence of what she will do in the hour of impending peril than the attack on Copenhagen?* That she prostrates all rights that come in collision with her self-preservation?

No, sir; let us pursue the steady line of rigid impartiality. Let us hold the scales of impartial neutrality with a high and steady hand, and export our products to, and bring back supplies from, all who will trade with us. Much of the world is yet open to us, and let us profit of the occasion.

* The British, seeking to forestall Napoleon, had bombarded and captured the neutral Danish capital in 1807.

At present we exercise no neutral rights. We have quit the ocean; we have abandoned our rights; we have retired to our shell. Sooner than thus continue, our merchantmen should arm to protect legitimate trade. Sir, I believe war itself, as we could carry it on, would produce more benefit and less cost than the millions lost by the continuance of the embargo.

2. A Jeffersonian (Giles) Upholds the Embargo (1808)

Stung by Federalist criticisms of the embargo, Senator W. B. Giles of Virginia sprang to its defense. A prickly personage but a brilliant debater, he had assailed or was to assail virtually every figure prominent in public life. Bitterly anti-Hamilton and anti-British, he was more Jeffersonian than Jefferson himself. Decide whether his argument for the coercive role of the embargo is as convincing as that for the precautionary role.

Sir, I have always understood that there were two subjects contemplated by the embargo laws. The first, precautionary, operating upon ourselves. The second, coercive, operating upon the aggressing belligerents. Precautionary, in saving our seamen, our ships, and our merchandise from the plunder of our enemies, and avoiding the calamities of war. Coercive, by addressing strong appeals to the interests of both the belligerents.

The first object has been answered beyond my most sanguine expectations. To make a fair and just estimate of this measure, reference should be had to our situation at the time of its adoption. At that time, the aggressions of both the belligerents were such as to leave the United States but a painful alternative in the choice of one of three measures, to wit, the embargo, war, or submission. . . .

It was found that merchandise to the value of one hundred millions of dollars was actually afloat, in vessels amounting in value to twenty millions more; that an amount of merchandise and vessels equal to fifty millions of dollars more was expected to be shortly put afloat; and that it would require fifty thousand seamen to be employed in the navigation of this enormous amount of property. The administration was informed of the hostile edicts of France previously issued, and then in a state of execution; and of an intention on the part of Great Britain to issue her orders [in Council], the character and object of which were also known. The object was to sweep this valuable commerce from the ocean. The situation of this commerce was as well known to Great Britain as to ourselves, and her inordinate cupidity could not withstand the temptation of the rich booty she vainly thought within her power. This was the state of information at the time this measure was recommended.

The President of the United States, ever watchful and anxious for the preservation of the persons and property of all our fellow citizens, but particularly of the merchants, whose property is most exposed to danger, and of the seamen, whose persons are also most exposed, recommended the embargo for the protection of both. And it has saved and protected

2. *Ibid.,* 10 Cong., 2 sess., III, cols. 96–106, *passim.*

both. . . . It is admitted by all that the embargo laws have saved this enormous amount of property and this number of seamen, which, without them, would have forcibly gone into the hands of our enemies, to pamper their arrogance, stimulate their injustice, and increase their means of annoyance.

I should suppose, Mr. President, this saving worth some notice. But, sir, we are told that, instead of protecting our seamen, it has driven them out of the country, and into foreign service. I believe, sir, that this fact is greatly exaggerated. But, sir, suppose for a moment that it is so, the government has done all, in this respect, it was bound to do. It placed these seamen in the bosoms of their friends and families, in a state of perfect security. And if they have since thought proper to abandon these blessings and emigrate from their country, it was an act of choice, not of necessity. . . .

DEATH OF THE TERRA-PIN, OR THE EMBARGO
The administration kills the embargo (turtle) before it kills the administration. B. J. Lossing, *Pictorial Field-Book of the War of 1812*, 1868.

. . . But, sir, these are not the only good effects of the embargo. It has preserved our peace—it has saved our honor—it has saved our national independence. Are these savings not worth notice? Are these blessings not worth preserving . . . ?

The gentleman next triumphantly tells us that the embargo laws have not had their expected effects upon the aggressing belligerents. That they have not had their complete effects; that they have not caused a revocation of the British orders and French decrees, will readily be admitted. But they certainly have not been without some beneficial effects upon those nations. . . .

The first effect of the embargo upon the aggressing belligerents was to lessen their inducements to war, by keeping out of their way the rich spoils of our commerce, which had invited their cupidity, and which was saved by those laws. . . .

The second effect which the embargo laws have had on the aggressing belligerents is to enhance the prices of all American produce, especially articles of the first necessity to them, to a considerable degree; and, if it be a little longer persisted in, will either banish our produce (which I believe indispensable to them) from their markets altogether, or increase the prices to an enormous amount; and, of course, we may hope will furnish irresistible inducements for a relaxation of their hostile orders and edicts.

[*The effects of the embargo ultimately proved disastrous. Confronted with anarchy and bankruptcy, Jefferson engineered its repeal in 1809 and the substitution of a more limited Non-Intercourse Act.*]

E. JEFFERSONIAN IDEALISM

1. Jefferson Spurns a Third Term (1805)

Still politically dominant, Jefferson probably could have arranged for a third election in 1808, but he decided to bow out. Washington had retired largely because of weariness; Jefferson retired primarily because he feared the entering wedge of dictatorship. In this remarkable letter, written four years in advance, assess Jefferson's capacity to change his mind in the light of experience, and his reason for not making his intentions public at once. The 22nd Amendment (anti-third term), at which he hinted, was adopted in 1951.

. . . My opinion originally was that the President of the United States should have been elected for seven years, and forever ineligible afterwards. I have since become sensible that seven years is too long to be irremovable, and that there should be a peaceable way of withdrawing a man in midway who is doing wrong. The service for eight years, with a power to remove at the end of the first four, comes nearly to my principle as corrected by experience. And it is in adherence to that that I determined to withdraw at the end of my second term.

The danger is that the indulgence and attachments of the people will keep a man in the chair after he becomes a dotard, that re-election through life shall become habitual, and election for life follow that.

General Washington set the example of voluntary retirement after eight years. I shall follow it, and a few more precedents will oppose the obstacle of habit to anyone after a while who shall endeavor to extend his term. Perhaps it may beget a disposition to establish it by an amendment of the Constitution.

I believe I am doing right, therefore, in pursuing my principle. I had determined to declare my intention, but I have consented to be silent on the opinion of friends, who think it best not to put a continuance out of my power in defiance of all circumstances. There is, however, but one circumstance which could engage my acquiescence in another election: to wit, such a division about a successor as might bring in a monarchist But this circumstance is impossible. While, therefore, I shall make no formal declarations to the public of my purpose, I have freely let it be understood in private conversation.

1. P. L. Ford, ed., *Writings of Thomas Jefferson* (1897), VIII, 339 (Jan. 6, 1805).

2. Jefferson Pens His Own Epitaph

Jefferson himself composed the inscription which is to be found over his grave at Monticello. One of his proudest achievements was his role in the struggle after the Revolution to abolish in Virginia the tax-supported established church. Note the idealistic nature of the deeds that he records, and speculate on why he did not list others, including the Louisiana Purchase.

The following would be to my manes [departed spirit] the most gratifying.

On the grave a plain die or cube of 3 feet without any mouldings, surmounted by an obelisk of 6 feet height, each of a single stone: on the faces of the obelisk the following inscription, and not a word more:

Here was buried
Thomas Jefferson
author of the Declaration of American Independence
of the Statute of Virginia for religious freedom
and Father of the University of Virginia.

because by these, as testimonials that I have lived, I wish most to be remembered.

THOUGHT PROVOKERS

1. To what extent did the Louisiana Purchase strengthen or weaken the no-alliance tradition? Did good diplomacy or good luck bring about the Purchase?
2. Did it take more courage on the part of Jefferson to accept Louisiana than not to accept it? What becomes of the Constitution if the Executive may resort to what he believes to be unconstitutional acts for the common good? What probably would have happened if, as the Federalists argued, the thirteen original states had kept all new territory in a permanent colonial status?
3. In the matter of impressment, were the Americans more sinned against than sinning? Why were the British so unwilling to give up impressment?
4. In what respects would war have been less costly in dollars and more satisfying to the national ego than the embargo? Do you find any inconsistency in the fact that the Americans, dedicated to freedom of the seas, temporarily abandoned their right to sail the high seas? Were the wholesale violations of the embargo in keeping with the American national character?
5. Woodrow Wilson said in 1916: "The immortality of Jefferson does not lie in any one of his achievements, but in his attitude toward mankind." Comment.

FURTHER EXPLORATION

General: Edward Channing, *The Jeffersonian System* (1906); C. G. Bowers, *Jefferson in Power* (1936); L. D. White, *The Jeffersonians* (1951); **Louisiana Purchase:** George Dangerfield, *Chancellor Robert R. Livingston of New York* (1960); E. W. Lyon, *Louisiana in French Diplomacy* (1934). **Approval:** Irving Brant, *James Madison: Secretary of State* (1953); A. P. Whitaker, *The Mississippi Question* (1934). **Sailors' Rights:** J. F. Zimmerman, *Impressment of American Seamen* (1925); Bradford Perkins, *The First Rapprochement* (1955). **Embargo:** L. M. Sears, *Jefferson and the Embargo* (1927). **Idealism:** M. D. Peterson, *The Jefferson Image in the American Mind* (1960). **Recent:** N. E. Cunningham, *The Jeffersonian Republicans in Power* (1963).

2. Facsimile in S. K. Padover, *The Complete Jefferson* (1943), p. 1300.

Chapter 11

The Second War with Britain

Every consideration of moral duty and political expedience seems to concur in warning the United States not to mingle in this hopeless and, to human eye, interminable European contest.

PROTEST OF FEDERALIST MINORITY IN CONGRESS, 1812

PROLOGUE: The Western War Hawks in Congress, bitter about maritime grievances against Britain and British-succored Indian raids, engineered a declaration of war on Britain in 1812. But the pro-British Federalists of New England vehemently opposed "Mr. Madison's War" as a scheme of the Jeffersonian Republicans to ruin them economically and politically. With the nation thus dangerously divided and wretchedly unprepared, the American invasions of Canada in 1812 and 1813 all collapsed, despite overconfident predictions of an easy conquest. In 1814 the British counter-invaded and burned Washington. The Americans won brilliant fleet victories on Lake Erie under Perry (1813) and on Lake Champlain under Macdonough (1814), but the tiny high-seas navy, although winning some spectacular single-ship victories, was virtually wiped out. When peace was signed, the British had the better of the fighting. The American coasts were tightly blockaded, the Redcoats were about to attack New Orleans, and British forces occupied about half of Maine and even larger areas on the northwestern frontier. Lucky to escape with a whole skin, the Americans gladly accepted a restoration of the *status quo* in the Treaty of Ghent (1814). Neither side won or lost or yielded anything.

A. ROOTS OF THE WAR OF 1812

1. Tecumseh Challenges Harrison (1810)

The American frontiersmen blamed the British for egging the Indians onto them, but actually American greed was goad enough. William Henry Harrison, the aggressive governor of Indiana Territory, had negotiated a series of land-grabbing agreements with the Indians, culminating in the Treaty of Fort Wayne (1809). Two Indian tribes, ignoring the rights of all others and succumbing to firewater, sold 3,000,000 acres of their ancestral lands for a pittance. The gifted Shawnee chief Tecumseh, together with his epileptic twin brother The Prophet, was then organizing the Indians ·against white encroachments. Absent when the Treaty of Fort Wayne was negotiated, he journeyed angrily to Vincennes (Indiana), where, in a stormy scene, he confronted Governor Harrison and threatened to resist white occupancy of the ceded lands. Form some judgment as to the validity of his main grievance.

I would not then come to Governor Harrison to ask him to tear the treaty and to obliterate the landmark. But I would say to him: Sir, you have liberty to return to your own country.

1. C. M. Depew, ed., *The Library of Oratory* (1902), IV, 363–64.

The Being within, communing with past ages, tells me that . . . until lately there was no white man on this continent; that it then all belonged to red men, children of the same parents, placed on it by the Great Spirit that made them, to keep it, to traverse it, to enjoy its productions, and to fill it with the same race—once a happy race, since made miserable by the white people, who are never contented, but always encroaching. The way—and the only way—to check and to stop this evil is for all the red men to unite in claiming a common equal right in the land, as it was at first, and should be yet. For it never was divided, but belongs to all for the use of each. That no part has a right to sell, even to each other, much less to strangers; those who want all, and will not do with less.

The white people have no right to take the land from the Indians, because they had it first. It is theirs. They may sell, but all must join. Any sale not made by all is not valid. The late sale is bad. It was made by a part only. Part do not know how to sell. It requires all to make a bargain for all. All red men have equal rights to the unoccupied land. The right of occupancy is as good in one place as in another. There cannot be two occupations in the same place. The first excludes all others. It is not so in hunting or traveling; for there the same ground will serve many, as they may follow each other all day. But the camp is stationary, and that is occupancy. It belongs to the first who sits down on his blanket or skins which he has thrown upon the ground; and till he leaves it no other has a right.

2. Representative Grundy Demands War (1811)

Following Tecumseh's speech and the subsequent Indian raids on the frontier, Governor Harrison led an army provocatively toward the red men's headquarters. On the night of November 7, 1811, at Tippecanoe near the Wabash River (Indiana), he succeeded in beating off an Indian attack. This hollow but costly victory further inflamed the West, from which rode Henry Clay and other leaders of the War Hawks in Congress in 1811. Among them was Felix Grundy of Tennessee, three of whose brothers had been butchered by the Indians. As the most famous criminal lawyer in the Southwest, he had often cheated the gallows by reducing the jury to tears. In this eloquent speech in Congress, note which grievances were peculiarly Western and which ones were nationwide. Historians used to think that the West had no direct stake in a free sea.* Observe how Grundy refutes this charge.

I will now state the reasons which influenced the Committee [on Foreign Affairs] in recommending the [war] measures now before us.

It is not the [Atlantic] carrying trade properly so called about which this nation and Great Britain are at present contending. Were this the only question now under consideration, I should feel great unwillingness (however clear our claim might be) to involve the nation in war for the assertion of a right in the enjoyment of which the community at large are not more deeply concerned.

2. *Annals of Congress,* 12 Cong., 1 sess., I, cols. 424–26 (Dec. 9, 1811).
* On the Western maritime stake, see G. R. Taylor, "Agrarian Discontent in the Mississippi Valley Preceding the War of 1812," *Journal of Political Economy,* XXXIX (1931), 471–505.

The true question in controversy is of a very different character; it involves the interest of the whole nation. It is the right of exporting the productions of our own soil and industry to foreign markets. Sir, our vessels are now captured when destined to the ports of France, and condemned by the British Courts of Admiralty, without even the pretext of having on board contraband of war, enemies' property, or having in any other respect violated the laws of nations.

These depredations on our lawful commerce, under whatever ostensible pretense committed, are not to be traced to any maxims or rules of public law, but to the maritime supremacy and pride of the British nation. This hostile and unjust policy of that country towards us is not to be wondered at, when we recollect that the United States are already the second commercial nation in the world. The rapid growth of our commercial importance has not only awakened the jealousy of the commercial interests of Great Britain, but her statesmen, no doubt, anticipate with deep concern the maritime greatness of this republic. . . .

What, Mr. Speaker, are we now called on to decide? It is whether we will resist by force the attempt, made by the [British] government, to subject our maritime rights to the arbitrary and capricious rule of her will. For my part I am not prepared to say that this country shall submit to have her commerce interdicted, or regulated, by any foreign nation. Sir, I prefer war to submission.

Over and above these unjust pretensions of the British government, for many years past they have been in the practice of impressing our seamen from merchant vessels. This unjust and lawless invasion of personal liberty calls loudly for the interposition of this government. To those better acquainted with the facts in relation to it, I leave it to fill up the picture.

My mind is irresistibly drawn to the West. Although others may not strongly feel the

HARRISON'S CAMPAIGN, 1811

bearing which the late transactions in that quarter [Tippecanoe] have on this subject, upon my mind they have great influence. It cannot be believed, by any man who will reflect, that the savage tribes, uninfluenced by other powers, would think of making war on the United States. They understand too well their own weakness and our strength. They have already felt the weight of our arms; they know they hold the very soil on which they live as tenants in sufferance. How, then, sir, are we to account for their late conduct? In one way only: some powerful nation must have intrigued with them, and turned their peaceful dispositions towards us into hostilities. Great Britain alone has intercourse with those Northern tribes. I therefore infer that if British gold has not been employed, their baubles and trinkets, and the promise of support and a place of refuge, if necessary, have had their effect.

If I am right in this conjecture, war is not to commence by sea or land. It is already begun; and some of the richest blood of our country has already been shed. . . . The whole Western country is ready to march; they only wait for our permission. And, sir, war once declared, I pledge myself for my people—they will avenge the death of their brethren. . . .

Ask the Northern man, and he will tell you that any state of things is better than the present. Inquire of the Western people why their crops are not equal to what they were in former years; they will answer that industry has no stimulus left, since their surplus products have no markets. . . .

This war, if carried on successfully, will have its advantages. We shall drive the British from our continent. They will no longer have an opportunity of intriguing with our Indian neighbors and setting on the ruthless savage to tomahawk our women and children. That nation will lose her Canadian trade, and, by having no resting place in this country, her means of annoying us will be diminished.

3. Representative Randolph Needles the War Hawks (1811)

Tall, gawky, and squeaky-voiced John Randolph of Virginia, an unsparing critic of President Madison and the War of 1812, was one of the most brilliant eccentrics ever to enter Congress. A tireless orator and horseman, he strode about the floor with riding whip in hand and quip on tongue. His contentious nature provoked two duels (one with Henry Clay), and he narrowly escaped another. Late in life he went completely insane. In reading his sardonic reply to Representative Grundy, form conclusions regarding his charge that the American pioneers themselves were more responsible for Indian troubles than the unproved plottings of the so-called British "hair buyers." The following text is not a direct quotation but a paraphrase in the third person.

An insinuation had fallen from the gentleman from Tennessee (Mr. Grundy) that the late massacre of our brethren on the Wabash [at Tippecanoe] had been instigated by the British government.

Has the President given any such information? Has the gentleman [Grundy] received any such, even informally, from any officer of this government? Is it so believed by the administration? He [Randolph] had cause to think the contrary to be the fact; that such was not their opinion. This insinuation was of the grossest kind—a presumption of the most rash, the most unjustifiable. Show but good ground for it, he would give up the question at the threshold—he was ready to march to Canada. It was indeed well calculated to excite the feelings of the Western people particularly, who were not quite so tenderly attached to our red brethren as some

3. *Annals of Congress,* 12 Cong., 1 sess., I, cols., 445–46, 449–50, 533.

modern philosophers. But it was destitute of any foundation, beyond mere surmise and suspicion. . . .

There was an easy and natural solution of the late transaction on the Wabash, in the well-known character of the aboriginal savage of North America, without resorting to any such mere conjectural estimate. He was sorry to say that for this signal calamity and disgrace the House [of Representatives] was, in part, at least, answerable. Session after session, their table had been piled up with Indian treaties, for which the appropriations had been voted as a matter of course, without examination. Advantage had been taken of the spirit of the Indians, broken by the war which ended in the Treaty of Greenville [1795]. Under the ascendancy then acquired over them, they had been pent up by subsequent treaties into nooks, straightened in their quarters by a blind cupidity seeking to extinguish their title to immense wildernesses, for which (possessing, as we do already, more land than we can sell or use) we shall not have occasion for half a century to come. It was our own thirst for territory, our own want of moderation, that had driven these sons of nature to desperation, of which we felt the effects. . . .

Our people will not submit to be taxed for this war of conquest and dominion. The government of the United States was not calculated to wage offensive foreign war—it was instituted for the common defense and general welfare.

[*Six days after his reply to Grundy, Randolph accused the War Hawks of wrapping their greed for Canada in the patriotic cloak of a free sea. Note to what extent his reference to Halifax (the prime British naval base) seems to prove the War Hawks guilty of hypocrisy. Actually, Canada was the only place where Britain could be attacked with reasonable prospects of success.*]

. . . Sir, if you go to war it will not be for the protection of, or defense of, your maritime rights. Gentlemen from the North have been taken up to some high mountain and shown all the kingdoms of the earth; and Canada seems tempting in their sight—that rich vein of Genesee land, which is said to be even better on the other side of the [Great] Lake[s] than on this.

Agrarian cupidity, not maritime right, urges the war. Ever since the [pro-war] report of the Committee on Foreign Relations came into the House, we have heard but one word—like the whip-poor-will, but one eternal monotonous tone—Canada! Canada! Canada! Not a syllable about Halifax [Nova Scotia], which unquestionably should be our great object in a war for maritime security.

It is to acquire a preponders Northern influence that you are to launch into war. For purposes of maritime safety, the barren rocks of Bermuda were worth more to us than all the deserts [of Canada] through which [explorers] Hearne and McKenzie had pushed their adventurous researches.

[*Randolph, in making his misleading charge of land-lust, conveniently overlooked the obvious fact that Canada was the one place where small-navy America could most effectively attack big-navy Britain.*]

B. THE BRINK OF HOSTILITIES

1. A Republican Editor Urges War (1812)

The ridiculous ease with which Canada could presumably be conquered added enthusiasm to the demands of the War Hawks for hostilities with Britain. Espousing this view was the *Daily National Intelligencer,* a leading Washington newspaper which enjoyed profitable printing contracts from the government. Loyal to the administration and conservative in tone, it was known as "the Court Paper." The Federalists charged that President Madison took advantage of Britain's necessities to stab her in the back. Determine whether or not this editorial in the *Daily National Intelligencer* supports such an accusation.

. . . It is said that we are not prepared for war, and ought therefore not to declare it. This is an idle objection, which can have weight with the timid and pusillanimous only. The fact is otherwise. Our preparations are adequate to every essential object.

Do we apprehend danger to ourselves? From what quarter will it assail us? From England, and by invasion? The idea is too absurd to merit a moment's consideration. Where are her troops? But lately she dreaded an invasion of her own dominions from her powerful and menacing neighbor [France]. That danger, it is true, has diminished, but it has not entirely and forever disappeared. . . .

The war in the [Spanish] Peninsula, which lingers, requires strong armies to support it. She [England] maintains an army in Sicily; another in India; and a strong force in Ireland, and along her own coast, and in the West Indies. Can anyone believe that, under such circumstances, the British government could be so infatuated, or rather mad, as to send troops here for the purpose of invasion?

The experience and the fortune of our Revolution, when we were comparatively in an infant state, have doubtless taught her a useful lesson which cannot have been forgotten. Since that period, our population has increased threefold, whilst hers has remained almost stationary. The condition of the civilized world, too, has changed. Although Great Britain has nothing to fear as to her independence, and her military operations are extensive and distant, the contest [against Napoleon] is evidently maintained by her rather for safety than for conquest.

Have we cause to dread an attack from her neighboring provinces [Canada]? That apprehension is still more groundless. Seven or eight millions of people have nothing to dread from 300,000. From the moment that war is declared, the British colonies will be put on the defensive, and soon after we get in motion must sink under the pressure.

2. A Federalist Editor Rejects War (1812)

William Coleman, a gifted protégé of Alexander Hamilton and editor of the influential New York *Evening Post,* was the leading Federalist journalist of the era.

1. *Daily National Intelligencer* (Washington), April 14, 1812.
2. New York *Evening Post,* April 21, 1812.

Sometimes abusive, he did not hesitate to call a rival editor a "vile reptile," and he was ultimately thrashed on the streets by a victim of his pen prickings. Hating President Madison, he fought the declaration of the "unjust war," and after it came he editorially discouraged enlistments. Analyze critically his strongest argument against war; his weakest. Evaluate his prophetic faculties.

Citizens, if pecuniary redress is your object in going to war with England, the measure is perfect madness. You will lose millions when you will gain a cent. The expense will be enormous. It will ruin our country. Direct taxes must be resorted to. The people will have nothing to pay. We once had a revenue; that has been destroyed in the destruction of our commerce [by embargoes]. For several years past you have been deceived and abused by the false pretenses of a full treasury. That phantom of hope will soon vanish.

You have lately seen fifteen millions of dollars wasted in the purchase of a province [Louisiana] we did not want, and never shall possess. And will you spend hundreds of millions in conquering a province which, were it made a present to us, would not be worth accepting? Our territories are already too large. The desire to annex Canada to the United States is as base an ambition as ever burned in the bosom of Alexander. What benefit will it ever be to the great body of the people, after their wealth is exhausted, and their best blood is shed in its reduction? . . . Canada, if annexed to the United States, will furnish offices to a set of hungry villains, grown quite too numerous for our present wide limits. And that is all the benefit we ever shall derive from it.

These remarks will have little weight with men whose interest leads them to advocate war. Thousands of lives, millions of money, the flames of cities, the tears of widows and orphans, with them are light expedients when they lead to wealth and power. But to the people who must fight, if fighting must be done—who must pay if money be wanted—who must march when the trumpet sounds, and who must die when the "battle bleeds"—to the people I appeal. To them the warning voice is lifted. From a war they are to expect nothing but expenses and suffering—expenses disproportionate to their means, and sufferings lasting as life.

In our extensive shores and numerous seaports, we know not where the enemy will strike; or more properly speaking, we know they will strike when a station is defenseless. Their fleets will hover on our coasts, and can trace our line from Maine to New Orleans in a few weeks. Gunboats cannot repel them, nor is there a fort on all our shores in which confidence can be placed. The ruin of our seaports and loss of all vessels will form an item in the list of expenses. Fortifications and garrisons numerous and strong must be added.

As to the main points of attack or defense, I shall only say that an efficient force will be necessary. A handful of men cannot run up and take Canada, in a few weeks, for mere diversion.

The conflict will be long and severe, resistance formidable, and the final result doubtful. A nation that can debar the conqueror of Europe [Napoleon] from the sea, and resist his armies in Spain, will not surrender its provinces without a struggle. Those who advocate a British war must be perfectly aware that the whole revenue arising from all British America for the ensuing century would not repay the expenses of that war.

3. Madison's Fateful War Message (1812)

Scholars once believed that Madison—mild-mannered and highly intellectual—was prodded into war by the purposeful War Hawks from the West. The truth is that the President, unable to wring concessions from the British, worked hand in glove with the War Hawks. In reading his following War Message, ascertain whether he seems more concerned with purely Western grievances than with national grievances. Decide which of his numerous charges against England carries the least conviction, and note the additional evidence that the West had an economic stake in a free sea.

British cruisers have been in the continued practice of violating the American flag on the great highway of nations, and of seizing and carrying off persons sailing under it, not in the exercise of a belligerent right founded on the law of nations against an enemy, but of a municipal [internal] prerogative over British subjects. British jurisdiction is thus extended to neutral vessels. . . .

The practice . . . is so far from affecting British subjects alone that, under the pretext of searching for these, thousands of American citizens, under the safeguard of public law and of their national flag, have been torn from their country and from everything dear to them; have been dragged on board ships of war of a foreign nation and exposed, under the severities of their discipline, to be exiled to the most distant and deadly climes, to risk their lives in the battles of their oppressors, and to be the melancholy instruments of taking away those of their own brethren.

Against this crying enormity, which Great Britain would be so prompt to avenge if committed against herself, the United States have in vain exhausted remonstrances and expostulations. And that no proof might be wanting of their conciliatory dispositions, and no pretext left for a continuance of the practice, the British government was formally assured of the readiness of the United States to enter into arrangements such as could not be rejected if the recovery of British subjects were the real and the sole object. The communication passed without effect.

British cruisers have been in the practice also of violating the rights and the peace of our coasts. They hover over and harass our entering and departing commerce. To the most insulting pretensions they have added the most lawless proceedings in our very harbors, and have wantonly spilt American blood within the sanctuary of our territorial jurisdiction. . . . [See Pierce case, p. 186.]

Under pretended blockades, without the presence of an adequate force and sometimes without the practicability of applying one, our commerce

3. J. D. Richardson, ed., *Messages and Papers of the Presidents* (1896), I, 500–04.

has been plundered in every sea, the great staples of our country have been cut off from their legitimate markets, and a destructive blow aimed at our agricultural and maritime interests. . . .

Not content with these occasional expedients for laying waste our neutral trade, the Cabinet of Britain resorted at length to the sweeping system of blockades, under the name of Orders in Council, which has been molded and managed as might best suit its political views, its commercial jealousies, or the avidity of British cruisers. . . .

It has become, indeed, sufficiently certain that the commerce of the United States is to be sacrificed, not as interfering with the belligerent rights of Great Britain; not as supplying the wants of her enemies, which she herself supplies; but as interfering with the monopoly which she covets for her own commerce and navigation. . . .

In reviewing the conduct of Great Britain toward the United States, our attention is necessarily drawn to the warfare just renewed by the savages on one of our extensive frontiers—a warfare which is known to spare neither age nor sex and to be distinguished by features peculiarly shocking to humanity. It is difficult to account for the activity and combinations which have for some time been developing themselves among tribes in constant intercourse with British traders and garrisons, without connecting their hostility with that influence, and without recollecting the authenticated examples of such interpositions heretofore furnished by the officers and agents of that government.

4. Federalist Congressmen Protest (1812)

A group of thirty-four anti-war Federalists, outvoted in the House, prepared the following remonstrance, which was widely circulated. A leading author was the unbridled Josiah Quincy, who, the year before, had declared that if the Territory of Louisiana was admitted as a state, the Union was "virtually dissolved," and that likeminded men must "prepare definitely for a separation—amicably, if they can; violently, if they must." The protest of the thirty-four Congressmen was in effect a reply to Madison's War Message. After minimizing or partially justifying Britain's provocative maritime practices and Indian policy, the statement continued as follows. Detect with what degree of plausibility it makes the points regarding the futility of the war and the folly of becoming a virtual ally of France; also to what extent the war was immoral.

If our ills were of a nature that war would remedy, if war would compensate any of our losses or remove any of our complaints, there might be some alleviation of the suffering in the charm of the prospect. But how will war upon the land protect commerce upon the ocean? What balm has Canada for wounded honor? How are our mariners benefited by a war which exposes those who are free, without promising release to those who are impressed?

But it is said that war is demanded by honor. Is national honor a prin-

ciple which thirsts after vengeance, and is appeased only by blood? . . .
If honor demands a war with England, what opiate lulls that honor to
sleep over the wrongs done us by France? On land, robberies, seizures,
imprisonments, by French authority; at sea, pillage, sinkings, burnings,
under French orders. These are notorious. Are they unfelt because they
are French? . . . With full knowledge of the wrongs inflicted by the French,
ought the government of this country to aid the French cause by engaging
in war against the enemy of France? . . .

It would be some relief to our anxiety if amends were likely to be made
for the weakness and wildness of the project by the prudence of the preparation. But in no aspect of this anomalous affair can we trace the great
and distinctive properties of wisdom. There is seen a headlong rushing into
difficulties, with little calculation about the means, and little concern about
the consequences. With a navy comparatively nominal, we are about to enter into the lists against the greatest marine [sea power] on the globe. With
a commerce unprotected and spread over every ocean, we propose to make
a profit by privateering, and for this endanger the wealth of which we are
honest proprietors. An invasion is threatened of the colonies of a power
which, without putting a new ship into commission, or taking another soldier
into pay, can spread alarm or desolation along the extensive range of our
seaboard. . . .

The undersigned cannot refrain from asking, what are the United States
to gain by this war? Will the gratification of some privateersmen compensate the nation for that sweep of our legitimate commerce by the
extended marine of our enemy which this desperate act invites? Will
Canada compensate the Middle states for New York; or the Western states
for New Orleans?

Let us not be deceived. A war of invasion may invite a retort of invasion.
When we visit the peaceable, and as to us innocent, colonies of Great
Britain with the horrors of war, can we be assured that our own coast will
not be visited with like horrors? At a crisis of the world such as the present,
and under impressions such as these, the undersigned could not consider
the war, in which the United States have in secret been precipitated, as
necessary, or required by any moral duty, or any political expediency.

C. DISLOYALTY IN NEW ENGLAND

1. A Boston Paper Obstructs the War (1813)

The anti-war bitterness of the New England Federalists found vigorous voice in
Major Benjamin Russell's *Columbian Centinel* (Boston). The editor, earlier fined
twenty shillings for spitting in the face of a journalistic adversary, believed that a
French-loving cabal of Virginia planter lordlings had provoked unnecessary hostilities.
He charged that this Jeffersonian Republican group, headed by President Madison,
was determined to ruin the Federalists by destroying their commerce and by carving
new states out of Canada—states that would outvote the New England bloc. Con-

1. *Columbian Centinel* (Boston), Jan. 13, 1813.

sidering that the United States had already been at war for six months, judge whether this editorial was treasonable. Assess the validity of its charges, and note how far it goes toward secession.

The sentiment is hourly extending, and in these Northern states will soon be universal, that we are in a condition no better in relation to the South than that of a conquered people. We have been compelled, without the least necessity or occasion, to renounce our habits, occupations, means of happiness, and subsistence. We are plunged into a war without a sense of enmity, or a perception of sufficient provocation; and obliged to fight the battles of a cabal which, under the sickening affectation of republican equality, aims at trampling into the dust the weight, influence, and power of commerce and her dependencies.

We, whose soil was the hotbed and whose ships were the nursery of sailors, are insulted with the hypocrisy of a devotedness to sailors' rights, and the arrogance of pretended skill in maritime jurisprudence, by those whose country furnishes no navigation beyond the size of a ferry boat or an Indian canoe. We have no more interest in waging this sort of war, at this period and under these circumstances, at the command of Virginia, than Holland in accelerating her ruin by uniting her destiny to France. . . .

We resemble Holland in another particular. The officer [offices] and power of government are engrossed [monopolized] by executive minions, who are selected on account of their known infidelity to the interest of their fellow citizens, to foment divisions and to deceive and distract the people whom they cannot intimidate. . . .

The consequence of this state of things must then be either that the Southern states must drag the Northern states farther into the war, or we must drag them out of it; or the chain will break. This will be the "imposing attitude" of the next year. We must no longer be deafened by senseless clamors about a separation of the states. It is an event we do not desire, not because we have derived advantages from the compact, but because we cannot foresee or limit the dangers or effects of revolution. But the states are separated in fact, when one section assumes an imposing attitude, and with a high hand perseveres in measures fatal to the interests and repugnant to the opinions of another section, by dint of a geographical majority.

2. The Hartford Convention Fulminates (1814)

As the war dragged on, the British extended their suffocating blockade to the coasts of New England. The New Englanders, forced to resort to costly defensive measures, complained bitterly that their federal tax payments were being used to fight the war elsewhere. Late in 1814, with Massachusetts and Connecticut as ringleaders, twenty-six delegates assembled secretly in a protest convention at Hartford, Connecticut. Although some of the Federalist extremists spoke brazenly of immediate secession, conservatives like the venerable George Cabot sat on the lid, saying, "We are going to keep you young hotheads from getting into mischief." The final resolutions, less treasonable than commonly supposed, were a manifesto of states' rights

2. Timothy Dwight, *History of the Hartford Convention* (1833), pp. 377–78.

and sectionalism designed to revive New England's slipping national power, avert Jeffersonian embargoes, and keep new Western states from outvoting the charter members. Determine which of these proposed amendments were most clearly sectional, and which one probably had the best chance of adoption at the time.

Resolved, That the following amendments of the Constitution of the United States be recommended to the states. . . .

First. Representatives and direct taxes shall be apportioned among the several states which may be included within this Union, according to their respective numbers of free persons, including those bound to serve for a term of years, and excluding Indians not taxed, and all other persons. [Aimed at reducing Southern representation based on slaves.]

Second. No new state shall be admitted into the Union by Congress, in virtue of the power granted by the Constitution, without the concurrence of two-thirds of both Houses.

Third. Congress shall not have power to lay any embargo on the ships or vessels of the citizens of the United States, in the ports or harbors thereof, for more than sixty days.

Fourth. Congress shall not have power, without the concurrence of two-thirds of both Houses, to interdict the commercial intercourse between the United States and any foreign nation, or the dependencies thereof.

Fifth. Congress shall not make or declare war, or authorize acts of hostility against any foreign nation, without the concurrence of two-thirds of both Houses, except such acts of hostility be in defense of the territories of the United States when actually invaded.

Sixth. No person who shall hereafter be naturalized shall be eligible as a member of the Senate or House of Representatives of the United States, nor capable of holding any civil office under the authority of the United States. [Aimed at men like Jefferson's Swiss-born Secretary of the Treasury Gallatin.]

Seventh. The same person shall not be elected President of the United States a second time; nor shall the President be elected from the same state two terms in succession. [Prompted by the successive two-term tenures of Jefferson and Madison, both from Virginia.]

Resolved, That if the application of these states to the government of the United States, recommended in a foregoing resolution, should be unsuccessful, and peace should not be concluded, and the defense of these states should be neglected, as it has been since the commencement of the war, it will, in the opinion of this convention, be expedient for the legislatures of the several states to appoint delegates to another convention, to meet at Boston . . . with such powers and instruction as the exigency of a crisis so momentous may require.

[*The legislatures of Massachusetts and Connecticut enthusiastically approved the Hartford Resolutions. Three emissaries from Massachusetts departed for Washington with their demands, confidently expecting to hear at any moment of a smashing British victory at New Orleans, the collapse of the peace negotiations at Ghent, and the dissolution of the Union. But instead came news of the* smashing British defeat at New Orleans and the signing of the peace treaty at Ghent. The Hartfordites were hooted off the stage of history, amid charges of treason that cling to this day.]

A MASSACHUSETTS ELECTION HANDBILL

Jeffersonians use taint of the Hartford Convention against the Federalists in next election. B. J. Lossing, *Pictorial Field-Book of the War of 1812*, 1868.

3. Adams Reproaches the Hartfordites (1815)

Independent-minded John Quincy Adams, son of the second President and destined to be the sixth President, rose above the sectional prejudices of his native New England. Entering the Senate from Massachusetts, he reluctantly voted for the Louisiana Purchase appropriation and subsequently supported Jefferson's unpopular embargo as preferable to war. The Federalists of New England now regarded him as an apostate. After serving as one of the five American negotiators of the Treaty of Ghent, he wrote the following spirited attack on the Hartford Convention. Note what, in his view, was the ultimate aim of the Hartfordites. This interpretation has been challenged by some scholars.

The [Hartford] Convention represented the extreme portion of the Federalism of New England—the party spirit of the school of Alexander Hamilton combined with the sectional Yankee spirit. . . .

This coalition of Hamiltonian Federalism with the Yankee spirit had produced as incongruous and absurd a system of politics as ever was exhibited in the vagaries of the human mind. It was compounded of the following prejudices:—

3. Henry Adams, ed., *Documents Relating to New England Federalism, 1800–1815* (1877), pp. 283–84, 321–22.

1. An utter detestation of the French Revolution and of France, and a corresponding excess of attachment to Great Britain, as the only barrier against the universal, dreaded empire of France.

2. A strong aversion to republics and republican government, with a profound impression that our experiment of a confederated republic had failed for want of virtue in the people.

3. A deep jealousy of the Southern and Western states, and a strong disgust at the effect of the slave representation in the Constitution of the United States.

4. A belief that Mr. Jefferson and Mr. Madison were servilely devoted to France, and under French influence.

Every one of these sentiments weakened the attachments of those who held them to the Union, and consequently their patriotism. . . .

It will be no longer necessary to search for the objects of the Hartford Convention. They are apparent from the whole tenor of their report and resolutions, compared with the journal of their proceedings. They are admitted in the first and last paragraphs of the report, and they were:

To wait for the issue of the negotiation at Ghent.

In the event of the continuance of the war, to take one more chance of getting into their own hands the administration of the general government.

On the failure of that, a secession from the Union and a New England confederacy.

To these ends, and not to the defense of this part of the country against the foreign enemy, all the measures of the Hartford Convention were adapted. . . .

D. THE DAWN OF PEACE

1. The London *Times* Cries Vengeance (1814)

Congress had declared war on Britain in the confident expectation that Napoleon would pin down British forces in Europe. After his power crumbled in 1814, three veteran armies of Redcoats were readied for invasions of the United States. The powerful London *Times*, eager for a thrashing of the Yankees, thundered against any reasonable peace terms. Ascertain why this journal believed that the Madison administration was untrustworthy and treacherous; why it was willing to trust the Federalists; and in what respects it was most conspicuously unfair.

. . . Let us direct our attention to the situation of America. By a gradual but entire subversion of the Constitution, the faction who are impregnated with the most deep and rancorous hatred of Britain had possessed themselves of the supreme power in the United States. They abused that sacred trust, to put, as they fondly hoped, the last hand to our ruin.

Let the memorable era of June, 1812, be ever had in remembrance, when these wretches joined with the Corsican tyrant [Napoleon] to overwhelm Russia and Britain at once. Scepticism itself cannot doubt of the infamous

1. London *Times*, May 24, 1814.

pre-concert. Charity, that hopeth all things, and believeth all things, cannot persuade itself that the motive was not most black and malignant.

Let us follow up their attack on Canada, the real object of their hostilities. Let us recall to mind their insidious proclamations to the British subjects to revolt, and their invitation to the Indians to join them. Foiled and defeated in these views, let us not forget that with the most unblushing effrontery they turned round and accused us of inhumanity in accepting the proffered cooperation of the very Indians whom they first courted to their standard. . . .

Is it possible that men who have carried on hostilities with so diabolical a spirit can have relaxed their whole system, and that so suddenly, from any other motive than fear? They are struck to the heart with terror for their impending punishment—and oh! may no false liberality, no mistaken lenity, no weak and cowardly policy interpose to save them from the blow! Strike. Chastise the savages; for such they are, in a much truer sense than the followers of Tecumseh or The Prophet.

Let us not be so foolishly confiding as to trust again to the honour or veracity of the Madisons, the Jeffersons, or any of the tribe, to whom we are well aware that those principles are altogether unknown. A real peace with them is impossible. But, as we predicted of Bonaparte, so, and with much more confidence, do we predict of them—their fall is at hand, if we do but persevere in a vigorous prosecution of hostilities. . . .

With Madison and his perjured set, no treaty can be made; for no oath can bind them. But his political antagonists are men not insensible of the many claims we have on their friendship, not unmindful of the common origin and common principles which they share with us.

2. The London *Times* Bemoans Peace (1814)

The British had expected to topple the United States by their invasion of northern New York in 1814, but the Redcoats were turned back at Plattsburg by Thomas Macdonough's spectacular victory on Lake Champlain. The hard-pressed Americans had meanwhile completely abandoned their demands on impressment and other issues, and gladly accepted the stalemate Treaty of Ghent. The grim reality was that the British had begun the war with over eight hundred ships in their navy, the Americans with sixteen. When the war ended, the British still dominated the seas, while the Americans, although they had won a dozen or so single-ship duels, were down to two or three warships. But one would hardly have thought so from the following anguished outburst in the London *Times*, which irresponsibly urged non-ratification of the treaty. Conclude why this influential journal was so unhappy, and whether it presented a false picture of British operations.

. . . [The European powers] will reflect that we have attempted to force our principles on America, and have failed. Nay, that we have retired from the combat with the stripes yet bleeding on our backs—with the recent defeats at Plattsburg and on Lake Champlain unavenged. To make peace at such a moment, they will think, betrays a deadness to the feelings of honour, and shows a timidity of disposition, inviting further insult.

2. *Ibid.,* Dec. 30, 1814.

John Bull, in the person of the king, indicates the pain which the fermented juice of the pear, called perry, will produce. This caricature refers to O. H. Perry's great victory on Lake Erie in 1813, with the names of his ships indicated. The "boxing match" refers to the capture of the British Boxer *by the American* Enterprise. *B. J. Lossing,* Pictorial Field-Book of the War of 1812, *1868.*

. . . "Two or three of our ships have struck to a force vastly superior!"—No, not two or three, but many on the ocean, and whole squadrons [to Perry and Macdonough] on the Lakes. And their numbers are to be viewed with relation to the comparative magnitude of the two navies. Scarcely is there one American ship of war which has not to boast a victory over the British flag; scarcely one British ship in thirty or forty that has beaten an American.

Our seamen, it is urged, have on all occasions fought bravely. Who denies it? Our complaint is that with the bravest seamen and the most powerful navy in the world, we retire from the contest when the balance of defeat is so heavily against us. Be it accident or be it misconduct, we enquire not now into the cause. The certain, the inevitable consequences are what we look to, and these may be summed up in few words—the speedy growth of an American navy—and the recurrence of a new and much more formidable American war. . . .

The [American] people—naturally vain, boastful, and insolent—have been filled with an absolute contempt of our maritime power, and a furious eagerness to beat down our maritime pretensions. Those passions, which have been inflamed by success, could only have been cooled by what in vulgar and emphatic language has been termed "a sound flogging." But, unfortunately, our Christian meekness has induced us rather to kiss the rod

than to retaliate its exercise. Such false and feeble humanity is not calculated for the guidance of nations.

War is, indeed, a tremendous engine of justice. But when justice wields
the sword, she must be inflexible. Looking neither to the right nor to the
left, she must pursue her blow until the evil is clean rooted out. This is not
blind rage, or blinder revenge; but it is a discriminating, a calm, and even
a tender calculation of consequences. Better is it that we should grapple
with the young lion when he is first fleshed with the taste of our flocks than
wait until, in the maturity of his strength, he bears away at once both
sheep and shepherd.

3. A Federalist Editor Welcomes Peace (1815)

The American people were so disunited, tax-burdened, and war-weary that they
greeted the news of the Treaty of Ghent with frenzied joy, even though they knew
nothing of its contents and rather expected to lose some territory to British occupiers.
The arch-Federalist New York *Evening Post* joined the happy chorus. Decide from
its editorial why the financial community was pleased, and how good a prophet the
editor was.

. . . [The treaty] has come, and the public expressions of tumultuous joy
and gladness that spontaneously burst forth from all ranks and degrees of
people on Saturday evening, without stopping to enquire the conditions,
evinced how really sick at heart they were of a war that threatened to
wring from them the remaining means of subsistence, and of which they
could neither see the object nor the end. . . .

In truth, the occasion called for the liveliest marks of sincere congratulation. Never, in our opinion, has there occurred so great a one since we
became an independent nation. Expresses of the glad tidings were instantly
dispatched in all directions—to Boston, Philadelphia, Providence, Albany,
etc., etc.

The country will now be convinced that the Federalists were right in
the opinion they have ever held, that during the despotism of Bonaparte
no peace was to be expected for their own country, and therefore they
publicly rejoiced at his downfall, and celebrated the restoration of the
Bourbons.

Men of property, particularly, should felicitate themselves, for they may
look back upon the perils they have just escaped with the same sensations
that the passenger in a ship experiences when, driving directly on the
breakers through the blunders of an ignorant pilot, he is unexpectedly
snatched from impending destruction by a sudden shifting of the wind.
Fears were entertained that it was really intended, like losing and desperate
gamblers, to find a pretense for never paying the public debt, in the magnitude of the sum: that a sponge would be employed in the last resort as the
favorite instrument to wipe off all scores at once. A principle nearly bordering on this was, not long ago, openly avowed on the floor of Congress by a

3. New York *Evening Post*, Feb. 13, 1815.

member from Virginia. Neither is it a small cause of congratulation that we are now to be delivered from that swarm of [Republican] leeches that have so long fastened upon the nation, and been sucking its blood. Their day is over. Let the nation rejoice.

What the terms of the peace are, we cannot tell. They will only be made known at Washington, by the dispatches themselves. But one thing I will venture to say now and before they are opened, and I will hazard my reputation upon the correctness of what I say, that when the terms are disclosed, it will be found that the government have not by this negotiation obtained one single avowed object for which they involved the country in this bloody and expensive war.

[*The editor did not risk much as a prophet; he had already been informed of the terms by London newspapers.*]

4. A Jeffersonian Journal Rejoices (1815)

The invading Redcoats had routed the militia and burned the government buildings in Washington in 1814. They also vengefully destroyed the press of the *Daily National Intelligencer,* the stalwart pro-administration newspaper (see p. 198) that had berated the British. But this disaster did not prevent the editor from joining the Federalist opposition in acclaiming the treaty. His enthusiasm was doubtless heightened by the fact that news of General Jackson's incredible victory at the Battle of New Orleans (fought two weeks after the signing of the Treaty of Ghent) arrived in Washington early in February, shortly before a copy of the peace pact. Note the most glaring evidences of partisanship and the most obvious warpings of the historical record, and account for them.

We will not mock the feelings of our readers at this moment by any diffuse comment on the exhilarating news the last eight-and-forty hours have announced to us. We will only say—

Americans! Rejoice!

For that, by the unsurpassed exploits of your army and navy, and the consummate wisdom of your statesmen, you have achieved an honorable peace with one of the most powerful nations on the globe, with whom you were at war—

Republicans, rejoice!

For that the men of your heart, those virtuous patriots whom you have cherished as the apple of your eye, have conducted you through a glorious contest, under every disadvantage, to an honorable peace with a powerful and arrogant enemy—

Federalists, rejoice!

For that your opposition has been unavailing in checking the measures of your government; and that your Hartford Conventions, your plots and counterplots, have not arrested the march of the republic to the heights of fame and glory—

Rejoice, all men, of whatever party ye be!

4. *Daily National Intelligencer* (Washington), Feb. 16, 1815.

For that, while the effusion of blood is stayed, and the blessings of peace restored to our beloved land, your country is proudly exalted among the Nations of the Earth by her success in an honorable struggle, commenced in self-defense, and terminating in a recognition of the justice of her cause.

THOUGHT PROVOKERS

1. It has been said that the Indians could no more sell their land than the birds could sell a piece of the sky. Comment. Why did the United States fight Britain in 1812? Was the war really one for a free sea? What single factor, if removed, would have averted hostilities? Discuss pro and con the charge that the War Hawks were hypocrites, and come to a conclusion.

2. Why were the Federalists so bitterly opposed to the war? Were their grievances legitimate? Did America really stab England in the back? How firmly united must a people be before it is safe to lead them into war?

3. Were the Federalists victims of the "tyranny of the majority" or just poor losers? Were they guilty of disloyalty during the war? How would you define disloyalty? treason? (See Constitution, Art. III, Sec. III.) How much free speech is permissible in wartime?

4. If the peace of Ghent was so unpopular in England and so popular in America, what conclusions would you draw as to which side won? Comment on the common statement that the United States has never won a peace or lost a war. How does one determine the victor in a war: by battles won, territory seized, casualties inflicted, or what?

FURTHER EXPLORATION

General: A. L. Burt, *The United States, Great Britain, and British North America* (1940); Bradford Perkins, *Prologue to War: England and the United States, 1805–1812* (1961); F. F. Beirne, *The War of 1812* (1925). **Roots of War:** J. W. Pratt, *Expansionists of 1812* (1925); Reginald Horsman, *The Causes of the War of 1812* (1962). **Brink of Hostilities:** Irving Brant, *James Madison: The President, 1809–1812* (1956). **Disloyalty:** S. E. Morison, *Life and Letters of Harrison Gray Otis* (2 vols., 1913). **Peace:** Henry Adams, *History of the United States* (1891), vol. IX; F. A. Updyke, *The Diplomacy of the War of 1812* (1915); Irving Brant, *James Madison: Commander in Chief, 1812–1835* (1961); F. L. Engelman, *The Peace of Christmas Eve* (1962).

Recent: R. H. Brown, *The Republic in Peril: 1812* (1964); H. L. Coles, *The War of 1812* (1965) [paperback]; P. C. T. White, *A Nation on Trial: America and the War of 1812* (1965).

Chapter 12

The Flowering of Nationalism

The war [of 1812] has renewed and reinstated the national feelings and character which the Revolution had given, and which were daily lessened.

ALBERT GALLATIN, 1816

PROLOGUE: Partly as a result of Jackson's exhilarating victory at New Orleans, an outburst of nationalism followed the otherwise frustrating War of 1812. The new unifying impulse revealed itself in a successful demand for the protective tariff of 1816; in the clamor for roads and canals at federal expense (partly thwarted by presidential vetoes); in the epochal decisions of Chief Justice Marshall that narrowed the limits of state sovereignty; and in President Monroe's stern warning to the European powers to keep their monarchical systems at home and their hands off the Americas. The chief damper on nationalism was the ominous sectional quarrel over slavery in Missouri. The stormy issue was at length sidetracked for a period of years by the Missouri Compromise of 1820, which enabled the nation to grow strong enough to resist the formidable attempts at disunion beginning in the late 1850's.

A. THE FIGHT OVER INTERNAL IMPROVEMENTS

1. Representative Calhoun Pleads for Federal Aid (1817)

John C. Calhoun of South Carolina, frontier-born and Yale-educated, became a plantation aristocrat by marrying his cousin. A tall, commanding figure, with a heavy shock of hair, a piercing eye, an eloquent tongue, and a steel-trap mind, he was the intellectual giant of his day. But there were two Calhouns. The ambitious young man was a fiery War Hawk of 1812, an ardent patriot and nationalist, a devoted Unionist, a tariff protectionist, a champion of a national bank, a loose constructionist of the Constitution at the expense of the states, and an advocate of internal improvements financed by federal sources. The older Calhoun of the 1830's and 1840's, his presidential ambitions frustrated, was an introverted South Carolinian, a Southern sectionalist, an inflexible states'-righter, a nullifier, an incipient secessionist, and a strict interpreter of the Constitution to the advantage of the states. In 1816, while still a flaming nationalist, he sponsored a bill in the House designed to provide a permanent fund for internal improvements from the bonus paid the federal government by the Bank of the United States. In analyzing the following speech by Calhoun in support of the bonus bill, ascertain his strongest argument for this type of internal improvement, and determine what is most surprising about his position in the light of his subsequent career.

Let it not be said that internal improvements may be wholly left to the enterprise of the states and of individuals. I know that much may justly be

1. R. K. Crallé, ed., *Speeches of John C. Calhoun* . . . (1888), II, 187–92 (Feb. 4, 1817).

expected to be done by them; but, in a country so new and so extensive as ours, there is room enough for all the general and state governments and individuals in which to exert their resources. But many of the improvements contemplated are on too great a scale for the resources of the states or individuals; and many of such a nature as the rival jealousy of the states, if left alone, would prevent. They require the resources and the general superintendence of this government to effect and complete them. . . .

In many respects, no country of equal population and wealth possesses equal materials of power with ours. The people, in muscular power, in hardy and enterprising habits, and in lofty and gallant courage, are surpassed by none. In one respect, and, in my opinion, in one only, are we materially weak. We occupy a surface prodigiously great in proportion to our numbers. The common strength is brought to bear with great difficulty on the point that may be menaced by any enemy. It is our duty, then, as far as in the nature of things it can be effected, to counteract this weakness.

Good roads and canals, judiciously laid out, are the proper remedy. In the recent war, how much did we suffer for the want of them! Besides the tardiness and the consequential inefficacy of our military movements, to what an increased expense was the country put for the article of transportation alone! In the event of another war, the saving, in this particular, would go far towards indemnifying us for the expense of constructing the means of transportation. . . .

But, on this subject of national power, what can be more important than a perfect unity in every part, in feelings and sentiments? And what can tend more powerfully to produce it than overcoming the effects of distance? No state enjoying freedom ever occupied anything like as great an extent of country as this republic. One hundred years ago, the most profound philosophers did not believe it to be even possible. They did not suppose it possible that a pure republic could exist on as great a scale even as the island of Great Britain.

What then was considered as chimerical, we now have the felicity to enjoy. And, what is more remarkable, such is the happy mould of our government— so wisely are the state and general powers arranged—that much of our political happiness derives its origin from the extent of our republic. It has exempted us from most of the causes which distracted the small republics of antiquity. Let it not, however, be forgotten—let it be forever kept in mind—that it exposes us to the greatest of all calamities—next to the loss of liberty—and even to that in its consequence—disunion.

We are great, and rapidly—I was about to say fearfully—growing. This is our pride and our danger; our weakness and our strength. Little does he deserve to be entrusted with the liberties of this people who does not raise his mind to these truths. We are under the most imperious obligation to counteract every tendency to disunion. . . . Whatever impedes the intercourse of the extremes with this, the center of the republic, weakens the union. The more enlarged the sphere of commercial circulation—the more extended that of social intercourse—the more strongly are we bound together —the more inseparable are our destinies.

Those who understand the human heart best, know how powerfully distance tends to break the sympathies of our nature. Nothing—not even dissimilarity of language—tends more to estrange man from man. Let us, then, bind the republic together with a perfect system of roads and canals. Let us conquer space. It is thus the most distant parts of the republic will be brought within a few days' travel of the center; it is thus that a citizen of the West will read the news of Boston still moist from the press. The mail and the press are the nerves of the body politic. By them, the slightest impression made on the most remote parts is communicated to the whole system. And the more perfect the means of transportation, the more rapid and true the vibration. . . .

Such, then, being the obvious advantages of internal improvements, why should the House hesitate to commence the system? I understand there are, with some members, constitutional objections. . . . It is mainly urged that the Congress can only apply the public money in execution of the [Constitution's] enumerated powers. I am no advocate for refined arguments on the Constitution. The instrument was not intended as a thesis for the logician to exercise his ingenuity on. It ought to be construed with plain, good sense; and what can be more express than the Constitution on this very point?

2. Representative Robertson Trusts the States (1817)

Virginia-born Thomas B. Robertson, educated like Thomas Jefferson at the College of William and Mary, moved to Louisiana and became the state's first representative in Congress. Tall, handsome, and eloquent, he retained his Jeffersonian attachment to a strict interpretation of the Constitution: he would reserve to the states all powers not specifically enumerated as within the purview of the federal government. He therefore replied as follows to Calhoun's speech, which favored federally supported internal improvements. Form conclusions as to the validity of his arguments, especially in the light of subsequent "pork barrel" and "logrolling" legislation.

Good roads and canals are of undisputed importance. I agree in all the advantages which have been attributed to them; there is indeed but one opinion in this regard. Are there no other public works of equal consequence? What will be objected to establishing schools, clearing out and embanking rivers, deepening harbors, draining marshes? Why appropriate exclusively for the objects embraced by the bill?

The question now is, by what power are these and other improvements of a similar kind to be effected? Gentlemen contend that they belong to the general government. I am inclined to the opinion that they had better be left to the regulation of the states. They are in their nature internal; they are minute and involved in detail; they require a close and ready supervision. They are of the nature of police; they require, in fact, the agency

2. *Annals of Congress,* 14 Cong., 2 sess., II, cols. 864–66 (Feb. 4, 1817).

of officers and laws which are to be found only in the institutions of the individual states.

The general government, from its nature, from the force of the term, should engage in business of a general description; should provide for the general welfare; should make peace and war. I will not recapitulate the broadly extended powers which it possesses, and to which it should confine itself. A clear line of demarcation ought to be drawn between the United States and state governments. Interference ought to be avoided. Let the one attend to internal improvement, the other to the great concern of this nation. . . .

Before we pass, then, finally on this proposition, it is necessary to be assured that it involves no violation of the Constitution. I cannot agree in the loose manner of construing that instrument which has been recommended and adopted by my friend from South Carolina [Calhoun]. . . . If the United States have money to spare, let it be distributed among the states to be applied to works of internal improvement. The states are better judges of their wants and interests; they know best whether they most require roads or canals, or schools, or dykes, or embankments. They can more conveniently, too, give that attention which objects of this nature demand. They can more successfully provide against profuse and wasteful expenditure.

This plan, too, possesses other advantages. It will prevent the disgraceful scene which will be exhibited in this House when we shall be called upon to designate the position and course of the contemplated roads and canals, when all our local feelings will be up in arms, and, under a pretense of general benefit, we shall have in view exclusively the interests of the state or district which we represent.

[*Calhoun's bonus bill for internal improvements passed Congress in February, 1817. But President Madison, in his last official act, March 3, 1817, killed it with a veto. Although conceding that internal improvements at federal expense could be of "signal advantage to the general prosperity," he was induced to take a negative view, "seeing that such a power is not expressly given by the Constitution, and believing that it cannot be deduced from any part of it without an inadmissible latitude of construction . . ." (Richardson,* Messages and Papers, *I, 585).*]

B. THE MISSOURI STATEHOOD CONTROVERSY

1. Representative Taylor Reviles Slavery (1819)

The slaveholding territory of Missouri applied to Congress for admission as a state in 1819. Representative Tallmadge of New York touched off the fireworks when he proposed an amendment to the Missouri statehood bill (a) prohibiting any further introduction of slaves and (b) freeing at age twenty-five all children born to slave parents after the admission of the state. During the ensuing debates, a leading role was played by Representative John W. Taylor, a prominent anti-slavery leader from

1. *Ibid.,* 15 Cong., 2 sess., III, cols. 1174–76.

New York who was to serve for twenty consecutive years in the House. The South never forgave him, and later engineered his defeat for election as Speaker. In the light of his speech for the Tallmadge amendment, explain the apparent contradictions in the attitude of the South toward the Negro.

Having proved . . . our right to legislate in the manner proposed, I proceed to illustrate the propriety of exercising it. And here I might rest satisfied with reminding my [Southern] opponents of their own declarations on the subject of slavery. How often, and how eloquently, have they deplored its existence among them! What willingness, nay, what solicitude have they not manifested to be relieved from this burden! How have they wept over the unfortunate policy that first introduced slaves into this country! How have they disclaimed the guilt and shame of that original sin, and thrown it back upon their ancestors!

I have with pleasure heard these avowals of regret and confided in their sincerity. I have hoped to see its effects in the advancement of the cause of humanity. Gentlemen now have an opportunity of putting their principles into practice. If they have tried slavery and found it a curse, if they desire to dissipate the gloom with which it covers their land, I call upon them to exclude it from the Territory in question. Plant not its seeds in this uncorrupt soil. Let not our children, looking back to the proceedings of this day, say of them, as they have been constrained to speak of their fathers, "We wish their decision had been different. We regret the existence of this unfortunate population among us. But we found them here; we know not what to do with them. It is our misfortune; we must bear it with patience."

History will record the decision of this day as exerting its influence for centuries to come over the population of half our continent. If we reject the amendment and suffer this evil, now easily eradicated, to strike its roots so deep in the soil that it can never be removed, shall we not furnish some apology for doubting our sincerity when we deplore its existence? . . .

Mr. Chairman, one of the gentlemen from Kentucky (Mr. Clay) has pressed into his service the cause of humanity. He has pathetically urged us to withdraw our amendment and suffer this unfortunate population to be dispersed over the country. He says they will be better fed, clothed, and sheltered, and their whole condition will be greatly improved. . . .

Sir, my heart responds to the call of humanity. I will zealously unite in any practicable means of bettering the condition of this oppressed people. I am ready to appropriate a territory to their use, and to aid them in settling it—but I am not willing, I never will consent, to declare the whole country west of the Mississippi a market overt for human flesh. . . .

To the objection that this amendment will, if adopted, diminish the value of a species of property in one portion of the Union, and thereby operate unequally, I reply that if, by depriving slaveholders of the Missouri market, the business of raising slaves should become less profitable, it would be an effect incidentally produced, but is not the object of the measure. The law prohibiting the importation of foreign slaves was not passed for the purpose

PROPAGANDA AGAINST THE GROWING SLAVE TRADE

Slavery and slave trade in sight of U. S. Capitol, 1830. Library of Congress. Reproduced in D. L. Dumond, *Anti-Slavery*, 1961.

of enhancing the value of those then in the country, but that effect has been incidentally produced in a very great degree. . . .

It is further objected that the amendment is calculated to disfranchise our brethren of the South by discouraging their emigration to the country west of the Mississippi. . . . The description of emigrants may be affected, in some measure, by the amendment in question. If slavery shall be tolerated, the country will be settled by rich planters, with their slaves. If it shall be rejected, the emigrants will chiefly consist of the poorer and more laborious classes of society. If it be true that the prosperity and happiness of a country ought to constitute the grand object of its legislators, I cannot hesitate for a moment which species of population deserves most to be encouraged by the laws we may pass.

2. Representative Pinckney Upholds Slavery (1820)

Angered Southerners spoke so freely of secession and "seas of blood" during the Missouri debate that the aging Thomas Jefferson likened the issue to "a fire bell in the night." The argument inevitably involved the general problem of slavery, and the view of the South was eloquently presented, in a justly famous speech, by Representative Charles Pinckney of South Carolina. Vain, demagogic, and of questionable morals, he was nevertheless touched with genius. As one of the few surviving members of the Philadelphia Convention that had framed the Constitution in 1787, and as South Carolina's former governor and United States Senator, he was in a position to command attention. Ascertain his most convincing argument for slavery, and determine whether both South and North had genuine grounds for apprehension. Note what is the most alarming aspect of the speech.

A great deal has been said on the subject of slavery: that it is an infamous stain and blot on the states that hold them, not only degrading the slave,

2. *Ibid.,* 16 Cong., 1 sess., II, cols. 1323–28, *passim.*

but the master, and making him unfit for republican government; that it is contrary to religion and the law of God; and that Congress ought to do everything in their power to prevent its extension among the new states.

Now, sir, . . . is there a single line in the Old or New Testament either censuring or forbidding it [slavery]? I answer without hesitation, no. But there are hundreds speaking of and recognizing it. .   Hagar, from whom millions sprang, was an African slave, brought out of Egypt by Abraham, the father of the faithful and the beloved servant of the Most High; and he had, besides, three hundred and eighteen male slaves. The Jews, in the time of the theocracy, and the Greeks and Romans, had all slaves; at that time there was no nation without them.

If we are to believe that this world was formed by a great and omnipotent Being, that nothing is permitted to exist here but by his will, and then throw our eyes throughout the whole of it, we should form an opinion very different indeed from that asserted, that slavery was against the law of God. . . .

It will not be a matter of surprise to anyone that so much anxiety should be shown by the slaveholding states, when it is known that the alarm, given by this attempt to legislate on slavery, has led to the opinion that the very foundations of that kind of property are shaken; that the establishment of the precedent is a measure of the most alarming nature. . . . For, should succeeding Congresses continue to push it, there is no knowing to what length it may be carried.

Have the Northern states any idea of the value of our slaves? At least, sir, six hundred millions of dollars. If we lose them, the value of the lands they cultivate will be diminished in all cases one half, and in many they will become wholly useless. And an annual income of at least forty millions of dollars will be lost to your citizens, the loss of which will not alone be felt by the non-slaveholding states, but by the whole Union. For to whom, at present, do the Eastern states, most particularly, and the Eastern and Northern, generally, look for the employment of their shipping, in trans-porting our bulky and valuable products [cotton], and bringing us the manufactures and merchandises of Europe?

Another thing, in case of these losses being brought on us, and our being forced into a division of the Union, what becomes of your public debt? Who are to pay this, and how will it be paid? In a pecuniary view of this subject, therefore, it must ever be the policy of the Eastern and Northern states to continue connected with us.

But, sir, there is an infinitely greater call upon them, and this is the call of justice, of affection, and humanity. Reposing at a great distance, in safety, in the full enjoyment of all their federal and state rights, unattacked in either, or in their individual rights, can they, with indifference, or ought they, to risk, in the remotest degree, the consequences which this measure may produce? These may be the division of this Union and a civil war. Knowing that whatever is said here must get into the public prints, I am

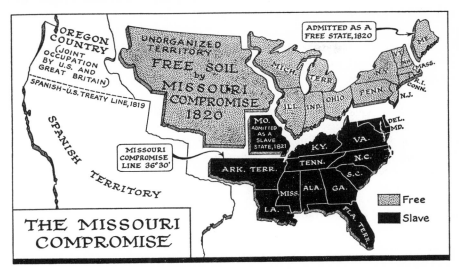

THE MISSOURI COMPROMISE

unwilling, for obvious reasons, to go into the description of the horrors which such a war must produce, and ardently pray that none of us may ever live to witness such an event.

[*Other Southerners, so reported Representative William Plumer, Jr., of New Hampshire, "throw out many threats, and talk loudly of separation." Even "Mr. [Henry] Clay declares that he will go home and raise troops, if necessary, to defend the people of Missouri." But the Tallmadge amendment was rejected and the famed Missouri Compromise was finally hammered out in 1820. The delicate sectional balance subsisting between the eleven free states and eleven slave states was cleverly preserved: Maine (a part of Massachusetts) was to come in as a free state and Missouri as a slave state. But henceforth slavery was forbidden elsewhere in the Louisiana Purchase territory north of the line of 36° 30'—the southern border of Missouri. John Quincy Adams wrote prophetically: "I take it for granted that the present question is a mere preamble—a title page to a great tragic volume."*]

3. A Connecticut Anti-Slavery Outcry (1820)

It would be an error to assume that the clash over Missouri was prompted solely by sectional and economic differences. The forebears of the extreme Garrisonian abolitionists in New England were deeply disturbed by human bondage. The Boston *Gazette* printed a "Black List" of the members of Congress from the free states who had supported the Missouri Compromise. A writer signing himself "Brutus," and attributing undue weight to three Connecticut members of Congress, published the following indictment in a New Haven newspaper. Judge what it reveals about abolitionism in New England eleven years before Garrison launched his *Liberator*.

Slavery is extended to Missouri, by a majority of three.

The deed is done. The galling chains of slavery are forged for myriads

3. New Haven *Journal*, March 14, 1820; facsimile reproduction in Glover Moore, *The Missouri Controversy, 1819–1821* (1953), p. 196.

yet unborn. Humble yourselves in the dust, ye high-minded citizens of Connecticut. Let your cheeks be red as crimson. On *your* representatives rests the stigma of this foul disgrace. It is a stain of blood, which oceans of tears and centuries of repentance can never obliterate. The names of LANMAN, STEVENS, and FOOT will go down to posterity with the name of Judas.* Their memory will be preserved in the execrations of the good, in the groans and sighs of the oppressed, and they will be remembered by the proud oppressor himself in THE DAY OF RETRIBUTION. That day will surely come, for God is just. But for *their* vote future millions now destined to the whips and scourges of the inhuman slavedealer might have breathed the air of freedom and of happiness.

* The writer does not mean to intimate that, like Judas, these men were *bribed*. The public will judge of their motives for themselves.

C. JOHN MARSHALL AND THE SUPREME COURT

1. Marshall Sanctions the Bank (1819)

Jefferson and Hamilton had clashed over the constitutionality of the monopolistic Bank of the United States in 1791 (see p. 151). Nearly three decades later Chief Justice John Marshall, a die-hard Hamiltonian Federalist, settled the issue judicially when he led a unanimous Supreme Court in a sweeping decision in the case of McCulloch *vs.* Maryland. Certain branches of the Second Bank of the United States, guilty of reckless speculation and even fraud, had incurred popular hatred. As a consequence, Maryland undertook to stamp out a branch of the Bank by a prohibitory tax. In upholding the constitutionality of the Bank and its branches, Marshall invoked the "necessary and proper" clause of the Constitution to the advantage of the national government. In fact, he used almost the exact words of Hamilton in 1791. In denying the right of a state to destroy by taxation an arm of the federal government, Marshall ringingly reasserted the supremacy of the central regime over the states. Ascertain his most convincing argument, and what probably would have happened to the federal authority if the Court had upheld Maryland.

That the power of taxation is one of vital importance; that it is retained by the states; that it is not abridged by the grant of a similar power to the government of the Union; that it is to be concurrently exercised by the two governments—are truths which have never been denied. But such is the paramount character of the Constitution that its capacity to withdraw any subject from the action of even this power is admitted. The states are expressly forbidden to lay any duties on imports or exports, except what may be absolutely necessary for executing their inspection laws. . . . The same paramount character would seem to restrain . . . a state from such other exercise of this power as is in its nature incompatible with, and repugnant to, the constitutional laws of the Union. A law absolutely repugnant to another, as entirely repeals that other as if express terms of repeal were used.

1. 4 Wheaton 316 (pp. 432–33, 436, 437).

On this ground the counsel for the Bank place its claim to be exempted from the power of a state to tax its operations. There is no express provision for the case, but the claim has been sustained on a principle which so entirely pervades the Constitution, is so intermixed with the materials which compose it, so interwoven with its web, so blended with its texture, as to be incapable of being separated from it without rending it into shreds.

This great principle is that the Constitution, and the laws made in pursuance thereof, are supreme; that they control the constitutions and laws of the respective states, and cannot be controlled by them. From this, which may be almost termed an axiom, other propositions are deduced as corollaries. . . . These are: 1. That a power to create implies a power to preserve. 2. That a power to destroy, if wielded by a different hand, is hostile to, and incompatible with, these powers to create and preserve. 3. That where this repugnancy exists, that authority which is supreme must control, not yield to that over which it is supreme. . . .

That the power to tax involves the power to destroy; that the power to destroy may defeat and render useless the power to create; that there is a plain repugnance in conferring on one government a power to control the constitutional measures of another . . . are propositions not to be denied. . . .

If we apply the principle for which the state of Maryland contends, to the Constitution generally, we shall find it capable of changing totally the character of that instrument. We shall find it capable of arresting all the measures of the government, and of prostrating it at the foot of the states. The American people have declared their Constitution, and the laws made in pursuance thereof, to be supreme; and this principle would transfer the supremacy, in fact, to the states.

If the states may tax one instrument employed by the government in the execution of its powers, they may tax any and every other instrument. They may tax the mail; they may tax the mint; they may tax patent rights; they may tax the papers of the custom-house; they may tax judicial process; they may tax all the means employed by the government, to an excess which would defeat all the ends of government. This was not intended by the American people. They did not design to make their government dependent on the states. . . .

The question is, in truth, a question of supremacy. And if the right of the states to tax the means employed by the general government be conceded, the declaration that the Constitution, and the laws made in pursuance thereof, shall be the supreme law of the land, is empty and unmeaning declamation.

2. A Maryland Editor Dissents (1819)

Maryland hotheads reacted vehemently against their setback in the famous Bank case. Outspoken Hezekiah Niles of Baltimore, editor from 1811 to 1836 of the most influential weekly in the country, expressed grave concern. He did not believe that

2. *Niles' Weekly Register*, XVI (1819), 41, 43.

Congress, in 1791, had been empowered to charter the first Bank of the United States. Assess the validity of his states'-rights argument, and determine whether he is more concerned about the monopolistic power of the Bank than he is about the encroachment on states' rights.

. . . A deadly blow has been struck at the sovereignty of the states, and from a quarter so far removed from the people as to be hardly accessible to public opinion. It is needless to say that we allude to the decision of the Supreme Court in the case of McCulloch *versus* the State of Maryland, by which it is established that the states cannot tax the Bank of the United States.

We are yet unacquainted with the grounds of this alarming decision, but of this are resolved—that nothing but the tongue of an angel can convince us of its compatibility with the Constitution of the United States, in which a power to grant acts of incorporation is not delegated [to the federal government], and all powers not delegated are retained.

Far be it from us to be thought as speaking disrespectfully of the Supreme Court, or to subject ourselves to the suspicion of a "contempt" of it. We do not impute corruption to the judges, nor intimate that they have been influenced by improper feelings. They are great and learned men; but still, only men. And, feeling as we do—as if the very stones would cry out if we did not speak on this subject—we will exercise our right to do it, and declare that, if the Supreme Court is not mistaken in its construction of the Constitution of the United States, or that [if] another definition cannot be given to it by some act of the states, their sovereignty is at the mercy of their creature—Congress. It is not on account of the Bank of the United States that we speak thus . . . it is but a drop in the bucket compared with the principles established by the decision, which appear to us to be these:

1. That Congress has an unlimited right to grant acts of incorporation!

2. That a company incorporated by Congress is exempted from the common operation of the laws of the state in which it may be located!! . . .

We repeat it: it is not on account of the Bank of the United States that we are thus moved. Our sentiments are on record that we did not wish the destruction of that institution but, fearing the enormous power of the corporation, we were zealous that an authority to arrest its deleterious influence might be vested in responsible hands, for it has not got any soul. Yet this solitary institution may *not* subvert the liberties of our country, and command every one to bow down to it as Baal. It is the principle of it that alarms us, as operating against the unresigned rights of the states.

3. Brickbats for John Marshall (1835)

The last Federalist administration expired with the departure of John Adams in 1801. Yet Chief Justice Marshall, an eleventh-hour Adams appointee, inflexibly handed down Federalist decisions for thirty-four years. Thomas Jefferson, resenting the centralizing and anti-states'-rights bias of his distant cousin, wrote despairingly

3. New York *Evening Post*, July 8, 1835. The long-time editor-in-chief of this newspaper, the eminent poet-journalist William Cullen Bryant, was then absent in Europe.

in 1821, "It is a misnomer to call a government republican in which a branch of the supreme power is independent of the nation." These views were shared by the New York *Evening Post,* the most influential Democratic newspaper in the metropolis. It was then being edited by the fiery and outspoken William Leggett, who during his career became involved in several dueling affairs. Decide what was most debatable about the following judgment (presumably Leggett's), and what was probably most offensive to Marshall's admirers.

The Philadelphia papers of yesterday bring us intelligence of the death of Chief Justice John Marshall, of Virginia, in the eightieth year of his age. He retained his faculties to the last, and a few days before his death is said to have composed an inscription for his own tomb.

Judge Marshall was a man of very considerable talents and acquirements, and great amiableness of private character. His political doctrines, unfortunately, were of the ultra-federal or aristocratic kind. He was one of those who, with Hamilton, distrusted the virtue and intelligence of the people, and was in favor of a strong and vigorous general government, at the expense of the rights of the states and of the people. His judicial decisions of all questions involving political principles have been uniformly on the side of implied powers and a free construction of the Constitution, and such also has been the uniform tendency of his writings.

That he was sincere in these views we do not express a doubt, nor that he truly loved his country. But that he has been, all his life long, a stumbling block and impediment in the way of democratic principles no one can deny. And his situation, therefore, at the head of an important tribunal, constituted in utter defiance of the very first principles of democracy, has always been to us, as we have before frankly stated, an occasion of lively regret. That he is at length removed from that station is a source of satisfaction, while at the same time we trust we entertain a proper sentiment for the death of a good and exemplary man.

D. LAUNCHING THE MONROE DOCTRINE

1. Jefferson Turns Pro-British (1823)

Stirred by the Napoleonic upheaval, most of Spain's colonies in the Americas threw off the monarchical yoke and set themselves up as independent republics. Late in 1823 rumors were afloat in Europe that the great powers—Russia, Austria, Prussia, France (loosely called the Holy Alliance)—were planning to crush the upstart colonials and restore Spanish misrule. British Foreign Secretary Canning, fearful that these newly opened markets would be lost to British merchants, proposed to the American minister in London, Richard Rush, that the United States and Britain issue a joint warning against foreign intervention in Spanish America. President Monroe sought the advice of ex-President Jefferson, the eighty-year-old Sage of Monticello. Remembering that Jefferson had been anti-alliance, anti-war, and anti-British, note what is curious about his response, and determine why he takes the stand that he does.

Dear Sir, The question presented by the letters you have sent me is the most momentous which has ever been offered to my contemplation since

1. P. L. Ford, ed., *Writings of Thomas Jefferson* (1899), X, 277–78 (Oct. 24, 1823).

that of Independence. That made us a nation; this sets our compass and points the course which we are to steer through the ocean of time opening on us. And never could we embark on it under circumstances more auspicious.

Our first and fundamental maxim should be never to entangle ourselves in the broils of Europe. Our second, never to suffer Europe to intermeddle with cis-Atlantic affairs. America—North and South—has a set of interests distinct from those of Europe, and peculiarly her own. She should therefore have a system of her own, separate and apart from that of Europe. While the last is laboring to become the domicile of despotism, our endeavor should surely be to make our hemisphere that of freedom.

One nation, most of all, could disturb us in this pursuit. She now offers to lead, aid, and accompany us in it. By acceding to her proposition, we detach her from the bands, bring her mighty weight into the scale of free government, and emancipate a continent [South America] at one stroke, which might otherwise linger in doubt and difficulty.

Great Britain is the nation which can do us the most harm of any one, or all on earth. And with her on our side, we need not fear the whole world. With her, then, we should most sedulously cherish a cordial friendship; and nothing would tend more to knit our affections than to be fighting once more, side by side, in the same cause.

Not that I would purchase even her amity at the price of taking part in her wars. But the war in which the present proposition might engage us, should that be its consequence, is not her war, but ours. Its object is to introduce and establish the American system of keeping out of our land all foreign powers, of never permitting those of Europe to intermeddle with the affairs of our nations. It is to maintain our own principle, not to depart from it. And if, to facilitate this, we can effect a division in the body of the European powers, and draw over to our side its most powerful member, surely we should do it.

But I am clearly of Mr. Canning's opinion that it will prevent instead of provoking war. With Great Britain withdrawn from their scale and shifted into that of our two continents, all Europe combined would not undertake such a war. For how would they propose to get at either enemy without superior fleets? . . .

But we have first to ask ourselves a question. Do we wish to acquire to our own confederacy any one or more of the Spanish provinces?

I candidly confess that I have ever looked on Cuba as the most interesting addition which could ever be made to our system of states. The control which, with Florida Point, this island would give us over the Gulf of Mexico . . . would fill up the measure of our political well-being. Yet, as I am sensible that this can never be obtained, even with her own consent, but by war; and its independence, which is our second interest (and especially its independence of England), can be secured without it, I have no hesitation in abandoning my first wish to future chances, and accepting its independence, with peace and the friendship of England, rather than its association at the expense of war and her enmity.

2. Adams Rejects a Joint Declaration (1823)

John Quincy Adams, Monroe's stiff-backed and lone-wolf Secretary of State, strongly suspected Canning's motives in approaching Minister Rush. Adams cleverly calculated that the potent British navy would not permit the newly opened Spanish-American markets to be closed, and he therefore concluded that the European monarchs were powerless to intervene, no matter what the United States did. He failed to share Secretary Calhoun's fear of the French army, which, acting as the avenging sword of the reactionary powers, was then crushing a republican uprising in Spain. Adams here records in his diary the relevant Cabinet discussion. Of the arguments that he advanced against cooperation with Canning, decide which was strongest, and why.

Washington, November 7th.—Cabinet meeting at the President's from half-past one till four. Mr. Calhoun, Secretary of War, and Mr. Southard, Secretary of the Navy, present. The subject for consideration was the confidential proposals of the British Secretary of State, George Canning, to Richard Rush, and the correspondence between them relating to the projects of the Holy Alliance upon South America. There was much conversation without coming to any definite point. The object of Canning appears to have been to obtain some public pledge from the government of the United States, ostensibly against the forcible interference of the Holy Alliance between Spain and South America, but really or especially against the acquisition to the United States themselves of any part of the Spanish-American possessions.

Mr. Calhoun inclined to giving a discretionary power to Mr. Rush to join in a declaration against the interference of the Holy Allies, if necessary, even if it should pledge us not to take Cuba or the province of Texas; because the power of Great Britain being greater than ours to seize upon them, we should get the advantage of obtaining from her the same declaration we should make ourselves.

I thought the cases not parallel. We have no intentions of seizing either Texas or Cuba. But the inhabitants of either or both may exercise their primitive rights, and solicit a union with us. They will certainly do no such thing to Great Britain. By joining with her, therefore, in her proposed declaration, we give her a substantial and perhaps inconvenient pledge against ourselves, and really obtain nothing in return.

Without entering now into the enquiry of the expediency of our annexing Texas or Cuba to our Union, we should at least keep ourselves free to act as emergencies may arise, and not tie ourselves down to any principle which might immediately afterwards be brought to bear against ourselves. . . .

I remarked that the communications recently received from the Russian

2. C. F. Adams, ed., *Memoirs of John Quincy Adams* (1875), VI, 177–79.

minister, Baron Tuyl, afforded, as I thought, a very suitable and convenient opportunity for us to take our stand against the Holy Alliance, and at the same time to decline the overture of Great Britain. It would be more candid, as well as more dignified, to avow our principles explicitly to Russia and France than to come in as a cockboat in the wake of the British man-of-war.

3. Monroe Warns the European Powers (1823)

Secretary Adams' cogent arguments helped turn President Monroe toward a go-it-alone policy. The President's annual message to Congress, quite surprisingly, contained several emphatic warnings. The Russians, who had caused some alarm by their push toward California, had privately shown a willingness to retreat to the southern bounds of present Alaska. But Monroe warned them and the other powers that there was now a closed season on colonizing in the Americas. On the other hand, the heroic struggle of the Greeks for independence from the Turks was creating some agitation in America for intervention, but Monroe made his "you stay out" warning seem fairer by volunteering a "we'll stay out" pledge. Note whether he aimed his main warning at non-colonization on the northwest coast or at the non-extension of monarchical systems to Spanish America; also to what extent he tied America's hands regarding the acquisition of Cuba or intervention in Greece. Did he actually threaten the European powers?

In the discussions to which this interest [Russia's on the northwest coast] has given rise, the occasion has been judged proper for asserting, as a principle in which the rights and interests of the United States are involved, that the American continents, by the free and independent condition which they have assumed and maintain, are henceforth not to be considered as subjects for the future colonization by any European powers. . . .

The political system of the Allied Powers [Holy Alliance] is essentially different . . . from that of America. This difference proceeds from that which exists in their respective [monarchical] governments; and to the defense of our own . . . this whole nation is devoted. We owe it, therefore, to candor and to the amicable relations existing between the United States and those powers to declare that we should consider any attempt on their part to extend their system to any portion of this hemisphere as dangerous to our peace and safety.

With the existing colonies or dependencies of any European power, we have not interfered and shall not interfere. But with the governments [of Spanish America] who have declared their independence and maintained it, and whose independence we have, on great consideration and on just principles, acknowledged, we could not view any interposition for the purpose of oppressing them, or controlling in any other manner their destiny, by any European power in any other light than as the manifestation of an unfriendly disposition toward the United States. . . .

Our policy in regard to Europe, which was adopted at an early stage of the wars which have so long agitated that quarter of the globe, nevertheless

3. J. D. Richardson, ed., *Messages and Papers of the Presidents* (1896), II, 209, 218–19.

remains the same, which is, not to interfere in the internal concerns of any of its powers; to consider the government *de facto* as the legitimate government for us; to cultivate friendly relations with it, and to preserve those relations by a frank, firm, and manly policy, meeting in all instances the just claims of every power, submitting to injuries from none.

But in regard to those [American] continents, circumstances are eminently and conspicuously different. It is impossible that the Allied Powers should extend their political system to any portion of either continent without endangering our peace and happiness. Nor can anyone believe that our southern brethren, if left to themselves, would adopt it of their own accord. It is equally impossible, therefore, that we should behold such interposition in any form with indifference.

E. REACTIONS TO THE MONROE DOCTRINE

1. A Baltimore Editor Exults (1823)

Monroe's defiant pronouncement touched a patriotic chord and evoked near-unanimous acclaim. The *Vermont Gazette*, with remarkable foresight, predicted that the message would "go down in our annals along with Washington's Farewell Address." Other journals guessed that the President must have had some secret information as to a possible hostile move by the "crowned conspirators" of Europe. The Baltimore *Morning Chronicle* gave vent to the following editorial bombast. Observe the evidences of blatant nationalism and particularly the world-dominating role envisaged for the United States.

We can tell . . . further that this high-toned, independent, and dignified message will not be read by the crowned heads of Europe without a revolting stare of astonishment. The conquerors of Bonaparte, with their laurels still green and blooming on their brows, and their disciplined animal machines, called armies, at their backs, could not have anticipated that their united force would so soon be defied by a young republic, whose existence, as yet, cannot be measured with the ordinary life of man.

This message itself constitutes an era in American history, worthy of commemoration. . . . We are confident that, on this occasion, we speak the great body of American sentiment, such as exulting millions are ready to re-echo. . . . We are very far from being confident that, if Congress occupy the high and elevated ground taken in the Message, it may not, under the smiles of Divine Providence, be the means of breaking up the Holy Alliance.

Of this we are positively sure: that all timidity, wavering, imbecility, and backwardness on our part will confirm these detested tyrants in their confederacy; paralyze the exertions of freedom in every country; accelerate the fall of those young sister republics whom we have recently recognized; and, perhaps, eventually destroy our own at the feet of absolute monarchy.

1. Baltimore *Morning Chronicle*, Dec. 5, 1823 in *Daily National Intelligencer* (Washington), Dec. 8, 1823.

2. Metternich Is Miffed (1824)

Only minor dissenting voices in the American press complained that the United States was not endangered and that the President had gone too far. A few surviving Federalist newspapers quibbled over the unwisdom of safeguarding the Patagonians and Eskimos from despotism. But the reaction in Continental Europe was uniformly unfavorable. The monarchical powers were not frightened away by Monroe's paper pronouncement; they were painfully aware that the thundering broadsides of the British navy stood between them and Spanish America. In their anger and frustration they vented their spleen against the upstart American republic, which had already given much unofficial aid and comfort to Spain's rebelling subjects. Prince Metternich, the Austrian chancellor and arch-priest of post-Napoleonic reaction, boiled over. Discover what seemed to bother him most and why.

These United States of America, which we have seen arise and grow, and which during their too short youth already meditated projects which they dared not then avow, have suddenly left a sphere too narrow for their ambition, and have astonished Europe by a new act of revolt, more unprovoked, fully as audacious, and no less dangerous than the former. They have distinctly and clearly announced their intention to set not only power against power, but, to express it more exactly, altar against altar. In their indecent declarations they have cast blame and scorn on the institutions of Europe most worthy of respect, on the principles of its greatest sovereigns, on the whole of those measures which a sacred duty no less than an evident necessity has forced our government to adopt to frustrate plans most criminal.

In permitting themselves these unprovoked attacks, in fostering revolutions wherever they show themselves, in regretting those which have failed, in extending a helping hand to those which seem to prosper, they lend new strength to the apostles of sedition, and reanimate the courage of every conspirator.

If this flood of evil doctrines and pernicious examples should extend over the whole of America, what would become of our religious and political institutions, of the moral force of our governments, and of that conservative system which has saved Europe from complete dissolution?

THOUGHT PROVOKERS

1. Explain how the drive for a protective tariff and internal improvements was a manifestation of post-war nationalism. It has been said that nationalism can be a force for both good and evil. Give illustrations of both types and form general conclusions.
2. If many leaders of the South acknowledged in 1820 that slavery was a baleful institution, why should they have fought its proposed abolition in Missouri?
3. Why was Marshall's famous Bank decision so unpopular in many parts of the country? Did it strengthen or weaken nationalism? Is a highly centralized government necessarily anti-democratic? Since Marshall was a Federalist, and

2. Quoted in Dexter Perkins, *The Monroe Doctrine, 1823–1826* (1927), p. 167. By permission of the Harvard University Press.

the Federalist Party had died out, was it consonant with democracy for him to be handing down Federalist decisions? Should he have been impeached?

4. It has been argued that in the long run the United States would have benefited more if Monroe had followed the advice of Jefferson and formed an accord with England. Argue both sides and come to a conclusion.

5. Why did the American public react so favorably to the Monroe Doctrine, and why did the European governments, then and later, never show any real liking for it?

FURTHER EXPLORATION

General: George Dangerfield, *The Era of Good Feelings* (1952). **Internal Improvements:** F. J. Turner, *Rise of the New West* (1906); G. R. Taylor, *The Transportation Revolution, 1815–1860* (1951). **Missouri Compromise:** Glover Moore, *The Missouri Controversy* (1953). **John Marshall:** A. J. Beveridge, *Life of John Marshall* (4 vols., 1916–1919); Charles Warren, *The Supreme Court in United States History* (2 vols., 1935). **Monroe Doctrine:** Dexter Perkins, *The Monroe Doctrine, 1823–1826* (1927); A. P. Whitaker, *The United States and the Independence of Latin America, 1800–1830* (1941); S. L. Falk, "Some Contemporary Views of the Monroe Doctrine: The United States Press in 1823," *The Americas*, XII (1955), 183–93; J. A. Logan, Jr., *No Transfer: An American Security Principle* (1961).

Recent: George Dangerfield, *The Awakening of American Nationalism, 1815–1828* (1965) [paperback]; F. S. Philbrick, *The Rise of the West, 1754–1830* (1965) [paperback]; P. C. Nagel, *One Nation Indivisible: The Union in American Thought, 1776–1861* (1964); G. M. Capers, *John C. Calhoun, Opportunist: A Reappraisal* (1960); R. N. Current, *John C. Calhoun* (1963) [paperback]; M. N. Rothbard, *The Panic of 1819* (1962); Frank Donovan, *Mr. Monroe's Message; The Story of the Monroe Doctrine* (1963); Bradford Perkins, *Castlereagh and Adams: England and the United States, 1812–1823* (1964).

Chapter 13

The Advent of Jacksonian Democracy, 1824-1830

The tendency of democracies is, in all things, to mediocrity.

JAMES FENIMORE COOPER, 1838

PROLOGUE: The explosive growth of the West, with its ocean of available land, weakened the old property qualifications for voting and stimulated the New Democracy of the "unwashed masses." General Jackson was the people's choice for President in 1824, but a disputed election and a so-called "corrupt bargain" with Speaker Henry Clay brought the austere J. Q. Adams to the White House for four frustrated years. The Jacksonites finally swept their military hero into the Presidency in 1829. Although Jefferson had introduced the "spoils system" on a minor scale, Jackson went much farther in his efforts to reward supporters, oust political enemies, and rid Washington of entrenched bureaucrats. Meanwhile Southern anger was boiling up over a tariff that had edged steadily upward in 1816, 1824, and 1828. One resulting flare-up was the turn taken by the classic Webster-Hayne debate of 1830 in the Senate. Webster immensely strengthened the ideal of Union by touching a nationalistic chord that vibrated in harmony with America's call to greatness.

A. BACKGROUNDS OF THE NEW DEMOCRACY

1. A Disgusting Spirit of Equality (1807)

Freedom of opportunity in America weakened class barriers and caused the "lower orders" to be more free and easy with their "betters." Such behavior was highly offensive to English visitors from a class-ridden society, especially to those who came in the 1830's and 1840's. C. W. Janson emigrated to America from England to make his fortune, lost his money, and vented his spleen in an ill-natured book which contained numerous unpleasant truths. Note what specific traits of the Americans he finds annoying, and which one the most annoying. Draw relevant conclusions as to whether manhood suffrage and bad manners necessarily went together.

Arrived at your [New England] inn, let me suppose, like myself, you had fallen in with a landlord who at the moment would condescend to take the trouble to procure you refreshment after the family hour. . . . He will sit by your side, and enter in the most familiar manner into conversation; which is prefaced, of course, with a demand of your business, and so forth. He will then start a political question (for here every individual is a politician), force your answer, contradict, deny, and, finally, be ripe for a quarrel, should you not acquiesce in all his opinions.

1. C. W. Janson, *The Stranger in America, 1793–1806* (1807), pp. 85–88.

When the homely meal is served up, he will often place himself opposite to you at the table, at the same time declaring that "though he thought he had eaten a hearty dinner, yet he will pick a bit with you."

Thus he will sit, drinking out of your glass, and of the liquor you are to pay for, belching in your face, and committing other excesses still more indelicate and disgusting. Perfectly inattentive to your accommodation, and regardless of your appetite, he will dart his fork into the best of the dish, and leave you to take the next cut.

If you arrive at the dinner hour, you are seated with "mine hostess" and her dirty children, with whom you have often to scramble for a plate, and even the servants of the inn. For liberty and equality level all ranks upon the road, from the host to the hostler.

The children, imitative of their free and polite papa, will also seize your drink, slobber in it, and often snatch a dainty bit from your plate. This is esteemed wit, and consequently provokes a laugh, at the expense of those who are paying for the board. . . .

The arrogance of domestics [servants] in this land of republican liberty and equality is particularly calculated to excite the astonishment of strangers. To call persons of this description servants, or to speak of their master or mistress, is a grievous affront.

Having called one day at the house of a gentleman of my acquaintance, on knocking at the door, it was opened by a servant-maid, whom I had never before seen, as she had not been long in his family. The following is the dialogue, word for word, which took place on this occasion:

"Is your master at home?"

"I have no master."

"Don't you live here?"

"I stay here."

"And who are you then?"

"Why, I am Mr. ———'s help. I'd have you to know, man, that I am no sarvant. None but negers are sarvants."

2. A Plea for Non-Property Suffrage (1841)

Until the days of Jacksonian democracy, property qualifications were generally demanded of all voters. In Virginia, where such restrictions discouraged immigration and encouraged emigration, a memorable convention met at Richmond in 1829–1830 to revise the state constitution. The result was a widening of the suffrage, in accord with the New Democracy, but a retention of certain property qualifications. One of the strongest arguments against change—and this argument was repeated in other conservative states—was that possession of property provided the surest guarantee of a permanent stake in the community. Grave dangers would presumably be courted if political power were put into the hands of the irresponsible, propertyless "bipeds of the forest." A popular author, George S. Camp, took sharp issue with the advocates of property qualifications in a long-lived book on democracy. In the light of his argument, decide whether it is true that the propertyless have as much of a stake in the community as the propertied.

2. George S. Camp, *Democracy* (1841), pp. 145–46.

All should have an equal voice in the public deliberations of the state, however unequal in point of circumstances, since human rights, by virtue of which alone we are entitled to vote at all, are the attributes of the man, not of his circumstances.

Should the right to vote, the characteristic and the highest prerogative of a freeman, be at the mercy of a casualty? I am rich today, worth my hundred thousands. But my wealth consists in stock and merchandise; it may be in storehouses, it may be upon the ocean. I have been unable to effect an insurance, or there is some concealed legal defect in my policy. The fire or the storms devour my wealth in an hour: am I the less competent to vote? Have I less of the capacity of a moral and intelligent being? Am I the less a good citizen? Is it not enough that I have been deprived of my fortune—must I be disfranchised by community?

My having a greater or less amount of property does not alter my rights. Property is merely the subject on which rights are exercised; its amount does not alter rights themselves. If it were otherwise, every one of us would be in some degree subject to some wealthier neighbor. And, if the representation of property were consistently carried out, the affairs of every community, instead of being governed by the majority of rational and intelligent beings, would be governed by a preponderance of houses, lands, stocks, plate, jewelry, merchandise, and money!

It is not true that one man has more at stake in the commonwealth than another. We all have our rights, and no man has anything more. If we look at the subject philosophically, and consider how much superior man is by nature to what he is by external condition, how much superior his real attributes are to what he acquires from the accidents of fortune, we shall then view the distinctions of rank and wealth in their true comparative insignificance, and make as little difference on these accounts with the political as with the moral man.

3. Crockett Advises Politicians (1836)

David Crockett—fabulous Tennessee frontiersman, Indian scout, rifleman, bear hunter, and braggart—was a homespun product of the New Democracy. His scanty six months of schooling led him to scorn both grammar and "book larnin'," although he became a justice of the peace, an elected militia colonel, and a member of the state legislature. When a joking remark prompted him to campaign for Congress, he overwhelmed his two opponents with a barrage of ridicule and humorous stories. Re-elected for two additional terms, he attracted wide attention in Washington with his backwoods dress, racy language, homely wit, shrewd common sense, and presumed naïveté regarding the aristocratic East. Ruggedly independent, he delighted Eastern conservatives by refusing to follow President Jackson on all issues. His advice to aspiring politicians, though offered in a jocular vein, reveals the debased tone of the new manhood-suffrage democracy. Note which of his recommended devices are still employed by politicians today.

3. David Crockett, *Exploits and Adventures in Texas* . . . (1836), pp. 56–59.

"Attend all public meetings," says I, "and get some friend to move that you take the chair. If you fail in this attempt, make a push to be appointed secretary. The proceedings of course will be published, and your name is introduced to the public. But should you fail in both undertakings, get two or three acquaintances, over a bottle of whisky, to pass some resolutions, no matter on what subject. Publish them, even if you pay the printer. It will answer the purpose of breaking the ice, which is the main point in these matters.

"Intrigue until you are elected an officer of the militia. This is the second step toward promotion, and can be accomplished with ease, as I know an instance of an election being advertised, and no one attending, the inn-keeper at whose house it was to be held, having a military turn, elected himself colonel of his regiment." Says I, "You may not accomplish your ends with as little difficulty, but do not be discouraged—Rome wasn't built in a day.

"If your ambition or circumstances compel you to serve your country, and earn three dollars a day, by becoming a member of the legislature, you must first publicly avow that the constitution of the state is a shackle upon free and liberal legislation, and is, therefore, of as little use in the present enlightened age as an old almanac of the year in which the instrument was framed. There is policy in this measure, for by making the constitution a mere dead letter, your headlong proceedings will be attributed to a bold and unshackled mind; whereas, it might otherwise be thought they arose from sheer mulish ignorance. 'The Government' has set the example in his [Jackson's] attack upon the Constitution of the United States, and who should fear to follow where 'the Government' leads?

"When the day of election approaches, visit your constituents far and wide. Treat liberally, and drink freely, in order to rise in their estimation, though you fall in your own. True, you may be called a drunken dog by some of the clean-shirt and silk-stocking gentry, but the real roughnecks will style you a jovial fellow. Their votes are certain, and frequently count double.

"Do all you can to appear to advantage in the eyes of the women. That's easily done. You have but to kiss and slabber [slobber over] their children, wipe their noses, and pat them on the head. This cannot fail to please their mothers, and you may rely on your business being done in that quarter.

"Promise all that is asked," said I, "and more if you can think of anything. Offer to build a bridge or a church, to divide a county, create a batch of new offices, make a turnpike, or anything they like. Promises cost nothing; therefore, deny nobody who has a vote or sufficient influence to obtain one.

"Get up on all occasions, and sometimes on no occasion at all, and make long-winded speeches, though composed of nothing else than wind. Talk of your devotion to your country, your modesty and disinterestedness, or on any such fanciful subject. Rail against taxes of all kinds, officeholders,

DAVY CROCKETT CONVULSES CONGRESSMEN
Davy Crockett Almanac for 1844. American Antiquarian Society.

and bad harvest weather; and wind up with a flourish about the heroes who fought and bled for our liberties in the times that tried men's souls. To be sure, you run the risk of being considered a bladder of wind, or an empty barrel. But never mind that; you will find enough of the same fraternity to keep you in countenance.

"If any charity be going forward, be at the top of it, provided it is to be advertised publicly. If not, it isn't worth your while. None but a fool would place his candle under a bushel on such an occasion.

"These few directions," said I, "if properly attended to, will do your business. And when once elected—why, a fig for the dirty children, the promises, the bridges, the churches, the taxes, the offices, and the subscriptions. For it is absolutely necessary to forget all these before you can become a thoroughgoing politician, and a patriot of the first water."

B. ADAMS AND THE "CORRUPT BARGAIN"

1. Adams Confers with Clay (1824–1825)

In the free-for-all presidential campaign of 1824, the popular vote pushed General Jackson well ahead. Strung out behind were Secretary of State J. Q. Adams, Secretary of the Treasury Crawford, and Speaker of the House Henry Clay, in that order. Since no candidate had won a majority in the Electoral College, the issue was thrown into the House of Representatives, with fourth-place Henry Clay eliminated. After a lengthy private conference with Adams, Clay, a former foe, threw his potent support to Adams, who consequently was declared elected, on February 9, 1825. Three days later President-elect Adams formally offered Clay the Secretaryship of State. Angry and suspicious Jacksonites promptly proclaimed that the Secretaryship was a part of

1 C. F. Adams, ed., *Memoirs of John Quincy Adams*, VI (1875), 444, 447, 457, 464–65.

the "corrupt bargain" by which Adams had purchased the Presidency of the United States. In reading the following relevant excerpts from Adams' diary, form conclusions as to whether some kind of deal was entered into for Clay's support.

[Dec. 15, 1824.] [Edward] Wyer [confidential informant] came also to the office [State Department], and told me that he had it from good authority that Mr. Clay was much disposed to support me, if he could at the same time be useful to himself. . . . I had conversation at dinner with Mr. Clay.

[Dec. 17, 1824, conversation with R. P. Letcher, member of the House of Representatives of Kentucky, Clay's state.] Letcher wished to know what my sentiments towards Clay were, and I told him without disguise that I harbored no hostility against him; that whatever of difference there had been between us had arisen altogether from him, and not from me. . . . He was sure Clay felt now no hostility to me. He had spoken respectfully of me, and was a man of sincerity. . . . The drift of all Letcher's discourse was much the same as Wyer had told me, that Clay would willingly support me if he could thereby serve himself, and the substance of his *meaning* was, that if Clay's friends could *know* that he would have a prominent share in the administration, that might induce them to vote for me, even in the face of instructions. But Letcher did not profess to have any authority from Clay for what he said, and he made no definite propositions. He spoke of his interview with me as altogether confidential, and in my answers to him I spoke in more general terms.

[Jan. 1, 1825, after a public dinner.] He [Clay] told me [in a whisper] that he should be glad to have with me soon some confidential conversation upon public affairs. I said I should be happy to have it whenever it might suit his convenience.

[Jan. 9, 1825.] Mr. Clay came at six, and spent the evening with me in a long conversation explanatory of the past and prospective of the future. He said that the time was drawing near when the choice must be made in the House of Representatives of a President from the three candidates presented by the electoral colleges; that he had been much urged and solicited with regard to the part in that transaction that he should take, and had not been five minutes landed at his lodgings before he had been applied to by a friend of Mr. Crawford's, in a manner so gross that it had disgusted him; that some of my friends also, disclaiming, indeed, to have any authority from me, had repeatedly applied to him, directly or indirectly, urging considerations personal to himself as motives to his cause.

He had thought it best to reserve for some time his determination to himself: first, to give a decent time for his own funeral solemnities as a candidate; and, secondly, to prepare and predispose all his friends to a state of neutrality between the three candidates who would be before the House, so that they might be free ultimately to take that course which

might be most conducive to the public interest. The time had now come
at which he might be explicit in his communication with me, and he had
for that purpose asked this confidential interview. He wished me, as far as
I might think proper, to satisfy him with regard to some principles of great
public importance, but without any personal considerations for himself.
In the question to come before the House between General Jackson, Mr.
Crawford, and myself, he had no hesitation in saying that his preference
would be for me.

[*At this point in his diary Adams, who was usually most painstaking, left a blank
space, as though he intended to fill in later the details of the conversation. Dr.
Samuel Flagg Bemis, his ablest biographer, states that "he let his conscience
slip." On January 23, 1825, two weeks after the secret conference, Clay wrote to
a correspondent that he believed he could enter the Cabinet "in any situation"
he desired. Both parties to the so-called "corrupt bargain" denied that they had
made any specific deal. But politics being politics, some kind of informal understanding was almost certainly reached in advance; and it brought to the Presidency
a man who was not the people's choice. Dr. Bemis concludes that the so-called
"corrupt bargain" was "the least questionable of the several deals" that Adams
made to secure his election.*]

2. Clay Protests His Innocence (1825)

Henry Clay, hard bitten by the presidential bug, probably would have favored Adams
in any event. He had quarreled bitterly with General Jackson, who remained his
lifelong foe. Crawford was now a paralytic wreck, unable to walk normally or speak
distinctly. Clay readily perceived that if Jackson, a fellow Westerner, entered the
White House, the country probably would not stomach another Westerner as his
successor. In passages from two letters, the first to Francis P. Blair, and the second
to Francis Brooke, Clay thus unbosomed himself. Note his ostensible reason for
opposing Jackson, his surprising attitude toward Adams, and whether these statements
support the contention that there was no "corrupt bargain."

[Jan. 29, 1825.] The friends of [Jackson?] have turned upon me, and
with the most amiable unanimity agree to vituperate me. . . . The knaves
cannot comprehend how a man can be honest. They cannot conceive that I
should have solemnly interrogated my conscience and asked it to tell me
seriously what I ought to do. That it should have enjoined me not to
establish the dangerous precedent of elevating, in this early stage of the
Republic, a military chieftain, merely because he has won a great victory.
That it should have told me that a public man is undeserving his station
who will not, regardless of aspersions and calumnies, risk himself for his
country.

I am afraid that you will think me moved by these abuses. Be not
deceived. I assure you that I never in my whole life felt more perfect
composure, more entire confidence in the resolutions of my judgment, and
a more unshakable determination to march up to my duty. And, my dear

2. Calvin Colton, ed., *The Works of Henry Clay* (1904), IV, 112–14.

sir, is there an intelligent and unbiased man who must not, sooner or later, concur with me?

Mr. Adams, you know well, I should never have selected, if at liberty to draw from the whole mass of our citizens for a President. But there is no danger in his elevation now, or in time to come. Not so of his competitor, of whom I cannot believe that killing two thousand five hundred Englishmen at New Orleans qualifies for the various, difficult, and complicated duties of the Chief Magistracy.

[Feb. 4, 1825.] I observe what you kindly tell me about the future Cabinet. My dear sir, I want no office. When have I shown an avidity for office? In rejecting the mission to Russia and the Department of War under one administration? In rejecting the same Department, the mission to England, or any other foreign mission under the succeeding administration? If Mr. Adams is elected, I know not who will be his Cabinet; I know not whether I shall be offered a place in it or not. If there should be an offer, I shall decide upon it, when it may be made, according to my sense of duty. But do you not perceive that this denunciation of me, by anticipation, is a part of the common system between the discordant confederates which I have above described? Most certainly, if an office should be offered to me under the new administration, and I should be induced to think that I ought to accept it, I shall not be deterred from accepting it, either by the denunciations of open or secret enemies, or the hypocrisy of pretended friends.

3. Plumer Dissects the "Bargain" (1825)

In a personal conference on February 12, 1825, President-elect Adams formally offered Clay the Secretaryship of State. After some hesitancy, the glamorous Kentuckian accepted the post. The cry of "corrupt bargain" had already been raised, in part to head off his acceptance. From the following private letter by William Plumer, Jr., a member of the House of Representatives, ascertain why Clay was sure to invite criticism, whatever he did.

The office of Secretary of State was, at the same time, offered to Mr. Clay. This was anticipated by everybody as a matter of course. The Western states, nine in number, with a population of two or three millions, have never had a President, a Secretary of State, or any other commanding station in the government. Upon every principle, they were entitled to notice. When to this we add that five of these states voted for Mr. Adams, and thereby pledged themselves to his support, and that all this was done by the friends of Mr. Clay, it is hardly necessary to suppose any corrupt bargain, or intrigue between Clay and Adams, to account for the promotion of a man who had already been twice offered a seat in the Cabinet by former Presidents.

Yet the peculiar state of things, at the present moment, makes it a ques-

3. E. S. Brown, *The Missouri Compromises and Presidential Politics, 1820–1825* (1926), pp. 140–42. By permission of the Missouri Historical Society.

tion of great delicacy to determine what he ought to do in this emergency. To accept will confirm, in the minds of his enemies, all those vulgar prejudices which have been so industriously circulated against him—and give them an opportunity to represent both Adams and Clay as unprincipled intriguers, who have sacrificed old resentments to present interests, and advanced their own views of personal aggrandizement at the expense of the public good.

Should he, on the other hand, decline, he will get no credit for this act. His conduct will be imputed to fear rather than to principle—and it will be said that he had not courage to accept the reward of his own perfidy. His friends are somewhat divided in opinion; but the greater part advise him to accept the offer—and I have very little doubt he will do so.

The interests of Clay and Adams are, at any rate, identified. If Adams is run down, Clay falls with him. If Clay loses his ground in the West, Adams loses also all foothold in that country. What is good for one is, therefore, good for both. On the whole, there are great difficulties on every side—and it will require no ordinary prudence to surmount them. The friends of Jackson, or rather of Calhoun, announce already their intention to commence a regular and steady opposition to the administration; and are determined to be satisfied with nothing which can be done.

C. THE RENEWAL OF THE TARIFF CONTROVERSY

1. Representative Strong Pleads for Wool (1828)

Tarred at the outset by the so-called "corrupt bargain," President Adams floundered from one embarrassment to another in domestic and foreign affairs. Most ominous of all for the Union was the frightening sectional clash over the Tariff of 1828 (the "Tariff of Abominations"). Designed largely as a measure to protect the wool growers, it was pushed up to ridiculous heights by the logrollers and political schemers in Congress. President Adams nevertheless signed it, thereby adding further to his overflowing cup of woes. Representative James Strong, from the wool-producing state of New York, presented his case as follows on the floor of the House of Representatives. Locate his weakest and strongest arguments, and decide whether the wool producer as well as the manufacturer needed tariff protection.

What, then, does the farmer require? What does he need, to enable him to produce and to continue the production of wool? He obviously needs, and must have, a market. Has he any abroad? None. He must therefore look, and can look only, to the home market. Who makes this market? The manufacturer of woolen goods. No one else can make it. How is this market to be secured? By protecting the fabric; by keeping the spindle and shuttle in motion. Is there any other, and is not this the only way? Destroy all the woolen factories, and what would your wool be worth? Where the market? Who would buy?

It has been assumed in the course of this debate—and much of the argument has rested upon the assumption—that the interests of the wool grower and of the woolen manufacturer are separate, at variance, not common to

1. *Congressional Debates* (1827–1828), IV, pt. 2, cols. 2269–70, 2273–74 (April 10, 1828).

each other, and that a high degree of protection to the manufacturer is rather an injury than a benefit to the producer of the wool. Sir, I think this wholly erroneous. It is plain to the commonest understanding that, without the aid of machinery, wool, essential as it is to human comfort, would be of little use and of less value. . . .

It is conceded, even by the advocates of the bill as reported, that the manufacture of woolen goods is valuable to the country; that the business is depressed, and needs further protection. . . .

England is our greatest competitor; and the existence of her power essentially depends upon the spindle and the anvil. Who, then, can doubt that she would sacrifice much in order to command a market like ours, in which the whole annual consumption of woolens, exclusive of household manufactures, is not less than twenty or twenty-five millions of dollars? The prostration of our woolen factories would give her this market. How can she accomplish it, in case the impost duty on woolens be too low? Why, sir, by adapting her goods to these low minimum points—forcing them into the country, and underselling our own manufacturers. In this way, a great foreign capital will be constantly acting upon a small American capital. The difference will be nearly as five hundred to one. The odds are fearful. The competition will be manifestly unequal. . . .

But it is alleged that the proposed duties, which are intended for the protection of our capital and industry, will tax and oppress the poor. Sir, it is true that an impost on an article not produced in the country, as on tea, for example, is a charge upon both the producer and the consumer. But, when the home manufacturer can, and does, supply the home market with any given article, no amount of impost will enhance its price, because the domestic competition will always keep it at the lowest rate for which it can be made, allowing to the maker a reasonable profit. This is a law of human labor that never varies.

2. A Carolinian Condemns the Tariff (1828)

Representative (later Senator) George McDuffie of South Carolina, an air-pawing orator of the old school, customarily packed the galleries with expectant listeners. Already hostile to protective duties, he assailed the towering "Tariff of Abominations" of 1828. He went so far as to advocate a prohibitory tax on Northern goods, and in 1830 propounded the "forty-bale" theory—namely, that each Southern cotton planter indirectly contributed forty bales out of every hundred to Northern manufacturers because of tariff inequities. In this speech in the House of Representatives, decide how convincing he is in arguing that the North should join the South in fighting a protective tariff. Why was free trade to the advantage of the cotton grower?

Mr. Speaker, it is distressing to witness the kind of aristocratic influence by which measures of this sort are obviously controlled. I have witnessed, with astonishment and regret, as a strong proof of the aristocratic tendency of every system of government, the melancholy fact that intelligent and honorable men upon this floor, in whose Congressional districts there is

2. *Ibid.*, cols. 2401–03 (April 19, 1828).

perhaps a single manufactory of iron, owned by perhaps the very wealthiest man in the county, will give their votes, without the least compunction, to impose an odious and oppressive tax upon the remaining thousands of their poor constituents, to increase the profits of one wealthy nabob.

And yet, sir, we hear gentlemen very gravely talking about promoting the interest of "a whole state," when they are in the very act of imposing a tax upon the great body of the people of that very state. Such, for example, was the language used by the gentleman from Missouri, when urging the expediency of increasing the duty on lead; when, I will venture to say, one hundred of his constituents would feel the tax, where one of them would realize the bounty of such an imposition. And yet, sir, we talk about a democratic government, and the responsibility of the representative to the people!

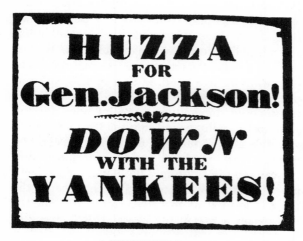

A CAMPAIGN POSTER

The Yankee protective tariff condemned by the South in the Adams-Jackson presidential campaign of 1828. Woodrow Wilson, *A History of the American People*, 1902, vol. III.

I speak not the language of the demagogue, but the grave and solemn language of historical and philosophical truth, when I say that it is the very genius of this system, as exhibited in this and every other country, to tax the many and the poor for the benefit of the few and the wealthy.

Take up the articles embraced in the scheme of protection, one by one, and I defy any man to point out a single one of them that does not specifically prove and illustrate the proposition I have laid down. Salt, for example, is an article of first necessity, equally consumed by the poor and the rich. The people of the United States now pay about 100 percent on every bushel of salt they consume, amounting in the aggregate to a tax of at least a million and a half dollars, paid by all classes, for the exclusive benefit of the owners of some one or two hundred salt works, at the most. The same remark is strictly applicable to the duty on iron. It imposes a universal tax, both heavy and permanent, for the benefit of not more than one or two hundred ironmasters in the United States. . . .

. . . I, sir, complain of the duty upon sugar as much as any other member of the House. It is obnoxious [open], in a peculiar manner, to the objection I have urged against the duties on salt and iron. It is a tax on the great body of the people, for the benefit of some two or three hundred sugar planters, who are men of immense wealth. For the fact is notorious that the business is almost exclusively confined to large capitalists. Every family in the United States that consumes 33⅓ pounds of sugar pays a tax of one dollar to these wealthy monopolists. And I know a single individual—he is a personal friend—worth between two and three millions of dollars, who receives annually about $30,000 as his dividend of this national bounty.

Can there be a more striking proof of the injustice, and impolicy, and anti-republican tendency of this system? It imposes a tax of at least four millions five hundred thousand dollars upon the mass of the people in every state in the Union, for the sole and exclusive benefit of the iron-masters, sugar planters, and owners of salt works, not amounting, in the whole Union, to more than from five hundred to one thousand persons. And if we add all the owners of cotton and woolen manufactories in the United States, it would not swell the number to two thousand. . . .

. . . But, sir, I shall be probably asked how it happens that the capitalists of the South, the wealthy cotton planters, are arrayed on the side of the great mass of the people in the contest between capital and labor? Have they more knowledge or more honesty than other capitalists? Sir, I set up no such pretension for them. We lay claim to no other intelligence and honesty than such as enables us to understand, and prompts us to defend, our own rights. I will not undertake to say that we might not be tempted to join this plundering expedition, if a tariff could be so regulated as to increase the price of cotton. But such is our position in this contest that our interest throws us into a natural alliance with the great body of the people in the farming states.

The wealthy cotton planter of the South fights by the side of the small farmer, the mechanic, the merchant, and the laborer, in New York and Pennsylvania, because they all have a similar interest in opposing a system of which the burden falls upon them and the benefit on others. . . . The Southern states, depending on free trade for their prosperity, must always be opposed to any attempts on the part of this government to build up, by commercial prohibitions, an aristocracy of favored monopolists.

Sir, this is not a contest, as some are anxious to represent it, between the Southern and Northern states. It is a contest of less than one hundred thousand manufacturers and farmers against all the other farmers and manufacturers in the Union, and against the whole population in the Southern states.

D. THE BLIGHT OF THE SPOILS SYSTEM

1. Jackson Deplores Patronage (1829)

Shouting "Jackson and Reform," the long-frustrated followers of "Old Hickory" finally enthroned their hero, after the bedeviled President Adams had served only one term.

1. J. S. Bassett, ed., *Correspondence of Andrew Jackson* (1929), IV, 39 (May 30, 1829). By permission of the Carnegie Institution of Washington.

Their concept of reform was to sweep out the Adams men and replace them with ardent (if sometimes illiterate) Jacksonites. Jackson is notorious as the President who widened the spoils system in a wholesale manner, although he did not engineer a clean sweep of the incumbents. In truth, many of the civil servants had become uncivil, incompetent, or dishonest. From Jackson's complaint in the following private letter, draw conclusions as to his general attitude toward the problem. Was he personally responsible for all bad appointments?

The most disagreeable duty I have to perform is the removals and appointments to office. There is great distress here [Washington], and it appears that all wno possess office depend upon the emolument for support, and thousands who are pressing for office do it upon the ground that they are starving, and their families, and must perish without [unless] they can be relieved by the emolument of some office.

These hungry expectants, as well as those who enjoy office, are dangerous contestants over the public purse, unless possessed of the purest principles of integrity and honesty; and when any and every man can get recommendations of the strongest kind, it requires great circumspection to avoid imposition and select honest men.

You will see from the public journals we have begun reform, and that we are trying to cleanse the Augean stables, and expose to view the corruption of some of the agents of the late administration.

2. Jackson Defends Rotation (1829)

A basic principle of Jacksonian democracy, and a potent stimulant of the spoils system, was rotation in office—that is, giving as many supporters as possible a chance at the hog-trough of patronage. One of the most plausible defenses of the practice appears in Jackson's first annual message to Congress. Note what light it sheds on his own concept of public service and his understanding of government. Explain why this reasoning would be less valid today than it was then.

There are, perhaps, few men who can for any great length of time enjoy office and power without being more or less under the influence of feelings unfavorable to the faithful discharge of their public duties. Their integrity may be proof against improper considerations immediately addressed to themselves, but they are apt to acquire a habit of looking with indifference upon the public interests, and of tolerating conduct from which an unpracticed man would revolt.

Office is considered as a species of property, and government rather as a means of promoting individual interests than as an instrument created solely for the service of the people. Corruption in some, and in others a perversion of correct feelings and principles, divert government from its legitimate ends and make it an engine for the support of the few at the expense of the many.

The duties of all public officers are, or at least admit of being made, so plain and simple that men of intelligence may readily qualify themselves

2. J. D. Richardson, ed., *Messages and Papers of the Presidents* (1896), II, 448–49.

A HINT TO OFFICE-HOLDERS

Pre-Civil War cartoon shows how rotation ax falls
with change of party. Albert Shaw, *Abraham Lincoln: A Cartoon History,* 1930, vol. II.

for their performance. And I cannot but believe that more is lost by the
long continuance of men in office than is generally to be gained by their
experience. I submit, therefore, to your consideration whether the efficiency
of the government would not be promoted, and official industry and
integrity better secured, by a general extension of the law which limits
appointments to four years.

In a country where offices are created solely for the benefit of the people,
no one man has any more intrinsic right to official station than another.
Offices were not established to give support to particular men at the public
expense. No individual wrong is, therefore, done by removal, since neither
appointment to, nor continuance in, office is matter of right.

The incumbent became an officer with a view to public benefits, and
when these require his removal, they are not to be sacrificed to private
interests. It is the people, and they alone, who have a right to complain
when a bad officer is substituted for a good one. He who is removed has the
same means of obtaining a living that are enjoyed by the millions who never
held office.

The proposed limitation [of four years] would destroy the idea of property now so generally connected with official station, and although individual distress may be sometimes produced, it would, by promoting that rotation which constitutes a leading principle in the republican creed, give healthful action to the system.

3. Emerson Ridicules Rotation (1851)

Ralph Waldo Emerson—poet, essayist, and Transcendentalist philosopher—recorded in a catch-all journal his musings on rotation in office. The following passage was inspired by the defeat of Senator Benton of Missouri for re-election because he had taken an unpopular stand on the slavery issue. Note both the strength and the weakness of Emerson's argument.

Rotation. What an excellent principle our favorite rule of rotation in office would be if applied in industrial matters. You have been watch-maker long enough, now it is my turn to make watches, and you can bake muffins. The carpenter is to make glass this year, and the glass-blower staircases. The blacksmith is to cut me a coat, and the tailor to take charge of the machine-shop. Mr. Benton [of Missouri] has served an apprenticeship of thirty years to the Federal Senate, has learned the routine, has opened his views to a national scope, and must now retire to give place to Johnny Raw.

4. Marcy Claims Spoils for the Victors (1832)

Senator Henry Clay of Kentucky, about to run again for the Presidency, attacked the spoils system under Jackson. Senator William L. Marcy, later to be Secretary of State, came back with a spirited defense of the system and of his own state of New York as the reputed initiator of it. Why was President Jackson under stronger compulsion than his three predecessors to wield the patronage ax?

It may be, sir, that the politicians of the United States are not so fastidious as some gentlemen are, as to disclosing the principles on which they act. They boldly preach what they practice. When they are contending for victory, they avow their intention of enjoying the fruits of it. If they are defeated, they expect to retire from office. If they are successful, they claim, as a matter of right, the advantages of success. They see nothing wrong in the rule, that to the victor belong the spoils of the enemy. . . .

When the Senator from Kentucky [Henry Clay] condemns the present administration for making removals from office, and then ascribes the act to the pernicious system of politics imported from New York, I fear he does not sufficiently consider the peculiar circumstances under which the present administration came into power. General Jackson did not come in under the same circumstances that Mr. Adams did, or Mr. Monroe, or Mr. Madison.

3. E. W. Emerson and W. E. Forbes, *Journals of Ralph Waldo Emerson* (1912), VIII, 165. By permission of Houghton Mifflin Company.
4. *Congressional Debates,* VIII, pt. 1, cols. 1325–26 (Jan. 24–25, 1832).

His accession was like that of Mr. Jefferson. He came in, sir, upon a political revolution. The contest was without a parallel. Much political bitterness was engendered. Criminations and recriminations were made. Slanders of a most extraordinary character flooded the land.

When the present Chief Magistrate took upon himself the administration of the government, he found almost all the offices, from the highest to the lowest, filled by political enemies. That his Cabinet was composed of his friends, no one will complain. The reasons for thus composing it will apply with considerable force to many of the officers under the heads of the several departments.

If some dismissals of the subordinate officers in these departments were made, it will not be asserted that all opposed to the administration were discharged. I have heard it confidently asserted, by those who I supposed spoke with knowledge on the subject, that many, perhaps a majority, of those retained—and almost all were retained—belong now to the opposition; they are the political supporters of the honorable Senator from Kentucky.

I have good reasons, very good reasons, for believing that it is the gentleman's [Clay's] rule of conduct to take care of his friends when he is in power. It requires not the foresight of a prophet to predict that, if he shall come into power, he will take care of his friends, and, if he does, I can assure him I shall not complain. Nor shall I be in the least surprised if he imitates the example which he now so emphatically denounces.

5. Swartwout the Swindler (1838)

Samuel Swartwout, a beneficiary of the spoils system, was the first man to steal a million dollars from the federal government. A personally charming and loyal supporter of Jackson, he was awarded the prize plum of Collectorship of the Port of New York, despite warnings as to his mania for speculation. In 1838 he left for England. Philip Hone—a wealthy New York City businessman, Whig politician, civic leader, patron of the arts, and dinner host of great men—records his disgust in one of the raciest secret diaries of the time. Making allowance for Hone's anti-Jackson bias, ascertain what this account reveals about the inconsistencies and other shortcomings of the administration.

November 13 [1838].—The city has been agitated today by reports of a defalcation in the accounts of the late Collector of the Port, Samuel Swartwout, to the amount of a million and a quarter of dollars. He has taken the public money and engaged with it in wild speculation of Texas lands, gold mines, and other humbugs, which have caused ruin for several years past to men of more means and greater judgment than Mr. Swartwout.

A large proportion of this abstraction of the public funds took place during the first two years of his collectorship, and the amount has been increasing ever since. How it was possible that so enormous a deficiency should never have been discovered until now is perfectly inconceivable! It is a dreadful commentary upon the manner of conducting business at

5. Bayard Tuckerman, ed., *The Diary of Philip Hone* (1889), I, 332–33.

Washington, and it would appear impossible that there should not have been connivance on the part of some of the coordinate branches of the department, either there or here. . . .

President Jackson, on his accession to office, made a great fuss about public defaulters; prosecuted several petty offenders, whom he got imprisoned, and swore in his usual amiable manner that they should never be released; and at the same time appointed his personal friends, who were notoriously irresponsible, to offices of the highest trust, whose claims consisted only in their unscrupulous devotion to him and his party. And when a committee of Congress was raised to investigate the affairs of the Treasury Department, which investigation would have naturally led to the discovery of this and other similar frauds, he interposed between his servants and the representatives of the people, would not allow them to answer questions, and took upon himself the responsibility.

E. THE WEBSTER–HAYNE DEBATE

1. Hayne Advocates Nullification (1830)

The restrictive "Tariff of Abominations" of 1828 had angered the South, especially the South Carolinians, who protested vehemently against an "unconstitutional" tax levied indirectly on them to support "greedy" Yankee manufacturers. An eruption finally occurred in the Senate when Senator Robert Y. Hayne of South Carolina— fluent, skillful, and personally attractive—attacked New England's inconsistency, greed, and selfishness, notably during the War of 1812. The only way to resist usurpations by the federal government, he insisted, was for the states to nullify unauthorized acts of Congress, as foreshadowed by Jefferson in the Kentucky Resolutions of 1798–1799 (see earlier, p. 173). In this peroration of his impressive speech, note whether Hayne is a disunionist and whether he is willing to let the Supreme Court pass upon the unconstitutionality of acts of Congress.

Thus it will be seen, Mr. President, that the South Carolina doctrine [of nullification] is the [Jeffersonian] Republican doctrine of 1798; that it was first promulgated by the Fathers of the Faith; that it was maintained by Virginia and Kentucky in the worst of times; that it constituted the very pivot on which the political revolution of that day turned; that it embraces the very principles the triumph of which at that time saved the Constitution at its last gasp, and which New England statesmen were not unwilling to adopt [at Hartford in 1814] when they believed themselves to be the victims of unconstitutional legislation.

Sir, as to the doctrine that the federal government is the exclusive judge of the extent as well as the limitations of its powers, it seems to me to be utterly subversive of the sovereignty and independence of the states. It makes but little difference in my estimation whether Congress or the Supreme Court are invested with this power. If the federal government

1. *Register of Debates in Congress* (1829–1830), VI, pt. 1, p. 58 (Jan. 25, 1830).

in all or any of its departments is to prescribe the limits of its own authority, and the states are bound to submit to the decision and are not allowed to examine and decide for themselves when the barriers of the Constitution shall be overleaped, this is practically "a government without limitation of powers." The states are at once reduced to mere petty corporations and the people are entirely at your mercy.

I have but one word more to add. In all the efforts that have been made by South Carolina to resist the unconstitutional [tariff] laws which Congress has extended over them, she has kept steadily in view the preservation of the Union by the only means by which she believes it can be long preserved—a firm, manly, and steady resistance against usurpation.

The [tariff] measures of the federal government have, it is true, prostrated her interests, and will soon involve the whole South in irretrievable ruin. But even this evil, great as it is, is not the chief ground of our complaints. It is the principle involved in the contest—a principle which, substituting the discretion of Congress for the limitations of the Constitution, brings the states and the people to the feet of the federal government and leaves them nothing they can call their own.

Sir, if the measures of the federal government were less oppressive, we should still strive against this usurpation. The South is acting on a principle she has always held sacred—resistance to unauthorized taxation.

These, sir, are the principles which induced the immortal [John] Hampden to resist the payment [in 1637] of a tax of twenty shillings [to the English government]. Would twenty shillings have ruined his fortune? No! but the payment of half twenty shillings on the principle on which it was demanded would have made him a slave.

Sir, if in acting on these high motives, if animated by that ardent love of liberty which has always been the most prominent trait in the Southern character, we should be hurried beyond the bounds of a cold and calculating prudence, who is there with one noble and generous sentiment in his bosom that would not be disposed, in the language of Burke, to exclaim, "You must pardon something to the spirit of liberty!"

2. Webster Pleads for the Union (1830)

Daniel Webster, native son of New Hampshire and adopted son of Massachusetts, sprang to the defense of New England and the Union in a running debate with Hayne that lasted two weeks and ranged over many subjects. The crowded Senate galleries thrilled to the eloquence of the two parliamentary gladiators, as the states'-rightism of the South clashed head-on with the buoyant nationalism of the North. Webster's main points were that the people and not the states had formed the Constitution of 1787 (here he was historically shaky); that while the people were sovereign, the national government was supreme in its sphere and the state governments were supreme in their spheres; that if each of the twenty-four states could defy the laws of Congress at will, there would be no Union but "a rope of sand"; and that there was a better

2. *The Works of Daniel Webster* (20th ed., 1890), III, 340–42 (Jan. 26. 1830).

If anything be found in the national Constitution, either by original provision or subsequent interpretation, which ought not to be in it, the people know how to get rid of it. If any construction be established, unacceptable to them, so as to become, practically, a part of the Constitution, they will amend it, at their sovereign pleasure. But while the people choose to maintain it as it is—while they are satisfied with it, and refuse to change it—who has given, or who can give, to the state legislatures a right to alter it, either by interference, construction, or otherwise? . . .

I profess, sir, in my career, hitherto, to have kept steadily in view the prosperity and honor of the whole country, and the preservation of our Federal Union. It is to that Union we owe our safety at home and our consideration and dignity abroad. It is to that Union that we are chiefly indebted for whatever makes us most proud of our country.

That Union we reached only by the discipline of our virtues in the severe school of adversity. It had its origin in the necessities of disordered finance, prostrate commerce, and ruined credit. Under its benign influence, these great interests immediately awoke us from the dead and sprang forth with newness of life. Every year of its duration has teemed with fresh proofs of its utility and its blessings; and although our territory has stretched out wider and wider, and our population spread farther and farther, they have not outrun its protection or its benefits. It has been to us all a copious fountain of national, social, and personal happiness.

I have not allowed myself, sir, to look beyond the Union to see what might lie hidden in the dark recess behind. I have not coolly weighed the chances of preserving liberty when the bonds that unite us together shall be broken asunder. I have not accustomed myself to hang over the precipice of disunion to see whether, with my short sight, I can fathom the depth of the abyss below. Nor could I regard him as a safe counselor in the affairs of this government whose thoughts should be mainly bent on considering not how the Union should be best preserved, but how tolerable might be the condition of the people when it shall be broken up and destroyed.

While the Union lasts we have high, exciting, gratifying prospects spread out before us—for us and our children. Beyond that, I seek not to penetrate the veil. God grant that in my day, at least, that curtain may not rise! God grant that, on my vision, never may be opened what lies behind!

When my eyes shall be turned to behold, for the last time, the sun in heaven, may I not see him shining on the broken and dishonored fragments of a once glorious Union; on states dissevered, discordant, belligerent; on a land rent with civil feuds, or drenched, it may be, in fraternal blood! Let their last feeble and lingering glance rather behold the gorgeous ensign of the Republic, now known and honored throughout the earth, still full high advanced, its arms and trophies streaming in their original luster, not a stripe erased or polluted, not a single star obscured, bearing for its motto no such miserable interrogatory as "What is all this worth?" nor those other words of delusion and folly, "Liberty first and Union afterward"; but everywhere, spread all over in characters of living light, blazing on all its ample folds, as they float over the sea and over the land, and in every wind under the whole heavens, that other sentiment, dear to every true American heart—Liberty *and* Union, now and forever, one and inseparable!

THOUGHT PROVOKERS

1. Is it true that the coming of manhood suffrage made for better government? In the days of Mussolini it was said that self-government was better than good government. Comment. Macaulay said, "The only way in which to fit a people for self-government is to entrust them with self-government." Comment. Metternich said, "Ten million ignorances do not constitute one knowledge." Comment.
2. In reference to the "Corrupt Bargain," is it possible for a man to go far in politics without stooping to deals of an unsavory nature?
3. How would subsequent American history have been changed if a protective tariff could have raised the price of cotton?
4. With reference to the New Democracy, it has been said that once we start counting heads we have to educate them. Comment. Does democracy have more to fear from ingrown bureaucrats than from inexperienced zealots holding office? It has been said that ignorance is more of a menace to American democracy than corruption and graft. Comment. Jefferson said, "Whenever a man has cast a longing eye on offices, a rottenness begins in his conduct." Comment.
5. Southern nullification did not succeed in the 1830's, yet it has been noted that informal nullification of unpopular federal laws, amendments, and court decisions has been going on for generations. Illustrate. What better or other safeguards have a minority of the states against the "tyranny of the majority"?

FURTHER EXPLORATION

General: A. M. Schlesinger, Jr., *The Age of Jackson* (1945); G. G. Van Deusen, *The Jacksonian Era* (1959). **The New Democracy:** F. J. Turner, *Rise of the New West* (1906); Chilton Williamson, *American Suffrage from Property to Democracy* (1960). **Corrupt Bargain:** S. F. Bemis, *John Quincy Adams and the Union* (1956). **Tariff:** F. W. Taussig, *Tariff History of the United States* (8th ed., 1931). **Spoils System:** L. D. White, *The Jacksonians* (1954); C. R. Fish, *The Civil Service and the Patronage* (1905). **Webster-Hayne:** C. M. Fuess, *Daniel Webster* (2 vols., 1930).

Recent: R. V. Remini, *The Election of Andrew Jackson* (1963) [paperback]; R. P. McCormick, *The Second American Party System: Party Formation in the Jacksonian Era* (1966); S. H. Aronson, *Status and Kinship in the Higher Civil Service* (1964); Lee Benson, *The Concept of Jacksonian Democracy: New York as a Test Case* (1961) [paperback].

Chapter 14

The Heyday of Jacksonian Democracy

I consider, then, the power to annul a law of the United States, assumed by one state, incompatible with the existence of the Union, contradicted expressly by the letter of the Constitution, unauthorized by its spirit, inconsistent with every principle on which it was founded, and destructive of the great object for which it was formed.

JACKSON'S SOUTH CAROLINA NULLIFICATION PROCLAMATION, 1832

PROLOGUE: President Jackson, idol and champion of the Democratic masses, was a direct-actionist. Despising Indians, he engineered their brutal uprooting from the East to the Western plains. Distrusting the monopolistic Bank of the United States, he crippled it in 1832 with his scorching veto of a re-charter bill, and then drove it to the wall. Resenting back talk from the states, he took a firm stand against South Carolina during the anti-high-tariff nullification crisis of 1832–1833. The state finally rescinded its nullification ordinance and gagged down the more reasonable rates of the compromise tariff of 1833. Ever popular with the poorer classes, Jackson was triumphantly re-elected over the Whig Henry Clay in 1832, with the Bank issue uppermost. Four years later "King Andrew" succeeded in enthroning his hand-picked crown prince, the wire-pulling "American Talleyrand," Martin Van Buren. But the paralyzing Panic of 1837, triggered partly by Jackson's roughshod finance, blighted the unhappy four years of the Van Buren administration.

A. TRANSPLANTING THE RED MEN

1. Jackson Endorses the Indian Removal (1829)

By the 1820's the once "inexhaustible" land east of the Mississippi was filling up with white men, and the luckless red men were being elbowed aside. Congress, responding to pressure for transplanting the tribes to a "permanent" home beyond the Mississippi River, took under consideration the Indian Removal Bill. President Jackson threw his powerful weight behind the movement in the following section of his first annual message to Congress. Note whether his anti-Indian bias shows through, what inconsistencies had developed in the white man's policies, and why the Indians would presumably choose to go West.

The condition and ulterior destiny of the Indian tribes within the limits of some of our states have become objects of much interest and importance. It has long been the policy of government to introduce among them the arts of civilization, in the hope of gradually reclaiming them from a wandering life. This policy has, however, been coupled with another wholly

1. J. D. Richardson, ed., *Messages and Papers of the Presidents* (1896), II, 456–59 (Dec. 8, 1829).

incompatible with its success. Professing a desire to civilize and settle them, we have at the same time lost no opportunity to purchase their lands and thrust them farther into the wilderness. By this means they have not only been kept in a wandering state, but been led to look upon us as unjust and indifferent to their fate. . . .

Our conduct toward these people is deeply interesting to our national character. Their present condition, contrasted with what they once were, makes a most powerful appeal to our sympathies. Our ancestors found them the uncontrolled possessors of these vast regions. By persuasion and force they have been made to retire from river to river and from mountain to mountain, until some of the tribes have become extinct and others have left but remnants to preserve for awhile their once terrible names. Surrounded by the whites with their arts of civilization, which, by destroying the resources of the savage, doom him to weakness and decay, the fate of the Mohegan, the Narragansett, and the Delaware is fast overtaking the Choctaw, the Cherokee, and the Creek. That this fate surely awaits them if they remain within the limits of the states does not admit of a doubt. Humanity and national honor demand that every effort should be made to avert so great a calamity. . . .

As a means of effecting this end, I suggest for your consideration the propriety of setting apart an ample district west of the Mississippi, and without [outside] the limits of any state or territory now formed, to be guaranteed to the Indian tribes as long as they shall occupy it, each tribe having a distinct control over the portion designated for its use. There they may be secured in the enjoyment of governments of their own choice, subject to no other control from the United States than such as may be necessary to preserve peace on the frontier and between the several tribes. There the benevolent may endeavor to teach them the arts of civilization, and, by promoting union and harmony among them, to raise up an interesting commonwealth, destined to perpetuate the race and to attest the humanity and justice of this government.

This emigration should be voluntary, for it would be as cruel as unjust to compel the aborigines to abandon the graves of their fathers and seek a home in a distant land. But they should be distinctly informed that if they remain within the limits of the states they must be subject to their laws.

2. Frelinghuysen Champions Justice (1830)

Senator Theodore Frelinghuysen, a distinguished New Jersey lawyer and later president of Rutgers College, shone so prominently as a lay leader as to be dubbed "the Christian statesman." Respected by both Whigs and Democrats in Congress, he gained nationwide recognition as a result of his magnificent six-hour speech opposing the Indian removal. Decide to what extent his arguments are valid insofar as they relate to law, justice, and humanity, and why they did not prevail with the conscience of America.

2. *Register of Debates in Congress,* 21 Cong., 1 sess., VI, pt. 1, pp. 311–12, 318.

I now proceed to the discussion of those principles which, in my humble judgment, fully and clearly sustain the claims of the Indians to all their political and civil rights, as by them asserted. And here I insist that, by immemorial possession, as the original tenants of the soil, they hold a title beyond and superior to the British Crown and her colonies, and to all adverse pretensions of our Confederation and subsequent Union. God, in his Providence, planted these tribes on this western continent, so far as we know, before Great Britain herself had a political existence. . . .

In the light of natural law, can a reason for a distinction exist in the mode of enjoying that which is my own? If I use it for hunting, may another take it because he needs it for agriculture? I am aware that some writers have, by a system of artificial reasoning, endeavored to justify, or rather excuse, the encroachments made upon Indian territory; and they denominate these abstractions the law of nations, and in this ready way the question is despatched. Sir, as we trace the sources of this law, we find its authority to depend either upon the conventions or common consent of nations. And when, permit me to inquire, were the Indian tribes ever consulted on the establishment of such a law? . . .

Our ancestors found these people, far removed from the commotions of Europe, exercising all the rights and enjoying the privileges of free and independent sovereigns of this new world. . . . The white men, the authors of all their wrongs, approached them as friends . . . and, being then a feeble colony and at the mercy of the native tenants of the soil, by presents and profession propitiated their good will.

The Indian yielded a slow but substantial confidence; granted to the colonists an abiding place; and suffered them to grow up to man's estate beside him. He never raised the claim of elder title; as the white man's wants increased, he opened the hand of his bounty wider and wider.

By and by conditions are changed. His people melt away; his lands are constantly coveted; millions after millions [of acres] are ceded. The Indian bears it all meekly. He complains, indeed, as well he may, but suffers on. And now he finds that this neighbor, whom his kindness had nourished, has spread an adverse title over the last remains of his patrimony, barely adequate to his wants, and turns upon him and says, "Away! we cannot endure you so near us! These forests and rivers, these groves of your fathers, these firesides and hunting grounds are ours by the right of power and the force of numbers."

Sir, . . . I ask who is the injured and who is the aggressor? Let conscience answer, and I fear not the result. . . . Do the obligations of justice change with the color of the skin? Is it one of the prerogatives of the white man that he may disregard the dictates of moral principles when an Indian shall be concerned? No, sir. . . .

Sir, . . . if the contending parties were to exchange positions; place the white man where the Indian stands; load him with all these wrongs; and what path would his outraged feelings strike out for his career? . . . A few pence of duty on tea—that invaded no fireside, excited no fears, disturbed no substantial interest whatever—awakened in the American colonies a spirit of firm resistance. And how was the tea tax met, sir? Just as it should be. . . . We successfully and triumphantly contended for the very rights and privileges that our Indian neighbors now implore us to protect and to preserve to them.

Sir, this thought invests the subject under debate with most singular and momentous interest. We, whom God has exalted to the very summit of prosperity—whose brief career forms the brightest page in history; the wonder and praise of the world; freedom's hope and her consolation—we, about to turn traitors to our principles and our fame, about to become the oppressors of the feeble and to cast away our birthright! Sir, I hope for better things. . . .

The end, however, is to justify the means. "The removal of the Indian tribes to the west of the Mississippi is demanded by the dictates of humanity." This is a word of conciliating import. But it often makes its way to the heart under very doubtful titles, and its present claims deserve to be rigidly questioned. Who urges this plea? They who covet the Indian lands— who wish to rid themselves of a neighbor that they despise, and whose state pride is enlisted in rounding off their territories.

[*The Indian Removal Bill passed Congress in 1830. The sequel was a sorry tale of greed, force, and fraud. Thousands of Indians of all ages and both sexes died on the tragic trek—perhaps as many as one-fourth of the 60,000 from the South. Hostile tribes in the West often did not welcome the newcomers; and the new home lost its "permanency" as soon as unscrupulous whites found the land worth grabbing.*]

B. THE WAR ON THE BANK

1. Jackson Vetoes the Bank Recharter (1832)

The charter of the Second Bank of the United States was due to expire in 1836. Senator Henry Clay, seeking a sure-fire issue in the presidential campaign of 1832 against Jackson, arranged in Congress for a premature recharter. The assumption was that if the President vetoed the bill, he would incur the wrath of the voters. But Jackson, his ire aroused, wielded the veto pen. He denounced the Bank as monopolistic, as the tool of a favored few stockholders, as a gold mine for certain foreign investors, as a citadel of special privilege, as a menace to basic liberties, and withal unconstitutional (although John Marshall's Supreme Court had decreed otherwise, p. 220). Jackson also complained that an incomplete investigation by a House committee had recently uncovered questionable practices that needed further probing. Judge whether Jackson, in his veto message, resorted to electioneering demagoguery, and to what extent he was Jeffersonian in his views toward states' rights and the rich.

As the [Bank] charter had yet four years to run, and as a renewal now was not necessary to the successful prosecution of its business, it was to

1. J. D. Richardson, ed., *Messages and Papers of the Presidents* (1896), II, 589–90 (July 10, 1832).

have been expected that the Bank itself, conscious of its purity and proud of its character, would have withdrawn its application for the present, and demanded the severest scrutiny into all its transactions. . . .

The Bank is professedly established as an agent of the Executive Branch of the government, and its constitutionality is maintained on that ground. Neither upon the propriety of present action nor upon the provisions of this act was the Executive consulted. It has had no opportunity to say that it neither needs nor wants an agent clothed with such powers and favored by such exemptions. There is nothing in its legitimate functions which makes it necessary or proper. Whatever interest or influence, whether public or private, has given birth to this act, it cannot be found either in the wishes or necessities of the Executive Department, by which present action is deemed premature, and the powers conferred upon its agent not only unnecessary but dangerous to the government and country.

It is to be regretted that the rich and powerful too often bend the acts of government to their selfish purposes. Distinctions in society will always exist under every just government. Equality of talents, of education, or of wealth cannot be produced by human institutions. In the full enjoyment of the gifts of heaven and the fruits of superior industry, economy, and virtue, every man is equally entitled to protection by law.

But when the laws undertake to add to these natural and just advantages artificial distinctions, to grant titles, gratuities, and exclusive privileges, to make the rich richer and the potent more powerful, the humble members of society—the farmers, mechanics, and laborers—who have neither the time nor the means of securing like favors to themselves, have a right to complain of the injustice of their government.

There are no necessary evils in government. Its evils exist only in its abuses. If it would confine itself to equal protection, and, as heaven does its rains, shower its favors alike on the high and the low, the rich and the poor, it would be an unqualified blessing. In the act before me there seems to be a wide and unnecessary departure from these just principles.

Nor is our government to be maintained or our Union preserved by invasions of the rights and powers of the several states. In thus attempting to make our General Government strong, we make it weak. Its true strength consists in leaving individuals and states as much as possible to themselves—in making itself felt, not in its power, but in its beneficence; not in its control, but in its protection; not in binding the states more closely to the center, but leaving each to move unobstructed in its proper orbit.

Experience should teach us wisdom. Most of the difficulties our government now encounters, and most of the dangers which impend over our Union, have sprung from an abandonment of the legitimate objects of government by our national legislation, and the adoption of such principles as are embodied in this act. Many of our rich men have not been content with equal protection and equal benefits, but have besought us to make them richer by act of Congress. By attempting to gratify their desires we have in the results of our legislation arrayed section against section, interest against interest, and man against man, in a fearful commotion which threatens to shake the foundations of our Union.

2. A Boston Journal Attacks Jackson (1832)

The Bank of the United States, as Jackson charged, had undoubtedly wielded its vast power ruthlessly, arrogantly, and at times unscrupulously. Its numerous "loans" to public men had often resembled bribes. The pro-Jackson men hated it as a despot-ism of wealth. The pro-Bank men suspected, especially after the veto message, that Jackson was trying to establish a despotism of the masses, with himself as chief despot. Senator Daniel Webster, a paid counsel for the Bank, shared these fears. The Boston *Daily Atlas*, a pro-Webster journal that was rapidly becoming the most influential Whig newspaper in New England, reacted with the following counter-blast against Jackson's veto message. Note which charge in this editorial would be most likely to arouse the anti-Jackson Whigs in the campaign then being fought between the Democrat Jackson and the Whig Clay.

The Bank veto . . . is the most wholly radical and basely Jesuitical docu-ment that ever emanated from any administration, in any country.

It violates all our established notions and feelings. It arraigns Congress for not asking permission of the Executive before daring to legislate on the matter, and fairly intimates a design to save the two Houses in future from all such trouble.

It impudently asserts that Congress have acted prematurely, blindly, and without sufficient examination.

It falsely and wickedly alleges that the rich and powerful throughout the country are waging a war of oppression against the poor and the weak; and attempts to justify the President on the ground of its being his duty thus to protect the humble when so assailed.

Finally, it unblushingly denies that the Supreme Court is the proper tribunal to decide upon the constitutionality of the laws!!

The whole paper is a most thoroughgoing electioneering missile, intended to secure the madcaps of the South, and as such deserves the execration of all who love their country or its welfare.

This veto seems to be the production of the whole Kitchen Cabinet—of hypocrisy and arrogance; of imbecility and talent; of cunning, falsehood, and corruption—a very firebrand, intended to destroy their opponents, but which now, thanks to Him who can bring good out of evil, bids fair to light up a flame that shall consume its vile authors.

If the doctrines avowed in this document do not arouse the nation, we shall despair that anything will, until the iron hand of despotism has swept our fair land, and this glorious Republic, if not wholly annihilated, shall have been fiercely shaken to its very foundations.

[*Form conclusions as to whether a more temperate statement by this partisan journal would have been more effective, and compare the tone of this editorial with that of President Jackson's veto message.*]

2. Boston *Daily Atlas,* quoted in the *Daily National Intelligencer* (Washington), Aug. 9, 1832.

Race over Uncle Sam's Course.
4ᵉ *March* 1833

Clay, with his American System, is supposed to gain the White House as Jackson, with Van Buren as running mate, comes a cropper on the Bank issue in 1832. An unduly optimistic Whig cartoon. Boston Public Library.

3. Biddle Rejoices Prematurely (1832)

Wealthy and aristocratic, Nicholas Biddle of Philadelphia was a rare combination of classical scholar, linguist, diplomat, world traveler, lawyer, minor poet, magazine editor, state legislator, and top-flight financier. As the conservative president of the plutocratic Bank of the United States, he incurred the wrath of the non-conservative President of the United States. But Jackson's veto message was not altogether displeasing to Whigs like Nicholas Biddle and candidate Henry Clay. Its financial absurdities, its constitutional fallacies, and its crass appeal to class hatred prompted the Whigs to circulate many thousands of copies as an anti-Jackson campaign document. From Biddle's private letter to Clay shortly after the veto message, form some conclusions as to Biddle's political insight and his attitude toward democracy. Is he Hamiltonian or Jeffersonian?

You ask what is the effect of the veto. My impression is that it is working as well as the friends of the Bank and of the country could desire. I have always deplored making the Bank a party question, but since the President will have it so, he must pay the penalty of his own rashness. As to the veto message, I am delighted with it. It has all the fury of a chained panther biting the bars of his cage. It is really a manifesto of anarchy—such as Marat or Robespierre might have issued to the [French revolutionary] mob

3. R. G. McGrane, ed., *Correspondence of Nicholas Biddle* . . . (1919), p. 196 (Aug. 1, 1832). By permission of the editor.

of the Faubourg St. Antoine [section of Paris]; and my hope is that it will contribute to relieve the country from the dominion of these miserable people. You are destined to be the instrument of that deliverance, and at no period of your life has the country ever had a deeper stake in you. I wish you success most cordially, because I believe the institutions of the Union are involved in it.

[*Biddle proved to be a poor prophet. The pro-Bank strategy backfired, and Jackson was triumphantly elected over Clay later that year.*]

C. THE NULLIFICATION CRISIS

1. South Carolina Threatens Secession (1832)

As if detonated by a delayed-action fuse, the tariff issue exploded during the Jackson-Clay campaign, and threatened to overshadow the Bank controversy. The recent tariff act of 1832, though watering down the "abominable" Tariff of 1828, aroused the South Carolinians by its reassertion of the protective principle. Excitedly summoning a special convention in Columbia, they formally declared that the two tariff acts "are unauthorized by the Constitution of the United States, and violate the true meaning and intent thereof, and are null, void, and no law, nor binding upon this State, its officers or citizens. . . ." The convention specifically forbade the enforcement of the federal tariff within the borders of the state, and bluntly threatened secession if the federal government employed force. Before adjourning, the delegates issued the following public appeal to the American people. Comment critically on the assumption that the other Southern states would have to follow South Carolina in dissolving the Union and that the tariff law was unconstitutional. Also form some judgment as to the earnestness of the South Carolinians.

If South Carolina should be driven out of the Union, all the other planting states, and some of the Western states, would follow by an almost absolute necessity. Can it be believed that Georgia, Mississippi, Tennessee, and even Kentucky, would continue to pay a tribute of 50 percent upon their consumption to the Northern states, for the privilege of being united to them, when they could receive all their supplies through the ports of South Carolina without paying a single cent for tribute?

The separation of South Carolina would inevitably produce a general dissolution of the Union, and, as a necessary consequence, the protecting system, with all its pecuniary bounties to the Northern states, and its pecuniary burdens upon the Southern states, would be utterly overthrown and demolished, involving the ruin of thousands and hundreds of thousands in the manufacturing states. . . .

With them, it is a question merely of pecuniary interest, connected with no shadow of right, and involving no principle of liberty. With us, it is a question involving our most sacred rights—those very rights which our common ancestors left to us as a common inheritance, purchased by their

1. *Daily National Intelligencer* (Washington), Dec. 7, 1832.

common toils, and consecrated by their blood. It is a question of liberty on the one hand, and slavery on the other.

If we submit to this system of unconstitutional oppression, we shall voluntarily sink into slavery, and transmit that ignominious inheritance to our children. We will not, we cannot, we dare not submit to this degradation; and our resolve is fixed and unalterable that a protecting tariff shall be no longer enforced within the limits of South Carolina. We stand upon the principles of everlasting justice, and no human power shall drive us from our position.

We have not the slightest apprehension that the General Government will attempt to force this system upon us by military power. We have warned our brethren of the consequences of such an attempt. But if, notwithstanding, such a course of madness should be pursued, we here solemnly declare that this system of oppression shall never prevail in South Carolina, until none but slaves are left to submit to it. We would infinitely prefer that the territory of the state should be the cemetery of freemen than the habitation of slaves. Actuated by these principles, and animated by these sentiments, we will cling to the pillars of the temple of our liberties, and, if it must fall, we will perish amidst the ruins.

2. Jackson Denounces Nullification (1832)

South Carolina's defiance of the federal government, combined with her feverish military preparations, angered her most famous native son, Commander-in-Chief General Andrew Jackson. Privately he issued orders to strengthen federal forces in Charleston harbor. Five days after his resounding re-election over Clay, he issued the following proclamation (ghostwritten by Secretary of State Edward Livingston) appealing to the Carolinians to forsake the treacherous paths of nullification and disunion. Note whether his appeal to practicalities is more convincing than that to patriotism, and whether he is prepared to negotiate with the South Carolinians.

For what would you exchange your share in the advantages and honor of the Union? For the dream of a separate independence—a dream interrupted by bloody conflicts with your neighbors and a vile dependence on a foreign power.

If your leaders could succeed in establishing a separation, what would be your situation? Are you united at home? Are you free from the apprehension of civil discord, with all its fearful consequences? Do our neighboring [Latin American] republics, every day suffering some new revolution or contending with some new insurrection, do they excite your envy?

But the dictates of a high duty oblige me solemnly to announce that you cannot succeed. The laws of the United States must be executed. I have no discretionary power on the subject; my duty is emphatically pronounced in the Constitution. Those who told you that you might peaceably prevent their execution deceived you; they could not have been deceived themselves. They know that a forcible opposition could alone prevent the

2. J. D. Richardson, ed., *Messages and Papers of the Presidents* (1896), II, 654–55.

execution of the laws, and they know that such opposition must be repelled. Their object is disunion.

But be not deceived by names. Disunion by armed force is *treason.* Are you really ready to incur its guilt? If you are, on the heads of the instigators of the act be the dreadful consequences; on their heads be the dishonor, but on yours may fall the punishment. On your unhappy state will inevitably fall all the evils of the conflict you force upon the government of your country. . . . The consequence must be fearful for you, distressing to your fellow citizens here and to the friends of good government throughout the world.

Its enemies have beheld our prosperity with a vexation they could not conceal. It was a standing refutation of their slavish doctrines, and they will point to our discord with the triumph of malignant joy. It is yet in your power to disappoint them. There is yet time to show that the descendants of the Pinckneys, the Sumters, the Rutledges, and of the thousand other names which adorn the pages of your Revolutionary history will not abandon that Union to support which so many of them fought and bled and died.

I adjure you, as you honor their memory, as you love the cause of freedom, to which they dedicated their lives, as you prize the peace of your country, the lives of its best citizens, and your own fair fame, to retrace your steps. Snatch from the archives of your state the disorganizing edict of its convention; bid its members to reassemble and promulgate the decided expressions of your will to remain in the path which alone can conduct you to safety, prosperity, and honor.

3. Jackson Fumes in Private (1832)

The Unionists of South Carolina, constituting perhaps two-fifths of the adult whites, were branded "submissionists, cowards, and Tories" by the nullifiers. But the Union men, undaunted, hanged John C. Calhoun and Governor Hamilton in effigy, held their own convention, and gathered weapons for their defense. One of their leaders in organizing the militia, Joel R. Poinsett, wrote of his activities to Jackson, even though the post office was infiltrated with nullifiers. The doughty General replied as follows in a letter whose original spelling, punctuation, and capitalization are here preserved as revealing of Jackson and his era. Article III, Section III of the Constitution states: "Treason against the United States shall consist only in levying war against them, or in adhering to their enemies, giving them aid and comfort." Was Jackson correct in branding the actions of the Carolinians "treason"? Was he more bellicose in this private letter than in his recently published proclamation?

Washington, December 9, 1832.

My D'r Sir, Your letters were this moment recd, from the hands of Col. Drayton, read and duly considered, and in haste I reply. The true spirit of patriotism that they breath fills me with pleasure. If the Union party unite

3. J. S. Bassett, ed., *Correspondence of Andrew Jackson* (1929), IV, 497–98. By permission of the Carnegie Institution of Washington. See also Fred Rippy, *Joel R. Poinsett, Versatile American* (1935).

with you, heart and hand in the text you have laid down, you will not only preserve the union, but save our native state, from that ruin and disgrace into which her treasonable leaders have attempted to plunge her. All the means in my power, I will employ to enable her own citizens, those faithful patriots, who cling to the Union to put it down.

The proclamation I have this day Issued, and which I inclose you, will give you my views, of the treasonable conduct of the convention and the Governors recommendation to the assembly—it is not merely rebellion, but the act of raising troops, positive treason, and I am assured by all the members of congress with whom I have conversed that I will be sustained by congress. If so, I will meet it at the threshold, and have the leaders arrested and arraigned for treason—I am only waiting to be furnished with the acts of your Legislature, to make a communication to Congress, ask the means necessary to carry my proclamation into compleat affect, and by an exemplary punishment of those leaders for treason so unprovoked, put down this rebellion, and strengthen our happy government both at home and abroad.

My former letter and the communication from the Dept. of War, will have informed you of the arms and equipments having been laid in Deposit subject to your requisition, to aid the civil authority in the due execution of the law, *whenever called on as the posse comitatus,* etc. etc.

The vain threats of resistance by those who have raised the standard of rebellion shew their madness and folly. You may assure those patriots who cling to their country, and this union, which alone secures our liberty prosperity and happiness, that in forty days, I can have within the limits of So. Carolina fifty thousand men, and in forty days more another fifty thousand—However potant the threat of resistance with only a population of 250,000 whites and nearly that double in blacks with our ships in the port to aid in the execution of our laws?—The wickedness, madness and folly of the leaders and the delusion of their followers in the attempt to destroy themselves and our union has not its paralel in the history of the world. The Union will be preserved. The safety of the republic, the supreme law, which will be promptly obeyed by me.

I will be happy to hear from you often, thro' Col. Mason or his son, if you think the postoffice unsafe   I am with sincere respect

yr mo. obdt. servt.

4. Hone Applauds Jackson's Vigor (1832)

Jackson's stirring proclamation, though greeted with jeers by South Carolina nullifiers, was roundly applauded in the North. Many anti-nullification mass meetings were held; the one in New York City alone attracted some 10,000 persons. The wealthy pro-Bank New York businessman Philip Hone, who had not "hurrahed" for Jackson in the recent Jackson-Clay presidential canvass, for once approved the irascible Hero

4. Bayard Tuckerman, ed., *The Diary of Philip Hone, 1828–1851* (1889), I, 68–69.

of New Orleans. In examining these entries from Hone's diary, note in what respects this staunch Whig accepts Jackson's interpretation of South Carolina's defiance, and what his only reservations are.

December 3 [1832].—The South Carolina convention have passed a number of resolutions, worse by far than the friends of union believed it possible for them to go. It is rank treason, and in my opinion the leaders deserve to be hanged. . . .

December 12.—Very much to the surprise of some and to the satisfaction of all our citizens, we have a long proclamation of President Jackson, which was published in Washington on the 12th inst., and is in all our papers this day. It is a document addressed to the nullifiers of South Carolina, occasioned by the late treasonable proceedings of their convention. The whole subject is discussed in a spirit of conciliation, but with firmness and decision, and a determination to put down the wicked attempt to resist the laws.

On the constitutionality of the laws which the nullifiers object to, and their right to recede from the Union, this able state paper is full and conclusive. The language of the President is that of a father addressing his wayward children, but determined to punish with the utmost severity the first open act of insubordination. As a composition it is splendid, and will take its place in the archives of our country, and will dwell in the memory of our citizens alongside of the Farewell Address of the "Father of His Country." It is not known which of the members of the Cabinet is entitled to the honor of being the author; it is attributed to Mr. Livingston, the Secretary of State, and to Governor Cass, the Secretary of War. Nobody, of course, supposes it was written by him whose name is subscribed to it. But whoever shall prove to be the author has raised to himself an imperishable monument of glory. The sentiments, at least, are approved by the President, and he should have the credit of it, as he would the blame if it were bad; and, possessing those sentiments, we have reason to believe that he has firmness enough to do his duty.

I say, Hurrah for Jackson! And so I am willing to say at all times when he does his duty. The only difference between the thoroughgoing Jackson men and me is that I will not "hurrah" for him right or wrong. And I think Jackson's [recent] election may save the Union. If he is sincere in this proclamation, he will put down this rebellion. . . . A majority of the people would have gone with him, right or wrong; they all will when he is right. In this able state paper he addresses the deluded people of South Carolina with tenderness, but seems to be gathering up his wrath to let it fall heavily on the heads of the ringleaders.

[*Jackson's stern words, both public and private, no doubt shook the South Carolinians. Supported by no other state, and riven by a Unionist minority, they finally came down off their high horse and accepted the lower schedules of the compromise Tariff of 1833.*]

D. THE VAN BUREN ERA

1. Crockett Caricatures Van Buren (1835)

Rifleman Davy Crockett, who perished at the Alamo early the next year (1836), permitted his name to be used by certain Whig politicians and ghost writers to cloak an anti-Jackson and anti-Van Buren campaign biography. A bitter foe of Jackson, Crockett feared that the "Gin'ral," seeking vengeance against political foes, would "appoint" the "little gentleman" from New York as his successor. This, essentially, is what happened in the campaign of 1836. Observe which alleged trait of Van Buren the Whigs seized upon most eagerly in this Crockett book. Actually Van Buren was a much stronger man than his foes would concede.

Van Buren is as opposite to General Jackson as dung is to a diamond. Jackson is open, bold, warm-hearted, confiding, and passionate to a fault. Van Buren is secret, sly, selfish, cold, calculating, distrustful, treacherous; and if he could gain an object just as well by openness as intrigue, he would choose the latter. . . .

But there is one thing in which I think *all* will agree, that Martin Van Buren is not the man he is cracked up to be; and that if he is made President of the United States, he will have reached a place to which he is not entitled, either by sense or sincerity; and that he owes his good luck to the hangers-on of office, who, to serve themselves, have used the popularity of General Jackson to abuse the country with Martin Van Buren. . . .

A pleasant anecdote is related of him when he was quite young. It is truly like him, and planted the principle upon which he has acted ever since. A warmly contested election was coming on, and the friends on both sides, being men of influence, used great exertions, and became much excited; our hero applied to quite a knowing politician for his opinion as to the result. The answer expressing much doubt, young Martin, casting his eyes wishfully towards the ground, said, "I do wish I knew which party would succeed, as I want to take a side, but don't like to be in the minority."

2. Hone Welcomes a Change (1837)

Balding little Martin Van Buren took the inaugural oath on March 4, 1837. Philip Hone, the wealthy New York Whig, although approving of Jackson's resolute stand against South Carolina, approved of little else done by "this terrible old man." Despite being a Whig, he expected better things of Van Buren's Democratic regime. In reading his diary entry, note why he had this confidence, and what most appalled him (and other aristocratic Whigs) about the Jackson administration.

March 4 [1837].—This is the end of General Jackson's administration— the most disastrous in the annals of the country, and one which will excite "the special wonder" of posterity. That such a man should have governed

---

1. David Crockett, *The Life of Martin Van Buren, Heir-Apparent to the "Government,"* *and the Appointed Successor of General Andrew Jackson* (16th ed., 1837), pp. 13, 20, 31–32.
2. Bayard Tuckerman, ed., *The Diary of Philip Hone, 1828–1851* (1889), I, 245–46.

this great country, with a rule more absolute than that of any hereditary monarch of Europe, and that the people should not only have submitted to it, but upheld and supported him in his encroachments upon their rights, and his disregard of the Constitution and the laws, will equally occasion the surprise and indignation of future generations. The people's indifference will prove that the love of liberty and independence is no longer an attribute of our people, and that the patriotic labors of the men of the Revolution have sunk like water in the sands, and that the vaunted rights of the people are considered by them as a "cunningly devised fable."

This is also the commencement of Mr. Van Buren's reign, the first New York President. He has said that it was "honor enough to have served [as Vice-President] under such a chief," and will no doubt for a time speak with reverence of the ladder by which he has risen to the summit of ambitious hopes. But I do not despair of him. He will be a party President, but he is too much of a gentleman to be governed by the rabble who surrounded his predecessor and administered to his bad passions. As a man, a gentleman, and a friend, I have great respect for Mr. Van Buren. I hate the cause, but esteem the man, and, although I differ in my expectations from some of my political friends, I am disposed to give him a fair chance.

THE DICTATORIAL JACKSON, 1837

The President, veto in hand, tramples on the people's rights. James Parton, *Caricature and Other Comic Art*, 1877.

3. Van Buren Opposes Handouts (1837)

President Van Buren, once described by a foreign diplomat as the most perfect imitation of a gentleman he had ever seen, was left to face the post-Jackson whirlwind. The frightful Panic of 1837, touched off in part by Jackson's bull-in-a-china-shop finance, brought bankruptcies, suicides, bank failures, shipping stagnation, mass unemployment, widespread hunger, and even food riots. In response to appeals for a helping hand from the federal government, Van Buren sent this Jeffersonian warning to Congress. Determine whether his reasoning is sound, why it could be adhered to in those times, and why the Democratic Party (Van Buren's party) departed from it so conspicuously during the Great Depression of the 1930's.

Those who look to the action of this Government for specific aid to the citizen to relieve embarrassments, arising from losses by revulsions in commerce and credit, lose sight of the ends for which it was created, and the powers with which it is clothed.

It was established to give security to us all in our lawful and honorable

3. J. D. Richardson, ed., *Messages and Papers of the Presidents* (1896), III, 344–45.

pursuits, under the lasting safeguard of republican institutions. It was not intended to confer special favors on individuals or on any classes of them; to create systems of agriculture, manufactures, or trade; or to engage in them either separately or in connection with individual citizens or organized associations. If its operations were to be directed for the benefit of any one class, equivalent favors must in justice be extended to the rest, and the attempt to bestow such favors with an equal hand, or even to select those who should most deserve them, would never be successful.

All communities are apt to look to government for too much. Even in our own country, where its powers and duties are so strictly limited, we are prone to do so, especially at periods of sudden embarrassment and distress.

But this ought not to be. The framers of our excellent Constitution, and the people who approved it with calm and sagacious deliberation, acted at the time on a sounder principle. They wisely judged that the less government interferes with private pursuits, the better for the general prosperity. It is not its legitimate object to make men rich, or to repair, by direct grants of money or legislation in favor of particular pursuits, losses not incurred in the public service. This would be substantially to use the property of some for the benefit of others. But its real duty—that duty the performance of which makes a good government the most precious of human blessings—is to enact and enforce a system of general laws commensurate with, but not exceeding, the objects of its establishment, and to leave every citizen and every interest to reap under its benign protection the rewards of virtue, industry, and prudence.

I cannot doubt that, on this as on all similar occasions, the Federal Government will find its agency most conducive to the security and happiness of the people when limited to the exercise of its conceded powers. In never assuming, even for a well-meant object, such powers as were not designed to be conferred upon it, we shall in reality do most for the general welfare. To avoid every unnecessary interference with the pursuits of the citizen will result in more benefit than to adopt measures which could only assist limited interests, and are eagerly, but perhaps naturally, sought for under the pressure of temporary circumstances.

If, therefore, I refrain from suggesting to Congress any specific plan for regulating the [stock and mercantile] exchanges of the country, relieving mercantile embarrassments, or interfering with the ordinary operations of foreign or domestic commerce, it is from a conviction that such measures are not within the constitutional province of the General Government, and that their adoption would not promote the real and permanent welfare of those they might be designed to aid.

4. Dickens Dislikes Yankee "Smartness" (1842)

Many British investors were hard hit by the Van Buren Panic of 1837. More than a half-dozen states, after plunging too deeply into debt, openly repudiated their

4. Charles Dickens, *American Notes,* Ch. 18.

outstanding bonds or defaulted on them. The world-famous novelist Charles Dickens, smarting from his losses in the Cairo [Illinois] City & Canal Company, made a memorable tour of America in 1842. The criticisms in his resulting book stirred up a storm of resentment in the United States, and contributed much ammunition to the verbal war with England discussed in the next chapter. Reconcile the American reputation for industry, morality, and churchgoing with the trait which, fairly or unfairly, Dickens here criticizes.

Another prominent feature [of America] is the love of "smart" dealing, which gilds over many a swindle and gross breach of trust, many a defalcation, public and private; and enables many a knave to hold his head up with the best, who well deserves a halter; though it has not been without its retributive operation, for this smartness has done more in a few years to impair the public credit, and to cripple the public resources, than dull honesty, however rash, could have effected in a century. The merits of a broken speculation, or a bankruptcy, or of a successful scoundrel, are not gauged by its or his observance of the golden rule, "Do as you would be done by," but are considered with reference to their smartness.

I recollect, on both occasions of our passing that ill-fated Cairo on the Mississippi, remarking on the bad effects such gross deceits must have when they exploded, in generating a want of confidence abroad, and discouraging foreign investment. But I was given to understand that this was a very smart scheme by which a deal of money had been made; and that its smartest feature was that they forgot these things abroad in a very short time, and speculated again, as freely as ever.

THE LAND OF LIBERTY

Sanctimonious Yankees pick the pockets of gullible British investors. Detail from cartoon. *Punch* (London), 1847.

The following dialogue I have held a hundred times:

"Is it not a very disgraceful circumstance that such a man as So-and-so should be acquiring a large property by the most infamous and odious means, and, notwithstanding all the crimes of which he has been guilty, should be tolerated and abetted by your citizens? He is a public nuisance, is he not?"

"Yes, sir."

"A convicted liar?"

"Yes, sir."

"He has been kicked, and cuffed, and caned?"

"Yes, sir."

"And he is utterly dishonorable, debased, and profligate?"

"Yes, sir."

"In the name of wonder, then, what is his merit?"

"Well, sir, he is a smart man."

5. Cooper Castigates Parties (1838)

The Jacksonian Democrats, heirs of the manhood-suffrage New Democracy, had hurrahed Jackson and Van Buren into the presidential chair with frothy, slogan-filled campaigns. The more aristocratic Whigs, finally stealing the thunder of the Jacksonites, hurrahed Van Buren out of the presidential chair and Harrison into it in the frothy hard-cider campaign of 1840. The political boss had now come into his own, and the national nominating conventions had become his to manipulate. The famed author of the Leatherstocking Tales, James Fenimore Cooper, after an extended sojourn abroad, returned to America and was shocked by what he found. The following blast that he published in 1838, two years before the hard-cider campaign, illustrates the bitterness that involved him in protracted public controversy, including numerous libel suits. Note how much of his indictment seems sound; how much of it is true today.

Party is known to encourage prejudice, and to lead men astray in the judgment of character. Thus it is we see one half the nation extolling those that the other half condemns, and condemning those that the other half extols. Both cannot be right, and as passions, interests, and prejudices are all enlisted on such occasions, it would be nearer the truth to say that both are wrong.

Party is an instrument of error, by pledging men to support its policy instead of supporting the policy of the state. Thus we see party-measures almost always in extremes, the resistance of opponents inducing the leaders to ask for more than is necessary.

Party leads to vicious, corrupt, and unprofitable legislation, for the sole purpose of defeating party. Thus have we seen those territorial divisions and regulations which ought to be permanent, as well as other useful laws, altered [gerrymandered], for no other end than to influence an election. . . .

The discipline and organization of party are expedients to defeat the intention of the institutions, by putting managers in the place of the people; it being of little avail that a majority elect, when the nomination rests in the hands of a few. . . .

Party pledges the representative to the support of the Executive, right or wrong, when the institutions intend that he shall be pledged only to justice, expediency, and the right, under the restrictions of the Constitution.

When party rules, the people do not rule, but merely such a portion of the people as can manage to get the control of party. The only method by which the people can completely control the country is by electing representatives known to prize and understand the institutions; and who, so far from being pledged to support an administration, are pledged to support nothing but the right, and whose characters are guarantees that this pledge will be respected.

The effect of party is always to supplant established power. In a monarchy it checks the king; in a democracy it controls the people.

Party, by feeding the passions and exciting personal interests, overshadows truth, justice, patriotism, and every other public virtue, completely

5. James F. Cooper, *The American Democrat* (1838), pp. 180–81.

reversing the order of a democracy by putting unworthy motives in the place of reason.

It is a very different thing to be a democrat, and to be a member of what is called a Democratic Party; for the first insists on his independence and an entire freedom of opinion, while the last is incompatible with either.

The great body of the nation has no real interest in party. Every local election should be absolutely independent of great party divisions, and until this be done, the intentions of the American institutions will never be carried out, in their excellence. . . .

No freeman who really loves liberty and who has a just perception of its dignity, character, action, and objects will ever become a mere party man. He may have his preferences as to measures and men, may act in concert with those who think with himself, on occasions that require concert. But it will be his earnest endeavor to hold himself a free agent, and most of all to keep his mind untrammeled by the prejudices, frauds, and tyranny of factions.

THOUGHT PROVOKERS

1. Explain why basically the Indians and the white men could not live peacefully side by side. What are the moral implications of the argument that the Indians were not putting their land to good use?

2. Why did Jackson's veto of the Bank recharter appeal so strongly to the masses? Was Jackson right? Should foreigners have been allowed to hold stock in the Bank? Is it better to have aristocratically controlled financial institutions that are sound than democratically controlled financial institutions that are less sound?

3. Should Jackson have taken a stronger position in public against South Carolina? Should he have used force? Who won in the struggle over nullification, especially in view of the forthcoming Civil War? Would a "preventive war" at this time have been wise policy for Jackson?

4. Would Van Buren have approved federal unemployment relief and price supports as we now know them? What would probably have happened during the Great Depression of the 1930's if President Franklin Roosevelt had pursued Van Buren's philosophy? Present a rebuttal to Cooper's case against political parties, and speculate on how our government would function today if Cooper's views were to prevail.

FURTHER EXPLORATION

General: G. G. Van Deusen, *The Jacksonian Era* (1959); A. M. Schlesinger, Jr., *The Age of Jackson* (1945). **Indian Removal:** Angie Debo, *The Road to Disappearance* (1941); Grant Foreman, *Indian Removal* (1932). **Bank War:** Bray Hammond, *Banks and Politics in America from the Revolution to the Civil War* (1957); R. C. H. Catterall, *The Second Bank of the United States* (1903); T. P. Govan, *Nicholas Biddle* (1959). **Nullification:** C. S. Boucher, *The Nullification Controversy in South Carolina* (1916); C. M. Wiltse, *John C. Calhoun: Nullifier, 1829–1839* (1949). **Van Buren:** Holmes Alexander, *The American Talleyrand* (1935); R. C. McGrane, *The Panic of 1837* (1924); R. G. Gunderson, *The Log Cabin Campaign* (1957).

Recent: W. W. Freehling, *Prelude to Civil War: The Nullification Controversy in South Carolina, 1816–1836* (1966); Robert Seager II, *And Tyler Too: A Biography of John and Julia Gardiner Tyler* (1963).

Chapter 15

Oregon, Texas, and War with Mexico

If you will take all the theft, all the assaults, all the cases of arson, ever committed in time of peace in the United States since the settlement of Jamestown in 1608 [1607], and add to them all the cases of violence offered to woman, with all the murders, they will not amount to half the wrongs committed in this war for the plunder of Mexico.

THEODORE PARKER, ABOLITIONIST CLERGYMAN, 1848

PROLOGUE: Hereditary British-American antipathy, inflamed by the poison pens of English critics, came to a head in 1846 over extreme American demands for the boundary line of 54° 40′ in the Oregon Country. The dispute was settled later that year by a compromise on the line of 49°. Meanwhile the overconfident Mexicans, not unwilling to fight and encouraged by the prospect of an Anglo-American conflict over Oregon, were threatening the United States with war over the annexation of the revolted province of Texas. President Polk, unable to buy coveted California from the Mexicans or to adjust other disputes with them, forced a showdown in 1846 by moving American troops provocatively close to the Mexican border. In the ensuing war the Americans were everywhere victorious—General Zachary Taylor in northern Mexico at Monterrey and Buena Vista; General Winfield Scott at Cerro Gordo and elsewhere in his spectacular drive toward Mexico City. By the terms of peace, Polk finally secured California —and an aggravated slavery problem to boot.

A. THE WAR OF WORDS WITH BRITAIN

1. Mrs. Trollope's Tart Comments (1832)

Notorious among the numerous English traveler-critics of America in the 1830's and 1840's was Mrs. Frances Trollope, later famous as a novelist and as the mother of two novelists. Seeking to repair the family fortunes, she set up a bazaar for fancy goods in crude Cincinnati—and failed miserably. After returning to England with the stench of the pork-packing plants in her nostrils, she dipped her pen in acid and wrote a book condemning the lack of culture and refinement in the United States. It was devoured in England, denounced in America. The cry "A Trollope! A Trollope!" was sometimes enough to shame the rabble into silence in American theaters and other public places. In this description of her coach trip in New York state, locate the half-dozen or more traits of Americans that Mrs. Trollope finds most offensive.

The coach stopped to take in "a lady" at Vernon. She entered, and completely filled the last vacant inch of our vehicle, for "we were eight" before.

But no sooner was she seated than her beau came forward with a most enormous best-bonnet box. He paused for a while to meditate the possi-

---

1. Frances Trollope, *Domestic Manners of the Americans* (1832), II, 277–80.

268

bilities—raised it, as if to place it in our laps—sunk it, as if to put it beneath our feet. Both alike appeared impossible; when, in true Yankee style, he addressed one of our party with,

"If you'll just step out a minute, I guess I'll find room for it."

"Perhaps so. But how shall I find room for myself afterwards?"

This was uttered in European accents, and in an instant half a dozen whiskey drinkers stepped from before the whiskey store, and took the part of the beau.

"That's because you'll be English travelers, I expect, but we have traveled in better countries than Europe—we have traveled in America—and the box will go, I calculate."

We remonstrated on the evident injustice of the proceeding, and I ventured to say that, as we had none of us any luggage in the carriage, because the space was so very small, I thought a chance passenger could have no right so greatly to incommode us.

"Right!—there they go—that's just their way—that will do in Europe, maybe; it sounds just like English tyranny, now—don't it? But it won't do here." And thereupon he began thrusting in the wooden box against our legs with all his strength.

"No law, sir, can permit such conduct as this."

"Law!" exclaimed a gentleman very particularly drunk; "we makes our own laws, and governs our own selves."

"Law!" echoed another gentleman of Vernon; "this is a free country; we have no laws here; and we don't want no foreign power to tyrannize over us."

I give the words exactly. It is, however, but fair to state that the party had evidently been drinking more than an usual portion of whiskey; but, perhaps, in whiskey, as in wine, truth may come to light. At any rate, the people of the Western Paradise follow the Gentiles in this, that they are a law unto themselves.

During this contest, the coachman sat upon the box without saying a word, but seemed greatly to enjoy the jokes. The question of the box, however, was finally decided in our favor by the nature of the human material, which cannot be compressed beyond a certain degree.

2. The *Democratic Review* Strikes Back (1844)

America in the 1830's and 1840's was the beacon light of democracy in a monarchy-ridden world. England was a stronghold of conservatism. The British upper class, as represented in American eyes by travelers like Captain Marryat, was interested in dampening democratic agitation at home by exposing the United States as the land of the boor, the blusterer, and the bully. Viewing the rustic scene through an amber spray of tobacco juice, English visitors wrote travel books that stressed shortcomings ranging from the horrors of Negro slavery to the eye gouging of no-holds-barred wrestling. One of the most nationalistic of the American magazines struck back in the following blistering article. Note what the writer finds most offensive about British

2. *United States Magazine and Democratic Review,* n.s., XIV (1844), 338–39.

criticisms, why he regards the traveler as ungrateful, and what the article reveals about American nationalism in a year when the nation was about to shout "Fifty-four forty or fight!"

The first words of the British critic indicate that we are about to encounter a foe; and the first page of a British traveler announces at once the spirit by which he is inspired. We feel instinctively that a stranger has been among us to spy out and exaggerate our foibles, faults, and weaknesses; to take advantage of our frankness and hospitality for the purpose of assailing us with sarcasm, ridicule, misrepresentation, and slander; to peep behind our doors, look under our beds, pry into our closets, and become the pimp of scandal for the purpose of collecting a mass of insignificant trash, which he may pervert to the dastardly, malignant purpose of administering to the imaginary superiority of one nation by pointing out the imaginary inferiority of another. They know that the sole object of these travelers in visiting the United States is to concoct a book that will be popular at home, which they can only do by following the example of the gallant Captain Marryat, R.N., as disclosed with such amiable simplicity and frankness in his letter to the *Edinburgh Review,* when he says, "My great object was to do serious injury to Democracy."

Hence, the people of the United States are little likely to receive any benefit from being told of their faults, real or imaginary, by such monitors as those who virtually say to them, "My good friends, you are a pack of gouging, spitting, boasting, ignorant, dishonest, impious, rascally republicans, who are going headlong into anarchy and ruin. This you can't deny, for we all agree in that particular. Now I am come on purpose to give you some good advice, namely, as soon as possible to discard your contemptible government, which in fact is no government at all, and return to the good old system of hereditary kings, hereditary nobility, and an established church. Above all, I advise you to abandon that disgusting, degrading, and abominable system of equality, the invariable tendency of which is to make all men equally vulgar, ignorant, and independent. Do this, my good friends, and there is some ground for hoping you will in time cease to be such a contemptible, degraded nation of gouging, spitting, boasting, ignorant, dishonest, impious cowards as I am sorry to say you are at present."

Surely this is not the way to discipline grown-up nations, correct their faults, or cure their foibles. The pride of human nature, however degraded, revolts at such a course of culture, which begins by wounding the feelings, and ends by generating an obstinate perseverance in error, rather than a disposition to reform. Yet this is the mode adopted by a great portion of British writers, and most especially British travelers, the latter of whom, from time to time, come among us, as it were, seeking whom they shall devour; receive our homage, partake our hospitalities, and despise us for that miserable subserviency by which we so often degrade ourselves.

It is not, however, my design to intimate that this absurd homage, which reminds me of a circle of Indians offering incense to a boar, or these liberal hospitalities, should operate as a bribe for the suppression of their opinions. Still, I confess I cannot help despising a man from the bottom of my soul who visits this country with a premeditated design of libeling it, and yet not only accepts but courts the attention of those he affects to despise. One who sits down at the table of his liberal entertainer, to partake of his fare and share in his social enjoyments, not as a friendly guest, but as an insidious, malignant spy, watching with ceaseless assiduity for some trifling lapse of etiquette, some insignificant departure from those arbitrary modes which he is pleased to consider the standard of taste, the criterion of refinement, and which he may trumpet to the world as the vulgar "spawn of Democracy."

B. THE DEBATE OVER OREGON

1. Senator McDuffie Belittles Oregon (1843)

British critics also aimed their shafts at alleged Yankee land-grabbing, which was highlighted by the Anglo-American dispute over the vast Oregon Country. The controversy came to a boil in 1843, when Congress heatedly debated but finally rejected a bill to fortify the overland route to Oregon and grant land to the Americans settling there. Senator McDuffie of South Carolina, an impassioned pro-slavery orator (see p. 239), vehemently opposed the acquisition of free-soil Oregon, although he had favored the annexation of slave-soil Texas. Observe in what respects his foresight and his geographical knowledge were faulty. Or was he just overstating his case?

What do we want with this [Oregon] territory? What are we to do with it? What is to be the consequence of our taking possession of it? What is the act we are called on now to do? Why, it is neither more nor less than an act of colonization, for the first time proposed since the foundation of this government.

If this were a question of gradual, and continuous, and progressive settlement—if the territory to which our citizens are invited were really to become a part of the Union, it would present a very different question. But, sir, does any man seriously suppose that any state which can be formed at the mouth of the Columbia River, or any of the inhabitable parts of that territory, would ever become one of the states of the Union?

I have great faith . . . in the power of the representative principle to extend the sphere of government. But I confess that, even in the most sanguine days of my youth, I never conceived the possibility of embracing within the same government people living five thousand miles apart.

But, sir, the worthy Senator from New Hampshire [Mr. Woodbury] seems to have discovered a principle much more potent than the representative principle. He refers you to steam, far more potent. I should doubt very much whether the elements or powers, or organization of the principles of government, will ever be changed by steam.

1. *Congressional Globe,* 27 Cong., 3 sess., XII, pp. 199–200.

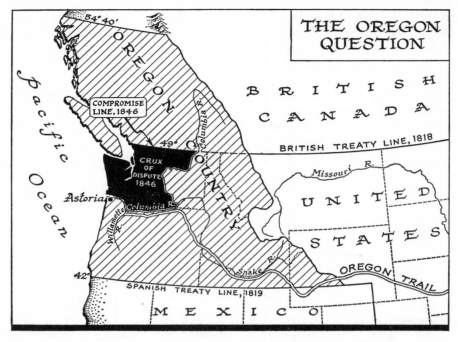

THE OREGON QUESTION

Steam! How are you to apply steam in this case? Has the Senator examined the character of the country? What is the character of the country? Why, as I understand it, that about seven hundred miles this side of the Rocky Mountains is uninhabitable, where rain scarcely ever falls—a barren sandy soil. On the other side—we have it from a very intelligent gentleman [Frémont?], sent to explore that country by the State Department, that there are three successive ridges of mountains extending towards the Pacific, and running nearly parallel; which mountains are totally impassable, except in certain parts, where there are gaps or depressions, to be reached only by going one hundred miles out of the direct course.

Well, now, what are we to do in such a case as this? How are we going to apply steam? Have you made anything like an estimate of the cost of a railroad running from here to the mouth of the Columbia? Why, the wealth of the Indies would not be sufficient. You would have to tunnel through mountains five hundred or six hundred miles in extent. It is true they [the British] have constructed a tunnel beneath the Thames, but at a vast expenditure of capital. With a bankrupt Treasury and a depressed and suffering people, to talk about constructing a railroad to the western shore of the continent manifests a wild spirit of adventure which I never expected to hear broached in the Senate of the United States. . . .

Why, sir, of what use will this be for agricultural purposes? I would not for that purpose give a pinch of snuff for the whole territory. I wish to

God we did not own it. I wish it was an impassable barrier to secure us against the intrusion of others.

2. Senator Hannegan Demands 54° 40′ (1846)

The Democratic Party, when nominating Polk for the Presidency at Baltimore in 1844, had demanded the annexation of the Republic of Texas and the acquisition of Oregon all the way to 54° 40′. Texas entered the Union as a slave state in 1845. A year later Congress, before acquiescing in the Oregon compromise line of 49°, was debating resolutions proclaiming American ownership of all the territory to the line of 54° 40′. Senator Hannegan, an intemperate orator (and drinker) from Indiana, was the most bellicose spokesman for the free-soil Northwest. From his Senate speech —reported in the third person—form conclusions as to the existing upsurge of nationalism and as to the logic of his charges of bad faith on the part of the South.

Now, if the adoption of the [Oregon] resolutions, which contained the immutable principles of truth, should bring war on us, let war come! What American was there who, through fear of war, would hesitate to declare the truth in this Chamber? He [Hannegan] also was for peace. He shrunk back from the thought of war as much as could the Senator from South Carolina [Calhoun]. He loved peace; but if it were only to be maintained on degrading and dishonorable terms, war, even of extermination, would be far preferable. . . .

There had been a singular course pursued on this Oregon question, and with reference to which he must detain the Senate a moment. It contrasted so strangely, so wonderfully, with a precisely similar question—the annexation of Texas. Texas and Oregon were born the same instant, nursed and cradled in the same cradle—the Baltimore Convention—and they were at the same instant adopted by the Democracy throughout the land. There was not a moment's hesitation, until Texas was admitted. But the moment she was admitted, the peculiar friends of Texas turned, and were doing all they could to strangle Oregon!

But the country were not blind or deaf. The people see, they comprehend, and he trusted they would speak. It was a most singular state of things. We were told that we must be careful not to involve ourselves in a war with England on a question of disputed boundary. There was a question of disputed boundary between us and Mexico. But did we hear, from the same quarter, any warning against a collision with Mexico when we were about to consummate the annexation of Texas? We were told by those who knew something of these matters that the Nueces [River] was the proper boundary of Texas! And how did they find the friends of Texas moving on that occasion? Did we, for a single instant, halt on the banks of the Nueces? No; at a single bound we crossed the Nueces, and the blasts of our trumpets, and the prancing of our war-horses, were heard on the banks of the Rio del Norte [Rio Grande], one hundred miles beyond.

2. *Ibid.,* 29 Cong., 1 sess., XV, Pt. 1, pp. 109–10.

"WHAT? YOU YOUNG YANKEE-NOODLE, STRIKE
YOUR OWN FATHER!"

The Yankee, with unkempt hair and slave-driver's
whip, ready to fight over Oregon. *Punch* (London),
1846.

Nearly one hundred miles of disputed territory gives no cause for a
moment's hesitation!

There was no negotiation then, so far as Mexico was concerned: we took
all. But when Oregon is brought into question, we are called on, as an act
proper and right, to give away a whole empire on the Pacific, if England
desire it. He never would consent to a surrender of any portion of the
country north of 49°, nor one foot, by treaty or otherwise, under 54° 40′.

C. PROVOKING WAR WITH MEXICO

1. Sumner Assails the Texas Grab (1847)

Boston-bred and Harvard-polished Charles Sumner, soon to be a United States
Senator, was one of the most impressive orators of his day. Six feet four inches in
height, and blessed with a powerful voice, he could sway vast audiences. An earnest
foe of war, he preached arbitration; an impassioned enemy of slavery, he demanded
abolition; a devoted champion of race equality, he fought the Massachusetts law
forbidding marriages between whites and blacks. In 1847, in the midst of the war
with Mexico, the Massachusetts legislature adopted this document which he had
prepared blasting the annexation of Texas. While he overplays the slave conspiracy

1. *Old South Leaflets* (Boston, 1904), VI, no. 132, pp. 2–4.

accusation, he makes a number of telling points. Assuming that his facts are correct, determine how many genuine grievances Mexico had against the United States.

The history of the annexation of Texas cannot be fully understood without reverting to the early settlement of that province by citizens of the United States.

Mexico, on achieving her independence of the Spanish Crown, by a general ordinance worthy of imitation by all Christian nations, had decreed the abolition of human slavery within her dominions, embracing the province of Texas. . . .

At this period, citizens of the United States had already begun to remove into Texas, hardly separated, as it was, by the River Sabine from the slave-holding state of Louisiana. The idea was early promulgated that this extensive province ought to become a part of the United States. Its annexation was distinctly agitated in the Southern and Western states in 1829; and it was urged on the ground of the strength and extension it would give to the "Slave Power," and the fresh market it would open for the sale of slaves.

The suggestion of this idea had an important effect. A current of emigration soon followed from the United States. Slaveholders crossed the Sabine with their slaves, in defiance of the Mexican ordinance of freedom. Restless spirits, discontented at home, or feeling the restraint of the narrow confines of our country, joined them; while their number was swollen by the rude and lawless of all parts of the land, who carried to Texas the love of license which had rendered a region of justice no longer a pleasant home to them. To such spirits, rebellion was natural.

It soon broke forth. At this period the whole [Texan] population, including women and children, did not amount to twenty thousand; and, among these, most of the older and wealthier inhabitants still favored peace. A Declaration of Independence, a farcical imitation of that of our fathers, was put forth, not by persons acting in a Congress or in a representative character, but by about ninety individuals—all, except two, from the United States—acting for themselves, and recommending a similar course to their fellow citizens. In a just cause the spectacle of this handful of adventurers, boldly challenging the power of Mexico, would excite our sympathy, perhaps our admiration. But successful rapacity, which seized broad and fertile lands while it opened new markets for slaves, excites no sentiment but that of abhorrence.

The work of rebellion sped. Citizens of the United States joined its fortunes, not singly, but in numbers, even in armed squadrons. Our newspapers excited the lust of territorial robbery in the public mind. Expeditions were openly equipped within our own borders. Advertisements for volunteers summoned the adventurous, as to patriotic labors. Military companies, with officers and standards, directed their steps to the revolted province.

During all this period the United States were at peace with Mexico. A proclamation from our government, forbidding these hostile preparations within our borders, is undeniable evidence of their existence, while truth compels us to record its impotence in upholding the sacred duties of neutrality between Mexico and the insurgents. . . .

The Texan flag waved over an army of American citizens. Of the six or eight hundred who won the [decisive] battle of San Jacinto, scattering the Mexican forces and capturing their general [Santa Anna], not more than fifty were citizens of Texas having grievances of their own to redress on that field.

The victory was followed by the recognition of the independence of Texas by the United States; while the new state took its place among the nations of the earth. . . .

Certainly our sister republic [Mexico] might feel aggrieved by this conduct. It might justly charge our citizens with disgraceful robbery, while, in seeking extension of slavery, they repudiated the great truths of American freedom.

Meanwhile Texas slept on her arms, constantly expecting new efforts from Mexico to regain her former power. The two combatants regarded each other as enemies. Mexico still asserted her right to the territory wrested from her, and refused to acknowledge its independence.

Texas turned for favor and succor to England. The government of the United States, fearing it might pass under the influence of this power, made overtures for its annexation to our country. This was finally accomplished by joint resolutions of Congress, in defiance of the Constitution [?], and in gross insensibility to the sacred obligations of amity with Mexico, imposed alike by treaty and by justice, "both strong against the deed." The Mexican minister regarded it as an act offensive to his country, and, demanding his passport, returned home.

2. Polk Justifies the Texas Coup (1845)

The United States had tried to wrest Texas from Spain under the vague terms of the Louisiana Purchase, but had at last abandoned such claims in the swap that netted the Floridas in 1819. The Texan-Americans finally staged a successful revolt against Mexico in 1835–1836, but for nine years lived in constant apprehension of a renewed Mexican invasion. Three days before President Polk took office on March 4, 1845, President Tyler had signed a joint resolution of Congress offering the Republic of Texas annexation to the United States. All that remained was for the Texans to accept the terms, and this they formally did on June 23, 1845. The tension was heightened by the keen interest of Britain and France in making Texas a satellite, with the consequent dangers of involving the United States in war. Polk, a purposeful and persistent expansionist, justified the annexation as follows in his inaugural address. List his arguments and determine which one is the most convincing from the standpoint of the United States; which the least convincing from the standpoint of Mexico. Note also whether he handles the slavery issue persuasively.

The Republic of Texas has made known her desire to come into our Union, to form a part of our Confederacy and enjoy with us the blessings

2. J. D. Richardson, ed., *Messages and Papers of the Presidents* (1897), IV, 379–81.

of liberty secured and guaranteed by our Constitution. Texas was once a part of our country—was unwisely ceded away to a foreign power [in 1819] —is now independent, and possesses an undoubted right to dispose of a part or the whole of her territory, and to merge her sovereignty as a separate and independent state in ours. . . .

I regard the question of annexation as belonging exclusively to the United States and Texas. They are independent powers, competent to contract; and foreign nations have no right to interfere with them or to take exception to their reunion. . . . Foreign powers should therefore look on the annexation of Texas to the United States, not as the conquest of a nation seeking to extend her dominions by arms and violence, but as the peaceful acquisition of a territory once her own, by adding another member to our Confederation, with the consent of that member, thereby diminishing the chances of war and opening to them new and ever-increasing markets for their products.

To Texas, the reunion is important because the strong protecting arm of our government would be extended over her, and the vast resources of her fertile soil and genial climate would be speedily developed, while the safety of New Orleans and of our whole southwestern frontier against hostile aggression, as well as the interests of the whole Union, would be promoted by it. . . .

None can fail to see the danger to our safety and future peace if Texas remains an independent state, or becomes an ally or dependency of some foreign nation more powerful than herself. Is there one among our citizens who would not prefer perpetual peace with Texas to occasional wars, which so often occur between bordering independent nations? Is there one who would not prefer free intercourse with her, to high duties on all our products and manufactures which enter her ports or cross her frontiers? Is there one who would not prefer an unrestricted communication with her citizens, to the frontier obstructions which must occur if she remains out of the Union?

Whatever is good or evil in the local [slave] institutions of Texas will remain her own, whether annexed to the United States or not. None of the present states will be responsible for them any more than they are for the local institutions of each other. They have confederated together for certain specified objects. Upon the same principle that they would refuse to form a perpetual union with Texas because of her local institutions, our forefathers would have been prevented from forming our present Union.

3. The Cabinet Debates War (1846)

The expansionist Polk, fearing that so-called British land-grabbers would forestall him, was eager to purchase California from Mexico. But the proud Mexicans, though bankrupt, refused to sell. They also threatened war over the annexation of Texas, and

3. M. M. Quaife, ed., *The Diary of James K. Polk* (1910), I, 384–86. By permission of the Chicago Historical Society.

defaulted on their payment of claims to Americans for damages during their recent revolutionary disturbances. Polk made a last-hope effort to buy California and adjust other disputes when he sent John Slidell to Mexico as a special envoy late in 1845. But the Mexicans refused to negotiate with him. Polk then ordered General Taylor to move his small army from Corpus Christi on the Nueces River (the traditional southwest border of Texas) to the Rio Grande del Norte (which the Texans extravagantly claimed as their new boundary). Still the Mexicans did not attack the provocative Yankee invader. Polk thereupon recommended to his Cabinet a declaration of war, presumably on the basis of (a) unpaid damage claims and (b) Slidell's rejection. Both were rather flimsy pretexts. From this passage in his diary, decide whether the President was really trying to avoid a fight, and whether his grounds for war were valid, even after sixteen American soldiers were killed or wounded.

Saturday, 9th May, 1846.—The Cabinet held a regular meeting today; all the members present.

I brought up the Mexican question, and the question of what was the duty of the administration in the present state of our relations with that country. The subject was very fully discussed.

All agreed that if the Mexican forces at Matamoros committed any act of hostility on Gen'l Taylor's forces, I should immediately send a message to Congress recommending an immediate declaration of war.

I stated to the Cabinet that up to this time, as they knew, we had heard of no open act of aggression by the Mexican army, but that the danger was imminent that such acts would be committed. I said that in my opinion we had ample cause of war, and that it was impossible that we could stand *in statu quo,* or that I could remain silent much longer; that I thought it was my duty to send a message to Congress very soon and recommend definitive measures. I told them that I thought I ought to make such a message by Tuesday next; that the country was excited and impatient on the subject; and if I failed to do so, I would not be doing my duty.

I then propounded the distinct question to the Cabinet, and took their opinions individually, whether I should make a message to Congress on Tuesday, and whether in that message I should recommend a declaration of war against Mexico.

All except the Secretary of the Navy [Bancroft] gave their advice in the affirmative. Mr. Bancroft dissented, but said if any act of hostility should be committed by the Mexican forces, he was then in favor of immediate war. Mr. Buchanan [Secretary of State] said he would feel better satisfied in his course if the Mexican forces had or should commit any act of hostility, but that as matters stood we had ample cause of war against Mexico, and he gave his assent to the measure.

It was agreed that the message should be prepared and submitted to the Cabinet in their meeting on Tuesday. . . .

About 6 o'clock P.M. Gen'l R. Jones, the Adjutant General of the Army, called and handed to me despatches received from Gen'l Taylor by the Southern mail which had just arrived, giving information that a part of [the] Mexican army had crossed . . . the [Rio Grande] Del Norte, and

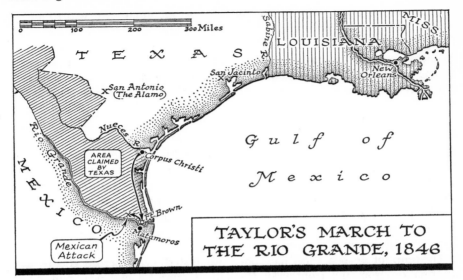

TAYLOR'S MARCH TO THE RIO GRANDE, 1846

attacked and killed and captured two companies of dragoons of Gen'l Taylor's army, consisting of 63 officers and men. . . .

I immediately summoned the Cabinet to meet at 7½ o'clock this evening. The Cabinet accordingly assembled at that hour; all the members present. The subject of the despatch received this evening from Gen'l Taylor, as well as the state of our relations with Mexico, were fully considered. The Cabinet were unanimously of opinion, and it was so agreed, that a message should be sent to Congress on Monday laying all the information in my possession before them, and recommending vigorous and prompt measure[s] to enable the Executive to prosecute the war.

4. The President Blames Mexico (1846)

The hundred-mile-wide expanse between the Nueces River and the Rio Grande, virtually uninhabited except for tens of thousands of wild horses, was clearly in dispute between the United States and Mexico, although the Mexicans still claimed all of revolted Texas. The blunt truth is that the Mexican title to the disputed area was then the stronger. The Whigs and other anti-slavery foes of the Democratic Polk, regarding him as a willing tool of the expansionist Southern "slavocracy," condemned him as a liar ("Polk the Mendacious") for his allegations that Mexico, rather than the United States, had provoked the war. In the President's war message to Congress, given herewith with italics inserted by the present editor, discover what warrant there is for this accusation. Did the United States have just grounds for war?

The grievous wrongs perpetrated by Mexico upon our citizens throughout a long period of years remain unredressed, and solemn [claims] treaties pledging her public faith for this redress have been disregarded. A government either unable or unwilling to enforce the execution of such treaties fails to perform one of its plainest duties.

4. J. D. Richardson, ed., *Messages and Papers of the Presidents* (1897), IV, 441–42.

Our commerce with Mexico has been almost annihilated. It was formerly highly beneficial to both nations, but our merchants have been deterred from prosecuting it by the system of outrage and extortion which the Mexican authorities have pursued against them, whilst their appeals through their own government for indemnity have been made in vain. Our forbearance has gone to such an extreme as to be mistaken in its character. Had we acted with vigor in repelling the insults and redressing the injuries inflicted by Mexico at the commencement, we should doubtless have escaped all the difficulties in which we are now involved.

Instead of this, however, we have been exerting our best efforts to propitiate her good will. Upon the pretext that Texas, a nation as independent as herself, thought proper to unite its destinies with our own, she has affected to believe that we have severed her rightful territory, and in official proclamations and manifestoes has repeatedly threatened to make war upon us for the purpose of reconquering Texas. In the meantime, we have tried every effort at reconciliation.

The cup of forbearance had been exhausted even before the recent information from the frontier of the [Rio Grande] Del Norte. But now, after reiterated menaces, Mexico has passed the boundary of the United States, has *invaded our territory*, and *shed American blood upon the American soil*. She has proclaimed that hostilities have commenced, and that the two nations are now at war.

As war exists, and, *notwithstanding all our efforts to avoid it*, exists by the act of Mexico herself, we are called upon by every consideration of duty and patriotism to vindicate with decision the honor, the rights, and the interests of our country.

D. OPPOSITION TO THE WAR

1. Massachusetts Voices Condemnation (1847)

The killing or wounding of sixteen American soldiers on American (?) soil precipitated war with Mexico. But the abolitionists and the free-soil Whigs of the North, resenting an alleged grab for more slave territory, gradually increased their clamor for peace. The following mid-war resolution, drafted by the orator Charles Sumner and passed by the legislature of Massachusetts in 1847, betrayed an ugly frame of mind. Ascertain in what respects this statement is sound in describing the outbreak of war, in what respects unsound, and in what respects it verges on treason.

This was the state of things when . . . General Taylor was directed, by the President of the United States, to occupy the east bank of the Rio Grande, being the extreme western part of the territory claimed by Texas, the boundaries of which had been designated as an "open question," to be determined by "negotiation." General Taylor broke up his quarters at Corpus Christi on the 11th March, and, proceeding across this disputed territory, established his post, and erected a battery, directly opposite the

1. *Old South Leaflets* (1904), VI, no. 132, pp. 10–11, 30–31.

Mexican city of Matamoros, and, under his directions, the mouth of the Rio Grande was blockaded, so as to cut off supplies from the Mexican army at Matamoros. . . .

These were acts of war, accomplished without bloodshed. But they were nevertheless acts of unquestioned hostility against Mexico. Blockade! and military occupation of a disputed territory! These were the arbiters of the "open question" of boundary. These were the substitutes for "negotiation."

It is not to be supposed that the Mexican army should quietly endure these aggressive measures, and regard with indifference cannon pointed at their position. . . . On the 26th of April a small body of American troops, under the command of Captain Thornton, encountered Mexican troops at a place twenty miles north of General Taylor's camp. Here was the first collision of arms. The report of this was hurried to Washington. Rumor, with a hundred tongues, exaggerated the danger of the American army under General Taylor, and produced an insensibility to the aggressive character of the movement. . . .

It was under the influence of this feeling that the untoward act of May 13th was pressed through Congress, by which it was declared that "war exists by the act of Mexico". . . . The passage of this act placed the whole country in hostile array against Mexico, and impressed upon every citizen of the United States the relation of enemy of every citizen of Mexico. This disastrous condition still continues. War is still waged; and our armies, after repeated victories achieved on Mexican soil, are still pursuing the path of conquest. . . .

Resolves. Concerning the Mexican War, and the Institution of Slavery.

Resolved, That the present war with Mexico has its primary origin in the unconstitutional annexation to the United States of the foreign state of Texas while the same was still at war with Mexico; that it was unconstitutionally commenced by the order of the President, to General Taylor, to take military possession of territory in dispute between the United States and Mexico, and in the occupation of Mexico; and that it is now waged ingloriously—by a powerful nation against a weak neighbor—unnecessarily and without just cause, at immense cost of treasure and life, for the dismemberment of Mexico, and for the conquest of a portion of her territory, from which slavery has already been excluded, with the triple object of extending slavery, of strengthening the "Slave Power," and of obtaining the control of the Free States, under the Constitution of the United States.

Resolved, That such a war of conquest, so hateful in its objects, so wanton, unjust, and unconstitutional in its origin and character, must be regarded as a war against freedom, against humanity, against justice, against the Union, against the Constitution, and against the Free States; and that a regard for the true interests and the highest honor of the country, not less than the impulses of Christian duty, should arouse all good citizens to join in efforts to arrest this gigantic crime, by withholding supplies, or other voluntary contributions, for its further prosecution; by calling for the withdrawal of our army within the established limits of the United States; and in every just way aiding the country to retreat from the disgraceful position of aggression which it now occupies towards a weak, distracted neighbor and sister republic.

Resolved, That our attention is directed anew to the wrong and "enormity" of slavery, and to the tyranny and usurpation of the "Slave Power," as displayed in the history of our country, particularly in the annexation of Texas and the present war with Mexico. . . .

2. Illinoians Censure Lincoln (1848)

A gangling, countrified, one-term Whig Congressman from Illinois, A. Lincoln, sharply challenged the truthfulness of the Democratic President Polk. (He little realized that one day he himself would be the victim of similar partisan attacks.) On the floor of the House he insisted that the war had been "unnecessarily and unconstitutionally commenced by the President," and in a series of "spot resolutions," which he persistently pushed, he demanded to know the exact "spot" on which American blood had been shed and whether that "spot" was in fact American soil. Certain citizens of Lincoln's Illinois district, presumably Democrats, passed the following resolution condemning the unpatriotic stand of their representative. Determine to what extent these criticisms seem warranted, and whether a Congressman should heed his conscience or his constituents in wartime.

[*Resolved,*]

That, as citizens of the Seventh Congressional District of Illinois, we can but express the deep mortification inflicted upon us by our representative in Congress in his base, dastardly, and treasonable assault upon President Polk; in his disgraceful speech on the present war; and in the resolutions offered by him against his own government, in flagrant violation of all expectation here, and direct opposition to the views of a majority of our Congressional electors [voters].

That this district has been often afflicted with inefficient *per diem* men, or unfortunate representation, but never until now has it known disgrace so black, so mortifying, so unanswerable. Such insulting opprobrium cast upon our citizens and soldiers, such black odium and infamy heaped upon the living brave and illustrious dead, can but excite the indignation of every true Illinoian, the disgust of republicans, and condemnation of men.

Therefore, henceforth will this Benedict Arnold of our district be known here only as the Ranchero Spotty of one term.

3. Abolitionists Libel General Taylor (1848)

One of the foulest murders of the century occurred in 1830. Captain Joseph White, a wealthy merchant of Salem, Massachusetts, was found dead in his bed with a fractured skull and thirteen stab wounds. Dick Crowningshield, who had been offered

2. *Illinois State Register,* March 10, 1848.
3. H. C. Wright, *Dick Crowningshield the Assassin and Zachary Taylor the Soldier: The Difference between Them* (1848), pp. 11–12.

$1000 by two expectant heirs, was the murderer. Henry C. Wright, an abolitionist and pacifist, compared the current war hero, General Zachary Taylor, to Crowningshield. After reading Wright's tirade entitled "The Assassin and the Soldier," form conclusions as to the nature of the opposition to the Mexican War by the pacifist-abolitionist extremists. Was this attack too overdrawn to be effective?

Zachary had millions of employers; the assassin had but two.

Zachary killed thousands; the assassin killed one.

Zachary's sword, balls, and bombshells were accounted Christian weapons to slay men; the assassin's bludgeon and dirk were considered un-Christian.

Zachary broke the limbs and tore the flesh of his victims, and left them to die in protracted agony; the assassin killed his instantly and without protracted pain.

Zachary's deeds are said by the priest and churches to be God-approved and Christlike; the assassin's are denounced by them as evil and only evil.

Zachary is hailed as a Christian patriot; Dick is shunned by all.

Zachary, as he returns from Monterrey, his face, his hands, and garments dripping with the blood of innocent women and children, is welcomed "by the smiles and kisses of his countrywomen"; they shrink from Dick with horror.

Zachary is held up by mothers, by teachers, by priests and politicians, as an example of piety and patriotism; Dick is held up by them to execration.

Zachary is made a life-member of a Missionary Society; Dick is cast out as a heathen.

Zachary is counted worthy of all honor by a professedly enlightened, civilized republican and Christian people, and is by them elevated to the Presidency; Dick, by the same people, is elevated to the gallows.

Such are the different results of killing one at the bidding and for the benefit of two, and killing thousands for the benefit and at the bidding of millions.

E. PEACE WITH MEXICO

1. Polk Submits the Trist Treaty (1848)

Hoping to win California with a minimum of bloodshed, President Polk sent special envoy Nicholas Trist to Mexico. There he was to join General Scott's army driving toward Mexico City. Trist bungled an attempt to bribe Santa Anna, the slippery Mexican dictator, and Polk recalled his negotiator in disgust. But Trist, who now saw a temporary opening, concluded a treaty anyhow. Polk was furious at such defiance, but he finally decided to submit Trist's Treaty of Guadalupe-Hidalgo to the Senate. By its terms Mexico formally yielded Texas, California, and the intervening territory; the United States bound itself to pay $18,250,000, including $3,250,000 in the damage claims owing to American citizens. In reading Polk's diary account, locate the argument for the treaty that seems strongest; the one that seems to carry the most weight with him.

1. M. M. Quaife, ed., *The Diary of James K. Polk* (1910), III, 347–48. By permission of the Chicago Historical Society.

Monday, 21st February, 1848.—I saw no company this morning. At 12 o'clock the Cabinet met; all the members present. I made known my decision upon the Mexican Treaty, which was that under all the circumstances of the case, I would submit it [to] the Senate for ratification. . . .

I assigned my reasons for my decision. They were, briefly, that the treaty conformed on the main question of limits and boundary to the instructions given to Mr. Trist in April last; and that though, if the treaty was now to be made, I should demand more territory, perhaps to make the Sierra Madre* the line, yet it was doubtful whether this could be ever obtained by the consent of Mexico.

I looked, too, to the consequences of its rejection. A [Whig] majority of one branch of Congress [the House] is opposed to my administration; they have falsely charged that the war was brought on and is continued by me with a view to the conquest of Mexico. And if I were now to reject a treaty made upon my own terms, as authorized in April last, with the unanimous approbation of the Cabinet, the probability is that Congress would not grant either men or money to prosecute the war. Should this be the result, the army now in Mexico would be constantly wasting and diminishing in numbers, and I might at last be compelled to withdraw them, and thus lose the two provinces of New Mexico and Upper California, which were ceded to the United States by this treaty.

Should the opponents of my administration succeed in carrying the next presidential election, the great probability is that the country would lose all the advantages secured by this treaty. I adverted to the immense value of Upper California; and concluded by saying that if I were now to reject my own terms, as offered in April last, I did not see how it was possible for my administration to be sustained.

2. A Whig Journal Accepts the Pact (1848)

The Washington *Daily National Intelligencer,* an opposition Whig newspaper, wry-facedly supported the Trist draft as an unsatisfactory way out of a bad mess. One reason for a speedy acceptance was the mounting popular clamor for all of Mexico, rather than the one-half actually taken. Ascertain the least convincing argument advanced; the most convincing. Note what additional objections to taking all of Mexico might have been voiced.

We regard with distrust and apprehension the proposed vast acquisition of territory by the United States. So far from paying twenty millions of dollars for it, we have not the smallest doubt that the acquisition of it will entail mischiefs upon this country which no supposed advantages to be derived from it will compensate, now or ever. Were these territories to be whelmed in the Pacific Ocean, instead of being incorporated in our Union, far better, in our opinion, would it be for the welfare and prosperity of the present population of the United States. . . .

* A mountain range bordering the central plateau of Mexico.
2. *Daily National Intelligencer* (Washington), Feb. 28, 1848.

That the annexation of *the whole* of Mexico to the United States would be fatal to this government, whoever may doubt it, we are well convinced. Add to our Senate the representation of some fifteen or twenty Mexican states, and the conservative character of that body will be destroyed. The increased representation in the other branch of the national legislature might, at first, be less injurious; but its evils cannot now be computed. Would our commercial, manufacturing, and agricultural states be content to be governed by Mexican generals, who are ignorant of civil government, and who could not understand the principles of our Constitution? *Pronunciamentos* at the head of a military array constitute the basis of their political knowledge. The Union of these states has withstood the shocks of war and of internal excitement, but it would be dissolved by the annexation of Mexico.

We would take the treaty, then, as it is, to avoid a greater national evil. We cannot reject it and continue our opposition to the war. Payment of the debts which Mexico owed our citizens at the commencement of the war is now hopeless; her means are exhausted. Her territory with its population will entail upon us increased expenditures, and evils moral and political. But it is all that Mexico can give. There *can* be no indemnity for the war expenses. We had better, then, as we have said, stop where we are; for if we go further, we shall only increase the evil.

The crisis should be met with firmness. By the continued prosecution of the war, we should in three months expend a larger sum than the treaty requires us to pay to our own citizens and to the Mexican government. And where is the individual so lost to a sense of justice and to the common sympathies of our nature who would not rather pay the money than to expend even that much (more likely ten times as much) in prosecuting the war to the annihilation of the Mexican government and name?

3. Democrats Hail a Glorious Achievement (1848)

A staunch pro-Polk newspaper, the Democratic Washington *Daily Union,* took sharp issue with its rival, the Whig *Daily National Intelligencer.* It hailed the outcome of the war as a magnificent triumph. Note what it seems to regard as the greatest intangible gain; the greatest tangible gain. Observe how the treaty would benefit both the security and the commerce of the United States.

It is true that the war has cost us millions of money, and, what is far more precious, the lives of some of our noblest citizens. But what great advantages has it not obtained for us? It has covered us with glory. It has extended our fame to the remotest corners of the earth. If the treaty be ratified, it will extend the area of freedom to the Southern Pacific.

The *National Intelligencer,* indeed, denies that it has "accomplished any one of the ostensible objects of the war." Yet surely nothing but the blindest party spirit could have made this extravagant assertion.

3. Washington *Daily Union,* March 16, 1848.

PLUCKED

Prophetic Yankee bumptiousness during the Mexican War. *Yankee Doodle,* 1847.

Have we not driven back the insolent enemy, who invaded Texas and shed the blood of our citizens upon our own soil? Have we not pursued him into the heart of his own country, seized all his strongholds upon the coast, and occupied his capital? Have we not subdued that vainglorious and arrogant spirit which has been productive of so many insults and so many aggressions? What has become of all those idle threats to drive us from Texas—of the silly boast of Santa Anna that he would gather his laurels upon the banks of the Sabine [River]!*

The London *Times,* in 1845, flattered the national vanity of the Mexicans with the hope that we should not be able to send men enough to encounter their troops. They were under the impression that our army dared not enter Mexico, or, if we made the attempt, that we should be driven back like chaff before the whirlwind. Their vanity deceived them; but their government flattered their arrogance and increased their infatuation.

Now they are tamed. Now they have consented to negotiate for peace, without requiring our ships to leave their coast and our troops to desert their territory. These changes in the popular sentiment have been produced by the brilliant achievements of Buena Vista and of Cerro Gordo, the capture of their castle and of their capital. Does anyone now believe that their spirit is not humbled, and that the sense of their own inferiority will not induce them to refrain from a repetition of the insults and aggressions which they had so repeatedly perpetrated upon us?

* The southwestern border of Louisiana.

They will be stripped, too, of a large portion of their territory. They may be stripped of more, if they should wantonly insult us again. Will not the lessons they have learned operate as a "security for the future"? Will not the moral force we have gained, and the military genius we have exhibited, go beyond Mexico, and produce their impression upon the other nations of the earth?

With ample "indemnity for the past," then, and with such "security for the future"—with achievements in arms which any nation might envy—with an extension of territory to the Pacific, which gives us some of the finest harbors in the world (for one of which alone—the bay of San Francisco—Gen. Jackson was willing to give five millions of dollars)—with an immense commerce opening upon us with the richest nations of Asia—with every facility secured for our whalers in the Pacific, and with the other advantages which we will have secured—with all these, we can truly say that we have every reason to be proud of the war, and proud of the peace which it has obtained us.

4. Mexico Remembers the Despoilers (1935)

Patriotic Mexicans can never forget the catastrophe that cost them about half of their country. Their resistance was weakened by internal political turmoil that amounted almost to civil war. The teen-age boys of the military academy at Chapultepec, near Mexico City, perished heroically; legend has several throwing themselves suicidally from the battlements. In 1935, after some of the bitterness had subsided, the Ministry of Education in Mexico City published an elementary survey of Mexican history in which there appears the following account of the war and the treaty—with a before-and-after map. Ascertain what is revealed of the weakness of Mexican resistance, and the grievances against the United States. Which one seems to rankle most deeply?

In the war with the United States, and in the military operations incidental thereto, we are unable to find a single outstanding figure to represent the defense of Mexico, in the form of a hero or military leader. Invasion first of all took place from the north, and the American troops defeated our armies, not beneath them in courage, but due to inferior organization, armaments, and high command. The classes that controlled material resources, and the groups at the head of the political situation, failed to rise to the occasion in that desperate situation.

A chronicle of the march of invasion makes painful reading. Our soldiers were defeated at Matamoros, at Resaca de Guerrero, and Monterrey, in spite of the sacrifices of the troops. . . .

When one follows, event by event, the military operations and the political happenings of this period, one's feelings are harrowed by the details.

In this swift historical sketch, we shall be content to mention, if no great captain representative of defense, the youthful heroes who saved the honor

4. Alfonso Teja Zabre, *Guide to the History of Mexico* (1935), pp. 299–304, *passim*.

of Mexico: the cadets of the Military College [at Chapultepec], who fell on September 13, 1847, when the school was stormed by the invading troops, then on the point of occupying the capital of the Republic. The glorious deaths of Francisco Marquez, Agustin Melgar, Juan Escutia, Fernando Montes de Oca, Vicente Suarez, and Juan de la Barrera, in an unequal contest, without hope, crushed by an overwhelming force, are as it were a symbol and image of this unrighteous war.

To Mexico, the American invasion contains a terrible lesson. In this war we saw that right and justice count but little in contests between one people and another, when material force, and organization, are wanting.

A great portion of Mexico's territory was lost because she had been unable to administer and settle those regions, and handed them over to alien colonization [Texas].

There is no principle nor law that can sanction spoliation. Only by force was it carried out, and only by force or adroit negotiation could it have been avoided. That which Spain had been unable to colonize, and the [Mexican] Republic to settle, was occupied by the stream of Anglo-American expansion.

The war of 1847 is not, so far as Mexico is concerned, offset by anything but the courage of her soldiers. At Matamoros, at Resaca de Guerrero, at La Angostura [Buena Vista], at Vera Cruz, at Cerro Gordo, at Padierna, at Churubusco, and at Chapultepec, victory was won by a well-organized and instructed General Staff; by longer-range rifles and cannon, better-fed soldiers, abundance of money and ammunition, and of horses and wagons. . . .

The American invasion cost Mexico the total loss of Texas, whose boundaries were, without the slightest right, brought down to the Rio Grande; the Province of New Mexico and Upper California; and an outpouring of blood, energy, and wealth, offset only by material compensation in the amount of fifteen million pesos, by way of indemnity.

[*In 1947 President Truman, on a good-will tour, laid a wreath on the monument at Chapultepec honoring the boy heroes. It was assumed that this gesture assuaged some of the anti-Yankee bitterness.*]

THOUGHT PROVOKERS

1. Why should Britain and America have been on friendly terms in the 1830's and 1840's, and why were they not?

2. Why was there so much lack of interest in Oregon during the early 1840's?

3. Polk claimed that no other power similarly situated would have refused the annexation of Texas. Do you agree or disagree? Explain how each side, at the outbreak of the Mexican War, could claim that the other was the aggressor. Were the annexation of Texas and the sending of General Taylor to the Rio Grande unconstitutional, as the abolitionists claimed? If England had held Mexico, like Canada, how would matters have been worked out differently?

4. Should a democratic government permit the kind of criticism that was indulged in by the Whigs and the abolitionists during the Mexican War? Compare the attitude of Massachusetts toward the War of 1812 with her attitude toward the Mexican War.

5. Did the advantages to the United States from the Mexican War outweigh the ultimate disadvantages? Emerson remarked that victory would be a dose of arsenic. Comment. Mexicans claim that they would now be a rich nation if they had not been robbed of the oil and other riches of California and Texas. Comment.

FURTHER EXPLORATION

General: R. A. Billington, *The Far Western Frontier, 1830–1860* (1956); G. G. Van Deusen, *The Jacksonian Era, 1828–1848* (1959); N. A. Graebner, *Empire on the Pacific* (1955); O. A. Singletary, *The Mexican War* (1960). **War of Words:** Allan Nevins, ed., *America through British Eyes* (1948). **Oregon:** M. C. Jacobs, *Winning Oregon* (1938). **Provoking War:** J. H. Smith, *The Annexation of Texas* (1911); E. I. McCormac, *James K. Polk* (1922). **Opposition to War:** J. H. Smith, *The War with Mexico* (2 vols., 1919). **Peace:** R. S. Henry, *The Story of the Mexican War* (1950); J. D. P. Fuller, *The Movement for the Acquisition of All Mexico, 1846–1848* (1936).

Recent: Charles Sellers, *James K. Polk: Continentalist, 1843–1846* (1966); Frederick Merk, *Manifest Destiny and Mission in American History* (1963) [paperback], and *The Oregon Question: Essays in Anglo-American Diplomacy and Politics* (1967); W. H. Goetzmann, *When the Eagle Screamed: The Romantic Horizon in American Diplomacy, 1800–1960* (1966) [paperback].

Chapter 16

Industry, Labor, and Transportation to 1860

Take not from the mouth of labor the bread it has earned.

THOMAS JEFFERSON, 1801

PROLOGUE: The Industrial Revolution spawned the factory, and in turn the factory-magnet drew from the hallowed home countless men, women, and even tiny children. Alexander Hamilton himself had stressed the spiritual value of training "the little innocents" in honest habits of industry. But the exploitation of "little innocents," as well as their elders, resulted in grave abuses. For more than a century, labor fought an uphill fight against employers for a gradual improvement of its lot. Meanwhile the spread of the factory was spurred by the canal network, by the river steamboat, and then by the railroad. The fast-growing states of the Ohio Valley and the Upper Mississippi Valley became less dependent on the mouth of the Mississippi as the outlet for their produce, because the new arteries of transportation carried their exports cheaply and swiftly to the cities of the Eastern seaboard. The ties of the Union, conspicuously in an East-West direction, were thus greatly strengthened.

A. THE SPREAD OF THE FACTORY

1. Wage Slavery in New England (1832)

Seth Luther, a poorly educated carpenter who helped construct New England textile factories, ranks as one of the most forceful of the early labor reformers. In numerous speeches and pamphlets he condemned such abuses as paternalistic control, "black lists" of troublemakers, low wages, and overlong hours. He especially deplored the exploitation of children, who were sometimes dragged to "whipping rooms." His deadly earnestness and biting sarcasm were partly responsible for America's first law to control child labor—that of Massachusetts enacted in 1842. It prohibited children under twelve from working more than ten hours a day. List the most serious abuses that Luther here discusses. Determine which was the most grievous, and why such practices were intellectually blighting.

A [Western] member of the United States Senate seems to be extremely pleased with cotton mills. He says in the Senate, "Who has not been delighted with the clockwork movements of a large cotton manufactory? He had visited them often, and always with increased delight." He says the women work in large airy apartments, well warmed. They are neatly dressed, with ruddy complexions, and happy countenances. They mend the broken threads and replace the exhausted balls or broaches, and at stated

---

1. Seth Luther, *An Address to the Working-Men of New-England* . . . (2nd ed., 1833), pp. 17–21.

periods they go to and return from their meals with light and cheerful step. (While on a visit to that pink of perfection, Waltham [Mass.], I remarked that the females moved with a very light step, and well they might, for the bell rang for them to return to the mill from their homes in nineteen minutes after it had rung for them to go to breakfast. Some of these females boarded the largest part of a half a mile from the mill.)

And the grand climax [says the Western Senator] is that at the end of the week, after working like slaves for thirteen or fourteen hours every day, "they enter the temples of God on the Sabbath, and thank him for all his benefits. . . ." We remark that whatever girls or others may do west of the Allegheny Mountains, we do not believe there can be a single person found east of those mountains who ever thanked God for permission to work in a cotton mill. . . .

We would respectfully advise the honorable Senator to travel incognito when he visits cotton mills. If he wishes to come at the truth, he must not be known. Let him put on a short jacket and trousers, and join the "lower orders" for a short time. . . . In that case we could show him, in some of the prisons in New England called cotton mills, instead of rosy cheeks, the pale, sickly, haggard countenance of the ragged child—haggard from the worse than slavish confinement in the cotton mill. He might see that child driven up to the "clockwork" by the cowskin [whip], in some cases. He might see, in some instances, the child taken from his bed at four in the morning, and plunged into cold water to drive away his slumbers and prepare him for the labors of the mill. After all this he might see that child robbed, yes, robbed of a part of his time allowed for meals by moving the hands of the clock backwards, or forwards, as would best accomplish that purpose. . . . He might see in some, and not infrequent, instances, the child, and the female child too, driven up to the "clockwork" with the cowhide, or well-seasoned strap of AMERICAN MANUFACTURE.

We could show him many females who have had corporeal punishment inflicted upon them; one girl eleven years of age who had her leg broken with a billet of wood; another who had a board split over her head by a heartless monster in the shape of an overseer of a cotton mill "paradise."

We shall for want of time . . . omit entering more largely into detail for the present respecting the cruelties practiced in some of the American mills. Our wish is to show that education is neglected, . . . because if thirteen hours' actual labor is required each day, it is impossible to attend to education among children, or to improvement among adults.

2. The Abuse of Female Workers (1836)

The factory girls of Lowell, Massachusetts, were a showpiece for visitors, notably Charles Dickens in 1842. Having seen the miserable working conditions in England, he wrote almost ecstatically of the fresh air, the cheerful faces, and the blooming

2. *The Harbinger*, Nov. 14, 1836, in H. R. Warfel *et al.*, eds., *The American Mind* (1937), pp. 390–91. In 1847 this journal became the official organ of the Brook Farm colony.

health. He also took favorable note of the girls' cleanliness, clothes, thrift, morals, and educational and recreational facilities. Perhaps he was unduly impressed by the contrast with English factories; certainly he did not investigate as carefully the less savory mills. Six years earlier, an associationist (Fourierist) writer in a contemporary American journal presented a strikingly different view. Note the evidence that belies the reports of good health, cheerful countenances, and educational activity.

We have lately visited the cities of Lowell [Mass.] and Manchester [N. H.] and have had an opportunity of examining the factory system more closely than before. We had distrusted the accounts which we had heard from persons engaged in the labor reform now beginning to agitate New England. We could scarcely credit the statements made in relation to the exhausting nature of the labor in the mills, and to the manner in which the young women—the operatives—lived in their boardinghouses, six sleeping in a room, poorly ventilated.

We went through many of the mills, talked particularly to a large number of the operatives, and ate at their boardinghouses, on purpose to ascertain by personal inspection the facts of the case. We assure our readers that very little information is possessed, and no correct judgments formed, by the public at large, of our factory system, which is the first germ of the industrial or commercial feudalism that is to spread over our land. . . .

In Lowell live between seven and eight thousand young women, who are generally daughters of farmers of the different states of New England. Some of them are members of families that were rich in the generation before. . . .

The operatives work thirteen hours a day in the summer time, and from daylight to dark in the winter. At half past four in the morning the factory bell rings, and at five the girls must be in the mills. A clerk, placed as a watch, observes those who are a few minutes behind the time, and effectual means are taken to stimulate to punctuality. This is the morning commencement of the industrial discipline (should we not rather say industrial tyranny?) which is established in these associations of this moral and Christian community.

At seven the girls are allowed thirty minutes for breakfast, and at noon thirty minutes more for dinner, except during the first quarter of the year, when the time is extended to forty-five minutes. But within this time they must hurry to their boardinghouses and return to the factory, and that through the hot sun or the rain or the cold. A meal eaten under such circumstances must be quite unfavorable to digestion and health, as any medical man will inform us. At seven o'clock in the evening the factory bell sounds the close of the day's work.

Thus thirteen hours per day of close attention and monotonous labor are exacted from the young women in these manufactories. . . . So fatigued— we should say, exhausted and worn out, but we wish to speak of the system in the simplest language—are numbers of girls that they go to bed soon after their evening meal, and endeavor by a comparatively long sleep to resuscitate their weakened frames for the toil of the coming day.

When capital has got thirteen hours of labor daily out of a being, it can get nothing more. It would be a poor speculation in an industrial point of view to own the operative; for the trouble and expense of providing for times of sickness and old age would more than counterbalance the difference between the price of wages and the expense of board and clothing. The far greater number of fortunes accumulated by the North in comparison with the South shows that hireling labor is more profitable for capital than slave labor.

Now let us examine the nature of the labor itself, and the conditions under which it is performed. Enter with us into the large rooms, when the looms are at work. The largest that we saw is in the Amoskeag Mills at Manchester. . . . The din and clatter of these five hundred looms, under full operation, struck us on first entering as something frightful and infernal, for it seemed such an atrocious violation of one of the faculties of the human soul, the sense of hearing. After a while we became somewhat inured to it, and by speaking quite close to the ear of an operative and quite loud, we could hold a conversation and make the inquiries we wished.

The girls attend upon an average three looms; many attend four, but this requires a very active person, and the most unremitting care. However, a great many do it. Attention to two is as much as should be demanded of an operative. This gives us some idea of the application required during the thirteen hours of daily labor. The atmosphere of such a room cannot of course be pure; on the contrary, it is charged with cotton filaments and dust, which, we are told, are very injurious to the lungs.

On entering the room, although the day was warm, we remarked that the windows were down. We asked the reason, and a young woman answered very naïvely, and without seeming to be in the least aware that this privation of fresh air was anything else than perfectly natural, that "when the wind blew, the threads did not work well." After we had been in the room for fifteen or twenty minutes, we found ourselves, as did the persons who accompanied us, in quite a perspiration, produced by a certain moisture which we observed in the air, as well as by the heat. . . .

The young women sleep upon an average six in a room, three beds to a room. There is no privacy, no retirement, here. It is almost impossible to read or write alone, as the parlor is full and so many sleep in the same chamber. A young woman remarked to us that if she had a letter to write, she did it on the head of a bandbox, sitting on a trunk, as there was no space for a table.

So live and toil the young women of our country in the boardinghouses and manufactories which the rich and influential of our land have built for them.

3. The "Utopian" Lowell Looms (1844)

Charles Dickens recorded three facts about the Lowell girls that he was sure would startle his English readers. First, many of the boardinghouses had joint-stock pianos; second, "nearly all" of the girls subscribed to circulating libraries; third, the operatives —ultimately about seventy of the more literate—published a journal called *The Lowell Offering.* The factory owners encouraged it, no doubt conscious of its public-relations value, and probably censored it as well. Actually, the matrons of the boarding-houses went to great lengths to keep "fallen women" from entering this "paradise" and tainting the virginal farm girls. The following imaginary and stilted conversation, published in *The Lowell Offering,* is a piece of propaganda probably inspired by the employers and certainly representing the employers' point of view. Detect the serious grievances that are not mentioned, and the ones that are least satisfactorily explained in the light of the testimony already presented.

Miss S: I am very happy to see you this evening, Miss Bartlett, for I have something particular to say to you. Now do tell me if you still persist in your resolution to return to your factory employment?

Miss B: I do. I have no objection, neither have I heard any sufficiently strong to deter me.

Miss S: The idea that it is degrading, in the opinion of many, would be objection enough for me without taking into the account its real tendency to promote ignorance and vice.

Miss B: By whom is factory labor considered degrading? It is by those who believe all labor degrading—by those who contemptuously speak of the farmer, the mechanic, the printer, the seamstress, and all who are obliged to toil as belonging to the lower orders—by those who seem to think the condition of labor excludes all the capacities of the mind and the virtues of humanity. They forget that circumstances, over which they have little or no control, place them above the necessity of labor; and that circumstances may yet compel them to engage in that at which they now scoff and spurn.

Miss S: There are objections to factory labor, which serve to render it degrading—objections which cannot be urged against any other kind of female employment. For instance, to be called and to be dismissed by the ringing of a bell savors of compulsion and slavery, and cannot cease to produce mortification without having been destructive to self-respect.

Miss B: In almost all kinds of employment it is necessary to keep regular established hours: more particularly so where there are as many connected as in the factories. Because we are reminded of those hours by the ringing of a bell, it is no argument against our employment, any more than it would be against going to church or to school. Our engagements are voluntarily entered into with our employers, with the understanding that they may be dissolved at our pleasure. However derogatory to our dignity and liberty you may consider factory labor, there is not a tinge of slavery existing in it,

3. *The Lowell Offering,* 1844, in Willard Thorp *et al.,* eds., *American Issues* (1941), I, 410–12.

THE LURE OF AMERICAN WAGES *c.* 1855
British employers resent loss of women workers to American factories. M. B.
Davidson, *Life in America,* 1951, vol. I.

unless there be in every kind of labor that is urged upon us by the force
of circumstances.

MISS S: Objections have been brought up against the boardinghouses,
and, I think, with much plausibility. The large number of females who are
there thrown together are, unavoidably, intimately connected with each
other. It cannot be denied that some, guilty of immoralities, find their way
into the factories and boardinghouses. The example and influence of such
must be pernicious, and terminate in the increase of vice.

MISS B: It is true that the example and influence of immorality, wherever
it exists, cannot be otherwise than evil. We know, also, that some exception-
able characters occasionally find a place among those employed in factories.
We know it from the fact that dismissals do, now and then, occur as the
consequence. But, my dear Miss S, did you ever know or hear of a class
of people who could boast of perfection? among whom wrong of any
description was never known?

MISS S: O, no! And, as I am no perfectionist, I never expect to know one.

MISS B: Then, if in one case the guilt of a few has not corrupted the
whole, why should it in the other? Living in a factory boardinghouse, and
working in a factory, changes not "human nature": it is susceptible of good,
and also of evil, there, as it is elsewhere.

MISS S: I agree with you in thinking that among all classes, and in every
condition in life, evil influences are at work. But in some situations in life

is not the exposure to these influences much more extensive, and, therefore, more dangerous, especially to the young?

MISS B: I believe there are many kinds of female employment offered in our large towns and cities far more dangerous in this respect than factory employment, although they may be considered more desirable and respectable. . . .

MISS S: You will not acknowledge that factory labor is degrading, or that it is productive of vice, but you must own that it fosters ignorance. When there are so many hours out of each day devoted to labor, there can be no time for study and improvement.

MISS B: It is true that too large a portion of our time is confined to labor. But, first, let me remark that this is an objection which cannot be said to exist only in factory labor. . . . We have abundant proof that un-remitted toil is not always derogatory to improvement. A factory girl's work is neither hard nor complicated. She can go on with perfect regularity in her duties while her mind may be actively employed on any other subject. There can be no better place for reflection, when there must be toil, than the factory. The patronage which newspapers and periodicals find in our city, our well-worn libraries, evening schools, crowded churches and sabbath schools, prove that factory operatives find leisure to use the means of improvement both in mind and heart.

4. "Slavers" for New England Girls (1846)

Many of the Lowell girls toiled only a few years—perhaps to help needy parents, to pay off a farm mortgage, to accumulate a dowry, or to send a brother through college. Dickens noted that 978 girls had deposits in the Lowell Savings Bank totaling an estimated $100,000. But conditions in other factories were less wholesome, and the following account in a labor journal, though no doubt overdrawn, contains a large element of truth. Determine how free these New England girls were to quit their jobs, and in what respects the analogy to slavery is too farfetched.

We were not aware, until within a few days, of the *modus operandi* of the factory powers in this village of forcing poor girls from their quiet homes to become their tools and, like the Southern slaves, to give up their life and liberty to the heartless tyrants and taskmasters.

Observing a singular-looking "long, low, black" wagon passing along the street, we made inquiries respecting it, and were informed that it was what we term a "slaver." She makes regular trips to the north of the state [Massachusetts], cruising around in Vermont and New Hampshire, with a "commander" whose heart must be as black as his craft, who is paid a dollar a head for all he brings to the market, and more in proportion to the distance —if they bring them from such a distance that they cannot easily get back.

This is done by "hoisting false colors," and representing to the girls that they can tend more machinery than is possible, and that the work is so very

4. *Voice of Industry*, Jan. 2, 1846, in H. R. Warfel *et al.*, eds., *The American Mind* (1937), p. 392.

neat, and the wages such that they can dress in silks and spend half their time in reading. Now, is this true? Let those girls who have been thus deceived, answer.

Let us say a word in regard to the manner in which they are stowed in the wagon, which may find a similarity only in the manner in which slaves are fastened in the hold of a vessel. It is long, and the seats so close that it must be very inconvenient.

Is there any humanity in this? Philanthropists may talk of Negro slavery, but it would be well first to endeavor to emancipate the slaves at home. Let us not stretch our ears to catch the sound of the lash on the flesh of the oppressed black while the oppressed in our very midst are crying out in thunder tones, and calling upon us for assistance.

5. Disaster in a Massachusetts Mill (1860)

The lot of women factory workers in New England seemed less idyllic after an appalling accident in the five-story Pemberton textile mill, herewith described. George T. Strong, a prominent New York lawyer and public-spirited citizen, poured his indignation into his diary. Ascertain who was at fault and why the South probably took some secret satisfaction in the tragedy.

January 11 [1860]. News today of a fearful tragedy at Lawrence, Massachusetts, one of the wholesale murders commonly known in newspaper literature as accident or catastrophe. A huge factory, long notoriously insecure and ill-built, requiring to be patched and bandaged up with iron plates and braces to stand the introduction of its machinery, suddenly collapsed into a heap of ruins yesterday afternoon without the smallest provocation. Some five or six hundred operatives went down with it—young girls and women mostly. An hour or two later, while people were working frantically to dig out some two hundred still under the ruins, many of them alive and calling for help, some quite unhurt, fire caught in the great pile of debris, and these prisoners were roasted. It is too atrocious and horrible to think of.

Of course, nobody will be hanged. Somebody has murdered about two hundred people, many of them with hideous torture, in order to save money, but society has no avenging gibbet for the respectable millionaire and homicide. Of course not. He did not want to or mean to do this massacre; on the whole, he would have preferred to let these people live. His intent was not homicidal. He merely thought a great deal about making a large profit and very little about the security of human life. He did not compel these poor girls and children to enter his accursed mantrap. They could judge and decide for themselves whether they would be employed there. It was a matter of contract between capital and labor; they were to receive cash payment for their services.

5. Reprinted with permission of the publisher from *The Diary of George Templeton Strong,* edited by Allan Nevins and M. H. Thomas, III, 4. Copyright 1952 by The Macmillan Company.

No doubt the legal representatives of those who have perished will be duly paid the fractional part of their week's wages up to the date when they became incapacitated by crushing or combustion, as the case may be, from rendering further service. Very probably the wealthy and liberal proprietor will add (in deserving cases) a gratuity to defray funeral charges. It becomes us to prate about the horrors of slavery! What Southern capitalist trifles with the lives of his operatives as do our philanthropes of the North?

B. MOUNTING LABOR UNREST

1. A One-sided Labor Contract (*c.* 1832)

The plight of the factory worker in the 1830's was such as to justify the term "wage slavery." Work contracts—often a pre-condition of employment—gave the employer blank-check power. The following contract was used by a textile company in Dover, New Hampshire. Note the feature of it that would be most offensive to an active labor-unionist today, and determine whether these arrangements could be called "collective bargaining."

We, the subscribers [the undersigned], do hereby agree to enter the service of the Cocheco Manufacturing Company, and conform, in all respects, to the regulations which are now, or may hereafter be adopted, for the good government of the institution.

We further agree to work for such wages per week, and prices by the job, as the Company may see fit to pay, and be subject to the fines as well as entitled to the premiums paid by the Company.

We further agree to allow two cents each week to be deducted from our wages for the benefit of the sick fund.

We also agree not to leave the service of the Company without giving two weeks' notice of our intention, without permission of an agent. And if we do, we agree to forfeit to the use of the Company two weeks' pay.

We also agree not to be engaged in any combination [union] whereby the work may be impeded or the Company's interest in any work injured. If we do, we agree to forfeit to the use of the Company the amount of wages that may be due to us at the time.

We also agree that in case we are discharged from the service of the Company for any fault, we will not consider ourselves entitled to be settled with in less than two weeks from the time of such discharge.

Payments for labor performed are to be made monthly.

2. Agitation for the Ten-Hour Day (1835)

A reduction of daily working hours from thirteen or more was a primary goal of labor in the 1830's. During a third unsuccessful strike for the ten-hour day, the Boston

1. Seth Luther, *An Address to the Working-Men of New-England* . . . (1833), p. 36.
2. Quoted in Irving Mark and E. I. Schwaab, *The Faith of Our Fathers* (1952), pp. 342–43.

artisans issued the following circular. It led to the successful general strike in Philadelphia on the coal wharves. Decide whether the main objection by employers to the
ten-hour day is convincingly met.

. . . In the name of the Carpenters, Masons, and Stone Cutters [we] do
respectfully represent—

That we are now engaged in a cause which is not only of vital importance
to ourselves, our families, and our children, but is equally interesting and
equally important to every mechanic in the United States and the whole
world. We are contending for the recognition of the natural right to dispose
of our own time in such quantities as we deem and believe to be most
conducive to our own happiness and the welfare of all those engaged in
manual labor.

The work in which we are now engaged is neither more nor less than
a contest between money and labor. Capital, which can only be made
productive by labor, is endeavoring to crush labor, the only source of all
wealth.

We have been too long subjected to the odious, cruel, unjust, and tyrannical system which compels the operative mechanic to exhaust his physical
and mental powers by excessive toil, until he has no desire to eat and
sleep, and in many cases he has no power to do either from extreme
debility. . . .

It is for the rights of humanity we contend. Our cause is the cause of
philanthropy. Our opposers resort to the most degrading obloquy to injure
us—not degrading to us, but to the authors of such unmerited opprobrium
which they attempt to cast upon us. They tell us, "We shall spend all our
hours of leisure in drunkenness and debauchery if the hours of labor are
reduced." We hurl from us the base, ungenerous, ungrateful, detestable,
cruel, malicious slander, with scorn and indignation. . . .

To show the utter fallacy of their idiotic reasoning, if reasoning it may be
called, we have only to say they employ us about eight months in the year
during the longest and the hottest days, and in short days hundreds of us
remain idle for want of work for three or four months, when our expenses
must of course be the heaviest during winter. When the long days again
appear, our guardians set us to work, as they say, "to keep us from getting
drunk." No fear has ever been expressed by these benevolent employers
respecting our morals while we are idle in short days, through their
avarice. . . . Further, they threaten to starve us into submission to their
will. Starve us to prevent us from getting drunk!! Wonderful wisdom!!
Refined benevolence!! Exalted philanthropy!!

3. The Tailors Strike in New York (1836)

Under existing laws, a strike for higher wages was a criminal conspiracy. The courts
dealt harshly with strikers, especially before the pro-labor decision in Massachusetts
in the case of Commonwealth *vs.* Hunt (1842). Philip Hone, a wealthy and con-

3. Bayard Tuckerman, ed., *Diary of Philip Hone* (1889), pp. 210–11.

servative New York businessman, quite approved of keeping laborers in their place, particularly the New York tailors, as the following diary entry reveals. In the light of present-day standards, decide whether Hone or the strikers expressed the more extreme views.

June 6 [1836].—In corroboration of the spirit of faction and contempt of the laws which pervades the community at this time is the conduct of the journeymen tailors, instigated by a set of vile foreigners (principally English), who, unable to endure the restraints of wholesome law well administered in their own country, take refuge here, establish trades-unions, and vilify Yankee judges and juries. Twenty odd of these were convicted at the Oyer and Terminer [Court] of a conspiracy to raise their wages and to prevent any of the craft from working at prices less than those for which they struck. Judge Edwards gave notice that he would proceed to sentence them this day. But, in consequence of the continuance of Robinson's trial, the Court postponed the sentence until Friday.

This, however, being the day on which it was expected, crowds of people have been collected in the park, ready for any mischief to which they may have been instigated, and a most diabolical and inflammatory hand-bill was circulated yesterday, headed by a coffin. The Board of Aldermen held an informal meeting this evening, at which a resolution was adopted authorizing the Mayor to offer a reward for the discovery of the author, printer, publisher, or distributor of this incendiary publication. The following was the hand-bill:

THE RICH AGAINST THE POOR!

Judge Edwards, the tool of the aristocracy, against the people! Mechanics and working men! A deadly blow has been struck at your liberty! The prize for which your fathers fought has been robbed from you! The freemen of the North are now on a level with the slaves of the South! with no other privilege than laboring, that drones may fatten on your lifeblood! Twenty of your brethren have been found guilty for presuming to resist a reduction of their wages! And Judge Edwards has charged an American jury, and, agreeably to that charge, they have established the precedent that workingmen have no right to regulate the price of labor, or, in other words, the rich are the only judges of the wants of the poor man. On Monday, June 6, 1836, at ten o'clock, these freemen are to receive their sentence, to gratify the hellish appetites of the aristocrats!

On Monday, the liberty of the workingmen will be interred! Judge Edwards is to chant the requiem! Go! Go! Go! every freeman, every workingman, and hear the hollow and melancholy sound of the earth on the coffin of equality! Let the courtroom, the City Hall, yea! the whole park, be filled with mourners. But remember, offer no violence to Judge Edwards, bend meekly, and receive the chain wherewith you are to be bound! Keep the peace! Above all things, keep the peace!

[*Judge Edwards fined the president of the "unlawful club" of tailors $150, the other defendants $50 or $100. In passing sentence, he scolded them for having "craftily" entered into "a conspiracy" to "injure trade," and declared: "The law leaves every individual [the] master of his own individual acts. But it will not suffer him to encroach upon the rights of others. He may work or not, as suits his pleasure, but he shall not enter into a confederacy with a view of controlling others, and take measures to carry it into effect." Contrary to this dictum, the tailors had not only resorted to a strike but had harassed the employers with picketing and other demonstrations, and had brought various kinds of pressures to bear on the strikebreakers.*]

4. Negro Slavery versus Wage Slavery (1840)

Orestes A. Brownson, a self-taught Vermonter, made his mark as a preacher, magazine editor, lecturer, reformer, Socialist, Transcendentalist, and writer (twenty volumes). Fearless and uncompromising, he began as a Presbyterian minister and wound up as a convert to Catholicism. While preaching to groups of workers he had become deeply interested in labor reform, and his blast, herewith given, was music to the ears of Southern slaveowners. Note his most obvious exaggerations, and determine whether the slaveowner was a greater hypocrite than the millowner.

In regard to labor, two systems obtain: one that of slave labor, the other that of free labor. Of the two, the first is, in our judgment, except so far as the feelings are concerned, decidedly the least oppressive. If the slave has never been a free man, we think, as a general rule, his sufferings are less than those of the free laborer at wages. As to actual freedom, one has just about as much as the other. The laborer at wages has all the disadvantages of freedom and none of its blessings, while the slave, if denied the blessings, is freed from the disadvantages.

We are no advocates of slavery. We are as heartily opposed to it as any modern abolitionist can be. But we say frankly that, if there must always be a laboring population distinct from proprietors and employers, we regard the slave system as decidedly preferable to the system at wages.

It is no pleasant thing to go days without food; to lie idle for weeks, seeking work and finding none; to rise in the morning with a wife and children you love, and know not where to procure them a breakfast; and to see constantly before you no brighter prospect than the almshouse.

Yet these are no infrequent incidents in the lives of our laboring population. Even in seasons of general prosperity, when there was only the ordinary cry of "hard times," we have seen hundreds of people in a not very populous village, in a wealthy portion of our common country, suffering for the want of the necessaries of life, willing to work and yet finding no work to do. Many and many is the application of a poor man for work, merely for his food, we have seen rejected. These things are little thought of, for the applicants are poor; they fill no conspicuous place in society, and they have no biographers. But their wrongs are chronicled in heaven.

4. *Boston Quarterly Review*, III (1840), 368–70.

It is said there is no want in this country. There may be less in some other countries. But death by actual starvation in this country is, we apprehend, no uncommon occurrence. The sufferings of a quiet, unassuming but useful class of females in our cities, in general seamstresses, too proud to beg or to apply to the almshouse, are not easily told. They are industrious; they do all that they can find to do. But yet the little there is for them to do, and the miserable pittance they receive for it, is hardly sufficient to keep soul and body together.

And yet there is a man who employs them to make shirts, trousers, etc., and grows rich on their labors. He is one of our respectable citizens, perhaps is praised in the newspapers for his liberal donations to some charitable institution. He passes among us as a pattern of morality and is honored as a worthy Christian. And why should he not be, since our Christian community is made up of such as he, and since our clergy would not dare question his piety lest they should incur the reproach of infidelity and lose their standing and their salaries? . . .

The average life—working life, we mean—of the girls that come to Lowell, for instance, from Maine, New Hampshire, and Vermont, we have been assured, is only about three years. What becomes of them then? Few of them ever marry; fewer still ever return to their native places with reputations unimpaired. "She has worked in a factory" is almost enough to damn to infamy the most worthy and virtuous girl. . . .

Where go the proceeds of their labors? The man who employs them, and for whom they are toiling as so many slaves, is one of our city nabobs, reveling in luxury; or he is a member of our legislature, enacting laws to put money in his own pocket; or he is a member of Congress, contending for a high tariff to tax the poor for the benefit of the rich; or in these times he is shedding crocodile tears over the deplorable condition of the poor laborer, while he docks his wages 25 percent. . . . And this man too would fain pass for a Christian and a republican. He shouts for liberty, stickles for equality, and is horrified at a Southern planter who keeps slaves.

One thing is certain: that, of the amount actually produced by the operative, he retains a less proportion than it costs the master to feed, clothe, and lodge his slave. Wages is a cunning device of the devil, for the benefit of tender consciences who would retain all the advantages of the slave system without the expense, trouble, and odium of being slaveholders.

C. STEAMBOATS AND CANALS

1. The First "Fire Canoe" in the West (1811)

Less well known than Fulton's epochal steamboat trip up the Hudson in 1807, but hardly less significant, was the first steamboat on the Mississippi. The *New Orleans* was built at Pittsburgh by Nicholas J. Roosevelt, an associate of Fulton and a distant

1. J. H. B. Latrobe, *The First Steamboat Voyage on the Western Waters* (1871), pp. 13–28, *passim.*

relative of two future Presidents. The vessel made the historic voyage from Pittsburgh to New Orleans in fourteen days, despite low water at the falls of the Ohio, a fire on board, the birth of a baby, and a series of tremendous earthquakes that changed the course of the river in places and so destroyed landmarks as to confuse the pilot. The story is here told by J. H. B. Latrobe, whose eldest sister, married to Roosevelt, made the trip. Enumerate and assess the significant revelations made by this account.

As the *New Orleans* approached completion, and when it came to be known that Mrs. Roosevelt intended to accompany her husband on the voyage, the numerous friends she had made in Pittsburgh united in endeavoring to dissuade her from what they regarded as utter folly, if not absolute madness. Her husband was appealed to. The criticisms that had been freely applied to the boat by the crowds of visitors to the shipyard were now transferred to the conduct of the builder. He was told that he had no right to peril his wife's life, however reckless he might be of his own. Mrs. Roosevelt, too, expected before long to become a mother; and this was held to enhance the offense which the good people of Pittsburgh fancied he was committing. But the wife believed in her husband; and in the latter part of September, 1811, the *New Orleans,* after a short experimental trip up the Monongahela, commenced her voyage . . . the voyage which changed the relations of the West—which may almost be said to have changed its destiny. . . .

On the second day after leaving Pittsburgh, the *New Orleans* rounded to opposite Cincinnati, and cast anchor in the stream. Levees and wharf boats were things unknown in 1811. Here, as at Pittsburgh, the whole town seemed to have assembled on the bank, and many of the acquaintances of the former visit came off in small boats. "Well, you are as good as your word; you have visited us in a steamboat," they said; "but we see you for the last time. Your boat may go *down* the river; but, as to coming up it, the very idea is an absurd one." This was one of those occasions on which seeing was not believing. . . .

The morning after the arrival of the vessel at Louisville, Mr. Roosevelt's acquaintances and others came on board, and here the same things were said that had been said at Cincinnati. Congratulations at having descended the river were, without exception, accompanied by regrets that it was the first and last time a steamboat would be seen above the Falls of the Ohio. Still, so far, certainly, Mr. Roosevelt's promises had been fulfilled; and there was a public dinner given to him a few days after his arrival. . . .

Not to be outdone in hospitality, Mr. Roosevelt invited his hosts to dine on board the *New Orleans,* which still lay anchored opposite the town. The company met in the forward or gentlemen's cabin, and the feast was at its height when suddenly there were heard unwonted rumblings, accompanied by a very perceptible motion in the vessel. The company had but one idea. The *New Orleans* had escaped from her anchor, and was drifting towards the Falls, to the certain destruction of all on board. There was an instant and simultaneous rush to the upper deck, when the company found

EXPLODING MISSISSIPPI STEAMBOAT, 1816

The *Washington,* on a maiden trip, suffered an explosion. It was the first of many steamboat disasters to cost lives.

that, instead of drifting towards the Falls of the Ohio, the *New Orleans* was making good headway up the river and would soon leave Louisville in the distance downstream. As the engine warmed to its work, and the steam blew off at the safety valve, the speed increased. Mr. Roosevelt, of course, had provided this mode of convincing his incredulous guests, and their surprise and delight may readily be imagined. After going up the river for a few miles, the *New Orleans* returned to her anchorage. . . .

Hitherto the voyage had been one of pleasure. Nothing had marred the enjoyment of the travelers. The receptions at Louisville and Cincinnati had been great events. But now were to come, to use the words of the letter already referred to, "those days of horror." The comet of 1811 had disappeared, and was followed by the earthquake of that year . . . , and the earthquake accompanied the *New Orleans* far on her way down the Mississippi. . . .

Sometimes the Indians attempted to approach the steamboat; and, again, fled on its approach. The Chickasaws still occupied that part of the state of Tennessee lying below the mouth of the Ohio. On one occasion, a large canoe, fully manned, came out of the woods abreast of the steamboat. The Indians, outnumbering the crew of the vessel, paddled after it. There was at once a race, and for a time the contest was equal. The result, however, was what might have been anticipated. Steam had the advantage of endurance; and the Indians with wild shouts, which might have been shouts of defiance, gave up the pursuit, and turned into the forest from whence they had emerged. . . .

Sometimes Indians would join the wood choppers [seeking fuel]; and occasionally one would be able to converse in English with the men. From these it was learned that the steamboat was called the "Penelore" or "Fire Canoe" and was supposed to have some affinity with the comet that had preceded the earthquake—the sparks from the chimney of the boat being likened to the train of the celestial visitant. Again, they would attribute the smoky atmosphere of the steamer and the rumbling of the earth to the beating of the waters by the fast-revolving paddles.

To the native inhabitants of the boundless forest that lined the river banks, the coming of the first steamboat was an omen of evil; and as it was the precursor of their own expulsion from their ancient homes, no wonder they continued for years to regard all steamboats with awe. As late as 1834, when the emigration of the Chickasaws to their new homes, west of the river, took place, hundreds refused to trust themselves in such conveyances but preferred making their long and weary pilgrimage on foot.

2. The Impact of the Erie Canal (1853)

The Erie Canal, completed in 1825, wrote epochal new chapters in the history of American transportation and industry. Projected by western-minded New Yorkers, it was bitterly opposed by New York City, which shortsightedly clung to its seaboard orientation. When the issue was debated in the state legislature, and the question arose of filling the canal with water, one eastern member exclaimed, "Give yourself no trouble—the tears of our constituents will fill it!" The most immediate result of the canal was to reduce sharply the cost of moving bulk shipments. Further results were analyzed as follows in a graphic report by the Secretary of the Treasury in 1853. Note why other cities lost out in competition with New York, and decide which section gained the most from the canal.

Although the rates of transportation over the Erie Canal, at its opening, were nearly double the present charges . . . it immediately became the convenient and favorite route for a large portion of the produce of the Northwestern states, and secured to the City of New York the position which she now holds as the emporium of the Confederacy [Union].

Previous to the opening of the Canal, the trade of the West was chiefly carried on through the cities of Baltimore and Philadelphia, particularly the latter, which was at that time the first city of the United States in population and wealth, and in the amount of its internal commerce.

As soon as the [Great] Lakes were reached, the line of navigable water was extended through them nearly one thousand miles farther into the interior. The Western states immediately commenced the construction of similar works, for the purpose of opening a communication, from the more remote portions of their territories, with this great water-line. All these works took their direction and character from the Erie Canal, which in this manner became the outlet for almost the greater part of the West.

It is difficult to estimate the influence which this Canal has exerted upon

2. *Senate Executive Documents*, 32 Cong., 1 sess., No. 112, pp. 278–79.

the commerce, growth, and prosperity of the whole country, for it is impossible to imagine what would have been the state of things without it.

But for this work, the West would have held out few inducements to the settler, who would have been without a market for his most important products, and consequently without the means of supplying many of his most essential wants. That portion of the country would have remained comparatively unsettled up to the present time; and, where now exist rich and populous communities, we should find an uncultivated wilderness.

The East would have been equally without the elements of growth. The Canal has supplied it with cheap food, and has opened an outlet and created a market for the products of its manufactures and commerce.

The increase of commerce, and the growth of the country, have been very accurately measured by the growth of the business of the Canal. It has been one great bond of strength, infusing life and vigor into the whole. Commercially and politically, it has secured and maintained to the United States the characteristics of a homogeneous people.

3. Steamboats Lose to the Railroads (*c.* 1857)

Samuel Clemens, whose pen name "Mark Twain" was a depth measurement, became apprenticed as a Mississippi pilot in 1857, when only twenty-two. Emerging as a full-fledged pilot, he remained on the river until the Civil War interrupted traffic in 1861. In 1883, at the height of his powers, he published his classic *Life on the Mississippi,* in which he described the spectacular races between river queens that foamed perilously against the current at an average of more than fourteen miles an hour. Ascertain what the following brief episode, as related by Clemens, reveals about changed conditions.

The locomotive is in sight from the deck of the steamboat almost the whole way from St. Louis to St. Paul—eight hundred miles. These railroads have made havoc with the steamboat commerce. The clerk of our boat was a steamboat clerk before these roads were built. In that day the influx of population was so great, and the freight business so heavy, that the boats were not able to keep up with the demands made upon their carrying capacity; consequently the captains were very independent and airy—pretty "biggity," as Uncle Remus would say. The clerk nutshelled the contrast between the former time and the present, thus:

"Boat used to land—captain on hurricane roof—mighty stiff and straight—iron ramrod for a spine—kid gloves, plug tile [hat], hair parted behind—man on shore takes off hat and says:

" 'Got twenty-eight tons of wheat, cap'n—be great favor if you can take them.'

"Captain says:

" 'I'll take two of them'—and don't even condescend to look at him.

"But nowadays the captain takes off his old slouch [hat], and smiles all the way around to the back of his ears, and gets off a bow which he hasn't got any ramrod to interfere with, and says:

3. Mark Twain, *Life on the Mississippi*, Ch. 58.

" 'Glad to see you, Smith, glad to see you—you're looking well—haven't seen you looking so well for years—what you got for us?'

" 'Nuth'n,' says Smith; and keeps his hat on, and just turns his back and goes to talking with somebody else.

"Oh, yes! eight years ago the captain was on top; but it's Smith's turn now. Eight years ago a boat used to go up the river with every stateroom full, and people piled five and six deep on the cabin floor; and a solid deckload of immigrants and harvesters down below, into the bargain. To get a first-class stateroom, you'd got to prove sixteen quarterings of nobility and four hundred years of descent, or be personally acquainted with the nigger that blacked the captain's boots. But it's all changed now; plenty staterooms above, no harvesters below—there's a patent self-binder now, and they don't have harvesters any more; they've gone where the woodbine twineth—and they didn't go by steamboat, either; they went by the train."

D. THE COMING OF THE IRON HORSE

1. A Canal Stockholder's Outburst (1830)

New methods of transportation naturally alarmed intrenched interests. Turnpike investors fought the canals; canal investors and teamsters fought the railroads; railroad investors were to fight the motor trucks and airlines; airline investors are presumably destined to fight rocket ships. In particular, teamsters objected to "the damned railroad" because it cut up farms; ruined the horse and hay market; deprived wheelwrights, blacksmiths, and mechanics of their employment; and brought in hordes of pick-and-shovel Irishmen, with ready fists, to work on the roadbeds. Canal boatmen and canal investors voiced similar grievances. Note what real substance there is in these obviously overdrawn objections that appeared in this item in an Indiana newspaper.

The following humorous argument was advanced by a canal stockholder, for the purpose of putting down railways:

"He saw what would be the effect of it; that it would set the whole world a-gadding. Twenty miles an hour, sir.—Why, you will not be able to keep an apprentice boy at his work! Every Saturday evening he must have a trip to Ohio to spend a Sunday with his sweetheart. Grave, plodding citizens will be flying about like comets. All local attachments will be at an end. It will encourage flightiness of intellect. Veracious people will turn into the most immeasurable liars: all conceptions will be exaggerated by the magnificent notions of distance.—Only a hundred miles off!—Tut, nonsense, I'll step across, madam and bring your fan! 'Pray, sir, will you dine with me today, at my little box on the Allegheny?' 'Why indeed I don't know—I shall be there, but you must let me off in time for the theater.'

"And then, sir, there will be barrels of pork, cargoes of flour, chaldrons of coal, and even lead and whiskey, and such-like sober things that have always been used to slow traveling—whisking away like a sky rocket. It will upset all the gravity of the nation. If a couple of gentlemen have an affair

1. Vincennes (Indiana) *Western Sun*, July 24, 1830.

of honor, it is only to steal off to the Rocky Mountains and there is no jurisdiction that can touch them. And then, sir; think of it—flying for debt! A set of bailiffs mounted on bombshells would never overtake an absconding debtor, only give him a fair start.

"Upon the whole, sir, it is a pestilential, topsy-turvy, harum-scarum whirligig. Give me the old, solemn, straightforward, regular Dutch canal— three miles an hour for expresses, and two-rod jogtrot journeys—with a yoke of oxen for heavy loads! I go for beasts of burden; it is more firmative and scriptural, and suits a moral and religious people better. None of your hop-skip-and-jump whimsies for me."

2. Railroads Link East and West (1849)

Alexander Mackay, a gifted British journalist and barrister, published in 1849 a three-volume description of his American travels. It ranks as the finest work of its kind for the era. Liberal, sympathetic, and friendly, Mackay struck up enlightening conversations with the Americans, as the following passage attests. Ascertain how much logic there was in his prognosis of an East-West split, and why such a division did not work out in actual practice.

"It is a common thing in Europe," said I [Mackay], "to speculate upon the probabilities of a speedy dissolution between the Northern and Southern divisions of the Union. But I confess that, for myself, I have for some time back been of opinion that, should a disseverance ever take place, the danger is that it will be between the East and the West."

"On what do you base such an opinion?" inquired my [American] companion.

"On referring to the map," replied I, "it will be found that fully one-third of the members [states] of the Confederation are situated in the same great basin, having one great interest in common between them, being irrigated by the same system of navigable rivers, and all united together into one powerful belt by their common artery, the Mississippi."

"Admitting this," observed my friend, "what danger arises therefrom to the stability of the Union?"

"Only that arising from a probable conflict of interests," replied I. "The great region drained by the Mississippi is pre-eminently agricultural, whilst much of the seaboard is manufacturing and commercial. The first-named region is being rapidly filled with an adventurous and energetic population, and its material resources are being developed at a ratio unexampled in the annals of human progress. The revolution [passing] of a very few years will find it powerful enough to stand by itself, should it feel so inclined. And then nothing can prevent a fatal collision of interests between it and the different communities on the seaboard but the recognition and adoption of a commercial policy which will afford it an ample outlet for its vast and varied productions." . . .

2. Alexander Mackay, *The Western World, or Travels in the United States in 1846–47* (1849), I, 236–40.

OPPOSITION TO THE RAILROADS

Canal and turnpike investors stressed damage to life, property, and business from railroad monopoly. Detail from a Philadelphia poster, 1839. Union Pacific Railroad Photo.

"I am free to admit," cried my friend, "the necessity for such an adjustment as an essential condition to the stability of the Union. . . . Antagonistic as they are in many respects in their interests, were the East and the West to be left physically isolated from each other, the difficulties in the way of a compromise of interests would indeed be insurmountable. Had the East no direct hold upon the West, and had the West no communication with the rest of the world but through the Mississippi, one might well despair of a permanent reconciliation. It is in obviating the physical obstructions . . . that the great barrier to a permanent good understanding between the East and the West has been broken down. It is by rendering each more necessary to the other that the foundation has been laid for that mutual concession which alone can ensure future harmony and give permanence to the Union."

"And how have you done this?" inquired I.

"We have tapped the West," replied he. . . .

"By tapping the West, then, you mean opening direct communications between the East and the West?"

"Exactly so," said he. "Had matters been left as nature arranged them, the whole traffic of the Mississippi valley would have been thrown upon the Gulf of Mexico. . . ."

"When I consider," said I, "the many parallel lines of artificial communication which you have established between the East and the West, I must say that, in tapping the latter, you have tapped it liberally."

"We have taken, or are taking, advantage of all our opportunities in this respect," replied he [referring to the East-West network of canals and railroads]. . . .

"And to these you look," observed I, "as your securities for the integrity of the republic?"

"As bonds," said he, "the existence of which renders improbable the severance of the East from the West. These four great parallel lines of intercommunication have effectually counteracted the political tendencies of the Mississippi. . . . Everything, too, which improves the position of the West, as regards the Atlantic seaports, renders the mutual dependence between the two sections of the Union, as respects their home trade, more intimate and complete. In addition to this, it strengthens more and more the sentiment of nationality, by bringing the denizens of the West and the East in constant communication with each other. They freely traverse each other's fields, and walk each other's streets, and feel equally at home, whether they are on the Wabash, the Arkansas, the Potomac, the Susquehanna, the Genesee, or the St. John's.

"This is what we have effected by tapping the West. We have united it to us by bonds of iron, which it cannot, and which, if it could, it would not, break. By binding it to the older states by the strong tie of material interests, we have identified its political sentiment with our own. We have made the twain one by our canals, our railroads, and our electric telegraphs, by making the Atlantic more necessary to the West than the Gulf; in short," said he, "by removing the Alleghenies."

THOUGHT PROVOKERS

1. Would American women (and society) be better off today if they had never been drawn into industry? Argue both sides. Could women have been kept out?

2. Were the rich men of the 1830's really exploiting the workers or providing them with job opportunities? Would you rather have been a Negro slave in the South than a wage slave in a New England factory? Argue both sides. Is a man really free if he is free to starve? In what noteworthy respects is labor better off today than it was in the 1830's, and why?

3. Compare and contrast the advantages and disadvantages of canals, river waterways, and railroads, and draw conclusions. Why could some canals, including the Erie Canal, continue to compete with the railroads?

4. Why can it be asserted with plausibility that the Erie Canal won the Civil War for the North? Would there have been a Civil War if there had been no Erie Canal? Do contrasting economies tend to divide sections or unite them because of their dependence on one another?

FURTHER EXPLORATION

General: T. C. Cochran and William Miller, *The Age of Enterprise* (1942); G. R. Taylor, *The Transportation Revolution, 1815–1860* (1951). **Factory Spread:** Caroline F. Ware, *The Early New England Cotton Manufacture* (1931). **Labor Unrest:** J. R. Commons *et al., History of Labor in the United States* (4 vols., 1918–1935); F. R. Dulles, *Labor in America: A History* (1960); J. G. Rayback, *A History of American Labor* (1959). **Inland Waterways:** Seymour Dunbar, *A History of American Travel* (4 vols., 1915); A. B. Hulbert, *The Paths of Inland Commerce* (1920); M. S. Waggoner, *The Long Haul West* (1958). **Iron Horse:** Slason Thompson, *A Short History of American Railways* (1925); Stewart Holbrook, *The Story of American Railroads* (1947). **Recent:** R. E. Shaw, *Erie Water West; A History of the Erie Canal, 1792–1854* (1966).

Chapter 17

Religion, Immigration, and Education to 1860

> *This country is filling up with thousands and millions of voters, and you must educate them to keep them from our throats.*
>
> POPULAR SAYING, QUOTED BY RALPH WALDO EMERSON, 1844

PROLOGUE: Both the War of Independence and the War of 1812, with their homebreaking and other demoralizing effects, helped dampen the hell-fire religion of colonial days. But church members were more numerous than ever. Orgiastic revivals—often as camp meetings on the frontier—served to check backsliding. The influx of famine-cursed Irish Catholics in the 1840's and 1850's alarmed the "native" Protestants already here, and resulted in ugly manifestations of intolerance. These outbursts of anti-foreignism were to some extent restrained by the spread of free public education, which came into its own in the second quarter of the 19th Century. The grade schools emphasized moral precepts through the high-quality textbooks of William H. McGuffey. They were hammered home by the hickory stick, and supplemented on the outside by moralistic tales like those of Parson Weems.

A. RELIGION AND MORALS

1. Thomas Paine's Unorthodoxy (1794)

Thomas Paine, famed author of *Common Sense* in 1776, turned his incendiary talents toward defending and participating in the French Revolution. In the 1790's he published his two-volume *Age of Reason*—the so-called "atheists' Bible"—which stirred up bitter condemnation in America through its attack on orthodox religion. Theodore Roosevelt later branded Paine "that filthy little atheist." The truth is that despite his great services during the American Revolution, Paine was dirty, slothful, boorish, opinionated, and unduly addicted to alcohol. From the following preface to his *Age of Reason*, determine whether he was really an atheist, and why the Christian clergy were more prone to condemn him than the Christian laity. What is his most valid criticism of orthodox religion?

I believe in one God, and no more; and I hope for happiness beyond this life.

I believe [in] the equality of man, and I believe that religious duties consist in doing justice, loving mercy, and endeavoring to make our fellow creatures happy.

But, lest it should be supposed that I believe many other things in addition to these, I shall, in the progress of this work, declare the things I do not believe, and my reasons for not believing them.

1. M. D. Conway, ed., *The Writings of Thomas Paine* (1896), IV, 21–22.

I do not believe in the creed professed by the Jewish church, by the Roman church, by the Greek church, by the Turkish church, by the Protestant church, nor by any church that I know of. My own mind is my own church.

All national institutions of churches [established churches], whether Jewish, Christian, or Turkish, appear to me no other than human inventions set up to terrify and enslave mankind, and monopolize power and profit.

I do not mean by this declaration to condemn those who believe otherwise; they have the same right to their belief as I have to mine. But it is necessary to the happiness of man that he be mentally faithful to himself. Infidelity does not consist in believing, or in disbelieving; it consists in professing to believe what he does not believe.

It is impossible to calculate the moral mischief, if I may so express it, that mental lying has produced in society. When a man has so far corrupted and prostituted the chastity of his mind as to subscribe his professional belief to things he does not believe, he has prepared himself for the commission of every other crime. He takes up the trade of a priest for the sake of gain, and, in order to qualify himself for that trade, he begins with a perjury. Can we conceive anything more destructive to morality than this?

Soon after I had published the pamphlet *Common Sense* in America, I saw the exceeding probability that a revolution in the system of government would be followed by a revolution in the system of religion. The adulterous connection of church and state, wherever it had taken place, whether Jewish, Christian, or Turkish, had so effectually prohibited, by pains and penalties, every discussion upon established creeds, and upon first principles of religion, that until the system of government should be changed, those subjects could not be brought fairly and openly before the world; but that whenever this should be done, a revolution in the system of religion would follow. Human inventions and priestcraft would be detected; and man would return to the pure, unmixed, and unadulterated belief of one God, and no more.

2. The Indians Rebuff a Missionary (1805)

Red Jacket—so called from a British gift—was a powerful Seneca (Iroquois) chief, born in present Seneca County, New York, and famed for his political wirepulling and oratory. In 1805 a young Protestant evangelist named Cram sought permission to establish a mission in the Seneca country. Red Jacket, who bitterly opposed missionaries, spurned him in this memorable speech. Twenty-five years later the eloquent chief, debauched by the white man's firewater, was buried—in violation of his express wish—in a Christian cemetery with a Christian funeral service. Ascertain which of his arguments was probably most embarrassing to the whites, and whether the Indians were in their conduct better Christians than the whites.

Brother, listen to what we say.

There was a time when our forefathers owned this great island [con-

2. C. M. Depew. ed., *Library of Oratory* (1902), III, 389–92.

tinent]. Their seats extended from the rising to the setting sun. The Great Spirit had made it for the use of Indians. . . .

But an evil day came upon us. Your forefathers crossed the great water and landed on this island. Their numbers were small. They found friends and not enemies. They told us they had fled from their own country for fear of wicked men, and had come here to enjoy their religion. They asked for a small seat. We took pity on them; granted their request; and they sat down amongst us. We gave them corn and meat; they gave us poison [liquor] in return.

The white people, brother, had now found our country. Tidings were carried back and more came amongst us. Yet we did not fear them. We took them to be friends. They called us brothers. We believed them and gave them a larger seat. At length their numbers had greatly increased. They wanted more land; they wanted our country. Our eyes were opened and our minds became uneasy. Wars took place. Indians were hired to fight against Indians, and many of our people were destroyed. They also brought strong liquor amongst us. It was strong and powerful and has slain thousands.

Brother, our seats were once large and yours were small. You have now become a great people, and we have scarcely a place left to spread our blankets. You have got our country, but are not satisfied. You want to force your religion upon us.

Brother, continue to listen.

You say that you are sent to instruct us how to worship the Great Spirit agreeably to his mind; and, if we do not take hold of the religion which you white people teach us, we shall be unhappy hereafter. You say that you are right and we are lost. How do we know this to be true? We understand that your religion is written in a book. If it was intended for us, as well as you, why has not the Great Spirit given to us, and not only to us, but why did he not give to our forefathers the knowledge of that book, with the means of understanding it rightly? We only know what you tell us about it. How shall we know when to believe, being so often deceived by the white people?

Brother, you say there is but one way to worship and serve the Great Spirit. If there is but one religion, why do you white people differ so much about it? Why not all agreed, as you can all read the book?

Brother, we do not understand these things. We are told that your religion was given to your forefathers, and has been handed down from father to son. We also have a religion, which was given to our forefathers and has been handed down to us, their children. We worship in that way. It teaches us to be thankful for all the favors we receive; to love each other and to be united. We never quarrel about religion.

Brother, the Great Spirit has made us all, but he has made a great difference between his white and red children. He has given us different complexions and different customs. To you he has given the arts. To these he has not opened our eyes. We know these things to be true. Since he has made so great a difference between us in other things, why may we not conclude that he has given us a different religion according to our understanding? The Great Spirit does right. He knows what is best for his children. We are satisfied.

Brother, we do not wish to destroy your religion or take it from you. We only want to enjoy our own.

Brother, you say you have not come to get our land or our money, but to enlighten our minds. I will now tell you that I have been at your meetings and saw you collect money from the meeting. I cannot tell what this money was intended for, but suppose that it was for your minister; and, if we should conform to your way of thinking, perhaps you may want some from us.

Brother, we are told that you have been preaching to the white people in this place. These people are our neighbors. We are acquainted with them. We will wait a little while and see what effect your preaching has upon them. If we find it does them good, makes them honest, and less disposed to cheat Indians, we will then consider again of what you have said.

Brother, you have now heard our answer to your talk and this is all we have to say at present. As we are going to part, we will come and take you by the hand, and hope the Great Spirit will protect you on your journey and return you safe to your friends.

3. A Catholic Views Camp Meetings (*c.* 1801)

Kentucky-born Martin J. Spalding was an eminent Catholic prelate who died as the Archbishop of Baltimore. He won many friends with his merry laugh, attractive speaking voice, and frank manner. Drawing on memoirs and oral testimony, he described some forty years later the great Protestant camp meetings in Kentucky, where thousands assembled for a week or so to repent of their sins and to find emotional release from a grinding, monotonous frontier life. The camp meeting, though not confined to the frontier, was a typically frontier phenomenon, and attracted camp followers who purveyed alcohol and sex. Note whether the participants were only ignorant Baptists and Methodists, and whether the effect was minor and short-lived. Consider why a Roman Catholic should take some satisfaction in these excesses, and account for the manifestations that developed.

To understand more fully how very "precious and astonishing" this great revival was, we must farther reflect: 1st, that it produced, not a mere momentary excitement, but one that lasted for several successive years. 2ndly, that it was not confined to one particular denomination, but, to a greater or less extent, pervaded all. 3rdly, that men of sense and of good judgment in other matters were often carried away by the same fanaticism which swayed the mob. 4thly, that this fanaticism was as widespread as it was permanent—not being confined to Kentucky, but pervading most of the adjoining states and territories. And 5thly, that though some were found who had good sense enough to detect the imposture, yet they were

3. M. J. Spalding, *Sketches of the Early Catholic Missions of Kentucky* . . . (1844), pp. 104–06.

A WESTERN CAMP MEETING

Henry Howe, *Historical Collections of the Great West*, 1851, vol. I.

comparatively few in number, and wholly unable to stay the rushing torrent of fanaticism, even if they had had the moral courage to attempt it.

Such are some of the leading features of a movement in religion (!) which is perhaps one of the most extraordinary recorded in history, and to which we know of but few parallels, except in some of the fanatical doings of the Anabaptists in Germany during the first years of their history. The whole matter furnishes one more conclusive evidence of the weakness of the human mind when left to itself; and one more sad commentary on the Protestant rule of faith.

Here we see whole masses of population, spread over a vast territory, boasting too of their enlightenment and Bible-learning, swayed for years by a fanaticism as absurd as it was blasphemous; and yet believing all this to be the work of the Holy Spirit!! Let Protestants after this talk about Catholic ignorance and superstition! Had Catholics ever played the "fantastic tricks" which were played off by Protestants during these years, we would perhaps never hear the end of it. . . .

Besides the "exercises" [described earlier] . . . there was also the jumping exercise. Spasmodic convulsions, which lasted sometimes for hours, were the usual sequel to the falling exercise. Then there were the "exercises" of screaming and shouting and crying. A camp meeting during that day exhibited the strangest bodily feats, accompanied with the most Babel-like sounds. An eyewitness of undoubted veracity stated to us that, in passing one of the camp-grounds, he noticed a man in the "barking exercise," clasping a tree with his arms, and dashing his head against it until it was all besmeared with blood, shouting all the time that he had "treed his Saviour"!! Another eyewitness stated that in casually passing by a camp in the night, while the exercises were at the highest, he witnessed scenes of too revolting a character even to be alluded to here.

One of the most remarkable features, perhaps, of these "exercises" is the apparently well-authenticated fact that many fell into them by a kind of sympathy, almost in spite of themselves, and some even positively against their own will! Some who visited the meetings to laugh at the proceedings, sometimes caught the contagion themselves. There seems to have then existed in Kentucky a kind of mental and moral epidemic—a sort of contagious frenzy—which spread rapidly from one to another.

Yet the charm was not so strong that it could not be broken, as the following incident, related to us by a highly intelligent Protestant gentleman, clearly proves. Some young ladies of his acquaintance came from one of those meetings to pass the night at his father's house. They were laboring under great nervous excitement, and, in the course of the evening, began to jerk most violently. The father, one of the most intelligent men in Kentucky, severely rebuked them, and told them bluntly that he would "have no such behavior as this in his house." The reproof was effectual, and the jerking spirit was exorcised! . . .

4. De Tocqueville Commends American Morals (1831)

Alexis de Tocqueville, an observant young Frenchman, came to America in 1831 when only twenty-six, on a government mission to study the penal system. Traveling widely and interrogating freely, he gathered enough material to fill fourteen notebooks. His findings were published in a two-volume classic, *Democracy in America*, which remains one of the most penetrating analyses of American government and society ever written. He was told that since no religion was dominant, all Americans supported toleration lest they become the victims of intolerance. He was also informed that sexual morality was at a higher level among all classes than in Europe. He recorded the explanation as follows in his notebook. Determine which of the reasons seems least convincing in the light of then existing conditions.

American morals are, I think, the most chaste that exist in any nation, a fact which can, it seems to me, be attributed to five chief causes:

1st. Physical constitution. They belong to a northern race, although they almost all live in a climate hotter than that of England.

2nd. Religion still holds great sway over their souls. They have even retained some of the traditions of the strictest religious sects.

3rd. They are entirely absorbed by their preoccupation with making a fortune. There are no idle ones among them. They have the *settled* habits of people who work the whole time.

4. Alexis de Tocqueville, *Journey to America*, trans. George Lawrence; ed. J. P. Mayer (1960), pp. 222–23. By permission of the Yale University Press.

4th. There is no trace of the prejudices of birth which prevail in Europe, and it is so easy to make a fortune that poverty is never an obstacle to marriage. As a result the individuals of both sexes are early joined in marriage, only marry because they are attracted one to another, and they find themselves tied at a time of life when a man is almost always more sensible of the pleasures of the heart than of the senses. It is rare for a man not to be married at twenty-one.

5th. The women generally receive a rational education (perhaps even a somewhat rationalistic one). The reasons listed above make it possible without great drawbacks to allow them extreme freedom; the transition from the status of girl to married woman has no dangers for them.

B. THE FLOCKING OF THE IMMIGRANTS

1. An English Radical Praises America (1818)

Economic hardship, begotten by the Industrial Revolution and the Napoleonic wars, laid a withering hand on England. Political reaction under the Tories was hardly less blighting; the Reform Bills of 1832 and 1867 lay in the future. Of the 24,000,000 souls in the British Isles in 1831, only 400,000 were qualified voters. "Pocket boroughs," controlled by the Crown or by aristocratic landowners, sent members to Parliament, while newly mushroomed industrial cities, like Manchester and Birmingham, enjoyed no direct representation. Favored placemen occupied high office. The tax-supported state Church of England rode high. Thomas Hulme, an English radical, here tells his story. Despairing of Parliamentary reform and chafing under the rule of "the great insolent" families, he decided to bring his children to America before he should die and leave them "the slaves of such a set of beings." Note his most violent prejudices and what features of America appealed to him most.

I was well pleased with America, over a considerable part of which I traveled. I saw an absence of human misery. I saw a government taking away a very, very small portion of men's earnings. I saw ease and happiness and a fearless utterance of thought everywhere prevail. I saw laws like those of the old laws of England, everywhere obeyed with cheerfulness and held in veneration. I heard of no mobs, no riots, no spies, no [penal] transportings, no hangings. I saw those very Irish, to keep whom in order such murderous laws exist in Ireland, here good, peaceable, industrious citizens. I saw no placemen and pensioners riding the people under foot. I saw no greedy Priesthood fattening on the fruits of labor in which they had never participated, and which fruits they seized in despite of the people. I saw a debt, indeed, but then it was so insignificant a thing; and, besides, it had been contracted for the people's use, and not for that of a set of tyrants who had used the money to the injury of the people. In short, I saw a state of things precisely the reverse of that in England, and very nearly what it would be in England if the Parliament were reformed. . . .

During the spring and early part of the summer of 1817, I made preparations for the departure of myself and family, and when all was ready, I bid an everlasting adieu to boroughmongers, sinecure placemen and

1. In William Cobbett, *A Year's Residence in America* (n.d.), pp. 201–04 (Pt. III).

placewomen, pensioned lords and ladies, standing armies in time of peace, and (rejoice, oh! my children) to a hireling, tithe-devouring Priesthood.

We arrived safe and all in good health, and which health has never been impaired by the climate. We are in a state of ease, safety, plenty; and how can we help being so happy as people can be? The more I see of my adopted country, the more gratitude do I feel towards it for affording me and my numerous offspring protection from the tyrants of my native country. There I should have been in constant anxiety about my family. Here I am in none at all. Here I am in fear of no spies, no false witnesses, no blood-money men. Here no fines, irons, no gallowses await me, let me think or say what I will about the government. Here I have to pay no people to be ready to shoot at me, or run me through the body, or chop me down. Here no vile priest can rob me and mock me in the same breath. . . .

I could mention numerous instances of Englishmen, coming to this country with hardly a dollar in their pocket, and arriving at a state of ease and plenty and even riches in a few years. And I explicitly declare that I have never known or heard of an instance of one common laborer who, with common industry and economy, did not greatly better his lot. Indeed, how can it otherwise be, when the average wages of agricultural labor is double what it is in England, and when the average price of food is not more than half what it is in that country? These two facts, undeniable as they are, are quite sufficient to satisfy any man of sound mind.

As to the manners of the people, they are precisely to my taste: unostentatious and simple. Good sense I find everywhere, and never affectation; kindness, hospitality, and never-failing civility. I traveled more than four thousand miles about this country, and I have never met with one single insolent or rude native American.

2. The Coming of the Shamrock (1836)

Charles J. Latrobe was a Londoner who achieved some fame as a minor poet, a travel writer, and a mountain climber in Switzerland. His two extensive trips to America came in 1832 and 1834, and he observed the swarming of the Irish even in those pre-potato-famine days. Note his prejudices and also the assets and liabilities of the Irish as residents of the United States. It has been said that they were "good to handle a pick or pick a fight." Comment.

Here comes a shipload of Irish. They land upon the wharfs of New York in rags and open-knee'd breeches, with their raw looks and bare necks. They flourish their cudgels, throw up their torn hats, and cry, "Hurrah for Gineral Jackson!" They get drunk and kick up a row, lend their forces to any passing disturbance, and make early acquaintance with the interior of the lock-ups [jails].

From New York they go in swarms to the canals, railroads, and public works, where they perform that labor which the Americans are not inclined

2. C. J. Latrobe, *The Rambler in North America* (1836), II, 222–23.

to do. Now and then they get up a fight among themselves in the style of old Ireland, and perhaps kill one another, expressing great indignation and surprise when they find that they must answer for it though they are in a free country. By degrees, the more thrifty get and keep money, and diving deeper into the continent, purchase lands; while the intemperate and irreclaimable vanish from the surface.

The Americans complain, and justly, of the disorderly population which Ireland throws into the bosom of the Union, but there are many reasons why they should be borne with. They, with the poor Germans, do the work which without them could hardly be done. Though the fathers may be irreclaimable, the children become good citizens—and there is no finer race in the world, both for powers of mind and body, than the Irish, when favored by education and under proper control.

In one thing the emigrant Irish of every class distinguish themselves above the people of other nations, and that is in the love and kindly feeling which they cherish towards their native land, and towards those whom they have left behind—a fact proved by the large sums which are yearly transmitted from them to the mother country, in aid of their poverty-stricken relatives.

3. The Burning of a Convent School (1834)

The swelling tide of Irish-Catholic immigrants in the Boston area intensified a long-festering prejudice against the Catholic Church. A half-dozen riots occurred before public indignation vented itself against an Ursuline convent school at Charlestown, outside Boston. Responding to ill-founded tales of abuse suffered by incarcerated nuns, a well-organized mob of about fifty men sacked and burned the four-storey brick building, on August 11, 1834. (Ironically, more than half of the fifty-seven pupils were Protestant girls.) Neither the authorities nor the hundreds of approving spectators made any attempt to restrain the mob. In retaliation, angry Irish laborers began to mobilize, but were restrained by Bishop Fenwick. The following editorial from the Boston *Atlas* expresses the widespread condemnation voiced in the press and among responsible citizens. Observe what this journal finds most disturbing about the outrage.

From all we can learn, the violence was utterly without cause. The institution was in its very nature unpopular, and a strong feeling existed against it. But there was nothing in the vague rumors that have been idly circulating to authorize or account for any the least act of violence. We should state, perhaps, that during the violent scenes that were taking place before the convent—while the mob were breaking the windows and staving in the doors of the institution—and while the fire was blazing upon the hill as a signal to the mob—one or two muskets were discharged from the windows of the nunnery, or some of the buildings in the vicinity.

What a scene must this midnight conflagration have exhibited—lighting up the inflamed countenances of an infuriated mob of demons—*attacking a*

3. Quoted in *Niles' Weekly Register*, XLVI, 437 (Aug. 23, 1834).

convent of women, a seminary for the instruction of young females; and turning them out of their beds half naked in the hurry of their flight, and half dead with confusion and terror. And this drama, too, to be enacted on the very soil that afforded one of the earliest places of refuge to the Puritans of New England—themselves flying from religious persecution in the Old World—that their descendants might wax strong and mighty, and in their turn be guilty of the same persecution in the New!

We remember no parallel to this outrage in the whole course of history. Turn to the bloodiest incidents of the French Revolution . . . and point us to its equal in unprovoked violence, in brutal outrage, in unthwarted iniquity. It is in vain that we search for it. In times of civil commotion and general excitement . . . there was some palliation for violence and outrage—in the tremendously excited state of the public mind. But here there was no such palliation. The courts of justice were open to receive complaints of any improper confinement, or unauthorized coercion. The civil magistrates were, or ought to be, on the alert to detect any illegal restraint, and bring its authors to the punishment they deserve. But nothing of the kind was detected. The whole matter was a cool, deliberate, systematized piece of brutality—unprovoked—under the most provoking circumstances totally unjustifiable—and visiting the citizens of the town, and most particularly its magistrates and civil officers, with indelible disgrace.

[*Local sentiment undoubtedly supported the mobsters. The subsequent trial of the ringleaders was a farce: insults were showered on the prosecution, the nuns, and the Catholic Church. Only one culprit was convicted, and he was pardoned following a petition by forgiving Catholics. The Massachusetts legislature, bowing to intimidation, dropped all efforts to provide financial recompense. Catholic churches in the area were forced to post armed guards, and for a time insurance companies refused to insure Catholic buildings built of inflammable materials. The Ursuline sisters of Charlestown finally moved to Canada, and for thirty-five years the blackened brick ruins of the school remained a monument to religious bigotry.*]

4. A Southerner Defends the Catholics (1854)

The great flood of Irish Catholics, uprooted by the potato famine of the mid-1840's, further aroused many "native Americans." The newcomers not only worsened already stinking slums but became willing voting tools of the corrupt political machines. "Nativist" resentment found vent in the powerful Know-Nothing (American) Party, which undertook to elect only "natives" to office; to raise the residence requirement for naturalization from 5 to 21 years; and to exclude Roman Catholics from office, on the popular assumption that orders from the Pope took precedence over their oath to support the Constitution. Yet Know-Nothingism found little support in the South. Relatively few Catholic immigrants went there; and in addition the Catholic Church did not cry out against slavery, as did the leading Protestant denominations of the North. Representative William T. S. Barry of Mississippi, a

4. *Congressional Globe*, 33 Cong., 2 sess., Appendix, pp. 58–59.

Presbyterian with Episcopalian leanings and one of the South's great orators, here defends the Catholics in a justly famous speech. In the light of his remarks, assess the following statements: persecution strengthens the persecuted; proscriptionists become the proscribed; intolerance has no logical half-way stopping point.

The last purpose to be achieved by the Know-Nothings is the exclusion of all Catholics from office. . . . How dare we talk of freedom of conscience, when more than a million of our citizens are to be excluded from office for conscience sake!

Yesterday, to have argued in favor of religious toleration in this country would have been absurd, for none could have been found to deny or question it. But today there is a sect [Know-Nothings] boasting that it can control the country, avowing the old Papist and monarchical doctrine of political exclusion for religious opinions' sake. The arguments by which they sustain themselves are those by which the Inquisition justified their probing the consciences and burning the bodies of men five hundred years ago, and against which Protestantism has struggled since the days of Luther.

You, sir, and I, and all of us, owe our own right to worship God according to our consciences to that very doctrine which this new [Know-Nothing] order abjures; and if the right of the Catholic is first assailed and destroyed, you, sir, or another member who believes according to a different Protestant creed, may be excluded from this House, and from other preferment, because of your religious faith.

The security of all citizens rests upon the same broad basis of universal right. Confederates who disfranchise one class of citizens soon turn upon each other. The strong argument of general right is destroyed by their united action, and the proscriptionist of yesterday is the proscribed of tomorrow. Human judgment has recognized the inexorable justice of the sentence which consigned Robespierre and his accomplices [of the French Revolution] to the same guillotine to which they had condemned so many thousand better men.

No nation can content itself with a single act of persecution; either public intelligence will reject that as unworthy of itself, or public prejudice will add others to it. If the Catholic be untrustworthy as a citizen, and the public liberty is unsafe in his keeping, it is but a natural logical consequence that he shall not be permitted to disseminate a faith which is adjudged hostile to national independence; that he shall not be allowed to set the evil example of the practice of his religion before the public; that it shall not be preached from the pulpit; that it shall not be taught in the schools; and that, by all the energy of the law, it shall be utterly exterminated.

If this [Catholic] faith be incompatible with good citizenship, and you set about to discourage it—destroy it utterly, uproot it from the land. Petty persecution will but irritate a sect which the Know-Nothings denounce as so powerful and so dangerous. This was the course which England pursued when she entertained the same fears of the Catholics three hundred years

THE NATURALIZATION OFFICE DAY BEFORE ELECTION

Citizen of undoubted respectability: "Did you happen to want a friend to swear you've been five years a resident?" Immigrant voters in New York illegally sworn in. *Harper's Weekly*, 1857.

ago, and which she has lived to see the absurdity of, and has removed almost, if not quite, every disability imposed. Perhaps, however, this new [Know-Nothing] sect will not startle the public mind by proposing too much at once, and holds that it will be time enough to propose further and more minute persecution when the national sentiment is debauched enough to entertain favorably this first great departure from the unbounded toleration of our fathers.

It is the experience of this country that persecution strengthens a new creed. . . . Perhaps it is true of all times and countries. . . . In my judgment, this attempt at proscription will do more to spread Catholicism here than all the treasures of Rome, or all the Jesuitism of the Cardinals.

C. THE FIGHT FOR PUBLIC EDUCATION

1. Mr. X Attacks Free Schools (1829)

The coming of universal manhood suffrage convinced many well-to-do citizens that they must educate the illiterate voter to his new responsibilities. Otherwise they would risk demagoguery, property seizures, and outright anarchy. But an anonymous North Carolinian, in an open letter to the state legislature, expressed contrary views. Analyze his concept of education and his motives for opposing more of it.

1. Raleigh *Register*, Nov. 9, 1829, in C. L. Coon, *The Beginnings of Public Education in North Carolina* (1908), I, 432–33.

... You may be solicited to take some steps with regard to the establishment among us of common schools. Should so rediculous [*sic*] a measure be propounded to you, you will unquestionably, for your own interest, as well as that of your constituents, treat it with the same contemptuous neglect which it has ever met with heretofore.

Common schools indeed! Money is very scarce, and the times are unusually hard. Why was such a matter never broached in better and more prosperous days?

Gentlemen, it appears to me that schools are sufficiently plenty, and that the people have no desire they should be increased. Those now in operation are not all filled, and it is very doubtful if they are productive of much real benefit. Would it not redound as much to the advantage of young persons, and to the honor of the state, if they should pass their days in the cotton patch, or at the plow, or in the cornfield, instead of being mewed up in a schoolhouse where they are earning nothing?

Such an ado as is made in these times about education surely was never heard of before. Gentlemen, I hope you do not conceive it at all necessary that *everybody* should be able to read, write, and cipher. If one is to keep a store or a school, or to be a lawyer or physician, such branches may, *perhaps*, be taught him; though I do not look upon them as by any means indispensable. But if he is to be a plain farmer, or a mechanic, they are of no manner of use, but rather a detriment. There need no arguments to make clear so self-evident a proposition.

Should schools be established by law in all parts of the state, as at the North, our taxes must be considerably increased, possibly to the amount of one percent and sixpence on a poll [person]; and I will ask any prudent, sane, saving man if he desires his taxes to be higher?

2. Philadelphians Demand Free Schools (1830)

The "lower orders" were painfully aware of their poor preparation for voting. The following excerpt from a report of a workingmen's committee in Philadelphia is a poignant reminder of their deficiencies. In the light of its assertions explain what is meant by the following: ignorance is the ally of despotism; ignorance is the mother of demagoguery; the ignorant are enchained.

The original element of despotism is a monopoly of talent, which consigns the multitude to comparative ignorance, and secures the balance of knowledge on the side of the rich and the rulers. . . .

In a republic, the people constitute the government, and by wielding its powers in accordance with the dictates either of their intelligence or their ignorance, of their judgment or their caprices, are the makers and the rulers of their own good or evil destiny. They frame the laws and create the institutions that promote their happiness or produce their destruction. If they be wise and intelligent, no laws but what are just and equal will

2. *Working Man's Advocate*, March 6, 1830, in J. R. Commons *et al.*, eds., *A Documentary History of American Industrial Society* (1910), V, 99–100, 102.

receive their approbation, or be sustained by their suffrages [votes]. If they be ignorant and capricious, they will be deceived by mistaken or designing rulers into the support of laws that are unequal and unjust.

It appears, therefore, to the committee that there can be no real liberty without a wide diffusion of real intelligence; that the members of a republic should all be alike instructed in the nature and character of their equal rights and duties, as human beings and as citizens; and that education, instead of being limited as in our public poor [charity] schools, to a simple acquaintance with words and ciphers, should tend, as far as possible, to the production of a just disposition, virtuous habits, and a rational self-governing character. . . .

The instruction afforded by common schools, . . . being only elementary, must of necessity produce but a very limited development of the human faculties. It would indeed diminish, but could not destroy, the present injurious monopoly of talent. While the higher branches of literature and science remain accessible only to the children of the wealthy, there must still be a balance of knowledge, and with it a "balance of power," in the hands of the privileged few, the rich and the rulers.

Another radical defect in the best system of common schools yet established will be found in its not being adapted to meet the wants and necessities of those who stand most in need of it. Very many of the poorest parents are totally unable to clothe and maintain their children while at school, and [the children] are compelled to employ their time, while yet very young, in aiding to procure a subsistence.

3. Mann Pleads for Public Libraries (1840)

Horace Mann, the most influential educational reformer of his day, sacrificed a lucrative law practice for a life of public service. His influence radiated out from Massachusetts, where he did much to improve the common schools by securing better buildings, higher salaries, and superior teaching methods through teachers' institutes and normal schools. A born reformer and a Puritan at heart, he also fought Negro slavery, lotteries, the liquor traffic, profanity, intemperance, smoking, and ballet dancing. In his famous lecture on public libraries, note the relationship he posits between ignorance and opinionatedness.

A library will produce one effect upon school children, and upon the neighborhood generally, before they have read one of the books, and even if they should never read one of them.

It is in this way: The most ignorant are the most conceited. Unless a man knows that there is something more to be known, his inference is, of course, that he knows everything. Such a man always usurps the throne of universal knowledge, and assumes the right of deciding all possible questions. We all know that a conceited dunce will decide questions extemporaneously which would puzzle a college of philosophers or a bench of judges. Ignorant and shallow-minded men do not see far enough to see the difficulty.

3. M. T. P. Mann, *The Life and Works of Horace Mann* (1891), II, 319–21.

But let a man know that there are things to be known of which he is ignorant, and it is so much carved out of his domain of universal knowledge. And for all purposes of individual character, as well as of social usefulness, it is quite as important for a man to know the extent of his own ignorance as it is anything else.

To know how much there is that we do not know is one of the most valuable parts of our attainments; for such knowledge becomes both a lesson of humility and a stimulus to exertion. Let it be laid down as a universal direction to teachers, when students are becoming proud of their knowledge, to spread open before them some pages of the tremendous volume of their ignorance.

Now those children who are reared without any advantages of intelligent company, or of travel, or of books—which are both company and travel—naturally fall into the error of supposing that they live in the center of the world, that all society is like their society, or, if different from theirs, that it must be wrong. They come, at length, to regard any part of this vast system of the works of man, and of the wisdom of God, which conflicts with their homebred notions, as baneful, or contemptible, or non-existent. They have caught no glimpse of the various and sublime sciences which have been discovered by human talent and assiduity; nor of those infinitely wise and beautiful laws and properties of the visible creation. . . .

Now, when this class of persons go out into the world and mingle with their fellow men, they are found to be alike useless on account of their ignorance, and odious for their presumption. And if a new idea can be projected with sufficient force to break through the incrustations of folly and prejudice which envelop their souls, . . . they appear as ridiculous, under its influence, as did the mouse which was born in the till of a chest, and, happening one day to rear itself upon its hind legs and to look over into the body of the chest, exclaimed, in amazement, that he did not think the universe so large!

A library, even before it is read, will teach people that there is something more to be known.

D. SCHOOLMASTERS OF THE REPUBLIC

1. Parson Weems and the Cherry Tree (1806)

The Reverend Mason L. Weems left his Episcopal pulpit in Maryland for the wider missionary field of selling "good books." He is best known for his moralizing tracts against such assorted sins as adultery and dueling, and especially for his semi-fictionalized biographies of American heroes. His life of George Washington, published about 1800, became an incredible best seller, and ran through over seventy editions, including five in German. Not until the fifth edition (1806) did he insert the inherently improbable tale of the cherry tree and the hatchet. To him, more than to any other man, we owe the bloodless, plaster-cast image of a priggishly perfect

1. M. L. Weems, *A History of the Life and Death, Virtues and Exploits of General George Washington* . . . (1918 ed.), pp. 20–23.

Washington. Decide what light this account casts on the reading habits and
morals of the day; what kind of reception such a book would have today; and what
part of the account seems most overdrawn.

Never did the wise Ulysses take more pains with his beloved [son]
Telemachus than did Mr. Washington with George, to inspire him with an
early love of truth.

"Truth, George," said he, "is the loveliest quality of youth. I would ride
fifty miles, my son, to see the little boy whose heart is so honest, and his
lips so pure, that we may depend on every word he says. Oh, how lovely
does such a child appear in the eyes of everybody! His parents dote on him.
His relations glory in him. They are constantly praising him to their children, whom they beg to imitate him. They are often sending for him to
visit them; and receive him, when he comes, with as much joy as if he
were a little angel, come to set pretty examples to their children.

"But oh! how different, George, is the case with the boy who is so given
to lying that nobody can believe a word he says! He is looked at with
aversion wherever he goes, and parents dread to see him come among
their children.

"Oh, George! my son! rather than see you come to this pass, dear as you
are to my heart, gladly would I assist to nail you up in your little coffin,
and follow you to your grave. Hard, indeed, would it be to me to give up
my son, whose little feet are always so ready to run about with me, and
whose fondly looking eyes and sweet prattle make so large a part of my
happiness. But still I would give him up, rather than see him a common
liar."

"Pa," said George very seriously, "do I ever tell lies?"

"No, George, I thank God you do not, my son; and I rejoice in the hope
you never will. At least, you shall never, from me, have cause to be guilty
of so shameful a thing. Many parents, indeed, even compel their children
to this vile practice by barbarously beating them for every little fault;
hence, on the next offense, the little terrified creature slips out a lie! just to
escape the rod. But as to yourself, George, you know I have always told
you, and now tell you again, that, whenever by accident you do anything
wrong, which must often be the case, as you are but a poor little boy yet,
without experience or knowledge, you must never tell a falsehood to conceal
it. But come bravely up, my son, like a little man, and tell me of it: and,
instead of beating you, George, I will but the more honor and love you
for it, my dear."

This, you'll say, was sowing good seed!—Yes, it was; and the crop, thank
God, was as I believe it ever will be where a man acts the true parent, that
is, the Guardian Angel, by his child.

The following anecdote is a case in point. It is too valuable to be lost,
and too true to be doubted; for it was communicated to me by the same
excellent lady to whom I am indebted for the last.

"When George," said she, "was about six years old, he was made the
wealthy master of a hatchet! of which, like most little boys, he was im-

DRUNKARDS BEWARE

Parson Weems also preaches against drunkenness. M. L. Weems, *The Drunkard's Looking Glass*, 1818.

moderately fond; and was constantly going about chopping everything that came in his way.

"One day, in the garden, where he often amused himself hacking his mother's pea-sticks, he unluckily tried the edge of his hatchet on the body of a beautiful young English cherry tree, which he barked so terribly that I don't believe the tree ever got the better of it.

"The next morning the old gentleman, finding out what had befallen his tree, which, by the by, was a great favorite, came into the house; and with much warmth asked for the mischievous author, declaring at the same time that he would not have taken five guineas for his tree. Nobody could tell him anything about it.

"Presently George and his hatchet made their appearance. 'George,' said his father, 'do you know who killed that beautiful little cherry tree yonder in the garden?'

"This was a tough question; and George staggered under it for a moment; but quickly recovered himself, and looking at his father with the sweet face of youth brightened with the inexpressible charm of all-conquering truth, he bravely cried out, 'I can't tell a lie, Pa; you know I can't tell a lie. I did it with my hatchet.'

" 'Run to my arms, you dearest boy,' cried his father in transports; 'run to my arms. Glad am I, George, that you killed my tree; for you have paid me for it a thousandfold. Such an act of heroism in my son is more worth than a thousand trees, though blossomed with silver, and their fruits of purest gold.' "

It was in this way, by interesting at once both his heart and head, that Mr. Washington conducted George with great ease and pleasure along the happy paths of virtue.

2. McGuffey Implants Morality (1844)

William H. McGuffey—preacher, lecturer, college professor, and college president—
was a fabulously successful compiler of grade-school readers. His texts altogether sold
an estimated 122,000,000 copies. In combining moralizing with human-interest stories
and good literature, he did more to shape the American character than any other
living man. In this supposed incident from the life of one of the Founding Fathers—
Roger Sherman, of New Haven, Connecticut—locate at least five object lessons for
the youth.

I cannot forbear adducing another instance of the power he [Sherman]
had acquired over himself. He was naturally possessed of strong passions;
but over these he at length obtained an extraordinary control. He became
habitually calm, sedate, and self-possessed.

Mr. Sherman was one of those men who are not ashamed to maintain
the forms of religion in their families. One morning he called them all
together, as usual, to lead them in prayer to God; the "old family Bible"
was brought out, and laid on the table.

Mr. Sherman took his seat, and placed beside him one of his children,
a child of his old age. The rest of the family were seated around the room;
several of these were now grown up. Besides these, some of the tutors of
the college [Yale] were boarders in the family, and were present at the
time alluded to. His aged and superannuated mother occupied a corner
of the room, opposite the place where the distinguished judge sat.

At length he opened the Bible and began to read. The child who was
seated beside him made some little disturbance, upon which Mr. Sherman
paused and told it to be still. Again he proceeded; but again he paused to
reprimand the little offender, whose playful disposition would scarcely
permit it to be still. And this time he gently tapped its ear. The blow, if
blow it might be called, caught the attention of his aged mother, who now,
with some effort, rose from the seat, and tottered across the room. At length
she reached the chair of Mr. Sherman, and, in a moment, most unexpectedly to him, she gave him a blow on the ear with all the force she
could summon. "There," said she, "you strike your child, and I will strike
mine."

For a moment the blood was seen mounting to the face of Mr. Sherman;
but it was only for a moment, when all was calm and mild as usual. He
paused; he raised his spectacles; he cast his eye upon his mother; again it
fell upon the book from which he had been reading. Not a word escaped
him; but again he calmly pursued the service, and soon after sought in
prayer an ability to set an example before his household which would be
worthy of their imitation. Such a victory was worth more than the proudest
one ever achieved on the field of battle.

[*McGuffey concluded, "No one has a temper naturally so good that it does not
need attention and cultivation, and no one has a temper so bad, but that, by
proper culture, it may become pleasant."*]

2. W. H. McGuffey, *Fifth Eclectic Reader* (1879 ed.), pp. 205–06.

3. Whitman Criticizes the Schools (1847)

Walt Whitman, later famed as the poet of Democracy, attended school until his eleventh or possibly thirteenth year. Between 1836 and 1841 he taught seven different schools in seven different towns. As a teacher he was described as "a dreamy, impracticable youth," "untidy," "inordinately indolent," and "morose." Entering the newspaper world and ultimately joining the staff of the Brooklyn *Eagle*, he penned the following editorial blast—based in part on sad experience—at the public schools. Note which complaints are still being made, which have been met, and why flogging was bad for all concerned.

As a general thing the faults of our public schools system are: crowding too many students together; insufficiency of books, and their cost being taxed directly on the pupil; and the flogging system, which in a portion of the schools still holds its wretched sway.

With pride we unite in the numerous commendations of the grand free school system of this state [New York]—with its twelve thousand seminaries, and its twenty thousand teachers, to whom each child, rich or poor, can come without money and without price! But we are none the less aware that the prodigious sum—hundreds of thousands of dollars—annually expended on these schools might be expended to more profit.

We have by no means ascended to the height of the great argument of education. The monotonous *old* still resists the fresh philosophical *new*. Form and precedent often are more thought of than reality. . . . To teach the child *book grammar* is nothing; to teach him by example, by practice, by thoroughly clarifying the principles of correct syntax, *how to talk and write harmoniously* is everything. To put him through the arithmetic is not much; to make him able to compare, calculate, and quickly seize the bearings of a practical figure-question, such as occurs in business every hour, is a good deal.

Mere atlas geography is a sham, too, unless the learner have the position of places in his mind, and *know* the direction, distances, bearings, etc., of the countries, seas, cities, rivers, and mountains whose names (as our miserable school geographies give them) he runs over so glibly.

We care very little indeed for—what is the pride of many teachers' hearts —the military discipline of their schools, and the slavish obedience of their pupils to the imperial nod or waved hand of the master. As to the flogging plan, it is the most wretched item yet left of the ignorance and inefficiency of schoolkeeping. It has surrounded the office (properly one of the noblest on earth) with a character of contemptibleness and petty malignance that will stick to it as long as whipping sticks among teachers' habits.

What nobleness can reside in a man who catches boys by the collar and cuffs their ears? What elevation or dignity of character can even a child's elastic thoughts connect with one who cuts him over the back with a rattan or makes him hold out his hand to receive the whack of a ferrule?

3. Brooklyn *Eagle*, Feb. 4, 1847, in Cleveland Rodgers and John Black, eds., *The Gathering of the Forces* [Whitman's contributions to the *Eagle*] (1920), I, 138–41.

For teachers' own sakes—for the true height and majesty of their office, hardly second to the priesthood—they should one and all unite in precluding this petty and foolish punishment—this degrader and bringer-down of their high standing. As things are, the word *schoolteacher* is identified with a dozen unpleasant and ridiculous associations—a sour face, a whip, hard knuckles snapped on tender heads, no gentle, fatherly kindness, no inciting of young ambition in its noble phases, none of the beautifiers of authority, but all that is small, ludicrous, and in after life productive of indignation.

We have reason to think that the flogging system still prevails in several of our Brooklyn schools to quite a wretched extent. In the school in Baltic Street under a former management, forty children in the boys' department were thrashed in the course of one morning! And in the female department a little girl was so cut and marked with the rattan over back, neck, and shoulders, for some trifling offense, that the livid marks remained there for several days.

4. Barnum Exhibits His Egress (1842)

Phineas T. Barnum, a shrewd Connecticut Yankee, ranks high among the most unusual schoolmasters of the republic. Prince of showmen, he taught Americans to relax—and also to chuckle over his barefaced hoaxes. His American Museum in New York City, though featuring freaks like the dwarf General Tom Thumb, also displayed minerals, fossils, and other curious specimens. He openly declared that the American public likes to be humbugged, and he lectured in England on "The Science of Money Making, and the Philosophy of Humbug." Less delicately he is supposed to have said, "There's a sucker born every minute." His own account of a worried day at his American Museum is self-explanatory.

Further investigation showed that pretty much all of my visitors had brought their dinners, with the evident intention of literally "making a day of it." No one expected to go home till night; the building was overcrowded; and meanwhile hundreds were waiting at the front entrance to get in when they could. In despair I sauntered upon the stage behind the scenes, biting my lips with vexation, when I happened to see the scenepainter at work and a happy thought struck me: "Here," I exclaimed, "take a piece of canvas four feet square, and paint on it, as soon as you can, in large letters—

☞ TO THE EGRESS."

Seizing the brush, he finished the sign in fifteen minutes, and I directed the carpenter to nail it over the door leading to the back stairs. He did so, and as the crowd, after making the entire tour of the establishment, came pouring down the main stairs from the third story, they stopped and looked at the new sign, while some of them read audibly [in Irish accents]: "To the Aigress."

4. P. T. Barnum, *Struggles and Triumphs* (1873), pp. 140–41.

"The Aigress," said others, "sure that's an animal we haven't seen," and the throng began to pour down the back stairs, only to find that the "Aigress" was the elephant, and that the elephant was all out o' doors, or so much of it as began with Ann Street. Meanwhile, I began to accommodate those who had long been waiting with their money at the Broadway entrance.

THOUGHT PROVOKERS

1. It has been said that Christianity has not failed, because it has never really been tried. Comment with reference to Indian-white relations. Do highly emotional revival meetings, such as those herein described, do more harm than good in the long run? Argue both sides and form a conclusion.

2. Compare the ways in which anti-foreignism manifests itself in America today with those of the 1850's and 1860's. Is the nation growing more tolerant?

3. Comment critically on Jefferson's remark that ignorance is incompatible with freedom in a civilized society. Why is it to the interest of the rich to support the public schools, even though they send their children to private schools? Why are the learned usually humble?

4. If the moralistic McGuffey readers were so popular and wholesome, why are they not being widely used today? Should we return to them? Would they help combat juvenile delinquency? Has the cherry-tree-and-hatchet fable done more good than harm?

FURTHER EXPLORATION

General: C. R. Fish, *The Rise of the Common Man, 1830–1850* (1927); R. B. Nye, *The Cultural Life of the New Nation, 1776–1830* (1960). **Religion:** W. W. Sweet, *The Story of Religion in America* (2nd rev. ed., 1950); A. O. Aldridge, *"Man of Reason": The Life of Thomas Paine* (1959); C. A. Johnson, *The Frontier Camp Meeting* (1955); B. A. Weisberger, *They Gathered at the River* (1958). **Immigration:** Carl Wittke, *We Who Built America* (1940); Carl Wittke, *The Irish in America* (1956); M. L. Hansen, *The Atlantic Migration, 1607–1860* (1940); R. A. Billington, *The Protestant Crusade, 1800–1860* (1952). **Education:** E. P. Cubberley, *Public Education in the United States* (1934); E. W. Knight, *Education in the United States* (1951); Merle Curti, *The Social Ideas of American Educators* (1935); Paul Monroe, *Founding of the American Public School System* (1940).

Recent: Richard Hofstadter, *Anti-intellectualism in American Life* (1963) [paperback]; Carleton Beals, *Brass-Knuckle Crusade; The Great Know-Nothing Conspiracy, 1820–1860* (1960).

Chapter 18

Culture and Reform, 1790-1860

I could readily see in Emerson, notwithstanding his merit, a gaping flaw. It was the insinuation that, had he lived in those days when the world was made, he might have offered some valuable suggestions.

HERMAN MELVILLE, 1849

PROLOGUE: The Americans, who boasted a high birth rate and magnificent acreage, were a people of destiny. They sought to bridge the gap between existing realities and future possibilities by loud and offensive boasting. In cultural achievement and social reform they had a little to brag about, but they overdid it. The theological works of Jonathan Edwards were well known in Europe, as was the *Autobiography* of Benjamin Franklin. In 1818 Professor Benjamin Silliman of Yale launched his long-lived *American Journal of Science and Arts*. Dorothea Dix, famous at home for her fight to improve the lot of the insane, also left a strong impact abroad. Badly needed crusades for temperance and woman's rights were likewise gathering steam. And talented American writers like Cooper and Irving, Hawthorne and Poe, Emerson and Thoreau, were beginning to supply an answer to the English taunt of intellectual sterility.

A. AMERICAN CULTURAL SELF-CONSCIOUSNESS

1. "Who Reads an American Book?" (1820)

American boastfulness got under the skin of Englishmen, notably the Reverend Sydney Smith. An English lecturer and preacher (often to standing-room-only congregations), he was esteemed as a writer and a social lion. Too witty and sarcastic for his own good, he failed to become a bishop of the Church of England. Herewith is reproduced a portion of one of his famous early pieces in the *Edinburgh Review*, which he helped found and which he kept afloat with his brilliant contributions. Note the few marks of friendliness, the obvious exaggerations, the undeniable truths, and the criticism that would be most offensive to the South.

Thus far we are the friends and admirers of Jonathan [the Yankee]. But he must not grow vain and ambitious; or allow himself to be dazzled by that galaxy of epithets by which his orators and newspaper scribblers endeavor to persuade their supporters that they are the greatest, the most refined, the most enlightened, and the most moral people upon earth. The effect of this is unspeakably ludicrous on this side of the Atlantic—and even on the other, we should imagine, must be rather humiliating to the reasonable part of the population.

The Americans are a grave, industrious, and acute people. But they have hitherto given no indications of genius, and made no approaches to the

1. *Edinburgh Review*, XXXIII (1820), 78–80.

heroic, either in their morality or character. They are but a recent offset indeed from England; and should make it their chief boast, for many generations to come, that they are sprung from the same race with Bacon and Shakespeare and Newton.

Considering their numbers, indeed, and the favorable circumstances in which they have been placed, they have yet done marvelously little to assert the honor of such a descent, or to show that their English blood has been exalted or refined by their republican training and institutions. Their Franklins and Washingtons, and all the other sages and heroes of their Revolution, were born and bred subjects of the King of England—and not among the freest or most valued of his subjects. And, since the period of their separation, a far greater proportion of their statesmen and artists and political writers have been foreigners than ever occurred before in the history of any civilized and educated people.

During the thirty or forty years of their independence, they have done absolutely nothing for the sciences, for the arts, for literature, or even for the statesmanlike studies of politics or political economy. Confining ourselves to our own country, and to the period that has elapsed since they had an independent existence, we would ask: Where are their . . . [Edmund] Burkes . . . their [James] Watts . . . their [Adam] Smiths . . . their [Sir Walter] Scotts . . . or their parallels to the hundred other names that have spread themselves over the world from our little island in the course of the last thirty years, and blest or delighted mankind by their works, inventions, or examples? In so far as we know, there is no such parallel to be produced from the whole annals of this self-adulating race.

In the four quarters of the globe, who reads an American book? or goes to an American play? or looks at an American picture or statue? What does the world yet owe to American physicians or surgeons? What new substances have their chemists discovered? or what old ones have they analyzed? What new constellations have been discovered by the telescopes of Americans? What have they done in the mathematics? Who drinks out of American glasses? or eats from American plates? or wears American coats or gowns? or sleeps in American blankets?

Finally, under which of the old tyrannical governments of Europe is every sixth man a slave, whom his fellow creatures may buy and sell and torture?

When these questions are fairly and favorably answered, their laudatory epithets may be allowed. But, till that can be done, we would seriously advise them to keep clear of superlatives.

2. Bryant Attacks Kowtowing (1839)

By the 1830's British critics were praising a few American writers like Irving and Cooper, but the general tone was one of condescension. It deepened the cultural inferiority complex that haunted many Americans. Ralph W. Emerson, in his famous

2. Parke Godwin, ed., *Prose Writings of William Cullen Bryant* (1889), II, 389–90.

address "The American Scholar" (1837), appealed to his countrymen to stand on their "own feet." One of America's most distinguished poets, William Cullen Bryant, who had published his first verses when only fourteen years of age, echoed these sentiments in the liberal New York *Evening Post*, on whose editorial staff he labored brilliantly for fifty-two years. Reconcile American boastfulness with the trait that he here bemoans. Assess his concept of "double despotism," and his view that adverse criticism helps the sale of a book.

[James F.] Cooper's last work, "Home as Found," has been fiercely attacked, in more than one quarter, for its supposed tendency to convey to the people of other countries a bad idea of our national character.

Without staying to examine whether all Mr. Cooper's animadversions on American manners are perfectly just, we seize the occasion to protest against this excessive sensibility to the opinion of other nations. It is no matter what they think of us. We constitute a community large enough to form a great moral tribunal for the trial of any question which may arise among ourselves. There is no occasion for this perpetual appeal to the opinions of Europe. We are competent to apply the rules of right and wrong, boldly and firmly, without asking in what light the superior judgment of the Old World may regard our decisions.

It has been said of Americans that they are vainglorious, boastful, fond of talking of the greatness and the advantages of their country, and of the excellence of their national character. They have this foible in common with other nations. But they have another habit which shows that, with all their national vanity, they are not so confident of their own greatness, or of their own capacity to estimate it properly, as their boasts would imply. They are perpetually asking: What do they think of us in Europe? How are we regarded abroad?

If a foreigner publishes an account of his travels in this country, we are instantly on the alert to know what notion of our character he has communicated to his countrymen. If an American author publishes a book, we are eager to know how it is received abroad, that we may know how to judge it ourselves. So far has this humor been carried that we have seen an extract from a third- or fourth-rate critical work in England, condemning some American work, copied into all our newspapers one after another, as if it determined the character of the work beyond appeal or question.

For our part, we admire and honor a fearless accuser of the faults of so thin-skinned a nation as ours, always supposing him to be sincere and well-intentioned. He may be certain that, where he has sowed animadversion, he will reap an abundant harvest of censure and obloquy. We will have one consolation, however, that if his book be written with ability, it will be read; that the attacks which are made upon it will draw it to the public attention; and that it may thus do good even to those who recalcitrate most violently against it.

If every man who writes a book . . . were first held to inquire what notions it conveys of Americans to persons abroad, we should pull the sinews out of our literature.

B. SOCIAL AND HUMANITARIAN REFORMERS

1. Dorothea Dix Succors the Insane (1843)

In 1840 there were only eight insane asylums in the twenty-six states. The overflow, regarded as perverse, were imprisoned or chained in poorhouses, jails, and houses of correction. Schoolteacher Dorothea Dix—a frail, soft-spoken spinster from New England who lived to be eighty-five despite incipient tuberculosis—almost single-handedly wrought a revolution. Filled with infinite compassion for these outcasts, she journeyed thousands of wearisome miles to investigate conditions and to appeal to state legislatures. Despite the powerful prejudice against women in public, she succeeded in securing modern facilities with trained attendants. Her horrifying report to the Massachusetts legislature is a classic. In the following excerpt from it, observe whom she blames for conditions, and why the use of jails and poorhouses by the insane was doubly bad.

I must confine myself to few examples, but am ready to furnish other and more complete details, if required. If my pictures are displeasing, coarse, and severe, my subjects, it must be recollected, offer no tranquil, refined, or composing features. The condition of human beings, reduced to the extremest states of degradation and misery, cannot be exhibited in softened language, or adorn a polished page.

I proceed, gentlemen, briefly to call your attention to the present state of insane persons confined within this Commonwealth, in cages, closets, cellars, stalls, pens! Chained, naked, beaten with rods, and lashed into obedience!

As I state cold, severe facts, I feel obliged to refer to persons, and definitely to indicate localities. But it is upon my subject, not upon localities or individuals, I desire to fix attention. And I would speak as kindly as possible of all wardens, keepers, and other responsible officers, believing that most of these have erred not through hardness of heart and willful cruelty so much as want of skill and knowledge, and want of consideration.

Familiarity with suffering, it is said, blunts the sensibilities, and where neglect once finds a footing, other injuries are multiplied. This is not all, for it may justly and strongly be added that, from the deficiency of adequate means to meet the wants of these cases, it has been an absolute impossibility to do justice to this matter. Prisons are not constructed in view of being converted into county hospitals, and almshouses are not founded as receptacles for the insane. And yet, in the face of justice and common sense, wardens are by law compelled to receive, and the masters of almshouses not to refuse, insane and idiotic subjects in all stages of mental disease and privation.

It is the Commonwealth, not its integral parts, that is accountable for most of the abuses which have lately [existed] and do still exist. I repeat it, it is defective legislation which perpetuates and multiplies these abuses. . . .

1. *Old South Leaflets* (1904), VI, 490–91, 493–94, 513, 518–19.

Danvers. November. Visited the almshouse. A large building, much out of repair. Understand a new one is in contemplation. Here are fifty-six to sixty inmates, one idiotic, three insane, one of the latter in close confinement at all times.

Long before reaching the house, wild shouts, snatches of rude songs, imprecations and obscene language, fell upon the ear, proceeding from the occupant of a low building, rather remote from the principal building to which my course was directed. Found the mistress, and was conducted to the place which was called "the home" of the forlorn maniac, a young woman, exhibiting a condition of neglect and misery blotting out the faintest idea of comfort, and outraging every sentiment of decency. She had been, I learned, "a respectable person, industrious and worthy. Disappointments and trials shook her mind, and, finally, laid prostrate reason and self-control. She became a maniac for life. She had been at Worcester Hospital for a considerable time, and had been returned as incurable." The mistress told me she understood that, "while there, she was comfortable and decent."

Alas, what a change was here exhibited! She had passed from one degree of violence to another, in swift progress. There she stood, clinging to or beating upon the bars of her caged apartment, the contracted size of which afforded space only for increasing accumulations of filth, a foul spectacle. There she stood with naked arms and disheveled hair, the unwashed frame invested with fragments of unclean garments, the air so extremely offensive, though ventilation was afforded on all sides save one, that it was not possible to remain beyond a few moments without retreating for recovery to the outward air. Irritation of body, produced by utter filth and exposure, incited her to the horrid process of tearing off her skin by inches. Her face, neck, and person were thus disfigured to hideousness. She held up a fragment just rent off. To my exclamation of horror, the mistress replied: "Oh, we can't help it. Half the skin is off sometimes. We can do nothing with her; and it makes no difference what she eats, for she consumes her own filth as readily as the food which is brought her." . . .

The conviction is continually deepened that hospitals are the only places where insane persons can be at once humanely and properly controlled. Poorhouses converted into madhouses cease to effect the purposes for which they were established, and instead of being asylums for the aged, the homeless, and the friendless, and places of refuge for orphaned or neglected childhood, are transformed into perpetual bedlams. . . .

Injustice is also done to the convicts. It is certainly very wrong that they should be doomed day after day and night after night to listen to the ravings of madmen and madwomen. This is a kind of punishment that is not recognized by our statutes, and is what the criminal ought not to be called upon to undergo. The confinement of the criminal and of the insane in the same building is subversive of the good order and discipline which should be observed in every well-regulated prison. . . .

Gentlemen, I commit to you this sacred cause. Your action upon this subject will affect the present and future condition of hundreds and of thousands.

2. Dana Witnesses a Flogging (1835)

Richard H. Dana, Jr., later a prominent Massachusetts lawyer, wrote the *Uncle Tom's Cabin* of the sea. His eyes weakened by measles, he left Harvard College temporarily in his sophomore year to ship as a common sailor around the Horn to California. His classic narrative, *Two Years before the Mast,* which presented the seaman's side of nautical tyranny, made a profound impression at home and abroad and helped promote overdue reforms. As the following selection opens, ill-tempered Captain Thompson has just flogged with a rope seaman Sam, who had complained, "I'm no Negro slave," and now prepares to punish John the Swede, who had dared speak up in protest. Note what redress the common sailor had against this kind of abuse, why such despotic power was vested in the captain, and why the South probably found some satisfaction in Dana's account.

When he [the Swede] was made fast, he turned to the captain [Thompson], who stood rolling up his sleeves and getting ready for the blow, and asked him what he was to be flogged for. "Have I ever refused my duty, sir? Have you ever known me to hang back, or to be insolent, or not to know my work?"

"No," said the captain, "it is not that that I flog you for. I flog you for your interference, for asking questions."

"Can't a man ask a question here without being flogged?"

"No," shouted the captain; "nobody shall open his mouth aboard this vessel but myself," and began laying the blows upon his back, swinging half round between each blow, to give it full effect. As he went on, his passion increased, and he danced about the deck, calling out, as he swung the rope: "If you want to know what I flog you for, I'll tell you. It's because I like to do it!—because I like to do it! It suits me! That's what I do it for!"

The man writhed under the pain until he could endure it no longer, when he called out, with an exclamation more common among foreigners than with us: "O Jesus Christ! O Jesus Christ!"

"Don't call on Jesus Christ," shouted the captain; "he can't help you. Call on Frank Thompson! He's the man! He can help you! Jesus Christ can't help you now!"

At these words, which I never shall forget, my blood ran cold. I could look on no longer. Disgusted, sick, I turned away, and leaned over the rail, and looked down into the water. A few rapid thoughts, I don't know what —our situation, a resolution to see the captain punished when we got home— crossed my mind; but the falling of the blows and the cries of the man called me back once more.

At length they ceased, and, turning round, I found that the mate, at a signal from the captain, had cast him loose. Almost doubled up with pain, the man walked slowly forward, and went down into the forecastle.

2. R. H. Dana, Jr., *Two Years before the Mast* (1887 ed.), pp. 115–17, 114.

Everyone else stood still at his post, while the captain, swelling with rage, and with the importance of his achievement, walked the quarter-deck, and at each turn, as he came forward, calling out to us: "You see your condition! You see where I've got you all, and you know what to expect!"— "You've been mistaken in me; you didn't know what I was! Now you know what I am!"—"I'll make you toe the mark, every soul of you, or I'll flog you all, fore and aft, from the boy up!"—"You've got a driver over you! Yes, a slave-driver—a nigger-driver! I'll see who'll tell me he isn't a NIGGER slave!" . . .

. . . What is there for sailors to do? If they resist, it is mutiny; and if they succeed, and take the vessel, it is piracy. If they ever yield again, their punishment must come; and if they do not yield, what are they to be for the rest of their lives? If a sailor resist his commander, he resists the law, and piracy or submission is his only alternative. Bad as it was, they saw it must be borne. It is what a sailor ships for.

3. Arthur's *Ten Nights in a Barroom* (1854)

T. S. Arthur, an ill-educated New Yorker, became the moralistic author of seventy books and countless articles. His lurid *Ten Nights in a Barroom* was the *Uncle Tom's Cabin* of the temperance crusade, and second only to *Uncle Tom's Cabin* as the best seller of the 1850's. Endorsed by the clergy, it was put on the stage for an incredible run. Although the author was a foe of saloons, he was not a teetotaler, and he consistently advocated temperance by education rather than prohibition by legislation. In his famous novel, Simon Slade's tavern ("Sickle and Sheaf") is portrayed as the ruination of quiet Cedarville. After numerous heart-tugging tragedies, the climax comes when the drunken tavern owner is murdered by his drunken son with a brandy bottle. Earlier in the book the following conversation takes place. Enumerate and assess the arguments on both sides, and evaluate this interchange as propaganda in the battle against the bottle.

The man, who had until now been sitting quietly in a chair, started up, exclaiming as he did so—

"Merciful heavens! I never dreamed of this! Whose sons are safe?"

"No man's," was the answer of the gentleman in whose office we were sitting; "no man's—while there are such open doors to ruin as you may find at the 'Sickle and Sheaf.' Did not you vote the anti-temperance ticket at the last election?"

"I did," was the answer, "and from principle."

"On what were your principles based?" was inquired.

"On the broad foundations of civil liberty."

"The liberty to do good or evil, just as the individual may choose?"

"I would not like to say that. There are certain evils against which there can be no legislation that would not do harm. No civil power in this country has the right to say what a citizen shall eat or drink."

"But may not the people, in any community, pass laws, through their delegated lawmakers, restraining evil-minded persons from injuring the common good?"

3. T. S. Arthur, *Ten Nights in a Barroom,* "Night the Sixth."

TEN NIGHTS IN A BARROOM

Frontispiece of first edition, 1854. Mary Morgan, who was killed in the subsequent brawl, tries to persuade her drunken father to leave Sam Slade's tavern.

"Oh, certainly—certainly."

"And are you prepared to affirm that a drinking shop, where young men are corrupted—ay, destroyed, body and soul—does not work an injury to the common good?"

"Ah! but there must be houses of public entertainment."

"No one denies this. But can that be a really Christian community which provides for the moral debasement of strangers, at the same time that it entertains them? Is it necessary that, in giving rest and entertainment to the traveler, we also lead him into temptation?"

"Yes—but—but—it is going too far to legislate on what we are to eat and drink. It is opening too wide a door for fanatical oppression. We must inculcate temperance as a right principle. We must teach our children the evils of intemperance, and send them out into the world as practical teachers of order, virtue, and sobriety. If we do this, the reform becomes radical, and in a few years there will be no barrooms, for none will crave the fiery poison.

"Of little value, my friend, will be, in far too many cases, your precepts, if temptation invites our sons at almost every step of their way through life. Thousands have fallen, and thousands are now tottering, soon to fall. Your sons are not safe, nor are mine. We cannot tell the day nor the hour when they may weakly yield to the solicitation of some companion, and enter the wide-open door of ruin. . . . Sir! while you hold back from the work of staying the flood that is desolating our fairest homes, the black waters are approaching your own doors."

There was a startling emphasis in the tones with which this last sentence was uttered, and I did not wonder at the look of anxious alarm that it called to the face of him whose fears it was meant to excite.

"What do you mean, sir?" was inquired.

"Simply, that your sons are in equal danger with others."

"And is that all?"

"They have been seen of late in the barroom of the 'Sickle and Sheaf.'"

"Who says so?"

"Twice within a week I have seen them going in there," was answered.

"Good heavens! No!"

"It is true, my friend. But who is safe? If we dig pits and conceal them from view, what marvel if our own children fall therein?"

"My sons going to a tavern!" The man seemed utterly confounded. "How *can* I believe it? You must be in error, sir."

"No. What I tell you is the simple truth."

4. Dr. Morton Administers Ether (1846)

After Sydney Smith sneered in 1820, "What does the world yet owe to American physicians and surgeons?" he finally got his answer in a dramatic form. Whiskey, opium, and mesmerism having failed as anesthetics, Dr. Crawford Long of Georgia performed the first known surgical operation with ether in 1842, when he removed a tumor from the back of a patient's neck. Unfortunately for his fame, his exploits were not publicized until 1849. Meanwhile Dr. William T. G. Morton, a Boston dentist working with Professor Charles T. Jackson of Harvard, independently experimented on patients seeking extractions. In 1846 he performed the "miracle" here described—the first public feat of its kind. Dr. Morton ultimately broke himself down and died in poverty while trying to monopolize his discovery. In this latter-day account, note what is remarkable about the skepticism shown.

Meanwhile, within, all necessary preparations for the operation had been made. The patient selected for the trial was Gilbert Abbott, who was suffering from a congenital but superficial vascular tumor just below the jaw on the left side of the neck. The announcement that the operation was to furnish a test of some preparation for which the astounding claim had been made that it would render the person treated with it temporarily incapable of feeling pain, had attracted a large number of medical men to the theater. It was inevitable that nearly all of those present should be skeptical as to the result. As the minutes slipped by without any sign of Dr. Morton, the

4. E. L. Snell, "Dr. Morton's Discovery of Anesthesia," *Century Illustrated Monthly Magazine*, XLVIII (1894), 589–91.

incredulous gave vent to their suspicions concerning him and his discovery.

"As Dr. Morton has not yet arrived," said Dr. Warren, after waiting fifteen minutes, "I presume that he is otherwise engaged."

The response was a derisive laugh, clearly implying the belief that Dr. Morton was staying away because he was afraid to submit his discovery to a critical test.

Dr. Warren grasped the knife. At that critical moment Dr. Morton entered. No outburst of applause, no smiles of encouragement, greeted him. Doubt and suspicion were depicted on the faces of those who looked down upon him from the tiers of seats that encircled the room. No actor about to assume a new role ever received a more chilling reception.

"Well, sir," exclaimed Dr. Warren abruptly, "your patient is ready."

Thus aroused from the bewilderment into which the novelty of his position had thrown him, he [Dr. Morton] spoke a few words of encouragement to the young man about to be operated on, adjusted the inhaler, and began to administer the ether. As the subtle vapor gradually took possession of the citadel of consciousness, the patient dropped off into a deep slumber.

Dr. Warren seized the bunch of veins and made the first incision with his knife.

Instead of awakening with a cry of pain, the patient continued to slumber peacefully, apparently as profoundly unconscious as before.

Then the spectators underwent a transformation. All signs of incredulity and indifference vanished. Not a whisper was uttered. As the operation progressed, men began to realize that they were witnessing something the like of which had never been seen before.

When the operation was over, and while the patient still lay like a log on the table, Dr. Warren, addressing the spectators, said, with solemn emphasis, "Gentlemen, this is no humbug."

But notwithstanding that Dr. Morton had thus demonstrated that a patient could be rendered completely insensible to suffering while undergoing an operation, yet for three weeks the employment of the ether at the hospital was discontinued, and surgery and agony still went hand in hand. In fact, instead of being hailed as a public benefactor, Dr. Morton found himself, for a short period immediately following the public announcement of his discovery, the target for indignant scorn and contempt. He was pilloried in the public prints by medical men and laymen as a charlatan.

C. THE CRUSADE FOR WOMAN'S RIGHTS

1. The Seneca Falls Manifesto (1848)

Mrs. Lucretia C. Mott, militant anti-slavery Quakeress, received her first harsh lesson in feminism when, as a teacher, she was paid half a man's salary. Mrs. Elizabeth C. Stanton, also a temperance and anti-slavery reformer, insisted on leaving "obey" out of her marriage ceremony. Both were aroused when, attending the World Anti-Slavery

1. E. C. Stanton *et al.*, eds., *History of Woman Suffrage* (1881), I, 70–71.

Convention in London in 1840, they were denied seats because of their sex. These two women sparked the memorable convention at Seneca Falls, New York, which formally launched the modern woman's rights movement. The embattled females issued a flaming pronouncement in the manner of the Declaration of Independence ("all men *and women* are created equal"). They not only proclaimed their grievances but passed eleven resolutions designed to improve their lot. In reading the list of grievances, determine which have been the least satisfactorily met.

The history of mankind is a history of repeated injuries and usurpations on the part of man toward woman, having in direct object the establishment of an absolute tyranny over her. To prove this, let facts be submitted to a candid world.

He has never permitted her to exercise her inalienable right to the elective franchise.

He has compelled her to submit to laws in the formation of which she had no voice.

He has withheld from her rights which are given to the most ignorant and degraded men—both natives and foreigners.

Having deprived her of this first right of a citizen, the elective franchise, thereby leaving her without representation in the halls of legislation, he has oppressed her on all sides.

He has made her, if married, in the eye of the law, civilly dead.

He has taken from her all right of property, even to the wages she earns.

He has made her, morally, an irresponsible being, as she can commit many crimes with impunity, provided they be done in the presence of her husband. In the covenant of marriage, she is compelled to promise obedience to her husband, he becoming, to all intents and purposes, her master—the law giving him power to deprive her of her liberty, and to administer chastisement.

He has so framed the laws of divorce as to what shall be the proper causes, and in case of separation to whom the guardianship of the children shall be given, as to be wholly regardless of the happiness of women—the law, in all cases, going upon a false supposition of the supremacy of man, and giving all power into his hands.

After depriving her of all rights as a married woman, if single, and the owner of property, he has taxed her to support a government which recognizes her only when her property can be made profitable to it.

He has monopolized nearly all the profitable employments; and from those she is permitted to follow, she receives but a scanty remuneration. He closes against her all the avenues to wealth and distinction which he considers most honorable to himself. As a teacher of theology, medicine, or law, she is not known.

He has denied her the facilities for obtaining a thorough education, all colleges being closed against her.

He allows her in church, as well as state, but a subordinate position, claiming apostolic authority for her exclusion from the ministry, and, with some exceptions, from any public participation in the affairs of the church.

He has created a false public sentiment by giving to the world a different code of morals for men and women, by which moral delinquencies which exclude women from society are not only tolerated but deemed of little account in man.

He has usurped the prerogative of Jehovah himself, claiming it as his right to assign for her a sphere òf action, when that belongs to her conscience and to her God.

He has endeavored, in every way that he could, to destroy her confidence in her own powers, to lessen her self-respect, and to make her willing to lead a dependent and abject life.

Now, in view of this entire disfranchisement of one-half the people of this country, their social and religious degradation—in view of the unjust laws above mentioned, and because women do feel themselves aggrieved, oppressed, and fraudulently deprived of their most sacred rights, we insist that they have immediate admission to all the rights and privileges which belong to them as citizens of the United States.

In entering upon the great work before us, we anticipate no small amount of misconception, misrepresentation, and ridicule. But we shall use every instrumentality within our power to effect our object. We shall employ agents, circulate tracts, petition the state and national legislatures, and endeavor to enlist the pulpit and the press in our behalf. We hope this convention will be followed by a series of conventions embracing every part of the country.

2. New Yorkers Ridicule Feminists (1856)

Masculine opponents of feminism claimed that the lady crusaders were frustrated old maids (many were married); that women would become coarsened and defeminized by entering the cutthroat arena of politics; that their husbands (if they were lucky enough to have husbands) would look after their rights; and that women, like Negro slaves, were divinely ordained to be inferior and would be happier in that status. An editorial in the New York *Herald* wondered what would happen if pregnant sea captains, generals, Congressmen, physicians, and lawyers were suddenly seized with birth pangs in critical situations. The following official report reveals the levity with which the New York legislature approached the problem. Discern what substance there is, if any, in this document.

Mr. Foote, from the Judiciary Committee, made a report on Women's Rights that set the whole House in roars of laughter:

"The Committee is composed of married and single gentlemen. The bachelors on the Committee, with becoming diffidence, have left the subject pretty much to the married gentlemen. They have considered it with the aid of the light they have before them and the experience married life has given them. Thus aided, they are enabled to state that the ladies always have the best place and choicest tidbit at the table. They have the best seat in the cars, carriages, and sleighs; the warmest place in the winter, and the coolest place in the summer. They have their choice on which side

2. *Ibid.*, I, 629–30.

HOW IT WOULD BE IF SOME LADIES HAD THEIR OWN WAY
Harper's Weekly, 1868.

of the bed they will lie, front or back. A lady's dress costs three times as much as that of a gentleman; and, at the present time, with the prevailing fashion, one lady occupies three times as much space in the world as a gentleman.

"It has thus appeared to the married gentlemen of your Committee, being a majority (the bachelors being silent for the reason mentioned, and also probably for the further reason that they are still suitors for the favors of the gentler sex), that, if there is any inequality or oppression in the case, the gentlemen are the sufferers. They, however, have presented no petitions for redress; having, doubtless, made up their minds to yield to an inevitable destiny.

"On the whole, the Committee have concluded to recommend no measure, except that as they have observed several instances in which husband and wife have both signed the same petition. In such case, they would recommend the parties to apply for a law authorizing them to change dresses, so that the husband may wear petticoats, and the wife the breeches, and thus indicate to their neighbors and the public the true relation in which they stand to each other."

D. TRANSCENDENTALISM AND EARTHLY UTOPIAS

1. Emerson Chides the Reformers (1844)

Dissatisfied Europeans let off steam in the 1840's in a series of armed revolts; dissatisfied Americans let off steam in various reformist protests. Every brain was seemingly gnawed by a "private maggot." Ralph Waldo Emerson—poet, essayist, Transcendentalist, and ever-popular lyceum lecturer—delivered this famous discourse on the New England reformers in 1844. A non-conformist himself, he had resigned his Unitarian pastorate in Boston after disagreeing with his congregation over the

1. R. W. Emerson, *Complete Works* (1884), III, 240–43.

sacrament of the Lord's Supper. Ascertain the probable connection between the phenomena that Emerson describes and the Southern spirit of political nullification. Note that he is not opposed to all reform—just to the absurdities or what he judged to be absurdities.

What a fertility of projects for the salvation of the world!

One apostle thought all men should go to farming, and another that no man should buy or sell, that the use of money was the cardinal evil; another that the mischief was in our diet, that we eat and drink damnation. These made unleavened bread and were foes to the death to fermentation.

It was in vain urged by the housewife that God made yeast as well as dough, and loves fermentation just as dearly as he loves vegetation; that fermentation develops the saccharine element in the grain, and makes it more palatable and more digestible. No; they wish the pure wheat, and will die but it shall not ferment. Stop, dear Nature, these incessant advances of thine; let us scotch these ever-rolling wheels!

Others attacked the system of agriculture, the use of animal manures in farming, and the tyranny of man over brute nature [animals]. These abuses polluted his food. The ox must be taken from the plow, and the horse from the cart; the hundred acres of the farm must be spaded. And the man must walk, wherever boats and locomotives will not carry him.

Even the insect world was to be defended—that had been too long neglected, and a society for the protection of ground-worms, slugs, and mosquitoes was to be incorporated without delay.

With these, appeared the adepts of homoeopathy, of hydropathy, of mesmerism, of phrenology, and their wonderful theories of the Christian miracles! Others assailed particular vocations, as that of the lawyer, that of the merchant, of the manufacturer, of the clergyman, of the scholar. Others attacked the institution of marriage as the fountain of social evils. Others devoted themselves to the worrying of churches and meetings for public worship, and the fertile forms of antinomianism* among the elder Puritans seemed to have their match in the plenty of the new harvest of reform.

With this din of opinion and debate, there was a keener scrutiny of institutions and domestic life than any we had known. There was sincere protesting against existing evils, and there were changes of employment dictated by conscience. . . .

In politics, for example, it is easy to see the progress of dissent. The country is full of rebellion; the country is full of kings. Hands off! Let there be no control and no interference in the administration of the affairs of this kingdom of me. Hence the growth of the doctrine and of the party of Free Trade, and the willingness to try that experiment in the face of what appear incontestable facts.

I confess the motto of the *Globe* newspaper is so attractive to me that I can seldom find much appetite to read what is below it in its columns:

---

* The belief that Christian faith alone, not obedience to moral law, insures salvation.

"The world is governed too much." So the country is frequently affording solitary examples of resistance to the government, solitary nullifiers who throw themselves on their reserved rights; nay, who have reserved all their rights; who reply to the [tax] assessor and to the clerk of the court that they do not know the state, and embarrass the courts of law by non-juring [refusing to take an oath] and the commander-in-chief of the militia by non-resistance.

2. The "Paradise" at Brook Farm (*c.* 1846)

Of the numerous communal schemes in the 1840's, Brook Farm (1841–1847) attractively combined "plain living with high thinking." Pooling their poverty, the members were to share the intellectual feast, while contributing enough manual labor to keep the enterprise going. But the sandy soil, combined with inexperience in farming, contributed to their undoing. Nathaniel Hawthorne, who extracted a delightful novel from the adventure (*The Blithedale Romance*), recorded in his diary: "Mr. Ripley put a four-pronged instrument into my hands, which he gave me to understand was called a pitchfork; and he and Mr. Farley being armed with similar weapons, we all commenced a gallant attack upon a heap of manure." The following description was written some years later by Robert Carter, a well-known writer who enjoyed the friendship of nearly all of the literary giants of his generation. Ascertain the purposes of Brook Farm and the general causes of its failure.

At Brook Farm the disciples of the "Newness" [Transcendentalism] gathered to the number, I think, of about a hundred. Among them were [George] Ripley, the founder of the institution, Charles A. Dana, W. H. Channing, J. S. Dwight, Warren Burton, Nathaniel Hawthorne, G. W. Curtis, and his brother Burrill Curtis. The place was a farm of two hundred acres of good land, eight miles from Boston, in the town of West Roxbury, and was of much natural beauty, with a rich and varied landscape. The avowed object of the association was to realize the Christian ideal of life by making such industrial, social, and educational arrangements as would promote economy, combine leisure for study with healthful and honest toil, avert collisions of caste, equalize refinements, diffuse courtesy, and sanctify life more completely than is possible in the isolated household mode of living.

It is a remarkable feature of this establishment that it was wholly indigenous, a genuine outgrowth of the times in New England, and not at all derived from Fourierism [French cooperative socialism], as many supposed. Fourier was, in fact, not known to its founders until Brook Farm had been a year or two in operation. They then began to study him, and fell finally into some of his fantasies, to which in part is to be ascribed the ruin of the institution.

Of the life of Brook Farm I do not intend to say much, for I was there only one day, though I knew nearly all the members. It was a delightful gathering of men and women of superior cultivation, who led a charming life for a few years, laboring in its fields and philandering in its pleasant woods. It was a little too much of a picnic for serious profit, and the young men and maidens were rather unduly addicted to moonlight wanderings in the pine-grove, though it is creditable to the sound moral training of New England that little or no harm came of these wanderings—at least not to the maidens. So far as the relation of the sexes is concerned, the Brook Farmers, in spite of their free manners, were as pure, I believe, as any other people.

The enterprise failed pecuniarily, after seeming for some years to have succeeded. Fourierism brought it into disrepute, and finally a great wooden phalanstery [main building], in which the members had invested all their means, took fire, and burned to the ground just as it was completed. Upon this catastrophe the association scattered (in 1847, I think), and Brook Farm became the site of the town poorhouse.

3. Thoreau Praises Spiritual Wealth (1854)

Henry David Thoreau, a leading Transcendentalist, had worn a green coat to the Harvard chapel because the rules required black. He tried his hand at teaching, but when the authorities criticized his use of moral suasion, he whipped a dozen surprised pupils, just to show the absurdity of flogging, and forthwith resigned. While the Brook Farmers sought stimulation in association, he sought it in solitude. Building a hut on the shore of Walden Pond, near Concord, Massachusetts, he spent over two years in philosophical introspection and in communion with the wild life, including fish and moles. His experiences unfold in his classic *Walden*, which was socialistic enough to become a textbook of the British Labour Party. James Russell Lowell accused Thoreau of trying to make a virtue out of his indolence and other defects of character. Comment. Determine which of Thoreau's observations in *Walden* have been weakened or strengthened by the passage of a hundred years. Which ones would we of today regard as absurd?

For more than five years I maintained myself thus solely by the labor of my hands, and I found that by working about six weeks in a year, I could meet all the expenses of living. The whole of my winters, as well as most of my summers, I had free and clear for study.

I have thoroughly tried schoolkeeping, and found that my expenses were in proportion, or rather out of proportion, to my income, for I was obliged to dress and train, not to say think and believe, accordingly, and I lost my time into the bargain. As I did not teach for the good of my fellow-men, but simply for a livelihood, this was a failure.

I have tried trade. But I found that it would take ten years to get under way in that, and that then I should probably be on my way to the devil. I was actually afraid that I might by that time be doing what is called a good business.

When formerly I was looking about to see what I could do for a living, . . . I thought often and seriously of picking huckleberries. That surely I could do, and its small profits might suffice—for my greatest skill has been to want but little—so little capital it required, so little distraction from my

3. H. D. Thoreau, *Walden* (1893 ed.), pp. 110–11, 112, 498, 505–06, 510.

wonted moods, I foolishly thought. While my acquaintances went unhesitantly into trade or the professions, I contemplated this occupation as most like theirs; ranging the hills all summer to pick the berries which came in my way, and thereafter carelessly dispose of them. . . . But I have since learned that trade curses everything it handles; and though you trade in messages from heaven, the whole curse of trade attaches to the business. . . .

For myself, I found that the occupation of a day-laborer was the most independent of any, especially as it required only thirty or forty days in a year to support one. The laborer's day ends with the going down of the sun, and he is then free to devote himself to his chosen pursuit, independent of his labor. But his employer, who speculates from month to month, has no respite from one end of the year to the other. . . .

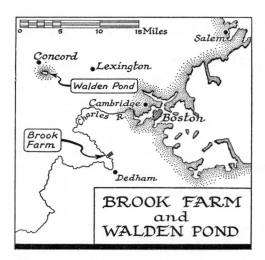

BROOK FARM
and
WALDEN POND

I left the woods for as good a reason as I went there. Perhaps it seemed to me that I had several more lives to live, and could not spare any more time for that one. It is remarkable how easily and insensibly we fall into a particular route, and make a beaten track for ourselves. I had not lived there a week before my feet wore a path from my door to the pond-side; and though it is five or six years since I trod it, it is still quite distinct. It is true, I fear, that others may have fallen into it, and so helped to keep it open.

The surface of the earth is soft and impressible by the feet of men; and so with the paths which the mind travels. How worn and dusty, then, must be the highways of the world, how deep the ruts of tradition and conformity! I did not wish to take a cabin passage, but rather to go before the mast and on the deck of the world, for there I could best see the moonlight amid the mountains. I do not wish to go below now. . . .

However mean your life is, meet it and live it; do not shun it and call it hard names. It is not so bad as you are. It looks poorest when you are richest. The fault-finder will find faults even in Paradise. Love your life, poor as it is. You may perhaps have some pleasant, thrilling, glorious hours even in a poorhouse. The setting sun is reflected from the windows of the almshouse as brightly as from the rich man's abode; the snow melts before its door as early in the spring. I do not see but a quiet mind may live as contentedly there, and have as cheering thoughts, as in a palace.

The town's poor seem to me often to live the most independent lives of any. Maybe they are simply great enough to receive without misgiving. Most think that they are above being supported by the town; but is oftener happens that they are not above supporting themselves by dishonest means, which should be more disreputable.

Cultivate poverty like a garden herb, like sage. Do not trouble yourself much to get new things, whether clothes or friends. Turn the old; return to them. Things do not change; we change. Sell your clothes and keep your thoughts. God will see that you do not want society. If I were confined to a corner of a garret all my days, like a spider, the world would be just as large to me while I had my thoughts about me. . . .

Rather than love, than money, than fame, give me truth.

4. Emersonisms and Thoreauisms

The following pithy sayings are culled from the writings of Emerson and Thoreau, who were close Transcendentalist friends and non-conformists. Note in what areas there seems to be a close similarity in thinking, and how many of these observations have been borne out by personalities or experiences in American history.

GOVERNMENT

The less government we have, the better—fewer laws, and the less confided power. EMERSON

I heartily accept the motto "That government is best which governs least". . . . Carried out, it finally amounts to this, which I also believe: "That government is best which governs not at all"; and when men are prepared for it, that will be the kind of government which they will have. THOREAU

Under a government which imprisons any unjustly, the true place for a just man is also a prison.* THOREAU

Of all debts men are least willing to pay the taxes. What a satire this [is] on government! EMERSON

REFORM

We are reformers in spring and summer; in autumn and winter we stand by the old; reformers in the morning, conservers at night. Reform is affirmative, conservatism negative; conservatism goes for comfort, reform for truth. EMERSON

Every reform was once a private opinion. EMERSON

Beware when the Great God lets loose a thinker on this planet. EMERSON

There is no strong performance without a little fanaticism in the performer. EMERSON

Every burned book enlightens the world. EMERSON

* In 1845 Thoreau was jailed for one night for refusing to pay his poll tax to a state (Massachusetts) which supported slavery. The tax, much to his disgust, was paid by an aunt. Legend has it that Emerson visited him in jail, saying, "Why are you here?" Thoreau allegedly replied, "Why are you not here?"

Every reform is only a mask under cover of which a more terrible reform, which dares not yet name itself, advances. EMERSON

If anything ail a man so that he does not perform his functions, if he have a pain in his bowels . . . he forthwith sets about reforming—the world. THOREAU

WEALTH

The greatest man in history [Jesus] was the poorest. EMERSON

If a man own land, the land owns him. EMERSON

Poverty consists in feeling poor. EMERSON

I would rather sit on a pumpkin, and have it all to myself, than to be crowded on a velvet cushion. THOREAU

They take their pride in making their dinner cost much; I take my pride in making my dinner cost little. THOREAU

Men have become the tools of their tools. THOREAU

To inherit property is not to be born—it is to be stillborn, rather. THOREAU

That man is the richest whose pleasures are the cheapest. THOREAU

GREAT MEN

To be great is to be misunderstood. EMERSON

Shallow men believe in luck. EMERSON

Every hero becomes a bore at last. EMERSON

If the single man plant himself indomitably on his instincts, and there abide, the huge world will come around to him. EMERSON

Great men are they who see that spiritual is stronger than any material force; that thoughts rule the world. EMERSON

The true test of civilization is, not the census, nor the size of cities, nor the crops—no, but the kind of man the country turns out. EMERSON

An institution is the lengthened shadow of one man. EMERSON

There are men too superior to be seen except by a few, as there are notes too high for the scale of most ears. EMERSON

If a man does not keep pace with his companions, perhaps it is because he hears a different drummer. Let him step to the music he hears, however measured or far away. THOREAU

LIVING

Nothing can bring you peace but yourself. EMERSON

The only gift is a portion of thyself. EMERSON

Hitch your wagon to a star. EMERSON

Nothing is so much to be feared as fear.* THOREAU

We do not quite forgive a giver. EMERSON

Do not be too moral. You may cheat yourself out of much life so. Aim above morality. Be not simply good; be good for something. THOREAU

* Perhaps Franklin D. Roosevelt's most famous saying, uttered in his inaugural address in 1933, was: "The only thing we have to fear is fear itself."

I never found the companion that was so companionable as solitude.
THOREAU

The mass of men lead lives of quiet desperation. THOREAU

THOUGHT PROVOKERS

1. Account for America's cultural backwardness in the early 19th Century. Why were the British so much farther ahead? What are the dangers of writing with one eye on the reviewers?
2. Article VIII of the Bill of Rights of the Constitution requires that "cruel and unusual punishments" shall not be "inflicted." In what respects did Dorothea Dix find the Constitution being widely violated? Why do reformers invariably encounter difficulties?
3. The observation has been made that it was a man's world in the 19th Century; now it is a woman's world. Comment critically and draw conclusions. Why did many women not want the ballot?
4. Why is there less reformism in America today than there was in the 1840's? Assess the soundness of Emerson's remark: "Men are conservative when they are least vigorous, or when they are most luxurious. They are conservatives after dinner." It has been said that the wise man reduces his wants; the fool increases his income. Comment in the light of Thoreau's philosophy. What would happen to our economic and social structure if large numbers of men literally followed Thoreau's teachings?

FURTHER EXPLORATION

General: R. B. Nye, *The Cultural Life of the New Nation, 1776–1830* (1960); C. R. Fish, *The Rise of the Common Man* (1927); A. F. Tyler, *Freedom's Ferment* (1944); R. E. Riegel, *Young America, 1830–1840* (1949); E. D. Branch, *The Sentimental Years, 1836–1860* (1934). **Cultural Self-Consciousness:** Van Wyck Brooks, *The Flowering of New England* (1936); F. O. Matthiessen, *American Renaissance* (1941). **Reformers:** H. E. Marshall, *Dorothea Dix* (1937); Blake McKelvey, *American Prisons* (1936). **Woman's Rights:** Eleanor Flexner, *Century of Struggle* (1959). **Transcendentalism:** R. L. Rusk, *The Life of Ralph Waldo Emerson* (1949); J. W. Krutch, *Henry David Thoreau* (1948); A. E. Bestor, *Backwoods Utopias* (1950); H. W. Sams, ed., *Autobiography of Brook Farm* (1958).

Recent: Loren Baritz, *City on a Hill; A History of Ideas and Myths in America* (1964) [paperback]; R. E. Riegel, *American Feminists* (1963); Norman Dain, *Concepts of Insanity in the United States, 1789–1865* (1964).

Chapter 19

The South and the Slave System

Whenever I hear anyone arguing for slavery, I feel a strong impulse to see it tried on him personally.

ABRAHAM LINCOLN, 1865

PROLOGUE: In slavery, the Southerners had a bear by the tail: to hang on was embarrassing; to let go would be costly and seemingly dangerous. So situated, they put the best face they could on their "peculiar institution," and freely quoted the Bible to defend an archaic practice which both God and Jesus had tolerated, if not sanctioned. The abolitionists, especially the Garrisonian extremists, harped on the evils of slavery; the Southerners stressed the less horrid aspects. The truth lay somewhere between. Certainly most Southerners were not sadists. Self-interest, if not humanity, was a strong though not infallible deterrent to mayhem. The bondsmen were seldom beaten to death, and as a rule families were not needlessly separated. But slaves were discouraged from learning to read and encouraged to embrace the Christian religion, which is often the solace of the oppressed. And countless Northerners, with a financial stake in slave-grown cotton, deplored the boat-rocking tactics of the abolitionists.

A. THE SORDID SIDE OF SLAVERY

1. A Mulatto Boy Learns a Lesson (*c.* 1827)

The amazing Frederick Douglass, sired by an unknown white father, was born in Maryland to a slave woman. He learned to read and write; and after suffering much cruel usage he escaped to the North, where, despite mobbings and beatings, he became a leading abolitionist orator and journalist. A commanding figure of a man, he raised Negro regiments during the Civil War, and in 1889 became United States Minister to the Negro republic of Haiti. He showed impartiality in his two marriages: his first wife, he quipped, was the color of his mother and his second (despite a storm of criticism) was that of his father. From the following passage in his autobiography, ascertain why the slaveholders were willing to have their slaves know the Bible but not to read it.

The frequent hearing of my mistress reading the Bible aloud—for she often read aloud when her husband was absent—awakened my curiosity in respect to this mystery of reading, and roused in me the desire to learn. Up to this time I had known nothing whatever of this wonderful art, and my ignorance and inexperience of what it could do for me, as well as my confidence in my mistress, emboldened me to ask her to teach me to read.

With an unconsciousness and inexperience equal to my own, she readily consented, and in an incredibly short time, by her kind assistance, I had mastered the alphabet and could spell words of three or four letters. My

1. *Life and Times of Frederick Douglass* (1882), pp. 94–97.

mistress seemed almost as proud of my progress as if I had been her own child, and supposing that her husband would be as well pleased, she made no secret of what she was doing for me. Indeed, she exultingly told him of the aptness of her pupil, and of her intention to persevere in teaching me, as she felt her duty to do, at least to read the Bible. . . .

Master Hugh was astounded beyond measure, and probably for the first time proceeded to unfold to his wife the true philosophy of the slave system, and the peculiar rules necessary in the nature of the case to be observed in the management of human chattels. Of course, he forbade her to give me any further instruction, telling her in the first place that to do so was unlawful, as it was also unsafe. "For," said he, "if you give a nigger an inch, he will take an ell. Learning will spoil the best nigger in the world. If he learns to read the Bible, it will forever unfit him to be a slave. He should know nothing but the will of his master, and learn to obey it. As to himself, learning will do him no good, but a great deal of harm, making him disconsolate and unhappy. If you teach him how to read, he'll want to know how to write, and this accomplished, he'll be running away with himself."

2. An Ex-Slave Exposes Slavery (1850)

Flogged without effect by his master, Douglass was hired out for one year to a notorious "slave breaker," who also professed to be a devout Methodist. Worked almost to death in all kinds of weather, allowed five minutes or less for meals, and brutally whipped about once a week, Douglass admitted that "Mr. Covey succeeded in *breaking* me—in body, soul, and spirit. My natural elasticity was crushed; my intellect languished, the disposition to read departed, the cheerful spark that lingered about my eye died out; the dark night of slavery closed in upon me; and behold a man transformed to a brute!" In this abolitionist speech in Rochester, New York, Douglass spoke from bitter experience. Note in what respects the non-physical abuses of slaves were worse than the physical ones, and where the system was most unjust.

More than twenty years of my life were consumed in a state of slavery. My childhood was environed by the baneful peculiarities of the slave system. I grew up to manhood in the presence of this hydra-headed monster —not as a master—not as an idle spectator—not as the guest of the slaveholder; but as A SLAVE, eating the bread and drinking the cup of slavery with the most degraded of my brother bondmen, and sharing with them all the painful conditions of their wretched lot. In consideration of these facts, I feel that I have a right to speak, and to speak strongly. Yet, my friends, I feel bound to speak truly. . . .

First of all, I will state, as well as I can, the legal and social relation of master and slave. A master is one (to speak in the vocabulary of the Southern states) who claims and exercises a right of property in the person of a fellow man. This he does with the force of the law and the sanction of Southern religion.

2. Quoted in Irving Mark and E. L. Schwaab, eds., *The Faith of Our Fathers* (1952), pp. 157–59.

FLOGGING NEGRO SLAVES
An example of anti-slavery propaganda. *Anti-Slavery Almanac,* 1838.

The law gives the master absolute power over the slave. He may work him, flog him, hire him out, sell him, and in certain contingencies kill him with perfect impunity.

The slave is a human being, divested of all rights—reduced to the level of a brute—a mere "chattel" in the eye of the law—placed beyond the circle of human brotherhood—cut off from his kind. His name, which the "recording angel" may have enrolled in heaven among the blest, is impiously inserted in a master's ledger with horses, sheep, and swine.

In law a slave has no wife, no children, no country, and no home. He can own nothing, possess nothing, acquire nothing, but what must belong to another. To eat the fruit of his own toil, to clothe his person with the work of his own hands, is considered stealing.

He toils, that another may reap the fruit. He is industrious, that another may live in idleness. He eats unbolted meal, that another may eat the bread of fine flour. He labors in chains at home, under a burning sun and biting lash, that another may ride in ease and splendor abroad. He lives in ignorance, that another may be educated. He is abused, that another may be exalted. He rests his toil-worn limbs on the cold, damp ground, that another may repose on the softest pillow. He is clad in coarse and tattered raiment, that another may be arrayed in purple and fine linen. He is sheltered only by the wretched hovel, that a master may dwell in a magnificent mansion. And to this condition he is bound down as by an arm of iron.

From this monstrous relation there springs an unceasing stream of most revolting cruelties. The very accompaniments of the slave system stamp it as the offspring of hell itself. To ensure good behavior, the slaveholder relies on the whip. To induce proper humility, he relies on the whip. To rebuke what he is pleased to term insolence, he relies on the whip. To supply the place of wages, as an incentive to toil, he relies on the whip. To bind down the spirit of the slave, to imbrute and destroy his manhood, he relies on the whip, the chain, the gag, the thumb-screw, the pillory, the bowie knife, the pistol, and the bloodhound. . . .

There is a still deeper shade to be given to this picture. The physical cruelties are indeed sufficiently harassing and revolting; but they are as a few grains of sand on the sea shore, or a few drops of water in the great ocean, compared with the stupendous wrongs which it inflicts upon the mental, moral, and religious nature of its hapless victims. It is only when we contemplate the slave as a moral and intellectual being that we can adequately comprehend the unparalleled enormity of slavery, and the intense criminality of the slaveholder.

3. Human Cattle for Sale (*c.* 1850)

Slave auctions, at best ugly affairs, received top billing in abolitionist propaganda. Here is an account, less sensational than many, by Solomon Northup, a free Negro of New York state. Kidnaped in Washington, D. C., and enslaved on a Louisiana plantation, he luckily managed to regain his freedom. His narrative, edited and perhaps ghostwritten by a New York lawyer, bears the earmarks of credibility. Discover what aspect of this New Orleans slave auction held by a Mr. Freeman would be most likely to wound Northern sensibilities.

Next day many customers called to examine Freeman's "new lot" [of slaves]. The latter gentleman was very loquacious, dwelling at much length upon our several good points and qualities. He would make us hold up our heads, walk briskly back and forth, while customers would feel of our hands and arms and bodies, turn us about, ask us what we could do, make us open our mouths and show our teeth, precisely as a jockey examines a horse which he is about to barter for or purchase.

Sometimes a man or woman was taken back to the small house in the yard, stripped, and inspected more minutely. Scars upon a slave's back were considered evidence of a rebellious or unruly spirit, and hurt his sale.

One old gentleman, who said he wanted a coachman, appeared to take a fancy to me. From his conversation with Freeman, I learned he was a resident of the city [New Orleans]. I very much desired that he would buy me, because I conceived it would not be difficult to make my escape from New Orleans on some Northern vessel. Freeman asked him $1500 for me. The old gentleman insisted it was too much, as times were very hard. Freeman, however, declared that I was sound and healthy, of a good constitution, and intelligent. He made it a point to enlarge upon my musical attainments. The old gentleman argued quite adroitly that there was nothing extraordinary about the nigger, and finally, to my regret, went out, saying he would call again.

During the day, however, a number of sales were made. David and Caroline were purchased together by a Natchez planter. They left us, grinning broadly, and in the most happy state of mind, caused by the fact of their not being separated. Lethe was sold to a planter of Baton Rouge, her eyes flashing with anger as she was led away.

3. Solomon Northup, *Twelve Years a Slave* (1853), pp. 79–82.

The same man also purchased Randall. The little fellow was made to jump, and run across the floor, and perform many other feats, exhibiting his activity and condition. All the time the trade was going on, Eliza [the mother] was crying aloud, and wringing her hands. She besought the man not to buy him unless he also bought herself and Emily. She promised, in that case, to be the most faithful slave that ever lived. The man answered that he could not afford it, and then Eliza burst into a paroxysm of grief, weeping plaintively.

Freeman turned round to her, savagely, with his whip in his uplifted hand, ordering her to stop her noise, or he would flog her. He would not have such work—such sniveling; and unless she ceased that minute, he would take her to the yard and give her a hundred lashes. Yes, he would take the nonsense out of her pretty quick—if he didn't, might he be d––d.

Eliza shrunk before him, and tried to wipe away her tears, but it was all in vain. She wanted to be with her children, she said, the little time she had to live. All the frowns and threats of Freeman could not wholly silence the afflicted mother. She kept on begging and beseeching them, most piteously, not to separate the three. Over and over again she told them how she loved her boy. A great many times she repeated her former promises—how very faithful and obedient she would be; how hard she would labor day and night, to the last moment of her life, if he would only buy them all together.

But it was of no avail; the man could not afford it. The bargain was agreed upon, and Randall must go alone. Then Eliza ran to him; embraced him passionately; kissed him again and again; told him to remember her —all the while her tears falling in the boy's face like rain.

4. Cohabitation in the Cabins (*c.* 1834)

As the once-fertile lands of Maryland and Virginia petered out, the producing of slaves often proved more profitable than the producing of tobacco. Selling the surplus into slavery "down the [Mississippi] River" presented no real problems. The marriage tie, if indeed there was a marriage, was lightly held. One slave preacher united couples with the formula "until death or distance do you part." Frederick Douglass, in his reminiscences, here recounts how his Maryland slave-breaker, Mr. Covey, laid the foundations of riches. Note whether this slaveowner was regarded or could be regarded as an immoral man.

In pursuit of this object [wealth], pious as Mr. Covey was, he proved himself as unscrupulous and base as the worst of his neighbors. In the beginning he was only able—as he said—"to buy one slave"; and scandalous and shocking as is the fact, he boasted that he bought her simply "as a breeder." But the worst of this is not told in this naked statement. This young woman (Caroline was her name) was virtually compelled by Covey to abandon herself to the object for which he had purchased her; and the result was the birth of twins at the end of the year. At this addition to

4. *Life and Times of Frederick Douglass* (1882), pp. 150–51.

his human stock Covey and his wife were ecstatic with joy. No one dreamed of reproaching the woman or finding fault with the hired man, Bill Smith, the father of the children, for Mr. Covey himself had locked the two up together every night, thus inviting the result.

But I will pursue this revolting subject no farther. No better illustration of the unchaste, demoralizing, and debasing character of slavery can be found than is furnished in the fact that this professedly Christian slaveholder, amidst all his prayers and hymns, was shamelessly and boastfully encouraging and actually compelling, in his own house, undisguised and unmitigated fornication, as a means of increasing his stock. It was the system of slavery which made this allowable, and which condemned the slaveholder for buying a slave woman and devoting her to this life no more than for buying a cow and raising stock from her; and the same rules were observed, with a view to increasing the number and quality of the one as of the other.

B. THE SOUTHERN VIEW OF SLAVERY

1. William Harper's Apology (1837)

William Harper was a distinguished South Carolina jurist, an anti-tariff zealot, and a nullification advocate who early predicted civil war. He is perhaps best remembered as the author of the memorable ordinance of nullification voted by South Carolina in 1832, and also of the *Memoir on Slavery*. This remarkable apology, a part of which is presented here, ranks as one of the ablest defenses of the "peculiar institution." Detect in what respects Harper's defense turns out to be an indictment. Decide which are the most absurd statements, and why. Locate the weakness in the argument that cotton could not be grown without slaves.

Slavery was forced upon us by the extremest exigency of circumstances in a struggle for very existence. Without it, it is doubtful whether a white man would be now existing on this continent—certain that, if there were, they would be in a state of the utmost destitution, weakness, and misery. I neither deprecate nor resent the gift of slavery.

The Africans brought to us had been slaves in their own country and only underwent a change of masters.

That there are great evils in a society where slavery exists, and that the institution is liable to great abuse, I have already said. But the whole of human life is a system of evils and compensations. The free laborer has few real guarantees from society, while security is one of the compensations of the slave's humble position.* There have been fewer murders of slaves than of parents, children, and apprentices in society where slavery does not exist. The slave offers no temptation to the murderer, nor does he really suffer injury from his master. Who but a driveling fanatic has

1. Quoted in A. C. McLaughlin *et al.*, eds., *Source Problems in United States History* (1918), pp. 419–24.
* For the evils of "wage slavery" see earlier, p. 301.

thought of the necessity of protecting domestic animals from the cruelty
of their owners?

. . . It is true that the slave is driven to labor by stripes [lashes]; and
if the object of punishment be to produce obedience or reformation with
the least permanent injury, it is the best method of punishment. Men claim
that this is intolerable. It is not degrading to a slave, nor is it felt to be so.
Is it degrading to a child?

Odium has been cast upon our legislation on account of its forbidding
the elements of education to be communicated to slaves. But in truth what
injury has been done them by this? He who works during the day with
his hands does not read in intervals of leisure for his amusement or the
improvement of his mind—or the exception is so rare as scarcely to need
the being provided for. If there were any chance of elevating their rank,
the denial of the rudiments of education might be a matter of hardship.
But this they know cannot be and that further attainments would be useless to them. . . .

It has been said that marriage does not exist among our slaves. But we
know that marriages among slaves are solemnized; but the law does not
make them indissoluble, nor could it do so. . . . Some suppose that a
slaveholding country is one wide stew [brothel] for the indulgence of
unbridled lust, and there are particular instances of brutal and shameless
debauches in every country. It is even true that in this respect the morals
of this class [slave women] are very loose and that the passions of men
of the superior caste tempt and find gratification in the easy chastity of
the females. . . .

[In countries where free labor prevails] the unmarried woman who
becomes a mother is an outcast from society—and though sentimentalists
lament the hardship of the case, it is justly and necessarily so. But with
us this female slave has a different status. She is not a less useful member
of society than before. She has not impaired her means of support nor
materially impaired her character or lowered her station in society; she
has done no great injury to herself or any other human being. Her offspring
is not a burden but an acquisition to her owner. . . .

Supposing finally that the abolitionists should effect their purpose. What
would be the result? The first and most obvious effect would be to put an
end to the cultivation of our great Southern staple [cotton]. . . . The cultivation of the great staple crops cannot be carried on in any portion of our
own country where there are not slaves. . . . Even if it were possible to
procure laborers at all, what planter would venture to carry on his operations? Imagine an extensive rice or cotton plantation cultivated by free
laborers who might perhaps strike for an increase of wages at a season
when the neglect of a few days would insure the destruction of the whole
crop. I need hardly say that these staples cannot be produced to any
extent where the proprietor of the soil cultivates it with his own hands.

And what would be the effect of putting an end to the cultivation of these staples and thus annihilating, at a blow, two-thirds or three-fourths of our foreign commerce? Can any sane mind contemplate such a result without terror? Our slavery has not only given existence to millions of slaves within our own territories; it has given the means of subsistence, and therefore of existence, to millions of freemen in our Confederate [United] States, enabling them to send forth their swarms to overspread the plains and forests of the West and appear as the harbingers of civilization. Not only on our continent but on the other it has given existence [in textile mills] to hundreds of thousands and the means of comfortable subsistence to millions. A distinguished citizen of our state has lately stated that our great staple, cotton, has contributed more than anything else of later times to the progress of civilization. By enabling the poor to obtain cheap and becoming clothing, it has inspired a taste for comfort, the first stimulus to civilization.

2. The "Blessings" of the Slave (1849)

Connecticut-born and Puritan-descended Solon Robinson became a Yankee peddler at eighteen. Moving to Indiana, he attained prominence as a trader and agriculturist. During the course of his extensive travels through practically every state, he wrote a series of discerning sketches for the foremost agricultural magazines. The following contribution to a leading Southern trade journal is hardly what one would expect from a Connecticut Yankee. Observe in what respects Robinson appears to be too soft on slavery and in what respects he provides a corrective to abolitionist propaganda.

A greater punishment could not be devised or inflicted upon the Southern slave at this day than to give him that liberty which God in his wisdom and mercy deprived him of. . . .

Free them from control, and how soon does poverty and wretchedness overtake them! . . . I boldly and truly assert that you may travel Europe over—yea, you may visit the boasted freemen of America—aye, you may search the world over—before you find a laboring peasantry who are more happy, more contented, as a class of people, or who are better clothed and fed and better provided for in sickness, infirmity, and old age, or who enjoy more of the essential comforts of life, than these so-called miserable, oppressed, abused, starved slaves. . . .

I doubt whether one single instance can be found among the slaves of the South where one has injured himself at long and excessive labor. Instead of a cruel and avaricious master being able to extort more than a very reasonable amount of labor from him, his efforts will certainly produce the contrary effect. This is a well-known fact, so much so indeed that an overseer of this character cannot get employment among masters, who know that over-driving a Negro, as well as a mule, is the poorest way to get work out of either of them. These facts are well understood by all observant masters and overseers: that neither mule nor Negro can be made to do more than a certain amount of work; and that amount so small in comparison

2. *De Bow's Review*, VII (n.s., I, 1849), pp. 217–21, 383–84.

to the amount done by white laborers at the North that it is a universal observation at the South. Northern men are always the hardest masters, in the vain attempt they make to force the Negro to do even half as much as a hireling in New England is compelled to do, or lose his place and wages. . . .

It is true that some men abuse and harshly treat their slaves. So do some men abuse their wives and children and apprentices and horses and cattle. . . .

The fact is notorious that slaves are better treated now than formerly, and that the improvement in their condition is progressing; partly from their masters becoming more temperate and better men, but mainly from the greatest of all moving causes in human actions—self-interest. For masters have discovered in the best of all schools—experience—that their true interest is inseparably bound up with the humane treatment, comfort, and happiness of their slaves.

And many masters have discovered, too, that their slaves are more temperate, more industrious, more kind to one another, more cheerful, more faithful, and more obedient under the ameliorating influences of religion than under all the driving and whipping of all the tyrannical taskmasters that have existed since the day when the children of Israel were driven to the task of making Egyptian brick without straw.

And I do most fearlessly assert, and defy contradiction, that in no part of this Union, even in Puritan New England, is the Sabbath better kept by master and slave, by employer and hireling, or by all classes, high and low, rich and poor, than in the state of Mississippi, where I have often been told that that thing so accursed of God [slavery] existed in all its most disgusting deformity, wretchedness, and sinful horror. From the small plantations, the slaves go more regularly, and better dressed and behaved, to church, often a distance of five or six miles, than any other class of laborers that I have ever been acquainted with. Upon many of the large plantations, divine service is performed more regularly, and to larger and more orderly audiences, than in some county towns. . . .

In all my tour during the past winter, I did not see or hear of but two cases of flogging: one of which was for stealing, and the other for running away from as good a master as ever a servant need to have, which is proved by the appearance and general good conduct of his Negroes. And that they are well fed I know from many days' personal observation; and I have seen some of them with better broadcloth suits on than I often wear myself; and more spare money than their master, as he will freely acknowledge. . . .

But I do seriously say that I did not see or hear of one place where the Negroes were not well fed; and I did not see a ragged gang of Negroes in the South. And I could only hear of one plantation where the Negroes were overworked or unjustly flogged, and on that plantation the master was a drunken, abusive wretch, as heartily despised by his neighbors as he was hated by his Negroes. And were it not for the consequences to themselves if they should rise upon and pull him limb from limb, his brother planters would rejoice that he had met the fate that cruelty to slaves, they are free to say, justly merits.

The two things that are most despised and hated in the South are masters that abuse and starve and ill-treat their slaves, and abolitionists, who seize upon every isolated case of the kind, and trumpet it through the land as evidence of the manner that all slaves are treated, and then call upon the people of the free states to aid the Negroes to free themselves from such inhuman bondage, peaceably if they can, forcibly if they must, no matter whose or how much blood shall flow.

3. Slaves Don't Strike (1846)

The South invested its capital in human muscle, not machinery; in the lash system, not the cash system. The slaveowners had one ace-in-the-hole argument against emancipation: it would wipe out that reliable supply of labor without which Southern agriculture (and Northern textile factories) would perish. These fears were not groundless, as the chaos which followed the Civil War amply demonstrated. Sir Charles Lyell, the distinguished British geologist and world traveler, was exposed to the Southern viewpoint. In his account, discern why the South clung to slavery while white day-labor was admittedly cheaper.

An intelligent Louisianian said to me, "Were we to emancipate our Negroes as suddenly as your government did the West Indians, they would be a doomed race. But there can be no doubt that white labor is more profitable even in this climate."

"Then, why do you not encourage it?" I asked.

"It must be the work of time," he replied. "The prejudices of owners have to be overcome, and the sugar and cotton crop is easily lost if not taken in at once when ripe; the canes being damaged by a slight frost, and the cotton requiring to be picked dry as soon as mature, and being ruined by rain. Very lately a planter, five miles below New Orleans, having resolved to dispense with slave labor, hired one hundred Irish and German emigrants at very high wages. In the middle of the harvest they all struck for double pay. No others were to be had, and it was impossible to purchase slaves in a few days. In that short time he lost produce to the value of $10,000."

C. THE ABOLITIONIST CRUSADE

1. Garrison Launches *The Liberator* (1831)

Mild-appearing William Lloyd Garrison, the most notorious of the extreme abolitionists, began publication of his incendiary weekly newspaper, *The Liberator*, with the following trumpet blast. Despite a subscription list of not more than 3000 and embarrassing annual deficits, he continued the journal for thirty-five years—until slavery was legally ended. The crude woodcut at the top of the front page showing a

---

3. Charles Lyell, *A Second Visit to the United States of North America* (1849), II, 126–27.
1. *The Liberator* (Boston), Jan. 1, 1831.

slave auction near the Capitol infuriated the South; the state of Georgia offered
$5000 for Garrison's arrest and conviction. Jailed in Baltimore for libel, mobbed in
Boston, and jeered at while on the lecture platform, he not only outraged the South
but angered Northern conservatives and even moderate abolitionists. Note the specific
extreme measures he was advocating, and whether he was addressing his appeal
exclusively to the South. Comment critically on his assertion that posterity would
vindicate him.

During my recent tour for the purpose of exciting the minds of the
people by a series of discourses on the subject of slavery, every place that
I visited gave fresh evidence of the fact that a greater revolution in public
sentiment was to be effected in the free states—*and particularly in New
England*—than at the South. I found contempt more bitter, opposition more
active, detraction more relentless, prejudice more stubborn, and apathy
more frozen, than among slaveowners themselves. Of course, there were
individual exceptions to the contrary.

This state of things afflicted but did not dishearten me. I determined, at
every hazard, to lift up the standard of emancipation in the eyes of the
nation, *within sight of Bunker Hill and in the birthplace of liberty*. That
standard is now unfurled; and long may it float, unhurt by the spoliations
of time or the missiles of a desperate foe—yea, till every chain be broken,
and every bondman set free! Let Southern oppressors tremble—let their
secret abettors tremble—let their Northern apologists tremble—let all the
enemies of the persecuted blacks tremble. . . .

Assenting to the "self-evident truth" maintained in the American Declaration of Independence "that all men are created equal, and endowed by
their Creator with certain
inalienable rights — among
which are life, liberty, and
the pursuit of happiness,"
I shall strenuously contend
for the immediate enfranchisement of our slave population. . . . In Park Street
Church, on the Fourth of
July, 1829, in an address
on slavery, I unreflectingly
assented to the popular but
pernicious doctrine of *gradual* abolition. I seize this
opportunity to make a full
and unequivocal recantation, and thus publicly to

ILLUSTRATION FROM GARRISON'S *Liberator*

ask pardon of my God, of my country, and of my brethren the poor slaves,
for having uttered a sentiment so full of timidity, injustice, and absurdity. . . .

I am aware that many object to the severity of my language; but is there not cause for severity? I *will be* as harsh as truth, and as uncompromising as justice. On this subject I do not wish to think, or speak, or write, with moderation. No! No! Tell a man whose house is on fire to give a moderate alarm; tell him to moderately rescue his wife from the hands of the ravisher; tell the mother to gradually extricate her babe from the fire into which it has fallen—but urge me not to use moderation in a cause like the present. I am in earnest—I will not equivocate—I will not excuse—I will not retreat a single inch—AND I WILL BE HEARD. The apathy of the people is enough to make every statue leap from its pedestal, and to hasten the resurrection of the dead.

It is pretended that I am retarding the cause of emancipation by the coarseness of my invective and the precipitancy of my measures. *The charge is not true.* On this question my influence—humble as it is—is felt at this moment to a considerable extent, and shall be felt in coming years—not perniciously, but beneficially—not as a curse, but as a blessing. And posterity will bear testimony that I was right.

2. Manifesto of the Anti-Slavery Society (1833)

About fifty abolitionist zealots, meeting in Philadelphia, launched the American Anti-Slavery Society with the following declaration. William L. Garrison, later elected its president twenty-two times, was chief architect of this manifesto. Later becoming more extreme and arrogant, he denounced the churches as "cages of unclean birds" (because they tolerated slavery), denied the full inspiration of the Bible (because it sanctioned slavery), publicly burned a copy of the Constitution (because it upheld slavery), and as early as 1841 advocated the disruption of the Union (because it legalized slavery). In examining this edict by the American Anti-Slavery Society, note why it demands immediate and uncompensated emancipation; what concessions it makes at this early date to the South; and wherein its arguments seem to be completely unreasonable.

We further maintain that no man has a right to enslave or imbrute his brother—to hold or acknowledge him, for one moment, as a piece of merchandise—to keep back his hire by fraud—or to brutalize his mind by denying him the means of intellectual, social, and moral improvement.

The right to enjoy liberty is inalienable. To invade it is to usurp the prerogative of Jehovah. Every man has a right to his own body—to the products of his own labor—to the protection of law—and to the common advantages of society. It is piracy to buy or steal a native African and subject him to servitude. Surely, the sin is as great to enslave an American as an African.

Therefore we believe and affirm that there is no difference, in principle, between the African slave trade and American slavery;

That every American citizen who retains a human being in involuntary bondage as his property is, according to Scripture (Exodus 21:16), a man-stealer;

2. W. P. Garrison and F. J. Garrison, *William Lloyd Garrison, 1805–1879* (1885), I, 410–11.

That the slaves ought instantly to be set free and brought under the protection of law; . . .

That all those laws which are now in force admitting the right of slavery are therefore, before God, utterly null and void. . . .

We further believe and affirm that all persons of color who possess the qualifications which are demanded of others ought to be admitted forthwith to the enjoyment of the same privileges, and the exercise of the same prerogatives, as others; and that the paths of preferment, of wealth, and of intelligence should be opened as widely to them as to persons of a white complexion.

We maintain that no compensation should be given to the planters emancipating their slaves:

Because it would be a surrender of the great fundamental principle that man cannot hold property in man;

Because slavery is a crime, and therefore [the slave] is not an article to be sold;

Because the holders of slaves are not the just proprietors of what they claim; freeing the slave is not depriving them of property, but restoring it to its rightful owner; it is not wronging the master, but righting the slave—restoring him to himself;

Because immediate and general emancipation would only destroy nominal, not real, property; it would not amputate a limb or break a bone of the slaves, but, by infusing motives into their breasts, would make them doubly valuable to the masters as free laborers; and

Because, if compensation is to be given at all, it should be given to the outraged and guiltless slaves, and not to those who have plundered and abused them.

We regard as delusive, cruel, and dangerous any scheme of expatriation [to Liberia] which pretends to aid, either directly or indirectly, in the emancipation of the slaves, or to be a substitute for the immediate and total abolition of slavery.

We fully and unanimously recognize the sovereignty of each state to legislate exclusively on the subject of the slavery which is tolerated within its limits; we concede that Congress, under the present national compact, has no right to interfere with any of the slave states in relation to this momentous subject;

But we maintain that Congress has a right, and is solemnly bound, to suppress the domestic trade between the several states, and to abolish slavery in those portions of our territory which the Constitution has placed under its exclusive jurisdiction [District of Columbia].

3. Weld Pillories Slavery (1839)

Theodore Dwight Weld assumed leadership of the New York abolitionist group, which objected to the extreme anti-Constitutional tactics of Garrison's New England

3. T. D. Weld, *American Slavery As It Is* (1839), p. 9.

following. He was one of the most influential of the abolitionists, and certainly one of the great men of his era. Preacher, lecturer (until he ruined his voice), pamphleteer, organizer, and inspirational genius, he founded numerous local abolitionist societies and won countless converts to abolition, including Congressmen and other public figures. His documented compilation of horror tales, published in 1839 in *American Slavery As It Is*, not only became the Bible of the cause but greatly influenced the writing of *Uncle Tom's Cabin*. The following statements in his Introduction have been criticized as grossly overdrawn. Locate the charges that appear to be most incredible, and form conclusions as to the soundness of the Southern rebuttal.

We will prove that the slaves in the United States are treated with barbarous inhumanity; that they are overworked, underfed, wretchedly clad and lodged, and have insufficient sleep; that they are often made to wear round their necks iron collars armed with prongs, to drag heavy chains and weights at their feet while working in the field, and to wear yokes, and bells, and iron horns; that they are often kept confined in the stocks day and night for weeks together, made to wear gags in their mouths for hours or days, have some of their front teeth torn out or broken off, that they may be easily detected when they run away; that they are frequently flogged with terrible severity, have red pepper rubbed into their lacerated flesh, and hot brine, spirits of turpentine, etc., poured over the gashes to increase the torture; that they are often stripped naked, their backs and limbs cut with knives, bruised and mangled by scores and hundreds of blows with the paddle, and terribly torn by the claws of cats, drawn over them by their tormentors; that they are often hunted with bloodhounds and shot down like beasts, or torn in pieces by dogs; that they are often suspended by the arms and whipped and beaten till they faint, and when revived by restoratives beaten again till they faint, and sometimes till they die; that their ears are often cut off, their eyes knocked out, their bones broken, their flesh branded with red-hot irons; that they are maimed, mutilated, and burned to death over slow fires.

All these things, and more, and worse, we shall prove. . . . We shall show, not merely that such deeds are committed, but that they are frequent; not done in corners, but before the sun; not in one of the slave states, but in all of them; not perpetrated by brutal overseers and drivers merely, but by magistrates, by legislators, by professors of religion, by preachers of the Gospel, by governors of states, by "gentlemen of property and standing," and by delicate females moving in the "highest circles of society."

We know, full well, the outcry that will be made by multitudes at these declarations; the multiform cavils, the flat denials, the charges of "exaggeration" and "falsehood" so often bandied; the sneers of affected contempt at the credulity that can believe such things; and the rage and imprecations against those who give them currency.

We know, too, the threadbare sophistries by which slaveholders and their apologists seek to evade such testimony. If they admit that such deeds are committed, they tell us that they are exceedingly rare, and therefore furnish no grounds for judging of the general treatment of slaves; that occasionally a brutal wretch in the free states barbarously butchers his wife, but that no one thinks of inferring from that the general treatment of wives at the North and West.

They tell us, also, that the slaveholders of the South are proverbially hospitable, kind, and generous, and it is incredible that they can perpetrate such enormities upon human beings; further, that it is absurd to suppose that they would thus injure their own property, that self-interest would prompt them to treat their slaves with kindness, as none but fools and madmen wantonly destroy their own property; further, that Northern visitors at the South come back testifying to the kind treatment of the slaves, and that the slaves themselves corroborate such representations. . . . We are not to be turned from our purpose by such vapid babblings.

D. JUDGMENTS ON THE ABOLITIONISTS

1. Webster Is Critical (1850)

The thunderously eloquent Daniel Webster was no abolitionist, though the abolitionists liked to think of him as in their camp. He sadly disillusioned them in his famed Seventh of March speech on the Compromise of 1850 (see later, p. 379). Pleading passionately for North-South harmony, he turned upon the anti-slavery zealots. Their pained outcry rent the heavens. At a public meeting in Faneuil Hall, in Boston, the Reverend Theodore Parker declared, "I know of no deed in American history done by a son of New England to which I can compare this but the act of Benedict Arnold. . . ." In this portion of Webster's speech, ascertain the most convincing argument as to the harm done by the abolitionists, and decide whether less extremism would have produced better results.

Then, sir, there are those abolition societies, of which I am unwilling to speak, but in regard to which I have very clear notions and opinions. I do not think them useful. I think their operations for the last twenty years have produced nothing good or valuable.

At the same time, I know thousands of them are honest and good men; perfectly well-meaning men. They have excited feelings; they think they must do something for the cause of liberty. And in their sphere of action, they do not see what else they can do than to contribute to an abolition press, or an abolition society, or to pay an abolition lecturer.

I do not mean to impute gross motives even to the leaders of these societies, but I am not blind to the consequences. I cannot but see what mischiefs their interference with the South has produced.

And is it not plain to every man? Let any gentleman who doubts of that recur to the debates in the Virginia House of Delegates in 1832, and he will see with what freedom a proposition made by Mr. Randolph for the gradual abolition of slavery was discussed in that body. Everyone spoke of slavery as he thought; very ignominious and disparaging names and epithets were applied to it.

The debates in the House of Delegates on that occasion, I believe, were

1. *Congressional Globe,* 31 Cong., 1 sess., Appendix, XXII, pt. 1, p. 275.

all published. They were read by every colored man who could read, and if there were any who could not read, those debates were read to them by others. At that time Virginia was not unwilling nor afraid to discuss this question, and to let that part of her population know as much of it as they could learn.

That was in 1832. . . . These abolition societies commenced their course of action in 1835. It is said—I do not know how true it may be—that they sent incendiary publications into the slave states. At any event, they attempted to arouse, and did arouse, a very strong feeling. In other words, they created great agitation in the North against Southern slavery.

Well, what was the result? The bonds of the slaves were bound more firmly than before; their rivets were more strongly fastened. Public opinion, which in Virginia had begun to be exhibited against slavery, and was opening out for the discussion of the question, drew back and shut itself up in its castle.

I wish to know whether anybody in Virginia can, now, talk openly as Mr. Randolph, Gov. McDowell, and others talked there, openly, and sent their remarks to the press, in 1832.

We all know the fact, and we all know the cause. And everything that this agitating people have done, has been, not to enlarge, but to restrain, not to set free, but to bind faster, the slave population of the South. That is my judgment.

2. Lincoln Appraises Abolitionism (1854)

Abolitionism and crackpotism were closely associated in the public mind, and the taint of abolitionism was almost fatal to a man aspiring to public office. Southerners commonly regarded Abraham Lincoln as an abolitionist, even though his wife's family in Kentucky were slaveholders. Lincoln set forth his views at some length in this memorable speech at Peoria, Illinois, in 1854. Determine how close he comes to being an abolitionist, and in what respects the South might resent his position.

Before proceeding, let me say that I have no prejudice against the Southern people. They are just what we would be in their situation. If slavery did not now exist among them, they would not introduce it. If it did now exist amongst us, we should not instantly give it up. This I believe of the masses North and South.

Doubtless there are individuals, on both sides, who would not hold slaves under any circumstances, and others who would gladly introduce slavery anew, if it were out of existence. We know that some Southern men do free their slaves, go North, and become tiptop abolitionists; while some Northern ones go South and become most cruel slave-masters.

When Southern people tell us they are no more responsible for the origin of slavery than we, I acknowledge the fact. When it is said that the institution exists, and that it is very difficult to get rid of it in any satisfactory way, I can understand and appreciate the saying. I surely will not blame them for not doing what I should not know how to do myself.

2. R. P. Basler, ed., *The Collected Works of Abraham Lincoln* (1953), II, 255–56.

COLORED SCHOOLS BROKEN UP, IN THE FREE STATES.
When schools have been established for colored scholars, the law-makers and the
mob have combined to destroy them ;—as at Canterbury, Ct., at Canaan, N. H.,
Aug. 10, 1835, at Zanesville and Brown Co., Ohio, in 1836.

Anti-abolitionist conservatives in North vent their wrath in attacks on school
for Negroes. *Anti-Slavery Almanac,* 1839.

If all earthly power were given me, I should not know what to do as to
the existing institution. My first impulse would be to free all the slaves and
send them to Liberia—to their native land. But a moment's reflection would
convince me that whatever of high hope (as I think there is) there may
be in this in the long run, its sudden execution is impossible. If they all
landed there in a day, they would all perish in the next ten days; and there
are not surplus shipping and surplus money enough to carry them there in
many times ten days.

What then? Free them all and keep them among us as underlings? Is it
quite certain that this betters their condition? I think I would not hold one
in slavery at any rate; yet the point is not clear enough for me to denounce
people upon.

What next? Free them, and make them politically and socially our
equals? My own feelings will not admit of this; and if mine would, we well
know that those of the great mass of white people would not. Whether this
feeling accords with justice and sound judgment is not the sole question,
if indeed it is any part of it. A universal feeling, whether well or ill founded,
cannot be safely disregarded. We cannot then make them equals.

It does seem to me that systems of gradual emancipation might be
adopted; but for their tardiness in this I will not undertake to judge our
brethren of the South.

When they remind us of their constitutional rights, I acknowledge them,
not grudgingly but fully and fairly. And I would give them any legislation
for the reclaiming of their fugitives which should not, in its stringency, be
more likely to carry a free man into slavery than our ordinary criminal laws
are to hang an innocent one.

3. The Abolitionists Provoke War (1882)

The fanatical abolitionists were often accused of having precipitated the Civil War. In his memoirs Frederick Douglass, the remarkable ex-slave and abolitionist agitator, pleads partly guilty to the indictment. Note whether he is correct in his assumption as to who were the aggressors.

The abolitionists of this country have been charged with bringing on the war between the North and South, and in one sense this is true. Had there been no anti-slavery agitation at the North, there would have been no active anti-slavery anywhere to resist the demands of the Slave Power at the South, and where there is no resistance there can be no war. Slavery would then have been nationalized, and the whole country would then have been subjected to its power. Resistance to slavery and the extension of slavery invited and provoked secession and war to perpetuate and extend the slave system.

Thus, in the same sense, England is responsible for our Civil War. The abolition of slavery in the West Indies gave life and vigor to the abolition movement in America. Clarkson of England gave us Garrison of America; Granville Sharpe of England gave us our Wendell Phillips; and Wilberforce of England gave us our peerless Charles Sumner.

These grand men and their brave co-workers here took up the moral thunderbolts which had struck down slavery in the West Indies, and hurled them with increased zeal and power against the gigantic system of slavery here, till, goaded to madness, the traffickers in the souls and bodies of men flew to arms, rent asunder the Union at the center, and filled the land with hostile armies and the ten thousand horrors of war. Out of this tempest, out of this whirlwind and earthquake of war, came the abolition of slavery, came the employment of colored troops, came colored citizens, came colored jurymen, came colored Congressmen, came colored schools in the South, and came the great amendments of our national Constitution.

E. THE RISING SOUTHERN TEMPER

1. Helper's Banned Book (1857)

Hinton R. Helper, an impoverished North Carolinian who hated Negroes, published a sensational book in 1857 in which he statistically contrasted the rapid economic growth of the North with the slower progress of the South. Concluding that the slaveless whites were the chief victims of the slave system, he urged upon them various means, some incendiary, to overthrow both slavery and the grip of the white oligarchy. Unable to find a publisher in the South, he aired his views in the North under the title *The Impending Crisis of the South*. The Southern aristocracy reacted violently, banning the book and roughly handling a few daring souls who had obtained smuggled copies. All told, about a million copies in one form or another were distributed. Determine why it was to the advantage of the slaveowners to treat the poor whites as Helper alleges they did.

3. *Life and Times of Frederick Douglass* (1882), p. 607.
1. H. R. Helper, *The Impending Crisis of the South* (1860 ed.), pp. 42–45.

Notwithstanding the fact that the white non-slaveholders of the South are in the majority as five to one, they have never yet had any part or lot in framing the laws under which they live. There is no legislation except for the benefit of slavery and slaveholders.

As a general rule, poor white persons are regarded with less esteem and attention than Negroes, and though the condition of the latter is wretched beyond description, vast numbers of the former are infinitely worse off. A cunningly devised mockery of freedom is guaranteed to them, and that is all. To all intents and purposes, they are disfranchised and outlawed, and the only privilege extended to them is a shallow and circumscribed participation in the political movements that usher slaveholders into office.

We have not breathed away seven and twenty years in the South without becoming acquainted with the demagogical maneuverings of the oligarchy. . . . To the illiterate poor whites—made poor and ignorant by the system of slavery—they hold out the idea that slavery is the very bulwark of our liberties, and the foundation of American independence! . . .

The lords of the lash are not only absolute masters of the blacks, who are bought and sold, and driven about like so many cattle, but they are also the oracles and arbiters of all non-slaveholding whites, whose freedom is merely nominal, and whose unparalleled illiteracy and degradation is purposely and fiendishly perpetuated. How little the "poor white trash"—the great majority of the Southern people—know of the real condition of the country is, indeed, sadly astonishing.

The truth is they know nothing of public measures, and little of private affairs, except what their imperious masters, the slave-drivers, condescend to tell—and that is but precious little. And even that little, always garbled and one-sided, is never told except in public harangues. For the haughty cavaliers of shackles and handcuffs will not degrade themselves by holding private converse with those who have neither dimes nor hereditary rights in human flesh.

Whenever it pleases . . . a slaveholder to become communicative, poor whites may hear with fear and trembling, but not speak.

Non-slaveholders are not only kept in ignorance of what is transpiring at the North, but they are continually misinformed of what is going on even in the South. Never were the poorer classes of a people, and those classes so largely in the majority, and all inhabiting the same country, so basely duped, so adroitly swindled, or so damnably outraged.

It is expected that the stupid and sequacious [servile] masses, the white victims of slavery, will believe—and, as a general thing, they do believe— whatever the slaveholders tell them. And thus it is that they are cajoled into the notion that they are the freest, happiest, and most intelligent people in the world, and are taught to look with prejudice and disapprobation upon every new principle or progressive movement. Thus it is that the South, woefully inert and inventionless, has lagged behind the North, and is now weltering in the cesspool of ignorance and degradation.

2. The South Condemns Helperites (1859)

Helper's appeal to the poor whites of the South fell on barren ground; most of them were illiterate or apathetic, while others could not get the book. But the free-soil Republicans of the North seized upon it for political purposes, and sixty-eight members of the House of Representatives signed an appeal for funds to distribute free 100,000 copies of a paperbacked abridgment. Following John Brown's fear-inspiring raid into Virginia in 1859, the Southerners were determined to keep from the Speakership of the House any endorser of Helper's book. For two months they filibustered successfully against Republican John Sherman, who had ill-advisedly signed the appeal, while the flames of sectional conflict roared higher and higher. Observe what the following speech by Representative Clark of Missouri presaged as to the preservation of the Union.

These [Helperite] gentlemen come in and say that the riches of the South are neglected by the bad management of the South; that the accursed plague of slavery does it; and that, therefore, non-slaveholders at the South should rise in their majesty—peaceably if they can, forcibly if they must—take their arms, subdue the slaveholders, drive out the plague of slavery, take possession of the country, and dedicate it to free labor.

That is the sentiment in the book which these gentlemen recommend to have circulated gratuitously all over the South. Are such men fit to preside over the destinies of our common country? Can the South expect from such men the maintenance of the integrity of the Constitution? Our slave property is as much our property under the Constitution, and under the guarantees of this government, as any property held at the North. Whether it is sinful to hold slaves, whether slavery is a plague and a loss, and whether it will affect our future destiny, is our own business. We suffer for that, and not they.

We ask none of their prayers. We need none of them. If we were in need of them, and if the only way to escape future punishment and misery were to receive benefit from the prayers of those [sixty-eight] who signed that recommendation, I should expect, after death, to sink into the nethermost Hell. [Laughter.]

Do gentlemen expect that they can distribute incendiary books, give incendiary advice, advise rebellion, advise non-intercourse in all the relations of life, spread such works broadcast over the country, and not be taken to task for it? I presume that the South has sufficient self-respect; that it understands the effect of its institutions well enough; that it has its rights, and dares to maintain them.

3. Hammond Proclaims Cotton King (1858)

As the resentment of the South rose, so did its confidence in its ability to stand alone as a Confederacy, if need be. It rode through the Panic of 1857 with flying colors; its enormous exports of "King Cotton" overshadowed all others from America. But the North might well have responded with the cry "Grass is King!" For, as

2. *Congressional Globe,* 36 Cong., 1 sess., p. 17 (Dec. 8, 1859).
3. *Ibid.,* 35 Cong., 1 sess., p. 961 (March 3, 1858).

Helper pointed out in his banned book, the value of the North's hay crop, though consumed at home, was greater than that of the South's cotton crop. Yet Senator Hammond of South Carolina, a bombastic owner of some three hundred slaves, voiced the cry "Cotton is King!" in this famous Senate speech. He had reference to the dangerous dependence of the enormous English textile industry on the huge imports from the South. Locate the fallacy or fallacies, if any, in his reasoning.

Why, sir, the South has never yet had a just cause of war. Every time she has seized her sword it has been on the point of honor, and that point of honor has been mainly loyalty to her sister colonies and sister states, who have ever since plundered and calumniated her.

But if there were no other reason why we should never have a war, would any sane nation make war on cotton? Without firing a gun, without drawing a sword, when they make war on us we can bring the whole world to our feet.

The South is perfectly competent to go on, one, two, or three years, without planting a seed of cotton. I believe that if she was to plant but half her cotton, it would be an immediate advantage to her. I am not so sure but that after three years' cessation she would come out stronger than ever she was before and better prepared to enter afresh upon her great career of enterprise.

What would happen if no cotton was furnished for three years? I will not stop to depict what everyone can imagine, but this is certain: old England would topple headlong and carry the whole civilized world with her. No, sir, you dare not make war on cotton. No power on earth dares make war upon it. Cotton is King!

[*It is not surprising that cotton should have deluded the South when the British themselves conceded their fatal dependence. A writer in* Blackwood's Edinburgh Magazine *(Feb., 1851, p. 216) confessed: ". . . We rest almost entirely on the supplies obtained from a single state* [nation]. *No one need be told that five-sixths, often nine-tenths, of the supply of cotton consumed in our manufactures come from America, and that seven or eight thousand persons are directly or indirectly employed in the operations which take place upon it. Suppose America wishes to bully us, to make us abandon Canada or Jamaica for example, she has no need to go to war. She has only to stop the export of cotton for six months, and the whole of our manufacturing counties are starving or in rebellion; while a temporary cessation of profit is the only inconvenience they experience on the other side of the Atlantic. Can we call ourselves independent in such circumstances?"*]

THOUGHT PROVOKERS

1. A favorite argument of the South was that the Negro slave was better off than the wage slave of the North or England. (See also earlier, p. 301.) In what respects was this true? false? J. Q. Adams said, "Misery is not slavery." Comment.

2. Why could persons viewing slavery in the South come away with such radically differing accounts? What would have been the future of slavery if it had been left alone?

3. It has been said that the Garrison abolitionists were right in principle but wrong in method. Comment. Garrison advocated disunion as a means of ending slavery. Explain the logic or illogic of his position. How would you have dealt with slavery if given "all earthly power"?
4. Why did the bulk of the conservatives in the North deplore the boat-rocking tactics of the abolitionists and often despise these extremists? Did the abolitionists do more harm than good?
5. In what respects did Hinton R. Helper cause the Civil War? In what respects did the "Cotton is King" complex cause the Civil War? It has been said that cotton was a king who enslaved his subjects. Comment.

FURTHER EXPLORATION

General: Allan Nevins, *Ordeal of the Union* (1947), I, chs. 13–15; W. E. Dodd, *The Cotton Kingdom* (1921). **Sordid Side:** K. M. Stampp, *The Peculiar Institution* (1956). **Southern View:** U. B. Phillips, *American Negro Slavery* (1918); U. B. Phillips, *Life and Labor in the Old South* (1929). **Abolition Crusade:** D. L. Dumond, *Anti-Slavery: The Crusade for Freedom in America* (1961); Louis Filler, *The Crusade against Slavery, 1830–1860* (1960); G. H. Barnes, *The Anti-Slavery Impulse* (1933). **Critics and Defenders:** W. S. Jenkins, *Pro-Slavery Thought in the Old South* (1935); S. M. Elkins, *Slavery* (1959). **Rising Tempers:** Allan Nevins, *The Emergence of Lincoln* (2 vols., 1950); D. L. Cohn, *The Life and Times of King Cotton* (1956).

Recent: W. R. Taylor, *Cavalier and Yankee: The Old South and American National Character* (1961) [paperback]; D. B. Davis, *The Problem of Slavery in Western Culture* (1966); Clement Eaton, *The Growth of Southern Civilization, 1790–1860* (1961) [paperback], *The Freedom-of-Thought Struggle in the Old South* (rev. ed. 1964) [paperback], *The Mind of the Old South* (1964); E. D. Genovese, *The Political Economy of Slavery* (1965); L. F. Litwack, *North of Slavery* (1961) [paperback]; W. M. Merrill, *Against Wind and Tide, a Biography of William Lloyd Garrison* (1963); J. L. Thomas, *The Liberator: William Lloyd Garrison* (1963); David Bertelson, *The Lazy South* (1967).

Chapter 20

The Fires of Sectional Conflict, 1848-1854

There is a higher law than the Constitution.

WILLIAM H. SEWARD, IN SENATE, 1850

PROLOGUE: The electrifying discovery of gold in California in 1848 brought a frantic inrush of population, a demand for statehood, and a showdown in Congress over the future of slavery in the territories. The fruit of these debates was the great Compromise of 1850, which purchased an uneasy truce between North and South. It left the Southerners unhappy over the gains of free soil, and the Northerners unhappy over being drafted as slave-catchers under the new Fugitive Slave Act of 1850. The short-lived truce was ruptured by the Kansas-Nebraska Act of 1854, which threw open the free soil of Kansas to possible slavery. To many Northerners this repeal of the time-sanctified Missouri Compromise line of 1820 seemed like bad faith on the part of the South; to many Southerners the open flouting of the Fugitive Slave Act, especially after 1854, seemed like bad faith on the part of the North. With distrust rapidly mounting on both sides, the days of the Union seemed numbered.

A. THE WILMOT PROVISO ISSUE

1. Wilmot Appeals for Free Soil (1847)

While the Mexican War was still being fought, President Polk, his eye on California, asked Congress for $2,000,000 with which to negotiate a peace. Representative David Wilmot of Pennsylvania proposed adding to the appropriation bill an amendment or proviso designed to bar slavery forever from any territory to be wrested from Mexico. Angry Southerners sprang to their feet; and the so-called Wilmot Proviso, though twice passing the House, was blocked in the Senate. But it became the cradle of the yet unborn Republican Party, and it precipitated a debate that continued until silenced by the guns of civil war. In examining the following speech in Congress by Wilmot, note what he conceives the moral issue to be; how effectively he meets the argument regarding "joint blood and treasure"; and whether he could properly be regarded as an abolitionist.

But, sir, the issue now presented is not whether slavery shall exist unmolested where it now is, but whether it shall be carried to new and distant regions, now free, where the footprint of a slave cannot be found. This, sir, is the issue. Upon it I take my stand, and from it I cannot be frightened or driven by idle charges of abolitionism.

I ask not that slavery be abolished. I demand that this government preserve the integrity of free territory against the aggressions of slavery—against its wrongful usurpations.

1. *Congressional Globe*, 29 Cong., 2 sess., Appendix, p. 315 (Feb. 8, 1847).

Sir, I was in favor of the annexation of Texas. . . . The Democracy [Democratic Party] of the North, almost to a man, went for annexation. Yes, sir, here was an empire larger than France given up to slavery. Shall further concessions be made by the North? Shall we give up free territory, the inheritance of free labor? Must we yield this also? Never, sir, never, until we ourselves are fit to be slaves. . . .

But, sir, we are told that the joint blood and treasure of the whole country being expended in this acquisition, therefore it should be divided, and slavery allowed to take its share. Sir, the South has her share already; the instalment for slavery was paid in advance. We are fighting this war for Texas and for the South. I affirm it—every intelligent man knows it— Texas is the primary cause of this war. For this, sir, Northern treasure is being exhausted, and Northern blood poured upon the plains of Mexico. We are fighting this war cheerfully, not reluctantly—cheerfully fighting this war for Texas; and yet we seek not to change the character of her institutions. Slavery is there; there let it remain. . . .

Now, sir, we are told that California is ours, that New Mexico is ours— won by the valor of our arms. They are free. Shall they remain free? Shall these fair provinces be the inheritance and homes of the white labor of freemen or the black labor of slaves? This, sir, is the issue—this the question. The North has the right, and her representatives here have the power. . . .

But the South contend that, in their emigration to this free territory, they have the right to take and hold slaves, the same as other property. Unless the amendment I have offered be adopted, or other early legislation is had upon this subject, they will do so. Indeed, they unitedly, as one man, have declared their right and purpose so to do, and the work has already begun.

Slavery follows in the rear of our armies. Shall the war power of our government be exerted to produce such a result? Shall this government depart from its neutrality on this question, and lend its power and influence to plant slavery in these territories?

There is no question of abolition here, sir. Shall the South be permitted, by aggression, by invasion of the right, by subduing free territory and planting slavery upon it, to wrest these provinces from Northern freemen, and turn them to the accomplishment of their own sectional purposes and schemes?

This is the question. Men of the North, answer. Shall it be so? Shall we of the North submit to it? If we do, we are coward slaves, and deserve to have the manacles fastened upon our own limbs.

2. Southerners Threaten Secession (1849)

After the Mexican War officially brought rich territorial plums, the Northern anti-slaveryites became more persistent. They introduced measures in Congress for abolishing slavery in the District of Columbia and for organizing California and New Mexico as territories without slavery—that is, on the basis of the unpassed Wilmot

2. *Ibid.,* 31 Cong., 1 sess., pt. 1, pp. 26, 28, 29.

Proviso. Outraged Southerners responded with cries of disunion. The following incendiary outbursts all occurred on the floor of the House on December 13, 1849. The most famous speaker was hale and hearty Robert Toombs of Georgia, a brilliant orator and one of the more moderate Southern planters. (He later became Secretary of State for the Confederacy). Observe the reasons why the South was so bitterly aroused over the question of slavery in the territories, and draw conclusions as to what these statements portended.

Mr. MEADE [of Va.]—But, sir, if the organization of this House is to be followed by the passage of these bills—if these outrages are to be committed upon my people—I trust in God, sir, that my eyes have rested upon the last Speaker of the House of Representatives. . . .

Mr. TOOMBS [of Ga.]—I do not, then, hesitate to avow before this House and the country, and in the presence of the living God, that if by your legislation you [Northerners] seek to drive us from the territories of California and New Mexico, purchased by the common blood and treasure of the whole people, and to abolish slavery in this District [of Columbia], thereby attempting to fix a national degradation upon half the states of this Confederacy, *I am for disunion*. And if my physical courage be equal to the maintenance of my convictions of right and duty, I will devote all I am and all I have on earth to its consummation.

From 1787 to this hour, the people of the South have asked nothing but justice—nothing but the maintenance of the principles and the spirit which controlled our fathers in the formation of the Constitution. Unless we are unworthy of our ancestors, we will never accept less as a condition of union. . . .

The Territories are the common property of the people of the United States, purchased by their common blood and treasure. You [the Congress] are their common agents. It is your duty, while they are in a territorial state, to remove all impediments to their free enjoyment by all sections and people of the Union, the slaveholder and the non-slaveholder. . . .

Mr. COLCOCK [of S. C.]— . . . I here pledge myself that if any bill should be passed at this Congress abolishing slavery in the District of Columbia, or incorporating the Wilmot Proviso in any form, I will introduce a resolution in this House declaring, in terms, *that this Union ought to be dissolved*.

B. THE COMPROMISE DEBATES OF 1850

1. Calhoun Demands Southern Rights (1850)

Two burning questions brought the sectional controversy to a furious boil in 1850. The first was the failure of Northerners loyally to uphold both the Constitution and the Fugitive Slave Law of 1793 regarding runaway slaves. The second was the effort of California to win admission as a free state, thus establishing a precedent for the rest of the Mexican Cession territory. The subsequent debate over the compromise measures of 1850 featured a galaxy of forensic giants: Henry Clay, John C. Calhoun, Daniel Webster, Thomas H. Benton, William H. Seward, Stephen A. Douglas,

1. *Ibid.,* pp. 453, 455 (March 4, 1850).

Jefferson Davis, and many others. Highly revealing was the following swan-song speech of Senator Calhoun. On the verge of death from tuberculosis, he authorized a colleague to read it for him. Note his views on the Constitution, the Union, and secession; how successfully he placed the onus of insincerity and aggression on the North; and how practicable his remedies for preserving the Union were.

. . . How can the Union be saved? To this I answer, there is but one way by which it can be, and that is by adopting such measures as will satisfy the states belonging to the Southern section that they can remain in the Union consistently with their honor and their safety. There is, again, only one way by which this can be effected, and that is by removing the causes by which this belief [that the South cannot honorably and safely remain in the Union] has been produced. Do that and discontent will cease, harmony and kind feelings between the sections be restored, and every apprehension of danger to the Union removed. The question, then, is, By what can this be done? But, before I undertake to answer this question, I propose to show by what the Union cannot be saved.

It cannot, then, be saved by eulogies on the Union, however splendid or numerous. The cry of "Union, Union, the glorious Union!" can no more prevent disunion than the cry of "Health, health, glorious health!" on the part of the physician can save a patient lying dangerously ill. So long as the Union, instead of being regarded as a protector, is regarded in the opposite character by not much less than a majority of the states, it will be in vain to attempt to conciliate them by pronouncing eulogies on it.

Besides, this cry of Union comes commonly from those whom we cannot believe to be sincere. It usually comes from our assailants. But we cannot believe them to be sincere; for, if they loved the Union, they would necessarily be devoted to the Constitution. It made the Union, and to destroy the Constitution would be to destroy the Union. But the only reliable and certain evidence of devotion to the Constitution is to abstain, on the one hand, from violating it, and to repel, on the other, all attempts to violate it. It is only by faithfully performing these high duties that the Constitution can be preserved, and with it the Union. . . .

Having now shown what cannot save the Union, I return to the question with which I commenced, How can the Union be saved? There is but one way by which it can, with any certainty; and that is by a full and final settlement, on the principle of justice, of all the questions at issue between the two sections.

The South asks for justice, simple justice, and less she ought not to take. She has no compromise to offer but the Constitution; and no concession or surrender to make. She has already surrendered so much that she has little left to surrender. Such a settlement would go to the root of the evil, and remove all cause of discontent by satisfying the South she could remain honorably and safely in the Union, and thereby restore the harmony and fraternal feelings between the sections which existed anterior to the Missouri [Compromise] agitation [1820]. Nothing else can, with any certainty,

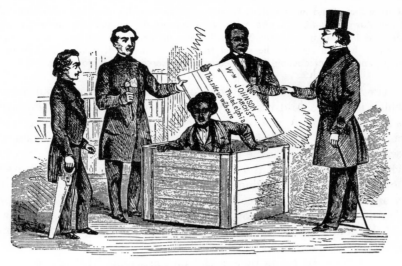

RESURRECTION OF HENRY BOX BROWN

Brown was shipped to Philadelphia abolitionists from Virginia in a box. Illustration in William Still, *The Underground Railroad,* 1872.

finally and forever settle the questions at issue, terminate agitation, and save the Union.

But can this be done? Yes, easily; not by the weaker party [the South], for it can of itself do nothing—not even protect itself—but by the stronger. The North has only to will it to accomplish it—to do justice by conceding to the South an equal right in the acquired territory, and to do her duty by causing the stipulations relative to fugitive slaves to be faithfully fulfilled— to cease the agitation of the slave question, and to provide for the insertion of a provision in the Constitution, by an amendment, which will restore to the South, in substance, the power she possessed of protecting herself, before the equilibrium between the sections was destroyed by the action of this government. There will be no difficulty in devising such a provision*— one that will protect the South, and which, at the same time, will improve and strengthen the government instead of impairing and weakening it.

But will the North agree to this? It is for her to answer the question. But, I will say, she cannot refuse if she has half the love of the Union which she professes to have, or without justly exposing herself to the charge that her love of power and aggrandizement is far greater than her love of the Union.

At all events, the responsibility of saving the Union rests on the North, and not the South. The South cannot save it by any act of hers, and the North may save it without any sacrifice whatever, unless to do justice, and to perform her duties under the Constitution, should be regarded by her as a sacrifice. . . .

If you, who represent the stronger portion, cannot agree to settle . . .

* Calhoun evidently had in mind two Presidents: one Northern, one Southern, each with crippling veto power.

[the question at issue] on the broad principle of justice and duty, say so; and let the states we both represent agree to separate and part in peace. If you are unwilling we should part in peace, tell us so; and we shall know what to do, when you reduce the question to submission or resistance.

If you remain silent, you will compel us to infer by your acts what you intend. In that case, California will become the test question. If you admit her, under all the difficulties that oppose her admission, you compel us to infer that you intend to exclude us from the whole of the acquired territories, with the intention of destroying, irretrievably, the equilibrium between the two sections. We would be blind not to perceive, in that case, that your real objects are power and aggrandizement, and infatuated not to act accordingly.

2. Webster Urges Concessions (1850)

On the anvil of Congressional debate was forged the great Compromise of 1850. California was admitted as a free state; the fate of slavery in the rest of the Mexican Cession territory was left to the inhabitants. The major sop to the South was the enactment of a more stringent Fugitive Slave Law. As a concession to the North, slave trade was abolished in the District of Columbia; as a concession to the South, slavery in the District was retained. Texas received $10,000,000 for yielding a disputed chunk of her territory to New Mexico.

Senator Daniel Webster's Seventh of March speech during these Congressional debates was distinguished by its emphasis on concession, compromise, moderation, and Union. He attacked the abolitionists (see earlier, p. 366) and deplored the agitation over the extension of slavery to the territories. A slave economy was geographically impossible there, he felt, and no legislative body should re-enact the law of God. Finally, he took sharp issue with Calhoun's threat of secession. Determine how good a prophet Webster was, and which of his arguments as to the impracticability of peaceful secession probably carried most weight in the North.

Mr. President, I wish to speak today, not as a Massachusetts man, nor as a Northern man, but as an American, and a member of the Senate of the United States. . . . I speak today for the preservation of the Union. "Hear me for my cause." . . .

Mr. President, I should much prefer to have heard, from every member on this floor, declarations of opinion that this Union should never be dissolved, than the declaration of opinion that in any case, under the pressure of circumstances, such a dissolution was possible. I hear with pain, and anguish, and distress, the word *secession*, especially when it falls from the lips of those who are eminently patriotic, and known to the country, and known all over the world, for their political services.

Secession! Peaceable secession! Sir, your eyes and mine are never destined to see that miracle. The dismemberment of this vast country without convulsion! The breaking up of the fountains of the great deep without ruffling the surface! Who is so foolish—I beg everybody's pardon—as to expect to see any such thing? . . .

There can be no such thing as a peaceable secession. Peaceable secession

2. *Ibid.*, 31 Cong., 1 sess., pp. 276, 482–83.

is an utter impossibility. Is the great Constitution under which we live here—covering this whole country—is it to be thawed and melted away by secession, as the snows on the mountain melt under the influence of a vernal sun—disappear almost unobserved, and die off? No, sir! No, sir! No, sir! I will not state what might produce the disruption of the states; but, sir, I see it as plainly as I see the sun in heaven—I see that disruption must produce such a war as I will not describe, in its twofold characters.

Peaceable secession! Peaceable secession! The concurrent agreement of all the members of this great Republic to separate! A voluntary separation, with alimony on one side and on the other! Why, what would be the result? Where is the line to be drawn? What states are to secede?—What is to remain American? What am I to be?—an American no longer? Where is the flag of the Republic to remain? Where is the eagle still to tower? or is he to cower, and shrink, and fall to the ground? . . .

What is to become of the army? What is to become of the navy? What is to become of the public lands? How is each of the thirty states to defend itself? I know, although the idea has not been stated distinctly, there is to be a Southern Confederacy. I do not mean, when I allude to this statement, that anyone seriously contemplates such a state of things. I do not mean to say that it is true, but I have heard it suggested elsewhere, that that idea has originated in a design to separate. I am sorry, sir, that it has ever been thought of, talked of, or dreamed of, in the wildest flights of human imagination. But the idea must be of a separation, including the slave states upon one side and the free states on the other.

Sir, there is not—I may express myself too strongly perhaps—but some things, some moral things, are almost as impossible as other natural or physical things. And I hold the idea of a separation of these states—those that are free to form one government, and those that are slaveholding to form another—as a moral impossibility.

We could not separate the states by any such line, if we were to draw it. We could not sit down here today and draw a line of separation that would satisfy any five men in the country. There are natural causes that would keep and tie us together, and there are social and domestic relations which we could not break if we would, and which we should not if we could. . . .

And now, Mr. President, instead of speaking of the possibility or utility of secession . . . let our comprehension be as broad as the country for which we act, our aspirations as high as its certain destiny. Let us not be pigmies in a case that calls for men.

Never did there devolve on any generation of men higher trusts than now devolve upon us for the preservation of this Constitution and the harmony and peace of all who are destined to live under it. Let us make our generation one of the strongest and brightest links in that golden chain which is destined, I fully believe, to grapple the people of all the states to this Constitution for ages to come.

3. Free-Soilers Denounce Webster (1850)

The new and more merciless Fugitive Slave Act of 1850 was the keystone of the Compromise of 1850, and Senator Webster's eloquent support of it scandalized the abolitionists. "The fame of Webster ends in this nasty law," wrote Ralph Waldo Emerson. But conservative-minded Northerners were well aware, as Emerson himself had recorded, that "Cotton thread holds the Union together." Bankers, shippers, and manufacturers—holding Southern mortgages, transporting cotton, or using it in their factories—praised Webster's course as statesmanlike. Verily, the abolitionists cried, the "Lords of the Loom" were joining hands with the "Lords of the Lash." A New Hampshire newspaper editor here assails the New England "cotton lords." Judging from this criticism, what were the political reactions to Webster's stand?

Some eight hundred of the "cotton lords" of State Street [Boston], with a few . . . Doctors of Divinity . . . of the Andover Theological Seminary, have signed a letter of thanks to Daniel Webster for his recent apostasy to freedom.

This was to be expected. There are, and always have been, men at the North whose habits, associations, and interests all lead them to love whatever degrades labor, and the man who lives by labor. Wherever Mammon is the great god, there flourishes the spirit of slavery. Wealth and luxury are ever the handmaids of oppression. The fastnesses of liberty have always been in the homes of the untitled masses. And hence the antagonism between capital and labor, which marks so strongly modern civilization.

In thanking Mr. Webster for his efforts in behalf of slavery, the "cotton" men of Boston are but signing a certificate of his servility to themselves. No such certificate, however, will commend him to the people of New England, nor of Massachusetts. Instead, it will have the very opposite effect. It is already doing a work far different from that intended.

The honest anti-slavery masses, upon whom Webster has heretofore relied,

VOTERS, Read This!

EXTRACT FROM A

SPEECH

DELIVERED BY THE

Hon. Daniel Webster,

IN THE SENATE OF THE UNITED STATES, ON THE 7th OF MARCH, 1850.

"If the infernal Fanatics and Abolitionists ever get the power in their hands, they will override the Constitution, set the Supreme Court at defiance, change and make Laws to suit themselves. They will lay violent hands on those who differ with them politically in opinion, or dare question their infallibility; bankrupt the country and finally deluge it with blood."

ANTI-WEBSTER HANDBILL IN MASSACHUSETTS Presumably issued by abolitionists, this is manifestly a fraud. For what Webster actually said, see p. 366. New-York Historical Society.

3. *Independent Democrat* (Concord, N. H.), in *The Liberator* (Boston), April 19, 1850.

see at once that it cannot be for any good thing done for freedom and humanity that such men praise him. To the representative of freemen, the "well done" of the enemies of freedom is the breath of infamy. That "well done" Daniel Webster has received, not only from the "cotton lords" of Massachusetts, but from the prince of cotton lords [Calhoun?] of South Carolina. He is doomed, withered, blasted; and the "thanks" of all the worshipers of Mammon and Wrong in the universe cannot save him.

[*Southerners, as indicated, were generally pleased by the unexpected show of fairness from the Yankee Webster, but their praise was a political kiss of death to the Senator. The Richmond* Enquirer *remarked that the Massachusetts abolitionists—"the miserable peddlers for notoriety"—would "defame and abuse him." It further stated that his "selfish and penurious constituency"—"the moneyed men and manufacturers of New England"—were finally "aroused to the dangers that threaten the Union and their interests . . ." (quoted in* The Liberator, *April 5, 1850).*]

C. REACTIONS TO THE FUGITIVE SLAVE LAW

1. Giddings Rejects Slave Catching (1850)

If the South had a grievance against Northern abettors of runaway slaves, the North had a grievance against the harsh Fugitive Slave Act of 1850. No single irritant of the 1850's proved to be more persistently galling. Among the numerous features of the law, federal officers could summon bystanders to form a posse to chase the fugitive. Citizens who prevented an arrest or aided the escapee were liable to six months' imprisonment and a fine of $1000. Few men were more deeply outraged by these stipulations than fiery Joshua R. Giddings, who served for twenty years as an uncompromising anti-slavery Congressman from Ohio. In his speech in Congress against the Fugitive Slave Act, note the parts that seem to be most grossly overdrawn; the parts most offensive to the South; the part that most strongly foreshadowed a dissolution of the Union. Does the accessory-to-murder analogy hold water?

Sir, what protection does this law lend to the poor, weak, oppressed, degraded slave, whose flesh has often quivered under the lash of his inhuman owner? whose youth has been spent in labor for another? whose intellect has been nearly blotted out? When he seeks an asylum in a land of freedom, this worse than barbarous law sends the officers of government to chase him down. The people are constrained to become his pursuers. Famishing, fainting, and benumbed with the cold, he drags his weary limbs forward, while the whole power of the government under the President's command, the army and navy, and all the freemen of the land, organized into a constabulary force, are on his track to drag him back to bondage, under this law. . . .

Sir, there is not a man in this body—there is not an intelligent man in the free states—but knows, if he delivers a fugitive into the custody of his pursuers, that he will be carried to the South and sold to the sugar and cotton plantations. And his life will be sacrificed in five years if employed on the sugar plantations, and in seven years on the cotton plantations. The

1. *Congressional Globe,* 31 Cong., 2 sess., p. 15 (Dec. 9, 1850).

men of the North, who look upon this as murder, would as soon turn out and cut the throats of the defenseless Negro as to send him back to a land of chains and whips. As soon would they do this as comply with a law which violates every principle of common justice and humanity.

The [common] law, sir, holds him who aids in a murder as guilty as he who strikes the knife to the heart of the victim. Under our law, a man is hanged if he fails to prevent a murder when it is plainly in his power to do so. Such man is held guilty of the act, and he is hanged accordingly. The man who should assist in the capture of a fugitive would be regarded by us as guilty as he under whose lash the victim expires.

I have compared this capture of a fugitive to a common murder. In doing that, I do injustice to the common murderer. To capture a slave and send him to the South, to die under a torture of five years, is far more criminal than ordinary murder.

Sir, we will not commit this crime. Let me say to the President, no power of government can compel us to involve ourselves in such guilt. No! The freemen of Ohio will never turn out to chase the panting fugitive—they will never be metamorphosed into bloodhounds, to track him to his hiding-place, and seize and drag him out, and deliver him to his tormentors. Rely upon it, they will die first. They may be shot down, the cannon and bayonet and sword may do their work upon them; they may drown the fugitives in their blood, but never will they stoop to such degradation.

Let no man tell me there is no higher law than this fugitive bill. We feel there is a law of right, of justice, of freedom, implanted in the breast of every intelligent human being, that bids him look with scorn upon this libel upon all that is called law.

2. Rhett Resents a Hoax (1851)

When Northerners began to obstruct the enforcement of the Fugitive Slave Law, the Southerners heatedly cried betrayal. Their only real gain from the Compromise of 1850 had presumably been this trouble-brewing statute. One of the loudest Southern voices was that of the impassioned Senator Robert B. Rhett, who had opposed the compromise measures of 1850 and who had fallen heir to the seat of Senator Calhoun of South Carolina. Sometimes referred to as "the Father of Secession," Rhett resigned from the Senate after two years because his state would not take an extreme position on withdrawal from the Union. Conclude from this Senate speech whether, in the light of American history, he was sound in his view of the relationship of law to public opinion, and whether he was justified in his belief that the Fugitive Slave Law was a deliberate hoax.

Sir, the law is not always a law. . . . A law to have its practical effect must move in harmony with the opinions and feelings of the community where it is to operate. In this case, no one can doubt that the feeling of the whole and entire North—whatever may be their submission to what they may consider to be the supreme law of the land—is opposed to the institution of slavery, and opposed to this law.

Now, you may multiply officers as much as you please; you may make

2. *Ibid.*, Appendix, pp. 317–18 (Feb. 24, 1851).

every ship a prison; you may make every custom-house a guard-room; you may, in all your great central points, make every effort you can for the purpose honestly of enforcing the law; nay, you may have a large majority in all the free states in favor of its enforcement. And yet, if there be a formidable minority that determine upon the defeat of the operation of the law, they can defeat it, and they will defeat it.

The recovery of the fugitive slave is not merely the case of a person coming into court. It is not merely a case in which the law should be enforced by courts. The fugitive slave may be concealed or sworn out of court; a thousand artifices and expedients may be resorted to, by which the slaveholder will be unable to recapture his slave, or the slave, when regained, will be rescued. Although the government may be perfectly honest in its determination to enforce the law, although you may legislate with the utmost rigor, yet, after all, the statutes may be nothing more than so much waste paper, of no use but to deceive those who are willing to be deceived.

As my honorable colleague very correctly said the other day, out of fifteen thousand slaves at the North—and I have seen a statement myself putting the number at thirty thousand—how many have been recaptured? Some fifteen have been taken in eight or nine months; and in every case in which there was any dispute it cost the master more than the worth of the slave.

I know of a case which has been communicated to me very recently. Several gentlemen in Maryland, on the Eastern Shore, knowing that they had fugitive slaves in Philadelphia, agreed that one should go and endeavor to recapture his slave, and, if he succeeded, the rest would endeavor to do so likewise. The gentleman went armed with the proof of the identity of his slave by the presence of several of his neighbors, but when he got to Philadelphia, embarrassments of one kind and another were thrown in his way—false swearing as to the identity of the person was resorted to, and he was defeated. . . .

It is on an examination of these facts that I have come to the conclusion that this law cannot and will not be so enforced as practically to secure the rights of the South. With this conviction, I have looked most carefully into this matter since it arose here in debate. And I have come to the conclusion that, from the beginning of the legislation of Congress on this whole subject to this day, we of the South have been wronged, and have been made to abandon a better and more efficient remedy [secession?], which the Constitution provides.

3. The South Threatens Retaliation (1855)

The Fugitive Slave Act of 1850 prompted a number of Northern states to strengthen their old "personal liberty laws" or enact new ones. Ostensibly these statutes were designed to protect the bona fide free Negro from the ever-present danger of being

3. New Orleans *Bulletin*, July, 1855, in Allan Nevins, ed., *American Press Opinion* (1928), pp. 205–06.

kidnaped and re-enslaved. Actually they operated to hamper or nullify the Fugitive Slave Act. Slaveholders who entered free states risked being sued for false arrest, jailed for kidnaping, or mobbed. Some states denied their jails to slave-catchers. Numerous attempts by Northern mobs to rescue Negro fugitives from the authorities led to riots and some loss of life. In 1854 maddened abolitionists in Boston stormed the courthouse and shot Deputy Marshal Batchelder in a vain attempt to rescue the escaped slave Anthony Burns. In the following New Orleans editorial, determine what merit there is in the argument that the North had consistently violated the Constitution; that retaliation in kind would be justified; and that one section of the nation had already seceded.

Under the Massachusetts "personal liberty law," no open action as yet has taken place. . . . Our people are scattered for the summer, hundreds spending their money in pleasure excursions or purchases in Massachusetts. No, my good friends of Bunker Hill and Lexington (and long may I be permitted to address you as such), there has been as yet no open action. Some of our [social] bees and butterflies have fluttered off among you, but we who are toiling here at home consult together about your "liberty law," and other movements, and I have leave to tell you some things which are more than hinted at, if such laws are to be enforced.

First.—Excluding your ships.

Second.—Excluding your manufactures.

Third.—Ceasing our visits to your borders, already unsafe and more or less unpleasant.

Fourth.—Requiring your citizens trading here at least to take out licenses, perhaps to furnish bond for good behavior.

How will such laws suit you? Of course not at all. They trench on that provision of the Constitution [Art. IV, Sec. II] which declares that the citizens of each state shall be entitled to all the privileges and immunities of citizens in the several states. They certainly do, my conscientious friends, and such laws operate against all other rights the people of the several states have in other states under the Federal Constitution. . . . We know it! But we also know that this is precisely our objection to this "liberty law," which has made all the trouble, and that its unconstitutionality has been pronounced by our highest tribunals.

All your reasoning would have done very well, so long as you held to your bargain—so long as you yourselves submitted to the paramount law, and recognized our rights under its guarantees—so long as Massachusetts held to her obligations and place in the great American family. But now you have repudiated a right of vital importance to us, and passed a law to fine and imprison as felons our citizens who may claim their rights under that Constitution.

Why wait for a formal rupture and separation from you? You have not done so. Our compact is broken by you. There is little obligation on us to respect the rights of your citizens or their property, when you openly trample on ours. There is as little to restrain a [New Orleans] mob from taking possession of one or more of your ships as there was to restrain your

[Boston] mob in the case of the Negro Burns from their assaults on the court and its officers, and from murdering the marshal Batchelder.

D. THE DEBATE OVER THE KANSAS–NEBRASKA BILL

1. Douglas' Popular-Sovereignty Plea (1854)

The Kansas-Nebraska Act of 1854 shattered the uneasy sectional truce. Senator Stephen Arnold Douglas of Illinois—a bouncy, stumpy, real estate booster and transcontinental railroad enthusiast—undertook to organize Nebraska into a territory. Hoping to enlist Southern support, he held out the bait of making Kansas a slave state by the operation of "squatter" or "popular" sovereignty. In short, he would let the people of the territories themselves democratically decide whether they wanted slaves or no slaves. But this meant an outright repeal, by means of the Kansas-Nebraska Act, of the time-hallowed Compromise of 1820—the compromise which had banned slavery in the Louisiana Purchase territory north of 36° 30' (see earlier, p. 219). Whatever his motives, Douglas infuriated Northern abolitionists and free-soilers by driving the Kansas-Nebraska Bill through the Senate with relentless energy. In this portion of his Senate speech, assess the merits of his proposal for laying the slavery issue to rest, and his powers as a prophet.

SENATOR STEPHEN A. DOUGLAS

Douglas' "squatter sovereignty" inspired this caricature of him as a well-armed squatter, 1860.

. . . When the people of the North shall all be rallied under one banner, and the whole South marshaled under another banner, and each section excited to frenzy and madness by hostility to the institutions of the other, then the patriot may well tremble for the perpetuity of the Union. Withdraw the slavery question from the political arena, and remove it to the states and territories, each to decide for itself, such a catastrophe can never happen. Then you will never be able to tell, by any Senator's vote for or against any measure, from what state or section of the Union he comes.

Why, then, can we not withdraw this vexed question from politics? Why can we not adopt the [popular sovereignty] principle of this [Kansas-Nebraska] bill as a rule of action in all new territorial organizations? Why can we not deprive these agitators of their vocation, and render it impossible for Senators to come here upon bargains on the slavery question? I believe that the peace, the harmony, and perpetuity of the Union require us to go back to the doctrines of the Revolution, to the principles of the Constitution, to the principles of the Compromise of 1850, and leave the people, under the

1. *Congressional Globe,* 33 Cong., 1 sess.. Appendix, p. 338.

Constitution, to do as they may see proper in respect to their own internal affairs.

Mr. President, I have not brought this question forward as a Northern man or as a Southern man. I am unwilling to recognize such divisions and distinctions. I have brought it forward as an American Senator, representing a state which is true to this principle, and which has approved of my action in respect to the Nebraska bill. I have brought it forward not as an act of justice to the South more than to the North. I have presented it especially as an act of justice to the people of those territories, and of the states to be formed therefrom, now and in all time to come.

I have nothing to say about Northern rights or Southern rights. I know of no such divisions or distinctions under the Constitution. The bill does equal and exact justice to the whole Union, and every part of it; it violates the rights of no state or territory, but places each on a perfect equality, and leaves the people thereof to the free enjoyment of all their rights under the Constitution. . . .

I say frankly that, in my opinion, this measure will be as popular at the North as at the South, when its provisions and principles shall have been fully developed and become well understood.

2. Chase Upholds Free Soil (1854)

Senator Salmon P. Chase of Ohio—later Lincoln's Secretary of the Treasury, and still later Chief Justice of the Supreme Court—was an ardent free-soiler. So active was he in defense of runaway Negroes that he was dubbed "Attorney General for the fugitive slaves." Pathologically ambitious for the Presidency, he was so handsome as to be "a sculptor's ideal of a President." He vehemently opposed both the Compromise of 1850 and the Kansas-Nebraska Act of 1854. These two measures, notably the second, aroused so much ill feeling between the sections as to make future compromise improbable, and led to the spontaneous formation of the Republican Party. In the light of Chase's remarks, decide whether he was justified in considering the slave power the aggressor, and whether all future compromise was now impossible. Was he a better prophet than Douglas?

Now, sir, who is responsible for this renewal of strife and controversy? Not we [free-soilers], for we have introduced no question of territorial slavery into Congress—not we who are denounced as agitators and factionists. No, sir; the quietists and the finalists have become agitators; they who told us that all agitation was quieted, and that the resolutions of the political conventions put a final period to the discussion of slavery.

This will not escape the observation of the country. It is slavery that renews the strife. It is slavery that again wants room. It is slavery, with its insatiate demands for more slave territory and more slave states.

And what does slavery ask for now? Why, sir, it demands that a time-honored and sacred compact [Missouri Compromise] shall be rescinded—a compact which has endured through a whole generation—a compact which has been universally regarded as inviolable, North and South—a compact

2. *Ibid.*, pp. 134, 140.

the constitutionality of which few have doubted, and by which all have consented to abide. . . .

You may pass it here. You may send it to the other House. It may become law. But its effect will be to satisfy all thinking men that no compromises with slavery will endure, except so long as they serve the interests of slavery; and that there is no safe and honorable ground for non-slaveholders to stand upon, except that of restricting slavery within state limits, and excluding it absolutely from the whole sphere of federal jurisdiction.

The old questions between political parties are at rest. No great question so thoroughly possesses the public mind as this of slavery. This discussion will hasten the inevitable reorganization of parties upon the new issues which our circumstances suggest. It will light up a fire in the country which may, perhaps, consume those who kindle it.

I cannot believe that the people of this country have so far lost sight of the maxims and principles of the Revolution, or are so insensible to the obligations which those maxims and principles impose, as to acquiesce in the violation of this compact. Sir, the Senator from Illinois [Douglas] tells us that he proposes a final settlement of all territorial questions in respect to slavery, by the application of the principle of popular sovereignty. What kind of popular sovereignty is that which allows one portion of the people to enslave another portion? Is that the doctrine of equal rights? Is that exact justice? Is that the teaching of enlightened, liberal, progressive democracy?

No, sir; no! There can be no real democracy which does not fully maintain the rights of man, as man.

3. Northwestern Support for Douglas (1854)

Critics have frequently maintained that the whole controversy over slavery in the territories rang hollow. It concerned a non-existent slave in an area where he could not exist—thanks to geography and climate. The ideal of popular sovereignty received some support in Douglas's own Northwest, as indicated by this editorial in the Detroit *Free Press*. Note the evidence that slavery would not go into the territories; also why the Northwest in particular should favor popular sovereignty.

Slavery, in this country, is the creature of statutory law. It exists, and can exist, nowhere except by positive enactment. It cannot go to Nebraska, or Kansas, or any other new territory, until it is established by the legislative power.

Now, is there a man in the whole country who supposes that the legislatures of either the territories of Nebraska or Kansas will legalize slavery? Under Mr. Douglas's bill, as it passed the Senate, those legislatures will have the sole and unlimited control of the subject. Is there the most distant probability that they will exercise that control in favor of slavery? Have

3. Detroit *Free Press,* March 16, 1854, in *Daily National Intelligencer* (Washington), March 21, 1854.

Utah and New Mexico, both further south than Nebraska, so exercised it? Did California, over which no restriction existed, so exercise it? In Utah and New Mexico, although they have been four years organized, no slavery has been established, or attempted to be established. In California, the convention which formed her state constitution voted unanimously for a slavery-prohibition clause.

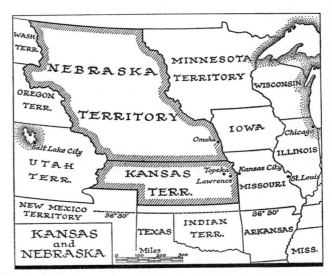

Mr. Douglas's bill is the greatest advance movement in the direction of human freedom that has been made since the adoption of the Constitution. Never before has the right of all American communities to self-government been fully recognized. The people of the territories have hitherto been held to a species of vassalage not less humiliating to them than it was inconsistent with popular rights. They have not been permitted to make their own laws or to manage their own domestic concerns. They have been treated as minors, incompetent to take care of themselves. Mr. Douglas's bill changes all this. The territories have the same privileges in respect to domestic legislation as the states, and their citizens are recognized as American freemen.

Ought not this bill to receive universal commendation? We believe it ought. And it would, were it not for the delusion that prevails in the minds of some, encouraged and excited by Whig and abolition demagogues, that there is danger of slavery extension.

4. The South Is Lukewarm (1854)

The anti-slavery North, as might have been expected, reacted violently against the gain for slavery (on paper) under the Kansas-Nebraska Act. Ominously, most of the opposition came not from wild-eyed abolitionists but from sober men who had reluctantly accepted the Compromise of 1850 but had now lost all confidence in the good faith of the South. "The day of compromise is over," warned the Hartford *Connecticut Courant.* Horace Greeley, editor of the potent New York *Tribune,* declared that Douglas and his co-conspirators had "made more abolitionists than

4. *Western Citizen* (Kentucky), April 21, 1854, in *Daily National Intelligencer* (Washington), April 24, 1854.

Garrison and Phillips could have made in half a century." Even the South, though on the whole mildly favorable, had its misgivings. The Columbia *South Carolinian* conceded that "practically" the Kansas-Nebraska Act would "scarcely ever benefit the South," but it would "render justice to the South" and serve as a "triumph" over abolitionism. A more realistic view was taken by an editorial in the slaveholding state of Kentucky. Observe why the editor, with uncanny insight, regards the Kansas-Nebraska Act as a thing of unmitigated evil.

The Nebraska Bill is advocated and denounced upon grounds the most opposite and for reasons the most diverse. There is the greatest contrariety of opinion as to what effect its passage will have upon the question of slavery. Southern men, of course, support it upon the ground that it will give slavery a chance to get into the territory from which it has hitherto been excluded; whilst others, with quite as much show of reason, take the ground occupied by the President, that the effect will be to prevent the admission of slave states into the Union forever.

A measure whose effects, in matters of so much consequence, are so uncertain; which proposes to violate and disannul a compact [Missouri Compromise] regarded by one section of our common country as sacred, and acquiesced in for a third of a century by the other—a compact the advantages of which the South has fully received on her part—should at least promise some decided practical good as the result of its passage, and should be chargeable with the production of as few evils as possible.

We believe that the adoption of the measure will be productive of evil, and only evil, continually. Even supposing that the Missouri Compromise is not a bargain that we of the slave states are bound to respect and stand to, and that we may declare it void without a breach of faith, what do we gain by its repeal? What but a revival, in a wilder and intenser and more dangerous form, of that agitation of the slavery question which was but yesterday allayed by the all but superhuman efforts of our noblest statesmen [in the Compromise of 1850]? The North regards the Missouri Compromise as a sacred compact, to the preservation of which the honor and faith of the South was pledged. If we now violate that pledge, what right have we to expect the North to respect any compromise that has been or may be made for our advantage? . . .

And what should we gain? A mere right to carry slaves into Nebraska, which we can never exercise; the mere gratification of having an old law [Missouri Compromise] repealed which the South now chooses to consider unjust to her, but which her wisest statesmen at the time of its passage regarded as highly advantageous to her—a law carried by Southern votes, and heretofore looked upon as one of the noblest achievements of Southern statesmanship.

THOUGHT PROVOKERS

1. If the Wilmot Proviso issue had not come up during the Mexican War, is it probable that the question of slavery in the territories would have been raised in an acute form?

2. It has been said that by the 1850's each side distrusted the other so greatly that disunion was inevitable: the North because of Southern grasping for more slave territory; the South because of Northern nullification of the Constitution and federal laws. Comment critically. Webster in 1850 was condemned as an appeaser or compromiser and hence not a statesman. Can a real statesman avoid all compromise?

3. Are a people ever justified in openly violating laws (like the Fugitive Slave Act) that they disapprove of and think immoral? What has been the fate of such laws in American history? Should the majority always rule?

4. Was it "immoral," as abolitionists alleged, for Congress to repeal the Missouri Compromise line of 1820? Why was further compromise between North and South impossible after 1854? Was the North or the South the "aggressor" in the 1850's with regard to the slavery issue? Which side was constitutionally right?

FURTHER EXPLORATION

General: Allan Nevins, *Ordeal of the Union* (2 vols., 1947); Avery Craven, *The Coming of the Civil War* (1957). **Wilmot Proviso:** C. B. Going, *David Wilmot, Free Soiler* (1924). **Compromise of 1850:** C. M. Fuess, *Daniel Webster* (2 vols., 1930). **Fugitive Slaves:** Louis Filler, *The Crusade against Slavery, 1830–1860* (1960); D. L. Dumond, *Anti-Slavery Origins of the Civil War* (1939); William Breyfogle, *Make Free: The Story of the Underground Railroad* (1958). **Kansas-Nebraska Act:** G. F. Milton, *The Eve of Conflict* (1934); P. O. Ray, *Repeal of the Missouri Compromise* (1909); R. F. Nichols, "The Kansas-Nebraska Act: A Century of Historiography," *Mississippi Valley Historical Review,* XLIII (1956), 187–212.

Recent: R. F. Nichols, *The Stakes of Power, 1845–1877* (1961) [paperback]; Holman Hamilton, *Prologue to Conflict; The Crisis and Compromise of 1850* (1964) [paperback].

Chapter 21

The Eve of Civil Conflict, 1854-1861

It is an irrepressible conflict between opposing and enduring forces.

WILLIAM H. SEWARD, 1858

PROLOGUE: Popular sovereignty in Kansas degenerated into unpopular savagery. Embattled free-soilers fought embittered pro-slaveryites, as the complaisant pro-Southern administrations of Presidents Pierce and Buchanan continued to drift. Irate Northerners, resenting the Kansas-Nebraska grab, increasingly turned the Fugitive Slave Act into a dead letter. At the same time the newly born Republican Party, sired by the same Kansas-Nebraska Act, gathered such amazing momentum in the North as to give the Democrats a real scare in the presidential election of 1856. The sectional tension was heightened by a series of inflammatory incidents, including Representative Brooks' brutal beating of Senator Sumner, the pro-slavery Dred Scott decision, and John Brown's fantastic raid at Harpers Ferry. Southerners also reacted angrily against the overwhelming approval in the North of such anti-slavery propaganda as *Uncle Tom's Cabin* and Helper's *Impending Crisis of the South* (see earlier, p. 369). And the imminent election of the Republican Lincoln in 1860 foreshadowed both secession and shooting.

A. THE IMPACT OF *UNCLE TOM'S CABIN*

1. Tom Defies Simon Legree (1852)

Mrs. Harriet Beecher Stowe, a busy mother and housewife then living in Maine, was aroused by the recent gains of slavery to write—partly on old wrapping paper— her heart-tugging novel *Uncle Tom's Cabin*. Reared in New England as the daughter of a Congregational preacher, and having lived for seventeen years in Ohio on the route of the Underground Railroad, she had developed an abhorrence of "the patriarchal institution." Oddly enough, her first-hand observations of slavery were limited to a brief visit to Kentucky. In her best-selling book she sought to mollify the South to some extent by representing the saintly slave Uncle Tom as having two kind masters; by featuring the whimsical Topsy and the angelic little Eva (who died); and by portraying the monster Simon Legree, who finally ordered Uncle Tom beaten to death, as a Yankee from Vermont. In the following scene, the cotton-picking slaves have just returned from the fields, and Legree orders Tom to flog one of the sickly women for not having picked enough. Decide what details of this episode would most offend the anti-slavery North; the pro-slavery South.

"And now," said Legree, "come here, you Tom. You see, I told ye I didn't buy ye jest for the common work. I mean to promote ye, and make a driver of ye; and tonight ye may jest as well begin to get yer hand in. Now, ye jest take this yer gal and flog her; ye've seen enough on't [of it] to know how."

1. Harriet B. Stowe, *Uncle Tom's Cabin*, Ch. 33.

"I beg Mas'r's pardon," said Tom; "hopes Mas'r won't set me at that. It's what I an't used to—never did—and can't do, no way possible."

"Ye'll larn a pretty smart chance of things ye never did know, before I've done with ye!" said Legree, taking up a cowhide and striking Tom a heavy blow across the cheek, and following up the infliction by a showei of blows.

"There!" he said, as he stopped to rest; "now, will ye tell me ye can't do it?"

"Yes, Mas'r," said Tom, putting up his hand, to wipe the blood that trickled down his face. "I'm willin' to work, night and day, and work while there's life and breath in me. But this yer thing I can't feel it right to do; and, Mas'r, I *never* shall do it—*never!*"

Tom had a remarkably smooth, soft voice, and a habitually respectful manner that had given Legree an idea that he would be cowardly and easily subdued. When he spoke these last words, a thrill of amazement went through everyone. The poor woman clasped her hands and said, "O Lord!" and everyone involuntarily looked at each other and drew in their breath, as if to prepare for the storm that was about to burst.

Legree looked stupefied and confounded; but at last burst forth:

"What! ye blasted black beast! tell *me* ye don't think it *right* to do what I tell ye! What have any of you cussed cattle to do with thinking what's right? I'll put a stop to it! Why, what do ye think ye are? May be ye think ye're a gentleman, master Tom, to be a telling your master what's right, and what an't! So you pretend it's wrong to flog the gal!"

"I think so, Mas'r," said Tom; "the poor crittur's sick and feeble; 'twould be downright cruel, and it's what I never will do, nor begin to. Mas'r, if you mean to kill me, kill me; but, as to my raising my hand agin any one here, I never shall—I'll die first!"

Tom spoke in a mild voice, but with a decision that could not be mistaken. Legree shook with anger; his greenish eyes glared fiercely, and his very whiskers seemed to curl with passion. But, like some ferocious beast, that plays with its victim before he devours it, he kept back his strong impulse to proceed to immediate violence, and broke out into bitter raillery.

"Well, here's a pious dog, at last, let down among us sinners!—a saint, a gentleman, and no less, to talk to us sinners about our sins! Powerful holy crittur, he must be! Here, you rascal, you make believe to be so pious—didn't you never hear, out of yer Bible, 'Servants, obey yer masters'? An't I yer master? Didn't I pay down twelve hundred dollars, cash, for all there is inside yer old cussed black shell? An't yer mine, now, body and soul?" he said, giving Tom a violent kick with his heavy boot; "tell me!"

In the very depth of physical suffering, bowed by brutal oppression, this question shot a gleam of joy and triumph through Tom's soul. He suddenly stretched himself up, and, looking earnestly to heaven, while the tears and blood that flowed down his face mingled, he exclaimed,

"No! no! no! my soul an't yours, Mas'r! You haven't bought it—ye can't

UNCLE TOM'S CABIN: FIRST ILLUSTRATED EDITION, 1853
Uncle Tom, sold to a slave trader, sadly takes leave of his wife (Aunt Chloe) and their children.

buy it! It's been bought and paid for by One that is able to keep it. No matter, no matter, you can't harm me!"

"I can't!" said Legree, with a sneer; "we'll see—we'll see! Here, Sambo, Quimbo, give this dog such a breakin' in as he won't get over this month!"

The two gigantic Negroes that now laid hold of Tom, with fiendish exultation in their faces, might have formed no unapt personification of powers of darkness. The poor woman screamed with apprehension, and all rose, as by a general impulse, while they dragged him unresisting from the place.

2. The South Scorns Mrs. Stowe (1852)

Northern abolitionists naturally applauded Mrs. Stowe's powerful tale; the poet Whittier now thanked God for the Fugitive Slave Act which had inspired the book. The few Northern journals that voiced criticism were drowned out by the clatter of the printing presses running off tens of thousands of new copies. Southern critics cried that this "wild and unreal picture" would merely arouse the "fanaticism" of the North while exciting the "indignation" of the South. They insisted that the slave beatings were libelously overstressed; that the worst slave-drivers were imported Northerners (like Legree); that the Southern Negro slave was better off than the Northern wage slave; and that relatively few families were broken up, fewer in fact than among soldiers on duty, Irish immigrants coming to America, sailors going to sea, and pioneers venturing West. Note why the *Southern Literary Messenger* of Richmond found it important to refute Mrs. Stowe's "slanders" as follows.

There are some who will think we have taken upon ourselves an unnecessary trouble in exposing the inconsistencies and false assertions of *Uncle*

2. *Southern Literary Messenger*, XVIII (1852). 638. 731.

Tom's Cabin. It is urged by such persons that in devoting so much attention to abolition attacks we give them an importance to which they are not entitled. This may be true in general. But let it be borne in mind that this slanderous work has found its way to every section of our country, and has crossed the water to Great Britain, filling the minds of all who know nothing of slavery with hatred for that institution and those who uphold it. Justice to ourselves would seem to demand that it should not be suffered to circulate longer without the brand of falsehood upon it.

Let it be recollected, too, that the importance Mrs. Stowe will derive from Southern criticism will be one of infamy. Indeed ⌐he is only entitled to criticism at all as the mouthpiece of a large and dangerous faction which, if we do not put down with the pen, we may be compelled one day (God grant that day may never come!) to repel with the bayonet.

There are questions that underlie the story of *Uncle Tom's Cabin* of far deeper significance than any mere false coloring of Southern society. . . . We beg to make a single suggestion to Mrs. Stowe—that, as she is fond of referring to the Bible, she will turn over, before writing her next work of fiction, to the twentieth chapter of Exodus and there read these words—"Thou shalt not bear false witness against thy neighbor." . . .

We have not had the heart to speak of an erring woman as she deserved, though her misconduct admitted of no excuse and provoked the keenest and most just

HAPPY UNCLE TOM

Pro-slavery illustration in the reply to *Uncle Tom's Cabin*, W. L. G. Smith, *Life at the South: or "Uncle Tom's Cabin" As It Is,* 1852.

reprobation. We have little inclination—and, if we had much, we have not the time—to proceed with our disgusting labor, to anatomize minutely volumes as full of poisonous vermin as of putrescence, and to speak in such language as the occasion would justify, though it might be forbidden by decorum and self-respect.

We dismiss *Uncle Tom's Cabin* with the conviction and declaration that every holier purpose of our nature is misguided, every charitable sympathy betrayed, every loftier sentiment polluted, every moral purpose wrenched to wrong, and every patriotic feeling outraged, by its criminal prostitution of the high functions of the imagination to the pernicious intrigues of sectional animosity, and to the petty calumnies of willful slander.

3. The London *Times* Demurs (1852)

Uncle Tom's Cabin was also a sensational success abroad. Some Russian noblemen were prompted by it to free their serfs. Lord Palmerston, who had not read a novel in thirty years, devoured this one three times. But the lordly London *Times*, reputedly the semi-official mouthpiece of the government, was one of the few important journals in England to express strong reservations. From this portion of the lengthy review in the *Times* assess the soundness of the argument that the book was self-defeating, in that, far from promoting, it would hinder the peaceful abolition of slavery.

The gravest fault of the book has, however, to be mentioned. Its object is to abolish slavery. Its effect will be to render slavery more difficult than ever of abolishment. Its very popularity constitutes its greatest difficulty. It will keep ill-blood at boiling point, and irritate instead of pacifying those whose proceedings Mrs. Stowe is anxious to influence on behalf of humanity.

Uncle Tom's Cabin was not required to convince the haters of slavery of the abomination of the "institution"; of all books, it is the least calculated to weigh with those whose prejudices in favour of slavery have yet to be overcome, and whose interests are involved in the perpetuation of the system. If slavery is to cease in America, and if the people of the United States, who fought and bled for their liberty and nobly won it, are to remove the disgrace that attaches to them for forging chains for others which they will not tolerate on their own limbs, the work of enfranchisement must be a movement, not forced upon slaveowners, but voluntarily undertaken, accepted, and carried out by the whole community.

There is no federal law which can compel the slave states to resign the "property" which they hold. The states of the South are as free to maintain slavery as are the states of the North to rid themselves of the scandal. Let the attempt be made imperiously and violently to dictate to the South, and from that hour the Union is at an end.

We are aware that to the mind of the "philanthropist" the alternative brings no alarm, but to the rational thinkers, to the statesman, and to all men interested in the world's programs, the disruption of the bond that holds the American states together is fraught with calamity, with which the present evil of slavery—a system destined sooner or later to fall to pieces under the weight of public opinion and its own infamy—bears no sensible comparison.

The writer of *Uncle Tom's Cabin* and similar well-disposed authors have yet to learn that to excite the passions of their readers in favour of their philanthropic schemes is the very worst mode of getting rid of a difficulty which, whoever may be to blame for its existence, is part and parcel of the whole social organization of a large proportion of the states, and cannot be forcibly removed without instant anarchy, and all its accompanying mischief.

3. London *Times*, Sept. 3, 1852.

B. BLEEDING KANSAS AND "BULLY" BROOKS

1. Sumner Assails the Slavocracy (1856)

The erasing of the Missouri Compromise line in 1854 touched off a frantic tug-of-war between South and North to make Kansas either a slave or a free state. "Border ruffians," pouring into Kansas from slaveholding Missouri by the hundreds, set up a fraudulent but legal government. Resolute pioneers from the North, some of them assisted by the New England Emigrant Aid Company, countered by founding Lawrence, by setting up an extra-legal free-soil government, and by seeking admission as a free state. Aroused by the resulting civil war, Senator Charles Sumner of Massachusetts —a handsome, egotistical, and violently outspoken abolitionist—assailed the slavery men in a savage two-day speech ("The Crime against Kansas"). He singled out the slaveholding state of South Carolina, and in particular her well-liked Senator Butler, who, declared Sumner, had taken as his "mistress" "the harlot, slavery." Note the aspects of the speech that would be most offensive to a South Carolina gentleman.

If the slave states cannot enjoy what, in mockery of the great Fathers of the Republic, he [Butler] misnames equality under the Constitution— in other words, the full power in the national territories to compel fellow men to unpaid toil, to separate husband and wife, and to sell little children at the auction block—then, sir, the chivalric Senator will conduct the state of South Carolina out of the Union! Heroic knight! Exalted Senator! A second Moses come for a second exodus!

But not content with this poor menace . . . the Senator, in the unrestrained chivalry of his nature, has undertaken to apply opprobrious words to those who differ from him on this floor. He calls them "sectional and fanatical"; and opposition to the usurpation in Kansas he denounces as "an uncalculating fanaticism." To be sure, these charges lack all grace of originality, and all sentiment of truth; but the adventurous Senator does not hesitate. He is the uncompromising, unblushing representative on this floor of a flagrant sectionalism, which now domineers over the Republic. . . .

With regret, I come again upon the Senator from South Carolina [Butler], who, omnipresent in this debate, overflowed with rage at the simple suggestion that Kansas had applied for admission as a state; and, with incoherent phrases, discharged the loose expectoration of his speech,* now upon her representative, and then upon her people. There was no extravagance of the ancient parliamentary debate which he did not repeat. Nor was there any possible deviation from truth which he did not make, with so much of passion, I am glad to add, as to save him from the suspicion of intentional aberration.

But the Senator touches nothing which he does not disfigure—with error, sometimes of principle, sometimes of fact. He shows an incapacity of accuracy, whether in stating the Constitution or in stating the law, whether in the details of statistics or the diversions of scholarship. He cannot ope his mouth but out there flies a blunder. . . .

1. *Congressional Globe,* 34 Cong., 1 sess., Appendix, pp. 530, 543 (May 19–20, 1856).
* Butler suffered from a slight paralysis of the mouth.

[*Sumner next attacks South Carolina, with her "shameful imbecility" of slavery, for presuming to sit in judgment over free-soil Kansas and block her admission as a free state.*]

South Carolina is old; Kansas is young. South Carolina counts by centuries; where Kansas counts by years. But a beneficent example may be born in a day; and I venture to say that against the two centuries of the older state may be already set the two years of trial, evolving corresponding virtue, in the younger community. In the one is the long wail of Slavery; in the other, the hymns of Freedom. And if we glance at special achievements, it will be difficult to find anything in the history of South Carolina which presents so much of heroic spirit in an heroic cause as appears in that repulse of the Missouri invaders by the beleaguered town of Lawrence, where even the women gave their efforts to Freedom. . . .

Were the whole history of South Carolina blotted out of existence, from its very beginning down to the day of the last election of the Senator to his present seat on this floor, civilization might lose—I do not say how little; but surely less than it has already gained by the example of Kansas, in its valiant struggle against oppression, and in the development of a new science of emigration. Already in Lawrence alone there are newspapers and schools, including a high school, and throughout this infant territory there is more mature scholarship far, in proportion to its inhabitants, than in all South Carolina. Ah, sir, I tell the Senator that Kansas, welcomed as a free state, will be a "ministering angel" to the Republic when South Carolina, in the cloak of darkness which she hugs, "lies howling."

2. The South Justifies Yankee-Beaters (1856)

Southern fire-eaters had already used abusive language in Congress, but Sumner's epithets infuriated Representative Brooks of South Carolina. Resenting the insults to his state and to his cousin (Senator Butler), he entered the Senate chamber and broke a heavy cane over the head of Sumner, then sitting at his desk. The Senator fell bleeding to the floor, while several other members of Congress, perhaps thinking that he was getting his just deserts, made no effort to rescue him. His nervous system shattered, Sumner was incapacitated for about three years; Brooks resigned his seat and was unanimously re-elected. A resolution passed by the citizens of his district applauded his exhibition of "the true spirit of Southern chivalry and patriotism" in "chastising, coolly and deliberately, the vile and lawless Sumner." The same group sent him a new cane inscribed "Use knock-down arguments." From the following editorial in an Alabama newspaper form conclusions as to the general attitude of the South and what it portended for the Union.

There are but two papers in the state that we have seen that denounce the chastisement of Sumner by Mr. Brooks as a shameful outrage. One of them is the *Mobile Tribune,* one of the editors of which is a Yankee, and the other is a sheet, the name of which we shall not mention.

With the exception of the papers alluded to, the press of the entire state have fully approved of the course Mr. Brooks pursued, under the circum-

2. Autauga (Alabama) *Citizen,* in *The Liberator* (Boston), July 4, 1856.

stances, and recommend that other Southern members of Congress adopt the same method of silencing the foul-mouthed abolition emissaries of the North. Indeed, it is quite apparent, from recent developments, that the shillalah [club] is the best argument to be applied to such low-bred mongrels.

More than six years ago, the abolitionists were told that if they intended to carry out their principles, they must fight. When the Emigrant Aid Societies began to send their [Yankee] tools to Kansas, they were told that if their object was to establish a colony of thieves under the name of "Free State Men," on the border of Missouri, for the purpose of keeping out Southerners and destroying slavery, they must fight. And let them understand that if they intend to carry their abolitionism into Congress, and pour forth their disgusting obscenity and abuse of the South in the Senate Chamber, and force their doctrines down the throats of Southerners, they must fight.

Let [editor Horace] Greeley be severely cowhided, and he will cease to publish his blackguardism about Southern men. Let [Senators] Wilson and Sumner and Seward, and the whole host of abolition agitators in Congress, be chastised to their heart's content, and, our word for it, they will cease to heap abuse upon our citizens.

We repeat, let our Representative in Congress use the cowhide and hickory stick (and, if need be, the bowie knife and revolver) more frequently, and we'll bet our old hat that it will soon come to pass that Southern institutions and Southern men will be respected.

3. Northerners Denounce Ruffianism (1856)

Northern members of Congress condemned "Bully" Brooks in such violent language that the hot-tempered Carolinian challenged at least two of them to duels. Senator Henry Wilson, Sumner's Massachusetts colleague, who had branded the attack as "brutal, murderous, and cowardly," flatly refused to meet the Honorable Preston Brooks on the "field of honor." The New York *Times*, referring to the well-armed pro-slavery "border ruffians" then pouring into Kansas from Missouri, here calls for stern measures. Determine how reasonable its fears are regarding the long-run effects of the assault, and what it foreshadows regarding further relations with the South.

It is disgraceful enough that any man living in a civilized community . . . should resort to the club as a mode of expressing a difference of opinion or of resenting an impeachment of political character. But that an assault of this kind should be made upon a man known to be unarmed, and under circumstances which rendered it impossible for him to make any resistance whatever, could not have been anticipated from any but the basest and most brutalized of the race. A New York dog-killer has notions of honor that would make it impossible for him to commit such an outrage.

It has been reserved for Preston S. Brooks, of South Carolina—member of Congress from a state which prides herself upon the chivalry of her sons

3. New York *Times*, May 24, 1856.

—to perpetrate the act. And it is stated in our dispatches from Washington that "his colleagues and the majority of the Southern men *justify*" him in it.

If this be so, it indicates a state of feeling at the Capitol which cannot be contemplated without horror and alarm. It shows that the Border Ruffian has become the type and the exemplar of a large portion of the lawmakers of the Republic; that the revolver, the club, and the bowie knife are to be the weapons by which the champions of slavery propose hereafter to silence their opponents; that assassination is to be employed, not only by private ruffians as a means of redressing private wrongs but by representatives of the slaveholding class as a mode of advancing their peculiar views and establishing their own ascendancy. It affords another and a very strong proof of the domineering insolence of the slaveholding interest . . . that it will stop at no extremity of violence in order to subdue the people of the Free States and force them into a tame subserviency to its own domination.

The success of Ruffianism in Kansas has emboldened the champions of slavery to introduce it at the federal capital; and everything indicates a purpose on their part to resort to force when argument fails.

What will be the result of such a policy remains to be seen. That men from the Free States will be cowed and conquered by it is very probable, unless it is met and resisted. If Southern members are to use the bludgeon and the pistol with impunity, and if their victims are to submit without resistance to all this brutality, as a matter of course, Northern men will avoid making issues or taking positions which involve the danger of such assaults. . . .

Both the Senate and the House of Representatives, as parliamentary bodies, seem utterly insensible to all considerations of their own dignity and self-respect. Unless some reform can be introduced in this particular . . . there is but this alternative: Northern men must suit their conduct to the company they are compelled to keep, and meet the pro-slavery bullies with their own weapons and upon their own ground, or they must continue to be the victims of their insolence and brutality.

C. THE DRED SCOTT DECISION

1. The Pro-Southern Court Speaks (1857)

Dred Scott, an illiterate Missouri slave, was taken by his master for several years (1834–1838) to the free state of Illinois and then to a portion of Wisconsin Territory now located in the state of Minnesota. The Minnesota area was then free territory, since it lay north of the line of 36° 30′ established by the Missouri Compromise of 1820, subsequently repealed in 1854. Scott, taken in hand by interested abolitionists, sued for his freedom on the grounds of residence on free soil. The case was appealed from the Circuit Court to the Supreme Court, which grappled with several basic

1. 19 Howard 393 (pp. 451–52, 454).

questions. Among them were these: Was a slave a citizen under the Constitution? (If not, he was not entitled to sue in the federal courts.) Was Dred Scott rendered free by residence in Minnesota, under the terms of the Missouri Compromise? The Court, headed by the pro-Southern Chief Justice Taney of the slaveholding state of Maryland, ruled as follows. Note how the basic questions were answered, and what their implications were for the future.

Now . . . the right of property in a slave is distinctly and expressly affirmed in the Constitution. The right to traffic in it, like an ordinary article of merchandise and property, was guaranteed to the citizens of the United States, in every state that might desire it, for twenty years. And the government in express terms is pledged to protect it in all future time, if the slave escapes from his owner. This is done in plain words—too plain to be misunderstood. And no word can be found in the Constitution which gives Congress a greater power over slave property, or which entitles property of that kind to less protection, than property of any other description. The only power conferred is the power coupled with the duty of guarding and protecting the owner in his rights.

Upon these considerations, it is the opinion of the Court that the Act of Congress [Missouri Compromise] which prohibited a citizen from holding and owning property of this kind in the territory of the United States north of the line [of 36° 30′] therein mentioned is not warranted by the Constitution, and is therefore void; and that neither Dred Scott himself, nor any of his family, were made free by being carried into this territory; even if they had been carried there by the owner with the intention of becoming a permanent resident. . . .

Upon the whole, therefore, it is the judgment of this Court that it appears by the record before us that the plaintiff in error [Dred Scott] is not a citizen of Missouri, in the sense in which that word is used in the Constitution; and that the Circuit Court of the United States for that reason had no jurisdiction in the case, and could give no judgment in it.

2. A Virginia Newspaper Gloats (1857)

The South was overjoyed at the Dred Scott decision. The sanctity of slave property was ringingly reaffirmed. The slave could be taken with impunity into the territories and perhaps also into the free states. Even if the territory of Kansas should vote slavery down under popular sovereignty, the slaveowner could still keep his slave. Also pleasing to the South was Chief Justice Taney's observation that *in 1776 the Negroes were "so far inferior that they had no rights which the white man was bound to respect. . . ."* This dictum, torn out of context and applied to the present, enraged the abolitionists. Decide what the following editorial in a Virginia newspaper portended for an amicable solution of the slave-race problem.

The highest judicial tribunal in the land has decided that the blackamoors, called by the extreme of public courtesy the colored population, are not citizens of the United States. This decision must be followed by other

2. Southside (Virginia) *Democrat*, in *The Liberator* (Boston), April 3, 1857.

decisions and regulations in the individual states themselves. Negro suffrage must, of course, be abolished everywhere.

Negro nuisances, in the shape of occupying promiscuous seats in our rail-cars and churches with those who are citizens, must be abated. Negro insolence and domineering arrogance must be rebuked; the whole tribe must be taught to fall back into their legitimate position in human society—the position that Divine Providence intended they should occupy. Not being citizens, they can claim none of the rights or privileges belonging to a citizen. They can neither vote, hold office, nor occupy any other position in society than an inferior and subordinate one—the only one for which they are fitted, the only one for which they have the natural qualifications which entitle them to enjoy or possess.

3. The North Breathes Defiance (1857)

The anti-slavery North was shocked by the Dred Scott decision. If slavery could not be barred from the territories, then the constitutional basis of popular sovereignty was in doubt, and the unpopular Kansas-Nebraska Act of 1854 was a gigantic hoax. Especially galling was the presence of several slaveholders on the Supreme Bench. Various Northern spokesmen denounced the decision as no more binding than that of a Southern debating society. Horace Greeley, editor of the influential New York *Tribune*, insisted that the Court's finding had no more "moral weight" than the judgment of "a Washington barroom." The rising politician Abraham Lincoln, referring to the "apparent partisan bias" and the numerous dissenting opinions of the Court, branded the decision "erroneous." From the following reaction in a Boston religious journal, judge whether the South was justified in feeling that the North was determined to break up the Union.

Shall this decision be submitted to? It need not be. A most righteous decision of the Supreme Court (as we believe), regarding the rights of the Cherokee nation, was made of none effect by the state of Georgia, with the connivance of President Jackson.

The people are mightier than courts or Presidents. The acts of Congress, though declared void, are not repealed. The acts of the free states, though pronounced invalid, still exist. If the people will, they can be maintained and enforced.

Is it said that this is revolutionary counsel? We answer, it is the Southern judges of the Supreme Court who are the authors of revolution. They have enacted a principle contrary to the most plain and obvious sense of the Constitution they pretend to interpret. . . . The most explicit allusion to slaves, in that instrument, describes them as held to service in the states "under the laws thereof," plainly deriving the rights of the master from local, not from common law.

The decision is also opposed to the unanimous judgment of the statesmen and jurists by whom the Constitution was formed, and to the amplest recorded testimony as to their intentions. It is a doctrine not twenty years old, which those judges, conspiring with the most desperate school of

3. *Christian Watchman and Reflector* (Boston), in *The Liberator* (Boston), March 27, 1857.

THE DIS-UNITED STATES—A BLACK BUSINESS
Slavery pulls U. S. apart. *Punch* (London), 1856.

Southern politicians, the men who have been for the space of a generation plotting against the Union, have dared to foist upon the Constitution. It is a sacrilege, against which the blood of our fathers cries from the ground. No man who has in his veins a drop kindred to the blood that bought our liberties can actively submit to their decree.

But if the free states will sit down in the dust, without an effort to vindicate their sovereign rights, if the majority of the people are so fallen away from the spirit of their fathers as to yield their birthright without a struggle, then it becomes the solemn duty of every conscientious freeman to regard the Union of these states as stripped henceforth of all title to his willing allegiance. If the Constitution is a charter to protect slavery, everywhere, then it is a sin against God and man to swear allegiance to it. Every man will be forced to choose between disunion and the guilt of an accomplice in the crime of slavery. May God avert such an alternative!

D. THE LINCOLN–DOUGLAS DEBATES

1. Douglas Opposes Negro Citizenship (1858)

With the Illinois Senatorship at stake, "Honest Abe" Lincoln boldly challenged Senator Douglas—the "Little Giant"—to a series of joint debates, presumably on current issues. He lost the ensuing election but placed his feet squarely on the path to the White House. The first forensic encounter occurred at Ottawa, Illinois, where

1. R. P. Basler, ed., *The Collected Works of Abraham Lincoln* (1953), III, 9–11.

the gladiators exchanged the following verbal blows before some 12,000 partisans. In examining Douglas' remarks on this occasion, determine wherein he both pleases and offends the South, and whether he is more anti-Negro than pro-slavery.

We are told by Lincoln that he is utterly opposed to the Dred Scott decision, and will not submit to it, for the reason that he says it deprives the Negro of the rights and privileges of citizenship. (Laughter and applause.) That is the first and main reason which he assigns for his warfare on the Supreme Court of the United States and its decision.

I ask you, are you in favor of conferring upon the Negro the rights and privileges of citizenship? ("No, no.") Do you desire to strike out of our state constitution that clause which keeps slaves and free Negroes out of the state, and allow the free Negroes to flow in ("Never.") and cover your prairies with black settlements? Do you desire to turn this beautiful state into a free Negro colony ("No, no.") in order that when Missouri abolishes slavery she can send one hundred thousand emancipated slaves into Illinois, to become citizens and voters, on an equality with yourselves? ("Never," "No.")

If you desire Negro citizenship, if you desire to allow them to come into the state and settle with the white man, if you desire them to vote on an equality with yourselves, and to make them eligible to office, to serve on juries, and to adjudge your rights, then support Mr. Lincoln and the Black [pro-Negro] Republican Party, who are in favor of the citizenship of the Negro. ("Never, never.")

For one, I am opposed to Negro citizenship in any and every form. (Cheers.) I believe this government was made on the white basis. ("Good.") I believe it was made by white men for the benefit of white men and their posterity for ever, and I am in favor of confining citizenship to white men, men of European birth and descent, instead of conferring it upon Negroes, Indians, and other inferior races. ("Good for you," "Douglas forever.")

Mr. Lincoln, following the example and lead of all the little abolition orators who go around and lecture in the basements of schools and churches, reads from the Declaration of Independence that all men were created equal, and then asks how can you deprive a Negro of that equality which God and the Declaration of Independence awards to him. He and they maintain that Negro equality is guaranteed by the laws of God, and that it is asserted in the Declaration of Independence. If they think so, of course they have a right to say so, and so vote. I do not question Mr. Lincoln's conscientious belief that the Negro was made his equal, and hence is his brother (Laughter.), but for my own part, I do not regard the Negro as my equal, and positively deny that he is my brother or any kin to me whatever. ("Never," "Hit him again," and cheers.) . . .

Now, I do not believe that the Almighty ever intended the Negro to be the equal of the white man. ("Never, never.") If he did, he has been a long time demonstrating the fact. (Cheers.) . . . He belongs to an inferior race, and must always occupy an inferior position. ("Good," "That's so," etc.)

I do not hold that because the Negro is our inferior that therefore he ought to be a slave. By no means can such a conclusion be drawn from what I have said. On the contrary, I hold that humanity and Christianity both require that the Negro shall have and enjoy every right, every privilege, and every immunity consistent with the safety of the society in which he lives. ("That's so.") On that point, I presume, there can be no diversity of opinion. . . . This is a question which each state and each territory must decide for itself—Illinois has decided it for herself. . . .

Now, I hold that Illinois had a right to abolish and prohibit slavery as she did, and I hold that Kentucky has the same right to continue and protect slavery that Illinois had to abolish it. I hold that New York had as much right to abolish slavery as Virginia has to continue it, and that each and every state of this Union is a sovereign power, with the right to do as it pleases upon this question of slavery, and upon all its domestic institutions.

2. Lincoln Denies Negro Equality (1858)

Lincoln, in his high-pitched voice, parried Douglas' charges, to the delight of his noisy Ottawa supporters, who outnumbered the Douglasites about two to one. When this particular debate ended, the Republicans bore their awkward hero in triumph from the platform—with his drawn-up trousers, said one observer, revealing the edges of his long underwear. Douglas later claimed that his opponent, beaten and exhausted, was unable to leave under his own power—a charge that angered Lincoln. From the following portion of Lincoln's contribution to the interchange at Ottawa, decide what portion of his stand was most offensive to Northern abolitionists; to the South in general.

My Fellow Citizens: When a man hears himself somewhat misrepresented, it provokes him—at least, I find it so with myself. But when the misrepresentation becomes very gross and palpable, it is more apt to amuse him. (Laughter.) . . .

. . . Anything that argues me into his [Douglas'] idea of perfect social and political equality with the Negro is but a specious and fantastic arrangement of words, by which a man can prove a horse chestnut to be a chestnut horse. (Laughter.)

I will say here, while upon this subject, that I have no purpose directly or indirectly to interfere with the institution of slavery in the states where it exists. I believe I have no lawful right to do so, and I have no inclination to do so. I have no purpose to introduce political and social equality between the white and the black races. There is a physical difference between the two, which in my judgment will probably forever forbid their living together upon the footing of perfect equality, and inasmuch as it becomes a necessity that there must be a difference, I, as well as Judge Douglas, am in favor of the race to which I belong having the superior position.

2. *Ibid.*, III, 13, 16.

I have never said anything to the contrary, but I hold that, notwithstanding all this, there is no reason in the world why the Negro is not entitled to all the natural rights enumerated in the Declaration of Independence, the right to life, liberty, and the pursuit of happiness. (Loud cheers.) I hold that he is as much entitled to these as the white man. I agree with Judge Douglas he is not my equal in many respects—certainly not in color, perhaps not in moral or intellectual endowment. But in the right to eat the bread, without leave of anybody else, which his own hand earns, *he is my equal and the equal of Judge Douglas, and the equal of every living man.* (Great applause.)

E. JOHN BROWN AT HARPERS FERRY

1. The Richmond *Enquirer* Is Outraged (1859)

The fanatical abolitionist John Brown plotted a large slave insurrection at Harpers Ferry in western Virginia. Purchasing arms with about $3000 provided by sympathetic Northern abolitionists, he launched his abortive enterprise with a score of men, including two of his own sons. Wounded and captured, after the loss of several innocent lives, he was given every opportunity to pose as a martyr while being tried. He was found guilty of three capital offenses: conspiracy with slaves, murder, and treason. Most of the abolitionists who had financed his enterprise ran for cover, though many of them had evidently not known of his desperate plan to attack a federal arsenal and bring down on himself the Washington government. The Southerners were angered by the widespread expressions of sympathy for Brown in the North. A week after the raid the influential Richmond *Enquirer* wrote as follows. Ascertain the most alarming aspect of this editorial.

The Harper's Ferry invasion has advanced the cause of Disunion more than any other event . . . since the formation of the government; it has rallied to that standard men who formerly looked upon it with horror; it has revived, with tenfold strength, the desire of a Southern Confederacy. The heretofore most determined friends of the Union may now be heard saying, "If under the form of a Confederacy [Union] our peace is disturbed, our state invaded, its peaceful citizens cruelly murdered . . . by those who should be our warmest friends, . . . and the people of the North sustain the outrage, then let disunion come."

2. Governor Wise Refuses Clemency (1859)

It is perhaps surprising that Brown was not lynched, instead of being hanged after an orderly, if hurried, trial. Ten of his own men had been killed; six more were tried and hanged. Other casualties that his raid inflicted included seven dead and ten wounded. Pressures of various kinds converged on Governor Wise to extend clemency, and he explained to the legislature as follows why he could not do so. Determine whether there was any reasonable middle ground, and what the proper punishment for Brown should have been.

---

1. Richmond *Enquirer,* Oct. 25, 1859, in Edward Stone, ed., *Incident at Harper's Ferry* (1956), p. 177.
2. Richmond *Enquirer,* Dec. 6, 1859 ; *ibid.,* pp. 152–53.

JOHN BROWN ARRAIGNED
Brown (the tallest) and his comrades (some wounded) appear in
court. Contemporary sketch, *Harper's Weekly,* 1859.

During the trial of . . . [the Harpers Ferry raiders] and since, appeals
and threats of every sort . . . have been made to the Executive. I lay before
you the mass of these, it being impossible to enter into their details.

Though the laws do not permit me to pardon in cases of treason, yet
pardons and reprieves have been demanded on the grounds of, 1st, insanity;
2nd, magnanimity; 3rd, the policy of not making martyrs.

As to the first, the parties themselves or counsel put in no plea of insanity.
No insanity was feigned even; the prisoner Brown spurned it. . . .

As to the second ground . . . : I know of no magnanimity which is
inhumane, and no inhumanity could well exceed that to our society, our
slaves as well as their masters, which would turn felons like these . . . loose
again on a border already torn by a fanatical and sectional strife. . . .

As to the third ground . . . : to hang would be no more martyrdom than
to incarcerate the fanatic. The sympathy would have asked on and on for
liberation, and to nurse and soothe him, while life lasted, in prison. His
state of health would have been heralded weekly, as from a palace . . . ; the
work of his hands would have been sought as holy relics. . . .

There is no middle ground of mitigation. To pardon or reprieve at all
was to proclaim a licensed impunity to the thousand fanatics who are mad
only in the guilt and folly of setting up their individual supremacy over
life, law, property, and civil liberty itself. The sympathy with the leader
was worse than the invasion itself. The appeal was: it is policy to make
no martyrs, but disarm murderers, traitors, robbers, insurrectionists, by free
pardon for wanton, malicious, unprovoked felons!

3. Horace Greeley Hails a Martyr (1859)

Reactions in the North to Brown's incredible raid ranged from execration to adulation. The extreme abolitionists, who believed that slavery was so black a crime as to
justify murder, defended Brown. The orator Wendell Phillips cried (amid cheers),
"John Brown has twice as much right to hang Governor Wise as Governor Wise has
to hang him." Emerson and Thoreau publicly likened the execution to the crucifixion of Jesus. Eccentric Horace Greeley, the influential anti-slavery editor of the New
York *Tribune,* was denounced by Southerners for having given editorial aid and
comfort to John Brown. Greeley replied as follows in an editorial which no doubt
reflected the views of countless moderate anti-slavery men—men who deplored the
method while applauding the goal. Ascertain how effectively Greeley makes the point
that Brown's crime was no ordinary felony, and to what extent he is anti-Brown.

John Brown knew no limitations in his warfare on slavery—why should
slavery be lenient to John Brown, defeated and a captive?

War has its necessities, and they are sometimes terrible. We have not
seen how slavery could spare the life of John Brown without virtually
confessing the iniquity of its own existence. We believe Brown himself has
uniformly taken this view of the matter, and discountenanced all appeals
in his behalf for pardon or commutation, as well as everything savoring of
irritation or menace. There are eras in which death is not merely heroic
but beneficent and fruitful. Who shall say that this was not John Brown's
fit time to die?

We are not those who say, "If slavery is wrong, then John Brown was
wholly right." There are fit and unfit modes of combating a great evil;
we think Brown at Harper's Ferry pursued the latter. . . . And, while we
heartily wish every slave in the world would run away from his master
tomorrow and never be retaken, we should not feel justified in entering a
slave state to incite them to do so, even if we were sure to succeed in the
enterprise. Of course, we regard Brown's raid as utterly mistaken and, in
its direct consequences, pernicious.

But his are the errors of a fanatic, not the crimes of a felon. It were
absurd to apply to him opprobrious epithets or wholesale denunciations.
The essence of crime is the pursuit of selfish gratification in disregard of
others' good; and that is the precise opposite of Old Brown's impulse and
deed. He periled and sacrificed not merely his own life—that were, perhaps,
a moderate stake—but the lives of his beloved sons, the earthly happiness
of his family and theirs, to benefit a despised and downtrodden race—to
deliver from bitter bondage and degradation those whom he had never seen.

Unwise, the world will pronounce him. Reckless of artificial yet palpable
obligations he certainly was, but his very errors were heroic—the faults of
a brave, impulsive, truthful nature, impatient of wrong, and only too
conscious that "Resistance to tyrants is obedience to God." Let whoever
would first cast a stone ask himself whether his own noblest act was equal
in grandeur and nobility to that for which John Brown pays the penalty of
a death on the gallows.

3. New York *Tribune,* Dec. 3, 1859.

And that death will serve to purge his memory of any stain which his errors might otherwise have cast upon it. Mankind are proverbially generous to those who have suffered all that can here be inflicted—who have passed beyond the portals of the life to come. John Brown dead will live in millions of hearts—will be discussed around the homely hearth of toil and dreamed of on the couch of poverty and trial. . . .

Admit that Brown took a wrong way to rid his country of the curse, his countrymen of the chains of bondage, what is the right way? And are we pursuing that way as grandly, unselfishly, as he pursued the wrong one? If not, is it not high time we were? Before censuring severely his errors, should we not abandon our own?

4. Lincoln Disowns Brown (1860)

The South quickly seized upon the John Brown raid as a stick with which to belabor the fast-growing Republican Party, which allegedly had connived with the conspirators. Rough-hewn Abraham Lincoln, Republican presidential aspirant, came east from Illinois for his make-or-break speech before a sophisticated Eastern audience at Cooper Union, in New York City. During the course of his address, which was a smashing success, he dealt with the Brown raid. Discover how convincingly he meets the accusation of Republican complicity, and to what extent he is both pro-Brown and anti-Brown.

You [Southerners] charge that we [Republicans] stir up insurrections among your slaves. We deny it; and what is your proof? Harper's Ferry! John Brown!!

John Brown was no Republican; and you have failed to implicate a single Republican in his Harper's Ferry enterprise. If any member of our party is guilty in that matter, you know it, or you do not know it. If you do know it, you are inexcusable for not designating the man and proving the fact. If you do not know it, you are inexcusable for asserting it, and especially for persisting in the assertion after you have tried and failed to make the proof. You need not be told that persisting in a charge which one does not know to be true is simply malicious slander.

Some of you admit that no Republican designedly aided or encouraged the Harper's Ferry affair, but still insist that our doctrines and declarations necessarily lead to such results. We do not believe it. . . .

Slave insurrections are no more common now than they were before the Republican Party was organized. What induced the Southampton [Nat Turner's] insurrection, twenty-eight years ago, in which at least three times as many lives were lost as at Harper's Ferry? You can scarcely stretch your very elastic fancy to the conclusion that Southampton was "got up by Black Republicanism." In the present state of things in the United States, I do not think a general, or even a very extensive, slave insurrection is possible. . . .

John Brown's effort was peculiar. It was not a slave insurrection. It was

4. J. G. Nicolay and John Hay, eds., *Complete Works of Abraham Lincoln* (1894), V, 314–19, *passim.*

an attempt by white men to get up a revolt among slaves, in which the slaves refused to participate. In fact, it was so absurd that the slaves, with all their ignorance, saw plainly enough it could not succeed. That affair, in its philosophy, corresponds with the many attempts, related in history, at the assassination of kings and emperors. An enthusiast broods over the oppression of a people till he fancies himself commissioned by Heaven to liberate them. He ventures the attempt, which ends in little else than his own execution.

F. THE PRESIDENTIAL CAMPAIGN OF 1860

1. Fire-Eaters Urge Secession (1860)

The surprise nomination of Abraham Lincoln for President on the Republican ticket in 1860 precipitated a crisis. Many Southern spokesmen served notice that the election of this backwoods "ape," whose opposition to slavery was grossly exaggerated, would prove that the North no longer wanted the South in the Union. The vitriolic Charleston *Mercury*, which had championed nullification as early as 1832, was perhaps the foremost newspaper advocating secession. Note the grievances that it presents which seem exaggerated, those which seem valid; and determine whether they justify the solution proposed.

The leaders and oracles of the most powerful party in the United States [Republican] have denounced us as tyrants and unprincipled heathens, through the civilized world. They have preached it from their pulpits. They have declared it in the halls of Congress and in their newspapers. In their schoolhouses they have taught their children (who are to rule this government in the next generation) to look upon the slaveholder as the special disciple of the devil himself. They have published books and pamphlets in which the institution of slavery is held up to the world as a blot and a stain upon the escutcheon of America's honor as a nation.

They have established abolition societies among them for the purpose of raising funds—first to send troops to Kansas to cut the throats of all the slaveholders there, and now to send emissaries among us to incite our slaves to rebellion against the authority of their masters, and thereby endanger the lives of our people and the destruction of our property.

They have brought forth an open and avowed enemy to the most cherished and important institution of the South, as candidate for election to the Chief Magistracy of this government—the very basis of whose political principles is an uncompromising hostility to the institution of slavery under all circumstances.

They have virtually repealed the Fugitive Slave Law, and declare their determination not to abide by the decision of the Supreme Court guaranteeing to us the right to claim our property wherever found in the United States.

And, in every conceivable way, the whole Northern people, as a mass,

1. Charleston (South Carolina) *Mercury,* Sept. 18, 1860.

have shown a most implacable hostility to us and our most sacred rights; and this, too, without the slightest provocation on the part of the South. . . .

Has a man's own brother, born of the same parents, a right to invade the sacred precincts of his fireside, to wage war upon him and his family, and deprive him of his property? And if he should do so, the aggrieved brother has not only a right, but it is his duty, sanctioned by every principle of right, to cut off all communication with that unnatural brother, to drive him from the sanctuary of his threshold, and treat him as an enemy and a stranger. Then why should we any longer submit to the galling yoke of our tyrant brother—the usurping, domineering, abolition North!

The political policy of the South demands that we should not hesitate, but rise up with a single voice and proclaim to the world that we will be subservient to the North no longer, but that we *will* be a free and an independent people. . . .

All admit that an ultimate dissolution of the Union is inevitable, and we believe the crisis is not far off. Then let it come now; the better for the South that it should be today; *she* cannot afford to wait.

2. The North Resents Threats (1860)

Outstanding among Northern newspapers was the Springfield (Massachusetts) *Republican.* Edited by the high-strung Samuel Bowles, who was known at times to drive himself forty-eight hours without sleep, it featured straightforward reporting and concise writing. Ascertain from the following editorial in the Springfield *Republican* to what extent the issue of majority rule was legitimately involved in the North-South dispute.

The South, through the mouth of many of its leading politicians and journals, defies the North to elect Abraham Lincoln to the Presidency. It threatens secession in case he shall be elected. It arrogantly declares that he shall never take his seat. It passes resolutions of the most outrageous and insolent character, insulting every man who dares to vote for what they call a "Black Republican." To make a long matter very short and plain, they claim the privilege of conducting the government in all the future, as they have in all the past, for their own benefit and their own way, with the alternative of dissolving the Union of the States.

Now, if the non-slaveholding people have any spirit at all, they will settle this question at once and forever. Look at the history of the last two administrations, in which the slave interest has had undisputed sway. This sway, the most disgraceful and shameless of anything in the history of the government, we are told must not be thrown off, else the Union will be dissolved. Let's try it! Are we forever to be governed by a slaveholding minority? Will the passage of four years more of misrule make it any easier for the majority to assume its legitimate functions?

There are many reasons why we desire to see this experiment tried this fall. If the majority cannot rule the country without the secession of the

2. Springfield *Republican*, Aug. 25, 1860.

minority, it is time the country knew it. If the country can only exist under the rule of an oligarchy [of slaveowners], let the fact be demonstrated at once, and let us change our institutions. We desire to see the experiment tried, because we wish to have the Southern people, who have been blinded and cheated by the politicians, learn that a "Black Republican" respects the requirements of the Constitution and will protect their interests. Harmony between the two sections of this country can never be secured until the South has learned that the North is not its enemy, but its best friend.

[The "Black Republican" Lincoln was elected President on November 6, 1860. Three days later a New Orleans newspaper declared, "The Northern people, in electing Mr. Lincoln, have perpetrated a deliberate, cold-blooded insult and outrage upon the people of the slaveholding states. . . ." On December 20, a special convention in South Carolina led the secessionist parade by voting 169 to 0 to leave the Union.]

THOUGHT PROVOKERS

1. Why was the South so deeply disturbed by *Uncle Tom's Cabin?* Did the novel do the Negro more harm than good in the short run? in the long run?
2. Did Sumner receive his just deserts for his "Crime against Kansas" speech? Argue both sides and come to a conclusion.
3. Compare the reaction of the North to the Dred Scott decision of 1857 with that of the South to the Supreme Court decision of 1954 ordering desegregation. To what extent is it true, as Republicans insisted in 1857, that the people are the court of last resort in this country?
4. Were both Douglas and Lincoln segregationists as regards the Negro? Was Douglas more pro-popular sovereignty than he was pro-slavery? Was Lincoln, as often charged, an abolitionist?
5. In what ways may John Brown's raid be regarded as one of the causes of the Civil War? Since John Brown in Kansas had murdered pro-slavery men and run off their horses and slaves, how could he be rationally compared to Jesus? Was slavery such a crime, as extreme abolitionists charged, as to justify theft and murder in fighting it? Compare this approach with the Communist rationalization that the end justifies the means.
6. Was Lincoln's election an excuse or a reason for secession? Were the Southerners, as charged, poor sportsmen? Did they have sound grounds for fearing a Republican administration?

FURTHER EXPLORATION

General: Allan Nevins, *Ordeal of the Union* (2 vols., 1947); Allan Nevins, *The Emergence of Lincoln* (2 vols., 1950). Uncle Tom's Cabin: Forrest Wilson, *Crusader in Crinoline* (1941). Brooks-Sumner Affair: David Donald, *Charles Sumner and the Coming of the Civil War* (1960). Dred Scott Decision: Vincent Hopkins, *Dred Scott's Case* (1951); Charles Warren, *The Supreme Court in United States History* (1923), vol. III. Lincoln-Douglas Debates: A. J. Beveridge, *Abraham Lincoln* (1928), vol. II; H. V. Jaffa, *Crisis of the House Divided* (1959); D. E. Fehrenbacher, *Prelude to Greatness: Lincoln in the 1850's* (1962). Brown's Raid: O. G. Villard, *John Brown* (1943); J. C. Furnas, *The Road to Harper's Ferry* (1959); Edward Stone, ed., *Incident at Harper's Ferry* (1956); Louis Ruchames, ed., *A John Brown Reader* (1959). Presidential Campaign: R. H. Luthin, *The First Lincoln Campaign* (1944).

Chapter 22

The War for the Union

Among freemen there can be no successful appeal from the ballot to the bullet, and . . . they who take such appeal are sure to lose their case and pay the cost.

ABRAHAM LINCOLN, 1863

PROLOGUE: The first seven Southern states seceded peacefully. Then, in a blunder comparable to that of the Japanese at Pearl Harbor in 1941, the South galvanized the North into retaliation by bombarding Fort Sumter. Thus began the War for the Union. The North's secondary war aim—the freeing of the slaves —could not be officially proclaimed until late in 1862; otherwise the crucial slave-holding Border States of Maryland, Kentucky, and Missouri would have been driven out. Even so, the final Emancipation Proclamation of January 1, 1863, angered the Border States and aroused much indignation in the North. Meanwhile the South had to be dragged back into the Union by brute force. The process was slow and frustrating, for Lincoln was compelled to employ costly trial-and-error methods until he found in U. S. Grant a general "who fights." General Sherman collaborated relentlessly in Georgia and the Carolinas by warring on civilian morale as well as on uniformed armies. The Confederates, finally forced to their knees by Grant's sledge-hammer blows in Virginia, surrendered in the spring of 1865.

A. LINCOLN AND THE SECESSION CRISIS

1. A Marylander Rejects Disunion (1861)

By early February, 1861, seven Southern states had seceded, taking over most of the federal forts, arsenals, mints, and other public property. Many Northerners were demanding that "in God's name" the "wayward sisters" be allowed to depart in peace. At this juncture a stirring cry of protest arose from Henry Winter Davis, a handsome, eloquent, and ambitious Maryland Congressman. He was especially provoked by the action of the South Carolinians in firing upon and driving off from Charleston harbor an unarmed merchant ship, *Star of the West*, sent to reinforce beleaguered Fort Sumter. His speech had a profound effect in slaveholding Maryland, and although it probably cost him his seat in the next election, it helped hold the state in the Union. List all of his arguments against secession, and assess those relating to commercial, military, and ideological considerations.

Mr. Speaker, we are driven to one of two alternatives. We must recognize what we have been told more than once upon this floor is an accomplished fact—the independence of the rebellious states—or we must refuse to acknowledge it, and accept all the responsibilities that attach to that refusal.

1. *Congressional Globe*, 36 Cong., 2 sess., Appendix, p. 182.

Recognize them! Abandon the Gulf and coast of Mexico; surrender the forts of the United States; yield the privilege of free commerce and free intercourse; strike down the guarantees of the Constitution for our fellow citizens in all that wide region; create a thousand miles of interior frontier to be furnished with internal customhouses, and armed with internal forts, themselves to be a prey to the next caprice of state sovereignty; organize a vast standing army, ready at a moment's warning to resist aggression; create upon our southern boundary a perpetual foothold for foreign powers, whenever caprice, ambition, or hostility may see fit to invite the despot of France [Napoleon III] or the aggressive power of England to attack us upon our undefended frontier; sever that unity of territory which we have spent millions, and labored through three generations, to create and establish; pull down the flag of the United States and take a lower station among the nations of the earth; abandon the high prerogative of leading the march of freedom, the hope of struggling nationalities, the terror of frowning tyrants, the boast of the world, the light of liberty—to become the sport and prey of despots whose thrones we consolidate by our fall—to be greeted by Mexico with the salutation: "Art thou also become weak as we? Art thou become like unto us?" This is recognition.

Refuse to recognize! We must not coerce a state in the peaceful process of secession. We must not coerce a state engaged in the peaceful process of firing into a United States vessel [*Star of the West*] to prevent the reinforcement of a United States fort. We must not coerce states which, without any declaration of war, or any act of hostility of any kind, have united, as have Mississippi, Florida, and Louisiana, their joint forces to seize a public fortress. We must not coerce a state which has planted cannon upon its shores to prevent the free navigation of the Mississippi. We must not coerce a state which has robbed the United States Treasury. This is peaceful secession!

Mr. Speaker, I do not design to quarrel with gentlemen about words. I do not wish to say one word which will exasperate the already too much inflamed state of the public mind. But I say that the Constitution of the United States and the laws made in pursuance thereof must be enforced; and they who stand across the path of that enforcement must either destroy the power of the United States or it will destroy them.

2. Fort Sumter Inflames the North (1861)

Fort Sumter, in Charleston harbor, still flaunted the Stars and Stripes when Lincoln took office in March, 1861. Unwilling either to goad the South into war or to see the garrison starved out, he compromised by announcing that he would send provisions but not reinforcements. The Southerners, who regarded provisioning as aggression, opened fire. The North rose in instant resentment. Especially important was the reaction of New York City, where the merchants and bankers involved in the cotton trade were plotting treacherous courses. In the light of the recollections of a contemporary Episcopal clergyman, form conclusions as to the patriotism of the financial world, and as to the importance of retaining New York's loyalty.

2. Morgan Dix, *Memoirs of John Adams Dix* (1883), II, 9.

"ALL WE ASK IS TO BE LET ALONE"

UNCLE SAM: "Hallo there, you rascal! Where are you going with my property, eh?"
JEFF. DAVIS: "Oh, dear Uncle! ALL I WANT IS TO BE LET ALONE."
(In an early message to the Confederate Congress, President Davis had said, "All we ask is to be let alone." Yet the seceding South took over federal mints, arsenals, post offices, customs houses, lighthouses, forts [Sum(p)ter], etc.) *Harper's Weekly*, 1861.

On Sunday, April 14 [1861], the fact became known that Fort Sumter had surrendered. The excitement created by the bombardment of that fortress and its magnificent defense by Anderson was prodigious. The outrage on the government of the United States thus perpetrated by the authorities of South Carolina sealed the fate of the new-born Confederacy and the institution of slavery.

Intelligent Southerners at the North were well aware of the consequences which must follow. In the city of New York a number of prominent gentlemen devoted to the interests of the South, and desirous to obtain a bloodless dissolution of the Union, were seated together in anxious conference, studying with intense solicitude the means of preserving the peace. A messenger entered the room in breathless haste with the news: "General Beauregard has opened fire on Fort Sumter!" The persons whom he thus addressed remained a while in dead silence, looking into each other's pale faces; then one of them, with uplifted hands, cried, in a voice of anguish, "My God, we are ruined!"

The North rose as one man. The question had been asked by those who were watching events, "How will New York go?" There were sinister hopes in certain quarters of a strong sympathy with the secession movements; dreams that New York might decide on cutting off from the rest of the country and becoming a free city. These hopes and dreams vanished in a day. The reply to the question how New York would go was given with an energy worthy of herself.

3. Fort Sumter Inspirits the South (1861)

If the Southern attack on Fort Sumter angered the North, it had an exhilarating effect on the South. Gala crowds in Charleston harbor cheered their cannonading heroes. The *Star-Spangled Banner* was rewritten to read:

The Star-Spangled Banner in disgrace shall wave
O'er the land of the tyrant, and the home of the knave.

The Virginia "Submissionists," who had resisted secession, were overwhelmed by the popular clamor. Note what the following account from the *Daily Richmond Examiner* reveals about the mood of the people, and what it portended for the secession of Virginia and the prolongation of the war.

The news of the capture of Fort Sumter was greeted with unbounded enthusiasm in this city. Everybody we met seemed to be perfectly happy. Indeed, until the occasion we did not know how happy men could be. Everybody abuses war, and yet it has ever been the favorite and most honored pursuit of men; and the women and children admire and love war ten times as much as the men. The boys pulled down the stars and stripes from the top of the Capitol (some of the boys were sixty years old), and very properly run [*sic*] up the flag of the Southern Confederacy in its place. What the women did we don't precisely know, but learned from rumor that they praised South Carolina to the skies, abused Virginia, put it to the Submissionists hot and heavy with their two-edged swords, and wound up the evening's ceremonies by playing and singing secession songs until fifteen minutes after twelve on Saturday night.—The boys exploded an infinite number of crackers; the price of tar has risen 25 percent, and sky-rockets and Roman candles can be had at no price, the whole stock in trade having been used up Saturday night. We had great firing of cannon, all sorts of processions, an infinite number of grandiloquent, hifaluting speeches, and some drinking of healths, which has not improved healths; for one half the people we have met since are hoarse from long and loud talking, and the other half have a slight headache, it may be, from long and patriotic libations.

4. A Catholic Bishop Justifies Secession (1861)

The globe-girdling Roman Catholic Church, unlike the leading Protestant denominations, remained officially neutral as the North-South quarrel intensified, despite private differences of opinion. Irish-born Bishop Patrick N. Lynch of Charleston, a commanding speaker and administrator, was ministering to some 10,000 Catholics in his diocese when war erupted. In a letter to Archbishop John Hughes of New York, who replied in the press, he cogently outlined the case for the South. Northerners have often claimed that the South had nothing to fear in 1860–1861: the

3. *Daily Richmond Examiner*, April 15, 1861, in W. J. Kimball, *Richmond in Time of War* (1960), p. 4.
4. J. T. Ellis, ed., *Documents of American Catholic History* (1956), pp. 357–64, *passim*. By permission of the Bruce Publishing Company.

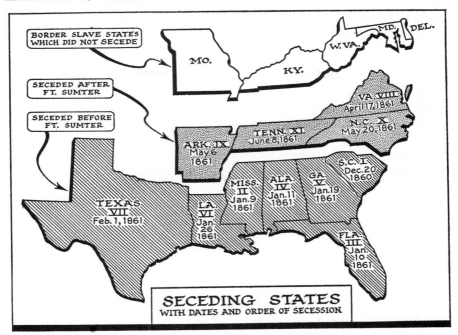

BORDER SLAVE STATES WHICH DID NOT SECEDE

SECEDED AFTER FT. SUMTER

SECEDED BEFORE FT. SUMTER

MD. DEL.

W. VA.

MO.

KY.

VA. VIII April 17, 1861

N.C. X May 20, 1861

ARK. IX May 6 1861

TENN. XI June 8, 1861

S.C. I Dec. 20 1860

MISS. II Jan. 9 1861

ALA. IV Jan. 11 1861

GA. V Jan. 19 1861

TEXAS VII Feb. 1, 1861

LA. VI Jan. 26 1861

FLA. III Jan. 10 1861

SECEDING STATES
WITH DATES AND ORDER OF SECESSION

victorious Republicans did not control the Supreme Court or Congress, and there were fifteen slave states to block a three-fourths vote on any amendment abolishing slavery. Comment critically in the light of Bishop Lynch's statement.

This war is generally dated from the bombardment of Fort Sumter. There we [the South] fired the first gun, and the responsibility is charged on us. But, in reality, that responsibility falls on those who rendered the conflict unavoidable. The South, years ago, and a hundred times, declared that the triumph of the abolition or anti-slavery policy would break up the Union. They were in earnest. When that [Republican] party, appealing to the people on the Chicago platform, elected their candidate by every free-state vote (excepting New Jersey, which was divided), South Carolina seceded, and other states were preparing to do so. . . .

Then came the special messenger of the President, announcing that he intended revictualing the fort, quietly, if permitted, forcibly, if resisted; then the account of the sailing of the fleet from New York. The fort was at once attacked and taken without waiting their arrival. The attack was not made until the offer of negotiation and peaceful arrangement had been rejected, and until the United States Government was in the act of sending an armed force. But it is of little use now to inquire on whom the responsibility rests; we have the war on us, with all its loss of life and long train of evils of every kind. . . .

Taking up anti-slavery, making it a religious dogma, and carrying it into politics, they [the Republicans] have broken up the Union. While it was merely an intellectual opinion, they might discuss it as they pleased; they might embrace it as they did any other ism. Even their virulent use and misrepresentation we scarcely heeded, provided they did not obtrude them upon us at home. . . . But when they carried it [anti-slavery] into politics, gaining one state government after another . . . and grasping the power of the Federal Government, what could the South do but consult its own safety by withdrawing from the Union?

What other protection had they? The Senate, which had still a Democratic majority? They had seen the House of Representatives pass into the hands of their enemies, and each session saw an increasing majority there. The Executive had gone for four years. Their own majority in the Senate was dwindling fast, while on the territorial question not a few of the Northern Democrats were unsound.

To the Supreme Court? That had spoken in the Dred Scott decision. The North would not sustain it, and the Black Republicans scouted it. And, moreover, in a few years President Lincoln would have the privilege of placing on the bench new judges from the ranks of his party.

To the sober thought of the people? But this [anti-slavery] was no new issue on which they were taken by surprise. For years and years it had been discussed; North and South it had been denounced as fraught with disunion and ruin; and yet the Northern people had gradually come to accept it. But the South had spoken so often and so strongly of disunion, without doing anything, that the Northern people had no real belief that any evil consequences would ensue. . . .

Well, South Carolina seceded—other states were preparing to follow her. The matter was taken up in Congress. Many Southerners hoped that then, when the seriousness of the questions could no longer be doubted, something might be done. How vainly they hoped, the Committees of Congress showed. The alternative was thus forced on the South either of tame submission or of resistance. They did not hesitate. They desired to withdraw in peace. This war has been forced upon them.

The separation of the Southern States is *un fait accompli* [an accomplished fact]. The Federal Government has no power to reverse it. Sooner or later it must be recognized. Why preface the recognition by a war equally needless and bloody? Men at the North may regret the rupture, as men at the South may do. The Black Republicans . . . are responsible. If there is to be fighting, let those who voted the Black Republican ticket shoulder their musket and bear the responsibility.

B. NORTHERN WAR AIMS

1. Congress Voices Its Views (1861)

John J. Crittenden of Kentucky—at various times a Cabinet member, a Senator, and a Congressman—achieved renown in 1860 by his efforts to work out a last-ditch compromise over slavery in the territories. After war broke out, one of his sons became a general in the Union army, another (to his father's sorrow) a general in the

1. *House Journal*, 37 Cong., 1 sess., p. 123.

Confederate army. The older Crittenden, determined not to force slaveholding Kentucky and her sister Border States out of the Union by a crusade against slavery, shepherded the following new resolution through the House of Representatives in 1861. Note how cleverly this statement is designed to quiet the fears of Confederates, Southern Unionists, and Border Staters.

Resolved by the House of Representatives of the Congress of the United States, That the present deplorable civil war has been forced upon the country by the disunionists of the Southern states, now in arms against the constitutional government, and in arms around the capital; that in this national emergency, Congress, banishing all feelings of mere passion or resentment, will recollect only its duty to the whole country; that this war is not waged on their part in any spirit of oppression, or for any purpose of conquest or subjugation, or purpose of overthrowing or interfering with the rights or established institutions of those states, but to defend and maintain the supremacy of the Constitution, and to preserve the Union with all the dignity, equality, and rights of the several states unimpaired; and that as soon as these objects are accomplished the war ought to cease.

2. Lincoln Answers Greeley's Prayer (1862)

Bespectacled little Horace Greeley, editor of the widely read New York *Tribune*, reached the heights of arrogance when he published an open letter to President Lincoln entitled "The Prayer of Twenty Millions." Professing to speak for virtually the entire population of the North, he thundered against the administration for hampering the war effort by not coming out bluntly for the emancipation of slaves. Lincoln replied as follows in a public letter. Analyze the qualities of his character that shine through this remarkable statement. Decide whether Lincoln was putting expediency above morality, and what he would have done if the South had been willing to surrender, subject only to the retention of its slaves.

Dear Sir: I have just read yours of the 19th, addressed to myself through the New York *Tribune*. If there be in it any statements, or assumptions of fact, which I may know to be erroneous, I do not, now and here, controvert them. If there be in it any inferences which I may believe to be falsely drawn, I do not now and here argue against them. If there be perceptible in it an impatient and dictatorial tone, I waive it in deference to an old friend, whose heart I have always supposed to be right.

As to the policy I "seem to be pursuing," as you say, I have not meant to leave anyone in doubt.

I would save the Union. I would save it the shortest way under the Constitution. The sooner the National authority can be restored, the nearer the Union will be "the Union as it was."

If there be those who would not save the Union unless they could at the same time save Slavery, I do not agree with them. If there be those who would not save the Union unless they could at the same time destroy Slavery, I do not agree with them. My paramount object in this struggle is to save the Union, and is not either to save or destroy Slavery.

2. R. P. Basler, ed., *The Collected Works of Abraham Lincoln* (1953), V, 388–89 (Aug. 22, 1862).

If I could save the Union without freeing any slave, I would do it; and if I could save it by freeing all the slaves, I would do it; and if I could do it by freeing some and leaving others alone, I would also do that. What I do about Slavery and the colored race, I do because I believe it helps to save this Union; and what I forbear, I forbear because I do not believe it would help to save the Union.

I shall do less whenever I shall believe what I am doing hurts the cause, and I shall do more whenever I shall believe doing more will help the cause. I shall try to correct errors when shown to be errors; and I shall adopt new views so fast as they shall appear to be true views.

I have here stated my purpose according to my view of official duty; and I intend no modification of my oft-expressed personal wish that all men, everywhere, could be free.

C. LINCOLN AND HIS GENERALS

1. McClellan Snubs the President (1861)

Stocky and well-built General George B. McClellan, a red-mustached West Pointer who sat his horse superbly, was given command of the Union Army of the Potomac in 1861, at the unusual age of thirty-four. A well-trained engineer and tactician, he was immensely popular with his men, who cheered and waved their caps as he galloped by. But the wine of responsibility and adulation went to his head. Youthful John Hay, Lincoln's private secretary who later became a world-famous Secretary of State, records in his diary the following astounding incident. Observe what it reveals about the characters of McClellan and Lincoln, as well as the general atmosphere of the time.

November 13 [1861]. I wish here to record what I consider a portent of evil to come. The President [Lincoln], Governor Seward, and I went over to McClellan's house tonight. The servant at the door said the General . . . would soon return. We went in, and after we had waited about an hour, McC. came in and without paying any particular attention to the porter, who told him the President was waiting to see him, went upstairs, passing the door of the room where the President and Secretary of State were seated. They waited about half an hour, and sent once more a servant to tell the General they were there, and the answer coolly came that the General had gone to bed.

I merely record this unparalleled insolence of epaulettes without comment. It is the first indication I have yet seen of the threatened supremacy of the military authorities.

Coming home I spoke to the President about the matter but he seemed not to have noticed it specially, saying it was better at this time not to be making points of etiquette and personal dignity.

1. Reprinted by permission of Dodd, Mead and Company from *Lincoln and the Civil War in the Diaries and Letters of John Hay,* ed. Tyler Dennett, pp. 34–35; copyright 1939 by Dodd, Mead and Company. It is possible that McClellan had been drinking too heavily at a party.

[*Although Lincoln remarked, "I will hold McClellan's horse, if he will only bring us success," thereafter the President summoned McClellan to the White House whenever he wanted to see him.*]

2. McClellan Upbraids His Superior (1862)

General McClellan, though a superb drillmaster and organizer of the Army of the Potomac, suffered from perfectionism and overcaution—"the slows," Lincoln once said. Relying on Pinkerton's Detective Agency, he habitually overestimated the number of his foes. He perceived difficulties more readily than possibilities. Finally prodded by Lincoln into moving, he assaulted the defenses of Richmond in the clumsily roundabout Peninsular Campaign. When he was driven back in bloody fighting by inferior forces (he reported "vastly superior numbers"), he blamed everybody but himself for his failures. He was particularly critical of the Lincoln administration for having failed to provide expected troops. Note what his report to Secretary of War Stanton reveals about his character. Determine to what extent, if any, he was guilty of insubordination, and what may be said in his defense.

. . . My regulars were superb, and I count upon what are left to turn another battle, in company with their gallant comrades of the volunteers. Had I 20,000, or even 10,000, fresh troops to use tomorrow, I could take Richmond. But I have not a man in reserve, and shall be glad to cover my retreat and save the material and personnel of the army.

If we have lost the day, we have yet preserved our honor; and no one need blush for the Army of the Potomac. I have lost this battle because my force was too small.

I again repeat that I am not responsible for this, and I say it with the earnestness of a general who feels in his heart the loss of every brave man who has been needlessly sacrificed today. I still hope to retrieve our fortunes; but to do this the government must view the matter in the same earnest light that I do. You must send me very large reinforcements, and send them at once. I shall draw back to this side of the Chickahominy [River], and think I can withdraw all our material. Please understand that in this battle we have lost nothing but men, and those the best we have.

In addition to what I have already said, I only wish to say to the President that I think he is wrong in regarding me as ungenerous when I said that my force was too weak. I merely intimated a truth which today has been too plainly proved. If, at this instant, I could dispose of 10,000 fresh men, I could gain the victory tomorrow.

I know that a few thousand more men would have changed this battle from a defeat to a victory. As it is, the government must not and cannot hold me responsible for the result.

I feel too earnestly tonight. I have seen too many dead and wounded comrades to feel otherwise than that the government has not sustained this army. If you do not do so now, the game is lost.

If I save the army now, I tell you plainly that I owe no thanks to you or to any other persons in Washington.

You have done your best to sacrifice this army.

2. G. B. McClellan, *McClellan's Own Story* (1887), pp. 424–25 (June 28, 1862).

[*The supervisor of military telegrams ordered this message toned down before it was shown to the Secretary of War. President Lincoln wrote to McClellan that the charge of withholding troops "pains me very much. I give you all I can, and act on the presumption that you will do the best you can with what you have, while you continue, ungenerously I think, to assume that I could give you more if I would. I have omitted, and shall omit, no opportunity to send you reënforcements whenever I possibly can." (J. G. Nicolay and John Hay, eds., Complete Works of Abraham Lincoln [1894], VII, 235.)*]

3. Lincoln Warns General Hooker (1863)

General McClellan was forced to yield the driver's seat to General Pope, whom General Lee vanquished at the Second Battle of Bull Run (1862). This setback caused McClellan to look better, and he was now restored to his active command. After holding Lee to only a draw at Antietam, he was replaced by General Burnside. Lee crushed his new adversary on the battlefield of Fredericksburg late in 1862. "Fighting Joe" Hooker now succeeded Burnside. Tall, robust, bronze-haired, and affable, this energetic West Pointer had already won laurels for his dash and courage amid hailstorms of bullets. Perhaps he was the dictatorial "man on horseback" who, many critics thought, was necessary for victory. Yet his army of 138,000 men was defeated by Lee's 62,500 at the battle of Chancellorsville, May 2–4, 1863. During much of the fray Hooker was in a daze from a near-hit by a cannon ball. The letter of appointment that Lincoln had earlier addressed to this ambitious general is one of the most remarkable ever written. Decide what it reveals of Lincoln's character, what he most fears from Hooker, and what he regards as Hooker's greatest disservice to the army.

General:—I have placed you at the head of the Army of the Potomac. Of course I have done this upon what appear to me to be sufficient reasons. And yet I think it best for you to know that there are some things in regard to which I am not quite satisfied with you.

I believe you to be a brave and skillful soldier, which, of course, I like. I also believe you do not mix politics with your profession, in which you are right. You have confidence in yourself, which is a valuable, if not an indispensable, quality. You are ambitious, which, within reasonable bounds, does good rather than harm. But I think that, during General Burnside's command of the army, you have taken counsel of your ambition, and thwarted him as much as you could, in which you did a great wrong to the country, and to a most meritorious and honorable brother officer.

I have heard, in such way as to believe it, of your recently saying that both the army and the government needed a dictator. Of course, it was not for this, but in spite of it, that I have given you the command. Only those generals who gain successes can set up dictators. What I now ask of you is military success, and I will risk the dictatorship. The government will support you to the utmost of its ability—which is neither more nor less than it has done and will do for all commanders.

I much fear that the spirit which you have aided to infuse into the army,

3. R. P. Basler, ed., *The Collected Works of Abraham Lincoln* (1953), VI, 78–79 (Jan. 26, 1863).

of criticizing their commander [Burnside], and withholding confidence from him, will now turn upon you. I shall assist you, as far as I can, to put it down. Neither you nor Napoleon, if he were alive again, could get any good out of an army while such a spirit prevails in it.

And now, beware of rashness. Beware of rashness, but, with energy and sleepless vigilance, go forward and give us victories.

D. THE PROCLAIMING OF EMANCIPATION

1. Lincoln Expresses Misgivings (1862)

Preserving the Union was the officially announced war aim of the North. But to many Northern abolitionists and free-soilers the unshackling of the slave was more important. An edict of emancipation would presumably quiet their clamor while strengthening the nation's moral position abroad. Yet such a stroke would antagonize the slaveholding but still loyal Border States, as well as countless Northern Democrats who were fighting for the Union and not for "a passel of slaves." The issuance of an emancipation proclamation after the current series of Northern defeats would, moreover, seem like a last-chance act of desperation. On September 13, 1862, four days before the crucial battle of Antietam and nine days before he issued his preliminary Emancipation Proclamation, Lincoln explained his position to a visiting delegation of Northern Christians from Chicago. List in parallel columns the arguments that he gives for and against an emancipation proclamation; decide which argument in each column is the strongest and which set of arguments is the weaker. Note whether Lincoln is concerned with moral considerations primarily, whether he has misgivings regarding the constitutionality of emancipation, and to what extent he regards slavery as the cause of the war.

What good would a proclamation of emancipation from me do, especially as we are now situated? I do not want to issue a document that the whole world will see must necessarily be inoperative, like the Pope's bull against the comet.* Would my word free the slaves, when I cannot even enforce the Constitution in the rebel states? Is there a single court, or magistrate, or individual that would be influenced by it there? And what reason is there to think it would have any greater effect upon the slaves than the late law of Congress, which I approved, and which offers protection and freedom to the slaves of rebel masters who come within our lines? Yet I cannot learn that that law has caused a single slave to come over to us.

And suppose they could be induced by a proclamation of freedom from me to throw themselves upon us, what should we do with them? How can we feed and care for such a multitude? General Butler [in New Orleans] wrote me a few days since that he was issuing more rations to the slaves who have rushed to him than to all the white troops under his command. They eat, and that is all; though it is true General Butler is feeding the whites also by the thousand, for it nearly amounts to a famine there.

1. J. G. Nicolay and John Hay, eds., *Complete Works of Abraham Lincoln* (1894), VIII, 30–33.
* The tale that a terrified Pope Calixtus III excommunicated Halley's comet by a papal bull in 1456 is baseless, but he did decree "several days of prayer for averting the wrath of God . . ." (A. D. White, *A History of the Warfare of Science with Theology* [1896], I, 177).

ABE LINCOLN'S LAST CARD: OR, ROUGE-ET-NOIR

The London *Punch*, 1862, regards the preliminary Emancipation Proclamation as an act of desperation. Jefferson Davis watches smugly while Lincoln plays his ace of spades (note Negro face on card) in the game of rouge-et-noir (red and black).

If, now, the pressure of the war should call off our forces from New Orleans to defend some other point, what is to prevent the masters from reducing the blacks to slavery again? For I am told that whenever the rebels take any black prisoners, free or slave, they immediately auction them off. They did so with those they took from a boat that was aground in the Tennessee River a few days ago. And then I am very ungenerously attacked for it! For instance, when, after the late battles at and near Bull Run, an expedition went out from Washington under a flag of truce to bury the dead and bring in the wounded, and the rebels seized the blacks who went along to help, and sent them into slavery, Horace Greeley said in his paper [New York *Tribune*] that the government would probably do nothing about it. What could I do?

Now, then, tell me, if you please, what possible result of good would follow the issuing of such a proclamation as you desire? Understand, I raise no objections against it on legal or constitutional grounds; for, as commander-in-chief of the army and navy, in time of war I suppose I have a right to take any measure which may best subdue the enemy. Nor do I urge objections of a moral nature, in view of possible consequences of insurrection and massacre at the South.

I view this matter as a practical war measure, to be decided on according to the advantages or disadvantages it may offer to the suppression of the rebellion.

I admit that slavery is the root of the rebellion, or at least its *sine qua non* [the factor without which it could not exist]. The ambition of politicians may have instigated them to act, but they would have been impotent without slavery as their instrument. I will also concede that emancipation would help us in Europe, and convince them that we are incited by something more than ambition. I grant, further, that it would help somewhat at the North, though not so much, I fear, as you and those you represent imagine. Still some additional strength would be added in that way to the war, and then, unquestionably, it would weaken the rebels by drawing off their laborers, which is of great importance; but I am not so sure we could do much with the blacks. If we were to arm them, I fear that in a few weeks the arms would be in the hands of the rebels; and, indeed, thus far we have not had arms enough to equip our white troops.

I will mention another thing, though it meet only your scorn and contempt. There are fifty thousand bayonets in the Union armies from the border slave states. It would be a serious matter if, in consequence of a proclamation such as you desire, they should go over to the rebels. I do not think they all would—not so many, indeed, as a year ago, or six months ago— not so many today as yesterday. Every day increases their Union feeling. They are also getting their pride enlisted, and want to beat the rebels.

Let me say one thing more: I think you should admit that we already have an important principle to rally and unite the people, in the fact that constitutional government [Union] is at stake. This is a fundamental idea going down about as deep as anything.

2. Davis Deplores Emancipation (1863)

Seeking to improve the military and moral position of the North, and taking advantage of the recent (limited) Union success at Antietam, Lincoln finally issued his preliminary Emancipation Proclamation on September 22, 1862, nine days after giving such excellent reasons for not doing so. Declaring anew that the preservation of the Union was still his primary goal, he announced that as of January 1, 1863, the slaves would be "forever free" in all areas still in rebellion—areas in fact where Lincoln was then powerless to free anybody. He further proclaimed that the Washington government would "do no act or acts to repress" the slaves "in any efforts they may make for their actual freedom." To Southerners, this seemed like an invitation to wholesale rape and insurrection. They upbraided Lincoln "the Fiend," while seriously discussing the advisability of shooting all Yankee prisoners of war, wounded or able-bodied. President Jefferson Davis reacted bitterly as follows in his message to the Confederate Congress. Assess the logic in his views that the Proclamation was inhumane, unethical, and unconstitutional, and that it revealed the impotence of the North and further justified the South in seceding.

We may well leave it to the instincts of that common humanity which a beneficent Creator has implanted in the breasts of our fellow men of all

2. J. D. Richardson, comp., *Messages and Papers of the Confederacy* (1904), I, 290–93, *passim* (Jan. 12, 1863).

countries to pass judgment on a measure by which several millions of human beings of an inferior race, peaceful and contented laborers in their sphere, are doomed to extermination, while at the same time they are encouraged to a general assassination of their masters by the insidious recommendation "to abstain from violence unless in necessary self-defense." Our own detestation of those who have attempted the most execrable measure recorded in the history of guilty man is tempered by profound contempt for the impotent rage which it discloses. . . .

In its political aspect this measure possesses great significance, and to it in this light I invite your attention. It affords to our whole people the complete and crowning proof of the true nature of the designs of the party which elevated to power the present occupant of the presidential chair at Washington, and which sought to conceal its purpose by every variety of artful device and by the perfidious use of the most solemn and repeated pledges on every possible occasion. I extract in this connection as a single example the following declaration, made by President Lincoln under the solemnity of his oath of Chief Magistrate of the United States, on the 4th of March, 1861: . . .

"I declare that I have no purpose, directly or indirectly, to interfere with the institution of slavery in the states where it exists. I believe I have no lawful right to do so; and I have no inclination to do so. . . ."

Nor was this declaration of the want of power or disposition to interfere with our social system confined to a state of peace. Both before and after the actual commencement of hostilities the President of the United States repeated in formal official communication to the Cabinets of Great Britain and France that he was utterly without constitutional power to do the act which he has just committed. . . .

This proclamation is also an authentic statement by the Government of the United States of its inability to subjugate the South by force of arms, and as such must be accepted by neutral nations, which can no longer find any justification in withholding our just claims to formal recognition.

3. Border Staters Are Alarmed (1862)

Lincoln did not dare issue his Emancipation Proclamation until he was reasonably sure that the crucial Border States would not be driven into the welcoming arms of their Confederate sisters. Even so, he was careful to exempt the slaves held in these states, and to hold out to their owners the hope of compensated emancipation. But the Border States were quick to perceive that the days of their own slave property were numbered. The fearless editor of the Louisville *Journal*, George D. Prentice, a South-adopted Connecticut Yankee who had two sons in the Confederate army, had labored mightily to keep Kentucky in the Union, but even he voiced strong dissent. In his editorial determine whether he is fair in his appraisal of the Proclamation, especially its moral implications, and why he does not advocate joining the Confederacy.

3. Quoted in the *Daily National Intelligencer* (Washington), Oct. 8, 1862.

It [the Proclamation] is evidently an arbitrary act of the President as Commander-in-Chief of the army and navy of the Union. In short, it is a naked stroke of military necessity.

We shall not stop now to discuss the character and tendency of this measure. Both are manifest. The one is as unwarrantable as the other is mischievous. The measure is wholly unauthorized and wholly pernicious. Though it cannot be executed in fact, and though its execution probably will never be seriously attempted, its moral influence will be decided, and purely hurtful. So far as its own purpose is concerned, it is a mere *brutum fulmen* [futile display of force], but it will prove only too effectual for the purposes of the enemy [the South]. It is a gigantic usurpation, unrelieved by the promise of a solitary advantage, however minute and faint, but on the contrary aggravated by the menace of great and unmixed evil.

Kentucky cannot and will not acquiesce in this measure. Never! As little will she allow it to chill her devotion to the cause thus cruelly imperiled anew. The government our fathers framed is one thing, and a thing above price; Abraham Lincoln, the temporary occupant of the Executive chair, is another thing, and a thing of comparatively little worth. The one is an individual, the sands of whose official existence are running fast, and who, when his official existence shall end, will be no more or less than any other individual. The other is a grand political structure, in which is contained the treasures and the energies of civilization, and upon whose lofty and shining dome, seen from the shores of all climes, center the eager hopes of mankind.

What Abraham Lincoln, as President, does or fails to do may exalt or lower our estimate of himself, but not of the great and beneficent government of which he is but the temporary servant. The temple is not the less sacred and precious because the priest lays an unlawful sacrifice upon the altar. The loyalty of Kentucky is not to be shaken by any mad act of the President. If necessary, she will resist the act, and aid in holding the actor to a just and lawful accountability, but she will never lift her own hand against the glorious fabric because he has blindly or criminally smitten it. She cannot be so false to herself as this. She is incapable of such guilt and folly.

4. Lincoln's Home Town Applauds (1862)

Northern responses to the Proclamation varied. Garrison's abolitionist *Liberator*, though complaining that Lincoln had not gone far enough fast enough, conceded that he had taken a major step in the right direction. Republican journals like the New York *Times* rejoiced that the Union cause was now strong enough to risk this act of military necessity. "God bless Abraham Lincoln!" cried the New York *Christian Inquirer*. Democratic critics were prone to condemn the unconstitutionality of the stroke and its shift of war aims to include freeing of the slaves. Others pointed out that Lincoln had indeed issued a "bull against a comet": in those areas where he

4. *Illinois State Journal* (Springfield), Sept. 24, 1862, in Herbert Mitgang, *Lincoln as They Saw Him* (1956), p. 306.

had no control he was freeing the slaves; in those (Border States) where he had control he refused to do so, for reasons of expediency. Lincoln himself confessed keen disappointment over the public reaction. But his home-town newspaper, the *Illinois State Journal* of Springfield, came through with a resounding endorsement. Evaluate its prophetic judgment as to the place of the document in history, and the legal grounds on which it justifies this drastic action.

President Lincoln has at last hurled against rebellion the bolt which he has so long held suspended. The act is the most important and the most memorable of his official career—no event in the history of this country since the Declaration of Independence itself has excited so profound attention either at home or abroad.

While its justice is indisputable, we may well suppose that the step has been taken reluctantly. A people waging a causeless and unholy war against a mild and just government has forfeited the right to protection by that government. No principle is clearer. Yet the President has repeatedly warned the people of the rebellious states to return to their allegiance without effect. He now employs the power with which Congress and the Constitution have clothed him.

There can be but one opinion among all true friends of the country. The President must and will be sustained. That extremists will condemn—one class because emancipation is not immediate and unconditional; the other because it is proclaimed even prospectively—is to be expected. But those who refuse to support the government in the exercise of its necessary and just authority are traitors and should be so treated, whatever name they may wear. True patriots of every name rally around the President, determined that the Union shall be preserved and the laws enforced.

E. THE EMANCIPATION PROCLAMATION IN ENGLAND

1. *Blackwood's* Blasts Servile War (1862)

President Jefferson Davis, seeking both the moral support and the active intervention of neutral Europe, predicted that the Emancipation Proclamation would aid the South. He was correct insofar as the ruling class of England was concerned. The London *Times* regarded the Proclamation as "an incitement to assassination": Lincoln would abolish slavery to punish the rebellious and preserve it to reward the loyal. A member of Parliament branded the President's edict "one of the most devilish acts of fiendish malignity which the wickedness of men could have conceived." The Tory *Blackwood's Edinburgh Magazine*, after letting go the following salvo, vainly besought the London government to intervene by force of arms. Ascertain why it regards the Proclamation as an act of bafflement and desperation beyond the pale of civilized warfare.

The past month has brought us to the veritable crisis of the great Civil War in America. Brought to bay upon their own soil, the Federals in desperation have invoked to their aid the unutterable horrors of a servile

1. *Blackwood's Edinburgh Magazine*, XCII (1862), 637.

war. With their armies baffled and beaten, and with the standards of the rebel army again within sight of Washington, the President has at length owned the impossibility of success in fair warfare, and seeks to paralyze the victorious armies of the South by letting loose upon their hearths and homes the lust and savagery of four million Negroes.

The die is cast. Henceforth it is a war of extermination. The North seeks to make of the South a desert—a wilderness of bloodshed and misery; for thus only, now, does it or can it hope to overcome the seceding Confederacy. Monstrous, reckless, devilish as the project is, we believe it will not succeed. But it at least marks the crisis and turning point of the war. It shows that the North has shot its last bolt—the effects of which we do not yet see, but beyond which there is no other. It proves what everyone in this country was loath to believe, that rather than let the Southern states be independent, rather than lose their trade and custom, the North would league itself with Beelzebub [the Devil], and seek to make a hell of half a continent.

In return, this atrocious act justifies the South in hoisting the black flag, and in proclaiming a war without quarter against the Yankee hosts. And thus, within the bosom of civilization, we are called upon to contemplate a war more full of horrors and wickedness than any which stands recorded in the world's history.

2. English Working Classes Cheer (1863)

The working classes of England, deeply concerned with the dignity of human labor, favored emancipation, despite heavy unemployment caused by the cotton famine. They hailed the Proclamation with spontaneous mass meetings. The city of Birmingham alone sent Lincoln a congratulatory address containing 10,000 signatures. Conspicuous among the British friends of the North was a wealthy low-tariff liberal and Member of Parliament, Richard Cobden, who had twice visited the United States. He wrote privately to his abolitionist friend, Senator Charles Sumner, as follows. Note why Cobden regards the Proclamation as a preventive of possible British intervention.

You know how much alarmed I was from the first lest our government should interpose in your affairs. The disposition of our ruling class, and the necessities of our cotton trade, pointed to some act of intervention; and the indifference of the great mass of our population to your struggle, the object of which they did not foresee and understand, would have made intervention easy, indeed popular, if you had been a weaker naval power.

This state of feeling existed up to the announcement of the President's emancipation policy. From that moment our old anti-slavery feeling began to arouse itself, and it has been gathering strength ever since. The great rush of the public to all the public meetings called on the subject shows how wide and deep the sympathy for personal freedom still is in the hearts of our people. I know nothing in my political experience so striking as a

2. Cobden to Sumner, Feb. 13, 1863, in *American Historical Review*, II (1897), 308–09.

display of spontaneous public action as that of the vast gathering at Exeter Hall when, without one attraction in the form of a popular orator, the vast building, its minor rooms and passages, and the streets adjoining were crowded with an enthusiastic audience. That meeting has had a powerful effect on our newspapers and politicians. It has closed the mouths of those who have been advocating the side of the South.

And I now write to assure you that any unfriendly act on the part of our government, no matter which of our aristocratic parties is in power, towards your cause is not to be apprehended. If an attempt were made by the government in any way to commit us to the South, a spirit would be instantly aroused which would drive our government from power. . . .

So much for the influence which your emancipation policy has had on the public opinion of England. But judging from the tone of your press in America, it does not seem to have gained the support of your masses. About this, however, I do not feel competent to offer an opinion. . . .

When I met [John C.] Frémont in Paris two years ago, just as you commenced this terrible war, I remarked to him that the total abolition of slavery in your northern continent was the only issue which could justify the war to the civilized world. Every symptom seems to point to this result. But at what a price is the Negro to be emancipated! I confess that if then I had been the arbiter of his fate, I should have refused him freedom at the cost of so much white men's blood and women's tears. I do not, however, blame the North. The South fired the first shot, and on them righteously falls the malediction that "they who take the sword shall perish by the sword."

F. THE UNCIVIL WAR

1. Sherman Dooms Atlanta (1864)

General William T. Sherman, a tall and red-bearded West Pointer from Ohio, understood and liked the South better than most Northerners. He was in fact teaching in a military academy in Louisiana when war erupted. Yet he became one of the earliest practitioners of "total war"—that is, breaking the morale of the civilians in order to break the backbone of the military. Before leaving captured Atlanta on his spectacular march to the sea, he ordered the inhabitants to evacuate the city, pending its destruction as a military measure. In response to an appeal from the city fathers that he would work a cruel hardship on pregnant women, invalids, widows, orphans, and others in an area already overflowing with refugees, he sent the following reply. Decide whether the South had actually brought these cruelties on itself, and whether its generals would have acted differently in Sherman's place.

Gentlemen: I have your letter of the 11th, in the nature of a petition to revoke my orders removing all the inhabitants from Atlanta. I have read it carefully, and give full credit to your statements of the distress that will be occasioned, and yet shall not revoke my orders, because they were not

1. *Memoirs of General William T. Sherman* (1887), II, 125–27. Letter of Sept. 12, 1864.

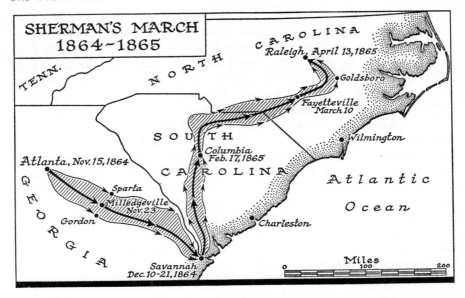

SHERMAN'S MARCH
1864~1865

designed to meet the humanities of the case, but to prepare for the future struggles in which millions of good people outside of Atlanta have a deep interest.

We must have peace, not only at Atlanta, but in all America. To secure this, we must stop the war that now desolates our once happy and favored country. To stop war, we must defeat the rebel armies which are arrayed against the laws and Constitution that all must respect and obey. To defeat those armies, we must prepare the way to reach them in their recesses, provided with the arms and instruments which enable us to accomplish our purpose.

Now, I know the vindictive nature of our enemy, that we may have many years of military operations from this quarter; and, therefore, deem it wise and prudent to prepare in time. The use of Atlanta for warlike purposes is inconsistent with its character as a home for families. There will be no manufactures, commerce, or agriculture here for the maintenance of families, and sooner or later want will compel the inhabitants to go. Why not go now, when all the arrangements are completed for the transfer, instead of waiting till the plunging shot of contending armies will renew the scenes of the past month? Of course, I do not apprehend any such thing at this moment, but you do not suppose this army will be here until the war is over. I cannot discuss this subject with you fairly, because I cannot impart to you what we propose to do, but I assert that our military plans make it necessary for the inhabitants to go away, and I can only renew my offer of services to make their exodus in any direction as easy and comfortable as possible.

You cannot qualify war in harsher terms than I will. War is cruelty, and you cannot refine it; and those who brought war into our country deserve all the curses and maledictions a people can pour out. I know I had no hand in making this war, and I know I will make more sacrifices today than any of you to secure peace. But you cannot have peace and a division of our country. If the United States submits to a division now, it will not stop, but will go on until we reap the fate of Mexico, which is eternal war.

The United States does and must assert its authority, wherever it once had power; for, if it relaxes one bit to pressure, it is gone, and I believe that such is the national feeling. This feeling assumes various shapes, but always comes back to that of Union. Once admit the Union, once more acknowledge the authority of the national Government, and, instead of devoting your houses and streets and roads to the dread uses of war, I and this army become at once your protectors and supporters, shielding you from danger, let it come from what quarter it may. I know that a few individuals cannot resist a torrent of error and passion, such as swept the South into rebellion, but you can point out, so that we may know those who desire a government, and those who insist on war and its desolation.

You might as well appeal against the thunderstorm as against these terrible hardships of war. They are inevitable, and the only way the people of Atlanta can hope once more to live in peace and quiet at home, is to stop the war, which can only be done by admitting that it began in error and is perpetuated in pride.

We don't want your Negroes, or your horses, or your houses, or your lands, or anything you have, but we do want and will have a just obedience to the laws of the United States. That we will have, and, if it involves the destruction of your improvements, we cannot help it.

You have heretofore read public sentiment in your newspapers, that live by falsehood and excitement; and the quicker you seek for truth in other quarters, the better. I repeat then that, by the original compact of government, the United States had certain rights in Georgia, which have never been relinquished and never will be; that the South began war by seizing forts, arsenals, mints, custom-houses, etc., etc., long before Mr. Lincoln was installed, and before the South had one jot or tittle of provocation.

I myself have seen in Missouri, Kentucky, Tennessee, and Mississippi, hundreds of thousands of women and children fleeing from your armies and desperadoes, hungry and with bleeding feet. In Memphis, Vicksburg, and Mississippi, we fed thousands upon thousands of the families of rebel soldiers left on our hands, and whom we could not see starve.

Now that war comes home to you, you feel very different. You deprecate its horrors, but did not feel them when you sent carloads of soldiers and ammunition, and molded shells and shot, to carry war into Kentucky and Tennessee, to desolate the homes of hundreds and thousands of good people who only asked to live in peace at their old homes, and under the government of their inheritance.

But these comparisons are idle. I want peace, and believe it can only be reached through union and war, and I will ever conduct war with a view to perfect and early success.

But, my dear sirs, when peace does come, you may call on me for anything. Then will I share with you the last cracker, and watch with you to shield your homes and families against danger from every quarter.

Now you must go, and take with you the old and feeble, feed and nurse them, and build for them, in more quiet places, proper habitations to shield them against the weather until the mad passions of men cool down, and allow the Union and peace once more to settle over your old homes at Atlanta. Yours in haste,

W. T. Sherman, Major-General commanding

2. Georgia Damns the Yankees (1864)

After burning much of Atlanta, General Sherman daringly cut loose from his base of supplies, and headed for the sea. Forced to live off the country, he detailed soldiers (loosely called "bummers") to round up poultry, livestock, and other provisions. This type of foraging degenerated at times into pillaging, which was worsened by bands of lawless civilians from both North and South. Ascertain what light this passage from the diary of a returning Georgia woman casts on the effectiveness of Sherman's methods, the state of Southern morale, and the prospect of North-South harmony after the war.

December 24, 1864.—About three miles from Sparta [Georgia] we struck the "Burnt Country," as it is well named by the natives, and then I could better understand the wrath and desperation of these poor people. I almost felt as if I should like to hang a Yankee myself. There was hardly a fence left standing all the way from Sparta to Gordon. The fields were trampled down and the road was lined with carcasses of horses, hogs, and cattle that the invaders, unable either to consume or to carry away with them, had wantonly shot down, to starve out the people and prevent them from making their crops. The stench in some places was unbearable; every few hundred yards we had to hold our noses or stop them with the cologne Mrs. Elzey had given us, and it proved a great boon.

The dwellings that were standing all showed signs of pillage, and on every plantation we saw the charred remains of the gin-house and packing-screw, while here and there lone chimney-stacks, "Sherman's sentinels," told of homes laid in ashes. The infamous wretches! I couldn't wonder now that these poor people should want to put a rope round the neck of every red-handed "devil of them" they could lay their hands on.

Hay ricks and fodder stacks were demolished, corn-cribs were empty, and every bale of cotton that could be found was burnt by the savages. I saw no grain of any sort, except little patches they had spilled when feeding their horses and which there was not even a chicken left in the country to

2. Eliza F. Andrews, *The War-Time Journal of a Georgia Girl* (1908), pp. 32–33. By permission of Appleton-Century-Crofts.

eat. A bag of oats might have lain anywhere along the road without danger from the beasts of the fields, though I cannot say it would have been safe from the assaults of hungry man.

Crowds of [Confederate] soldiers were tramping over the road in both directions; it was like traveling through the streets of a populous town all day. They were mostly on foot, and I saw numbers seated on the roadside greedily eating raw turnips, meat skins, parched corn—anything they could find, even picking up the loose grains that Sherman's horses had left. I felt tempted to stop and empty the contents of our provision baskets into their laps, but the dreadful accounts that were given of the state of the country before us made prudence get the better of our generosity.

Before crossing the Oconee [River] at Milledgeville we ascended an immense hill, from which there was a fine view of the town, with Governor Brown's fortifications in the foreground and the river rolling at our feet. The Yankees had burnt the bridge; so we had to cross on a ferry. There was a long train of vehicles ahead of us, and it was nearly an hour before our turn came; so we had ample time to look about us. On our left was a field where thirty thousand Yankees had camped hardly three weeks before. It was strewn with the debris they had left behind, and the poor people of the neighborhood were wandering over it, seeking anything they could find to eat, even picking up grains of corn that were scattered around where the Yankees had fed their horses. We were told that a great many valuables were found there at first, plunder that the invaders had left behind, but the place had been picked over so often by this time that little now remained except tufts of loose cotton, piles of half-rotted grain, and the carcasses of slaughtered animals, which raised a horrible stench. Some men were plowing in one part of the field, making ready for next year's crop.

3. Grant Displays Generosity (1865)

While Sherman was ravaging Georgia and the Carolinas, General Grant was slowly grinding his way into Virginia. Superior Union forces finally drove General Lee into a corner, and at Appomattox the sloppily dressed General Grant met with the handsomely attired General Lee to discuss terms of surrender. The following version is taken from Grant's *Memoirs*, which he completed on his deathbed in 1885 while suffering agony from cancer of the throat. (Although he did not live to see the two volumes published, they netted his indebted widow more than $400,000 in royalties.) At the time of the surrender negotiations there were still several Confederate armies in the field, and there was a real possibility that the Civil War would degenerate into a protracted guerrilla war. In the light of these circumstances, comment on Grant's generosity as described in his *Memoirs*.

Then, after a little further conversation, General Lee remarked to me again that their army was organized a little differently from the army of the United States (still maintaining by implication that we were two countries); that in their army the cavalrymen and artillerists owned their own horses;

3. *Personal Memoirs of U. S. Grant* (1886), II, 492–93.

and he asked if he was to understand that the men who so owned their horses were to be permitted to retain them. I told him that as the terms were written they would not; that only the officers were permitted to take their private property. He then, after reading over the terms a second time, remarked that that was clear.

I then said to him that I thought this would be about the last battle of the war—I sincerely hoped so; and I said further I took it that most of the men in the ranks were small farmers. The whole country had been so raided by the two armies that it was doubtful whether they would be able to put in a crop to carry themselves and their families through the next winter without the aid of the horses they were then riding. The United States did not want them and I would, therefore, instruct the officers I left behind to receive the paroles of his troops to let every man of the Confederate army who claimed to own a horse or mule take the animal to his home. Lee remarked again that this would have a happy effect.

[*On the day that Lee asked Grant for surrender terms (April 7, 1865), the* Richmond Evening Whig *published the following obituary notice:*

DIED: CONFEDERACY,
SOUTHERN.—At the late resi-
dence of his father, J. Davis,
Richmond, Virginia, Southern
Confederacy, aged 4 years.
Death caused by strangulation.
No funeral.]

THOUGHT PROVOKERS

1. Why did the South secede? Would the North have acquiesced in peaceful coexistence if the South had not fired on Fort Sumter? Which side was really the aggressor in starting the war?
2. Why was the ideal of Union more important than that of freeing the slave? Which had the greater emotional appeal, and why?
3. Why was there danger of a military dictatorship in the North during the Civil War? Should there have been a dictatorship?
4. In what respects did the Emancipation Proclamation prove to be statesmanlike? in what respects more productive of harm than good?
5. In view of the earlier British emancipation of slaves, why should Britain's ruling class have criticized Lincoln's Emancipation Proclamation?
6. It has been argued that Sherman was a humane general in that in the long run he reduced civilian suffering by bringing the war to a more speedy end. Comment. Could the same argument be used to support the dropping of atomic bombs on two Japanese cities in 1945? Argue both sides of the ethics of making war on civilians.

FURTHER EXPLORATION

General: J. G. Randall and David Donald, *The Civil War and Reconstruction* (2nd ed., 1961); Allan Nevins, *The War for the Union: The Improvised War, 1861–1862* (1959); Allan Nevins, *The War for the Union: War Becomes Revolution, 1862–1863* (1960).

Secession Crisis: R. N. Current, *The Lincoln Nobody Knows* (1959). **War Aims:** B. P. Thomas, *Abraham Lincoln* (1952). **Lincoln's Generals:** T. H. Williams, *Lincoln and His Generals* (1952); K. P. Williams, *Lincoln Finds a General* (5 vols., 1952–1959); W. W. Hassler, Jr., *General George B. McClellan* (1957); D. S. Freeman, *R. E. Lee* (4 vols., 1934–1935). **Emancipation Proclamation:** J. G. Randall, *Lincoln the President* (1945), vol. II; Carl Sandburg, *Abraham Lincoln: The War Years* (1939), vols. I, II; E. D. Adams, *Great Britain and the American Civil War* (2 vols., 1925). **Uncivil War:** Lloyd Lewis, *Sherman: Fighting Prophet* (1932); J. G. Barrett, *Sherman's March through the Carolinas* (1956).

Recent: R. N. Current, *Lincoln and the First Shot* (1963) [paperback]; R. A. Wooster, *The Secession Conventions of the South* (1962); P. S. Klein, *President James Buchanan* (1962); Edward Wagenknecht, *Harriet Beecher Stowe: The Known and the Unknown* (1965); A. D. Kirwan, *John J. Crittenden: The Struggle for the Union* (1962); Philip Stern, *When the Guns Roared: World Aspects of the American Civil War* (1965); J. M. McPherson, *The Negro's Civil War: How American Negroes Felt and Acted During the War for the Union* (1965); J. A. Rawley, *Turning Points of the Civil War* (1966); Bruce Catton, *Never Call Retreat* (1965).

Chapter 23

The Civilian Front: North and South

It has long been a grave question whether any government not too strong for the liberties of its people can be strong enough to maintain its existence in great emergencies.

ABRAHAM LINCOLN, 1864

PROLOGUE: The seven seceding states formed a provisional government about a month before the firing on Fort Sumter forced the remaining four laggard sisters into their camp. In the ensuing conflict the civilian front, both at home and abroad, was no less important than the fighting front. Northern diplomats strove to keep the European powers out; the Southern diplomats strove to drag them in. Britain, the key nation, remained officially neutral because of self-interest. Meanwhile in America, with dollars pouring into the maw of the war machine, conscienceless grafters and profiteers on each side grew fat. The Washington and Richmond regimes were both forced to override constitutional guarantees and deal harshly with critics. Lincoln, who had failed to bring military victory, was in grave danger of being unhorsed in the presidential election of 1864 by dissatisfied Democrats, but his ultimate triumph insured a bitter-end prosecution of the war. His assassination in 1865 brought deification in the North and grave forebodings in the South.

A. FRAMING A NEW GOVERNMENT

1. Two Constitutions Compared (1861)

A spirit of high adventure permeated the atmosphere of Montgomery, Alabama, on February 4, 1861, when a convention of Southern delegates assembled to launch a new experiment in government. A committee of two men from each of the seven seceded states, headed by fiery R. B. Rhett of South Carolina, set to work upon a permanent constitution. After five weeks of labor the assembled delegates, now forming a Congress. As each state claimed to be entering into a compact in its sovereign capacity, the right of subsequent secession could be inferred, though three proposals were quashed that specifically guaranteed such a right. The more significant parts of the Confederate Constitution that differed substantially from the United States Constitution are given in italics in the right-hand column below (with editorial commentary, also in italics, placed opposite in the left-hand column). The emphasis upon slavery prompted the English magazine *Punch* to brand the new government "Slave-ownia." After eliminating all references to slaves, direct and indirect, ascertain which features of the Confederate Constitution, if engrafted upon the United States Constitution, would definitely strengthen the latter; definitely weaken it. Determine to what extent the Confederate innovations reflected the traditional position of the South before 1861.

1. Complete texts of both constitutions in parallel columns appear in Woodrow Wilson, *A History of the American People* (1902), IV (Appendix).

CONSTITUTION OF THE
UNITED STATES OF AMERICA

We, the people of the United States, in order to form a more perfect union, establish justice, insure domestic tranquillity, provide for the common defense, promote the general welfare, and secure the blessings of liberty to ourselves and our posterity, do ordain and establish this Constitution for the United States of America.

Article I

Section II. . . . The House of Representatives . . . shall have the sole power of impeachment.

[*A greater grant of power to the states over the central government.*]

Section VI. . . . and no person holding any office under the United States shall be a member of either House during his continuance in office.

[*Presumably a gain for democratic government, and a possible entering wedge for a parliamentary form. The Confederacy collapsed before this innovation had a proper trial.*]

Section VII. [Provisions for the President's veto power and for Congress' power to override.]

[*This "item veto," now employed by many states, was designed to prevent the logrolling addition of pork-barrel schemes to essential appropriation bills.*]

Section VIII. The Congress shall have power—

To lay and collect taxes, duties, imposts, and excises, to pay the debts

CONSTITUTION OF THE CONFEDERATE STATES OF AMERICA

We, the people of the *Confederate* States, *each State acting in its sovereign and independent character,* in order to form *a permanent federal government,* establish justice, insure domestic tranquillity, and secure the blessings of liberty to ourselves and our posterity—*invoking the favor and guidance of Almighty God*—do ordain and establish this Constitution for the Confederate States of America.

Article I

Section II. . . . The House of Representatives . . . shall have the sole power of impeachment; *except that any judicial or other Federal officer, resident and acting solely within the limits of any State, may be impeached by a vote of two-thirds of both branches of the Legislature thereof.*

Section VI. . . . and no person holding any office under the Confederate States shall be a member of either House during his continuance in office. *But Congress may, by law, grant to the principal officer in each of the Executive Departments a seat upon the floor of either House, with the privilege of discussing any measures appertaining to his department.*

Section VII. [Identical provisions with the following addition:] *The President may approve any appropriation and disapprove any other appropriation in the same bill. In such case he shall, in signing the bill, designate the appropriations disapproved; and shall return a copy of such appropriations, with his objections, to the House in which the bill shall have originated; and the same proceedings shall then be had as in case of other bills disapproved by the President. . . .*

Section VIII. The Congress shall have power—

To lay and collect taxes, duties, imposts, and excises, *for revenue nec-*

and provide for the common defense and general welfare of the United States; but all duties, imposts, and excises shall be uniform throughout the United States. . . .

[*A reflection of traditional Southern antipathy to protective tariffs; tariffs for revenue permissible.*]

essary to pay the debts, provide for the common defense, *and carry on the government* of the Confederate States; *but no bounties shall be granted from the Treasury; nor shall any duties or taxes on importations from foreign nations be laid to promote or foster any branch of industry;* and all duties, imposts, and excises shall be uniform throughout the Confederate States. . . .

To regulate commerce with foreign nations, and among the several States, and with the Indian tribes. . . .

[*A reflection of traditional Southern antipathy to taxing all the states to construct internal improvements in a selected few; a safeguard of states' rights.*]

To regulate commerce with foreign nations, and among the several States, and with the Indian tribes; *but neither this, nor any other clause contained in the Constitution, shall ever be construed to delegate the power of Congress to appropriate money for any internal improvement intended to facilitate commerce; except for the purpose of furnishing lights, beacons, and buoys, and other aids to navigation upon the coasts, and the improvement of harbors and the removing of obstructions in river navigation, in all which cases such duties shall be laid on the navigation facilitated thereby, as may be necessary to pay the costs and expenses thereof.* . . .

Section IX. The migration or importation of such persons [slaves] as any of the States now existing shall think proper to admit shall not be prohibited by the Congress prior to the year 1808, but a tax or duty may be imposed on such importation, not exceeding $10 for each person. . . .

[*Gestures to the civilized world, presumably to speed recognition by France and Britain; also to spur secession of other slave states.*]

Section IX. The importation of *negroes of the African race, from any foreign country other than the slaveholding States or Territories of the United States of America, is hereby forbidden; and Congress is required to pass such laws as shall effectually prevent the same.*

Congress shall also have power to prohibit the introduction of slaves from any State not a member of, or Territory not belonging to, this Confederacy. . . .

No bill of attainder or ex post facto law shall be passed. . . .

No bill of attainder, or ex post facto law, *or law denying or impairing the right of property in negro slaves* shall be passed . . .

No tax or duty shall be laid on articles exported from any State. . . .

[*A new source of revenue to be tapped. The South had opposed an export duty in 1787.*]

No tax or duty shall be laid on articles exported from any State, *except by a vote of two-thirds of both Houses.* . . .

No money shall be drawn from the Treasury but in consequence of appropriations made by law; and a regular statement and account of the receipts and expenditures of all public money shall be published from time to time. . . .

[*For more businesslike financing, and to prevent logrolling bills.*]

No money shall be drawn from the Treasury but in consequence of appropriations made by law; and a regular statement and account of the receipts and expenditures of all public money shall be published from time to time.

Congress shall appropriate no money from the Treasury except by a vote of two-thirds of both Houses, taken by yeas and nays, unless it be asked and estimated for by some one of the heads of departments, and submitted to Congress by the President; or for the purpose of paying its own expenses and contingencies; or for the payment of claims against the Confederate States, the justice of which shall have been judicially declared by a tribunal for the investigation of claims against the government, which it is hereby made the duty of Congress to establish.

All bills appropriating money shall specify in federal currency the exact amount of each appropriation and the purposes for which it is made; and Congress shall grant no extra compensation to any public contractor, officer, agent, or servant, after such contract shall have been made or such service rendered. . . .

Article II

Section I. The executive power shall be vested in a President of the United States of America. He shall hold his office during the term of four years, and, together with the Vice-President, chosen for the same term, be elected as follows: . . . [Changed in 1951 by the 22nd Amendment, which limits the President to two terms of four years each.]

Article II

Section I. The executive power shall be vested in a President of the Confederate States of America. He and the Vice-President shall hold their offices for the term of *six* years; *but the President shall not be re-eligible.* The President and the Vice-President shall be elected as follows: . . .

Article IV

Section II. The citizens of each State shall be entitled to all privileges and immunities of citizens in the several States. . . .

[*The South reaffirms the Dred Scott decision, 1857.*]

Article IV

Section II. The citizens of each State shall be entitled to all the privileges and immunities of citizens in the several States; *and shall have the right of transit and sojourn in any State of this Confederacy, with their slaves and other property; and the right of property in said slaves shall not be thereby impaired. . . .*

Section III. . . . The Congress shall have power to dispose of and make all needful rules and regulations respecting the territory or other property belonging to the United States. . . .

[*A safeguard against the type of controversy that arose after 1848 regarding the extension of slavery into the territories.*]

Section III. . . . The Congress shall have power to dispose of and make all needful rules and regulations concerning the property of the Confederate States, including the lands thereof.

The Confederate States may acquire new territory; and Congress shall have power to legislate and provide governments for the inhabitants of all territory belonging to the Confederate States, lying without the limits of the several States; and may permit them, at such times and in such manner as it may by law provide, to form States to be admitted into the Confederacy. In all such territory, the institution of negro slavery, as it now exists in the Confederate States, shall be recognized and protected by Congress and by the territorial government, and the inhabitants of the several Confederate States and Territories shall have the right to take to such territory any slaves lawfully held by them in any of the States or Territories of the Confederate States. . . .

2. Stephens' Cornerstone Speech (1861)

The same convention at Montgomery, Alabama, that framed the Confederate Constitution chose Jefferson Davis as President and Alexander Hamilton Stephens of Georgia, an ex-Congressman, as Vice-President. Stephens was a sallow-complexioned, emaciated figure (seldom weighing more than one hundred pounds) with a piping voice and a fighting spirit. Although opposing secession, he loyally (or disloyally) went along with his state. In this famous speech at Savannah, three weeks before the blowup at Fort Sumter, he spelled out the philosophical basis of the Confederate Constitution. From it decide whether the Confederacy looked upon slavery as an evolutionary institution that would gradually fade away in consonance with the spirit of the age.

The new Constitution has put at rest forever all the agitating questions relating to our peculiar institution, African slavery, as it exists amongst us —the proper status of the Negro in our form of civilization. This was the immediate cause of the late rupture and present revolution. Jefferson, in his forecast, had anticipated this as the "rock upon which the old Union would split." He was right. What was conjecture with him is now a realized fact. But whether he fully comprehended the great truth upon which that

2. Henry Cleveland, *Alexander H. Stephens* (1866), p. 721 (March 21, 1861).

rock stood and stands may be doubted. The prevailing ideas entertained
by him and most of the leading statesmen at the time of the formation of
the old Constitution were that the enslavement of the African was in violation of the laws of nature; that it was wrong in principle, socially, morally,
and politically.

It was an evil they knew not well how to deal with, but the general
opinion of the men of that day was that, somehow or other, in the order
of Providence, the institution would be evanescent and pass away. This
idea, though not incorporated in the Constitution, was the prevailing idea
at the time. . . .

Our new government is founded upon exactly the opposite idea; its
foundations are laid, its cornerstone rests, upon the great truth that the
Negro is not equal to the white man; that slavery—subordination to the
superior race—is his natural and normal condition. [Applause.]

This, our new government, is the first, in the history of the world, based
upon this great physical, philosophical, and moral truth.

3. The New York *Times* Dissents (1861)

The unabashed prominence that Stephens gave to slavery, though applauded by his
audience, was probably a mistaken tactic. Determine why from this direct editorial
response in the New York *Times*. Note how Stephens has misled this journal with
regard to the general motives for secession.

Mr. Stephens is quite right in saying that this is the *first* government in
the history of the world based upon slavery. This present year is the first
time in the history of the world when a great community has overthrown
a free Constitution, not because of its oppressions, but in order to perpetuate the abject slavery of four millions of its people.

Mr. Stephens apparently sees nothing in this fact of evil omen to the
success of his experiment. Indeed, he makes it the chief glory of the new
nation that its cornerstone is slavery. He may rest assured the civilized
world will take a very different view of this matter. He will find in that
declaration a barrier mountain-high against the sympathies of every nation
on earth. There is no power so utterly dead to all the impulses of humanity,
and to all the influences of Christian civilization, as to look with anything
but horror and detestation upon a nation commencing its career for such
a motive and with such an aim.

B. BRITISH INVOLVEMENT

1. The London *Times* Breathes Easier (1862)

The British government tried to preserve a cold neutrality during the Civil War.
But the landed aristocracy, with a kindred feeling for the plantation aristocracy of
the South, generally hoped for a Confederate victory. Some Britons even argued that

3. New York *Times*, March 27, 1861.
1. London *Times*, Aug. 15, 1862.

their Christian duty required them to intervene and stop the senseless bloodshed. The pontifical London *Times* on the whole supported the official policy of non-intervention, and the North could rejoice that it did. So influential was this journal that when it took snuff, the quipsters said, the rest of England sneezed. From this *Times* editorial determine why, as between humanitarian intervention and realistic non-intervention, the British government chose non-intervention.

The prevalent expectation is that both North and South will suffer unexampled injury, and finally settle down into two or more states, much the wiser and sadder for their bitter experience. Many politicians are only too content to see things take this course.

Indeed, people are breathing more freely, and talking more lightly of the United States, than they have done any time these thirty years. We don't now hear once a twelvemonth that England has complied with some ridiculous demand, or endured some high-flying specimen of American impudence, or allowed them to draw their boundary lines [Maine, Oregon?] as they please. We are no longer stunned every quarter of a year with the tremendous totals of American territory, population, and wealth, computed to come due thirty, sixty, a hundred years hence; when, of course, the tallest empire of the Old World will easily walk between the legs of the American colossus.

Nevertheless, the riddance of a nightmare is purchased very dearly at the cost of present suffering. Great as that suffering is, we have assured the Americans over and over again that we have no intention of interfering. If there is any fault to be found with this country, it is that we are too well resigned to the suicidal work of which we are the safe, but not unconcerned, witnesses. It is the old story of the traveller frightened by the tiger and relieved by seeing him immediately afterwards in deadly conflict with some other monster.

2. Britons Hail Democracy's Collapse (1862)

Many British aristocrats derived satisfaction from recalling 1776. Then thirteen colonies, struggling for freedom against King George III, were trying to secede from the British Empire. Now eleven states, struggling for freedom against King Abraham I, were trying to secede from the American Empire. Ascertain why the London *Times* believed that the South, in these weeks before Emancipation, had the better moral (if not legal) case, and why this newspaper could maintain that democracy had broken down.

In this respect, as in others, the South has an immense advantage over the North. The Confederates are fighting in a cause which is at once plain and popular, which they have always avowed, and of which they have never despaired. They are fighting for independence—for possession and enjoyment of their own territories under their own laws, apart from any connection with a people from whom they always differed, and whom they now most cordially detest. . . .

2. *Ibid.,* Sept. 13, 1862.

LATEST FROM SPIRIT-LAND

GHOST OF KING GEORGE III: "Well, Mr. Washington, what
do you think of your fine republic now, eh?—What
d'ye think? What d'ye think, eh?"
GHOST OF MR. WASHINGTON: "Humph!"
The Confederates revolt against the rebels of yesteryear.
Punch (London), 1863.

But with the Northerners all is different. They are not content with their
own. They are fighting to coerce others, and to retain millions of people
in political union with them against their will. This, too, they are doing
in spite of the principles on which all American institutions have been
notoriously based—principles inculcating the most extreme doctrines of
freedom, and deriving all governments from the mere will and assent of
the governed. . . .

The principles on which the President and the majority, perhaps, of his
coadjutors undertook the war are in themselves by no means indefensible.
Mr. Lincoln held that the Constitution of the Union, which he was bound
to preserve, did not permit the secession of any of its states, and, though
the point is not very clear, it may be allowed that this view of the legal
merits of the case was shared in England. We were of opinion that South
Carolina had no title, under the provisions of the American Constitution,
to proclaim her own independence, and it follows, therefore, that the Supreme Government was entitled to restrain her in such a proceeding.

But when South Carolina was followed by other states, when nine
millions of people asserted their claims to self-government, and when it
became evident that these claims were based, if not upon law, at any rate

upon facts, we were unable to see how the Northerners could with any consistency resist the demand. That they did resist it, and even made an appeal to the sword, was simply a proof that democracies, in this respect, are influenced by the same passions as the most despotic monarchies.

Here, in fact, it was that republicanism broke down. The real collapse was not in the secession of the South, but in the resistance of the North. If the Northerners, on ascertaining the resolution of the South, had peaceably allowed the seceders to depart, the result might fairly have been quoted as illustrating the advantages of democracy. But when republicans put empire above liberty, and resorted to political oppression and war rather than suffer any abatement of national power, it was clear that nature at Washington was precisely the same as nature at St. Petersburg.

There was not, in fact, a single argument advanced in defense of the war against the South which might not have been advanced with exactly the same force for the subjugation of Hungary or Poland [by Russia].

Democracy broke down, not when the Union ceased to be agreeable to all its constituent states, but when it was upheld, like any other empire, by force of arms.

3. Southern Resentment against England (1862)

"Cotton is King!" the Southern fire-eaters had exulted before secession. For England was so heavily dependent on the Southern fiber for her vast textile industry that in the event of a North-South clash the British would presumably be forced to intervene on the side of the Confederacy. The Confederates even tried to hasten that day, to the annoyance of Britishers, by burning cotton. Late in the second year of the Civil War, England was in the grip of a cotton famine, but, much to the disappointment of the South, the London regime refused to go even so far as to extend recognition to the Confederates. President Davis openly condemned British partiality toward the North. Determine why, in the view of the Southern journal quoted below, Britain wanted the Union to break up but refused to intervene. Which of the arguments seems most farfetched?

The Confederate States are the only new power she [England] has refused to recognize, and yet they have manifested a degree of strength greater than all those we have enumerated [*e.g.,* Belgium] put together. We have, under these circumstances, we think, some right to be indignant. We have not the smallest right to be astonished.

Great Britain has been trying to bring about the very state of things now existing here ever since the United States became a recognized power of the earth. She never could find it in her heart to forgive the successful revolt of the colonies. . . . In latter days England has been jealous of the growing power of the United States to an inordinate degree. She has clearly foreseen that, if they continue united, they must become, before the close of this century, the first nation of the world, with an invincible army, a navy that must assume the empire of the seas, and a commerce that must swallow up all the commerce of the Old World.

3. *Southern Illustrated News,* Oct. 4, 1862.

Thus, in addition to the old grudge, she has been stimulated by the fear of losing her position among the powers of the earth. Cost what it might, she has felt that for her the greatest of all objects has been to destroy the Union. She has succeeded at last, and it is not wonderful that she should desire to see the war carried on as long as both parties may have the strength to maintain themselves. She feels that intervention would follow recognition, and this she is by no means disposed to undertake, because it might have the effect of shortening the war.

The war in question, besides removing a powerful rival from her path, is useful to her in another respect. If it should last long enough, it may be the means of getting her cotton from India into demand, and it may stimulate the production in Australia. When we consider that cotton constitutes the very basis upon which her enormous power is built, we shall see at once the importance of having it all under her own control. This she hopes to accomplish by destroying the culture in this country, which can only be done by destroying the labor which produces it. The abolition of slavery in her West India possessions was but the preliminary step to the abolition of slavery in this country. . . .

In addition to these causes, it may be that the British Government feels itself in no condition to intervene, because of the present condition in Europe. Affairs are far from satisfactory in Italy, and any moment may witness the outbreak of a general war. As we have already observed, recognition might bring on intervention as a necessary consequence, and intervention would be sure to bring on war. This the British Government will avoid if it can. It already has a most exaggerated opinion of the strength of the Yankee Government, and is evidently very unwilling—we might almost say afraid—to come into collision with it. A late debate in Parliament plainly revealed an extraordinary degree of alarm on the subject of Canada. . . .

These, we think, are the reasons why Great Britain—meaning the British Government—is averse to recognize us. That the majority of the people sympathize with us, while they detest the Yankees, we do not doubt.

4. A Northerner Lambasts Britain (1863)

The South was disillusioned because England did not seem sympathetic enough; the North was angered because England seemed too sympathetic to the South. Several diplomatic crises between London and Washington were narrowly surmounted —the *Trent* affair, the building of the cruiser *Alabama*, the Laird rams threat—but the construction of destructive Confederate commerce-raiders in England rankled most deeply. Despite the serious shortage of cotton, the British prospered from an enormously expanded two-way trade with the North. George T. Strong, a prominent New York lawyer, here expresses a common view. Judge whether his assessment of England's alleged unneutrality seems fair, and why he is more bitter toward England than his Southern counterpart in the preceding article.

4. Reprinted with permission of the publisher from *The Diary of George Templeton Strong*, edited by Allan Nevins and M. H. Thomas, III, 311. Copyright 1952 by The Macmillan Company.

NEUTRALITY

MRS. NORTH: "How about the *Alabama,* you wicked old man?"
MRS. SOUTH: "Where's my rams? Take back your precious consuls—there!!!"
Lincoln scolds John Bull for too much interference; Davis for not enough. *Punch*
(London), 1863.

April 14 [1863]. We drift fast toward war with England, but I think we shall not reach that point. The shopkeepers who own England want to do us all the harm they can and to give all possible aid and comfort to our slave-breeding and woman-flogging adversary, for England has degenerated into a trader, manufacturer, and banker, and has lost all the instincts and sympathies that her name still suggests. She would declare war against us fast enough if she dared follow her sordid impulses, but there are dirty, selfish considerations on the other side.

She cannot ally herself with slavery, as she inclines to do, without closing a profitable market, exposing her commerce to [Yankee] privateers, and diminishing the supply of [Northern] breadstuffs on which her operatives depend for life. On the other side, however, is the consideration that by allowing piratical *Alabamas* to be built, armed, and manned in her ports to prey on our commerce, she is making a great deal of money.

It's fearful to think that the sympathies of England—the England of Shakespeare and Hooker, Cowper, Milton, Somers, Erskine, and others— with North or South, freedom or slavery, in this great continental battle of her children, are guided by mere considerations of profit and loss. Anglomaniac [pro-English] Americans, like myself, are thoroughly "disillusionated."

C. GRAFT AND SHORTAGES NORTH AND SOUTH

1. Shoddy Wool in Yankeeland (1861–1865)

Great wars invariably inspire devotion and self-sacrifice; they also spawn grafters and chiselers. The Civil War, with all its noble ideals, was no exception. The orgy of greed, which begot the "shoddy millionaires," is here described by General de Trobriand, a French émigré and New York newspaper editor who served as a volunteer officer in the United States army for four years. Account for the existence and persistence of the conditions he describes.

But besides the army formed to act against the enemy, there was another army—of lobbyists, contractors, speculators—which was continually renewed and never exhausted. These hurried to the assault on the Treasury, like a cloud of locusts alighting down upon the capital to devour the substance of the country. They were everywhere; in the streets, in the hotels, in the offices, at the Capitol, and in the White House. They continually besieged the bureaus of administration, the doors of the Senate and House of Representatives, wherever there was a chance to gain something.

Government, obliged to ask the aid of private industry for every kind of supply that the army and navy must have without delay, was really at the mercy of these hungry spoilers, who combined with one another to make the law for the government. From this arose contracts exceedingly burdensome, which impoverished the Treasury to enrich a few individuals.

As a matter of course, these latter classes, strangers to every patriotic impulse, saw in the war only an extraordinary opportunity of making a fortune. Every means of obtaining it was a good one to them; so that corruption played a great part in the business of contracting. Political protection was purchased by giving an interest in the contracts obtained. . . .

The government . . . was, then, fleeced by the more moderate and robbed by the more covetous. The army suffered from it directly, as the supplies, which were furnished at a price which was much above their value if they had been of a good quality, were nearly all of a fraudulent inferiority. For example, instead of heavy woolen blankets, the recruits received, at this time, light, open fabrics, made I do not know of what different substances, which protected them against neither the cold nor the rain. A very short wear changed a large part of the uniform to rags, and during the winter spent at Tenallytown the ordinary duration of a pair of shoes was not longer than twenty or thirty days.

This last fact, well attested in my regiment, was followed by energetic remonstrances, on account of which the general commanding the brigade appointed, according to regulations, a special Board of Inspection, with the object of obtaining the condemnation of the defective articles. Amongst the members of the board was an officer expert in these matters, having been employed, before the war, in one of the great shoe factories of Massachusetts. The report was very precise. It showed that the shoes were made

1. Régis de Trobriand, *Four Years with the Army of the Potomac* (1889), pp. 134–36.

of poor leather, not having been properly tanned; that the inside of the soles was filled with gray paper; and that the heels were so poorly fastened that it needed only a little dry weather following a few days of rain to have them drop from the shoes. In fine, the fraud was flagrant in every way.

The report was duly forwarded to the superior authorities. Did it have any consideration? I never knew. However, it was necessary to exhaust the stock in hand before obtaining a new supply, and the price charged the soldier was not altered.

2. Chiselers in the South (1862–1863)

The myth that the Southern "Cavaliers" gave their all with selfless dedication must be discarded. There was magnificent devotion to the Lost Cause, but human nature is not changed by Mason and Dixon lines. In proportion to numbers, desertion was about as rampant in the South as in the North, especially after Yankee invaders burned the homes of absent soldiers. And in proportion to the amount of graft obtainable, the number of grafters was probably about the same. John B. Jones, a prolific and popular Maryland novelist, worked as a clerk for the Confederate government in Richmond and recorded some bitter observations. Determine his chief grievance and what it reveals this early of the South's capacity to resist.

[Dec. 1, 1862] God speed the day of peace! Our patriotism is mainly in the army and among the ladies of the South. The avarice and cupidity of the men at home could only be excelled by ravenous wolves; and most of our sufferings are fully deserved. Where a people will not have mercy on one another, how can they expect mercy? They depreciate the Confederate notes [currency] by charging from $20 to $40 per bbl. for flour; $3.50 per bushel for meal; $2 per lb. for butter; $20 per cord for wood, etc. When we shall have peace, let the extortionists be remembered! Let an indelible stigma be branded upon them.

A portion of the people look like vagabonds. We see men and women and children in the streets in dingy and dilapidated clothes; and some seem gaunt and pale with hunger—the speculators, and thieving quartermasters and commissaries only, looking sleek and comfortable. If this state of things continue a year or so longer, they will have their reward. There will be governmental bankruptcy, and all their gains will turn to dust and ashes, dust and ashes! . . .

[Feb. 11, 1863] Some idea may be formed of the scarcity of food in this city from the fact that, while my youngest daughter was in the kitchen today, a young rat came out of its hole and seemed to beg for something to eat; she held out some bread, which it ate from her hand, and seemed grateful. Several others soon appeared, and were as tame as kittens. Perhaps we shall have to eat them! . . .

[Oct. 22, 1863] A poor woman yesterday applied to a merchant in Carey Street to purchase a barrel of flour. The price he demanded was $70.

2. E. S. Miers, ed., *A Rebel War Clerk's Diary* [John B. Jones] (1958), pp. 126, 257, 296. By permission of the Sagamore Press.

"My God!" exclaimed she, "how can I pay such prices? I have seven children; what shall I do?"

"I don't know, madam," said he, coolly, "unless you eat your children."

3. The Pinch of the Blockade (1861–1865)

The Yankee blockade, which created acute shortages, played into the hands of Southern profiteers. Not all the blockade runners carried munitions of war exclusively. Dr. Paul Barringer, then a small boy in North Carolina, later recalled that an ornately bound copy of Johnson's *Rasselas* came through to his family early in 1865. From recollections edited after his death in 1941, form conclusions as to the effect of the blockade on Southern armies and civilian morale.

Almost at once we began to feel the pinch of war. White sugar disappeared immediately; not only were there no more lumps for gun-shy horses, but there was no sugar for the table. There was, however, an unlimited quantity of sorghum syrup, and around the barrels of sorghum a thick crust of brown sugar often formed. This was carefully scraped off to be served with coffee and berries, the fluid product going to the servants [slaves]. . . .

In a very short time I noticed that matches had disappeared, and I have learned that at the outbreak of the war there was not one match factory in the South. However, flint and steel had passed out of use so recently that many of these old relics, which were sticking around in closets and hidden recesses in attics, were taken out and returned to use. . . .

Other shortages threatened of which I, as a child, saw only the signs and could not realize the seriousness. Paper was getting so scarce that my elders feared that even the dreaded death lists might cease to come. Then it was discovered that wallpaper could be used, and if properly removed from the walls and bleached, it could be printed on both sides. At the last, they used wallpaper that could not be bleached, printing on one side only. I still have one of these old journals. Framed under glass, it shows pink flowers on one side, while the bloody harvest of war is recorded on the other. . . .

The Federal Government declared all drugs contraband of war, and almost no morphine or quinine came through the blockade. As a substitute for the latter, as I have already stated, we used boneset tea, which helped but did not cure malaria. To supply opiate we grew our own poppies, making incisions into the sides of the ovaries of these plants and with the flat of a case knife scraping up the exuded gum. The knife was then scraped off on the edge of a glass jar, and thus we found that we could raise gum opium that was 10 or 12 percent morphine.

There was a poppy bed in every garden planted for this purpose, and when I was seven years old I worked daily for the soldiers, scraping the inspissated juice of the poppy from the bulbar ovaries which had been punctured a few days before, and, like everyone else, I worked under the

---

3. *The Natural Bent: The Memories of Dr. Paul B. Barringer* (1949), pp. 48–53, *passim.*
By permission of the University of North Carolina Press.

eternal mandate, "Don't taste it!" On some fifty poppy heads it was a morning's work to get a mass about as big as a small peanut.

The time came when no more Chilean nitre could run the blockade, and the South must depend on its own resources for this essential element of explosives. It was then that the urine cart began to make its rounds, collecting the night's urine and hauling it to the boiling vats, where the urea and other nitrogenous constituents were extracted and shipped to Augusta, Georgia, for the manufacture of gunpowder. That plant was never more than a few days ahead of the needs of the firing line.

Later on the need became so great that many old cabins which stood up on four corner posts were raised by levers, so that men could crawl under them to scrape the ground for the thin layer of nitrogen-charged clay at the top. As wondering children, we saw men crawling under old barns to scrape up the dry dust, and we saw old plaster taken from the walls and leached in the ash hopper. We heard that in Virginia and Kentucky searching parties invaded the caves where bats roosted, to scrape the bat manure from the floor. All such gleanings were likewise sent to the plant in Augusta.

Looking back at it now, I can see the reason for that persistent and unceasing call to save and extend every natural resource in every section of the South. The need was desperate, and the toil in the homes, the fields, and the improvised factories was unceasing.

4. Self-sacrificing Southern Belles (*c.* 1865)

Food shortages produced a serious bread riot in Richmond in 1863; by 1864 a "Starvation Club" was organized for entertainment without refreshment. As the end neared, hoarders would conceal groceries under the coverlets of their bedrooms. But in general the Southern women showed remarkable devotion and self-sacrifice, even to making dresses out of old curtains. George C. Eggleston, later a distinguished author, was an Indiana-born Virginian who served as an officer in the Confederate forces. From this passage in his reminiscences, determine in what respects it is true that Southern women prolonged the war.

Many of . . . [the women of the South] denied themselves not only delicacies, but substantial food also, when by enduring semi-starvation they could add to the stock of food at the command of the subsistence officers. I myself knew more than one houseful of women who, from the moment that food began to grow scarce, refused to eat meat or drink coffee, living thenceforth only upon vegetables of a speedily perishable sort, in order that they might leave the more for the soldiers in the field.

When a friend remonstrated with one of them, on the ground that her health, already frail, was breaking down utterly for want of proper diet, she replied, in a quiet, determined way, "I know that very well; but it is little that I can do, and I must do that little at any cost. My health and my life are worth less than those of my brothers, and if they give theirs to the cause, why should not I do the same? I would starve to death cheerfully

4. G. C. Eggleston, *A Rebel's Recollections* (1878), pp. 67–68.

if I could feed one soldier more by doing so, but the things I eat can't be sent to camp. I think it a sin to eat anything that can be used for rations."

And she meant what she said, too, as a little mound in the churchyard testifies.

D. CIVIL LIBERTIES NORTH AND SOUTH

1. Vallandigham Flays Despotism (1863)

To preserve the Constitution, Lincoln was forced to take liberties with it. His arbitrary acts included a suspension of the writ of *habeas corpus*, and a consequent imprisonment without trial of scores of Southern sympathizers. Many Democrats in the North—dubbed Copperheads—condemned such highhanded action. The most notorious of these was Clement L. Vallandigham, an eloquent and outspoken critic of this "wicked and cruel" war. He regarded it as a diabolical attempt to end slavery and inaugurate a Republican despotism. Convicted by a military tribunal in Cincinnati of treasonable utterances, he was banished by Lincoln to the Confederacy. After a short stay, he made his way by ship to Canada. From there he ran for the governorship of Ohio in 1863 and, though defeated, polled a heavy vote. Some two months before his arrest in 1863 he delivered this flaming speech in New York to a Democratic group, assailing the recent act of Congress which authorized the President to suspend *habeas corpus* during the war. Decide whether this speech is treasonable, and form conclusions as to whether *habeas corpus* should have been suspended.

. . . [The Habeas Corpus Act] authorizes the President whom the people made, whom the people had chosen by the ballot box under the Constitution and laws, to suspend the writ of *habeas corpus* all over the United States; to say that because there is a rebellion in South Carolina, a man shall not have freedom of speech, freedom of the press, or any of his rights untrammeled in the state of New York, or a thousand miles distant. That was the very question upon which the people passed judgment in the recent [Congressional] elections, more, perhaps, than any other question. . . .

The Constitution gives the power to Congress, and to Congress alone, to suspend the writ of *habeas corpus*, but it can only be done in case of invasion or rebellion, and then only when the public safety requires it. And in the opinion of the best jurists of the land, and indeed of every one previous to these times, Congress could only suspend this writ in places actually in rebellion or actually invaded. That is the Constitution. [Cheers.] And whenever this question shall be tried before a court in the state of New York, or Ohio, or Wisconsin, or anywhere else, before honest and fearless judges worthy of the place they occupy, the decision will be that it is unconstitutional.* [Loud applause.] . . .

Was it this which you were promised in 1860, in that grand [Lincoln] "Wide Awake" campaign, when banners were borne through your streets inscribed "Free speech, free press, and free men"? And all this has been accomplished, so far as the forms of the law go, by the Congress which has just expired. Now, I repeat again that if there is anything wanting to

1. C. L. Vallandigham, *Speeches, Arguments, Addresses, and Letters* (1864), pp. 486–89.
* The Supreme Court did not hold the Habeas Corpus Act unconstitutional.

THE YANKEE GUY FAWKES

Lincoln represented as destroying American liberties by the draft, the suspension of habeas corpus,
and the Emancipation Proclamation. *Fun* (London), 1863.

make up a complete and absolute despotism, as iron and inexorable in its
character as the worst despotisms of the old world, or the most detestable
of modern times, . . . I am unable to comprehend what it is.

All this, gentlemen, infamous and execrable as it is, is enough to make
the blood of the coldest man who has one single appreciation in his heart
of freedom, to boil with indignation. [Loud applause.] Still, so long as they
leave to us free assemblages, free discussion, and a free ballot, I do not
want to see, and will not encourage or countenance, any other mode of
ridding ourselves of it. ["That's it," and cheers.] We are ready to try these
questions in that way. But . . . when the attempt is made to take away
those other rights, and the only instrumentalities peaceably of reforming
and correcting abuses—free assemblages, free speech, free ballot, and free
elections—THEN THE HOUR WILL HAVE ARRIVED WHEN IT WILL BE THE DUTY
OF FREEMEN TO FIND SOME OTHER AND EFFICIENT MODE OF DEFENDING THEIR
LIBERTIES. [Loud and protracted cheering, the whole audience rising to
their feet.]

Our fathers did not inaugurate the Revolution of 1776, they did not
endure the sufferings and privations of a seven years' war to escape from
the mild and moderate control of a constitutional monarchy like that of
England, to be at last, in the third generation, subjected to a tyranny equal
to that of any upon the face of the globe. [Loud applause.]

2. Brownlow Scolds the Secessionists (1861)

If President Lincoln had his pro-Confederate Copperheads, President Davis had his pro-Union "Tories," chiefly among the mountain whites. If Lincoln had his Vallandigham, Davis had his William G. ("Parson") Brownlow, the fiery and fearless Methodist preacher with a foghorn voice who had become editor of the Knoxville *Whig*. This journal was the most influential paper in East Tennessee, and the last Union paper in the South. Though not anti-slavery, Brownlow was anti-secession. His newspaper was suppressed late in 1861, his press was destroyed, and he was imprisoned for treason. The Confederates banished him to the Federal lines—a Vallandigham case in reverse—but he returned to be elected Reconstruction governor of Tennessee in 1865. His defiant flying of a United States flag over his home led him to publish the following statement in his paper on May 25, 1861, two weeks before Tennessee seceded by a popular vote of 104,913 to 47,238. Considering the time of the incident, note who acted treasonably: Brownlow or those who displayed the Confederate flag. Ascertain also what this episode reveals of the strength of Unionism in Tennessee during those anxious weeks.

It is known to this community and to the people of this county that I have had the Stars and Stripes, in the character of a small flag, floating over my dwelling, in East Knoxville, since February. This flag has become very offensive to certain leaders of the Secession party in this town, and to certain would-be leaders, and the more so as it is about the only one of the kind floating in the city. Squads of troops, from three to twenty, have come over to my house within the last several days, cursing the flag in front of my house, and threatening to take it down, greatly to the annoyance of my wife and children. No attack has been made upon it, and consequently we have had no difficulty.

It is due to the Tennessee troops to say that they have never made any such demonstrations. Other troops from the Southern states, passing on to Virginia, have been induced to do so by certain cowardly, sneaking, white-livered scoundrels residing here, who have not the melt [guts] to undertake what they urge strangers to do. One of the Louisiana squads proclaimed in front of my house, on Thursday, that they were told to take it down by citizens of Knoxville.

Now, I wish to say a few things to the public in connection with this subject. This flag is private property, upon a private dwelling, in a state that has never voted herself out of the Union or into the Southern Confederacy, and is therefore lawfully and constitutionally under these same Stars and Stripes I have floating over my house. Until the state, by her citizens, through the ballot box, changes her federal relations, her citizens have a right to fling this banner to the breeze. Those who are in rebellion against the government represented by the Stars and Stripes have up the Rebel flag, and it is a high piece of work to deny loyal citizens of the Union the privilege of displaying their colors! . . .

If these God-forsaken scoundrels and hell-deserving assassins want satis-

---

2. W. G. Brownlow, *Sketches of the Rise, Progress, and Decline of Secession* (1862), pp. 55-58, *passim*.

faction [a duel] out of me for what I have said about them—and it has been no little—they can find me on these streets every day of my life but Sunday. I am at all times prepared to give them satisfaction. I take back nothing I have ever said against the corrupt and unprincipled villains, but reiterate all, cast it in their dastardly faces, and hurl down their lying throats their own infamous calumnies.

Finally, the destroying of my small flag or of my town property is a small matter. The carrying out of the state upon the mad wave of secession is also a small matter, compared with the great PRINCIPLE involved. Sink or swim, live or die, survive or perish, I am a Union man, and owe my allegiance to the Stars and Stripes of my country. Nor can I, in any possible contingency, have any respect for the government of the Confederate States, originating as it did with, and being controlled by, the worst men in the South. And any man saying—whether of high or low degree—that I am an abolitionist or a Black Republican, is a LIAR and a SCOUNDREL.

3. A North Carolinian Is Defiant (1863)

States' rights proved about as harmful to the South as Yankee bayonets. Many Southerners, with their strong tradition of localism, resented or resisted the arbitrary central government in Richmond. William W. Holden, who attacked conscription and other harsh measures, was the recklessly outspoken editor of the Raleigh *North Carolina Standard*. Probably the most influential paper in the state, it allegedly inspired wholesale desertions. In 1863, when a Georgia regiment destroyed Holden's office, he and his associates retaliated by wrecking the headquarters of a rival secessionist organ. (Scores of similar mob demonstrations occurred in the North against Copperhead journals.) Note what is ironical and fantastic about the extreme remedy that Holden here proposes, and what extraordinary conditions he is overlooking.

We were told, when the government was broken up by the states south of us, that the contest was to be for liberty; that the civil power was to prevail over the military; that the common government was to be the agent of the states, and not their master; and that free institutions, not an imperial despotism, were to constitute the great object of our toils and sufferings. But the official paper [the Richmond *Enquirer*] has declared otherwise. That paper is opposed to a nobility to be established by law, but it favors a military despotism like that of France. . . .

We know that a military despotism is making rapid strides in these [Confederate] states. We know that no people ever lost their liberties at once, but step by step, as some deadly disease steals upon the system and gradually but surely saps the fountain of life. . . . The argument now is, we hate Lincoln so bitterly that in order to resist him successfully we must make slaves of ourselves. The answer of our people is, we will be slaves neither to Lincoln, nor Davis, nor France, nor England.

North Carolina is a state, not a province, and she has eighty thousand of as brave troops as ever trod the earth. When she calls them they will come.

3. *North Carolina Standard* (Raleigh), May 6, 1863.

If the worst should happen that can happen, she will be able to take care of herself as an independent power. She will not submit, in any event, to a law of [the Confederate] Congress, passed in deliberate violation of the Constitution, investing Mr. Davis with dictatorial powers; but will resist such a law by withdrawing, if necessary, from the Confederation, and she will fight her way out against all comers. . . . For one, we are determined not to exchange one despotism for another.

E. LINCOLN'S RE-ELECTION AND ASSASSINATION

1. The South Bemoans Lincoln's Election (1864)

President Lincoln, though savagely criticized by many, was renominated in 1864. His opponent was slow-moving General McClellan, the deposed war hero, whom the Democrats nominated on a peace-at-almost-any-price platform, and for whose election the Confederates were praying. Leaving nothing to chance, the Republicans rounded up the soldier vote and, aided by timely military successes, swept Lincoln to victory. Northern newspapers hailed the result as a triumph for the democratic processes. Southern journals reacted differently, notably the jaundiced Richmond *Dispatch*, which had branded Lincoln "the Ape." Account for this newspaper's extreme bitterness, and for its conviction that the election had not been a free one.

Yesterday [election day] will be long remembered in the annals of mankind. On yesterday, twenty millions of human beings, but four years ago esteemed the freest population on earth, met at various points of assemblage for the purpose of making a formal surrender of their liberties . . . to a vulgar tyrant who has never seen a shot fired in anger; who has no more idea of statesmanship than as a means of making money; whose career has been one of unlimited and unmitigated disaster, whose personal qualities are those of a low buffoon, and whose most noteworthy conversation is a medley of profane jests and obscene anecdotes—a creature who has squandered the lives of millions without remorse and without even the decency of pretending to feel for their misfortunes; who still cries for blood and for money in the pursuit of his atrocious designs. . . .

It seems strange to us that he should have condescended to submit to an election at all; and we are convinced he would never have done so had he not been convinced beforehand that it would result in his favor. How McClellan could ever have been so infatuated as to thrust himself in his way, we are unable to conceive. The light punishment he had to expect was to be crushed, for he might have felt assured that, even had he been elected, he would not have been allowed to take his seat.

All the preparations of Lincoln indicate a determination to take possession of the government by force—his military arrangements; the stationing of soldiers about the polls; the arrest of the New York commissioners; the

1. Richmond *Dispatch*, Nov. 9, 1864.

prohibition against any tickets but his own in the fleet; his jealous supervision of the voting in the army—all these indicate a determination to conquer by the ballot box if possible, but, in any event, to conquer. How could McClellan expect to weather such a storm as his adversary had it in his power to raise at any moment of the day? . . .

We are prone to believe that every nation enjoys the exact proportion of freedom to which it is entitled. If the Yankees have lost their liberties, therefore, we think it self-evident that it is because they never deserved to have them. If they are slaves, it is because they are fit for the situation. Slaves they have been for years to all the base passions that are indicative of a profligate and degenerate race; and when nations advance to that point, the transition to material bondage costs but a single step.

2. Davis Deplores Lincoln's Murder (1881)

On Good Friday, April 14, 1865, Lincoln was shot in the head at close range by a half-crazed actor, John Wilkes Booth. The North was outraged. Frenzied mobs wrecked the headquarters of a number of Copperhead newspapers that displayed unconvincing grief or unconcealed satisfaction. Many unthinking Southerners expressed secret or open joy. But others had sobering second thoughts. Jefferson Davis, who was then fleeing and who was falsely suspected of plotting the foul deed, recorded his impressions some sixteen years later. Determine why some Southerners cheered, and why Davis regarded the assassination as a great misfortune.

We arrived at Charlotte [North Carolina] on April 18, 1865, and I there received, at the moment of dismounting, a telegram from General Breckinridge announcing, on information received from General Sherman, that President Lincoln had been assassinated.

An influential citizen of the town, who had come to welcome me, was standing near me, and, after remarking to him in a low voice that I had received sad intelligence, I handed the telegram to him. Some troopers encamped in the vicinity had collected to see me; they called to the gentleman who had the dispatch in his hand to read it, no doubt supposing it to be army news. He complied with their request, and a few, only taking in the fact but not appreciating the evil it portended, cheered, as was natural at news of the fall of one they considered their most powerful foe. The man who invented the story of my having read the dispatch with exultation had free scope for his imagination, as he was not present, and had no chance to know whereof he bore witness, even if there had been any foundation of truth for his fiction.

For an enemy so relentless in the war for our subjugation, we could not be expected to mourn; yet, in view of its political consequences, it could not be regarded otherwise than as a great misfortune to the South. He had power over the Northern people, and was without personal malignity toward the people of the South. His successor [Johnson of Tennessee] was without

2. Jefferson Davis, *The Rise and Fall of the Confederate Government* (1881), II, 683.

power in the North, and the embodiment of malignity toward the Southern people, perhaps the more so because he had betrayed and deserted them in the hour of their need.

3. The British Press Recants (1865)

The British journals, which had been highly critical of Lincoln, were shocked by his assassination into substituting commendation for criticism. A conspicuous exception was the Tory London *Standard,* which ungraciously declared, "He was not a hero while he lived, and therefore his cruel murder does not make him a martyr." The magisterial London *Times,* which had referred to the President as "Lincoln the Last," ate crow in generous amounts. From its editorial comment ascertain whether Britain's concern was wholly sentimental.

. . . A space of twenty-four hours has sufficed not only to fill the country with grief and indignation, but to evoke almost unprecedented expression of feeling from constituted bodies. . . . In the House of Lords the absence of precedent for such a manifestation was actually made the subject of remark.

That much of this extraordinary feeling is due to the tragical character of the event and the horror with which the crime is regarded is doubtless true, nor need we dissemble the fact that the loss which the Americans have sustained is also thought our own loss in so far as one valuable guarantee for the amity of the two nations may have been thus removed.

But, upon the whole, it is neither the possible embarrassment of international relations nor the infamous wickedness of the act itself which has determined public feeling. The preponderating sentiment is sincere and genuine sympathy—sorrow for the chief of a great people struck down by an assassin, and sympathy for that people in the trouble which at a crisis of their destinies such a catastrophe must bring.

Abraham Lincoln was as little of a tyrant as any man who ever lived. He could have been a tyrant had he pleased, but he never uttered so much as an ill-natured speech. . . . In all America there was, perhaps, not one man who less deserved to be the victim of this revolution than he who has just fallen.

4. A Kentucky Editor Laments (1865)

The Border State of Kentucky, precariously loyal during the Civil War, reacted to the murder of her most famous son with mixed emotions. Some seventy miles from the site of the log cabin in which the infant Lincoln had first seen the light of day, the editor of the Frankfort *Commonwealth* penned the following sad tribute to "our noble and beloved President," "stricken down, unarmed, defenceless, and unwarned, by the hand of a rebel assassin." Note why this newspaper regarded the tragedy as a calamity for the South, and decide in what respect this eulogy seems overdrawn.

3. London *Times,* April 29, 1865.
4. Frankfort *Commonwealth,* April 18, 1865, in Herbert Mitgang, *Lincoln as They Saw Him* (1956), pp. 474–75.

LINCOLN IS DEAD. The awful fact which these few words convey has filled the land with mourning. How suddenly had it turned our joy to sadness, our gladness to grief. In the very midst of our rejoicing over the late triumph of the Union over the rebellion, of our joy in view of the ending of our civil strife, and of our thoughts and purposes of love towards those who have brought all these troubles upon us at whose hands we have so greatly suffered, this crushing blow has come upon us, turning the light to darkness, our happiness to misery, our laughter to tears. God in mercy grant it may not, too, turn our thoughts of peace and love towards our enemies into purposes of deadly hate and implacable revenge.

LINCOLN IS DEAD. They have conspired against his life, have sought and taken it, towards whom he had not one thought of hate, to whom he had again and again made most gracious offers of peace and pardon, and for whose kind and merciful reception back to their old places in the Union, his last thoughts and work were given. Truly they knew not what they did —when Abraham Lincoln fell, the South lost its best and truest friend.

LINCOLN IS DEAD. He has fallen at his post, working for the restoration of the Union to its old harmony and prosperity. And in this work there was an earnest desire to serve his whole country. In his heart there was no hate of the rebellious South, no feeling of revenge on account of the terrible wrongs it had inflicted upon our happy land, no bitterness of spirit towards those who continually maligned and traduced him. By the bands of love he would draw back those of rebellion to their old allegiance. Thus have they rewarded him.

LINCOLN IS DEAD. He has given his life a sacrifice for ours. That the Union might be preserved and the enjoyment of life, liberty and property be insured to us and our posterity, he called the people to arms after the blow struck at Sumter. For that, and for all that he has done well and wisely for the suppression of the rebellion, he has incurred the hatred of rebels in arms and their sympathizers in our midst. This hatred has bred vengeance, and vengeance has done its base, cowardly work in the assassination of our President. Thus he has laid down his life for ours—he has fallen a martyr to his country's cause, and in his country's memory his praise shall ever live.

THOUGHT PROVOKERS

1. The Confederate Constitution has been described as a conservative and unoriginal document that liberally plagiarized the Constitution of the United States. Comment. Explain why there were fewer changes than one might have expected.
2. Why did both North and South regard Britain as unduly partial to the other side? What would probably have happened if the British fleet had intervened to break the blockade? To what extent was democracy an issue in the Civil War?
3. Why was the government on both sides unable to stop profiteering, graft, and corruption? What special circumstances during the Civil War encouraged such practices?

4. Explain why, in all of America's major wars, constitutional guarantees of freedom have suffered infringement. What conditions during the Civil War caused them to be more endangered than during other wars?

5. During his lifetime Lincoln was widely regarded in the South and among many Northern Democrats as an inept, joke-telling buffoon. Account for his ranking today as perhaps our greatest President. Is he overrated?

FURTHER EXPLORATION

General: J. G. Randall and David Donald, *The Civil War and Reconstruction* (2nd ed., 1961). **New Government:** A. H. Stephens, *A Constitutional View of the Late War between the States* (2 vols., 1868–1870); W. B. Yearns, *The Confederate Congress* (1960). **British Involvement:** F. L. Owsley, *King Cotton Diplomacy* (2nd ed., 1959); E. D. Adams, *Great Britain and the American Civil War* (2 vols., 1925). **Grafters:** E. D. Fite, *Social and Industrial Conditions in the North during the Civil War* (1910); C. W. Ramsdell, *Behind the Lines in the Southern Confederacy* (1944). **Civil Liberties:** J. G. Randall, *Constitutional Problems under Lincoln* (2nd ed. rev., 1929); F. L. Owsley, *State Rights in the Confederacy* (1925). **Election and Assassination:** W. F. Zornow, *Lincoln and the Party Divided* (1954); R. N. Current, *The Lincoln Nobody Knows* (1958).

Recent: C. R. Lee, Jr., *The Confederate Constitutions* (1963); G. M. Frederickson, *The Inner Civil War: Northern Intellectuals and the Crisis of the Union* (1965); Benjamin Quarles, *Lincoln and the Negro* (1962); J. H. Franklin, *The Emancipation Proclamation* (1963) [paperback]; Frank Donovan, *Mr. Lincoln's Proclamation* (1964); Hudson Strode, *Jefferson Davis, Tragic Hero, . . . 1864–1889* (1964); Carleton Beals, *War Within a War: The Confederacy Against Itself* (1965); Edmund Wilson, *Patriotic Gore: Studies in the Literature of the American Civil War* (1962) [paperback]; J. M. McPherson, *The Struggle for Equality: Abolitionists and the Negro in the Civil War and Reconstruction* (1964); P. W. Gates, *Agriculture and the Civil War* (1965).

Chapter 24

The Negro and Reconstruction

The years of war tried our devotion to the Union; the time of peace may test the sincerity of our faith in democracy.

HERMAN MELVILLE, *c.* 1866

PROLOGUE: President Johnson, a rough-hewn Tennessean, favored reconstruction of the seceded states on a "soft" basis. But he soon ran afoul of the Radical Republicans, who would not readmit the wayward sisters until they had adopted the 14th Amendment. This amendment (ratified in 1868) would guarantee civil rights to the Negro, while reducing Congressional representation in states where the ex-slave was denied a vote. But such terms were spurned by ten of the eleven high-spirited Southern states. The Radical-dominated Congress thereupon passed the drastic military reconstruction acts of 1867, under which Negro suffrage was forced upon the South. The Radicals also came within a hairsbreadth, in 1868, of removing the obstructive President Johnson by impeachment. Meanwhile the part-Negro Southern legislatures, despite grievous excesses, passed stacks of long-overdue social and economic legislation. The whites struck back through secret terrorist organizations, and ultimately secured control of their state governments by fraud, fright, and force.

A. THE STATUS OF THE SOUTH

1. Schurz Reports Southern Defiance (1865)

President Johnson sent Carl Schurz—the lanky, bewhiskered, and bespectacled German-American reformer—into the devastated South to report objectively on conditions there. But Schurz was predisposed to see continued defiance. He was on intimate terms with the Radical Republican leaders, who favored a severe reconstruction of the South, and in addition he was financially obligated to the Radical Charles Sumner. President Johnson, evidently hoping for evidence that would support his lenient policies, brushed aside Schurz's elaborate report with ill-concealed annoyance. Schurz partially financed his trip by selling a series of letters under an assumed name to the Boston *Advertiser*, which presumably welcomed his pro-Radical bias. In reading the letter which he wrote from Savannah to the newspaper, note what class of people he deems responsible for the trouble, what motivated them, and why their outbursts were not more serious.

But there is another class of people here [in Savannah], mostly younger men, who are still in the swearing mood. You can overhear their conversations as you pass them on the streets or even sit near them on the stoop of a hotel. They are "not conquered but only overpowered." They are only smothered for a time. They want to fight the war over again, and they

1. *Georgia Historical Quarterly*, XXXV (1951), 244–47 (July 31, 1865). Reprinted by permission.

are sure in five years they are going to have a war bigger than any we have seen yet. They are meaning to get rid of this d——d military despotism. They will show us what stuff Southern men are made of. They will send their own men to Congress and show us that we cannot violate the Constitution with impunity.

They have a rope ready for this and that Union man when the Yankee bayonets are gone. They will show the Northern interlopers that have settled down here to live on their substance the way home. They will deal largely in tar and feathers. They have been in the country and visited this and that place where a fine business is done in the way of killing Negroes. They will let the Negro know what freedom is, only let the Yankee soldiers be withdrawn.

Such is their talk. You can hear it every day, if you have your ears open. You see their sullen, frowning faces at every street corner. Now, there may be much of the old Southern braggadocio in this, and I do not believe that such men will again resort to open insurrection. But they will practice private vengeance whenever they can do it with impunity, and I have heard sober-minded Union people express their apprehension of it. This spirit is certainly no evidence of true loyalty.

It was this spirit which was active in an occurrence which disgraced this city on the Fourth of July. Perhaps you have heard of it. The colored firemen of this city desired to parade their engine on the anniversary of our independence. If nobody else would, they felt like celebrating that day. A number will deny that it was a legitimate desire. At first the engineer of the fire department, who is a citizen of this town, refused his permission. Finally, by an interposition of an officer of the "Freedmen's Bureau,"* he was prevailed upon to give his consent, and the parade took place. In the principal street of the city the procession was attacked with clubs and stones by a mob opposed to the element above described, and by a crowd of boys all swearing at the d——d niggers. The colored firemen were knocked down, some of them severely injured, their engine was taken away from them, and the peaceable procession dispersed. Down with the d——d niggers. A Northern gentleman who loudly expressed his indignation at the proceeding was in danger of being mobbed, and had to seek safety in a house. . . .

To return to the "unconquered" in Savannah—the occurrence of the Fourth of July shows what they are capable of doing even while the Yankee bayonets are still here. If from this we infer what they will be capable of doing when the Yankee bayonets are withdrawn, the prospect is not altogether pleasant, and Union people, white and black, in this city and neighborhood may well entertain serious apprehensions. . . .

Unfortunately, this spirit receives much encouragement from the fair sex. We have heard so much of the bitter resentment of the Southern ladies that the tale becomes stale by frequent repetition, but when inquiring into the feelings of the people, this element must not be omitted. There are certainly

* A federal agency designed to adjust the freed Negro.

PRIMARY SCHOOL FOR FREEDMEN IN VICKSBURG, MISSISSIPPI
Note the wide range of ages. *Harper's Weekly,* 1866.

a good many sensible women in the South who have arrived at a just appreciation of the circumstances with which they are surrounded. But there is a large number of Southern women who are as vindictive and defiant as ever, and whose temper does not permit them to lay their tongues under any restraint. You can see them in every hotel, and they will treat you to the most ridiculous exhibitions whenever an occasion offers.

A day or two ago a Union officer, yielding to an impulse of politeness, handed a dish of pickles to a Southern lady at the dinner-table of a hotel in this city. A look of unspeakable scorn and indignation met him. "So you think," said the lady, "a Southern woman will take a dish of pickles from a hand that is dripping with the blood of her countrymen?"

It is remarkable upon what trifling material this female wrath is feeding and growing fat. In a certain district in South Carolina, the ladies were some time ago, and perhaps are now, dreadfully exercised about the veil question. You may ask me what the veil question is. Formerly, under the old order of things, Negro women were not permitted to wear veils. Now, under the new order of things, a great many are wearing veils. This is an outrage which cannot be submitted to; the white ladies of the neighborhood agree in being indignant beyond measure. Some of them declare that whenever they meet a colored woman wearing a veil they will tear the veil from her face. Others, mindful of the consequences which such an act of violence might draw after it, under this same new order of things, declare their resolve never to wear veils themselves as long as colored women wear veils. This is the veil question, and this is the way it stands at present.

Such things may seem trifling and ridiculous. But it is a well-known fact that a silly woman is sometimes able to exercise a powerful influence over a man not half as silly, and the class of "unconquered" above described is undoubtedly in a great measure composed of individuals that are apt to be influenced by silly women. It has frequently been said that had it not been for the spirit of the Southern women, the rebellion would have broken down long ago, and there is, no doubt, a grain of truth in it.

2. General Grant Is Optimistic (1865)

President Johnson, hoping to capitalize on Grant's enormous prestige, also sent the General on a fact-finding trip to the South. Grant spent less than a week hurriedly visiting leading cities in four states. Schurz had ranged far more widely over a longer period, from July to September, 1865. But just as Schurz was predisposed to see defiance, Grant was predisposed to see compliance. In examining the portion of Grant's report that follows, determine whether his findings are entitled to more credence than those of Schurz. Bear in mind also that Schurz was an idealist, strongly pro-Negro, and a leading Republican politician closely in touch with the Radicals. Grant was none of these.

I am satisfied that the mass of thinking men of the South accept the present situation of affairs in good faith. The questions which have heretofore divided the sentiment of the people of the two sections—slavery and state rights, or the right of a state to secede from the Union—they regard as having been settled forever by the highest tribunal—arms—that man can resort to. I was pleased to learn from the leading men whom I met that they not only accepted the decision arrived at as final, but, now that the smoke of battle has cleared away and time has been given for reflection, that this decision has been a fortunate one for the whole country, they receiving like benefits from it with those who opposed them in the field and in council.

Four years of war, during which law was executed only at the point of the bayonet throughout the states in rebellion, have left the people possibly in a condition not to yield that ready obedience to civil authority the American people have generally been in the habit of yielding. This would render the presence of small garrisons throughout those states necessary until such time as labor returns to its proper channel, and civil authority is fully established. I did not meet anyone, either those holding places under the government or citizens of the Southern states, who think it practicable to withdraw the military from the South at present. The white and the black mutually require the protection of the general government.

There is such universal acquiescence in the authority of the general government throughout the portions of country visited by me that the mere presence of a military force, without regard to numbers, is sufficient to maintain order. . . .

My observations lead me to the conclusion that the citizens of the Southern states are anxious to return to self-government, within the Union, as

2. *Senate Executive Documents,* 39 Cong., 1 sess., I, No. 2, pp. 106–07

soon as possible; that whilst reconstructing they want and require protection from the government; that they are in earnest in wishing to do what they think is required by the government, not humiliating to them as citizens, and that if such a course were pointed out they would pursue it in good faith.

B. IMPEACHING THE PRESIDENT

1. Johnson's Cleveland Speech (1866)

A tactless and stubborn President Johnson clashed openly with the Radical Republicans in Congress, including embittered Thaddeus Stevens, when he vetoed a series of Radical-sponsored bills. Two of the measures designed to help the Negro—the Civil Rights Bill and the New Freedmen's Bureau Bill—were speedily repassed over his veto. Nothing daunted, Johnson embarked upon a speech-making tour to urge the election of anti-Radical Congressmen favorable to his policies. But the public was in an ugly mood. Ex-President Jefferson Davis, though still in prison, was untried and unhanged, as were other ex-Confederates. A recent anti-Negro riot in New Orleans had resulted in some two hundred casualties. Johnson had earlier distinguished himself as a rough-and-ready stump speaker in Tennessee, but, as Secretary Seward remarked, the President of the United States should not be a stump speaker. His undignified harangue in Cleveland contained passages (here italicized) which formed the basis of some of the impeachment charges later brought by the House. Enumerate the criticisms that may be leveled against this speech, and decide which one is the most serious.

Notwithstanding the subsidized gang of hirelings and traducers [in Congress?], I have discharged all my duties and fulfilled all my pledges, and I say here tonight that if my predecessor had lived, the vials of wrath would have been poured out upon him. [Cries of "Never!" "Three cheers for the Congress of the United States!"]

. . . Where is the man or woman who can place his finger upon one single act of mine deviating from any pledge of mine or in violation of the Constitution of the country? [Cheers.] . . . Who can come and place his finger on one pledge I ever violated, or one principle I ever proved false to? [A voice, "How about New Orleans?" Another voice, "Hang Jeff Davis."] Hang Jeff Davis, he says. [Cries of "No," and "Down with him!"] . . . Hang Jeff Davis. Why don't you hang him? [Cries of "Give us the opportunity."] Have not you got the court? Have not you got the Attorney General? . . .

I will tell you what I did do. I called upon your Congress that is trying to break up the government. [Cries, "You be d——d!" and cheers mingled with hisses. Great confusion. "Don't get mad, Andy!"] Well, I will tell you who is mad. "Whom the gods wish to destroy, they first make mad." Did your Congress order any of them to be tried? [Three cheers for Congress.] . . .

You pretend now to have great respect and sympathy for the poor brave fellow who has left an arm on the battlefield. [Cries, "Is this dignified?"] I understand you. . . . I care not for dignity. . . . [A voice, "Traitor!"] I wish I could see that man. I would bet you now that if the light fell

1. Edward McPherson, *The Political History of the United States of America during the Period of Reconstruction* (3rd ed., 1880), pp. 134–36.

on your face, cowardice and treachery would be seen in it. Show yourself. Come out here where I can see you. [Shouts of laughter.] If you ever shoot a man you will do it in the dark, and pull the trigger when no one is by to see you. [Cheers.]

I understand traitors. I have been fighting them at the south end of the line, and we are now fighting them in the other direction. [Laughter and cheers.] I come here neither to criminate or recriminate, but when attacked, my plan is to defend myself. [Cheers.] . . . As Chief Magistrate, I felt so after taking the oath to support the Constitution, and when I saw encroachments upon your Constitution and rights, as an honest man I dared to sound the tocsin of alarm. [Three cheers for Andrew Johnson.] . . .

("HANG JEFF DAVIS.") "THEN I WOULD ASK YOU WHY NOT HANG THAD STEVENS AND WENDELL PHILLIPS?"

Thomas Nast represents Johnson's remarks to a heckler to mean that he would pardon Jeff Davis (imprisoned at Fortress Monroe) and hang the abolitionists Stevens and Phillips. *Harper's Weekly,* 1866.

I love my country. Every public act of my life testifies that is so. Where is the man that can put his finger upon any one act of mine that goes to prove the contrary? And what is my offending? [A voice, "Because you are not a Radical," and cry of "Veto."] Somebody says veto. Veto of what? What is called the Freedmen's Bureau Bill? . . . I might refer to the Civil Rights Bill, the results of which are very similar. I tell you, my countrymen, that though the powers of hell and Thad Stevens and his gang were by, they could not turn me from my purpose. . . .

In conclusion, beside that, Congress had taken such pains to poison their constituents against him.[*] *But what had Congress done? Had they done anything to restore the Union of these states? No; on the contrary, they had done everything to prevent it; and because he stood now where he did when the rebellion commenced, he had been denounced as a traitor. Who had run greater risks or made greater sacrifices than himself? But Congress, factious and domineering, had [under]taken to poison the minds of the American people.*

[*] The reporter now lapses into the third person.

2. Senator Trumbull Defends Johnson (1868)

Johnson's unrestrained oratory backfired, and at the polls in November the Radicals won control of a two-thirds majority in both Houses of Congress. They proceeded to pass the Tenure of Office Act, which was designed to entrap Johnson. Doubting its constitutionality (by indirection it was later judged unconstitutional) and seeking to bring a test case, he deliberately challenged it by removing Secretary Stanton. The House thereupon impeached Johnson for "high crimes and misdemeanors." Most of its indictment related to Johnson's alleged violation of the Tenure of Office Act; other charges related to his "scandalous harangues." Particularly objectionable was a speech at the White House in which the President had declared that acts of Congress were not binding upon him because the South did not enjoy proper representation in it. One of the ablest of those who spoke for Johnson was Senator Lyman Trumbull of Illinois, a brilliant constitutional lawyer and a former associate of Lincoln. As one who followed principle rather than partisanship, he changed parties three times during his career. Ascertain his main reason for thinking that Johnson's removal would be unfortunate.

In coming to the conclusion that the President is not guilty of any of the high crimes and misdemeanors with which he stands charged, I have endeavored to be governed by the case made, without reference to other acts of his not contained in the record, and without giving the least heed to the clamor of intemperate zealots who demand the conviction of Andrew Johnson as a test of party faith, or seek to identify with and make responsible for his acts those who from convictions of duty feel compelled, on the case made, to vote for his acquittal.

His speeches and the general course of his administration have been as distasteful to me as to anyone, and I should consider it the great calamity of the age if the disloyal element, so often encouraged by his measures, should gain political ascendancy. If the question was, Is Andrew Johnson a fit person for President? I should answer, no; but it is not a party question, nor upon Andrew Johnson's deeds and acts, except so far as they are made to appear in the record, that I am to decide.

Painful as it is to disagree with so many political associates and friends whose conscientious convictions have led them to a different result, I must, nevertheless, in the discharge of the high responsibility under which I act, be governed by what my reason and judgment tell me is the truth, and the justice and law of this case. . . .

Once set the example of impeaching a President for what, when the excitement of the hour shall have subsided, will be regarded as insufficient causes, as several of those now alleged against the President were decided to be by the House of Representatives only a few months since, and no future President will be safe who happens to differ with a majority of the House and two-thirds of the Senate on any measure deemed by them important, particularly if of a political character. Blinded by partisan zeal, with such an example before them, they will not scruple to remove out of the way any obstacle to the accomplishment of their purposes, and what then becomes of the checks and balances of the Constitution, so carefully devised and so vital to its perpetuity? They are all gone.

2. *Congressional Globe,* 40 Cong., 2 sess., Supplement, p. 420 (May 7, 1868).

In view of the consequences likely to flow from this day's proceedings, should they result in conviction on what my judgment tells me are insufficient charges and proofs, I tremble for the future of my country. I cannot be an instrument to produce such a result; and at the hazard of the ties even of friendship and affection, till calmer times shall do justice to my motives, no alternative is left me but the inflexible discharge of duty.

[*President Johnson escaped removal by the margin of a single vote, and only because seven conscientious Republican Senators, including Trumbull, risked political suicide by refusing to go along with the Radical majority.*]

C. ENTHRONING THE NEGRO VOTER

1. Stevens Demands Negro Suffrage (1867)

The most influential Radical Republican in the House, crippled and vindictive Thaddeus Stevens of Pennsylvania, loathed slavery, slaveholders, and slave-breeders. He felt a deep compassion for the Negro, lived in open sin with a colored mistress, and arranged to be buried in a Negro cemetery. But in his demands for Negro suffrage he was motivated, like many other Radicals, by a mixture of idealism and realism. Enumerate the arguments for Negro voting that he set forth in the following speech in the House, and judge which ones were the most selfish; the least selfish.

There are several good reasons for the passage of this bill [for reconstructing the South].

In the first place, it is just. I am now confining my argument to Negro suffrage in the rebel states. Have not loyal blacks quite as good a right to choose rulers and make laws as rebel whites?

In the second place, it is a necessity in order to protect the loyal white men in the seceded states. The white Union men are in a great minority in each of those states. With them the blacks would act in a body; and it is believed that in each of said states, except one, the two united would form a majority, control the states, and protect themselves. Now they are the victims of daily murder. They must suffer constant persecution, or be exiled. . . .

Another good reason is, it would insure the ascendancy of the Union [Republican] Party. "Do you avow the party purpose?" exclaims some horror-stricken demagogue. I do. For I believe, on my conscience, that on the continued ascendancy of that party depends the safety of this great nation.

If impartial suffrage is excluded in the rebel states, then every one of them is sure to send a solid rebel representative delegation to Congress, and cast a solid rebel electoral vote. They, with their kindred Copperheads of the North, would always elect the President and control Congress. While Slavery sat upon her defiant throne, and insulted and intimidated the trembling North, the South frequently divided on questions of policy between Whigs and Democrats, and gave victory alternately to the sections.

1. *Congressional Globe,* 39 Cong., 2 sess., p. 252 (Jan. 3, 1867).

Now, you must divide them between loyalists, without regard to color, and disloyalists, or you will be the perpetual vassals of the free-trade, irritated, revengeful South.

For these, among other reasons, I am for Negro suffrage in every rebel state. If it be just, it should not be denied; if it be necessary, it should be adopted; if it be a punishment to traitors, they deserve it.

2. Black-and-White Legislatures (*c.* 1876)

Negro suffrage was finally forced upon the Southern whites by their new state constitutions and by the 15th Amendment to the federal Constitution (1870). Tension grew worse as designing Northern "carpetbaggers" and Unionist Southern whites ("scalawags") moved in to exploit the confused Negro. Inexperienced colored men (in several states in a majority) sat in the newly constituted Southern legislatures, in some instances with feet on desks, reading newspapers bottom side up. The resulting horseplay, profanity, parliamentary irrelevance, and blatant corruption were fully advertised by ex-Confederates. They neglected to add that certain white legislatures of the era, North and South, were guilty of some of these same excesses. J. W. Leigh, an English clergyman turned Georgia rice planter, recorded the following observations in a personal letter. Note the conditions he describes that were most galling to the ex-Confederates, and determine which of them was the most galling.

The fact is, the poor Negro has since the war been placed in an entirely false position, and is therefore not to be blamed for many of the absurdities he has committed, seeing that he has been urged on by Northern "carpetbaggers" and Southern "scalawags," who have used him as a tool to further their own nefarious ends.

The great mistake committed by the North was giving the Negroes the franchise so soon after their emancipation, when they were not the least prepared for it. In 1865 slavery was abolished, and no one even among the Southerners, I venture to say, would wish it back. In 1868 they [Negroes] were declared citizens of the United States, and in 1870 they had the right of voting given them, and at the same time persons concerned in the rebellion were excluded from public trusts by what was called the "iron-clad" oath. And as if this was not enough, last year [1875] the Civil Rights Bill was passed, by which Negroes were to be placed on a perfect equality with whites, who were to be compelled to travel in the same cars with them, and to send their children to the same schools.

The consequence of all this is that where there is a majority of Negroes, as is the case in the states of Louisiana, Mississippi, and South Carolina, these states are placed completely under Negro rule, and scenes occur in the state legislatures which baffle description.

I recollect at the beginning of 1870 being at Montgomery, the capital of Alabama, and paying a visit to the State House there, when a discussion was going on with respect to a large grant which was to be made for the building of the Alabama and Chattanooga Railway, the real object of

2. Frances B. Leigh, *Ten Years on a Georgia Plantation since the War* (1883), pp. 286–92 (Appendix).

which was to put money into the pockets of certain carpetbaggers, who, in order to gain their object, had bribed all the Negroes to vote for the passing of the bill.

The scene was an exciting one. Several Negro members were present, with their legs stuck up on the desks in front of them, and spitting all about them in free and independent fashion. One gentleman having spoken for some time against the bill, and having reiterated his condemnation of it as a fraudulent speculation, a stout Negro member from Mobile sprung up and said, "Mister Speaker, when yesterday I spoke, I was not allowed to go on because you said I spoke twice on the same subject. Now what is sauce for the goose is sauce for the gander. Dis Member is saying over and over again de same thing; why don't you tell him to sit down? for what is sauce for," etc. To which the Speaker said, "Sit down yourself, sir." Another member (a carpetbagger) jumped up and shook his fist in the speaking member's face, and told him he was a liar, and if he would come outside he would give him satisfaction.

This is nothing, however, to what has been going on in South Carolina this last session. Poor South Carolina, formerly the proudest state in America, boasting of her ancient families, remarkable for her wealth, culture, and refinement, now prostrate in the dust, ruled over by her former slaves, an old aristocratic society replaced by the most ignorant democracy that mankind ever saw invested with the functions of government. Of the 124 representatives, there are but 23 representatives of her old civilization, and these few can only look on at the squabbling crowd amongst whom they sit as silent enforced auditors. Of the 101 remaining, 94 are colored, and 7 their white allies. The few honest amongst them see plundering and corruption going on on all sides, and can do nothing. . . .

The Negroes have it all their own way, and rob and plunder as they please. The Governor of South Carolina lives in luxury, and treats his soldiers to champagne, while the miserable planters have to pay taxes amounting to half their income, and if they fail to pay, their property is confiscated.

Louisiana and Mississippi are not much better off. The former has a Negro barber for its Lieutenant-Governor, and the latter has just selected a Negro steamboat porter as its United States Senator, filling the place once occupied by Jefferson Davis.

3. Du Bois Justifies Negro Legislators (1910)

Dr. W. E. B. Du Bois, a Massachusetts-born Negro of French Huguenot extraction, received his Ph.D. from Harvard University in 1895. Distinguished as a teacher, lecturer, historian, economist, sociologist, novelist, poet, and propagandist, he became a militant advocate of equal rights for Negroes. A founder of the National Association for the Advancement of Colored People, he served for twenty-four years as editor of its chief organ. Du Bois, who was born the day before the House impeached

3. *American Historical Review*, XV (1910), 791–99, *passim*. By permission of the editor. See also F. L. Broderick, *W. E. B. Du Bois* (1959).

Johnson, here writes as a scholar. Observe the important respects in which the Negro legislatures have been unfairly represented, and the most convincing evidence that these bodies were responsible for significant achievements.

Undoubtedly there were many ridiculous things connected with Reconstruction governments: the placing of ignorant field-hands who could neither read nor write in the legislature, the gold spittoons of South Carolina, the enormous public printing bill of Mississippi—all these were extravagant and funny; and yet somehow, to one who sees, beneath all that is bizarre, the real human tragedy of the upward striving of downtrodden men, the groping for light among people born in darkness, there is less tendency to laugh and jibe than among shallower minds and easier consciences. All that is funny is not bad.

Then, too, a careful examination of the alleged stealing in the South reveals much. First, there is repeated exaggeration. For instance, it is said that the taxation in Mississippi was fourteen times as great in 1874 as in 1869. This sounds staggering until we learn that the state taxation in 1869 was only ten cents on one hundred dollars, and that the expenses of government in 1874 were only twice as great as in 1860, and that too with a depreciated currency. . . .

The character of the real thieving shows that white men must have been the chief beneficiaries. . . . The frauds through the manipulation of state and railway bonds and of banknotes must have inured chiefly to the benefit of experienced white men, and this must have been largely the case in the furnishing and printing frauds. . . .

That the Negroes, led by astute thieves, became tools and received a small share of the spoils is true. But . . . much of the legislation which resulted in fraud was represented to the Negroes as good legislation, and thus their votes were secured by deliberate misrepresentation. . . .

Granted, then, that the Negroes were to some extent venal but to a much larger extent ignorant and deceived, the question is: Did they show any signs of a disposition to learn better things? The theory of democratic governments is not that the will of the people is always right, but rather that normal human beings of average intelligence will, if given a chance, learn the right and best course by bitter experience. This is precisely what Negro voters showed indubitable signs of doing. First, they strove for schools to abolish ignorance, and, second, a large and growing number of them revolted against the carnival of extravagance and stealing that marred the beginning of Reconstruction, and joined with the best elements to institute reform. . . .

We may recognize three things which Negro rule gave to the South:

1. Democratic government.
2. Free public schools.
3. New social legislation. . . .

In South Carolina there was before the war a property qualification for officeholders, and, in part, for voters. The [Reconstruction] constitution of

1868, on the other hand, was a modern democratic document . . . preceded by a broad Declaration of Rights which did away with property qualifications and based representation directly on population instead of property. It especially took up new subjects of social legislation, declaring navigable rivers free public highways, instituting homestead exemptions, establishing boards of county commissioners, providing for a new penal code of laws, establishing universal manhood suffrage "without distinction of race or color," devoting six sections to charitable and penal institutions and six to corporations, providing separate property for married women, etc. Above all, eleven sections of the Tenth Article were devoted to the establishment of a complete public-school system.

So satisfactory was the constitution thus adopted by Negro suffrage and by a convention composed of a majority of blacks that the state lived twenty-seven years under it without essential change. And when the constitution was revised in 1895, the revision was practically nothing more than an amplification of the constitution of 1868. No essential advance step of the former document was changed except the suffrage article. . . .

There is no doubt but that the thirst of the black man for knowledge—a thirst which has been too persistent and durable to be mere curiosity or whim—gave birth to the public free-school system of the South. It was the question upon which black voters and legislators insisted more than anything else, and while it is possible to find some vestiges of free schools in some of the Southern states before the war, yet a universal, well-established system dates from the day that the black man got political power. . . .

Finally, in legislation covering property, the wider functions of the state, the punishment of crime, and the like, it is sufficient to say that the laws on these points established by Reconstruction legislatures were not only different from and even revolutionary to the laws in the older South, but they were so wise and so well suited to the needs of the new South that in spite of a retrogressive movement following the overthrow of Negro governments, the mass of this legislation, with elaboration and development, still stands on the statute books of the South.

D. TERRORISM IN THE SOUTH

1. The K.K.K. in Kentucky (1871)

The ex-Confederates deeply resented both their own disfranchisement and the enfranchisement of ill-prepared Negroes. In their desperation they formed night-riding organizations, notoriously the Ku Klux Klan, which discouraged the freedmen from exercising their newly granted political rights. Although Kentucky had not seceded, the besheeted Klansmen were active in that state. The following is a pathetic petition to Congress from Negroes of the Frankfort area praying for the enactment of protective laws, and listing 116 separate instances of outrages, including the burning of buildings. Note what groups were allegedly responsible, either actively or passively, for this sad state of affairs.

1. *Senate Miscellaneous Documents,* 42 Cong., 1 sess., No. 49.

To the Senate and House of Representatives in Congress assembled:

We, the colored citizens of Frankfort and vicinity, do this day memorialize your honorable bodies upon the condition of affairs now existing in the state of Kentucky.

We would respectfully state that life, liberty, and property are unprotected among the colored race of this state. Organized bands of desperate and lawless men, mainly composed of soldiers of the late rebel armies, armed, disciplined, and disguised, and bound by oath and secret obligations, have, by force, terror, and violence, subverted all civil society among colored people; thus utterly rendering insecure the safety of persons and property, overthrowing all those rights which are the primary basis and objects of the government, which are expressly guaranteed to us by the Constitution of the United States as amended [by the 13th and 14th Amendments].

We believe you are not familiar with the description of the Ku Klux Klans riding nightly over the country, going from county to county, and in the county towns, spreading terror wherever they go by robbing, whipping, ravishing, and killing our people without provocation, compelling colored people to break the ice and bathe in the chilly waters of the Kentucky River.

The [state] legislature has adjourned. They refused to enact any laws to suppress Ku-Klux disorder. We regard them [the Ku-Kluxers] as now being licensed to continue their dark and bloody deeds under cover of the dark night. They refuse to allow us to testify in the state courts where a white man is concerned. We find their deeds are perpetrated only upon colored men and white Republicans. We also find that for our services to the government and our race we have become the special object of hatred and persecution at the hands of the Democratic Party. Our people are driven from their homes in great numbers, having no redress only [except] the United States court, which is in many cases unable to reach them.

We would state that we have been law-abiding citizens, pay our taxes, and in many parts of the state our people have been driven from the polls, refused the right to vote. Many have been slaughtered while attempting to vote. We ask, how long is this state of things to last?

We appeal to you as law-abiding citizens to enact some laws that will protect us, and that will enable us to exercise the rights of citizens. We see that the Senator [Stevenson] from this state denies there being organized bands of desperadoes in the state. For information, we lay before you a number of violent acts [that] occurred during his administration. Although he, Stevenson, says half a dozen instances of violence did occur, these are not more than one-half the acts that have occurred.

The Democratic Party has here a political organization composed only of Democrats; not a single Republican can join them. Where many of these acts have been committed, it has been proven that they were the men, done with arms from the state arsenal.

We pray you will take some steps to remedy these evils.

[Within a month after the above petition was presented, Congress passed the Force Act (Ku Klux Act) of 1871. It authorized the President to suspend the writ of habeas corpus *and to employ federal troops to crush disturbances in the South. The act was enforced with considerable success.]*

2. Tillman's Anti-Negro Tirade (1907)

Reared in a slaveowning family, Senator Benjamin R. Tillman of South Carolina had participated in anti-Negro outrages during Reconstruction days. His face contorted, his one good eye glowing like a live coal, and his voice rising to a whine, "Tillman the Terrible" shocked the Senate and the nation with wild speeches in which he boasted that "we took the government away [from Negroes]," we "stuffed the ballot boxes," we used "tissue ballots," "we shot them," "we are not ashamed of it," and "we will do it again." Ascertain whom he blames most for the alleged conditions to which he refers, and which of these grievances would come closest to justifying the measures employed by the whites.

It was in 1876, thirty years ago, and the people of South Carolina had been living under Negro rule for eight years. There was a condition bordering upon anarchy. Misrule, robbery, and murder were holding high carnival. The people's substance was being stolen, and there was no incentive to labor. Our legislature was composed of a majority of Negroes, most of whom could neither read nor write. They were the easy dupes and tools of as dirty a band of vampires and robbers as ever preyed upon a prostrate people. . . . Life ceased to be worth having on the terms under which we were living, and in desperation we determined to take the government away from the Negroes.

We reorganized the Democratic Party [of South Carolina] with one plank, and only one plank, namely, that "this is a white man's country, and white men must govern it." Under that banner we went to battle.

We had 8000 Negro militia organized by carpetbaggers. . . . They used to drum up and down the roads with their fifes and their gleaming bayonets, equipped with new Springfield rifles and dressed in the regulation uniform. It was lawful, I suppose, but these Negro soldiers—or this Negro militia, for they were never soldiers—growing more and more bold, let drop talk among themselves where the white children might hear their purpose, and it came to our ears. This is what they said: "The President [Grant] is our friend. The North is with us. We intend to kill all the white men, take the land, marry the white women, and then these white children will wait on us." . . .

We knew—who knew better?—that the North then was a unit in its opposition to Southern ideas, and that it was their purpose to perpetuate Negro governments in those states where it could be done by reason of there being a Negro majority. Having made up our minds, we set about it as practical men. . . .

Clashes came. The Negro militia grew unbearable and more and more insolent. I am not speaking of what I have read; I am speaking of what I know, of what I saw. There were two militia companies in my township

2. *Congressional Record,* 59 Cong., 2 sess., p. 1440 (Jan. 21, 1907).

IN SELF-DEFENSE

Southern Chiv. [Chivalrous gentleman] "Ef I hadn't-er killed
you, you would hev growd up to rule me."
A brutally unfair Northern reference to the fact that a few
adult Negroes were killed during the Hayes-Tilden Presidential
campaign. *Harper's Weekly,* 1876.

and a regiment in my county. We had clashes with these Negro militiamen.
The Hamburg riot was one clash, in which seven Negroes and one white
man were killed. A month later we had the Ellenton riot, in which no one
ever knew how many Negroes were killed, but there were forty or fifty
or a hundred. It was a fight between barbarism and civilization, between
the African and the Caucasian, for mastery.

It was then that "we shot them"; it was then that "we killed them"; it was
then that "we stuffed ballot boxes." After the [federal] troops came and
told us, "You must stop this rioting," we had decided to take the government away from men so debased as were the Negroes. . . .

[President] Grant sent troops to maintain the carpetbag government in
power and to protect the Negroes in the right to vote. He merely obeyed the
law. . . . Then it was that "we stuffed ballot boxes," because desperate
diseases require desperate remedies, and having resolved to take the state
away, we hesitated at nothing. . . .

I want to say now that we have not shot any Negroes in South Carolina
on account of politics since 1876. We have not found it necessary. Eighteen
hundred and seventy-six happened to be the hundredth anniversary of the
Declaration of Independence, and the action of the white men of South

Carolina in taking the state away from the Negroes we regard as a second declaration of independence by the Caucasian from African barbarism.

E. THE BLUNDERS OF RECONSTRUCTION

1. Editor Godkin Grieves (1871)

Irish-born E. L. Godkin, a fearless liberal, founded the distinguished and long-lived New York *Nation* in 1865. So biting were his criticisms that the magazine was dubbed "the weekly day of judgment." His views on the blunders of Reconstruction were aired with incisiveness. He argued that there were two ways of dealing with the post-war South: (1) reorganize the section "from top to bottom"; (2) treat the whole community as made up of "unfortunate Americans, equally entitled to care and protection, demoralized by an accursed institution for which the whole Union was responsible, and which the whole Union had connived at, and, down to 1860, had profited by. . . ." But the North, wrote Godkin, followed neither course. Note the blunders that he points out, and form some judgment as to whether they could have been avoided, given the inflamed state of mind in the North.

The condition of the Negro after emancipation . . . attracted the carpetbagger as naturally as a dead ox attracts the buzzard. The lower class of demagogue scents an unenlightened constituency at an almost incredible distance, and travels towards it over mountain, valley, and river with the certainty of the mariner's compass.

But then we hastened his coming by our legislation. We deliberately, and for an indefinite period, excluded all the leading Southern men from active participation in the management of their local affairs, by a discrimination not unlike that which would be worked in this city [New York], but very much worse, if every man who had not at some time belonged to the Tammany Society were declared incapable of holding office.

It was before the war the time-honored custom of the Southern states, and a very good custom too, to put their ablest men, and men of the highest social standing and character, in office. The consequence was that it was these men who figured most prominently in the steps which led to the rebellion, and in the rebellion itself. When the war was over, we singled these men out, and not unnaturally, for punishment by the 14th Amendment and other legislation.

But we forgot that, as the President points out, they were no worse, so far as disloyalty went, than the rest of the community. They broke their oaths of allegiance to the United States, but the other white men of the South would have done the same thing if they had got the chance of doing it by being elevated to office, either under the United States or under the Confederacy. We forgot, too, that when putting a mutinous crew in irons, the most justly indignant captain leaves at liberty enough able-bodied seamen to work the ship. . . .

The results . . . have been positively infernal. In the idea that we were befriending the Negroes, we gave them possession of the government, and deprived them of the aid of all the local capacity and experience in the

1. *The Nation* (New York), XIII, 364 (Dec. 7, 1871).

management of it, thus offering the states as a prey to Northern adventurers, and thus inflicting on the freedmen the very worst calamity which could befall a race newly emerged from barbarism—that is, familiarity, in the very first moments of enfranchisement, with the processes of a corrupt administration, carried on by gangs of depraved vagabonds, in which the public money was stolen, the public faith made an article of traffic, the legislature openly corrupted, and all that the community contained of talent, probity, and social respectability put under a legal ban as something worthless and disreputable.

We do not hesitate to say that a better mode of debauching the freedmen, and making them permanently unfit for civil government, could hardly have been hit on had the North had such an object deliberately in view Instead of establishing equal rights for all, we set up the government of a class, and this class the least competent, the most ignorant and inexperienced, and a class, too, whose history and antecedents made its rule peculiarly obnoxious to the rest of the community.

Out of this state of things Ku-Kluxing has grown . . . naturally. . . . We cannot gainsay anything anybody says of the atrocity of riding about the country at night with one's face blackened, murdering and whipping people. But we confess we condemn Ku-Kluxing very much as we condemn the cholera. . . . There is no more use in getting in a rage with Ku-Kluxery, and sending cavalry and artillery after it, than of legislating against pestilence, as long as nothing is done to remove the causes.

2. Frederick Douglass Complains (1882)

The incredible ex-slave Frederick Douglass (see earlier, p. 352) raised two famous colored regiments in Massachusetts during the Civil War. Among the first recruits were his own sons. Continuing his campaign for civil rights and suffrage for the freedmen, he wrote the following bitter commentary in his autobiography. One of his keenest regrets was that the federal government, despite the urgings of Thaddeus Stevens and others, failed to provide land for the Negro. In the light of his observations, determine how free land would have alleviated the conditions he describes, and why the former slaveowners made life extremely difficult for the ex-slaves.

Though slavery was abolished, the wrongs of my people were not ended. Though they were not slaves, they were not yet quite free. No man can be truly free whose liberty is dependent upon the thought, feeling, and action of others, and who has himself no means in his own hands for guarding, protecting, defending, and maintaining that liberty. Yet the Negro after his emancipation was precisely in this state of destitution.

The law on the side of freedom is of great advantage only where there is power to make that law respected. I know no class of my fellow men, however just, enlightened, and humane, which can be wisely and safely trusted absolutely with the liberties of any other class. Protestants are excellent people, but it would not be wise for Catholics to depend entirely upon them to look after their rights and interests. Catholics are a pretty

2. *Life and Times of Frederick Douglass* (1882), pp. 458–59.

good sort of people (though there is a soul-shuddering history behind them); yet no enlightened Protestants would commit their liberty to their care and keeping.

And yet the government had left the freedmen in a worse condition than either of these. It felt that it had done enough for him. It had made him free, and henceforth he must make his own way in the world, or, as the slang phrase has it, "root, pig, or die." Yet he had none of the conditions for self-preservation or self-protection.

He was free from the individual master, but the slave of society. He had neither money, property, nor friends. He was free from the old plantation, but he had nothing but the dusty road under his feet. He was free from the old quarter that once gave him shelter, but a slave to the rains of summer and the frosts of winter. He was, in a word, literally turned loose, naked, hungry, and destitute, to the open sky.

The first feeling toward him by the old master classes was full of bitterness and wrath. They resented his emancipation as an act of hostility toward them, and, since they could not punish the emancipator, they felt like punishing the object which that act had emancipated. Hence they drove him off the old plantation, and told him he was no longer wanted there. They not only hated him because he had been freed as a punishment to them, but because they felt that they had been robbed of his labor.

An element of greater bitterness still came into their hearts: the freedman had been the friend of the government, and many of his class had borne arms against them during the war. The thought of paying cash for labor that they could formerly extort by the lash did not in any wise improve their disposition to the emancipated slave, or improve his own condition.

Now, since poverty has, and can have, no chance against wealth, the landless against the landowner, the ignorant against the intelligent, the freedman was powerless. He had nothing left him but a slavery-distorted and diseased body, and lame and twisted limbs, with which to fight the battle of life.

3. Booker T. Washington Reflects (1901)

Booker T. Washington, the son of a Negro mother and an unidentified white father, was reared in a one-room, dirt-floored shanty, and never slept on a bed until after Emancipation. Obtaining an education under grave hardships, he ultimately became the head of the famed Negro industrial institute at Tuskegee, Alabama. Acknowledged leader of his race after Frederick Douglass died in 1895, he won additional fame as an orator and as an apostle of "gradualism" in achieving equality with the whites. He believed that the Negro should acquire manual skills and otherwise prove himself worthy of a place beside white men. Negro intellectuals like Du Bois (see earlier, p. 470) criticized this conservative "Uncle Tomism" as condemning the race to a permanent bootblack inferiority. Note in the following selection from Washington's justly famous autobiography what the author regards as the chief mistakes made by both whites and Negroes in handling Reconstruction, and why they were mistakes.

3. B. T. Washington, *Up from Slavery* (1901), pp. 83–86.

Though I was but little more than a youth during the period of Reconstruction, I had the feeling that mistakes were being made, and that things could not remain in the condition that they were in then very long. I felt that the Reconstruction policy, so far as it related to my race, was in a large measure on a false foundation, was artificial and forced. In many cases it seemed to me that the ignorance of my race was being used as a tool with which to help white men into office, and that there was an element in the North which wanted to punish the Southern white men by forcing the Negro into positions over the heads of the Southern whites. I felt that the Negro would be the one to suffer for this in the end. Besides, the general political agitation drew the attention of our people away from the more fundamental matters of perfecting themselves in the industries at their doors and in securing property.

The temptations to enter political life were so alluring that I came very near yielding to them at one time, but I was kept from doing so by the feeling that I would be helping in a more substantial way by assisting in the laying of the foundation of the race through a generous education of the hand, head, and heart. I saw colored men who were members of the state legislatures, and county officers, who, in some cases, could not read or write, and whose morals were as weak as their education.

Not long ago, when passing through the streets of a certain city in the South, I heard some brick-masons calling out, from the top of a two-story brick building on which they were working, for the "Governor" to "hurry up and bring up some more bricks." Several times I heard the command, "Hurry up, Governor!" "Hurry up, Governor!" My curiosity was aroused to such an extent that I made inquiry as to who the "Governor" was, and soon found that he was a colored man who at one time had held the position of Lieutenant-Governor of his state.

But not all the colored people who were in office during Reconstruction were unworthy of their positions, by any means. Some of them, like the late Senator B. K. Bruce, Governor Pinchback, and many others, were strong, upright, useful men. Neither were all the class designated as carpetbaggers dishonorable men. Some of them, like ex-Governor Bullock of Georgia, were men of high character and usefulness.

Of course the colored people, so largely without education, and wholly without experience in government, made tremendous mistakes, just as any people similarly situated would have done. Many of the Southern whites have a feeling that, if the Negro is permitted to exercise his political rights now to any degree, the mistakes of the Reconstruction period will repeat themselves. I do not think this would be true, because the Negro is a much stronger and wiser man than he was thirty-five years ago, and he is fast learning the lesson that he cannot afford to act in a manner that will alienate his Southern white neighbors from him. . . .

During the whole of the Reconstruction period our people throughout the South looked to the federal government for everything, very much as a child looks to its mother. This was not unnatural. The central government gave them freedom, and the whole nation had been enriched for more than two centuries by the labor of the Negro. Even as a youth, and later in manhood, I had the feeling that it was cruelly wrong in the central government, at the beginning of our freedom, to fail to make some provision for the general education of our people in addition to what the states might do, so that the people would be the better prepared for the duties of citizenship.

It is easy to find fault, to remark what might have been done, and perhaps, after all, and under all the circumstances, those in charge of the conduct of affairs did the only thing that could be done at the time. Still, as I look back now over the entire period of our freedom, I cannot help feeling that it would have been wiser if some plan could have been put in operation which would have made the possession of a certain amount of education or property, or both, a test for the exercise of the franchise, and a way provided by which this test should be made to apply honestly and squarely to both the white and black races.

THOUGHT PROVOKERS

1. Was the South ever really defeated in spirit? Would the results have been more satisfactory from its point of view if it had accepted the rule of the conqueror with better grace?
2. It has been said that Johnson was his own worst enemy, and that the Southerners were damaged by his determination to befriend them with a "soft" policy. Comment critically.
3. Present the case for and against *immediate* Negro suffrage; *gradual* Negro suffrage. Form conclusions. Why have the excesses of the Negro-white legislatures been overplayed and their achievements downgraded? What analogies can one find in the disorders of the newly freed nations of Africa in the 20th Century?
4. Were organizations like the Ku Klux Klan justifiable? Was there any other way by which the whites could regain control?
5. Would it have been as dangerous to employ leading ex-Confederates in Reconstruction as leading ex-Nazis in the reconstruction of Hitler's Germany? What was the most serious long-run mistake made in dealing with the Negro after the war? Has the Southern Negro ever been free?

FURTHER EXPLORATION

General: J. G. Randall and David Donald, *The Civil War and Reconstruction* (2nd ed., 1961); Hodding Carter, *The Angry Scar* (1959); Fawn M. Brodie, *Thaddeus Stevens* (1959). Status of South: E. M. Coulter, *The South during Reconstruction* (1947). Impeachment: H. K. Beale, *The Critical Year* (1930); E. L. McKitrick, *Andrew Johnson and Reconstruction* (1960). Negro Voter: F. B. Simkins and R. H. Woody, *South Carolina during Reconstruction* (1932); W. E. B. Du Bois, *Black Reconstruction* (1935). Terrorism: S. F. Horn, *The Invisible Empire* [K.K.K.] (1939). Blunders: J. H. Franklin, *From Slavery to Freedom* (2nd ed., 1956); R. W. Logan, *The Negro in American Life and Thought* (1954); J. H. Franklin, *Reconstruction* (1961). Recent: K. M. Stampp, *The Era of Reconstruction, 1865–1877* (1965); R. W. Patrick, *The Reconstruction of the Nation* (1967) [paperback].

Chapter **25**

The Republican Doldrums, 1869-1881

The phrase "public office is a public trust" has of late become common property.

SENATOR CHARLES SUMNER, 1872

PROLOGUE: War hero U. S. Grant came to the White House in 1869, when the lowered moral tone engendered by the war was producing a series of nauseous scandals. A great general, the politically inexperienced Grant proved to be a great disappointment as President. Yet his administration could claim credit for the Geneva arbitration of 1872, which smoothed over the *Alabama* claims controversy with Britain. Republican critics, unable to stomach their naïve general for a second term, organized the Liberal Republican Party in 1872, and chose the politically preposterous editor Horace Greeley as their presidential standard-bearer. Grant's ultimate triumph at the polls was rather a vote of no confidence in Greeley than of confidence in himself. His successor, Rutherford B. Hayes, elected in 1877 after a bitterly disputed contest, restored a degree of respectability to the Republican Party. He ended the carpetbag governments in the South by withdrawing the support of federal troops, and made some progress toward civil service reform despite last-ditch opposition from the bosses of his own party.

A. THE ALABAMA CLAIMS CONTROVERSY

1. Sumner Presents an Outrageous Bill (1869)

Confederate commerce-raiders like the "British pirate" *Alabama*, built with dubious legality in "neutral" England, had embittered the North by destroying scores of Yankee merchant ships. An unpopular Anglo-American treaty, designed to settle mutual claims for damages, was flatly rejected in 1869 by a Senate vote of 54 to 1. No speech was needed, but the influential Senator Charles Sumner, though professing friendship for England, delivered the following harangue. It caused Henry Adams to entertain the "gravest doubts of Sumner's sanity." The Senator claimed direct damages in the amount of $15,000,000 (the value of the shipping destroyed) and indirect damages in the amount of $110,000,000 (the cost of such items as increased insurance and transferred registry). He then went on to detail "national losses." Determine what degree of plausibility, if any, there was in his most exaggerated claim.

This is what I have to say for the present on national losses through the destruction of commerce. These are large enough; but there is another chapter where they are larger far. I refer, of course, to the national losses caused by the prolongation of the war, and traceable directly to England. Pardon me if I confess the regret with which I touch this prodigious item;

1. *The Works of Charles Sumner* (1880), XIII, 84–86, 90.

for I know well the depth of feeling which it is calculated to stir. But I cannot hesitate. It belongs to the case.

No candid person who studies this eventful period can doubt that the Rebellion was originally encouraged by hope of support from England; that it was strengthened at once by the concession of belligerent rights on the ocean; that it was fed to the end by British supplies; that it was encouraged by every well-stored British ship that was able to defy our blockade; that it was quickened into frantic life with every report from the British pirates, flaming anew with every burning ship.

Nor can it be doubted that without British intervention the Rebellion would have soon succumbed under the well-directed efforts of the National Government. Not weeks or months, but years, were added in this way to our war, so full of costly sacrifice. The subsidies which in other times England contributed to [allies in] Continental wars were less effective than the aid and comfort which she contributed to the Rebellion.

It cannot be said too often that the naval base of the Rebellion was not in America, but in England. The blockade runners and the pirate ships were all English. England was the fruitful parent, and these were the "hell hounds." . . . Mr. Cobden boldly said in the House of Commons that England made war from her shores on the United States, with "an amount of damage to that country greater than would be produced by many ordinary wars." According to this testimony, the conduct of England was war; but it must not be forgotten that this war was carried on at our sole cost. The United States paid for a war waged by England upon the National Unity.

There was one form that this war assumed which was incessant, most vexatious, and costly, besides being in itself a positive alliance with the Rebellion. It was that of blockade runners, openly equipped and supplied by England under the shelter of that baleful Proclamation [extending belligerent rights]. Constantly leaving English ports, they stole across the ocean, and then broke the blockade. These active agents of the Rebellion could be counteracted only by a network of vessels stretching along the coast, at great cost to the country. Here is another distinct item, the amount of which may be determined by the Navy Department.

The sacrifice of precious life is beyond human compensation; but there may be an approximate estimate of the national loss in treasure. Everybody can make the calculation. I content myself with calling attention to the elements which enter into it.

Besides the blockade, there was the prolongation of the war. The Rebellion was suppressed at a cost of more than four thousand million dollars, a considerable portion of which has been already paid, leaving twenty-five hundred millions as a national debt to burden the people. If, through British intervention, the war was doubled in duration, or in any way extended, as cannot be doubted, then is England justly responsible for the additional expenditure to which our country was doomed. And whatever may be the final settlement of these great accounts, such must be the judgment. . . .

If the case against England is strong, and if our claims are unprecedented in magnitude, it is only because the conduct of this power at a trying period was most unfriendly, and the injurious consequences of this conduct were on a scale corresponding to the theater of action. . . . The attempt to close this great international debate without a complete settlement is little short of puerile.

2. British Tories Are Poor Losers (1872)

Sumner's tirade angered the British, who nevertheless began to develop increasingly troubled consciences. The *Alabama*, moreover, had created a dangerous precedent which might one day be used against Britain's merchant marine by a navyless foe (Ireland?). London finally gave way when, in the Treaty of Washington (1871), it consented to a five-man arbitral tribunal. The British also agreed to stringent new rules for neutral conduct which virtually insured the loss of their case. When the arbitrators met at Geneva the United States infuriated the British by resurrecting Sumner's indirect damages, but the storm blew over and the tribunal assessed Great Britain $15,500,000. The London *Times*, though critical of the tribunal's methods, put on the best possible face when it remarked, "We simply wanted the judgment of five men of sense and honour; we have obtained it, and we cheerfully abide by it." Less cheerful were the following remarks of the Tory *Saturday Review*. Comment critically on its belief that if the British had been partial to the North they would have created a dangerous precedent.

The decision of the Geneva Court of Arbitration is profoundly mortifying to Englishmen, although it is neither ruinous in the amount of awarded damages nor unexpected in substance. The favourite organ of the Government [London *Times*] exceeds the license of irresponsible levity when it boasts of the arbitration and its result as a triumph to both the litigants. Neither the reference [referral to arbitration] nor the manner in which it has been conducted on the part of the United States has been gratifying to English feeling.

The best consolation for the painful result is that the humiliation which it involves had been virtually incurred when the English Government consented [in the Treaty of Washington] to the invention of an *ex post facto* law by which its responsibility was to be determined. The amount of damages is of secondary, though not of trivial, importance, and the calculated rudeness of the American representatives afforded no sufficient reason for repudiating the wide obligations of the Treaty [of Washington]. . . .

The litigation has been made as nearly as possible to resemble war in the constant attempt to inflict injury and annoyance on the opponent. The attempt to extort an enormous penalty for the pretended prolongation of the Civil War fortunately afforded an opportunity of proving that there were limits to the English capacity of submission. . . .

2. *Saturday Review* (London), XXXIV, 327–28 (Sept. 14, 1872).

The Americans have from the first discussed the question on the assumption that in their Civil War there was only one lawful belligerent. Although they are also in the habit of boasting that their final victory was attained in the face of almost unsurmountable obstacles, they have never admitted that a formidable adversary must have been engaged in the conduct of a serious war. It was possible, and for a long time it appeared probable, that the Southern states would establish their independence, and that consequently neutrals would have to justify their conduct on both sides to a regular and lawful government.

The Confederate authorities, not without a certain show of plausibility, accused England of gross partiality to the North, and at one time they announced their intention of abstaining from further diplomatic intercourse. Having been finally defeated and destroyed, the Confederate Government has no rights to enforce and no complaints to urge, but in future wars it will often happen that both combatants survive the struggle. It will then become necessary to account for every refusal to acknowledge a commission or to afford hospitality to a man-of-war; and England may perhaps be summoned before a court of arbitration to defend the omission of acts identical with those which have now involved the payment of damages.

3. Greeley Is Aggrieved (1872)

The Geneva award, unquestionably a landmark in the history of international arbitration, was the most significant single achievement of Grant's scandal-smeared two terms. The regular Republicans, who were running Grant for re-election, clucked delightedly over their Geneva triumph. But supporters of Horace Greeley, Grant's Liberal Republican opponent, naturally assailed the "Geneva farce." The New York *Herald* sneered, "England in truth laughs in her sleeve at her triumph over the shrewd Yankees. . . ." Greeley's own New York *Tribune* took a dim view of the award. The British were authorized at Geneva to collect counter-damages for American encroachments on the Canadian fisheries and for illegal seizures of British merchant ships during the war. The bill finally presented to the United States amounted to $7,429,819, which watered down the *Alabama* award of $15,500,000 to approximately $8,000,000. Note Greeley's complaints, and decide which one carried the most weight.

So much has been done by our own government to neutralize all the good results which might have been attained by this experiment of international arbitration that there will be a general feeling of surprise and possibly even of congratulation that anything has been given in satisfaction of the claims of the United States. The controversy has grown stale, and everyone will be glad to hear that it is at an end. But it could scarcely have ended worse. We have lost every point we tried to make.

By asking too much we have gained nothing. The thousand millions which would have made our case sublime, if they had not made it ridiculous, have dwindled to fifteen and a half. This petty sum will doubtless be

3. New York *Tribune*, Sept. 16, 1872.

greatly diminished by the English claims against the United States which are yet to be allowed.

Of course the mere matter of money is the least important feature of so grave and authoritative a decision, which forms a sort of epoch in international proceedings. But this trifling sum is positively all we have gained.

In every point of view the great moral advantage is with England, and against us. In their anxiety to convict England of negligence, our attorneys have persistently urged the propriety and necessity of the employment of arbitrary powers by the [London] government, to prevent possible violations of the neutrality laws. As we are to pass the greater portion of our national life as neutrals, and as we all expect our shipbuilding interests to revive some day, it is easy to see how jealous belligerents could annoy our legitimate industries by the weapons we have thus put into their hands. . . .

The cheerfulness of the London papers over the award is, therefore, easy to understand. It will be difficult for us to extract any satisfaction from the conclusion of the matter. We are to have a few millions, it is true, at the end of a year, provided there is anything left of the sum awarded after it is decided what English claims we are to pay. Otherwise we have nothing on our side of the account.

B. THE LIBERAL REPUBLICAN REVOLT

1. Schurz Exposes the Spoilsmen (1871)

The whiteness of the White House was blackened by the scramble for offices under the gullible Grant. Cigar-chomping politicians, like hogs at the swill-box, grunted and shoved for soft jobs. The reformers, soon to organize the Liberal Republican Party, were prodded into protest. Conspicuous among them was the angular gadfly Carl Schurz (see earlier, p. 461), who had grown up under the efficient German civil service. Now a liberal Senator from Missouri, he delivered the following indictment in the Senate. Enumerate the evils that he finds in the existing spoils system, and determine which one he regards as the most serious.

After the incoming of this administration, a gentleman of my acquaintance who had strong "claims" desired to be appointed postmaster in a Western city. But the President happened to put one of his own friends into that office; and so the man to be provided for could not be postmaster. Then the [Congressional] delegation of his state agreed to make him pension agent at the same place; but an influential member of that delegation opposed it, and so he could not be pension agent.

Then he took his case into his own hands, for he knew that he was a man to be provided for, and the President nominated him as minister resident to a South American republic. Having obtained that, he thought he could obtain more. He saw a chance to be appointed minister plenipotentiary to another government, and, sure enough, he received the nomination for that

1. *Congressional Globe*, 41 Cong., 3 sess., Appendix, p. 70.

also. Then his nomination came into the Senate, and was rejected. There was a terrible disappointment! And yet the man to be provided for was provided for. He was finally sent as a governor to a territory.

Thus, sir, under the present intelligent system of making appointments, the same man aspired to a post office, a pension agency, a minister resident-ship, a full mission, and finally landed in the governorship of a territory. And the appointing power, yielding to the peculiar pressure characteristic of the existing system, declared him fit for all these places consecutively. And all this in seven days, save the territorial governorship, which was discovered for him afterward.

And with him there were a multitude of men to be provided for at the same time; there always are a good many more than places to put them in. Do you complain of the unnecessary multiplication of offices? That evil is unavoidable as long as we suffer under the system which recognizes men to be provided for.

Must it not be clear to every observing mind that our present mode of making appointments is a blindfold game, a mere haphazard proceeding? Was Mr. Lincoln very wrong when once, in a moment of despair, he said with grim humor: "I have discovered a good way of providing officers for the government: put all the names of the applicants into one pepper-box and all the offices into another, and then shake the two, and make appointments just as the names and the offices happen to drop out together."

2. Greeley Praises Greeley (1872)

The voices of the liberals, including that of Carl Schurz, swelled to a roar. With scandals bursting like popcorn, the reformers clamored for a renovation of the civil service. With the cruelest phase of Reconstruction going forward, they demanded more lenient treatment of the vanquished. When the spoilsmen and regulars of the Republican Party insisted on renominating the "old man" Grant, the reformers bolted and formed the short-lived Liberal Republican Party. Meeting in a chaotic convention in Cincinnati, they emerged with a most unlikely nominee in the erratic and politically inept editor Horace Greeley. His own influential paper published the following appeal on the eve of the election. In reading this statement, note the extent to which the Southern question was involved. What did the slogan "Reunion and Reform" mean?

We ask those who are accustomed to read and trust the *Tribune* to vote today for Horace Greeley for President of the United States—

Because he is the best man for the place. He is incomparably abler, better informed, safer than his antagonist.

Because his election would mean reconciliation with the South, an end of the war, a revival of Southern industry, increased markets for Northern products, a homogeneous country, with consequent safety and prosperity.

Because his election would mean reform at the North—an end of government patronage in elections, an end of administering the civil service

2. New York *Tribune*, Nov. 5, 1872.

"WHOEVER SAYS THIS ISN'T A REAL ELEPHANT
IS 'A LIAR'"

Greeley tries to make a Republican elephant of states'
righters, Northern Tammany Democrats, and Southern
Ku Kluxers. *Harper's Weekly*, 1872.

not to do the government work but to defeat one party and help another—
an investigation of the corruptions which have seemed to pervade all
branches of the national government, and have made the rule at Washington as much worse than Tweed's[*] rule as its scope was wider and its power
more resistless.

Because his election would mean an end of carpetbag governments at
the South, propped up by Washington interference for yet longer robbery
of already bankrupt communities.

Because, in a word, it would secure those great ends of Reunion and
Reform for which the Cincinnati [Liberal Republican] movement was
begun, and the triumph of which, whether today hastened or delayed, is as
sure to come as the Republic is to endure.

3. The *Herald* Hails Grant's Victory (1872)

"Not all Democrats are horse thieves, but all horse thieves are Democrats." So
Greeley had earlier written. But the success-starved Democrats, in the hope of defeating the Republicans, "ate crow" and formally endorsed him. Such dubious bed-
fellows merely increased Greeley's vulnerability. The rebellion-tainted Democrats were
accused of plotting a repeal of the 14th Amendment (civil rights) and the 15th
Amendment (Negro vote). They were also accused of seeking to ruin the financial

[*] Tweed was the corrupt "boss" of New York City who filched millions of dollars.
3. New York *Herald,* Nov. 6, 1872.

structure by paying off the government bonds in depreciated greenbacks. Moreover, ex-Confederates like Alexander H. Stephens, who had been Vice-President of the Confederacy, were too actively associated with the Democratic Party for the good of the Liberal Republicans. Grant's sweeping triumph in November was acclaimed by the New York *Herald* as "another Appomattox." Assess the arguments advanced in behalf of Grant by this journal, and determine which one probably carried the greatest weight with the voters.

But the case against General Grant was too weak. . . . Made up of charges of corruption not established nor generally believed; of promises of civil service reform too shadowy to attract public attention; of an acceptance of the 14th and 15th Amendments widely distrusted; and of a plea for universal amnesty and Southern reconciliation so broad and comprehensive as to excite suspicion of a meditated surrender to Southern rights as expounded by Alexander H. Stephens, the case of the opposition coalition against General Grant is swept away by his case against the coalition.

The administration party [Republicans] presented, in their case for General Grant, his practical reforms and retrenchments; his payment of hundreds of millions of the public debt, with reductions amounting to hundreds of millions of our national taxations; his foreign policy of peace and arbitration [at Geneva]; his humane Indian policy; his conciliatory treatment of the Southern ex-rebel whites while executing the Ku Klux laws of Congress for the protection of the Southern blacks; and, above all, the safety under Grant of our established financial system—bonds, banks, currency, and all the stupendous business affairs of the country depending upon this financial system; and, on the other hand, the dangers of a financial convulsion and collapse that would follow the election of Greeley, with a party at his back intent upon various quixotic financial experiments, including the immediate resumption of specie payments at all hazards.*

This case for the administration was too strong for the cloudy and unsubstantial case of the opposition. The American people have accordingly decreed in favor of the safety of their general interests under the existing administration, and against the doubts and dangers involved in the indefinite and uncertain designs and tendencies of an opposing coalition, charged with no higher bond of union in their late canvass than the spoilsman's shibboleth of "anything to beat Grant!"

C. THE END OF GRANTISM

1. The House Protests a Third Term (1875)

Grant's victory over Greeley delayed a house-cleaning. More scandals broke during the General's second term than during his first, although he was not personally re-

---

* During the Civil War the Treasury had gone off the gold standard. The Liberal Republicans demanded a redemption of paper money with hard money.
1. *Congressional Record,* 44 Cong., 1 sess., p. 228 (Dec. 15, 1875). Several Republican state legislatures also passed anti-third term resolutions.

sponsible for many of them. The Republican spoilsmen were naturally eager to run their benefactor a third time. And Grant, twice elected by substantial majorities and still largely unaware of his ineptitude, betrayed a disturbing willingness. But the Democratic House of Representatives, by a smashing bipartisan vote of 233 to 18, approved the following resolution introduced by Springer of Illinois. Ascertain what "peril" was feared.

Resolved, That, in the opinion of this House, the precedent established by Washington and other Presidents of the United States, in retiring from the presidential office after their second term, has become, by universal concurrence, a part of our republican system of government, and that any departure from this time-honored custom would be unwise, unpatriotic, and fraught with peril to our free institutions.

2. The Democrats Arraign Grant (1876)

"Eight long years of scandal" was the tag that the Democrats tellingly attached to the Grant era. Meeting in their national convention in St. Louis and nominating the reformer Samuel J. Tilden, they flayed the Republican regime as follows in their platform. Appraise the assumption that a change of administration would eliminate the evils described.

Reform is necessary in the civil service. Experience proves that efficient, economical conduct of the government is not possible if its civil service be subject to change at every election, be a prize fought for at the ballot-box, be an approved reward of party zeal instead of posts of honor assigned for proved competency and held for fidelity in the public employ; that the dispensing of patronage should neither be a tax upon the time of our public men nor an instrument of their ambition. Here, again, profession falsified in the performance attest that the party in power can work out no practical or salutary reform.

Reform is necessary even more in the higher grades of the public service. President, Vice-President, judges, Senators, Representatives, Cabinet officers —these and all others in authority are the people's servants. Their offices are not a private perquisite; they are a public trust. When the annals of this Republic show disgrace and censure of a Vice-President [Schuyler Colfax]; a late Speaker of the House of Representatives [James G. Blaine] marketing his rulings as a presiding officer; three Senators profiting secretly by their votes as law-makers; five chairmen of the leading committees of the late House of Representatives exposed in jobbery; a late Secretary of the Treasury [W. A. Richardson] forcing balances in the public accounts; a late Attorney-General [G. H. Williams] misappropriating public funds; a Secretary of the Navy [G. M. Robeson] enriched and enriching friends by a percentage levied off the profits of contractors with his department; an Ambassador to England [R. C. Schenck] censured in a dishonorable speculation; the President's Private Secretary [O. E. Babcock] barely

2. K. H. Porter, comp., *National Party Platforms* (1924), pp. 89–90.

escaping conviction upon trial for guilty complicity in frauds upon the revenue; a Secretary of War [W. W. Belknap] impeached for high crimes and misdemeanors—the demonstration is complete that the first step in reform must be the people's choice of honest men from another party, lest the disease of one political organization infect the body politic, and lest by making no change of men or parties we get no change of measures and no real reform.

All these abuses, wrongs, and crimes, the product of sixteen years' ascendancy of the Republican Party, create a necessity for reform, confessed by Republicans themselves; but their reformers are voted down in convention and displaced from the Cabinet. The party's mass of honest voters is powerless to resist the eighty thousand office-holders, its leaders and guides. Reform can only be had by a peaceful civic revolution. We demand a change of system, a change of administration, a change of parties, that we may have a change of measures and of men.

[*The Republican platform of 1876 naturally praised Grant's "honorable work" as President, while stressing the rebellion-stained record of the Democrats. The scandals were dismissed in one brief paragraph: "We rejoice in the quickened conscience of the people concerning political affairs. We will hold all public officers to a rigid responsibility, and engage that the prosecution and punishment of all who betray official trusts shall be speedy, thorough, and unsparing." Yet precisely here Grant had failed tragically. In 1876 he had shielded his private secretary, Babcock (when tried for graft involving the whiskey revenue frauds), and also his Secretary of War, Belknap (when involved in graft regarding Indian supplies). But Grant had nothing whatever to do with the scandals besmirching Speaker Blaine and Vice-President Colfax. Cabinet members Richardson, Williams, and Robeson were all his appointees, and to that extent he was responsible for their shortcomings. Minister Schenck in London, who used his popularity as the "high priest of draw poker" to sell bogus mining stock, also falls into this category.*]

3. Grant's Farewell Apology (1876)

Grant had voted only once for a President prior to his own nomination (though a Republican, he had backed the Democrat Buchanan in the hope of averting secession). A regimented military life had not fitted him for civilian administration, and his blind loyalty to his thieving appointees was carried to an incredible point. Into his last annual message to Congress he inserted a farewell apology which indicated that he was becoming aware of his own shortcomings. This remarkable statement has been called both naïve and lacking in manliness. Comment. Discover whom or what he blamed for his failures.

It was my fortune, or misfortune, to be called to the office of Chief Executive without any previous political training. From the age of seventeen, I had never even witnessed the excitement attending a presidential campaign but twice antecedent to my own candidacy, and at but one of them was I eligible as a voter.

3. J. D. Richardson, ed., *Messages and Papers of the Presidents* (1897), VII, 399–401.

Under such circumstances, it is but reasonable to suppose that errors of judgment must have occurred. Even had they not, differences of opin-ion between the Ex-ecutive, bound by an oath to the strict performance of his duties, and writers and debaters must have arisen. It is not necessarily evidence of blunder on the part of the Executive be-cause there are these differences of views. Mistakes have been made, as all can see and I admit, but it seems to me oftener in the selections made of the assistants ap-pointed to aid in car-rying out the various duties of administer-ing the government —in nearly every case selected without a personal acquaintance

IN FOR IT

U. S. [Grant]: "I hope I shall get to the bottom soon." Grant, after promising a probe, has not reached bottom yet. *Harper's Weekly*, 1876.

with the appointee, but upon recommendations of the representatives chosen directly by the people.

It is impossible, where so many trusts are to be allotted, that the right parties should be chosen in every instance. History shows that no admin-istration from the time of Washington to the present has been free from these mistakes. But I leave comparisons to history, claiming only that I have acted in every instance from a conscientious desire to do what was right, constitutional, within the law, and for the very best interests of the whole people. Failures have been errors in judgment, not of intent.

My civil career commenced, too, at a most critical and difficult time. Less than four years before, the country had emerged from a conflict such as no other had ever survived. . . . Immediately on the cessation of hos-tilities the then noble President, who had carried the country so far through its perils, fell a martyr to his patriotism at the hands of an assassin.

The intervening time of my first inauguration was filled up with wran-gling between Congress and the new Executive [Johnson] as to the best mode of "reconstruction," or, to speak plainly, as to whether the control of the government should be thrown immediately into the hands of those who had so recently and persistently tried to destroy it, or whether the victors should continue to have an equal voice with them in this control. Reconstruction, as finally agreed upon, means this and only this, except that the late slave was enfranchised, giving an increase, as was supposed, to the Union-loving and Union-supporting votes. If *free* in the full sense of the word, they would not disappoint this expectation.

Hence, at the beginning of my first administration, the work of Reconstruction, much embarrassed by the long delay, virtually commenced. It was the work of the legislative branch of the government. My province was wholly in approving their acts, which I did most heartily, urging the legislatures of states that had not yet done so to ratify the 15th Amendment [Negro vote] to the Constitution.

The country was laboring under an enormous debt, contracted in the suppression of rebellion, and taxation was so oppressive as to discourage production. Another danger also threatened us—a foreign war. The last difficulty had to be adjusted, and was adjusted without a war and in a manner highly honorable to all parties concerned.

D. HAYES AND THE SOUTHERN PROBLEM

1. Hayes Believes Himself Defrauded (1876)

In 1876 the Republicans nominated, as Grant's successor, Governor Rutherford B. Hayes of Ohio. Hayes was a political Puritan so serious-minded that at the age of twelve he had written in his diary of the necessity of reading law books rather than the frivolous newspapers. The Democrats nominated a multimillionaire bachelor, Governor Samuel J. Tilden of New York, a prominent corporation lawyer and a noted but overrated reformer. The first electoral returns, although not the later ones, indicated a Democratic landslide, and Hayes privately conceded defeat in his diary. Observe why he felt that he would have won in a fair election.

Sunday, November 12.—The news this morning is not conclusive. The headlines of the morning papers are as follows: the *News*, "Nip and Tuck"; "Tuck has it"; "The Mammoth National Doubt"; and the *Herald* heads its news column, "Which?" But to my mind the figures indicate that Florida has been carried by the Democrats. No doubt both fraud and violence intervened to produce the result. But the same is true in many Southern states.

We shall, the fair-minded men of the country will, history will hold that the Republicans were by fraud, violence, and intimidation, by a nullification of the 15th Amendment, deprived of the victory which they fairly won. But we must, I now think, prepare ourselves to accept the inevitable. I do it with composure and cheerfulness. To me the result is no personal calamity.

1. C. R. Williams, ed., *Diary and Letters of Rutherford Birchard Hayes* (1924), III. 377–78. By permission of the Ohio Historical Society.

I would like the opportunity to improve the civil service. It seems to me I could do more than any Democrat to put Southern affairs on a sound basis. I do not apprehend any great or permanent injury to the financial affairs of the country by the victory of the Democrats. The hard-money wing of the party is at the helm. . . .

We are in a minority in the electoral colleges; we lose the administration. But in the former free states—the states that were always loyal—we are still in a majority. We carry eighteen of the twenty-two and have two hundred thousand majority of the popular vote. In the old slave states, if the recent Amendments were cheerfully obeyed, if there had been neither violence nor intimidation nor other improper interference with the rights of the colored people, we should have carried enough Southern states to have held the country and to have secured a decided popular majority in the nation.

Our adversaries are in power, but they are supported by a minority only of the lawful voters of the country. A fair election in the South would undoubtedly have given us a large majority of the electoral votes, and a decided preponderance of the popular vote.

2. Chandler Assails the Solid South (1879)

With the electoral vote of three carpetbag states of the South in hot dispute, the Hayes-Tilden deadlock of 1876 was broken in 1877 by the specially constituted Electoral Commission of fifteen men. Its questionable decision for Hayes was grudgingly accepted by the Democrats. But they did not yield until they had received assurances that federal bayonets would no longer prop up Republican regimes in Louisiana and South Carolina—the last of the states under military reconstruction. Hayes honored this pledge and withdrew the troops, despite Republican outcries. The two states then went over to the Democratic Solid South. The spoilsman Senator Zachariah Chandler of Michigan, who had been a violent anti-slaveryite, deplored these developments in a fiery speech in Chicago. (He died the next day.) The Democrats at that time controlled both Houses of Congress. Note why Chandler regarded the Southern states as grossly overrepresented, and to what extent his objection is still relevant.

They [the Confederates] have forfeited all their property—we gave it back to them. We found them naked, and we clothed them. They were without the rights of citizenship, and we restored to them those rights. We took them to our bosoms as brethren, believing that they had repented of their sins. We killed for them the fatted calf and invited them to the feast, and they gravely informed us that they had always owned that animal, and were not grateful for the invitation.

By the laws of war, and by the laws of nations, they were bound to pay every dollar of the expense incurred in putting down that rebellion. But we forgave them that debt, and today you are being taxed heavily to pay the interest on the debt that they ought to have paid. Such magnanimity

2. C. M. Depew, ed., *The Library of Oratory* (1902), VIII, 448–51 (Oct. 31, 1879).

"OF COURSE HE WANTS TO VOTE THE DEMOCRATIC TICKET!"

Democratic "Reformer": "You're free as air, ain't you? Say you are, or I'll
blow yer black head off!"
A satire on the Southern claim that the Negroes of the South were "free as
air" in the Hayes-Tilden campaign. *Harper's Weekly*, 1876.

as was exhibited by this nation to these rebels has never been witnessed
on the earth since God made it, and, in my humble judgment, it will never
be witnessed again.

Mistakes we undoubtedly made, errors we committed, but, in my judgment, the greatest mistake we made, and the gravest error we committed,
was in not hanging enough of these rebels to make treason forever odious.

Today, in Congress, the men have changed but not the measures. Twenty
years ago they said: "Do this, or fail to do that, and we will shoot your
government to death." If I am to die, I would rather be shot to death with
musketry than starved to death. These rebels (for they are just as rebellious
now as they were twenty years ago; there is not a particle of difference—
I know them better than any other living mortal man; I have summered
and wintered with them)—these rebels today have thirty-six members on
the floor of the House of Representatives. Without one single constituent,
and in violation of law, those thirty-six members represent 4,000,000 people,

lately slaves, who are as absolutely disfranchised as if they lived in another sphere, through shotguns, and whips, and tissue-ballots. For the law [14th Amendment] expressly says that wherever a race or class is disfranchised, they shall not be represented upon the floor of the House. And these thirty-six members thus elected constitute three times the whole of their majority upon the floor.*

This is not only a violation of the law, but it is an outrage upon all the loyal men of the United States. It ought not to be. It must not be. And it shall not be. Twelve members of the Senate—more than their whole majority—occupy their seats upon the floor by fraud and violence; and I am saying no more to you than I said to those rebel generals. With majorities thus obtained by fraud and violence in both Houses, they dared to dictate terms to the loyal men of these United States. . . .

What they want is not free elections, but free fraud at elections. They have got a Solid South by fraud and violence. Give them permission to perpetrate the same fraud and violence in New York City and Cincinnati, and New York and Ohio, with the Solid South, will give them the Presidency, and that once obtained by fraud and violence, they would hold it for a generation. Today 8,000,000 of people in the Southern states control the legislation of the country through caucus dictation, as they controlled their slaves when slavery existed.

[*Chandler was partially correct. The Democratic Party that finally won the White House under Cleveland, Wilson, and Franklin Roosevelt was basically the Solid South plus the Democratic machines of the large Northeastern and Middle Western cities.*]

E. HAYES AND CIVIL SERVICE REFORM

1. The President Issues New Rules (1877)

"His Honesty" President Hayes was pledged to a long-overdue renovation of the civil service. The scandal-ridden New York Custom House, with some 1300 voter-employees, was a well-greased political machine controlled by the imperious New York boss, Senator Roscoe Conkling. After a federal commission had investigated the Custom House, Hayes wrote this refreshing letter to Secretary of the Treasury John Sherman. Determine which of the new rules would be most objectionable to the bosses, and to what extent political activity would thereafter be permitted.

My dear Sir: I have read the partial report of the commission appointed to examine the New York Custom House. I concur with the commission in their recommendations.

It is my wish that the collection of the revenues should be free from partisan control, and organized on a strictly business basis, with the same

* The House numbered 149 Democrats and 130 Republicans; the Senate, 42 Democrats and 33 Republicans.
1. C. R. Williams, ed., *Diary and Letters of Rutherford Birchard Hayes* (1924), III, 435–36 (May 26, 1877). By permission of the Ohio Historical Society.

guaranties for efficiency and fidelity in the selection of the chief and sub-ordinate officers that would be required by a prudent merchant. Party leaders should have no more influence in appointments than other equally respectable citizens. No [monetary] assessments for political purposes, on officers or subordinates, should be allowed. No useless officer or employee should be retained. No officer should be required or permitted to take part in the management of political organizations, caucuses, conventions, or election campaigns. Their right to vote, and to express their views on public questions, either orally or through the press, is not denied, provided it does not interfere with the discharge of their official duties.

2. Hayes Tightens the Regulations (1879)

The Collector of the Port of New York was the dudish, side-whiskered Chester A. Arthur, a stooge of the powerful Senator Conkling, and a future (accidental) President of the United States. He felt secure enough to defy Hayes' new orders forbidding political activity. The President thereupon dismissed him. The outraged Senator Conkling put up a prolonged fight in the Senate against the confirmation of Arthur's successor, General Merritt, but finally lost out when the Custom House scandals were thoroughly aired. Ascertain the most surprising aspects of Hayes' new instructions to General Merritt.

Dear General: I congratulate you on your confirmation. It is a great gratification to your friends, very honorable to you, and will prove, I believe, of signal service to the country. My desire is that your office shall be conducted on strictly business principles, and according to the rules which were adopted on the recommendation of the Civil Service Com-mission by the administration of General Grant.

In making appointments and removals of subordinates, you should be perfectly independent of mere influence. Neither my recommendation, nor that of the Secretary of the Treasury, nor the recommendation of any member of Congress, or other influential person, should be specially re-garded. Let appointments and removals be made on business principles and by fixed rules. There must be, I assume, a few places, the duties of which are confidential, and which would be filled by those whom you personally know to be trustworthy; but restrict the area of patronage to the narrowest possible limits. Let no man be put out merely because he is a friend of the late collector [Arthur], and no man be put in merely because he is our friend.

3. *The Nation* Finds Fault (1881)

A woman who wants to be reputed chaste must always be chaste; a single lapse will destroy her good name. President Hayes made commendable progress toward civil service reform, but the demands of practical politics forced him on a distressing number of occasions to depart from the narrow path of virtue. Notoriously, he had

2. *Ibid.*, III, 520 (Feb. 4, 1879). By permission of the Ohio Historical Society.
3. *The Nation* (New York), XXXII, 144 (March 3, 1881).

given federal jobs to every one of the four Republican members of the Louisiana Returning Board who had invalidated enough Democratic votes to insure his election. The reformist editor of the New York *Nation*, E. L. Godkin, remembered these lapses when appraising the Hayes administration. It has been said that Hayes could please neither the reformers, the Republicans, nor the Democrats. Explain why in the light of Godkin's remarks.

He [Hayes] actually came to the conclusion, as soon as he entered the White House—we do not know under what influence—that his first duty was, not by an exhibition of unswerving integrity, to relieve the honest souls all over the country who had supported him with misgiving . . . but to provide the Louisiana and Florida politicians who had counted him in with substantial rewards for their services. As soon as he did this, he delivered himself into the hands of his enemies. He discarded the warranty which he had received from the Electoral Commission, and confessed obligation to the Returning Boards.

Under the best of circumstances, it would have been hard for him to live up to the standard of reform set out in his letter of acceptance; after this fatal compliance it became impossible. He could only have conquered by the aid of a sincerity which no man dared to doubt. After using the civil service to reward the Southern Republican counters, his enemies were able to deny his sincerity with the aid of proofs which his warmest friends found it difficult to meet. In fact, the battle was lost before a shot had been fired. . . .

That his administration has been very pure as contrasted with that of his predecessor, there is no doubt. Its freedom from all scandals, and the general sweetness of the social atmosphere with which it has surrounded the White House, must always give it strong claims on public gratitude. . . . And assuredly when the Democrats do come into power, if they come before long, they will find in the history of Mr. Hayes's administration plenty of excuse for persistence in the practices which were the disgrace of Grant's.

It is true Mr. Hayes leaves behind some good precedents, such as the withdrawal of the New York Custom House and Post Office from politics. But it is one of the misfortunes of a President's position, as it is of a clergyman's, that when he sets up as a reformer he cannot afford a single lapse from virtue. He has to be a reformer, as they say in the conventions, "first, last, and all the time" in order to save himself from the reproach of hypocrisy.

THOUGHT PROVOKERS

1. Why were both North and South displeased with Britain's policy during the Civil War? If criticism of an arbitral award by both parties means that it is fair, what may be said of the Geneva award?

2. To what extent would the difficulties of the Grant period have occurred under an experienced non-military man? What good can be said of Grant's administration?

3. Some have argued that the 22nd Amendment (no third term) would have been especially desirable in the days of Grant. Argue both sides and come to a conclusion.

4. Was it fair to the Southern Republicans, both white and Negro, for Hayes to withdraw the troops and permit the Democrats to take over? If Tilden, the Democrat, had won in 1876, could he have taken this action as quickly as Hayes did?

5. Explain why Hayes' commendable new rules for civil service reform encountered such furious opposition. To what extent are these rules commonplace today?

FURTHER EXPLORATION

General: L. D. White, *The Republican Era, 1869–1901* (1958). **Alabama Claims:** Goldwin Smith, *The Treaty of Washington, 1871* (1941); Allan Nevins, *Hamilton Fish* (1936). **Liberal Republicans:** E. D. Ross, *The Liberal Republican Movement* (1919). **Grantism:** W. B. Hesseltine, *Ulysses S. Grant, Politician* (1935). **Hayes and the South:** C. V. Woodward, *Reunion and Reaction* (1951); C. V. Woodward, *Origins of the New South* (1951). **Hayes and Reform:** Harry Barnard, *Rutherford B. Hayes and His America* (1954).

Recent: T. Harry Williams, ed., *Hayes: The Diary of a President, 1875–1881* (1964); William Gillette, *The Right to Vote: Politics and the Passage of the Fifteenth Amendment* (1965); Irwin Unger, *The Greenback Era* (1964).

Chapter 26

Republicans and Democrats, 1881-1889

Public officers are the servants and agents of the people, to execute the laws which the people have made.

GROVER CLEVELAND, 1882

PROLOGUE: Mounting agitation for civil service reform, following the scandals of the Grant era and the assassination of President Garfield, finally forced the passage of the pathbreaking Pendleton Act of 1883. It was only a modest beginning, but it halted and partially reversed the spoils-system tide that had risen shamefully since Jackson's day. The ex-spoilsman President Arthur, who had succeeded Garfield, cooperated with commendable energy in launching the Pendleton Act. The widening reform movement was further strengthened by the outcome of the presidential election of 1884. In a gutter-low contest, Republican James G. Blaine lost out to Democratic Grover Cleveland. Cleveland's incumbency —the first Democratic administration since the end of Buchanan's in 1861—was distinguished for upright and economical government, and for a determination to face up to the explosive issues of tariff reduction and Civil War pensions.

A. THE BEGINNINGS OF CIVIL SERVICE REFORM

1. Morton Praises the Spoils System (1871)

Oliver P. Morton, Indiana's able war governor, had labored so zealously against hostile Copperhead Democrats that his exertions were blamed for the paralytic stroke that crippled him in 1865. As a fanatical Republican, he could see little good in the Democrats, and consequently favored appointing fellow partisans to office. His speech in the United States Senate in 1871 against the proposed civil service reform is a classic argument for the spoils system. Locate his strongest and weakest points, and assess them critically.

The Senator [Trumbull of Illinois] says that he is in favor of organizing the civil service so that officers shall be appointed without regard to politics. . . . Now, sir, to have appointments made without regard to politics will suit our Democratic friends remarkably well while they are not in power, but it would not suit them one moment after they came into power. . . .

The Senator from Illinois praises the civil service system of Great Britain. A system that might be appropriate to Great Britain would not be appropriate here; our institutions are different. In England the tenure of office in the civil service is for life. They hold their offices during good behavior; that is to say, during life. Can we adopt the life tenure here?

---

1. *Congressional Globe,* 41 Cong., 3 sess., Pt. I, pp. 458, 460–61 (Jan. 12, 1871).

Why, sir, ten thousand men in this city [Washington] holding office for life would form a privileged class that would revolutionize the very foundation principle of this government. We have but one life tenure under our Constitution, and if we had it to make over again we would not have that. I refer to the Supreme Court of the United States. . . . If a man has an office for life, it takes a very serious cause to get him out. An ordinary delinquency, an ordinary neglect or abuse or failure, is never sufficient to oust a man who holds an office for life.

CAN A MAN BE A NURSE?

U. S. Grant holds the baby as he finds neither party wanting it. *Harper's Weekly,* 1875.

No, sir, we cannot afford to adopt the English system under any circumstances; it is anti-republican; it is contrary to the fundamental principles of this government; and yet the Senator held up to us the beauties of the English system!

Sir, what is the fact there? Are the English clerks better qualified than those in our departments are? From the evidence I have, they are not. But they have one quality that our clerks have not got: that is, they have "the insolence of office" that results from a life tenure. I could refer to the facts on this point. You have all read *Little Dorrit,* by Charles Dickens, where he described the Circumlocution Office and the Somerset House. . . .

I am not arguing against competitive examinations. I am in favor of them; but they are not infallible by any means. Men may pass an examination, and a first-rate examination, and yet be utterly unqualified for the position. How does it happen so often that the young men who graduate at law schools and carry off the first prizes fail in the practice of the law? So in regard to medicine. And how often does it happen that those who take the honors of the class at West Point do not succeed upon the field of battle or in the Army? You can adopt no system that will guard against exceptional cases. . . .

But the Senator says that officers ought to be appointed without regard to politics. Whenever you can carry on this government without regard to politics, that doctrine will do. But this is a government of the people and a government of public opinion, in which the mass of the people take a deep interest, as they do not in England and in countries on the continent of Europe. Just so long as the character of this government continues as it is, appointments will continue to be made with reference to politics; and no system can be devised that will prevent it. I do not care how many competitive examinations you institute, or whether you make the tenure for life or a tenure for ten years, you cannot change that thing unless you change the character of the government.

But what propriety is there in it? A man high in office, who has climbed up the political ladder, may then turn around and slap the faces of his friends who helped him up, if they should want appointments, and call that virtue! Would it make it a virtue? . . .

I have been in the Senate now nearly four years, and, so far as I know, there have been but three clerks appointed upon my recommendation. . . . As far as I am personally concerned, I would be glad to be relieved of all this labor. But what right have I to be relieved? My friends have the same right to call upon me that I have had in times past to call upon them, and, if they are respectable, and capable, and honest, why should I refuse to give them that legitimate aid which may be within my power? Why, sir, men act upon this principle in all conditions of life, whether in regard to politics or in regard to business; and you cannot change it by any enactment which you can make.

2. *The Nation* Analyzes the Assassination (1881)

President Garfield, the Republican Congressman who succeeded President Hayes, appointed an arch-foe of Senator Roscoe Conkling of New York to head the New York Custom House. Both Senator Conkling and his colleague Senator Thomas ("Me Too") Platt resigned in protest, and then sought re-election and vindication by the Albany legislature. (Until the 17th Amendment of 1913, legislatures elected Senators.) With excitement at fever pitch, a disappointed office seeker and half-crazed Conklingite, Charles Guiteau, fatally shot President Garfield. Both Conkling and Platt, now thoroughly discredited, failed of re-election. Ascertain from this editorial in the New York *Nation* the most important result of Garfield's assassination.

A . . . source of consolation is the way in which the tragedy has brought home to the public the need of some change in the mode of appointment and in the tenure-of-office in the civil service. Thousands who did not see it before now see that it will not do to lead great hordes of shiftless, half-cracked ne'er-do-wells to look to the government for a living when their friends get tired of supporting them; that it will not do to expose a President, to whom all have access, first to their solicitations and then to their resentment; and, finally, that it will not do to leave it in the power of

2. *The Nation* (New York), XXXIII, 1 (July 7, 1881).

disappointed politicians to denounce the President in the vilest billingsgate, and hold him up to popular execration, because he does not satisfy them with collectorships, gaugerships, and consulates.

Guiteau's shot did much for civil service reform. Nothing that the Conklingite faction can accomplish, even if they come into power during the next four years, will do away with the impression it has made.

3. A Democrat Attacks Reform (1882)

Many envious Democrats had clamored for civil service reform during the long and unbroken drought of Republican ascendancy from 1861 to 1885. But the sweeping Democratic victory in the Congressional elections of 1882 foreshadowed a Democratic President in 1885. The Democrats now grew hostile toward proposals for "freezing" resolute Republicans in the civil service, from which they could not be dislodged by deserving Democrats. Senator Brown of Georgia, a Democrat, here voices his displeasure on the Senate floor. Assess his argument that since government by party is necessary, the spoils system is desirable.

Now, I am going [to] talk plainly to Democrats. . . . The Republican Party have had the offices of this government for the last twenty-two years consecutively. The Executive has been Republican, and they have had the distribution of the offices and places. They still have it. True, an avalanche has swept over the country, and with it the strongest condemnation of the practices of that party. . . . If we make no great blunders . . . there can be, to my mind, and I think to the minds of Senators generally, but little doubt that the next President of this Republic will be a Democrat.

I am speaking now to Democrats. How do you go into that campaign? Suppose you put my honorable and worthy friend from Ohio [Mr. Pendleton] or my honorable friend from Delaware [Mr. Bayard], or any other one of the prominent and able gentlemen mentioned for the place, in nomination for the Presidency, and you go before the Democratic masses of the United States and tell them that you are handicapped; that all the offices that amount to anything, the higher and more important places, are already disposed of.

"Disposed of how?" they will inquire.

"Why, the Republican Party have had them for twenty-two years, and seeing that there was a probability of a change of administration"—to put it in no stronger light—"they have hedged, and they have taken good care of themselves; they have passed a civil service bill, and Democrats have helped them to enact it; and we have it on the statute book now that there is no Democrat to be put into office in any of the Executive Departments except in the lowest positions. Above them the Republicans alone may compete with each other for the places; but there is no chance for a Democrat."

In a free republican government like this, those who belong to both parties fight for office as well as principle. Do you believe that the Demo-

3. *Congressional Record,* 47 Cong., 2 sess., pp. 277, 278 (Dec. 14, 1882).

cratic leaders in all the different states would work with the same energy, and zeal, and ability, as they would if you held out to them a chance of a change of the offices with the change of the Executive? It would be contrary to all the history of the past to expect any such work. . . . They would vote the ticket patriotically as true Democrats, but they would not exert themselves as they would do if they believed there would be a general change or even a change of one-half the persons holding the offices. . . .

I do not laud the sentiment mentioned by the honorable Senator from Massachusetts [Hoar], which he attributes to Mr. Marcy, that "to the victors belong the spoils." He said it was rather coarse. Probably it was; but yet to a very great extent it has been the system practiced from the first day of the inauguration of this government; and whatever you may put upon the statute book it will be the system practiced until its funeral knell is sounded. And no party in this government ever practiced the spoils system with more zeal and energy than the Republican Party has. "To the victors belong the spoils" has been its constant motto in practice; and still would be, if impending defeat did not stare it in the face. There may be some reforms, some of the worst features may be cut off; but in the main the Executive who comes into power when his party has long been deprived of power will find a way, and the heads of departments under him will find a way, to give to his followers the benefit of the offices or a large proportion of them.

B. THE AFTERMATH OF THE PENDLETON ACT

1. *Harper's Weekly* Hails a New Era (1883)

The Pendleton Civil Service Reform Act finally passed Congress in 1883. Most of the opposition came from spoils-hungry Democrats, who now resented the death-bed repentance of the Republicans. The new law forbade obligatory political contributions from officeholders, and authorized competitive examinations to ascertain fitness. But the act was initially applied to only about 10,000 officials in the "classified service," out of some 130,000 federal employees. The passage of the measure was unwittingly assisted by Congressman J. A. Hubbell, chairman of the Republican Congressional Committee, who had given ammunition to the reformers by brazenly demanding contributions from federal officers as office insurance. *Harper's Weekly*, whose editor (George W. Curtis) was a leading civil service reformer, here comments on the passage of the bill by the Senate, before its approval by the House. Form conclusions as to why the measure was enacted at this particular time.

The passage of the Pendleton bill by the Senate is an important event in our political history. It is the first practical legislative step toward the correction of abuses of administration involving dangerous consequences which are plainly perceived and universally acknowledged. It is a measure which, should it become law, will overthrow the aristocracy of patronage and spoils, and open the public service to all the people.

It will not, indeed, purify politics at a blow. There will still be corruption

1. *Harper's Weekly*, XXVII, 3 (Jan. 6, 1883).

and demagogism, and no good citizen can put off his armor of diligent watchfulness and effort. But it is not an argument against sanitary regulations that they do not abolish disease, nor against penal laws that crime still continues. It is no reason for refusing to try to improve a situation that still further improvement may be possible.

The passage of this bill by the Senate is a prompt response to a public demand unmistakably expressed at the autumn election, and it is a significant sign of the immediate influence of sound public opinion upon legislation. . . .

The awakening of public sentiment which has produced this great result is largely due to two very different events—the murder of Garfield and the assessments of Hubbell. Last spring Mr. Hubbell issued his circulars as a matter of course. The storm that followed showed how truly the public mind attributed the murder of Garfield to the spoils system. The result was impressive. Before the year ended, the action of Hubbell had been condemned by the Supreme Court, and the Senate of the United States had unanimously made it a penal offense.

The history of the year upon this subject exhorts every friend of wise progress to trust the people, and never to despair.

2. Schurz Applauds Partial Gains (1893)

The liberal German-American reformer and orator Carl Schurz (see earlier, p. 485) was regarded by spoilsmen as a foreign busybody trying to "Prussianize" the civil service. Here he speaks eloquently in New York City as president of the Civil-Service Reform League. Ten years after the much heralded birth of the Pendleton Act, he finds much to deplore and something to praise. Ascertain his chief satisfaction and his chief concern, and whether the gains now outweighed the drawbacks.

The Fourth of March last [1893] a new administration went into power. Untold thousands of men poured into the national capital clamoring for office; not for offices that were vacant, but to be vacated in order to make room for the clamorers. No matter whether he was ever so good a public servant, the man who was in was to be kicked out, to let him in who was out, no matter whether he would be not half so good a public servant.

The office-hunting throng swept into the White House and into the departments like a cloud of locusts. . . . The Cabinet ministers, all new men in their places, who felt the urgent need of studying somewhat their departmental duties, were hunted down so that they had hardly time to eat and to sleep, much less to study. When their cry for pity availed nothing, they at last barricaded their doors with strict regulations. They went into hiding in order to save some hours for the business of the government.

The Post Office Department was not only overrun by the crowd, but snowed under with written applications and recommendations for office, which in huge heaps covered the floors of the rooms, and the whole force of the department had to work after business hours merely to open and

2. National Civil-Service Reform League, *Proceedings* (1893), pp. 7–8, 10, 11–12, 16–17.

assort them. Senators and members of the House of Representatives ran wildly about like whipped errand boys to press the claims of greedy constituents or mercenary henchmen. . . .

But there is one part of the public service which now remains untouched by the tumultuous debauch of the spoils carnival. It is like a quiet, peaceable island, with a civilized, industrious population, surrounded by the howling sea. The President and the chiefs of the government departments contemplate this part of the service with calmness and contentment, for it gives them no trouble while the turmoil of the office hunt rages all around it. The good citizen, anxious for the honor of his country, beholds it with relief and satisfaction, for here he finds nothing to be ashamed of, and much that is worthy of this free and great nation. This is the "classified service," covered by the Civil Service Law, the creation of Civil Service Reform. On the portals the words are written: "Nobody enters here who has not proved his fitness for the duties to be performed." The office-hunting mob reads this and recoils. The public servant within it calmly walks the paths of his duty, undisturbed by the thought of the greedy cormorant hungering for his place. He depends upon his merit for his security and advancement, and this consciousness inspires his work. This is the application of common sense and common honesty to the public service. It is Civil Service Reform. . . .

At the close of President Arthur's administration in 1885 the number of places classified—that is, covered by the Civil Service Law—was about 15,500. At the close of President Cleveland's administration in 1889, it was about 27,300. At the close of President Harrison's administration in 1893 it was about 43,400, to which should be added several thousand laboring men in the navy yards placed under similar rules by the voluntary and most laudable act of Secretary Tracy.

As the whole number of places under the national government amounts to about 180,000, we may say that more than one-fourth of the service of the national government has ceased to be treated as mere spoils of party warfare. In one-fourth the party boss has lost his power. One-fourth is secure from the quadrennial loot. In one-fourth influence and favoritism go for nothing. One-fourth has been rescued from barbarism. One-fourth is worthy of a civilized country. So much, Civil Service Reform has accomplished in the time of three presidential terms.

But great and encouraging as its progress has been, Civil Service Reform, having conquered only one-fourth of the service, has done only one-fourth of its work. . . . Civil Service Reform has undertaken to open the offices to all according to their ability to serve the people.

The spoils system asks the candidate for office: "Does your member of Congress recommend you, or does the party boss in your state or your county ask for your appointment? Or are you backed by a man who gives much money to our campaign fund? What men of influence have you behind you? If you have none, you can have no place." Civil Service Reform asks the candidate: "Are you a man of good character, and what can you show to prove it? What do you know? What can you do? What qualifications have you for serving the people? Have you more than other candidates for the place?"

On the one side, under the spoils system, the aristocracy of influence—and a very vulgar aristocracy it is—robbing the man who has only merit, unbacked by power, of his rightful chance. On the other hand, Civil Service Reform, inviting all freely to compete, and then giving the best chance to the best man, be that man ever so lowly, and be his competitor ever so great a favorite of wealth and power. On that side the aristocracy of "pull"; on this the democracy of merit. . . .

The spoils politician is fond of objecting that civil service examinations do not always point out the fittest man for the place. Perhaps not always. The best marksman does not hit the bull's-eye every time; but he misses it rarely. The civil service examinations may have a small record of failures. But what the system, fairly conducted, *always* does is to snatch public office from the undemocratic control of influence and favoritism. And there is the point which stings the spoils politician.

C. THE BLAINE–CLEVELAND MUDSLINGERS

1. The Moralists Condemn Cleveland (1884)

The Republicans nominated for the Presidency in 1884 their premier personality and orator, James G. Blaine of Maine. In so doing they brushed aside suspicions that he had prostituted the Speakership of the House for private gain. Republican reformers, sneeringly dubbed "Mugwumps," turned their backs on the nominee. The Democrats gleefully nominated their reformist New York governor, bachelor Grover Cleveland. The crusade of the Clevelandites against immorality in public life faltered badly when Republican scandal-seekers revealed that Cleveland had fathered an illegitimate son eight years earlier in Buffalo. The accused candidate, courageously confessing his guilt, responded, "Tell the truth." The burning issue then became one of alleged public immorality versus private immorality. A leading Republican religious journal, *The Independent*, righteously turned its back on both candidates, especially Cleveland. Decide what force there is in the argument that weakness of character in private life indicates weakness in public life, and that the Democrats, in their own interests and in the interests of the high office, should have replaced Cleveland as soon as the scandal broke.

Some of Mr. Cleveland's supporters try to comfort themselves with the idea that the offense charged against him, being a delinquency in his private life, has nothing to do with the question of his fitness or unfitness for the Presidency. Though his morals in this respect may be bad, he may, nevertheless, be trusted with the duties of the office. . . .

The plain truth is that licentiousness is one of the very worst of vices, that a man's real character is the one shown by his private life, and that this is the character which he will carry with him into his public life, if elected thereto. The connection between the two lives is direct and

1. *The Independent*, XXXVI, 16 (Oct. 30, 1884).

intimate; and, hence, no one who is bad in his private character is fit to be trusted with public duties.

No decent man surely would think of voting for a horse-thief; and, for an equally good reason, no one should vote for the lecherous corrupter of womanhood. Both are essentially rotten at the seat of moral life. It is bad enough to have them in private life, and will be much worse to have them in public life, especially when the latter would carry with it the virtual acceptance and indorsement of a gross immorality. A nation that, with its eyes open, will select a libertine for its chief magistrate must be in the worst stage of moral decay.

It is, however, urged by some of the Cleveland supporters, who find it difficult to adopt this new philosophy, that he has sincerely repented of what the law of God makes a grievous sin, and the law of man in some states makes a crime.

The first answer is that there is no evidence before the public to show the fact of such repentance, and that, in the absence of such evidence, the presumption is exactly the reverse. It will be time enough to reason from Mr. Cleveland's assumed repentance when the fact itself is established.

A second answer is that, if we admit the repentance alleged, this would not cancel the wrong to such an extent as to render him a fit candidate for President. We take it that repentant debauchees, though they may be forgiven by both God and man, are not, any more than repentant thieves and robbers, to be deemed morally eligible to the supreme magistracy of this great nation. Their past record is a fatal objection to them. The people can and should do better with the office than to burlesque it with such a palpable incongruity. The interests of sound morality sternly demand that this office should not be associated with an admitted bastardy on the part of its incumbent.

It was, hence, the duty of the Democratic Party, the moment the uncleanness in Mr. Cleveland's private character was made known, to withdraw him from the field, and put a decent, pure, and competent candidate in his place. The continuance of his candidacy with this knowledge is a disgrace to the party; and his election would be a burning disgrace to the whole country. The example of his success would be a moral calamity. His defeat is an imperative duty.

2. The Mugwumps Condone Cleveland (1884)

Blaine, in sharp contrast to bachelor Cleveland, appears to have been a model husband and father. A Democratic orator, noting that the allegedly dishonest Blaine was a splendid family man and that the once-immoral Cleveland was a spotless public servant, proposed that "we should elect Cleveland to the public office which he is so admirably qualified to fill and remand Mr. Blaine to the private life which he is so eminently fitted to adorn." *Harper's Weekly*, a leading Mugwump journal, here puts the best face it can on the dilemma. Evaluate its most convincing argument in support of Cleveland. Would a throw-away vote for a third-party candidate have been the proper course?

2. *Harper's Weekly*, XXVIII, 528 (Aug. 16, 1884).

THE "MAGNETIC" BLAINE: OR, A VERY HEAVY "LOAD"-STONE
[MAGNET] FOR THE REPUBLICAN PARTY TO CARRY

Blaine's personal magnetism, which was famous, here attracts to himself assorted
scandals of the Grant era, including his own involvement in the railroad bonds
and the Mulligan letters. *Harper's Weekly,* 1880.

Undoubtedly every good citizen would prefer a choice between two
candidates absolutely irreproachable in every respect, and there are many
honest persons who will prefer not to vote for a candidate of whom any
kind of irregularity at any time can be justly alleged. Such voters, however,
if they cannot support Mr. Cleveland, who said at once, "Tell the truth,"
can still less support Mr. Blaine, who said, "Let my private [financial]
affairs alone," and tried in vain to deceive the country.*

In the actual situation the practical alternative seems to us to lie between
a candidate whose offense is wholly in the past, and was of a kind which
does not necessarily disqualify him for the highest public trusts, and a
candidate who deliberately prostituted public office to private gain. No
such man . . . has ever been nominated or elected to a great office in this
country. But Franklin and Hamilton and Jefferson and Webster and Clay,
and other eminent men still nearer our own time, were held by their fellow
citizens to be worthy of the highest public responsibilities, although it was
known that their private lives had not been always without stain. It was not
that the people were indifferent to morality, but that they wisely discrimi-
nated between conduct which justly and necessarily unfits a man for public

---

* Blaine had acquired wealth out of all proportion to his known salaries, and had resisted
all attempts "to expose his private business." A decision that he had rendered as Speaker
of the House in 1869 had saved a grant of land for the Little Rock and Fort Smith Railroad.
He subsequently sought and secured a financial favor from the company. The accusation was
that he had made his ruling *after* entering into the secret deal. Proof of his guilt or innocence presumably lay in a packet of letters ("Mulligan letters") which he had written,
but which he refused to make public in their entirety.

trusts, and that which experience and the general consciousness prove to be compatible with the utmost personal honesty and official fidelity.

The allegation that Mr. Cleveland is at this time a libertine and a drunkard is unquestionably, upon any kind of evidence known to us, false. His official career has been open to the eyes of all men, and if during the time that he has faithfully executed great public trusts his private life has disgraced his public office, the fact is wholly unknown to us, and certainly no evidence of it has been submitted to the public.

No honest man will mistake us as defending moral irregularities of any kind, nor, on the other hand, will he doubt our hearty contempt of those who affect horror at private immorality in order to divert public attention from official corruption. . . . The supporters of Mr. Blaine have chosen by his nomination to raise the question of official integrity as an indispensable qualification for the chief office in the government. Such an issue cannot be evaded, and it is the paramount issue of this election. But if those who are utterly unable to impeach Mr. Cleveland's official integrity, or to establish that of Mr. Blaine, should invite a contest of the comparative decency of their past and private lives, the contest must be declined for the honor of the American name. A controversy for the Presidency which should turn upon such a discussion would be the most disgusting and degrading in our history.

[*The hope expressed by this journal proved futile. Panicky Democrats, with no encouragement from Cleveland, discovered a disconcerting date on the headstone over the grave of the first-born Blaine child. It indicated that the baby had arrived within three months of the marriage. Blaine hastened to explain this irregularity by pointing to two wedding ceremonies several months apart. He also brought a libel suit against an Indiana newspaper, but subsequently dropped it. Someone—presumably a Republican—thoughtfully and surreptitiously destroyed the evidence by chiseling away the offensive date.*]

D. THE PRESIDENT AND THE PENSIONERS

1. Cleveland Wields the Veto Pen (1886)

Cleveland, who defeated Blaine by the narrowest of margins, found himself in no bed of roses. Pensions for Civil War veterans proved to be persistently embarrassing. First of all, Cleveland, who had hired a substitute while supporting his widowed mother, had not served in the army. Second, the bulk of his voting support came from the ex-Confederate Solid South. Finally, the Northern wing of his own party was tainted with anti-Lincoln Copperheadism, while most of the organized veterans of the Grand Army of the Republic (G.A.R.) were pressure-group Republicans. Scores of private pension bills passed Congress and piled up on the White House desk. The country was prosperous and the sums involved were petty, but a con-

1. J. D. Richardson, ed., *Messages and Papers of the Presidents* (1897), VIII, 443, 451. "King Andrew" Jackson, who was condemned for an excessive use of the veto, vetoed 12 bills in eight years; Cleveland vetoed 584 in eight years, 414 of them in his first term. Franklin Roosevelt vetoed 631 in a little more than twelve years, leaving Cleveland ahead on a per annum basis. Third place must be awarded to Eisenhower, with 169 in eight years; fourth place to Grant, with 92 in eight years.

scientious Cleveland read the bills and vetoed those (123 out of 977) that he deemed improper. Two representative veto messages follow. Note what is particularly offensive about the first; and decide whether Cleveland is too harsh in the second.

Executive Mansion, June 23, 1886

To the House of Representatives:

I hereby return without approval House bill No. 6688, entitled "An act for the relief of William Bishop."

This claimant was enrolled as a substitute on the 25th day of March, 1865. He was admitted to a post hospital at Indianapolis on the 3rd day of April, 1865, with the measles; was removed to the City General Hospital, in Indianapolis, on the 5th day of May, 1865; was returned to duty May 8, 1865; and was mustered out with a detachment of unassigned men on the 11th day of May, 1865.

This is the military record of this soldier, who remained in the Army one month and seventeen days, having entered it as a substitute at a time when high bounties were paid.

Fifteen years after this brilliant service and this terrific encounter with the measles, and on the 28th day of June, 1880, the claimant discovered that his attack of measles had some relation to his army enrollment and that this disease had "settled in his eyes, also affecting his spinal column."

This claim was rejected by the Pension Bureau, and I have no doubt of the correctness of its determination.

Grover Cleveland

Executive Mansion, June 23, 1886

To the House of Representatives:

I return without approval House bill No. 7162, entitled "An act granting a pension to Martha McIlwain."

R. J. McIlwain, the husband of the claimant, enlisted in 1861, and was discharged in 1862 because of the loss of his right leg by a gunshot wound. He was pensioned for his disability. He died May 15, 1883, from an overdose of morphia. It is claimed by the widow that her husband was in the habit of taking morphia to alleviate the pain he endured from his stump, and that he accidentally took too much.

The case was investigated by a special examiner upon the widow's application for pension, and his report shows that the deceased had been in the habit of taking morphia and knew how to use it; that he had been in the habit of buying 6 grains at a time, and that his death was caused by his taking one entire purchase of 6 grains while under the influence of liquor.

In any event it is quite clear that the taking of morphia in any quantity was not the natural result of military service or injury received therein.

I concur in the judgment of the Pension Bureau, which rejected the widow's claim for the pension on the ground that "the death of the soldier was not due to his military service."

Grover Cleveland

[*When Cleveland ran for re-election in 1888, the* National Tribune *(Sept. 27), with a wide readership among veterans, urged: "An unprecedented number of these [pension bills] have been presented to Mr. Cleveland for his signature, and he has found in them a boundless field for ridicule, cheap wit, sarcasm, satire, and vituperation of the unfortunates who were so indiscreet as to go into the army and lose their health or lives. . . . The President has been amusing himself for years writing vetoes. The veterans now have a chance to use their hands at vetoing. Let them improve the opportunity." (Quoted in W. H. Glasson,* Federal Military Pensions in the United States *[1918], p. 278 n.)*]

2. Ex-Confederates Praise Cleveland (1887)

A generous Congress finally passed the Dependent Pension Bill in 1887. It provided pensions for Union veterans unable to earn their living, regardless of any service-connected disability. Cleveland, who felt that the Washington government should not take over the role of local poorhouses, resolutely vetoed the measure—and it stayed vetoed. He regarded the pension list as an honor roll of service-disabled veterans, and not a refuge for deadbeats and frauds. Republican newspapers openly accused Cleveland of vetoing the bill because it would not benefit the ex-Confederate South, where the bulk of his political strength lay. Southerners naturally sprang to his defense. Note what is most surprising about the ex-Confederate view as here expressed in the Mobile (Alabama) *Register.*

Had that iniquitous measure [Dependent Pension Bill] prevailed, the Treasury would have become bankrupt in a very few years. The burden of it would have fallen upon the North. The South cares very little about it practically, but we have a right as citizens of a common country to protest against a measure which is based upon an empty sentimentality, and is utterly devoid of justice. The Southern soldier is willing to see pensions voted to the Federal soldier who was disabled by reason of his military service. He fought as well, and we respect him. We were vanquished, and without murmuring we pay our quota of the pension fund.

Our own old soldiers are getting along very well without pensions. They came back to ruined homes, but they have struggled along and win their bread without calling upon their neighbors for assistance. They have as much right to look to their own states for pensions as the Northern soldier has to look to the Federal Treasury. But the old Confederate looks to nobody for support. Even though with one leg, he intends to stump it through life without being dependent upon anybody's bounty.

Still he does not say a word against his old enemy getting a pension if he has been a victim of war. He does object, however, to this Dependent Pension Act, which gives a pension to any old soldier who has become incompetent for work not from wounds of war, but from advancing age or any other reason. To carry the pension business to that extent is to bankrupt the government. The President has done a true and brave act in vetoing the bill, and we hope the Northern people will sustain him.

2. Mobile *Register,* Feb. 13, 1887, in *Public Opinion,* II, 393 (Feb. 19, 1887).

E. THE TARIFF AND THE SURPLUS

1. Cleveland Pleads for Tariff Reduction (1885)

The financial embarrassments of Cleveland's first administration, oddly enough, stemmed from too much money in the Treasury. The great bulk of federal revenue then came from tariff duties, which the consumer repaid as a hidden tax in the increased price of the import. The only feasible way to reduce the unnecessarily large inflow to the Treasury was to reduce the tariff, and such a reduction was bound to arouse the high-protectionists, mostly Republicans but some Democrats. Cleveland, never one to shrink from disagreeable duty, courageously recommended such a remedy in his first annual message to Congress. Determine whether he is really hostile to protection, and why he singles out a certain class of items for reduction.

The fact that our revenues are in excess of the actual needs of an economical administration of the government justifies a reduction in the amount exacted from the people for its support. Our government is but the means established by the will of a free people, by which certain principles are applied which they have adopted for their benefit and protection. And it is never better administered, and its true spirit is never better observed, than when the people's taxation for its support is scrupulously limited to the actual necessity of expenditure, and distributed according to a just and equitable plan.

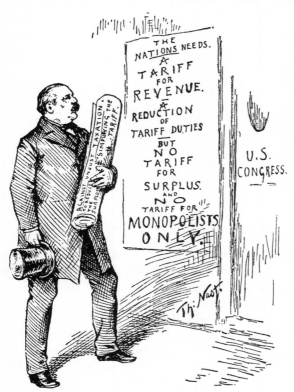

CLEVELAND DEMANDS TARIFF REDUCTION

Thomas Nast cartoon. Roger Butterfield, *The American Past*, 1947.

The proposition with which we have to deal is the reduction of the revenue received by the government, and indirectly paid by the people, from customs duties. The question of free trade is not involved, nor is there now any occasion for the general discussion of the wisdom or expediency of a protective system.

1. J. D. Richardson, ed., *Messages and Papers of the Presidents* (1897), VIII, 341.

Justice and fairness dictate that, in any modification of our present laws relating to revenue, the industries and interests which have been encouraged by such laws, and in which our citizens have large investments, should not be ruthlessly injured or destroyed.

We should also deal with the subject in such manner as to protect the interests of American labor, which is the capital of our workingmen. Its stability and proper remuneration furnish the most justifiable pretext for a protective policy.

Within these limitations a certain reduction should be made in our customs revenue. The amount of such reduction having been determined, the inquiry follows: Where can it best be remitted and what articles can best be released from duty in the interest of our citizens?

I think the reductions should be made in the revenue derived from a tax upon the imported necessaries of life. We thus directly lessen the cost of living in every family of the land, and release to the people in every humble home a larger measure of the rewards of frugal industry.

2. Philadelphians Criticize Cleveland (1887)

To Cleveland's repeated pleas for tariff reduction, the protectionists, both Republicans and Democrats, turned a deaf ear. The President finally decided to arouse the country by taking the unprecedented step of devoting his entire annual message to one subject—the tariff and its implications. Old-line Democratic politicians, fearful that such boat-rocking tactics would lose the next presidential election, vainly urged him to reconsider. But, one of his critics remarked, he would rather be wrong than President. In his sensational tariff message of 1887, he declared that the surplus confronted the nation with a "condition," and "not a theory." He called for a "slight reduction" of the tariff, and branded as "irrelevant" and "mischievous" Republican charges of "free trade." Ascertain in what particular the following reaction of the Philadelphia *Press* (Republican) is most unfair.

A thousand thanks to President Cleveland for the bold, manly, and unequivocal avowal of his extreme free-trade purposes! And a thousand rebukes and defeats for the false, dangerous, and destructive policy which he thus frankly and unreservedly proclaims!

The message deserves all the glory of courage, all the praise of high public issue, all the condemnation of utter, ruinous heresy.

It is a surprise in its method and a still greater surprise in its matter. It comes like the sudden, echoing boom of a great gun signaling a crucial fight on unexpected ground. In its immediate flash of light and in its broad bearings it looms up as one of the most momentous political events since the war.

It plants the President and his party squarely on free trade; it clarifies the next presidential battle as by a lightning stroke; it makes free trade *vs.* protection the overshadowing issue; it dwarfs and dismisses all other questions; it clears away all cowardly evasions and juggling subterfuges; it ends all pitiful personal bespattering; and it summons the American

2. Quoted in *Public Opinion*, IV, 193 (Dec. 10, 1887).

people to decide the supreme question whether the grand protective system which has built up our splendid industries shall be overthrown or not!

For the distinct and emphatic manner in which the President has faced and forced this paramount issue he deserves all credit; for the wrongs, the perils, and the inevitable disasters of his policy he must be crushed unless the people would have their own vital interests crushed.

3. The New York *Times* Acclaims Courage (1887)

The New York *Times*, an independent newspaper with Democratic leanings, regarded Cleveland's tariff message as statesmanlike but politically unwise. Explain why, in the light of this editorial.

Mr. Cleveland has done an act of statesmanship in the best sense. Recognizing a great duty, he has performed it with courage, with firmness, and at the right time. And he has performed it so that every honest man must see that it is an honest act—disinterested, faithful to the requirements of conscience, without hope or purpose of personal or party advantage except such as comes from the public recognition of public service.

Judged by an ordinary standard of political expediency, the President's act is inexpedient. He has forced upon his party an issue as to which the party is divided, and so divided that unless the minority yield, it can defeat the will of the majority. He has done this on the eve of a national contest in which a considerable number of men of influence in the party have been urging him to avoid this issue, and threatening him and the party with disaster if he did not avoid it.

On the other hand, there is nothing in this issue, thus presented, by which Mr. Cleveland could hope to draw from the Republican Party any votes to compensate those he is in danger of losing, and which he has been warned over and again by leaders of his own party that he would lose.

Nor this alone, for if the protectionist faction in the Democratic Party carry out their own desires, or do what they have continually declared that they would do, Mr. Cleveland has done the one thing by which he could imperil the prospect of his own renomination. From the point of view of the politician, he has shown a courage that is temerity in the pursuit of an end of no value to himself.

[*The Cleveland-Harrison presidential canvass of 1888 hinged on the tariff, not the private morals of the candidates, and the Republican Harrison won. The tariff message of 1887 is commonly blamed for the Democratic defeat. But Cleveland actually polled in excess of 100,000 more popular votes than his opponent, and he showed increased strength in states like New Jersey and Rhode Island, where manufacturing was strong. Other factors were no doubt important in tipping the scales, notably the blundering interference of the British minister in Washington, Sackville-West. He declared in effect that a vote for Cleveland was a vote for England.*]

3. New York *Times*, Dec. 7, 1887.

THOUGHT PROVOKERS

1. Could a better case be made out for the spoils system in 1883 than now? Explain. What can be said for and against partisanship in public life? Can a Republican administration function better with only Republicans in office?

2. Many Republicans who supported the Civil Service Reform Act were accused of hypocrisy. Explain. Is it desirable to have federal officials, including Supreme Court justices, hold office for life?

3. Why is there not likely to be another presidential campaign as low as that of 1884? Were Blaine's shortcomings more reprehensible than Cleveland's?

4. With a surplus in the Treasury, why should not the government have been generous in dealing with the aging veterans who had fought many years earlier to preserve the Union? What did Cleveland have in mind when he said that the pension list should be an honor roll?

5. With reference to the tariff-surplus problem, what did Cleveland mean when he said that "unnecessary taxation is unjust taxation"? In the light of experience in recent decades, how could the surplus have been disposed of advantageously without causing serious political repercussions?

FURTHER EXPLORATION

General: L. D. White, *The Republican Era, 1869–1901* (1958); H. S. Merrill, *Bourbon Leader: Grover Cleveland and the Democratic Party* (1957). Civil Service Reform: C. R. Fish, *The Civil Service and the Patronage* (1904); Ari Hoogenboom, *Outlawing the Spoils: A History of the Civil Service Reform Movement, 1865–1883* (1961). Pendleton Act: A. B. Sageser, *The First Two Decades of the Pendleton Act* (1935). Blaine-Cleveland Mudslingers: H. T. Peck, *Twenty Years of the Republic, 1885–1905* (1919); E. P. Oberholtzer, *A History of the United States* (1931), vol. IV. Pensions: J. W. Oliver, *History of the Civil War Military Pensions, 1861–1885* (1917). Tariff and Surplus: Allan Nevins, *Grover Cleveland* (1932).

Recent: S. P. Hirshson, *Farewell to the Bloody Shirt* (1962); D. M. Pletcher, *The Awkward Years: American Foreign Relations under Garfield and Arthur* (1962).

Chapter 27

The Growing Pains of Industry

That is the most perfect government in which an injury to one is the concern of all.

MOTTO OF THE KNIGHTS OF LABOR

PROLOGUE: A few of the railroad companies after 1865 had more employees than a number of the state governments—and more power to inflict harm. When cutthroat competition failed to eliminate abuses, Congress finally passed the precedent-shattering Interstate Commerce Act of 1887. But this pioneer measure fell far short of providing adequate safeguards. Competing industries had meanwhile been merging as monopolistic trusts, notably Rockefeller's Standard Oil Company. Congress belatedly tried to restrain these monsters with the rather toothless Sherman Anti-Trust Act of 1890. As the new industrial giants grew, their power over their unorganized employees increased. The Knights of Labor, who in the 1870's and 1880's made the most successful attempt until then to organize the nation's army of toilers, amassed considerable numerical strength. But they overreached themselves in the 1880's, and the wage-conscious American Federation of Labor, with its component skilled unions, forged to the front.

A. THE PROBLEM OF THE RAILROADS

1. A Defense of Long-Haul Rates (1885)

A serious grievance against the "railroad rascals" was discrimination. Their rates would often be lower where a line had competition, and higher elsewhere. Charges were sometimes heavier for a short haul than for a long haul over the same track. At one time the freight rate on cotton goods shipped from Boston to Denver was $1.79 a hundredweight; if the shipment went 1400 miles farther to San Francisco, the total charge was only $1.50. Ascertain whether the following justification of this practice by a Southern railroad manager (H. S. Haines) is convincing, and why certain farmers favored this type of discrimination.

If it costs $600,000 per annum to keep up a [rail]road, then the money must come out of the freight and passengers that are obliged to pass over it. Whether the amount of business be small or large, the money to keep up the road must be forthcoming, or it will go to decay.

If 100,000 bales of cotton were the only freight that passed over a road which carried no passengers, that cotton would have to pay a freight of $6 per bale if it cost $600,000 per annum to maintain the road, and no legislation could make it otherwise. But if the quantity of cotton to be transported could be increased to 200,000 bales, then the cost of trans-

---

1. Report of the Senate Select Committee on Interstate Commerce," 49 Cong., 1 sess., *Senate Reports*, No. 46, II, pt. 1, Appendix, pp. 130–31.

portation could be fixed at $3 per bale, to the great joy and relief of the shippers of the first 100,000 bales; and yet the $600,000 required to operate the road would be forthcoming.

Now, suppose that the community which raised this second 100,000 bales had a water route to market and said to the railroad company, "It only costs a dollar per bale to ship our cotton by water, but we prefer to ship it by rail at the same price." Who would be benefited if the company took the cotton at a dollar per bale? Who but the local shippers themselves, for without this addition to the business of the road they would have to pay $600,000 per year, or $6 per bale, to keep up the road, while with the $100,000 obtained from the other 100,000 bales of competitive or through cotton they would have to pay but $500,000 or $5 per bale on their own cotton. Should they turn around upon the managers of the railroad and say that it was unjust to the local shippers to charge only a dollar per bale on the through cotton?

No, it is not only just, but to the benefit of the local shippers, that the railroad which they are obliged to use should get all the business it can from those who are not obliged to use it, and at any rate the latter choose to pay, provided—and it is a very important provision—that such competitive business adds something to the net revenue of the road; or, in other words, if it be carried at anything above the actual cost of transportation.

2. The Free-Pass Evil (1885)

Dishonest railroad operators would use cash bribes with state legislators to secure favorable legislation or to avert undesirable taxation or vexatious controls. This kind of bribery was supplemented by the lavish issuance of passes—the equivalent of money —to Congressmen, governors, state legislators, county auditors, and others. A Supreme Court justice applied for free transportation worth, in a single instance, about $300. One railroad company took an entire board of tax commissioners and their families on an extensive trip in a private Pullman car, and in return received a reduction in tax appraisals worth thousands of dollars a year. The demands of these free riders grew in an ever-widening circle, as they offered inducements or issued threats. If the railroad, no matter how generous in the past, refused such favors, it laid itself open to reprisals by legislative and administrative bodies. Charles F. Adams (grandson of J. Q. Adams), the high-minded president of the Union Pacific Railroad, here testifies before a Senate committee in behalf of legislation to curb passes. Note what additional pressures were being brought to bear on his railroad; why Adams could not unilaterally give up the issuance of passes; and how the pass evil affected the public.

Mr. ADAMS. If you would, in a way that will be effective, forbid the issuing of passes, I would agree at once to make a considerable reduction in our passenger rates.

Senator PLATT. Would you like to have it done, if it could be done?

Mr. ADAMS. Nothing would please me more. I should like to have a heavy penalty imposed for every pass issued. I do not, as a rule, like to work through legislation in these matters, but if you will pass a law prohibiting

2. *Ibid.*, pp. 1219–20.

all free passes and subjecting to fine and imprisonment any man who signs a pass or any conductor who takes a pass up—

Senator PLATT (*interposing*). Or any man who rides on a pass.

Mr. ADAMS (*continuing*).—or any man who rides on a pass, it would make a happy day for railroads and railroad managers. . . .

Senator PLATT. Have not some railroads in this country largely cut down that business of issuing passes?

Mr. ADAMS. Ever since I have been president of the Union Pacific I have been laboring to cut it down. It has been one of the great annoyances I have met with, but I have been foiled at nearly every attempt.

The CHAIRMAN. People who have been in the habit of getting them still insist upon having them?

Mr. ADAMS. They not only insist upon having them, but the pass system mixes itself up with newspapers, politics, and everything. For instance, if tomorrow I gave an order that such and such a system of passes should be cut off, I would be met with the answer, "Very well, our competitors give them. These people have been accustomed to having passes, and we will simply lose our traffic by refusing to give them longer."

The CHAIRMAN. That is said by whom?

Mr. ADAMS. By our freight agents. For instance, Mr. Kimball here would undoubtedly say just that to me.

The CHAIRMAN. And the merchants and farmers?

Mr. ADAMS. Mr. Kimball would say to me at once, "Very well, Mr. Adams, I will obey your orders and cut off those passes, but the company will lose business."

The CHAIRMAN. Why would it lose business?

Mr. ADAMS. It would go by the other route which gave the passes.

The CHAIRMAN. Who is it that would say this to you?

Mr. KIMBALL. The shipper would say it.

The CHAIRMAN. Whether he was shipping merchandise or corn or wheat or what not?

Mr. KIMBALL. Yes, sir.

Mr. ADAMS. The pass system is an outrage. There is no reason whatever why anyone should be carried free over a railroad any more than why he should be boarded and lodged free at a hotel, drive free in public carriages, or order goods without paying for them in shops. Yet, and especially in the West, things are getting to such a pass that no man who has money, or official position, or influence—especially political or newspaper influence—thinks he ought to pay anything for riding on a railroad.

3. President Dillon Supports Stock Watering (1891)

Critics of the railroads especially condemned "stock watering"—the practice of issuing stocks and bonds grossly in excess of the value of the property. The more the stock was "watered," the higher the freight and passenger rates would have to be

3. Sidney Dillon, "The West and the Railroads," *North American Review*, CLII, 445–48, *passim* (April, 1891).

to insure a normal return on the investment. Sidney Dillon, a later president of the Union Pacific Railroad, stoutly defended stock watering. Beginning his career at the age of seven as a "water boy"—appropriately enough—on a New York railway, he ultimately amassed a fortune by building railroads, including the Union Pacific. Present at the "wedding of the rails" in Utah in 1869, he retained one of the final silver spikes until his death. He here attacks regulatory legislation in an article for a popular magazine. Comment critically on his social philosophy, on his view of the citizens' impertinence, and on his faith in competition and the courts.

Statutory enactments interfere with the business of the railway, even to the minutest details, and always to its detriment. This sort of legislation proceeds on the theory that the railroad is a public enemy; that it has its origin in the selfish desire of a company of men to make money out of the public; that it will destroy the public unless it is kept within bounds; and that it is impossible to enact too many laws tending to restrain the monster. The advocates of these statutes may not state their theory in these exact words. But these words certainly embody their theory, if they have any theory at all beyond such prejudices as are born of the marriage between ignorance and demagogism.

Many of the grievances that are urged against railways are too puerile to be seriously noticed, but the reader will pardon a few words as to "overcapitalization". . . .

Now, it is impossible to estimate in advance the productive power of this useful and untiring servant. Sometimes a railway is capitalized too largely, and then it pays smaller dividends; sometimes not largely enough, and then the dividends are much in excess of the usual interest of money. In the former case stockholders are willing to reduce the face of their shares, or wait until increase of population increases revenue; in the latter they accept an enlarged issue. But, as a matter of reason and prin-

THE SENATORIAL ROUND-HOUSE

Railroad attorneys in Senate let off steam against a bill to prevent members of Congress from accepting fees from government-subsidized railroads. *Harper's Weekly*, 1886.

ciple, the question of capitalization concerns the stockholders, and the stockholders only. A citizen, simply as a citizen, commits an impertinence when he questions the right of any corporation to capitalize its properties at any sum whatever. . . .

Then as to prices, these will always be taken care of by the great law of competition, which obtains wherever any human service is to be performed for a pecuniary consideration. That any railway, anywhere in a republic, should be a monopoly is not a supposable case. If between two points, A and B, a railway is constructed, and its charges for fares and freight are burdensome to the public and unduly profitable to itself, it will not be a long time before another railway will be laid between these points, and then competition may be safely trusted to reduce prices. We may state it as an axiom that no common carrier can ever maintain burdensome and oppressive rates of service permanently or for a long period. . . .

Given a company of men pursuing a lawful and useful occupation,—why interfere with them? Why empower a body of other men, fortuitously assembled, not possessing superior knowledge, and accessible often to unworthy influences, to dictate to these citizens how they shall manage their private affairs? Wherever such management conflicts with public policy or private rights, there are district attorneys and competent lawyers and upright courts to take care that the commonwealth or the citizen shall receive no detriment. . . .

4. General Weaver Deplores Stock Watering (1892)

General James B. Weaver, a walrus-mustached veteran of the Civil War, had early experienced extortion when he had to borrow $100 at 33⅓% interest to finish law school. Fiery orator and relentless foe of the railroads and other "predatory" corporations, he won the presidential nomination of the People's Party (Populists) in 1892. His book entitled *A Call to Action*, published during the campaign, condemned stock waterers. Ascertain to what extent the following excerpt from it casts doubts on the testimony of President Dillon, whose article, presented in the previous selection, he sharply attacks. Note especially Weaver's view of the citizens' "impertinence."

In their delirium of greed the managers of our transportation systems disregard both private right and the public welfare. Today they will combine and bankrupt their weak rivals, and by the expenditure of a trifling sum possess themselves of properties which cost the outlay of millions. Tomorrow they will capitalize their booty for five times the cost, issue their bonds, and proceed to levy tariffs upon the people to pay dividends upon the fraud.

Take for example the Kansas Midland. It cost $10,200 per mile. It is capitalized at $53,024 per mile. How are the plain plodding people to defend themselves against such flagrant injustice?

Mr. Sidney Dillon, president of the Union Pacific, . . . is many times a millionaire, and the road over which he presides was built wholly by public

4. J. B. Weaver, *A Call to Action* (1892), pp. 412–13.

funds and by appropriations of the public domain. The road never cost Mr. Dillon nor his associates a single penny. It is now capitalized at $106,000 per mile! This company owes the government $50,000,000 with accruing interest which is destined to accumulate for many years. The public lien exceeds the entire cost of the road, and yet this government, which Mr. Dillon defies, meekly holds a second mortgage to secure its claim. . . .

It is pretty clear that it would not be safe for the public to take the advice of either Mr. Dillon or Mr. Gould [railroad promoter] as to the best method of dealing with the transportation problem.

[*Responding to a mounting public outcry, Congress passed the Interstate Commerce Act in 1887—the first regulatory legislation of its kind in American history. Among various reforms it forbade unreasonable or unjust rates, discriminatory rates or practices, the payment of rebates, the pooling of profits among competing lines, and a higher charge for a short haul than for a long haul. In practice, the law proved to be riddled with loopholes, and subsequent legislation was required to provide adequate safeguards.*]

B. THE TRUSTS AND MONOPOLY

1. Rockefeller Justifies Rebates (1909)

John D. Rockefeller, who amassed a fortune of nearly one billion dollars, lived to give away more than half of his "oil-gotten gains" in philanthropy. A prominent lay Baptist, he early donated a tenth of his income to charities, and in 1859 helped a Cincinnati Negro to buy his slave wife. As a founding father of the mighty Standard Oil Company, he here puts the best possible face on railroad rebates, which were finally banned by the Interstate Commerce Act. He tactfully neglects to add that at one time his company also extorted secret payments ("drawbacks") from the railways on shipments by his competitors. Enumerate the advantages to the railroads of the rebate system, and determine to what extent they, rather than Standard Oil, profited from these under-the-counter deals.

Of all the subjects which seem to have attracted the attention of the public to the affairs of the Standard Oil Company, the matter of rebates from railroads has perhaps been uppermost. The Standard Oil Company of Ohio, of which I was president, did receive rebates from the railroads prior to 1880, but received no advantages for which it did not give full compensation.

The reason for rebates was that such was the railroads' method of business. A public rate was made and collected by the railroad companies, but, so far as my knowledge extends, was seldom retained in full; a portion of it was repaid to the shippers as a rebate.

By this method the real rate of freight which any shipper paid was not known by his competitors nor by other railroad companies, the amount being a matter of bargain with the carrying company. Each shipper made

1. J. D. Rockefeller, *Random Reminiscences of Men and Events* (1909), pp. 107–09, 111–12. Copyright 1909, Doubleday & Company, Inc.; copyright renewed 1936, John D. Rockefeller. By permission of the Executors of the Estate of John D. Rockefeller, Jr.

the best bargain that he could, but whether he was doing better than his competitor was only a matter of conjecture. Much depended upon whether the shipper had the advantage of competition of carriers.

The Standard Oil Company of Ohio, being situated at Cleveland, had the advantage of different carrying lines, as well as of water transportation in the summer. Taking advantage of those facilities, it made the best bargains possible for its freights. Other companies sought to do the same.

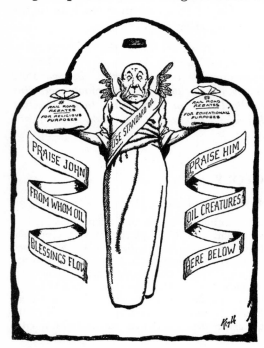

THE SANCTIFICATION OF ROCKEFELLER

A muckraking satire on Rockefeller's donating part of his rebate-swollen oil fortune for religious and educational purposes. *Collier's*, 1905.

The Standard gave advantages to the railroads for the purpose of reducing the cost of transportation of freight. It offered freights in large quantity, carloads and trainloads. It furnished loading facilities and discharging facilities at great cost. It provided regular traffic, so that a railroad could conduct its transportation to the best advantage and use its equipment to the full extent of its hauling capacity without waiting for the refiner's convenience. It exempted railroads from liability for fire and carried its own insurance. It provided at its own expense terminal facilities which permitted economies in handling. For these services it obtained contracts for special allowances on freights. But notwithstanding these special allowances, this traffic from the Standard Oil Company was far more profitable to the railroad companies than the smaller and irregular traffic, which might have paid a higher rate.

To understand the situation which affected the giving and taking of rebates, it must be remembered that the railroads were all eager to enlarge their freight traffic. They were competing with the facilities and rates offered by the boats on lake and canal and by the pipe lines. All these means of transporting oil cut into the business of the railroads, and they were desperately anxious to successfully meet this competition. . . .

The profits of the Standard Oil Company did not come from advantages given by railroads. The railroads, rather, were the ones who profited by the traffic of the Standard Oil Company, and whatever advantage it received in its constant efforts to reduce rates of freight was only one of the many elements of lessening cost to the consumer which enabled us to increase our volume of business the world over because we could reduce the selling price.

How general was the complicated bargaining for rates can hardly be imagined; everyone got the best rate that he could. After the passage of the Interstate Commerce Act, it was learned that many small companies which shipped limited quantities had received lower rates than we had been able to secure, notwithstanding the fact that we had made large investments to provide for terminal facilities, regular shipments, and other economies.

I well remember a bright man from Boston who had much to say about rebates and drawbacks. He was an old and experienced merchant, and looked after his affairs with a cautious and watchful eye. He feared that some of his competitors were doing better than he in bargaining for rates, and he delivered himself of this conviction:

"I am opposed on principle to the whole system of rebates and drawbacks —unless I am in it."

2. An Oil Man Goes Bankrupt (1899)

Rockefeller's great passion was not so much love of power or money as a dislike of waste and inefficiency. Having begun as a $3.50-a-week employee, he ultimately moved into the chaotically overproduced oil business with a vision that enabled him to see far ahead, and then "around the corner." Overlooking no detail, he insisted that every drop of solder used on his oil cans be counted. By acquiring or controlling warehouses, pipe lines, tankers, railroads, oil fields, and refineries, he helped forge America's first great trust in 1882. He produced a superior product at a lowered price but, in line with existing ethics, resorted to such "refined robbery" as ruthless price cutting, dictation to dealers, deception, espionage, and rebates. George Rice, one of his ill-starred competitors, here complains to the United States Industrial Commission. Ascertain his two principal grievances and evaluate them critically.

I am a citizen of the United States, born in the state of Vermont. Producer of petroleum for more than thirty years, and a refiner of same for twenty years. But my refinery has been shut down during the past three years, owing to the powerful and all-prevailing machinations of the Standard Oil Trust, in criminal collusion and conspiracy with the railroads to destroy my business of twenty years of patient industry, toil, and money in building up, wholly by and through unlawful freight discriminations.

I have been driven from pillar to post, from one railway line to another, for twenty years, in the absolutely vain endeavor to get equal and just freight rates with the Standard Oil Trust, so as to be able to run my refinery at anything approaching a profit, but which I have been utterly unable to do. I have had to consequently shut down, with my business absolutely ruined and my refinery idle.

This has been a very sad, bitter, and ruinous experience for me to endure, but I have endeavored to the best of my circumstances and ability to combat it the utmost I could for many a long waiting year, expecting

2. *Report of the U. S. Industrial Commission,* I (1899), 687, 704.

relief through the honest and proper execution of our laws, which have [has] as yet, however, never come. But I am still living in hopes, though I may die in despair. . . .

Outside of rebates or freight discriminations, I had no show with the Standard Oil Trust, because of their unlawfully acquired monopoly, by which they could temporarily cut only my customers' prices, and below cost, leaving the balance of the town, nine-tenths, uncut. This they can easily do without any appreciable harm to their general trade, and thus effectually wipe out all competition, as fully set forth. Standard Oil prices generally were so high that I could sell my goods 2 to 3 cents a gallon below their prices and make a nice profit, but these savage attacks and [price] cuts upon my customers' goods . . . plainly showed . . . their power for evil, and the uselessness to contend against such odds. . . .

3. Weaver Attacks the Trusts (1892)

Rockefeller's Standard Oil of Ohio was not authorized to operate outside the state, so in 1882 the Standard Oil Trust, the first of its kind, was born. "A corporation of corporations," it secretly merged forty-one different concerns. In 1892 the courts held this trust to be illegally in restraint of trade, but Rockefeller and his associates were able to achieve their semi-monopolistic ends by less formal agreements. General Weaver, the fiery Populist candidate for President in 1892 (see later, p. 569), here assails the trusts, whose unwritten motto was said to be "Let us prey." Note his enumeration of the evils of the trusts, and examine the monopolist's claim that the elimination of wasteful competition is advantageous to the consumer.

The trust is organized commerce with the Golden Rule excluded and the trustees exempted from the restraints of conscience.

They argue that competition means war and is therefore destructive. The trust is eminently docile and hence seeks to destroy competition in order that we may have peace. But the peace which they give us is like that which exists after the leopard has devoured the kid. This professed desire for peace is a false pretense. They dread the war of competition because the people share in the spoils. When rid of that, they always turn their guns upon the masses and depredate without limit or mercy.

The main weapons of the trust are threats, intimidation, bribery, fraud, wreck, and pillage. Take one well-authenticated instance in the history of the Oat Meal Trust as an example. In 1887 this trust decided that part of their mills should stand idle. They were accordingly closed. This resulted in the discharge of a large number of laborers who had to suffer in consequence. The mills which were continued in operation would produce seven million barrels of meal during the year. Shortly after shutting down, the trust advanced the price of meal one dollar per barrel, and the public was forced to stand the assessment. The mills were more profitable when idle than when in operation.

The Sugar Trust has it within its power to levy a tribute of $30,000,000

3. J. B. Weaver, *A Call to Action* (1892), pp. 392–93.

upon the people of the United States by simply advancing the price of sugar one cent per pound for one year. If popular tumult breaks out and legislation in restraint of these depredations is threatened, they can advance prices, extort campaign expenses and corruption funds from the people, and force the disgruntled multitude to furnish the sinews of war for their own destruction. They not only have the power to do these things, but it is their known mode of warfare, and they actually practice it from year to year.

The most distressing feature of this war of the trusts is the fact that they control the articles which the plain people consume in their daily life. It cuts off their accumulations and deprives them of the staff upon which they fain would lean in their old age.

C. THE RISE OF THE NEW SOUTH

1. Grady Issues a Challenge (1889)

The industrialized South—the New South—was slow to rise from the ashes of civil conflict. A kind of inferiority complex settled over the area. Henry W. Grady, eloquent editor of the Atlanta *Constitution,* did more than anyone else to break the spell. With Irish wit he preached the need for diversified crops, a readjustment of the Negro, the encouragement of manufacturing, and the development of local resources. In demand as a speaker, he broadcast his message widely and with demonstrable effect. The South of the 1880's was experiencing a marvelous economic boom, and new industries were spreading like its own honeysuckle. The following is a selection from a speech in Boston in which Grady contrasted the broken-down South of Reconstruction days with the new industrialized South. Determine what major lesson this passage must have impressed upon his Northern listeners.

I attended a funeral once in Pickens county in my state [Georgia]. A funeral is not usually a cheerful object to me unless I could select the subject. I think I could, perhaps, without going a hundred miles from here, find the material for one or two cheerful funerals. Still, this funeral was peculiarly sad. It was a poor "one-gallus" fellow, whose breeches struck him under the armpits and hit him at the other end about the knee—he didn't believe in décolleté clothes.

They buried him in the midst of a marble quarry—they cut through solid marble to make his grave—and yet a little tombstone they put above him was from Vermont. They buried him in the heart of a pine forest, and yet the pine coffin was imported from Cincinnati. They buried him within the touch of an iron mine, and yet the nails in his coffin and the iron in the shovel that dug his grave were imported from Pittsburgh. They buried him by the side of the best sheep-grazing country on earth, and yet the wool in the coffin bands and the coffin bands themselves were brought from the North. The South didn't furnish a thing on earth for that funeral but the corpse and the hole in the ground.

1. Joel C. Harris, *Life of Henry W. Grady* (1890), pp. 204–05. Shortly after delivering this speech, Grady contracted pneumonia and died.

There they put him away and the clods rattled down on his coffin, and they buried him in a New York coat and a Boston pair of shoes and a pair of breeches from Chicago and a shirt from Cincinnati, leaving him nothing to carry into the next world with him to remind him of the country in which he lived, and for which he fought for four years, but the chill of blood in his veins and the marrow in his bones.

Now we have improved on that. We have got the biggest marble-cutting establishment on earth within a hundred yards of that grave. We have got a half-dozen woolen mills right around it, and iron mines, and iron furnaces, and iron factories. We are coming to meet you. We are going to take a noble revenge, as my friend Mr. Carnegie said last night, by invading every inch of your territory with iron, as you invaded ours [in the Civil War] twenty-nine years ago.

2. A Yankee Visits the New South (1887)

New England-born Charles Dudley Warner—lecturer, newspaper editor, essayist, and novelist—shone as one of the literary lights of the post-Civil War years. World traveler and humorist, he collaborated with his friend and neighbor Mark Twain in writing an uneven novel, *The Gilded Age* (1873). He revisited the South, after a two-year absence, on an extensive six-week tour. The result was the charming magazine article from which the following section is excerpted. Note what is most remarkable about the industrial flowering of the South, and who or what was primarily responsible for it.

When we come to the New Industrial South, the change is marvelous. . . . Instead of a South devoted to agriculture and politics, we find a South wide awake to business, excited and even astonished at the development of its own immense resources in metals, marbles, coal, timber, fertilizers, eagerly laying lines of communication, rapidly opening mines, building furnaces, founderies, and all sorts of shops for utilizing the native riches.

It is like the discovery of a new world. When the Northerner finds great founderies in Virginia using only (with slight exceptions) the products of Virginia iron and coal mines; when he finds Alabama and Tennessee making iron so good and so cheap that it finds ready market in Pennsylvania, and founderies multiplying near the great furnaces for supplying Northern markets; when he finds cotton mills running to full capacity on grades of cheap cottons universally in demand throughout the South and Southwest; when he finds small industries, such as paper box factories and wooden bucket and tub factories, sending all they can make into the North and widely over the West; when he sees the loads of most beautiful marbles shipped North; when he learns that some of the largest and most important engines and mill machinery were made in Southern shops; when he finds in Richmond a "pole locomotive," made to run on logs laid end to end, and

2. C. D. Warner, "The South Revisited," *Harper's New Monthly Magazine*, LXXIV, 638–39 (March, 1887).

drag out from Michigan forests and Southern swamps lumber hitherto inaccessible; when he sees worn-out highlands in Georgia and Carolina bear more cotton than ever before by help of a fertilizer the base of which is the cotton seed itself (worth more as a fertilizer than it was before the oil was extracted from it); when he sees a multitude of small shops giving employment to men, women, and children who never had any work of that sort to do before; and when he sees Roanoke iron cast in Richmond into car irons, and returned to a car factory in Roanoke which last year sold three hundred cars to the New York and New England Railroad—he begins to open his eyes.

The South is manufacturing a great variety of things needed in the house, on the farm, and in the shops, for home consumption, and already sends to the North and West several manufactured products. With iron, coal, timber contiguous and easily obtained, the amount sent out is certain to increase as the labor becomes more skillful. The most striking industrial development today is in iron, coal, lumber, and marbles; the more encouraging for the self-sustaining life of the Southern people is the multiplication of small industries in nearly every city I visited.

When I have been asked what impressed me most in this hasty tour, I have always said that the most notable thing was that everybody was at work. In many cities this was literally true: every man, woman, and child was actively employed, and in most there were fewer idlers than in many Northern towns. There are, of course, slow places, antiquated methods, easygoing ways, a-hundred-years-behind-the-time makeshifts, but the spirit in all the centers, and leavening the whole country, is work. Perhaps the greatest revolution of all in Southern sentiment is in regard to the dignity of labor. Labor is honorable, made so by the example of the best in the land. There are, no doubt, fossils or Bourbons, sitting in the midst of the ruins of their estates, martyrs to an ancient pride; but usually the leaders in business and enterprise bear names well known in politics and society. The nonsense that it is beneath the dignity of any man or woman to work for a living is pretty much eliminated from the Southern mind. It still remains true that the purely American type is prevalent in the South, but in all the cities the business signboards show that the enterprising Hebrew is increasingly prominent as merchant and trader, and he is becoming a plantation owner as well.

It cannot be too strongly impressed upon the public mind that the South, to use a comprehensible phrase, "has joined the procession." Its mind is turned to the development of its resources, to business, to enterprise, to education, to economic problems; it is marching with the North in the same purpose of wealth by industry. It is true that the railways, mines, and furnaces could not have been without enormous investments of Northern capital, but I was continually surprised to find so many and important local industries the result solely of home capital, made and saved since the war.

D. THE KNIGHTS OF LABOR

1. Powderly Battles for Larger Goals (1893)

The blue-eyed and ruddy-complexioned Terence V. Powderly, a nimble-witted son of Irish immigrants, became a machinist and joined the secret order of the all-embracing Knights of Labor. He ultimately rose to be its influential head as Grand Master Workman, and saw the organization attain a maximum strength of some 700,000 members—skilled and unskilled, white and colored. But lawyers, bankers, gamblers, and liquor dealers were barred. The Knights strove primarily for social and economic reform on a broad front, rather than the piecemeal raising of wages that was the chief concern of the skilled-crafts unions. Powderly favored the substitution of arbitration for strikes, the regulation of trusts and monopolies, and the replacement of the wage system with producers' cooperatives. Shot at from the front by conservatives, who accused him of communism, he was sniped at from the rear by some of his own following. From this account in his autobiography, ascertain why.

I have held a most anomalous position before the public for the last twenty years. All of this time I have opposed strikes and boycotts. I have contended that the wage question was of secondary consideration; I have contended that the short-hour question was not the end but merely the means to an end; I have endeavored to direct the eyes of our members to the principal parts of the preamble of our Order—government ownership of land, of railroads, or regulation of railroads, telegraphs, and money. But all of this time I have been fighting for a raise in wages, a reduction in the hours of labor, or some demand of the trade element in our Order, to the exclusion of the very work that I have constantly advocated and which the General Assembly of the Order commanded me to advocate.

Just think of it! Opposing strikes and always striking; battling for short hours for others, obliged to work long hours myself, lacking time to devote to anything else. Battling with my pen in the leading journals and magazines of the day for the great things we are educating the people on, and fighting with might and main for the little things.

Our Order has held me in my present position because of the reputation I have won in the nation at large by taking high ground on important national questions, yet the trade element in our Order has always kept me busy at the base of the breastworks throwing up earth which they trample down.

2. Gompers Condemns the Knights (c. 1886)

Samuel Gompers, a stocky Jewish cigarmaker who had been born in a London tenement, emerged as the potent leader of the skilled-crafts American Federation of Labor. Once asked what organized labor wanted, he is said to have replied, "More"— more wages, more power, more liberty, more leisure, more benefits. He and his skilled crafts battled the unskilled of the Knights of Labor against revolutionary schemes for

1. T. V. Powderly, *The Path I Trod* (1940), p. 401. By permission of the Columbia University Press.
2. Samuel Gompers, *Seventy Years of Life and Labor* (1925), II, 244–45, 284. Copyright, 1925, by E. P. Dutton and Co., Inc. Renewal, 1952, by Gertrude Cleaves Gompers. Reprinted by permission of the publishers.

remaking American society. After reading his own account, enumerate the weaknesses of the Knights of Labor from the skilled-union point of view, and try to determine which one was the most serious in the eyes of Gompers.

In 1886 a definite order went out from D. A. [District Assembly No.] 49 [of the Knights of Labor] to make war on the International Cigarmakers' Unions. It was the culmination of years of friction developing over Knights of Labor encroachments on trade union functions.

The two movements were inherently different. Trade unions endeavored to organize for collective responsibility persons with common trade problems. They sought economic betterment in order to place in the hands of wage-earners the means to wider opportunities.

The Knights of Labor was a social or fraternal organization. It was based upon a principle of cooperation, and its purpose was reform. The Knights of Labor prided itself upon being something higher and grander than a trade union or political party. Unfortunately, its purposes were not always exemplified through the declarations and the acts of its members.

The order admitted to membership any person, excluding only lawyers and saloonkeepers. This policy included employers among those eligible. Larger employers gradually withdrew

BETWEEN TWO FIRES

Employer: "If you don't go to work, I must fill your place."
Anarchist: "If you go to work, I'll make it hot for you." *Harper's Weekly*, 1886.

from the order, but the small employers and small businessmen and politicians remained.

The order was a hodgepodge with no basis for solidarity, with the exception of a comparatively few trade assemblies. The aggressive policy inaugurated in 1886 [against the Cigarmakers' Unions] was not due to any change of heart or program, but solely to the great increase in the membership of the Knights of Labor that made it seem safe to put declarations into effect.

When the order began to encroach upon the economic field, trouble was inevitable, for such invasion was equivalent to setting up a dual organization to perform a task for which they were entirely unfitted. It was particularly unfortunate when it endeavored to conduct strikes. The Knights of Labor was a highly centralized organization, and this often placed decision upon essential trade policies in the hands of officers outside the trade concerned. Strikes are essentially an expression of collective purpose of workers who perform related services and who have the spirit of union growing out of joint employment. . . .

Talk of harmony with the Knights of Labor is bosh. They are just as great enemies of trade unions as any employer can be, only more vindictive. I tell you they will give us no quarter, and I would give them their own medicine. It is no use trying to placate them or even to be friendly. They will not cooperate with a mere trades union, as they call our organization. The time will come, however, when the workingmen of the country will see and distinguish between a natural and an artificial organization.

3. Chicago Anarchists Demand Blood (1886)

The rank and file of the Knights of Labor favored an eight-hour day, and their agitation for this goal came to a boil in Chicago on May Day, 1886. The McCormick Harvesting Machine Company, involved with strikers on other issues, had hired strikebreakers. These "scabs" were attacked by the displaced men, whereupon the police killed or injured several of the aroused strikers. August Spies, a German-born anarchist and newspaper editor, angrily issued a circular containing the following appeal in German and English. Note how, in expressing the radicalism of the anarchists, it grossly exaggerates the situation.

REVENGE!

WORKINGMEN, TO ARMS!!!

Your masters sent out their bloodhounds—the police; they killed six of your brothers at McCormick's this afternoon. They killed the poor wretches, because they, like you, had the courage to disobey the supreme will of your bosses. They killed them, because they dared ask for the shortening of the hours of toil. They killed them to show you, "Free American Citizens," that you must be satisfied and contented with whatever your bosses condescend to allow you, or you will get killed!

You have for years endured the most abject humiliations; you have for years suffered unmeasurable iniquities; you have worked yourself to death; you have endured the pangs of want and hunger; your children you have sacrificed to the factory-lords. In short, you have been miserable and obedient slave[s] all these years. Why? To satisfy the insatiable greed, to fill the coffers of your lazy thieving master! When you ask them now to lessen your burden, he sends his bloodhounds out to shoot you, kill you!

If you are men, if you are the sons of your grand sires, who have shed

3. B. R. Kogan, *The Chicago Haymarket Riot* (1959), p. 9 (reproduction of a copy of the circular in the Chicago Historical Society collection).

their blood to free you, then you will rise in your might, Hercules, and destroy the hideous monster that seeks to destroy you. To arms we call you, to arms!

YOUR BROTHERS

[*Responding to such inflammatory appeals, a protest meeting against police brutality assembled at Haymarket Square in Chicago, May 4, 1886. It was about to break up peaceably when some 180 policemen advanced, to be met by an exploding bomb which killed several persons (including a policeman) and injured many others. To this day no one has revealed who threw the bomb, but eight alleged anarchists, accused of preaching incendiary doctrines, were tried and found guilty. Four of them, including August Spies, were hanged.*]

4. Powderly Denies a Breakup (1887)

The Knights of Labor suffered a lasting black eye when the public erroneously associated them with the Chicago anarchists and the "Haymarket Massacre." In addition, many of the May Day strikes of 1887 had failed, internal friction was multiplying, and unwise producers' cooperatives were draining away union funds. Visionary schemes, rather than down-to-earth projects, preoccupied the leaders. Powderly's own denial of a decline was whistling in the dark, but the following statement by him is highly revealing of the broad social objectives of the Knights. Ascertain how many of these objectives the hardheaded Samuel Gompers and his skilled-crafts unions would have approved.

This prophecy, so long deferred of fulfillment, approaches its realization: "The Knights are breaking up" at last. The Philadelphia *Chronicle,* in a late issue, notes the approach of their dissolution without one word of sympathy or regret. Others of our esteemed contemporaries seem just as callous to our approaching dissolution, and watch the coming of the fatal moment of the fleeting breath with the same degree of insensibility.

It is true, the Knights are breaking up. We are at last forced to acknowledge the truth so long, so stubbornly, resisted. We are breaking up— breaking up as the plowman breaks up the soil for the sowing of new seed. We are breaking up old traditions. We are breaking up hereditary rights, and planting everywhere the seed of universal rights. We are breaking up the idea that money makes the man and not moral worth. We are breaking up the idea that might makes right. We are breaking up the idea that legislation is alone for the rich. We are breaking up the idea that the Congress of the United States must be run by millionaires for the benefit of millionaires. We are breaking up the idea that a few men may hold millions of acres of untilled land while other men starve for the want of one acre. We are breaking up the practice of putting the labor of criminals [convict labor] into competition with honest, industrious labor and starving it to death. We are breaking up the practice of importing [European] ignorance, bred of monarchies and dynamite, in order to depreciate intelligent, skilled labor at home. We are breaking up the practice of employing

4. *Journal of United Labor,* July 16, 1887, in *Public Opinion,* III, 318 (July 23, 1887).

little children in factories, thus breeding a race of deformed, ignorant, and profligate. We are breaking up the idea that a man who works with his hands has need neither of education nor of civilized refinements. We are breaking up the idea that the accident of sex puts one-half of the human race beyond the pale of constitutional rights. We are breaking up the practice of paying woman one-third the wages paid man simply because she is a woman. We are breaking up the idea that a man may debauch an infant [minor] girl and shield himself from the penalty behind a law he himself has made. We are breaking up ignorance and intemperance, crime and oppression, of whatever character and wherever found.

Yes, the Knights of Labor are breaking up, and they will continue their appointed work of breaking up until universal rights shall prevail; and while they may not bring in the millennium, they will do their part in the evolution of moral forces that are working for the emancipation of the race.

[*With Samuel Gompers at the helm, the skilled-crafts American Federation of Labor emerged in 1886. By 1890 it had overshadowed the fast-fading Knights of Labor. Skilled carpenters, striking for their own narrow objectives, could not easily be replaced by strikebreakers. Unskilled workers could be. The skilled crafts became weary of sacrificing themselves on the altar of large social objectives. This, in brief, was the epitaph of the Knights of Labor.*]

THOUGHT PROVOKERS

1. Which of the so-called railroad abuses of the post-Civil War are the easiest to justify and which are the hardest? In view of the fact that the railway rates were becoming progressively lower when the Interstate Commerce Act was passed in 1887, why should the public have complained? The free-pass evil allegedly did much to undermine America's moral fiber. Comment.

2. Comment critically on the advantages and disadvantages of the monopolistic trust from the standpoint of the consumer. Was the attempted distinction between "good" and "bad" trusts a valid one?

3. Why was the South, which has many natural resources and is being rapidly industrialized today, so slow to be industrialized after the Civil War?

4. Is organized labor today tending toward the Gompers or the Powderly approach? Explain. Why does the United States not have a Labor Party?

FURTHER EXPLORATION

General: Ida M. Tarbell, *The Nationalizing of Business, 1878–1898* (1936); S. P. Hays, *The Response to Industrialism, 1885–1914* (1957). **Railroads:** J. F. Stover, *American Railroads* (1961); R. W. Fogel, *The Union Pacific Railroad* (1960); R. E. Riegel, *The Story of the Western Railroads* (1926). **Trusts:** Eliot Jones, *The Trust Problem in the United States* (1921); Allan Nevins, *Study in Power: John D. Rockefeller, Industrialist and Philanthropist* (2 vols., 1953). **New South:** C. V. Woodward, *The Origins of the New South, 1877–1913* (1951); Broadus and G. S. Mitchell, *The Industrial Revolution in the South* (1930). **Labor:** Norman Ware, *The Labor Movement in the United States, 1860–1895* (1929); J. G. Rayback, *A History of American Labor* (1959); Philip Taft, *The A. F. of L. in the Time of Gompers* (1957). **Recent:** James McCague, *Moguls and Iron Men* [railroads] (1964); Philip Taft, *Organized Labor in American History* (1964); Bernard Mandel, *Samuel Gompers* (1963).

Chapter 28

The Social Ferment, 1865-1900

Th' worst thing ye can do fr anny man is to do him good.
F. P. DUNNE ("MR. DOOLEY"), PARAPHRASING ANDREW CARNEGIE, 1906

PROLOGUE: The inpouring of the New Immigration from southern and eastern Europe, beginning conspicuously in the 1880's, aggravated existing social ills. It further crowded the melting pot, worsened slum conditions, stimulated agitation to halt cheap foreign labor, and revived anti-Catholic outcries. Protestant denominations, already disturbed by the numerical primacy of the Roman Catholic Church in America, were alarmed by its hundreds of thousands of new communicants. At the same time Protestantism was profoundly shaken by the impact of Darwinism. One manifestation was a heated debate between the rock-ribbed Fundamentalists and the more adaptable Modernists, who came to see in evolution a more glorious revelation of a wonder-working God. Private philanthropy was flourishing, particularly when conscience-pricked millionaires like Rockefeller and Carnegie donated unprecedented sums to worthy causes. American society in general, despite the curse of the saloon, continued to show substantial gains.

A. IMMIGRATION AND URBANIZATION

1. Mary Antin Praises America (1894)

The bomb-assassination of Czar Alexander II in 1881 touched off an outburst of anti-Semitism in Russia that resulted in countless riots, burnings, pillagings, rapings, and murders. Tens of thousands of Jewish refugees fled to America then and later. Mary Antin, a Polish Jewess thirteen years of age, joined her father in Boston in 1894. She later distinguished herself as an author and a welfare worker. In her autobiographical account, excerpted herewith, note what these Jewish immigrants found most gratifying in America.

In our flat we did not think of such a thing as storing the coal in the bathtub. There was no bathtub. So in the evening of the first day my father conducted us to the public baths. As we moved along in a little procession, I was delighted with the illumination of the streets. So many lamps, and they burned until morning, my father said, and so people did not need to carry lanterns.

In America, then, everything was free, as we had heard in Russia; the streets were as bright as a synagogue on a holy day. Music was free; we had been serenaded, to our gaping delight, by a brass band of many pieces, soon after our installation on Union Place.

Education was free. That subject my father had written about repeatedly,

---

1. Mary Antin, *The Promised Land* (1911), pp. 185–86. By permission of Houghton Mifflin Company.

as comprising his chief hope for us children, the essence of American opportunity, the treasure that no thief could touch, not even misfortune or poverty. It was the one thing that he was able to promise us when he sent for us; surer, safer, than bread or shelter.

On our second day I was thrilled with the realization of what this freedom of education meant. A little girl from across the alley came and offered to conduct us to school. My father was out, but we five between us had a few words of English by this time. We knew the word *school*. We understood. This child, who had never seen us till yesterday, who could not pronounce our names, who was not much better dressed than we, was able to offer us the freedom of the schools of Boston! No application made, no questions asked, no examinations, rulings, exclusions; no machinations, no fees. The doors stood open for every one of us. The smallest child could show us the way.

This incident impressed me more than anything I had heard in advance of the freedom of education in America. It was a concrete proof—almost the thing itself. One had to experience it to understand it.

[*Distressingly common was the experience of Anzia Yezierska, whose impoverished family came from Russia to New York City in 1901. Buoyed up by the hope of finding green fields and open places, she found herself in a smelly, crowded slum. God's blue sky was not visible; the landscape was the brick wall of the next building; and there was no place for the pasty-faced children to play. One of her despairing companions said, "In Russia, you could hope to run away from your troubles to America. But from America where can you go?"*]

2. Jacob Riis Goes Slumming (1890)

Police reporter Jacob A. Riis, a Danish-born immigrant who had known rat-infested tenements in Denmark, aimed his talented pen at the scandalous slums of New York. He was shocked by the absence of privacy, sanitation, and playgrounds, and by the presence of dirt, stench, and vermin. One tenement area in New York was known as the "Lung Block" because of the prevalence of tuberculosis. Despite the opposition of heartless landlords, who worked hand-in-glove with corrupt politicians, Riis helped to eliminate some of these foul firetraps, especially the dark "rear tenements." Form conclusions from his personal observations about the chief obstacles to good health and good morals in these slums.

Suppose we look into one? No. — Cherry Street. Be a little careful, please! The hall is dark and you might stumble over the children pitching pennies back there. Not that it would hurt them; kicks and cuffs are their daily diet. They have little else.

Here where the hall turns and dives into utter darkness is a step, and another, another. A flight of stairs. You can feel your way, if you cannot see it. Close? Yes! What would you have? All the fresh air that ever enters these stairs comes from the hall-door that is forever slamming, and from the windows of dark bedrooms that in turn receive from the stairs their sole supply of the elements God meant to be free, but man deals out with such niggardly hand.

2. J. A. Riis, *How the Other Half Lives* (1890), pp. 43–44.

That was a woman filling her pail by the hydrant you just bumped against. The sinks are in the hallway, that all the tenants may have access— and all to be poisoned alike by their summer stenches.

Hear the pump squeak! It is the lullaby of tenement-house babes. In summer, when a thousand thirsty throats pant for a cooling drink in this block, it is worked in vain. But the saloon, whose open door you passed in the hall, is always there. The smell of it has followed you up.

Here is a door. Listen! That short hacking cough, that tiny, helpless wail —what do they mean? They mean that the soiled bow of white you saw on the door downstairs will have another story to tell—oh! a sadly familiar story—before the day is at an end. The child is dying with measles. With half a chance it might have lived; but it had none. The dark bedroom killed it.

"It was took all of a suddint," says the mother, smoothing the throbbing little body with trembling hands. There is no unkindness in the rough voice of the man in the jumper, who sits by the window grimly smoking a clay pipe, with the little life ebbing out in his sight, bitter as his words sound: "Hush, Mary! If we cannot keep the baby, need we complain—such as we?"

Such as we! What if the words ring in your ears as we grope our way up the stairs and down from floor to floor, listening to the sounds behind the closed doors—some of quarreling, some of coarse songs, more of profanity. They are true. When the summer heats come with their suffering, they have meaning more terrible than words can tell.

Come over here. Step carefully over this baby—it is a baby, spite of its rags and dirt—under these iron bridges called fire-escapes, but loaded down, despite the incessant watchfulness of the firemen, with broken household goods, with washtubs and barrels, over which no man could climb from a fire.

This gap between dingy brick walls is the yard. That strip of smoke-colored sky up there is the heaven of these people. Do you wonder the name does not attract them to the churches?

That baby's parents live in the rear tenement here. She is at least as clean as the steps we are now climbing. There are plenty of houses with half a hundred such in. The tenement is much like the one in front we just left, only fouler, closer, darker—we will not say more cheerless. The word is a mockery. A hundred thousand people lived in rear tenements in New York last year.

B. THE REVIVAL OF ANTI–FOREIGNISM

1. The A.P.A. Hates Catholics (1893)

The flood of cheap South European labor in the 1880's, predominantly Roman Catholic, rearoused nativist bigots. The most powerful group, the secretive American Protective Association (A.P.A.), claimed a million members by 1896. Among various

---

1. John T. Ellis, ed., *Documents of American Catholic History* (1956), pp. 500–01. By permission of the Bruce Publishing Company.

activities, it circulated forged documents revealing alleged papal orders to "exterminate" non-Catholics. In Toledo, Ohio, the local branch gathered Winchester rifles
for defense. The A.P.A. was especially alarmed by the Irish-Catholic political machines, which in cities like New York and Chicago had secured a semi-monopoly of
public offices, including the fire department and the police department. In examining
the following secret oath of the A.P.A., determine whether the economic prohibitions
were more vicious than the political.

I do most solemnly promise and swear that I will always, to the utmost
of my ability, labor, plead, and wage a continuous warfare against ignorance
and fanaticism; that I will use my utmost power to strike the shackles and
chains of blind obedience to the Roman Catholic Church from the hampered and bound consciences of a priest-ridden and church-oppressed
people; that I will never allow anyone, a member of the Roman Catholic
Church, to become a member of this order, I knowing him to be such; that
I will use my influence to promote the interest of all Protestants everywhere
in the world that I may be; that I will not employ a Roman Catholic in any
capacity, if I can procure the services of a Protestant.

I furthermore promise and swear that I will not aid in building or maintaining, by my resources, any Roman Catholic church or institution of their
sect or creed whatsoever, but will do all in my power to retard and break
down the power of the Pope, in this country or any other; that I will not
enter into any controversy with a Roman Catholic upon the subject of this

THE UNSEEN SIGNAL OF THE JESUITS

Anti-Catholic cartoon showing a government official at confession betraying state
secrets that are being relayed to Rome by secret wire. New York Public Library

order, nor will I enter into any agreement with a Roman Catholic to strike or create a disturbance whereby the Catholic employees may undermine and substitute their Protestant co-workers; that in all grievances I will seek only Protestants, and counsel with them to the exclusion of all Roman Catholics, and will not make known to them anything of any nature matured at such conferences.

I furthermore promise and swear that I will not countenance the nomination, in any caucus or convention, of a Roman Catholic for any office in the gift of the American people, and that I will not vote for, or counsel others to vote for, any Roman Catholic, but will vote only for a Protestant, so far as may lie in my power (should there be two Roman Catholics in opposite tickets, I will erase the name on the ticket I vote); that I will at all times endeavor to place the political positions of this government in the hands of Protestants, to the entire exclusion of the Roman Catholic Church, of the members thereof, and the mandate of the Pope.

To all of which I do most solemnly promise and swear, so help me God. Amen.

2. Lodge Urges a Literacy Test (1896)

The continued influx of hordes of impoverished and illiterate South Europeans during the depression of the 1890's intensified outcries for their exclusion. Organized labor objected to their low wages; religious bigots, to their Catholicism; city planners, to their slum residence; racial purists, to their "degenerate" stock. Senator Henry Cabot Lodge, a Massachusetts blue blood and later the arch-foe of Woodrow Wilson, here argues for a bill that would establish a literacy test. Note the group which he was trying to exclude, and whether the best interests of the nation would have been served by his proposal.

It is found, in the first place, that the illiteracy test will bear most heavily upon the Italians, Russians, Poles, Hungarians, Greeks, and Asiatics, and very lightly, or not at all, upon English-speaking emigrants or Germans, Scandinavians, and French.

In other words, the races most affected by the illiteracy test are those whose emigration to this country has begun within the last twenty years and swelled rapidly to enormous proportions, races with which the English-speaking people have never hitherto assimilated, and who are most alien to the great body of the people of the United States.

On the other hand, emigrants from the United Kingdom and of those races which are most closely related to the English-speaking people, and who with the English-speaking people themselves founded the American colonies and built up the United States, are affected but little by the proposed test. These races would not be prevented by this law from coming to this country in practically undiminished numbers.

These kindred races also are those who alone go to the Western and Southern states, where immigrants are desired, and take up our unoccupied

2. *Congressional Record,* 54 Cong., 1 sess., p. 2817 (March 16, 1896).

lands. The races which would suffer most seriously by exclusion under the proposed bill furnish the immigrants who do not go to the West or South, where immigration is needed, but who remain on the Atlantic seaboard, where immigration is not needed and where their presence is most injurious and undesirable.

The statistics prepared by the committee show further that the immigrants excluded by the illiteracy test are those who remain for the most part in congested masses in our great cities. They furnish, as other tables show, a large proportion of the population of the slums. The committee's report proves that illiteracy runs parallel with the slum population, with criminals, paupers, and juvenile delinquents of foreign birth, or parentage, whose percentage is out of all proportion to their share of the total population when compared with the percentage of the same classes among the native-born.

It also appears from investigations which have been made that the immigrants who would be shut out by the illiteracy test are those who bring least money to the country, and come most quickly upon private or public charity for support.

3. Cleveland Vetoes a Literacy Test (1897)

In 1897 Congress finally passed a bill excluding all prospective immigrants who could not read or write twenty-five words of the Constitution of the United States in some language. One of the several goals of the exclusionists was to bar anarchists and other radical labor agitators. Cleveland, ever ruggedly independent, vetoed the bill. Evaluate his most effective argument against it, and decide whether his objections were strong enough to justify his successful veto.

It is not claimed, I believe, that the time has come for the further restriction of immigration on the ground that an excess of population overcrowds our land.

It is said, however, that the quality of recent immigration is undesirable. The time is quite within recent memory when the same thing was said of immigrants who, with their descendants, are now numbered among our best citizens.

It is said that too many immigrants settle in our cities, thus dangerously increasing their idle and vicious population. This is certainly a disadvantage. It cannot be shown, however, that it affects all our cities, nor that it is permanent; nor does it appear that this condition, where it exists, demands as its remedy the reversal of our present immigration policy.

The claim is also made that the influx of foreign laborers deprives of the opportunity to work those who are better entitled than they to the privilege of earning their livelihood by daily toil. An unfortunate condition is certainly presented when any who are willing to labor are unemployed, but so far as this condition now exists among our people, it must be conceded to be a result of phenomenal business depression and the stag-

3. J. D. Richardson, ed., *Messages and Papers of the Presidents* (1897), IX, 758–59.

nation of all enterprises in which labor is a factor. With the advent of settled and wholesome financial and economic governmental policies, and consequent encouragement to the activity of capital, the misfortunes of unemployed labor should, to a great extent at least, be remedied. If it continues, its natural consequences must be to check the further immigration to our cities of foreign laborers and to deplete the ranks of those already there. In the meantime those most willing and best entitled ought to be able to secure the advantages of such work as there is to do. . . .

The best reason that could be given for this radical restriction of immigration is the necessity of protecting our population against degeneration and saving our national peace and quiet from imported turbulence and disorder.

I cannot believe that we would be protected against these evils by limiting immigration to those who can read and write in any language twenty-five words of our Constitution. In my opinion, it is infinitely more safe to admit a hundred thousand immigrants who, though unable to read and write, seek among us only a home and opportunity to work than to admit one of those unruly agitators and enemies of governmental control who can not only read and write, but delight in arousing by inflammatory speech the illiterate and peacefully inclined to discontent and tumult.

Violence and disorder do not originate with illiterate laborers. They are, rather, the victims of the educated agitator. The ability to read and write, as required in this bill, in and of itself affords, in my opinion, a misleading test of contented industry and supplies unsatisfactory evidence of desirable citizenship or a proper apprehension of the benefits of our institutions.

If any particular element of our illiterate immigration is to be feared for other causes than illiteracy, these causes should be dealt with directly, instead of making illiteracy the pretext for exclusion, to the detriment of other illiterate immigrants against whom the real cause of complaint cannot be alleged.

[*President Taft, following Cleveland's example of 1897, successfully vetoed a literacy test in 1913, as did President Wilson in 1915. Finally, in 1917, such a restriction was passed over Wilson's veto. Wilson had declared that the prohibition was "not a test of character, of quality, or of personal fitness." In fact, a literacy test denied further opportunity to those who had already been denied opportunity.*]

C. THE CHURCH ON THE DEFENSIVE

1. The Shock of Darwinism (1896)

The theory of evolution, popularized by Charles Darwin's *On the Origin of Species* (1859), directly challenged the Biblical story of creation. (In 1654 a distinguished English scholar had declared the date of creation to be "the 26th of October, 4004

1. A. D. White, *A History of the Warfare of Science with Theology in Christendom* (1896), I, 70, 71–72, 79–80

B.C. at 9 o'clock in the morning.") Orthodox religionists flooded the New York publishers of Darwin's volume with letters demanding its suppression. Andrew D. White, a prominent American educator, scholar, and diplomat, here describes in a famous book some of the reactions in the United States. Account for the violence of these comments.

Darwin's *Origin of Species* had come into the theological world like a plough into an anthill. Everywhere those thus rudely awakened from their old comfort and repose had swarmed forth angry and confused. Reviews, sermons, books light and heavy, came flying at the new thinker from all sides. . . .

Echoes came from America. One review, the organ of the most widespread of American religious sects, declared that Darwin was "attempting to befog and to pettifog the whole question"; another denounced Darwin's views as "infidelity"; another, representing the American branch of the Anglican Church, poured contempt over Darwin as "sophistical and illogical," and then plunged into an exceedingly dangerous line of argument in the following words: "If this hypothesis be true, then is the Bible an unbearable fiction; . . . then have Christians for nearly two thousand years been duped by a monstrous lie. . . . Darwin requires us to disbelieve the authoritative word of the Creator."

A leading journal representing the same church took pains to show the evolution theory to be as contrary to the explicit declarations of the New Testament as to those of the Old, and said: "If we have all, men and monkeys, oysters and eagles, developed from an original germ, then is St. Paul's grand deliverance—'All flesh is not the same flesh; there is one kind of flesh of men, another of beasts, another of fishes, and another of birds'—untrue." . . .

But a far more determined opponent was the Rev. Dr. Hodge, of Princeton. His anger toward the evolution doctrine was bitter: he denounced it as thoroughly "atheistic"; he insisted that Christians "have a right to protest against the arraying of probabilities against the clear evidence of the Scriptures"; he even censured so orthodox a writer as the Duke of Argyll, and declared that the Darwinian theory of natural selection is "utterly inconsistent with the Scriptures," and that "an absent God, who does nothing, is to us no God"; that "to ignore design as manifested in God's creation is to dethrone God"; that "a denial of design in Nature is virtually a denial of God"; and that "no teleologist can be a Darwinian."

Even more uncompromising was another of the leading authorities at the same university—the Rev. Dr. Duffield. He declared war not only against Darwin but even against men like Asa Gray, Le Conte, and others, who attempted to reconcile the new theory with the Bible. He insisted that "evolutionism and the Scriptural account of the origin of men are irreconcilable"—that the Darwinian theory is "in direct conflict with the teaching of the apostle, 'All Scripture is given by inspiration of God.'" He pointed out, in his opposition to Darwin's *Descent of Man* and Lyell's *Antiquity of Man,* that in the Bible "the genealogical links which connect the Israelites in Egypt with Adam and Eve in Eden are explicitly given."

These utterances of Prof. Duffield culminated in a declaration which deserves to be cited as showing that a Presbyterian minister can "deal damnation round the land" *ex cathedra* in a fashion quite equal to that of popes and bishops. It is as follows: "If the development theory of the origin of man," wrote Dr. Duffield in the *Princeton Review,* "shall in a little while take its place—as doubtless it will—with other exploded scientific speculations, then they who accept it with its proper logical consequences will in the life to come have their portion with those who in this life 'know not God and obey not the gospel of His Son.'"

2. Beecher Accepts Evolution (1886)

The Reverend Henry Ward Beecher, a famed Congregational minister, was the most popular and influential preacher of his day. Like his sister, Harriet Beecher Stowe, he crusaded against slavery, and in a mock auction in his Brooklyn church raised money to redeem a Negro girl from slavery. Although besmirched by a notorious adultery trial which ended in a hung jury, he continued to preach religion and discuss public issues with eloquence and boldness. His disbelief in a literal hell, combined with his belief in evolution, generated friction with orthodox clergymen and led to his withdrawal from the Association of Congregational Ministers. He customarily preached to 2500 people; after he died, 40,000 viewed his body. Comment critically on his view that evolution was bound to command acceptance, and that evolution would help true religion.

As thus set forth, it may be said that Evolution is accepted as the method of creation by the whole scientific world, and that the period of controversy is passed and closed. A few venerable men yet live with many doubts; but it may be said that 99 percent—as has been declared by an eminent physicist—99 percent of scientific men and working scientists of the world are using this theory without any doubt of its validity. . . .

This science of Evolution is taught in all advanced academies, in all colleges and universities, in all medical and surgical schools, and our children are receiving it as they are the elements of astronomy or botany or chemistry. That in another generation Evolution will be regarded as uncontradictable as the Copernican system of astronomy, or the Newtonian doctrine of gravitation, can scarcely be doubted. Each of these passed through the same contradiction by theologians. They were charged by the Church, as is Evolution now, with fostering materialism, infidelity, and atheism.

We know what befell Galileo for telling the truth of God's primitive revelation. We know, or do not know, at least, how Newton stood charged with infidelity and with atheism when he announced the doctrine of gravitation.

Who doubts the heliocentric theory [of Copernicus] today? Who doubts whether it is the sun which is moving round the earth or the earth round

2. H. W. Beecher, *Evolution and Religion* (1886), pp. 50–54.

the sun? Who doubts that the law of attraction, as developed by Newton, is God's material law universally? The time is coming when the doctrine of Evolution, or the method of God in the creation of the world, will be just as universally accepted as either of these great physical doctrines. The whole Church fought them; yet they stand, conquerors. . . .

Evolution is substantially held by men of profound Christian faith: by the now venerable and universally honored scientific teacher, Professor Dana of Yale College, a devout Christian and communicant of a Congregational Church; by Professor Le Conte of the University of California, an elder in the Presbyterian Church; by President McCosh of Princeton College, a Presbyterian of the Presbyterians, and a Scotch Presbyterian at that; by Professor Asa Gray of Harvard University, a communicant of the Christian Church; by increasing numbers of Christian preachers in America; by Catholics like Mivart, in England. . . .

To the fearful and the timid let me say that while Evolution is certain to oblige theology to reconstruct its system, it will take nothing away from the grounds of true religion. It will strip off Saul's unmanageable armor from David, to give him greater power over the giant. Simple religion is the unfolding of the best nature of man towards God, and man has been hindered and embittered by the outrageous complexity of unbearable systems of theology that have existed. If you can change theology, you will emancipate religion; yet men are continually confounding the two terms, religion and theology. . . .

Evolution, applied to religion, will influence it only as the hidden temples are restored, by removing the sands which have drifted in from the arid deserts of scholastic and medieval theologies. It will change theology, but only to bring out the simple temple of God in clearer and more beautiful lines and proportions. . . .

In every view, then, it is the duty of the friends of simple and unadulterated Christianity to hail the rising light and to uncover every element of religious teaching to its wholesome beams. Old men may be charitably permitted to die in peace, but young men and men in their prime are by God's providence laid under the most solemn obligations to thus discern the signs of the times, and to make themselves acquainted with the knowledge which science is laying before them. And above all, those zealots of the pulpit who make faces at a science which they do not understand, and who reason from prejudice to ignorance; who not only will not lead their people, but hold up to scorn those who strive to take off the burden of ignorance from their shoulders—these men are bound to open their eyes and see God's sun shining in the heavens.

3. Ingersoll Spurns Orthodoxy (1896)

Colonel Robert G. Ingersoll ("the Great Agnostic") was a brilliant political orator who gained renown as a Civil War officer, a Congressman, a clever debater, a big-time lawyer, and above all a popular lecturer. His doubts deepened by Darwin, he spoke to numerous freethinking audiences on such subjects as "Some Mistakes of Moses" and "Why I Am an Agnostic." He might have become President if he had kept his doubts to himself. Although a lovable personality and an upright character, he became the favorite whipping boy of orthodox clergymen. Of them he reportedly said, "I know that they know that I know that they know that they do not know." On Thanksgiving Day, 1895, groups of earnest young Christians held well-publicized prayer meetings for his conversion. He replied in the press as follows. Note which of his points was most difficult for his orthodox adversaries to answer.

I take it for granted that the people praying for me are sincere, and that they have a real interest in my welfare. Of course, I thank them one and all. They believe in a God of infinite power, of infinite wisdom, and of infinite goodness. If they are right in this, then their God knows what ought to be done and has the goodness and power to do it. It is not necessary for a finite being to enlighten infinite wisdom or to soften the heart of infinite goodness or to assist the infinitely powerful. Certainly an infinite God needs no advice.

These Christians also believe in another great being called the Devil. They do not think he is quite as strong as God, but somewhat quicker; not as wise as God, but altogether more cunning. This Devil does all he can to keep people from being converted. God knits and the Devil ravels. God sews and the Devil rips.

Why does not God convert the Devil? Why did he create the Devil? These things, I know, are sacred mysteries that we should not try to understand. At the same time it is hard to see why a wise and good God would create living suffering fuel for eternal fire.

I think that I had better remain as I am. I had better follow the light of my reason, be true to myself, express my honest thoughts, and do the little I can for the destruction of superstition, the little I can for the development of the brain, for the increase of intellectual hospitality, and the happiness of my fellow beings. One world at a time.

D. THE NEW MATERIALISM

1. Carnegie's Gospel of Wealth (1889)

Andrew Carnegie, the ambitious little Scottish steel magnate, spent the first part of his life in America making a half-billion or so dollars, and the rest of it giving his fortune away. Not a gambler or speculator at heart, he gambled everything on the future prosperity of America. His social conscience led him to preach "The Gospel of Wealth," notably in the following magazine article. Comment critically on his argument that the millionaire is a trustee for the poor, and that direct charity is an evil.

This, then, is held to be the duty of the man of wealth: first, to set an example of modest, unostentatious living, shunning display or extravagance; to provide moderately for the legitimate wants of those dependent

1. Andrew Carnegie, "Wealth," *North American Review*, CXLVIII, 661–64 (June, 1889).

upon him; and after doing so to consider all surplus revenues which come to him simply as trust funds, which he is called upon to administer, and strictly bound as a matter of duty to administer in the manner which, in his judgment, is best calculated to produce the most beneficial results for the community—the man of wealth thus becoming the mere agent and trustee for his poorer brethren, bringing to their service his superior wisdom, experience, and ability to administer, doing for them better than they would or could do for themselves. . . .

Those who would administer wisely must, indeed, be wise, for one of the serious obstacles to the improvement of our race is indiscriminate charity. It were better for mankind that the millions of the rich were thrown into the sea than so spent as to encourage the slothful, the drunken, the unworthy. Of every thousand dollars spent in so-called charity today, it is probable that $950 is unwisely spent; so spent, indeed, as to produce the very evils which it proposes to mitigate or cure.

THE MACMILLION

The Scotsman Carnegie in 1901 provided £2,000,000 for establishing free education at four Scottish universities, each of which is represented by an upturned hat. *Punch* (London), 1901.

A well-known writer of philosophic books admitted the other day that he had given a quarter of a dollar to a man who approached him as he was coming to visit the house of his friend. He knew nothing of the habits of this beggar; knew not the use that would be made of this money, although he had every reason to suspect that it would be spent improperly. This man professed to be a disciple of Herbert Spencer; yet the quarter-dollar given that night will probably work more injury than all the money which its thoughtless donor will ever be able to give in true charity will do good. He only gratified his own feelings, saved himself from annoyance

—and this was probably one of the most selfish and very worst actions of his life, for in all respects he is most worthy.

In bestowing charity, the main consideration should be to help those who will help themselves; to provide part of the means by which those who desire to improve may do so; to give those who desire to rise the aids by which they may rise; to assist, but rarely or never to do all. Neither the individual nor the race is improved by almsgiving. Those worthy of assistance, except in rare cases, seldom require assistance. The really valuable men of the race never do, except in cases of accident or sudden change. Everyone has, of course, cases of individuals brought to his own knowledge where temporary assistance can do genuine good, and these he will not overlook.

But the amount which can be wisely given by the individual for individuals is necessarily limited by his lack of knowledge of the circumstances connected with each. He is the only true reformer who is as careful and as anxious not to aid the unworthy as he is to aid the worthy, and, perhaps, even more so, for in almsgiving more injury is probably done by rewarding vice than by relieving virtue.

The rich man is thus almost restricted to following the examples of Peter Cooper, Enoch Pratt of Baltimore, Mr. Pratt of Brooklyn, Senator Stanford,* and others, who know that the best means of benefiting the community is to place within its reach the ladders upon which the aspiring can rise—parks, and means of recreation, by which men are helped in body and mind; works of art, certain to give pleasure and improve the public taste; and public institutions of various kinds, which will improve the general condition of the people;—in this manner returning their surplus wealth to the mass of their fellows in the forms best calculated to do them lasting good. . . .

The man who dies leaving behind him millions of available wealth, which was his to administer during life, will pass away "unwept, unhonored, and unsung," no matter to what uses he leaves the dross which he cannot take with him. Of such as these the public verdict will then be: "The man who dies thus rich dies disgraced."

Such, in my opinion, is the true Gospel concerning Wealth, obedience to which is destined some day to solve the problem of the Rich and the Poor, and to bring "Peace on earth, among men good will."

2. *The Nation* Challenges Carnegie (1901)

Carnegie died "disgraced" by dying rich. He managed to give away only $350,000,-000, from both income and principal. A total of $60,000,000 went to public municipal libraries, many named after himself. Finley Peter Dunne ("Mr. Dooley") poked fun at this immodest arrangement, especially the feature that required the community to

---

* Cooper founded an institute in New York City for educating the working classes; Enoch Pratt established a free library in Baltimore; Charles Pratt created an institute in Brooklyn for training skilled workers; and Leland Stanford endowed Stanford University.
2. *The Nation* (New York), LXII, 55 (Jan. 17, 1901).

provide the site, the books, the upkeep: "Ivry time he [Carnegie] dhrops a dollar, it makes a noise like a waither [waiter] fallin' downstairs with a tray iv dishes." The New York *Nation* reviewed rather critically Carnegie's essay on the Gospel of Wealth when it was published in book form. Decide whether Carnegie or *The Nation* has the better of the argument as to the baleful effects of inherited riches. Note how the problem has been partially solved since Carnegie's day.

Mr. Carnegie's philosophy is perfectly simple, and it is stated clearly and forcibly. He holds, first, that the present competitive system, which necessarily creates millionaires, or allows men to get rich, is essential to progress, and should not be altered. Secondly, rich men should not leave their fortunes to their children, because their children will be demoralized by having money to spend which they have not earned. Thirdly, rich men should not indulge in luxury. Fourthly, they should dispose of their fortunes while living, or the government should confiscate them at their death. Fifthly, the only practical way of disposing of them is to found libraries and other public institutions, requiring the public to contribute to their support.

Evidently, this system assumes that millionaires are sinners above other men. The number of persons who have wealth sufficient to maintain their children in idleness is very large, and such persons are able to indulge in many luxuries. We cannot concede that the children of millionaires will go straight to perdition if they inherit their parents' wealth, while those who get but a hundred thousand shall be immune. Everyone familiar with the life of the common people knows that an inheritance of a very few thousand dollars may demoralize a young man, and this principle has been illustrated on a prodigious scale in our pension largesses.

On the other hand, virtue among the children of millionaires is not quite so rare as Mr. Carnegie intimates. Instances are known where inherited wealth has been wisely administered by men of respectable and even irreproachable habits. Mr. Carnegie's dictum, "I would as soon leave to my son a curse as the almighty dollar," is too sweeping. Millions of people who are not millionaires desire to give their children the advantages of wealth, and this desire is one of the greatest incentives to accumulation. Provided they educate their children wisely, it is impossible to maintain that the gift of these advantages is necessarily injurious.

On this point Mr. Carnegie and Mr. Gladstone [British statesman] had some debate; the latter contending that "the hereditary transmission of wealth and position, in conjunction with the calls of occupation and of responsibility, is a good and not an evil thing." Of course, this is nothing but the old conflict between the ideals of democracy and aristocracy, and we need not restate it. . . .

Probably we shall see the experiment of confiscating large fortunes at the death of their owners tried on an increasing scale, together with progressive taxes on incomes.

3. Conwell Deifies the Dollar (*c.* 1900)

The Reverend Russell H. Conwell was a remarkable Baptist preacher of Philadelphia who founded Temple University and had a large hand in establishing three hospitals. He delivered his famous lecture, *Acres of Diamonds*, more than six thousand times. The proceeds went to the educating of some ten thousand young men. His basic theme was that in seeking riches people were apt to overlook the opportunities in their own backyards (acres of diamonds). Critics charged that Conwell was merely throwing the cloak of religion about the materialistic ideals of his time, especially since he combined philanthropy with dollar-chasing. In reading the following excerpt from his famous lecture, form conclusions as to the soundness of his attitude toward the poor. Reconcile this brand of Christianity with the teachings of Christ, who said to the young man, "Go and sell that thou hast, and give to the poor . . ." (Matthew 19:21).

You have no right to be poor. It is your duty to be rich.

Oh, I know well that there are some things higher, sublimer than money! Ah, yes, there are some things sweeter, holier than gold! Yet I also know that there is not one of those things but is greatly enhanced by the use of money.

"Oh," you will say, "Mr. Conwell, can you, as a Christian teacher, tell the young people to spend their lives making money?"

Yes, I do. Three times I say, I do, I do, I do. You ought to make money. Money is power. Think how much good you could do if you had money now. Money is power, and it ought to be in the hands of good men. It would be in the hands of good men if we comply with the Scripture teachings, where God promises prosperity to the righteous man. That means more than being goody-good—it means the all-round righteous man. You should be a righteous man. If you were, you would be rich.

I need to guard myself right here. Because one of my theological students came to me once to labor with me, for heresy, inasmuch as I had said that money was power.

He said: "Mr. Conwell, I feel it my duty to tell you that the Scriptures say that money 'is the root of all evil.' ". . .

So he read: "The *love* of money is the root of all evil." Indeed it is. The *love* of money is the root of all evil. The love of money, rather than the love of the good it secures, is a dangerous evil in the community. The desire to get hold of money, and to hold on to it, "hugging the dollar until the eagle squeals," is the root of all evil. But it is a grand ambition for men to have the desire to gain money, that they may use it for the benefit of their fellow men.

Young man! you may never have the opportunity to charge at the head of your nation's troops on some Santiago's heights. Young woman! you may never be called on to go out in the seas like Grace Darling to save suffering humanity. But every one of you can earn money honestly, and

3. R. H. Conwell, *Acres of Diamonds* (1901), pp. 145–47, 151. Reprinted from *Modern Eloquence*.

with that money you can fight the battles of peace; and the victories of peace are always grander than those of war. I say then to you that you ought to be rich. . . .

No man has a right to go into business and not make money. It is a crime to go into business and lose money, because it is a curse to the rest of the community. No man has a moral right to transact business unless he makes something out of it. He has also no right to transact business unless the man he deals with has an opportunity also to make something. Unless he lives and lets live, he is not an honest man in business. There are no exceptions to this great rule. . . .

It is cruel to slander the rich because they have been successful. It is a shame to "look down" upon the rich the way we do. They are not scoundrels because they have gotten money. They have blessed the world. They have gone into great enterprises that have enriched the nation and the nation has enriched them. It is all wrong for us to accuse a rich man of dishonesty simply because he secured money. Go through this city and your very best people are among your richest people. Owners of property are always the best citizens. It is all wrong to say they are not good.

E. THE ANTI–SALOON CRUSADE

1. Frances Willard Prays in a Saloon (1874)

An independent girl, Frances E. Willard defied her novel-hating father by openly reading Scott's *Ivanhoe* on her eighteenth birthday. At first an educator of females, she gained fame as an advocate of temperance and woman suffrage. She was one of the founders of the Woman's Christian Temperance Union, which grew out of the praying-in-saloons crusade of 1873–1874. Miss Willard stressed not so much the social and economic evils of drinking as the need for protecting the home and the Christian way of life. The saloon, often in league with gambling and prostitution, was riding high from 1870 to 1900. Some towns had one for every two hundred inhabitants; and the swinging doors, the heavy brass rails, and the nude Venus over the huge gilded mirror were all familiar sights. Miss Willard here describes her experiences in Pittsburgh. Judge how effective this approach probably was, and how it would be received today.

We paused in front of the saloon that I have mentioned. The ladies ranged themselves along the curbstone, for they had been forbidden in any wise to incommode the passers-by, being dealt with much more strictly than a drunken man or a heap of dry-goods boxes would be.

At a signal from our gray-haired leader, a sweet-voiced woman began to sing, "Jesus the water of life will give," all our voices soon blending in that sweet song. I think it was the most novel spectacle that I recall. There stood women of undoubted religious devotion and the highest character, most of them crowned with the glory of gray hairs. Along the stony pave-

1. Frances E. Willard, *Glimpses of Fifty Years* (1880), pp. 340–41.

ment of that stoniest of cities rumbled the heavy wagons, many of them carriers of beer; between us and the saloon in front of which we were drawn up in line, passed the motley throng, almost every man lifting his hat and even the little newsboys doing the same. It was American manhood's tribute to Christianity and to womanhood, and it was significant and full of pathos.

The leader had already asked the saloonkeeper if we might enter, and he had declined, else the prayer meeting would have occurred inside his door. A sorrowful old lady, whose only son had gone to ruin

HERE THEY COME

Praying ladies about to descend on a saloon. *Harper's Weekly*, 1874.

through that very death-trap, knelt on the cold, moist pavement and offered a broken-hearted prayer, while all our heads were bowed.

At a signal we moved on and the next saloonkeeper permitted us to enter. I had no more idea of the inward appearance of a saloon than if there had been no such place on earth. I knew nothing of its high, heavily corniced bar, its barrels with the ends all pointed towards the looker-on, each barrel being furnished with a faucet, its shelves glittering with decanters and cut glass, its floors thickly strewn with sawdust, and here and there a round table with chairs—nor of its abundant fumes, sickening to healthful nostrils.

The tall, stately lady who led us placed her Bible on the bar and read a psalm, whether hortatory or imprecatory I do not remember, but the spirit of these crusaders was so gentle, I think it must have been the former.

Then we sang "Rock of Ages" as I thought I had never heard it sung before, with a tender confidence to the height of which one does not rise in the easy-going, regulation prayer meeting, and then one of the older women whispered to me softly that the leader wished to know if I would pray. It was strange, perhaps, but I felt not the least reluctance, and kneeling on that sawdust floor, with a group of earnest hearts around me, and behind them, filling every corner and extending out into the street, a crowd of unwashed, unkempt, hard-looking drinking men, I was conscious that perhaps never in my life, save beside my sister Mary's dying bed, had I prayed as truly as I did then. This was my Crusade baptism. The next day I went on to the West and within a week had been made president of the Chicago W.C.T.U.

2. Gompers Defends the Saloon (*c.* 1886)

The Knights of Labor, joining the foes of the saloon, refused to admit liquor sellers to their membership. Their leader, Terence V. Powderly, even accused certain employers of encouraging drink so that the employees would become more content with their underpaid lot. (This argument assumes that docility is preferable to efficiency.) But Samuel Gompers of the American Federation of Labor had a good word to say for the attractively lighted "poor man's club," even though it drained away the family's grocery money. Form some judgment as to whether these advantages offset the disadvantages.

The saloon was the only club the workingmen had then. For a few cents we could buy a glass of beer and hours of congenial society. Talk in these meeting places had a peculiar freedom from formality that engendered good-fellowship and exchange of genuine intimacies.

The saloon rendered a variety of industrial services. Frequently, wages were paid there—in checks which the saloonkeeper cashed. Of course, it was embarrassing to accept that service without spending money with him.

All too frequently the saloonkeeper also served as an employment agent. But on the other hand the saloonkeeper was often a friend in time of strikes and the free lunch [salty foods to stimulate thirst] he served was a boon to many a hungry striker.

Nearly every saloon had a room or a hall back of it or over it that could be rented for a nominal sum. Of course, the saloon was counting on increased receipts due to gatherings held in the hall. These rooms were practically the only meeting places available to unions, which were poor and small in numbers.

[The continued callousness of "booze barons" resulted in the launching of the Anti-Saloon League in 1893. It supplemented the efforts of the Prohibition Party, organized in 1869, and the Woman's Christian Temperance Union, organized in 1874. With mounting zeal the reformers harped on the following arguments: (1) Alcohol was a debauching force in American politics. (2) The rapid mechanization of industry required sobriety for safety and efficiency. (3) The liquor sellers were saddling the taxpayers with the occupants of prisons and poorhouses. But prohibition in the localities and the states was slow in coming. By 1905 only four

2. Samuel Gompers, *Seventy Years of Life and Labor* (1925), II, 176. Copyright, 1925, by E. P. Dutton and Co., Inc. Renewal, 1952, by Gertrude Cleaves Gompers. Reprinted by permission of the publishers.

states had entered the "dry" column: Kansas, Maine, Nebraska, and North Dakota. Success was slowest in the large urban areas, where huge colonies of undigested immigrants had brought with them Old World drinking habits.]

THOUGHT PROVOKERS

1. If the New Immigrants were disillusioned by America, why did they not return to the Old Country? Why did they flock to the slums? Why did so many of them rise from the slums to respectability?

2. Was a literacy test fairer than restricting immigrants, as now, by quota? Why was the immigrant less welcome in the 1890's than in the 1790's?

3. It has been said that Darwin jolted orthodox Christianity more severely than Copernicus did three hundred years earlier with his discoveries regarding the solar system. Explain. Why was it so difficult to reconcile evolution with a literal reading of the Bible?

4. To what extent was Carnegie selfish in his Gospel of Wealth? Is it better to have large private benefactions or to have the government tax wealth and engage in benefactions itself? Why is it difficult to give away large sums of money intelligently?

5. Critics have charged that one reason why the saloon prospered was that the churches and the community failed to provide wholesome alternatives. Discuss.

FURTHER EXPLORATION

General: A. M. Schlesinger, *The Rise of the City, 1878–1898* (1933). **Immigration and Urbanization:** Oscar Handlin, *The Uprooted* (1953); John Higham, *Strangers in the Land* (1955); M. A. Jones, *American Immigration* (1960). **Anti-Foreignism:** Michael Williams, *The Shadow of the Pope* (1932); H. J. Desmond, *The A.P.A. Movement* (1912). **The Church:** Richard Hofstadter, *Social Darwinism in American Thought* (1944); Cameron Rogers, *Colonel Bob Ingersoll* (1927). **Carnegie:** *Autobiography of Andrew Carnegie* (1920); B. J. Hendrick, *The Life of Andrew Carnegie* (2 vols., 1932). **Saloons:** E. H. Cherrington, *History of the Anti-Saloon League* (1913).

Recent: Blake McKelvey, *The Urbanization of America, 1860–1915* (1963); T. D. Clark and A. D. Kirwan, *The South Since Appomattox: A Century of Regional Change* (1967); Ray Ginger, *Age of Excess: The United States from 1877 to 1914* (1965) [paperback]; D. L. Kinzer, *An Episode in Anti-Catholicism: The American Protective Association* (1964); F. P. Weisenburger, *Triumph of Faith* (1962); August Meier, *Negro Thought in America, 1880–1915* (1963) [paperback].

Chapter 29

Westward Expansion

Many, if not most, of our Indian wars have had their origin in broken promises and acts of injustice upon our part. . . .

PRESIDENT HAYES, 1877

PROLOGUE: The fence-erecting white men inevitably clashed with the wide-roaming red men of the plains. As land-greed undermined ethical standards, many settlers acted as though the Indians had no more rights than the buffalo, which were also ruthlessly slaughtered. The seemingly endless frontier wars ended finally when the red men, cooped up in "human zoos" called reservations, were forced to adopt in part the economic life of their conquerors. The honest farmer and the fraudulent speculator were now free to open the Far West under the Homestead Act of 1862—America's first big give-away program. Much of the settlement occurred in areas with only scanty rainfall; and when crops failed, or when overproduction came, the farmer was trapped. Agitation for relief vented itself most spectacularly in 1892, when the Populist Party waged a colorful campaign for the Presidency under General James B. Weaver. Although he carried six Western states, he ran well behind the second-place Republicans as the Democrats again swept Grover Cleveland to victory.

A. THE PLIGHT OF THE RED MAN

1. Custer's Last Stand (1876)

As the white men closed in, the Western Indians were forced to make numerous treaties with Washington which confined them to reservations and guaranteed needed supplies. But rascally government contractors cheated them with moldy flour, rotten beef, and moth-eaten blankets. In 1875 the discovery of gold on the Sioux reservation in the Dakotas brought stampeding thousands of miners, who brutally ignored treaty guarantees. The Indians took to the warpath, and the dashing General George Custer with only 264 men rashly attacked a hostile force that turned out to number several thousand braves. Custer and his entire command were wiped out near the Little Big Horn River (Montana), in what the white men call a "massacre" and the Indians a "battle." Many of the whites were stripped, scalped, and unspeakably mutilated. From this account in the reformist *Harper's Weekly*, enumerate the mistakes in dealing with the Indians, and determine who was basically responsible for the situation that had developed.

The fate of the brave and gallant Custer has deeply touched the public heart, which sees only a fearless soldier leading a charge against an ambushed [lurking] foe, and falling at the head of his men and in the thick of the fray. A monument is proposed, and subscriptions have been made. But a truer monument, more enduring than brass or marble, would be an

1. *Harper's Weekly*, XX, 630–31 (Aug. 5, 1876).

Indian policy intelligent, moral, and efficient. Custer would not have fallen in vain if such a policy should be the result of his death.

It is a permanent accusation of our humanity and ability that over the Canadian line the relations between Indians and whites are so tranquil, while upon our side they are summed up in perpetual treachery, waste, and war. When he was a young lieutenant on the frontier, General Grant saw this, and watching attentively, he came to the conclusion that the reason of the difference was that the English respected the rights of the Indians and kept faith with them, while we make solemn treaties with them as if they were civilized and powerful nations, and then practically regard them as vermin to be exterminated.

The folly of making treaties with the Indian tribes may be as great as treating with a herd of buffaloes. But the infamy of violating treaties when we have made them is undeniable, and we are guilty both of the folly and the infamy.

We make treaties—that is, we pledge our faith—and then leave swindlers and knaves of all kinds to execute them. We maintain and breed pauper colonies. The savages, who know us, and who will neither be pauperized nor trust our word, we pursue, and slay if we can, at an incredible expense. The flower of our young officers is lost in inglorious forays, and one of the intelligent students of the whole subject rises in Congress and says, "The fact is that these Indians, with whom we have made a solemn treaty that their territory should not be invaded, and that they should receive supplies upon their reservations, have seen from one thousand to fifteen hundred [gold] miners during the present season entering and occupying their territory, while the Indians, owing to the failure of this and the last Congress to make adequate appropriations for their subsistence, instead of being fattened, as the gentleman says, by the support of this government, have simply been starved." . . .

It is plain that so long as we undertake to support the Indians as paupers, and then fail to supply the food; to respect their rights to reservations, and then permit the reservations to be overrun; to give them the best weapons and ammunition, and then furnish the pretense of their using them against us; to treat with them as men, and then hunt them like skunks—so long we shall have the most costly and bloody Indian wars, and the most tragical ambuscades, slaughters, and assassinations.

The Indian is undoubtedly a savage, and a savage greatly spoiled by the kind of contact with civilization which he gets at the West. There is no romance, there is generally no interest whatever, in him or his fate. But there should be some interest in our own good faith and humanity, in the lives of our soldiers and frontier settlers, and in the taxation to support our Indian policy. All this should certainly be enough to arouse a public demand for a thorough consideration of the subject, and the adoption of a system which should neither be puerile nor disgraceful, and which would tend to spare us the constant repetition of such sorrowful events as the slaughter of Custer and his brave men.

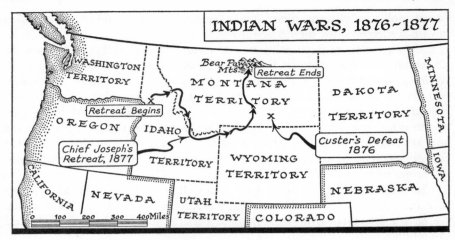

2. Chief Joseph's Lament (1879)

Chief Joseph, a noble-featured and humane Nez Percé (Pierced Nose) Indian, refused to be removed from his ancestral lands in Oregon and penned up on a reservation in Idaho. After an amazing strategic retreat of about 1000 miles, he was finally captured in 1877 near the Canadian border. The miserable remnants of his band were deported to Indian Territory (now Oklahoma), where many died of malaria and other afflictions. Chief Joseph appealed personally to the President, and subsequently the Nez Percés were returned to the Pacific Northwest. After reading his narrative, assess critically his formula for ending white-Indian wars.

At last I was granted permission to come to Washington and bring my friend Yellow Bull and our interpreter with me. I am glad I came. I have shaken hands with a good many friends, but there are some things I want to know which no one seems able to explain. I cannot understand how the government sends a man out to fight us, as it did General Miles, and then breaks his word. Such a government has something wrong about it. . . .

I have heard talk and talk, but nothing is done. Good words do not last long unless they amount to something. Words do not pay for my dead people. They do not pay for my country, now overrun by white men. They do not protect my father's grave. They do not pay for my horses and cattle.

Good words do not give me back my children. Good words will not make good the promise of your war chief, General Miles. Good words will not give my people good health and stop them from dying. Good words will not get my people a home where they can live in peace and take care of themselves.

I am tired of talk that comes to nothing. It makes my heart sick when I remember all the good words and all the broken promises. There has been too much talking by men who had no right to talk. Too many misinterpretations have been made; too many misunderstandings have come up between the white men and the Indians.

If the white man wants to live in peace with the Indian, he can live in peace. There need be no trouble. Treat all men alike. Give them the same laws. Give them all an even chance to live and grow.

All men are made by the same Great Spirit Chief. They are all brothers. The earth is the mother of all people, and all people should have equal rights upon it. You might as well expect all rivers to run backward as that any man who was born a free man should be contented penned up and denied liberty to go where he pleases. If you tie a horse to a stake, do you expect he will grow fat? If you pen an Indian up on a small spot of earth and compel him to stay there, he will not be contented nor will he grow and prosper.

I have asked some of the Great White Chiefs where they get their authority to say to the Indian that he shall stay in one place, while he sees white men going where they please. They cannot tell me.

I only ask of the government to be treated as all other men are treated. If I cannot go to my own home, let me have a home in a country where my people will not die so fast. I would like to go to Bitter Root Valley [western Montana]. There my people would be healthy; where they are now, they are dying. Three have died since I left my camp to come to Washington. When I think of our condition, my heart is heavy. I see men of my own race treated as outlaws and driven from country to country, or shot down like animals.

I know that my race must change. We cannot hold our own with the white men as we are. We only ask an even chance to live as other men live. We ask to be recognized as men. We ask that the same law shall work alike on all men. If an Indian breaks the law, punish him by the law. If a white man breaks the law, punish him also.

Let me be a free man—free to travel, free to stop, free to work, free to trade where I choose, free to choose my own teachers, free to follow the religion of my fathers, free to think and talk and act for myself—and I will obey every law or submit to the penalty.

Whenever the white man treats the Indian as they treat each other, then we shall have no more wars. We shall all be alike—brothers of one father and mother, with one sky above us and one country around us and one government for all. Then the Great Spirit Chief who rules above will smile upon this land and send rain to wash out the bloody spots made by brothers' hands upon the face of the earth. For this time the Indian race are waiting and praying. I hope no more groans of wounded men and women will ever go to the ear of the Great Spirit Chief above, and that all people may be one people.

3. Roosevelt Downgrades the Indians (1885)

Sickly and bespectacled young Theodore Roosevelt, the future President, invested more than $50,000 of his patrimony in ranch lands in Dakota Territory. He lost

3. Theodore Roosevelt, *Hunting Trips of a Ranchman* (1885), pp. 17–19. In the Dawes Act of 1887, Congress made provision for granting the Indians individual allotments, as Roosevelt here suggests.

most of his investment, but gained robust health and valuable experience. Wasting little sympathy on the Indians, he felt that the government had "erred quite as often on the side of too much leniency as on the side of too much severity." The following account, based in part on firsthand observations, appears in one of his earliest books. Note what light his observations cast on the allegation that the white man robbed the Indian of his lands, and appraise critically his proposed solution of the problem.

There are now no Indians left in my immediate neighborhood, though a small party of harmless Grosventres occasionally passes through. Yet it is but six years since the Sioux surprised and killed five men in a log station just south of me, where the Fort Keogh trail crosses the river; and, two years ago, when I went down on the prairies toward the Black Hills, there was still danger from Indians. That summer the buffalo hunters had killed a couple of Crows, and while we were on the prairie a long-range skirmish occurred near us between some Cheyennes and a number of cowboys. In fact, we ourselves were one day scared by what we thought to be a party of Sioux; but on riding toward them they proved to be half-breed Crees, who were more afraid of us than we were of them.

During the past century a good deal of sentimental nonsense has been talked about our taking the Indians' land. Now, I do not mean to say for a moment that gross wrong has not been done the Indians, both by government and individuals, again and again. The government makes promises impossible to perform, and then fails to do even what it might toward their fulfilment; and where brutal and reckless frontiersmen are brought into contact with a set of treacherous, revengeful, and fiendishly cruel savages a long series of outrages by both sides is sure to follow.

But as regards taking the land, at least from the Western Indians, the simple truth is that the latter never had any real ownership in it at all. Where the game was plenty, there they hunted; they followed it when it moved away to new hunting-grounds, unless they were prevented by stronger rivals; and to most of the land on which we found them they had no stronger claim than that of having a few years previously butchered the original occupants.

When my cattle came to the Little Missouri the region was only inhabited by a score or so of white hunters; their title to it was quite as good as that of most Indian tribes to the lands they claim; yet nobody dreamed of saying that these hunters owned the country. Each could eventually have kept his own claim of 160 acres, and no more.

The Indians should be treated in just the same way that we treat the white settlers. Give each his little claim; if, as would generally happen, he declined this, why then let him share the fate of the thousands of white hunters and trappers who have lived on the game that the settlement of the country has exterminated, and let him, like these whites, who will not work, perish from the face of the earth which he cumbers.

The doctrine seems merciless, and so it is; but it is just and rational for all that. It does not do to be merciful to a few, at the cost of justice to

THE INDIAN'S PORTION
Puck, 1880.

the many. The cattlemen at least keep herds and build houses on the land; yet I would not for a moment debar settlers from the right of entry to the cattle country, though their coming in means in the end the destruction of us and our industry.

4. Morgan Proposes Fair Treatment (1891)

The last significant Indian uprising occurred in South Dakota in 1890 among the Teton Sioux, whose reservations the government had cut in half. Half-starved by corrupt white agents, and faced with a searing drought, they engaged in frenzied "ghost dances" to bring back the good old days. A bungling intervention by the United States Army resulted in the massacre of some two hundred Sioux of both sexes and all ages at the "Battle" of Wounded Knee. Rapid-fire Hotchkiss guns rendered resistance hopeless. The next year Thomas Jefferson Morgan, an able and energetic Baptist minister serving as Commissioner of Indian Affairs, published the following recommendations, many of which were subsequently adopted. Observe whom he blames most for existing conditions; which of his proposed courses of action he regards as most important; and what his long-range goals are.

. . . There are certain things which the people of the United States will do well to remember.

First.—The people of this country during the past hundred years have spent enormous sums of money in Indian wars. These wars have cost us vast quantities of treasure and multitudes of valuable lives (besides greatly hindering the development of the country), have destroyed great numbers of Indians, and have wrought upon them incalculable disaster. The record which the nation has made for itself in this sanguinary conflict is not one to be proud of.

Second.—So long as the Indians remain in their present condition, the

4. T. J. Morgan, *The Present Phase of the Indian Question* (1891), pp. 18–21.

possibility of other wars, costly and dreadful, hangs over us as a perpetual menace. The recent [Ghost Dance] events have shown us how easy it is to spread alarm throughout our entire borders, and what fearful possibilities there are in store for us.

Third.—Indian wars are unnecessary, and if we will but take proper precautions, they may be entirely avoided in the future. Justice, firmness, kindness, and wisdom will not only prevent future wars, but will promote the prosperity and welfare of the Indians, as well as of the entire commonwealth.

Fourth.—We should remember that the circumstances surrounding the Indians are constantly, in many cases, aggravating the difficulties in the way of their procuring a proper supply of food; and that unless wise precautions are taken at once to assist them in the development of the resources of the lands upon which they are compelled to live, they will be confronted more and more with the dread spectre of hunger, and we with that of war. We are called upon not so much to feed them, as we are to make it possible for them to feed themselves.

Fifth.—The only possible solution of our Indian troubles lies in the suitable education of the rising generation. So long as the Indians remain among us aliens, speaking foreign languages, unable to communicate with us except through the uncertain and often misleading medium of interpreters, so long as they are ignorant of our ways, are superstitious and fanatical, they will remain handicapped in the struggle for existence, will be an easy prey to the medicine man and the false prophet, and will be easily induced, by reason of real or imaginary wrongs, to go upon the warpath. An education that will give them the mastery of the English language, train their hands to useful industries, awaken within them ambition for civilized ways, and develop a consciousness of power to achieve honorable places for themselves, and that arouses within them an earnest and abiding patriotism, will make of them American citizens, and render future conflicts between them and the government impossible.

Sixth.—Let it be especially remembered that the recent troubles [in South Dakota], deplorable as they have been, have been very small and insignificant compared with what they might have been; and that this has been brought about largely by the influence exerted upon the Indians through the schools of learning which have been established, and have already accomplished so much for their enlightenment and elevation. The influence for good exerted by the great school at Carlisle [Pennsylvania] alone, throughout the whole country, has been beyond estimate, and has repaid the government many times over every dollar that has been put into that institution.

Seventh.—It should be remembered that the time for making provision for the education of the entire body of Indian youth is now, and that any delay or postponement in the matter is hazardous and unwise.

Eighth.—In our judgment of the Indians and of the difficulties of the Indian question, we should remember that the most perplexing element in the problem is not the Indian, but the white man. The white man furnishes the Indian with arms and ammunition; the white man provides him with whiskey; the white man encroaches upon his reservation, robs him of his stock, defrauds him of his property, invades the sanctity of his home, and treats him with contempt, thus arousing within the Indian's breast those feelings of a sense of wrong, and dishonor, and wounded manhood that prepare him to vindicate his honor and avenge his wrongs.

In the late troubles in Dakota, the wrongs and outrages inflicted upon the Indians have vastly exceeded those inflicted by them upon the whites.

Ninth.—We should not forget that the prime object to be aimed at is the civilization of the Indians and their absorption into our national life, and that the agencies for the accomplishment of this work are not bayonets, but books. A schoolhouse will do vastly more for the Indians than a fort. It is better to teach the Indian to farm than to teach him to fight. Civil policemen are in every way to be preferred to Indian scouts, and we can much better afford to spend money in the employment of the Indians in useful industries, than to enroll them as soldiers in the army.

Tenth.—Finally, let us not forget what progress has already been made in this work of civilization; how potent are the forces now at work in preparing them for citizenship; how hopeful is the outlook if we, as a people, simply do our duty. Let us keep our faith with the Indian; protect him in his rights to life, liberty, and the pursuit of happiness; provide for all his children a suitable English and industrial education; throw upon them the responsibilities of citizenship, and welcome them to all the privileges of American freemen.

The end at which we aim is that the American Indians shall become as speedily as possible Indian-Americans; that the savage shall become a citizen; that the nomad shall cease to wander, and become a resident in a fixed habitation; that hunting shall cease to be a necessity, and become a pastime; that the smouldering fires of war shall become extinguished; that tribal animosities shall end; that the Indians, no longer joining in the "Sun Dance," or the "Ghost Dance," or other ceremonies in which they recount their wrongs and glory in the deeds of blood of their ancestors, shall gather at their firesides to talk of the memory of their days in school, and assemble in their places of worship to thank the Great Father above for the blessings of a Christian civilization vouchsafed to them in common with us all.

B. THE CRUSADE FOR FREE HOMESTEADS

1. "Vote Yourself a Farm" (1846)

Free homesteads from the public domain found a powerful champion in George H. Evans, an immigrant from England who became a pioneer editor of American labor journals. A confirmed atheist, he was preoccupied with "natural rights" to the

1. J. R. Commons *et al.*, eds., *A Documentary History of American Industrial Society* (1910), VII, 305–07. "Vote Yourself a Farm" was a Republican slogan in the Lincoln campaign of 1860.

soil. He hoped particularly to increase the wages of Eastern laborers by luring surplus workers onto free lands in the West. Characterize the general nature of his arguments in this handbill statement, and determine which of them seem least convincing.

Are you an American citizen? Then you are a joint-owner of the public lands. Why not take enough of your property to provide yourself a home? Why not vote yourself a farm?

Remember Poor Richard's saying: "Now I have a sheep and a cow, every one bids me 'good morrow.'" If a man have a house and a home of his own, though it be a thousand miles off, he is well received in other people's houses; while the homeless wretch is turned away. The bare right to a farm, though you should never go near it, would save you from many an insult. Therefore, Vote yourself a farm.

Are you a party follower? Then you have long enough employed your vote to benefit scheming office-seekers; use it for once to benefit yourself—Vote yourself a farm.

Are you tired of slavery—of drudging for others—of poverty and its attendant miseries? Then, Vote yourself a farm.

Are you endowed with reason? Then you must know that your right to life hereby includes the right to a place to live in—the right to a home. Assert this right, so long denied mankind by feudal robbers and their attorneys. Vote yourself a farm.

Are you a believer in the Scriptures? Then assert that the land is the Lord's, because He made it. Resist then the blasphemers who exact money for His work, even as you would resist them should they claim to be worshiped for His holiness. Emancipate the poor from the necessity of encouraging such blasphemy—Vote the freedom of the public lands.

Are you a man? Then assert the sacred rights of man—especially your right to stand upon God's earth, and to till it for your own profit. Vote yourself a farm.

Would you free your country, and the sons of toil everywhere, from the heartless, irresponsible mastery of the aristocracy of avarice? Would you disarm this aristocracy of its chief weapon, the fearful power of banishment from God's earth? . . . Therefore forget not to Vote yourself a farm.

2. A Texan Scorns Futile Charity (1852)

Agitation for free land continued to mount, and a homestead bill was introduced in Congress designed to donate 160 acres of land to every landless head of a family needing it. Easterners objected that this was a give-away scheme to benefit a few new Western states at the expense of the old states. It would drain off factory workers and hence push up wages and jeopardize prosperity. Critics further argued that the public domain, which was then being sold to replenish the Treasury, was the property of all the taxpayers and should not be given away to a favored few. Representa-

2. *Congressional Globe,* 32 Cong., 1 sess., Appendix, pp. 583–84. The safety-valve theory, popularly attributed to the historian Frederick J. Turner, antedated him by many years. As early as 1843 a British journal referred to "the safety-valve of western emigration" in America (*Quarterly Review,* LXXI, 522). Only a few Eastern mechanics moved to the West, but many incoming immigrants were attracted there who otherwise would have further congested the seaboard cities.

tive Howard of Texas aired additional objections in Congress. Assess them. Note what light his remarks cast on the "safety-valve theory": that is, that impoverished Eastern families could reduce economic distress and relieve class conflict by moving West and taking up cheap land.

But, sir, I deny the constitutional power of Congress to grant away the public property in donations to the poor. This government is not a national almshouse. We have no right to collect money by taxation and then divide the proceeds among the people generally, or those who are destitute of land, food, or raiment. . . .

There is no sound distinction between giving money by direct appropriations from the Treasury, and land, in the purchase of which [*e.g.*, Louisiana Purchase] that money has been invested. It is no more the property of the nation in one case than in the other, nor less an appropriation. What right have we to tax the property and industry of all classes of society to purchase homesteads, and enrich those who may not be the possessors of the soil? . . .

It is a great mistake to suppose that you will materially better the condition of the man in the old states, or the Atlantic cities, by giving him 160 acres of land in the Far West. The difficulty with him is not that of procuring the land, but to emigrate himself and family to the country where it is, and to obtain the means of cultivating it. Without this the grant is useless to the poor man.

The gift, to make it efficient, should be followed up by a further donation to enable the beneficiary to stock and cultivate it. It would be a far greater boon to all our citizens, of native and foreign origin, to furnish them, for a few dollars, a rapid means of reaching the land states in the West; and this, in my opinion, may be accomplished by exercising the legitimate powers of the government, and without drawing upon the Treasury, or diminishing the value of the public domain as a source of revenue.

3. Buchanan Kills a Homestead Bill (1860)

Free-soilers continued to argue that settlers not only had a "natural right" to Western land but that they should receive it as recompense for their own expense and sweat in taming the wilderness. In the 1850's homestead bills thrice passed the House, where the North was dominant, but all met defeat in the Senate, where the South was entrenched. Senator Wade of Ohio cried inelegantly in 1859 that it was "a question of land to the landless" while the Southern-sponsored bill to buy Cuba was "a question of niggers to the niggerless." Finally, in 1860, a compromise measure staggered through both Houses of Congress. It granted 160 acres of land to bona fide settlers who would pay the nominal sum of 25 cents an acre at the end of five years. President Buchanan, a Pennsylvanian under Southern influence, vetoed the measure. Comment critically on his views regarding unfairness to non-farmers and to the older states. Was he correct in arguing that such a law would undermine the nation's moral fiber?

4. This bill will prove unequal and unjust in its operation, because from its nature it is confined to one class of our people. It is a boon exclusively

3. J. D. Richardson, ed., *Messages and Papers of the Presidents* (1897), V, 611–14, *passim.*

conferred upon the cultivators of the soil. Whilst it is cheerfully admitted that these are the most numerous and useful class of our fellow citizens, and eminently deserve all the advantages which our laws have already extended to them, yet there should be no new legislation which would operate to the injury or embarrassment of the large body of respectable artisans and laborers. The mechanic who emigrates to the West and pursues his calling must labor long before he can purchase a quarter section of land, whilst the tiller of the soil obtains a farm at once by the bounty of the government. The numerous body of mechanics in our large cities cannot, even by emigrating to the West, take advantage of the provisions of this bill without entering upon a new occupation for which their habits of life have rendered them unfit.

5. This bill is unjust to the old states of the Union in many respects; and amongst these states, so far as the public lands are concerned, we may enumerate every state east of the Mississippi, with the exception of Wisconsin and a portion of Minnesota.

It is a common belief within their limits that the older states of the confederacy [Union] do not derive their proportionate benefit from the public lands. This is not a just opinion. It is doubtful whether they could be rendered more beneficial to these states under any other system than that which at present exists. Their proceeds go into the common Treasury to accomplish the objects of the government, and in this manner all of the states are benefited in just proportion. But to give this common inheritance away would deprive the old states of their just proportion of this revenue without holding out any, the least, corresponding advantage. Whilst it is our common glory that the new states have become so prosperous and populous, there is no good reason why the old states should offer premiums to their own citizens to emigrate from them to the West. That land of promise presents in itself sufficient allurements to our young and enterprising citizens without any adventitious aid.

The offer of free farms would probably have a powerful effect in encouraging emigration, especially from states like Illinois, Tennessee, and Kentucky, to the west of the Mississippi, and could not fail to reduce the price of property within their limits. An individual in states thus situated would not pay its fair value for land when, by crossing the Mississippi, he could go upon the public lands and obtain a farm almost without money and without price.

6. This bill will open one vast field for speculation. . . . Large numbers of actual settlers will be carried out by capitalists upon agreements to give them half of the land for the improvement of the other half. This cannot be avoided. Secret agreements of this kind will be numerous.* In the entry of graduated lands the experience of the Land Office justifies this objection. . . .

---

* Buchanan was right. Under the Homestead Act as finally passed, about ten acres were secured by speculators for every acre secured by a bona fide settler.

10. The honest poor man, by frugality and industry, can in any part of our country acquire a competence for himself and his family, and in doing this he feels that he eats the bread of independence. He desires no charity, either from the government or from his neighbors. This bill, which proposes to give him land at an almost nominal price out of the property of the government, will go far to demoralize the people and repress this noble spirit of independence. It may introduce among us those pernicious social theories which have proved so disastrous in other countries.

C. THE HOMESTEAD HOAX

1. Pre-emption Grafters (1858)

The Homestead Act at last passed in 1862, after Southern obstructionists had left Congress—and the Union. Actual settlers might obtain 160 acres of land free, if they lived on it for five years, cultivated it, and paid a fee of $10. They could also continue to pre-empt 160 acres by paying $1.25 an acre, and by swearing that the land was for their exclusive use and cultivation. After the required five years the settler would have to prove "by two credible witnesses" that he had lived on and cultivated the grant, and he would have to swear that he had not alienated it to others by secret sale or other collusion. This open invitation to fraud led to grave abuses of the type that A. D. Richardson had discovered in Kansas in 1858. Why was so much perjury tolerated on the frontier among presumably law-respecting people?

During this fall many residents were pre-empting their claims. The law contemplates a homestead of 160 acres at a nominal price for each actual settler and no one else; but land is plenty and everybody pre-empts. A young merchant, lawyer, or speculator rides into the interior, to the un-occupied public lands, pays some settler five dollars to show him the vacant claims, and selects one upon which he places four little poles around a hollow square upon the ground, as children commence a cob house. Then he files a notice in the land office that he has laid the foundation of a house upon this claim and begun a settlement for actual residence. He does not see the land again until ready to "prove up," which he may do after thirty days. Then he revisits his claim, possibly erects a house of rough slabs, costing from ten to twenty dollars, eats one meal, and sleeps for a single night under its roof. More frequently, however, his improvements consist solely of a foundation of four logs. . . .

In three cases out of four, after "proving up," the pre-emptor never visits his land again unless for the purpose of selling it. Says the Spanish proverb, "Oaths are words, and words are wind." Thus this unequivocal perjury is regarded upon the frontier. The general feeling is that it wrongs no one, and that the settlers have a right to the land.

Hundreds of men whose families are still in the East find witnesses to testify that their wives and children are residing upon the land. I have known men to pre-empt who had never been within twenty miles of their

1. A. D. Richardson, *Beyond the Mississippi* (1866), pp. 137–38, 140–41.

A BONA FIDE RESIDENCE

A removable house for fraudulent purposes. Illustration in A. B.
Richardson's *Beyond the Mississippi,* 1866.

claims, facile witnesses swearing with the utmost indifference that they
were residing upon them.

The pre-emptors must state under oath that they have made no agreement, direct or indirect, for selling any part of the land. But in numberless
instances these statements are falsehoods, connived at by the officers.

In most land offices a man cannot pre-empt unless he has a house at least
twelve feet square. I have known a witness to swear that the house in
question was twelve by fourteen when actually the only building upon the
claim was one whittled out with a penknife, twelve inches by fourteen.

Some officers require that the house must have a glass window. While
traveling in the interior I stopped at a little slab cabin where I noticed a
window sash without lights hanging upon a nail. As I had seen similar
frames in other cabins, I asked the owner what it was for.

"To pre-empt with," was the reply.

"How?"

"Why, don't you understand? To enable my witness to swear that there
is a window in my house!"

Sometimes the same cabin is moved from claim to claim until half a
dozen different persons have pre-empted with it. In Nebraska a little frame
house . . . was built for this purpose on wheels and drawn by oxen.
It enabled the pre-emptor to swear that he had a bona fide residence upon
his claim. It was let at five dollars a day, and scores of claims were proved
up and pre-empted with it. The discovery of any such malpractice and
perjury would invalidate the title. But I never knew of an instance where
the pre-emptor was deprived of his land after once receiving his title.

No woman can pre-empt unless she is a widow or the "head of a family."
But sometimes an ambitious maiden who wishes to secure 160 acres of land
borrows a child, signs papers of adoption, swears that she is the head of a
family, and pre-empts her claim, then annuls the papers and returns her
temporary offspring to its parents with an appropriate gift.

2. Going Broke in Kansas (1895)

The Homestead Act proved to be a bitter trap for thousands of honest settlers who pushed West to their "ultimate destitution." A farm of 160 acres could support a family in well-watered Illinois, but often not in the semi-arid West. A common saying on the frontier was that homesteading was a gamble: the government was "betting you 160 acres of land that you can't live on it five years." William Allen White, then twenty-seven years of age and just entering upon a distinguished journalistic career in Kansas, here describes a tragic scene. Comment critically on the observation that the homesteaders got their 160 acres "free."

There came through Emporia yesterday two old-fashioned "mover wagons," headed east. The stock in the caravan would invoice four horses, very poor and very tired; one mule, more disheartened than the horses; and one sad-eyed dog, that had probably been compelled to rustle his own precarious living for many a long and weary day.

A few farm implements of the simpler sort were in the wagon, but nothing that had wheels was moving except the two wagons. All the rest of the impedimenta had been left upon the battlefield, and these poor stragglers, defeated but not conquered, were fleeing to another field, to try the fight again.

These movers were from western Kansas—from Gray County, a county which holds a charter from the state to officiate as the very worst, most desolate, God-forsaken, man-deserted spot on the sad old earth. They had come from that wilderness only after a ten years' hard, vicious fight, a fight which had left its scars on their faces, had beat their bodies, had taken the elasticity from their steps, and left them crippled to enter the battle anew.

For ten years they had been fighting the elements. They had seen it stop raining for months at a time. They had heard the fury of the winter wind as it came whining across the short burned grass, and their children huddling in the corner. They have strained their eyes watching through the long summer days for the rain that never came. They have seen that big cloud roll up from the southwest about one o'clock in the afternoon, hover over the land, and stumble away with a few thumps of thunder as the sun went down. They have tossed through hot nights wild with worry, and have arisen only to find their worst nightmares grazing in reality on the brown stubble in front of their sun-warped doors.

They had such high hopes when they went out there; they are so desolate now—no, not now, for now they are in the land of corn and honey. They have come out of the wilderness, back to the land of promise. They are now in God's own country down on the Neosho, with their wife's folks, and the taste of apple butter and good cornbread and fresh meat and pie—pieplant pie like mother used to make—gladdened their shrunken palates last night. And real cream, curdling on their coffee saucers last night for supper, was a sight so rich and strange that it lingered in their dreams, wherein they walked beside the still water, and lay down in green pastures.

2. Emporia (Kansas) *Gazette*, June 15, 1895.

3. Wheat Bowls Become Dust Bowls (1883)

The topsoil of the semi-arid great plains, especially beyond the 100th meridian, was held down by tough prairie grass. Gradually much of this protective covering was eroded by overgrazing cattle and by the plainsman's plow. In periods of drought, dust storms blew up with increasing intensity. They culminated in the 1930's in the great dust-bowl tragedy, which ruined vast areas in a half-dozen or so states. A Western journalist here reconstructs the details of a scene which has long been legendary in the West.

One day in the spring of 1883 as a Scandinavian farmer, John Christiansen, plowed his fields in Montana's neighbor state of North Dakota, he looked up to find that he was being watched . . . by an old and solemn Sioux Indian.

Silently the old Indian watched as the dark soil curled up and the prairie grass was turned under. Christiansen stopped, leaned against the plow handle, pushed his black Stetson back on his head, rolled a cigarette. He watched amusedly as the old Indian knelt, thrust his fingers into the plow furrow, measured its depth, fingered the sod and the buried grass.

Then the old Indian straightened up, looked at the farmer.

"Wrong side up," he said, and went away.

For a number of years that was regarded as a very amusing story indeed, betraying the ignorance of the poor Indian. Now there's a marker on Highway No. 10 in North Dakota on the spot where the words were spoken—a little reminder to the white man that his red brother was not so dumb.

D. THE FARMERS' PROTEST MOVEMENT

1. An Iowan Assesses Discontent (1893)

Farm distress increased during the 1890's, to a large extent in the South but more spectacularly on the Western plains. The four "d's"—drought, debt, deflation, and depression—played their dismal role, but the basic trouble was overproduction of grain. The farmer simply could not control prices that were determined by the world supply, and he vented his spleen on whipping boys nearer at hand, notably the railroads. Freight rates had fallen substantially since the Civil War, but no rates seemed fair to a farmer whose grain prices were so low that he could not make a profit. And inequities persisted, despite the Interstate Commerce Act of 1887. A prominent Iowa journalist here analyzes some of the grievances which caused these hardy sons of the soil to beat their Farmers' Alliances into a political plowshare. Enumerate his complaints, and determine which one seems to be the most pressing.

Nothing has done more to injure the [Western] region than these freight rates. The railroads have retarded its growth as much as they first hastened it. The rates are often four times as large as Eastern rates. . . . The extortionate character of the freight rates has been recognized by all parties, and all have pledged themselves to lower them, but no state west of the Missouri has been able to do so.

3. J. K. Howard, *Montana: High, Wide, and Handsome* (1943), p. 14. By permission of the Yale University Press.
1. F. B. Tracy, "Why the Farmers Revolted," *The Forum*, XVI, 242–43 (Oct., 1893).

In the early days, people were so anxious to secure railways that they would grant any sort of concession which the companies asked. There were counties in Iowa and other Western states struggling under heavy loads of bond-taxes, levied twenty-five years ago, to aid railways of which not one foot has been built. Perhaps a little grading would be done, and then the project would be abandoned, the bonds transferred, and the county called upon by the "innocent purchaser" to pay the debt incurred by blind credulity. I have known men to sacrifice fortunes, brains, and lives in fighting vainly this iniquitous bond-swindle.

Railways have often acquired mines and other properties by placing such high freight rates upon their products that the owner was compelled to sell at the railroad company's own terms. These freight rates have been especially burdensome to the farmers, who are far from their selling and buying markets, thus robbing them in both directions.

Another fact which has incited the farmer against corporations is the bold and unblushing participation of the railways in politics. At every political convention their emissaries are present with blandishments and passes and other practical arguments to secure the nomination of their friends. The sessions of these legislatures are disgusting scenes of bribery and debauchery. There is not an attorney of prominence in Western towns who does not carry a pass or has not had the opportunity to do so. The passes, of course, compass the end sought. By these means, the railroads have secured an iron grip upon legislatures and officers, while no redress has been given to the farmer.

The land question, also, is a source of righteous complaint. Much of the land of the West, instead of being held for actual settlers, has been bought up by speculators and Eastern syndicates in large tracts. They have done nothing to improve the land and have simply waited for the inevitable settler who bought cheaply a small "patch" and proceeded to cultivate it. When he had prospered so that he needed more land, he found that his own labor had increased tremendously the value of the adjacent land. . . .

Closely connected with the land abuse are the money grievances. As his pecuniary condition grew more serious, the farmer could not make payments on his land. Or he found that, with the ruling prices, he could not sell his produce at a profit. In either case he needed money, to make the payment or maintain himself until prices should rise. When he went to the moneylenders, these men, often dishonest usurers, told him that money was very scarce, that the rate of interest was rapidly rising, etc., so that in the end the farmer paid as much interest a month as the moneylender was paying a year for the same money. In this transaction, the farmer obtained his first glimpse of the idea of "the contraction of the currency at the hands of Eastern money sharks."

Disaster always follows the exaction of such exorbitant rates of interest, and want or eviction quickly came. Consequently, when demagogues went among the farmers to utter their calamitous cries, the scales seemed to drop from the farmer's eyes, and he saw gold bugs, Shylocks, conspiracies, and criminal legislation *ad infinitum*. Like a lightning flash, the idea of political action ran through the Alliances. A few farmers' victories in county campaigns the previous year became a promise of broader conquest, and with one bound the Farmers' Alliance went into politics all over the West.

2. Mrs. Lease Raises More Hell (*c.* 1890)

As the plains seethed with protest, the Populist Party emerged from the Farmers' Alliance. Kansas spawned the most picturesque and vocal group of orators. A flaming speaker in great demand was the Irish-born Mrs. Mary E. Lease, a tall, magnetic lawyer known as a "Patrick Henry in Petticoats." Noting that corn was so cheap that it was being burned as fuel, she demanded the raising of less corn and "more hell." Noting also the disparity between the wealthy families and the people allegedly living out of garbage cans, she insisted on drastic measures. Separate her substantial grievances from her demagogic outpourings, and decide which of her complaints seem to be the most serious.

This is a nation of inconsistencies. The Puritans fleeing from oppression became oppressors. We fought England for our liberty and put chains on four million of blacks. We wiped out slavery and by our tariff laws and national banks began a system of white wage slavery worse than the first.

Wall Street owns the country. It is no longer a government of the people, by the people, and for the people, but a government of Wall Street, by Wall Street, and for Wall Street.

The great common people of this country are slaves, and monopoly is the master. The West and South are bound and prostrate before the manufacturing East.

Money rules, and our Vice-President is a London banker. Our laws are the output of a system which clothes rascals in robes and honesty in rags.

The parties lie to us and the political speakers mislead us. We were told two years ago to go to work and raise a big crop, that was all we needed. We went to work and plowed and planted; the rains fell, the sun shone, nature smiled, and we raised the big crop that they told us to; and what came of it? Eight-cent corn, ten-cent oats, two-cent beef, and no price at all for butter and eggs—that's what came of it.

Then the politicians said we suffered from overproduction. Overproduction, when 10,000 little children, so statistics tell us, starve to death every year in the United States, and over 100,000 shopgirls in New York are forced to sell their virtue for the bread their niggardly wages deny them.

Tariff is not the paramount question. The main question is the money question. . . . Kansas suffers from two great robbers, the Santa Fe Railroad and the loan companies. The common people are robbed to enrich their masters. . . .

We want money, land, and transportation. We want the abolition of the

2. Elizabeth N. Barr, "The Populist Uprising," in W. E. Connelley, ed., *History of Kansas, State and People* (1928), II, 1167. By permission of the Lewis Historical Publishing Company.

national banks, and we want the power to make loans direct from the government. We want the accursed foreclosure system wiped out. Land equal to a tract thirty miles wide and ninety miles long has been foreclosed and bought in by loan companies of Kansas in a year.

We will stand by our homes and stay by our fireside by force if necessary, and we will not pay our debts to the loan-shark companies until the government pays its debts to us. The people are at bay; let the bloodhounds of money who have dogged us thus far beware.

3. Godkin Sneers at the Populists (1892)

The embittered farmers and laborites, organized into the People's (Populist) Party, met in a frenzied convention in Omaha, Nebraska, in July, 1892. They nominated General James B. Weaver for President and adopted a scorching platform. In addition to other grievances, they pilloried corruption among politicians and judges, the subsidized and "muzzled" press, the impoverishment of labor, the shooting of strikers, and the hypocrisy of the two major parties. More specifically, the platform demanded distribution of monopolized land to actual settlers; government ownership of the telegraphs, telephones, and railroads ("the railroad corporations will either own the people or the people must own the railroads"); reduction of bloated fortunes by a graduated income tax; and inflation of the currency by issuing more paper money and coining all silver produced. Editor Godkin of the New York *Nation* viewed many of these schemes with the intolerant eye of a smug Easterner. How does his basic philosophy regarding the government square with that in vogue today?

The People's Party convention, which has just completed its sessions at Omaha, was the most largely attended and most thoroughly representative national gathering which any third party has ever got together. All sections of the country sent delegates, and the delegates were full of enthusiasm.

The dominant tone of the assembly was discontent with existing conditions. A large part of this discontent was the vague dissatisfaction which is always felt by the incompetent and lazy and "shiftless" when they contemplate those who have got on better in the world. But there was also manifested that spirit of doubt as to the tendencies of our social development of late years which is shared by many thoughtful and philosophic observers, and which causes such observers to question whether something should not be done to check these tendencies.

Practically the platform declares that everybody could be made happy if the government would print a vast quantity of paper currency, allow free coinage and foist light-weight silver dollars upon the country, establish an immense loaning agency, and take control of the railroads. In other words, the fundamental theory of the party is that the federal government is an institution of such omniscience and omnipotence, such a repository of wealth and wisdom, that it can be trusted with limitless power. In short, the theory holds that a paternal government can make all its children "healthy, wealthy, and wise."

General Weaver is the proper candidate for President of such a party.

3. *The Nation* (New York), LV, 1 (July 7, 1892).

He is a demagogue who came to the surface in the Greenback period, and was nominated for President by that element in 1880. He is the sort of man who is always ready to take up with any new organization which can give him either office or prominence, and no platform could be constructed so ridiculous that he would not gladly stand upon it.

[*In the presidential election of 1892 General Weaver suffered the fate of all third-party candidates in American history—overwhelming defeat at the hands of the old-line parties.*]

THOUGHT PROVOKERS

1. It has been said that there was no Indian problem, but a white problem; no Negro problem, but a white problem. Comment critically. Why did Canada have less trouble with the Indians than the United States? Has the Indian been treated fairly in our school textbooks?
2. Did the American people have a "natural right" to the free lands? Was selling the public land to replenish the Treasury sound in principle?
3. Would you agree that the Homestead Act was class legislation? How can you account for the wholesale fraud in connection with the Western lands? Why was the Homestead Act so long delayed? Did the East and South both have legitimate objections to it?
4. Farmers, to be successful, had to be good businessmen, and many failed because they were not. It was charged that they illogically put the blame for their failures on other factors. Comment. Other critics accused them of not doing well because they had fallen into habits of indolence. Would greater energy and larger harvests have cured the basic ills?

FURTHER EXPLORATION

General: R. A. Billington, *Westward Expansion* (1960); T. D. Clark, *Frontier America* (1959). **Red Man:** Paul Radin, *The Story of the American Indian* (1937); W. P. Webb, *The Great Plains* (1931); Francis Haines, *The Nez Percés* (1955); W. T. Hagan, *American Indians* (1961). **Free Homesteads:** R. M. Robbins, *Our Landed Heritage* (1950). **Homestead Hoax:** B. H. Hibbard, *A History of the Public Land Policies* (1924). **Farmers' Protest:** J. D. Hicks, *The Populist Revolt* (1955); F. A. Shannon, *The Farmers' Last Frontier* (1945); C. C. Taylor, *The Farmers' Movement, 1620–1920* (1953); Theodore Saloutos, *Farmer Movements in the South, 1865–1913* (1960).

Recent: G. C. Fite, *The Farmers' Frontier, 1865–1900* (1966); W. H. Leckie, *The Military Conquest of the Southern Plains* (1963); R. K. Andrist, *The Long Death; The Last Days of the Plains Indian* (1964); H. E. Fritz, *The Movement for Indian Assimilation, 1860–1890* (1963); Lewis Atherton, *The Cattle Kings* (1961); Rodman Paul, *Mining Frontiers of the Far West, 1848–1880* (1963); W. S. Greever, *The Bonanza West* (1963); C. V. Woodward, *The Strange Career of Jim Crow* (2nd ed. rev., 1966) [paperback]; Norman Pollack, *The Populist Response to Industrial America* (1962) [paperback]; R. F. Durden, *The Climax of Populism: The Election of 1896* (1965) [paperback]; Martin Ridge, *Ignatius Donnelly* (1962).

Chapter 30

Hard Times and Free Silver, 1889-1900

Bryan . . . has every crank, fool, and putative criminal in the country behind him, and a large proportion of the ignorant and honest class.

THEODORE ROOSEVELT, 1896

PROLOGUE: The Big Business Republicans, capitalizing on President Harrison's victory over Cleveland in 1888, passed the highly protective McKinley Tariff in 1890. It wiped out the troublesome surplus by putting sugar on the free list. It also supplemented Harrison's lavish pension program, which further depleted dwindling Treasury reserves. Reacting unfavorably to these extravagant Republican policies, the voters reinstated Cleveland in 1893. The panic which burst that year led to violent labor disturbances, notably the Pullman strike centering in Chicago. Cleveland incurred much abuse by sending federal troops there to restore order, and by making a secret bond deal with Wall Street to stem the alarming leakage of gold from the Treasury. To his unconcealed annoyance, all attempts at genuine tariff reform were frustrated by entrenched lobbyists in 1894. As the depression deepened, the underprivileged clutched desperately at the cure-all of free silver. It became the overshadowing issue in the class-struggle presidential campaign of 1896, in which the Republican McKinley emerged victorious over the Democratic (and allegedly demagogic) Bryan.

A. THE TARIFF ISSUE

1. McKinley Pleads for Protection (1890)

The amiable Republican Congressman McKinley, chairman of the House Ways and Means Committee, sponsored the tariff bill that bears his name. It carried protection to a new extreme. It not only protected "infant" industries but, in the case of tinplate, it extended protection to an industry yet unborn. The free list was delusively large, for it contained such inconsequential items as arsenic, stuffed birds, bladders, fossils, broken glass, salted guts, orchids, turtles, and manufactured teeth. As a sop to the farmer, new duties—largely unneeded—were levied on agricultural products. It has been said that for McKinley the tariff was a religious rather than an economic issue. Comment in the light of this excerpt from his speech in the House. Locate the fallacy in his argument in behalf of a tariff for American grain producers.

It has been asserted in the views of the [Democratic] minority that the duty put upon wheat and other agricultural products would be of no value to the agriculturists of the United States. The committee, believing differently, have advanced the duty upon these products.

As we are the greatest wheat-producing country of the world, it is

1. *Congressional Record*, 51 Cong., 1 sess., pp. 4249, 4255 (May 7, 1890).

571

habitually asserted and believed by many that this product is safe from foreign competition. We do not appreciate that while the United States last year raised 490,000,000 bushels of wheat, France raised 316,000,000 bushels, Italy raised 103,000,000 bushels, Russia 189,000,000 bushels, and India 243,000,000 bushels. . . . Our sharpest competition [in the world market] comes from Russia and India . . . and if we will only reflect on the difference between the cost of labor in producing wheat in the United States and in competing countries, we will readily perceive how near we are, if we have not quite reached, the danger line so far even as our own markets are concerned. . . .

It is also to be noted, Mr. Chairman, that having increased the duties on wools we have also increased the duties on the product—the manufactures of wool—to compensate for the increased duty on the raw product. . . .

If our trade and commerce are increasing and profitable within our own borders, what advantage can come from passing it by, confessedly the best market, that we may reach the poorest by distant seas? In the foreign market the profit is divided between our own citizen and the foreigner, while with the trade and commerce among ourselves the profit is kept in our own family and increases our national wealth and promotes the welfare of the individual citizen. Yet in spite of all the croaking about foreign trade, our exports were never so great as they are today. We send abroad what is not consumed at home, and we could do no more under any system. . . .

Experience has demonstrated that for us and ours, and for the present and the future, the protective system meets our wants, our conditions, promotes the national design, and will work out our destiny better than any other.

With me this position is a deep conviction, not a theory. I believe in it, and thus warmly advocate it because enveloped in it are my country's highest development and greatest prosperity. Out of it come the greatest gains to the people, the greatest comforts to the masses, the widest encouragement for manly aspirations, with the largest rewards, dignifying and elevating our citizenship, upon which the safety, and purity, and permanency of our political system depend.

2. Mills Challenges McKinley (1890)

Colonel Roger Q. Mills of Texas, twice severely wounded during his service in the Confederate army, had recently been chairman of the House Ways and Means Committee. A lawyer, a Democrat, and long an earnest advocate of a lowered tariff, he here contradicts the Republican McKinley in the simple yet eloquent style for which he was famous. Enumerate and evaluate his arguments against higher duties on agricultural products, and determine how convincingly he meets McKinley's allegation that a higher duty was needed to protect American grain.

The [Republican members of the] committee are greatly alarmed about our wheat-growers. That great industry is imperiled by "a most damaging

2. *Ibid.*, pp. 4260–61 (May 7, 1890).

competition". . . . They have increased the duty on wheat and that great product is safe.

How many bushels of wheat are imported into this country? We exported last year 90,000,000 bushels in wheat and flour . . . and last year . . . imported the inconsiderable amount of 1,946 bushels of wheat. And that duty has been put on to protect America's farmers against the damaging foreign competition from India and Russia.

What did that 1,946 bushels of wheat cost? Our wheat was at an average price of 89 cents per bushel, and the average price of the 1,946 bushels which we imported was $2.05. . . . What do you suppose that wheat was imported for? Do not all speak at once, please.

It was seed wheat, imported by the wheat-grower of the West to improve his seed. Does not every man know that? And you have made it cost him that much more to improve his agricultural product so that he can raise a better character of wheat and better compete in the markets of the world, where he has to meet all comers in free competition. . . .

We exported 69,000,000 bushels of corn last year and we imported into this country 2,388 bushels, an amount, we are told, that imperils the market of those who raise 2,000,000,000 bushels. . . .

How much rye did we import last year? Sixteen bushels! It could all have been raised on a turnip patch. . . .

The Germans, French, English, Spaniards, Austrians, and others with whom we are trading are dissatisfied with our discriminations against their products, and they have been taking steps to retaliate upon us. They have increased the duty on wheat in Germany two or three times since 1880. . . .

Why have we not the prices of 1881? Because we have cut off importation from our European customers, and they have cut off importation from us. Our surplus is increasing with our population, and we have no markets to consume it. What ought we to do?

We should reduce the duties on imports, put all raw materials on the free list, increase our importation four or five hundred millions more if we could, and thus increase our exports to that extent. That would raise the prices of agricultural products and the aggregate value of our annual crops $1,500,000,000 or $2,000,000,000 per year. That would distribute a large amount of wealth that would be expended in the employment of labor, and thus unbounded prosperity would be brought to the whole country.

Instead of this the committee have prepared a bill increasing taxes, raising duties, restricting importations, shutting in our farm products, and decreasing prices. They are going in the opposite direction and struggling to intensify the distress of the country.

3. The Sugar Trust Lobby (1894)

The high-duty McKinley Tariff of 1890 boomeranged against the Republicans, and the Democrat Grover Cleveland returned triumphantly to the White House in 1893.

3. *Senate Reports,* 53 Cong., 2 sess., X, pp. 656–57 (June 13, 1894).

An attempt to put sugar on the free list provoked powerful opposition from the lobby of the so-called Sugar Trust, and the "sugar Senators" succeeded in forcing a protective duty into the new Wilson-Gorman Tariff Bill of August, 1894. Ugly charges that the giant American Sugar Refining Company was exerting improper influence to secure tariff changes led to a grilling, by a Senate committee, of its president, the multimillionaire Henry O. Havemeyer. Note what was surprising about his revelations. Assess their propriety.

Senator ALLEN. I do understand you, however, to say and repeat that in states where you have a financial interest, at least where the sugar refining company has an interest as refiners, you do contribute to either the Democratic or Republican Party as one or the other may be in the ascendancy in that state?

Mr. HAVEMEYER. We do for local and state purposes, but not national.

Senator ALLEN. You never contribute to the campaign fund of a party in the minority?

Mr. HAVEMEYER. We may; I will not say we do not.

Senator ALLEN. Your policy, however, is to stand in with the ruling power?

Mr. HAVEMEYER. Not to "stand in" but to contribute to the campaign expenses of that party, for the reason that, they being in power and control, it could give us the protection we should have.

Senator ALLEN. And by that means you placate—

Mr. HAVEMEYER. Oh, no; there is no placation or obligation at all; nothing more than we consider the proper thing to do; everybody does it.

THE SOW THAT BREEDS THE LITTER

In Populist eyes the Wall Street Money Trust bred and fattened the other trusts, while the little pig representing the people lay dead. W. H. Harvey, *Coin's Financial School up to Date*, 1895.

Senator ALLEN. Does any other corporation in these same states do the same thing, that you know?

Mr. HAVEMEYER. I understand every individual, corporation, and firm in existence does it in their respective states.

Senator ALLEN. So the American Sugar Refining Company's politics, so far as its contributions to the campaign fund are concerned, is controlled by the political complexion of the state in which it happens to have a particular refinery?

Mr. HAVEMEYER. The American Sugar Refining Company has no politics of any kind.

Senator ALLEN. Only the politics of business?

Mr. HAVEMEYER. Only the politics of business.

Senator LINDSAY. You say the company is separate and distinct from the officers and stockholders; each man has his own politics?

Mr. HAVEMEYER. We have nothing to do with politics in any shape or manner. Our business is the refining of sugar at a slight profit that is consistent with a reasonable return on the industry.

[*The scandalous pressures of the various lobbies ("the third house of Congress") became so notorious that President Cleveland refused to sign the new Wilson-Gorman Tariff Bill. Additional scandals were aired in response to rumors that certain United States Senators had speculated in sugar stocks while the duty on sugar was under consideration. After an investigation, Senators McPherson of New Jersey and Quay of Pennsylvania admitted the charge. Senator Quay, a powerful and unsavory political boss, declared defiantly: "I do not feel that there is anything in my connection with the Senate to interfere with my buying or selling the stock when I please; and I propose to do so." Contrast this with present-day conflict-of-interest practices.*]

B. THE PULLMAN STRIKE

1. A Populist Condemns Pullman (1894)

George M. Pullman, who invented the popular upper-and-lower-berth Pullman Palace Car, made a fortune in manufacturing and controlling his brain child. A generous philanthropist with his millions, he built for his employees the model town of Pullman (now in Chicago). But when the depression came and the company slashed wages about 25 percent, the workers struck. They were joined by Eugene V. Debs' powerful American Railway Union. According to Debs, the management had said, "There is nothing to arbitrate." Senator Peffer, a Populist from Kansas who combed his long whiskers with his fingers while delivering even longer speeches, here presents his views. Ascertain what the two main grievances of the Pullman workers were, and whether they were legitimate.

Without going into all the details, I will state by way of preface that the Pullman Company established what most people in this world believed to be an ideal community, in which all the citizens should have equal rights, in which none should have special privileges. The object was to build a

1. *Congressional Record*, 53 Cong., 2 sess., p. 7231 (July 10, 1894).

community where the best modern scientific principles of hygiene, drainage, sewerage, grading, lighting, watering, and every other convenience should abound.

But while the company was doing that, while the world was looking on applauding, the company, like every other corporation of which I have ever known anything, held all of the power, all of the reins within its own grasp. That is to say, while there was sewerage, while there was light, while there was water, while there were parks, and all those desirable things, at the end of every month or of every week, as the case might be, when pay day came around, the charges that were set up against the residents of the town of Pullman for their lots and for their conveniences were deducted from their pay (just as the clothing of a soldier or extra rations or a lost gun were deducted from his pay) and the balance found to be due was paid to these people. Among these charges were rents and stated dues for the purchase of property.

After a while hard times began to pinch the company as it did everybody else, and it began to reduce the pay of the men. The men submitted patiently. Another reduction came and the men again submitted, only asking, however, that their rent charges should be reduced, that their taxes should be reduced, to correspond to the amount of reduction in their wages.

Then it was found that these poor people were absolutely defenseless, absolutely powerless in the hands of a corporation that had no soul. They asked to have a reduction of their rent charges and of other charges; they asked for a little time to turn around.

All these things were denied them. Finally, the Pullman citizens came to the conclusion that they might as well starve in defense of their rights as to starve while the proprietors of the town, the organizers and controllers of the corporation, were feasting on the fat things that these men had made for them. Now the trouble is on hand, and the leader of this great corporation [George M. Pullman] is off at the seashore, or on a lake, or on an island, or somewhere, refusing to entertain even a newspaper man, except to say, "I have nothing to say; the company at Chicago will look after the company's interest there"—heartless, soulless, conscienceless, Mr. President, this tyrant of tyrants.

2. Pullman Defends His Company (1894)

The bloody disorders attending the Pullman strike led to an investigation by the United States Strike Commission. George M. Pullman took the stand and testified that his company had undertaken to manufacture cars at a loss so as to keep his men employed. But he conceded that it was better to operate at a slight loss than to incur the larger losses resulting from idle factories. He also testified that the salaries of management (including his own) had not been cut; that the Pullman Company still had about $25,000,000 in undivided profits; and that the dividends paid to stockholders had ranged from 12% to the current 8%. United States Commissioner Worthington extracted the following information from Pullman. Evaluate

2. *Senate Executive Documents*, 53 Cong., 3 sess., II, No. 7, pp. 555–56.

the soundness of Pullman's position on arbitration. How does his general business philosophy square with that prevalent today in America?

Commissioner WORTHINGTON. Now, let me ask you right there, Mr. Pullman, what do you see that is objectionable, in a business point of view, under the existing state of affairs, . . . in submitting to disinterested persons the question as to whether under all the circumstances wages might not be increased somewhat of your employees?

Mr. PULLMAN. I think I have made that as plain in this [written] statement as I can make it if I should repeat it a thousand times.

Commissioner WORTHINGTON. Is that the only reason you can give?

Mr. PULLMAN. What do you mean by that, "The only reason"?

Commissioner WORTHINGTON. The reason you give here (in the statement), "It must be clear to every businessman and to every thinking workman that no prudent employer could submit to arbitration the question whether he should commit such a piece of business folly." Is that the only answer to it?

Mr. PULLMAN. Well, now, I have a little memorandum here which is practically the same thing on the question of arbitration. Of course there are matters which are proper subjects of arbitration—matters of opinion.

Commissioner WORTHINGTON. What are those matters that are proper subjects for arbitration?

Mr. PULLMAN. A matter of opinion would be a proper subject of arbitration, as, for instance, a question of title, or a disagreement on a matter of opinion. . . . But as to whether a fact that I know to be true is true or not, I could not agree to submit to arbitration. Take the case in hand: the question as to whether the shops at Pullman shall be continuously operated at a loss or not is one which it was impossible for the company, as a matter of principle, to submit to the opinion of any third party; and as to whether they were running at a loss on contract work in general, as explained to the committee of the men in my interview with them—that was a simple fact that I knew to be true, and which could not be made otherwise by the opinion of any third party.

Commissioner WORTHINGTON. You use the expression, "Impossible to be submitted." Why is it impossible?

Mr. PULLMAN. Because it would violate a principle.

Commissioner WORTHINGTON. What principle?

Mr. PULLMAN. The principle that a man should have the right to manage his own property.

Commissioner WORTHINGTON. The decision of arbitrators would not be compulsory, would it?

Mr. PULLMAN. I still think, having managed the property of the Pullman Company for twenty-seven years, that I am perhaps as well calculated to manage it for the interests of its stockholders and for the interests of the public—for the general interest—as some man who is not interested, who comes in to arbitrate certain points.

3. Starvation at Pullman (1894)

The Pullman strike was finally broken by federal bayonets, and the Company allegedly imported more docile workers to replace those who had struck. A group signing themselves "The Starving Citizens of Pullman" appealed to Governor Altgeld of Illinois for relief. After examining conditions personally, the Governor wrote the following letter to George M. Pullman. Ascertain whether the evidence here given supports the charge of discrimination.

Sir: I examined the conditions at Pullman yesterday, visited even the kitchens and bedrooms of many of the people. Two representatives of your company were with me and we found the distress as great as it was represented. The men are hungry and the women and children are actually suffering. They have been living on charity for a number of months and it is exhausted. Men who had worked for your company for more than ten years had to apply to the relief society in two weeks after the work stopped.

I learn from your manager that last spring there were 3,260 people on the payroll; yesterday there were 2,220 at work, but over 600 of these are new men, so that only about 1,600 of the old employees have been taken back, thus leaving over 1,600 of the old employees who have not been taken back. A few hundred have left, the remainder have nearly all applied for work, but were told that they were not needed. These are utterly destitute. The relief committee on last Saturday gave out two pounds of oatmeal and two pounds of cornmeal to each family. But even the relief committee has exhausted its resources.

Something must be done and at once. The case differs from instances of destitution found elsewhere, for generally there is somebody in the neighborhood able to give relief; this is not the case at Pullman. Even those who have gone to work are so exhausted that they cannot help their neighbors if they would. I repeat now that it seems to me your company cannot afford to have me appeal to the charity and humanity of the state to save the lives of your old employees. Four-fifths of those people are women and children. No matter what caused this distress, it must be met.

[*Mr. Pullman turned a deaf ear to appeals for relief, and humane citizens were forced to help the destitute. "Mr. Dooley" (F. P. Dunne) referred to the time "whin God quarried his heart. . . ." Reconcile Pullman's attitude in this instance with his large private philanthropies, including a bequest of $1,200,000 for a free manual training school in Pullman.*]

C. THE FREE–SILVER MIRAGE

1. Coin's Financial School (1894)

By the 1880's and 1890's indebted Americans, especially the farmers, were caught in a deflationary pinch. A cry arose for inflating the currency by abandoning the

---

3. John P. Altgeld, *Live Questions* (1899), pp. 422–23 (Aug. 21, 1894).
1. W. H. Harvey, *Coin's Financial School* (1894), pp. 130–33, *passim.*

single gold standard and restoring the bimetallic gold-silver standard, dropped by Congress in 1873 ("the Crime of '73"). The silverites specifically demanded the free and unlimited coinage of silver in the ratio of sixteen ounces of silver to one ounce of gold, despite Britain's adherence to the gold standard. William Hope Harvey, a frustrated silver-mine operator from Colorado, came to Chicago and in 1894 published his best-selling tract *Coin's Financial School.* His fictional account tells how Coin, the boy wizard of Chicago, conducted a six-day financial school attended by many leading figures, whom he converted to the gospel of free silver. The 174-page booklet, cleverly but deceptively illustrated, sold upwards of a million copies and was a major propaganda weapon in the free-silver crusade. From Harvey's inflammatory pamphlet determine why he (like other silverites) was bitter against England, and why the proposed international agreement on bimetallism had little prospect of realization.

His [Coin's] appearance upon the platform was the signal for an ovation. He had grown immensely popular in those last five days.

He laid his silk hat on the table, and at once stepped to the middle of the platform. He raised his eyes to the audience, slowly turned his head to the right and left, and looked into the sea of faces that confronted him.

"In the midst of plenty, we are in want," he began. "Helpless children and the best womanhood and manhood of America appeal to us for release from a bondage that is destructive of life and liberty. All the nations of the Western Hemisphere turn to their great sister republic for assistance in the emancipation of the people of at least one-half the world.

"The Orient, with its teeming millions of people, and France, the cradle of science and liberty in Europe, look to the United States to lead in the struggle to roll back the accumulated disasters of the last twenty-one years [since "the Crime of '73"]. What shall our answer be? [Applause.]

"If it is claimed we must adopt for our money the metal England selects [gold], and can have no independent choice in the matter, let us make the test and find out if it is true. It is not American to give up without trying. If it is true, let us attach England to the United States and blot her name out from among the nations of the earth. [Applause.]

"A war with England would be the most popular ever waged on the face of the earth. [Applause.] If it is true that she can dictate the money of the world, and thereby create world-wide misery, it would be the most just war ever waged by man. [Applause.]

"But fortunately this is not necessary. Those who would have you think that we must wait for England, either have not studied this subject, or have the same interest in continuing the present conditions as England. It is a vain hope to expect her voluntarily to consent. England is the creditor nation of the globe, and collects hundreds of millions of dollars in interest annually in gold from the rest of the world. We are paying her two hundred millions yearly in interest. She demands it in gold; the contracts call for it in gold. Do you expect her to voluntarily release any part of it? It has a purchasing power twice what a bimetallic currency would have. She knows it. . . .

"Whenever property interests and humanity have come in conflict,

UNCLE SAM: "IT WON'T WORK WITHOUT
A NEW WHEEL."

A specious argument for bimetallism. W. H. Harvey, *Coin's Financial School Up to Date*, 1895.

England has ever been the enemy of human liberty. All reforms with those so unfortunate as to be in her power have been won with the sword. She yields only to force. [Applause.]

"The moneylenders in the United States, who own substantially all of our money, have a selfish interest in maintaining the gold standard. They, too, will not yield. They believe that if the gold standard can survive for a few years longer, the people will get used to it—get used to their poverty—and quietly submit.

"To that end they organize international bimetallic committees and say, 'Wait on England, she will be forced to give us bimetallism.' Vain hope! Deception on this subject has been practiced long enough upon a patient and outraged people."

2. A "Gold Bug" Defends Britain (1895)

"Coin" Harvey's pamphlets inspired both imitations and rebuttals. Among the more prominent critics was a New York international lawyer, Everett P. Wheeler, who, despite an interest in a silver mine, attacked Harvey. He had served as counsel for a company doing business in Central America, where the silver standard had caused his clients inconvenience and loss. How convincing is his argument that the ruin of England would not operate to the benefit of America?

Coin [Harvey] resorts to the familiar and well-worn appeal to the prejudice which some people in this country are supposed to feel against England.

The people of that country have the same religion, the same laws, and the same language as ourselves. We did fight in years gone by, but we are now united by the close ties of business and friendship. The English octopus, as Coin calls it, is really a country that is our best customer for wheat, for cotton, for beef, for petroleum, and for Yankee notions.

He says it "feeds on nothing but gold." In fact, however, it feeds on the wheat, the coffee, the sugar of South America, the tea of China; in short,

2. E. P. Wheeler, *Real Bi-Metallism or True Coin versus False Coin* (1895), pp. 69–70, 73.

the natural or manufactured products of every part of the world, all of which it pays for. Along its arms, steamers ply, freighted with the merchandise which is the subject of this mutual trade, which benefits both parties. Telegraphic cables thread the bottom of the sea to its head, carrying messages of business and of friendship. American investors draw great sums in royalties from this "octopus". . . .

In short, the whole octopus business, like the other delectable illustrations in Coin's school, is a delusion and a snare. The worst thing that could happen to this country would be the ruin of England. No merchant would look with satisfaction on the ruin of his best customer or want to quarrel with him.

Another favorite argument of the free-silver advocates is that England first adopted the gold standard and has grown rich by it, and that therefore it must be bad for other countries.

Let us note two things in this connection.

1. England first adopted trial by jury, and the writ of *habeas corpus*. She first enforced the principle of freedom that no man should be deprived of life, liberty, or property but by the judgment of his peers, or the law of the land. Shall we discard these sacred muniments of liberty because they are of English origin?

2. If England has prospered under the gold standard, why not the United States? Certainly no country ever became really prosperous by the ruin of its neighbors. In the great commonwealth of nations, the prosperity of one makes trade with all, and helps to enrich all.

D. THE FREE–SILVER CONVENTION

1. Tillman Repudiates Cleveland (1896)

Negro-baiting Benjamin R. Tillman (see p. 474) had recently emerged as the demagogic champion of the poor white farmers of South Carolina. Rabidly opposed to President Cleveland's conservative gold policy, he had run successfully for the United States Senate in 1894, shouting, "Send me to Washington and I'll stick my pitchfork into his [Cleveland's] old ribs!" He was vehement in denouncing Cleveland's secret bond deal with the Wall Street bankers. Aspiring to the Democratic presidential nomination as a silverite, he ruined his chances at the Chicago convention by the following violent speech attacking the Cleveland administration. During this harangue he paced the platform like a madman. Enumerate his grievances against Cleveland, and ascertain which one seems to rankle the deepest.

When this convention disperses, I hope my fellow citizens will have a different opinion of the man with the pitchfork from South Carolina. I am from South Carolina, which was the home of secession. [Great hissing.] Oh, hiss if you like. There are only three things on earth which can hiss— a goose, a serpent, and a man, and the man who hisses the name of South Carolina has no knowledge whatever of its grand history.

But I tell you I do not come from the South Carolina of 1860, which you

1. *Public Opinion*, XXI, 69–70 (July 16, 1896). The speech was delivered on July 9.

charge brought about the disruption of the Democratic Party. The war there declared was for the emancipation of the black slaves. I come now from a South Carolina which demands the emancipation of the white slaves. You charge that in 1860 South Carolina brought about the disruption of the Democratic Party. I say to you now that I am willing to see the Democratic Party disrupted again to accomplish the emancipation of the white slaves.

New York for twenty years or more has been the one dominant factor and dictator of the National Democratic Party. While we want to thank New York and Connecticut and New Jersey for the aid extended to us in the past, I want to say to you here that we have at last recognized in the South that we are mere hewers of wood and drawers of water, while the great states I have named have eaten up our substance. My friends say this is not a sectional issue. I say it is. . . .

[*Great scenes of disorder then ensued, and quiet was restored with difficulty. Many times the Senator was interrupted, but he went on:*]

As Grover Cleveland stands for gold monometallism, we have repudiated him. We are diametrically opposed to his policy, and why should we write ourselves down as asses and liars? They ask us to say that he is honest. Well, in reply I say he signed a contract for bonds in secret, with one of his partners as a witness. Nobody disputes his boldness or obstinacy. He had the courage to overthrow the Constitution of the United States when he overrode the rights of the citizens of Illinois [during the Pullman strike] and sent federal troops into this state. You ask us to indorse his fidelity. In reply, I say he has been faithful unto death—the death of the Democratic Party. We have denounced him in South Carolina as a tool of Wall Street, and what was prophecy then is history now. . . .

I tell you that the Democratic Party of the United States will turn out the party in this fall's election if it dares indorse Grover Cleveland here. I tell you you dare not go before this country after indorsing the Cleveland administration. We of the South have burned our bridges behind us so far as the Eastern Democrats are concerned. We have turned our faces to the West and they have responded.

2. Senator Hill Urges Sanity (1896)

The gold-standard Democrats, supporting Cleveland, were clearly outnumbered in the wildly shouting Chicago convention. The ranks of the silverite majority were swelled by Populists and by free-silver men who had deserted the gold-standard Republican Party. The Chicago "assembly of lunatics"—so called by the Republican New York *Tribune*—uproariously endorsed the platform reported by a majority of the resolutions committee. It endorsed the well-known Populist scheme of freely coining, at the ratio of 16 to 1, all silver mined. Dissenting Senator David B. Hill of New York, an adroit machine politician bitten by the presidential bug, here speaks

2 *Ibid.,* XXI, 70 (July 16, 1896). The speech was delivered on July 9.

logically but vainly for the gold-standard minority on the resolutions committee. After the convention, he reputedly said, "I am a Democrat still—very still." Note what his solution of the problem is and why he proposes it.

I am a Democrat, but I am not a revolutionist. My mission here today is to unite, not to divide—to build up, not to destroy—to plan for victory, not to plot for defeat. The question which this convention is to decide is: What is the best position to take at this time on the financial question? In a word, the question presented is between international bimetallism and local bimetallism. If there are any different points in it, they are not represented either in the majority or in the minority report.

I therefore start out with this proposition, that the Democratic Party stands today in favor of gold and silver as the money of the country; that it stands in favor neither of a silver standard nor of a gold standard, but that we differ as to the means to bring about the result.

Those whom I represent and for whom I speak—the sixteen minority members of the committee—insist that we should not attempt the experiment of the free and unlimited coinage of silver without cooperation of other great nations. It is not a question of patriotism, it is not a question of courage, it is not a question of loyalty, as the majority platform speaks of it. The minority has thought it was simply a question as to whether we were able to enter on this experiment. It is a question of business. It is a question of finance. . . .

I think, Mr. President, that the safest and best course for this convention to have pursued was to take the first step forward in the great cause of monetary reform by declaring in favor of international bimetallism. I know that it is said by enthusiastic friends that America can mark out a course for herself. I know that that idea appeals to the pride of the average American, but I beg to remind you that if that suggestion be carried out to its legitimate conclusion, you might as well do away with our international treaties. . . .

Be not deceived. Do not attempt to drive those Democrats out of the party who have grown gray in its service, in order to make room for a lot of Republicans and Populists who will not vote your ticket at all. My friends, I speak more in sorrow than in anger.

[*A resolution backed by Hill and approving the Democratic administration of President Cleveland was voted down by a face-slapping vote of 564 to 357.*]

3. Bryan's Cross of Gold (1896)

The dramatic assignment of replying to Senator Hill and closing the debate on the platform fell to William Jennings Bryan of Nebraska. Although a well-known ex-Congressman and free-silver orator, he was not then regarded as one of the front runners for the presidential nomination. Tall, lean, smooth-shaven, hawk-nosed, and wide-mouthed, "the Boy Orator of the Platte" hushed the vast assemblage of some 15,000 with his masterful presence. The "cross of gold" analogy to the crucifixion of

3. C. M. Depew, ed., *The Library of Oratory* (1902), XIV, 415, 418, 420–25, *passim.*

Christ he had already used a number of times, but never so effectively. Projecting his organ-like voice to the outer reaches of the vast hall, he had the frenzied crowd cheering his every sentence as he neared the end. The climax swept the delegates off their feet and won Bryan the presidential nomination the next day. In accounting for the success of his memorable speech, analyze the different kinds of prejudice to which Bryan appeals.

I would be presumptuous, indeed, to present myself against the distinguished gentlemen to whom you have listened if this were a mere measuring of abilities. But this is not a contest between persons. The humblest citizen in all the land, when clad in the armor of a righteous cause, is stronger than all the hosts of error. I come to speak to you in defense of a cause as holy as the cause of liberty—the cause of humanity. . . .

We [silverites] do not come as aggressors. Our war is not a war of conquest. We are fighting in the defense of our homes, our families, and posterity. We have petitioned, and our petitions have been scorned. We have entreated, and our entreaties have been disregarded. We have begged, and they have mocked when our calamity came. We beg no longer; we entreat no more; we petition no more. We defy them! . . .

The gentleman from New York [Senator Hill] . . . says he wants this country to try to secure an international agreement. Why does he not tell us what he is going to do if he fails to secure an international agreement? . . . Our opponents have tried for twenty years to secure an international agreement, and those are waiting for it most patiently who do not want it at all. . . .

We go forth confident that we shall win. Why? Because upon the paramount issue of this campaign there is not a spot of ground upon which the enemy will dare to challenge battle. If they [the Republicans] tell us that the gold standard is a good thing, we shall point to their platform and tell them that their platform pledges the party to get rid of the gold standard and substitute bimetallism. If the gold standard is a good thing, why try to get rid of it? . . .

Mr. Carlisle* said in 1878 that this was a struggle between "the idle holders of idle capital" and "the struggling masses, who produce the wealth and pay the taxes of the country"; and, my friends, the question we are to decide is: upon which side will the Democratic Party fight—upon the side of "the idle holders of idle capital" or upon the side of "the struggling masses"? That is the question which the party must answer first, and then it must be answered by each individual hereafter. The sympathies of the Democratic Party, as shown by the platform, are on the side of the struggling masses who have ever been the foundation of the Democratic Party.

There are two ideas of government. There are those who believe that, if you will only legislate to make the well-to-do prosperous, their prosperity will leak through on those below. The Democratic idea, however, has been

---

* John G. Carlisle of Kentucky, formerly a distinguished member of Congress, was Cleveland's Secretary of the Treasury in 1896.

that if you legislate to make the masses prosperous, their prosperity will find its way up through every class which rests upon them.

You come to us and tell us that the great cities are in favor of the gold standard. We reply that the great cities rest upon our broad and fertile prairies. Burn down your cities and leave our farms, and your cities will spring up again as if by magic. But destroy our farms, and the grass will grow in the streets of every city in the country.

My friends, we declare that this nation is able to legislate for its own people on every question, with-

"YOU SHALL NOT PRESS DOWN UPON THE BROW OF LABOR *this* CROWN"

A parody of Bryan's famous crown-of-thorns speech, with Bryan pressing down the fifty-cent "bunco dollar." *Harper's Weekly,* 1896.

out waiting for the aid or consent of any other nation on earth; and upon that issue we expect to carry every state in the Union. I shall not slander the inhabitants of the fair state of Massachusetts nor the inhabitants of the state of New York by saying that, when they are confronted with the proposition, they will declare that this nation is not able to attend to its own business. It is the issue of 1776 over again. Our ancestors, when but three millions in number, had the courage to declare their political independence of every other nation. Shall we, their descendants, when we have grown to seventy millions, declare that we are less independent than our forefathers?

No, my friends, that will never be the verdict of our people. Therefore, we care not upon what lines the battle is fought. If they say bimetallism is good but that we cannot have it until other nations help us, we reply that, instead of having a gold standard because England has, we will restore bimetallism, and then let England have bimetallism because the United States has it. If they dare to come out in the open field and defend the gold standard as a good thing, we will fight them to the uttermost.

Having behind us the producing masses of this nation and the world, supported by the commercial interests, the laboring interests, and the toilers everywhere, we will answer their demand for a gold standard by saying to them: You shall not press down upon the brow of labor this crown of thorns; you shall not crucify mankind upon a cross of gold.

[*The Cleveland Democrats, with their devotion to the gold standard, were appalled by the nomination of Bryan. "What a burlesque on a Democratic convention," wrote Postmaster General Wilson in his diary. "May God help the country!" He stressed the youth, ambition, and Populist leanings of the candidate, while noting that Bryan's "utter ignorance of the great diplomatic, financial, and other questions a President has constantly to dispose of, will be lost sight of in the fanaticism of the one idea he represents." (F. P. Summers,* The Cabinet Diary of William L. Wilson, 1896–1897 *[1957], p. 116.) Conservatives, then and later, generally agreed that Bryan was strong on sound but weak on substance.*]

E. THE TRIUMPH OF McKINLEY

1. The "Anarchists" Lose Out (1896)

Bryan's whirlwind campaign for free silver gained such momentum in the early stages that he might have won if the election had been held two months earlier. But frightened "gold-bug" Republicans opened wide their purses, and the subsequent deluge of propaganda helped bring victory to William McKinley, the Republican candidate. Many of the gold-standard Cleveland Democrats spurned Bryan and contributed actively to McKinley's victory. The "gold-bug" East stressed the presence in Bryan's camp of such radicals as Eugene V. Debs, who had headed the Pullman strike of 1894, and Governor Altgeld of Illinois, who had pardoned the three surviving Haymarket Riot anarchists. Note in what respects this editorial in the New York *Nation* is least fair.

We have escaped from what a large number of people supposed was an immense danger, the danger of having our currency adulterated and our form of government changed, and a band of ignoramuses and anarchists put at the head of what remained of the great American republic. Probably no man in civil life has succeeded in inspiring so much terror, without taking life, as Bryan. Attila and Tamerlane frightened more people, but they killed or threatened to kill them; they hardly destroyed more property.

Bryan succeeded in persuading hundreds of thousands that the great fabric of government which was built up by the wisdom of experience of a thousand years, and cemented by hundreds of thousands of lives, was, almost in the first century of its existence, about to be handed over by the vote of its own people to a knot of silly, half-taught adventurers and anarchists. We were to exchange the Constitution and the Supreme Court for the decrees of Altgeld and Debs and Bryan and Teller, whose principal occupation was to be striking off "cheap money for the poor man."

The whole episode has been utterly discreditable to our politics, as conducted by politicians. Could anything better reveal the character of our nominating system than the fact that the nominating convention of one of our two great parties could be taken possession of by a few adventurers,

1. *The Nation* (New York), LXIII, 337 (Nov. 5, 1896).

that the platform could be drawn, in the main, by a noted anarchist [Altgeld], and an unknown young man nominated on it simply because the audience was pleased with one of his metaphors, and that it should drive away from it all the party's men of light and leading before going to the country?

2. Bryan's Afterthoughts (1896)

While his memory of the campaign was still fresh, Bryan recorded his impressions. His then unprecedented 600 speeches and his 18,000 miles of sweaty travel must have left him in something of a daze. On the basis of his account comment critically on the ethics of the opposition, on the intellectual level of the campaign, and on the assumption that the canvass was a crusade rather than a campaign.

The reminiscences of the campaign of 1896 form such a delightful chapter in memory's book that I am constrained to paraphrase a familiar line and say that it is better to have run and lost than never to have run at all. . . .

Unless I am mistaken, the deep awakening among the people during the campaign just closed will result in a more careful study of political questions by both men and women, and in a more rigid scrutiny of the conduct of public officials by those whom they serve. No matter what may be the ultimate outcome of the struggle over the financial question, better government will result from the political interest which has been aroused. . . .

During the campaign I ran across various evidences of coercion, direct and indirect. One of the most common means of influencing voters was the advertising of orders placed with manufacturers, conditioned upon Republican success at the polls. The following is an illustration. Tuesday morning, November 3rd, there appeared at the head of the last column of the first page of the *Morning News*, of Wilmington, Del.:

CONTINGENT ORDERS.

The Harlan and Hollingsworth Company, of this city, have received a contract for a boat costing $300,000. One clause in the contract provides that in the event of Bryan's election the contract shall be canceled. If the boat is built here, $160,000 of its cost would be paid to Wilmington workmen for wages. The corporation wanting the boat feel that it would not be justified in having it constructed if Bryan should become President. . . .

I may mention a still more forcible means adopted by many employers. The workingmen were paid off Saturday night before election and notified

2. W. J. Bryan, *The First Battle* (1896), pp. 612–24, *passim*.

that they might expect work Wednesday morning in case of Mr. McKinley's election, but that they need not return if I was elected. Whether the employers themselves were actually afraid or whether they merely intended to frighten their employees, the plan worked admirably and exerted a most potent influence on election day....

MONEY TALKS

"No, Mr. McKinley will not make any campaign speeches, but there will be other eloquent speakers in the field." Mark Hanna [Republican National Chairman]. A reference to the common assumption that Hanna's lavish use of money swung the election. Buffalo *Times*, 1896.

The ratio of 16 to 1 was scrupulously adhered to during the campaign, and illustrated with infinite variety. At one place our carriage was drawn by sixteen white horses and one yellow horse; at any number of places we were greeted by sixteen young ladies dressed in white and one dressed in yellow, or by sixteen young men dressed in white and one dressed in yellow. But the ratio was most frequently represented in flowers, sixteen white chrysanthemums and one yellow one being the favorite combination....

It is impossible to chronicle all the evidences of kindly feeling given during the campaign; in fact the good will manifested and the intense feeling shown impressed me more than any other feature of the campaign. When the result was announced my composure was more endangered by the sorrow exhibited by friends than it was during all the excitement of the struggle. Men broke down and cried as they expressed their regret, and there rises before me now the face of a laboring man of Lincoln, who, after he dried his tears, held out his hand from which three fingers were missing, and said: "I did not shed a tear when those were taken off."

People have often lightly said that they would die for a cause, but it may be asserted in all truthfulness that during the campaign just closed there were thousands of bimetallists who would have given their lives, had their lives been demanded, in order to secure success to the principles which they advocated. Surely, greater love hath no man than this....

I am proud of the character of my support. Those who voted for me did so of their own volition; neither coercion nor purchase secured their suffrages; their confidence and good will robbed defeat of all its pangs.

3. The London *Standard* Rejoices (1896)

William McKinley, the high priest of high protection, had expected to emphasize the tariff in the campaign, but Bryan took the play away from him with free silver. The business world on both sides of the Atlantic, unwilling to be paid off in fifty-cent silver dollars, rejoiced over the Republican triumph. London reported that mil-

3. Quoted in *Public Opinion*, XXI, 623 (Nov. 12, 1896).

lions of dollars' worth of orders from the United States had been placed in England contingent on Bryan's defeat. In examining the comments of the London *Standard*, explain why this journal was not altogether happy.

The complete rejection of Bryan's tempting program, addressed to indolence, incapacity, and cupidity, shows that these qualities are less widely distributed in the United States than Bryan would have us believe. There has been a revolt of the honest and loyal citizens, who are solicitous for the fair name and fame of the Republic, and the Bryanites astonished the world by the comparative paucity of their numbers. The hopelessly ignorant and savagely covetous waifs and strays of American civilization voted for Bryan, but the bulk of the solid sense, business integrity, and social stability sided with McKinley. The nation is to be heartily congratulated. The victory has drawbacks for Englishmen, and, indeed, for every country in Europe engaged in manufacturing industries. It is a triumph of good faith, but also a triumph of [tariff] protection.

THOUGHT PROVOKERS

1. Since the evidence is strong that a tariff on grain was not really needed, and that such tariffs in the long run would hurt the American farmer, why did it? Was it improper for the Sugar Trust to lobby for a tariff on sugar?

2. Is a company like Pullman's justified in cutting wages when it has a large surplus of money? Does management have a higher obligation to the investor than to the laborer? Is the businessman the best interpreter of the public interest? Is a large-scale business a purely private matter?

3. Explain how the money question increased anti-British bitterness. Was this feeling rational? irrational? To what extent is the United States today the victim of such envy?

4. Explain why the free-silver craze developed the momentum that it did. Comment on the common assumption that the silverites were all ignorant, poor, and basically dishonest.

5. Would disaster have befallen America if Bryan had been elected and the Treasury had coined many dollars with the purchasing power of fifty cents each? Did Bryan's defeat help improve or worsen British-American relations?

FURTHER EXPLORATION

General: H. U. Faulkner, *Politics, Reform, and Expansion, 1890–1900* (1959); Allan Nevins, *Grover Cleveland* (1932); Margaret Leech, *In the Days of McKinley* (1959). **McKinley Tariff:** F. W. Taussig, *The Tariff History of the United States* (8th ed., 1931). **Pullman Strike:** Almont Lindsey, *The Pullman Strike* (1942); Grover Cleveland, *Presidential Problems* (1904). **Free Silver:** F. B. Simkins, *Pitchfork Ben Tillman* (1944); Paxton Hibben, *The Peerless Leader* (1929). **McKinley's Triumph:** Herbert Croly, *Marcus Alonzo Hanna* (1919); M. R. Werner, *Bryan* (1929); P. W. Glad, *The Trumpet Soundeth: William Jennings Bryan and His Democracy, 1896–1912* (1960).

Recent: S. L. Jones, *The Presidential Election of 1896* (1964); J. R. Hollingsworth, *The Whirligig of Politics* (1963); P. W. Glad, *McKinley, Bryan and the People* (1964) [paperback]; P. E. Coletta, *William Jennings Bryan . . . 1860–1908* (1964). See references for previous chapter.

Chapter 31

The Birth of Imperialism

It has been a splendid little war [with Spain]; begun with the highest motives, carried on with magnificent intelligence and spirit, favored by that fortune which loves the brave.

JOHN HAY, 1898

PROLOGUE: As the century neared its sunset, the American people felt a strange restlessness. The frontier was filling up; factories and farms were pouring out exportable surpluses; the nation had not had a rousing war for a generation. Spain, trying desperately to crush a rebellion in Cuba with brutal measures, proved to be the whipping boy. The Big Business administration of McKinley did not want war; but public opinion, inflamed by the racy new yellow journalism, did. Spain made important eleventh-hour diplomatic concessions, but an impatient and outraged Congress declared hostilities. The United States navy was ready, and smashed two badly outmatched Spanish fleets, one at Manila, the other off Cuba. But the army was most unready. After some sharp and confused fighting in Cuba, the Spaniards hoisted the white flag. The imperialistic virus had meanwhile attacked the American people, and McKinley, their ever-obedient servant, demanded and obtained all of the Philippines in the treaty of peace signed at Paris in December, 1898.

A. YELLOW JOURNALISM IN FLOWER

1. Pulitzer Demands Intervention (1897)

The oppressed Cubans revolted in 1895, and the Spanish commander, General ("Butcher") Weyler, tried to crush them by herding them into pesthole concentration camps. Atrocities on both sides were inevitable, but the United States heard little of Cuban misdeeds. The American yellow press, with Joseph Pulitzer's New York *World* and William Randolph Hearst's New York *Journal* competing in sensationalism, headlined lurid horror tales. The basic principle of the "new journalism" seemed to be "Anything to Sell a Paper," regardless of the truth. A *World* reporter wrote from Cuba that slaughtered rebels were fed to dogs, and that children of high-ranking Spanish families clamored for Cuban ears as playthings. The following editorial in Pulitzer's *World* demanded action. Note what point or points probably made the heaviest impact on the American public.

How long are the Spaniards to drench Cuba with the blood and tears of her people?

How long is the peasantry of Spain to be drafted away to Cuba to die miserably in a hopeless war, that Spanish nobles and Spanish officers may get medals and honors?

1. New York *World*, Feb. 13, 1897.

590

How long shall old [Cuban] men and women and children be murdered by the score, the innocent victims of Spanish rage against the patriot armies they cannot conquer?

How long shall the sound of rifles in Castle Morro at sunrise proclaim that bound and helpless prisoners of war have been murdered in cold blood?

How long shall Cuban women be the victims of Spanish outrages and lie sobbing and bruised in loathsome prisons?

How long shall women passengers on vessels flying the American flag be unlawfully seized and stripped and searched by brutal, jeering Spanish officers, in violation of the laws of nations and of the honor of the United States?*

How long shall American citizens, arbitrarily arrested while on peaceful and legitimate errands, be immured in foul Spanish prisons without trial?†

How long shall the navy of the United States be used as the sea police of barbarous Spain?

How long shall the United States sit idle and indifferent within sound and hearing of rapine and murder?

How long?

2. Hearst Stages a Rescue (1897)

William R. Hearst, the irresponsible California playboy who had inherited some $20,000,000 from his father, was even more ingenious than his arch-rival Joseph Pulitzer. He is said to have boasted (with undue credit to himself) that it cost him $3,000,000 to bring on the Spanish-American War. He outdid himself in the case of Evangelina Cisneros, a "tenderly nurtured" Cuban girl of eighteen imprisoned in Havana on charges of rebellion, and reportedly facing a twenty-year incarceration with depraved Negresses. The yellow press pictured her as a beautiful young woman whose only crime had been to preserve her virtue against the lustful advances of a "lecherous" Spanish officer. Hearst's New York *Journal* whipped up a storm of sympathy for the girl, and inspired appeals to the Spanish Queen and to the Pope. All else failing, a *Journal* reporter rented a house next to the prison, drugged the inmates, sawed through the cell bars, and, using a forged visa, escaped with Señorita Cisneros disguised as a boy. Form conclusions as to the nature of the new yellow journalism from this account in the *Journal*.

EVANGELINA CISNEROS RESCUED BY THE JOURNAL

AN AMERICAN NEWSPAPER ACCOMPLISHES AT A SINGLE
STROKE WHAT THE RED TAPE OF DIPLOMACY
FAILED UTTERLY TO BRING ABOUT IN
MANY MONTHS

By Charles Duval
(Copyright, 1897, by W. R. Hearst)

---

* The most highly publicized case actually involved an examination by a police matron.
† By 1897 there were few, if any, American citizens in Cuban prisons, even naturalized Americans of Cuban birth.
2. New York *Journal*, Oct. 10, 1897.

Havana, Oct. 7, via Key West, Fla., Oct. 9.—Evangelina Cosio y Cisneros is at liberty, and the *Journal* can place to its credit the greatest journalistic coup of this age. It is an illustration of the methods of new journalism and it will find an indorsement in the heart of every woman who has read of the horrible sufferings of the poor girl who has been confined for fifteen long months in Recojidas Prison.

The *Journal*, finding that all other methods were unavailing, decided to secure her liberation through force, and this, as the specially selected commissioner of the *Journal*, I have succeeded in doing.

I have broken the bars of Recojidas and have set free the beautiful captive of monster Weyler, restoring her to her friends and relatives, and doing by strength, skill, and strategy what could not be accomplished by petition and urgent request of the Pope.

Weyler could blind the Queen to [the] real character of Evangelina, but he could not build a jail that would hold against *Journal* enterprise when properly set to work.

Tonight all Havana rings with the story. It is the one topic of conversation; everything else pales into insignificance.

B. THE CRISIS WITH SPAIN

1. The *Maine* Is Threatened (1898)

Tension over Cuba eased late in 1897 when "Butcher" Weyler was removed, to be succeeded by General Blanco, and a species of autonomy was granted to the Cubans. But conservative Spaniards in Havana, incensed by these concessions to the rebels, vented their wrath in furious riots. Fearful that Americans there would have to be evacuated to a place of safety, Washington dispatched the battleship *Maine* to the harbor on a "friendly" visit in January, 1898. Shortly after arriving, Captain Sigsbee was handed a leaflet, evidently printed by the conservative Spanish faction, containing the following insults. Form relevant judgments from its content, its innuendo, and its tone.

SPANIARDS!

Long Live Spain with Honor!

What are you doing that you allow yourselves to be insulted in this way? Do you not see what they have done to us in withdrawing our brave and beloved Weyler, who at this very time would have finished with this unworthy, rebellious rabble who are trampling on our flag and on our honor?

Autonomy is imposed on us to cast us aside and give places of honor and authority to those who initiated this rebellion, these lowbred auton-

1. C. D. Sigsbee, "Personal Narrative of the *Maine.*" *Century Magazine,* LVII. 87 (November, 1898).

omists, ungrateful sons of our beloved country!

And, finally, these Yankee pigs* who meddle in our affairs, humiliating us to the last degree, and, for a still greater taunt, order to us a man-of-war of their rotten squadron, after insulting us in their newspapers with articles sent from our own home!

Spaniards! The moment of action has arrived. Do not go to sleep! Let us teach these vile traitors that we have not yet lost our pride, and that we know how to protest with the energy befitting a nation worthy and strong, as our Spain is, and always will be!

Death to the Americans! Death to autonomy!

Long live Spain! Long live Weyler!

THE GREAT WEYLER APE

"Butcher" Weyler, a distinguished though ruthless Spanish soldier, was unfairly caricatured in America as an ape-like glutton and windbag. Maurice and Cooper, *The History of the 19th Century in Caricature*, 1904.

2. De Lôme's Indiscreet Letter (1898)

The roaring flames of jingoism received fresh fuel in February, 1898. Dupuy de Lôme, the Spanish minister in Washington, had written an indiscreet private letter which was stolen from the post office in Havana and emblazoned in the American yellow press. The crestfallen envoy resigned before he could be dismissed. Hearst's New York *Journal*, which itself had attacked McKinley in unbridled terms, led the outcry. It even dug up a book written by de Lôme in 1876 in which he had reflected upon the chastity of American women, before and after marriage. Enumerate the disturbing features of this letter from the American viewpoint, and detect what portion was probably most offensive to the McKinley administration.

The situation here [in Washington] remains the same. Everything depends on the political and military outcome in Cuba. . . .

The [annual] message [of President McKinley] has been a disillusion-

---

* The Americans, who exported vast quantities of pork, were routinely cartooned in the Spanish press as pigs.

2. *Foreign Relations of the United States, 1898*, pp. 1007–08. The letter was probably written about the middle of December, 1897.

ment to the insurgents, who expected something different; but I regard it as bad (for us).

Besides the ingrained and inevitable bluntness (*grosería*) with which is repeated all that the press and public opinion in Spain have said about Weyler, it once more shows what McKinley is: weak and a bidder for the admiration of the crowd, besides being a would-be politician (*politicastro*) who tries to leave a door open behind himself while keeping on good terms with the jingoes of his party.

Nevertheless, whether the practical results of it [the annual message] are to be injurious and adverse depends only upon ourselves.

I am entirely of your opinions; without a military end of the matter nothing will be accomplished in Cuba, and without a military and political settlement there will always be the danger of encouragement being given to the insurgents by a part of the [Spanish] public opinion, if not by the [Madrid] government. . . .

It would be very advantageous to take up, even if only for effect, the question of commercial relations, and to have a man of some prominence sent hither in order that I may make use of him here to carry on a propaganda among the Senators and others in opposition to the [Cuban] junta, and to try to win over the [Cuban] refugees. . . .

3. A Madrid Paper Talks Back (1898)

All other headlines paled when, on February 15, 1898, the United States battleship *Maine* mysteriously blew up in Havana harbor with heavy loss of life. A host of Americans, inflamed by jingoistic yellow journals, leaped to the unproved conclusion that Spanish officials had diabolically destroyed the vessel. The following editorial in a Madrid journal was aimed at the bacon-exporting Yankee "pigs." Note what it reveals most clearly of Spanish character and of Spanish misunderstanding of American government and institutions, including the free press.

It would be losing our time to discuss the American theory that the *Maine* was blown up by the explosion of a mine connected by means of wires with our shipyard. Infamies should not be discussed, but punished. Spain's honor stands too high to be soiled by the squeamish drivel of those toads filled with nastiness and bold enough to pretend to sully it. The best way to get rid of these toads is to crush them with the feet, not to protect ourselves against them, but merely to prevent the carrying of their nastiness further.

We shall not question the good faith of the American jingoes who imagine us capable of the most foul villainies and cowardly actions. Scoundrels by nature, the American jingoes believe that all men are made like themselves. What do they know about noble and generous feelings? Did they ever hear of any such thing? We should not in any way heed the jingoes: they are not even worth our contempt, or the saliva with which we might honor them in spitting at their faces.

3. *El País* (Madrid), March 1, 1898, in *Public Opinion*, XXIV, 328–29 (March 17, 1898).

But there are not only jingoes in the United States. There is also the government, which represents the nation, and which has not so far had the courage to throw off its mask and confess to its jingoism. It is not enough for a man to say that he is honest. Whenever a man's honesty is questioned, that man has to prove it, or else nobody will believe that he is honest. This applies also to friendship.

The government of the United States, which almost looked upon Dupuy de Lôme's private letter to Canalejas as a *casus belli* [cause of war], and which, by taking advantage of the stealing of that letter, became a shelterer of thieves, that government, we repeat, has to do something besides exchanging compliments with our minister of foreign affairs, if we are to believe in the affectionate friendship of which it constantly speaks. McKinley, "the pothouse politician and caterer to the rabble," could well boast of having obtained Dupuy de Lôme's dismissal, and yet Dupuy de Lôme never said that McKinley was a dastardly murderer, as perhaps is thought by the [Spanish] mothers of the men who die by the hundred in the Cuban woods without being able to face their real enemy. Our women do not give expression to such thoughts. The privilege to do so was reserved to the jingo newspapers of the United States in their savage attacks upon Spain [over the *Maine*]. Do the Yankees think that we are going to receive as a caress what they themselves consider to be an outrage? Of what do they believe our epidermis to be made? Do they imagine that bacon is the best transmitter of moral impressions?

If not out of respect for himself, at least for the sake of his country, it was McKinley's duty to see that Spain should not be so grossly insulted by the jingo newspapers. Since he did not do so, nor does he do it now, McKinley is as much of a jingo and as great a slanderer as the jingo newspapers themselves.

Aside from this, we must declare that the persistency in saying that the *Maine* was blown up by us is laughable. What interest could we have in destroying the American battleship? It is not one ship nor ten ships which might enable the United States to triumph over Spain. Ships have to be manned, and there are very few men in the United States. The inhabitants of that country lack the stuff men are made of.

The United States seem to believe that war with us is something easy and feasible. This is perhaps why they wish it. We do not blame them. The *Maine* disaster must have inspired them with the belief that luck will accompany them all through the war. They surely could not have been luckier when the *Maine* blew up! Hundreds of men were then killed, but the ship's officers were all saved, as though they had known what was going to happen.

[*The theory was often voiced, especially later in unfriendly Cuban quarters, that unprincipled American officials blew up the* Maine *in order to have an excuse to intervene. Other excuses already existed; and besides a smaller warship would have sufficed.*]

4. Senator Proctor's Damning Report (1898)

The American public, though prodded by the yellow press, remained remarkably restrained pending an official investigation of the *Maine*. On March 21, 1898, a United States commission formally reported that the battleship had been destroyed by an external mine—and to most Americans this meant Spanish treachery. The resulting demand for revenge was reinforced by a remarkable speech in the Senate four days earlier. Senator Proctor of Vermont, having made a firsthand investigation of four of the six provinces of Cuba, reported as follows. Many Americans had distrusted the gory accounts in the yellow press, and the impact produced by this temperate, matter-of-fact account was profound. Proctor first speaks of the conditions resulting from General Weyler's reconcentration order, as modified by General Blanco. Determine what aspect of this report would most incline the American people to war.

Their huts are about 10 by 15 feet in size, and for want of space are usually crowded together very closely. They have no floor but the ground, no furniture, and, after a year's wear, but little clothing, except such stray substitutes as they can extemporize, and with large families, or more than one, in this little space, the commonest sanitary provisions are impossible. Conditions are unmentionable in this respect. Torn from their homes, with foul earth, foul air, foul water, and foul food or none, what wonder that one-half have died and that one-quarter of the living are so diseased that they cannot be saved?

A form of dropsy is a common disorder resulting from these conditions. Little children are still walking about with arms and chest terribly emaciated, eyes swollen, and abdomen bloated to three times the natural size. The physicians say these cases are hopeless.

Deaths in the streets have not been uncommon. I was told by one of our consuls that they have been found dead about the markets in the morning, where they had crawled, hoping to get some stray bits of food from the early hucksters, and that there had been cases where they had dropped dead inside the market surrounded by food. . . .

I could not believe that out of a population of 1,600,000, two hundred thousand had died within these Spanish forts [camps], practically prison walls, within a few months past from actual starvation and diseases caused by insufficient and improper food. My inquiries were entirely outside of sensational sources. They were made of our medical officers, of our consuls, of city alcaldes (mayors), of relief committees, of leading merchants and bankers, physicians and lawyers. Several of my informants were Spanish-born, but every time the answer was that the case had not been overstated. What I saw I cannot tell so that others can see it. It must be seen with one's own eyes to be realized. . . .

I do not impugn General Blanco's motives, and believe him to be an amiable gentleman, and that he would be glad to relieve the condition of

4. *Congressional Record*, 55 Cong., 2 sess., pp. 2917–19. Senator Proctor was the so-called "marble king" of Vermont, and Speaker T. B. Reed sneered, "A war will make a large market for gravestones."

Spain claimed that the *Maine* incident was an accident, but clearly the starvation in Cuba was not. Minneapolis *Journal,* 1898.

the *reconcentrados* if he could do so without loss of any military advantage. But he knows that all Cubans are insurgents at heart, and none now under military control will be allowed to go out from under it. . . .

I have endeavored to state in not intemperate mood what I saw and heard, and to make no argument thereon, but leave everyone to draw his own conclusions. To me the strongest appeal is not the barbarity practiced by Weyler nor the loss of the *Maine,* if our worst fears should prove true, terrible as are both of these incidents, but the spectacle of a million and a half of people, the entire native population of Cuba, struggling for freedom and deliverance from the worst misgovernment of which I ever had knowledge. . . .

C. THE DECLARATION OF WAR

1. Madrid's Diplomatic Concessions (1898)

General Stewart L. Woodford, a New Yorker of distinguished bearing and ingratiating manner, had served as a Civil War officer, a lawyer, and a Congressman. Although an amateur diplomat, he revealed surprising skill as the American minister in Madrid. He was under instructions from the State Department to secure from Spain (a) an immediate end to the (modified) reconcentration policy, (b) the granting of an armistice to the insurgents, and (c) acknowledgment of Cuba's independence if the President deemed it necessary. After long haggling, the Madrid government ordered an end to reconcentration, March 30, 1898. Two of Woodford's subsequent cablegrams to Washington, reprinted herewith, reveal his further progress. Note what pressures were being exerted for peace in Madrid, and whether Spain's concessions offered hope of an amicable adjustment in Cuba.

1. *Foreign Relations of the United States, 1898,* pp. 746—

Madrid, April 9, 1898

Assistant Secretary Day, Washington:

Spanish minister for foreign affairs has just sent for me. The representatives of the European powers called upon him this morning and advised acquiescence in Pope's request for an armistice [in Cuba]. Armistice has been granted. Spanish minister in Washington instructed to notify our Department of State and yourself. Authority has been cabled to General Blanco [in Cuba] to proclaim armistice. I send verbatim memorandum just handed me by Spanish minister for foreign affairs, as follows:

"In view of the earnest and repeated request of His Holiness [the Pope], supported resolutely by declarations and friendly counsels of the representatives of the six great European powers, who formulated them this morning in a collective visit to the minister of state, as corollary of the efforts of their Governments in Washington, the Spanish Government has resolved to inform the Holy Father that on this date it directs the general-in-chief [Blanco] of the army in Cuba to grant immediately a suspension of hostilities for such length of time as he may think prudent to prepare and facilitate the peace earnestly desired by all."

I hope that this dispatch may reach you before the President's message goes to Congress.

Woodford

Madrid, April 10, 1898

President McKinley, Washington:

[Referring to] My personal [dispatch] No. 66. In view of action of Spanish Government, as cabled Saturday, April 9, I hope that you can obtain full authority from Congress to do whatever you shall deem necessary to secure immediate and permanent peace in Cuba by negotiations, including the full power to employ the Army and Navy, according to your own judgment, to aid and enforce your action. If this be secured, I believe you will get final settlement before August 1 on one of the following bases: either such autonomy as the insurgents may agree to accept, or recognition by Spain of the independence of the island, or cession of the island to the United States.

I hope that nothing will now be done to humiliate Spain, as I am satisfied that the present Government is going, and is loyally ready to go, as fast and as far as it can. With your power of action sufficiently free you will win the fight on your own lines. I do not expect immediate reply, but will be glad to have an early acknowledgment of receipt.

Woodford

2. Spain Regrets the *Maine* (1898)

The American commission investigating the *Maine* had not permitted Spanish officials to examine the wreck, no doubt out of fear that the evidence might be tampered with. The Spaniards nevertheless ran their own inquiry, and concluded

2. *Ibid.*, pp. 748–49 (April 10, 1898).

that the explosion was internal. When the Spanish minister in Washington reported to the State Department his nation's recent concessions regarding Cuba, he added the following plea regarding the *Maine*. Observe what light it casts on the theory of Spanish official culpability, and what is the most convincing evidence of Spain's good faith.

The Government of Her Majesty doubts not that this [granting of concessions to Cuba] will be recognized by the United States Government, even as it must recognize the manifest injustice with which a portion of the public opinion of this country [U.S.] claims to discover responsibilities on the part of Spain for the horrible catastrophe which took place on the calamitous night of the 15th of February last. Her Majesty the Queen Regent, her responsible government, the Governor-General of Cuba, the insular government, and all the higher authorities of Habana displayed from the first moment the profound sorrow and sentiments of horror which that measureless misfortune caused to them, as well as the sympathy which on that melancholy occasion linked them to the American Government and people.

Proof of this is found in the visits of Her Majesty's chargé d'affaires to the illustrious President of the United States, the visits made by the highest officers of the Spanish State to Mr. Woodford, the assistance unsparingly given to the victims, the funeral obsequies which were provided for them by the municipal council of Habana, and the notes addressed to the Department of State by this legation. . . .

The officers and crews of Her Majesty's war vessels lying near the *Maine*, heedless of the evident peril that menaced them, as is testified by the officers of that American ironclad, immediately lowered their boats, saving a large number of the wrecked ship's men, who alone owe their lives to the instant and efficient aid of the Spanish sailors.

It is singular that these well-known facts and impressive declarations seem to have been forgotten by [American] public opinion, which instead lends credence to the most absurd and offensive conjectures.

The Government of Her Majesty would very greatly esteem the sense of justice and the courtesy of the United States Government were an official statement to set the facts in their true light, for it would seem that they are ignored, and the failure to appreciate them is potentially contributing to keep up an abnormal excitement in the minds of the people that imperils, causelessly and most irrationally, the friendly relations of the two countries.

As for the question of fact which springs from the diversity of views between the reports of the Spanish and American boards, the Government of Her Majesty, although not yet possessed of the official text of the two reports, has hastened to declare itself ready to submit to the judgment of impartial and disinterested experts, accepting in advance the decision of the arbitrators named by the two parties, which is obvious proof of the frankness and good faith which marks the course of Spain on this as on all occasions.

[The United States government failed to accept Spain's offer of arbitration.]

3. McKinley Submits a War Message (1898)

Despite the belated concessions of Spain, McKinley sent his war message to Congress on April 11, 1898. His nerves were giving way under the constant clamor for war; his heart went out to the mistreated Cubans. (He had anonymously contributed $5000 for their relief.) He realized that Spain's offer of an armistice, at the discretion of her commander, did not guarantee peace. The rebels had to agree on terms; and Spain had shown a talent for breaking promises and protracting negotiations. Further delay would only worsen the terrible conditions. In analyzing the reasons that McKinley here gives Congress for intervention, note which ones are the soundest and which the weakest. Comment on the dangers of intervention for humanitarian reasons.

The grounds for such intervention may be briefly summarized as follows:

First. In the cause of humanity and to put an end to the barbarities, bloodshed, starvation, and horrible miseries now existing there, and which the parties to the conflict are either unable or unwilling to stop or mitigate. It is no answer to say this is all in another country, belonging to another nation, and is therefore none of our business. It is specially our duty, for it is right at our door.

Second. We owe it to our citizens in Cuba to afford them that protection and indemnity for life and property which no government there can or will afford, and to that end to terminate the conditions that deprive them of legal protection.

Third. The right to intervene may be justified by the very serious injury to the commerce, trade, and business of our people and by the wanton destruction of property and devastation of the island.

Fourth, and which is of the utmost importance. The present condition of affairs in Cuba is a constant menace to our peace, and entails upon this government an enormous expense. With such a conflict waged for years in an island so near us and with which our people have such trade and business relations; when the lives and liberty of our citizens are in constant danger and their property destroyed and themselves ruined; where our trading vessels are liable to seizure and are seized at our very door by warships of a foreign nation; the expeditions of filibustering [freebooting] that we are powerless to prevent altogether, and the irritating questions and entanglements thus arising—all these and others that I need not mention, with the resulting strained relations, are a constant menace to our peace and compel us to keep on a semi-war footing with a nation with which we are at peace.

These elements of danger and disorder already pointed out have been strikingly illustrated by a tragic event which has deeply and justly moved the American people. I have already transmitted to Congress the report of the Naval Court of Inquiry on the destruction of the battleship *Maine* in the harbor of Havana during the night of the 15th of February. The destruction of that noble vessel has filled the national heart with inexpressible

3. J. D. Richardson, ed., *Messages and Papers of the Presidents* (1899), X, 147–50, *passim.*

horror. Two hundred and fifty-eight brave sailors and marines and two officers of our Navy, reposing in the fancied security of a friendly harbor, have been hurled to death, [and] grief and want brought to their homes and sorrow to the nation.

The Naval Court of Inquiry, which, it is needless to say, commands the unqualified confidence of the government, was unanimous in its conclusion that the destruction of the *Maine* was caused by an exterior explosion—that of a submarine mine.* It did not assume to place the responsibility. That remains to be fixed.

In any event, the destruction of the *Maine,* by whatever exterior cause, is a patent and impressive proof of a state of things in Cuba that is intolerable. That condition is thus shown to be such that the Spanish government cannot assure safety and security to a vessel of the American Navy in the harbor of Havana on a mission of peace, and rightfully there. . . .

[*McKinley here refers to the offer by the Spanish minister to arbitrate the* Maine, *and simply adds, "To this I have made no reply."*]

The long trial has proved that the object for which Spain has waged the war cannot be attained. The fire of insurrection may flame or may smolder with varying seasons, but it has not been, and it is plain that it cannot be, extinguished by present methods. The only hope of relief and repose from a condition which can no longer be endured is the enforced pacification of Cuba. In the name of humanity, in the name of civilization, in behalf of endangered American interests which give us the right and the duty to speak and to act, the war in Cuba must stop. . . .

The issue is now with the Congress. It is a solemn responsibility. I have exhausted every effort to relieve the intolerable condition of affairs which is at our doors. Prepared to execute every obligation imposed upon me by the Constitution and the law, I await your action.

Yesterday, and since the preparation of the foregoing message, official information was received by me that the latest decree of the Queen Regent of Spain directs General Blanco, in order to prepare and facilitate peace, to proclaim a suspension of hostilities, the duration and details of which have not yet been communicated to me.

This fact, with every other pertinent consideration, will, I am sure, have your just and careful attention in the solemn deliberations upon which you are about to enter. If this measure attains a successful result, then our aspirations as a Christian, peace-loving people will be realized. If it fails, it will be only another justification for our contemplated action.

[*The President had prepared the foregoing war message a week or so before he submitted it; the delay was primarily to permit American citizens to flee Cuba. A few hours before McKinley finally moved, the cablegrams on pp. 597–*

---

* Assuming that the outside-explosion theory is correct—and it has been challenged—the *Maine* might have been blown up by Cuban insurgents seeking to involve the United States in the war.

598, *above, arrived from Minister Woodford in Madrid. They brought the news that Spain, having already revoked reconcentration, had met the rest of the President's demands by authorizing an armistice. So, at the end of a message that urged war, McKinley casually tacked on the two foregoing paragraphs hinting that hostilities might be avoided. Eight days later a bellicose Congress overwhelmingly passed what was in effect a declaration of war. Several years after the event General Woodford told O. G. Villard, "When I sent that last cable to McKinley, I thought I should wake up the next morning to find myself acclaimed all over the United States for having achieved the greatest diplomatic victory in our history. . . ." Instead, he learned of the war message. (O. G. Villard,* Fighting Years [1939], *p. 136.)]*

4. Professor Norton's Patriotic Protest (1898)

Lovable and immensely popular, Charles Eliot Norton served for many years at Harvard as professor of the history of the fine arts. After war broke out, he shocked public opinion with a speech in Cambridge urging young men not to enlist. The press denounced him as one of the "intellectual copperheads." McKinley had recommended war in the interests of civilization; Norton here urges an opposite course. Determine who had the sounder arguments; also whether a tiny minority such as Norton represented should be silenced in wartime. Was it more patriotic to protest than to acquiesce?

And now of a sudden, without cool deliberation, without prudent preparation, the nation is hurried into war, and America, she who more than any other land was pledged to peace and good will on earth, unsheathes her sword, compels a weak and unwilling nation to a fight, rejecting without due consideration her [Spain's] earnest and repeated offers to meet every legitimate demand of the United States. It is a bitter disappointment to the lover of his country; it is a turning back from the path of civilization to that of barbarism.

"There never was a good war," said Franklin. There have indeed been many wars in which a good man must take part. . . . But if a war be undertaken for the most righteous end, before the resources of peace have been tried and proved vain to secure it, that war has no defense. It is a national crime. The plea that the better government of Cuba, and the relief of the *reconcentrados,* could only be secured by war is the plea either of ignorance or of hypocrisy.

But the war is declared; and on all hands we hear the cry that he is no patriot who fails to shout for it, and to urge the youth of the country to enlist, and to rejoice that they are called to the service of their native land. The sober counsels that were appropriate before the war was entered upon must give way to blind enthusiasm, and the voice of condemnation must be silenced by the thunders of the guns and the hurrahs of the crowd.

Stop! A declaration of war does not change the moral law. "The Ten Commandments will not budge" at a joint resolve of Congress. . . . No! the voice of protest, of warning, of appeal is never more needed than when

4. *Public Opinion,* XXIV, 775–76 (June 23, 1898).

the clamor of fife and drum, echoed by the press and too often by the pulpit, is bidding all men fall in and keep step and obey in silence the tyrannous word of command. Then, more than ever, it is the duty of the good citizen not to be silent, and spite of obliquity, misrepresentation, and abuse, to insist on being heard, and with sober counsel to maintain the everlasting validity of the principles of the moral law.

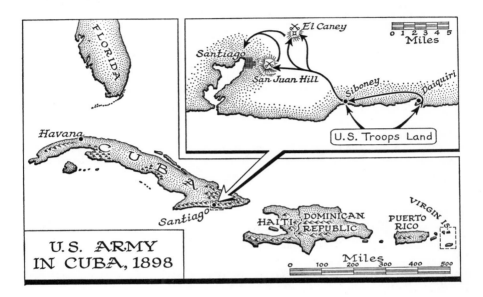

D. THE SORDID LITTLE WAR

1. Rough Times for Rough Riders (1898)

Fight-thirsty Theodore Roosevelt was so determined to get into action that he resigned his post as Assistant Secretary of the Navy. He hastily raised a volunteer cavalry outfit and, as lieutenant colonel of these Rough Riders, managed to reach Cuba—without the horses. Exposing himself with reckless courage, he got into the thick of the fray and won renown near Santiago. But commanding General Shafter was too fat for active duty, the "embalmed beef" was vomit-inducing, and most of the volunteers were poorly trained and equipped. They betrayed their position with old-fashioned, smoke-emitting powder; and one outfit dragged around a captive balloon, thereby revealing its movements. The easy naval victories, combined with the nation's holiday mood and John Hay's reference to the "splendid little war," left a false impression of glamour. Correct it in the light of Roosevelt's letter to his close friend, Senator Henry Cabot Lodge.

Outside Santiago, July 3, 1898

Dear Cabot: Tell the President for Heaven's sake to send us every regiment and, above all, every battery possible. We have won so far at a heavy

1. E. E. Morison, ed., *The Letters of Theodore Roosevelt* (1951), II, 846 (July 3, 1898). By permission of the Harvard University Press.

cost; but the Spaniards fight very hard, and charging these intrenchments against modern rifles is terrible. We are within measurable distance of a terrible military disaster; we *must* have help—thousands of men, batteries, and *food* and ammunition. The other volunteers are at a hideous disadvantage owing to their not having smokeless powder. Our General [Shafter] is poor; he is too unwieldy to get to the front. I commanded my regiment, I think I may say, with honor. We lost a quarter of our men. For three days I have been at the extreme front of the firing line; how I have escaped I know not; I have not blanket or coat; I have not taken off my shoes even; I sleep in the drenching rain, and drink putrid water. Best love to Nannie.

2. The Mutinous Round Robin (1898)

After Santiago surrendered to the encircling American troops, new dangers loomed from disease. But army red tape hampered prompt action. Colonel Roosevelt, who had no regular army career to jeopardize, drafted a round robin appeal to General Shafter, signed by himself and by seven other officers. It was promptly published and caused consternation in Washington, which was then negotiating the terms of an armistice with beaten Spain. Explain why the McKinley administration was alarmed.

Santiago, August 3, 1898

To William Rufus Shafter:

We, the undersigned officers commanding the various brigades, divisions, etc., of the Army of Occupation in Cuba, are of the unanimous opinion that this army should be at once taken out of the island of Cuba and sent to some point on the northern seacoast of the United States; that [this] can be done without danger to the people of the United States; that yellow fever in the army at present is not epidemic; that there are only a few sporadic cases; but that the army is disabled by malarial fever to the extent that its efficiency is destroyed, and that it is in a condition to be practically entirely destroyed by an epidemic of yellow fever, which is sure to come in the near future.

We know from the reports of competent officers and from personal observations that the army is unable to move into the interior, and that there are no facilities for such a move if attempted, and that it could not be attempted until too late. Moreover, the best medical authorities of the island say that with our present equipment we could not live in the interior during the rainy season without losses from malarial fever, which is almost as deadly as yellow fever.

The army must be moved at once, or perish. As the army can be safely moved now, the persons responsible for preventing such a move will be responsible for the unnecessary loss of many thousands of lives.

Our opinions are the result of careful personal observation, and they are also based on the unanimous opinion of our medical officers with the army, who understand the situation absolutely.

2. *Ibid.*, II, 865 (Aug. 3, 1898). By permission of the Harvard University Press. The term *round robin* stems from the practice of signing dangerous documents in a circle so as not to reveal who had signed first.

[*The round robin appeal, though angering the War Department, aroused public opinion. Shortly thereafter the enervated and demoralized American troops were moved to the chilly shores of Long Island. Ironically, the Secretary of War had issued the orders for the transfer several hours before the appeal was published.*]

3. Disillusionment over the Cubans (1898)

The American press, in playing up Spanish atrocities, had idealized the nondescript Cuban insurgents and their shadowy government. The liberating United States troops were speedily disillusioned. They had to restrain their ragged allies from pillaging towns, shooting Spanish prisoners, and butchering the wounded. The insurgents flatly refused to help their deliverers with such menial tasks as building roads and carrying American wounded from the battlefield. American anger and contempt naturally bred Cuban resentment. In the Teller Amendment, passed by Congress in 1898, the United States had pledged itself to free Cuba; in the Platt Amendment, passed by Congress in 1902, Washington reserved the right to intervene to preserve order. Establish the relationship between the Platt Amendment and the views expressed in the following Virginia editorial.

Day by day the news from Santiago brings out more clearly the real character of the majority of the Cuban insurgents. Men who have to be prevented by force from killing prisoners and plundering surrendered cities are not likely to make admirable citizens of an independent country. Liberty, according to their conception of it, would truly be synonymous with many crimes.

In the meanwhile, let us be thankful that the President [McKinley] stood so strongly against the recognition of the alleged insurgent government—a step which was urged with ceaseless vehemence by many influential members of Congress, and by innumerable orators and periodicals. Wouldn't we have been in a pretty predicament if we had found ourselves obliged at every point to bow to the wishes

PEACE! — AND AFTER?

Spain (to Uncle Sam): "Well, you wanted him! You've got him! And I wish you joy of him!!" *Punch* (London), 1898.

3. Norfolk (Va.) *Landmark,* in *Public Opinion,* XXV, 104 (July 28, 1898).

of the undisciplined, bloodthirsty guerrillas who seem to compose the majority of the insurgent forces?

Of course, we believe that Cuba will rise from her ruin and show herself fully worthy of the attempt that has been made to save her, but a good many years will pass before it will be safe for the United States to withdraw their troops and leave the island to her own devices. Even then, it is a question whether Cuban independence outside of the Union will be a success or a failure.

E. THE SIREN SONG OF IMPERIALISM

1. McKinley Prays for Guidance (1898)

What to do with the conquered Philippines? At first McKinley considered taking only a foothold at Manila, on the main island of Luzon. But this would be rendered militarily untenable if the remaining islands should fall into the hands of an unfriendly power, possibly Germany. The decision then lay between all or nothing. To hand back the islands to Spain was unthinkable. After fighting a war to free Cuba from Spanish misrule, America could hardly return the Filipinos, who had likewise risen in revolt, to Spanish misrule. To cut them completely loose might result in a mad scramble among the powers that would touch off a world war into which America might be drawn. McKinley had to make the decision while badly upset by the murder of his brother-in-law at the hands of a betrayed woman. He later told a group of fellow Methodists how he sought divine guidance, presumably late in October, 1898. In analyzing this statement, locate the part that seems least likely to have come from the Almighty; also note the application of the five "d's": duty, destiny, dollars, defense, and deity.

When next I realized that the Philippines had dropped into our laps, I confess I did not know what to do with them. I sought counsel from all sides—Democrats as well as Republicans—but got little help. I thought first we would take only Manila; then Luzon; then other islands, perhaps, also.

I walked the floor of the White House night after night until midnight; and I am not ashamed to tell you, gentlemen, that I went down on my knees and prayed Almighty God for light and guidance more than one night. And one night late it came to me this way—I dont know how it was, but it came:

(1) That we could not give them back to Spain—that would be cowardly and dishonorable;

(2) That we could not turn them over to France or Germany, our commercial rivals in the Orient—that would be bad business and discreditable;

(3) That we could not leave them to themselves—they were unfit for

1. This document is a report of an interview with McKinley at the White House, November 21, 1899, written by one of the interviewers and confirmed by others present. Published in *The Christian Advocate*, Jan. 22, 1903, it is here reprinted from C. S. Olcott, *The Life of William McKinley* (1916), II, 110–11.

self-government, and they would soon have anarchy and misrule worse than Spain's was; and

(4) That there was nothing left for us to do but to take them all, and to educate the Filipinos, and uplift and civilize and Christianize them and by God's grace do the very best we could by them, as our fellow men, for whom Christ also died.

And then I went to bed and went to sleep, and slept soundly, and the next morning I sent for the chief engineer of the War Department (our map-maker), and I told him to put the Philippines on the map of the United States (pointing to a large map on the wall of his office), and there they are and there they will stay while I am President!

2. Professor Sumner Spurns Empire (1898)

The "magnificently bald" and "iron-voiced" Professor William G. Sumner, of Yale, was an immensely popular lecturer and a leading anti-imperialist. Fearlessly outspoken, he offended influential alumni by opposing tariff protection and by turning a cynical eye on America's "civilizing mission" in the Philippines. The truth is that the more obvious the natural resources of the islands became, the less capable the inhabitants seemed of self-rule. The moral obligation of the "White Man's Burden," which the British poet Kipling urged the United States to shoulder, had many of the earmarks of the loot sack. The British welcomed Americans as fellow civilizers, no doubt in part because imperialistic misery loved company. From Sumner's statement ascertain why the conquered peoples would be unlikely to accept American rule, and why such rule was a perversion of American principles.

There is not a civilized nation which does not talk about its civilizing mission just as grandly as we do. The English, who really have more to boast of in this respect than anybody else, talk least about it, but the Phariseeism with which they correct and instruct other people has made them hated all over the globe. The French believe themselves the guardians of the highest and purest culture, and that the eyes of all mankind are fixed on Paris, whence they expect oracles of thought and taste. The Germans regard themselves as charged with a mission, especially to us Americans, to save us from egoism and materialism. The Russians, in their books and newspapers, talk about the civilizing mission of Russia in language that might be translated from some of the finest paragraphs in our imperialistic newspapers.

The first principle of Mohammedanism is that we Christians are dogs and infidels, fit only to be enslaved or butchered by Moslems. It is a corollary that wherever Mohammedanism extends it carries, in the belief of its votaries, the highest blessings, and that the whole human race would be enormously elevated if Mohammedanism should supplant Christianity everywhere.

2. W. G. Sumner, *War and Other Essays* (1919), pp. 303–05. By permission of the Yale University Press.

To come, last, to Spain, the Spaniards have, for centuries, considered themselves the most zealous and self-sacrificing Christians, especially charged by the Almighty, on this account, to spread true religion and civilization over the globe. They think themselves free and noble, leaders in refinement and the sentiments of personal honor, and they despise us as sordid money-grabbers and heretics. I could bring you passages from peninsular authors of the first rank about the grand rôle of Spain and Portugal in spreading freedom and truth.

Now each nation laughs at all the others when it observes these manifestations of national vanity. You may rely upon it that they are all ridiculous by virtue of these pretensions, including ourselves. The point is that each of them repudiates the standards of the others, and the outlying nations, which are to be civilized, hate all the standards of civilized men.

We assume that what we like and practice, and what we think better, must come as a welcome blessing to Spanish-Americans and Filipinos. This is grossly and obviously untrue. They hate our ways. They are hostile to our ideas. Our religion, language, institutions, and manners offend them. They like their own ways, and if we appear amongst them as rulers, there will be social discord in all the great departments of social interest. The most important thing which we shall inherit from the Spaniards will be the task of suppressing rebellions.

If the United States takes out of the hands of Spain her mission, on the ground that Spain is not executing it well, and if this nation in its turn attempts to be schoolmistress to others, it will shrivel up into the same vanity and self-conceit of which Spain now presents an example. To read our current literature one would think that we were already well on the way to it.

Now, the great reason why all these enterprises which begin by saying to somebody else, "We know what is good for you better than you know yourself and we are going to make you do it," are false and wrong is that they violate liberty; or, to turn the same statement into other words, the reason why liberty, of which we Americans talk so much, is a good thing is that it means leaving people to live out their own lives in their own way, while we do the same.

If we believe in liberty, as an American principle, why do we not stand by it? Why are we going to throw it away to enter upon a Spanish policy of dominion and regulation?

3. Beveridge Trumpets Imperialism (1898)

Albert J. Beveridge delivered this famous speech, "The March of the Flag," at Indianapolis, Indiana, on September 16, 1898, before McKinley had decided to keep the Philippines. Born to an impoverished family, Beveridge had spent his youth at hard manual labor, but ultimately secured a college education with prizes

3. C. M. Depew, ed., *The Library of Oratory* (1902), XIV, 438–40.

won in oratorical contests. The cadences of his spellbinding oratory were such that "Mr. Dooley" (F. P. Dunne) said you could waltz to them. The year after making this address Beveridge was elected to the United States Senate from Indiana at the remarkably youthful age of thirty-six. Note how convincingly he replies to the anti-imperialists' warnings against the annexation of non-contiguous territory and to their argument that no more land was needed. Assess his powers as a prophet.

Distance and oceans are no arguments. The fact that all the territory our fathers bought and seized is contiguous is no argument. In 1819 Florida was further from New York than Porto Rico is from Chicago today; Texas, further from Washington in 1845 than Hawaii is from Boston in 1898; California, more inaccessible in 1847 than the Philippines are now. . . . The ocean does not separate us from lands of our duty and desire—the oceans join us, a river never to be dredged, a canal never to be repaired.

Steam joins us; electricity joins us—the very elements are in league with our destiny. Cuba not contiguous! Porto Rico not contiguous! Hawaii and the Philippines not contiguous! Our navy will make them contiguous. [Admirals] Dewey and Sampson and Schley have made them contiguous, and American speed, American guns, American heart and brain and nerve will keep them contiguous forever.

But the Opposition is right—there is a difference. We did not need the western Mississippi Valley when we acquired it, nor Florida, nor Texas, nor California, nor the royal provinces of the far Northwest. We had no emigrants to people this imperial wilderness, no money to develop it, even no highways to cover it. No trade awaited us in its savage fastnesses. Our productions were not greater than our trade. There was not one reason for the land-lust of our statesmen from Jefferson to Grant, other than the prophet and the Saxon within them.

But today we are raising more than we can consume. Today we are making more than we can use. Today our industrial society is congested; there are more workers than there is work; there is more capital than there is investment. We do not need more money—we need more circulation, more employment. Therefore we must find new markets for our produce, new occupation for our capital, new work for our labor. And so, while we did not need the territory taken during the past century at the time it was acquired, we do need what we have taken in 1898, and we need it now.

Think of the thousands of Americans who will pour into Hawaii and Porto Rico when the republic's laws cover those islands with justice and safety! Think of the tens of thousands of Americans who will invade mine and field and forest in the Philippines when a liberal government, protected and cont.... this republic, if not the government of the republic itself, shall es.... er and equity there! Think of the hundreds of thousands of Amer.... will build a soap-and-water, common-school civilization of energy .... try in Cuba, when a government of law replaces the double reign of anarchy and tyranny!—think of the prosperous millions that Empress of Islands will support when, obedient to the law of political gravitation, her people ask for the highest honor liberty can bestow, the sacred Order of the Stars and Stripes, the citizenship of the Great Republic!

What does all this mean for every one of us? It means opportunity for all the glorious young manhood of the republic—the most virile, ambitious, impatient, militant manhood the world has ever seen. It means that the resources and the commerce of these immensely rich dominions will be increased as much as American energy is greater than Spanish sloth; for Americans henceforth will monopolize those resources and that commerce.

[*The Treaty of Paris, by which the United States acquired the Philippines received Senate approval by a close vote on February 6, 1899. The imperialists had little to add to the materialistic-humanitarian arguments herein presented by McKinley and Beveridge. The anti-imperialists stressed the unwisdom of annexing non-contiguous areas in the tropics thickly populated by alien peoples. They also harped on the folly of departing from the principles of freedom and non-intervention as set forth in the Declaration of Independence, Washington's Farewell Address, the Monroe Doctrine, and the Emancipation Proclamation. Senator Hoar of Massachusetts assailed the imperialists with these words: "If you ask them what they want, you are answered with a shout: 'Three cheers for the flag! Who will dare to haul it down? Hold on to everything you can get. The United States is strong enough to do what it likes. The Declaration of Independence and the counsel of Washington and the Constitution of the United States have grown rusty and musty. They are for little countries and not for great ones. There is no moral law for strong nations. America has outgrown Americanism.'"* (Congressional Record, 55 Cong., 3 sess., p. 495.)]

THOUGHT PROVOKERS

1. Have the newspapers in a democracy an ethical responsibility to pursue sober policies, even though such tactics hurt circulation? Has the press shown more responsibility in recent years than in 1898?

2. Should a diplomat be dismissed because of a *private* letter stolen from the mails? Were patriotic Spaniards justified in resenting American attitudes and accusations in 1897–1898? Should the United States have accepted arbitration of the *Maine* dispute?

3. It has been said that a joint-power intervention in Cuba for humanitarian reasons would have been on sounder ground than America's unilateral intervention. Explain. Using McKinley's reasoning, would Spain have been justified in intervening in the American Civil War to prevent continued bloodshed off Cuba's shores? Would a grant of autonomy have solved the Cuban problem?

4. Are army officers justified in appealing to the press over the heads of their superiors to correct conditions that would otherwise remain uncorrected? Argue both sides and form conclusions.

5. In the long run would the United States have been better off if it had kept Cuba and relinquished the Philippines? Did intervention solve the Cuban problem? Has the White Man's Burden proved to be unselfish or a cover for selfishness?

FURTHER EXPLORATION

General: E. R. May, *Imperial Democracy* (1961). **Yellow Journalism:** M. M. Wilkerson, *Public Opinion and the Spanish-American War* (1932); J. E. Wisan, *The Cuban Crisis as Reflected in the New York Press, 1895–1898* (1934). **Spanish Crisis:** F. E. Chadwick, *The Relations of the United States and Spain: Diplomacy* (1909); Orestes Ferrara, *The Last Spanish War* (1937). **Declaration of War:** Margaret Leech, *In the Days of McKinley* (1959). **The War:** Walter Millis, *The Martial Spirit* (1931); Frank Freidel, *The Splendid Little War* (1958). **Imperialism:** J. W. Pratt, *Expansionists of 1898* (1936); F. R. Dulles, *The Imperial Years* (1956).

Recent: Walter LaFeber, *The New Empire: An Interpretation of American Expansion, 1860–1898* (1963) [paperback]; H. W. Morgan, *William McKinley and His America* (1963), and *America's Road to Empire* (1965) [paperback].

Chapter 32

America as a Great Power, 1899-1909

The mission of the United States is one of benevolent assimilation.

PRESIDENT MC KINLEY, 1898

PROLOGUE: The resentful Filipinos, unwilling to be caged by American overlords, revolted in 1899. The insurrection dragged on scandalously for seven years. In 1900 the Democratic Bryan, trumpeting anti-imperialism as the "paramount issue," again ran unsuccessfully against the prosperity President, William McKinley. The victor was fatally shot late in 1901 after serving only six months of his second term. Theodore Roosevelt, moving up from the Vice-Presidency, promptly launched a two-fisted, Big Stick foreign policy. By strong-arm methods, he secured a canal zone at Panama, and then "made the dirt fly." By devising the Roosevelt corollary to the Monroe Doctrine, he intervened in the bankrupt Dominican Republic to prevent other powers from intervening. By mediating a settlement at the end of the Russo-Japanese War in 1905, he won the Nobel Peace Prize. And by interceding in the quarrel between California and Japan over Japanese immigrants, he worked out the Gentlemen's Agreement for amicably halting the inflow.

A. THE BITTER FRUITS OF IMPERIALISM

1. Beveridge Deplores Unpatriotic Talk (1900)

The Filipino troops, under their leader Emilio Aguinaldo, had cooperated loyally with the Americans in capturing Manila. They had received informal promises of freedom, but when these were not honored, they rose in revolt. The fighting between Filipinos and Americans rapidly degenerated into brutal guerrilla warfare. Albert J. Beveridge of Indiana (see p. 608), recently elected to the United States Senate, went to the Philippines on a personal tour of inspection and reported his findings in an impressive Senate speech. Assuming that his main accusation is sound, determine what attitude the anti-imperialists should have taken toward the insurrection.

It has been charged that our conduct of the war has been cruel. Senators, it has been the reverse. I have been in our hospitals and seen the Filipino wounded as carefully, tenderly cared for as our own. Within our lines they may plow and sow and reap and go about the affairs of peace with absolute liberty. And yet all this kindness was misunderstood, or rather not understood. Senators must remember that we are not dealing with Americans or Europeans. We are dealing with Orientals. We are dealing with Orientals who are Malays. We are dealing with Malays instructed in Spanish methods. They mistake kindness for weakness, forbearance for fear. . . .

1. *Congressional Record,* 56 Cong., 1 sess., p. 708 (Jan. 9, 1900).

SENATOR BEVERIDGE URGES PHILIPPINE IMPERIALISM
America ignores Puerto Rico bound hand and foot with tariffs.
Brooklyn *Daily Eagle*, 1900.

Mr. President, reluctantly and only from a sense of duty am I forced to say that American opposition to the war has been the chief factor in prolonging it. Had Aguinaldo not understood that in America, even in the American Congress, even here in the Senate, he and his cause were supported; had he not known that it was proclaimed on the stump and in the press of a faction in the United States that every shot his misguided followers fired into the breasts of American soldiers was like the volleys fired by Washington's men against the soldiers of King George, his insurrection would have dissolved before it entirely crystallized.

The utterances of American opponents of the war are read to the ignorant soldiers of Aguinaldo, and repeated in exaggerated form among the common people. Attempts have been made by wretches claiming American citizenship to ship arms and ammunition from Asiatic ports to the Filipinos, and these acts of infamy were coupled by the Malays with American assaults on our government at home.

The Filipinos do not understand free speech, and therefore our tolerance of American assaults on the American President and the American government means to them that our President is in the minority or he would not permit what appears to them such treasonable criticism. It is believed and stated in [the islands of] Luzon, Panay, and Cebu that the Filipinos have only to fight, harass, retreat, break up into small parties, if necessary, as they are doing now, but by any means hold out until the next presidential election, and our forces will be withdrawn.

All this has aided the enemy more than climate, arms, and battle. Senators, I have heard these reports myself; I have talked with the people; I have seen our mangled boys in the hospital and field; I have stood on the firing line and beheld our dead soldiers, their faces turned to the pitiless southern sky, and in sorrow rather than anger I say to those whose voices in America have cheered those misguided natives on to shoot our soldiers down, that the blood of those dead and wounded boys of ours is on their hands, and the flood of all the years can never wash that stain away. In sorrow rather than anger I say these words, for I earnestly believe that our brothers knew not what they did.

2. Bryan Vents His Bitterness (1901)

In 1900 the Republican President McKinley, who favored keeping the Philippines, again ran against the Democrat William J. Bryan, who favored giving them independence. Republicans accused Bryan of prolonging the insurrection by holding out false hopes. One popular magazine published a picture of the Filipino leader on its front cover, with the query, "Who is behind Aguinaldo?" The curious reader lifted a flap and saw the hawklike features of Bryan. McKinley triumphed by a handsome margin, and Republicans misleadingly hailed the results as a national mandate to retain the islands. The next year Bryan expressed his bitterness as follows, several months after the Americans had captured Aguinaldo. Ascertain his strongest point in rebutting Republican charges that the Democrats were responsible for prolonging the insurrection. How good a prophet was Bryan?

In the campaign of 1900 the Republican leaders denied that their party contemplated a permanent increase in the standing army. They asserted that a large army was only necessary because of the insurrection in the Philippines, and they boldly declared that the insurrection would cease immediately if the Republican ticket was successful. The Democratic platform and Democratic speakers were blamed for the prolongation of the war. "Just re-elect President McKinley," they said, "and let the Filipinos know they are not to have independence, and they will lay down their arms and our soldiers can come home."

Well, the Republican ticket was elected, and the Filipinos were notified that they were not to have independence. But a month after the election the Republicans rushed through Congress a bill authorizing the President to raise the regular army to 100,000, and now, after a year has elapsed, the insurrection is still in progress and the end is not yet. Some of the worst losses of the year have been suffered by our troops within two months. . . .

After the Republican victory made it impossible for the imperialists to blame the anti-imperialists for the continuation of hostilities, the Republican leaders declared that Aguinaldo, actuated by selfish ambition, was compelling his countrymen to continue the war. But even after his capture and imprisonment—yes, even after his captors had secured from him an address advising his comrades to surrender—the insurrection continued.

How long will it take the imperialists to learn that we can never have peace in the Philippine Islands? That we can suppress open resistance is certain, although the cost may be far beyond any gain that can be derived from a colonial government, but that we can ever make the Filipinos love us or trust us while we rule them through a carpetbag government is absurd.

2. *The Commoner,* Nov. 22, 1901.

If the Republicans had read the speeches of Abraham Lincoln as much recently as they did in former years, they would have known that hatred of an alien government is a natural thing and a thing to be expected everywhere. Lincoln said that it was God himself who placed in every human heart the love of liberty. . . .

3. *The Nation* Denounces Atrocities (1902)

Many of the Filipino tribesmen were primitive peoples who knew little of so-called "civilized warfare." Some of them would horribly mutilate and torture American captives, sometimes fastening them down to be eaten alive by insects. The infuriated white soldiers retaliated by shooting a few prisoners and by administering the "water cure"—that is, pouring buckets of dirty water into Filipinos, deflating them with rifle butts, and repeating the painful process. In certain areas, the Americans herded the populace into reconcentration camps, somewhat after the manner of "Butcher" Weyler in Cuba. General Jacob ("Hell Roaring Jake") Smith was "admonished" by the War Department for an order (not carried out) to kill all males over ten years of age on the island of Samar. Reflect on the aptness of the parallel that the New York *Nation* here draws regarding the causes of America's intervention in Cuba.

Even if the condemnation of barbarous warfare in the Philippines by the imperialist press is somewhat belated, we welcome it, as we welcome everything that compels Americans to give attention to a subject to which too many of them have become increasingly indifferent. Silence, we know, is consistent with shame, and may be one of the signs of its existence; and the fact that only a few of the more unblushing or foolish newspapers have defended Gen. Smith's policy of extermination shows what the general sentiment is.

To allege the provocation which our soldiers had is to set up a defense which President Roosevelt brushed aside in advance. To fall back on the miserable sophistry that "war is hell" is only another way of making out those who engage in that kind of war to be fiends. It is, besides, to offer an excuse for ourselves which we did not tolerate for an instant in the case of Spanish atrocities. That is our present moral humiliation in the eyes of the world.

We made war on Spain four years ago for doing the very things of which we are now guilty ourselves. As the Chicago *News* pointedly observes, we are giving Spain as good reason to interfere with us on the ground of humanity as we had to interfere with her. Doubtless she would interfere if she were strong enough and thought she could acquire some islands in the virtuous act.

4. A San Francisco Weekly Defends the Army (1902)

Moderate defenders of the Republican administration replied that the charges of cruelty were grossly exaggerated, that atrocity stories were being used by Democrats

3. *The Nation* (New York), LXXIV, 357 (May 8, 1902).
4. San Francisco *Argonaut*, L, 342 (May 26, 1902).

for partisan advantage, and that in any event such tales did not affect the question of America's duty in the Philippines. The *Outlook* (April 26, 1902) concluded: "The humanity of the army as a whole cannot be discredited by single acts of cruelty, no matter how abhorrent these may be in their character." The extreme imperialists openly avowed a policy of brutality. Shockingly frank was the San Francisco *Argonaut*, a respectable and long-lived weekly magazine. Comment critically on its apportionment of the blame for the existing situation, as between Republicans and Democrats, and note what force there is in its case for the army.

There has been too much hypocrisy about this Philippine business—too much snivel—too much cant. Let us all be frank.

WE DO NOT WANT THE FILIPINOS.

WE WANT THE PHILIPPINES.

All of our troubles in this annexation matter have been caused by the presence in the Philippine Islands of the Filipinos. Were it not for them, the Treaty of Paris would have been an excellent thing; the purchase of the archipelago for twenty millions of dollars would have been cheap. The islands are enormously rich; they abound in dense forests of valuable hardwood timber; they contain mines of the precious metals; their fertile lands will produce immense crops of sugar cane, rice, and tobacco. Touched by the wand of American enterprise, fertilized with American capital, these islands would speedily become richer than Golconda was of old.

But, unfortunately, they are infested by Filipinos. There are many millions of them there, and it is to be feared that their extinction will be slow. Still, every man who believes in developing the islands must admit that it cannot be done successfully while the Filipinos are there. They are indolent. They raise only enough food to live on; they don't care to make money; and they occupy land which might be utilized to much better advantage by Americans. Therefore the more of them killed, the better.

It seems harsh. But they must yield before the superior race, and the American syndicate. How shortsighted, then, to check the army in its warfare upon these savages; particularly when the army is merely carrying out its orders and the duly expressed wishes of the American people, as shown through their elections and their representatives.

Doubtless, many of the excellent gentlemen now in Congress would repudiate these sentiments as brutal. But we are only saying what they are doing. We believe in stripping all hypocritical verbiage from national declarations, and telling the truth simply and boldly. We repeat—the American people, after thought and deliberation, have shown their wishes. THEY DO NOT WANT THE FILIPINOS. THEY WANT THE PHILIPPINES.

It is no one party, no one class, that is responsible for our Philippine policy. It is the people of the United States. The Democratic Party shares equally the responsibility with the Republican Party. The Democratic Party voted for the war with Spain. Had it opposed the fifty-million [arms] appropriation, the war could not have taken place. The Democrats advocated the purchase of the Philippines. For a time the confirmation of the Philippine treaty was in doubt. It was the direct personal lobbying of William J. Bryan with the Democratic Senators which led to the confirmation of the Philippine purchase, and which also led to the present bloody war. Mr. Bryan said at the time that he advocated the confirmation of the treaty in order to put "the Republicans into a hole." He has certainly put his country into a hole. Is he proud of his work?

We are all responsible. You, reader, are responsible. If you are a Republican, your party has made this action part of its national policy. If you are a Democrat, your party, by its vote in the House of Representatives, made the war possible, and by its vote in the Senate turned the scales for the purchase of the Philippines.

But if we, the people of the United States, are responsible for the Philippine campaign, the American army is not. The army is only seventy thousand out of seventy millions. The army did not ask to go there. It was sent. It has fought for four years under tropic suns and torrential rains, in pestilential jungles and miasmatic swamps, patiently bearing the burdens placed upon it by the home country, and with few laurels to be gained as a result of hard and dangerous duty. Nearly every general officer returning from the Philippines has returned to either a wrecked reputation, newspaper odium, or public depreciation. Look at Merritt, Otis, Merriam, MacArthur, Funston. The best treatment that any of them has received is not to be abused. And yet, with these melancholy examples before them, our army toils on uncomplainingly doing its duty.

The army did not bring on the war. We civilians did it. The army is only doing our bidding as faithful servants of their country. And now that they have shown a perfectly human tendency to fight the devil with fire, we must not repudiate their actions, for their actions are our own. They are receiving the fire of the enemy from the front. It is shameful that there should be a fire upon them from the rear.

B. THE PANAMA REVOLUTION

1. Hay Twists Colombia's Arm (1903)

The Spanish-American War, which netted a far-flung empire, increased public pressure for an isthmian canal. Nicaragua had long been the favored route, but in 1902 Congress approved Colombia's Isthmus of Panama. Secretary of State Hay, by threatening to revert to the Nicaragua route, finally secured a treaty from the reluctant Colombian envoy in Washington. But the Senate of Colombia delayed ratification, for it was dissatisfied with the rather niggardly financial terms offered for this priceless asset—$10,000,000 plus an annual payment of $250,000. Secretary Hay thereupon sent the following telegram to the American minister in Bogotá, the capital of Colombia. Critics have contended that this statement contained an intolerable threat to a sovereign republic. Comment.

1. *Foreign Relations of the United States, 1903*, p. 146.

Department of State
Washington, June 9, 1903

The Colombian Government apparently does not appreciate the gravity of the situation. The canal negotiations were initiated by Colombia, and were energetically pressed upon this Government for several years. The propositions presented by Colombia, with slight modifications, were finally accepted by us. In virtue of this agreement our Congress reversed its previous judgment [favoring Nicaragua] and decided upon the Panama route. If Colombia should now reject the treaty or unduly delay its ratification, the friendly understanding between the two countries would be so seriously compromised that action might be taken by the Congress next winter which every friend of Colombia would regret. Confidential. Communicate substance of this verbally to the minister of foreign affairs. If he desires it, give him a copy in form of memorandum.

Hay

[*When the American envoy in Bogotá conveyed this stern message to the foreign minister, the latter asked whether the threat meant hostile measures against Colombia or the adoption of the Nicaragua route. The American was unable to answer. Actually, Secretary Hay took liberties with the truth when he stated that Colombia had "energetically pressed" canal negotiations for several years. Washington had done the pressing.*]

2. Roosevelt Hopes for Revolt (1903)

The Colombian Senate unanimously rejected the canal-zone treaty on August 12, 1903. Among other motives, it hoped to secure for Colombia an additional $40,000,-000—the sum that Washington was proposing to pay the heirs of the French company that had started the canal in the 1870's. The Panamanians feared that the United States would now turn to Nicaragua, as the law required Roosevelt to do if blocked, and thus deprive the Panamanians of the anticipated prosperity that the canal would bring. They had revolted against Colombia's misrule fifty-three times in the past fifty-seven years (by Roosevelt's count), and they were now riper than ever for rebellion. The following letter that Roosevelt sent to Dr. Albert Shaw, editor of the *Review of Reviews,* is often cited as evidence that he connived at the revolt. Assess it critically.

My dear Dr. Shaw: I enclose you, purely for your own information, a copy of a letter of September 5th from our Minister to Colombia. I think it might interest you to see that there was absolutely not the slightest chance of securing by treaty any more than we endeavored to secure. The alternatives were to go to Nicaragua, against the advice of the great majority of competent engineers—some of the most competent saying that we had better have no canal at this time than go there—or else to take the territory by force without any attempt at getting a treaty.

2. E. E. Morison, ed., *The Letters of Theodore Roosevelt* (1951), III, 628 (Oct. 10, 1903). By permission of the Harvard University Press.

I cast aside the proposition made at this time to foment the secession of Panama. Whatever other governments can do, the United States cannot go into the securing by such underhand means, the secession. Privately, I freely say to you that I should be delighted if Panama were an independent State, or if it made itself so at this moment; but for me to say so publicly would amount to an instigation of revolt, and therefore I cannot say it.

3. The President's Unsent Message (1903)

Never a patient man, Roosevelt became violent in his denunciation of the "cut-throats" of Bogotá. He was eager to get the canal started at once so as to strengthen his bid for election to the Presidency "in his own right" in 1904. To offer more money to the "blackmailers of Bogotá" would delay "making the dirt fly." In his anger and frustration, he failed to note that the United States Senate had often rejected treaties, and that the terms granted Colombia were not overgenerous. He went so far as to draft the following message to Congress, which fortunately for his reputation he did not send. Note its most remarkable feature, and decide whether an unsent message can properly be used to implicate him in the Panama revolution. (He wrote on November 12 that he had drafted it "less than a week before the outbreak occurred.")

The refusal of Colombia properly to respond to our sincere and earnest efforts to come to an agreement, or to pay heed to the many concessions we have made, renders it in my judgment necessary that the United States should take immediate action on one of two lines: either we should drop the Panama canal project and immediately begin work on the Nicaraguan canal, or else we should purchase all the rights of the French company, and, without any further parley with Colombia, enter upon the completion of the canal which the French company has begun. I feel that the latter course is the one demanded by the interests of this Nation, and I therefore bring the matter to your attention for such action in the premises as you may deem wise. If in your judgment it is better not to take such action, then I shall proceed at once with the Nicaraguan canal.

4. Official Connivance in Washington (1903)

The conspirators in Panama, encouraged by Roosevelt's ill-concealed anger, revolted on November 3, 1903. Under the ancient treaty of 1846 with Colombia, the United States had guaranteed the neutrality of the Isthmus, obviously against *foreign invaders*. In this case Roosevelt guaranteed the neutrality of the Isthmus by having orders issued to the *Nashville* and other United States naval units to prevent Colombian troops from landing and crossing from the Atlantic port of Colón to Panama City and crushing the rebellion. On November 4, 1903, Panama proclaimed her independence. A little more than an hour after receiving the news, Roosevelt hastily authorized *de facto* recognition, which was extended on November 6, 1903. This

3. J. B. Bishop, *Theodore Roosevelt and His Time* (1920), I, 289. By permission of Charles Scribner's Sons.
4. *Senate Documents,* 58 Cong., 2 sess., No. 51, p. 104.

unseemly haste suggested improper connivance by Washington, and in response to a public demand Roosevelt sent the following official documents to Congress. They consist of interchanges between Acting Secretary of State Loomis (Hay was then absent) and the American Vice Consul General at Panama City, Felix Ehrman. Comment critically on the alleged connivance, precipitancy, and unneutrality of the United States.

Mr. Loomis to Mr. Ehrman
Department of State
Washington, November 3, 1903
(Sent 3:40 P.M.)

Uprising on Isthmus reported. Keep Department promptly and fully informed.

Loomis, Acting

Mr. Ehrman to Mr. Hay
Panama, November 3, 1903
(Received 8:15 P.M.)

No uprising yet. Reported will be in the night. Situation is critical.

Ehrman

Mr. Ehrman to Mr. Hay
Panama, November 3, 1903
(Received 9:50 P.M.)

Uprising occurred [at Panama City] tonight, 6; no bloodshed. [Colombian] Army and navy officials taken prisoners. Government will be organized tonight, consisting three consuls, also cabinet. Soldiers changed. Supposed same movement will be effected in Colón. Order prevails so far. Situation serious. Four hundred [Colombian] soldiers landed Colón today [from] Barranquilla.

Ehrman

Mr. Loomis to Mr. Ehrman
Department of State
Washington, November 3, 1903
(Sent 11:18 P.M.)

Message sent to *Nashville* to Colón may not have been delivered. Accordingly see that following message is sent to *Nashville* immediately:
Nashville, Colón:
In the interests of peace make every effort to prevent [Colombian] Government troops at Colón from proceeding to Panama. The transit of the Isthmus must be kept open and order maintained. Acknowledge.

(signed) Darling, Acting [Secretary of Navy]

Secure special train [to deliver message], if necessary. Act promptly.

Loomis, Acting

[*Resolute action by Commander Hubbard of the* Nashville, *in response to his instructions from Washington, forced the Colombian troops to sail away from Colón on November 5, two days after the revolutionists had seized Panama City.*]

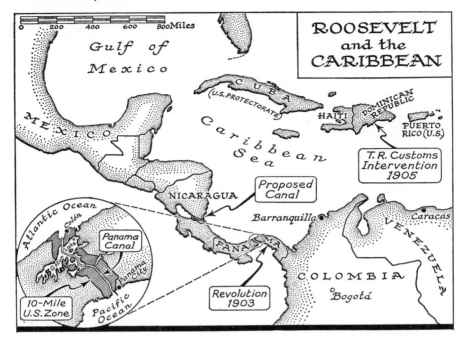

C. THE PANAMA AFTERTASTE

1. T.R.'s "Mandate" from Civilization (1904)

Americans were eager to get the Big Ditch started, and most newspaper editors, especially loyal Republicans, approved Roosevelt's rush-order tactics. But partisan Democrats and liberal journals alike spoke of "indecent haste," "piracy," "scandal, disgrace, and dishonor." The liberal New York *Evening Post*, condemning "this miserable intrigue—this cooked-up republic," concluded that "this mad plunge" was "a vulgar and mercenary venture, without a rag to cover its sordidness and its shame." Critics were also quick to point out that a canal in Nicaragua would be about as desirable, despite volcanoes, and would have required no revolution. Roosevelt struck back in the following message to Congress. After referring to the bloodshed of previous revolutions in Panama, he congratulated himself on having kept order under the antiquated treaty of 1846. Determine whether his hands were as clean as he represents; whether long-established rules of recognition should be set aside in the interests of immediate gain; and whether Roosevelt actually had a "mandate from civilization."

The fact that in this last revolution not a life was lost, save that of the man killed by the shells of the Colombian gunboat, and no property destroyed, was due to the action which I have described. We, in effect, policed the Isthmus in the interest of its inhabitants and of our own national needs, and for the good of the entire civilized world. Failure to act as the Administration acted would have meant great waste of life, great suffering,

---

1. *A Compilation of the Messages and Papers of the Presidents* (n.d.), XVI, 6918–19, 6921, 6923 (Jan. 4, 1904).

THE MAN BEHIND THE EGG

The clever Frenchman Bunau-Varilla, about to sell the rights of the defunct French Panama Canal Company to the U.S. for $40,000,000, intrigues to hatch the Panamanian revolt from the Colombian egg. He then has himself made Panama's minister to the U.S. and negotiates a canal treaty highly favorable to the U.S. New York *Times,* 1903.

great destruction of property; all of which was avoided by the firmness and prudence with which Commander Hubbard [of the *Nashville*] carried out his orders and prevented either party from attacking the other.

Our action was for the peace both of Colombia and of Panama. It is earnestly to be hoped that there will be no unwise conduct on our part which may encourage Colombia to embark on a war which can not result in her gaining control of the Isthmus, but which may cause much bloodshed and suffering.

I hesitate to refer to the injurious insinuations which have been made of complicity by this Government in the revolutionary movement in Panama. They are as destitute of foundation as of propriety. The only excuse for my mentioning them is the fear lest unthinking persons might mistake for acquiescence the silence of mere self-respect. I think proper to say, therefore, that no one connected with this Government had any part in preparing, inciting, or encouraging the late revolution on the Isthmus of Panama, and that save from the reports of our military and naval officers, given above, no one connected with this Government had any previous knowledge of the revolution except such as was accessible to any person of ordinary intelligence who read the newspapers and kept up a current acquaintance with public affairs.

By the unanimous action of its people, without the firing of a shot—with a unanimity hardly before recorded in any similar case—the people of Panama declared themselves an independent Republic. Their recognition by this Government was based upon a state of facts in no way dependent for its justification upon our action in ordinary cases.

I have not denied, nor do I wish to deny, either the validity or the propriety of the general rule that a new state should not be recognized as independent till it has shown its ability to maintain its independence. This rule is derived from the principle of non-intervention, and as a corollary of that principle has generally been observed by the United States. But, like the principle from which it is deduced, the rule is subject to exceptions; and there are in my opinion clear and imperative reasons why a departure from it was justified and even required in the present instance. These reasons embrace, first, our treaty rights; second, our national interests and safety; and, third, the interests of collective civilization. . . .

[After discussing the first reason, Roosevelt continues:] This recognition was, in the second place, further justified by the highest considerations of our national interests and safety. In all the range of our international relations, I do not hesitate to affirm that there is nothing of greater or more pressing importance than the construction of an inter-oceanic canal. Long acknowledged to be essential to our commercial development, it has become, as the result of the recent extension of our territorial dominion, more than ever essential to our national self-defense. . . .

In the third place, I confidently maintain that the recognition of the Republic of Panama was an act justified by the interests of collective civilization. If ever a government could be said to have received a mandate from civilization to effect an object the accomplishment of which was demanded in the interest of mankind, the United States holds that position with regard to the inter-oceanic canal.

2. Roosevelt Blasts the "Blackmail" Treaty (1914)

As time wore on, Roosevelt became more indiscreet in defense of his conduct. In a speech at Berkeley, California, in 1911 he boasted: " . . . I took the Canal Zone and let Congress debate; and while the debate goes on, the canal does also." Three years later, when the Democrats returned to power, they negotiated a treaty with Colombia expressing "sincere regret" and providing for an indemnity of $25,000,000 ("canalimony"). With the canal about to be opened to shipping (August 15, 1914), an angry ex-President Roosevelt wrote the following letter to the chairman of the Senate Committee on Foreign Relations. Decide whether it was more honorable to pay the indemnity or to keep quiet, and whether such a payment could be properly described as "belated blackmail."

Sir: If there is any intention of your Committee to act favorably on the proposed Treaty with Colombia by which we are to pay Colombia twenty-five million dollars and to express regret for the action taken in the past, I respectfully request to be heard thereon.

I was President throughout the time of the negotiations, first with Colombia and then with Panama, by which we acquired the right to build the Panama Canal. Every act of this Government in connection with these negotiations and the other proceedings for taking possession of the Canal Zone and beginning the building of the Canal was taken by my express direction or else in carrying out the course of conduct I had laid down. I

2. E. E. Morison, ed., *The Letters of Theodore Roosevelt* (1954), VII, 777–79 (July 11, 1914). By permission of the Harvard University Press.

had full knowledge of everything of any importance that was done in connection with the transaction by any agent of the Government and I am solely responsible for what was done. The then Secretary of State, John Hay, had almost as complete a firsthand knowledge of what occurred, but no man living, except myself, has this firsthand knowledge; and no man, living or dead, shared the responsibility for the action with me, save in a wholly minor degree.

I ask for this hearing because I regard the proposed Treaty as a crime against the United States, an attack upon the honor of the United States, which, if true, would convict the United States of infamy, and a serious menace to the future well-being of our people. Either there is warrant for paying this enormous sum and for making the apology, or there is not. If there is no warrant for it, then the payment is simply the payment of belated blackmail. If there is warrant for it, then we have no business to be on the Isthmus at all. The payment can only be justified upon the ground that this nation has played the part either of a thief or of the receiver of stolen goods. In such case the only proper course is to restore everything to the original owner. In such case it is a crime to remain on the Isthmus and it will be much worse than an absurdity for the President, the Secretary of State, and other officials of the Government to take part in opening the Canal. . . .

As a matter of fact every action we took was not only open but was absolutely straight and was rendered absolutely necessary by the misconduct of Colombia and the dignity of the United States and the interests not only of the United States but of the world in having the Canal built. Every action we took was in accordance with the highest principles of public and private morality.

[*Roosevelt's friends in the Senate rallied to his support, and the apologetic treaty with Colombia was blocked. But by 1921 Roosevelt was dead, and American promoters were avidly interested in recently discovered Colombian oil. Washington thereupon concluded a treaty under which the United States paid the $25,000,000 without any formal expression of regret, but this much money was an apology in any language.*]

D. THE MONROE DOCTRINE IN THE CARIBBEAN

1. Roosevelt Launches a Corollary (1904)

The corrupt and bankrupt "banana republics" of the Caribbean were inclined to overborrow, and Roosevelt believed that they could properly be "spanked" by European creditors. But the British-German "spanking" of Venezuela in 1902 resulted in the sinking of two Venezuelan gunboats and the bombardment of a fort and village. Such interventions foreshadowed a possible permanent foothold and a consequent violation of the Monroe Doctrine. Sensing this danger, Roosevelt, in his annual message

1. *A Compilation of the Messages and Papers of the Presidents* (n.d.), XVI, 7053–54 (Dec. 6, 1904).

to Congress of 1904, sketched out his famous corollary to the Monroe Doctrine. Monroe had in effect warned the European powers in 1823, "Hands Off." Roosevelt was now saying that since the United States would not permit the powers to lay their hands on, he had an obligation to do so himself. In short, he would intervene to keep them from intervening. In the statement embodied in his annual message, note what assurances he gives the Latin American countries, and to what extent he seems justified in making the United States an international policeman.

It is not true that the United States feels any land hunger or entertains any projects as regards the other nations of the Western Hemisphere, save such as are for their welfare. All that this country desires is to see the neighboring countries stable, orderly, and prosperous. Any country whose people conduct themselves well can count upon our hearty friendship. If a nation shows that it knows how to act with reasonable efficiency and decency in social and political matters, if it keeps order and pays its obligations, it need fear no interference from the United States.

Chronic wrongdoing, or an impotence which results in a general loosening of the ties of civilized society, may in America, as elsewhere, ultimately require intervention by some civilized nation, and in the Western Hemisphere the adherence of the United States to the Monroe Doctrine may force the United States, however reluctantly, in flagrant cases of such wrongdoing or impotence, to the exercise of an international police power. If every country washed by the Caribbean Sea would show the progress in stable and just civilization which, with the aid of the Platt amendment, Cuba has shown since our troops left the island, and which so many of the republics in both Americas are constantly and brilliantly showing, all question of interference by this Nation with their affairs would be at an end.

Our interests and those of our southern neighbors are in reality identical. They have great natural riches, and if within their borders the reign of law and justice obtains, prosperity is sure to come to them. While they thus obey the primary laws of civilized society, they may rest assured that they will be treated by us in a spirit of cordial and helpful sympathy. We would interfere with them only in the last resort, and then only if it became evident that their inability or unwillingness to do justice at home and abroad had violated the rights of the United States or had invited foreign aggression to the detriment of the entire body of American nations. It is a mere truism to say that every nation, whether in America or anywhere else, which desires to maintain its freedom, its independence, must ultimately realize that the right of such independence cannot be separated from the responsibility of making good use of it.

2. A Latin American Protests (1943)

Following up his new corollary to the Monroe Doctrine, Roosevelt arranged with the local authorities to take over and administer the customhouses of the bankrupt Santo Domingo. The European creditors then had no real excuse for interfering,

2. Luis Quintanilla, *A Latin American Speaks* (1943), pp. 125–26. By permission of the author.

for they received their regular payments. In his annual message of 1905, Roosevelt added a refinement to his corollary to the Monroe Doctrine: to prevent European creditors from taking over customhouses (and perhaps staying), the United States had an obligation to take over the customhouses itself. In subsequent years, and pursuant to the Roosevelt corollary to the Monroe Doctrine, the marines landed and acted as international policemen, notably in Haiti, Santo Domingo, and Nicaragua. The Latin Americans, cherishing their sovereign right to revolution and disorder, bitterly resented this bayonet-enforced twisting of Monroe's protective dictum. Below, an outspoken Mexican diplomat, with a Ph.D. from Johns Hopkins University, expresses his wrath. It has been said that the Roosevelt corollary was so radically different from the original Monroe Doctrine (see earlier, p. 226) that the two should never have been associated. Comment critically in the light of the following remarks.

No document has proved more harmful to the prestige of the United States in the Western Hemisphere [than the Roosevelt corollary]. No White House policy could be more distasteful to Latin Americans—not even, perhaps, outspoken imperialism. Latin Americans are usually inclined to admire strength, force, a nation *muy hombre* [very manly]. This was imperialism without military glamour. . . . Moreover, it was a total distortion of the original Message. Monroe's Doctrine was defensive and negative: defensive, in that it was essentially an opposition to eventual aggression from Europe; negative, in that it simply told Europe what it should not do—not what the United States should do.

The Monroe Doctrine of later corollaries became aggressive and positive: aggressive, because, even without actual European attack, it urged United States "protection" of Latin America—and that was outright intervention; positive, because instead of telling Europe what not to do, it told the United States what it should do in the Western Hemisphere. From a case of America vs. Europe, the corollaries made of the Doctrine a case of the United States vs. America.

President Monroe had merely shaken his head, brandished his finger, and said to Europe, "Now, now, gentlemen, if you meddle with us, we will not love you any more," while Teddy Roosevelt, brandishing a big stick, had shouted, "Listen, you guys, don't muscle in—this territory is ours."

In still another corollary, enunciated to justify United States intervention [in Santo Domingo], the same Roosevelt said: "It is far better that this country should put through such an arrangement [enforcing fulfillment of financial obligations contracted by Latin American states] rather than to allow any foreign country to undertake it." To intervene in order to protect: to intervene in order to prevent others from so doing. It is the "Invasion for Protection" corollary, so much in the limelight recently, in other parts of the world.

[*Latin American bitterness against this perversion of the Monroe Doctrine festered for nearly three decades. A sharp turn for the better came in 1933. President Franklin D. Roosevelt, implementing a policy initiated by President Hoover, formally renounced the doctrine of intervention in Latin America. Thus what the first Roosevelt gave, the second Roosevelt took away.*]

E. ROOSEVELT AND JAPAN

1. The President Anticipates Trouble (1905)

Secretary of State John Hay, attempting to halt European land-grabbing in China, had induced the reluctant powers to accept his famed Open Door policy in 1899–1900. But Russia's continued encroachments on China's Manchuria led to the exhausting Russo-Japanese War of 1904–1905, during which the underdog Japanese soundly thrashed the Russian army and navy. President Roosevelt, who was finally drafted as peace mediator, wrote the following letter to his close friend Senator Henry Cabot Lodge. Victory-drunk, Japan was becoming understandably cocky, while the race-conscious California legislature was preparing to erect barriers against Japanese immigrants. Note why Roosevelt regarded the attitude of Californians as bigoted, foolish, and dangerous.

That Japan will have her head turned to some extent I do not in the least doubt, and I see clear symptoms of it in many ways. We should certainly as a nation have ours turned if we had performed such feats as the Japanese have in the past sixteen months; and the same is true of any European nation. Moreover, I have no doubt that some Japanese, and perhaps a great many of them, will behave badly to foreigners. They cannot behave worse than the State of California, through its Legislature, is now behaving toward the Japanese.

The feeling on the Pacific slope, taking it from several different standpoints, is as foolish as if conceived by the mind of a Hottentot. These Pacific Coast people wish grossly to insult the Japanese and to keep out the Japanese immigrants on the ground that they are an immoral, degraded, and worthless race; and at the same time that they desire to do this for the Japanese, and are already doing it for the Chinese, they expect to be given advantages in Oriental markets; and with besotted folly are indifferent to building up the navy while provoking this formidable new power— a power jealous, sensitive, and warlike, and which if irritated could at once take both the Philippines and Hawaii from us if she obtained the upper hand on the seas.

Most certainly the Japanese soldiers and sailors have shown themselves to be terrible foes. There can be none more dangerous in all the world. But our own navy, ship for ship, is I believe at least as efficient as theirs, although I am not certain that our torpedo boats would be handled as well as theirs. At present we are superior to them in number of ships, and this superiority will last for some time. It will of course come to an end if [Senator] Hale has his way, but not otherwise.

I hope that we can persuade our people on the one hand to act in a spirit of generous justice and genuine courtesy toward Japan, and on the other hand to keep the navy respectable in numbers and more than respectable in the efficiency of its units. If we act thus we need not fear the Japanese. But if, as Brooks Adams says, we show ourselves "opulent, aggressive, and unarmed," the Japanese may sometime work us an injury.

1. E. E. Morison, ed., *The Letters of Theodore Roosevelt* (1951), IV, 1205–06 (June 5, 1905). By permission of the Harvard University Press.

2. Japan Resents Discrimination (1906)

The San Francisco Board of Education precipitated a crisis in 1906 by ordering all Oriental students to attend a specially segregated school. The sensitive Japanese rose in instant resentment against what they regarded as a deliberate and insulting act of discrimination. The Tokyo *Mainichi Shimbun*, a reputable journal, reacted as follows. Draw relevant conclusions in the light of Roosevelt's foregoing letter.

The whole world knows that the poorly equipped army and navy of the United States are no match for our efficient army and navy. It will be an easy work to awake the United States from her dream of obstinacy when one of our great admirals appears on the other side of the Pacific. . . . The present situation is such that the Japanese nation cannot rest easy by relying only upon the wisdom and statesmanship of President Roosevelt. The Japanese nation must have a firm determination to chastise at any time the obstinate Americans.

Stand up, Japanese nation! Our countrymen have been HUMILIATED on the other side of the Pacific. Our poor boys and girls have been expelled from the public schools by the rascals of the United States, cruel and merciless like demons.

At this time we should be ready to give a blow to the United States. Yes, we should be ready to strike the Devil's head with an iron hammer for the sake of the world's civilization. . . . Why do we not insist on sending [war]ships?

3. The Gentlemen's Agreement (1908)

The San Francisco school incident revealed anew that a municipality or a state could take perfectly legal action that might involve the entire nation in war. Roosevelt soothed the Japanese, but not the Californians, by adopting the Oriental side of the dispute. He publicly branded the action of the School Board as a "wicked absurdity," and he brought that entire body to Washington, where he persuaded the members to come to terms. The San Franciscans agreed to readmit Japanese children of the proper age to the public schools, on condition that Roosevelt would arrange to shut off the influx of coolies. This he did in the famous Gentlemen's Agreement, which consisted of an understanding growing out of an extensive exchange of diplomatic notes. These were officially summarized as follows in the annual report of the United States Commissioner-General of Immigration. Note how the inflow of coolies was to be halted by a face-saving device.

In order that the best results might follow from an enforcement of the regulations, an understanding was reached with Japan that the existing policy of discouraging the emigration of its subjects of the laboring classes to continental United States should be continued and should, by cooperation of the governments, be made as effective as possible.

This understanding contemplates that the Japanese Government shall issue passports to continental United States only to such of its subjects as are non-laborers or are laborers who, in coming to the continent, seek to

2. Oct. 22, 1906, in T. A. Bailey, *Theodore Roosevelt and the Japanese-American Crises* (1934), p. 50. By permission of the Stanford University Press.
3. *Annual Report of the Secretary of Commerce and Labor, 1908* (1908), pp. 221–22.

resume a formerly acquired domicile, to join a parent, wife, or children residing there, or to assume active control of an already possessed interest in a farming enterprise in this country; so that the three classes of laborers entitled to receive passports have come to be designated "former residents," "parents, wives, or children of residents," and "settled agriculturists."

With respect to Hawaii, the Japanese Government stated that, experimentally at least, the issuance of passports to members of the laboring classes proceeding thence would be limited to "former residents" and "parents, wives, or children of residents." The said government has also been exercising a careful supervision over the subject of the emigration of its laboring class to foreign contiguous territory [Mexico, Canada].

[*The honor-system Gentlemen's Agreement worked reasonably well until 1924, when Congress in a fit of pique slammed the door completely in the faces of the Japanese (see later, p. 750). The resulting harvest of ill will had much to do with the tragic events that led to Pearl Harbor and World War II.*]

THOUGHT PROVOKERS

1. Critics said that while the Filipinos might not have been able to govern themselves, Americans were incapable of governing them if true to the "consent of the governed" philosophy of the Declaration of Independence. Comment. Why do atrocity stories come out of all protracted wars? Has the United States been more humane than other nations in conducting warfare, whether against Indians or "civilized" peoples?

2. Would it have been better to delay construction of the Panama Canal for ten or so years rather than have the scandal that attended the Panama coup? Was the scandal really necessary?

3. With the Panama revolution in mind, assess the dangers of assuming self-chosen mandates from civilization.

4. With reference to Roosevelt's corollary to the Monroe Doctrine, are small nations entitled to complete sovereignty if they fail to exercise it properly? When certain states of the United States defaulted on their debts to British creditors in the 1830's, Britain did not attempt to take over American customhouses. Comment critically on the parallel afforded by Roosevelt's Dominican intervention.

5. Why did Japan especially resent California's discrimination in 1906, and why was the Gentlemen's Agreement better than exclusion by act of Congress?

FURTHER EXPLORATION

General: F. R. Dulles, *America's Rise to World Power, 1898–1954* (1955); Margaret Leech, *In the Days of McKinley* (1959). **Imperialism:** J. H. Blount, *The American Occupation of the Philippines* (1912); J. A. LeRoy, *Americans in the Philippines* (1914). **Panama Revolution:** D. C. Miner, *The Fight for the Panama Route* (1940). **Panama Aftertaste:** H. F. Pringle, *Theodore Roosevelt, A Biography* (1931). **Monroe Doctrine:** H. C. Hill, *Roosevelt and the Caribbean* (1927); H. K. Beale, *Theodore Roosevelt and the Rise of America to World Power* (1956). **Japan:** T. A. Bailey, *Theodore Roosevelt and the Japanese-American Crises* (1934); Yamato Ichihashi, *Japanese in the United States* (1932). **Recent:** R. A. Esthus, *Theodore Roosevelt and Japan* (1966); R. A. Hart, *The Great White Fleet* (1965); W. H. Harbaugh, *Power and Responsibility* [T.R.] (1961) [paperback].

Chapter *33*

Roosevelt and the Reformers

Men with the muckrake are often indispensable to the well-being of society, but only if they know when to stop raking the muck.

THEODORE ROOSEVELT, 1906

PROLOGUE: The wholesale exposure of iniquities during the Roosevelt years led to a wave of reform in the Progressive era, which crested about 1908. A group of professional writers (muckrakers) pilloried sweatshop conditions, municipal graft, adulterated food and drugs, and other kinds of skulduggery. At first Roosevelt was not hostile to the revelations of the muckrakers. But he finally came to believe that they were corrupting public taste by overstressing the bad to the exclusion of the good. His own major contribution as a reformer was to reinvigorate the movement for conserving the nation's fast-melting natural resources, especially the forests. As brandisher of the Big Stick, he won a great reputation for trust busting. But the truth is that he regarded the Sherman Anti-Trust Act as ineffective, and he did not bestir himself as mightily as all the uproar indicated.

A. THE PLIGHT OF LABOR

1. Baer's Divine Right of Plutocrats (1902)

The anthracite coal miners of Pennsylvania, who were frightfully exploited and accident-cursed, struck for higher wages in 1902. About 140,000 men were idled, and the chilled East was threatened with paralysis. George F. Baer, the multimillionaire spokesman for the owners, refused to permit intervention, arbitration, or even negotiation. He believed that mining was a "business," not a "religious, sentimental, or academic proposition." In response to a complaining letter from a Mr. W. F. Clark, he sent the following reply. Comment critically on the social philosophy of Big Business as here revealed.

17th July 1902

My dear Mr. Clark:—

I have your letter of the 16th instant.

I do not know who you are. I see that you are a religious man; but you are evidently biased in favor of the right of the working man to control a business in which he has no other interest than to secure fair wages for the work he does.

I beg of you not to be discouraged. The rights and interests of the laboring man will be protected and cared for—not by the labor agitators,

1. *Literary Digest*, XXV, 258 (Aug. 30, 1902). A photostatic copy of the letter is in Caro Lloyd, *Henry Demarest Lloyd* (1912), II, 190.

but by the Christian men to whom God in His infinite wisdom has given the control of the property interests of the country, and upon the successful management of which so much depends.

Do not be discouraged. Pray earnestly that right may triumph, always remembering that the Lord God Omnipotent still reigns, and that His reign is one of law and order, and not of violence and crime.

Yours truly,

Geo. F. Baer
President

[*When the Baer letter was published, the press assailed its "arrant hypocrisy," "egregious vanity," and "ghastly blasphemy." Roosevelt nevertheless finally brought the disputants together late in 1902. Although he admittedly lost his temper and did not behave "like a gentleman," he had a large hand in working out the resulting compromise wage increase.*]

2. Child Labor in the Coal Mines (1906)

The arrogant attitude of the coal operators seems even less excusable in the light of John Spargo's book *The Bitter Cry of the Children*—another significant contribution to the "muckraking" movement. An English-born Socialist, Spargo had come to America in 1901 at the age of twenty-five. He was especially stirred by the rickety children of the New York tenement districts. Their mothers had no time to prepare proper meals; needlework labor in the sweatshops ran from twelve to twenty hours a day, at a wage ranging from ten cents to a cent and a half an hour. From Spargo's description of work in the coal mines, ascertain the various kinds of hazards involved, and form relevant conclusions.

Work in the coal breakers is exceedingly hard and dangerous. Crouched over the chutes, the boys sit hour after hour, picking out the pieces of slate and other refuse from the coal as it rushes past to the washers. From the cramped position they have to assume, most of them become more or less deformed and bent-backed like old men. When a boy has been working for some time and begins to get round-shouldered, his fellows say that "He's got his boy to carry round wherever he goes."

The coal is hard, and accidents to the hands, such as cut, broken, or crushed fingers, are common among the boys. Sometimes there is a worse accident: a terrified shriek is heard, and a boy is mangled and torn in the machinery, or disappears in the chute to be picked out later smothered and dead. Clouds of dust fill the breakers and are inhaled by the boys, laying the foundations for asthma and miners' consumption.

I once stood in a breaker for half an hour and tried to do the work a twelve-year-old boy was doing day after day, for ten hours at a stretch, for sixty cents a day. The gloom of the breaker appalled me. Outside the sun shone brightly, the air was pellucid, and the birds sang in chorus with the trees and the rivers. Within the breaker there was blackness, clouds of deadly dust enfolded everything, the harsh, grinding roar of the machinery

2. John Spargo, *The Bitter Cry of the Children* (1906), pp. 163–65.

UNCLE SAM: "HE'S GOOD ENOUGH FOR ME." Millions of copies of this pro-Roosevelt cartoon by Davenport were circulated during the presidential campaign of 1904. New York *Evening Mail,* 1904.

and the ceaseless rushing of coal through the chutes filled the ears. I tried to pick out the pieces of slate from the hurrying stream of coal, often missing them; my hands were bruised and cut in a few minutes; I was covered from head to foot with coal dust, and for many hours afterwards I was expectorating some of the small particles of anthracite I had swallowed.

I could not do that work and live, but there were boys of ten and twelve years of age doing it for fifty and sixty cents a day. Some of them had never been inside of a school; few of them could read a child's primer. True, some of them attended the night schools, but after working ten hours in the breaker the educational results from attending school were practically nil. "We goes fer a good time, an' we keeps de guys wot's dere hoppin' all de time," said little Owen Jones, whose work I had been trying to do. . . .

As I stood in that breaker I thought of the reply of the small boy to Robert Owen [British social reformer]. Visiting an English coal mine one day, Owen asked a twelve-year-old lad if he knew God. The boy stared vacantly at his questioner: "God?" he said, "God? No, I don't. He must work in some other mine." It was hard to realize amid the danger and din and blackness of that Pennsylvania breaker that such a thing as belief in a great All-good God existed.

From the breakers the boys graduate to the mine depths, where they become door tenders, switch boys, or mule drivers. Here, far below the surface, work is still more dangerous. At fourteen or fifteen the boys assume the same risks as the men, and are surrounded by the same perils. Nor is it in Pennsylvania only that these conditions exist. In the bituminous mines of West Virginia, boys of nine or ten are frequently employed. I met one little fellow ten years old in Mt. Carbon, W. Va., last year, who was employed as a "trap boy." Think of what it means to be a trap boy at ten years of age. It means to sit alone in a dark mine passage hour after hour, with no human soul near; to see no living creature except the mules as they pass with their loads, or a rat or two seeking to share one's meal; to stand in water or mud that covers the ankles, chilled to the marrow by the cold draughts that rush in when you open the trap door for the mules to pass through; to work for fourteen hours—waiting—opening and shutting a door—then waiting again—for sixty cents; to reach the surface when all is wrapped in the mantle of night, and to fall to the earth exhausted and have to be carried away to the nearest "shack" to be revived before it is possible to walk to the farther shack called "home."

Boys twelve years of age may be *legally* employed in the mines of West Virginia, by day or by night, and for as many hours as the employers care to make them toil or their bodies will stand the strain. Where the disregard of child life is such that this may be done openly and with legal sanction, it is easy to believe what miners have again and again told me—that there are hundreds of little boys of nine and ten years of age employed in the coal mines of this state.

3. Sweatshop Hours for Bakers (1905)

The abuse of labor in dangerous or unhealthful occupations prompted an increasing number of state legislatures, exercising so-called "police powers," to pass regulatory laws. In 1898 the Supreme Court upheld a Utah statute prohibiting miners from working more than eight hours a day, except in emergencies. But in 1905 the Court, by a 5-to-4 decision in the case of Lochner *vs.* New York, overthrew a state law forbidding bakers to work more than ten hours a day. The majority held that the right of both employers and employees to make labor contracts was protected by the 14th Amendment. Characterize the social conscience of the majority of the Supreme Court in the light of this memorable decision written by Mr. Justice Peckham.

The question whether this act is valid as a labor law, pure and simple, may be dismissed in a few words. There is no reasonable ground for interfering with the liberty of person or the right of free contract, by determining the hours of labor, in the occupation of a baker. There is no contention that bakers as a class are not equal in intelligence and capacity to men in other trades or manual occupations, or that they are not able to assert their rights and care for themselves without the protecting arm of the state interfering with their independence of judgment and of action. They are in no sense wards of the state.

Viewed in the light of a purely labor law, with no reference whatever to the question of health, we think that a law like the one before us involves neither the safety, the morals, nor the welfare of the public, and that the interest of the public is not in the slightest degree affected by such an act.

3. 198 *U.S. Reports* 57, 59, 61.

The law must be upheld, if at all, as a law pertaining to the health of the individual engaged in the occupation of a baker. It does not affect any other portion of the public than those who are engaged in that occupation. Clean and wholesome bread does not depend upon whether the baker works but ten hours per day or only sixty hours a week. The limitation of the hours of labor does not come within the police power on that ground. . . .

We think that there can be no fair doubt that the trade of a baker, in and of itself, is not an unhealthy one to that degree which would authorize the legislature to interfere with the right to labor, and with the right of free contract on the part of the individual, either as employer or employee.

In looking through statistics regarding all trades and occupations, it may be true that the trade of baker does not appear to be as healthy as some other trades, and is also vastly more healthy than still others. To the common understanding the trade of a baker has never been regarded as an unhealthy one. Very likely physicians would not recommend the exercise of that or of any other trade as a remedy for ill health. Some occupations are more healthy than others, but we think there are none which might not come under the power of the legislature to supervise and control the hours of working therein, if the mere fact that the occupation is not absolutely and perfectly healthy is to confer that right upon the legislative department of the government. . . .

. . . We do not believe in the soundness of the views which uphold this law. On the contrary, we think that such a law as this, although passed in the assumed exercise of the police power, and as relating to the public health, or the health of the employees named, is not within that power, and is invalid. The act is not, within any fair meaning of the term, a health law, but is an illegal interference with the rights of individuals, both employers and employees, to make contracts regarding labor upon such terms as they may think best, or which they may agree upon with the other parties to such contracts.

Statutes of the nature of that under review, limiting the hours in which grown and intelligent men may labor to earn their living, are mere meddlesome interferences with the rights of the individual, and they are not saved from condemnation by the claim that they are passed in the exercise of the police power and upon the subject of the health of the individual whose rights are interfered with, unless there be some fair ground, reasonable in and of itself, to say that there is material danger to the public health, or to the health of the employees, if the hours of labor are not curtailed.

[Mr. Justice Holmes, the great dissenter, filed a famous protest in the bakers' case. He argued that a majority of the people of New York State evidently wanted the law, and that the Court ought not to impose its own social philosophy. "The 14th Amendment," he solemnly declared, "does not enact Mr. Herbert Spencer's Social Statics." As for the right to work more than ten hours, Mayor Gaynor of New York remarked, "There were no journeymen bakers that I know of clamoring for any such liberty." Possibly chastened by Holmes' vigorous views,

*the Court relented and in 1908 unanimously approved an Oregon statute pro-
hibiting the employment of women in factories, laundries, and other establishments more than ten hours in one day. In 1917 the Court upheld an Oregon
ten-hour law for both men and women.*]

B. CORRUPTION IN THE CITIES

1. Steffens Bares Philadelphia Bossism (1904)

A California-born journalist, (Joseph) Lincoln Steffens, after serving as a "gentleman reporter" in New York, emerged as one of the first and most influential of the
reforming muckrakers. Associated with *McClure's Magazine*, the leading muckraking
journal, he published a sensational series of articles on municipal graft, later collected in book form as *The Shame of the Cities* (1904). After the muckraking
craze ended, Steffens became disillusioned, visited Russia, interviewed Lenin, and
developed a warm admiration for the Soviet Union. In reading his famous exposé
of Philadelphia, note what is most ironical about conditions; what is most shocking.
Who was responsible for the existence and continuation of these irregularities?

Other American cities, no matter how bad their own condition may be,
all point with scorn to Philadelphia as worse—"the worst-governed city in
the country." St. Louis, Minneapolis, Pittsburgh submit with some patience
to the jibes of any other community; the most friendly suggestion from
Philadelphia is rejected with contempt. The Philadelphians are "supine,"
"asleep"; hopelessly ring-ruled, they are "complacent." "Politically be-
nighted," Philadelphia is supposed to have no light to throw upon a state
of things that is almost universal.

This is not fair. Philadelphia is, indeed, corrupt; but it is not without
significance. Every city and town in the country can learn something from
the typical political experience of this great representative city. New York
is excused for many of its ills because it is the metropolis; Chicago, because
of its forced development; Philadelphia is our "third largest" city and its
growth has been gradual and natural.

Immigration has been blamed for our municipal conditions. Philadelphia,
with 47 percent of its population native-born of native-born parents, is the
most American of our greater cities.

It is "good," too, and intelligent. I don't know just how to measure the
intelligence of a community, but a Pennsylvania college professor who
declared to me his belief in education for the masses as a way out of
political corruption, himself justified the "rake-off" of preferred contractors
on public works on the ground of a "fair business profit."

Another plea we [Americans] have made is that we are too busy to
attend to public   siness, and we have promised, when we come to wealth
and leisure, to do better. Philadelphia has long enjoyed great and widely
distributed prosperity. It is the city of homes. There is a dwelling house
for every five persons—men, women, and children—of the population; and

1. Lincoln Steffens, *The Shame of the Cities* (1904), pp. 193–201, *passim.*

the people give one a sense of more leisure and repose than any community
I ever dwelt in. Some Philadelphians account for their political state on the
ground of their ease and comfort. . . .

Then we hear that we are a young people and that when we are older
and "have traditions," like some of the old countries, we also will be honest.
Philadelphia is one of the oldest of our cities and treasures for us scenes
and relics of some of the noblest traditions of "our fair land." Yet I was
told once, "for a joke," a party of boodlers [grafters] counted out the
"divvy" [division] of their graft in unison with the ancient chime of
Independence Hall. . . .

Philadelphia is proud; good people there defend corruption and boast
of their machine. My college professor, with his philosophic view of "rake-
offs," is one Philadelphia type. Another is the man who, driven to bay with
his local pride, says: "At least you must admit that our machine is the best
you have ever seen." . . .

PHILADELPHIA
REFORM BUTTON

An uprising of hon-
est voters blocked a
scheme to lease the
municipal gas plant
for seventy-five years.
Literary Digest, 1905.

Disgraceful? Other cities say so. But I say that if
Philadelphia is a disgrace, it is a disgrace not to
itself alone, nor to Pennsylvania, but to the United
States and to American character. For this great city,
so highly representative in other respects, is not
behind in political experience, but ahead, with New
York.

Philadelphia is a city that has had its reforms. . . .
The present condition of Philadelphia, therefore, is
not that which precedes, but that which follows
reform, and in this distinction lies its startling general significance. What has happened . . . in Philadelphia may happen in any American city "after
the reform is over."

For reform with us is usually revolt, not govern-
ment, and is soon over. Our people do not seek, they avoid self-rule, and
"reforms" are spasmodic efforts to punish bad rulers and get somebody that
will give us good government or something that will make it. A self-acting
form of government is an ancient superstition. We are an inventive people,
and we all think that we shall devise some day a legal machine that will
turn out good government automatically. The Philadelphians have treasured
this belief longer than the rest of us and have tried it more often. . . .

The Philadelphia machine isn't the best. It isn't sound, and I doubt if it
would stand in New York or Chicago. The enduring strength of the typical
American political machine is that it is a natural growth—a sucker, but
deep-rooted in the people. The New Yorkers vote for Tammany Hall. The
Philadelphians do not vote; they are disfranchised, and their disfranchisement is one anchor of the foundation of the Philadelphia organization.

This is no figure of speech. The honest citizens of Philadelphia have no
more rights at the polls than the Negroes down South. Nor do they fight

very hard for this basic privilege. You can arouse their Republican ire by talking about the black Republican votes lost in the Southern states by white Democratic intimidation, but if you remind the average Philadelphian that he is in the same position, he will look startled, then say, "That's so, that's literally true, only I never thought of it in just that way." And it is literally true.

The machine controls the whole process of voting, and practices fraud at every stage. The [tax] assessor's list is the voting list, and the assessor is the machine's man. . . . The assessor pads the list with the names of dead dogs, children, and non-existent persons. One newspaper printed the picture of a dog, another that of a little four-year-old Negro boy, down on such a list. A "ring" orator, in a speech resenting sneers at his ward as "low down," reminded his hearers that that was the ward of Independence Hall, and, naming over the signers of the Declaration of Independence, he closed his highest flight of eloquence with the statement that "these men, the fathers of American liberty, voted down here once. And," he added with a catching grin, "they vote here yet."

Rudolph Blankenburg, a persistent fighter for the right and the use of the right to vote (and, by the way, an immigrant), sent out just before one election a registered letter to each voter on the rolls of a certain selected division. Sixty-three percent were returned marked "not at," "removed," "deceased," etc. . . .

The repeating [voting more than once] is done boldly, for the machine controls the election officers, often choosing them from among the fraudulent names; and when no one appears to serve, assigning the heeler [political hanger-on] ready for the expected vacancy. The police are forbidden by law to stand within thirty feet of the polls, but they are at the [ballot] box and they are there to see that the machine's orders are obeyed and that repeaters whom they help to furnish are permitted to vote without "intimidation" on the names they, the police, have supplied. . . .

The business proceeds with very few hitches; there is more jesting than fighting. Violence in the past has had its effect; and is not often necessary nowadays, but if it is needed the police are there to apply it. Several citizens told me that they had seen the police help to beat citizens or election officers who were trying to do their duty, then arrest the victim. . . .

2. Plunkitt Defends "Honest Graft" (1905)

Tammany Hall was the powerful and corrupt Democratic political machine that dominated New York City politics for many years. One of its cleverest officials, who became a millionaire through "honest graft," was George Washington (!) Plunkitt. According to his account as here recorded by a newspaper reporter, he was above such dirty work as "shaking down" houses of prostitution ("disorderly houses"). Comment critically on the distinction between the two kinds of graft, and ascertain what light this statement throws on the continuing power of Tammany Hall.

2. William L. Riordan, *Plunkitt of Tammany Hall* (1948 ed.), pp. 3–8. By permission of Alfred A. Knopf, Inc.

"Everybody is talkin' these days about Tammany men growin' rich on graft, but nobody thinks of drawin' the distinction between honest graft and dishonest graft. There's all the difference in the world between the two. Yes, many of our men have grown rich in politics. I have myself. I've made a big fortune out of the game, and I'm gettin' richer every day, but I've not gone in for dishonest graft—blackmailin' gamblers, saloon-keepers, disorderly people, etc.—and neither has any of the men who have made big fortunes in politics.

"There's an honest graft, and I'm an example of how it works. I might sum up the whole thing by sayin': 'I seen my opportunities and I took 'em.'

"Just let me explain by examples. My party's in power in the city, and it's goin' to undertake a lot of public improvements. Well, I'm tipped off, say, that they're goin' to lay out a new park at a certain place.

"I see my opportunity and I take it. I go to that place and I buy up all the land I can in the neighborhood. Then the board of this or that makes its plan public, and there is a rush to get my land, which nobody cared particular for before.

"Ain't it perfectly honest to charge a good price and make a profit on my investment and foresight? Of course it is. Well, that's honest graft.

"Or, supposin' it's a new bridge they're goin' to build. I get tipped off and I buy as much property as I can that has to be taken for approaches. I sell at my own price later on and drop some more money in the bank.

"Wouldn't you? It's just like lookin' ahead in Wall Street or in the coffee or cotton market. It's honest graft, and I'm lookin' for it every day in the year. I will tell you frankly that I've got a good lot of it, too.

"I'll tell you of one case. They were goin' to fix up a big park, no matter where. I got on to it, and went lookin' about for land in that neighborhood.

"I could get nothin' at a bargain but a big piece of swamp, but I took it fast enough and held on to it. What turned out was just what I counted on. They couldn't make the park complete without Plunkitt's swamp, and they had to pay a good price for it. Anything dishonest in that?

"Up in the watershed I made some money, too. I bought up several bits of land there some years ago and made a pretty good guess that they would be bought up for water purposes later by the city.

"Somehow, I always guessed about right, and shouldn't I enjoy the profit of my foresight? It was rather amusin' when the condemnation commissioners came along and found piece after piece of the land in the name of George Plunkitt of the Fifteenth Assembly District, New York City. They wondered how I knew just what to buy. The answer is—I seen my opportunity and I took it. I haven't confined myself to land; anything that pays is in my line. . . .

"I've told you how I got rich by honest graft. Now, let me tell you that most politicians who are accused of robbin' the city get rich the same way.

"They didn't steal a dollar from the city treasury. They just seen their opportunities and took them. That is why, when a reform administration comes in and spends a half million dollars in tryin' to find the public robberies they talked about in the campaign, they don't find them.

"The books are always all right. The money in the city treasury is all right. Everything is all right. All they can show is that the Tammany heads of departments looked after their friends, within the law, and gave them what opportunities they could to make honest graft. Now, let me tell you that's never goin' to hurt Tammany with the people. Every good man looks after his friends, and any man who doesn't isn't likely to be popular. If I have a good thing to hand out in private life, I give it to a friend. Why shouldn't I do the same in public life? . . .

"Tammany was beat in 1901 because the people were deceived into believin' that it worked dishonest graft. They didn't draw a distinction between dishonest and honest graft, but they saw that some Tammany men grew rich, and supposed they had been robbin' the city treasury or levyin' blackmail on disorderly houses, or workin' in with the gamblers and lawbreakers.

"As a matter of policy, if nothing else, why should the Tammany leaders go into such dirty business when there is so much honest graft lyin' around when they are in power? Did you ever consider that?

"Now, in conclusion, I want to say that I don't own a dishonest dollar. If my worst enemy was given the job of writin' my epitaph when I'm gone, he couldn't do more than write:

" 'George W. Plunkitt.
He Seen His Opportunities and He Took 'Em.' "

C. THE HEYDAY OF MUCKRAKING

1. Exposing the Meat Packers (1906)

Upton Sinclair, the youthful and prolific Socialist writer, published his novel *The Jungle* in 1906. It was a damning exposure of conditions in the Chicago meat-packing plants. Seeking to turn people to socialism, he turned their stomachs. The uproar that followed publication of his novel caused President Roosevelt to initiate an official investigation, and the following sober report was hardly less shocking than *The Jungle*. It confirmed the essential truth of Sinclair's exposé, except for such lurid scenes as men falling into vats and emerging as lard. Determine which aspect of this official investigation revealed conditions most detrimental to the public health.

. . . Meat scraps were also found being shoveled into receptacles from dirty floors, where they were left to lie until again shoveled into barrels or into machines for chopping. These floors, it must be noted, were in most cases damp and soggy, in dark, ill-ventilated rooms, and the employees in utter ignorance of cleanliness or danger to health expectorated at will upon them. In a word, we saw meat shoveled from filthy wooden floors, piled on tables rarely washed, pushed from room to room in rotten box carts, in all of which processes it was in the way of gathering dirt, splinters, floor filth, and the expectoration of tuberculous and other diseased workers.

1. *Congressional Record,* 59 Cong., 1 sess., p. 7801 (June 4, 1906).

Where comment was made to floor superintendents about these matters, it was always the reply that this meat would afterwards be cooked, and that this sterilization would prevent any danger from its use. Even this, it may be pointed out in passing, is not wholly true. A very considerable portion of the meat so handled is sent out as smoked products and in the form of sausages, which are prepared to be eaten without being cooked. . . .

As an extreme example of the entire disregard on the part of employees of any notion of cleanliness in handling dressed meat, we saw a hog that had just been killed, cleaned, washed, and started on its way to the cooling room fall from the sliding rail to a dirty wooden floor and slide part way into a filthy men's privy. It was picked up by two employees, placed upon a truck, carried into the cooling room and hung up with other carcasses, no effort being made to clean it. . . .

In one well-known establishment we came upon fresh meat being shoveled into barrels, and a regular proportion being added of stale scraps that had lain on a dirty floor in the corner of a room for some days previous. In another establishment, equally well known, a long table was noted covered with several hundred pounds of cooked scraps of beef and other meats. Some of these meat scraps were dry, leathery, and unfit to be eaten; and in the heap were found pieces of pigskin, and even some bits of rope strands and other rubbish. Inquiry evoked the frank admission from the man in charge that this was to be ground up and used in making "potted ham."

All of these canned products bear labels, of which the following is a sample:

ABATTOIR NO. —

THE CONTENTS OF THIS PACKAGE HAVE BEEN
INSPECTED ACCORDING TO THE ACT OF
CONGRESS OF MARCH 3, 1891.

[*The agitation and investigation inspired by Sinclair's* The Jungle *had much to do with bringing about the passage by Congress of the Meat Inspection Act and the Pure Food and Drug Act of 1906.*]

2. Roosevelt Roasts Muckrakers (1906)

President Roosevelt, though recognizing some unpalatable truth in Upton Sinclair's *The Jungle,* was critical. He wrote the author bluntly that he had said things which should not have been written unless backed up "with testimony that would satisfy an honest man of reasonable intelligence." Privately he declared that Sinclair had reflected unfairly on both honest and dishonest capitalism in Chicago. Finally nauseated by excessive sensationalism, Roosevelt made the following famous attack (which gave rise to the term "muckraker") in a Washington speech. Analyze critically the strengths and weaknesses of his argument that hysterical and indiscriminate muckraking was doing more harm than good.

In Bunyan's *Pilgrim's Progress* you may recall the description of the Man with the Muck-rake [manure rake], the man who could look no way

2. Theodore Roosevelt, "The Man with the Muck-Rake," *Putnam's Monthly and The Critic,* I, 42–43 (October, 1906).

but downward, with the muck-rake in his hand; who was offered a celestial crown for his muck-rake, but who would neither look up nor regard the crown he was offered, but continued to rake to himself the filth of the floor.

In *Pilgrim's Progress* the Man with the Muck-rake is set forth as the example of him whose vision is fixed on carnal instead of on spiritual things. Yet he also typifies the man who in this life consistently refuses to see aught that is lofty, and fixes his eyes with solemn intentness only on that which is vile and debasing.

Now it is very necessary that we should not flinch from seeing what is vile and debasing. There is filth on the floor, and it must be scraped up with the muck-rake: and there are times and places where this service is the most needed of all the services that can be performed. But the man who never does anything else, who never thinks or speaks or writes save of his feats with the muck-rake, speedily becomes, not a help to society, not an incitement to good, but one of the most potent forces for evil.

WELL BRANDED! THE BEEF TRUST!
Equipped with the official Neill-Reynolds investigative report, Roosevelt brands the beef trust "Dangerous, Unclean, Revolting." Philadelphia *Press*, 1906.

There are—in the body politic, economic, and social—many and grave evils, and there is urgent necessity for the sternest war upon them. There should be relentless exposure of and attack upon every evil man, whether politician or businessman; every evil practice, whether in politics, in business, or in social life. I hail as a benefactor every writer or speaker, every man who, on the platform, or in book, magazine, or newspaper, with merciless severity makes such attack, provided always that he in his turn remembers that the attack is of use only if it is absolutely truthful. The liar is no whit better than the thief, and if his mendacity takes the form of slander, he may be worse than most thieves. It puts a premium upon knavery untruthfully to attack an honest man, or even with hysterical exaggeration to assail a bad man with untruth. An epidemic of indiscriminate assault upon character does no good, but very great harm. The soul of every scoundrel is gladdened whenever an honest man is assailed, or even when a scoundrel is untruthfully assailed.

Now, it is easy to twist out of shape what I have just said. . . . Some persons are sincerely incapable of understanding that to denounce mudslinging does not mean the indorsement of whitewashing, and both the interested individuals who need whitewashing and those others who practice mudslinging like to encourage such confusion of ideas. One of the chief counts against those who make indiscriminate assault upon men in business or men in public life is that they invite a reaction which is sure to tell powerfully in favor of the unscrupulous scoundrel who really ought to be attacked, who ought to be exposed, who ought, if possible, to be put in the penitentiary. If Aristides is praised overmuch as just, people get tired of hearing it;[*] and overcensure of the unjust finally and from similar reasons results in their favor.

Any excess is almost sure to invite a reaction; and, unfortunately, the reaction, instead of taking the form of punishment of those guilty of the excess, is very apt to take the form either of punishment of the unoffending or of giving immunity, and even strength, to offenders. The effort to make financial or political profit out of the destruction of character can only result in public calamity. Gross and reckless assaults on character, whether on the stump or in newspaper, magazine, or book, create a morbid and vicious public sentiment, and at the same time act as a profound deterrent to able men of normal sensitiveness and tend to prevent them from entering the public service at any price.

[*Roosevelt thus threw muck at the muckrakers. They resented his attack, claiming that even if they exaggerated they were exposing evil conditions and promoting desired legislation. (At the same time, they made money selling their magazine articles and books.) But Roosevelt was unconvinced. In 1911 he went so far as to write privately: ". . . I think the muckrakers stand on a level of infamy with the corruptionists in politics. After all, there is no great difference between violation of the eighth [no stealing] and the ninth [no lying] commandments; and to sell one's vote for money is morally, I believe, hardly as reprehensible as to practice slanderous mendacity for hire." (Roosevelt Letters, VII, 447.) The truth is that he continued with intemperate muckraking himself, attacking "malefactors of great wealth," "nature fakers," and others. "You're the chief muckraker," Speaker Cannon told him flatly in 1906.]*

D. THE CONSERVATION CRUSADE

1. Roosevelt Saves the Forests (1907)

Greedy or shortsighted Americans had plundered their forests and mineral resources with incredible rapacity. President Roosevelt, one-time Dakota cattle rancher, provided the lagging conservation movement with dynamic leadership. Under the

---

[*] An allusion to Plutarch's story of the Athenian who voted for the banishment of Aristides (called "The Just") because he was tired of hearing everyone call him just.

1. E. E. Morison, ed., *The Letters of Theodore Roosevelt* (1952), V, 683–84 (Roosevelt to Secretary of Agriculture Wilson, June 7, 1907). By permission of the Harvard University Press.

Forest Reserve Act of 1891, he set aside about 150,000,000 acres of government timberland as national forest reserves—more than three times as much as his three predecessors had saved. The "predatory interests" complained bitterly, and in this private letter Roosevelt took them to task. Actually the worst offenders among the "skinners" were the small-fry lumbermen. The big trusts, though grasping, were in some degree governed by the reforestation needs of long-range lumbering. Note what advantages would result from Roosevelt's policy, as he describes it in the following letter.

As to the forest reserves, their creation has damaged just one class, that is, the great lumber barons: the managers and owners of those lumber companies which by illegal, fraudulent, or unfair methods have desired to get possession of the valuable timber of the public domain, to skin the land, and to abandon it when impoverished well-nigh to the point of worthlessness.

There are some small men who have wanted to get hold of this lumber land for improper purposes, but they are not powerful or influential, and though they have sometimes been put forward to cause an agitation, the real beneficiaries of the destruction of the forest reserves would be the great lumber companies, which would speedily monopolize them.

If it had not been for the creation of the present system of forest reserves, practically every acre of timberland in the West would now be controlled or be on the point of being controlled by one huge lumber trust. The object of the beneficiaries of this trust would be to exhaust the resources of the country for their own immediate pecuniary benefit, and then when they had rendered it well-nigh worthless to turn it contemptuously over to settlers, who would find too late that those responsible for such conditions had betrayed them and had been false to the public.

The policy of the Government is to put actual settlers on every plot of agricultural ground within the forest reserves, and then, instead of turning these forests over to great corporations or standing by with supine indifference while they are raided by timber thieves, to enforce the law with strict honesty against all men, big or little, who try to rob the public domain; and all the time to permit the freest use of the timber, consistent with preserving the forests for the benefit of the next generation. . . .

It is absolutely necessary to ascertain in practical fashion the best methods of reforestation, and only the National Government can do this successfully.

In the East, the states are now painfully, and at great expense, endeavoring to undo the effects of their former shortsighted policy in throwing away their forest lands. Congress has before it bills to establish by purchase great forest reserves in the White Mountains and the Southern Appalachians, and the only argument against the bills is that of their great expense. New York and Pennsylvania are now, late in the day, endeavoring themselves to protect the forests which guard the headwaters of their streams. Michigan and Wisconsin have already had their good timber stripped from their forests by the great lumber companies. But the Western states, far more fortunate than their Eastern sisters in this regard, can now reserve their forests for the good of all their citizens, without expense, if they choose to show the requisite foresight.

2. The West Protests Conservation (1907)

The new forest-reserve policies often worked a hardship on honest Western settlers, who sometimes had to get permission from a federal official before they could lawfully cut a stick of firewood. The government, they charged, was more concerned with preserving trees than people. The Governor of Colorado, disturbed by the large-scale withdrawals of Western timber and coal lands by Washington, summoned a Public Lands Convention to meet in Denver in 1907. The deliberations of this body inspired the following editorial in a San Francisco newspaper. Ascertain whether the West really opposed conservation, and whether the East was unfair in its demands.

The convention which has just adjourned at Denver is the first body of importance that has dealt with the subject of the disposal of the public lands of the United States. Considering the fact that the country has been in the real estate business for more than a century, and that during that period it has, by hook and crook, chiefly by crook, disposed of the major part of its holdings, it seems like a case of locking the stable door after nearly all of the horses have been stolen. The only question left to determine is whether the people who have permitted the theft of the horses, and who lent a hand in the stealing, shall be allowed to enjoy the most of the benefits which may accrue from taking good care of the steeds which still remain in the stalls.

The Far West, in which all the lands—coal-bearing, forest, pasture, and agricultural—still remaining in the possession of the government are to be found, has formally gone on record in this matter, and demands that the new states be treated with the same consideration as those commonwealths which have already divided their patrimony among their individual citizens. The Denver Convention in its resolutions recognizes the wisdom of treating the lands of the nation as a public trust, but it insisted that this trust should be administered for the benefit of the states wherein the lands still remaining are situated and not for the benefit of the people of the older states of the Union, who have no lands, forests, mines, or pastures that are not in the possession of private individuals.

Congress will be unable to resist the justice of this contention. As a rule, that body is not overswift to recognize the rights of those sections of the Union with a small representation in the Lower House, but the American people, when they understand the matter thoroughly, may be depended upon to prevent an injustice. Just now the popular impression at the East is that the Far West is opposed to the conservation of its forests, and that it supports the efforts of unscrupulous grabbers to steal the public domain. But the campaign of education inaugurated by the Public Lands Convention will soon convince it that all that is asked for is even justice for the new states, and that demands that the profits arising from the eleventh-hour

2. San Francisco *Chronicle,* June 22, 1907.

reform shall not be absorbed by the states that have eaten their cake and now wish to share with those who have scarcely had a chance to nibble theirs.

E. THE ERA OF TRUST BUSTING

1. Roosevelt Attacks the Anti-Trust Act (1908)

Early in his thinking about trusts, Roosevelt concluded that bigness was not necessarily badness. He favored destroying the evils in trusts rather than the trusts themselves, and he had no sympathy with the "utter folly" of the "quacks" who cried, "Destroy the Trusts." Corporate organizations that used their power with a proper regard for the public welfare were necessary for the nation's prosperity, he believed, and should not be harassed; those that were guilty of malpractices should be curbed or broken up. Roosevelt instituted proceedings under the Sherman Act against the giant Standard Oil Company, and in 1911 the Supreme Court ordered it dissolved. But the pro rata distribution of stock among the new components left the combined power equal to what it had previously been, with stock values much higher. Explain why Roosevelt in this message to Congress wanted a drastic revision of the Sherman Act, and whether his position was sound.

In reference to the Sherman anti-trust law, I repeat the recommendations made in my message at the opening of the present Congress, as well as in my message to the previous Congress. The attempt in this law to provide in sweeping terms against all combinations of whatever character, if technically in restraint of trade as such restraint has been defined by the courts, must necessarily be either futile or mischievous, and sometimes both.

The present law makes some combinations illegal, although they may be useful to the country. On the other hand, as to some huge combinations which are both noxious and illegal, even if the action

THE TRUSTS: "HE'S GOOD ENOUGH FOR ME."

A famous anti-Roosevelt parody of the original Davenport cartoon (see p. 632) by Opper in the Hearst press.

1. *A Compilation of the Messages and Papers of the Presidents* (n.d.), XVII, 7511 (Jan. 31, 1908).

undertaken against them under the law by the Government is successful, the result may be to work but a minimum benefit to the public. Even though the combination be broken up and a small measure of reform thereby produced, the real good aimed at cannot be obtained, for such real good can come only by a thorough and continuing supervision over the acts of the combination in all its parts, so as to prevent stock watering, improper forms of competition, and, in short, wrongdoing generally.

The law should correct that portion of the Sherman Act which prohibits all combinations of the character above described, whether they be reasonable or unreasonable. But this should be done only as a part of a general scheme to provide for this effective and thoroughgoing supervision by the National Government of all the operations of the big interstate business concerns.

2. La Follette Exposes Roosevelt (1912)

Prior to Roosevelt's day the trusts had flourished, in part because successive Attorneys General were friendly to Big Business. Roosevelt noisily inaugurated a new era of "trust busting." The relative results are revealed by this seventeen-year table of federal prosecutions against Big Business under the Sherman Anti-Trust Act of 1890:

PRESIDENTIAL ADMINISTRATION	BILLS IN EQUITY	INDICTMENTS	CONTEMPT PROCEEDINGS	FORFEITURE PROCEEDINGS	TOTAL ACTIONS
Harrison (1890–1893)	4	3	0	0	7
Cleveland (1893–1897)	4	2	2	0	8
McKinley (1897–1901)	3	0	0	0	3
Roosevelt (1901–1909)	18	25	0	1	44
Taft (1909–1913)	46	43	1	0	90
Wilson (1913–1920)	35	45	0	0	80

The fiery Progressive Robert M. La Follette, United States Senator from Wisconsin, took sharp exception to Roosevelt's view that the Sherman Act ought to be modified so as to differentiate more sharply between "good" and "bad" trusts. La Follette believed that the Sherman Act was quite adequate if the administration would only bestir itself properly. Comment on Roosevelt's reputation as a "trust buster" in the light of the above table and La Follette's following criticism.

Thus it was that Roosevelt put the Sherman Anti-Trust Law under the ban of executive disapproval. It was the only federal statute for the protection of the public against these plundering combinations. His denunciation of the law was an executive sanction to violate the law. It opened the floodgates for trust organization, and upon Theodore Roosevelt, more than any other man, must rest the responsibility for the gravest problem which ever menaced the industrial freedom of the American people. He prosecuted on an average six cases a year against a carefully selected list of these

2. R. M. La Follette, *Autobiography* (1960 ed.), pp. 296–97. By permission of the University of Wisconsin Press. The tabular data are from Eliot Jones, *The Trust Problem in the United States* (1928), pp. 441–45.

combinations. He went just far enough to give color to the claim that he was upholding the law, but not far enough seriously to injure those prosecuted or deter in the slightest degree the hundreds that were organizing every month throughout his entire administration.

A study of the more important of these cases against combinations under the Sherman Act shows that the actions were so brought that the government would, at best, win only a nominal victory; and that the decree of the court would be so limited by the allegation of the complaint as to leave the defendant combination in a position, under its existing form or by an easy shift, to continue its wrongdoing.

. . . When Roosevelt became President there were 149 combinations and trusts, including railways, the entire 149 having a total stock and bond issue of only $3,784,000,000. When he left the White House there were 10,020 of these monster plants in combination, including, with the combined railroads, a total capitalization amounting to the enormous sum of $31,672,-000,000—more than 70 percent of which was water. The power of these combinations was so extensive, and so completely did they suppress competition, that they were able to advance prices on transportation, and on the products of the mines and factories, to enable them to pay dividends on this fictitious and fraudulent overcapitalization.

[*The accusation by Senator La Follette and others that Roosevelt, the Trust Buster, merely flourished a padded stick is not altogether fair. He inaugurated a significant movement, and some of his most important prosecutions, notably the Standard Oil case, were not concluded until the days of his successor, President Taft.*]

THOUGHT PROVOKERS

1. What would be the attitude of organized labor today toward George F. Baer's view that the only interest of the workingman in a business is to secure "fair wages for the work he does"?

2. It has been said that no community has any better government than it deserves. Comment. Account for the failure of honest citizens to participate more actively in city government.

3. Vested interests opposed the Pure Food and Drug Law of 1906 on the ground that one of our basic freedoms is the freedom to eat what we want to. Comment. Does overemphasis on the seamy side of life develop a depraved taste or callousness or both? Which reaction is the more dangerous?

4. The federal government owns over 20 percent of the land surface of the country today (exclusive of Alaska), chiefly in the West. Is this situation healthy or unhealthy? Should Americans be seriously concerned about conserving oil and other mineral resources when modern science has uncovered uranium and other fantastic new sources of energy?

5. Would there be fewer or more trusts today if Theodore Roosevelt had never been President?

FURTHER EXPLORATION

General: G. E. Mowry, *The Era of Theodore Roosevelt, 1900–1912* (1958); E. F. Goldman, *Rendezvous with Destiny* (1952); Richard Hofstadter, *The Age of Reform* (1955). **Labor:** R. J. Cornell, *The Anthracite Coal Strike of 1902* (1957). **Corruption:** G. E. Mowry, *Theodore Roosevelt and the Progressive Movement* (1946); John Chamberlain, *Farewell to Reform* (1932). **Muckraking:** Louis Filler, *Crusaders for American Liberalism* (1950); C. C. Regier, *The Era of the Muckrakers* (1932); O. E. Anderson, Jr., *The Health of a Nation: Harvey W. Wiley and the Fight for Pure Food* (1958). **Conservation:** E. L. Peffer, *The Closing of the Public Domain* (1951); R. M. Robbins, *Our Landed Heritage* (1942); S. P. Hays, *Conservation and the Gospel of Efficiency* (1959).

Recent: W. H. Harbaugh, *Power and Responsibility: The Life and Times of Theodore Roosevelt* (1961) [paperback]; R. H. Wiebe, *Businessmen and Reform* (1962); Gabriel Kolko, *Railroads and Regulation, 1877–1916* (1965); J. H. Timberlake, *Prohibition and the Progressive Movement, 1900–1920* (1963); Roy Lubove, *The Progressives and the Slums: Tenement House Reform in New York City, 1890–1917* (1962); R. C. Bannister, Jr., *Ray Stannard Baker: The Mind and Thought of a Progressive* (1966); J. H. Young, *The Toadstool Millionaires: A Social History of Patent Medicines in America before Federal Regulation* (1961); M. L. Fausold, *Gifford Pinchot: Bull Moose Progressive* (1961); Elmo R. Richardson, *The Politics of Conservation* (1962).

Chapter 34

Taft and the Progressive Tide

Taft is utterly hopeless. . . . It would be a misfortune to have him in the presidential chair for another term, for he has shown himself an entirely unfit President. . . .

THEODORE ROOSEVELT, 1911

PROLOGUE: President Taft, the hard-luck conservative, early floundered into hot water. Honestly attempting to revise the tariff, he had to accept a bill (Payne-Aldrich) clearly shaped by the "predatory interests." Seeking to conserve natural resources, he was forced to end a bureaucratic quarrel by dismissing the Chief Forester, Gifford Pinchot, a leading conservationist. He might have weathered such setbacks if the country had not been agitated by the reformist Progressive movement, which attained irresistible momentum between 1908 and 1912. The Progressives strove to achieve overdue reforms by instituting such innovations as woman suffrage, the direct election of United States Senators, and the initiative, the referendum, and the recall. The Progressive crusade reached near-hysterical levels in 1912, when ex-President Roosevelt broke with President Taft, split the Republican Party, and headed a new ("Bull Moose") Progressive ticket. His rebellion insured victory for the Democrat Woodrow Wilson, who carried forward the Progressive tradition under the flaming banner of the New Freedom.

A. THE CRUSADE FOR WOMAN SUFFRAGE

1. Senator Owen Supports Women (1910)

Wedded to the tried and true, President Taft was no enthusiast for woman suffrage. He believed that the issue was one which should be handled by the individual states. As late as 1912 he wrote privately, "I cannot change my view . . . just to suit the exigencies of the campaign, and if it is going to hurt me, I think it will have to hurt me." But the embattled females now had an increasingly strong argument. The rapid industrialization after the Civil War had lured millions of women from the home into the office and the factory, where they were competing with men. By 1910 four states—Wyoming, Colorado, Utah, and Idaho—had granted unrestricted suffrage to women, and the Progressive upheaval of the era added great impetus to the reform. Senator Robert L. Owen, of Oklahoma, who had earlier demanded citizenship for Indians, here makes a speech to a learned society favoring woman suffrage. Locate his strongest argument; his weakest argument. Note what good arguments he does not develop.

Women compose one-half of the human race. In the last forty years, women in gradually increasing numbers have been compelled to leave the

1. *Annals of the American Academy of Political and Social Science,* Supplement, XXXV (May, 1910), pp. 6–9, *passim.* By permission of the American Academy of Political and Social Science.

649

home and enter the factory and workshop. Over seven million women are so employed, and the remainder of the sex are employed largely in domestic services. A full half of the work of the world is done by women. A careful study of the matter has demonstrated the vital fact that these working women receive a smaller wage for equal work than men do, and that the smaller wage and harder conditions imposed on the woman worker are due to the lack of the ballot.

Many women have a very hard time, and if the ballot would help them, even a little, I should like to see them have it. . . . Equal pay for equal work is the first great reason justifying this change of governmental policy.

There are other reasons which are persuasive: First, women, take it all in all, are the equals of men in intelligence, and no man has the hardihood to assert the contrary. . . .

The man is usually better informed with regard to state government, but women are better informed about house government, and she can learn state government with as much facility as he can learn how to instruct children, properly feed and clothe the household, care for the sick, play on the piano, or make a house beautiful. . . .

The woman ballot will not revolutionize the world. Its results in Colorado, for example, might have been anticipated. First, it did give women better wages for equal work; second, it led immediately to a number of laws the women wanted, and the first laws they demanded were laws for the protection of the children of the state, making it a misdemeanor to contribute to the delinquency of a child; laws for the improved care of defective children; also, the Juvenile Court for the conservation of wayward boys and girls; the better care of the insane, the deaf, the dumb, the blind; the curfew bell to keep children off the streets at night; raising the age of consent for girls; improving the reformatories and prisons of the state; improving the hospital services of the state; improving the sanitary laws affecting the health of the homes of the state. Their [women's] interest in the public health is a matter of great importance. Above all, there resulted laws for improving the school system.

Several important results followed. Both political parties were induced to put up cleaner, better men, for the women would not stand a notoriously corrupt or unclean candidate. The headquarters of political parties became more decent, and the polling places became respectable. The bad women, enslaved by mercenary vice, do not vote, and good women do vote in as great proportion as men. Every evil prophecy against granting the suffrage has failed. The public men of Colorado, Wyoming, Utah, and Idaho give it a cordial support.

The testimony is universal:

First, it has not made women mannish; they still love their homes and children just the same as ever, and are better able to protect themselves and their children because of the ballot.

Second, they have not become office-seekers, nor pothouse politicians.

They have not become swaggerers and insolent on the streets. They still teach good manners to men, as they always have done. It [suffrage] has made women broader and greatly increased the understanding of the community at large of the problems of good government; of proper sanitation, of pure food, of clean water, and all such matters in which intelligent women would naturally take an interest.

It has not absolutely regenerated society, but it has improved it. It has raised the educational qualification of the suffrage, and has elevated the moral standard of the suffrage, because there are more criminal men than criminal women. . . .

The great doctrine of the American Republic that "all governments derive their just powers from the consent of the governed" justifies the plea of one-half of the people, the women, to exercise the suffrage. The doctrine of the American Revolutionary War that taxation without representation is unendurable justifies women in exercising the suffrage.

2. A Woman Assails Woman Suffrage (1910)

As late as 1910 many women plainly did not want to shoulder the heavy civic responsibilities that would come with the ballot. One argument was that each sex was superior in its own sphere—women in the home, men in the outside world— and that a separation was best for all concerned. Agitators for woman suffrage feared that if their cause were submitted to a vote by all women, it would be defeated. The suffragists argued that those females who did want the vote ought to have it. Mrs. Gilbert E. Jones, an opponent of votes for women, here pleads her case before a scholarly group. Ascertain to what extent she riddles the arguments of Senator Owen, just given, especially in regard to "taxation without representation," the improvement of wages, and the elevation of morals. In what respects is her logic faulty?

The anti-suffragists are not organizing or rushing into committees, societies, or associations, and their doings are not being cried out from the house-tops. Yet they show by undeniable facts, easily verified, that woman suffrage bills and proposals have been defeated and turned down at the rate of once in every twenty-seven days in the state legislatures for the last twelve years. . . .

A great many states have granted to women school suffrage, but only a partisan or sectarian issue will bring out the woman's vote. In Massachusetts women have voted on school boards, and after thirty years' training, only 2 or 3 percent of the women register to vote. This hardly can be pronounced "success," or worth while. . . .

Taxation without representation is tyranny, but we must be very careful to define what we mean by the phrase. If we adopt the suffrage attitude, "I pay taxes, therefore I should vote," the natural conclusion is that everybody who pays taxes should vote, or we have a tyrannical form of government. Remember that this argument is used in an unqualified way. We have a "tyranny" here, we are told, because some women pay taxes, yet do not

2. *Ibid.,* pp. 16–21, *passim.* By permission of the American Academy of Political and Social Science.

THE CHURCH VOTE DISFRANCHISED

Woman-suffrage propaganda issued by the National American Woman
Suffrage Association, *Headquarters News Letter,* October 25, 1916.

vote. If this is true without any qualification, it must be true not only of
women, but of everybody. Accordingly, this government is tyrannical if
corporations pay taxes, but do not vote; if aliens pay taxes, but do not vote;
if minors pay taxes, but do not vote; if anybody pays taxes, but does not
vote. The only correct conclusion is, not that women should vote because
some of them pay taxes, but that every taxpayer should be given the
privilege of the ballot. . . .

A very conscientious investigation by this League cannot find that the
ballot will help the wage-earning woman. Women must resort to organization, association, and trade unions, and then they can command and maintain a standard wage. Supply and demand will do the rest. Women are not
well trained and often very deficient and unskilled in most of their occupations. They are generally only supplementary workers and drop their
work when they marry. When married, and home and children are to be
cared for, they are handicapped way beyond their strength. Married women
should be kept out of industry, rather than urged into it, as scientists, physicians, and sociologists all state that as women enter into competitive
industrial life with men, just so does the death rate of little children increase and the birth rate decrease.

Anti-suffragists deplore the fact that women are found in unsuitable
occupations. But the suffragists glory in the fact that there are women
blacksmiths, baggage masters, brakemen, undertakers, and women political
"bosses" in Colorado.

The suffragists call this progress, independence, and emancipation of women. "Anti's" ask for more discrimination and better selection of indus-trial occupations for wage-earning women. Knowing that the average woman has half of the physical strength of the average man, and the price she must pay when in competition with him is too great for her ultimate health and her hope of motherhood, the "Anti's" ask for caution and extreme consideration before new activities are entered upon. . . .

The suffrage leaders say that a woman without the vote has no self-respect. We must then look to the suffrage states to find the fulfillment of the woman's true position, complete—worthy, exalted, and respected. But what do we find when we look at Utah! Women have voted there for forty years. Mormonism and woman suffrage were coincident. By the very nature of its teachings, as indicated by Brigham Young, the basis of the Mormon Church is woman—and the Mormon Church is the greatest political machine in the four suffrage States. . . .

The question of woman suffrage should be summed up in this way: Has granting the ballot to women in the two suffrage states where they have had it for forty years brought about any great reforms or great results? No—Wyoming has many more men than women, so the results cannot be measured. The Mormon women of Utah are not free American citizens. They are under the Elder's supreme power, and vote accordingly, and po-lygamy has been maintained by the woman's vote, and is still to be found, although forbidden, because women have political power.

Have the saloons been abolished in any of the suffrage states? No.

Do men still drink and gamble? Yes, without a doubt.

Have the slums been done away with? Indeed no.

Are the streets better cleaned in the states where women vote? No, they are quite as bad as in New York City and elsewhere.

Have the red-light districts been cleared away? Decidedly not, and they can be reckoned upon as a political factor, when they are really needed.

Have women purified politics? No, not in the least.

Have women voted voluntarily? Some do; but thousands are carried to the polls in autos and carriages; otherwise they would not vote.

Has pure food and pure milk been established by the woman's vote? Not at all.

Have women's wages been increased because women vote? No, indeed.

Have women equal pay for equal work? Not any more than in New York City.

Are there laws on the statute books that would give women equal pay for equal work? No, and never will be.

Are women treated with more respect in the four suffrage states than elsewhere? Not at all—certainly not in Utah. . . .

[*The "Anti's" also argued that womenfolk were adequately represented by their menfolk; that women already exercised a strong influence indirectly ("harem government"); that suffrage would end chivalry; that women were already over-burdened in the home; that family quarrels over partisan issues would increase the divorce rate; that females were too emotional; and that women, if allowed to*

vote, would soon be serving on juries and forced to hear "indecent testimony."
Despite such objections, some of them frivolous, nationwide woman suffrage
finally triumphed with the 19th Amendment in 1920. The victory was largely the
result of the increased importance of women's role during the World War of
1917–1918.]

B. THE POPULAR ELECTION OF SENATORS

1. Woodrow Wilson Favors Reform (1912)

The popular election of United States Senators was a favorite goal of the Progressives, and, somewhat surprisingly, President Taft did not come out publicly against it. Election by state legislatures, as required by the Constitution, had resulted in grave abuses. Some wealthy but unfit men were securing their seats by wirepulling and outright vote buying. At one time three Senators were under federal indictment for accepting bribes. Millionaires, like the powerful Senator Aldrich of Rhode Island, were more responsive to the demands of Big Business than to those of the people. Voting deadlocks in the legislatures over Senators often led to a paralysis of state business, to various unsavory "deals," and to a prolonged lack of representation in the Senate. For nearly two years, from 1895 to 1897, Delaware had only one Senator. Woodrow Wilson of New Jersey, the Democratic nominee for the Presidency in 1912, here delivers a "folksy" campaign speech for the direct election of Senators. Determine why, in his view, the state legislatures had not sent better men to the Senate.

Then there is another thing that the conservative people are concerned about: the direct election of United States Senators. I have seen some thoughtful men discuss that with a sort of shiver, as if to disturb the original constitution of the United States Senate was to do something touched with impiety, touched with irreverence for the Constitution itself. But the first thing necessary to reverence for the United States Senate is respect for United States Senators.

I am not one of those who condemn the United States Senate as a body; for, no matter what has happened there, no matter how questionable the practices or how corrupt the influences which have filled some of the seats in that high body, it must in fairness be said that the majority in it has all the years through been untouched by stain, and that there has always been there a sufficient number of men of integrity to vindicate the self-respect and the hopefulness of America with regard to her institutions.

But you need not be told, and it would be painful to repeat to you, how seats have been bought in the Senate; and you know that a little group of Senators holding the balance of power has again and again been able to defeat programs of reform upon which the whole country had set its heart; and that whenever you analyzed the power that was behind those little groups you have found that it was not the power of public opinion, but some private influence, hardly to be discerned by superficial scrutiny, that had put those men there to do that thing.

1. Woodrow Wilson, *The New Freedom* (1913), pp. 231–34. By permission of Mrs. Edith Bolling Wilson.

Now, returning to the original principles upon which we profess to stand, have the people of the United States not the right to see to it that every seat in the Senate represents the unbought United States of America? Does the direct election of Senators touch anything except the private control of seats in the Senate?

We remember another thing: that we have not been without our suspicions concerning some of the legislatures which elect Senators. Some of the suspicions which we entertained in New Jersey about them turned out to be founded upon very solid facts indeed. Until two years ago New Jersey had not in half a generation been represented in the United States Senate by the men who would have been chosen if the process of selecting them had been free and based upon the popular will.

We are not to deceive ourselves by putting our heads into the sand and saying, "Everything is all right." Mr. Gladstone declared that the American Constitution was the most perfect instrument ever devised by the brain of man. We have been praised all over the world for our singular genius for setting up successful institutions, but a very thoughtful Englishman, and a very witty one, said a very instructive thing about that: he said that to show that the American Constitution had worked well was no proof that it is an excellent constitution, because Americans could run any constitution —a compliment which we laid like sweet unction to our soul; and yet a criticism which ought to set us thinking.

While it is true that when American forces are awake they can conduct American processes without serious departure from the ideals of the Constitution, it is nevertheless true that we have had many shameful instances of practices which we can absolutely remove by the direct election of Senators by the people themselves. And therefore I, for one, will not allow any man who knows his history to say to me that I am acting inconsistently with either the spirit or the essential form of the American government in advocating the direct election of United States Senators.

2. Senator Root Opposes Change (1911)

Senator Elihu Root of New York was probably the most influential conservative of his generation. Onetime Secretary of War and Secretary of State under Theodore Roosevelt, he shunned elective office, partly because public opinion was turning against wealthy corporation lawyers. Root instinctively took a strong position against the popular election of Senators. In analyzing his arguments, assess his ability as a prophet, and determine how sound he was in preferring the scheme of the Founding Fathers.

There are specific reasons against this change. The first great reason, in my mind, is that it is inconsistent with the fundamental design of the Senate. The purpose of the Constitution was to create in the Senate a body which would be as unlike as possible to the other House. It was to be a body more secure in tenure, different in the manner of its election, different in its responsibility, more conservative, more deliberate than the other

2. *The Independent,* LXX, 497–98, 500 (March 9, 1911).

House, which responds year by year to every movement of the public mind and the public feeling.

The Senate was established by the Constitution to protect the American democracy against itself. The framers of the Constitution realized that the weakness of democracy is the liability to continual change; they realized that there needed to be some guardian of the sober second thought, and so they created the Senate. This change is to decrease the difference between the two Houses; to make the two more alike; to make the function of the Senate less distinctive, and to reduce the benefit which the Senate can render to the public service. . . .

. . . By the change we should also prevent the Senate from having the benefit of the service of a large class of citizens who are specifically qualified by character and training to render a peculiar kind of service especially needed for the purposes of the Senate, men who by lives of experience and effort have attained the respect of their fellow citizens and who are willing to undertake the burdens of public office, but who are unwilling to seek it; men who will accept the burden as a patriotic duty, with mingled feelings of satisfaction at the honor and dissatisfaction with the burden, the disturbance of life, the abuse of the press, the controversies about performance of duty, but who never would subject themselves to the disagreeable incidents, the strife, the personalities of a political campaign. This change will exile from the floor of the Senate men who answer closely to many of the greatest names in the glorious history of this body.

It is wholly unnecessary to provide for or demand a reform in the constitution of the Senate upon the theory that the existing system has failed. It is true that occasionally bad men are sent to the Senate; occasionally a man is sent who would not have been chosen in a fair and honest election by the people of the State. But they find their level and they find it in innocuous insignificance. . . .

There is no weaker course for men to take than to endeavor to make up for failure to do their duty by changing the form of the duty. It is a proposition that the people who cannot elect honest men from their own neighbors to their state legislatures can elect honest men to the Senate of the United States. But how can men who are unable or unwilling to perform the duty of selecting an honest and faithful legislator from their own vicinage improve upon their performance in the selection of a candidate in a statewide election of candidates whom most of them know little or nothing about except what they get from the newspapers?

Why should we consent to any attempt at an evasion of duty? The pathway lies clear before us under the Constitution. If we will do our duty the Constitution needs no amendment. If we do not do our duty you can amend the Constitution a thousand times without any utility.

[The direct election of Senators (17th Amendment) became a part of the Constitution on May 31, 1913, less than three months after Woodrow Wilson entered the White House. The proposal had passed Congress ,in June, 1911,

during the Taft administration. The reform put an end to the scandalous dead-locks in the state legislatures and to the open buying of seats by millionaires. Senators with more popular appeal became the people's choice. But the eminence and dignity of the Senate have declined to more nearly the level of the House; direct primaries sap both the energy and the money of candidates; many able men refuse to subject themselves to electioneering abuse; buyers of seats, dem-agogues, and a few men of questionable honesty continue to find their way into the Senate.]

C. THE INITIATIVE AND THE REFERENDUM

1. Wilson Urges Popular Control (1912)

President Taft was definitely unfriendly to the initiative and the referendum. But these devices were enthusiastically sponsored by the Progressives as means of coping with state legislatures that were failing to pass needed reform or were passing laws dictated by "the interests." Under the initiative, a stipulated percentage of the electorate (often 5 percent) could petition to have a proposed law placed on the ballot and then voted on at a general election. Under the referendum, a requisite percentage of the voters could petition to have a legislature-enacted law referred to the electorate for approval or disapproval. Candidate Woodrow Wilson, who as a professor of government at Princeton had long derided such schemes as "bosh," favored them in his down-to-earth speeches in the presidential campaign of 1912. Comment critically on his assumption that where the initiative and referendum exist, they serve as both a prod and a club.

Why do you suppose that in the United States, the place in all the world where the people were invited to control their own government, we should set up such an agitation as that for the initiative and referendum and the recall? When did this thing begin?

I have been receiving circulars and documents from little societies of men all over the United States with regard to these matters for the last twenty-five years. But the circulars for a long time kindled no fire. Men felt that they had representative government and they were content. But about ten or fifteen years ago the fire began to burn—and it has been sweep-ing over wider and wider areas of the country—because of the growing consciousness that something intervenes between the people and the gov-ernment, and that there must be some arm direct enough and strong enough to thrust aside the something that comes in the way.

I believe that we are upon the eve of recovering some of the most im-portant prerogatives of a free people, and that the initiative and referendum are playing a great part in that recovery. I met a man the other day who thought that the referendum was some kind of an animal, because it had a Latin name; and there are still people in this country who have to have it explained to them. But most of us know and are deeply interested. Why? Because we have felt that in too many instances our government did not represent us, and we have said: "We have got to have a key to the door of our own house. The initiative and referendum and the recall afford such

1. Woodrow Wilson, *The New Freedom* (1913), pp. 235–37. By permission of Mrs. Edith Bolling Wilson.

a key to our own premises. If the people inside the house will run the place as we want it run, they may stay inside and we will keep the latchkeys in our pockets. If they do not, we shall have to re-enter upon possession."

Let no man be deceived by the cry that somebody is proposing to substitute direct legislation by the people, or the direct reference of laws passed in the legislature to the vote of the people, for representative government. The advocates of these reforms have always declared, and declared in unmistakable terms, that they were intending to recover representative government, not supersede it; that the initiative and referendum would find no use in places where legislatures were really representative of the people whom they were elected to serve. The initiative is a means of seeing to it that measures which the people want shall be passed—when legislatures defy or ignore public opinion. The referendum is a means of seeing to it that the unrepresentative measures which they do not want shall not be placed upon the statute book.

2. Taft Scorns the Initiative and Referendum (1915)

South Dakota blazed the trail in 1898 by adopting both the initiative and the referendum for ordinary state laws. A score or more of sister states ultimately followed in her footsteps. Several states, spurning the more dangerous initiative, espoused only the referendum, which the cynical Ambrose Bierce described as a means of determining "the nonsensus of public opinion." The radical West, more than the conservative East, embraced these Progressive schemes. Ex-President Taft spelled out his disapproval in a lecture at Yale University. In the light of his remarks, compare and contrast the weaknesses of the initiative and the referendum as lawmaking machinery.

Now what is the initiative? In practice, it means that if 5 percent of the electorate can get together and agree on a measure, they shall compel all the rest of the electorate to vote as to whether it shall become law or not. There is no opportunity for amendment, or for discussion. The whole legislative program is put into one act to be voted on by the people.

Speakers will get up and claim that the millennium will be brought about by some measure that they advocate. Suppose it is voted in? It never has had the test of discussion and amendment that every law ought to have. I am not complaining of the movement that brings about this initiative and referendum, for that is prompted by a desire to clinch the movement against corruption, on the theory that you cannot corrupt the whole people and that the initiative and referendum mean detailed and direct government by the whole people. But the theory is erroneous. The whole people will not vote at an election, much less at a primary. When the people are thus represented at the polls by a small minority, there is nothing that the politicians will not be able to do with that minority when they get their hands in. . . .

2. W. H. Taft, *Ethics in Service* (1915), pp. 78–82. By permission of the Yale University Press.

Now what is the referendum? It is a reference of the thing proposed by the initiative to the people who are to vote on it. . . .

What answer do the people themselves give with reference to the wisdom of the referendum? At many elections candidates run at the same time that questions are referred to the people, and what is the usual result of the vote? In Oregon, where they have tried it most, and where the people are best trained, they do sometimes get as much as 70 percent of those who vote on candidates to vote on the referendum. But generally, as in Colorado, the vote at the same election upon the referendum measures is not more than 50 percent—sometimes as low as 25 or 20 percent—of those who vote for candidates. . . .

They have tried it in Switzerland. We get a good many of these new nostrums from that country. They said in Switzerland, "These men vote for candidates, they shall vote on referendums." What was the result? The electors went up to the polls and solemnly put in tickets. When they opened the ballots, they were blanks. What does that mean? It means that the people themselves believe that they do not know how to vote on those issues, and that such issues ought to be left to the agents whom they select as competent persons to discuss and pass upon them in accordance with the general principles that they have laid down in party platforms.

In Oregon, at the last presidential election, the people were invited to vote on thirty-one statutes, long, complicated statutes, and in order to inform them, a book of two hundred and fifty closely printed pages was published to tell them what the statutes meant.

I ask you, my friends, you who are studious, you who are earnest men who would like to be a part of the people in determining what their policy should be, I ask you to search yourselves and confess whether you would have the patience to go through that book of two hundred and fifty closely printed pages to find out what those acts meant? You would be in active business, you would go down to the polls and say, "What is up today?" You would be told: "Here are thirty-one statutes. Here are two hundred and fifty pages that we would like to have you read in order that you may determine how you are to vote on them." You would not do it.

There was once a Senator from Oregon named Jonathan Bourne, who advocated all this system of more democracy. He served one term in the Senate, and then sent word back to his constituents that he was not coming home at the time of the primary. He said that he was not on trial, for a man who had worked as hard as he had for the people could not be on trial. Instead, he said, it was the people of Oregon who were on trial, to say whether they appreciated a service like this. They did not stand the test, and he was defeated at the primary. Then he concluded that after all he would have to forgive them and take pity on them in their blindness. So he went out to Oregon and ran on another ticket to give them the benefit of his service. But still they resisted the acid test. He himself went to the polls to vote at this election where there were thirty-one statutes to be approved or rejected. How many of the thirty-one submitted to him do you suppose he voted for? The newspapers reported him as admitting that he voted on just three, and the other twenty-eight he left to fate. Now, gentlemen, is not that a demonstration? Is not that a *reductio ad absurdum* for this system of pure and direct democracy?

D. POPULAR CONTROL OF THE JUDICIARY

1. Taft Lambasts the Recall of Judges (1911)

Hand in glove with the initiative and referendum went the recall of elected officials. The theory was that inept or corrupt public servants should be summarily removed by a special election. Oregon, the first state to adopt this scheme, was followed by about a dozen others. But several of the "recall" states specifically exempted elected judges. In 1911 the territory of Arizona applied for admission with a state constitution that provided for the recall of the judiciary. A scandalized President Taft, himself an ex-judge, sternly vetoed the resolution. Arizona removed the offensive provision and was admitted the next year. It thereupon defiantly restored the innovation, and the federal government was powerless to act. After reading Taft's veto message, determine why the recall of judges is more dangerous than that of other elective officials.

By the recall in the Arizona constitution it is proposed to give to the majority power to remove arbitrarily, and without delay, any judge who may have the courage to render an unpopular decision. By the recall it is proposed to enable a minority of 25 percent of the voters of the district or state, for no prescribed cause, after the judge has been in office six months, to submit the question of his retention in office to the electorate.

The petitioning minority must say on the ballot what they can against him in two hundred words, and he must defend as best he can in the same space. Other candidates are permitted to present themselves and have their names printed on the ballot, so that the recall is not based solely on the record or the acts of the judge, but also on the question whether some other more popular candidate has been found to unseat him.

Could there be a system more ingeniously devised to subject judges to momentary gusts of popular passion than this? We cannot be blind to the fact that often an intelligent and respectable electorate may be so roused upon an issue that it will visit with condemnation the decision of a just judge, though exactly in accord with the law governing the case, merely because it affects unfavorably their contest. Controversies over elections, labor troubles, racial or religious issues as to the construction or constitutionality of liquor laws, criminal trials of popular or unpopular defendants, the removal of county seats, suits by individuals to maintain their constitutional rights in obstruction of some popular improvement—these and many other cases could be cited in which a majority of a district electorate would be tempted by hasty anger to recall a conscientious judge if the opportunity were open all the time.

1. *Congressional Record*, 62 Cong., 1 sess., p. 3965 (Aug. 15, 1911).

No period of delay is interposed for the abatement of popular feeling. The recall is devised to encourage quick action, and to lead the people to strike while the iron is hot. The judge is treated as the instrument and servant of a majority of the people and subject to their momentary will, not after a long term in which his qualities as a judge and his character as a man have been subjected to a test of all the varieties of judicial work and duty so as to furnish a proper means of measuring his fitness for continuance in another term. On the instant of an unpopular ruling, while the spirit of protest has not had time to cool and even while an appeal may be pending from his ruling in which he may be sustained, he is to be haled before the electorate as a tribunal, with no judicial hearing, evidence, or defense, and thrown out of office, and disgraced for life because he has failed, in a single decision, it may be, to satisfy the popular demand.

Think of the opportunity such a system would give to unscrupulous political bosses in control, as they have been in control, not only of conventions but elections! Think of the enormous power for evil given to the sensational, muckraking portion of the press in rousing prejudice against a just judge by false charges and insinuations, the effect of which in the short period of an election by recall it would be impossible for him to meet and offset!

Supporters of such a system seem to think that it will work only in the interest of the poor, the humble, the weak, and the oppressed; that it will strike down only the judge who is supposed to favor corporations and be affected by the corrupting influence of the rich.

Nothing could be further from the ultimate result. The motive it would offer to unscrupulous combinations to seek to control politics in order to control judges is clear. Those would profit by the recall who have the best opportunity of rousing the majority of the people to action on a sudden impulse. Are they likely to be the wisest or the best people in a community? Do they not include those who have money enough to employ the firebrands and slanderers in a community and the stirrers-up of social hate? Would not self-respecting men well hesitate to accept judicial office with such a sword of Damocles hanging over them? What kind of judgments might those on the unpopular side expect from courts whose judges must make their decisions under such legalized terrorism? The character of the judges would deteriorate to that of trimmers and time-servers, and independent judicial action would be a thing of the past.

As the possibilities of such a system pass in review, is it too much to characterize it as one which will destroy the judiciary, its standing, and its usefulness?

2. Roosevelt and Judicial Decisions (1912)

Ex-President Roosevelt, returning from shooting lions in Africa, became increasingly disturbed by President Taft's association with Old Guard reactionaries. Enthusi-

2. *Senate Documents,* 62 Cong., 2 sess., No. 348, XXXVI, pp. 14–15 (Feb. 21, 1912).

astically embracing the program of the Progressives, he went so far in a flaming speech at Columbus, Ohio, as to advocate the recall of judicial decisions at the state level. This extreme proposal shocked conservatives, and ultimately contributed to his defeat in the presidential race of 1912. Ascertain whether he regarded the recall of judicial decisions as more radical than the recall of judges, and form conclusions as to which was actually the more objectionable.

I do not believe in adopting the recall [of judges] save as a last resort, when it has become clearly evident that no other course will achieve the desired result. But either the recall will have to be adopted or else it will have to be made much easier than it now is to get rid, not merely of a bad judge, but of a judge who, however virtuous, has grown so out of touch with social needs and facts that he is unfit longer to render good service on the bench.

It is nonsense to say that impeachment meets the difficulty. In actual practice we have found that impeachment does not work, that unfit judges stay on the bench in spite of it, and indeed because of the fact that impeachment is the only remedy that can be used against them. Where such is the actual fact it is idle to discuss the theory of the case. Impeachment as a remedy for the ills of which the people justly complain is a complete failure. . . .

A RADICAL ROOSEVELT DEMANDS A THIRD TERM

New York *World*, 1912.

But there is one kind of recall in which I very earnestly believe, and the immediate adoption of which I urge. There are sound reasons for being cautious about the recall of a good judge who has rendered an unwise and improper decision. Every public servant, no matter how valuable, and not omitting Washington or Lincoln or Marshall, at times makes mistakes. Therefore we should be cautious about recalling the judge, and we should be cautious about interfering in any way with the judge in decisions which he makes in the ordinary course as between individuals. But when a judge decides a constitutional question, when he decides what the people as a whole can or cannot do, the people should have the right to recall that decision if they think it wrong. We should hold the judiciary in all respect; but it is both absurd and degrading to make a fetish of a judge or of anyone else. . . .

When the supreme court of the state declares a given statute unconstitutional, because in conflict with the state or the national constitution, its opinion should be subject to revision by the people themselves. Such an opinion ought always to be treated with great respect by the people, and unquestionably in the majority of cases would be accepted and followed by them. But actual experience has shown the vital need of the people reserving to themselves the right to pass upon such opinion. If any considerable number of the people feel that the decision is in defiance of justice, they should be given the right by petition to bring before the voters at some subsequent election, special or otherwise, as might be decided, and after the fullest opportunity for deliberation and debate, the question whether or not the judges' interpretation of the Constitution is to be sustained. If it is sustained, well and good. If not, then the popular verdict is to be accepted as final, the decision is to be treated as reversed, and the construction of the Constitution definitely decided—subject only to action by the Supreme Court of the United States.

3. The *World* Denounces Roosevelt (1912)

Frank I. Cobb, who wore a shabby coat in his office to put the common people at ease, was the distinguished editor-in-chief of the New York *World*, probably the most influential Democratic newspaper of the period. A powerful supporter of Woodrow Wilson for the Presidency, he deplored the antics of the Republican Theodore Roosevelt. He here attacks the Rough Rider's proposed recall of judicial decisions. Assess his contention that the recall of judicial decisions would in effect wipe out state constitutions and install mob rule.

This [recall of judicial decisions] is a frank repudiation of the principles upon which American institutions were established. It is another way of saying that the power of the majority ought always to be absolute, and that the minority has no rights which the majority is bound to respect. . . .

According to his [Roosevelt's] scheme of a Constitution, if the majority happens to think it will better "social and industrial conditions" to take away the minority's property without due process of law, it should have that power. . . .

To carry out his theory of government, Mr. Roosevelt would not only destroy constitutional guarantees but he would destroy the Constitution as well. . . . In other words, the majority is to enact the laws through the initiative and referendum, and the majority is to interpret the laws through another initiative and referendum. If a state court undertakes to protect the rights of a minority, if a state court ventures to say that an act of the majority transcends the constitution or transgresses against human rights and human liberties, the judge may be recalled, and the decision reversed, by the majority which enacted the law.

3. New York *World*, Feb. 22, 1912. By permission. For full text see J. L. Heaton, ed., *Cobb of "The World"* (1924), pp. 57–60.

In these circumstances there would be no state constitution except from day to day. No man would have any stable guarantee that the majority would respect his rights, and no man would know today what his constitutional rights might be tomorrow. Every instrument that makes for stability of government would have been crippled or destroyed. State government would become a matter of mob rule—a quiet, orderly mob, perhaps, but a mob that was lawless and unrestrained and responsible only to itself for its actions.

We shall pay Mr. Roosevelt the compliment of saying that we do not think he believes a word of the nonsense that he uttered in his Columbus speech. He is too experienced, he is too well informed, he has been too long a student of government to believe in such folly.

E. THE PROGRESSIVE CAMPAIGN OF 1912

1. Roosevelt Turns against Taft (1912)

As Roosevelt's enthusiasm for the Progressive movement mounted, his distrust of Taft deepened. The portly President was not moving fast enough with the reformist tide. "What a floppy-souled creature he is!" lamented Roosevelt privately late in 1911. Among other sins, Taft seemed to be selling out the conservation movement to the "predatory interests." Roosevelt, in this private letter written less than two weeks after formally announcing his willingness to accept the Republican nomination, reveals a determination to fight for a so-called third term. Form some judgment as to the validity of his chief grievance against Taft, and determine whether such a grievance was inevitable.

You oblige me to speak frankly by what you say about Mr. Taft—I would not say this for publication. I have never been so bitterly disappointed in any man.

I care not one whit as to his attitude toward me. But I care immensely as to his attitude toward the people. He has completely reversed the position he held when he was my lieutenant. Everything I said of Taft as member of the Cabinet and Governor of the Philippines was deserved. I have not reversed my position. He has reversed his. I care not a whit as to what he has said about me. I care what he has done in abandoning the policies for the benefit of the people for which I stood and in allying himself with the closest enemies of those policies.

He has not a chance of being nominated if he relies merely on the people. His sole chance, and an excellent one, lies in having the wish of the people thwarted by the activity of the federal officeholders under him, by the unscrupulous use of patronage, and by the successful efforts of his and my former foes, his present allies—Penrose, Crane, McKinley, Aldrich, Barnes, and all the other bosses to whom he seems to have surrendered himself.

1. E. E. Morison, ed., *The Letters of Theodore Roosevelt* (1954), VII, 520 (to Andrew Carnegie, March 5, 1912). By permission of the Harvard University Press.

That Mr. Taft should feel grateful because I put him in the Presidency, and should so express himself to you, is of very little consequence; but it is of great consequence that his deeds should falsify his words. I wish for no gratitude personally. I did wish that he should try to carry out for the benefit of the people the policies in which I believed, and this he has not only failed to do but has instead reversed those policies.

2. The Third-Term Issue (1912)

President Taft resented the attempt of Roosevelt, his former benefactor, to wrest the nomination from him. He insisted that he was a "man of peace," but added with characteristic clumsiness, "Even a rat in a corner will fight." Roosevelt was the people's choice at the Republican convention in Chicago, but when Taft's boss-driven steamroller ran over him, he deserted the Republican Party and headed the new Progressive Party. The Democrats wisely chose an outstanding liberal, ex-Professor Woodrow Wilson. With the Republican Party thus split, the election of the Democratic candidate was inevitable. Foes of Roosevelt charged that he was violating both the third-term tradition and his solemn pledge, impulsively given after his sweeping electoral victory in 1904, never to run again. His defenders replied that the third-term tradition applied only to consecutive terms, that Roosevelt had never served two full terms, and that his statement of 1904 was not an agreement with anybody. He had merely changed his mind. Appraise the fairness of the following deadly parallel run by the New York *Sun* repeatedly during the campaign.

THE DEADLIEST OF ALL PARALLELS

President Roosevelt's Decision on November 8, 1904: "Under no circumstances will I be a candidate for or accept another nomination."

Ex-President Roosevelt's Decision on February 25 [24], 1912: "I will accept the nomination for President if it is tendered to me."

3. Roosevelt's Post-Mortems (1912)

During the embittered campaign of 1912, both Taft and Roosevelt had privately conceded the inevitability of defeat. A few days after the election, Roosevelt analyzed the results with unusual detachment in two personal letters. Note evidences of unselfishness, egotism, and vindictiveness. Explain why Roosevelt was more vulnerable to attack than any other possible Progressive candidate and why he wanted to keep the party alive.

[November 5, 1912] I am immensely pleased that you so clearly grasp just what we have been doing in this Progressive fight. It would be more accurate to say what we have been *trying* to do, for there is no use disguising the fact that the defeat at the polls is overwhelming.

I had expected defeat, but I had expected that we would make a better showing. For instance, I thought that in New York and Massachusetts we would come second to Wilson, whereas Taft beat us. But I suppose that I

2. Quoted in D. C. Coyle, *Ordeal of the Presidency* (1960), p. 280.
3. E. E. Morison, ed., *The Letters of Theodore Roosevelt* (1954), VII, 633–34, 639. By permission of the Harvard University Press.

"HE'S GOOD ENOUGH FOR ME"

Roosevelt the ex-Rough Rider approves the third-term candidacy of Roosevelt the ex-President. Parody of the famous Davenport cartoon (see p. 632). New York *World*, 1912.

ought not to expect that in three months we could form a new Party that would do as well as we have actually done. We had all the money, all the newspapers, and all the political machinery against us and, above all, we had the habit of thought of the immense mass of dull unimaginative men who simply vote according to the party symbol.

Whether the Progressive Party itself will disappear or not, I do not know; but the Progressive movement must and will go forward even though its progress is fitful. It is essential for this country that it should go forward. The alternative is oscillation between the greedy arrogance of a party directed by conscienceless millionaires and the greedy envy of a party directed by reckless and unscrupulous demagogues.

As things were this year, there was no human being who could have made any fight or have saved the whole movement from collapse if I had not been willing to step in and take the hammering. But it doesn't seem to me as if I ever could make up my mind to repeat the experiment. Not only do I shrink from it personally but at present it seems to me that I cannot accomplish enough to warrant the damage that another candidacy of mine would do. I try not to think of the damage to myself personally; but I feel torn in two ways from the public standpoint; for while the fight could only have been made under my leadership, yet it is also true that an infinitely stronger attack was made upon me than would have been made upon any other Progressive leader, and that there is a strong tendency, among even respectable people, to feel that it is only my own personal ambition which I am desirous of gratifying.

[November 12, 1912] I feel that the Progressive Party has come to stay. We must keep up our organization. Above all, there must be no combination with any of the crooked bosses against whom this movement is a protest on behalf of all honest men. Every boss who was directly or indirectly concerned in the theft of the Chicago Convention, or in condoning it or approving it, has forfeited all right of association with decent men. I trust that the Progressives will see to it that not merely the National and State, but the Town and County officers are Progressives, and not tainted by any touch of subserviency to bosses of such a character.

[*Four years later, in 1916, the Progressive Party again nominated Roosevelt. He declined the honor. Despising President Wilson, he did not want to contribute to his re-election by again splitting Republican votes. The Progressive Party thereupon withered on the vine.*]

THOUGHT PROVOKERS

1. In what ways could women defend their rights before they received the ballot? Why has woman suffrage not improved conditions as much as anticipated? A study published in 1960 revealed that women voters are worse informed than men, have less party loyalty, are swayed more by personalities, are more isolationist, are more concerned about war, and are more inclined to be conservative. Comment.

2. Why has the direct election of Senators failed to achieve some of the changes that its most optimistic advocates predicted? Would we be better off under the old system?

3. Which is the least vulnerable to criticism: the initiative, the referendum, or the recall? Explain.

4. In the absence of recall, what means has the public to protect itself against incompetent, arbitrary, corrupt, or senile judges? Do greater evils flow from non-regulation than from popular regulation of the judiciary? Explain. Woodrow Wilson said: "Judges . . . determine not what the law should be, but what the law is." Comment.

5. In the light of our experience with third parties, including the Progressive, is it better to try to reform the party from within or to secede from the party? Is it ever wise for a President to handpick a successor to carry out his policies?

FURTHER EXPLORATION

General: G. E. Mowry, *The Era of Theodore Roosevelt, 1900–1912* (1958); A. S. Link, *Woodrow Wilson and the Progressive Era, 1910–1917* (1954); H. F. Pringle, *The Life and Times of William Howard Taft* (2 vols., 1939). **Woman Suffrage:** E. C. Stanton *et al.*, eds., *The History of Woman's Suffrage* (6 vols., 1881–1922). **Senate Elections:** G. H. Haynes, *The Election of Senators* (1906). **Initiative:** W. B. Munro, ed., *The Initiative, Referendum, and Recall* (1912). **Judiciary:** B. P. De Witt, *The Progressive Movement* (1915). **Progressive Campaign:** G. E. Mowry, *Theodore Roosevelt and the Progressive Movement* (1946); A. S. Link, *Wilson: The Road to the White House* (1947); Amos Pinchot, *History of the Progressive Party, 1912–1916* (1958).

Recent: Aileen S. Kraditor, *The Ideas of the Woman Suffrage Movement, 1890–1920* (1965). See also references for previous chapter.

Chapter 35

Wilsonian Idealism

We dare not turn from the principle that morality and not expediency is the thing that must guide us. . . .

PRESIDENT WILSON, 1913

PROLOGUE: Ex-Professor Wilson was spectacularly successful in inducing Congress to do the homework necessary to launch the New Freedom—that is, the economic freedom that would result from curbing monopoly and encouraging free competition. Legislative landmarks of 1913–1914 were the Underwood-Simmons Act (to lower the tariff), the Federal Reserve Act (to reform banking and currency), the Federal Trade Commission Act (to halt unfair practices), and the Clayton Anti-Trust Act (to restrain monopoly). But harsh necessity forced Wilson, the idealist, to return to the tactics of Taft, the realist, in pursuing dollar diplomacy in Latin America and China. He nevertheless insisted on fair play for Britain in connection with the Panama Canal tolls. His moralistic Mexican policy of "watchful waiting," despite the wholesale murder of Americans, evoked vehement demands for war. But Wilson, with the struggling masses of Mexico ever in mind, managed to avoid a full-dress intervention.

A. BATTLING FOR TARIFF REFORM

1. A President Appears before Congress (1913)

Woodrow Wilson, a lifelong foe of a highly protective tariff, had refused to uphold the "wrong side" of the question as a student debater at Princeton. As President, he was determined to redeem his campaign pledges and lower the existing Republican rates. Regarding himself as a colleague rather than a competitor of Congress, he decided to bridge the mile-long gap between Capitol Hill and the White House by presenting his messages in person. (President Jefferson, shy and weak-voiced, had discontinued personal appearances in 1801.) Wilson's shattering of precedent struck many Senators as effrontery. Secretary of Agriculture Houston, an ex-university president himself, here recaptures the tension in his diary entry. Note the distinction that Wilson makes between "protection" and "patronage," and why, basically, he urges a lowering of the tariff.

The discussion [in the Cabinet] was interrupted because the President had to leave at twelve o'clock to go to the Capitol to read his Tariff Message. I had a distinct sensation when this departure was brought thus sharply to my mind. I recognized both its political and historical significance. Some members of the Cabinet seemed to be a trifle shaky about the venture. The President showed no sign that he was aware, as of course he was, that anything unusual was about to happen.

1. D. F. Houston, *Eight Years with Wilson's Cabinet* (1926), I, 52–55.

668

The President regards himself as the head of his party and its political leader. He believes that he can lead better, can get nearer to Congress, and convey his message more impressively to the people by delivering his message in person. He is right; and his example will probably be followed till we get a President who is timid and a poor or indifferent speaker.

Most of the members of the Cabinet went to the Capitol to hear the President read his message. . . . There seemed to me to be a distinctly tense atmosphere, as if strange things were about to happen. Members of Congress appeared to be a trifle nervous, and something of a chill pervaded the air. Some members of Congress, I thought, had a sullen look. Suddenly the President of the United States was announced, and the Speaker rapped loudly with his gavel. The whole body stood up. . . .

The beauty of the President's English was instantly felt; and his first sentences relieved the strain and made for easier feeling. They were:

"I am very glad indeed to have this opportunity to address the two Houses directly and to verify for myself the impression that the President of the United States is a person, not a mere department of the government, hailing Congress from some isolated island of jealous power, sending messages, not speaking naturally and with his own voice—that he is a human being trying to cooperate with other human beings in a common service. After this pleasant experience I shall feel quite normal in all our dealings with one another."

The message was short. It pointed out that the tariff burden should be lightened; that, while the whole face of our commercial life had altered, tariff schedules had remained the same or had moved in the direction they had been given when no large circumstance of our industrial development was what it appeared today, and that our task was to square them with the facts. Tariff legislation had wandered very far afield. We had passed beyond the notion of protecting industry. We had come to hold that it was entitled to the direct patronage of the government. We were giving to each group of manufacturers what they thought they needed to maintain a closed market. We had built a set of privileges and fostered monopoly, "until at last nothing is normal, nothing is obliged to stand the test of efficiency and economy, in our world of big business, but everything thrives by concerted agreement.

"We must abolish everything that bears even the semblance of privilege or of any kind of artificial advantage, and put our businessmen and our producers under the stimulation of a constant necessity to be efficient, economical, and enterprising, masters of competitive supremacy, better merchants and better traders than any in the world." The object of duties henceforth must be to promote effective competition. We must accomplish our purpose without reckless haste. We must build up our foreign trade. We more than ever need an outlet for our energies. . . .

The next time I saw the President was at Cabinet meeting on Friday, April 11th. When he came in, I congratulated him on his address and on the success of his personally appearing before Congress. He thanked me and smilingly remarked: "Congress looked embarrassed. I did not feel so."

2. Wilson Tackles the Tariff Lobby (1913)

The new low-tariff Underwood Bill passed the Democratic House without undue difficulty, but when it reached the Senate the fast-talking lobbyists descended in droves. Buttonholing Senators, they resorted to high-pressure persuasion. The bill was in grave danger of being mutilated, as similar measures had been in the days of Presidents Cleveland and Taft. Wilson thereupon appealed over the heads of the lobbyists to the people in the following remarkable statement issued to the press. A snowstorm of approving telegrams and letters descended upon the White House and Congress. The lobbyists scurried for cover, and the Underwood-Simmons Bill passed in substantially its original form. Ascertain whether the Senate could properly regard this statement as a reflection on its integrity.

I think that the public ought to know the extraordinary exertions being made by the lobby in Washington to gain recognition for certain alterations of the Tariff bill. Washington has seldom seen so numerous, so industrious, or so insidious a lobby. The newspapers are being filled with paid advertisements calculated to mislead the judgment of public men not only, but also the public opinion of the country itself. There is every evidence that money without limit is being spent to sustain this lobby and to create an appearance of a pressure of opinion antagonistic to some of the chief items of the Tariff bill.

It is of serious interest to the country that the people at large should have no lobby and be voiceless in these matters, while great bodies of astute men seek to create an artificial opinion and to overcome the interests of the public for their private profit. It is thoroughly worth the while of the people of this country to take knowledge of this matter. Only public opinion can check and destroy it.

The Government in all its branches ought to be relieved from this intolerable burden and this constant interruption to the calm progress of debate. I know that in this I am speaking for the members of the two Houses, who would rejoice as much as I would to be released from this unbearable situation.

3. Senator Cummins Defends Lobbying (1913)

Wilson's routing of the lobbyists aroused the Senate to a four-hour debate, during which some Republicans professed to be insulted. Certain Senators attempted to draw a distinction between the professional lobbyist, who would espouse any cause for money, and the legitimate representatives of endangered interests. Senator Cummins of Iowa, a progressive Republican who had voted against the high Republican tariff of 1909, here recounts his own experience. Form conclusions as to whether this was lobbying in the accepted sense.

. . . I represent a state that probably has as little direct concern in the tariff as any state in the Union. I represent a state that can probably care

2. *Congressional Record,* 63 Cong., 1 sess., p. 1804 (statement of May 26, 1913).
3. *Ibid.,* pp. 1802–03 (May 29, 1913).

for itself without any assistance whatever from legislation as well or as completely as any state in the Union.

Yet this bill had barely reached the Senate until there came into my office a committee composed of three of the best-known and the most estimable men in my state. They constituted a committee raised by what is known as the Corn Belt Meat Producers' Association, an association made up of the farmers of my state, who would be horrified if from any source they were characterized as lobbyists attempting to improperly influence legislation. They came here to protest against admitting meat free and at the same time putting a duty on cattle.

I acted simply as their guide to the subcommittee room presided over so graciously and, I am sure, so fairly by my distinguished friend from Mississippi [Senator Williams]. They were received in a perfectly proper way; they were received kindly and decently, and they stated their case to the members of the subcommittee.

What impression they made I do not know, nor need I inquire. They did not confine the submission of their case to the subcommittee in formal session. They laid the facts, as they understood them, before every Senator with whom they could secure an audience; and having done so, like the good people they are, they went home.

I do not know whether their visit here accomplished anything or not; that is yet to be ascertained. But I do not want the people of this country to receive the impression that there was anything wrong in those men from my state coming to Washington for the purpose of putting before individual Senators or a committee of Senators their case as they understood it, and explaining how the proposed change in the tariff law would affect them.

[*The Democratic press generally acclaimed the new low-tariff Underwood-Simmons law. The New York* World *exulted: "It is the first tariff in fifty years which was passed by the representatives of the people, and not by the representatives of privilege and plutocracy." On the other hand, the Republican Boston* Evening Transcript *sourly remarked, "Framed unscientifically, and inspired by partisanship, the new tariff will of necessity encounter political and industrial opposition."*]

B. CAMPAIGNING FOR MONETARY REFORM

1. Brandeis Indicts Interlocking Directorates (1914)

Populists, muckrakers, Progressives, and Wilsonian Democrats alike had condemned the monopolistic "Money Trust." In 1912 the Democratic House of Representatives appointed the famed Pujo Committee, which launched a searching investigation. The next year it released a sensational report stating that 341 directorships in 112 corporations controlled resources amounting to $22,245,000,000. Many of these directorships, including the Wall Street House of Morgan, were interlocking. Louis D. Brandeis, a brilliant young liberal destined to be a Supreme Court justice, develops this aspect in the following partial summary of the Pujo Committee's

1. L. D. Brandeis, *Other People's Money* (1914), pp. 51–53. By permission of J. B. Lippincott Company.

findings. Determine the most objectionable feature of interlocking directorates from the standpoint of the public.

The practice of interlocking directorates is the root of many evils. It offends laws human and divine. Applied to rival corporations, it tends to the suppression of competition and to violation of the Sherman [anti-trust] law. Applied to corporations which deal with each other, it tends to disloyalty and to violation of the fundamental law that no man can serve two masters. In either event it tends to inefficiency; for it removes incentive and destroys soundness of judgment. It is undemocratic, for it rejects the platform: "A fair field and no favors," substituting the pull of privilege for the push of manhood. It is the most potent instrument of the Money Trust. Break the control so exercised by the investment bankers over railroads, public-service and industrial corporations, over banks, life-insurance and trust companies, and a long step will have been taken toward attainment of the New Freedom.

The term "interlocking directorates" is here used in a broad sense as including all intertwined conflicting interests, whatever the form, and by whatever device effected. The objection extends alike to contracts of a corporation, whether with one of its directors individually, or with a firm of which he is a member, or with another corporation in which he is interested as an officer or director or stockholder. The objection extends likewise to men holding the inconsistent position of director in two potentially competing corporations, even if those corporations do not actually deal with each other.

A single example will illustrate the vicious circle of control—the endless chain—through which our financial oligarchy now operates:

J. P. Morgan (or a partner), a director of the New York, New Haven & Hartford Railroad, causes that company to sell to J. P. Morgan & Co. an issue of bonds. J. P. Morgan & Co. borrow the money with which to pay for the bonds from the Guaranty Trust Company, of which Mr. Morgan (or a partner) is a director. J. P. Morgan & Co. sell the bonds to the Penn Mutual Life Insurance Company, of which Mr. Morgan (or a partner) is a director. The New Haven spends the proceeds of the bonds in purchasing steel rails from the United States Steel Corporation, of which Mr. Morgan (or a partner) is a director. The United States Steel Corporation spends the proceeds of the rails in purchasing electrical supplies from the General Electric Company, of which Mr. Morgan (or a partner) is a director. The General Electric Company sells supplies to the Western Union Telegraph Company, a subsidiary of the American Telephone and Telegraph Company; and in both Mr. Morgan (or a partner) is a director.

2. Morgan Denies a Money Trust (1913)

J. Pierpont Morgan, bulbous-nosed but august, appeared before the Pujo Committee with eight attorneys. (Their estimated fees for two days were $45,000.) He

2. *Letter from Messrs. J. P. Morgan & Co.* . . . (privately printed, Feb. 25, 1913), pp. 8–9, 12, 17–18. Reproduced by permission.

denied not only the existence of a "Money Trust" but the possibility of its existence. Less convincing was his claim that he neither possessed nor desired great financial power. A subsequent letter from the House of Morgan to the Pujo Committee summarized the influential financier's point of view. Judge to what extent this statement either partially or completely refutes the charges against the bankers.

. . . There have been spread before your Committee elaborate tables of so-called interlocking directorates, from which exceedingly mistaken inferences have been publicly drawn. In these tables it is shown that 180 bankers and bank directors serve upon the boards of corporations having resources aggregating $25,000,000,000, and it is implied that this vast aggregate of the country's wealth is at the disposal of these 180 men.

But such an implication rests solely upon the untenable theory that these men, living in different parts of the country, in many cases personally unacquainted with each other, and in most cases associated only in occasional transactions, vote always for the same policies and control with united purpose the directorates of the 132 corporations on which they serve.

The testimony failed to establish any concerted policy or harmony of action binding these 180 men together, and, as a matter of fact, no such policy exists. The absurdity of the assumption of such control becomes more apparent when one considers that, on the average, these directors represent only one quarter of the memberships of their boards. It is preposterous to suppose that every "interlocking" director has full control in every organization with which he is connected, and that the majority of directors who are not "interlocking" are mere figureheads, subject to the will of a small minority of their boards.

Perhaps the greatest harm in the presentation referred to lay in the further unwarranted inference, to which has been given wide publicity, that the vast sum of $25,000,000,000 was in cash or liquid form, subject to the selfish use or abuse of individuals. Such an idea excites the public mind to demand the correction of a fancied situation which does not and, in our belief, never can exist. . . .

Such growth in the size of banks in New York and Chicago has frequently been erroneously designated before your Committee as "concentration," whereas we have

HIS ALIBI
New York *World*, 1913.

hitherto pointed out [that] the growth of banking resources in New York City has been less rapid than that of the rest of the country. But increase of capital, and merger of two or more banks into one institution (with the same resources as the aggregate of the banks merging into it), has been frequent, especially since January 1, 1908.

These mergers, however, are a development due simply to the demand for larger banking facilities to care for the growth of the country's business. As our cities double and treble in size and importance, as railroads extend and industrial plants expand, not only is it natural, but it is necessary, that our banking institutions should grow in order to care for the increased demands put upon them. Perhaps it is not known as well as it should be that in New York City the largest banks are far inferior in size to banks in the commercial capitals of other and much smaller countries. . . .

For a private banker to sit upon . . . a directorate is in most instances a duty, not a privilege. Inquiry will readily develop the fact that the members of the leading banking houses in this country—and it was the leading houses only against which animadversions were directed—are besought continually to act as directors in various corporations, whose securities they may handle, and that in general they enter only those boards which the opinion of the investing public requires them to enter, as an evidence of good faith that they are willing to have their names publicly associated with the management.

Yet, before your Committee, this natural and eminently desirable relationship was made to appear almost sinister, and no testimony whatever was adduced to show the actual working of such relationships.

3. McAdoo Exposes the Bankers (*c.* 1913)

President Wilson, the foe of special privilege, was determined to break the so-called money monopoly. The need for a more flexible currency had been brought home to the nation by the disastrous "Bankers' Panic" of 1907. Wilson therefore threw the weight of his dynamic personality behind the Federal Reserve Bill introduced in Congress in 1913. The big bankers, mostly conservative Republicans, fought it passionately. They favored a huge new central bank with themselves in control; they were forced to accept a twelve-district Federal Reserve System, with a government-appointed Federal Reserve Board in control. Lanky, black-haired William G. McAdoo, Wilson's Secretary of the Treasury (and son-in-law), here describes the initial opposition of the bankers. Note in what respect they were most seriously wrong, and explain why.

As time went by, we observed that the public generally—I mean the ordinary, average citizen—was in favor of the Federal Reserve Bill. The bankers in the larger money centers were almost to a man bitterly opposed to it, and many businessmen shared their views. Sentiment among the smaller banks was divided—those against the bill being largely in the majority.

At the national convention of the American Bankers' Association, held in Boston, October, 1913, only two delegates attempted to speak in favor of the legislation; each was howled down until the chairman managed to

3. W. G. McAdoo, *Crowded Years* (1931), pp. 247–48. By permission of Houghton Mifflin Company.

make himself heard, and begged the convention to give them the courtesy of attention.

Dr. Joseph French Johnson, professor of political economy at New York University, said at a dinner of the Academy of Political Science that the bill, if passed, would bring on a dangerous credit expansion and that it would cause "a collapse of the banking system." He added that "blacksmiths could not be expected to produce a Swiss watch." The blacksmiths were, in this case, I suppose, the Democrats, and the Federal Reserve Bill was the Swiss watch. So I infer, and I fancy that another meaning, to the effect that Professor Johnson himself was an excellent watchmaker, lurked in the background.

And from Chicago came reports of a speech of Senator Lawrence Y. Sherman, Republican member of the Senate from Illinois. In addressing the Illinois Bankers' Association he said: "I would support a law to wind a watch with a crowbar as cheerfully as I will support any such bill."

But James B. Forgan, banking magnate of Chicago, was more direct in his expression of opinion. He said nothing about crowbars and blacksmiths and Swiss watches. He declared that the bill was "unworkable, impractical, and fundamentally bad." It would bring about, he said, "the most damnable contraction of currency ever seen in any country."

Forgan's idea that the currency would be damnably contracted was not shared by all the opponents of the Glass-Owen [Federal Reserve] Bill. Many bankers and economists proved, to their own satisfaction by figures and diagrams, that the Federal Reserve System would produce an extraordinary inflation. These vast and irreconcilable differences of opinion between the various groups of our adversaries had the effect of lessening my respect for so-called banking experts. I found that they could take the same set of facts and reach two diametrically opposite conclusions.

For example, Forgan estimated that the currency would be contracted to the extent of $1,800,000,000, while Senator Elihu Root, using the same data, predicted an inflation of at least $1,800,000,000.

President Arthur T. Hadley, of Yale, who had a high reputation as an economist, believed that the bill, if passed, would lead to inflation on an unparalleled scale, with a consequent depreciation. He was so deeply moved that he wrote a personal letter to President Wilson on July 1, 1913, for the purpose of pointing out to the President that the Act would "involve the country in grave financial danger." Practically all of our gold would leave for Europe, he thought. He was greatly mistaken. There is now in the United States about 45 percent of all the gold in the world.

Frank A. Vanderlip, president of the National City Bank of New York, declared that the notes of the Federal Reserve Banks would be "fiat money," and James J. Hill, the famous railroad builder and financier, said the plan was "socialistic." James R. Mann, Republican leader of the House, condemned the bill as all wrong, badly conceived, and impossible as a practical measure. However, he added bitterly, it did not matter; the national banks would not go into the system, anyway. Most of them would become state banks, and the Federal Reserve would just lie down and die for lack of support. Saying this, he washed his hands of the whole affair.

[*The Federal Reserve System, approved by Congress late in 1913, not only carried the nation triumphantly through World War I but remains the bulwark of the nation's financial structure. The sneers of the bankers gave way to cheers. Currency expansion to meet growing needs was abundantly provided by the issuance of Federal Reserve notes, backed in part by promissory notes and other assets held by the member banks. The national banks, authorized during the Civil War, were required to join the Federal Reserve System. The grip of Wall Street on money and credit was thus weakened, and interlocking directorates were curbed the next year (1914) by the Clayton Anti-Trust Act.*]

C. THE CANAL TOLLS EXEMPTION CONTROVERSY

1. Wilson Pleads for Repeal (1914)

As the Panama Canal neared completion, agitation mounted for exempting American coastwise traffic from paying tolls. A favorite anti-monopoly argument was that the lower the tolls were, the more the competing transcontinental railroad lines would have to lower their rates. In 1912, during the Taft administration, Congress approved such an exemption. Great Britain protested vigorously on the ground that this discrimination violated the Anglo-American treaty of 1901. In that year the British had granted the United States a free hand to build the canal, with the stipulation that it be open to *all nations* on equal terms. The legalistic Taft administration argued that this meant all *other nations.* Candidate Wilson had publicly upheld this narrow view, as had the Democratic platform. But the more he studied the problem, the more his Presbyterian conscience asserted itself; and he finally went before Congress with the following brief message. Ascertain the reasons why he took this step in the face of violent opposition within his own party. Observe also what this message reveals of his character.

I have come to you upon an errand which can be very briefly performed, but I beg that you will not measure its importance by the number of sentences in which I state it. No communication I have addressed to the Congress carried with it graver or more far-reaching implications as to the interest of the country, and I come now to speak upon a matter with regard to which I am charged in a peculiar degree, by the Constitution itself, with personal responsibility.

I have come to ask you for the repeal of that provision of the Panama Canal Act of August 24, 1912, which exempts vessels engaged in the coastwise trade of the United States from payment of tolls, and to urge upon you the justice, the wisdom, and the large policy of such a repeal with the utmost earnestness of which I am capable.

In my own judgment, very fully considered and maturely formed, that exemption constitutes a mistaken economic policy from every point of view, and is, moreover, in plain contravention of the treaty with Great Britain concerning the canal concluded on November 18, 1901.

But I have not come to urge upon you my personal views. I have come

1. *Congressional Record,* 63 Cong., 2 sess., p. 4313 (March 5, 1914).

UNCLE SAM'S CANAL

Many Americans felt that since Uncle Sam had built the canal, he could do what he wanted with it, despite treaty commitments to protesting John Bull. *Irish World* (New York), 1912.

to state to you a fact and a situation. Whatever may be our own differences of opinion concerning this much debated measure, its meaning is not debated outside the United States. Everywhere else the language of the treaty is given but one interpretation, and that interpretation precludes the exemption I am asking you to repeal. We consented to the treaty; its language we accepted, if we did not originate it; and we are too big, too powerful, too self-respecting a nation to interpret with a too strained or refined reading the words of our own promises just because we have power enough to give us leave to read them as we please. The large thing to do is the only thing we can afford to do, a voluntary withdrawal from a position everywhere questioned and misunderstood. We ought to reverse our action without raising the question whether we were right or wrong, and so once more deserve our reputation for generosity and for the redemption of every obligation without quibble or hesitation.

I ask this of you in support of the foreign policy of the administration. I shall not know how to deal with other matters [Mexico?] of even greater delicacy and nearer consequence if you do not grant it to me in ungrudging measure.

2. Champ Clark Demands Exemption (1914)

Embittered Champ Clark of Missouri, Speaker of the House, had been narrowly defeated by Wilson for the Democratic presidential nomination in 1912. He now clashed sharply with Wilsonian idealism on the floor of Congress. Appealing to the Irish-Americans and other anti-British groups, he declaimed, "I would rather see that canal blown up than to give the English any control over it." Note how much of his argument is relevant to the question of whether tolls exemption was a violation of the treaty of 1901 with Britain. Note also in what respects he was arguing that two wrongs make a right, and what aspect of his argument would have the greatest appeal to anti-monopoly sentiment.

To whom does the Panama Canal belong, anyway? To the United States of America. [Applause.] We built it at the enormous cost of $400,000,000. We built it on American soil. We built it by the genius of American engineers. We have fortified it; we will control it.

In order to get a chance to build it we created a Republic. [Applause.] Of course, we used to abuse Colonel Roosevelt and poke fun at his fly-by-night Republic; but he was the American President; we are responsible for him. He may have been a little hasty—I think he was—in the recognition of that newborn Republic, but nevertheless it is our Republic. We created it and we cannot escape its paternity. [Applause and laughter.]

For whose benefit did we build the canal? We are not such numbskulls as not to know what we built it for. We built it primarily for our own benefit. That is what we did, and nobody can lie out of it. [Applause and laughter.] Secondarily, we built it for the benefit of the world, but it was to be used under rules and conditions that we and nobody else prescribe. [Applause.] The British Government has just as much right to prescribe the rules for the government of that canal as it has to prescribe that I shall wear a white flannel suit in midwinter, as Mark Twain used to wear in the coldest weather. [Applause and laughter.]

Why did we build it? There is the crux of the whole situation. What did we do it for? Why did we violate the integrity of Colombia? Because that is exactly what we did. What did we spend $400,000,000 for? What did we want with the canal anyhow? I will tell you what we wanted. We wanted to get cheap freight water rates. [Applause.] And we wanted to fix it so that we can get both parts of our fleet into the Pacific or the Atlantic at the same time, wherever we want them and when we want them. [Applause.]

Who fought the building of that canal and defeated it for fifteen long, wearisome years? The transcontinental railroads. [Applause.] Who would be the chief beneficiaries of this repeal bill? The same transcontinental railroads—the Canadian Pacific and the Tehuantepec [Mexican] National Railway heading the list. It would be many millions of dollars in their capacious pockets annually. To do a thing to enable them to hold up their old rates is altruistic generosity run mad and an outrage on the American people. I refuse to indorse any such program.

2. *Ibid.,* pp. 6057–58 (March 31, 1914).

As a party pledged to encouragement of competition, we long ago took our stand unequivocally in favor of freeing transportation between our own ports, and, so far as I am informed, no change in conditions has taken place that could possibly justify a reversal of that policy.

[*Despite such wildly applauded pleas, the House passed the repeal of the tolls exemption by a vote of 247 to 162 on March 31, 1914. On June 11, 1914, the Senate followed suit, amid near fistfights, by a vote of 50 to 35.*]

D. MORAL MEDDLING IN MEXICO

1. Wilson Asks for War on Huerta (1914)

The decade-long despotic rule of dictator Díaz in Mexico crumbled during the upheaval of 1910–1911. But the revolution took an ugly turn in 1913, when General Huerta—a full-blooded Indian who was an alcoholic and a drug addict—connived at the murder of the liberal President Madero and forthwith seized power. Wilson, whose heart went out to the oppressed masses of Mexico, refused to recognize this bloody-handed dictator, and thereby departed from the traditional American policy of recognizing established regimes. Pursuing a plan of "watchful waiting," he modified America's arms embargo to the advantage of Huerta's foes. The crisis came to a boil in April, 1914, when Mexican officials seized two men from a United States navy boat at Tampico. The local officials promptly tendered apologies. But Admiral Mayo, acting without specific authorization from Washington, demanded a twenty-one-gun salute to the American flag. When Huerta refused to comply, Wilson went before Congress to ask for authority (which he already had as Commander-in-Chief) to use force. Observe how he attempts to reconcile his friendship for the Mexican people with a request to fight them. What other inconsistencies emerge?

The [Tampico] incident cannot be regarded as a trivial one, especially as two of the men arrested were taken from the boat itself—that is to say, from the territory of the United States. But had it stood by itself, it might have been attributed to the ignorance or arrogance of a single officer. Unfortunately, it was not an isolated case. A series of incidents have recently occurred which cannot but create the impression that the representatives of General Huerta were willing to go out of their way to show disregard for the dignity and rights of this Government,* and felt perfectly safe in doing what they pleased, making free to show in many ways their irritation and contempt. . . . So far as I can learn, such wrong and annoyances have been suffered to occur only against representatives of the United States. . . .

The manifest danger of such a situation was that such offenses might grow from bad to worse until something happened of so gross and intolerable a sort as to lead directly and inevitably to armed conflict. It was necessary that the apologies of General Huerta and his representatives should go much further; that they should be such as to attract the attention

1. *Ibid.,* pp. 6908–09 (April 20, 1914).
* Professor A. S. Link concludes that this statement misrepresents the facts; Huerta had shown "extraordinary concern" for American interests (*Wilson: The New Freedom* [1956], p. 398).

of the whole population to their significance, and such as to impress upon General Huerta himself the necessity of seeing to it that no further occasion for explanations and professed regrets should arise. I, therefore, felt it my duty to sustain Admiral Mayo in the whole of his demand, and to insist that the flag of the United States should be saluted in such a way as to indicate a new spirit and attitude on the part of the Huertistas.

Such a salute General Huerta has refused, and I have come to ask your approval and support in the course I now propose to pursue.

This Government can, I earnestly hope, in no circumstances be forced into war with the people of Mexico. Mexico is torn by civil strife. If we are to accept the tests of its own constitution, it has no government. General Huerta has set his power up in the City of Mexico, such as it is, without right and by methods for which there can be no justification. Only part of the country is under his control. If armed conflict should unhappily come as a result of his attitude of personal resentment toward this Government, we should be fighting only General Huerta and those who adhere to him and give him their support, and our object would be only to restore to the people of the distracted Republic the opportunity to set up again their own laws and their own government.

But I earnestly hope that war is not now in question. I believe that I speak for the American people when I say that we do not desire to control in any degree the affairs of our sister Republic. Our feeling for the people of Mexico is one of deep and genuine friendship, and everything that we have so far done or refrained from doing has proceeded from our desire to help them, not to hinder or embarrass them. We would not wish even to exercise the good offices of friendship without their welcome and consent. The people of Mexico are entitled to settle their own domestic affairs in their own way, and we sincerely desire to respect their right. The present situation need have none of the grave implications of interference if we deal with it promptly, firmly, and wisely.

No doubt I could do what is necessary in the circumstances to enforce respect for our Government without recourse to the Congress, and yet not exceed my constitutional powers as President. But I do not wish to act in a manner possibly of so grave consequence except in close conference and cooperation with both the Senate and House. I, therefore, come to ask your approval that I should use the armed forces of the United States in such ways and to such an extent as may be necessary to obtain from General Huerta and his adherents the fullest recognition of the rights and dignity of the United States, even amidst the distressing conditions now unhappily obtaining in Mexico.

There can in what we do be no thought of aggression or of selfish aggrandizement. We seek to maintain the dignity and authority of the United States, only because we wish always to keep our great influence unimpaired for the uses of liberty, both in the United States and wherever else it may be employed for the benefit of mankind.

2. A Republican Assails "Watchful Waiting" (1916)

A patriotic Congress promptly granted Wilson the authority to intervene. But a day earlier (April 21, 1914) American forces, under emergency orders from the White House, had bombarded and occupied Vera Cruz in a vain attempt to prevent a German ship from landing munitions that might be used against United States troops. With a Louisville paper crying "On to the Isthmus!" and with a full-blown war imminent, the ABC powers (Argentina, Brazil, and Chile) offered to mediate. Wilson gladly accepted this escape hatch, on April 25, 1914. Nearly three months later Huerta was forced to abdicate, but American businessmen clamored for full-dress intervention as United States citizens continued to lose both their property and their lives. The European war erupted later in 1914, and Republicans criticized Wilson for being "too proud to fight." They also condemned him for insisting that Americans leave the Mexican danger zone while he permitted others to sail through submarine-infested danger zones on the high seas. Here Representative William E. Humphrey, a prominent Congressman from Washington, voices typical Republican complaints. Determine how effectively he supports his charges that Wilson's policy was meddling, vacillating, hypocritical, inconsistent, and futile.

The President's policy in Mexico is not based upon his party platform. It is characterized by weakness, uncertainty, vacillation, and uncontrollable desire to intermeddle in Mexican affairs. He has not had the courage to go into Mexico nor the courage to stay out.

The President has repeatedly declared that he would not interfere in Mexico nor permit others to do so. . . . At Columbus, Ohio, in his recent speech he said:

"The Mexicans may not know what to do with their government; but that is none of our business, and, so long as I have the power to prevent it, nobody shall 'butt in' to alter it for them."

At the notable talk in the White House not long ago to the Democratic National Committee, where he referred to other people "talking through their hat," if he is correctly reported, he declared "that the Mexicans can raise all the h - - - they please; it is none of our business." Remember, the language I am using is not mine but the reported language of the President. Certainly their ability to raise what he so delicately described ought to satisfy even the President and that wing of the Democratic Party that believes in "watchful waiting."

But if the President had followed these declarations, however un-American and indefensible they may be, it would have been far better for us and probably for Mexico. But his deeds have been strangers to his words. Instead of a policy of "hands off," it has been a policy of constant interference in Mexican affairs.

The President told Huerta that he must not be a candidate; that he would not be recognized. He talked about fair elections and constitutional government, and showed a strong desire not only to control Mexican politics but to go into Mexico and regulate the land system of that country. He sent his secret special agents to Mexico City and became involved in a

2. *Congressional Record,* 64 Cong., 1 sess., pp. 1636–38, *passim* (Jan. 27, 1916).

personal quarrel with Huerta. This controversy reached its climax in the most grotesque and stupendous piece of folly in the history of civilized nations when the President appeared here before Congress and virtually asked that the United States declare war against Huerta, the individual. And, what was even more ridiculous and absurd, it was done. And for what reason? Who today will tell us the cause of that action? Americans had been driven from Mexico; American property had been destroyed in Mexico; American men had been murdered in Mexico; American women had been outraged in Mexico. But all these did not disturb the serenity of "watchful waiting," or recall to the mind of the President the Democratic platform declarations about protecting life and property of American citizens along the border and on foreign soil.

We were told that Huerta was a murderer, an assassin, a usurper, and a traitor, and a man that we would never under any circumstances recognize. But Huerta, the individual, not representing Mexico but himself, had refused to salute the American flag on a gasoline launch in a place where it had no right to be; or, to be exact, for the sake of history, Huerta agreed to fire six guns in salute, while the President, as I recall, demanded twenty-one.*

This insult from an assassin and a murderer that we would not in any way recognize was more than this administration, too proud to fight, could endure. Our magnificent battleship squadron was hurried to Mexican waters, although at that time the Mexican Navy consisted of one old antiquated gunboat. The Army was sent to Mexico, and, after Vera Cruz was bombarded by our Navy, it was landed on Mexican soil. Seventeen [nineteen] of our own soldiers lost their lives and more than a hundred Mexicans were killed. We seized the customhouse and carried away more than a million dollars.

And all this for what purpose? Why did we go to Mexico and what did we accomplish and why did we return? We were told that a German vessel was about to land a cargo of guns and ammunition, and this was the reason for hurrying our Navy to Mexican waters. But that same German vessel landed its cargo in Mexico. We are told that our Army and Navy went to Mexico to make Huerta apologize. Has anyone read that apology? We are told that our Army and Navy went to Mexico to make Huerta salute the flag. Has anyone heard that salute? . . .

Our policy in Mexico has earned us the contempt of the world, and beyond question has greatly influenced the warring nations of Europe in their present attitude toward us. . . .

We make a tremendous bluster about the killing of American citizens upon the high seas and fill the air with the tumult and the noise of many typewriters, although the killing is only accidental and undoubtedly really regretted by those who did the act. But so far we have looked with

---

* Huerta had agreed to a twenty-one-gun salute if returned on a gun-for-gun basis, but this was unacceptable to Wilson.

equanimity undisturbed while hundreds of Americans have been purposely foully murdered in Mexico in a most cruel and fiendish manner. . . .

Speaking for myself, but believing that I voice the sentiment of the American people, there are some things that I would do in regard to Mexico if upon me rested the responsibility. I would either go into Mexico and pacify the country or I would keep my hands entirely out of Mexico. If we are too proud to fight, we should be too proud to quarrel. I would not choose between murderers. I would not permit either side to procure guns or ammunition in this country that may hereafter be used to murder Americans. I would not depend upon secret personal agents for my information. I would deal openly and in the light of day with the Mexican situation. I would practice pitiless publicity as well as preach it. I would give the American people the facts. I would let them know the truth, and if that is done the American people will quickly decide what shall be done.

And, above all, I would do this—the thing that should have been done more than three years ago, and if it had been done, the letting of American blood in Mexico would not have occurred: I would serve notice upon all factions that no longer would any of them be permitted, under any pretense whatever, to destroy American property, or to murder American men, or to ravish American women, and back of that notice I would place the power of this great Republic.

3. Wilson Serves Mankind (1914)

"My ideal," Wilson had remarked in 1914, "is an orderly and righteous government in Mexico; but my passion is for the submerged eighty-five percent of the people of that Republic, who are now struggling toward liberty. . . ." He feared that those investors in the United States who were clamoring for "order" had in view the "old order" of despotism. In 1916 he was reluctantly forced to send General Pershing's army into Mexico in pursuit of the bandit Villa, whose raiders had shot up the town of Columbus, New Mexico. Yet on this occasion, as on others, Wilson avoided a full-fledged war. He realized that German plotters were seeking to involve the United States in Mexico so as to leave Germany with a freer hand in Europe. During the funeral services at the Brooklyn Navy Yard for the nineteen men who had fallen at Vera Cruz, Wilson thus bared his soul. Form conclusions as to his character from these remarks. Discover to what extent this speech is self-justification, and how the ideal of service can be extended to shooting Mexicans.

. . . We have gone down to Mexico to serve mankind if we can find out the way. We do not want to fight the Mexicans. We want to serve the Mexicans if we can, because we know how we would like to be free, and how we would like to be served, if there were friends standing by in such case ready to serve us. A war of aggression is not a war in which it is a proud thing to die, but a war of service is a thing in which it is a proud thing to die. . . .

War, gentlemen, is only a sort of dramatic representation, a sort of

3. Woodrow Wilson, *The New Democracy,* ed. R. S. Baker and W. E. Dodd (1926), I, 104–06, *passim.* By permission of Harper and Brothers.

A SORT OF WAR

President Wilson: "I hope you are not shooting at my
dear friends the Mexicans?"
U.S.A. Gunner: "Oh, no, sir. We have strict orders only
to aim at one Huerta." *Punch* (London), 1914.

dramatic symbol, of a thousand forms of duty. I never went into battle;
I never was under fire, but I fancy that there are some things just as hard
to do as to go under fire. I fancy that it is just as hard to do your duty
when men are sneering at you as when they are shooting at you. When they
shoot at you, they can only take your natural life; when they sneer at you,
they can wound your living heart, and men who are brave enough, steadfast enough, steady in their principles enough, to go about their duty with
regard to their fellow men, no matter whether there are hisses or cheers,
men who can do what Rudyard Kipling in one of his poems wrote, "Meet
with triumph and disaster and treat those two impostors just the same," are
men for a nation to be proud of. Morally speaking, disaster and triumph
are impostors. The cheers of the moment are not what a man ought to
think about, but the verdict of his conscience and of the consciences of
mankind.

When I look at you, I feel as if I also and we all were enlisted men. Not enlisted in your particular branch of the service, but enlisted to serve the country, no matter what may come, even though we may sacrifice our lives in the arduous endeavor. We are expected to put the utmost energy of every power that we have into the service of our fellow men, never sparing ourselves, not condescending to think of what is going to happen to ourselves, but ready, if need be, to go to the utter length of complete self-sacrifice.

THOUGHT PROVOKERS

1. Was the revival of personal appearances before Congress by the President desirable or undesirable? Argue both sides of the proposition that lobbies are useful and necessary. What advantages would American manufacturers have without a protective tariff in competing with low-wage European industry?

2. Are interlocking directorates of some kind inevitable in the American economy? Why are experts, like the bankers, often faulty in their prognoses? Should the bankers have been permitted to write the Federal Reserve Act?

3. Why should the British have been disturbed by the canal tolls exemption for coastwise American traffic, especially since they were not permitted to engage in this trade themselves?

4. Why did Wilson ask for authority to use the armed forces in Mexico when he already had that authority? Would the prestige of the United States have been better served by a disavowal of Admiral Mayo's unauthorized demand than by the bombardment of Vera Cruz? Should the President of the United States be the moral judge of foreign governments? Should Americans who live and invest in foreign countries be told that they do so purely at their own risk?

FURTHER EXPLORATION

General: A. S. Link, *Woodrow Wilson and the Progressive Era, 1910–1917* (1954), Woodrow Wilson, *The New Freedom* (1913); J. M. Blum, *Woodrow Wilson and the Politics of Morality* (1956). **Tariff Reform:** A. S. Link, *Wilson: The New Freedom* (1956). **Monetary Reform:** Carter Glass, *An Adventure in Constructive Finance* (1927). **Canal Tolls:** R. S. Baker, *Woodrow Wilson: Life and Letters* (1931), vol. IV. **Mexico:** J. F. Rippy, *The United States and Mexico* (rev. ed., 1931); H. F. Cline, *The United States and Mexico* (1953); R. E. Quirk, *An Affair of Honor: Woodrow Wilson and the Occupation of Vera Cruz* (1962); C. C. Clendenen, *The United States and Pancho Villa* (1961).

Recent: E. D. Cronon, ed., *The Cabinet Diaries of Josephus Daniels, 1913–1921* (1963).

Chapter 36

Waging Neutrality, 1914-1917

We must be impartial in thought as well as in action.

WOODROW WILSON, 1914

PROLOGUE: When World War I erupted in 1914, the American people were overwhelmingly determined to stay out. But their Anglo-Saxon heritage on the one hand, and German aggressions on the other, caused their sympathies to go out to Britain, France, and their allies (the Allied Powers) against Germany, Austria-Hungary, and their allies (the Central Powers). In consequence, the United States acquiesced the more readily in the unorthodox British naval blockade of Germany, while protesting the more sternly against the irregular German submarine blockade of Britain. America further offended the Germans by immense sales of munitions to their enemies, and by insisting that American citizens should continue to have the right to travel on munitions-laden belligerent liners. Facing ultimate starvation, the Germans finally proclaimed a desperate all-out submarine campaign in January, 1917. When they sank four unarmed American merchant ships in mid-March, 1917, they were indubitably making war on the United States, and President Wilson reluctantly concluded that the nation had no choice but to fight back.

A. ACQUIESCING IN THE BRITISH BLOCKADE

1. Lord Bryce's Propaganda Report (1915)

The American people were so deeply shocked by Germany's brutal invasion of Belgium that they uncritically swallowed large doses of Allied propaganda. British propagandists stressed the medically preposterous stories of Belgian babies (still living) with their hands hacked off and the alleged German practice of converting battlefield corpses into fertilizer and soap. The Germans, with much less persuasiveness, charged that the Allies gouged out the eyes of prisoners, that French soldiers put cholera germs in wells used by Germans, and that a Belgian priest had placed a machine gun behind his altar and mowed down German Catholic soldiers who came to mass. Lord Bryce, admired in America for his sympathetic two-volume *The American Commonwealth*, served his country by lending his name to a sensational report on atrocities in Belgium. In reading the following incident (one of many involving arson, rape, mayhem, and murder) determine what part is least worthy of belief, and assess the probable effect of the Bryce report in predisposing the American people to accept British infractions of neutral rights.

The [German] officer spoke Flemish. He knocked at the door; the peasant did not come. The officer ordered the soldiers to break down the door,

1. Viscount Bryce, *Report of the Committee on Alleged German Outrages* (1915), p. 51. Many of the incidents in the Bryce report were later proved to have been grossly exaggerated or completely fabricated.

BABES ON BAYONETS

An exaggerated stereotype in America of German atrocities in Belgium. *Life,* 1915.

which two of them did. The peasant came and asked what they were doing. The officer said he did not come quickly enough, and that they had "trained up" [disciplined] plenty of others. His hands were tied behind his back, and he was shot at once without a moment's delay.

The wife came out with a little sucking child. She put the child down and sprang at the Germans like a lioness. She clawed their faces. One of the Germans took a rifle and struck her a tremendous blow with the butt on the head. Another took his bayonet and fixed it and thrust it through the child. He then put his rifle on his shoulder with the child up it, its little arms stretched out once or twice.

The officers ordered the houses to be set on fire, and straw was obtained, and it was done. The man and his wife and the child were thrown on the top of the straw. There were about forty other peasant prisoners there also, and the officer said: "I am doing this as a lesson and example to you. When a German tells you to do something next time you must move more quickly." The regiment of Germans was a regiment of Hussars, with crossbones and a death's-head on the cap.

2. Page Plays Britain's Game (*c.* 1915)

The British, with their powerful navy, undertook to starve Germany into submission with a blockade. But the ancient practice of stationing warships off the three-mile line proved hazardous, primarily because of new long-range guns and lurking submarines. The British therefore took "liberties" with international law. They mined the North Sea and forced neutral ships into their ports to be searched for munitions and other contraband of war. They arbitrarily broadened the normal contraband lists to include such necessities as food and cotton. They halted the slippage of supplies into Ger-

2. Viscount Grey, *Twenty-five Years* (1925), II, 109–10. By permission of J. B. Lippincott Company.

many through neighboring neutrals like Denmark by limiting these small countries to their pre-war imports. Even though London paid for many of the intercepted cargoes, Washington protested against these disagreeable practices as violations of international law. Foreign Secretary Grey here tells how he dealt with Ambassador Page, the ex-journalist who became Wilson's ardently pro-British representative in London. Decide whether Page should be praised or blamed.

We got a list of absolute contraband that was not seriously challenged. But there was much more difficulty to come. We were now entitled to seize such things as copper and rubber in any ship on the high seas, if they were consigned to a German port. This alone was of little use. Germany could import goods as easily through Dutch, Danish, or Swedish ports as through her own, and in Sweden especially there were people disposed to make Sweden a source of supply for Germany. It was therefore as essential to Britain and the Allies to seize copper or rubber going to a Swedish or neutral port as when going to a German port.

It was on this point that controversy arose with the United States. The very fact that the United States was, in a sense, the trustee for the right of weaker neutrals made its Government disposed to champion those rights. Was a peaceful Swede desiring copper for innocent purposes to have it stopped? On the other hand, was the British Navy to let copper pass under its very guns to a Swede who was importing it for the German Government, and going to send it straight to Germany to be made into munitions to kill British soldiers?

The argument between these two opposite points of view was long, voluminous, and extensive. It was published, and anyone who has enough curiosity and time may read it.

The Navy acted and the Foreign Office had to find the argument to support the action; it was anxious work. British action provoked American argument; that was met by British counter-argument. British action preceded British argument; the risk was that action might follow American argument. In all this [Ambassador] Page's advice and suggestion were of the greatest value in warning us when to be careful or encouraging us when we could safely be firm.

One incident in particular remains in my memory. Page came to see me at the Foreign Office one day, and produced a long despatch from Washington contesting our claim to act as we were doing in stopping contraband going to neutral ports. "I am instructed," he said, "to read this despatch to you." He read, and I listened. He then said: "I have now read the despatch, but I do not agree with it; let us consider how it should be answered!"

3. Lansing's Pro-Ally Tactics (*c.* 1916)

International law required a blockading power to stop and search all merchant ships before seizing or sinking them. If they were unresisting enemy merchantmen, they could lawfully be destroyed only if proper provision was made for the safety of

3. *War Memoirs of Robert Lansing* (1935), pp. 110–12. Copyright 1935 by the Bobbs-Merrill Company, Inc.; used by special permission of the publishers.

passengers and crew. The blockading British, because of the menace of new weapons, were taking "liberties" with the old rules. The Germans, unable to sustain an orthodox blockade of the British Isles with fragile submarines vulnerable to ramming or gunfire, began to sink enemy merchantmen without warning. Berlin argued that Germany was forced to take such "liberties" because Allied merchant ships had first sunk German submarines attempting to stop them. Secretary of State Lansing, a fussily precise legalist who was warmly pro-Ally at heart, here explains his reactions. From his account enumerate and evaluate the various reasons why the United States turned against Germany rather than Britain.

Sifted down to the bare facts the position was this: Great Britain insisted that Germany should conform her conduct of naval [submarine] warfare to the strict letter of the rules of international law, and resented even a suggestion that there should be any variation of the rules to make them reasonably applicable to new conditions. On the other hand, Great Britain was herself repeatedly departing from the rules of international law, on the plea that new conditions compelled her to do so, and even showed resentment because the United States refused to recognize her right to ignore or modify the rules whenever she thought it necessary to do so.

Briefly, the British Government wished international law enforced when they believed that it worked to the advantage of Great Britain, and wished the law modified when the change would benefit Great Britain.

There is no doubt that the good relations between the United States and Great Britain would have been seriously jeopardized by this unreasonable attitude, which seems unworthy of British statesmanship, except for the fact that the British violations of law affected American property, while the German violations affected American lives. Nothing else saved our relations with Great Britain from becoming strained to the breaking point. Even as it was, there were many Americans, both in public and in private life, who considered that we were unjust, or at least unfair, because we differentiated between the illegal acts of the belligerents on the basis of their results.

These complaints against the conduct of the British were increasing in the United States, were gaining more and more converts in Congress, and were exerting more and more pressure upon the government to adopt vigorous measures to compel Great Britain to cease her illegal practices, when the Germans, with their genius for always doing the wrong thing in the wrong way and at the wrong time, perpetrated new crimes in their submarine campaign. These events made the complaints against the British seem insignificant and ill-timed, and aroused anew the indignation of the American people toward the ruthless commanders of Germany's undersea corsairs.

The British have only the stupidity of the Germans to thank for saving them from having a very serious situation develop in their relations with this country in the spring of 1916. It was luck on their part and nothing more. They had done everything that they could to make the position of this government difficult; and the worst of it was that they did not appear to realize it, for which our Embassy at London, it must be admitted, was by no means blameless.

Sympathetic as I felt toward the Allies and convinced that we would in the end join with them against the autocratic governments of the Central Empires, I saw with apprehension the tide of resentment against Great Britain rising higher and higher in this country. It was becoming increasingly difficult to avoid bringing the controversies between our two governments to a head, and to keep from assuming positions which went beyond the field of discussion.

I did all that I could to prolong the disputes by preparing, or having prepared, long and detailed replies, and introducing technical and controversial matters in the hope that, before the extended interchange of arguments came to an end, something would happen to change the current of American public opinion, or to make the American people perceive that German absolutism was a menace to their liberties and to democratic institutions everywhere.

Fortunately, this hope and effort were not in vain. Germany did the very thing which she should not have done. The tide of sentiment in the United States turned, and it was possible to prevent a widespread demand being made that the Allied Powers be "brought to book" without further delay for their illegal treatment of our commerce.

B. MERCHANTS OF DEATH

1. Bryan Backs the Munitions Business (1915)

Germany and Austria-Hungary, anticipating a blockade, had begun the war with adequate supplies of arms. Britain and her allies, counting on keeping the sea lanes open, were less well stocked. American factories soon began to provide the Allies with mountainous quantities of munitions. Meanwhile some of the small neutral countries, seeking to conserve their scanty supplies, had forbidden the export of arms. Berlin urged the United States to do likewise. Congress could have embargoed arms, as it later did in the neutrality laws of the 1930's. But taking such a step would have worked so greatly to the disadvantage of the Allies as to be virtually an unneutral act. Refusal to take such a step worked so heavily to the disadvantage of the Germans and their allies as to seem no less unneutral. Rather than slip back into the recent depression, the United States followed the profitable path of letting trade take its course. The silver-tongued orator William J. Bryan, Lansing's predecessor as Secretary of State, here defends official policy in a letter to Senator Stone. Note the weakest aspect of the German position. Was the obligation of the United States to stop the munitions traffic legal or moral?

There is no power in the Executive to prevent the sale of ammunition to the belligerents.

The duty of a neutral to restrict trade in munitions of war has never been imposed by international law or by municipal statute [domestic law]. It has never been the policy of this Government to prevent the shipment of arms

1. *Foreign Relations of the United States, 1914, Supplement,* pp. x, xiv (Jan. 20, 1915).

or ammunition into belligerent territory, except in the case of neighboring American Republics [*e.g.*, Mexico], and then only when civil strife prevailed. Even to this extent the belligerents in the present conflict, when they were neutrals, have never, so far as the records disclose, limited the sale of munitions of war. It is only necessary to point to the enormous quantities of arms and ammunition furnished by manufacturers in Germany to the belligerents in the Russo-Japanese war [1904–1905] and in the recent Balkan wars [1912–1913] to establish the general recognition of the propriety of the trade by a neutral nation. . . .

If any American citizens, partisans of Germany and Austria-Hungary, feel that this administration is acting in a way injurious to the cause of those countries, this feeling results from the fact that on the high seas the German and Austro-Hungarian naval power is thus far inferior to the British. It is the business of a belligerent operating on the high seas, not the duty of a neutral, to prevent contraband from reaching an enemy.

Those in this country who sympathize with Germany and Austria-Hungary appear to assume that some obligation rests upon this Government, in the performance of its neutral duty, to prevent all trade in contraband, and thus to equalize the difference due to the relative naval strength of the belligerents. No such obligation exists; it would be an unneutral act, an act of partiality on the part of this Government, to adopt such a policy if the Executive had the power to do so. If Germany and Austria-Hungary cannot import contraband from this country, it is not, because of that fact, the duty of the United States to close its markets to the Allies. The markets of this country are open upon equal terms to all the world, to every nation, belligerent or neutral.

2. Berlin Condemns the Munitions Traffic (1915)

The Germans were angered when America became a prime munitions factory of the Allies, all the more so when Wall Street bankers loaned hundreds of millions of dollars to finance the cargoes of death. The United States, on the other hand, stopped shipping foodstuffs and other commodities to the Germans. It was thwarted by the unconventional British blockade, in which the State Department protestingly acquiesced. Berlin, in this official protest in 1915, insisted that America was violating the true spirit of neutrality. Determine whether the Germans were reasonable in claiming that the unusual conditions of this war obligated Washington to embargo arms.

Then there is also the attitude of the United States in the question of the exportation of arms. The Imperial [German] Government feels sure that the United States Government will agree that, in questions of neutrality, it is necessary to take into consideration not only the formal aspect of the case, but also the spirit in which the neutrality is carried out.

The situation in the present war differs from that of any previous war. Therefore any reference to arms furnished by Germany in former wars is

2. *Ibid., 1915, Supplement,* pp. 157–58 (April 4, 1915).

not justified, for then it was not a question *whether* war material should be supplied to the belligerents, but *who* should supply it in competition with other nations. In the present war, all nations having a war material industry worth mentioning are either involved in the war themselves or are engaged in perfecting their own armaments, and have therefore laid an embargo against the exportation of war material.

The United States is accordingly the only neutral country in a position to furnish war materials. The conception of neutrality is thereby given a new purport, independently of the formal question of hitherto existing law. In contradiction thereto, the United States is building up a powerful arms industry in the broadest sense, the existing plants not only being worked but enlarged by all available means, and new ones built.

The international conventions [treaties] for the protection of the rights of neutral nations doubtless sprang from the necessity of protecting the existing industries of neutral nations as far as possible from injury in their business. But it can in no event be in accordance with the spirit of true neutrality if, under the protection of such international stipulations, an entirely new industry is created in a neutral state, such as is the development of the arms industry in the United States, the business whereof, under the present conditions, can benefit only the belligerent powers.

This industry is actually delivering goods only to the enemies of Germany. The theoretical willingness to supply Germany also, if shipments thither were possible, does not alter the case. If it is the will of the American people that there shall be a true neutrality, the United States will find means of preventing this one-sided supply of arms or at least of utilizing it to protect legitimate trade with Germany, especially that in foodstuffs.

This view of neutrality should all the more appeal to the United States Government because the latter enacted a similar [arms-embargo] policy toward Mexico. On February 4, 1914, President Wilson . . . declared that "we should stand for genuine neutrality. . . ." He then held that "in that case, because Carranza had no ports, while Huerta had them and was able to import these materials, that it was our duty as a nation to treat them [Carranza and Huerta] upon an equality. . . ." If this view were applied to the present case, it would lead to an embargo on the exportation of arms.

[*Representative Stephen G. Porter of Pennsylvania, pleading for true neutrality, added another argument to the German case in his speech of March 3, 1915:* "Our population is composed of former citizens of all the belligerent nations, and our position in the matter of these shipments is entirely different from that of any other country. They can sell these deadly materials to other nations without being a party to the death or wounding of those who are kin to their own people. Many a bullet made in an American factory, by an American workman, has found its deadly resting place in the body of that workman's brother, nephew, cousin, or even his father or son—the mere thought of which is horrible to contemplate." (*Congressional Record, 63 Cong., 3 sess., Appendix, p. 585.*)]

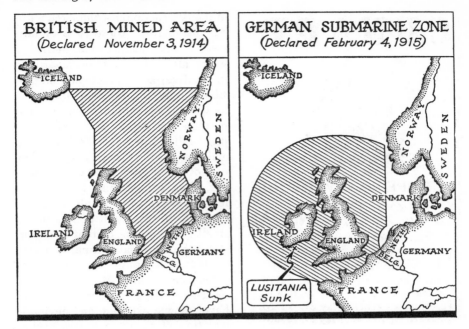

C. THE SINKING OF THE *LUSITANIA*

1. Wilson Demands Muzzled U-Boats (1915)

Late in 1914 the British, taking an unprecedented "liberty" with freedom of the seas, proclaimed the North Sea a military area and proceeded to mine it. (Washington did not protest, though more than two years later it formally declared that it had not abandoned its rights.) In retaliation, the Germans declared an unprecedented war zone around the British Isles, and announced that they would sink all enemy craft within those waters. Washington vigorously protested that it would hold Berlin to "strict accountability" if American ships were incidentally sunk and American lives were lost. But United States citizens continued to sail into the submarine-infested waters, as they had a perfect legal right to do. On May 1, 1915, the day the giant Cunard liner *Lusitania* left New York, an advertisement appeared in the local newspapers, over the name of the German Embassy, warning passengers of their danger. A week later the vessel was torpedoed without warning by a German submarine off the Irish coast and sank with the loss of 1198 persons, many of them women and children, and 128 of them Americans. Secretary Bryan signed the following stern protest. Ascertain whether the United States was fair to Germany in its position on the submarine, and also in taking notice of the newspaper advertisement.

The Government of the United States . . . desires to call the attention of the Imperial German Government, with the utmost earnestness, to the fact that the objection to their present method of attack against the trade of their enemies lies in the practical impossibility of employing submarines

1. *Foreign Relations of the United States, 1915, Supplement,* pp. 394–95.

CUNARD

EUROPE VIA LIVERPOOL

LUSITANIA

Fastest and Largest Steamer
now in Atlantic Service Sails
SATURDAY, MAY 1, 10 A. M.

Transylvania - Fri , May 7, 5 P.M.
Orduna, - - - Tues., May 18, 10 A.M.
Tuscania, - - - Fri., May 21, 5 P.M.
LUSITANIA, - Sat., May 29, 10 A.M.
Transylvania, - Fri., June 4, 5 P.M.

Gibraltar—Genoa—Naples—Piraeus
S.S. Carpathia, Thur., May 13, Noon

ROUND THE WORLD TOURS
Through bookings to all principal Ports
of the World.
Company's Office, 21-24 State St., N. Y.

New York *World,* May 1, 1915.

in the destruction of commerce without disregarding those rules of fairness, reason, justice, and humanity which all modern opinion regards as imperative. It is practically impossible for the officers of a submarine to visit a merchantman at sea and examine her papers and cargo. It is practically impossible for them to make a prize of her; and, if they cannot put a prize crew on board of her, they cannot sink her without leaving her crew and all on board of her to the mercy of the sea in her small boats. These facts it is understood the Imperial German Government frankly admit. . . . Manifestly submarines cannot be used against merchantmen, as the last few weeks have shown, without an inevitable violation of many sacred principles of justice and humanity.

American citizens act within their indisputable rights in taking their ships and in traveling wherever their legitimate business calls them upon the high seas, and exercise those rights in what should be the well-justified confidence that their lives will not be endangered by acts done in clear violation of universally acknowledged international obligations, and certainly in the confidence that their own Government will sustain them in the exercise of their rights.

There was recently published in the newspapers of the United States, I regret to inform the Imperial German Government, a formal warning, purporting to come from the Imperial German Embassy at Washington, addressed to the people of the United States, and stating, in effect, that any citizen of the United States who exercised his right of free travel upon the seas would do so at his peril if his journey should take him within the zone of waters within which the Imperial German Navy was using submarines against the commerce of Great Britain and France, notwithstanding the respectful but very earnest protest of his Government, the Government of the United States.

I do not refer to this for the purpose of calling the attention of the Imperial German Government at this time to the surprising irregularity of a communication from the Imperial German Embassy at Washington addressed to the people of the United States through the newspapers, but only for the purpose of pointing out that no warning that an unlawful and inhumane act will be committed can possibly be accepted as an excuse or palliation for that act or as an abatement of the responsibility for its commission.

2. Germany Justifies the Sinking (1915)

Berlin, though regretting the loss of innocent life, stoutly defended the torpedoing of the *Lusitania.* But the German Foreign Office was mistaken on several counts. The Cunarder was not armed, as charged (though many British merchantmen were); it was not carrying an organized body of Canadian troops; and it had not demonstrably violated the American law which forbade carrying powerful explosives. The fact that the vessel was transporting 4200 (not 5400) cases of small-arms ammunition had no bearing on the time-honored rule that unarmed and unresisting passenger ships could not be sunk without warning and without proper provision for the safety of passengers and crew. Warships could lawfully be destroyed without warning, and in several respects, especially in secret orders to ram at sight, the *Lusitania* could technically be regarded as an offensively armed warship. In reading Berlin's official reply to Washington's protest, judge whether the Germans had a sound moral case, if not a legal one.

The Government of the United States proceeds on the assumption that the *Lusitania* is to be considered as an ordinary unarmed merchant vessel. The Imperial Government begs, in this connection, to point out that the *Lusitania* was one of the largest and fastest English commerce steamers, constructed with Government funds as auxiliary cruisers, and is expressly included in the navy list published by British Admiralty. It is moreover known to the Imperial Government, from reliable information furnished by its officials and neutral passengers, that for some time practically all the more valuable English merchant vessels have been provided with guns, ammunition, and other weapons, and reinforced with a crew specially practiced in manning guns. According to reports at hand here, the *Lusitania*, when she left New York, undoubtedly had guns on board which were mounted under decks and masked.

The Imperial Government further-

2. *Ibid.,* p. 420 (May 28, 1915).

NOTICE!

TRAVELLERS intending to embark on the Atlantic voyage are reminded that a state of war exists between Germany and her allies and GreatBritian and her allies; that the zone of war includes the waters adjacent to the British Isles; that, in accordance with formal notice given by the Imperial German Government, vessels flying the flag of Great Britian, or of any of her allies, are liable to destruction in those waters and that travellers sailing in the war zone on ships of Great Britian or her allies do so at their own risk.

IMPERIAL GERMAN EMBASSY,
WASHINGTON. D. C., APRIL 22, 1915.

When Washington refused to warn U.S. citizens to keep off belligerent ships, the German Embassy inserted the above notice in the leading New York papers. New York *World,* May 1, 1915.

more has the honor to direct the particular attention of the American Government to the fact that the British Admiralty, by a secret instruction of February of this year, advised the British merchant marine not only to seek protection behind neutral flags and markings, but even, when so disguised, to attack German submarines by ramming them. High rewards have been offered by the British Government as a special incentive for the destruction of the submarines by merchant vessels, and such rewards have already been paid out.

In view of these facts, which are satisfactorily known to it, the Imperial Government is unable to consider English merchant vessels any longer as "undefended territory" in the zone of maritime war designated by the Admiralty Staff of the Imperial German Navy. The German commanders are consequently no longer in a position to observe the rules of capture otherwise usual, and with which they invariably complied before this.

Lastly, the Imperial Government must specially point out that on her last trip the *Lusitania,* as on earlier occasions, had Canadian troops and munitions on board, including no less than 5400 cases of ammunition destined for the destruction of brave German soldiers who are fulfilling with self-sacrifice and devotion their duty in the service of the Fatherland. The German Government believes that it acts in just self-defense when it seeks to protect the lives of its soldiers by destroying ammunition destined for the enemy with the means of war at its command.

The English steamship company must have been aware of the dangers to which passengers on board the *Lusitania* were exposed under the circumstances. In taking them on board in spite of this, the company quite deliberately tried to use the lives of American citizens as protection for the ammunition carried, and violated the clear provisions of American laws which expressly prohibit, and provide punishment for, the carrying of passengers on ships which have explosives on board. The company thereby wantonly caused the death of so many passengers. According to the express report of the submarine commander concerned, which is further confirmed by all other reports, there can be no doubt that the rapid sinking of the *Lusitania* was primarily due to the explosion of the cargo of ammunition caused by the torpedo. Otherwise, in all human probability, the passengers of the *Lusitania* would have been saved.*

3. Viereck Upholds the Torpedoing (1915)

America was shocked and outraged by the *Lusitania* slaughter. But many Germans, picturing the Cunarder as an arms-carrying warship, rejoiced when her lethal cargo sank. An unauthorized German struck off a medal showing the *Lusitania* bristling with guns. He distributed a few copies; Allied propagandists distributed some 250,000

---

* The *Lusitania* sank in eighteen minutes with unexpected rapidity, and there was a second explosion (possibly boilers). American officials had interpreted the law against munitions on passenger vessels as not applying to small-arms ammunition, which it was believed could not be exploded en masse. Other munitions may have been smuggled aboard.
3. *The Fatherland,* II, 5 (June 9, 1915).

more. George S. Viereck, a German-born poet, playwright, and propagandist who had come to America at the age of eleven, here presents a German point of view in his outspoken propaganda magazine published in New York. Many Germans believed with Secretary Bryan that permitting civilians to sail on munitions-carrying passenger ships was like "putting women and children in front of an army." Comment critically on Viereck's view that the torpedoing of the *Lusitania* was really a humanitarian act.

In spite of heavy provocation on the part of the United States, Germany has kept her temper. Not content with furnishing implements of murder to Germany's enemies, we [Americans] actually ask Germany to commit suicide. For a modification of submarine warfare as suggested in Mr. Bryan's note would be tantamount to self-destruction on Germany's part. . . .

We prattle about humanity, while we manufacture poisoned shrapnel and picric acid for profit. Ten thousand German widows, ten thousand orphans, ten thousand graves bear the legend "Made in America." . . .

Perhaps the captain of the submarine that sank the *Lusitania* to the bottom had a vision of a thousand passengers drowned. But above that vision he must have seen another vision of German armies mowed down by the deadly cargo within her hold, and of ten times ten thousand widows and orphans pointing an accusing finger at him if he failed to destroy the ammunition on its passage to England. The dictates of humanity demanded the destruction of the death-carrying vessel.

However we may deplore the loss of innocent lives, the *Lusitania* deserved her doom. The Cunard Line deliberately inveigled American passengers to imperil their lives. . . .

4. Secretary Houston Argues Both Sides (1915)

Wilson followed up the first *Lusitania* protest with another so strong that the pacifist Secretary Bryan spectacularly resigned rather than sign it. (He was succeeded by the more manageable Lansing.) Bryan, in his efforts to hold the scales even, had urged the sending of a parallel note of protest to Britain against her unconventional blockade practices. Secretary of Agriculture Houston here records his contribution to the Cabinet discussion immediately following Bryan's resignation. Assess the soundness of his argument that food could properly be cut off from Germany. In the light of his statement, how would the United States have acted if cast in the role of either Britain or Germany?

How far do you propose to go? Do you demand that Germany give up the use of the submarine in her efforts to destroy British trade? You speak of the practical impossibility of her using it in accordance with the rules of justice and humanity. I agree that it is unlikely that she can do so; but that is a matter she will have to resolve. We can insist that she observe such rules, but can we demand specifically that she give up the use of this new device? I do think that we can demand that she strictly comply with the rule of visit and search. We can demand that she make no mistakes and that she safeguard the lives of passengers and crew.

4. D. F. Houston, *Eight Years with Wilson's Cabinet* (1926), I, 143–44 (June 8, 1915).

This war will present many new problems. England is violating the three-mile blockade. She is blockading at a distance. The long-range gun and the submarine make the three-mile rule obsolete. If I were England, I would do just as England is doing, and if I were Germany, I would use the submarine if I could justly and humanely do so to stop English trade. I would not, if I were England, let any supplies of any sort reach Germany if I could prevent it.

It is silly for the Germans to cry that England is starving her women and children. It is impossible in modern war to separate, in the matter of food and other supplies, the civilian from the soldier. War now is the war of whole nations. Conditions are different from what they were when a few thousand men went to war and passed back and forth. You cannot feed a mass of civilians and not feed armies also. If you cripple the civilian population, you cripple the army. The contest is one of resources. Nobody knows this better than the Germans, and they know that they are being cut off from the outside world. What they demand is, in effect, that the Allies be prevented from using their fleets. They ought to have thought of this and of their women and children before they entered upon their present enterprise.

D. THE BELLIGERENT PASSENGER SHIP CONTROVERSY

1. Bryan Pleads for Self-Denial (1915)

Berlin at length agreed to make monetary reparation for the loss of Americans on the *Lusitania*. But a prickly problem remained. Should the United States government warn its citizens to stay off belligerent passenger liners venturing into torpedo-infested waters? Ex-Secretary Bryan aired his views as follows in a statement to the press shortly after his resignation. Evaluate his argument regarding rights and responsibilities, and note the most serious inconsistency in the American position.

Why should an American citizen be permitted to involve his country in war by traveling upon a belligerent ship when he knows that the ship will pass through a danger zone? The question is not whether an American citizen has a right under international law to travel on a belligerent ship; the question is whether he ought not, out of consideration for his country, if not for his own safety, avoid danger when avoidance is possible.

It is a very one-sided citizenship that compels a government to go to war over a citizen's rights, and yet relieves the citizen of all obligations to consider his nation's welfare. I do not know just how far the President can go legally in actually preventing Americans from traveling on belligerent ships, but I believe the Government should go as far as it can, and that in case of doubt it should give the benefit of the doubt to the Government.

But even if the Government could not legally prevent citizens from traveling on belligerent ships, it could, and in my judgment should, earnestly advise American citizens not to risk themselves or the peace of their country, and I have no doubt that these warnings would be heeded.

1. New York *Times*, June 10, 1915.

President Taft advised Americans to leave Mexico when insurrection broke out there, and President Wilson has repeated the advice. This advice, in my judgment, was eminently wise, and I think the same course should be followed in regard to warning Americans to keep off vessels subject to attack.

I think, too, that American passenger ships should be prohibited from carrying ammunition. The lives of passengers ought not to be endangered by cargoes of ammunition, whether that danger comes from possible explosions within or from possible attacks from without. Passengers and ammunition should not travel together. The attempt to prevent American citizens from incurring these risks is entirely consistent with the effort which our Government is making to prevent attacks from submarines.

The use of one remedy does not exclude the use of the other. The most familiar illustration is to be found in the action taken by municipal authorities during a riot. It is the duty of the mayor to suppress the mob and to prevent violence, but he does not hesitate to warn citizens to keep off the streets, but, for their own protection and in the interest of order, he warns them not to incur the risks involved in going upon the streets when men are shooting at each other.

2. Wilson Insists on American Rights (1916)

The folly of voyaging on belligerent passenger ships impressed others besides Bryan, and two resolutions designed to prevent such travel found strong backing in Congress. But President Wilson helped scuttle them by publicizing the following appeal to Chairman Stone of the Senate Committee on Foreign Relations. Comment critically on the validity of his argument in the light of the fact that Congress in the 1930's passed several laws forbidding Americans to sail on belligerent passenger ships.

For my own part, I cannot consent to any abridgment of the rights of American citizens in any respect. The honor and self-respect of the nation is involved. We covet peace, and shall preserve it at any cost but the loss of honor. To forbid our people to exercise their rights for fear we might be called upon to vindicate them would be a deep humiliation indeed. It would be an implicit, all but an explicit, acquiescence in the violation of the rights of mankind everywhere, and of whatever nation or allegiance. It would be a deliberate abdication of our hitherto proud position as spokesmen, even amidst the turmoils of war, for the law and the right. It would make everything this Government has attempted, and everything that it has achieved during this terrible struggle of nations, meaningless and futile.

It is important to reflect that if, in this instance, we allowed expediency to take the place of principle, the door would inevitably be opened to still further concessions. Once accept a single abatement of right, and many other humiliations would certainly follow, and the whole fine fabric of international law might crumble under our hands piece by piece. What we are contending for in this matter is of the very essence of the things

2. *Foreign Relations of the United States, 1916, Supplement*, pp. 177–78 (Feb. 24, 1916).

that have made America a sovereign nation. She cannot yield them without conceding her own impotency as a nation, and making virtual surrender of her independent position among the nations of the world.

E. WAR WITH GERMANY

1. Wilson Breaks Diplomatic Relations (1917)

After the *Lusitania* uproar, Germany generally avoided sinking unresisting passenger ships without warning. But in March, 1916, a German submarine torpedoed a French liner, the *Sussex*, and inflicted some eighty casualties, including injuries to several Americans. Wilson indignantly presented an ultimatum to Berlin threatening a severance of diplomatic relations—an almost certain prelude to war—unless Germany discontinued these inhumane tactics. The Germans reluctantly acquiesced. But finally driven to the wall by the British blockade, they dramatically announced, on January 31, 1917, the opening of an unrestricted submarine warfare on virtually all ships plying the war zone, including American vessels. Wilson, whose hand had now been called, went sorrowfully before Congress to deliver this speech. Judge whether he was naïve or idealistic, and whether he seemed hasty in accepting the German U-boat challenge.

I think that you will agree with me that, in view of this [submarine] declaration, . . . this Government has no alternative, consistent with the dignity and honor of the United States, but to take the course which . . . it announced that it would take. . . .

I have, therefore, directed the Secretary of State to announce to His Excellency the German Ambassador that all diplomatic relations between the United States and the German Empire are severed. . . .

Notwithstanding this unexpected action of the German Government, this sudden and deeply deplorable renunciation of its assurances, given this Government at one of the most critical moments of tension in the relations of the two governments, I refuse to believe that it is the intention of the German authorities to do in fact what they have warned us they will feel at liberty to do. I cannot bring myself to believe that they will indeed pay no regard to the ancient friendship between their people and our own, or to the solemn obligations which have been exchanged between them, and destroy American ships and take the lives of American citizens in the willful prosecution of the ruthless naval program they have announced their intention to adopt. Only actual overt acts on their part can make me believe it even now.

If this inveterate confidence on my part in the sobriety and prudent foresight of their purpose should unhappily prove unfounded—if American ships and American lives should in fact be sacrificed by their naval commanders in heedless contravention of the just and reasonable understandings of international law and the obvious dictates of humanity—I shall take the liberty of coming again before the Congress, to ask that authority be given me to use any means that may be necessary for the protection of our seamen

1. *Congressional Record*, 64 Cong., 2 sess., pp. 2578–79 (Feb. 3, 1917).

and our people in the prosecution of their peaceful and legitimate errands on the high seas. I can do nothing less. I take it for granted that all neutral governments will take the same course.

We do not desire any hostile conflict with the Imperial German Government. We are the sincere friends of the German people, and earnestly desire to remain at peace with the Government which speaks for them. We shall not believe that they are hostile to us unless and until we are obliged to believe it; and we purpose nothing more than the reasonable defense of the undoubted rights of our people.

We wish to serve no selfish ends. We seek merely to stand true alike in thought and in action to the immemorial principles of our people which I sought to express in my address to the Senate only two weeks ago—seek merely to vindicate our right to liberty and justice and an unmolested life. These are the bases of peace, not war. God grant we may not be challenged to defend them by acts of willful injustice on the part of the Government of Germany!

[*Wilson first undertook to arm American merchantmen ("armed neutrality") against the submarines. But when this tactic failed and German U-boats began to sink American vessels, he again went before Congress, on April 2, 1917. Referring principally to these sinkings, he asked for a formal resolution acknowledging the fact that Germany had "thrust" war on the United States. "We have no quarrel with the German people," he declared—only with their government. With militaristic forces rampant, "there can be no assured security for the democratic governments of the world." Hence "The world must be made safe for democracy." War is "terrible." "But the right is more precious than peace, and we shall fight for the things which we have always carried nearest our hearts—for democracy, for the right of those who submit to authority to have a voice in their own governments, for the rights and liberties of small nations, for a universal dominion of right by such a concert of free peoples as shall bring peace and safety to all nations and make the world itself at last free."*]

2. Representative Kitchin Assails the War Resolution (1917)

Congress responded promptly to Wilson's request for a war resolution. But the lopsided vote—82 to 6 in the Senate and 373 to 50 in the House—did not conceal a widespread opposition to hostilities, especially in the German-American areas. A flaming anti-war speech came from the lips of Representative Claude Kitchin of North Carolina, an eloquent and beloved string-tie Congressman, whose outburst produced a deluge of unflattering letters and telegrams. "Go to Germany," demanded one detractor. "They need fertilizer!" Ascertain what truth there is in Kitchin's allegation that Wilson's inconsistent and unneutral policies were taking the nation into war. Did Kitchin deserve to be called a pro-German?

Great Britain every day, every hour, for two years has violated American rights on the seas. We have persistently protested. She has denied us not only entrance into the ports of the Central Powers but has closed to us by force the ports of neutrals. She has unlawfully seized our ships and our

2. *Congressional Record*, 65 Cong., 1 sess., pp. 332–33 (April 5, 1917).

WAR AGAINST EVERYBODY

The German announcement of unrestricted submarine
warfare (January 31) was interpreted in America as war
on the entire civilized world by the Kaiser. New York
World, 1917.

cargoes. She has rifled our mails. She has declared a war zone sufficiently
large to cover all the ports of her enemy. She made the entire North Sea a
military area—strewed it with hidden mines and told the neutral nations
of the world to stay out or be blown up. We protested.* No American ship
was sunk, no American life was destroyed, because we submitted and did
not go in. We kept out of war. We sacrificed no honor. We surrendered
permanently no essential rights. We knew that these acts of Great Britain,
though in plain violation of international law and of our rights on the
seas, were not aimed at us. They were directed at her enemy. They were
inspired by military necessity. Rather than plunge this country into war, we
were willing to forgo for the time our rights. I approved that course then;
I approve it now.

Germany declares a war zone sufficiently large to cover the ports of her
enemy. She infests it with submarines and warns the neutral world to stay
out, though in plain violation of our rights and of international law. We
know that these acts are aimed not directly at us but intended to injure
and cripple her enemy, with which she is in a death struggle.

We refuse to yield; we refuse to forgo our rights for the time. We insist
upon going in.

In my judgment, we could keep out of the war with Germany as we kept

* Kitchin was mistaken. The United States did not formally protest against the British
mined zone; more than two years later it merely reserved its rights.

out of the war with Great Britain, by keeping our ships and our citizens out of the war zone of Germany as we did out of the war zone of Great Britain. And we would sacrifice no more honor, surrender no more rights, in the one case than in the other. Or we could resort to armed neutrality, which the President recently urged and for which I voted on March 1.

But we are told that Germany has destroyed American lives while Great Britain destroyed only property. Great Britain destroyed no American lives because this nation kept her ships and her citizens out of her war zone which she sowed with hidden mines.

But are we quite sure that the real reason for war with Germany is the destruction of lives as distinguished from property, that to avenge the killing of innocent Americans and to protect American lives war becomes a duty?

Mexican bandits raided American towns, shot to death sleeping men, women, and children in their own homes. We did not go to war* to avenge these deaths. . . .

We were willing to forgo our rights rather than plunge this country into war while half the world was in conflagration. I approved that course then; I approve it now.

Why can we not, why should we not, forgo for the time being the violation of our rights by Germany, and do as we did with Great Britain, do as we did with Mexico, and thus save the universe from being wrapped in the flames of war?

I have hoped and prayed that God would forbid our country going into war with another for doing that which perhaps under the same circumstances we ourselves would do.

THOUGHT PROVOKERS

1. It has been said that truth is the first casualty in any war. Explain. What would have happened if the United States had demanded, with arms, that both Britain and Germany conform to the conventional rules of war? Would such a course have been to America's advantage?

2. In what way did the American policy on loans and munitions finally involve the United States in the war? Explain why Congress refused to enact an embargo on arms in 1916 but did so in the 1930's.

3. Legalities aside, did self-interest alone justify the German sinking of the *Lusitania*? Why was the *Sussex* more important than the *Lusitania*?

4. Was there any real inconsistency between Wilson's warning Americans to get out of Mexico and his refusing to warn them to stay out of the European danger zone? Does a failure to exercise national rights mean that they are lost forever?

5. It has been said that the United States got involved in World War I because it was not truly neutral. Explain. How could America have kept out? If you had been a German, would you have been willing to lose the war rather than use the submarine inhumanely?

* Technically, the United States did not go to war, but Wilson sent General Pershing into Mexico in 1916–1917 to pursue the bandit Villa.

FURTHER EXPLORATION

General: A. S. Link, *Woodrow Wilson and the Progressive Era, 1910–1917* (1954). **British Blockade:** H. C. Peterson, *Propaganda for War* (1939); J. M. Read, *Atrocity Propaganda, 1914–1919* (1941); Marion C. Siney, *The Allied Blockade of Germany, 1914–1916* (1957); Alice M. Morrissey, *The American Defense of Neutral Rights, 1914–1917* (1939). **Merchants of Death:** A. S. Link, *Wilson: The Struggle for Neutrality, 1914–1915* (1960). **Lusitania:** T. A. Bailey, "The Sinking of the *Lusitania*," *American Historical Review*, XLI (1935), 54–73. **Belligerent Ships:** C. C. Tansill, *America Goes to War* (1938). **War with Germany:** E. R. May, *The World War and American Isolation, 1914–1917* (1959).

Recent: D. M. Smith, *The Great Departure: The United States and World War I, 1914–1920* (1965) [paperback]; A. S. Link, *Wilson: Confusions and Crises, 1915–1916* (1964), *Wilson: Campaigns for Progressivism and Peace, 1916–1917* (1965).

Chapter 37

America in World War I

It is a fearful thing to lead this great peaceful people into war. . . .
WOODROW WILSON, WAR MESSAGE, APRIL 2, 1917

PROLOGUE: While the war-weary Allies held back the Germans, the United States belatedly, and with vast confusion, raised an army. More than a year passed before substantial forces under General Pershing got "over there" to France, where they helped turn the tide in the autumn of 1918. Back home, the current "Hang the Kaiser" hysteria had resulted in emotional crusades to raise money, produce food, build ships, conserve fuel, and silence dissent. The Espionage Act of 1917, stiffened by the Sedition Act of 1918, provided penalties up to $10,000 in fines and 20 years in prison for disloyal speech and writing. Especially noteworthy was the sensationally successful propaganda machine of George Creel, who featured Wilson's war aims as capsuled in the Fourteen Points. By November, 1918, the Germans were through. Their morale undermined by Allied propaganda, their belts tightened by the enemy blockade, and their armies reeling in the field, they sued for peace and were granted an armistice based on the Fourteen Points.

A. THE RAISING OF ARMIES

1. Houston Urges a Draft (1917)

The United States needed to create a huge army without delay, but the unhappy experience with conscription during the Civil War provided ready-made arguments against a draft. On the eve of the declaration of war, Secretary of Agriculture Houston met with the Council of National Defense, and then recorded his views. Comment critically on his reasoning that volunteering was actually less democratic than conscripting.

The majority of the members of the Council strongly objected to the volunteer idea and advocated the draft. One member questioned the wisdom of resorting to the draft, and another emphatically opposed it.

I advocated compulsory training. I strongly objected to volunteering on the ground that it was undemocratic and wasteful. It is unjust to allow those to fight our battles who have the vision to see and appreciate the issues, and the character and patriotism to offer their lives; and to permit those who are slow to remain in security. We cannot afford to have our most eager men swept away as England did. Volunteering is unjust. It is also inadequate and unsafe in modern war, especially where great numbers have to be raised and trained quickly. It has been ruinous in every other war in which we have engaged. It is likewise much more costly in dollars

1. D. F. Houston, *Eight Years with Wilson's Cabinet* (1926), I, 246.

and cents. Compulsion alone permits the requisite selection of men and their designation for tasks which are essential and for which they are best fitted.

2. The Rough Rider Is Rejected (1917)

Following heated debate, Congress passed a draft law six weeks *after* the declaration of war. This dangerous delay was partly due to Theodore Roosevelt's plea that he be authorized to raise a volunteer division forthwith and take it to France. Allied morale was sagging, and the presence of the world-famous Rough Rider would be electrifying. But the Democratic Wilson, whom the Republican Roosevelt had publicly condemned, followed the advice of the military in vetoing the scheme. The Colonel, now nearly fifty-nine, had never commanded a force larger than a regiment, and that was in a brief horse-and-saber war twenty years earlier. He had then proved markedly insubordinate. He was now blind in one eye, rheumatic, and subject to recurrent attacks of fever. General Pershing, who had no taste for Rough Rider heroics in a modern war, here sets forth the reasons for the rejection. Ascertain what additional arguments he might have used, and whether politics probably influenced the decision.

The appeal of Colonel Roosevelt for permission to raise a volunteer division aroused popular sentiment in his favor throughout the country. But approval would have opened the door for many similar requests, and the policy would have interfered materially with the orderly and businesslike enforcement of the Draft Law. Moreover, the regular establishment would have suffered from the loss of an undue proportion of the best officers, who inevitably would have been selected for important positions in these special units at a time when their services were urgently needed in building more largely.

Another important reason for disapproving Colonel Roosevelt's application was that in such a war it was necessary that officers, especially those in high command, should be thoroughly trained and disciplined. Furthermore, he was not in the best of health, and could not have withstood the hard work and exposure of the training camps and trenches. The Secretary of War, much to the disappointment of Colonel Roosevelt, wisely made an adverse decision in his case, which was confirmed by the President. It was evident that both Mr. Wilson and Secretary Baker were looking for trained leaders, and were determined to avoid the embarrassment Mr. Lincoln experienced in the Civil War, when he was more or less driven to fill many high positions with political appointees who, in the end, had to be replaced by men trained in the military profession.

3. T.R. Lambasts Broomstick Preparedness (1917)

Bitterly disappointed, Roosevelt accepted an editorial post with the Kansas City *Star* (salary $25,000) and flailed away at lagging military preparations. His complaint was that if Wilson had earlier supported military preparedness and had created a Big

2. J. J. Pershing, *My Experiences in the World War* (1931), I, 22. By permission of J. B. Lippincott Company.
3. Kansas City *Star*, Dec. 27, 1917. By permission of the Kansas City *Star*.

Stick, the contemptuous German war lords would not have forced America into the conflict. He also attributed the confusion in raising an army to the President's ineptitude, and charged that shipments of coffins and clay pigeons were being sent to France instead of military supplies urgently needed by the troops. General Leonard Wood, a Republican who had pioneered with Roosevelt for preparedness, was not given command of the American expeditionary force, although he was the senior general. But there were several reasons for such a snub: Wood, like T.R., was a notorious troublemaker, and like T.R. he was physically below par. Locate the most incredible part of this blistering editorial by Roosevelt in the Kansas City *Star*, and assess his apportionment of the blame.

It is earnestly to be hoped that the [current] Congressional investigation into the fruits of our military unpreparedness will keep two objects clearly in mind. First, the aim must be to speed up the work of efficient war preparation by doing away with all the present practices that are wrong. Second, the aim should be to make evident to all our people that our present shameful shortcomings are due to failure to prepare in advance, and that never again ought we to allow our governmental leaders to put us in such a humiliating and unworthy position.

It will be quite impossible to get at all the facts of our unpreparedness. Most officers will be very reluctant to testify to the whole truth. They know that they will suffer if they do so, because they have seen the punishment inflicted by the administration on Major General Wood for the sole reason that he dared to tell the truth about our shortcomings, and dared to advocate preparedness in advance. For this reason I am not at liberty to quote the generals, colonels, captains, and lieutenants of the artillery, infantry, medical corps, and quartermaster corps who have told me of their troubles with unheated hospitals, insufficient drugs, summer underclothes in winter weather, lack of overcoats, of shoes, of rifles, of ammunition, of cannon. But in the camps I visited I saw some things so evident that no harm can come to any officer from my speaking of them.

Last fall I saw thousands of men drilling with broomsticks. I have such a broomstick now before me. Last fall I saw thousands of men drilling with rudely whittled wooden guns. I have one such before me now. I saw them drilling with wooden machine guns as late as the beginning of December. I saw barrels mounted on sticks, on which zealous captains were endeavoring to teach their men how to ride a horse. I saw in the national army camps in Illinois and Ohio scores of wooden cannon. Doubtless any man can see them now if he goes there.

The excellent officers in the camps are as rapidly as possible remedying these deficiencies. I hope and believe that by spring they will all be remedied. But let our people not forget that for one year after Germany went to war with us, we were wholly unable to defend ourselves, and owed our safety only to the English and French ships and armies.

The cause was our refusal to prepare in advance. President Wilson's message of December, 1914, in which he ridiculed those who advocated preparedness, was part of the cause. His Presidential campaign [in 1916] on the "He kept us out of war" issue was part of the cause. We paid the price later with broomstick rifles, logwood cannon, soldiers without shoes, and epidemics of pneumonia in the camps. We are paying the price now. We pay the price in the doubled cost of necessary war supplies. We pay the price in shortage of coal and congested transportation. The refusal to prepare and the price we now pay because of the refusal stand in the relation of cause and effect.

B. WARTIME HYSTERIA

1. Un-Christlike Preachers (1918)

Ministers of the gospel, swallowing Allied propaganda and falling prey to the wartime hysteria, engaged in un-Christian excesses. "It is religious to hate the Kaiser," declared the Reverend James R. Day, Chancellor of Syracuse University, "because the Bible teaches us to hate the Devil and all his works." Less elegantly a prominent Baptist pastor in Cleveland cried, "To hell with the Kaiser!" Here a prominent Methodist bishop and author, Dr. William A. Quayle, pays his disrespects to Germany in a magazine article. Comment critically on the gullibility of this clergyman, after noting the most improbable parts of this statement. Observe also how he rejects Wilson's view that America was fighting only Germany's rulers.

Let us set down sternly that we are at war with the Germans, not the Junkers [German aristocrats], not autocracy, not Prussianism, not the Kaiser. . . . The German people is what we war with. The German people is committing the unspeakable horrors which set the whole world aghast. The German people is not and has not been conducting war. It is and has been conducting murder. Hold fast to that. The Supreme Court of New York declared the sinking of the *Lusitania* an act of piracy. Piracy is not war. All decencies, honors, humanities, international agreements, and laws have been smashed by them day and night from the first rape of Belgium to now. The new atrocity which appeared this week was spraying prisoners with burning oil. This is Germany's most recent jest. It makes them laugh so!

They have violated every treaty with the United States; they have lied from start to finish and to everybody. A treaty was a scrap of paper.* . . .

Germany has ravished the women of Belgium, Servia, Roumania, Poland, Armenia. Germany murdered the passengers of the *Lusitania* and struck a medal to celebrate that German triumph, dating it two days before the horrible occurrence. Germany has ruined cathedrals and cities in sheer wanton fury, in such fashion as has not been done in all the wars waged in Europe since the days of the building of the cathedrals. Germany has poisoned wells, crucified inhabitants and soldiers, burned people in their

1. *Northwestern Christian Advocate,* quoted in *Literary Digest,* LIX, 28 (Oct. 19, 1918).
* The phrase "scrap of paper" became one of the great propaganda weapons of the war. The German Chancellor, Bethmann-Hollweg, had defended Germany's invasion of Belgium in 1914 by referring to the treaty of 1839 guaranteeing her neutrality as a "scrap of paper."

EDITOR   CAPITALIST   POLITICIAN   MINISTER

HAVING THEIR FLING

In 1918 the editors of the anti-war Socialist journal, *The Masses,* were tried under the Espionage Act for obstructing the war. The above cartoon was Exhibit F for the prosecution. *The Masses* (New York), 1917.

houses, and this by system. Germany has denatured men and boys, has wantonly defaced the living and the dying and the dead. An eye-witness tells of seeing women dead at a table with their tongues nailed to the table and left to die.

Germany has stolen things little and big: playthings from children, finery from women, pictures of incalculable worth, bank-deposits, railroads, factories. Germany has sunk hospital-ships, has bombed hospitals and Red Cross camps. Germany has disclosed neither decency nor honor from the day it started war, nor has a single voice in Germany to date been lifted up against the orgies of ruthlessness which turn the soul sick and which constitute the chief barbarity of history. Germany remains unblushing and unconscious of its indecency. Germany's egotism still struts like a Kaiser. And to climax its horrid crimes, Germany has inflicted compulsory polygamy on the virgins of its own land.

[If such tales were given currency by well-educated clergymen schooled in Christian forbearance, one can hardly blame rank-and-file Americans for believing the same accounts. Actually there were cases of rape and violence affecting civilians on both sides; the Germans were involved to a greater extent because they fought almost the entire war on enemy territory. The Lusitania medal was struck off after the sinking; the story of the "Crucified Canadian" was a complete hoax; the French cathedral at Rheims was damaged after the towers had been used for military observation. The rest of this account reflects an uncritical belief in the thoroughly unreliable stories in the Bryce report (see earlier, p. 687).]

2. Abusing the Pro-Germans (1918)

The several million enemy aliens in the United States were under suspicion, especially those who did not buy Liberty Bonds. One of them was Robert Paul Prager, a young German residing in Illinois. He had tried to enlist in the Navy but was rejected because he had lost an eye. After he had spoken out for socialism, he was seized by a drunken mob in 1918, stripped of his clothes, wrapped in an American flag, and hanged. A patriotic jury acquitted the ringleaders. This was the worst outrage of its kind, but another almost occurred, as Secretary of War Baker related in the following letter. Note what it reveals of the American state of mind at this time, and explain why such an incident was much less likely to have happened in World War II.

The spirit of the country seems unusually good, but there is a growing frenzy of suspicion and hostility toward disloyalty. I am afraid we are going to have a good many instances of people roughly treated on very slight evidence of disloyalty. Already a number of men and some women have been "tarred and feathered," and a portion of the press is urging with great vehemence more strenuous efforts at detection and punishment. This usually takes the form of advocating "drum-head courts-martial"* and "being stood up against a wall and shot," which are perhaps none too bad for real traitors, but are very suggestive of summary discipline to arouse mob spirit, which unhappily does not take time to weigh evidence.

In Cleveland a few days ago a foreign-looking man got into a street car and, taking a seat, noticed pasted in the window next to him a Liberty Loan poster, which he immediately tore down, tore into small bits, and stamped under his feet. The people in the car surged around him with the demand that he be lynched, when a Secret Service man showed his badge and placed him under arrest, taking him in a car to the police station, where he was searched and found to have two Liberty Bonds in his pocket and to be a non-English-speaking Pole. When an interpreter was procured, it was discovered that the circular which he had destroyed had had on it a picture of the German Emperor, which had so infuriated the fellow that he destroyed the circular to show his vehement hatred of the common enemy. As he was unable to speak a single word of English, he would undoubtedly

2. Frederick Palmer, *Newton D. Baker* (1931), II, 162–63. Copyright 1931 by Frederick D. Palmer. Reprinted by permission of Dodd, Mead and Company.
* Originally a hasty court-martial in the field, around a drum as a table.

have been hanged but for the intervention and entirely accidental presence of the Secret Service agent.

I am afraid the grave danger in this sort of thing, apart from its injustice, is that the German Government will adopt retaliatory measures. While the Government of the United States is not only not responsible for these things, but very zealously trying to prevent them, the German Government draws no fine distinctions.

3. Mistreating Conscientious Objectors (*c.* 1918)

During the Civil War the Quakers and other conscientious objectors were excused from military service after making money payments. During the hysterical years of World War I there was no such alternative. Some four thousand conscientious objectors, whose "yellow streak" Roosevelt denounced, fell afoul of the law. About 450 were finally sent to military prison for terms averaging sixteen years. Here Jane Addams, the famed social worker, describes what happened there to a member of one religious sect, the Dukhobors. Form conclusions as to whether such treatment was likely to induce these people to put on the uniform more readily.

Because years before I had been somewhat identified with the immigration of the Doukhobortsi [Dukhobors], a non-resistant Russian sect in whom Tolstoy had been much interested, I found myself appealed to on behalf of a frightened little widow, who was at the moment desperately holding at bay the entire military prison system. Her husband had been one of "those obstinate cases who cling to a scriptural text and will not listen to reason." During his long imprisonments he had been treated in all sorts of barbarous ways and finally, after a prolonged ducking under a faucet in the prison yard on a freezing day, had contracted pneumonia and died. He had originally and continuously taken his stand against putting on the uniform, and when his wife arrived at Leavenworth to take away the body, to her horror she found that body, at last unable to resist, dressed in a soldier's uniform. Her representative who came to see me, with his broken English, could convey but feebly the sense of outrage, of unfairness, of brutal disregard of the things of the spirit, of the ruthless overriding of personality which this incident had aroused among thousands of Doukhobortsi.

C. FREE SPEECH IN WARTIME

1. La Follette Demands His Rights (1917)

Senator Robert M. La Follette of Wisconsin—undersized, pompadoured, and fiery— was one of the most eloquent reformers of his generation. Representing a state with

---

3. Jane Addams, *Peace and Bread in Time of War* (1922), pp. 125–26. By permission of John A. Brittain.
1. *Congressional Record*, 65 Cong., 1 sess., pp. 7878–79.

a heavy concentration of German-Americans, he had spoken out vehemently against war with Germany and had voted against it. He and his five dissenting colleagues were pilloried in the press as traitors for voting their consciences. On October 6, 1917, La Follette rose and quoted (from the press) a charge to a federal grand jury in Texas by a district judge. The jurist reportedly had said that these six Senators ought to be convicted of treason and shot. "I wish I could pay for the ammunition," he continued. "I would like to attend the execution, and if I were in the firing squad I would not want to be the marksman who had the blank shell." La Follette then went on to present this classic defense of free speech. Explain why representative government breaks down without free speech, and why public criticism is especially important in wartime.

But, sir, it is not alone Members of Congress that the war party in this country has sought to intimidate. The mandate seems to have gone forth to the sovereign people of this country that they must be silent while those things are being done by their Government which most vitally concern their well-being, their happiness, and their lives.

Today—and for weeks past—honest and law-abiding citizens of this country are being terrorized and outraged in their rights by those sworn to uphold the laws and protect the rights of the people. I have in my possession numerous affidavits establishing the fact that people are being unlawfully arrested, thrown into jail, held incommunicado for days, only to be eventually discharged without ever having been taken into court, because they have committed no crime. Private residences are being invaded, loyal citizens of undoubted integrity and probity arrested, cross-examined, and the most sacred constitutional rights guaranteed to every American citizen are being violated.

It appears to be the purpose of those conducting this campaign to throw the country into a state of terror, to coerce public opinion, to stifle criticism, and suppress discussion of the great issues involved in this war.

I think all men recognize that in time of war the citizen must surrender some rights for the common good which he is entitled to enjoy in time of peace. *But, sir, the right to control their own Government, according to constitutional forms, is not one of the rights that the citizens of this country are called upon to surrender in time of war.*

Rather, in time of war, the citizen must be more alert to the preservation of his right to control his Government. He must be most watchful of the encroachment of the military upon the civil power. He must beware of those precedents in support of arbitrary action by administrative officials which, excused on the plea of necessity in wartime, become the fixed rule when the necessity has passed and normal conditions have been restored.

More than all, the citizen and his representative in Congress in time of war must maintain his right of free speech. More than in times of peace, it is necessary that the channels for free public discussion of governmental policies shall be open and unclogged.

I believe, Mr. President, that I am now touching upon the most important question in this country today—and that is the right of the citizens of this country and their representatives in Congress to discuss in an orderly

way, frankly and publicly and without fear, from the platform and through the press, every important phase of this war; its causes, the manner in which it should be conducted, and the terms upon which peace should be made. . . .

I am contending for this right, because the exercise of it is necessary to the welfare, to the existence, of this Government, to the successful conduct of this war, and to a peace which shall be enduring and for the best interest of this country. . . .

Mr. President, our Government, above all others, is founded on the right of the people freely to discuss all matters pertaining to their Government, in war not less than in peace. . . . How can that popular will express itself between elections except by meetings, by speeches, by publications, by petitions, and by addresses to the representatives of the people?

FOR SERVICES RENDERED

German Kaiser hangs Iron Cross on Senator La Follette for speech opposing declaration of war. Los Angeles *Daily Times,* 1917.

Any man who seeks to set a limit upon those rights, whether in war or peace, aims a blow at the most vital part of our Government. And then as the time for election approaches, and the official is called to account for his stewardship—not a day, not a week, not a month, before the election, but a year or more before it, if the people choose—they must have the right to the freest possible discussion of every question upon which their representative has acted, of the merits of every measure he has supported or opposed, of every vote he has cast and every speech that he has made. And before this great fundamental right every other must, if necessary, give way, for in no other manner can representative government be preserved.

2. A Midwesterner Assails the War (1917)

The Socialist-tinged Nonpartisan League of Minnesota voiced strong opposition to the war. One of its organizers allegedly had told a young enlistee, "You are a damn fool to enlist in the navy to fight in the interest of the rich." For thus violating the Espionage Act by hampering the war effort, he was sentenced to two years in Leavenworth penitentiary. A colleague, Joseph Gilbert, after being convicted of making the following observations, was sentenced to a year in prison and fined $500. Note the most objectionable part of his statement, and judge whether these remarks, made in wartime, justified such a severe sentence.

We are going over to Europe to make the world safe for democracy, but I tell you we had better make America safe for democracy first. You say, What is the matter with our democracy? I tell you what is the matter with it: Have you had anything to say as to who should be President? Have you had anything to say as to who should be Governor of this state? Have you had anything to say as to whether we should go into this war? You know you have not. If this is such a great democracy, for Heaven's sake why should we not vote on conscription of men? We were stampeded into this war by newspaper rot to pull England's chestnuts out of the fire for her. I tell you, if they conscripted wealth like they have conscripted men, this war would not last over 48 hours.

3. Chafee Upholds Free Speech (1919)

The Socialists, many of whom were anti-war, ran afoul of the Espionage Act of 1917. Prominent among them was Mrs. Rose Pastor Stokes, a Russian-born Jewess who had worked in America as a cigarmaker and who became a prominent social worker and propagandist for socialism. Referring to American soldiers, she remarked that they were "not fighting for democracy but for the protection and safeguarding of Morgan's millions." In a letter to the Kansas City *Star* she wrote: "No government which is for the profiteers can also be for the people, and I am for the people, while the Government is for the profiteers." She was sentenced to ten years in prison, though a higher court later reversed the decision. President Wilson approved of her original conviction. Professor Zechariah Chafee, Jr., of the Harvard Law School, a prominent liberal, made the following comments on these espionage cases shortly after the war had ended. Analyze critically his assumption that the suppression of free speech can be self-defeating and dangerous in the long run.

Never in the history of our country, since the Alien and Sedition Laws of 1798, has the meaning of free speech been the subject of such sharp controversy as to-day. Over two hundred prosecutions and other judicial proceedings during the war, involving speeches, newspaper articles, pamphlets, and books, have been followed since the armistice by a widespread legislative consideration of bills punishing the advocacy of extreme radicalism. . . .

The courts have treated opinions as statements of fact, and then condemned them as false because they differed from the President's speech or the resolution of Congress declaring war. They have made it impossible

2. *State v. Gilbert,* 141 Minn. 263, 169 N.W. 790 (1918).
3. *Harvard Law Review,* XXXII, 923–33, 965, 971–73 (June, 1919). By permission of the publishers.

for an opponent of the war to write an article or even a letter in a newspaper of general circulation, because it will be read in some training camp where it might cause insubordination, or interfere with military success. He cannot address a large audience, because it is liable to include a few men in uniform; and some judges have held him punishable if it contains men between eighteen and forty-five; while Judge Van Valkenburgh, in *United States* v. *Rose Pastor Stokes,* would not even require that, because what is said to mothers, sisters, and sweethearts may lessen their enthusiasm for the war, and "our armies in the field and our navies upon the seas can operate and succeed only so far as they are supported and maintained by the folks at home." . . .

Although we have not gone so far as Great Britain in disregarding constitutional guarantees, we have gone much farther than in any other war, even in the Civil War, with the enemy at our gates. Undoubtedly some utterances had to be suppressed. We have passed through a period of danger, and have reasonably supposed the danger to be greater than it actually was, but the prosecutions in Great Britain during a similar period of peril in the French Revolution have not since been regarded with pride.

Action in proportion to the emergency was justified, but we have censored and punished speech which was very far from direct and dangerous interference with the conduct of the war. The chief responsibility for this must rest, not upon Congress, which was content for a long period with the moderate language of the Espionage Act of 1917, but upon the officials of the Department of Justice and the Post Office, who turned that statute into a drag-net for pacifists, and upon the judges who upheld and approved this distortion of law.

It may be questioned, too, how much has actually been gained. Men have been imprisoned, but their words have not ceased to spread. The poetry in *The Masses* was excluded from the mails only to be given a far wider circulation in two issues of the *Federal Reporter*. The mere publication of Mrs. Stokes' statement in the Kansas City *Star,* "I am for the people and the Government is for the profiteers," was considered so dangerous to the morale of the training camps that she was sentenced to ten years in prison, and yet it was repeated by every important newspaper in the country during the trial. There is an unconscious irony in all suppression. . . .

Those who gave their lives for freedom would be the last to thank us for throwing aside so lightly the great traditions of our race. Not satisfied to have justice and almost all the people with our cause, we insisted on an artificial unanimity of opinion behind the war. Keen intellectual grasp of the President's aims by the nation at large was very difficult when the opponents of his idealism ranged unchecked, while the men who urged greater idealism went to prison. In our efforts to silence those who advocated peace without victory, we prevented at the very start that vigorous threshing out of fundamentals which might to-day have saved us from a victory without peace.

D. THE PROPAGANDA FRONT

1. Creel Spreads Fear Propaganda (*c.* 1918)

George Creel—a young, dynamic, but tactless journalist—headed the nation's great propaganda engine, the Committee on Public Information. He not only prepared documentary movies and unleashed tens of thousands of orators, but issued some 75,000,000 copies of pamphlets. He also employed a galaxy of distinguished historians and other scholars to prepare these propaganda booklets, many of them in paper covers of red, white, and blue. One title, *How the War Came to America,* enjoyed a fantastic distribution of 7,000,000 copies. Professor J. S. P. Tatlock, a Chaucer specialist at Stanford University, wrote the following highly imaginative account, inspired in part by Allied propaganda like the Bryce report. Distributed as a part of a pamphlet entitled *Why America Fights Germany,* it boasted a circulation of about 750,000 copies. Some of these scholars were criticized for prostituting their skills to patriotism. Comment in the light of the following.

Now let us picture what a sudden invasion of the United States by these Germans would mean; sudden, because their settled way is always to attack suddenly.

First, they set themselves to capture New York City. While their fleet blockades the harbor and shells the city and the forts from far at sea, their troops land somewhere near and advance toward the city in order to cut its rail communications, starve it into surrender, and then plunder it.

One body of from 50,000 to 100,000 men lands, let us suppose, at Barnegat Bay, New Jersey, and advances without meeting resistance, for the brave but small American army is scattered elsewhere. They pass through Lakewood, a station on the Central Railroad of New Jersey. They first demand wine for the officers and beer for the men. Angered to find that an American town does not contain large quantities of either, they pillage and burn the post office and most of the hotels and stores. Then they demand $1,000,000 from the residents. One feeble old woman tries to conceal $20 which she has been hoarding in her desk drawer; she is taken out and hanged (to save a cartridge). Some of the teachers in two district schools meet a fate which makes them envy her. The Catholic priest and Methodist minister are thrown into a pig-sty, while the German soldiers look on and laugh. Some of the officers quarter themselves in a handsome house on the edge of the town, insult the ladies of the family, and destroy and defile the contents of the house.

By this time some of the soldiers have managed to get drunk; one of them discharges his gun accidentally, the cry goes up that the residents are firing on the troops, and then hell breaks loose. Robbery, murder, and outrage run riot. Fifty leading citizens are lined up against the First National Bank Building, and shot. Most of the town and the beautiful pinewoods are burned, and then the troops move on to treat New Brunswick in the same way—if they get there.

1. J. S. P. Tatlock, *Why America Fights Germany,* War Information Series No. 15, Cantonment Edition (1918), pp. 9–10.

This is not just a snappy story. It is not fancy. The general plan of campaign against America has been announced repeatedly by German military men. *And every horrible detail is just what the German troops have done in Belgium and France.*

2. Wilson Unveils His Fourteen Points (1918)
3. Roosevelt Blunts Wilson's Points (1918)

President Wilson's war-aims speeches were lofty and eloquent, but rather vague and long-winded. An American journalist in Russia suggested that he compress his views into crisp, placard-like paragraphs. This he did in his famed Fourteen Points address to Congress on January 8, 1918. By promising independence (self-determination) to minority groups under enemy rule, and by raising up hopes everywhere for a better tomorrow, the Fourteen Points undermined the foe's will to resist. Simultaneously they inspirited the Allies. George Creel's propaganda machine broadcast the Points in leaflet form throughout the world, while Allied rockets and shells showered them over enemy lines. German desertions multiplied. Form some judgment as to whether Wilson's aims were completely clear and consistent. Determine which ones would be most likely to weaken the resistance of Germany and Austria-Hungary. The frustrated Colonel Roosevelt fulminated against the Fourteen Points in the Kansas City *Star*. Remembering that before 1917 he had been anti-Wilson, pro-tariff, anti-Germany, pro-Ally, and internationalist-minded, detect the most important inconsistencies in his position.

WILSON'S POINTS

I. Open covenants of peace, openly arrived at, after which there shall be no private international understandings of any kind, but diplomacy shall proceed always frankly and in the public view.

[Wilson finally meant *secret* negotiations but *public* commitments. He had earlier laid himself open to criticism by landing the marines in Haiti and Santo Domingo in 1915 and 1916 to restore order.]

II. Absolute freedom of navigation upon the seas, outside territorial waters, alike in peace and in war, except as the seas may be closed in whole or in part by international action [of the League of Nations] for the enforcement of international covenants.

[Big-navy Britain, fearing to blunt her blockade weapon, refused to accept this point.]

ROOSEVELT'S COMPLAINTS

The President has recently waged war on Haiti and San Domingo, and rendered democracy within these two small former republics not merely unsafe, but non-existent. He has kept all that he has done in the matter absolutely secret. If he means what he says, he will at once announce what open covenant of peace he has openly arrived at with these two little republics, which he has deprived of their right of self-determination.

It makes no distinction between freeing the seas from murder, like that continually practiced by Germany, and freeing them from blockade of contraband merchandise, which is the practice of a right universally enjoyed by belligerents, and at this moment practiced by the United States. Either this proposal is meaningless, or it is a mischievous concession to Germany.

2. *Congressional Record*, 65 Cong., 2 sess., p. 691.
3. Kansas City *Star*, Oct. 30, 1918. By permission of the Kansas City *Star*. The full text may also be found in Ralph Stout, ed., *Roosevelt in the Kansas City "Star"* (1921), pp. 241–42, 243–46.

America in World War I

III. The removal, so far as possible, of all economic barriers, and the establishment of an equality of trade conditions among all the nations consenting to the peace, and associating themselves [in the League of Nations] for its maintenance.

[This meant, although not too clearly put, that the United States could still maintain tariffs but could not discriminate among fellow members of the League of Nations. Any commercial favors granted to one fellow member would automatically be extended to all.]

IV. Adequate guarantees given and taken that national armaments will be reduced to the lowest point consistent with domestic safety.

[This meant a force no larger than necessary to control domestic disorders and prevent foreign invasion.]

V. A free, open-minded, and absolutely impartial adjustment of all [wartime] colonial claims, based upon a strict observance of the principle that, in determining all such questions of sovereignty, the interests of the populations concerned must have equal weight with the equitable claims of the Government whose title is to be determined.

[German colonies captured by Britain and Japan might be returned, if this course seemed "equitable."]

VI. The evacuation of all Russian territory [inhabited by Russians], and such a settlement of all questions affecting Russia as will secure the best and freest cooperation of the other nations of the world in obtaining for her an unhampered and unembarrassed opportunity for the independent determination of her own political development and national policy, and assure her of a sincere welcome into the society of free nations, under institutions of her own choosing; and, more than a welcome, assistance also of every kind. . . .

The third point promises free trade among all the nations, unless the words are designedly used to conceal President Wilson's true meaning. This would deny to our country the right to make a tariff to protect its citizens, and especially its workingmen, against Germany or China or any other country. Apparently this is desired on the ground that the incidental domestic disaster to this country will prevent other countries from feeling hostile to us. The supposition is foolish. England practiced free trade and yet Germany hated England particularly. . . .

Either this is language deliberately used to deceive, or else it means that we are to scrap our army and navy, and prevent riot by means of a national constabulary, like the state constabulary of New York or Pennsylvania.

Unless the language is deliberately used to deceive, this means that we are to restore to our brutal enemy the colonies taken by our allies while they were defending us from this enemy. The proposition is probably meaningless. If it is not, it is monstrous.

Point VI deals with Russia. It probably means nothing, but if it means anything, it provides that America shall share on equal terms with other nations, including Germany, Austria, and Turkey [the Central Powers], in giving Russia assistance. The whole proposition would not be particularly out of place in a college sophomore's exercise in rhetoric.

[Wilson had in mind having the German invader evacuate Russian territory, and helping the Russian Poles and other non-Russian nationalities to achieve self-determination. He would also lend a helping hand to the new Bolshevik government.]

VII. Belgium, the whole world will agree, must be evacuated and restored, without any attempt to limit the sovereignty which she enjoys in common with all other free nations. No other single act will serve as this will serve to restore confidence among the nations in the laws which they have themselves set and determined for the government of their relations with one another. Without this healing act the whole structure and validity of international law is forever impaired.

[Germany, disregarding a neutrality treaty of 1839, had struck through Belgium at France in 1914. The war-minded Roosevelt at first approved this act as one of military necessity, but he soon changed his views. The word "restored" in Point VII implied that the Germans would be assessed an indemnity for the damage they had done.]

Point VII deals with Belgium and is entirely proper and commonplace.

VIII. All French territory should be freed and the invaded portions restored, and the wrong done to France by Prussia in 1871 in the matter of Alsace-Lorraine, which has unsettled the peace of the world for nearly fifty years, should be righted, in order that peace may once more be made secure in the interest of all.

[Wilson intended that Alsace-Lorraine, seized by Prussia [Germany] in 1871, should be returned to France.]

Point VIII deals with Alsace-Lorraine and is couched in language which betrays Mr. Wilson's besetting sin—his inability to speak in a straightforward manner. He may mean that Alsace and Lorraine must be restored to France, in which case he is right. He may mean that a plebiscite must be held, in which case he is playing Germany's evil game.

IX. A readjustment of the frontiers of Italy should be effected along clearly recognizable lines of nationality.

[Wilson would extend "self-determination" to nearby Italian peoples not under the Italian flag.]

Point IX deals with Italy, and is right.

X. The peoples of Austria-Hungary, whose place among the nations we wish to see safeguarded and assured, should be accorded the freest opportunity of autonomous development.

[This point raised difficulties because of the quarreling minorities of the "succession states" that rose from the ruins of Austria-Hungary.]

XI. Rumania, Serbia, and Montenegro should be evacuated; occupied territories restored; Serbia accorded free and secure access to the sea; and the relations of the several Balkan states to one another determined by friendly counsel along historically established lines of allegiance and nationality; and international guarantees of the political and economic independence and territorial integrity of the several Balkan states should be entered into.

[This point was also invalidated by the "succession states," including Yugoslavia, which embraced Serbia.]

XII. The Turkish portions of the present Ottoman Empire should be assured a secure sovereignty, but the other nationalities which are now under Turkish rule should be assured an undoubted security of life and an absolutely unmolested opportunity of autonomous development, and the Dardanelles should be permanently opened as a free passage to the ships and commerce of all nations under international guarantees.

[Wilson's ideal was self-determination for the Greeks, Armenians, Arabs, and other non-Turks in the Turkish empire, much of whose land became mandates of France and Britain under the League of Nations.]

XIII. An independent Polish state should be erected which should include the territories inhabited by indisputably Polish populations, which should be assured a free and secure access to the sea, and whose political and economic independence and territorial integrity should be guaranteed by international covenant.

Point X deals with the Austro-Hungarian Empire, and is so foolish that even President Wilson has abandoned it.

[Wilson later stressed independence rather than local autonomy.]

Point XI proposes that we, together with other nations, including apparently Germany, Austria, and Hungary, shall guarantee justice in the Balkan Peninsula. As this would also guarantee our being from time to time engaged in war over matters in which we had no interest whatever, it is worth while inquiring whether President Wilson proposes that we wage these wars with the national constabulary to which he desired to reduce our armed forces.

Point XII proposes to perpetuate the infamy of Turkish rule in Europe, and as a sop to the conscience of humanity proposes to give the subject races autonomy, a slippery word which in a case like this is useful only for rhetorical purposes.

Point XIII proposes an independent Poland, which is right; and then proposes that we guarantee its integrity in the event of future war, which is preposterous unless we intend to become a military nation more fit for overseas warfare than Germany is at present.

[Poland was to be restored from the territory of Germany, Russia, and Austria-Hungary, despite injustices to German and other minorities.]

XIV. A general association [League] of nations must be formed under specific covenants for the purpose of affording mutual guarantees of political independence and territorial integrity to great and small states alike.

In regard to these essential rectifications of wrong and assertions of right, we feel ourselves to be intimate partners of all the governments and peoples associated together against the Imperialists. We cannot be separated in interest or divided in purpose. We stand together until the end.

In its essence Mr. Wilson's proposition for a League of Nations seems to be akin to the Holy Alliance of the nations of Europe a century ago, which worked such mischief that the Monroe Doctrine was called into being especially to combat it. If it is designed to do away with nationalism, it will work nothing but mischief. If it is devised in sane fashion as an addition to nationalism and as an addition to preparing our own strength for our own defense, it may do a small amount of good. But it will certainly accomplish nothing if more than a moderate amount is attempted, and probably the best first step would be to make the existing league of the Allies a going concern.

E. THE COLLAPSE OF GERMANY

1. T.R. Demands Unconditional Surrender (1918)

In October, 1918, the reeling Germans asked President Wilson for peace terms based on the Fourteen Points. After he had forced them to overthrow the Kaiser and set up a more democratic regime, the Allies consented to an armistice. Based on twelve of the Fourteen Points, it resulted in the disarmament of Germany. Ex-President Roosevelt, one of the more vehement on-to-Berlin zealots, protested against negotiations. "Let us dictate peace by the hammering guns," he insisted, "and not chat about peace to the accompaniment of the clicking of typewriters." On the basis of his following editorial blast, form some judgment as to the moral soundness of his position, and as to his vision as a prophet.

When the American people speak for unconditional surrender, it means that Germany must accept whatever terms the United States and its allies think necessary in order to right the dreadful wrongs that have been committed, and to safeguard the world for at least a generation to come from another attempt by Germany to secure world dominion.

Unconditional surrender is the reverse of a negotiated peace. The interchange of notes, which has been going on between our Government and the Governments of Germany and Austria during the last three weeks, means, of course, if persisted in, a negotiated peace. It is the abandonment of force and the substitution of negotiation. This fact should be clearly and truth-

1. Kansas City *Star*, Oct. 26, 1918. By permission of the Kansas City *Star*. See also Ralph Stout, ed., *Roosevelt in the Kansas City "Star"* (1921), pp. 239–41.

GERMAN "REPENTANCE"

A prophetic reflection of the view that the failure to smash Germany
completely would lead to another world war. Dallas *News,* 1918.

fully stated by our leaders, so that the American people may decide with
their eyes open which course they will follow.

Those of us who believe in unconditional surrender regard Germany's
behavior during the last five years as having made her the outlaw among
nations. In private life sensible men and women do not negotiate with an
outlaw or grow sentimental about him, or ask for a peace with him on terms
of equality if he will give up his booty. Still less do they propose to make
a league with him for the future, and on the strength of this league to
abolish the sheriff and take the constable. On the contrary, they expect
the law officers to take him by force and to have him tried and punished.
They do not punish him out of revenge, but because all intelligent persons
know punishment to be necessary in order to stop certain kinds of criminals
from wrongdoing and to save the community from such wrongdoing.

We ought to treat Germany in precisely this manner. It is a sad and
dreadful thing to have to face some months or a year or so of additional
bloodshed, but it is a much worse thing to quit now and have the children
growing up obliged to do the job all over again, with ten times as much
bloodshed and suffering, when their turn comes. The surest way to secure

a peace as lasting as that which followed the downfall of Napoleon is to overthrow the Prussianized Germany of the Hohenzollerns as Napoleon was overthrown. If we enter into a league of peace with Germany and her vassal allies, we must expect them to treat the arrangement as a "scrap of paper" whenever it becomes to their interest to do so.

2. The *New Republic* Favors Negotiations (1918)

Liberal spokesmen, like the *New Republic*, were concerned with morality. Why fight to disarm the enemy, they argued, when the same result could be achieved by "political" means—that is, by negotiation? The Democratic New York *World* agreed that the outcry for unconditional surrender was "thoughtless and irresponsible." The New York *Nation* declared that the Americans were succumbing to the very Prussian militarism against which they were fighting when they demanded an unnecessary continuation of the shooting. The *New Republic* here argues that Roosevelt and his crowd were guilty of a species of disloyalty for which men had already been imprisoned during the war. Comment critically on its reasoning.

Yet just when the government of the United States is most in need of a united public support in order to pluck the political fruits of this great effort of the national will, a powerful faction consisting of people who proclaim themselves to be super-patriots deliberately agitate to divide the nation morally against itself. They confront and embarrass the President with embittered, unscrupulous, and irreconcilable opposition. . . .

Nor is that all. They are openly accusing the President of prosecuting the war, of demanding prodigious sacrifices of the American people, and of shedding the blood of thousands of the best beloved of our fellow-countrymen for the sake of benefiting the German people and presenting them with a political victory.

If the accusations of Mr. Roosevelt and the others are true, the President of the United States is treacherously cheating the people of America and Europe out of the fruits of their sufferings and losses. Could the most malevolent pro-German propagandist invent and disseminate a charge which, if true or false, is better calculated to blast to pieces the American nation as a moral unit? Yet it is being uttered by people who were most clamorous a few months ago ruthlessly to stamp out every suspicious and discordant utterance of opinion, and who have denounced all who then differed from them as contemptible disloyalists.

What has the President done to justify the terrible accusations of political treachery and pro-Germanism now being leveled against him by Mr. Roosevelt and others? Nothing, except to act loyally upon an interpretation of political victory in the war, which he delineated with the utmost conceivable clarity and emphasis in his speech recommending the declaration of war against Germany, and which he has reiterated in all his subsequent addresses. From the very beginning he has insisted that the future security and orderly democratic progress of France, Great Britain, and America

2. *New Republic*, XVII, 27–29 (Nov. 9, 1918). By permission of the *New Republic*.

after the war depended on the detachment of the German people from their government and their conversion to democracy. . . .

In the light of this record the present behavior of the Republican leaders, in condemning the fulfillment of the President's political pledges as "unconditional surrender to Germany," is nothing less than an unscrupulous factious attack on the national moral unity.

[*Germany was not invaded, but the Armistice terms left her helpless. The New York* Herald, *which had clamored for a bitter-end struggle, rejoiced, "German militarism is not only defeated but crushed; not only prone but bound hand and foot." Yet the German armies came marching home to be greeted with garlands. The legend took root that Germany had not been defeated, merely stabbed in the back by Jews and other saboteurs. The American people were frustrated and disillusioned as a result of not marching on to Berlin. And the Germans complained bitterly when the Treaty of Versailles failed to embody most of the Fourteen Points, on the basis of which Germany had laid down its arms. Partly to avoid such misunderstanding, President Franklin D. Roosevelt in 1943 proclaimed the controversial policy of unconditional surrender (see later, p. 851).*]

THOUGHT PROVOKERS

1. Discuss the shortcomings of volunteering, and explain why it would have been more dangerous in World War I than in preceding wars. In what ways can unpreparedness be more costly, financially and otherwise, than preparedness?
2. Why was there more anti-enemy hysteria in the United States in 1917–1918 than in World War II, when the nation was in graver danger? Why was not America's sense of fair play aroused in behalf of conscientious objectors? How are they dealt with today?
3. Is it safer to be too intolerant of disloyalty than too tolerant in an all-out war? Are there circumstances in which the vote of a Senator can be equated with disloyalty? Why was there less tolerance of opposition during World War I than during the Civil War? Why was the Kaiser, a Christian gentleman, attacked more violently in America than the depraved Hitler?
4. In connection with Point I, why is it impossible to conduct diplomacy with complete openness at all stages of the negotiations? Criticize Roosevelt's criticisms of the Fourteen Points.
5. In the light of subsequent events, would an unconditional surrender of Germany, after a march on Berlin, have worked out more happily than the conditional surrender based on unkept promises regarding the Fourteen Points?

FURTHER EXPLORATION

General: Mark Sullivan, *Our Times* (1933), vol. V; P. W. Slosson, *The Great Crusade and After* (1930); F. L. Paxson, *America at War* (1939). **Raising Armies:** Frederick Palmer, *Newton D. Baker* (2 vols., 1931); E. H. Crowder, *The Spirit of Selective Service* (1920). **Wartime Hysteria:** Norman Thomas, *The Conscientious Objector in America* (1923); H. C. Peterson and G. C. Fite, *Opponents of War* (1957). **Free Speech:** Zechariah Chafee, Jr., *Freedom of Speech* (1920); H. N. Scheiber, *The Wilson Administration and Civil Liberties, 1917–1921* (1960). **Propaganda:** J. R. Mock and Cedric Larson, *Words That Won the War* (1939); George Creel, *How We Advertised America* (1920). **German Collapse:** D. F. Fleming, *The United States and the League of Nations, 1918–1920* (1932); H. R. Rudin, *Armistice, 1918* (1944).

Chapter *38*

Wilson and the Lost Peace

Dare we reject it [the League of Nations] and break the heart of the world?

WOODROW WILSON, JULY 10, 1919

PROLOGUE: Wilson blundered when in October, 1918, he bluntly appealed for a Democratic Congress. Repudiated at the polls the next month, he further antagonized the Republicans by his decision to attend the Paris Peace Conference. The resulting Treaty of Versailles, with the League of Nations riveted in, was disillusioning. Wilson had been forced to compromise away many of his Fourteen Points in order to save his Fourteenth—the League. Returning to America, he bitterly opposed the nationalistic reservations to the Treaty sponsored by his arch-foe, Senator Lodge. With deadlock imminent, Wilson embarked upon a barnstorming appeal to the country, during which he collapsed. When the time came for a vote, the invalid President twice instructed the Democratic Senators to reject the Treaty with the hated Lodge reservations attached. This they dutifully did. Rather than yield to Lodge, Wilson appealed to the country for a "solemn referendum" in the 1920 presidential election. In a highly confused campaign, the Republican Harding won by a tremendous plurality. The League, as far as America was concerned, perished in a snowstorm of votes.

A. THE OCTOBER APPEAL

1. Wilson Asks for a Democratic Congress (1918)

President Wilson, now at the peak of his prestige, planned to attend the Paris Peace Conference. The mid-term November elections were nearing, and he feared that a Democratic defeat would weaken his hand. He therefore decided to issue the following appeal on October 25, 1918, more than two weeks before the Armistice with Germany. The Republicans in Congress had supported Wilson's war effort with conspicuous loyalty, and their leaders now reacted angrily to this "challenge" and "insult." Determine whether they had good reason to be indignant, and ascertain the strongest argument for Wilson's unusual course.

My fellow countrymen: The Congressional elections are at hand. They occur in the most critical period our country has ever faced or is likely to face in our time. If you have approved of my leadership and wish me to continue to be your unembarrassed spokesman in affairs at home and abroad, I earnestly beg that you will express yourselves unmistakably to that effect by returning a Democratic majority to both the Senate and the House of Representatives. I am your servant and will accept your judgment without cavil, but my power to administer the great trust assigned me by

1. *Congressional Record,* 65 Cong., 2 sess., p. 11494.

the Constitution would be seriously impaired should your judgment be adverse, and I must frankly tell you so because so many critical issues depend upon your verdict. . . .

I have no thought of suggesting that any political party is paramount in matters of patriotism. I feel too keenly the sacrifices which have been made in this war by all our citizens, irrespective of party affiliations, to harbor such an idea. I mean only that the difficulties and delicacies of our present task are of a sort that makes it imperatively necessary that the Nation should give its undivided support to the Government under a unified leadership, and that a Republican Congress would divide the leadership.

The leaders of the minority in the present Congress have unquestionably been pro-war, but they have been anti-administration. At almost every turn, since we entered the war, they have sought to take the choice of policy and the conduct of the war out of my hands and put it under the control of instrumentalities of their own choosing. This is no time either for divided counsel or for divided leadership. . . .

The return of a Republican majority to either House of the Congress would, moreover, certainly be interpreted on the other side of the water as a repudiation of my leadership. Spokesmen of the Republican Party are urging you to elect a Republican Congress in order to back up and support the President, but even if they should in this way impose upon some credulous voters on this side of the water, they would impose on no one on the other side. It is well understood there as well as here that the Republican leaders desire not so much to support the President as to control him. . . .

I need not tell you, my fellow countrymen, that I am asking your support not for my own sake or for the sake of a political party, but for the sake of the Nation itself, in order that its inward unity of purpose may be evident to all the world. In ordinary times I would not feel at liberty to make such an appeal to you. In ordinary times divided counsels can be endured without permanent hurt to the country. But these are not ordinary times.

2. Roosevelt Assails Wilson's Appeal (1918)

The aroused Republicans carried both Houses of Congress in November, and Wilson, having needlessly laid his prestige on the line, was a repudiated leader. Ex-President Roosevelt, who remembered that the Republican minority had supported crucial war measures like conscription in the teeth of considerable Democratic opposition, let fly this editorial blast. Form conclusions as to whether this criticism probably weakened Wilson as a negotiator in Paris, and if so, whether it was unpatriotic.

Ten days before election Mr. Wilson issued an appeal to the American people, in which he frankly abandoned the position of President of the whole people; assumed the position, not merely of party leader, but of party dictator; and appealed to the voters as such. . . .

2. *Kansas City Star*, Nov. 26, 1918. By permission of the Kansas City *Star*. The full text may also be found in Ralph Stout, ed., *Roosevelt in the Kansas City "Star"* (1921), pp. 272–77.

The Americans refused to sustain Mr. Wilson. They elected a heavily Republican House and, to the surprise of everyone, carried a majority in the Senate. On Mr. Wilson's own say-so they repudiated his leadership. In no other free country in the world to-day would Mr. Wilson be in office. He would simply be a private citizen like the rest of us.

Under these circumstances our allies and our enemies, and Mr. Wilson himself, should all understand that Mr. Wilson has no authority whatever to speak for the American people at this time. His leadership has just been emphatically repudiated by them. The newly elected Congress comes far nearer than Mr. Wilson to having a right to speak the purposes of the American people at this moment.

Mr. Wilson and his fourteen points and his four supplementary points and his five complementary points and all his utterances every which way have ceased to have any shadow of right to be accepted as expressive of the will of the American people. He is President of the United States, he is part of the treaty-making power, but he is only part. If he acts in good faith to the American people, he will not claim on the other side of the water any representative capacity in himself to speak for the American people. He will say frankly that his personal leadership has been repudiated and that he now has merely the divided official leadership which he shares with the Senate.

B. THE TREATY OF VERSAILLES

1. General Smuts Lectures Wilson (1919)

Wilson battled valiantly for his Fourteen Points at Paris, but the grasping Allies and harsh realities forced him to compromise. The result was that only about four of his original Fourteen Points and principles were found intact in the final Treaty. He consoled himself with the hope that the new League of Nations, which he had forced into the pact as its very first section, would iron out injustices. But the Germans, who had laid down their arms on the strength of promises that they would be granted a peace based on the Fourteen Points, complained bitterly of betrayal as they criticized the draft Treaty of Versailles. General Jan C. Smuts, who had fought the British in the Boer War but who had recently fought for them against Germany, was a South African delegate to the Paris Peace Conference. As a distinguished liberal leader and friend of the League of Nations, he made this last-minute appeal to Wilson. Determine why he was so deeply concerned about the ethical aspects of the draft Treaty of Versailles.

Dear President Wilson,

Even at the risk of wearying you I venture to address you once more. The German answer to our draft Peace Terms seems to me to strike the fundamental note which is most dangerous to us, and which we are bound to consider most carefully. They say in effect that we are under solemn obligation to them to make a Wilson Peace, a peace in accordance with your Fourteen Points and other Principles enunciated in 1918. To my mind there is absolutely no doubt that this is so. Subject to the two reservations made

1. Smuts to Wilson, May 30, 1919, in R. S. Baker, *Woodrow Wilson and World Settlement* (1923), III, 466–68. By permission of Mrs. Rachel Baker Napier.

by the Allies before the Armistice,* we are bound to make a peace within the four corners of your Points and Principles, and any provisions of the Peace Treaty which either go contrary to or beyond their general scope and intent would constitute a breach of agreement.

NOT FOURTEEN—ONLY TWO—POINTS LEFT

Although the promised 14 Points were not satisfactorily embodied in the treaty, Germany had no alternative but to sign or be invaded. Cincinnati *Post*, 1919.

This seems to my mind quite clear, and the question of fact remains whether there are any such provisions. If there are, then our position is indeed serious, as I understand it.

This war began with a breach of a solemn international undertaking [regarding Belgium], and it has been one of our most important war aims to vindicate international law and the sanctity of international engagements. If the Allies end the war by following the example of Germany at the beginning, and also confront the world with a "scrap of paper," the discredit on us will be so great that I shudder to think of its ultimate effect on public opinion. We would indeed have done a worse wrong than Germany because of all that has happened since August, 1914, and the fierce light which has been concentrated on this very point.

The question becomes, therefore, most important whether there are important provisions of the Treaty which conflict with or are not covered by, but go beyond, your Points and Principles. I notice a tendency to put the whole responsibility for deciding this question on you, and to say that after all President Wilson agrees to the Treaty and he knows best what the Points and Principles mean. This is most unfair to you, and I think we should all give the gravest consideration to the question whether our Peace Treaty is within the four corners of your Speeches of 1918.

Frankly I do not think this is so, and I think the Germans make out a good case in regard to a number of provisions. All the one-sided provisions, which exclude reciprocity or equality, and all the pinpricks, with which the Treaty teems, seem to me to be both against the letter and the spirit of your Points.

* The British had entered a reservation regarding freedom of the seas; the French, a reservation regarding the collection of reparations.

I cannot find anything in the Points or the Principles which should cover, for instance, the one-sided internationalization of German rivers, and the utterly bad and one-sided administration arranged in respect of them. Reparation by way of coal cannot cover the arrangements made in respect of the Saar Basin and its people. I even doubt whether the Occupation of the Rhine for fifteen years could be squared either with the letter or the spirit of your Points and Principles. And there are many other points to which I shall not refer, but which no doubt your Advisers will consider.

There will be a terrible disillusion if the peoples come to think that we are not concluding a Wilson Peace, that we are not keeping our promises to the world or faith with the public. But if in so doing we appear also to break the formal agreement deliberately entered into (as I think we do), we shall be overwhelmed with the gravest discredit, and this Peace may well become an even greater disaster to the world than the war was.

Forgive me for troubling you with this matter, but I believe it goes to the root of our whole case.

2. Colonel House Appraises the Conference (1919)

Colonel (honorary) E. M. House, a quiet and self-effacing Texan who had retired from cotton planting, became Wilson's intimate adviser in 1912—"the strangest friendship in history." As an influential member of the five-man American delegation at Paris, House acted as the President's deputy during Wilson's absence or incapacity. House's diary analysis of what went wrong is a classic. After reading it explain why Wilson personally failed, and why disappointment was inevitable.

June 29, 1919: I am leaving Paris, after eight fateful months, with conflicting emotions. Looking at the Conference in retrospect, there is much to approve and much to regret. It is easy to say what should have been done, but more difficult to have found a way for doing it.

The bitterness engendered by the war, the hopes raised high in many quarters because of victory, the character of the men having the dominant voices in the making of the Treaty, all had their influence for good or for evil, and were to be reckoned with. There seemed to be no full realization of the conditions which had to be met.

An effort was made to enact a peace upon the usual lines. This should never have been attempted. The greater part of civilization had been shattered, and history could guide us but little in the making of this peace.

How splendid it would have been had we blazed a new and better trail! However, it is to be doubted whether this could have been done, even if those in authority had so decreed, for the peoples back of them had to be reckoned with. It may be that Wilson might have had the power and influence if he had remained in Washington and kept clear of the Conference. When he stepped from his lofty pedestal and wrangled with

2. Charles Seymour, *The Intimate Papers of Colonel House* (1928), IV, 487–89. By permission of Houghton Mifflin Company.

representatives of other states upon equal terms, he became as common clay. . . .

To those who are saying that the Treaty is bad and should never have been made and that it will involve Europe in infinite difficulties in its enforcement, I feel like admitting it. But I would also say in reply that empires cannot be shattered and new states raised upon their ruins without disturbance. To create new boundaries is always to create new troubles. The one follows the other. While I should have preferred a different peace, I doubt whether it could have been made, for the ingredients for such a peace as I would have had were lacking at Paris. And even if those of us like Smuts, Botha, and Cecil* could have had our will, as much trouble might have followed a peace of our making as seems certain to follow this.

The same forces that have been at work in the making of this peace would be at work to hinder the enforcement of a different kind of peace, and no one can say with certitude that anything better than has been done could be done at this time. We have had to deal with a situation pregnant with difficulties and one which could be met only by an unselfish and idealistic spirit, which was almost wholly absent and which was too much to expect of men come together at such a time and for such a purpose.

And yet I wish we had taken the other road, even if it were less smooth, both now and afterward, than the one we took. We would at least have gone in the right direction, and if those who follow us had made it impossible to go the full length of the journey planned, the responsibility would have rested with them and not with us.

3. Editor Villard Reproaches Wilson (1939)

Oswald Garrison Villard, grandson of the abolitionist William Lloyd Garrison, was a fearless crusader in his own right. As editor and owner of the ultra-liberal New York *Nation*, he flailed away at the illiberal Treaty of Versailles. His earlier criticisms of Allied practices and Wilsonian unneutrality had already earned him the label "pro-German." Suspicion was increased by the fact of his birth in Germany while his parents were temporarily residing abroad, and by his ownership of a brown dachshund named Fritz. The following latter-day condemnation of the Conference appeared in his memoirs, published the year Hitler started World War II. Assess the validity of Villard's argument that America should have browbeaten the Allies instead of betraying the enemy.

As one who at the time approved of Mr. Wilson's going to Paris, I have come to realize the fatal mistake it was. What the occasion needed was a much more determined man. He had the whip hand; in fact, every card in the deck. He had the freshest, best-equipped, and only increasing army in France; he had all the money left in the world and controlled the bulk of the food. Without him the Allies could do nothing. Some of the money

---

* Louis Botha, South African Prime Minister, was a liberal colleague of General Smuts at the Conference; Lord Robert Cecil, a British liberal, was at Paris as one of the chief architects of the League of Nations.
3. O. G. Villard, *Fighting Years* (1939), p. 453. By permission of Henry H. Villard.

they owe us was still being poured out to them. A threat to make the separate treaty with Germany which we afterwards did make, a threat to withdraw our army at once and to loan not a dollar more, would have reduced the Allied leaders to pulp.

Against this, some defenders of Woodrow Wilson protest. It would have been outrageous, they say, thus arrogantly to have dictated the peace. But it would not have been dictation, only a righteous demand that the Allies live up to their pledges made to us and to Germany to make peace on the fourteen peace points. Our failure to insist upon this, whether politely or arrogantly, put us in the position of having broken faith with our enemy, of having tricked them.

Can anyone look at the world today and deny that this policy would have been better than to do what we did: help frame a wicked peace which has revived in worse form the German militarism which we set out to destroy, given rise to Fascism in Italy and elsewhere, and completely disappointed the hopes and the ambitions of millions everywhere for a better world?

C. THE ISSUE OF ARTICLE X

1. The Text of Article X (1919)

Wilson regarded the League of Nations as the backbone of the Treaty of Versailles, and Article X of the League Covenant, which he had partly authored, as the heart of the League. He envisaged the members of the League constituting a kind of police force to prevent aggression. Point out the basic weakness in the wording of this article.

The Members of the League undertake to respect and preserve, as against external aggression, the territorial integrity and existing political independence of all Members of the League. In case of any such aggression, or in case of any threat or danger of such aggression, the Council shall advise upon the means by which this obligation shall be fulfilled.

[*All member nations were represented in the Assembly of the League of Nations; only the Great Powers (originally Britain, France, Italy, and Japan) were represented in the Council. The same general scheme was adopted by the United Nations in 1945.*]

2. Editor Harvey Belittles Article X (1919)

The journalist George Harvey, who had launched a Wilson-for-President boom as early as 1906, ultimately became a venomous Wilson-hater. Founding *Harvey's Weekly* in 1918 as a vehicle for his barbed irony, he consistently jeered at "The Fourteen Commandments." After rereading Article X, comment critically on his view that this device was completely toothless.

1. *Senate Executive Documents,* 67 Cong., 4 sess., VIII, No. 348, p. 3339.
2. *Harvey's Weekly,* Aug. 9, 1919, pp. 6–7. This short-lived journal was published between 1918 and 1921.

If Article X of the League Covenant means what Mr. Wilson says it means, then it means nothing. If it means nothing, then its proper destination is the wastebasket. It should be stricken out *in toto* as so much sheer surplusage.

The first sentence of the Article provides that "the members of the League undertake to respect and preserve as against external aggression the territory and existing political independence of all members of the League." The second sentence provides that the League Council shall advise upon the means by which the obligation involved in the first sentence shall be fulfilled.

Mr. Wilson's interpretation of this second sentence, as presented in his message transmitting the Franco-American alliance treaty,* is that after the League Council's advice has been duly given, the League members will do precisely as they please about following it. In the first sentence, the members of the League solemnly agree to respect and protect each other as against external aggression. In the second sentence—according to Mr. Wilson's interpretation—a League member will act upon the League Council's advice in a given aggression case "only if its own judgment justifies such action." In other words, the second sentence of the Article completely cancels the first sentence, leaving zero as the remaining total.

Mr. Hughes [Republican nominee in 1916] said of Article X that it was an "illusory engagement." Mr. Wilson goes Mr. Hughes one better. He says, in substance, that it is no engagement at all, illusory or otherwise. The League Council may advise until it is black in the face, and the League members may go serenely on their respective ways without giving the slightest heed to this advice. And both League members and League Council will equally have done their full duty under Article X.

If Article X be interpreted to mean anything, that meaning necessarily is that we engage to send our armed forces wherever and whenever a super-government of foreigners sitting in Switzerland orders us to send them. If it be interpreted as Mr. Wilson interprets it, the foreign super-government's powers extend only to the giving of advice which we agree to heed or ignore as our judgment dictates. One interpretation is an insult to our self-respect as a nation. The other reduces the whole of Article X to a vacuum.

The way to treat Article X is to strike it out.

3. Wilson Testifies for Article X (1919)

The already ominous mood of the Senate had grown uglier when Wilson conspicuously snubbed that body in framing the peace. The Republican majority was led by the aristocratic Senator Lodge of Massachusetts, who was also chairman of the potent

* This alliance, signed by Wilson at Paris, was designed to defend France against future German aggression. The Senate pigeonholed it.
3. *Senate Documents*, No. 76, 66 Cong., 1 sess., XIII, pp. 6, 19.

Committee on Foreign Relations. He was determined to Republicanize and American-ize the pact by adding reservations which would adequately safeguard American in-terests. To avert such a watering-down, Wilson met with the entire Foreign Relations Committee at the White House on August 19, 1919, and underwent about three and a half hours of grilling. Much of the discussion revolved about Article X. In examining Wilson's statement, note the apparent contradictions; also the evidences of idealism.

Article X is in no respect of doubtful meaning, when read in the light of the Covenant as a whole. The Council of the League can only "advise upon" the means by which the obligations of that great article are to be given effect to. Unless the United States is a party to the policy or action in question, her own affirmative vote in the Council is necessary before any advice can be given, for a unanimous vote of the Council is required. If she is a party, the trouble is hers anyhow. And the unanimous vote of the Council is only advice in any case. Each Government is free to reject it if it pleases.

Nothing could have been made more clear to the [Paris] conference than the right of our Congress under our Constitution to exercise its independent judgment in all matters of peace and war. No attempt was made to question or limit that right.

The United States will, indeed, undertake under Article X to "respect and preserve as against external aggression the territorial integrity and existing political independence of all members of the League," and that engagement constitutes a very grave and solemn moral obligation. But it is a moral, not a legal, obligation, and leaves our Congress absolutely free to put its own interpretation upon it in all cases that call for action. It is bind-ing in conscience only, not in law.

Article X seems to me to constitute the very backbone of the whole Covenant. Without it the League would be hardly more than an influential debating society. . . .

Senator [Warren G.] HARDING. Right there, Mr. President, if there is nothing more than a moral obligation on the part of any member of the League, what avail Articles X and XI?

The PRESIDENT. Why, Senator, it is surprising that that question should be asked. If we undertake an obligation we are bound in the most solemn way to carry it out. . . . There is a national good conscience in such a matter. . . .

When I speak of a legal obligation, I mean one that specifically binds you to do a particular thing under certain sanctions. That is a legal obliga-tion. Now a moral obligation is of course superior to a legal obligation, and, if I may say so, has a greater binding force. . . .

[Never too respectful of the "bungalow-minded" members of the Senate, Wilson remarked several days later that Senator Harding, destined to be his successor, "had a disturbingly dull mind, and that it seemed impossible to get any explana-tion to lodge in it."]

4. The Lodge-Hitchcock Reservations (1919)

Wilson finally agreed to accept mildly interpretative Senate reservations which the other powers would not have to approve. But he balked at the more restrictive terms of the fourteen Lodge reservations. These were made a part of the resolution of ratification, and would require the assent of three of the four other major powers (Britain, France, Italy, Japan). To Wilson, such a course was unmanly and humiliating; besides, he detested Senator Lodge. He insisted that the Republican Lodge reservations, notably the one on Article X, devitalized the entire treaty. Below, on the left, appears the Lodge reservation to Article X, which Wilson resentfully rejected. On the right appears the Democratic interpretative reservation, which Senator Hitchcock (the Senate minority leader) had drafted after consulting Wilson. This version Wilson was willing to accept. Ascertain the essential difference, if any, between the two reservations; and form conclusions as to the existence of personal pride.

LODGE RESERVATION
TO ARTICLE X
(November, 1919)

The United States assumes no obligation to preserve the territorial integrity or political independence of any other country or to interfere in controversies between nations — whether members of the League or not — under the provisions of Article X, or to employ the military or naval forces of the United States under any article of the treaty for any purpose, unless in any particular case the Congress, which, under the Constitution, has the sole power to declare war or authorize the employment of the military or naval forces of the United States, shall by act or joint resolution so provide.

HITCHCOCK RESERVATION
TO ARTICLE X
(November, 1919)

That the advice mentioned in Article X of the covenant of the League which the Council may give to the member nations as to the employment of their naval and military forces is merely advice which each member nation is free to accept or reject according to the conscience and judgment of its then existing Government, and in the United States this advice can only be accepted by action of the Congress at the time in being, Congress alone under the Constitution of the United States having the power to declare war.

D. THE DEFEAT OF THE TREATY

1. Mrs. Wilson as Assistant President (1919)

Rather than knuckle under to Lodge, a weary Wilson spurned the advice of doctors and embarked upon a spectacular speechmaking appeal to the country. He journeyed as far west as the Pacific Coast, and on the return trip collapsed after delivering an emotional speech at Pueblo, Colorado. Shortly thereafter he suffered a stroke, which paralyzed the left side of his body and left him bedridden for many weeks. He did not meet his Cabinet for more than seven months. His devoted wife tells how the government was run. Form conclusions as to whether Wilson should have resigned, and whether the interests of an individual were put above those of the country. To what extent was Mrs. Wilson actually President of the United States?

4. Quoted in T. A. Bailey, *Woodrow Wilson and the Great Betrayal* (1945), pp. 388, 393–94. The Hitchcock reservation follows almost verbatim a reservation that Wilson had himself secretly drafted in September, 1919, and on which Hitchcock had based his. *Ibid.*, p. 393.
1. Edith B. Wilson, *My Memoir* (1939), pp. 288–90. Copyright 1938, 1939 by Edith Bolling Wilson; reprinted by special permission of the publishers. The Bobbs-Merrill Company, Inc.

Once my husband was out of immediate danger, the burning question was how Mr. Wilson might best serve the country, preserve his own life, and, if possible, recover. Many people, among them some I had counted as friends, have written of my overwhelming ambition to act as President; of my exclusion of all advice, and so forth. I am trying here to write as though I had taken the oath to tell the truth, the whole truth, and nothing but the truth—so help me God.

I asked the doctors to be frank with me; that I must know what the outcome would probably be, so as to be honest with the people. They all said that, as the brain was as clear as ever, with the progress made in the past few days there was every reason to think recovery possible. Dr. Dercum told me of the history of Pasteur, who had been stricken exactly in this way, but who recovered and did his most brilliant intellectual work afterwards. He sent me a copy of a remarkable book, *The Life of Pasteur.*

But recovery could not be hoped for, they said, unless the President were released from every disturbing problem during these days of Nature's effort to repair the damage done.

"How can that be," I asked the doctors, "when everything that comes to an Executive is a problem? How can I protect him from problems when the country looks to the President as the leader?"

Dr. Dercum leaned towards me and said: "Madam, it is a grave situation, but I think you can solve it. Have everything come to you: weigh the importance of each matter, and see if it is possible by consultations with the respective heads of the Departments to solve them without the guidance of your husband. In this way you can save him a great deal. But always keep in mind that every time you take him a new anxiety or problem to excite him, you are turning a knife in an open wound. His nerves are crying out for rest, and any excitement is torture to him."

"Then," I said, "had he better not resign, let Mr. [Vice-President] Marshall succeed to the Presidency, and he himself get that complete rest that is so vital to his life?"

"No," the Doctor said, "not if you feel equal to what I suggested. For Mr. Wilson to resign would have a bad effect on the country, and a serious effect on our patient. He has staked his life and made his promise to the world to do all in his power to get the Treaty ratified and make the League of Nations complete. If he resigns, the greatest incentive to recovery is gone; and as his mind is clear as crystal, he can still do more with even a maimed body than anyone else. He has the utmost confidence in you. Dr. Grayson [Wilson's personal physician] tells me he has always discussed public affairs with you; so you will not come to them uninformed."

So began my stewardship. I studied every paper, sent from the different Secretaries or Senators, and tried to digest and present in tabloid form the things that, despite my vigilance, had to go to the President. I, myself, never made a single decision regarding the disposition of public affairs. The only decision that was mine was what was important and what was not, and the *very* important decision of when to present matters to my husband.

He asked thousands of questions, and insisted upon knowing everything, particularly about the Treaty. He would dictate notes to me to send to Senator Hitchcock, who was leading the fight for the Treaty in the Senate. Or he would tell me what Senators to send for, and what suggestions he had to make to them. These directions I made notes of, so, in transmitting his views, I should make no mistake; and I would read them to him before going to the interviews.

This method of handling interviews was another suggestion of the doctors. It is always an excitement for one who is ill to see people. The physicians said that if I could convey the messages of Cabinet members and others to the President, he would escape the nervous drain audiences with these officials would entail. Even the necessary little courteous personal conversations that go with an official interview would consume the President's strength.

These instructions from the medical men were far from easy to carry out. Picture the situation when my husband was stricken: his tour a success; public sentiment which had been worked upon incessantly by the enemies of the League once more responding to Mr. Wilson's logic; the initiative again in the hands of friends of the Treaty; Mr. Hitchcock and the other pro-Treaty Senators eager to push their advantage. And then—the President laid low, ruled out of the fight which he would have continued though he knew it would cost him his life.

Upon all sides I was literally besieged by those who "must" see the President. But I carried out the directions of the doctors—and my heart was in it. Woodrow Wilson was first my beloved husband whose life I was trying to save, fighting with my back to the wall—after that he was the President of the United States.

2. The Aborted Lodge Compromise (1919)

Colonel House, Wilson's onetime intimate adviser, had likewise fallen ill and was confined to his bed in New York. He turned to Stephen Bonsal, a distinguished newspaper correspondent who had been attached to the American peace mission in Paris. Bonsal was instructed to go to Washington, confer with Lodge, and ascertain the Senator's minimum terms for compromise. The meeting took place late in October, 1919, and on November 16 Bonsal recorded the following account of the conference. Note in what respects this version changes the traditional concept of a vindictive and uncompromising Senator Lodge, the ex-student from Harvard who was locking horns with the ex-professor from Princeton.

The Senator and I went over the [League] Covenant, Article by Article. Here are some of the details. In our final session there was an official copy of the Treaty on the library table, also one of the so-called Lodge Reservations before the Senate but, so far as I can remember, we did not once

2. Stephen Bonsal, *Unfinished Business* (1944), pp. 274–75. By permission of Doubleday and Company and Michael Joseph, Ltd., publishers.

refer to them. It was on the printed copy of the Covenant that I brought with me that the Senator made the changes and inserted the interlineations which, if accepted, he thought would smooth the way to ratification.

The changes ran to about forty words, the "inserts" to about fifty. It seemed to me they were more concerned with verbiage than with the object and the intent of the instrument. In my judgment, they were complementary to, rather than limiting, any substantial purpose of the Covenant. In this they differed sharply from the Reservations Lodge had introduced into the Senate and which are now blocking the path to ratification.

The Senator, frankly and repeatedly, stated that his interest, or, as he put it several times, his anxiety, centered around Article X, which the President often refers to as the "heart of the Covenant," and his suggestion, indeed his demand, was to the effect that none of the obligations or commitments incurred under this provision should be undertaken without the approval of the Senate and the concurrence of the House.

When Lodge had finished what he had to say, I expressed my pleasure at the helpful collaboration of the chairman of the Committee, and with rea-

TEACHING HIM WHAT TO SAY

Democratic cartoon stressing Lodge's partisan obstructionism. The Republicans stressed Wilson's uncompromising stubbornness. New York *World*, 1920.

son, I think. What he asked for now was decidedly milder than the reservations before the Senate, but there was, I ventured to point out, one drawback to any change, even if merely of verbiage, because, in this case, the document would have to be referred back to all the co-signers of the Covenant, and this might open the gates to other changes and would certainly result in delay.

I also ventured to say that the clarification of Article X which he urged was implicit in the Article itself. I argued "it goes without saying," for a variety of obvious reasons, that the sanction of the Senate and the approval of the House, which alone can furnish the money, would have to be forthcoming before aggressive or even defensive action against an aggressor nation could be undertaken.

"If it goes without saying," commented the Senator somewhat tartly, "there is no harm in saying it—and much advantage."

Good-naturedly the Senator now chaffed me about the expression I had used, "it goes without saying," which he thought was a "barbarism." He then went on to express his opinion of the language in which the world charter was drawn, and it was a poor one.

"As an English production it does not rank high." Then, more in chaff than in earnest, he said: "It might get by at Princeton but certainly not at Harvard."

[*With high hopes, Colonel House dispatched the new Lodge concessions to the White House. There was no reply, no acknowledgment. Perhaps Mrs. Wilson thought the memorandum unimportant or too important. Wilson might be upset and suffer a relapse. Or Wilson may have decided merely to treat Lodge's proffered hand with the contempt that he felt for the Senator. Rebuffed and perhaps humiliated, Lodge now fought even more adamantly for his Fourteen Reservations.*]

3. Wilson Defeats Lodge's Reservations (1919)

The debate in the Senate ended in November, 1919, and Lodge was ready for a vote on the Treaty of Versailles with his Fourteen Reservations attached. In general, these reaffirmed American traditional or constitutional safeguards. But Wilson believed that if the odious Lodge reservations were voted down, the Treaty would then be approved without "crippling" reservations. Yet the Democrats, now a minority, could not muster a simple majority, much less the two-thirds vote needed to approve a treaty. The naturally stubborn Wilson, shielded from disagreeable realities by his anxious wife, believed that the great body of public opinion was behind him and would prevail. He evidently had not been told, or would not believe, that public opinion was shifting around in favor of reservations. When the Democratic Senator Hitchcock suggested compromise, Wilson sternly replied, "Let Lodge compromise." Mrs. Wilson again tells the story. Comment critically on the President's basic position.

All this time the fight for the reservations to the Covenant of the League was being pressed in the Senate. Deprived of Executive leadership because of the illness of my husband, friends of the Treaty were on the defensive. The ground gained on the Western tour had been gradually lost until things were worse than when he started. Friends, including such a valued and persuasive friend as Mr. Bernard M. Baruch, begged Mr. Wilson to accept a compromise, saying "half a loaf is better than no bread." I cannot be unsympathetic with them, for in a moment of weakness I did the same. In my anxiety for the one I loved best in the world, the long-drawn-out fight was eating into my very soul, and I felt nothing mattered but to get the Treaty ratified, even with those reservations.

On November 19th the Senate was to vote on the reservations. Senator Hitchcock came to tell me that unless the Administration forces accepted

3. Edith B. Wilson, *My Memoir* (1939), pp. 296–97. Copyright 1938, 1939 by Edith Bolling Wilson; reprinted by special permission of the publishers, The Bobbs-Merrill Company, Inc.

them, the Treaty would be beaten—the struggle having narrowed down to a personal fight against the President by Lodge and his supporters. In desperation I went to my husband. "For my sake," I said, "won't you accept these reservations and get this awful thing settled?"

He turned his head on the pillow and stretching out his hand to take mine answered in a voice I shall never forget: "Little girl, don't you desert me; that I cannot stand. Can't you see that I have no moral right to accept any change in a paper I have signed without giving to every other signatory, even the Germans, the right to do the same thing? It is not I that will not accept; it is the Nation's honor that is at stake."

His eyes looked luminous as he spoke, and I knew that he was right. He went on quietly: "Better a thousand times to go down fighting than to dip your colours to dishonorable compromise."

I felt like one of his betrayers to have ever doubted. Rejoining Senator Hitchcock outside, I told him that for the first time I had seen the thing clearly and I would never ask my husband again to do what would be manifestly dishonorable. When I went back to the President's room, he dictated a letter to Senator Hitchcock, saying: "In my opinion the resolution in that form [embodying the reservations] does not provide for ratification but rather for nullification of the Treaty. . . . I trust that all true friends of the Treaty will refuse to support the Lodge resolution."

That same day the Senate voted. The Administration forces, voting against ratification *with* the Lodge reservations, defeated it. The vote was then on the ratification of the Treaty without reservations—the Treaty as Mr. Wilson had brought it from France. The result was defeat.

When the word came from the Capitol, I felt I could not bear it and that the shock might be serious for my husband. I went to his bedside and told him the fatal news. For a few moments he was silent, and then he said: "All the more reason I must get well and try again to bring this country to a sense of its great opportunity and greater responsibility."

4. Lodge Blames Wilson (1919)

The crucial vote had come in the Senate on November 19, 1919, when the Treaty with the Lodge reservations commanded only 39 yeas to 55 nays. The bulk of the Democrats, heeding Wilson's plea, voted against it. The vote for the Treaty without any reservations was 38 yeas to 53 nays. The bulk of the Republicans voted against it. Lodge wrote in bitterness as follows to his friend ex-Secretary of State Root. Determine whether he was correct in his assessment of the blame.

If Wilson had not written his letter to the Democratic caucus, calling on them to kill the treaty rather than accept the reservations, the treaty would have been ratified on the 19th of November. There would have been enough Democrats voting with us to have done it. It was killed by Wilson. He has been the marplot from the beginning. All the delays and all the troubles have been made by him. . . . We have worked for more than two months over those reservations, and they represent an amount of labor

4. J. A. Garraty, *Henry Cabot Lodge* (1953), p. 379. By permission of Henry Cabot Lodge, Jr.

and modification and concession that it would take me a long time to explain to you. He can have the treaty ratified at any moment if he will accept the reservations, and if he declines to do so we are not in the least afraid to meet him at the polls on that issue.

[*A shocked public forced the Senate to reconsider the Treaty, which now emerged with fifteen revamped Lodge reservations tacked on. Wilson refused to budge an inch from his previous position, and sent another stern letter to the Democrats in the Senate urging them to vote down the odious package. Lodge, no less stubborn, made it clear that the Senate would have to gag down the Treaty with his reservations or there would be no treaty. Faced with naked realities, twenty-one Democrats parted company with Wilson and supported ratification. The vote on March 19 was 49 yeas to 35 nays, or seven short of the necessary two-thirds. A total of twenty-three loyal Democrats voted "nay." Senator Ashurst of Arizona, a "disloyal" Democrat, declared bitterly, "As a friend of the President, as one who has loyally followed him, I solemnly declare to him this morning: If you want to kill your own child because the Senate straightens out its crooked limbs, you must take the responsibility and accept the verdict of history"* (Congressional Record, 66 Cong., 2 sess., p. 4164).]

E. THE PRESIDENTIAL CAMPAIGN OF 1920

1. Wilson Suggests a "Solemn Referendum" (1920)

Wilson had long been addicted to the habit of appealing directly to the people. Unwilling to compromise with Lodge, he was prepared to force the infant League to run in the presidential campaign of 1920. On January 8, 1920, some two months before the second rejection of the Treaty, he sent the following plea to the Democratic National Chairman. He was evidently blind to the fact that even if all of the anti-League Senators up for re-election in 1920 were defeated, and replaced by pro-League Senators, he would still lack a two-thirds vote for the unreserved Treaty. Note further evidence that Wilson was out of touch with reality, especially since three and one-half months had elapsed since his speechmaking tour.

Personally, I do not accept the action of the Senate of the United States as the decision of the Nation.

I have asserted from the first that the overwhelming majority of the people of this country desire the ratification of the treaty, and my impression to that effect has recently been confirmed by the unmistakable evidences of public opinion given during my visit to seventeen of the States.

I have endeavored to make it plain that if the Senate wishes to say what the undoubted meaning of the League is, I shall have no objection. There can be no reasonable objection to interpretations accompanying the act of ratification itself. But when the treaty is acted upon, I must know whether it means that we have ratified or rejected it.

We cannot rewrite this treaty. We must take it without changes which alter its meaning, or leave it, and then, after the rest of the world has signed it, we must face the unthinkable task of making another and separate treaty with Germany.

1. *Congressional Record*, 66 Cong., 2 sess., p. 1249.

But no mere assertions with regard to the wish and opinion of the country are credited. If there is any doubt as to what the people of the country think on this vital matter, the clear and single way out is to submit it for determination at the next election to the voters of the Nation, to give the next election the form of a great and solemn referendum, a referendum as to the part the United States is to play in completing the settlements of the war and in the prevention in the future of such outrages as Germany attempted to perpetrate.

2. Harding Sidetracks the League (1920)

The pro-League Democrats chose as their 1920 presidential standard-bearer James M. Cox, an Ohio newspaperman. The Old Guard Republicans, supremely confident of victory, nominated the handsome Senator Harding, likewise an Ohio newspaper-man. His catch-all platform was artfully designed to attract both anti-League and pro-League Republicans. "Wobbly Warren" Harding straddled over various positions on the League, but in his Des Moines speech he put both feet under himself. In the light of his assertions, determine why he opposed clarifying reservations, and whether a pro-League Republican could conscientiously vote for him. Was his proposed substitute for the League of Nations feasible?

The [Democratic] platform, to be sure, approaches its indorsement [of the League] with winding words and sly qualifications . . . but it does, nevertheless, indorse the League as it stands. It does not advocate or favor any reservations or amendments or changes or qualifications. It goes no further than to suggest that reservations will not be opposed which make clearer or more specific the obligations of the United States and the League.

But there is no need of reservations of this character. The obligations are clear enough and specific enough. I

THE SAME PLATFORM

The Republican platform was so ambiguous that the anti-League Senator Johnson could promise defeat of *the* League while the pro-League ex-President Taft could promise *a* League. Dallas *News*, 1920.

2. New York *Times,* Oct. 8, 1920.

oppose the League not because I fail to understand what . . . "we are being let in for," but because I believe I understand precisely what we are being let in for.

I do not want to clarify these obligations; I want to turn my back on them. It is not interpretation but rejection that I am seeking. My position is that the present League strikes a deadly blow at our constitutional integrity and surrenders to a dangerous extent our independence of action. . . .

The issue therefore is clear. I understand the position of the Democratic candidate and he understands mine. . . . In simple words, it is that he favors going into the Paris League and I favor staying out. . . .

As soon as possible after my election I shall advise with the best minds in the United States. . . . I shall do this to the end that we shall have an association of nations for the promotion of international peace, but one which shall so definitely safeguard our sovereignty and recognize our ultimate and unmortgaged freedom of action that it will have back of it not a divided and distracted sentiment, but the united support of the American people.

3. The "Illustrious Thirty-one" (1920)

By election day in 1920 some thirty countries had already joined the new-born League of Nations. Only blockheads or blind partisans could expect them to abandon the organization in favor of some vaguely conceived Association of Nations dreamed up by the United States. A group of eminent Republicans, fearing a heavy loss of votes to Cox following Harding's blunt condemnation, issued the following declaration signed by thirty-one persons (mostly Republicans), who were later joined by twenty-five more. Prominent among the sponsors were Charles E. Hughes and Herbert C. Hoover, both destined to sit in the Harding Cabinet. Note whether they favored amending the League or forming Harding's Association of Nations, and assess the probable effect of this appeal on pro-League Republicans.

The undersigned, who desire that the United States shall do her full part in association with the other civilized nations to prevent war, have earnestly considered how we may contribute most effectively to that end by our votes in the coming election.

The question between the candidates is not whether our country shall join in such an association. It is whether we shall join under an agreement containing the exact provisions negotiated by President Wilson at Paris, or under an agreement which omits or modifies some of those provisions that are very objectionable to great numbers of the American people. . . .

The principal change proposed concerns Article X of the League Covenant as negotiated at Paris. Mr. Wilson declares this to be "the heart of the League" and the chief controversy is about this.

Article X provides that the nations agreeing to the treaty shall "preserve as against external aggression the territorial integrity and existing political independence of all members of the League."

3. *Ibid.*, Oct. 15, 1920.

That is an obligation of the most vital importance and it certainly binds every nation entering into it to go to war whenever war may be necessary to preserve the territorial integrity or political independence of any member of the League against external aggression.

It is idle to say that Congress has power to refuse to authorize such a war, for whenever the treaty calls for war a refusal by Congress to pass the necessary resolution would be a refusal by our Government to keep the obligation of the treaty. The alternatives would be war or a breach of the solemnly pledged faith of the United States.

We cannot regard such a provision as necessary or useful for a league to preserve peace.

We have reached the conclusion that the true course to bring America into an effective league to preserve peace is not by insisting with Mr. Cox upon the acceptance of such a provision as Article X, thus prolonging the unfortunate situation created by Mr. Wilson's insistence upon that article, but by frankly calling upon the other nations to agree to changes in the proposed agreement which will obviate this vital objection and other objections less the subject of dispute.

For this course we can look only to the Republican Party and its candidate; the Democratic Party and Mr. Cox are not bound to follow it. The Republican Party is bound by every consideration of good faith to pursue such a course until the declared object is attained.

4. An Editor Dissects the "Referendum" (1920)

Wilson had asked for a referendum on the League. The sovereign voters rose up and swept the anti-League Harding into the White House by the unprecedented plurality of more than 7,000,000 votes. The Republicans exulted that Wilson now had his mandate—in reverse. Disheartened Democrats replied that the results could be no true mandate. The pro-Democratic New York *Times* stated that with pro-League Democrats voting for Cox and pro-League Republicans (reassured by the "Illustrious Thirty-one") voting for Harding, the result could be interpreted, if anything, as a mandate *for* the League. Determine from the following editorial in the New York *Evening Post* why any incumbent administration probably would have been repudiated, how "opposites" contributed to the same result, and why Harding could not have received a clear-cut mandate on the League.

We are in the backwash from the mighty spiritual and physical effort to which America girded herself when she won the war for the Allies and saved the world from a fate which America would again challenge if the need arose. The war has not been repudiated, tho the administration that fought it has been overwhelmed. We are now in the chill that comes with the doctor's bills.

As we see it now, any man in the Presidency, and any party in power, would have met the same punishment that was meted out to Woodrow Wilson and the Democratic party. Any Administration that conducted the

4. New York *Evening Post,* quoted in *Literary Digest,* LXVII, 13 (Nov. 13, 1920).

war would now be the target of the bewildering number of protests that merged into one gigantic protest.

There entered into Harding's majorities the votes of those who were against war with Germany in 1917 and the votes of those who were for war with Germany in 1914; the votes of those who think the peace imposed upon Germany too crushing, and the votes of those who think the treatment of Germany not drastic enough; the votes of those who resent the restriction upon the liberties of the American people resulting from the war, and the votes of those who resent the Administration's supposed tenderness for "Bolshevism." Opposites combined to swell Harding's majorities.

But these were by no means the principal factors. The American people as a whole was tired of the Administration. Resentment both against the Treaty and against delay in the Treaty, resentment both against the high prices which were here until the other day and against falling prices to-day, resentment against the "exactions" of labor up to the other day and against the industrial decline and rising unemployment to-day—all these opposites combined in one great weariness, into one mighty desire for a change.

Warren G. Harding and the Republican party have profited thereby. They have come into power upon a mighty wave of protest. It is now for them to decide just what that protest means when it comes to satisfying it in specific concrete terms. The votes of mutually hostile interests count if thrown into the same ballot-box. They can not all be honored by an Administration that hopes to shape anything like a policy and a program.

[*Neither of the two among the "Illustrious Thirty-one" who became members of President Harding's Cabinet staged a revolt to implement their implicit pledge to join an amended League. Secretary of State Hughes recoiled before the threats of the irreconcilable anti-League Senators to tear the administration to pieces. So the United States joined neither a League nor an Association of Nations.*]

THOUGHT PROVOKERS

1. The party in power normally loses seats during the mid-term Congressional elections. What would Wilson's position have been if he had issued no October appeal and had still lost Congress? Such presidential appeals are now commonplace. Why do they not arouse the same resentment as in 1918?

2. In what sense was the Treaty of Versailles a betrayal of Germany? Would Wilson have achieved a better treaty if he had directed the negotiations by wire from Washington? Argue both sides and come to a conclusion.

3. With reference to Article X, is a moral obligation more binding on a person or a nation than a legal one? Is it more binding on a great nation than on a weaker one?

4. It has been said that if Wilson had resigned after his collapse, the United States would have joined the League of Nations. Explain. Would the results have been better if the United States had had a law on the books under which Wilson could have been declared disabled and temporarily out of the Presidency? Why was no such law passed following President Eisenhower's three

major illnesses? In the last analysis who was more responsible for keeping America out of the League of Nations, Wilson or Lodge?

5. It has been said that no presidential election can ever be a true mandate on an issue of foreign affairs, or on any single issue. Explain.

FURTHER EXPLORATION

General: Arthur Walworth, *Woodrow Wilson* (2 vols., 1958). **October Appeal:** D. F. Fleming, *The United States and the League of Nations, 1918–1920* (1932); T. A. Bailey, *Woodrow Wilson and the Lost Peace* (1944). **Versailles:** Paul Birdsall, *Versailles Twenty Years After* (1941); Harold Nicolson, *Peacemaking, 1919* (1939). **Article X:** J. C. Vinson, *Referendum for Isolation: Defeat of Article Ten of the League of Nations Covenant* (1961); T. A. Bailey, *Woodrow Wilson and the Great Betrayal* (1945). **Defeat of Treaty:** J. A. Garraty, *Henry Cabot Lodge* (1953); H. C. Lodge, *The Senate and the League of Nations* (1925). **1920 Campaign:** Fleming, *op. cit.*; Bailey, *Woodrow Wilson and the Great Betrayal;* J. M. Cox, *Journey through My Years* (1946).

Recent: S. W. Livermore, *Politics Is Adjourned: Woodrow Wilson and the War Congress, 1916–1918* (1966); L. E. Gelfand, *The Inquiry: American Preparations for Peace, 1917–1919* (1963); R. N. Stromberg, *Collective Security and American Foreign Policy* (1963); Ferdinand Czernin, *Versailles, 1919* (1964) [paperback]; Gene Smith, *When the Cheering Stopped* (1964) [paperback]; W. M. Bagby, *The Road to Normalcy: The Presidential Campaign and Election of 1920* (1962).

Chapter 39

The Era of Normalcy

[Harding is] a fitting representative of the common aspirations of his fellow citizens.

CALVIN COOLIDGE, 1920

He [Harding] is the archtype of the Homo boobus. *Put him into the White House, and you will put every president of every Chamber of Commerce into the White House. . . .*

H. L. MENCKEN, 1920

PROLOGUE: Post-war reconstruction lurched forward haphazardly during the Harding-Coolidge era of "wonderful nonsense." President Harding, awed by his so-called popular mandate, turned his back on former allies and made a separate peace with recent enemies. But he did respond to pressures from the pro-League Republicans by issuing the call for the Washington Conference on the Limitation of Armament (1921–1922). The disarmament results were illusory, but the temporary halting of the frantic naval race helped clear the fetid atmosphere in the Pacific. Dangerous new tensions developed when Congress, erecting immigration dikes in 1924 against the hordes of Europe, grievously affronted the Japanese by excluding them completely. The anti-Red scare of the late Wilson years finally fizzled out, but not until the wave of anti-foreignism had vented itself in the protracted Sacco-Vanzetti case and in the revived Ku Klux Klan. Harding died as the oil scandals were about to besmirch an already floundering administration.

A. HARDING AND THE WASHINGTON CONFERENCE

1. Harding Hates His Job (c. 1922)

The Old Guard Republicans had nominated President Harding largely because he was a second-rater whom they could easily manage. The times, one of them said, did not demand "first-raters." Harding, according to Alice Roosevelt, "was not a bad man. He was just a slob." In beyond his depth, Harding privately moaned that the job was too big for him. William Allen White, the peppery Kansas journalist, visited the White House and talked with the President's secretary, Jud Welliver, an old friend, who (as White remembered it) burst out with the following monologue. Determine what characteristics Harding had that are desirable in a President; undesirable.

"Lord, Lord, man! You can't know what the President is going through. You see he doesn't understand it; he just doesn't know a thousand things that he ought to know. And he realizes his ignorance, and he is afraid. He has no idea where to turn.

1. W. A. White, *Autobiography* (1946), p. 616. By permission of The Macmillan Company.

"Not long ago, when the first big tax bill came up, you remember there were two theories of taxation combating for the administration's support. He would listen for an hour to one side, become convinced; and then the other side would get him and overwhelm him with its contentions. Some good friend would walk into the White House all cocked and primed with facts and figures to support one side, and another man who he thought perhaps ought to know would reach him with a counter argument which would brush his friend's theory aside.

"I remember he came in here late one afternoon after a long conference, in which both sides appeared, talked at each other, wrangled over him. He was weary and confused and heartsick, for the man really wants to do the right and honest thing. But I tell you, he doesn't know. That afternoon he stood at my desk and looked at me for a moment and began talking out loud:

" 'Jud,' he cried, 'you have a college education, haven't you? I don't know what to do or where to turn in this taxation matter. Somewhere there must be a book that tells all about it, where I could go to straighten it out in my mind. But I don't know where the book is, and maybe I couldn't read it if I found it! And there must be a man in the country somewhere who could weigh both sides and know the truth. Probably he is in some college or other. But I don't know where to find him. I don't know who he is, and I don't know how to get him. My God, but this is a hell of a place for a man like me to be!' "

2. Hearst Blasts Disarmament at Washington (1922)

The infant League of Nations was designed in part to bring about disarmament. But with the powerful United States not a cooperating member, a feverish naval race was clattering forward. Rich Uncle Sam, though still slightly behind Britain, could outstrip all others. But the American taxpayers balked, and a popular clamor forced Harding to summon a multi-power conference at Washington for arms limitation. After prolonged wrangling, the conferees agreed that certain capital ships of the major powers—America, Britain, Japan, France, Italy—were to be scrapped and the remainder pegged at a tonnage ratio of 5–5–3–1.7–1.7. The sensitive Japanese were induced to accept an inferior ratio after receiving pledges from America and Britain not to fortify further their Far Eastern bases, including the Philippines and Guam. The surrender of potential (but expensive) naval supremacy by "Uncle Sap" aroused much criticism in America. The influential Hearst newspapers, traditionally anti-Japanese and anti-British, protested vehemently as follows. Detect the statement most obviously exaggerated; the criticism most patently valid. Note in what respects Hearst's bias is most evident.

Great Britain and Japan are the ones who gain in this Conference, the ones who are going home satisfied.

England, a naval empire, and Japan, a militaristic empire, have won all the points at the expense of the Republic of France, the Republic of China, the Republic of Russia, and the United States. . . .

2. *Selections from the Writings and Speeches of William Randolph Hearst* (1948), pp. 193–94. By permission.

We have surrendered Guam and the fortifications of our island possessions, so that the American Navy would have no bases for naval operations in case war should ever be forced upon us.

We have surrendered the naval supremacy that lay within our grasp, and which would always have protected us from any attack by overseas nations. . . .

We have surrendered the adequate development of our merchant marine, and not even the battleships to be put out of commission by the decision of this Conference can be transformed into merchant vessels.

The United States, the one first-class Power of the world, in wealth, in potential strength, in strategic position and condition, has been transformed into distinctly a second-class Power by the subordinate position it has voluntarily taken with regard to England and Japan.

But worst of all is the fact that Japan, by the recognition formally accorded it in this Conference, has been made the dominant nation among the yellow nations of the world, the militaristic leader of a thousand million racial enemies of the white peoples.

Not only the people of the United States but the peoples of Europe, the white race throughout the world, will pay dearly for this act of criminal folly in times to come.

3. Japan Resents the Washington Setback (1922)

If the Japanese won a great diplomatic victory at Washington, they were unaware of it. A Tokyo newspaper (*Yorodzu*) lamented that Uncle Sam, a "hateful and haughty" "international boor," though professing to work for peace, had invited the nations to Washington, where he had "tricked them one and all." Indignant mass meetings were held at various places in Japan. The consensus of the Japanese press was that Britain had gained the most, while Japan had lost the most. Japan was forced to junk the formidable Anglo-Japanese military alliance, which seemed to menace the United States, and accept for the Pacific a weak four-power consultative pact (U.S., Britain, Japan, France). "We have discarded whiskey and accepted water," moaned one Nipponese diplomat. Enumerate the grievances that the Tokyo newspaper *Kokumin* here expresses, and determine which one seems to rankle most deeply.

Our Navy will not have more than 60 percent of the American naval strength hereafter. We must think of some way of improving our relations with America.

Our Government and delegates have brought forth a quadruple agreement [Four Power Pact], replacing the Anglo-Japanese Alliance. It now becomes clear that Japan's claims will not be granted in future without a judgment by the four Powers. Although there are four nations, England is now in a state so that she cannot oppose the will of America. Any decision in a trial of the court of four Powers will be rendered as America sees fit.

Under the circumstances, no Japanese, however optimistic, will have the heart to be optimistic of Japan's future. No one will be able to deny that Japan has [had] her hands and feet cut off in Washington.

3. Tokyo *Kokumin,* quoted in *Literary Digest,* LXXII, 18 (Jan. 28, 1922).

We do not advocate pessimistic views by choice. If there be any material by which we can be optimistic, we [should] like to know what it is. If Japan's position has been improved in any way by the Washington Conference, we [should] like to be informed of it. Reflecting upon Japan, which was thus reduced to a state of blockade on all sides, we cannot but deeply sigh with despair. . . .

American public opinion makes it believed that benefits have been conferred upon Japan. Japan was in a position wherein she was obliged to abandon the Anglo-Japanese Alliance. In place of the Alliance, a quadruple agreement was given to Japan. Thus America has saved Japan's face, American public opinion claims.

By virtue of the quadruple entente, Japan decided not to make an issue out of a race discrimination in America. Our Government and delegates are so magnanimous that they would not raise an issue out of the race discrimination which is insulting to the Japanese race. Nay, our governing classes are never magnanimous. They have never been magnanimous to our countrymen. They are magnanimous to Western peoples. Because they are afraid of Western peoples, they feign to be magnanimous. While being governed by such weak-kneed statesmen, the Japanese race cannot expect to rise above water.

B. THE JAPANESE IMMIGRATION PROBLEM

1. Ambassador Hanihara's Blunder (1924)

The bad taste left in Japanese mouths by the Washington Disarmament Conference was partially washed away by the generous outpouring of American aid to Japan's earthquake sufferers in 1923. Meanwhile the Gentlemen's Agreement, fashioned by President Theodore Roosevelt in 1908, was working smoothly. Under this self-denying arrangement the Tokyo government was issuing passports to a severely limited number of non-laborers. But the anti-Japanese Americans on the Pacific Coast were determined to wipe out the Gentlemen's Agreement in an ungentlemanly fashion, and deny the Japanese even a nominal quota in the general immigration act then pending. Fearful of this slap-in-the-face legislation, the Japanese Ambassador in Washington, M. Hanihara, lodged the following protest. Assess his arguments in favor of a quota for the Japanese, and determine which one is the most convincing. Locate the most undiplomatic part of the note, and decide whether it can properly be regarded as a threat of war.

It is needless to add that it is not the intention of the Japanese Government to question the sovereign right of any country to regulate immigration to its own territories. Nor is it their desire to send their nationals to the countries where they are not wanted. On the contrary, the Japanese Government showed from the very beginning of this problem their perfect willingness to cooperate with the United States Government to effectively prevent by all honorable means the entrance into the United States of such Japanese nationals as are not desired by the United States, and have given

1. *Foreign Relations of the United States, 1924,* II, 372–73 (April 10, 1924).

ample evidences thereof [in the Gentlemen's Agreement], the facts of which are well-known to your Government.

To Japan, the question is not one of expediency but of principle. To her, the mere fact that a few hundreds or thousands of her nationals will or will not be admitted into the domains of other countries is immaterial, so long as no question of national susceptibilities is involved. The important question is whether Japan as a nation is or is not entitled to the proper respect and consideration of other nations. In other words, the Japanese Government ask of the United States Government simply that proper consideration ordinarily given by one nation to the self-respect of another, which after all forms the basis of amicable international intercourse throughout the civilized world. . . .

. . . The manifest object of the said Section 12 (*b*) [of the pending bill] is to single out Japanese as a nation, stigmatizing them as unworthy and undesirable in the eyes of the American people. And yet the actual result of that particular provision, if the proposed bill becomes the law as intended, would be to exclude only 146 Japanese per year.

On the other hand, the Gentlemen's Agreement is, in fact, accomplishing all that can be accomplished by the proposed Japanese exclusion clause, except for those 146. It is indeed difficult to believe that it can be the intention of the people of your great country, who always stand for high principles of justice and fair play in the intercourse of nations, to resort— in order to secure the annual exclusion of the 146 Japanese—to a measure which would not only seriously offend the just pride of a friendly nation, that has been always earnest and diligent in its efforts to preserve the friendship of your people, but would also seem to involve the question of the good faith and therefore of the honor of their Government, or at least of its executive branch.

Relying upon the confidence you have been good enough to show me at all times, I have stated, or rather repeated, all this to you very candidly and in a most friendly spirit, for I realize, as I believe you do, the grave consequences which the enactment of the measure retaining that particular provision would inevitably bring upon the otherwise happy and mutually advantageous relations between our two countries.

2. Lodge Regrets Japan's "Threat" (1924)

The unfortunate phrase "grave consequences" immediately produced grave consequences. Taken out of context, it was, in diplomatic language, a threat of war. One California newspaper branded the note an "insult." A Seattle journal called it "the most insolent message this Government has ever received." Using this so-called threat as a reason (or perhaps a pretext), Congress rejected a quota and by overwhelming majorities cut off Japanese immigration completely. Senator Lodge, who had been an American delegate to the Washington Disarmament Conference, here expresses concern over precedent in a Senate speech. Determine whether his argument seems sincere or farfetched.

2. *Congressional Record,* 68 Cong., 1 sess., p. 6305 (April 14, 1924).

Mr. LODGE. Mr. President . . . I think it proper that I should state very briefly what I said behind closed doors.

I have always been very friendly to the Japanese people. I have tried to do everything in my power to promote good relations between their country and ours. I think that may be said to have been shown in the negotiation of the treaties of the Washington conference. I had intended to do all in my power to make the legislation in the present bill as easy for them and their feelings as possible. But, Mr. President, the question of immigration—and I am only about to repeat what has been often said—is perhaps the greatest of fundamental sovereign rights. If a country cannot say who shall come into the country, it has ceased to be a sovereign country; it has become a subject country.

Mr. President, I regret to say that the letter addressed to our State Department by the ambassador from Japan seems to me a letter improper to be addressed by the representative of one great country to another friendly country. It contains, I regret much to say, a veiled threat. Now, Mr. President, the United States cannot legislate by the exercise by any other country of veiled threats. Owing to this, what we are now doing assumes the character of an international precedent; and I think it should be understood, and understood by the whole world, that the United States alone is to say who shall come into the United States to form part of its citizenship. What our country determines as to its immigration is neither a just cause of offense nor a subject for war or threats of war. It is an undoubted sovereign right and nothing else.

Mr. MOSES. Mr. President—

The PRESIDING OFFICER. Does the Senator from Massachusetts yield to the Senator from New Hampshire?

Mr. LODGE. I yield.

Mr. MOSES. May I inquire of the Senator why he repeatedly uses the words "veiled threat"? The Senator knows perfectly well that in the composition of diplomatic communications the two words "grave consequences" are not veiled. They are well known in their implication.

Mr. LODGE. They are just as well known as the phrase "the United States could not regard with indifference" the violation of the Monroe Doctrine. Everybody knows what "cannot regard with indifference" means. Both phrases are the well-recognized language of diplomacy.

The letter of the Japanese ambassador, Mr. President, has created a situation which makes it impossible for me to support the pending amendment [favorable to Japan]. When I was interrupted I was about to say that this amendment has now assumed the dignity of a precedent, and I never will consent to establish any precedent which will give any nation the right to think that they can stop by threats or by compliments the action of the United States when it determines who shall come within its gates and become part of its citizenship. That is a decision which belongs to the United States alone, and from that decision there can be no appeal.

3. Japan Denounces Discrimination (1924)

Tiny Japan had blossomed fantastically in a few short decades—economically, politically, territorially, and militarily. But the hypersensitive Japanese, who set much store by "face," were suffering from a national inferiority complex, all the more so because they were undersized and yellow-complexioned. The Immigration Act of 1924 denied the peoples of China and India, among other Orientals, even a token quota, but they did not respond with comparable bitterness. The Tokyo newspaper *Nichi Nichi* described the Americans as "devils to the peace of the world." Spontaneous boycotts featured signs like: "HATE EVERYTHING AMERICAN" and "DON'T ASK AMERICAN GOODS & AMERICAN DO NOT ASK ME. I DON'T LIKE YANKEE MONKEY." Riotous demonstrations occurred against American imports, including dancing. Several Japanese committed honorable suicide (hara-kiri); one unknown patriot disemboweled himself near the American Embassy in Tokyo. The following editorial, entitled "The Senate's Declaration of War," appeared in a Tokyo journal published in English. Ascertain why, in Japanese eye, the American "insult" was peculiarly ill timed.

There is no denying that the adoption by the American Senate of the exclusion amendment to the Immigration Bill has given a shock to the whole Japanese race such as has never before been felt, and which will undoubtedly be remembered for a long time to come. The wonder is, rather, that the shock has not found expression in a louder outburst of indignation than is the case. The knowledge that Senators Johnson, Shortridge [both of California], and company do not necessarily represent the entire American nation in offering an unnecessary affront is largely responsible for the spirit of forbearance which seems to be generally ruling the mind of the nation for the present. . . .

TWO-FACED UNCLE SAM

After the face-slapping Immigration Act of 1924, the Japanese regarded Uncle Sam as a fiend wearing the mask of a gentleman. Tokyo *Miyako*, 1924.

Nevertheless, the fact remains that the Senate has passed, with an overwhelming majority, an amendment which they know is a most humiliating one to the Japanese race. And the event cuts the Japanese minds deep—a wound that will hurt and rankle for generations and generations.

How came it to pass that the Senate should have chosen to act in so extraor-

3. *Japan Times & Mail* (Weekly Edition), April 26, 1924, pp. 431–32.

dinary a manner? The exclusion Senators themselves would have it believed that their ire was roused by Ambassador Hanihara's "grave consequences" threat. They contend that the "veiled menace" was an insult that no Power so great as the United States could bear, and its injured dignity could be vindicated only by a retaliation in kind, as by insulting Japan by way of return. Yet it is inconceivable that they did not know that, in view of the distortion of facts and misrepresentation of figures so freely resorted to by the exclusionists, the Ambassador could pen his note of protest in no other tone, and that read in a rational spirit there was nothing in it to constitute an international offence.

The whole thing cannot but lend itself to a theory that the Senators were looking for some excuse to get angry; and insinuations and falsifications were so engineered as to entrap Ambassador Hanihara into committing himself with words such as could be turned into a most effective weapon by them.

Even if this be going too far behind the show, it may not be gainsaid that the Senate has been most unfortunate in the choice of time for taking its action. While professing to be jubilant over the increased prospects of permanency of peace in consequence of the Washington Conference, all Japanese have ever since felt in the secret recesses of their heart that their country has been considerably weakened in its naval strength. To add to this there came that great devastating earthquake of last year, with its far-reaching effect in all directions, seen especially in the ever-increasing balance of the country's trade on the wrong side. It has been said openly more than once in different quarters abroad that Japan is as good as crushed to a naval and economic helplessness, from which there will be no recovering at least for a generation or two. Mark, then, it is at such a time that the Senate has said practically this: "We deliberately offer you this insult, knowing that you can do no more than make a wry face."

No Japanese takes any stock in the excuse that Ambassador Hanihara's "uncalled-for words" provoked the Senators to resentment to teach Japan manners.

The impression is not unnatural, therefore, on the Japanese side, that the American Senators took advantage of the adverse plight of Japan in developing and carrying into effect their scheme of making Japan and the Japanese victims of their political manoeuvring.

C. THE REVIVAL OF ANTI–FOREIGNISM

1. William A. White Condemns Deportations (1922)

Russian Bolshevism inspired a wave of hysteria which swept the United States after World War I and continued into 1920–1921. Strikes, bomb explosions, and other acts of violence were branded the work of alien "Reds," scores of whom were rounded up and deported. In 1919 a total of 249 undesirables were loaded onto a ship known as the "Soviet Ark" and bundled off to the Russian "paradise." Guy

1. Emporia (Kansas) *Gazette*, Jan. 8, 1922. By permission of the Emporia *Gazette*.

Empey, who applauded the "deportation delirium," wrote: "My motto for the Reds is S.O.S.—ship or shoot. I believe we should place them all on a ship of stone, with sails of lead, and that their first stopping place should be hell." By early 1922 newspaper editor William Allen White was calling for sanity. Comment critically on his view that deportation is not the American way of dealing with those who criticize the government. Note when, in his view, criticism becomes un-American.

The Attorney General seems to be seeing red. He is rounding up every manner of radical in the country; every man who hopes for a better world is in danger of deportation by the Attorney General. The whole business is un-American. There are certain rules which should govern in the treason cases.

First, it should be agreed that a man may believe what he chooses.

Second, it should be agreed that when he preaches violence he is disturbing the peace and should be put in jail. Whether he preaches violence in politics, business, or religion, whether he advocates murder and arson and pillage for gain or for political ends, he is violating the common law and should be squelched—jailed until he is willing to quit advocating force in a democracy.

Third, he should be allowed to say what he pleases so long as he advocates legal constitutional methods of procedure. Just because a man does not believe this government is good is no reason why he should be deported.

Abraham Lincoln did not believe this government was all right seventy-five years ago. He advocated changes, but he advocated constitutional means, and he had a war with those who advocated force to maintain the government as it was.

Ten years ago [Theodore] Roosevelt advocated great changes in our American life—in our Constitution, in our social and economic life. Most of the changes he advocated have been made, but they were made in the regular legal way. He preached no force. And if a man desires to preach any doctrine under the shining sun, and to advocate the realization of his vision by lawful, orderly, constitutional means—let him alone. If he is Socialist, anarchist, or Mormon, and merely preaches his creed and does not preach violence, he can do no harm. For the folly of his doctrine will be its answer.

The deportation business is going to make martyrs of a lot of idiots whose cause is not worth it.

2. Brickbats for Sacco and Vanzetti (1926)

The most notorious case associated with the Red Scare involved Nicola Sacco, a shoemaker, and Bartolomeo Vanzetti, a fish peddler. They were convicted of the 1920 murder of a paymaster and his guard at South Braintree, Massachusetts. When arrested, both men were carrying revolvers and both told numerous lies. Moreover, they were both aliens (Italians), atheists, conscientious objectors ("draft dodgers"),

2. Dearborn (Michigan) *Independent,* XXVII, 11 (Dec. 11, 1926). By permission.

and radicals. Their conviction by a jury in the anti-Red atmosphere of the time, despite serious flaws in the evidence, raised grave doubts as to the fairness of the trial and the presiding judge, Webster Thayer. Many critics believed that the accused had been found guilty of radicalism rather than murder; that they were martyrs in the "class struggle." Numerous demonstrations in their favor were staged by radical groups in foreign countries. The conservative Dearborn *Independent* (then published by the billionaire Henry Ford) here entitles an editorial "Government by Bomb." Determine whether American judicial procedures should in any degree be swayed by the type of pressure herein described, even though the foreign relations of the United States are damaged.

Partisans of Nicola Sacco and Bartolomeo Vanzetti, under sentence of death for murder, are attempting to persuade Governor Fuller of Massachusetts to pardon them by the classic argument of the bomb. The highest courts of Massachusetts have decided that they were granted a fair trial. The presiding judge [Thayer] has declared likewise, and has refused to reopen the case. The accused men have enjoyed a stay of execution for five years while eminent attorneys have argued the case on every conceivable technicality in the hope of finding a flaw in the verdict. The defendants have been afforded every opportunity before the law to prove their innocence. And the law has adjudged them guilty.

But because Sacco and Vanzetti happen to be members of a revolutionary party a great hue and cry is raised in their behalf. Charges of "persecution" fill the air. Demands for their freedom are made by radical organizations and newspapers throughout the land. Nor is this all. Bombs are exploded in front of United States embassies the world over. American diplomats are menaced. The homes of witnesses who testified against Sacco and Vanzetti are blown to atoms. The judge and jury who tried them are victims of retaliatory acts. Governor Fuller, visiting in Paris, is threatened with death unless he accedes to the demands. Substitution of the bomb for ordered law is a dangerous experiment.

3. Vanzetti Condemns Judge Thayer (1927)

After six years of fruitless appeal, the conviction of Sacco and Vanzetti was upheld, and they were condemned to death in the electric chair. Vanzetti's defiant words to Judge Thayer upon being sentenced are a classic. Note why, in his view, he was being executed.

You see, it is seven years that we are in jail. What we have suffered during these seven years no human tongue can say; and yet you see me before you, not trembling, you see me looking you in your eyes straight, not blushing, nor changing color, not ashamed or in fear.

Eugene Debs [the Socialist] say that not even a dog—something like that—not even a dog that kill the chickens would have been found guilty by American jury with the evidence that the Commonwealth have pro-

3. *The Sacco-Vanzetti Case; Transcript of the Record of the Trial* . . . *and Subsequent Proceedings, 1920–27* (5 vols., New York, 1928–1929), pp. 4898–99, 4904.

duced against us. I say that not even a leprous dog would have his appeal refused two times by the Supreme Court of Massachusetts—not even a leprous dog. . . .

We have proved that there could not have been another Judge on the face of the earth more prejudiced and more cruel than you [Thayer] have been against us. We have proven that. Still they refuse the new trial. We know, and you know in your heart, that you have been against us from the very beginning, before you see us. Before you see us you already know that we were radicals, that we were underdogs, that we were the enemy of the institution that you can believe in good faith in their goodness— I don't want to condemn that—and that it was easy on the time of the first trial to get a verdict of guiltiness.

We know that you have spoke yourself and have spoke your hostility against us, and your despisement against us with friends of yours on the train, at the University Club of Boston, on the Golf Club of Worcester, Massachusetts. I am sure that if the people who know all what you say against us would have the civil courage to take the stand, maybe your Honor—I am sorry to say this because you are an old man, and I have an old father—but maybe you would be beside us in good justice at this time. . . .

This is what I say: I would not wish to a dog or to a snake, to the most low and misfortunate creature of the earth—I would not wish to any of them what I have had to suffer for things that I am not guilty of. But my conviction is that I have suffered for things that I am guilty of. I am suffering because I am a radical and indeed I am a radical; I have suffered because I was an Italian, and indeed I am an Italian; I have suffered more for my family and for my beloved than for myself; but I am so convinced to be right that if you could execute me two times, and if I could be reborn two other times, I would live again to do what I have done already.

[*The most recent investigator, using ballistic tests and other evidence, concludes that Vanzetti probably was innocent, while Sacco may have been guilty. See Francis Russell, "Sacco Guilty, Vanzetti Innocent?"* in American Heritage, *XIII, 5–9, 107–11 (June, 1962); also the same author's* Tragedy in Dedham (1962)].

4. Lippmann Pleads for Sacco and Vanzetti (1927)

Four days before the execution, which was scheduled for August 23, 1927, the militant New York *World* ran a full-page editorial, written by its chief editorial writer, pundit Walter Lippmann, pleading for a stay of execution. Analyze his basic arguments against further delay and those for it, and form some judgment as to the strength of his over-all position.

We recognize perfectly well that no government can with self-respect yield to the clamor of ignorance and sentimentality and partisanship. We realize perfectly well how much more difficult it is for the Governor to

4. New York *World*, Aug. 19, 1927. By permission. A longer extract appears in R. P. Weeks, ed., *Commonwealth vs. Sacco and Vanzetti* (1958), pp. 240–46.

commute these sentences in the face of organized threats and of sporadic outrages. It will take greatness of mind and heart for the Governor and his Council to choose the wiser course. . . .

If Governor Fuller commutes these sentences, the Communists and Anarchists will shout that they coerced him. They will make the most of it for a day, a week, a month. The extremists on the other side will call him a weakling, and sneer. They will make the most of it for a day, a week, a month. But in the meantime moderate and disinterested opinion, which is never very talkative, will mobilize behind him and will recognize that he did a wise and a brave thing. . . .

Therefore we plead with the Governor to see this matter in the light, not of to-day and to-morrow, but of years to come. We plead with him to stay the execution because it will defeat the only purpose for which the death penalty can be exacted. We plead with him to remember that, however certain he may be in his own mind that the two men are guilty, no such certainty exists in the minds of his fellow-citizens. . . .

The Sacco-Vanzetti case is clouded and obscure. It is full of doubt. The fairness of the trial raises doubt. The evidence raises doubt. The inadequate review of the evidence raises doubt. The Governor's inquiry has not appeased these doubts. The report of his Advisory Committee has not settled these doubts. Everywhere there is doubt so deep, so pervasive, so unsettling, that it cannot be denied and it cannot be ignored. No man, we submit, should be put to death where so much doubt exists.

The real solution of this case would be a new trial before a new judge under new conditions. Fervently we hope that the Supreme Judicial Court of Massachusetts will decide that under the law such a new trial can be held. But if it does not, then to the Governor, to his Council, and to the friends of justice in Massachusetts we make this plea:

Stay the execution. Wait. The honor of an American Commonwealth is in your hands. Listen, and do not put an irrevocable end upon a case that is so full of doubt. It is human to err, and it is possible in the sight of God that the whole truth is not yet known.

[*As the condemned men were being prepared for execution, mobs stoned American embassies in European and South American capitals, while aroused workers went on strike in Italy, France, and the United States. As Sacco was strapped to the electric chair he cried out in Italian, "Long live anarchy!" Some five months earlier a reporter for the New* World *had visited Vanzetti in his cell and recorded the following remarks by the prisoner, which were published in the* World *on May 13, 1927, and which have become famous:*

"If it had not been for these thing, I might have live out my life, talking at street corners to scorning men. I might have die, unmarked, unknown, a failure. Now we are not a failure. This is our career and our triumph. Never in our full life can we hope to do such work for tolerance, for joostice, for man's onderstanding of man, as now we do by an accident.

"Our word—our lives—our pains—nothing! The taking of our lives—lives of a good shoemaker and a poor fish peddler—all! That last moment belong to us— that agony is our triumph!"]

D. THE RECONSTITUTED KU KLUX KLAN

1. Tar-Bucket Terror in Texas (1921)

The hysterical atmosphere of the Red Scare was also partly responsible for the revival of the Ku Klux Klan in the 1920's. The bed sheets, hoods, and lashes were old, but the principles, aside from anti-Negroism, were new. The revamped Klan was anti-foreign, anti-Catholic, anti-Jewish, and anti-Communist. It professed to uphold Christianity, the Bible, prohibition, clean movies, the law, the Constitution, the public schools, the home, the marriage vows. It undertook to persuade unchaste people, especially women, to mend their ways by giving them a dose of the lash and a coat of tar and feathers. The press reported in 1921 that a Negro bellboy had been branded on the forehead with the letters K.K.K.; that in Florida an Episcopal archdeacon had been whipped, tarred, and feathered; and that there had been forty-three tar-bucket parties in Texas in six months. The Houston *Chronicle* here addresses a protest to the Klan members. Assuming that the Klan had proper objectives, determine why its methods were basically undemocratic. Comment on the view that the Klan was responsible for all other night-riding outrages.

Boys, you'd better disband. You'd better take your sheets, your banners, your masks, your regalia, and make one fine bonfire.

Without pausing to argue over the objects you have in mind, it is sufficient to say that your methods are hopelessly wrong. Every tradition of social progress is against them. They are opposed to every principle on which this Government is founded. They are out of keeping with civilized life.

You seem to forget that the chief advantage of democracy is to let in the daylight, to prevent secret punishment, to insure a fair hearing for every person, to make impossible that kind of tyranny which can only flourish in the dark.

The newspapers of last Sunday were disgraced with the account of four illegal, unnecessary, and wholly ineffectual outrages. Without assuming that your organization was directly responsible for any or all of them, it was, in large measure, indirectly responsible. Your organization has made the thought of secretly organized violence fashionable.

It matters not who can get into your organization or who is kept out; any group of men can ape your disguise, your methods, and your practices. If outrages occur for which you are not accountable—and they will—you have no way of clearing yourselves, except by throwing off your disguise and invoking that publicity you have sought to deny. Your rôle of masked violence, of purification by stealth, of reform by terrorism is an impossible one. Your position is such that you must accept responsibility for every offense which smacks of disguised tryanny. . . .

Who was responsible for the Tenaha case, where a woman was stripped naked and then covered with tar and feathers? Has there ever been any crime committed in this state so horrible or one that brought such shame on Texas? Is there any member of the Ku Klux Klan in Texas so pure and holy that he can condemn even the vilest woman to such disgrace and torture?

1. Houston *Chronicle,* quoted in *Literary Digest,* LXX, 12 (Aug. 27, 1921).

Masked men did it, and the world was told in press dispatches that they were the hooded Klansmen of Texas.

If that outrage was done by Ku Klux Klansmen, then every decent man who was inveigled into the order should resign immediately. If it was not the work of the real order, its members should disband because of this one act, if for no other reason.

The Ku Klux Klan, as recently rejuvenated, serves no useful purpose. On the other hand, it makes room for innumerable abuses. The community—meaning the whole nation—is against it, and the community will grow more resolutely against it as time goes on. Those who brought it into being, no matter what their intentions, would better bring about its dissolution before the storm breaks.

"PUT IT ON AGAIN!"

The highest type of citizen did not wear bed sheets. Baltimore *Sun*, 1928.

2. A Methodist Editor Clears the Klan (1923)

The brutal excesses of the Ku Klux Klan (or its imitators) brought it into disrepute, and by the mid-1920's it was rapidly disintegrating. But for several years, with its hundreds of thousands of members, it remained a potent political force. The Reverend Bob Shuler (Methodist), editor of *Shuler's Magazine* and the Fundamentalist pastor of a large Los Angeles church, published the following advertisement in the Eugene (Oregon) *Register*. Note what biases form the basis of his pro-Klan views. Comment critically on the argument that when law-enforcement agencies fail, groups like the Klan should move in.

This editor has repeatedly affirmed privately and publicly that he is not a member of the Ku Klux or any other secret organization. But when it comes to secret societies, he sees no difference absolutely between the Ku Klux and many others, the Knights of Columbus,* for instance. The Knights of Columbus has an oath, just as binding, or more so, than the Ku Klux oath. Moreover, the Knights of Columbus' oath is not one-half so American as the Ku Klux. If you charge that the Ku Klux has put over mobs, I answer that the Knights of Columbus has put over two mobs to where any other secret organization on earth has ever put over one.

2. Eugene *Register,* quoted in *Literary Digest,* LXXVI, 18–19 (Jan. 20, 1923). By permission of the Eugene *Register.*
* An American Roman Catholic society for men, founded in 1882.

This editor has been favored recently by being permitted to look over documentary evidence as to the tenets, principles, and aims of the Ku Klux Klan. He finds that this organization stands with positive emphasis for Americanism as opposed to foreign idealism; for the principles of the Christian religion as opposed to Roman Catholicism and infidelity; for the American public schools and for the placing of the Holy Bible in the schoolrooms of this nation; for the enforcement of the laws upon the statute books and for a wholesome respect for the Constitution of the United States; for the maintenance of virtue among American women, sobriety and honor among American men, and for the eradication of all agencies and influences that would threaten the character of our children. So the principles of the Klan are not so damnable as pictured, it would seem.

This organization is opposing the most cunning, deceitful, and persistent enemy that Americanism and Protestant Christianity have ever had—the Jesuits. Speaking of "invisible empires," of forces that creep through the night and do their dirty work under cover, influences that are set going in the secret places of darkness, the Jesuits are the finished product. They have burned, killed, defamed, blackmailed, and ruined their enemies by the hundreds. History reeks with it. Though I disagree with the logic of the Klan, the members of that organization declare that they can only fight such a foe by using his own fire.

As to the charge that the Ku Klux Klan has functioned in mob violence in their efforts to correct conditions, I have this to say: I am convinced that most of the mobs reported have not been ordered and directed by the Klan as an organization. I am moreover convinced that many of them have been put over by forces opposed to the Klan and for the purpose of seeking to place the guilt for mob rule upon the Klan. The most of these mobs have been, according to investigation, not Ku Klux mobs at all, but gatherings of indignant citizens, bent on correcting conditions that the officers of the law refused to correct. The way to cause the Ku Klux to retire from the field is for the officers of the law to take that field and occupy it.

The Ku Klux has the same right to exist so long as it obeys the law that any other organization has. We have not heard of any investigation of the Knights of Columbus, although their un-American oaths are historic and their mob activities have been repeatedly published and heralded from platforms far and near.

E. THE HARDING OIL SCANDALS

1. Doheny Defends Ex-Secretary Fall (1924)

An oily scandal, involving the priceless Teapot Dome naval reserve in Wyoming and the Elk Hills naval reserve in California, blackened the administration of Harding. Secretary of the Interior Albert B. Fall had secretly (and without competitive bidding) leased these reserves to the companies of two millionaire oilmen, Harry F. Sinclair

1. *Hearings before the Committee on Public Lands and Surveys, United States Senate,* 68 Cong., 1 sess., pt. VI, pp. 1778–80 (Jan. 24, 1924).

and Edward F. Doheny. But Fall did not complete the transactions until he had received hush-hush loans of $25,000 from Sinclair and $100,000 from Doheny (who was reputed to be worth $60,000,000). Doheny's sworn testimony before a Senate committee appears below. Note what aspects of it raise the most serious doubts as to the innocent nature of the "loan."

Mr. DOHENY. I had known Senator Fall for about thirty years or more. We had been old-time friends. We both worked in the same mining district in New Mexico in 1885. In those days the Indian troubles were still on the country, and we were bound together by the same ties that men usually are, especially after they leave camp where they have lived under trying circumstances and conditions. Sometimes when men are in camp where their conditions are hard, and where the struggle for a living is precarious and the danger from Indians is bad, they do not have such a very great feeling for each other; but after they leave there they become warmer friends by reason of having associated under the same conditions.

Furthermore, I studied law at the same time that Senator Fall did. I practiced for a short time in the same district that he did. I watched his career all through the development of it, as district attorney, United States judge, and United States Senator. I was very much interested in him on account of our old associations. I, myself, followed prospecting. I was fortunate and accumulated quite a large amount of money. Senator Fall was unfortunate, and when he was telling me about his misfortunes, and at a time when it was coupled with his misfortune of having to bear the loss of his two children—two grown children—I felt greatly in sympathy with him. He was telling me about his hope of acquiring this ranch, and being of an impulsive nature I said to him, "Whenever you need some money to pay for that ranch I will lend it to you."

He spoke to me at that time about possibly borrowing it from Ned McLean. And he said something at that time about giving the ranch as security. I said, "I will lend it to you on your note. You do not need to give the ranch as security."

That relieved Senator Fall greatly. Later on he telephoned to me that the time had come when the ranch could be purchased. When he telephoned to me about it, I sent him the money. Whether he asked for the money in the form that I sent it, or whether I sent it in that form of my own election, I do not know. But I sent it in cash. . . .

Senator WALSH of Montana. How did you transmit the money to him?

Mr. DOHENY. In cash.

Senator WALSH. How did you transport the cash?

Mr. DOHENY. In a satchel. The cash was put up in a regular bank bundle, and taken over and delivered to him.

Senator WALSH. Who acted as your messenger in the matter?

Mr. DOHENY. My son. . . .

Senator WALSH. How did you come to make this remittance to Senator Fall in cash?

Mr. DOHENY. That is just what I said a moment ago. I do not remember whether it was the result of his request or whether it was my own idea of sending it to him in cash to pay for the property. But he was going to use it down in New Mexico, and I thought perhaps—well, I do not know exactly how that was, as my memory is not good on that point.

Senator WALSH. You are a man of very large affairs, and of great business transactions, so that it was not unusual for you to have large money transactions, perhaps, but it was, was it not, an extraordinary way of remitting money? . . .

Mr. DOHENY. Well, it was not unusual in my business, Senator Walsh, to make a remittance in that way. And I might say here that in making the decision to lend this money to Mr. Fall, I was greatly affected by his extreme pecuniary circumstances, which resulted, of course, from a long period, a lifetime of futile efforts. I realized that the amount of money I was loaning him was a bagatelle to me; that it was no more than $25 or $50 perhaps to the ordinary individual. Certainly a loan of $25 or $50 from one individual to another would not be considered at all extraordinary, and a loan of $100,000 from me to Mr. Fall is no more extraordinary.

Senator WALSH. I can appreciate that on your side, but looking at it from Senator Fall's side it was quite a loan.

Mr. DOHENY. It was, indeed; there is no question about that. And I am perfectly willing to admit that it probably caused him to have such a feeling that he would have been willing to favor me, but under the circumstances he did not have a chance to favor me. He did not carry on these [oil] negotiations. That is the point I would like for you to understand; that Senator Fall, in my opinion, was not influenced in any way by this loan, because the negotiations were carried on by men who were not under his control.

2. The *New Republic* Is Horrified (1924)

The Teapot Dome oil scandal provoked sober comments from the high-minded *New Republic*. It expressed grave concern over the health of the conservation movement, over the silence of "Silent Cal" Coolidge while Vice-President, and over President Coolidge's evident determination to soft-pedal the affair lest the good name of the Republican Party be further damaged. Comment critically on this journal's estimate of the effect of the scandal on democratic government.

Not in a generation have such shocking revelations of betrayal of trust by a high public official come to light as those regarding the relations of former Secretary Fall with the lease of public oil lands to H. F. Sinclair and E. L. Doheny. Whether Mr. Fall was technically guilty of accepting a bribe is not yet established; but the facts already made public are sufficient to shake in a grave degree the confidence of the American people in the integrity of those to whom have been delegated the tasks of responsible government.

2. *New Republic*, XXXVII, 266 (Feb. 6, 1924). By permission of the *New Republic*.

THE EMPTY CELL

The millionaire Teapot Dome bribers escape jail. New York *World*,
c. 1928, in M. R. Werner and John Starr, *Teapot Dome*.

Mr. Fall received $100,000 from Mr. Doheny, $35,000 [$25,000] from Mr.
Sinclair, and from sources not yet revealed at least $52,000 more. Mr. Fall,
Mr. Doheny, and Mr. Sinclair all publicly and formally lied about these
transactions. Mr. Edward B. McLean lied about the $100,000 which he
either did or didn't lend to Mr. Fall. The whole affair has been conducted
by every individual implicated with the grossest, most brazen contempt
for the truth and for the right of the American people to know that truth.

Mr. Doheny and Mr. Sinclair, who testified that they expected to make
a combined total of $125,000,000 out of the public lands Mr. Fall obligingly
handed over to them, take the attitude that the purchase of a member of
the Cabinet of the President of the United States is a matter of private
business, no one's concern but their own. Ten thousand Communists, armed
with unlimited gold from Moscow, could not in a decade do the democratic
theory of government so much harm as has been accomplished by this
precious crew.

[*Ex-Secretary Fall, convicted of accepting a bribe, was fined $100,000 and
sentenced to one year in jail. A jury acquitted both Doheny and Sinclair of
wrongdoing, though Sinclair was fined $1000 and sentenced to nine months in*

prison for refusing to answer questions put by a Senate committee, and for contemptuously hiring detectives to "shadow" his jury. The jailing of the broken bribe-taker and the freeing of the insolent bribe-givers, both of them millionaires, evoked acid comment about the injustice of American justice.]

THOUGHT PROVOKERS

1. It is said that a fair compromise of an international problem leads to some dissatisfaction on all sides. Comment critically with reference to the Washington disarmament parley of 1921–1922.

2. Is immigration, as alleged, a "purely domestic issue"? To what extent has the line between domestic and foreign issues broken down in recent decades, and why? In view of the fact that the Japanese received their long-sought quota in 1952, could they not better have received it in 1924?

3. Should aliens in America be allowed to criticize the American government? Should advocacy of violence be considered the same as violence itself? Was the seven-year delay in executing Sacco and Vanzetti evidence of justice or injustice?

4. Were the procedures of the K.K.K. in harmony with the American tradition of rough-and-ready justice? What can be said for and against secret "justice"? Was the Klan of Reconstruction days more justifiable than that of the 1920's?

5. Why was it easier to convict Secretary Fall of accepting a bribe than oilmen Doheny and Sinclair of giving one?

FURTHER EXPLORATION

General: J. D. Hicks, *Republican Ascendancy, 1921–1933* (1960); F. L. Allen, *Only Yesterday* (1931); P. W. Slosson, *The Great Crusade and After, 1914–1928* (1930). **Washington Conference:** J. C. Vinson, *The Parchment Peace* (1955); C. L. Hoag, *Preface to Preparedness* (1941). **Japanese Immigration:** R. W. Paul, *The Abrogation of the Gentlemen's Agreement* (1936); M. J. Pusey, *Charles Evans Hughes* (2 vols., 1951). **Anti-Foreignism:** R. K. Murray, *Red Scare* (1955); G. L. Joughin and E. M. Morgan, *The Legacy of Sacco and Vanzetti* (1948); R. P. Weeks, ed., *Commonwealth vs. Sacco and Vanzetti* (1958). **Ku Klux Klan:** J. M. Mecklin, *The Ku Klux Klan* (1924). **Oil Scandals:** M. R. Werner and John Starr, *Teapot Dome* (1959); Mark Sullivan, *Our Times* (1935), vol. VI; S. H. Adams, *Incredible Era* (1939).

Recent: Andrew Sinclair, *The Available Man: The Life Behind the Masks of Warren Gamaliel Harding* (1965); William Preston, Jr., *Aliens and Dissenters: Federal Suppression of Radicals, 1903–1933* (1963) [paperback]; Burl Noggle, *Teapot Dome: Oil and Politics in the 1920's* (1962) [paperback] J. L. Bates, *The Origins of Teapot Dome; Progressives, Parties, and Petroleum, 1909–1921* (1963); David Felix, *Protest: Sacco-Vanzetti and the Intellectuals* (1965); D. M. Chalmers, *Hooded Americanism: The First Century of the Ku Klux Klan, 1865–1965* (1965); A. S. Rice, *The Ku Klux Klan in American Politics* (1962).

Chapter 40

Coolidge and the Opulent Twenties

The country is in the midst of an era of prosperity more extensive and of peace more permanent than it has ever before experienced.

PRESIDENT COOLIDGE, 1928

PROLOGUE: The jazz-mad, slaphappy, prosperity-flushed 1920's wore on under complacent Calvin Coolidge. His administration forced the now unpopular Allies to pay a substantial part of their war debt, despite economic dislocations abroad that boomeranged upon the United States. Religious Fundamentalism waged its last spectacular campaign, notably under the banner of anti-evolution Protestants in the South. The post-war moral sag was accelerated by the prohibition amendment, which spawned a bloated brood of bootleggers, gangsters, rumrunners, home brewers, speakeasy proprietors, still-snoopers, and corrupt enforcement officials. America was rapidly becoming a nation of scofflaws and hypocrites. In 1928 the Republican Herbert Hoover triumphed over the Democrat Al Smith in a presidential contest that featured anti-foreignism, anti-Catholicism, anti-wetism, anti-big-cityism, and just plain snobbery. More decisive, probably, were continuing prosperity and Hoover's exalted reputation.

A. CAUTIOUS CALVIN COOLIDGE

1. Hoover Remembers His Chief (1952)

Tight-fisted and tight-lipped Calvin Coolidge once remarked, "I have never been hurt by anything I didn't say." His Secretary of Commerce, inherited from Harding, was the wealthy mining engineer Herbert Hoover, who had first fed the Belgians and then had directed the feeding of the Americans during World War I. Hoover's personal recollections modify the image of a dour, silent, and humorless Coolidge. In the light of this Hooverian version, account for Coolidge's reputation for silence and do-nothingism, and comment critically on his administrative techniques.

Before Mr. Coolidge came to the Presidency, I had only a secondary acquaintance with him—such as one gets by dinner contacts. He was reputed to be a most taciturn man. This was true in his relations with the general run of people and with the press. With his associates there was little of taciturnity. Many times over the five years he sent for men to come to the White House after dinner just to talk an hour or two. He had a fund of New England stories and a fine, dry wit.

After my election in 1928, he undertook to give me some fatherly advice as to how to run the White House. He said: "You have to stand every day

1. Herbert Hoover, *The Memoirs of Herbert Hoover: The Cabinet and the Presidency, 1920–1933* (1952), pp. 55–57. Reprinted with permission of The Macmillan Company. Copyright 1952, 1961 by Herbert Hoover.

three or four hours of visitors. Nine-tenths of them want something they ought not to have. If you keep dead-still they will run down in three or four minutes. If you even cough or smile they will start up all over again."

Mr. Coolidge was well equipped by education, experience, and moral courage for the Presidency. He was the incarnation of New England horse sense and was endowed with certain Puritan rigidities that served the nation well. He possessed New England thrift to the ultimate degree, and his tight hold on government expenditures and his constant reduction of public debt were its fine expression.

He was most reluctant to take any action in advance of the actual explosion of trouble. One of his sayings was, "If you see ten troubles coming down the road, you can be sure that nine will run into the ditch before they reach you and you have to battle with only one of them." It was a philosophy that served well while the nation was making a rapid convalescence from its war wounds. The trouble with this philosophy was that when the tenth trouble reached him he was wholly unprepared, and it had by that time acquired such momentum that it spelled disaster. The outstanding instance was the rising boom and orgy of mad speculation which began in 1927, in respect to which he rejected or sidestepped all our anxious urgings and warnings to take action. The country was prosperous and I suspect that he enjoyed the phrase "Coolidge prosperity" more than any other tag which the newspapers and the public pinned on him.

Mr. Coolidge was a real conservative, probably the equal of [President] Benjamin Harrison. He quickly dissolved our controls over foreign loans. He was a fundamentalist in religion, in the economic and social order, and in fishing. On one of his summer vacations, when he started in that art to which he was a stranger, he fished with worms—to the horror of all fly fishermen. . . .

Any summation of Mr. Coolidge's services to the country must conclude that America is a better place for his having lived in it.

2. Mencken Sneers at Coolidge (1933)

Acid-tongued Henry L. Mencken, editor of the *American Mercury*, was the most notorious gadfly of the 1920's. He attacked religion, marriage, women, Rotary Clubs, the K.K.K., the American Legion, Puritans, Babbitts, the "Bible Belt" Protestant South, farmers ("yokels"), the masses ("the boobery"), democracy, patriotism, and idealism. He had kind words for atheism, booze, bootleggers, evolution, anarchists, the German Kaiser, sin, suicide, and prostitution. The victims of his barbs responded with epithets ranging from "mangy ape" to "literary stink-pot." Ex-President Coolidge, who had taken long daily naps in the White House, died unexpectedly in 1933, and Mencken penned this charitable (for him) obituary. Note to what extent his characterization confirms that of Hoover, just given. Analyze both the weak and strong aspects of Coolidge's philosophy of governing.

The achievements of the deceased, in fact, almost always turn out on inspection to have been no achievements at all. Did he [as governor of

2. Baltimore *Evening Sun*, Jan. 30, 1933. By permission of the Baltimore *Evening Sun*. The full text is published in Malcolm Moos, ed., *A Carnival of Buncombe* (1956), pp. 132–36.

Massachusetts] actually break up the celebrated Boston police strike? He did not. It was broken up by other men, most of whom were not even in his confidence; all he did was to stand on the side lines until the tumult was over.* Did he tackle and settle any of the grave problems that confronted the country during his years in the White House? He tackled few of them and settled none of them. Not a word came out of him on the subject of Prohibition. Not once did he challenge the speculative lunacy that finally brought the nation to bankruptcy. And all he could be induced to do about the foreign debts was to hand the nuisance on to poor Hoover.

His record as President, in fact, is almost a blank. No one remembers anything that he did or anything that he said. His chief feat during five years and seven months in office was to sleep more than any other President —to sleep more and to say less. Wrapped in a magnificent silence, his feet upon his desk, he drowsed away the lazy days. He was no fiddler like Nero; he simply yawned and stretched. And while he yawned and stretched the United States went slam-bang down the hill—and he lived just long enough to see it fetch up with a horrible bump [of depression] at the bottom.

It was this snoozing, I suspect, that was at the bottom of such moderate popularity as he enjoyed. The American people, though they probably do not know it, really agree with Jefferson: they believe that the least government is the best. Coolidge, whatever his faults otherwise, was at all events the complete antithesis of the bombastic pedagogue, Wilson. The itch to run things did not afflict him; he was content to let them run themselves. Nor did he yearn to teach, for he was plainly convinced that there was nothing worth teaching. So the normalcy that everyone longed for began to come back in his time, and if he deserved no credit for bringing it in, he at least deserved credit for not upsetting it.

That this normalcy was itself full of dangers did not occur to anyone. The people generally believed that simple peace was all that was needed to cure the bruises and blisters of war time, and simple peace was what Dr. Coolidge gave them. He never made inflammatory speeches. He engaged in no public combats with other statesmen. He had no ideas for the overhauling of the government. He read neither the *Nation* nor the *New Republic,* and even in the New York *Times* he apparently read only the weather report. Wall Street got no lecturing from him. No bughouse professors, sweating fourth-dimensional economics, were received at the White House. The President's chosen associates were prosperous storekeepers, professional politicians, and the proprietors of fifth-rate newspapers. When his mind slid downhill toward the fine arts, he sent for a couple of movie actors.

Is anything to be said for this *Weltanschauung* [philosophy of life]? Perhaps a lot. . . . We suffer most when the White House busts with ideas. With a World Saver preceding him (I count out Harding as a mere hallu-

---

* After the Boston police strike was evidently broken in 1919, Governor Coolidge won an exaggerated reputation by wiring Samuel Gompers, of the American Federation of Labor, "There is no right to strike against the public safety by anybody, anywhere, any time." This ringing declaration probably won him the vice-presidential nomination in 1920.

cination) and a Wonder Boy following him, he begins to seem, in retrospect, an extremely comfortable and even praiseworthy citizen. His failings are forgotten; the country remembers only the grateful fact that he let it alone.

Well, there are worse epitaphs for a statesman. If the day ever comes when Jefferson's warnings are heeded at last, and we reduce government to its simplest terms, it may very well happen that Cal's bones now resting inconspicuously in the Vermont granite will come to be revered as those of a man who really did the nation some service.

B. DUNNING THE DEBTORS

1. Hoover Opposes Cancellation (1922)

During the war to make the world "safe for democracy," the United States advanced to its associates nearly $10 billion in credits (not gold). The expectation was that these sums would be repaid at 5% interest, although at the time there was some talk of an outright gift. The then deserving Allies were holding back the common enemy while America was belatedly raising an army. When the war ended with the world definitely not "safe for democracy," disillusionment with the "imperialistic" Allies set in. Demands for repayment more than canceled out those for cancellation. Secretary of Commerce Hoover, a hardheaded businessman who shared the current disillusionment, was dead set against cancellation. He was technically right in insisting that the debts were not connected with reparations, but the Allies were counting on reparations from Germany to pay their debts to America. Hoover expressed his views forcefully in this 1922 speech in Toledo. Enumerate his arguments against cancellation, and evaluate the strongest one. Comment on his view that the debts were not owed to the Washington government.

Proposals have been repeatedly made over the last three years that the loans from our government to foreign countries during the war should in part or in whole be canceled, either for moral reasons or in the interest of economic stability. Less sweeping proposals have been made that the payments of interest and installments, as required by Congress, should be further postponed or moderated. . . .

These loans are often spoken of as debts to our government. They are, in fact, debts owing to our taxpayers. These loans were made at the urgent request of the borrowers and under their solemn assurance of repayment. The loans were individual to each nation. They have no relation to other nations or other debts [reparations]. The American taxpayer did not participate in reparations and acquired no territory or any other benefits under the treaty, as did our debtors.

There is no question as to the moral or contractual obligation. The repudiation of these loans would undermine the whole fabric of international good faith. I do not believe any public official, either of the United States or any other country, could or should approve their cancellation. Certainly I do not. . . .

1. *Excerpts from Speeches and Writings of Herbert Hoover* (Hoover-for-President Washington Committee, 1928), pp. 38–39.

UNCLE SAM BECOMES UNCLE SHYLOCK

The Allied debt wrangle changes attitudes. St. Louis
Post-Dispatch, 1926.

America earnestly wishes to be helpful to Europe, but economic matters
require a degree of realism that will do justice to the American people, as
well as be helpful to peoples abroad.

[*Hoover consistently stressed the theme that if the debts were canceled, the
American taxpayer would have to assume the burden (which was all too true),
and that the debtors should pay off their obligation with the money they were
spending on armaments. The European arms race was largely a product of
America's desertion of the Allies; and, as one journal pointed out, no city was
going to dismiss its police force to meet payments on its bonded indebtedness.*]

2. Baker Urges Cancellation (1926)

The ex-Allies regarded the debts not as loans but as subsidies to comrades-in-arms.
The war-ravaged French argued that they were not asking for their dead soldiers
back; America should not ask for her dead dollars back. Washington nevertheless
used economic pressure to force the debtors to sign installment-payment agreements
spread over sixty-two years. No reduction of the principal sums was granted, but in
all cases the interest was lowered from the expected 5%, with a consequent cancellation of a large part of the over-all indebtedness. Americans preened themselves on

2. *Trade Winds* (Cleveland), quoted in *Literary Digest*, XC, 10 (Sept. 18, 1926).

their generosity, while the Allies complained bitterly about two generations of "USury" to "Uncle $am." Newton D. Baker, who had been Secretary of War under Wilson and was now associated with Cleveland bankers, published the following appeal. Ascertain why the best interests of both the American bankers and the United States would have been served by an all-around cancellation.

The fact is that not a penny of this money would have been lent by us, or have been borrowed by any of our debtor nations, but for the war. Their need for it arose out of the contributions and sacrifices made by them in the war, and our willingness to supply it arose out of our belief that it was necessary, to our own interest, to sustain their military efficiency until the Armistice, and their economic stability after the Armistice, in order to prevent a collapse which would have cost us vastly more than the money which we supplied.

Nor is it very important to inquire whether, at the time of the making of these so-called loans, there was an expectation that they should be repaid. The question is not what did somebody think in 1917, but what is it wise to think now?

In the modern world, industrial nations are so integrated, by mutual investment and by trade relations, that political isolation is an illusion. . . . The overseas investments of the people of the United States now aggregate perhaps eleven billions of dollars, and we are investing annually overseas at the rate of a billion a year.

Europe to-day is, and long has been, our best customer, consuming of our total exports more than double the amount of any other continent. In a very real sense, therefore, European buying in the world markets is a decisive factor in maintaining the price of our entire home product. It is not conceivable that the rest of the world will continue to trade with us during sixty-two years in which every one of them would have its own industries burdened by crushing taxes.

Every country in the world has had the experience of a vast and hopeless debtor class, and has realized that every so often it is necessary to wipe off the slate and start afresh, as in a Scriptural year of Jubilee. This releases the energies of men, restores hope, cures political disorder, and gives life a fresh start. The analogy applies perfectly to the present international situation. The United States needs, not dollars, but a confident, prosperous, and peaceful world as a field for its industrial and commercial operations. That condition cannot be brought about so long as we continue to exact payments up to the capacity of the debtors to pay.

If the foregoing observations are sound, the United States is not justified either in morals, or in a long view of its own best industrial and commercial interests, in adhering to its present policy with regard to the settlement of the inter-allied debts. The time has come when these questions, including the British settlement, ought to be reopened.

Personally, I believe that a mutual cancellation policy will be wise. Such a policy ought to relieve England, France, Italy, Belgium, and the rest of our war allies both as to their debts to us and their debts among themselves, and in turn ought to require the release of some part of the [reparations] burdens imposed upon Germany. This should be done at a round table, where a representative of the United States should be authorized to speak with authority and to demonstrate to the rest of the world that America's interest is not in dollars but in a reconstructed international order.

3. Lippmann Foresees Default (1926)

The debtors, though grumbling, kept up their payments until the early 1930's, when the Great Depression descended with devastating force. Then they all defaulted (save for "brave little Finland") and the debts were dead, except to the American taxpayer and the Treasury bookkeepers. The brilliantly prophetic Walter Lippmann, then on the editorial staff of the New York *World*, predicted what would happen. Enumerate his reasons for believing that the debts would never be paid, and evaluate his view that there was an essential difference between a war debt and an ordinary debt. What additional events of the 1930's and 1940's made for default?

The fundamental reason why these great international war debts cannot be regarded as ordinary debts is that they are dead. They do not represent capital invested in a living enterprise, which produces as it goes along the interest and the principal to repay the money which was loaned. An ordinary debt is productive for the debtor, but these international debts are like bills submitted to pay for the damage done on a wild party by one's grandfather. The payment seems to the debtor like a pure loss, and when it is paid by one nation to another it seems like tribute by the conquered to the conqueror. Money borrowed to build a railroad earns money to pay for itself. But money borrowed to fight a war produces nothing, and if it has to be paid it becomes a dead mortgage superimposed upon all the living credits of a nation.

The United States has engaged itself to collect for the next two generations the sum of $400,000,000 a year on a dead debt. Most of the veterans of the war will be gone. Their children born after the war, knowing no more of its reality than an American college boy knows of the Civil War, will be elderly men, their children in turn will be approaching middle age, and still the huge payments will go on. The last instalments will be paid out of the earnings of the great-grandsons of the men who directed the war. Is it conceivable that for the rest of the century this thing will go on? Does anybody really think he lives in a world where such things are possible?

Let us not deceive ourselves. Mr. Coolidge and Mr. Mellon [Secretary of the Treasury] and Mr. [Senator] Borah and Mr. Baldwin [of Britain] and M. Briand [of France] and the other gentlemen who have made these arrangements will not bind posterity nor mortgage the future in any such fashion as this. To us the war was a great event. But already there is a

3. New York *World*, July 29, 1926. By permission.

generation out in the world which has almost no knowledge of it. In a few years those of us who lived through the war will seem like reminiscent old bores to young people who will have many better things to do than hash over the rights and wrongs of 1914–18. Yet here we are deluding ourselves with the preposterous idea that from now until about 1984 people and governments are going to be bothered with carrying out what to them will be perfectly meaningless settlements.

Already Mr. Mellon and Mr. [Winston] Churchill can't quite remember what the money was spent for. The next generation certainly—our own if it is wise—will say in face of the endless bother and animosity that these settlements entail: Let the past be the past, let the dead bury the dead, let us forget, let us forgive, let us have peace.

C. MONKEY BUSINESS IN TENNESSEE

1. Darrow Grills Bryan (1925)

The Fundamentalists—or believers in a literal interpretation of the Bible—were still strong in the 1920's, especially in the Protestant ("Bible Belt") South. The legislature of Tennessee passed a law forbidding teachers in the state-supported (but not private) schools to teach the Darwinian theory of evolution. John T. Scopes, a pleasant young biology teacher and football coach, was brought to trial in the back-woods hamlet of Dayton. Aiding the defense was the famed agnostic and champion of the underdog, Clarence G. Darrow; aiding the prosecution was the famed orator and Fundamentalist William J. Bryan, who was spearheading a nationwide crusade against evolution. Bryan was induced to take the stand as an expert witness on the Bible, and Darrow sailed into him and his "fool religion." Form conclusions from this interchange as to whether such testimony helped or hurt the Fundamentalists.

Q—Do you believe the story of the temptation of Eve by the serpent?
A—I do.

Q—Do you believe that after Eve ate the apple, or gave it to Adam, which-ever way it was, that God cursed Eve, and at that time decreed that all womankind thenceforth and forever should suffer the pains of childbirth in the reproduction of the earth?

A—I believe what it says, and I believe the fact as fully—

Q—That is what it says, doesn't it?

A—Yes.

Q—And for that reason, every woman born of woman, who has to carry on the race, the reason they have childbirth pains is because Eve tempted Adam in the Garden of Eden?

A—I will believe just what the Bible says. I ask to put that in the language of the Bible, for I prefer that to your language. Read the Bible and I will answer.

Q—All right, I will do that.

[Darrow reads from Genesis 3:15–16.]

A—I accept it as it is.

1. *The World's Most Famous Court Trial: Tennessee Evolution Case* (1925), pp. 303–04.

GATHERING DATA FOR THE TENNESSEE TRIAL
Bryan finds no proof of evolution in the zoo. New York *World*, 1925.

Q—And you believe that came about because Eve tempted Adam to eat the fruit?

A—Just as it says.

Q—And you believe that is the reason that God made the serpent to go on his belly after he tempted Eve?

A—I believe the Bible as it is, and I do not permit you to put your language in the place of the language of the Almighty. You read that Bible and ask me questions, and I will answer them. I will not answer your questions in your language.

Q—I will read it to you from the Bible: "And the Lord God said unto the serpent, because thou hast done this, thou art cursed above all cattle, and above every beast of the field; upon thy belly shalt thou go and dust shalt thou eat all the days of thy life." Do you think that is why the serpent is compelled to crawl upon its belly?

A—I believe that.

Q—Have you any idea how the snake went before that time?

A—No, sir.

Q—Do you know whether he walked on his tail or not?

A—No, sir. I have no way to know. (*Laughter in audience.*)

Q—Now, you refer to the cloud that was put in the heaven after the flood, the rainbow. Do you believe in that?

A—Read it.

Q—All right, I will read it for you.

Mr. BRYAN—Your Honor, I think I can shorten this testimony. The only purpose Mr. Darrow has is to slur at the Bible, but I will answer his question. I will answer it all at once, and I have no objection in the world, I want the world to know that this man, who does not believe in a God, is trying to use a court in Tennessee—

Mr. DARROW—I object to that.

Mr. BRYAN (*continuing*)—to slur at it, and while it will require time, I am willing to take it.

Mr. DARROW—I object to your statement. I am examining you on your fool ideas that no intelligent Christian on earth believes.

2. *The Nation* Supports Local Opinion (1925)

The trial continued in a circus atmosphere; one promoter rented a store window to display an ape. Judge Raulston, himself a Methodist lay preacher, ruled that the truth of evolution was completely irrelevant, and that the only question was whether Scopes had violated the law. This he admittedly had. The jury found him guilty after only nine minutes of deliberation. (One juror could not read; three others admitted to having read no book but the Bible.) Scopes was fined $100 and costs under circumstances that precluded an ultimate appeal to higher courts. Darrow tried to make the issue the right of the teacher to teach the truth. The New York *Nation* perceived a larger issue. Comment critically on its views, and determine whether this journal or Darrow was basically correct.

To the trial in Tennessee newspapers all over the country are sending special correspondents; a great blare of publicity resounds. But it is not certain that anything of much importance will be accomplished there or in higher courts. Many people think that Mr. Scopes has clearly violated the law and must inevitably be convicted in Dayton, but that he will win eventually on appeal to the higher courts on the ground that the law provides for the interpretation of science according to a particular religious belief. . . .

But no decision of the Dayton or a higher court will resolve the problem. *The Nation,* as its readers know, is opposed to the continual nullification of the popular will by the courts, even in a direction which it approves. Truth cannot be established by vote of the courts any more than by vote of the legislature. In the end, a sustained public opinion will have its way.

We can hardly question the right of any people to decide how and what the youth in its schools should be taught. We ought to contest not the right but the wisdom of any limitation which prevents the teacher from presenting all sides of every question, of opening up for the young mind every possible avenue to truth. . . .

Thus the case of the State of Tennessee *vs.* Truth will not be settled by legislature or courts. It is rather a challenge to our churches and our edu-

2. *The Nation* (New York), CXXI, 58 (July 8, 1925). By permission of *The Nation.*

cators. It is, above all, a challenge to the intelligence and the leadership that center in our great cities and an indictment of a civilization that sucks into them the best, materially and morally, that the nation produces—leaving the rest of the country bankrupt and then expressing ridicule and surprise at the consequences.

[*Four decades later the Tennessee anti-evolution law was still on the books, but evolution was being taught in the public schools. The statute was largely a dead letter in the face of increased enlightenment, as* The Nation *had hoped. It was formally repealed in 1967. For the reminiscences of the forgotten man of the trial, John T. Scopes, see his article, "The Trial That Rocked the Nation,"* Reader's Digest, *LXXVIII, 136–44 (March, 1961).*]

D. THE WETS VERSUS THE DRYS

1. A German Observes Bootlegging (1928)

Before the end of World War I most of the states had decreed the prohibition of alcoholic beverages. Nationwide prohibition, authorized by the 18th Amendment in 1919, resulted largely from the spirit of self-sacrifice aroused by the war. A militant majority was thus able to force its will upon a large and vocal minority, especially in the big cities, where the foreign-born population was accustomed to the regular consumption of alcohol. "The Sea Devil" Felix von Luckner, a German naval hero who had destroyed some $25,000,000 worth of Allied commerce with his raider the *Seeadler (Sea Eagle)* during World War I, visited America as a lecturer and recorded his curious experiences with alcohol. Note the good and bad features of prohibition, and ascertain what conditions made enforcement peculiarly difficult.

My first experience with the ways of prohibition came while we were being entertained by friends in New York. It was bitterly cold. My wife and I rode in the rumble seat of the car, while the American and his wife, bundled in furs, sat in front. Having wrapped my companion in pillows and blankets so thoroughly that only her nose showed, I came across another cushion that seemed to hang uselessly on the side. "Well," I thought, "this is a fine pillow; since everyone else is so warm and cozy, I might as well do something for my own comfort. This certainly does no one any good hanging on the wall." Sitting on it, I gradually noticed a dampness in the neighborhood that soon mounted to a veritable flood. The odor of fine brandy told me I had burst my host's peculiar liquor flask.

In time, I learned that not everything in America was what it seemed to be. I discovered, for instance, that a spare tire could be filled with substances other than air, that one must not look too deeply into certain binoculars, and that the Teddy Bears that suddenly acquired tremendous popularity among the ladies very often had hollow metal stomachs.

"But," it might be asked, "where do all these people get the liquor?" Very

1. Reprinted by permission of the publishers from Oscar Handlin, ed., *This Was America* (Cambridge, Mass.: Harvard University Press, copyright 1949 by the President and Fellows of Harvard College), pp. 495–96.

simple. Prohibition has created a new, a universally respected, a well-beloved, and a very profitable occupation, that of the bootlegger who takes care of the importation of the forbidden liquor. Everyone knows this, even the powers of government. But this profession is beloved because it is essential, and it is respected because its pursuit is clothed with an element of danger and with a sporting risk. . . .

Yet it is undeniable that prohibition has in some respects been signally successful. The filthy saloons, the gin mills which formerly flourished on every corner and in which the laborer once drank off half his wages, have disappeared. Now he can instead buy his own car, and ride off for a week-end or a few days with his wife and children in the country or at the sea. But, on the other hand, a great deal of poison and methyl alcohol has taken the place of the good old pure whiskey. The number of crimes and misdemeanors that originated in drunkenness has declined. But by contrast, a large part of the population has become accustomed to disregard and to violate the law without thinking. The worst is that, precisely as a consequence of the law, the taste for alcohol has spread ever more widely among the youth. The sporting attraction of the forbidden and the dangerous leads to violations. My observations have convinced me that many fewer would drink were it not illegal.

2. La Guardia Pillories Prohibition (1926)

The wholesale violations of the prohibition law became so notorious that in 1926 a Senate judiciary subcommittee held extended hearings. It uncovered shocking conditions. Stubby, turbulent, fiery Fiorello ("The Little Flower") La Guardia, then a Congressman from New York and later to be the controversial reform mayor of New York City, expressed characteristically vigorous views. Note which of his statistics seem least susceptible of proof, and determine which of his arguments would probably carry the most weight with the average taxpayer.

It is impossible to tell whether prohibition is a good thing or a bad thing. It has never been enforced in this country.

There may not be as much liquor in quantity consumed to-day as there was before prohibition, but there is just as much alcohol.

At least 1,000,000 quarts of liquor is consumed each day in the United States. In my opinion such an enormous traffic in liquor could not be carried on without the knowledge, if not the connivance, of the officials entrusted with the enforcement of the law.

I am for temperance; that is why I am for modification.

I believe that the percentage of whisky drinkers in the United States now is greater than in any other country of the world. Prohibition is responsible for that. . . .

At least $1,000,000,000 a year is lost to the National Government and

2. *Hearings before the Subcommittee of the Committee on the Judiciary, United States Senate, Sixty-ninth Congress, First Session, on . . . Bills to Amend the National Prohibition Act,* I, 649–51.

the several states and counties in excise taxes. The liquor traffic is going on just the same. This amount goes into the pockets of bootleggers and into the pockets of the public officials in the shape of graft. . . .

I will concede that the saloon was odious, but now we have delicatessen stores, pool rooms, drug stores, millinery shops, private parlors, and 57 other varieties of speakeasies selling liquor and flourishing.

I have heard of $2,000 a year prohibition agents who run their own cars with liveried chauffeurs.

It is common talk in my part of the country that from $7.50 to $12 a case is paid in graft from the time the liquor leaves the 12-mile limit until it reaches the ultimate consumer. There seems to be a varying market price for this service created by the degree of vigilance or the degree of greed of the public officials in charge.

It is my calculation that at least $1,000,000 a day is paid in graft and corruption to Federal, state, and local officers. Such a condition is not only intolerable, but it is demoralizing and dangerous to organized government. . . .

The Prohibition Enforcement Unit has entirely broken down. It is discredited; it has become a joke. Liquor is sold in every large city. . . .

Only a few days ago I charged on the floor of the House that 350 cases of liquor of a seizure of 1,500 made by Federal officials and

THE NATIONAL GESTURE

Every official seemingly had his hand out for a bribe. *Judge*, c. 1930, in Andrew Sinclair, *Prohibition*, 1962.

stored in the Federal building at Indianapolis, Ind., had been removed. The Department of Justice, under date of April 9, 1926, confirmed my charge. The Attorney General admits that since this liquor was in the possession of the Federal authorities in the Federal building at Indianapolis, 330 cases are missing. If bootleggers can enter Federal buildings to get liquor, the rest can be easily imagined. . . .

I have been in public office for a great many years. I have had the opportunity to observe first the making of the present prohibition laws as a member of Congress, and later as president of the Board of Aldermen of the largest city in this country its attempted enforcement. In order to enforce prohibition in New York City I estimated at the time would require a police force of 250,000 men and a force of 200,000 men to police the police.

3. The W.C.T.U. Upholds Prohibition (1926)

Before the same Senate judiciary subcommittee, and from the same metropolitan area as La Guardia, appeared Mrs. Ella A. Boole, president of the National Woman's Christian Temperance Union. A member of the D.A.R., a Ph.D. from the University of Wooster, and a Presbyterian, she had run unsuccessfully for the United States Senate on the Prohibition ticket in 1920. Locate the parts of her testimony that are least susceptible of proof, and comment critically on her views as to the desirability of enforcing unpopular laws, despite widespread flouting.

You have listened to testimony of shocking conditions due to corruption of officials, and lack of enforcement, some of which suggested no remedy except a surrender to those who violate the law, while the propaganda of all these organizations is encouraging continued violation. Permit me to show another side of the picture, and propose that instead of lowering our standards we urge that the law be strengthened, and in that way notice be served on law violators that America expects her laws to be enforced and to be obeyed. . . .

Enforcement has never had a fair trial. Political patronage, leakage through the permit system, connivance at the violation of law, and spread of the propaganda that it is not obligatory to obey a law unless you believe in it, and to the effect that the responsibility for the enforcement of law rested with the officers alone, when it should be shared by the individual citizen, have materially hindered the work of enforcement—all this with the result that the United States has not derived from prohibition what it would have derived had all the people observed the law and had there been hearty cooperation of the press and the people. . . .

It is not easy to get at the facts about the effect of prohibition on health, morals, and economic [life] because they are interwoven with other causes, and partial statistics may be misleading. But the elimination of a preventable cause of poverty, crime, tuberculosis, the diseases of middle life, unhappy homes, and financial depression brings results insofar as the law is observed and enforced. . . .

The closing of the open saloon with its doors swinging both ways, an ever-present invitation for all to drink—men, women, and boys—is an outstanding fact, and no one wants it to return. It has resulted in better national health, children are born under better conditions, homes are better, and

3. *Ibid.,* pp. 1068–71.

the mother is delivered from the fear of a drunken husband. There is better food. Savings-banks deposits have increased, and many a man has a bank account to-day who had none in the days of the saloon.

The increase in home owning is another evidence that money wasted in drink is now used for the benefit of the family. Improved living conditions are noticeable in our former slum districts. The Bowery and Hell's Kitchen are transformed.

Safety-first campaigns on railroads and in the presence of the increasing number of automobiles are greatly strengthened by prohibition.

The prohibition law is not the only law that is violated. Traffic laws, anti-smuggling laws, as well as the Volstead [prohibition] Act, are held in contempt. It is the spirit of the age.

Life-insurance companies have long known that drinkers were poor risks, but they recognize the fact that prohibition has removed a preventable cause of great financial loss to them.

The wonderful advances in mechanics in the application of electricity and in transportation demand brains free from the fumes of alcohol, hence law enforcement and law observance contribute to this progress. . . .

Your attention has been called to the failures. We claim these have been the result of lax enforcement. The machinery of enforcement should be strengthened.

[*The federal enforcement machinery finally broke down, and the 18th Amendment was repealed in 1933. Prohibition had done much good but at a staggering cost. In addition to the evils already noted, gangsterism was flourishing; the courts and jails were clogged; non-bulky hard liquor was replacing light wines and beer; and the cause of temperance was receiving a severe setback. With repeal, the control of liquor went back to state and local governments.*]

E. THE MUDSLINGERS OF 1928

1. Al Smith Denounces Bigotry (1928)

Coolidge cautiously bowed out in 1928, and the Republicans nominated Herbert Hoover, the famed humanitarian. The Democrats chose Governor Alfred E. Smith of New York, a Catholic and a "wet," in the face of furious opposition from the normally Democratic Solid South—a stronghold of anti-Catholic Ku Klux Klanism, of Protestant Fundamentalism, and of prohibition (at least for Negroes). Smith was falsely accused of being so drunk when he gave radio speeches that he had to be held up by two men. Pictures showing him present at the opening of the Holland Tunnel (under the Hudson River) were used to "prove" that he was constructing a secret passageway to the Vatican under the ocean. In a flaming speech at Oklahoma City, before a hostile Protestant crowd, Smith openly tackled the religious issue. Determine how convincingly he answers the main charge of his critics.

I feel that I owe it to the Democratic Party to talk out plainly. If I had listened to the counselors that advised political expediency I would prob-

1. New York *Times,* Sept. 21, 1928.

ably keep quiet, but I'm not by nature a quiet man. [Laughter and applause.]

I never keep anything to myself. I talk it out. And I feel I owe it, not only to the party, but I sincerely believe that I owe it to the country itself to drag this un-American propaganda out into the open. Because this country, to my way of thinking, cannot be successful if it ever divides on sectarian lines. [Applause.]

If there are any considerable number of our people that are going to listen to appeals to their passion and to their prejudice, if bigotry and intolerance and their sister vices are going to succeed, it is dangerous for the future life of the Republic, and the best way to kill anything un-American is to drag it out into the open; because anything un-American cannot live in the sunlight. [Applause.] . . .

Now there is another lie, or series of lies, being carefully put out around the country, and it is surprising to find the number of people who seem to believe it. I would have refrained from talking about this if it were not for the avalanche of letters that have poured into the National Committee, and have poured into my own office in the Executive Department at Albany, asking for the facts.

And that is the lie that has been spread around that since I have been Governor of the State of New York nobody has even been appointed to office but Catholics. [Loud noises.]

We are losing time on the radio. Please wait.

The cabinet of the Governorship is made up of fourteen men. Three of them are Catholics, ten of them are Protestants, and one of them is a Jew. [Applause.]

Outside of the cabinet members, the Governor appoints two boards and commissions under the cabinet, twenty-six people. Twelve of them are Protestants.

Aside from that, various other State officials, making up boards and commissions, were appointed by the Governor, making a total of 157 appointments, of which 35 were Catholics, 106 were Protestants, 12 were Jewish, and four we were unable to find out about. . . .

Now just another word and I am going to finish. Here [a circular] is the meanest thing that I have seen in the whole campaign. This is the product of the lowest and most cunning mind that could train itself to do something mean or dirty.

This was sent to me by a member of the Masonic Order, a personal friend of mine. It purports to be a circular sent out under Catholic auspices to Catholic voters, and tells how "we have control in New York; stick together and we'll get control of the country."

And designedly, it said to the roster of the Masonic Order in my State, because so many members of that order are friends of mine and have been voting for me for the last ten years, "Stand together."

Now, I disown that circular; the Democratic Party disowns it; and I have no right to talk for the Catholic Church, but I'll take a chance and say that nobody inside the Catholic Church has been stupid enough to do a thing like that. [Applause.]

Let me make myself perfectly clear. I do not want any Catholic in the United States of America to vote for me on the 6th of November because I am a Catholic. [Applause.]

If any Catholic in this country believes that the welfare, the well-being, the prosperity, the growth, and the expansion of the United States is best conserved and best promoted by the election of Hoover, I want him to vote for Hoover and not for me. [Applause.]

But, on the other hand, I have the right to say that any citizen of this country that believes I can promote its welfare, that I am capable of steering the ship of State safely through the next four years, and then votes against me because of my religion, he is not a real, pure, genuine American. [Applause.]

2. Hoover Analyzes the Campaign (1952)

Mud was also flung at Hoover, who had spent much of his adult life abroad. He was accused of being a naturalized British subject ("Lord Hoover," sneered Mencken), of having acquired his mining fortune by crooked means, and of hiring cheap Oriental labor. A faked photograph showed a sign on a gatepost of his California ranch: "NO WHITE HELP WANTED." In his *Memoirs* Hoover notes that he was reared a Quaker—a sect that has suffered much persecution—and that he came out bluntly for tolerance in his speech of acceptance. He then gives his assessment of the campaign. (He modestly refrains from saying that his stature as a candidate, buttressed by world fame, was much more impressive than his opponent's.) Comment critically on Hoover's interpretation, and explain why the religious issue has been given too much blame for the outcome.

Governor Smith unwittingly fanned the flame in an address in Oklahoma against intolerance. He insisted that religious faith did not disqualify any man from public office. He was right. But up to that moment it had been an underground issue. The Governor thought that he would gain by bringing it out into the open. The result, however, was to embattle the bigoted Protestants in the open, particularly in the South.

I reprimanded many of those who agitated this question. On the occasion of a violent letter sent out from a Virginia organization,* I issued the following public statement: "Whether this letter is authentic or a forgery, it does violence to every instinct that I possess. I resent and repudiate it.

---

2. *The Memoirs of Herbert Hoover: The Cabinet and the Presidency, 1920–1933* (1952), pp. 208–09. Reprinted with permission of The Macmillan Company. Copyright 1952, 1961 by Herbert Hoover.

* Mrs. W. W. Caldwell, Republican National Committeewoman from Virginia, published a letter in the Washington *Post* saying: "We must save the United States from being Romanized and rum-ridden, and the call is to the women to do so." (Quoted in *Literary Digest*, XCIX, 9 [Oct. 13, 1928].) The allusion is evidently to the cry "Rum, Romanism, and Rebellion" during the Cleveland-Blaine campaign of 1884.

Such an attitude is entirely opposed to every principle of the Republican party. I made my position clear in my acceptance speech. I meant that then and I mean it now."

Later in the campaign I said on September 28, with reference to circulars in other parts of the country: "I cannot fully express my indignation at any such circulars. Nor can I reiterate too strongly that religious questions have no part in this campaign. I have repeatedly stated that neither I nor the Republican party want support on that basis. There are important and vital reasons for the return of the Republican administration, but this is not one of them."

Governor Smith was a prominent member of Tammany.* During the campaign he made a speech at the Hall eulogizing the organization, apparently believing that he could whitewash it. In so doing he certainly made it fair game for grass-roots debate. I never referred to it.

The issues which defeated the Governor were general prosperity, prohibition, the farm tariffs, Tammany, and the "snuggling" up of the Socialists. Had he been a Protestant, he would certainly have lost and might even have had a smaller vote. An indication of the small importance of the religious issue in final results was the vote in New York State. Here Governor Smith, a Catholic, had been twice elected Governor, and therefore no great amount of religious bigotry could have existed. It was for other reasons than his Catholicism that his own state rejected him for President.

In fact, the religious issue had no weight in the final result. I carried all but eight states. In four or five Southern states it may have had weight on my side, although the prohibition and Tammany issues were of far more influence there. As against this the Catholic votes in all states no doubt went preponderantly for Governor Smith, as evidenced by the fact that he carried Massachusetts, traditionally a Republican state, where the Catholics were stronger than in any other state in the Union.

THOUGHT PROVOKERS

1. Observers spoke of "the Coolidge luck." Comment. Would Coolidge have been regarded as a successful President if he had served at any other time?

2. It has been said that cancellation of the Allied war debts was theoretically desirable but practically impossible. Explain. Is it true that the United States (unlike the Allies) got nothing out of the war?

3. Should the taxpayer determine what shall be taught in the public schools, even false doctrines? If not, who should have this power?

4. What grounds are there for the complaint of the prohibitionists that prohibition was never given a fair trial? Could it have been given a fair trial in the America of that era (1919–1933)? Is a citizen morally bound to accept a law that he regards as wrong, even though passed by the majority?

5. In what respects is a Catholic presidential candidate both helped and hurt by his religious affiliation? The Constitution says (Art. VI, para. 3): ". . . No

---

* Tammany Hall: a powerful Democratic organization in New York City, often associated with unsavory politics.

religious test shall ever be required as a qualification to any office or public trust under the United States." Was this provision violated in the election of 1928?

FURTHER EXPLORATION

General: J. D. Hicks, *Republican Ascendancy, 1921–1933* (1960); F. L. Allen, *Only Yesterday* (1931); P. W. Slosson, *The Great Crusade and After, 1914–1928* (1930). **Coolidge:** C. M. Fuess, *Calvin Coolidge* (1940); W. A. White, *A Puritan in Babylon* (1938). **Debtors:** H. G. Moulton and Leo Pasvolsky, *War Debts and World Prosperity* (1932); B. H. Williams, *Economic Foreign Policy of the United States* (1929). **Monkey Business:** S. N. Grebstein, ed., *Monkey Trial* (1960); Ray Ginger, *Six Days or Forever?* (1958). **Wets:** Charles Merz, *The Dry Decade* (1931); J. H. Lyle, *The Dry and Lawless Years* (1960); Andrew Sinclair, *Prohibition* (1962). **Mudslingers:** E. A. Moore, *A Catholic Runs for President* (1956); A. E. Smith, *Up to Now* (1929); Oscar Handlin, *Al Smith and His America* (1958).

Recent: Selig Adler, *The Uncertain Giant: 1921–1941, American Foreign Policy Between the Wars* (1965); D. R. McCoy, *Calvin Coolidge* (1967); L. W. Levine, *Defender of the Faith, William Jennings Bryan: The Last Decade, 1915–1925* (1965); J. R. Tompkins, ed., *D-Days at Dayton: Reflections on the Scopes Trial* (1965); Ruth C. Silva, *Rum, Religion, and Votes: 1928 Re-examined* (1962).

Chapter 41

Hooverism and the Depression

While I can make no claim for having introduced the term "rugged individualism," I should be proud to have invented it.

HERBERT HOOVER, 1934

PROLOGUE: The stock market crash of 1929 heralded the first phase of the Great Depression. The Hoover administration sponsored a new tariff designed to help the farmer, but the resulting Hawley-Smoot hodgepodge merely worsened the stagnation. Economic catastrophe came with the financial collapse of Europe in 1931. The Allied debtors defaulted, the dictators rose, Japan staged imperialistic coups in the Far East, and naval disarmament broke down. Hoover grimly strove to alleviate the distress produced by the Depression. But he was handicapped by his philosophy of rugged individualism, by the time-sanctified policy of hands off in Washington, and, during his last two years, by a Democratic majority in the House. Desperately trying to balance the budget, he opposed bonus handouts to veterans and extravagant public works projects for the unemployed. As the ragged army of jobless mounted to some 15,000,000, he was swept out of office by Franklin Roosevelt in the electoral landslide of 1932.

A. THE HAWLEY-SMOOT TARIFF CONTROVERSY

1. Roosevelt Attacks Tariff Hikers (1932)

During the presidential campaign of 1928, the politically naïve Hoover was stampeded into promising a special session of Congress for "farm relief and limited changes in the tariff." But the manufacturers' lobbyists moved in, including the notorious Joseph R. Grundy of Pennsylvania, whom the governor appointed to the United States Senate in the midst of the fight. The resulting Hawley-Smoot Tariff of 1930, passed some nine months *after* the start of the Great Depression, was one of the highest thus far in the average percentage of rates on dutiable goods. Governor Franklin Roosevelt of New York, then grooming himself for the Democratic presidential nomination, declared in the following speech that the new tariff law had plunged America (and the world) deeper into the doldrums. Locate the ten criticisms that Roosevelt makes of the tariff, and determine which one or ones are most unfair to Hoover, the Great Engineer in politics.

The Republican Administration has greatly intensified the depression by its tariff policy. The Hawley-Smoot tariff law of 1930 was a drastic revision of the tariff upward. The existing tariff levels were already high enough to protect American industries which needed protection. The increases which the Hawley-Smoot bill made were not based on any scientific analysis

1. *The Public Papers and Addresses of Franklin D. Roosevelt* (1938), I, 636–37 (speech at St. Paul, April 18, 1932). By permission of Random House.

784

of tariffs. The increases were political favors—in large measure to contributors to the Republican campaign fund.

The consequences of the Hawley-Smoot bill have been tremendous, both directly and indirectly. Directly, American foreign trade has been steadily dwindling. Indirectly, the high schedules of the Hawley-Smoot bill caused European Nations to raise their own tariff walls, and those walls were raised not only against us but against each other. The result has been that the value of goods exchanged internationally in the last year or so has been less than fifty percent of what it was three or four years ago.

When the Hawley-Smoot bill was passed, European States were endeavoring to negotiate reciprocal arrangements which might have caused the lowering of European tariff walls. Our action prevented such an arrangement, and since 1930, when Congress acted and the President signed the law, European tariff barriers have gone higher and higher. This means a lower standard of living in many quarters, because prosperity exists only when goods are exchanged internationally.

Just before the Hawley-Smoot bill was presented to President Hoover for his signature, a thousand American economists told President Hoover that he should not sign the law. I am told that never before in history have so many economists been able to agree upon anything. But the faults of this bill were so open and palpable that they found easy agreement. With really prophetic insight they warned him in detail of what would happen, and the detail that they gave him is the detail of what has happened: no benefit to the farmers; injury to American export trade; weakening of the security of American investments abroad; increase of unemployment; and encouragement of a world-wide tariff war.

President Hoover ignored this warning. Would he have ignored a warning by a thousand engineers that a bridge which the national Government was building was unsafe?

2. Hoover Defends the Tariff (1932)

Hoover had signed the Hawley-Smoot tariff bill in the face of protests from domestic producers and some thirty foreign governments. At the same time he praised its few redeeming features, including the flexibility introduced by the Tariff Commission. By averaging the dutiable goods with those that came in free, he argued that this tariff was one of the lowest in America's recent history. But if a nation levies such high tariffs on certain goods that they can no longer be imported, then the percentage of dutiable goods falls while that of non-dutiable goods rises. Hoover deeply resented Roosevelt's attacks on the "Hoover-Grundy tariff" in the presidential campaign of 1932. He warned the people that "the grass will grow in the streets of a hundred cities" if tariff protection were removed. In a campaign speech he defended himself as follows. Discover the most serious fallacy and the most telling point in this speech. Did the new tariff cause the world-wide depression, worsen it, or leave it unaffected?

2. New York *Times,* Oct. 16, 1932 (speech at Cleveland, Oct. 15, 1932).

I now come to the amazing statements that the tariff bill of 1930 has borne a major influence in this débâcle.

I quote from the Democratic candidate [Roosevelt]:

"The Hawley-Smoot tariff is one of the most important factors in the present world-wide depression."

"It has destroyed international commerce."

"The tariff has done so much to destroy foreign trade as to make foreign trade virtually impossible."

I shall analyze the accuracy of these statements, not only because I should like to get before my countrymen a picture of the lack of understanding which the Democratic party has of world trade, but also for the further reason that it is of vital importance to labor. . . . It means that if they [the Democrats] are intrusted with control of our government they intend to break down the protective tariff, which is the very first line of defense of the American standard of living against these new forces.

It requires a collection of dull facts to demonstrate the errors in these bald assertions by Democratic leaders.

At the beginning, I may repeat that this tariff bill was not passed until nine months after the economic depression began in the United States, and also not until twenty other countries had already gone into the depression.

The Democratic party seldom mentions that 66 per cent of our imports are free of duty, but that is the fact. From half to two-thirds of the trade of the world is in non-dutiable goods—that is, mostly raw materials; another part is in luxuries, upon which all nations collect tariffs for revenue; another part, and probably less than one-third of the whole, is in competitive goods so far as the importing nation is concerned, and therefore subject to protective tariffs.

The trade of the world has distressingly diminished under the impact of these successive dislocations abroad. But the decrease is almost exactly the same in the free goods everywhere as in the dutiable goods. That is the case in the United States. If the Smoot-Hawley tariff reduced our imports of dutiable goods, what was it that reduced the two-thirds of non-dutiable goods? . . .

I can explore this in still another direction. I remind you that we levy tariffs upon only one-third of our imports. I also remind you that the actual increases made in the Smoot-Hawley Act covered only one-quarter of the dutiable imports. I may also remind you that our import trade is only one-eighth of the import trade of the world. So they would have us believe this world catastrophe and this destruction of foreign trade happened because the United States increased tariffs on one-fourth of one-third of one-eighth of the world's imports. Thus we pulled down the world, so they tell us, by increasing duties on less than 1 per cent of the goods being imported by the world.

[*During the 1932 campaign Roosevelt declared that the Hoover tariff had resulted in retaliatory barriers, including those of Canada on both asparagus and peaches from the state of Washington. Hoover replied that 2,000,000 cheap Mexican cattle were ready to stampede across the border as soon as the tariff fences fell. He also insisted that a number of countries had raised their tariffs before the Hawley-Smoot Act was passed. Roosevelt agreed, but contended that such action was retaliation for the hardly less high Republican Fordney-McCumber Tariff of 1922. He correctly added that the new legislation had forced numerous American companies to go abroad and locate their factories inside the new tariff walls. At all events, the Hawley-Smoot Tariff seems to have accelerated a world-wide trend toward tariff spite fences.]*

B. THE DEEPENING DEPRESSION

1. The Plague of Plenty (1932)

In his acceptance speech of 1928, delivered in the Stanford University football stadium, Hoover optimistically envisioned the day when poverty would be banished from America. A popular Republican slogan was "A Chicken in Every Pot, a Car in Every Garage." The next year the stock market collapsed and depression descended. Hoover was a "rugged individualist" who had pulled himself up by his own bootstraps, and he was unwilling to turn Washington into a gigantic soup kitchen for the unemployed. He struggled desperately to halt the Depression, but in general his efforts were too little and too late. To boost morale, he issued a number of cheery statements to the effect that prosperity was just around the corner. The following testimony of a newspaper editor, Oscar Ameringer of Oklahoma City, was given in 1932 before a House committee. Note the numerous paradoxical features of his description, and locate the greatest paradox of all.

During the last three months I have visited, as I have said, some twenty states of this wonderfully rich and beautiful country. Here are some of the things I heard and saw:

In the state of Washington I was told that the forest fires raging in that region all summer and fall were caused by unemployed timber workers and bankrupt farmers in an endeavor to earn a few honest dollars as fire-fighters. The last thing I saw on the night I left Seattle was numbers of women searching for scraps of food in the refuse piles of the principal market of that city. A number of Montana citizens told me of thousands of bushels of wheat left in the fields uncut on account of its low price that hardly paid for the harvesting. In Oregon I saw thousands of bushels of apples rotting in the orchards. Only absolute[ly] flawless apples were still salable, at from 40 to 50 cents a box containing 200 apples. At the same time, there are millions of children who, on account of the poverty of their parents, will not eat one apple this winter.

While I was in Oregon the Portland *Oregonian* bemoaned the fact that thousands of ewes were killed by the sheep raisers because they did not bring enough in the market to pay the freight on them. And while Oregon sheep raisers fed mutton to the buzzards, I saw men picking for meat scraps in the garbage cans in the cities of New York and Chicago. I talked to one

---

1. *Unemployment in the United States. Hearings before a Subcommittee of the Committee on Labor, House of Representatives, Seventy-second Congress, First Session, on H. R. 206 . . .* (1932), pp. 98–99.

TWO CHICKENS IN EVERY GARAGE

The "Hoover Depression" brought a parody of the Republican slogan
of 1928: "A chicken in every pot and two cars in every garage."
Reprinted courtesy New York *World-Telegram,* copyright 1932.

man in a restaurant in Chicago. He told me of his experience in raising
sheep. He said that he had killed 3,000 sheep this fall and thrown them
down the canyon, because it cost $1.10 to ship a sheep, and then he would
get less than a dollar for it. He said he could not afford to feed the sheep,
and he would not let them starve, so he just cut their throats and threw
them down the canyon.

The roads of the West and Southwest teem with hungry hitchhikers.
The camp fires of the homeless are seen along every railroad track. I saw
men, women, and children walking over the hard roads. Most of them
were tenant farmers who had lost their all in the late slump in wheat and
cotton. Between Clarksville and Russellville, Ark., I picked up a family.
The woman was hugging a dead chicken under a ragged coat. When I
asked her where she had procured the fowl, first she told me she had found
it dead in the road, and then added in grim humor, "They promised me a
chicken in the pot, and now I got mine."

In Oklahoma, Texas, Arkansas, and Louisiana I saw untold bales of cotton
rotting in the fields because the cotton pickers could not keep body and
soul together on 35 cents paid for picking 100 pounds. . . .

As a result of this appalling overproduction on the one side and the staggering underconsumption on the other side, 70 per cent of the farmers of Oklahoma were unable to pay the interests on their mortgages. Last week one of the largest and oldest mortgage companies in that state went into the hands of the receiver. In that and other states we have now the interesting spectacle of farmers losing their farms by foreclosure and mortgage companies losing their recouped holdings by tax sales.

The farmers are being pauperized by the poverty of industrial populations, and the industrial populations are being pauperized by the poverty of the farmers. Neither has the money to buy the product of the other, hence we have overproduction and underconsumption at the same time and in the same country.

I have not come here to stir you in a recital of the necessity for relief for our suffering fellow citizens. However, unless something is done for them and done soon, you will have a revolution on hand. And when that revolution comes it will not come from Moscow, it will not be made by the poor Communists whom our police are heading up regularly and efficiently. When the revolution comes it will bear the label "Laid in the U.S.A." and its chief promoters will be the people of American stock.

2. Distress in the South (1932)

As the Depression deepened, "Hooverville" shack towns sprang up and millions of footsore men sought non-existent jobs. Some sold apples on wind-swept street corners. Hoover, in his *Memoirs*, advances the improbable thesis that these people were exploited by the apple producers and that "Many persons left their jobs for the more profitable one of selling apples." The Negro—"the last hired and the first fired"—was especially hard hit, but the white sharecropper in the South was scarcely better off. Hoover's policy was that "no one shall starve in this country," but he was criticized for being more willing to use federal funds to supply seed for farmers and feed for animals than food for human beings. Congressman George Huddleston of Alabama thus described conditions in his state before a Senate committee. Form conclusions as to whether anyone really starved and as to what kinds of physical and psychic scars were inflicted.

We have a great many tenant farmers there [Alabama]. We have a great many Negro farmers, and practically all of them are tenants. Their ability to survive, to eat, to have a shelter, depends upon the ability of the landlord to supply them with the necessaries of life. They have a system under which they make a contract with the landlord to cultivate his land for the next year, and in the meantime he feeds them through the winter; and at the end of the year they gather their crops and pay for their supplies and rent, if they are able to do so. Conditions in agriculture have been such for several years that the landlords have been gradually impoverished, and their farms are mortgaged to the farm-loan system and to the mortgage companies in a multitude of instances.

2. *Unemployment Relief. Hearings before a Subcommittee of the Committee on Manufactures, United States Senate, Seventy-second Congress, First Session, on S. 174 . . .* (1932), pp. 244–45.

In a very large percentage [of cases] the landlord is now unable to finance these tenants for another year. He is unable to get the supplies. He has no security and no money with which to feed and clothe his tenants until they can make another crop. . . .

Many of these people, especially the Negro tenants, are now in the middle of a winter, practically without food and without clothes, and without anything else, and how are they going to live? Many of these local counties have no charitable organizations. They are poor people and impoverished. They have no county funds. There is no place to turn, nobody that has any money that they can turn to and ask for help.

Many white people are in the same kind of a situation. They beg around among their neighbors. The neighbors are poor and they have no means of helping them. They stray here and there.

Any thought that there has been no starvation, that no man has starved, and no man will starve, is the rankest nonsense. Men are actually starving by the thousands to-day, not merely in the general sections that I refer to, but throughout this country as a whole, and in my own district. I do not mean to say that they are sitting down and not getting a bite of food until they actually die, but they are living such a scrambling, precarious existence, with suffering from lack of clothing, fuel, and nourishment, until they are subject to be swept away at any time, and many are now being swept away.

The situation has possibilities of epidemics of various kinds. Its consequences will be felt many years. The children are being stunted by lack of food. Old people are having their lives cut short. The physical effects of the privations that they are forced to endure will not pass away within fifty years, and when the social and civic effects will pass away, only God knows. That is something that no man can estimate.

3. Rumbles of Revolution (1932)

Franklin Roosevelt was later acclaimed as the Messiah whose New Deal saved America for capitalism by averting armed revolution. He was quoted as saying that if he failed he would not be the worst but the last President of the United States. Certainly in 1932 the signs were ominous. Hundreds of Middle Western farmers were picketing the highways to keep their underpriced produce from reaching market, overturning milk trucks, overawing armed deputies, releasing prisoners from jail. With increasing millions of desperate men out of work, and with thousands defying the police, the worst might have happened. The testimony of Oscar Ameringer, the Oklahoma newspaperman, is impressive. Determine from it whether the talk of revolution was to be taken seriously.

Some time ago a cowman came into my office in Oklahoma City. He was one of these double-fisted gentlemen, with the gallon hat and all. He said, "You do not know me from Adam's ox."

3. *Unemployment in the United States. Hearings before a Subcommittee of the Committee on Labor, House of Representatives, Seventy-second Congress, First Session, on H. R. 206 . . .* (1932), pp. 100–01.

I said, "No; I do not believe I know you." . . .

He said, "I came to this country without a cent, but, knowing my onions, and by tending strictly to business, I finally accumulated two sections of land and a fine herd of white-faced Hereford cattle. I was independent."

I remarked that anybody could do that if he worked hard and did not gamble and used good management.

He said, "After the war, cattle began to drop, and I was feeding them corn, and by the time I got them to Chicago the price of cattle, considering the price of corn I had fed them, was not enough to even pay my expenses. I could not pay anything."

Continuing, he said, "I mortgaged my two sections of land, and to-day I am cleaned out; by God, I am not going to stand for it."

I asked him what he was going to do about it, and he said, "We have got to have a revolution here like they had in Russia and clean them up."

I finally asked him, "Who is going to make the revolution?"

He said, "I just want to tell you I am going to be one of them, and I am going to do my share in it."

I asked what his share was and he said, "I will capture a certain fort. I know I can get in with twenty of my boys," meaning his cowboys, "because I know the inside and outside of it, and I [will] capture that with my men."

I rejoined, "Then what?"

He said, "We will have 400 machine guns, so many batteries of artillery, tractors, and munitions and rifles, and everything else needed to supply a pretty good army."

Then I asked, "What then?"

He said, "If there are enough fellows with guts in this country to do like us, we will march eastward and we will cut the East off. We will cut the East off from the West. We have got the granaries; we have the hogs, the cattle, the corn; the East has nothing but mortgages on our places. We will show them what we can do."

That man may be very foolish, and I think he is, but he is in dead earnest; he is a hard-shelled Baptist and a hard-shelled Democrat, not a Socialist or a Communist, but just a plain American cattleman whose ancestors went from Carolina to Tennessee, then to Arkansas, and then to Oklahoma. I have heard much of this talk from serious-minded prosperous men of other days.

As you know, talk is always a mental preparation for action. Nothing is done until people talk and talk and talk it, and they finally get the notion that they will do it.

I do not say we are going to have a revolution on hand within the next year or two, perhaps never. I hope we may not have such; but the danger is here. That is the feeling of our people—as reflected in the letters I have read. I have met these people virtually every day all over the country. There is a feeling among the masses generally that something is radically wrong. They are despairing of political action. They say the only thing you do in Washington is to take money from the pockets of the poor and put it into the pockets of the rich. They say that this Government is a conspiracy against the common people to enrich the already rich. I hear such remarks every day.

I never pass a hitchhiker without inviting him in and talking to him. Bankers even are talking about that. They are talking in irrational tones. You have more Bolshevism among the bankers to-day than the hod carriers, I think. It is a terrible situation, and I think something should be done and done immediately.

C. HOOVER CLASHES WITH ROOSEVELT

1. On Public versus Private Power

a. Hoover Upholds Free Enterprise (1932)

Hoover, the wealthy conservative, instinctively shied away from anything suggesting socialism. In 1931 he emphatically vetoed the Muscle Shoals Bill, which would have put the federal government in the electric power business on the Tennessee River. (An expanded version later created the Tennessee Valley Authority [TVA] under President Roosevelt.) Hoover ringingly reaffirmed his basic position in a speech during the Hoover–Roosevelt presidential campaign of 1932. Explain why he is so strongly opposed to federally owned electric power, and why he would find local community ownership more acceptable.

I have stated unceasingly that I am opposed to the Federal Government going into the power business. I have insisted upon rigid regulation. The Democratic candidate has declared that under the same conditions which may make local action of this character desirable, he is prepared to put the Federal Government into the power business. He is being actively supported by a score of Senators in this campaign, many of whose expenses are being paid by the Democratic National Committee, who are pledged to Federal Government development and operation of electrical power.

I find in the instructions to campaign speakers issued by the Democratic National Committee that they are instructed to criticize my action in the veto of the bill which would have put the Government permanently into the operation of power at Muscle Shoals, with a capital from the Federal Treasury of over $100,000,000. In fact thirty-one Democratic Senators, being all except three, voted to override that veto.

In that bill was the flat issue of the Federal Government permanently in competitive business. I vetoed it because of principle and not because it especially applied to power business. In that veto, I stated that I was firmly opposed to the Federal Government entering into any business, the major purpose of which is competition with our citizens. . . .

From their utterances in this campaign and elsewhere it appears to me

1a. New York *Times,* Nov. 1, 1932 (speech at Madison Square Garden, New York, Oct. 31, 1932).

IT'S MIGHTY LUCKY FOR YOU SOME DEMOCRAT WASN'T DRIVING!

HOOVER'S CONSOLATION

The Republican argument that a less experienced Democratic driver might have fared worse had some plausibility. Omaha *World-Herald*, 1932.

that we are justified in the conclusion that our opponents propose to put the Federal Government in the power business.

b. Roosevelt Pushes Public Power (1932)

Franklin Roosevelt, who as governor of New York had shown much concern for the Niagara–St. Lawrence River power resources, had already locked horns with the private utility magnates. As President, he later had a large hand in launching the TVA project, which also involved fertilizer, flood control, and improved navigation. He presented his views on public power as follows during the campaign of 1932. Determine which of his points is the strongest, and whether his arguments are more convincing than Hoover's.

I therefore lay down the following principle: That where a community— a city or county or a district—is not satisfied with the service rendered or the rates charged by the private utility, it has the undeniable basic right, as one of its functions of government, one of its functions of home rule, to set up, after a fair referendum to its voters has been had, its own governmentally owned and operated service. . . .

My distinguished opponent is against giving the Federal Government, in any case, the right to operate its own power business. I favor giving the

1b. *Roosevelt's Public Papers*, I, 738, 741–42 (speech at Portland, Oregon, Sept. 21, 1932). By permission of Random House.

people this right where and when it is essential to protect them against inefficient service or exorbitant charges.

As an important part of this policy, the natural hydro-electric power resources belonging to the people of the United States, or the several States, shall remain forever in their possession.

To the people of this country I have but one answer on this subject. Judge me by the enemies I have made. Judge me by the selfish purposes of these utility leaders who have talked of radicalism while they were selling watered stock to the people, and using our schools to deceive the coming generation.

My friends, my policy is as radical as American liberty. My policy is as radical as the Constitution of the United States.

I promise you this: Never shall the Federal Government part with its sovereignty or with its control over its power resources, while I am President of the United States.

2. On Government in Business

a. Hoover Assails Federal Intervention (1932)

Hoover's conservative nature recoiled from the prospect of government in business, especially on the scale envisaged by the TVA. Annoyed by Democratic charges that he was a complete reactionary, he struck back in a major campaign speech at Madison Square Garden. Laboriously written by himself (he was the last President to scorn ghost writers), it was perhaps the best-conceived of his campaign. "Every time the Federal Government extends its arm," he declared, "531 Senators and Congressmen become actual boards of directors of that business." Decide what truth there is in his charge that government in business invites a species of servitude.

There is one thing I can say without any question of doubt—that is, that the spirit of liberalism is to create free men. It is not the regimentation of men. It is not the extension of bureaucracy. I have said in this city [New York] before now that you can not extend the mastery of government over the daily life of a people without somewhere making it master of people's souls and thoughts.

Expansion of government in business means that the Government, in order to protect itself from the political consequences of its errors, is driven irresistibly, without peace, to greater and greater control of the Nation's press and platform. Free speech does not live many hours after free industry and free commerce die.

It is a false liberalism that interprets itself into Government operation of business. Every step in that direction poisons the very roots of liberalism. It poisons political equality, free speech, free press, and equality of opportunity. It is the road not to liberty but to less liberty. True liberalism is found not in striving to spread bureaucracy, but in striving to set bounds to it. . . .

Even if the Government conduct of business could give us the maximum

2a. New York *Times,* Nov. 1, 1932 (speech at Madison Square Garden, New York, Oct. 31, 1932).

of efficiency instead of least efficiency, it would be purchased at the cost of freedom. It would increase rather than decrease abuse and corruption, stifle initiative and invention, undermine development of leadership, cripple mental and spiritual energies of our people, extinguish equality of opportunity, and dry up the spirit of liberty and progress.

Men who are going about this country announcing that they are liberals because of their promises to extend the Government in business are not liberals; they are reactionaries of the United States.

b. Roosevelt Attacks Business in Government (1932)

The Reconstruction Finance Corporation (R.F.C.), established late in the Hoover administration, was designed primarily to bail out hard-pressed banks and other big businesses—"a bread line for bankers." Charles G. Dawes, former Vice-President of the United States, hastily resigned as the head of the R.F.C. so that his Chicago bank might secure an emergency loan of $80,000,000 to stave off bankruptcy. The Democrats, who argued that loans to ordinary citizens were no less imperative, attacked this presumed favoritism. In the light of the following campaign speech by Roosevelt, assess the consistency of the Republican cry that government should be divorced from business.

Some of my friends tell me that they do not want the Government in business. With this I agree; but I wonder whether they realize the implications of the past. For while it has been American doctrine that the Government must not go into business in competition with private enterprises, still it has been traditional, particularly in Republican administrations, for business urgently to ask the Government to put at private disposal all kinds of Government assistance.

The same man who tells you that he does not want to see the Government interfere in business—and he means it, and has plenty of good reasons for saying so—is the first to go to Washington and ask the Government for a prohibitory tariff on his product. When things get just bad enough, as they did two years ago, he will go with equal speed to the United States Government and ask for a loan; and the Reconstruction Finance Corporation is the outcome of it.

Each group has sought protection from the Government for its own special interests, without realizing that the function of Government must be to favor no small group at the expense of its duty to protect the rights of personal freedom and of private property of all its citizens.

3. On Balancing the Budget

a. Hoover Stresses Economy (1932)

Hoover, the Iowa orphan, was dedicated to strict economy, a sound dollar, and the balanced budget. He was alarmed by proposals in the Democratic House to unbalance the budget further by voting huge sums to provide jobs for the unemployed. One proposed public works scheme called for the construction of 2300 new

2b. *Roosevelt's Public Papers*, I, 748 (Commonwealth Club speech, San Francisco, Sept. 23, 1932). By permission of Random House.
3a. New York *Times*, May 28, 1932 (Washington press conference of May 27, 1932).

post offices. The upkeep and interest charges on these would cost $14,000,000 a year, whereas, as he noted, "the upkeep and rent of buildings at present in use amounts to less than $3,000,000." Hoover unburdened himself as follows at a press conference. In the light of subsequent developments, determine whether he over-stresses the effects of an unbalanced budget in relation to uneconomical public works. (Since 1932 the federal Treasury has more often than not shown an annual deficit.)

The urgent question today is the prompt balancing of the Budget. When that is accomplished, I propose to support adequate measures for relief of distress and unemployment.

In the meantime, it is essential that there should be an understanding of the character of the draft bill made public yesterday in the House of Representatives for this purpose. That draft bill supports some proposals we have already made in aid to unemployment, through the use of the Reconstruction Finance Corporation, to make loans for projects which have been in abeyance and which proposal makes no drain on the taxpayer. But in addition it proposes to expend about $900,000,000 for Federal public works.

I believe the American people will grasp the economic fact that such action would require appropriations to be made to the Federal Departments, thus creating a deficit in the Budget that could only be met with more taxes and more Federal bond issues. That makes balancing of the Budget hopeless.

The country also understands that an unbalanced budget means the loss of confidence of our own people and of other nations in the credit and stability of the Government, and that the consequences are national demoralization and the loss of ten times as many jobs as would be created by this program, even if it could be physically put into action. . . .

This is not unemployment relief. It is the most gigantic pork barrel ever proposed to the American Congress. It is an unexampled raid on the public Treasury.

b. Roosevelt Stresses Humanity (1932)

The Democratic platform of 1932, which assailed Republican extravagance and deficits, had come out squarely for a balanced budget. A favorite slogan of the Democrats was "Throw the Spenders Out." When Roosevelt died thirteen years later, the national debt (including war costs) had risen from some $19 billion to $258 billion. During the campaign of 1932 Roosevelt expressed his views on a balanced budget as follows. Decide whether he later kept faith with the voters.

Let us have the courage to stop borrowing to meet continuing deficits. Stop the deficits! Let us have equal courage to reverse the policy of the Republican leaders and insist on a sound currency. . . .

This dilemma can be met by saving in one place what we would spend in others, or by acquiring the necessary revenue through taxation. Revenues must cover expenditures by one means or another. Any Government, like

3b. *Roosevelt's Public Papers,* I, 662, 663, 810. (The first two paragraphs are taken from a radio address from Albany, July 30, 1932; the last paragraph is taken from a speech at Pittsburgh, Oct. 19, 1932.) By permission of Random House.

any family, can for a year spend a little more than it earns. But you and I know that a continuation of that habit means the poorhouse. . . .

The above two categorical statements are aimed at a definite balancing of the budget. At the same time, let me repeat from now to election day so that every man, woman, and child in the United States will know what I mean: If starvation and dire need on the part of any of our citizens make necessary the appropriation of additional funds which would keep the budget out of balance, I shall not hesitate to tell the American people the full truth and ask them to authorize the expenditure of that additional amount.

4. On Restricted Opportunity

a. Roosevelt Urges Welfare Statism (1932)

"Why Change?" cried Republicans in the campaign of 1932. "Things Could Be Worse." A slight business upturn did occur in the summer, but a sag soon followed, owing, claimed Hoover, to fear of a Rooseveltian revolution. Roosevelt himself jeered that the "No Change" argument was like saying, "Do not swap toboggans while you are sliding downhill." He set forth his own concept of change in his memorable Commonwealth Club speech in San Francisco. Ascertain whether his argument regarding the overbuilding of America's industrial plant is sound in the light of subsequent history.

A glance at the situation today only too clearly indicates that equality of opportunity, as we have known it, no longer exists. Our industrial plant is built; the problem just now is whether under existing conditions it is not overbuilt.

Our last frontier has long since been reached, and there is practically no more free land. More than half of our people do not live on the farms or on lands, and cannot derive a living by cultivating their own property. There is no safety valve in the form of a Western prairie, to which those thrown out of work by the Eastern economic machines can go for a new start.* We are not able to invite the immigration from Europe to share our endless plenty. We are now providing a drab living for our own people. . . .

Recently a careful study was made of the concentration of business in the United States. It showed that our economic life was dominated by some six hundred odd corporations, who controlled two-thirds of American industry. Ten million small business men divided the other third. More striking still, it appeared that if the process of concentration goes on at the same rate, at the end of another century we shall have all American industry controlled by a dozen corporations, and run by perhaps a hundred men. Put plainly, we are steering a steady course toward economic oligarchy, if we are not there already.

Clearly, all this calls for a re-appraisal of values. A mere builder of more industrial plants, a creator of more railroad systems, an organizer of more

4a. *Ibid.,* I, 750–53 (speech of Sept. 23, 1932). By permission of Random House.
* For the safety-valve notion, see earlier, p. 560.

corporations, is as likely to be a danger as a help. The day of the great promoter or the financial Titan, to whom we granted anything if only he would build, or develop, is over.

Our task now is not discovery or exploitation of natural resources, or necessarily producing more goods. It is the soberer, less dramatic business of administering resources and plants already in hand, of seeking to re-establish foreign markets for our surplus production, of meeting the problem of underconsumption, of adjusting production to consumption, of distributing wealth and products more equitably, of adapting existing economic organizations to the service of the people. The day of enlightened administration has come.

b. Hoover Calls for New Frontiers (1932)

Roosevelt's annoying vagueness prompted Hoover to refer to "a chameleon on plaid." Smarting from the New Dealish overtones of the Commonwealth Club speech, Hoover struck back in his Madison Square Garden speech. Decide whether he interpreted America's past and future with greater fidelity than Roosevelt.

1932's SOAP BOX

The Republicans shift ground from 1928 to 1932. St. Louis *Post-Dispatch*, 1932.

But I do challenge the whole idea that we have ended the advance of America, that this country has reached the zenith of its power, the height of its development. That is the counsel of despair for the future of America. That is not the spirit by which we shall emerge from this depression. That is not the spirit that made this country. If it is true, every American must abandon the

4b. New York *Times*, Nov. 1, 1932 (speech at Madison Square Garden, New York, Oct. 31, 1932).

road of countless progress and unlimited opportunity. I deny that the promise of American life has been fulfilled, for that means we have begun the decline and fall. No nation can cease to move forward without degeneration of spirit.

I could quote from gentlemen who have emitted this same note of pessimism in economic depressions going back for a hundred years. What Governor Roosevelt has overlooked is the fact that we are yet but on the frontiers of development of science, and of invention. I have only to remind you that discoveries in electricity, the internal-combustion engine, the radio —all of which have sprung into being since our land was settled—have in themselves represented the greatest advances in America.

This philosophy upon which the Governor of New York proposes to conduct the Presidency of the United States is the philosophy of stagnation, of despair. It is the end of hope. The destinies of this country should not be dominated by that spirit in action. It would be the end of the American system.

D. AN APPRAISAL OF HOOVER

1. Hoover Defends His Record (1932)

Hoover smarted under charges that he had not fought the "Hoover depression" with every ounce of energy for the benefit of all the people. Such accusations, he asserted, were "deliberate, intolerable falsehoods." At times he put in an eighteen-hour day, remarking that his office was a "compound hell." When he spoke wearily at St. Paul during the last stages of the campaign of 1932, a man was stationed behind him ready to thrust forward an empty chair if he collapsed. In a major speech at Des Moines, Iowa, he thus refuted charges that he was a "see-nothing, do-nothing President." Note what is the least convincing part of this recital.

We have fought an unending war against the effect of these calamities upon our people. This is no time to recount the battles on a thousand fronts. We have fought the good fight to protect our people in a thousand cities from hunger and cold.

We have carried on an unceasing campaign to protect the Nation from that unhealing class bitterness which arises from strikes and lockouts and industrial conflict. We have accomplished this through the willing agreement of employer and labor, which placed humanity before money through the sacrifice of profits and dividends before wages.

We have defended millions from the tragic result of droughts.

We have mobilized a vast expansion of public construction to make work for the unemployed.

We [have] fought the battle to balance the Budget.

We have defended the country from being forced off the gold standard, with its crushing effect upon all who are in debt.

We have battled to provide a supply of credits to merchants and farmers and industries.

1. *Ibid.,* Oct. 5, 1932 (speech of Oct. 4, 1932).

We have fought to retard falling prices.

We have struggled to save homes and farms from foreclosure of mortgages; battled to save millions of depositors and borrowers from the ruin caused by the failure of banks; fought to assure the safety of millions of policyholders from failure of their insurance companies; and fought to save commerce and employment from the failure of railways.

We have fought to secure disarmament and maintain the peace of the world; fought for stability of other countries whose failure would inevitably injure us. And, above all, we have fought to preserve the safety, the principles, and ideals of American life. We have builded the foundations of recovery. . . .

Thousands of our people in their bitter distress and losses today are saying that "things could not be worse." No person who has any remote understanding of the forces which confronted this country during these last eighteen months ever utters that remark. Had it not been for the immediate and unprecedented actions of our government, things would be infinitely worse today.

2. Roosevelt Indicts Hoover (1932)

Roosevelt did not use kid gloves in his ghostwritten campaign speeches. (That at Topeka represented his own efforts and those of some twenty-five assistants.) Although crediting Hoover with "unremitting efforts," he assailed him for having claimed credit for prosperity while disclaiming discredit for the Depression; for having placed the blame for the Depression on wicked foreigners instead of on shortsighted Republican economic policies; for having marked time and issued airily optimistic statements when he should have grasped the bull by the horns. At Pittsburgh, Roosevelt cried, "I do indict this Administration for wrong action, for delayed action, for lack of frankness and for lack of courage." At Columbus, Ohio, he presented the following bill of particulars. Ascertain the unfairest part of his indictment.

Finally, when facts could no longer be ignored and excuses had to be found, Washington discovered that the depression came from abroad. In October of last year, the official policy came to us as follows: "The depression has been deepened by events from abroad which are beyond the control either of our citizens or our Government"—an excuse, note well, my friends, which the President still maintained in his acceptance speech last week.

Not for partisan purposes, but in order to set forth history aright, that excuse ought to be quietly considered. The records of the civilized Nations of the world prove two facts: first, that the economic structure of other Nations was affected by our own tide of speculation, and the curtailment of our lending helped to bring on their distress; second, that the bubble burst first in the land of its origin—the United States.

The major collapse in other countries followed. It was not simultaneous with ours. Moreover, further curtailment of our loans, plus the continual

2. *Roosevelt's Public Papers*, I, 677 (speech of Aug. 20, 1932). By permission of Random House.

stagnation in trade caused by the Grundy [Hawley-Smoot] tariff, has continued the depression throughout international affairs.

So I sum up the history of the present Administration in four sentences:

First, it encouraged speculation and overproduction, through its false economic policies.

Second, it attempted to minimize the [1929 stock market] crash and misled the people as to its gravity.

Third, it erroneously charged the cause to other Nations of the world.

And finally, it refused to recognize and correct the evils at home which had brought it forth; it delayed relief; it forgot reform.

THOUGHT PROVOKERS

1. Should the United States heed the protests of foreigners when it writes its tariff laws? The Hawley-Smoot Tariff has been called "a declaration of economic war against the whole of the civilized world." Comment critically.
2. Hoover urged self-help, private generosity, and local benefactions in handling the hungry unemployed, for he feared that federal handouts would impair "something infinitely valuable in the life of the American people" while striking at "the roots of self-government." Comment.
3. Would the objections to the government's entering the electric power business be applicable also in the case of the mail-carrying business? Do the people have a "natural right" to power sites pre-empted by private enterprise?
4. What truth is there in Hoover's accusation that liberals who demand more government in business are guilty of illiberalism?
5. Have unbalanced budgets and extravagant public works done more harm than good? Should Roosevelt have adhered strictly to the Democratic platform and his campaign promises?
6. What new frontiers have been opened since Roosevelt said that all frontiers were closed?
7. To what extent was Hoover to blame for the continuance of the Depression?

FURTHER EXPLORATION

General: J. D. Hicks, *Republican Ascendancy, 1921–1933* (1960); A. M. Schlesinger, Jr., *The Crisis of the Old Order, 1919–1933* (1957); F. L. Allen, *Since Yesterday* (1939); Dixon Wecter, *The Age of the Great Depression* (1948). **Tariff:** J. M. Jones, Jr., *Tariff Retaliation: Repercussions of the Hawley-Smoot Bill* (1934); Herbert Hoover, *Memoirs* (3 vols., 1952). **Depression:** Broadus Mitchell, *Depression Decade* (1947); J. K. Galbraith, *The Great Crash, 1929* (1955). **The Clash:** W. S. Myers and W. H. Newton, *The Hoover Administration* (1936); R. L. Wilbur and Arthur Hyde, *The Hoover Policies* (1937); Frank Freidel, *Franklin Roosevelt: The Triumph* (1956); R. V. Peel and T. C. Donnelly, *The 1932 Campaign* (1935). **Appraisal:** H. G. Warren, *Herbert Hoover and the Great Depression* (1959); Harold Wolfe, *Herbert Hoover* (1956).

Recent: A. U. Romasco, *The Poverty of Abundance: Hoover, the Nation, the Depression* (1965).

Chapter 42

Battling for the New Deal

I pledge you, I pledge myself, to a new deal for the American people.
FRANKLIN D. ROOSEVELT, ACCEPTING NOMINATION
OF DEMOCRATIC NATIONAL CONVENTION, 1932

PROLOGUE: Roosevelt boldly set up numerous New Deal agencies to provide relief, recovery, and reform. Ignored were the campaign pledges that he
would reduce government expenses, balance the budget, prune the bureaucracy,
maintain a sound currency, and eliminate the improper use of money in politics.
But Roosevelt honored other promises, directly or indirectly, in the reciprocal
tariff program, the Tennessee Valley Authority, the repeal of prohibition, the
insurance of bank deposits, and the encouragement of labor unions. Critics of the
New Deal cried that Roosevelt promoted class hatred by setting the poor against
the rich. New Dealers retorted that they were merely putting need above greed.
The voters endorsed Roosevelt so resoundingly at the polls in 1934 and 1936
that he was emboldened to unveil his scheme for "packing" the Supreme Court
in 1937. Although soundly rebuffed, he won an unprecedented third-term election
in 1940, with a strong assist from the crisis in Europe and a new war-born prosperity.

A. AN ENIGMA IN THE WHITE HOUSE

1. The Agreeable F.D.R. (1949)

The gay, smiling, wisecracking Franklin Roosevelt could occasionally be brutal
when he got his "Dutch up," but ordinarily he recoiled from hurting people's feelings.
Senator Huey Long complained, "I wonder if he says 'Fine!' to everybody." This
trait of ultra-agreeableness led visitors to suspect a lack of candor and truthfulness.
In the following account from Mrs. Roosevelt's memoirs, note particularly why the
President was often misunderstood.

The few books that have already been written about Franklin show quite
plainly that everyone writes from his own point of view, and that a man
like my husband, who was particularly susceptible to people, took color
from whomever he was with, giving to each one something different of
himself. Because he disliked being disagreeable, he made an effort to give
each person who came in contact with him the feeling that he understood
what his particular interest was. . . .

Often people have told me that they were misled by Franklin. Even

1. Eleanor Roosevelt, *This I Remember* (1949), p. 2. Reprinted by permission of Harper
and Brothers and Mr. Elliott Roosevelt.

when they have not said it in so many words, I have sometimes felt that he left them, after an interview, with the idea that he was in entire agreement with them. I would know quite well, however, that he was not, and that they would be very much surprised when later his actions were in complete contradiction to what they thought his attitude would be.

This misunderstanding not only arose from his dislike of being disagreeable, but from the interest that he always had in somebody else's point of view and his willingness to listen to it. If he thought it was well expressed and clear, he nodded his head and frequently said, "I see," or something of the sort. This did not mean that he was convinced of the truth of the arguments, or even that he entirely understood them, but only that he appreciated the way in which they were presented.

2. Coffee for the Veterans (1933)

In 1932, during Hoover's last year as President, some 30,000 unemployed veterans had descended upon Washington to obtain advance bonus payments from Congress. They occupied vacant buildings, erected makeshift camps without proper sanitation, and posed a threat to the public health and safety. A fearful Hoover, having doubled the White House guard, finally gave orders that resulted in their eviction by federal troops with bayonets, tear gas, and torches. A second, smaller bonus army came early in the Roosevelt administration, and Secretary of Labor Frances Perkins (the first woman Cabinet member) describes how Roosevelt welcomed them. Contrast the political instincts of Roosevelt with those of Hoover.

Like other kindhearted, liberal people, Roosevelt had been shocked by President Hoover's orders to drive veterans of World War I out of Anacostia Flats in Washington and to burn their encampment when they had marched there in protest in 1931 [1932]. He had been shocked that the President should fear his fellow citizens. His instinct had cried out that veterans in an illegal encampment in Washington, even if difficult and undesirable, must all be faced in a humane and decent way. He had said little, had just shaken his head and shuddered, when the incident took place.

When the veterans came to Washington in March 1933, in a similar, if smaller, march on the capital followed by an encampment, Roosevelt drove out and showed himself, waving his hat at them. He asked Mrs. Roosevelt and Louis Howe to go. "Above all," he said to them, "be sure there is plenty of good coffee. No questions asked. Just let free coffee flow all the time. There is nothing like it to make people feel better and feel welcome."

After the veterans in 1933 had the free coffee and a visit from Mrs. Roosevelt, they were willing to send a committee to talk with Howe. Gradually they began to go home, and relief funds were found to help them start back.

[*This was the last demonstration of its kind during these years.*]

2. Frances Perkins, *The Roosevelt I Knew* (1946), pp. 111–12. By permission of the Viking Press.

3. F.D.R. the Administrative "Artist" (1948)

The numerous and overlapping agencies of the New Deal created an atmosphere of indescribable confusion. Roosevelt was generally reputed to be a wretchedly bad administrator. Rather than face a disagreeable scene by dismissing an incompetent subordinate, he would set up a competing agency. Robert E. Sherwood, playwright and winner of three Pulitzer prizes, served with a government agency (Office of War Information) during World War II. He was forced to discharge one of his employees, and he here tells what happened when he reported this unpleasant incident to the President. Determine in what sense Roosevelt was both a poor administrator and a superior one.

Roosevelt now had an expression of open amazement and said, "I can't believe it. I can't believe you had the courage to fire anybody. I thought you were a complete softy—like me."

That scrap of highly unimportant conversation can indicate why those who knew Roosevelt well could never imagine him assuming the role of dictator. He could be and was ruthless and implacable with those whom he considered guilty of disloyalty; but with those in his Administration who were inefficient or even recalcitrant or hopelessly inept, but loyal, he was "a complete softy." He wasted precious hours of time and incalculable quantities of energy and ingenuity trying to find face-saving jobs—or "kicking upstairs" methods—for incompetents who should have been thrown out unceremoniously.

Roosevelt's methods of administration—typified in his handling of the work relief organization—were, to say the least, unorthodox. They filled some practical-minded observers with apprehension and dismay, and some with disgust; they filled others with awe and wonder. I am sure that no final appraisal of them can be made for a long time to come; but there is one thing that can be said about these methods—whether they were good or bad, sensible or insane, they *worked*.

While preparing this book I interviewed Harold Smith, who was Director of the Budget from 1939 to 1946. Smith was a modest, methodical, precise man, temperamentally far removed from Roosevelt and Hopkins. But I know of no one whose judgment and integrity and downright common sense the President trusted more completely. In the course of a long conversation, Smith said to me:

"A few months ago, on the first anniversary of Roosevelt's death, a magazine asked me to write an article on Roosevelt as an administrator. I thought it over and decided I was not ready to make such an appraisal. I've been thinking about it ever since. When I worked with Roosevelt—for six years—I thought, as did many others, that he was a very erratic administrator. But now, when I look back, I can really begin to see the size of his programs. They were by far the largest and most complex programs that any President ever put through. People like me who had the respon-

3. Robert E. Sherwood, *Roosevelt and Hopkins* (1948), pp. 72–73. Copyright 1948 by Robert E. Sherwood. Reprinted by permission of Harper and Brothers and Eyre and Spottiswoode, Ltd.

sibility of watching the pennies could only see the five or six or seven per cent of the programs that went wrong, through inefficient organization or direction. But now I can see in perspective the ninety-three or -four or -five per cent that went right—including the winning of the biggest war in history—because of unbelievably skillful organization and direction. And if I were to write that article now, I think I'd say that Roosevelt must have been one of the greatest geniuses as an administrator that ever lived. What we couldn't appreciate at the time was the fact that he was a real *artist* in government."

That word "artist" was happily chosen, for it suggests the quality of Roosevelt's extraordinary creative imagination. I think that he would have resented the application of the word as implying that he was an impractical dreamer; he loved to represent himself as a prestidigitator who could amaze and amuse the audience by "pulling another rabbit out of a hat." But he was an artist and no canvas was too big for him.

B. PLOWING THE SURPLUSES UNDER

1. The Planned-Scarcity Scandal (1934)

The surest way to raise the prices of farm produce to a profit-making level was to reduce the mountainous surpluses. Under the Agricultural Adjustment Act of 1933 ("Triple A"), six million pigs were slaughtered and one-fourth of the cotton acreage (already planted) was plowed under. The proverbially stubborn mules, trained to walk between rows of cotton, balked at trampling on them. Critics of the New Deal sneered that the mules had more sense than the New Dealers. Norman Thomas —ex-Presbyterian clergyman, orator, author, editor, and six times Socialist candidate for the Presidency (1928–1948)—here vents his indignation. Decide what alternatives there were, given the existing economic and social framework.

Poverty and insecurity are, alas, old stories for men. It remained for this generation, and particularly this generation of Americans, to invent a new and most bitter type of poverty. Pearl Buck's moving description of famine in a Chinese village is the kind of thing which, with minor changes, could have been written about agricultural villages over and over again in almost all parts of the world ever since the dim dawn of history. It remained for us to invent "bread lines knee-deep in wheat."

Other generations have been poor because they could not produce enough. We are told that we are poor because we have produced too much.

For thousands of years man had to accept the inevitability of scarcity. Society would have had the poor always with it, no matter how just and kind might have been its institutions, for the simple reason that man had not learned to harness the powers of nature to help him wrest an abundant living from the earth. It was on the basis of inevitable scarcity that the Greek philosophers tried to justify chattel slavery.

1. Reprinted with permission of The Macmillan Company from *The Choice before Us* by Norman Thomas, pp. 5–7. Copyright 1934 by Norman Thomas.

Today, as everybody admits, the machine is our slave. We depend not upon the energy of men but upon the energy of electricity to give us at once abundance and leisure. And still in a nation like our own, blessed by every gift man's skill and nature's abundance can bestow, millions of children go hungry. Their fathers vainly seek work that does not exist. They and their families are crowded together in shacks and slums and hovels while the builders of skyscrapers are idle.

No satirist ever penned such an indictment of a cruel and lunatic order of society as was written by the author of the Agricultural Adjustment Act in America who saw no way to restore a partial prosperity to farmers except to produce an artificial scarcity by paying agricultural producers from the proceeds of a tax on consumers to destroy the abundance of foodstuffs which men had struggled thousands upon thousands of years to be able to create.

And this, be it remembered, in the midst of a cold and hungry world. The more sincerely one believes that such legislation was an emergency necessity, the more terrible is the indictment of the civilization which brought it about.

2. Wallace Puts People above Pigs (1935)

Henry A. Wallace, a Republican convert to the New Deal, served as Roosevelt's first Secretary of Agriculture. An Iowan who had edited a farm journal and made a fortune in the hybrid-seed business, Wallace was destined to have a controversial career as Vice-President under Roosevelt and as presidential candidate on the Communist-backed Progressive ticket of 1948. Capable administrator, prolific author, and dynamic orator, Wallace was also a starry-eyed idealist who later proposed a quart of milk for all people. In this spirited radio defense of his New Deal policies, ascertain why the producers of pig iron were more blameworthy than the New Dealers, and in what way the policy of planned scarcity actually saved food from destruction.

People are still interested in the six million pigs that were killed in September of 1933. In letters I have received following these radio talks, the pigs are mentioned more often than any one thing except potatoes. One letter says:

"It just makes me sick all over when I think how the government has killed millions and millions of little pigs, and how that has raised pork prices until today we poor people cannot even look at a piece of bacon." . . .

So six million little pigs were killed in September of 1933. They were turned into one hundred million pounds of pork. That pork was distributed for relief. It went to feed the hungry. Some very small pigs could not be handled as meat by the packers. These were turned into grease and tankage for fertilizer.

If those six million pigs had grown up they would have been marketed in January, February, and March of 1934. They probably would have

2. Henry A. Wallace, *Democracy Reborn* (1944), pp. 103–06 (speech of Nov. 12, 1935). Copyright 1944 by Harcourt, Brace & World, Inc. Reprinted by permission of Harcourt, Brace & World, Inc., and Hammond, Hammond and Co., Ltd.

brought around $2.50 a hundredweight. Instead of that the price of hogs at that time averaged [a profitable] $3.60. . . .

Strange to say, I find myself in strong sympathy with the attitude of many folks who held up their hands in horror about the killing of little pigs. I will go further than most of them in condemning scarcity economics. We want an economy of abundance, but it must be balanced abundance of those things we really want.

The pig-iron reduction control of the big steel companies in 1933 was in principle one thousand times as damnable as the pig-reduction campaign of 1933. Pig-iron production in 1932 was about twenty percent of that in 1929. Pig production in 1933 in pounds was ninety-seven percent of that of 1929. In 1934 pig-iron production was about forty-five percent of that of 1929. Pig production in 1934, the drought year, was eighty percent of that of 1929.

In other words, farmers cut pig production three percent when steel companies cut pig-iron production eighty percent. That sort of industrial reduction program plowed millions of workers out into the streets. It is because of that industrial reduction program that we have to spend billions for relief to keep the plowed-out workers from starvation. I hope industry in future reduction programs will not find it desirable to plow millions of workers out of their jobs. People are more important than pigs. . . .

My attention has been called to a statement by a minister out in the Corn Belt before the district conference of his faith. Concerning the actions of the New Deal he says: ". . . some of them are downright sinful as the destruction of foodstuffs in the face of present want."

I have been used to statements of this sort by partisans, demagogues, politicians, and even newspaper columnists. To men of this sort I pay no attention, because I know that their interest in a cause makes it impossible for them to distinguish truth from falsehood. But when a minister of the gospel makes a statement, we expect it to be the truth.

Just what food does he think this administration has destroyed? We would like to know the specific instances. If he is merely referring to acreage control which enabled us to keep out of use in 1935 some thirty million of the fifty million acres which have produced in the past for markets in foreign countries, I would say, "Yes, we are guilty of acreage control and, depending on variations in weather, we shall continue to be until foreign purchasing power is restored by the breaking down of tariff and quota barriers."

We have not destroyed foodstuffs. We do not contemplate destroying them. However, foodstuffs *were* destroyed back in 1932 by farmers who found it profitable to burn their corn for fuel rather than to sell it for ten cents a bushel (which amounted to $3.33 a ton). It was cheaper for many farmers in the northwest Corn Belt to burn food for fuel at those pitiful prices than to burn coal.

People who believe that we ordered the destruction of food are merely the victims of their prejudices and the misinformation that has been fed to them by interested persons. What we actually did was to stop the destruction of foodstuffs by making it worth while for farmers to sell them rather than to destroy them.

Agricultural Adjustment of the past two years has been a million times as warranted as the industrial reduction policy of the past five years. Why does not the minister attack the industrial reduction which was made possible by corporate and tariff laws? It was this reduction by industry that created the *unemployment* and destroyed the farmers' markets.

C. THE TENNESSEE VALLEY AUTHORITY (TVA)

1. Norris Plays Down Electric Power (1933)

George W. Norris, for thirty years United States Senator from Nebraska, shone as one of the foremost liberals and reformers of his generation. He opposed war with Germany in 1917, fought the Treaty of Versailles, and authored the anti-lame duck (20th) Amendment. Best known as "the Father of the TVA," he fought tirelessly for this revolutionary high-dam project. (His fellow Republicans, finally fed up with his New Deal liberalism, read him out of the party in 1936.) The power companies attacked the TVA as primarily an effort to put the government in the electric power business. Norris replied that power was always secondary to navigation and flood control. He declared that the power trust, which favored a large number of obstructing small dams, "had no fundamental objection to making the Tennessee River navigable, but in pursuance of its own interest it preferred an unnavigable river to any interference with its monopolistic control of the generation and sale of electric power." In the final stages of the debate on the TVA bill, Norris spoke as follows. Explain why electric power could not have been the primary consideration in all instances.

We are confronted here, however, with the Government undertaking in the Tennessee Valley a great project, what we might call "a reclamation project." We are going to try to control the flow of the streams, particularly of the Tennessee River. We are going to try to control the floods. We are going to try to make the great stream navigable. We are going to reforest some of the land. We are going to put to better use some of the so-called "marginal lands." We are going to develop power. The development of power is only one of a large list of things we are going to try to do. They are all interlocked. In many of these improvements every one of these things will enter as a component part.

As to Dam No. 2,* which we own down there now, nobody that I know of has ever said how much of that dam should be allocated to navigation and how much to power. Most people think of it as a power dam only. They do not realize that if that dam had not been built, some similar improvement would have had to be constructed in order to make the Tennessee River navigable. A great lake has been constructed there over

1. *Congressional Record,* 73 Cong., 1 sess., p. 2684 (May 2, 1933).
* Today's Wilson Dam.

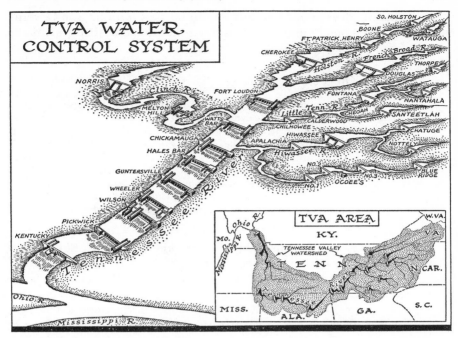

a portion of the river which at times in the year is just a rippling stream running over the rocks. . . .

Other dams—smaller dams, without any power—could have been built. Dam No. 3,* some twelve or fourteen miles above, a well-known dam provided for in the original plan, was never constructed. It strikes me . . . that no business man would construct Dam No. 3 as a power proposition. It would not pay; it would not be a good investment; but as a navigation proposition it is absolutely essential that we shall make the river navigable during portions of the year at least.

The difficulty arises because all this business is so interlocked and so interwoven that it is difficult to tell where one begins and the other ends, but when we put them together as a whole we know what we are going to get. We are going to get a navigable stream; we are going to get flood control; we are going to get power as an incident. But while the object of this bill is to get the maximum amount of flood control, it does not say the maximum amount of power, as will be noted by anyone who will read the bill. It provides for securing the maximum amount of flood control, the maximum amount of navigation—flood control and navigation—and the maximum amount of power "not inconsistent with navigation and flood control." That, I think, is the language of the bill.

The power is really a secondary proposition. It comes about because it would be sinful to build all these dams and not develop some power.

* Today's Wheeler Dam.

When it shall be developed, what is going to be done with it? The Government has it on its hands, and why should not the people of that great basin have the benefit of it?

2. Willkie Exposes the Rubber Yardstick (1937)

The aroused power companies fought the TVA all the way to the Supreme Court. They contended that expensive high dams would not check erosion, that inexpensive low dams would better serve navigation and flood control, and that the loss to individuals from floods was less than the cost of the grandiose project. Dynamic, tousle-haired, and eloquent Wendell Willkie, later an outspoken liberal and the opponent of Roosevelt in the presidential campaign of 1940, complained as follows in 1937 as president of the competing Commonwealth and Southern power corporation. (In 1939 it sold its Tennessee Electric Power Company to the TVA for some $78,000,000.) Form conclusions as to the fairness or unfairness of the so-called yardstick.

Like England's once famous military formation, the British Square, the TVA has had four fronts to present to the public, and it uses the front most suitable to the group which it is addressing. Before the courts it claims that it is not really a power enterprise, but primarily a *conservation* activity: it is a project to prevent floods, promote navigation on the Tennessee River, and check soil erosion in the great Tennessee Valley. Only before a more sympathetic audience is it frankly an instrument for the electrification of America. . . .

The TVA has therefore appeared to be on the side of the angels in the controversy between it and the utilities. But the conservation programme of the TVA is only a masquerade. It has no functional connection with the power programme of the Authority, and the amount spent on it is only an insignificant portion of the Authority's total expenditures. Other departments of government, both state and national, are charged with the duty of caring for soil erosion and are doing such work effectively without the building of dams and power facilities. . . .

The American people, therefore, are paying more than half a billion dollars for eleven dams, chiefly designed to supply power to one area. But this power, as will shortly be demonstrated, is to be supplied to this area at *less than cost*. In other words, the TVA will operate annually at a deficit, and these annual deficits must, of course, be paid for out of the pockets of the taxpayers.

The sponsors of the TVA maintained at the beginning that this vast programme was not designed to create a competitive power system, but to set up a yardstick by which the rates of the private companies could be judged. The yardstick idea was undoubtedly attractive, since, after all, the average consumer did not understand much about electric rates and had no way of personally checking their relative highness or lowness.

2. *Atlantic Monthly*, CLX, 211–14 (Aug., 1937). By permission of the *Atlantic Monthly*.

Unfortunately, the yardstick is rubber from the first inch to the last.

From the generation of power at the beginning to its distribution to the ultimate consumer at the end, the TVA enjoys privileges and exemptions which are denied to the private utility, which conceal the true cost of TVA power, and the cost of which comes out of the pockets of you and me as taxpayers. These can be best illustrated by a direct comparison between the TVA and the Tennessee Electric Power Company, one of the typical companies in the Commonwealth and Southern System operating in that area.

The first advantage given to the TVA is exemption from practically all taxes. For the fiscal year ended June 30, 1936, the TVA paid only $45,347 in taxes. The Tennessee Electric Power Company (with approximately the same capital investment) paid $2,339,284 in taxes. Here is a difference in this item alone of $2,293,937.

Let us turn to the item of depreciation. This is an expense, a cost of operation, just as much as labor and fuel. This cost to the Tennessee Company, fixed and determined by the Tennessee Railroad and Public Utilities Commission, amounts to $1,260,000 per year. The books of the TVA, however, carry no item for depreciation.

The same is true with respect to interest charges. The Tennessee Company properties were built only in part with borrowed capital. During the twelve months ended June 30, 1936, this company paid interest and preferred dividends amounting to $4,299,022. On the other hand, the property of the TVA is built entirely with borrowed capital. The United States Government is paying interest and will continue to pay interest on such borrowings. The TVA books, however, show no item to cover this interest. It got its property from the Federal Government, which in turn, of course, collected its money from the taxpayer. . . .

Since the TVA is apparently selling its power at less than cost, it should say so. If the people who live in New York City, for example, are to pay part of the electric bill of people who live in Corinth, Mississippi, the people in New York should know about it. Perhaps they will not object. On more than one occasion the American people as a whole have contributed, through taxes, to a development designed to serve only a limited area. Often that is socially desirable. But if we are to pay part of the electric light bills of the Tennessee Valley, the TVA should honestly tell us so.

Also, if the TVA is attempting to force the utilities into public ownership, it should employ means that will neither deceive nor injure the public and will not jeopardize the interests of utility investors. It should announce its intention and proceed, by condemnation proceedings duly instituted in the courts of the land, to take over utility properties with fair compensation to the owners. This is both the honest and the humane method of action. Also, it gives the people a fair chance to protest if they don't like the change; or if they are still skeptical of political management of a major industry. . . .

3. Displaced Tennesseans (1935)

Architects of the New Deal also designed the TVA to provide employment and to raise the living standards of an impoverished area. Electric lights and appliances were incredibly scarce. Before the valley bottoms were turned into lakes by the high dams, federal agents had to buy out the owners. More than one doughty Tennessean threatened to "shoot them TVA fellers." Form conclusions from this contemporary account as to the need for a TVA, and as to whether the social gains justified the cost.

. . . On Cedar Creek lives Isabel Brantley.

"I was born in this house and so was my pappy before me, and here I've lived and here I'll die, even if I have to bolt the door and let the flood come—but there hain't a-goin' to be no flood!"

This was her greeting to the TVA appraiser, prepared to offer twelve hundred dollars for her log cabin and eroded acres. In the end she was won over by the generosity of TVA's laborers, who offered to move the house in their spare time, without cost to her, to a site below the dam. Persuaded but not softened, she declared, "You got to find me a place with a spring or a well. I don't want none of this newfangled pipe water runnin' into my house."

Such is the sales resistance encountered by Government agents.

When Ezra Hill saw the plans for the home which was to replace his old one in the flood area, he pointed to the place on the print showing the circles and ovals of bathroom fixtures. "What's all this? . . . I won't have it! I guess a privy is still good enough for me."

[*The TVA brought improvement but not paradise; the per capita income of the region remained well below the national average. But the demands of both the government and the people grew so rapidly that by 1962 the TVA had supplementary steam plants capable of producing more than twice the amount of electricity generated by water power.*]

D. LITTLE STEEL VERSUS THE C.I.O.

1. Tom Girdler Girds for Battle (1937)

The New Dealers, with their strong appeal to the low-waged voter, encouraged the unionization of labor, notably through the Wagner Act of 1935. "Big Steel" (including the U.S. Steel Corporation) reluctantly accepted unionization by the C.I.O. (Committee for Industrial Organization). "Little Steel," led by the tough-fisted but mild-appearing Tom Girdler, who became a hero to conservatives, struck back. At his Republic Steel Company's plant in Chicago on Memorial Day, 1937, the police fired upon and killed ten strikers, while wounding many others. Several additional

3. Drew and Leon Pearson, "The Tennessee Valley Experiment," *Harper's Magazine*, CLXX, 707 (May, 1935). Reproduced by permission of *Harper's Magazine*.
1. "Delivery or Non-Delivery of Mail in Industrial Strife Areas," Senate Committee on Post Offices, *Hearings*, 75 Cong., 1 sess., pp. 207–10.

lives were lost in Ohio cities. Girdler, before a Senate committee, here justifies his opposition. Note whether the tactics of the C.I.O. were defensible (if correctly reported), and whether the accusations regarding Communism are convincing.

First of all let me make it clear that the fundamental issue in this strike is not one involving wages, hours, or working conditions in Republic [Steel Company] plants. This is not a strike in the sense that a large body of our employees quit work because of grievances against the company. What has happened is that an invading army descended upon our plants and forced many of our employees from their jobs.

Fully 23,000 of our employees have remained at work throughout the strike despite threats and violence, and many additional thousands have been kept from work against their will.

The basic issue of this strike is the right of American citizens to work, free from molestation, violence, coercion, and intimidation by a labor organization whose apparent policy is either to rule or to ruin American industry. . . .

The difficulties in the present dispute arise from the fact that the company will not enter into a contract, oral or written, with an irresponsible party; and the C.I.O., as presently constituted, is wholly irresponsible. . . .

The irresponsibility of the C.I.O. is well established by the fact that 200 strikes and walk-outs have taken place in the plants of the General Motors Corporation since that corporation signed an agreement with the C.I.O. which called for an end of strikes during the period of the agreement. . . .

Further evidence of the irresponsible character of the C.I.O. is to be seen in the lawless and terroristic conduct of its members since the beginning of the present strike. Republic plants have been surrounded by armed crowds who call themselves pickets and who, by force and violence, have imprisoned in the plants thousands of employees who refused to heed the strike call and remained at work. These men have been prevented from returning to their families when their work is done, and other employees who want to work have been prevented from getting into the plants.

Airplanes delivering food to workers besieged in the plants have been fired upon by armed mobs about the gates. The delivery of the United States mails has been interfered with. Railroad tracks have been dynamited. Families of men who are at work in the plants in certain communities have been threatened, coerced, and stoned. Defiance of law and order has been so flagrant that in some communities law enforcement has completely collapsed.

These illegal practices have not been peculiar to the Republic strike. They have characterized C.I.O. methods since the beginning of its organization drive in many industries. They have more than confirmed the conclusion reached by this company before the present strike ever started that the C.I.O. was and is an irresponsible and dangerous force in America. . . .

SURE, I'LL WORK FOR BOTH SIDES
Both management and labor resorted to violence. Milwaukee *Journal,* 1935.

We believe that the C.I.O. with its terroristic methods and Communistic technique of picketing constitutes the most dangerous threat to the preservation of democracy in the United States. . . .

Now, let me state a few fundamental conclusions which I have reached about the C.I.O.

First. The C.I.O. has denied to free American citizens who refuse to pay tribute to it the right to work.

Second. The C.I.O. encourages and promotes violence and disregard of law. If this is done under instructions and approval of its leaders, it amounts to a confession on their part that they are deliberately adopting the methods of force and terrorism which have proved so successful for the dictators of Europe. If this is done without their approval and occurs because they cannot control their own men, it is a confession that the C.I.O. is an irresponsible party and that a contract with it would not be worth the paper upon which it is written.

Third. The C.I.O. is associated with Communism. Many of its leaders and organizers are avowed Communists. The *Daily Worker,* the official newspaper of the Communist Party of the United States, gives the C.I.O. its full support. Can any organization which welcomes the support of the International Communist Party still claim that it adheres to the principles of democracy?

2. Lewis Lambasts Girdler (1937)

John L. Lewis—gruff, domineering, shaggy-browed—had risen from the depths of the coal mines to the headship of the potent United Mine Workers of America. Seeking new worlds to conquer, he undertook to unionize mass-production industries through his Committee for Industrial Organization (C.I.O.). The clash between him and Tom Girdler—both strong-minded men—became so noisy that F.D.R. himself burst out, "A plague on both your houses." Four years later, in 1941, Girdler's Little Steel was forced to accept unionization. In this impassioned speech over a radio hookup, Lewis betrays his anger. Locate his most serious grievances, and assess the truth of his observation that men like Girdler are more dangerous than Communists.

Five of the corporations in the steel industry elected to resist collective bargaining and undertook to destroy the steel-workers' union. These companies filled their plants with industrial spies, assembled depots of guns and gas bombs, established barricades, controlled their communities with armed thugs, leased the police power of cities, and mobilized the military power of a state to guard them against the intrusion of collective bargaining within their plants.

During this strike eighteen steel workers were either shot to death or had their brains clubbed out by police, or armed thugs in the pay of the steel companies. . . .

The steel workers have now buried their dead, while the widows weep and watch their orphaned children become objects of public charity. The murder of these unarmed men has never been publicly rebuked by any authoritative officer of the state or federal government. Some of them, in extenuation, plead lack of jurisdiction, but murder as a crime against the moral code can always be rebuked without regard to the niceties of legalistic jurisdiction by those who profess to be the keepers of the public conscience.

[Tom] Girdler, of Republic Steel, in the quiet of his bedchamber, doubtless shrills his psychopathic cackles as he files notches on his corporate gun and views in retrospect the ruthless work of his mercenary killers. . . .

The United States Chamber of Commerce, the National Association of Manufacturers, and similar groups representing industry and financial interests are rendering a disservice to the American people in their attempts to frustrate the organization of labor and in their refusal to accept collective bargaining as one of our economic institutions.

These groups are encouraging a systematic organization of vigilante groups to fight unionization under the sham pretext of local interests. They equip these vigilantes with tin hats, wooden clubs, gas masks, and lethal weapons, and train them in the arts of brutality and oppression. They bring in snoops, finks [strikebreakers], hatchet gangs, and Chowderhead Cohens to infest their plants and disturb the communities.

Fascist organizations have been launched and financed under the shabby pretext that the C.I.O. movement is Communistic. The real breeders of

2. *Vital Speeches,* III, 731 (Sept. 15, 1937 ; speech of Sept. 3, 1937).

discontent and alien doctrines of government and philosophies subversive of good citizenship are such as these who take the law into their own hands. No tin-hat brigade of goose-stepping vigilantes or bibble-babbling mob of blackguarding and corporation-paid scoundrels will prevent the onward march of labor, or divert its purpose to play its natural and rational part in the development of the economic, political, and social life of our nation. . . .

Do those who have hatched this foolish cry of Communism in the C.I.O. fear the increased influence of labor in our democracy? Do they fear its influence will be cast on the side of shorter hours, a better system of distributed employment, better homes for the underprivileged, social security for the aged, a fairer distribution of the national income?

Certainly the workers that are being organized want a voice in the determination of these objectives of social justice.

E. THE SUPREME COURT FIGHT AND AFTER

1. Ickes Defends His Chief (1937)

The ultra-conservative Supreme Court had repeatedly overthrown crucial New Deal measures for economic and social reform. Roosevelt, intoxicated by his heady majorities of 1932, 1934, and 1936, concluded that in a true democracy the "horse-and-buggy" Court ought to catch up with the will of the people. Two weeks after his second inauguration, he sprang his clever Supreme Court scheme on a surprised Congress and nation. Among other changes, he proposed increasing the membership of the Court from nine to fifteen by appointing additional (New Deal) justices to offset those aged seventy or more who were unwilling to retire. Critics cried that this was "packing" the Court; supporters replied that this was "unpacking" the Court by offsetting reactionaries. "Honest Harold" Ickes, the acid-tongued Secretary of the Interior, here tells how he defended Roosevelt before an audience of Texans. Bearing in mind that the Court scheme had not received mention in the Democratic platform or in Roosevelt's speeches during the recent campaign of 1936, analyze the strength of Ickes' argument regarding a popular mandate.

Then I switched to a discussion of the constitutional situation, with special reference to the recent proposal of the President to change the judiciary system. I could hear a gasp go up as I disclosed my purpose to discuss this issue. A week or ten days ago the Texas State Senate, with only three or four votes opposing, had gone on record as being against the President's proposal. The House decided neither to approve nor disapprove.

I waded right into the constitutional issue with both feet. In my first sentence I asked where had the Supreme Court gotten its supposed power to pass upon the constitutionality of acts of Congress. I read the Tenth Amendment and then I said that this power had been usurped.*

I then went on to discuss the supposed checks and balances in our

1. *The Secret Diary of Harold L. Ickes* (1954), II, 80. Copyright 1954 by Simon and Schuster, Inc. By permission of Simon and Schuster, Inc.
* The 10th Amendment reserved undelegated powers to the states, but the function of judicial review, "usurped" by the Supreme Court, is generally regarded as implicit in the views of the Founding Fathers and in the Constitution.

TO FURNISH THE SUPREME COURT PRACTICAL ASSISTANCE

Roosevelt's proposal to assist the Court by adding a maximum
of six new members was interpreted by critics as an attempt to
"pack" it with his mouthpieces. Washington *Post,* 1937.

tripartite Federal system, pointing out that while there were ample checks
and balances with respect to the legislative and executive branches, there
wasn't a single check on the judiciary except that of impeachment, which
was slow and cumbersome and of doubtful efficacy when it came to a
court of nine men. I remarked in passing that one could not be impeached
for being too old, that that was not a crime but merely a misfortune.

I argued that the people had given the President a mandate at the last
election to provide them with such social and economic legislation as is
implicit in the term "New Deal." I said that he would be recreant to his
trust if he didn't do all within his power to give the people what he had
promised them and what they had shown so unmistakably that they wanted.

I expressed the opinion that the people wanted the benefits of the New
Deal now. I pointed out that while those who are opposing the President
pretend to do it on the basis that a constitutional amendment is the proper
procedure, it would take all of twenty years to get such an amendment
through.

With respect to an act or acts of Congress limiting the powers of the
Supreme Court so as to provide, for instance, that no law could be held
to be unconstitutional except on a two-thirds or three-quarters majority,
I ventured to predict that any such law would be declared unconstitutional
by the Supreme Court and therefore would be ineffective.

2. Dorothy Thompson Dissents (1937)

As the battle over the Supreme Court mounted, critics accused Roosevelt of perverting the Constitution by destroying the delicate checks and balances, of undermining the integrity and independence of the judiciary, and of grooming himself for dictatorship. Even many New Dealers preferred an unhurried constitutional amendment to a hurried act of Congress. Perhaps most damaging was the suggestion of "slickness," together with Roosevelt's argument, based on false information, that the aged justices were behind in their work. Dorothy Thompson, the foremost woman columnist of her day, sounded the following clarion call. Evaluate her view that the people must be protected against fickle majorities, and that haste was not necessary.

If the American people accept this last audacity of the President without letting out a yell to high heaven, they have ceased to be jealous of their liberties and are ripe for ruin.

This is the beginning of pure personal government. Do you want it? Do you like it? Look around about the world—there are plenty of examples [*e.g.*, Hitler]—and make up your mind.

The Executive is already powerful by reason of his overwhelming victory in November, and will be strengthened even more if the reorganization plan for the administration, presented some weeks ago, is adopted. We have, to all intents and purposes, a one-party Congress, dominated by the President. Although nearly 40 percent of the voters repudiated the New Deal at the polls, they have less than 20 percent representation in both houses of Congress. And now the Supreme Court is to have a majority determined by the President and by a Senate which he dominates.

When that happens we will have a one-man Government. It will all be constitutional. So, he claims, is Herr Hitler.

Leave the personality and the intentions of the President out of the picture. They are not the crux of this issue. He may be as wise as Solon, lofty as Plato, and pure as Parsifal. He may have the liberties of the American people deeply at heart. But he will have a successor who may be none of these things. There have been benevolent dictatorships and benevolent tyrannies. They have even, at times in history, worked for the popular welfare. But that is not the welfare which, up to now, the American people have chosen.

And let us not be confused by the words "liberal" and "conservative" or misled into thinking that the expressed will of the majority is the essence of democracy. By that definition Hitler, Stalin, and Mussolini are all great democratic leaders. The essence of democracy is the protection of minorities.

Nor has a majority of this generation the right to mortgage a majority of the next. In the Constitution of the United States are incorporated the rights of the people, rights enjoyed by every American citizen in perpetuity, which cannot be voted away by any majority, ever.

2. Washington *Star,* Feb. 10, 1937, quoted in *Congressional Digest,* XVI, 96 (March, 1937). By permission of the Bell Syndicate.

Majorities are temporary things. The Supreme Court is there to protect the fundamental law even against the momentary "will of the people." That is its function. And it is precisely because nine men can walk out and say: "You can't do that!" that our liberties are protected against the mob urge that occasionally overcomes democracies. That is why the Supreme Court has been traditionally divorced from momentary majorities. . . .

The Constitution can be changed. There are ways provided for doing so. To change it will require much deliberation, debate, time. And what is wrong with deliberation and debate and time? What is the hurry? Under what threat are we living at this instant?

This is no proposal to change the Constitution. This is no proposal to limit the powers of the Supreme Court. This is a proposal to capture the Supreme Court. . . .

If, of the six men over 70, four had been "liberals" and two "conservatives," instead of the other way around, do you think that this program would have been proposed? . . .

Don't talk of liberalism! The liberal does not believe that the end justifies the means. Long experience has taught him that the means usually determine the end. No human being can believe in the sincerity of this proposal. It is clever, in a world sick of cleverness and longing for plain talk and simple honesty. Must we begin to examine every message from the President to see whether there is a trick in it somewhere?

[*Roosevelt threw all his weight behind the Supreme Court reform, but suffered his most severe political setback when he lost out on the "packing" feature. He underestimated popular reverence for the Court. But he did win certain other judicial reforms; the Supreme Court did shift to a more liberal position; and within four years he did fill seven vacancies with younger men. He lost a battle but in the end won the war.*]

3. Republicans Roast Roosevelt (1940)

The Roosevelt-Willkie presidential campaign of 1940 generated new bitterness. Roosevelt's challenge to the third-term tradition, combined with his unsuccessful attempt to "pack" the Supreme Court and "purge" certain Congressmen hostile to him, accentuated fears of dictatorship. The Democrats argued that Roosevelt had saved capitalism by averting, whatever the monetary cost and confusion, a revolutionary uprising. The Republican platform, invoking the Preamble of the Constitution, found the New Deal wanting on many counts. In the light of subsequent developments determine which was the most valid accusation.

Instead of leading us into More Perfect Union, the Administration has deliberately fanned the flames of class hatred.

Instead of the Establishment of Justice the Administration has sought the subjection of the Judiciary to Executive discipline and domination.

3. K. H. Porter and D. B. Johnson, eds., *National Party Platforms, 1840–1956* (1956), pp. 389–90. By permission of the University of Illinois Press.

Instead of insuring Domestic Tranquillity, the Administration has made impossible the normal friendly relation between employers and employees, and has even succeeded in alienating both the great divisions of Organized Labor.

Instead of Providing for the Common Defense, the Administration, notwithstanding the expenditure of billions of our dollars, has left the Nation unprepared to resist foreign attack.

Instead of promoting the General Welfare, the Administration has Domesticated the Deficit, Doubled the Debt, Imposed Taxes where they do the greatest economic harm, and used public money for partisan political advantage.

Instead of the Blessings of Liberty, the Administration has imposed upon us a Regime of Regimentation which has deprived the individual of his freedom and has made of America a shackled giant.

Wholly ignoring these great objectives, as solemnly declared by the people of the United States [in the Constitution], the New Deal Administration has for seven long years whirled in a turmoil of shifting, contradictory, and overlapping administrations and policies. Confusion has reigned supreme. The only steady undeviating characteristic has been the relentless expansion of the power of the Federal government over the everyday life of the farmer, the industrial worker, and the businessman. The emergency demands organization—not confusion. It demands free and intelligent cooperation—not incompetent domination. It demands a change.

The New Deal Administration has failed America.

It has failed by seducing our people to become continuously dependent upon government, thus weakening their morale and quenching the traditional American spirit.

THOUGHT PROVOKERS

1. Compare and contrast the presidential leadership of Hoover and Roosevelt. Temperamentally, could Roosevelt ever have been a true dictator?
2. What probably would have happened if the federal government had refused to provide relief for the 15,000,000 unemployed, as well as for the impoverished farmers? Was planned scarcity immoral?
3. Did the social gains resulting from the TVA more than offset the blow that was directed at legitimate private enterprise? If the TVA was designed as a yardstick, what could it accurately measure? If the TVA has been a success, why has it not been copied more widely elsewhere in the United States?
4. Is the right to work without first joining a union a basic right? Why did the C.I.O. call management Fascist, and why did management call the C.I.O. Communist?
5. Why did Roosevelt's Supreme Court proposal stir up such a hornets' nest? Was Roosevelt justified in breaking his platform promises regarding economy and a balanced budget? Did the New Deal change the basic character of the American people?

FURTHER EXPLORATION

General: Dixon Wecter, *The Age of the Great Depression* (1948); A. M. Schlesinger, Jr., *The Coming of the New Deal* (1959) and *The Politics of Upheaval* (1960). **Enigma:** J. M. Burns, *Roosevelt: The Lion and the Fox* (1956). **Surplus:** E. G. Nourse *et al.*, *Three Years of the Agricultural Adjustment Administration* (1937); Russell Lord, *The Wallaces of Iowa* (1947). **TVA:** D. E. Lilienthal, *TVA: Democracy on the March* (1953); P. J. Hubbard, *Origins of the T.V.A.* (1961). **Little Steel:** Selig Perlman, *Labor in the New Deal Decade* (1945); Milton Derber *et al.*, *Labor under the New Deal* (1957). **Supreme Court:** R. H. Jackson, *The Struggle for Judicial Supremacy* (1941); Joseph Alsop and Turner Catledge, *The 168 Days* (1938); M. J. Pusey, *Charles Evans Hughes* (1951), vol. II.

Recent: W. E. Leuchtenburg, *Franklin D. Roosevelt and the New Deal, 1932–1940* (1963) [paperback]; S. F. Charles, *Minister of Relief: Harry Hopkins and the Depression* (1963); E. W. Hawley, *The New Deal and the Problem of Monopoly* (1966); O. L. Graham, Jr., *An Encore for Reform: The Old Progressives and the New Deal* (1967) [paperback]; D. E. Conrad, *The Forgotten Farmers: The Story of Sharecroppers in the New Deal* (1965); N. L. Zucker, *George W. Norris: Gentle Knight of American Democracy* (1966); W. H. Droze, *High Dams and Slack Waters: TVA Rebuilds a River* (1965); P. J. Hubbard, *Origins of the TVA: The Muscle Shoals Controversy, 1920–1932* (1961).

Chapter 43

Franklin D. Roosevelt and Neutrality

The epidemic of world lawlessness is spreading. . . . There must be positive endeavors to preserve peace.

FRANKLIN D. ROOSEVELT, 1937

PROLOGUE: The same depression that generated the New Deal at home accelerated the rise of power-hungry dictators abroad: Hitler, Mussolini, and the Japanese war lords. Congress tried to insulate the nation from the imminent world war by arms embargoes and other presumed safeguards. But when Hitler attacked Poland in 1939, the American people found themselves torn between two desires: they wanted to avoid involvement, but they feared for their future security if they did not get involved to the extent of bolstering the democracies. Under Roosevelt's prodding, Congress repealed the arms embargo in 1939, and the administration gradually took a series of steps which removed any pretense of neutrality. Most Americans—but not the die-hard isolationists—were willing to risk hostilities in an effort to help the democracies and halt the aggressors. Roosevelt took the gamble but lost when a shooting war developed with Germany in the Atlantic, and when Japan struck a devastating aerial blow at Pearl Harbor.

A. THE ARMS EMBARGO DEBATE

1. Senator Connally Rejects Rigidity (1935)

By the mid-1930's Hitler was on the rise in Germany and Mussolini was on the loose in Ethiopia. An apprehensive American public was determined to legislate itself out of the next world war by a strait-jacket neutrality law. A special Senate investigation launched in 1934 and headed by the notoriety-seeking Senator Nye had left the impression that the manufacturers of arms had dragged America into World War I. If Congress would only embargo munitions, the nation would (on paper) keep out of World War II. Senator Connally, the long-haired, string-tie Texan orator who headed the Senate Foreign Relations Committee, showed himself unswayed by this logic in the following speech. Determine whether the proposed neutrality legislation provided for true neutrality.

Is it an expression of neutrality to say to two warring nations, one of which has ambitions for territorial conquest, the other unprepared, the other weak, the other trying to pursue its own destiny—is it neutral to say to those nations, "We shall give arms to neither of you," thereby insuring the triumph of the prepared nation, the covetous nation, the ambitious nation, the nation which seeks by force of arms to impose its will on a weaker and defenseless nation?

1. *Congressional Record,* 74 *Cong.,* 1 sess., p. 14432 (Aug. 24, 1935).

Mr. President, that is not neutrality; that is a form of unneutrality. That is a form of declaration which announces that the United States will take the side of the strong and powerful against the weak, the unprepared, and the defenseless. Why not leave that determination to the President of the United States when and if, in his conduct of our foreign relations, it becomes a sound American policy for him to take a position in a crisis of that kind? . . .

We cannot now put the United States into an international strait jacket and thereby keep out of war. We cannot by an act of Congress put the United States into a concrete cast internationally which will fit all future occasions and solve all future problems.

2. Roosevelt Pleads for Repeal (1939)

Despite Connally's urging, the arms-embargoing Neutrality Acts of 1935 and 1937 made no distinction between aggressor and victim. When Hitler wantonly launched World War II in September, 1939, the United States could not legally sell munitions to the unprepared democracies, even though American sentiment and self-interest both cried aloud for aid to Britain and France. A worried Roosevelt summoned Congress into special session and made the following dramatic appeal. He was wrong on two counts. First, the arms embargo, as purely domestic legislation, was not a departure from long-established international law. Second, the Jeffersonian embargo and non-intercourse acts did not cause the War of 1812; they came within a few days of averting it. Form conclusions as to Roosevelt's techniques as a politician and as to the most dangerous loophole in the existing legislation.

Beginning with the foundation of our constitutional Government in the year 1789, the American policy in respect to belligerent nations, with one notable exception, has been based on international law. . . .

The single exception was the policy adopted by this nation during the Napoleonic Wars, when, seeking to avoid involvement, we acted for some years under the so-called Embargo and Non-Intercourse Acts. That policy turned out to be a disastrous failure—first, because it brought our own nation close to ruin, and, second, because it was the major cause of bringing us into active participation in European wars in our own War of 1812. It is merely reciting history to recall to you that one of the results of the policy of embargo and non-intercourse was the burning in 1814 of part of this Capitol in which we are assembled.

Our next deviation by statute from the sound principles of neutrality, and peace through international law, did not come for 130 years. It was the so-called Neutrality Act of 1935—only 4 years ago—an Act continued in force by the Joint Resolution of May 1, 1937, despite grave doubts expressed as to its wisdom by many Senators and Representatives and by officials charged with the conduct of our foreign relations, including myself.

I regret that the Congress passed that Act. I regret equally that I signed that Act.

On July 14th of this year, I asked the Congress, in the cause of peace

2. *Ibid.,* 76 Cong., 2 sess., pp. 10–11 (Sept. 21, 1939).

and in the interest of real American neutrality and security, to take action to change that Act.

I now ask again that such action be taken in respect to that part of the Act which is wholly inconsistent with ancient precepts of the law of nations —the [arms] embargo provisions. I ask it because they are, in my opinion, most vitally dangerous to American neutrality, American security, and American peace.

These embargo provisions, as they exist today, prevent the sale to a belligerent by an American factory of any completed implements of war, but they allow the sale of many types of uncompleted implements of war, as well as all kinds of general material and supplies. They, furthermore, allow such products of industry [e.g., copper] and agriculture [e.g., cotton] to be taken in American-flag ships to belligerent nations. There in itself— under the present law—lies definite danger to our neutrality and our peace.

3. Senator Vandenberg Fights Repeal (1939)

Senator Arthur H. Vandenberg of Michigan—voluble orator, long-time newspaperman, and author of books on Alexander Hamilton—was a leader of the Republican isolationists and a serious contender for the presidential nomination in 1940. Later, in 1945, he underwent a spectacular conversion to internationalism, and rose to heights of statesmanship in supporting the Marshall Plan for the rehabilitation of post-war Europe. While fighting against the repeal of the arms embargo in 1939, he wrote in his diary that he deplored Roosevelt's "treacherous" and "cowardly" idea that America could be "half in and half out of this war." Hating Hitlerism, he felt that the manly course would be to go in or to stay out—and he much preferred to stay out. In his speech in the Senate against the repeal of the arms embargo, note what he regarded as both unneutral and unethical, and comment critically on his views.

Mr. President, I believe this debate symbolically involves the most momentous decision, in the eyes of America and of the world, that the United States Senate has confronted in a generation.

In the midst of foreign war and the alarms of other wars, we are asked to depart basically from the neutrality which the American Congress has twice told the world, since 1935, would be our rule of conduct in such an event. We are particularly asked to depart from it through the repeal of existing neutrality law establishing an embargo on arms, ammunition, and implements of war. We are asked to depart from it in violation of our own officially asserted doctrine, during the [first] World War, that the rules of a neutral cannot be prejudicially altered in the midst of a war.

We are asked to depart from international law itself, as we ourselves have officially declared it to exist. Consciously or otherwise, but mostly consciously, we are asked to depart from it in behalf of one belligerent whom our personal sympathies largely favor, and against another belligerent whom our personal feelings largely condemn. In my opinion, this is the road that may lead us to war, and I will not voluntarily take it. . . .

3. *Ibid.,* p. 95 (Oct. 4, 1939).

The proponents of the change vehemently insist that their steadfast purpose, like ours, is to keep America out of the war, and their sincere assurances are presented to our people. But the motive is obvious, and the inevitable interpretation of the change, inevitably invited by the circumstances, will be that we have officially taken sides.

Somebody will be fooled—either the America which is assured that the change is wholly pacific, or the foreigners who believe it is the casting of our die. Either of these disillusionments would be intolerable. Each is ominous. Yet someone will be fooled—either those at home who expect too much, or those abroad who will get too little.

There is no such hazard, at least to our own America, in preserving neutrality in the existing law precisely as we almost unanimously notified the world was our intention as recently as 1935 and 1937. There is no such jeopardy, at least to our own America, in maintaining the arms embargo as it is. No menace, no jeopardy, to us can thus be persuasively conjured.

Therefore millions of Americans and many members of the Congress can see no reason for the change, but infinite reason to the contrary, if neutral detachment is our sole objective. I am one who deeply holds this view. If I err, I want to err on America's side.

[*Despite such pleas, the arms embargo was repealed early in November, 1939. The vote was 55 to 24 in the Senate; 243 to 172 in the House.*]

B. THE INTERVENTION ISSUE

1. Lindbergh Argues for Isolation (1941)

After France fell to Hitler in 1940, the embattled British stood alone. American interventionists called for a helping hand to Britain; the isolationists called for hands off. The isolationist "America First" group proclaimed, "We have nothing to fear from a Nazi-European victory." Boyish-faced, curly-haired Colonel Charles A. Lindbergh, who had narrowed the Atlantic with his historic solo flight in 1927, stressed the width of the ocean in his new role as a leading isolationist orator. After inspecting Germany's aircraft facilities in 1938, he stoutly maintained that Hitler (who decorated him) could never be conquered in the air. If Lindbergh proved so wrong in an area in which he was a specialist, form some judgment as to the assessment of America's strategic position that he made in this speech before a New York mass meeting in April, 1941. Decide also to what extent interventionism was undemocratic, assuming that Lindbergh's figures were correct. Was his analysis of public opinion trustworthy?

We have weakened ourselves for many months, and still worse, we have divided our own people, by this dabbling in Europe's wars. While we should have been concentrating on American defense, we have been forced to argue over foreign quarrels. We must turn our eyes and our faith back to our own country before it is too late. And when we do this, a different vista opens before us.

1. New York *Times*, April 24, 1941, p. 12.

NEW NEUTRALITY LEGISLATION

Dual crises required drastic action. *Philadelphia Inquirer*, 1939.

Practically every difficulty we would face in invading Europe becomes an asset to us in defending America. Our enemy, and not we, would then have the problem of transporting millions of troops across the ocean and landing them on a hostile shore. They, and not we, would have to furnish the convoys to transport guns and trucks and munitions and fuel across three thousand miles of water. Our battleships and our submarines would then be fighting close to their home bases. We would then do the bombing from the air and the torpedoing at sea. And if any part of an enemy convoy should ever pass our navy and our air force, they would still be faced with the guns of our coast artillery, and behind them the divisions of our Army.

The United States is better situated from a military standpoint than any other nation in the world. Even in our present condition of unpreparedness no foreign power is in a position to invade us today. If we concentrate on our own defenses and build the strength that this nation should maintain, no foreign army will ever attempt to land on American shores.

War is not inevitable for this country. Such a claim is defeatism in the true sense. No one can make us fight abroad unless we ourselves are willing to do so. No one will attempt to fight us here if we arm ourselves as a great nation should be armed. Over a hundred million people in this nation are opposed to entering the war. If the principles of democracy mean anything at all, that is reason enough for us to stay out. If we are forced into a war against the wishes of an overwhelming majority of our people, we will have proved democracy such a failure at home that there will be little use fighting for it abroad.

The time has come when those of us who believe in an independent American destiny must band together and organize for strength. We have been led toward war by a minority of our people. This minority has power. It has influence. It has a loud voice. But it does not represent the American people. During the last several years I have traveled over this country from one end to the other. I have talked to many hundreds of men and women, and I have letters from tens of thousands more, who feel the same way as you and I.

[*Public-opinion polls during these months showed contradictory desires. A strong majority of the American people wanted to stay out of war, but a strong majority favored helping Britain even at the risk of war. The Lend-Lease Act of 1941 received about two-to-one support in the public-opinion polls, and more than that in the Congressional voting.*]

2. The New York *Times* Rejects Insulationism (1941)

The New York *Times* challenged Lindbergh's views in a lengthy and well-reasoned editorial which brilliantly set forth the case for intervention. Determine from this argument whether the greater future menace to the United States lay in direct or indirect aggression, and whether American democracy would be affected, in the first stages, directly or indirectly.

Those who tell us now that the sea is still our certain bulwark, and that the tremendous forces sweeping the Old World threaten no danger to the New, give the lie to their own words in the precautions they would have us take.

To a man they favor an enormous strengthening of our defenses. Why? Against what danger would they have us arm if none exists? To what purpose would they have us spend these almost incredible billions upon billions for ships and planes, for tanks and guns, if there is no immediate threat to the security of the United States? Why are we training the youth of the country to bear arms? Under pressure of what fear are we racing against time to double and quadruple our industrial production?

No man in his senses will say that we are arming against Canada or our Latin-American neighbors to the south, against Britain or the captive states of Europe. We are arming solely for one reason. We are arming against Hitler's Germany—a great predatory Power in alliance with Japan.

It has been said, times without number, that if Hitler cannot cross the English Channel he cannot cross three thousand miles of sea. But there is only one reason why he has not crossed the English Channel. That is because forty-five million determined Britons, in a heroic resistance, have converted their island into an armed base, from which proceeds a steady stream of sea and air power. As Secretary Hull has said: "It is not the water that bars the way. It is the resolute determination of British arms. Were the control of the seas by Britain lost, the Atlantic would no longer

2. *Ibid.*, April 30, 1941. By permission of the New York *Times*.

be an obstacle—rather, it would become a broad highway for a conqueror moving westward."

That conqueror does not need to attempt at once an invasion of continental United States in order to place this country in deadly danger. We shall be in deadly danger the moment British sea power fails; the moment the eastern gates of the Atlantic are open to the aggressor; the moment we are compelled to divide our one-ocean Navy between two oceans simultaneously.

The combined Axis fleets [German, Italian, Japanese] outmatch our own: they are superior in numbers to our fleet in every category of vessel, from warships and aircraft-carriers to destroyers and submarines.* The combined Axis air strength will be much greater than our own if Hitler strikes in time—and when has he failed to strike in time? The master of Europe will have at his command shipways that can outbuild us, the resources of twenty conquered nations to furnish his materials, the oil of the Middle East to stoke his engines, the slave labor of a continent—bound by no union rules, and not working on a forty-hour week—to turn out his production.

Grant Hitler the gigantic prestige of a victory over Britain, and who can doubt that the first result, on our side of the ocean, would be the prompt appearance of imitation Nazi regimes in a half-dozen Latin-American nations, forced to be on the winning side, begging favors, clamoring for admission to the Axis? What shall we do then? Make war upon these neighbors, send armies to fight in the jungles of Central or South America; run the risk of outraging native sentiment and turning the whole continent against us? Or shall we sit tight while the area of Nazi influence draws ever closer to the Panama Canal, and a spreading checkerboard of Nazi airfields provides ports of call for German planes that may choose to bomb our cities?

But even if Hitler gave us time, what kind of "time" would we have at our disposal?

There are moral and spiritual dangers for this country as well as physical dangers in a Hitler victory. There are dangers to the mind and heart as well as to the body and the land.

Victorious in Europe, dominating Africa and Asia through his Axis partners, Hitler could not afford to permit the United States to live an untroubled and successful life, even if he wished to. We are the arch-enemy of all he stands for: the very citadel of that "pluto-democracy" which he hates and scorns. As long as liberty and freedom prevailed in the United States there would be constant risk for Hitler that our ideas and our example might infect the conquered countries which he was bending to his will. In his own interest he would be forced to harry us at every turn. Who can doubt that our lives would be poisoned every day by chal-

---

* Three foreign fleets are not necessarily equal to the sum of all their parts. There are different languages and signals, different-caliber guns and ammunition, different types of maneuvers, etc.

lenges and insults from Nazi politicians; that Nazi agents would stir up anti-American feeling in every country they controlled; that Nazi spies would overrun us here; that Hitler would produce a continual series of lightning diplomatic strokes—alliances and "non-aggression pacts" to break our will; in short, that a continuous war of nerves, if nothing worse, would be waged against us?

And who can doubt that, in response, we should have to turn our own nation into an armed camp, with all our traditional values of culture, education, social reform, democracy and liberty subordinated to the single, all-embracing aim of self-preservation? In this case we should indeed experience "regimentation." Every item of foreign trade, every transaction in domestic commerce, every present prerogative of labor, every civil liberty we cherish, would necessarily be regulated in the interest of defense.

3. F.D.R. Pledges No Foreign War (1940)

During the hotly contested third-term campaign of 1940, the Republican candidate Wendell Willkie harped on Roosevelt's broken promises. The President's re-election, he charged, would spell war by April 1, 1941. Smarting from this attack, Roosevelt replied as follows in a memorable Boston speech, which later came back to plague him. Inasmuch as Willkie himself later dismissed his own prediction as "a bit of campaign oratory," decide whether Roosevelt was bound by this campaign pledge, regardless of subsequent circumstances.

And while I am talking to you fathers and mothers, I give you one more assurance.

I have said this before, but I shall say it again and again and again:

Your boys are not going to be sent into any foreign wars.

They are going into training to form a force so strong that, by its very existence, it will keep the threat of war far away from our shores.

Yes, the purpose of our defense is defense.

[*In previous speeches Roosevelt had ordinarily followed the no-war pledge with the words "except in case of attack." To blunt the force of Willkie's accusation, he now left out the qualification. When asked why he was going to do so, he replied somewhat lamely, "It's not necessary. If we're attacked, it's no longer a foreign war."*]

C. THE LEND-LEASE CONTROVERSY

1. F.D.R. Drops the Dollar Sign (1940)

A serious student of history, Roosevelt was determined to avoid the blunders of World War I. The post-war quarrel with the Allies over debts lingered in his memory as he groped for some means of bolstering the hard-pressed British without getting involved in a repayment wrangle. Keeping his new brainstorm under his hat until

---

3. *Ibid.*, Oct. 31, 1940 (speech of Oct. 30, 1940).
1. *The Public Papers and Addresses of Franklin D. Roosevelt, 1940 Volume* (1941), pp. 606–08. By permission of The Macmillan Company.

his triumphant re-election over Willkie—he might have lost if he had revealed it before then—he outlined his scheme at one of his breezy, off-the-cuff press conferences. Note how the root of the debt-row difficulty was to be neatly eliminated.

It is possible—I will put it that way—for the United States to take over British [war] orders, and, because they are essentially the same kind of munitions that we use ourselves, turn them into American orders. We have got enough money to do it. And thereupon, as to such portion of them as the military events of the future determine to be right and proper for us to allow to go to the other side, either lease or sell the materials, subject to mortgage, to the people on the other side. That would be on the general theory that it may still prove true that the best defense of Great Britain is the best defense of the United States, and therefore that these materials would be more useful to the defense of the United States if they were used in Great Britain than if they were kept in storage here.

Now, what I am trying to do is to eliminate the dollar sign. That is something brand new in the thoughts of practically everybody in this room, I think—get rid of the silly, foolish old dollar sign.

Well, let me give you an illustration: Suppose my neighbor's home catches fire, and I have a length of garden hose four or five hundred feet away. If he can take my garden hose and connect it up with his hydrant, I may help him to put out his fire. Now, what do I do? I don't say to him before that operation, "Neighbor, my garden hose cost me $15; you have

HANDS ACROSS THE SEA

F.D.R. extends a fist to Hitler and a hand to Britain through lend-lease.
Orr in *Scottish Daily Record* (Glasgow), 1941.

got to pay me $15 for it." What is the transaction that goes on? I don't want $15—I want my garden hose back after the fire is over. All right. If it goes through the fire all right, intact, without any damage to it, he gives it back to me and thanks me very much for the use of it. But suppose it gets smashed up—holes in it—during the fire; we don't have to have too much formality about it, but I say to him, "I was glad to lend you that hose; I see I can't use it any more, it's all smashed up." He says, "How many feet of it were there?" I tell him, "There were 150 feet of it." He says, "All right, I will replace it." Now, if I get a nice garden hose back, I am in pretty good shape.

In other words, if you lend certain munitions and get the munitions back at the end of the war, if they are intact—haven't been hurt—you are all right. If they have been damaged or have deteriorated or have been lost completely, it seems to me you come out pretty well if you have them replaced by the fellow to whom you have lent them.

[*After the United States entered the war, supplies provided by foreign countries to American forces were credited to their account as reverse lend-lease. The total value of American lend-lease was over $50 billion, less some $7 billion in reverse lend-lease. Some cash was involved in the final settlement of accounts.*]

2. Senator Wheeler Assails Lend-Lease (1941)

Like the interventionists, Roosevelt believed that the salvation of Britain through large-scale military aid was crucial for the defense of the United States. But so strong was isolationist opposition that the proposed lend-lease act could not be entitled "An Act to Intervene in World War II for the Defense of Britain." The official title was "An Act Further to Promote the Defense of the United States." As finally passed, the new law virtually pledged the United States to the full extent of its economic resources to provide military supplies for those who were fighting aggression. Fiery Senator Burton K. Wheeler of Montana, "a born prosecutor" who had run for Vice-President on the left-wing La Follette Progressive ticket of 1924, was one of the most vehement isolationists. In analyzing this radio speech, locate his most pertinent and his most overdrawn arguments, and draw conclusions as to his foresight as a prophet.

The lend-lease policy, translated into legislative form, stunned a Congress and a nation wholly sympathetic to the cause of Great Britain. . . . It warranted my worst fears for the future of America, and it definitely stamps the President as war-minded.

The lend-lease-give program is the New Deal's Triple-A foreign policy; it will plow under every fourth American boy.

Never before have the American people been asked or compelled to give so bounteously and so completely of their tax dollars to any foreign nation. Never before has the Congress of the United States been asked by any President to violate international law. Never before has this Nation resorted to duplicity in the conduct of its foreign affairs. Never before has

2. Reprinted in *Congressional Record*, 77 Cong.. 1 sess., Appendix, pp. 178–79 (speech of Jan. 12, 1941).

the United States given to one man the power to strip this Nation of its defenses. Never before has a Congress coldly and flatly been asked to abdicate.

If the American people want a dictatorship—if they want a totalitarian form of government and if they want war—this bill should be steam-rollered through Congress, as is the wont of President Roosevelt.

Approval of this legislation means war, open and complete warfare. I, therefore, ask the American people before they supinely accept it, Was the last World War worth while?

If it were, then we should lend and lease war materials. If it were, then we should lend and lease American boys. President Roosevelt has said we would be repaid by England. We will be. We will be repaid, just as England repaid her war debts of the first World War—repaid those dollars wrung from the sweat of labor and the toil of farmers with cries of "Uncle Shylock." Our boys will be returned—returned in caskets, maybe; returned with bodies maimed; returned with minds warped and twisted by sights of horrors and the scream and shriek of high-powered shells.

Considered on its merits and stripped of its emotional appeal to our sympathies, the lend-lease-give bill is both ruinous and ridiculous. . . .

It gives to one man—responsible to no one—the power to denude our shores of every warship. It gives to one individual the dictatorial power to strip the American Army of our every tank, cannon, rifle, or anti-aircraft gun. No one would deny that the lend-lease-give bill contains provisions that would enable one man to render the United States defenseless, but they will tell you, "The President would never do it." To this I say, "Why does he ask the power if he does not intend to use it?" Why not, I say, place some check on American donations to a foreign nation? . . .

I say in the kind of language used by the President—shame on those who ask the powers—and shame on those who would grant them.

[*Talk of "plowing under every fourth American boy" spurred Roosevelt into declaring at his press conference of January 14, 1941, that this was "the most untruthful, as the most dastardly, unpatriotic thing that has ever been said. Quote me on that. That really is the rottenest thing that has been said in public life in my generation." Determine what measure of truth there was in Wheeler's charge.*]

3. Hearst Denounces Aid to Russia (1941)

The fateful lend-lease bill became law in March, 1941. Three months later Hitler treacherously attacked Stalin, his co-conspirator in the non-aggression pact of 1939. Isolationists rejoiced that the two arch-menaces would now bleed each other white, and thus reduce the danger of American involvement. Catholics expressed relief at the weakening of the atheistic menace of Soviet Russia. But Roosevelt, fearful that the Russians could not stem Hitler's mechanized might, promised them lend-lease aid and ultimately delivered supplies worth $11 billion. The Hearst press here expresses distaste for "Bloody Joe" Stalin as a bedfellow. Note to what extent its apprehensions were justified by events.

3. New York *Journal-American*, Sept. 5, 1941. By permission.

If we are fighting against totalitarianism as a foul principle and oppressive policy, why in the name of high heaven should we not desire to see the two totalitarian powers exterminate each other and destroy not only the principle but the practice of despotic government?

If we are citizens—or subjects—of a genuine democracy and if we are devoted to the ideals of democracy, and honestly desirous of preserving and perpetuating those ideals, why should we not desire to see the enemies of democracy destroy each other? . . .

Is our free country piling up deficits, bleeding its citizens white with confiscatory taxation, rushing headlong into national bankruptcy, shoveling out our wealth abroad, and shipping our war materials to alien nations to bolster up Bolshevism in Russia to spread it over all of Europe, including Britain, and to breed it and broadcast it in our own America?

We may not think that this is what we want to do, but this is exactly what we are doing with our Bolshevist alliance, and no smoke screen of fine phrases can obscure that outstanding fact.

No country which fights for Russia can claim to be honestly opposed to tyranny, since Bolshevism is the basest and bloodiest tyranny that has disgraced the supposed civilization of Europe since the time of Ivan the Terrible.

No country can truthfully claim to be crusading for democracy and the four freedoms when it is supporting a tyranny which is the most evil enemy of democracy—a tyranny where all the four freedoms have been brutally suppressed—a tyranny with no liberty, no opportunity, no morality, and no God.

D. WAR IN THE ATLANTIC

1. Framing the Atlantic Charter (1941)

Roosevelt finally met with Prime Minister Churchill in deepest secrecy off the coast of Newfoundland in August, 1941. Major items of discussion were lend-lease shipments, common defense, and the halting of Japanese aggression. Churchill later wrote that for Roosevelt—the head of a technically neutral state—to meet in this way with the prime minister of a belligerent state was "astonishing" and amounted to "warlike action." The most spectacular offspring of the conference was the unofficial Atlantic Charter, which in 1942 became the cornerstone of Allied war aims. An admixture of the old Wilson Fourteen Points (see p. 717) and the new New Deal, it held out seductive hope to the victims of the dictators. Observe the aspect or aspects of the Atlantic Charter that came closest to "warlike action."

. . . The President of the United States of America and the Prime Minister, Mr. Churchill, representing His Majesty's Government in the United Kingdom, being met together, deem it right to make known certain common principles in the national policies of their respective countries on which they base their hopes for a better future for the world.

First, their countries seek no aggrandizement, territorial or other;

1. *Department of State Bulletin,* V, 125–26 (Aug. 14, 1941).

Second, they desire to see no territorial changes that do not accord with the freely expressed wishes of the peoples concerned [*i.e.*, self-determination, one of the later 14 Points; in part Points V and XII of the 14];

Third, they respect the right of all peoples to choose the form of government under which they will live; and they wish to see sovereign rights and self-government restored to those who have been forcibly deprived of them [cf. territorial restoration, Points VI, VII, VIII, XI of the 14];

Fourth, they will endeavor, with due respect for their existing obligations, to further the enjoyment by all states, great or small, victor or vanquished, of access, on equal terms, to the trade and to the raw materials of the world which are needed for their economic prosperity [*i.e.*, Point III of 14];

Fifth, they desire to bring about the fullest collaboration between all nations in the economic field with the object of securing, for all, improved labor standards, economic advancement, and social security [a combination of the objectives of the League of Nations and the New Deal];

Sixth, after the final destruction of the Nazi tyranny, they hope to see established a peace which will afford to all nations the means of dwelling in safety within their own boundaries, and which will afford assurance that all the men in all the lands may live out their lives in freedom from fear and want;

Seventh, such a peace should enable all men to traverse the high seas and oceans without hindrance [*i.e.*, freedom of the seas, Point II of 14];

Eighth, they believe that all of the nations of the world, for realistic as well as spiritual reasons, must come to the abandonment of the use of force. Since no future peace can be maintained if land, sea, or air armaments continue to be employed by nations which threaten, or may threaten, aggression outside of their frontiers, they believe, pending the establishment of a wider and permanent system of general security [United Nations, replacing League of Nations], that the disarmament of such nations is essential. They will likewise aid and encourage all other practicable measures which will lighten for peace-loving peoples the crushing burden of armaments [*i.e.*, Point IV of 14].

2. The Chicago *Tribune* Is Outraged (1941)

A highly influential mouthpiece of Middle Western isolationism was the Chicago *Tribune*, self-elected "The World's Greatest Newspaper." Violently anti-Roosevelt and anti-intervention, it resorted to extreme measures, including the publication of Washington's secret war plans three days before Pearl Harbor. In analyzing the *Tribune's* editorial on the Atlantic Conference, determine in what respects this newspaper would support Churchill's later observation that the deliberations amounted to "warlike action."

Mr. Roosevelt's dangerous ambition always to do what no other President ever did, and to be the man who shakes the world, led him to meet

2. Chicago *Tribune*, Aug. 15, 1941, as quoted in *A Century of Tribune Editorials* (1947), pp. 129–30. By permission of the Chicago *Tribune*.

Mr. Churchill, as is now disclosed, at sea. There, he, the head of a nation which is not at war, and the head of the British empire, which is at war, signed their names to an eight-point war and peace program, as if both countries not only were fighting side by side but saw their way to victory. . . .

For Mr. Churchill the event would be, he could hope, that last step which would bring him what he has awaited as his salvation—the final delivery on Mr. Roosevelt's commitments, the delivery of the United States with all its man power into the war at all points. Mr. Churchill would appreciate that Mr. Roosevelt in the eyes of the world became his full ally. . . .

Mr. Roosevelt himself had that end in view. As head of a nation at peace he had no right to discuss war aims with the ruler of a country at war. He had no right to take a chair at such a conference. He had no regard for his constitutional duties or his oath of office when he did so. He not only likes to shatter traditions, he likes to shatter the checks and restraints which were put on his office. He is thoroly un-American. His ancestry is constantly emerging. He is the true descendant of that James Roosevelt, his great-grandfather, who was a Tory in New York during the Revolution and took the oath of allegiance to the British king.* . . .

He comes of a stock that has never fought for the country and he now betrays it, altho it has repudiated his program and him with it. . . .

The American people can rest assured that Mr. Churchill was paying little attention to the rehash of the Wilsonian futilities, to the freedom of the seas and the freedom of peoples such as the [British-ruled] people of India, for instance. What he wanted to know of Mr. Roosevelt was: When are you coming across? And it is the answer to that question that concerns the American people, who have voted 4 to 1 that they are not going across at all unless their government drags them in against their will.

One phrase in the statement would have Mr. Churchill's complete approval—"after final destruction of the Nazi tyranny." To that he committed the President of the United States in circumstances as spectacular and theatrical as could be arranged. Mr. Roosevelt pledged himself to the destruction of Hitler and the Nazis. In the circumstances in which this was done Mr. Churchill would insist that it was the pledge of a government, binding upon the country.

The country repudiates it. Mr. Roosevelt had no authority and can find none for making such a pledge. He was more than outside the country. He was outside his office. The spectacle was one of two autocratic rulers, one of them determining the destiny of his country in the matter of war or peace absolutely in his own will, as if his subjects were without voice.

The country rejects that idea of its government.

* James Roosevelt, only fifteen years old when the fighting began, was a student at Princeton from 1776 to 1780. His father, a staunch Patriot, was forced to flee New York City. There is no evidence that young James took the alleged oath; the probabilities are strong that he did not. (Information provided by Elizabeth B. Drewry, Director of the Franklin D. Roosevelt Library.)

3. F.D.R. Proclaims Shoot-at-Sight (1941)

Lend-lease carried an implied commitment that the United States would guarantee delivery of arms, even though the law specifically forbade "convoying vessels by naval vessels of the United States." Roosevelt got around this restriction by setting up a system of patrols by American warships working in collaboration with the British. On September 4, 1941, the U.S. destroyer *Greer* in Icelandic waters trailed a German submarine for three and one-half hours, while radioing its position to nearby British aircraft. The U-boat finally fired two torpedoes (which missed), whereupon the *Greer* retaliated with depth bombs (which also missed). Seven days later, after presumably taking time to verify the facts, Roosevelt went on the radio with this sensational shoot-at-sight speech. Notice the liberties he took with the truth, and decide whether the crisis was such as to justify his doing so.

The Navy Department of the United States has reported to me that, on the morning of September fourth, the United States destroyer *Greer*, proceeding in full daylight toward Iceland, had reached a point southeast of Greenland. She was carrying American mail to Iceland. She was flying the American flag. Her identity as an American ship was unmistakable.

She was then and there attacked by a submarine. Germany admits that it was a German submarine. The submarine deliberately fired a torpedo at the *Greer*, followed later by another torpedo attack. In spite of what Hitler's propaganda bureau has invented, and in spite of what any American obstructionist organization may prefer to believe, I tell you the blunt fact that the German submarine fired first upon this American destroyer without warning, and with deliberate design to sink her.

Our destroyer, at the time, was in waters which the Government of the United States has declared to be waters of self-defense—surrounding outposts of American protection in the Atlantic.

In the north, outposts have been established by us in Iceland, Greenland, Labrador, and Newfoundland. Through these waters there pass many ships of many flags. They bear food and other supplies to civilians; and they bear [lend-lease] matériel of war, for which the people of the United States are spending billions of dollars, and which, by Congressional action, they have declared to be essential for the defense of our own land.

The United States destroyer, when attacked, was proceeding on a legitimate mission. . . .

Generation after generation, America has battled for the general policy of the freedom of the seas.* That policy is a very simple one—but a basic, fundamental one. It means that no nation has the right to make the broad oceans of the world, at great distances from the actual theater of land war, unsafe for the commerce of others. . . .

It is no act of war on our part when we decide to protect the seas which are vital to American defense. The aggression is not ours. Ours is solely defense.

3. *Department of State Bulletin*, V, 193, 195, 197 (Sept. 13, 1941).
* The traditional American concept of freedom of the seas did not include the armed convoying of gift lend-lease munitions through German-proclaimed war zones to the enemies of Germany.

But let this warning be clear. From now on, if German or Italian vessels of war enter the waters, the protection of which is necessary for American defense, they do so at their own peril.

THE NORTH ATLANTIC 1941

GREER attacked Sept. 4

KEARNY torpedoed Oct. 17

REUBEN JAMES Sunk Oct. 31

German Blockade Zone

GREENLAND

ICELAND

SCOTLAND ENGLAND

IRELAND

CANADA

NEWFOUNDLAND

NOVA SCOTIA

Roosevelt–Churchill Meeting, Aug. 9–12

[*Patrolling led to convoying by presidential edict, despite the express terms of the Lend-Lease Act, and convoying led to shooting. In October, 1941, the U.S. destroyer* Kearny *suffered torpedo damage and a loss of eleven lives in a battle with German submarines southeast of Iceland. Later that month the U.S. destroyer* Reuben James *was torpedoed and sunk off Iceland while on convoy duty. An undeclared shooting war with Hitler was now being waged in the Atlantic.*]

E. BLOWUP IN THE PACIFIC

1. Ickes Prepares to "Raise Hell" (1941)

New Japanese aggression in south Indochina, despite warnings from Washington, finally prompted Roosevelt to clamp down a complete embargo on shipments going to Japan when he froze all Japanese assets in the United States on July 25, 1941. Faced with the loss of critical oil supplies, the Tokyo war lords were confronted with agonizing alternatives: yielding some of the fruits of their aggression in the Far East or fighting the United States and its allies. America was by no means ready for war in the vast Pacific, and the administration seriously considered a three-month truce— Roosevelt favored six months. But this proposal was never formally presented to Japan. The outspoken Secretary of the Interior Harold Ickes records in his secret diary the story as he heard it. Note what this account (November 30) reveals of the inner workings of the Washington government, and determine basically why the truce scheme failed.

1. *The Secret Diary of Harold Ickes* (1954), III, 654–55. Copyright 1954 by Simon and Schuster, Inc. By permission of Simon and Schuster, Inc.

Our State Department has been negotiating for several days with Saburo Kurusu, the special envoy sent over from Japan, and with Ambassador Kichisaburo Nomura. I have had a suspicion for a long time that the State Department would resume a policy of appeasement toward Japan, if it could get away with it.

Our State Department, according to a story that I have heard, had actually proposed what it called a "truce" for three months with Japan. We were to resume shipments of cotton and other commodities, but the most important item on the list was gasoline for "civilian" purposes. Now anyone who knows anything about Japan and about the situation there knows that there is very little, if any, civilian use of gasoline. . . . Then a strong protest came in from General Chiang Kai-shek to the effect that to do this would destroy the morale of the Chinese. It was the intention of the State Department to crowd the thing through without even giving Halifax [British ambassador] a chance to refer it to Churchill. However, the British fought for and obtained a sufficient delay to consult Churchill, and he was strongly opposed.

The strong opposition of China and Britain caused the appeasers of the State Department to pause. They went to the White House, and in the end the President refused to go through with the deal.

If it had not been for the strenuous intervention of Churchill and Chiang Kai-shek, the appeasers in the State Department, with the support of the President, would have resumed at least a partial commercial relationship with Japan, as the result of which we would have sent Japan cotton and gasoline and other commodities. . . .

If this negotiation with Japan had been consummated, I would have promptly resigned from the Cabinet with a ringing statement attacking the arrangement and raising hell generally with the State Department and its policy of appeasement. I have no doubt that the country would have reacted violently. As a matter of fact, some of the newspapers indicated that they were uneasy and printed editorials deprecating any attempt at even a partial resumption of relationship with Japan. I believe that the President would have lost the country on this issue and that hell would have been to pay generally.

Now matters are very tense indeed so far as Japan is concerned. The morning papers carry headlines announcing that Japan has solemnly declared her determination "to purge American and British influence from East Asia for the honor and pride of mankind." So it may be, after all, that there will be a clash in the Pacific.

2. Tōgō Blames the United States (1952)

Instead of appeasement, Secretary Hull presented stern terms to the two Japanese envoys in his note of November 26, 1941. Japan would have to withdraw her armed

2. Tōgō Shigenori, *The Cause of Japan* (1956), pp. 186–88. Copyright © 1956 by Simon and Schuster, Inc. By permission of the publishers.

forces from China, after four years of aggression, and from Indochina as well. In return, the United States would unfreeze Japanese assets and make some other secondary concessions. Such loss of face was so abhorrent to the Japanese war lords that Hull had little hope that the terms would be accepted. The next day he told Secretary of War Stimson, "I have washed my hands of it, and it is now in the hands of you and [Secretary of the Navy] Knox—the Army and Navy." The reaction of Japan is described by the then Foreign Minister, Tōgō Shigenori, who later died in prison while serving a twenty-year sentence as a war criminal. Determine what warrant there was for the blame expressed by this official for the breakdown of negotiations.

Ambassador Grew, then in Tokyo, later said that when the note of 26 November was sent, the button which set off the war had been pushed.

On the 26th and 27th Secretary Hull held special press conferences at which he gave a full account of the Japanese-American negotiations; the American press responded by reporting almost unanimously that it was Japan's choice whether to accept the Hull Note or go to war. Later—in wartime—an American chronicler wrote that even a Monaco or a Luxemburg would have taken up arms against the United States if it had been handed such a memorandum as that which the State Department presented to the Japanese government. . . .

It is therefore no longer arguable at this time of day that the American authorities, having made all necessary preparations in the expectation that the negotiations would break down and a war ensue, delivered the Hull Note anticipating that Japan would reject it, thus compelling her to elect between total surrender and war. Indeed, remembering that the question of how to insure that Japan should fire the first shot had been in the forefront in the War Cabinet's discussions in Washington, it seems not unwarrantable to construe the note as going beyond the forcing of a choice —it is not too much to say that it was the throwing down of a challenge to Japan, or at the least constituted an ultimatum without time limit.

This we knew in Tokyo—though we could not then know of the words and acts of the high American officials which confirmed our deduction— from the drastic terms of the note and the inclusion among them of conditions never theretofore suggested. Our interpretation was confirmed by the reaction to Hull's disclosures by the American press—which played up, as if at the urging of the governmental authorities, the choice between the terms of the Hull Note and war—and by the plainly visible tightening of the encirclement of Japan.

So far as concerns my own state of mind upon receipt of the Hull Note, I can never forget the despair which overpowered me. I had fought and worked unflaggingly until that moment; but I could feel no enthusiasm for the fight thereafter. I tried as it were to close my eyes and swallow the Hull Note whole, as the alternative to war, but it stuck in the craw. In contrast to my dejection, many of the military men were elated at the uncompromising attitude of the United States, as if to say, "Didn't we tell you so?"—they were by no means easy to be patient with.

"GIVE 'EM BOTH BARRELS"

Uncle Sam aroused by Japanese sneak attack at
Pearl Harbor. New Orleans *Times-Picayune*, 1941.

[*The Japanese later
argued that they were
forced to break out of
the economic encircle-
ment resulting from
Roosevelt's embargo-
freezing order of July
25, 1941. This view
found surprising sup-
port in 1944 from one
of America's allies, Cap-
tain Oliver Lyttleton,
British Minister of Pro-
duction. In a London
speech he declared,
"Japan was provoked
into attacking the Amer-
icans at Pearl Harbor.
It is a travesty on his-
tory ever to say that
America was forced into
the war. . . . It is in-
correct to say that
America was ever truly
neutral. . . ." The sub-
sequent uproar in the*
United States forced Lyttleton hastily to soften his remarks. (*New York Times,
June 21, 22, 1944.*)]

3. Hull Justifies His Stand (1948)

Isolationist Senator Vandenberg, writing in his diary just after Pearl Harbor, felt
that the United States would have had to yield "relatively little" to pacify Japan,
and feared that "we may have *driven* her *needlessly* into hostilities through our dogmatic diplomatic attitudes. . . ." "We 'asked for it,' " he added, "and we 'got it.' "
Secretary of State Hull, the soft-spoken Tennessean, here outlines three possible alternatives in his *Memoirs*. Assuming that the ultimate security of the United States
required the halting of the Japanese, and knowing that America's navy was not ready
for Japan, form conclusions as to the wisdom of Hull's choice among the three possibilities. Were other courses open?

There were three methods to meet the danger from Japan. One was by
a preventive attack. But democracies do not engage in preventive attacks
except with greatest difficulty. Had I suggested to the President that he go
to Congress and ask for a declaration of war against Japan at some time
after the invasion of southern Indo-China, he could have made a good case
concerning the dangers to us inherent in Japan's course of aggression. But,

3. Reprinted with permission of The Macmillan Company from *The Memoirs of Cordell Hull*
(1948), II, 1104–05. Copyright 1948 by Cordell Hull.

remembering the fact that on August 13, 1941, only three weeks after Japan invaded southern Indo-China, the House of Representatives sustained the Selective Service Act by a majority of just one vote, it seems most unlikely that the President could have obtained a declaration.

Nor would the military and naval authorities have been ready for a preventive attack. The fact that they pleaded for more time solely to prepare our defenses in the Pacific was proof in itself that they were not prepared to take the offensive.

A preventive attack, moreover, would have run counter to our determination to pursue the course of peace to the end, with the hope, however microscopic, that even at the last hour the Japanese might have a change of heart.

The second method to meet the danger was to agree to Japan's demands. This would have given us peace—that is, until Japan, after strengthening herself through the concessions we should have made, was ready to move again. But it would have denied all the principles of right living among nations which we had supported; it would have betrayed the countries [China, Britain] that later became our allies; and it would have given us an infamous place in history.

When we realize that Japan was ruthlessly invading peaceful countries, that the United States had pleaded with her from the beginning to cease her course of military conquest in partnership with Hitler, and that all problems in the Pacific would have practically settled themselves if Japan had adopted a policy of peace, it is evident that Japan had no right to make demands upon us. Japan negotiated as if we, too, were an aggressor, as if both countries had to balance their aggressions. Japan had no more right to make demands upon us than an individual gangster has to make demands upon his intended victim.

The third method was simply to continue discussions with Japan, to convince her that her aggressions cost her more than they were worth, to point out to her that her partnership with Hitler could be as dangerous to her as it was to the rest of the world, to lay before her proposal after proposal which in the long run would have given her in peace the prosperity her military leaders were seeking in conquest.

It was this third that we chose. Of the three, it was the only American method.

[*The Tokyo war lords claimed that they had only two choices—surrender or war. Actually they had a third choice—accommodation. Loss of considerable face would have been better than loss of the war. The argument that Hull's note of November 26 provoked the Japanese into an attack is weakened by two facts. First, the naval force that attacked Pearl Harbor had left its rendezvous in Japan twenty-four hours earlier. Second, early in November the imperial conference had unanimously decided on war, provided that diplomacy had not produced a satisfactory settlement by December 1.*]

THOUGHT PROVOKERS

1. What would have happened if the United States had been truly neutral during World War II, and would the results have been to the nation's best interests? Is it unneutral to change the rules (laws) after the game (war) has started? It has been said that there is no inequality so great as the equal treatment of unequals. Comment.

2. Have the events since 1945 given support to the view that a democratic United States could exist as a kind of fortified island?

3. Lend-lease was designed to defend the United States by helping others fight America's potential enemies with America's weapons. Was there an element of immorality in this policy? Would the United States have kept out of the war if the Lend-Lease Act had not been passed?

4. Assuming that the Atlantic Charter was a warlike step, was it justified? Roosevelt believed that a Hitler victory would be ruinous for the United States, and to combat isolationist pressures he repeatedly misrepresented facts (*Greer* case) or usurped powers (convoying). Was he justified in using such methods to arouse the American people to an awareness of their danger?

5. With regard to the diplomatic breakdown preceding Pearl Harbor, it has been said that both Japan and America were right if one conceded their major premises. Explain fully and form a conclusion. Would the position of the United States be better today if Hitler had conquered Russia and Japan had crushed China?

FURTHER EXPLORATION

General: W. L. Langer and S. E. Gleason, *The Challenge to Isolation, 1937–1940* (1952); *The Undeclared War, 1940–1941* (1953). **Arms Embargo:** D. F. Drummond, *The Passing of American Neutrality, 1937–1941* (1955). **Intervention:** Walter Johnson, *The Battle against Isolationism* (1944); W. S. Cole, *America First* (1953). **Lend-Lease:** C. A. Beard, *President Roosevelt and the Coming of the War, 1941* (1948) [unfavorable]; Basil Rauch, *Roosevelt from Munich to Pearl Harbor* (1950) [favorable]. **Atlantic War:** S. E. Morison, *The Battle of the Atlantic, 1939–1943* (1947). **Pacific Blowup:** Herbert Feis, *The Road to Pearl Harbor* (1950); Toshikazu Kase, *Journey to the Missouri* (1950); Walter Lord, *Day of Infamy* (1957); H. L. Trefousse, ed., *What Happened at Pearl Harbor?* (1958); Roberta Wohlstetter, *Pearl Harbor: Warning and Decision* (1962); R. J. C. Butow, *Tojo and the Coming of the War* (1961).

Recent: W. E. Leuchtenburg, *Franklin D. Roosevelt and the New Deal, 1932–1940* (1963) [paperback]; R. A. Divine, *The Illusion of Neutrality* (1962) and *The Reluctant Belligerent: American Entry into World War II* (1965) [paperback]; W. L. Neumann, *America Encounters Japan* (1963) [paperback]; Manfred Jonas, *Isolationism in America, 1935–1941* (1966).

Chapter 44

Waging World War II

No matter how long it may take us to overcome this premeditated invasion [Pearl Harbor], the American people in their righteous might will win through to absolute victory.

FRANKLIN D. ROOSEVELT, WAR MESSAGE, 1941

PROLOGUE: The nation was plunged into war with the worst naval disaster in its history, and many agonizing months were to pass before the tide in the Pacific began to turn. The American conquest of bomber bases in the Marianas Islands in 1944 insured that Japan would be blasted into surrender. Meanwhile the Battle of Production at home and the Battle of the Atlantic against German submarines had to be won, as they narrowly were. The hard-pressed and ever-suspicious Soviets, anxious to have the Western allies share equally in the blood-letting, clamored ceaselessly for a second front. Following two widely spaced postponements, the invasion was launched on French soil in 1944, and it teetered so long in the balance as to indicate that earlier invasions would have failed. After Germany was hammered into submission in May, 1945, Japan was atom-bombed into prostration in August, 1945. The Great War ended as the Nuclear Age dawned, ushered in by an ominous mushroom-shaped cloud.

A. THE BLAME FOR PEARL HARBOR

1. War Warnings from Washington (1941)

The military officials in Washington had "cracked" Tokyo's secret code. They therefore knew from intercepted messages, especially after Secretary Hull's final note of November 26, that Japan was about to attack. But they could only guess where. The following war warnings were dispatched to Pacific commanders, including General MacArthur, who was caught with his planes down in the Philippines some eight hours *after* the Pearl Harbor attack on December 7, 1941. The messages from Washington did not mention Hawaii, evidently because of the belief, fortified by reports of massed ship movements, that the Japanese were about to strike in Southeast Asia. The surprised American commanders later complained that they had not been properly warned. Comment critically in the light of these warnings. Note also what grounds existed for the assumption that the attack would not come at Pearl Harbor.

[Navy Department to Pacific Commanders, November 24, 1941]

Chances of favorable outcome of negotiations with Japan very doubtful. This situation, coupled with statements of Japanese Government and movements their naval and military forces, indicates in our opinion that a surprise aggressive movement in any direction, including attack on Philippines or Guam, is a possibility. Chief of Staff has seen this dispatch; concurs

1. *Pearl Harbor Attack; Hearings before the Joint Committee on the Investigation of the Pearl Harbor Attack,* 79 Cong., 1 sess., pt. XIV, pp. 1405, 1406.

and requests action [by the respective addressees] to inform senior Army officers their areas. Utmost secrecy necessary in order not to complicate an already tense situation or precipitate Japanese action.

[Navy Department to Asiatic and Pacific Fleets, November 27, 1941]

This despatch is to be considered a war warning. Negotiations with Japan looking toward stabilization of conditions in the Pacific have ceased, and an aggressive move by Japan is expected within the next few days. The number and equipment of Japanese troops, and the organization of naval task forces, indicates an amphibious expedition against either the Philippines, Thai [Siam] or Kra [Malay] peninsula, or possibly Borneo [Dutch East Indies]. . . .

2. Admiral Kimmel Defends Himself (1946)

In 1942, after carrier-based Japanese bombers had crippled the American fleet at Pearl Harbor on that fateful Sunday morning, the special Roberts commission found Admiral H. E. Kimmel and General W. C. Short guilty of "dereliction of duty." But the Army and the Navy conducted their own investigations and concluded that there were no grounds for a court-martial. After the war a full-dress joint Congressional investigation (ten million words) elicited the following testimony from Admiral Kimmel, who must be judged in the light of three points. First, as early as 1932 the Navy had staged a successful mock (Japanese) raid on Pearl Harbor *on a Sunday morning* with carrier-based aircraft. Second, the attacking Japanese carriers had been lost to American naval intelligence for some days. Third, four hours and thirteen minutes before the surprise attack the Navy sighted an enemy submarine off the mouth of Pearl Harbor; an hour and ten minutes before the strike the Navy fired upon and sank a Japanese submarine off the mouth of Pearl Harbor. In view of the essential facts assess the strengths and weaknesses of Kimmel's defense, and form a judgment.

The so-called "war warning" dispatch of November 27 did not warn the Pacific Fleet of an attack in the Hawaiian area. It did not state expressly or by implication that an attack in the Hawaiian area was imminent or probable. It did not repeal or modify the advice previously given me by the Navy Department that no move against Pearl Harbor was imminent or planned by Japan.

The phrase "war warning" cannot be made a catch-all for all the contingencies hindsight may suggest. It is a characterization of the specific information which the dispatch contained. . . .

In brief, on November 27, the Navy Department suggested that I send from the immediate vicinity of Pearl Harbor the carriers of the fleet, which constituted the fleet's main striking defense against an air attack.[*]

On November 27, the War and Navy Departments suggested that we send from the island of Oahu [site of Pearl Harbor] 50 percent of the Army's resources in pursuit planes.

2. *Ibid.*, pt. VI, pp. 2518, 2520, 2521.
[*] Fortunately for the United States, the three great carriers were not at Pearl Harbor when the attack came.

These proposals came to us on the very same day of the so-called "war warning."

In these circumstances no reasonable man in my position would consider that the "war warning" was intended to suggest the likelihood of an attack in the Hawaiian area.

From November 27 to the time of the attack, all the information which I had from the Navy Department or from any other source, confirmed, and was consistent with, the Japanese movement in southeast Asia described in the dispatch of November 27. . . .

In short, all indications of the movements of Japanese military and naval forces which came to my attention confirmed the information in the dispatch of 27 November—that the Japanese were on the move against Thailand or the Kra [Malay] Peninsula in southeast Asia.

3. Secretary Stimson Charges Negligence (1946)

General Short, the Army commander in Hawaii, complained that the warnings from Washington were not specific enough regarding a possible Japanese attack. He felt that he should have been advised that Washington was intercepting Japanese coded messages (despite the need for secrecy in using these "magic" intercepts). Yet on November 30—a week early—the Honolulu *Advertiser* had headlined a story "JAPA-NESE MAY STRIKE OVER WEEKEND." Newly installed Army radar actually picked up the attacking Japanese planes fifty-three minutes in advance, but this evidence stirred no defensive action. Secretary of War Stimson, who had served in three presidential Cabinets, here defends his office before the joint Congressional committee. Determine whether or not his analogy to a sentinel is convincing.

Many of the discussions on this subject indicated a failure to grasp the fundamental difference between the duties of an outpost command and those of the commander in chief of an army or nation and his military advisers.

The outpost commander is like a sentinel on duty in the face of the enemy. His fundamental duties are clear and precise. He must assume that the enemy will attack at his particular post; and that the enemy will attack at the time and in the way in which it will be most difficult to defeat him. It is not the duty of the outpost commander to speculate or rely on the possibilities of the enemy attacking at some other outpost instead of his own. It is his duty to meet him at his post at any time, and to make the best possible fight that can be made against him with the weapons with which he has been supplied.

On the other hand, the Commander in Chief of the Nation (and his advisers) . . . has much more difficult and complex duties to fulfill. Unlike the outpost commander, he must constantly watch, study, and estimate where the principal or most dangerous attack is most likely to come, in order that he may most effectively distribute his insufficient forces and munitions to meet it. He knows that his outposts are not all equally sup-

3. *Ibid.*, pt. XI, pp. 5428–29.

plied or fortified, and that they are not all equally capable of defense. He knows also that from time to time they are of greatly varying importance to the grand strategy of the war. . . .

From the foregoing I believe that it was inevitable and proper that a far greater number of items of information coming through our Intelligence should be collected and considered and appraised by the General Staff at Washington than those which were transmitted to the commander of an outpost.

General Short had been told the two essential facts: (1) A war with Japan is threatening. (2) Hostile action by Japan is possible at any moment. Given those two facts, both of which were stated without equivocation in the message of November 27, the outpost commander should be on the alert to make his fight.

Even without any such message, the outpost commander should have been on the alert. If he did not know that the relations between Japan and the United States were strained and might be broken at any time, he must have been almost the only man in Hawaii who did not know it, for the radio and the newspapers were blazoning out those facts daily, and he had a chief of staff and an intelligence officer to tell him so. And if he did not know that the Japanese were likely to strike without warning, he could not have read his history of Japan or known the lessons taught in Army schools in respect to such matters.*

Under these circumstances, which were of general knowledge and which he must have known, to cluster his airplanes in such groups and positions that in an emergency they could not take to the air for several hours, and to keep his anti-aircraft ammunition so stored that it could not be promptly and immediately available, and to use his best reconnaissance system, the radar, only for a very small fraction of the day and night, in my opinion betrayed a misconception of his real duty which was almost beyond belief.

[*The joint Congressional committee investigating Pearl Harbor was a partisan body which submitted two reports. The majority (six Democrats, joined by two Republicans) generally absolved the Democratic Roosevelt administration of responsibility for the surprise attack, while finding the Hawaii commanders guilty of "errors of judgment and not derelictions of duty." Two Republican Senators filed a minority report highly critical of the Roosevelt administration.*]

4. Roosevelt Awaits the Blow (1941)

On the evening of December 6—the day before Pearl Harbor—American naval intelligence intercepted and decoded the bulk of Tokyo's warlike reply to Secretary Hull's last "tough" note (November 26). Commander Lester Schulz, a naval aide at the White House, promptly delivered these intercepts to the White House. Five years later he testified before the joint Congressional committee as to the President's reac-

---

* Attacking without warning had been a feudal practice in Japan. The Japanese attacked the Chinese without warning in 1894 and 1931 and the Russians in 1904. In the Age of Hitler, attacks without warning were commonplace.
4. *Ibid.*, pt. X, pp. 4662–63.

tion. Certain critics of Roosevelt claim that he now knew of the Japanese plan to strike Pearl Harbor the next day, and that he deliberately exposed the fleet so as to lure the Japanese into an act of aggression which would unify American opinion. Comment critically on this interpretation in the light of Commander Schulz's testimony.

Commander Schulz. The President read the papers, which took perhaps ten minutes. Then he handed them to Mr. [Harry] Hopkins. . . . Mr. Hopkins then read the papers and handed them back to the President. The President then turned toward Mr. Hopkins and said in substance . . . "This means war." Mr. Hopkins agreed, and they discussed then, for perhaps five minutes, the situation of the Japanese forces, that is, their deployment and—

Mr. Richardson [committee counsel]. Can you recall what either of them said?

Commander Schulz. In substance I can. . . . Mr. Hopkins . . . expressed a view that since war was undoubtedly going to come at the convenience of the Japanese, it was too bad that we could not strike the first blow and prevent any sort of surprise. The President nodded and then said in effect, "No, we can't do that. We are a democracy and a peaceful people." Then he raised his voice, and this much I remember definitely. He said, "But we have a good record."

The impression that I got was that we would have to stand on that record; we could not make the first overt move. We would have to wait until it came.

During this discussion there was no mention of Pearl Harbor. The only geographic name I recall was Indochina. The time at which war might begin was not discussed, but from the manner of the discussion there was no indication that tomorrow was necessarily the day.

B. SOVIET-AMERICAN FRICTION

1. Communists Distrust Capitalists (1946)

General John R. Deane, the chief United States military liaison officer in Moscow, found the hard-pressed Russians willing to accept American arms but not American personnel. He concluded that the Communist regime did not want its people tainted by exposure to capitalistic Americans; that it desired the prestige of winning solo victories; and that it regarded World War II as only one campaign in the long war against capitalism. Why permit possible future adversaries like the Americans to spy out the terrain and probe Russia's military weaknesses? In this post-war account, General Deane cites specific cases. Note which ones seem to be least credible, and form conclusions as to what they foreshadowed regarding cooperation with Moscow after the war.

Whatever the reasons, the fact that Russia desired, insofar as possible, to play a lone hand was proved by undeniable evidence. In her darkest

1. J. R. Deane, *The Strange Alliance* (1946), pp. 296, 160–61. By permission of the Viking Press.

days she refused to allow a group of Allied bombers to base in the Caucasus in order to assist her at Stalingrad. Our well-meant voluntary efforts to support her advance in the Balkans with our Air Force operating from Italy brought forth protests rather than gratitude. No single American was allowed to enter the Soviet Union without pressure from the Ambassador or me, and then a visa was granted only after an exhaustive study of the background of the individual involved. Under these circumstances it was clear that nothing much could come of a partnership in which one of the principals was not only reluctant, but proficient in sabotaging its effectiveness. . . .

When General Eisenhower visted Moscow after the war, he held a press conference at which he stated that after January 1945 he was kept fully informed at all times of the essentials of the Red Army's plans, particularly the timing of their offensives, their objectives, and the direction of their main efforts. This was true, but his possession of such information was a far cry from the co-operative action that might normally be expected between allies. All the information Eisenhower had concerning the Red Army's plans was the result of our initiative in seeking to obtain it, and then it was only obtained after continuous pressure at the highest levels.

Not once during the war did Stalin or his subordinates seek a meeting with British or American authorities in order to present proposals for improving our co-operative effort. It was either the President or the Prime Minister [Churchill] who proposed [conferences at] Teheran, Yalta, and Potsdam. No single event of the war irritated me more than seeing the President of the United States lifted from wheel chair to automobile, to ship, to shore, and to aircraft, in order to go halfway around the world as the only possible means of meeting J. V. Stalin.

There were innumerable little ways in which our joint war effort could have been made more effective. We might have learned something of immeasurable value in defeating the German submarines had we been allowed to see Gdynia [naval base] as soon as it was taken; we might have brought Germany to her knees quicker had we been allowed to establish radar triangulation stations in Russia as navigational aids to our bomber formations in eastern Germany. We might have defeated Germany more quickly had we shared our operational experience by having observers on each other's fronts. We might have, we might have—on and on. No! In Soviet Russia each such venture would have meant a closer association with capitalistic foreigners. Well, perhaps we were among friends, but it was difficult to believe it.

[*Deane further relates (p. 154) that when the British Military Mission in Moscow was disbanded at war's end, it was discovered that the place was "infested with well-concealed dictaphones." Everything said by these British allies of the Russians was evidently recorded for the information of the Soviet secret police.*]

2. Stalin Resents Second-Front Delays (1943)

The one kind of help that Stalin consistently demanded was the opening of a second front in France which would draw German divisions off the backs of the reeling Russians. As Stalingrad tottered, Communists and other groups in America demanded a morale-boosting second front in 1942, even though it might end in bloody failure. Conservatives insisted that the two menaces be left alone to cut each other's throats. Drew Pearson, the keyhole columnist, declared in 1943 that this brutal course was the policy of Washington. Secretary Hull thereupon branded such allegations "monstrous and diabolical falsehoods." Stalin was not unaware of such talk when he angrily sent the following secret message to Winston Churchill (June 24, 1943), just after Churchill had again backed down on his promise of a second front in 1943. From the viewpoint of the Allies, ascertain the most alarming aspect of Stalin's heated response.

. . . When you now write that "it would be no help to Russia if we threw away a hundred thousand men in a disastrous cross-Channel attack," all I can do is remind you of the following:

First, your own Aide-Mémoire of June 1942, in which you declared that preparations were under way for an invasion, not by a hundred thousand, but by an Anglo-American force exceeding one million men at the very start of the operation.

Second, your February [1943] message, which mentioned extensive measures preparatory to the invasion of Western Europe in August or September 1943, which, apparently, envisaged an operation, not by a hundred thousand men, but by an adequate force.

So when you now declare: "I cannot see how a great British defeat and slaughter would aid the Soviet armies," is it not clear that a statement of this kind in re-

NOW!

The *Daily Worker*, a Communist newspaper, began clamoring for an immediate second front less than four months after Pearl Harbor, so as to divert Hitler from his attack on Russia. New York *Daily Worker*, April 9, 1942.

2. Ministry of Foreign Affairs of the U.S.S.R., *Correspondence between the Chairman of the Council of Ministers of the U.S.S.R. and the Presidents of the U.S.A. and the Prime Ministers of Great Britain during the Great Patriotic War of 1941–1945* (1957), II, 75–76.

lation to the Soviet Union is utterly groundless and directly contradicts your previous and responsible decisions, listed above, about extensive and vigorous measures by the British and Americans to organise the invasion this year, measures on which the complete success of the operation should hinge?

I shall not enlarge on the fact that this responsible decision, revoking your previous decisions on the invasion of Western Europe, was reached by you and the President without Soviet participation and without inviting its representatives to the Washington conference, although you cannot but be aware that the Soviet Union's role in the war against Germany and its interest in the problems of the second front are great enough.

There is no need to say that the Soviet Government cannot become reconciled to this disregard of vital Soviet interests in the war against the common enemy.

You say that you "quite understand" my disappointment. I must tell you that the point here is not just the disappointment of the Soviet Government, but the preservation of its confidence in its Allies, a confidence which is being subjected to severe stress. One should not forget that it is a question of saving millions of lives in the occupied areas of Western Europe and Russia, and of reducing the enormous sacrifices of the Soviet armies, compared with which the sacrifices of the Anglo-American armies are insignificant.

3. Roosevelt Manages "Uncle Joe" (1943)

Roosevelt was eager to meet Stalin and soften his suspicions with the famous "Roosevelt charm." "I can handle that old buzzard," he allegedly boasted in private. Late in 1943 the two men met for the first time, together with Prime Minister Churchill, at Teheran, the capital of Persia, which was as far away as Stalin would venture from his direction of the Soviet armies. Roosevelt reported his experiences to his Secretary of Labor, Frances Perkins, who recalls them as follows. Account for Stalin's attitude early in the sessions, and form some conclusions as to Roosevelt's skill as a diplomat.

"You know [reported Roosevelt], the Russians are interesting people. For the first three days I made absolutely no progress. I couldn't get any personal connection with Stalin, although I had done everything he asked me to do. I had stayed at his Embassy, gone to his dinners, been introduced to his ministers and generals. He was correct, stiff, solemn, not smiling, nothing human to get hold of. I felt pretty discouraged. If it was all going to be official paper work, there was no sense in my having made this long journey which the Russians had wanted. They couldn't come to America or any place in Europe for it. I had come there to accommodate Stalin. I felt pretty discouraged because I thought I was making no personal headway. What we were doing could have been done by the foreign ministers.

3. Frances Perkins, *The Roosevelt I Knew* (1946), pp. 83–85. By permission of the Viking Press.

"I thought it over all night and made up my mind I had to do something desperate. I couldn't stay in Teheran forever. I had to cut through this icy surface so that later I could talk by telephone or letter in a personal way. I had scarcely seen Churchill alone during the conference. I had a feeling that the Russians did not feel right about seeing us conferring together in a language which we understood and they didn't.

"On my way to the conference room that morning we caught up with Winston [Churchill] and I had just a moment to say to him, 'Winston, I hope you won't be sore at me for what I am going to do.'

"Winston just shifted his cigar and grunted. I must say he behaved very decently afterward.

"I began almost as soon as we got into the conference room. I talked privately with Stalin. I didn't say anything that I hadn't said before, but it appeared quite chummy and confidential, enough so that the other Russians joined us to listen. Still no smile.

"Then I said, lifting my hand up to cover a whisper (which of course had to be interpreted), 'Winston is cranky this morning, he got up on the wrong side of the bed.'

"A vague smile passed over Stalin's eyes, and I decided I was on the right track. As soon as I sat down at the conference table, I began to tease Churchill about his Britishness, about John Bull, about his cigars, about his [drinking?] habits. It began to register with Stalin. Winston got red and scowled, and the more he did so, the more Stalin smiled. Finally Stalin broke out into a deep, hearty guffaw, and for the first time in three days I saw light. I kept it up until Stalin was laughing with me, and it was then that I called him 'Uncle Joe.' He would have thought me fresh the day before, but that day he laughed and came over and shook my hand.

"From that time on our relations were personal, and Stalin himself indulged in an occasional witticism. The ice was broken and we talked like men and brothers.

"You know . . . he was deeply touched by the presentation of the sword which Churchill brought him from the British people."

[*Relations between Roosevelt and Stalin remained friendly until several weeks before Roosevelt's death in April, 1945. Then Stalin abusively charged bad faith in connection with the surrender of German troops in Italy, while Roosevelt came back with protests against Stalin's violations of his Yalta pledges, notably in connection with Poland.*]

C. THE "UNCONDITIONAL SURRENDER" CONTROVERSY

1. Sherwood Defends F.D.R. (1948)

Late in 1942 the Allies launched a side-issue invasion of French North Africa, but Stalin refused to recognize it as a genuine second front. Shortly thereafter Roosevelt

1. Robert E. Sherwood, *Roosevelt and Hopkins* (1948), pp. 695–97. Copyright 1948 by Robert E. Sherwood. Reprinted by permission of Harper and Brothers and Eyre and Spottiswoode, Ltd.

flew to Casablanca, in French Morocco, for a conference with Prime Minister
Churchill, his eighth cousin once removed. Roosevelt knew that the embittered
Stalin was deeply suspicious of a possible "deal" between Hitler and the Allies. The
Russians might even make a separate peace with the Germans, as they had done with
disastrous effect in 1918. At Roosevelt's instigation, the Casablanca conference pro-
claimed a policy of "unconditional surrender"—that is, the unconditional surrender
of the Axis regimes but not "the destruction of the German populace, nor of the
Italian or Japanese populace." Robert E. Sherwood, the ghost-writer associate of
Roosevelt, here gives his version. Note how many different objectives the President
had in view, and why one can argue that "unconditional surrender" did not prolong
German resistance.

There were many propaganda experts, both British and American, who
believed that the utterance of these words ["unconditional surrender"]
would put the iron of desperate resistance into the Germans, Japanese, and
Italians and thereby needlessly prolong the war and increase its cost; there
are some who still believe that it did so. These critics were not necessarily
opposed to the principle of total defeat—but they considered it a disastrous
mistake for the President to announce it publicly. . . .

I wrote Winston Churchill asking him if he had discussed the unconditional surrender statement with Roosevelt before the press conference at
Casablanca, and his reply was as follows: "I heard the words 'Unconditional
Surrender' for the first time from the President's lips at the Conference.
It must be remembered that at that moment no one had a right to proclaim
that Victory was assured. Therefore, Defiance was the note. I would not
myself have used these words, but I immediately stood by the President
and have frequently defended the decision. It is false to suggest that it
prolonged the war. Negotiation with Hitler was impossible. He was a maniac
with supreme power to play his hand out to the end, which he did; and
so did we."

Roosevelt himself absolved Churchill from all responsibility for the
statement. Indeed, he suggested that it was an unpremeditated one on his
own part. He said, "We had so much trouble getting those two French
generals together that I thought to myself that this was as difficult as
arranging the meeting of Grant and Lee—and then suddenly the press
conference was on, and Winston and I had had no time to prepare for it,
and the thought popped into my mind that they had called Grant 'Old
Unconditional Surrender' and the next thing I knew, I had said it."

Roosevelt, for some reason, often liked to picture himself as a rather
frivolous fellow who did not give sufficient attention to the consequences
of chance remarks. In this explanation, indicating a spur-of-the-moment
slip of the tongue, he certainly did considerably less than justice to himself.
For this announcement of unconditional surrender was very deeply deliberated. Whether it was wise or foolish, whether it prolonged the war or
shortened it—or even if it had no effect whatsoever on the duration (which
seems possible)—it was a true statement of Roosevelt's considered policy

and he refused all suggestions that he retract the statement or soften it and continued refusal to the day of his death. In fact, he restated it a great many times. . . .

What Roosevelt was saying was that there would be no negotiated peace, no compromise with Nazism and Fascism, no "escape clauses" provided by another Fourteen Points which could lead to another Hitler. (The ghost of Woodrow Wilson was again at his shoulder.) Roosevelt wanted this uncompromising purpose to be brought home to the American people and the Russians and the Chinese, and to the people of France and other occupied nations, and he wanted it brought

WILLST DU DER LETZTE TOTE DES KRIEGES SEIN?

("Do you want to be the last dead of the war?") U.S. propaganda leaflet of World War II directed at German soldiers. Hoover Institution, Stanford University.

home to the Germans—that neither by continuance of force nor by contrivance of a new spirit of sweet reasonableness could their present leaders gain for them a soft peace. He wanted to ensure that when the war was won it would stay won.

2. Hull Opposes "Unconditional Surrender" (1948)

"Unconditional surrender" had its warm supporters. In addition to the advantages already indicated, it would hearten German-conquered peoples like the Poles; it would key the Allies up for greater sacrifices; it would postpone disruptive arguments among the Allies as to surrender terms; it would avert a quarrel like that with Germany after 1918 over the Armistice terms. Yet critics like Senator Wheeler of

2. Reprinted with permission of The Macmillan Company from *The Memoirs of Cordell Hull* (1948), II, 1570–71. Copyright 1948 by Cordell Hull.

Montana branded "unconditional surrender" as "brutal" and "asinine." It was vague and easily misinterpreted; it would provide ammunition for enemy propagandists; it would close the door to negotiations with Germany; it would pave the way for Soviet ascendancy in Eastern Europe. Secretary of State Hull, somewhat miffed, advances additional arguments in his *Memoirs*. Notice what he reveals about relations between the President and the State Department, and ascertain whether the alternative policy that he suggests would have made more sense.

The principle of unconditional surrender overshadowed our policy toward the Axis and their satellites and our planning for their future.

Originally this principle had not formed part of the State Department's thinking. We were as much surprised as Mr. Churchill when, for the first time, the President, in the Prime Minister's presence, stated it suddenly to a press conference during the Casablanca Conference in January, 1943. I was told that the Prime Minister was dumbfounded.

Basically, I was opposed to the principle for two reasons, as were many of my associates. One was that it might prolong the war by solidifying Axis resistance into one of desperation. The people of the Axis countries, by believing they had nothing to look forward to but unconditional surrender to the will of their conquerors, might go on fighting long after calmer judgment had convinced them that their fight was hopeless.

The President himself had qualified his unconditional surrender phrase by stating at Casablanca that this did not mean the destruction of the people of Germany, Japan, and Italy, but the ending of a philosophy based on conquest and subjugation of other peoples. Nevertheless the phrase itself spread more widely than the qualification, and it became a weapon in the hands of Nazi propagandists.

The second reason was that the principle logically required the victor nations to be ready to take over every phase of the national and local Governments of the conquered countries, and to operate all governmental activities and properties. We and our Allies were in no way prepared to undertake this vast obligation.

I thought that our principle of surrender should be flexible. In some cases the most severe terms should be imposed. I had Germany and Japan in mind in this connection. In other cases we would have preliminary informal conversations that would result in substantial adjustments away from the terms of unconditional surrender. Here I had in mind Italy and the Axis satellite states, Rumania, Hungary, Bulgaria, and Finland.

In our postwar-planning discussions in the State Department, which had begun more than three years prior to the Casablanca Conference, we had not embraced the idea of unconditional surrender. In the United Nations Declaration of January 1, 1942, each Government simply pledged itself not to make a separate armistice or peace with the enemies. Nevertheless, after the President had stated the principle so emphatically at Casablanca, there was nothing we could do except to follow it at least in form. It was to rise on numerous occasions to plague us and to require explanation.

[*Ironically, Japan did not surrender unconditionally in 1945. She held out for the retention of the Emperor.*]

D. JAPANESE FANATICISM

1. The *Kamikaze* Human Bombs (*c.* 1945)

The desperate nature of the naval war against Japan was perhaps best illustrated by the *kamikaze* suicide pilots. They were trained to crash their bomb-laden aircraft directly onto the deck of an enemy warship, without the slightest possibility of saving their own lives. Determine what is most revealing about the Japanese character in this first official order to the *kamikaze* fighters.

The Empire stands at the cross-roads between victory and defeat. The first suicide-unit determined to triumph through the power of the spirit will inspire, by its success, one unit after another to follow its example. It is absolutely out of the question for you to return alive. Your mission involves certain death. Your bodies will be dead, but not your spirits. The death of a single one of you will be the birth of a million others. Neglect nothing that may affect your training or your health. You must not leave behind you any cause for regret, which would follow you into eternity. And, lastly: do not be in too much of a hurry to die. If you cannot find your target, turn back; next time you may find a more favourable opportunity. Choose a death which brings about the maximum result.

2. Halsey Fears the Suicide Planes (1945)

The damage inflicted by the *kamikaze* flyers on the advancing American fleets was almost fatal: 34 vessels sunk (none a capital ship), 288 damaged, and heavy casualties inflicted. A little more Japanese persistence might have forced withdrawal of the attackers at Okinawa. At the time of Tokyo's surrender, Japan reportedly had about 5000 *kamikaze* planes left (some 2500 expended). A foreknowledge of the damage they could inflict had much to do with President Truman's decision to drop the atomic bomb. Admiral W. F. ("Bull") Halsey, a rough-and-ready naval hero, here describes his first encounter with the suicide planes. Note why at the outset he regarded them lightly.

I didn't know the term at the time, but I had seen a *kamikaze* before— the plane that had tried to crash the *Enterprise* during the Marshalls [Islands] raid in February, 1942. That plane was already doomed; its pilot would have been killed anyhow. But the plane that struck the *Intrepid* had not been damaged; the dive was obviously a deliberate sacrifice.

Intelligence had warned us that "the Divine Wind Special Attack Corps" had been organized, but even after we had seen this sample performance, I think that most of us took it as a sort of token terror, a tissue-paper dragon. The psychology behind it was too alien to ours; Americans, who

1. Desmond Flower and James Reeves, eds., *The Taste of Courage* (1960), p. 743.
2. W. F. Halsey and J. Bryan III, *Admiral Halsey's Story* (1947), pp. 229–30. Published by McGraw-Hill (Whittlesey House). Reprinted by permission of Brandt & Brandt.

fight to live, find it hard to realize that another people will fight to die. We could not believe that even the Japanese, for all their *hara-kiri* traditions, could muster enough recruits to make such a corps really effective.

We were violently disillusioned the very next day. They missed the *Enterprise,* in Davison's group, but they hit two of his other carriers, the *Franklin* and *Belleau Wood,* killing a total of 158 men, destroying forty-five planes, and requiring the withdrawal of both ships for repairs. Our CVs [aircraft carriers] were obvious targets: their huge tanks of aviation gasoline were as vulnerable as they were inflammable, their fire power was light, their armor was thin, and damage to their flight decks meant the neutralization of around a hundred planes. . . .

We had dismissed the Special Attack Corps as a flash in the pan. Now it seemed less a flash than a blast.

E. DROPPING THE ATOMIC BOMB
1. Japan's Horrified Reaction (1945)

With Germany knocked out of the war, President Truman journeyed to Potsdam, near Berlin, in July, 1945, to concert plans with Stalin and the British leaders. He was there informed that American scientists had experimentally detonated the first atomic bomb in history. The conferees now called upon the Japanese to surrender or be destroyed, although the Potsdam ultimatum made no reference, as perhaps it should have, to the existence of the fantastic new weapon. When Tokyo brushed aside the demand for surrender, Truman ordered the dropping of atomic bombs (the only two the United States then had) on Hiroshima (August 6) and Nagasaki (August 9). The horrified reaction of the *Nippon Times* is herewith given. Determine whether there was force in the Japanese charge of hypocrisy, and whether there is any moral difference between atomic bombing and large-scale incendiary bombing of civilian centers. (The Japanese had already bombed civilian centers, beginning with Shanghai in 1932.) Did the Japanese refusal to respond to the Potsdam ultimatum justify the bombing?

How can a human being with any claim to a sense of moral responsibility deliberately let loose an instrument of destruction which can at one stroke annihilate an appalling segment of mankind? This is not war; this is not even murder; this is pure nihilism. This is a crime against God and humanity which strikes at the very basis of moral existence. What meaning is there in any international law, in any rule of human conduct, in any concept of right and wrong, if the very foundations of morality are to be overthrown as the use of this instrument of total destruction threatens to do?

The crime of the Americans stands out in ghastly repulsiveness all the more for the ironic contradiction it affords to their lying pretensions. For in their noisy statements, they have always claimed to be the champions of

1. *Nippon Times* (Tokyo), Aug. 10, 1945. The third bomb was not scheduled to be ready until about Aug. 24, two weeks after the dropping of the second one.

fairness and humanitarianism. In the early days of the China Affair [beginning 1937], the United States repeatedly protested against the bombing operations of the Japanese forces, notwithstanding the fact that the Japanese operations were conducted on a limited scale against strictly military objectives. But where its own actions are concerned, the United States seems to see no inconsistency in committing on an unimaginably vast scale the very same crime it had falsely accused others of committing.

This hypocritical character of the Americans had already been amply demonstrated in the previous bombings of Japanese cities. Strewing explosives and fire bombs indiscriminately over an extensive area, hitting large cities and small towns without distinction, wiping out vast districts which could not be mistaken as being anything but strictly residential in character, burning or blasting to death countless thousands of helpless women and children, and machine-gunning fleeing refugees, the American raiders had already shown how completely they violate in their actual deeds the principles of humanity which they mouth in conspicuous pretense.

But now beside the latest technique of total destruction which the Americans have adopted, their earlier crimes pale into relative insignificance. What more barbarous atrocity can there be than to wipe out at one stroke the population of a whole city without distinction*—men, women, and children; the aged, the weak, the infirm; those in positions of authority, and those with no power at all; all snuffed out without being given a chance of lifting even a finger in either defense or defiance!

The United States may claim, in a lame attempt to raise a pretext in justification of its latest action, that a policy of utter annihilation is necessitated by Japan's failure to heed the recent demand for unconditional surrender. But the question of surrendering or not surrendering certainly can have not the slightest relevance to the question of whether it is justifiable to use a method which under any circumstance is strictly condemned alike by the principles of international law and of morality. For this American outrage against the fundamental moral sense of mankind, Japan must proclaim to the world its protest against the United States, which has made itself the arch-enemy of humanity.

2. The *Christian Century* Deplores the Bombing (1945)

The use of the atomic bomb was reluctantly but overwhelmingly recommended by Truman's large corps of expert advisers. Some of the scientists at first proposed test demonstrations in an uninhabited place, but the United States had only two bombs, and they might prove to be humiliating duds. They could not wreak much damage in desert areas, and might leave the Japanese unimpressed. If the cities to be bombed

---

* At Hiroshima about 150,000 people were killed and wounded out of a total population of some 350,000. The fire-bomb raid on Tokyo of March 10, 1945, killed an estimated 83,000 people.
2. *Christian Century*, LXII, 974 (Aug. 29, 1945). Copyright 1945 by the Christian Century Foundation. Reprinted by permission of the *Christian Century*.

were warned in advance, the Japanese might move American prisoners of war to them, and at the same time "ambush" the American bombers. Japan was reeling, but she perhaps had enough suicide resistance left to exact a million casualties, while losing more than a million of her own people. The atomic bomb, indicating that supernatural forces were working against the Japanese, might stun them into a quick surrender, as it did. (A dry-run demonstration would have weakened this effect.) The cost was perhaps 150,000 Japanese lives, as against 2,000,000—Japanese, American, and British. The *Christian Century*, a prominent Protestant journal published in Chicago, did not accept the philosophy of a "mercy bombing." Note which, if any, of its *practicable* suggestions would have strengthened the moral position of the United States.

Something like a moral earthquake has followed the dropping of atomic bombs on two Japanese cities. Its continued tremors throughout the world have diverted attention even from the military victory itself. . . . It is our belief that the use made of the atomic bomb has placed our nation in an indefensible moral position.

We do not propose to debate the issue of military necessity, though the facts are clearly on one side of this issue. The atomic bomb was used at a time when Japan's navy was sunk, her air force virtually destroyed, her homeland surrounded, her supplies cut off, and our forces poised for the final stroke. Recognition of her imminent defeat could be read between the lines of every Japanese communiqué. Neither do we intend to challenge Mr. Churchill's highly speculative assertion that the use of the bomb saved the lives of more than one million American and 250,000 British soldiers.

We believe, however, that these lives could have been saved had our government followed a different course, more honorable and more humane. Our leaders seem not to have weighed the moral considerations involved. No sooner was the bomb ready than it was rushed to the front and dropped on two helpless cities, destroying more lives than the United States has lost in the entire war.

Perhaps it was inevitable that the bomb would ultimately be employed to bring Japan to the point of surrender. . . . But there was no military advantage in hurling the bomb upon Japan without warning. The least we might have done was to announce to our foe that we possessed the atomic bomb; that its destructive power was beyond anything known in warfare; and that its terrible effectiveness had been experimentally demonstrated in this country. We could thus have warned Japan of what was in store for her unless she surrendered immediately. If she doubted the good faith of our representations, it would have been a simple matter to select a demonstration target in the enemy's own country at a place where the loss of human life would be at a minimum.

If, despite such warning, Japan had still held out, we would have been in a far less questionable position had we then dropped the bombs on Hiroshima and Nagasaki. At least our record of deliberation and ample warning would have been clear. Instead, with brutal disregard of any principle of humanity, we "demonstrated" the bomb on two great cities, utterly extinguishing them.* This course has placed the United States in a bad light throughout the world. What the use of poison gas did to the reputation of Germany in World War I, the use of the atomic bomb has done for the reputation of the United States in World War II. Our future security is menaced by our own act, and our influence for justice and humanity in international affairs has been sadly crippled.

IN THE PALM OF HIS HAND

The atomic bomb portends much for civilized man. Jerry Doyle in the Philadelphia *Record*, 1945.

3. Truman Justifies the Bombing (1945)

German scientists were known to be working on an atomic bomb, and Roosevelt was persuaded to push forward with an ultra-secret competing project that ultimately cost some $2.5 billion. The charge was made—without proof—that Truman had to use the new weapon or face an investigation of squandered money. More probable was his desire to end the Far Eastern war speedily before the bothersome Russians came in. The evidence is strong that they hurried up their six-day participation following the dropping of the first bomb. At all events, President Truman accepted full responsibility for his decision, and later defended it in his *Memoirs*, as excerpted herewith. Observe whether he made the decision by himself and whether he tried to use the bomb as a lawful weapon. Determine whether, in the light of conditions at the time rather than hindsight, he was justified in his action.

My own knowledge of these [atomic] developments had come about only after I became President, when Secretary [of War] Stimson had given

---

* Hiroshima was about three-fourths devastated, Nagasaki, one-third.
3. *Memoirs by Harry S. Truman* (1955), I, 419–20. Published by Doubleday and Company. Copyright 1955 by Time, Inc. Reprinted by permission of Time, Inc.

me the full story. He had told me at that time that the project was nearing completion, and that a bomb could be expected within another four months. It was at his suggestion, too, that I had then set up a committee of top men and had asked them to study with great care the implications the new weapon might have for us. . . .

It was their recommendation that the bomb be used against the enemy as soon as it could be done. They recommended further that it should be used without specific warning, and against a target that would clearly show its devastating strength. I had realized, of course, that an atomic bomb explosion would inflict damage and casualties beyond imagination. On the other hand, the scientific advisers of the committee reported, "We can propose no technical demonstration likely to bring an end to the war; we see no acceptable alternative to direct military use." It was their conclusion that no technical demonstration they might propose, such as over a deserted island, would be likely to bring the war to an end. It had to be used against an enemy target.

The final decision of where and when to use the atomic bomb was up to me. Let there be no mistake about it. I regarded the bomb as a military weapon, and never had any doubt that it should be used. The top military advisers to the President recommended its use, and when I talked to Churchill, he unhesitatingly told me that he favored the use of the atomic bomb if it might aid to end the war.

In deciding to use this bomb I wanted to make sure that it would be used as a weapon of war in the manner prescribed by the laws of war. That meant that I wanted it dropped on a military target. I had told Stimson that the bomb should be dropped as nearly as possibly upon a war production center of prime military importance. . . .

Four cities were finally recommended as targets: Hiroshima, Kokura, Niigata, and Nagasaki. They were listed in that order as targets for the first attack. The order of selection was in accordance with the military importance of these cities, but allowance would be given for weather conditions at the time of the bombing.

[*The devastating impact of the atomic bomb, together with Russia's sudden entry into the war against Japan, undoubtedly forced the Japanese surrender sooner than otherwise would have been possible. Even so, the fanatical military men in Tokyo almost won out for a last-ditch stand.*

In 1959, during interchanges with the students of Columbia University, ex-President Truman vigorously justified his action. He noted that "When we asked them to surrender at Potsdam, they gave us a very snotty answer. That is what I got. . . . They told me to go to hell, words to that effect." Mr. Truman insisted that the dropping of the bomb was "just a military maneuver, that is all," because "We were destroying the factories that were making more munitions." He then concluded: "All this uproar about what we did and what could have been stopped —should we take these wonderful Monday morning quarterbacks, the experts who are supposed to be right? They don't know what they are talking about. I was there. I did it. I would do it again." (Truman Speaks [1960], pp. 73–74.)]

THOUGHT PROVOKERS

1. Basically why were the defenders at Pearl Harbor caught by surprise, and who deserves the most blame for the surprise?
2. If the situation had been reversed, would Stalin have been more willing than the other Allies to open a second front? Explain.
3. Wilsonian propaganda in 1917–1918 drove a wedge between the German people and their government. Why was this technique less effective in World War II? On balance, and with the benefit of hindsight, was the policy of unconditional surrender "perhaps the biggest political mistake of the war" (Hanson W. Baldwin)?
4. Would Americans ever employ suicide tactics? Were such tactics a blind waste of trained manpower?
5. Does the probability that the Germans or the Japanese would have used the atomic bomb against the United States, if they had developed it first, strengthen the moral position of the United States? If Truman had announced at Potsdam that America had the atomic bomb, would the Japanese have been likely to surrender at once? Was the United States shortsighted in establishing a precedent that might one day be used against it? Comment on Secretary Stimson's view that the dropping of the bomb would prove war to be so horrible that there could never be another.

FURTHER EXPLORATION

General: L. L. Snyder, *The War: A Concise History* (1960). **Pearl Harbor:** H. L. Trefousse, ed., *What Happened at Pearl Harbor?* (1958); Walter Lord, *Day of Infamy* (1957). **Soviet Friction:** J. R. Deane, *The Strange Alliance* (1946); Herbert Feis, *Churchill, Roosevelt, Stalin* (1957). **Unconditional Surrender:** H. W. Baldwin, *Great Mistakes of the War* (1949); Anne Armstrong, *Unconditional Surrender* (1961). **Japanese Fanaticism:** S. E. Morison, *Victory in the Pacific, 1945* (1960). **Atomic Bomb:** Herbert Feis, *Japan Subdued* (1961); H. L. Stimson and M. Bundy, *On Active Service in Peace and War* (1947); K. R. Greenfield, ed., *Command Decisions* (1959); R. C. Batchelder, *The Irreversible Decision, 1939–1950* (1962).

Recent: A. R. Buchanan, *The United States and World War II* (2 vols., 1964) [paperback]; S. E. Morison, *The Two-Ocean War* (1963); Gaddis Smith, *American Diplomacy during the Second World War, 1941–1945* (1965) [paperback]; K. S. Davis, *Experience of War: The United States in World War II* (1965).

Chapter 45

Truman and the Rift with Russia

When they [the Russians] make agreements, they make them only to break them.

PRESIDENT TRUMAN, 1950

PROLOGUE: In February, 1945, while Germany was still fighting desperately and Japan was far from finished, an ailing Roosevelt arrived at Yalta in the Russian Crimea. There, in collaboration with Prime Minister Churchill, he thrashed out final agreements with Stalin. Nine weeks later Roosevelt was dead. The ultimate Communist take-over of the satellite governments of Central Europe, contrary to Stalin's pledges at Yalta, deepened American fears. To halt the southward surge of Communism, President Truman proclaimed the Truman Doctrine in 1947, designed to protect Greece and Turkey. To halt the westward infiltration of the Communists, he implemented the Marshall Plan in 1948, designed to rehabilitate war-torn Western Europe. The Marshall Plan proved conspicuously successful in attaining its objectives. But the continued aggressions of the Soviets forced the United States, despite its hoary anti-alliance tradition, to negotiate in 1949 an epochal military defense alliance in the form of the North Atlantic Treaty Organization.

A. THE YALTA AGREEMENTS

1. Roosevelt "Betrays" China and Japan (1945)

One of Roosevelt's primary objectives at the Yalta Conference was to coordinate with Stalin the final blows of the war. The American people were eager to induce Russia to enter the conflict against Japan so as to reduce their anticipated losses in the final stages of the assault. The Soviets had already suffered millions of casualties in fighting Hitler, and Stalin told Roosevelt that he would have to receive concessions if he were to justify another war to his war-weary people. The following one of the "Top Secret" Yalta agreements, hammered out between Roosevelt and Stalin, was not made public until exactly a year later. The basic reason for secrecy was that Russia and Japan were not then at war, and a publication or even leakage of the terms might prompt a Japanese attack before Russia was ready. A need for the utmost secrecy was the excuse given for not then notifying China, an ally of the United States, that her rights were being bartered away in Outer Mongolia and in Manchuria (the Manchurian railroads and the ports of Dairen and Port Arthur). Comment critically on the ethics of this deal, and note what stipulations made it less harsh than it seemed to be.

The leaders of the three Great Powers—the Soviet Union, the United States of America, and Great Britain—have agreed that in two or three

1. *Foreign Relations of the United States: The Conferences at Malta and Yalta, 1945* (1955), p. 984.

862

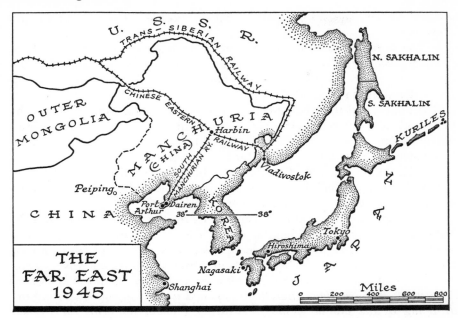

months* after Germany has surrendered and the war in Europe has terminated, the Soviet Union shall enter into the war against Japan on the side
of the Allies on condition that:

1. The *status quo* in Outer Mongolia (the Mongolian People's Republic) shall be preserved; [*This area, twice the size of Texas, had been
under China's sway until 1912; it had become a Soviet satellite in 1924.*]

2. The former rights of Russia violated by the treacherous attack of
Japan in 1904 shall be restored, *viz.*:

a) The southern part of Sakhalin, as well as all the islands adjacent
to it, shall be returned to the Soviet Union, [*Japan and Russia had shared
control until 1905, when Japan secured South Sakhalin.*]

b) The commercial port of [China's] Dairen shall be internationalized,
the preeminent interests of the Soviet Union in this port being safeguarded,
and the lease of [China's] Port Arthur as a naval base of the USSR restored,
[*F.D.R. here recognized Russia's age-old need for an ice-free port. Dairen
was internationalized, and the Port Arthur naval base was leased to Russia.
Both were ultimately restored to Communist China.*]

c) The Chinese Eastern Railroad and the South Manchurian Railroad,
which provides an outlet to Dairen, shall be jointly operated by the establishment of a joint Soviet-Chinese Company, it being understood that the
preeminent interests of the Soviet Union shall be safeguarded and that
China shall retain full sovereignty in Manchuria; [*The Yalta agreement*

* Russia entered the Far Eastern war exactly three months after Germany surrendered, but
her entrance was almost certainly hastened by the dropping of the atomic bomb.

insured Russia temporary control of these two key railroads in China's Manchuria.]

3. The Kurile Islands [of Japan] shall be handed over to the Soviet Union. [*Though colonized by both Russians and Japanese, these islands had become a Japanese possession in 1875. Giving away the territory of enemy Japan raised little protest at the time.*]

It is understood that the agreement concerning Outer Mongolia, and the ports and railroads referred to above, will require concurrence of Generalissimo Chiang Kai-shek. The President will take measures in order to obtain this concurrence on advice from Marshal Stalin.

The Heads of the three Great Powers have agreed that these claims of the Soviet Union shall be unquestionably fulfilled after Japan has been defeated [*that is, whether China consented or not*].

For its part, the Soviet Union expresses its readiness to conclude with the National Government of China a pact of friendship and alliance between the USSR and China in order to render assistance to China with its armed forces for the purpose of liberating China from the Japanese yoke. [*The pact of friendship was concluded after some demur by the Chinese on August 14, 1945, six days after Russia opened war on Japan. Following the dropping of the atomic bomb, the Russians could not wait for China's acquiescence.*]

> I. [J.] Stalin
> Franklin D. Roosevelt
> Winston S. Churchill

2. *The Freeman's* Bill of Indictment (1953)

Roosevelt left Yalta pleased with the victory for Allied unity. He had secured Stalin's consent to a conference at San Francisco to frame the United Nations Charter, and he had won a concession from him limiting the use of the veto. But Roosevelt and Churchill had been forced to agree to Russia's retention of eastern Poland, with compensating western territory to be given to the Poles at the expense of Germany. All this did violence to the rights of millions of Poles and Germans, as well as to the plain terms of the Atlantic Charter of 1941. On the other hand, Stalin had promised free elections for dismembered Poland and for the other satellite nations of Central Europe—a pledge which he later flouted. Critics have charged that Roosevelt should have known by this time that the Russians did not honor agreements which they found inconvenient, and that he should have stood firm for principle. *The Freeman*, a critical journal, published the following attack eight years later. Judge which of the allegedly immoral arrangements seems least defensible; most defensible.

Yalta was the most cynical and immoral international transaction to which the United States was ever a partner. It was a repudiation of all the

2. *The Freeman* (New York), III, 403 (March 9, 1953). By permission of The Foundation for Economic Education. Admiral Leahy reported in 1950 that at Yalta he had complained to Roosevelt about the vagueness of the agreement regarding a free Poland: " 'Mr. President, this is so elastic that the Russians can stretch it all the way from Yalta to Washington without ever technically breaking it.' The President replied, 'I know, Bill—I know it. But it's the best I can do for Poland at this time.' " W. D. Leahy, *I Was There* (1950), pp. 315–16.

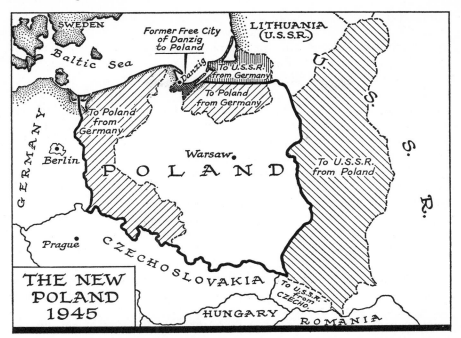

ideals for which the war against Nazism was supposedly being fought. America came very close to losing its soul at Yalta. What was even more ominous than the provisions of the agreement was the absence, at the time of its publication, of any loud or audible outcry of protest.* It would seem that the normal American ability to distinguish between right and wrong, freedom and slavery, had been badly blurred.

From the practical standpoint, most of our serious international difficulties at the present time can be traced back to a deal which gave Stalin the keys to Eastern Europe and East Asia in exchange for paper promises which, as anyone with reasonable knowledge of the Soviet record and Soviet psychology could have anticipated, were broken almost as soon as the ink on the Yalta document was dry.

The principle of self-determination for all peoples, spelled out in the first three clauses of the Atlantic Charter [see p. 833], was completely scrapped at Yalta, although there were hypocritical professions of respect for Atlantic Charter principles in the pact. The Soviet annexation of eastern Poland, definitely sanctioned, and the Polish annexation of large slices of ethnic German territory, foreshadowed in the agreement, were obviously against the will of the vast majority of the peoples concerned. There was no pretense of an honest plebiscite. These decisions have created millions of destitute, embittered refugees and have drawn frontier lines which are a very probable cause of future conflict.

* Polish-Americans did protest vigorously at the time; the unpublished secret agreements came out piecemeal later.

Both the freedom and the territorial independence of Poland were offered as sacrifices on the altar of appeasement. The treatment of Poland, carved up territorially and made ripe for a foreign dictatorship, its fate determined by outsiders without even the presence of a Polish spokesman, was similar in many ways to the treatment of Czechoslovakia at Munich. . . .

Two features of the Yalta agreement represent endorsement by the United States of the legitimacy of human slavery—scarcely fit news for the birthday of Abraham Lincoln. There was recognition that German labor could be used as a source of "reparations," which could be invoked as justification for the detention at forced labor of large numbers of German war prisoners in the Soviet Union and also in France and Great Britain. And there was a self-assumed obligation by the United States and Great Britain to repatriate all Soviet citizens in their zones of occupation. So long as this was carried out (it has now, fortunately, long been stopped), there were tragic scenes of actual and attempted suicide on the part of Soviet citizens who feared above everything else to return to their homeland of concentration camps.

Finally, the secret clauses of the Yalta agreement, which offered Stalin extensive territorial and economic concessions in the Far East at the expense of China and Japan, were immoral, unnecessary, and unwise. They were immoral because they gave away the rights and interests of an ally, the Nationalist government of China, without consulting or even informing Chiang Kai-shek. They were unnecessary, because Stalin's eagerness to be in at the kill in the Far East was beyond serious doubt or question.

[The Freeman *was more sympathetic toward Germans than were most Americans. Putting Germans under Polish rule and using German slave labor in Russia for reparations did not seem immoral to many Americans in 1945, especially in view of Hitler's diabolical slaughter of some 6,000,000 Jews. As for returning tens of thousands of anti-Communist refugees to Soviet tyranny, many Americans felt that this was not an unreasonable request to grant to their good Russian ally. Eight years later, perspectives had radically changed, as regards both Germany and Russia.*]

3. Secretary Stettinius Defends Yalta (1949)

Handsome Secretary of State Stettinius—he of the prematurely white hair and flashing white teeth—replaced the aged and ailing Secretary Hull late in 1944. Without political influence or diplomatic experience, he was expected to be a kind of errand boy for President Roosevelt, who took him along to Yalta. Stettinius here presents a spirited defense of the controversial agreements. Note what conditions existing *at the time* cause the Yalta decisions to appear in a less sinister light than has since been cast upon them.

What did the Soviet Union gain in eastern Europe which she did not already have as the result of the smashing victories of the Red Army?

3. E. R. Stettinius, Jr., *Roosevelt and the Russians: The Yalta Conference* (1949), pp. 303–06. Copyright 1949 by The Stettinius Fund, Inc. Reprinted by permission of Doubleday and Company, Inc., and Harold Ober Associates, Inc.

Great Britain and the United States secured pledges at Yalta, unfortunately not honored, which did promise free elections and democratic governments.

What, too, with the possible exception of the Kuriles, did the Soviet Union receive at Yalta which she might not have taken without any agreement? If there had been no agreement, the Soviet Union could have swept into North China, and the United States and the Chinese would have been in no real position to prevent it.

It must never be forgotten that, while the Crimea Conference was taking place, President Roosevelt had just been told by his military advisers that the surrender of Japan might not occur until 1947, and some predicted even later. The President was told that without Russia it might cost the United States a million casualties to conquer Japan.

It must be remembered, too, that at the time of the Yalta Conference it was still uncertain whether the atomic bomb could be perfected and that, since the Battle of the Bulge had set us back in Europe, it was uncertain how long it might take for Germany to crack. There had been immense optimism in the autumn of 1944, as Allied troops raced through France, that the war was nearly over. Then came the Battle of the Bulge, which was more than a military reversal. It cast a deep gloom over the confident expectation that the German war would end soon. In Washington, for instance, the procurement agencies of the armed services immediately began placing orders on the basis of a longer war in Europe than had been estimated.

With hindsight, it can be said that the widespread pessimism was unwarranted. The significant fact is not, however, this hindsight but the effect of this thinking on the strategy and agreements made in the Crimea. It was important to bring the Soviet Union into the united sphere of action. Russian co-operation in the Japanese war ran parallel to their co-operation in the world organization and to united action in Europe.

Furthermore, critics of the Far Eastern agreement have tended to overlook the fact that in the agreement the Soviet Union pledged that China was to retain "full sovereignty in Manchuria" and that the Soviet Union would conclude a pact of friendship with the Chinese Nationalist Government.

It is my understanding that the American military leaders felt that the war had to be concluded as soon as possible. There was the fear that heavy casualties in Japan or the possible lack of continuous victories would have an unfortunate effect on the attitude of the American people.

President Roosevelt had great faith in his Army and Navy staffs, and he relied wholeheartedly upon them. Their insistent advice was that the Soviet Union had to be brought into the Far Eastern war soon after Germany's collapse. The President, therefore, in signing the Far Eastern agreement, acted upon the advice of his military advisers. He did not approve the agreement from any desire to appease Stalin and the Soviet Union.

It is apparently the belief of some critics of the Yalta Conference that it would have been better to have made no agreements with the Soviet Union. Yet if we had made no agreements at Yalta, the Russians still would have been in full possession of the territory in Europe that President Roosevelt is alleged to have given them. The failure to agree would have been a serious blow to the morale of the Allied world, already suffering from five years of war; it would have meant the prolongation of the German and Japanese wars; it would have prevented the establishment of the United Nations; and it would probably have led to other consequences incalculable in their tragedy for the world.

[*The legend has taken root that an ailing Roosevelt, advised by the sickly Harry Hopkins and the Communist-employed Alger Hiss (his role has been exaggerated), was sold a gold brick by crafty "Uncle Joe" Stalin. The secret intelligence reports as to Japan's powers of resistance were faulty, but Roosevelt had to rely on such information as was given him. And if he was sick, what of the hale and hearty Churchill, who signed the agreements? Five months after Yalta, President Truman journeyed to Potsdam, where one of his primary purposes was to hold Stalin to his promise to enter the war against Japan. Truman was not sick, and he had further information as to Japanese powers of resistance. When Russia finally entered the war six days before its end, great was the rejoicing in the United States. As for the charge that America "lost" China because of the Yalta agreements, the fact is that China was never America's to lose. The "salvation" of Nationalist China would probably have involved large numbers of United States troops, and public opinion was unwilling to provide them. As for Japan, there was little opposition at the time of Yalta to depriving a savage enemy of the Kurile Islands and handing them over to a resolute ally.*]

B. THE SENATE DEBATE OVER THE UN

1. Senator Connally Urges Speedy Action (1945)

Even before Japan surrendered, the representatives of fifty nations met at San Francisco in the spring of 1945 to hammer out the framework of a new league of nations. When the Charter of the United Nations emerged, there was considerable fear that the Wilson-Lodge deadlock might be re-enacted in the Senate. But after only five days of hearings the Senate Committee on Foreign Relations reported the Charter without a single reservation or amendment. The chairman, impassioned Senator Tom Connally of Texas, concluded his opening remarks with the following dramatic appeal, rendered all the more forceful by his having been a delegate at the San Francisco Conference. Observe why he deemed it especially important that the United States should be the first to ratify.

Those who want to join a league that is magic, that requires no care, that requires no fuel, that requires no sacrifice on our part, that requires the sending of no troops by us if it comes to that point, are doomed to disappointment. There is no such league; there never has been such a league; and there never will be such a league. There has got to be constant

1. *Congressional Record*, 79 Cong., 1 sess., p. 7954 (July 23, 1945).

cooperation of the nations of the earth in support of the spirit as well as the letter of the Charter and the high purposes which it envisions.

Mr. President, these are the general principles upon which we base our appeal for the ratification of this Charter. Let me say . . . that ratification of the Charter by the Senate may well give a tremendous impulse to its ratification by the other nations of the earth. It will mean that we shall be the first of the great powers to ratify the treaty.

Strange as it may seem, in view of the practical unanimity of the people of the United States in support of the Charter, many representatives of foreign nations are still doubtful as to what the vote on the Charter will be here in the Senate. They remember 1919. They know how the League of Nations was slaughtered here on the floor. Can you not still see the blood on the floor? Can you not see upon the walls the marks of the conflict that raged here in the Chamber where the League of Nations was done to death? They fear that the same sentiment may keep the United States from ratifying this Charter. Our ratification of it will instill hope into the hearts of the peoples of the earth. We heard it constantly at San Francisco. Not publicly in debate but privately delegates would approach us and inquire what we thought about the prospects of the ratification of the Charter.

So I trust that the Senate, after such debate as it sees fit to indulge upon the subject, will ratify this Charter by a vote so overwhelming as to carry the conviction over the earth that the United States expects to assume its obligations for the purpose of keeping them, for the purpose of living up to them, for the purpose of supporting a world organization for peace with all our spirit and with all our hearts.

2. Senator Wheeler Is Dubious (1945)

Beneath the pressure of an overwhelming public opinion the opposition in the Senate collapsed. After only six days of debate (in contrast with the futile eight months of 1919–1920) the Charter was approved by the near-unanimous vote of 89 to 2. Fiery Senator Wheeler of Montana, a leading pre-1942 isolationist (see p. 831), provided about the only excitement with a three-hour speech. Ascertain what his most serious fears were, and whether they have been justified by events.

Mr. President, if some Members of the Senate have their way I greatly fear that this Charter would take away from America the right to be heard on the crucial issues of war and peace in the future, even though it is claimed by the proponents of this Charter that by some strange miracle it will bring about at least a partial restoration of sanity, decency, and law in international relations. Indeed, we have even been told that it is the greatest document ever conceived by the mind of man, that it insures world peace and prosperity, and that as the only hope of the world, we must ratify or chaos will prevail.

2. *Ibid.*, p. 7994 (July 24, 1945).

With these statements I do not agree, but I am going to vote for it very reluctantly on the strength of the statements made by Mr. Dulles* and concurred in by my able and distinguished colleagues, who helped frame the Charter, that all the questions of the specific duties and powers of our delegates will be spelled out in supplementary agreements and that these agreements will come back to the Senate for ratification.

Let me say that I cannot subscribe to the idea that the President of the United States now has, or ever has had, the right to send American forces anywhere, or for any reason that he desired, without a declaration of war by Congress. An examination of the authorities in this field suffices to show that, whatever the reason lurking in the mind of the President, it has always been claimed by the Chief Executive that every such act was to protect American lives and property, and not the property or lives of some foreign nations or combination of nations.

I stand upon that interpretation of the Chief Executive's power, and shall oppose any other theory or philosophy which tends to undermine in the slightest degree the plain provisions of the Constitution. Personally, I am convinced that the American people are going to want more to say as to when and where their boys are going to fight on foreign soil in the future, rather than less. . . .

Mr. President, this United Nations Charter being, as it is, a declaration of pious intentions and designed as it is for purposes not yet known to the American people, I will reluctantly—very reluctantly—vote for it. . . .

What I am doing by supporting this measure is to give the framers of this document an opportunity to prove their good faith and their good intentions. But I want to serve notice, here and now, that when the peace treaties are made, when any question of further appeasement arises, and when any threat to the continued democratic representation of the people of America comes before this body, I shall be in the vanguard of citizens and Members of this body who will feel it to be their duty exhaustively to scrutinize, analyze, and prove the wisdom of the creators of this Charter, to the end that the sovereignty of this people's Government and its Constitution may be preserved.

C. THE TRUMAN DOCTRINE

1. Truman Appeals to Congress (1947)

A crisis developed early in 1947 when the bankrupt British served notice on Washington that they could no longer afford to support the "rightist" government of Greece against Communist guerrillas. If Greece fell, Turkey and all the eastern Mediterranean countries would presumably collapse like falling dominoes. After hurried consultations in Washington, President Truman courageously went before Congress to ask for $400,000,000 to provide military and economic assistance to both Greece and Turkey. This was a great deal of money, he conceded, but a trifling

* John Foster Dulles, later Secretary of State.
1. *Congressional Record,* 80 Cong., 1 sess., p. 1981 (March 12, 1947).

sum compared with the more than a third of a trillion dollars already expended in the recent war to guarantee freedom. Note the grounds on which he bases his appeal, and which of his arguments would be most persuasive with Congress.

I am fully aware of the broad implications involved if the United States extends assistance to Greece and Turkey, and I shall discuss these implications with you at this time.

One of the primary objectives of the foreign policy of the United States is the creation of conditions in which we and other nations will be able to work out a way of life free from coercion. This was a fundamental issue in the war with Germany and Japan. Our victory was won over countries which sought to impose their will, and their way of life, upon other nations.

To insure the peaceful development of nations, free from coercion, the United States has taken a leading part in establishing the United Nations. The United Nations is designed to make possible lasting freedom and independence for all its members. We shall not realize our objectives, however, unless we are willing to help free peoples to maintain their free institutions and their national integrity against aggressive movements that seek to impose upon them totalitarian regimes. [Applause.] This is no more than a frank recognition that totalitarian regimes imposed upon free peoples, by direct or indirect aggression, undermine the foundations of international peace and hence the security of the United States.

TURKISH DELIGHTS

The *Daily Worker*, a Moscow-inspired newspaper, condemned the Truman Doctrine for assistance to Greece and Turkey as Truman's pipe dream of a dollar-based world empire. New York *Daily Worker*, 1947.

The peoples of a number of countries of the world have recently had totalitarian regimes forced upon them against their will. The Government of the United States has made frequent protests against coercion and intimidation, in violation of the Yalta Agreement, in Poland, Rumania, and Bulgaria. I must also state that in a number of other countries there have been similar developments. . . .

I believe that it must be the policy of the United States to support free peoples who are resisting attempted subjugation by armed minorities or by outside pressures.

I believe that we must assist free peoples to work out their own destiny in their own way.

I believe that our help should be primarily through economic and financial aid, which is essential to economic stability and orderly political processes.

The world is not static and the status quo is not sacred. But we cannot allow changes in the status quo in violation of the Charter of the United Nations by such methods as coercion, or by such subterfuge as political infiltration. In helping free and independent nations to maintain their freedom, the United States will be giving effect to the principles of the Charter of the United Nations. . . .

This is a serious course upon which we embark. I would not recommend it except that the alternative is much more serious. [Applause.] . . .

The free peoples of the world look to us for support in maintaining their freedoms.

If we falter in our leadership, we may endanger the peace of the world—and we shall surely endanger the welfare of our own Nation.

Great responsibilities have been placed upon us by the swift movement of events.

I am confident that the Congress will face these responsibilities squarely. [Applause, the members rising.]

2. The Chicago *Tribune* Dissents (1947)

The nation was momentarily stunned by Truman's bombshell. Critics complained that the initial appropriation would be but a drop in the bucket (as it was), that the Soviet Union (though not mentioned by name) would be gravely offended, and that the UN was being rudely bypassed. (Speed was of the essence, and the administration concluded that the Soviets would paralyze action in the UN.) The Chicago *Tribune*, a powerful isolationist newspaper, was vehemently anti-British, anti-Communist, and anti-Roosevelt. Decide which of its arguments against the Truman Doctrine had considerable weight and which were most obviously farfetched.

Mr. Truman made as cold a war speech yesterday against Russia as any President has ever made except on the occasion of going before Congress to ask for a declaration of war. . . .

The outcome will inevitably be war. It probably will not come this year

2. Chicago *Daily Tribune*, March 13, 1947. By permission of the Chicago *Tribune*

or next year, but the issue is already drawn. The declaration of implacable hostility between this country and Russia is one which cannot be tempered or withdrawn. . . .

Mr. Truman's statement constituted a complete confession of the bankruptcy of American policy as formulated by Mr. Roosevelt and pursued by himself. We have just emerged from a great war which was dedicated to the extinction of the three nations [Germany, Italy, Japan] which were as vocally opposed to Russia as Mr. Truman proclaims himself to be now. If communism was the real danger all along, why did Mr. Roosevelt and Mr. Truman adopt Russia as an ally, and why, at Teheran, Yalta, and Potsdam, did they build up Russia's power by making her one concession after another?

The Truman speech also leaves the United Nations as a meaningless relic of mistaken intentions. The world league to insure a lasting peace is a fraud and a sham, so impotent that Mr. Truman proposes that the United States ignore it and seek peace by force and threat of force—the very means which U. N. was intended to exclude in international dealings.

The one hope that is left is Congress, but even its peremptory refusal to follow Truman into his anti-communist crusade will not wholly undo the damage which the President has already done. His words cannot be unsaid, nor can their effect upon Russia be canceled out. Already, as witness Moscow's recall of the Soviet Ambassador from Washington, the nations are engaging in the usual preliminaries to war.

When the country views the terrible predicament in which it now finds itself, it cannot avoid the conclusion that wisdom at all times counseled the United States to follow Americanism only, to dedicate itself to the pursuit of its own interests, and to let Europe's wars alone. We have fought two of them without avail, and Mr. Truman is calling upon us to fight a third.

We were drawn into these wars primarily at the behest of Britain, and that nation, by dumping the Greek and Turkish problems into Mr. Truman's lap, is summoning us to the struggle again. If the United States can be induced to crush Russia, Britain again will rise to a station of security and comparative eminence, for it will be the only other surviving major nation.

For 10 years the United States has been dominated by alien interests. These interests, primarily financial, have bought up every newspaper, radio station, columnist, and commentator, and every so-called organization of public opinion that could be purchased. It has killed our sons by the hundreds of thousands and brought the nation to bankruptcy. It will use whatever tactics seem best to rush into World War III. It will coerce the timid and fool the stupid.

Congress must cease being a catspaw for this movement and think of America's interest first—even exclusively.

[*The dangers involved in the Truman Doctrine were great. but the dangers of drifting seemed greater. Congress, by better than a two-to-one vote in both Houses, finally approved the initial appropriation early in 1948.*]

D. THE MARSHALL PLAN

1. Secretary Marshall Speaks at Harvard (1947)

By June of 1947 it was painfully evident that the Truman Doctrine was merely a small boy on a man's errand. The hunger and economic prostration produced by the war were providing an alarming hotbed for the propagation of Communism in Europe, especially in Italy and France. A Russian-Communist take-over of all Western Europe impended. At this critical juncture the Secretary of State, General George C. Marshall, speaking at the Harvard University commencement exercises, made the following breath-taking proposal. Note to what extent it was both selfish and unselfish, and how, basically, it differed from the Truman Doctrine.

The truth of the matter is that Europe's requirements for the next three or four years of foreign food and other essential products—principally from America—are so much greater than her present ability to pay that she must have substantial additional help or face economic, social, and political deterioration of a very grave character. . . .

Aside from the demoralizing effect on the world at large and the possibilities of disturbances arising as a result of the desperation of the people concerned, the consequences to the economy of the United States should be apparent to all. It is logical that the United States should do whatever it is able to do to assist in the return of normal economic health in the world, without which there can be no political stability and no assured peace. Our policy is directed not against any country or doctrine but against hunger, poverty, desperation, and chaos. Its purpose should be the revival of a working economy in the world so as to permit the emergence of political and social conditions in which free institutions can exist.

Such assistance, I am convinced, must not be on a piecemeal basis as various crises develop. Any assistance that this Government may render in the future should provide a cure rather than a mere palliative. Any government that is willing to assist in the task of recovery will find full cooperation, I am sure, on the part of the United States Government. Any government which maneuvers to block the recovery of other countries cannot expect help from us. Furthermore, governments, political parties, or groups which seek to perpetuate human misery in order to profit therefrom politically or otherwise will encounter the opposition of the United States.

It is already evident that, before the United States Government can proceed much further in its efforts to alleviate the situation and help start the European world on its way to recovery, there must be some agreement among the countries of Europe as to the requirements of the situation and the part those countries themselves will take in order to give proper effect to whatever action might be undertaken by this Government.

It would be neither fitting nor efficacious for this Government to undertake to draw up unilaterally a program designed to place Europe on its feet economically. This is the business of the Europeans. The initiative, I

1. *Department of State Bulletin*, XVI, 1159–60 (June 15, 1947; speech of June 5, 1947).

think, must come from Europe. The role of this country should consist of friendly aid in the drafting of a European program and of later support of such a program so far as it may be practical for us to do so. The program should be a joint one, agreed to by a number, if not all, European nations.

2. Senator Vandenberg Is Favorable (1947, 1948)

Tax-burdened Americans, having spent billions in World War II, were reluctant to pour more treasure down the "European rathole." Eloquent Senator Vandenberg of Michigan (see p. 824), a recent convert from isolationism to internationalism, was one of the foremost champions in Congress of the Marshall Plan. In reading the following excerpts from letters to his constituents, enumerate his arguments for the Marshall Plan and observe how many and which of them were concerned with the self-interest of the United States.

I have no illusions about this so-called "Marshall Plan." . . . Furthermore, I certainly do not take it for granted that American public opinion is ready for any such burdens as would be involved unless and until it is far more effectively demonstrated to the American people that this (1) is within the latitudes of their own available resources and (2) serves their own intelligent self-interest.

. . . I am entirely willing to admit that America herself cannot prosper in a broken world. But it is equally true that if America ever sags, the world's hopes for peace will sag with her. Meanwhile, however, there are some very realistic problems which we must face—including the basic fact that even our friends in Western Europe will soon be totally devoid of dollar exchange and therefore unable to buy commodities from us which are indispensable to their own self-rehabilitation. I must confess that this poses a tough conundrum in international economics entirely aside from considerations of "charity" or "communism." . . .

So we have no alternative but to do the best we can, in the absence of certified knowledge, and to balance one "calculated risk" against another. . . .

You are entirely right that an "international WPA"* can't save Europe from communism or anything else. Is somebody proposing one? I hadn't heard about it. The so-called "Marshall Plan" is the exact opposite, if it runs true to form—and it's our business to see that it does. It is a program geared to self-help. It requires beneficiary countries to proceed specifically to do the things for themselves which will put them on their own feet (and off ours) by 1951—and our aid is progressively contingent upon concurrent results.

. . . I respectfully submit that we do "know enough" to know what will happen if it, or something like it, doesn't work. We know that independent

2. A. H. Vandenberg, Jr., *The Private Papers of Senator Vandenberg* (1952), pp. 381–83, 386–87. By permission of Houghton Mifflin Company.
* Works Progress Administration—a New Deal agency designed to provide employment on public works.

governments, whatever their character otherwise, will disappear from Western Europe; that aggressive communism will be spurred throughout the world; and that our concept of free men, free government, and a relatively free international economy will come up against accumulated hazards which can put our own, precious "American way of life" in the greatest, kindred hazard since Pearl Harbor. . . .

Let's be equally frank in our "calculations" as to what happens if the iron curtain reaches the Atlantic; if peace and justice are at the mercy of expanding, hostile totalitarian aggression, and if the greatest creditor and capitalist nation on earth should find itself substantially isolated in a communist world where the competition would force us into complete regimentation of ourselves beyond anything we have ever experienced.

This question of "what the Bill will cost" is a very interesting one. Unfortunately, the critics of the Bill have nothing to say about what the failure to pass the Bill will cost. You can get some direct and specific idea on this latter point by reading the testimony before our Senate Foreign Relations Committee by Secretary of Defense Forrestal and Secretary of the Army Royall, who both assert that without legislation of this character they would find it necessary immediately to ask for heavily increased appropriations for military defense. Why? Because it is infinitely cheaper to defend ourselves by economic means.

In other words, in the final analysis, peace is cheaper than war. War has no bargains. Peace does. There is no guarantee that this European Recovery Plan will "work." But certainly there is an even chance that it can succeed. In my opinion, we cannot afford not to take that chance.

3. Moscow's Misrepresentations (*c.* 1947)

> Winston Churchill praised the Marshall Plan as "the most unsordid act in history." But it certainly would not have received Congressional approval if the American people had not been convinced that their security depended on preventing Western Europe from falling under the sway of Soviet Communism. Humanitarian instincts, gratitude to former allies, the creation of prosperous customers for surplus goods— all these points were argued, but security was unquestionably paramount. American critics of the Marshall Plan charged that the poor people of the United States needed help, and that Washington should not subsidize socialism (in Britain and elsewhere). The following distorted description of the Marshall Plan was prepared by Soviet propagandists for a children's magazine. List the basic misrepresentations, and note which ones chime in most neatly with the Communist "line."

The American papers immediately raised a great noise about this [Marshall] plan. In different terms, they emphasized "the magnanimity" of America which had decided to help war-stricken Europe.

However, actually, this cunning plan pursued entirely different aims. The American capitalists want to use the help of the Marshall Plan to overwhelm Europe and bring it into subjection to themselves. The govern-

3. Quoted in W. B. Smith, *My Three Years in Moscow* (1949), pp. 198–200. By permission of J. B. Lippincott Company.

ment of the Soviet Union at once recognized the real meaning of the Marshall Plan, and definitely refused to take part in setting it up. So also did the governments of the other democratic lands—Poland, Czechoslovakia, Bulgaria, Yugoslavia, Rumania, Hungary, and also Finland.* But sixteen European states adopted the Marshall Plan against the wishes of their peoples.

Let us see now how the U.S.A. is preparing to carry out the Marshall Plan, and what it promises the European countries which have fallen for the American bait.

Representatives of these sixteen European states met together and calculated that they had to receive from the U.S.A. 29 billion dollars to restore their economies. The Americans answered that this sum was too high, and asked for its reduction to 20–22 billion dollars.

The Americans, moreover, attached the following condition: they themselves will dictate to each European country what branch of economy it must develop and what it must curtail. For example, they say to Britain: "You Britishers, build fewer ships for yourselves; you will buy ships from us in America." They propose to the French a reduction in the production of automobiles—American factories can make automobiles for France.

It goes without saying that this was very useful for American capitalists. In America everybody is fearfully awaiting "the economic crisis," i.e., the time when many factories and industries suddenly close and millions of people are left without work. At that time it will be difficult for the manufacturers to get rid of their output. A man out of work has nothing with which to buy them. So the American capitalists are greatly concerned how to sell profitably their output in Europe. Further, the European countries inevitably will become dependent on America: once they make a few machines, tools, and automobiles, it means that willy-nilly they must defer to the Americans.

According to the Marshall Plan, the American capitalists want to restore all the great factories of Western Germany. In other countries they are hastening to close many factories, while in Germany, on the contrary, they are opening them up. Their purpose there, too, is quite understandable: clearly, the U.S.A. considers Western Germany as its colony. By controlling the big industries there which can also make armaments, it will be easy for the Americans to frighten the European countries dependent on them.

The American capitalists counted on using the Marshall Plan to stir up trouble between the peoples of the democratic countries and the Soviet Union. The Americans proposed to these countries as follows: "We will give you dollars if only you will abandon your friendship with the Soviet Union. But if you don't, we won't give you anything." But the peoples of these countries did not fall for the American capitalists' trick. They answered the Americans: "We will not exchange our freedom and independence for dollars." . . .

* Soviet pressures on these satellite countries kept them from accepting the Marshall Plan.

But this isn't all. The American capitalists have still another dastardly aim. After using the Marshall Plan to reduce the European countries, they want to unite them in a military alliance for a future war against the democratic states.

The Marshall Plan is highly profitable to the United States. For the European countries it brings only poverty. Any land which wants to receive "aid" by means of this plan will be entirely dependent on America. Its economy will not be assisted: on the contrary, it will fall into greater ruin because the country will have to close many of its industries and plants, and hundreds of thousands of people will be out of work. That is why both in America itself and in all other lands progressive people are opposing the Marshall Plan with all their strength.

[*Soviet charges of economic dictation by Wall Street proved ill-founded. The sixteen nations gladly accepted the Marshall Plan, and within a few years were not only back on their feet but were exceeding their output of the pre-war years.*]

E. THE NORTH ATLANTIC PACT

1. Senator Connally Pleads for Support (1949)

The Soviet propagandists were right on one count: economic union under the Marshall Plan paved the way for a military alliance. The brutal Communist rape of democratic Czechoslovakia in 1948 accelerated the machinery. In 1949, the representatives of ten Western European nations, plus the United States and Canada, met in Washington, there to sign the epochal North Atlantic Pact. It stipulated that an attack on one was an attack on all, and that such an attack would cause each signatory to take "such action as it deems necessary," including "armed force." Senator Connally, the spellbinding chairman of the Senate Committee on Foreign Relations, here pleads for approval of the treaty. Comment critically on his view that the warning implicit in the pact was far-visioned policy, and that the pact itself was a logical supplement to the Marshall Plan.

It is obvious that the United States gains much by declaring now, in this written pact, the course of action we would follow even if the treaty did not exist. Without a treaty, we were drawn into two world wars to preserve the security of the North Atlantic community. Can anyone doubt that we would become involved in a third world conflict if it should ever come?

After the United States is involved in war, it cooperates with and coordinates its activities with its allies. A joint enterprise to win the war and defend its cause in union with its associates is launched with all of its power and might. If it is wise and desirable to cooperate with our partners after we shall have been involved in a war, why should it be wrong or unwise to cooperate with them prior to the outbreak of war for the purpose of preventing war?

From now on, no one will misread our motives or underestimate our determination to stand in defense of our freedom. By letting the world know exactly where we stand, we erect a fundamental policy that outlasts the

1. *Congressional Record*, 81 Cong., 1 sess., p. 8818 (July 5, 1949).

daily fluctuations of diplomacy, and the twists and turns of psychological warfare which the Soviet Union has chosen to wage against us. This public preview of our intentions has a steadying effect upon the course of human events both at home, where our people want no more Normandy beach-heads, and abroad, where men must work and live in the sinister shadow of aggression.

The treaty, in thus encouraging a feeling of confidence and security, will provide an atmosphere in which the European recovery program can move forward with new vitality. We know that encouraging progress has already been made. We know, too, that momentum of confidence has been building up in Europe as a direct result of our assistance.

But that is not enough. The greatest obstacle that stands in the way of complete recovery is the pervading and paralyzing sense of insecurity. The treaty is a powerful antidote to this poison. It will go far in dispelling the fear that has plagued Europe since the war.

LIGHTNING ATTRACTOR?

Isolationists argued that the NATO alliance would attract war to the U.S. Akron *Beacon-Journal,* 1949.

With this protection afforded by the Atlantic Pact, western Europe can breathe easier again. It can plan its future with renewed hope. New business enterprises, increased trade, and planning for long-range recovery should be the direct results.

The treaty is thus a logical and necessary complement to the recovery program. Through it we shall protect our past and future investments in that famous calculated risk which already has paid remarkable dividends. We might even look forward to the time when we can anticipate rather substantial savings in our ECA* expenditures, once the full impact of the treaty has been felt in Europe.

* Economic Cooperation Administration, which administered Marshall Plan aid.

2. Senator Taft Spurns Entanglements (1949)

Balding and bespectacled Senator Robert A. Taft of Ohio, a dyed-in-the-wool
isolationist who was dubbed "Mr. Republican," vigorously opposed the pact. A critic
quipped that he had the most brilliant mind in Washington until he made it up.
Evaluate the strengths and weaknesses of his argument that the United States was
embarking upon a war policy rather than a peace policy.

So, Mr. President, I am opposing the treaty. . . . This whole program in
my opinion is not a peace program; it is a war program. Mr. President, I
do not wish to make so didactic a statement as that, so I shall say that with
the arms factor the whole tendency of this program is toward a third world
war, instead of away from a third world war; because we are in the first
place committing ourselves to a vast program of foreign aid.

In the second place, we are committing ourselves to a policy of war,
not a policy of peace. We are building up armaments. We are undertaking
to arm half the world against the other half. We are inevitably starting an
armament race. The more the pact signatories arm, the more the Russians
are going to arm. It is said they are armed too much already. Perhaps
that is true. But that makes no difference. The more we arm, the more they
will arm, the more they will devote their whole attention to the building
up of arms. The general history of armament races in the world is that they
have led to war, not to peace.

In the third place, we are going back to the old balance-of-power theory.
Every American has denounced that theory. Every man who has thoroughly
thought out the question of international organization has said the only
ultimate hope of peace depends upon the establishment of law and justice
among nations, with international action by joint force against an aggressor.
We abandon that theory under the treaty and arms program; and we go
back to the old balance-of-power theory, which England followed for
years. . . . It always led to a series of wars in Europe, and it will lead to
a series of wars in the world, if that is all we develop.

[*The New York* Daily Worker, *a Communist sheet that slavishly echoed the
Moscow "line," blasted the Atlantic Pact as "terrible hypocrisy," a "criminal
scheme," and "Murder, Inc." It fumed that "even a reactionary like Taft" saw
through the "evil conspiracy," which involved "Marshall Plan stooges" groomed
for "war on the Soviet Union." The Senate nevertheless approved the twenty-year
pact, on July 21, 1949, by a vote of 82 to 13. Friends of the treaty credit it with
having played a leading role in preventing a Soviet engulfment of Western
Europe.*]

THOUGHT PROVOKERS

1. Is it justifiable for a nation to acquiesce in unethical decisions because it needs
   the cooperation of an ally during a war, and because it cannot prevent that
   ally from taking what it wants? Should Roosevelt have broken with Stalin at
   Yalta by opposing his demands, or was he right in gambling on Russian good

2. *Ibid.,* pp. 9887–88 (July 21, 1949).

behavior? If the President cannot rely on his military experts for military advice, on whom should he rely?

2. Is there evidence that a guilty conscience entered into the speedy approval of the UN Charter by the Senate? Were the Senators under illusions as to the ability of the UN to usher in the millennium?

3. Does the record since 1947 indicate that Truman's attempts to "contain" the Soviet Union spurred aggressive action by the Russians or, on balance, averted more disastrous aggressive action?

4. To what extent should the nations of Western Europe feel grateful for the Marshall Plan? Are nations that receive charity ordinarily grateful?

5. Explain why the United States relied on the Atlantic Pact rather than the United Nations to form a barrier against Soviet aggression. Were the risks in forming the North Atlantic Treaty Organization worth the benefits in security that have accrued to the United States? Why have the Russians proved uncooperative in realizing the avowed aims of the UN?

FURTHER EXPLORATION

General: J. W. Spanier, *American Foreign Policy since World War II* (1960). **Yalta:** J. L. Snell, ed., *The Meaning of Yalta* (1956); E. R. Stettinius, Jr., *Roosevelt and the Russians: The Yalta Conference* (1949); Herbert Feis, *The China Tangle* (1953) and *Churchill, Roosevelt, Stalin* (1957). **UN Debate:** *Congressional Record*, 79 Cong., 1 sess. **Truman Doctrine:** J. F. Byrnes, *Speaking Frankly* (1947); H. S. Truman, *Year of Decisions* (1955) and *Years of Trial and Hope* (1956). **Marshall Plan:** J. M. Jones, *The Fifteen Weeks* (1955); H. B. Price, *The Marshall Plan and Its Meaning* (1955). **Atlantic Pact:** J. C. Campbell, *The United States in World Affairs, 1948–1949* (1949); R. A. Taft, *A Foreign Policy for Americans* (1951).

Recent: W. G. Carleton, *The Revolution in American Foreign Policy* (1963) [paperback]; Cabell Phillips, *The Truman Presidency: The History of a Triumphant Succession* (1966); Alfred Steinberg, *The Man from Missouri* (1962); Tang Tsou, *America's Failure in China, 1941–1950* (1963); B. J. Bernstein and A. J. Matusow, *The Truman Administration: A Documentary History* (1966).

Chapter 46

Truman and the Fateful Fifties

I have been asked whether I have any regrets about any of the major decisions I had to make as President. I have none.

HARRY S. TRUMAN, 1960

PROLOGUE: The American policy of "containing" Russia suffered disaster when China fell to the Communists in 1949. Republicans blamed Truman's soft-on-Communism tactics; Democrats retorted that Chiang's regime was so rotten that it fell apart. A frontal challenge to the United Nations came in 1950 when the North Koreans, joined later by the Chinese, lunged into South Korea. Hoping to save collective security and avert World War III, Truman responded to the appeal of the UN and intervened. The United States and the South Koreans, with rather incidental aid from fifteen allies, fought the Communists to a standstill. Truman's unwillingness to risk a general war with China and Russia resulted in the dismissal of General MacArthur, revived charges of a Communist conspiracy in Washington, and accelerated Senator McCarthy's fanatical drive against Communists in government. The resulting witch hunt weakened America's prestige abroad, as did Southern resistance to the Supreme Court's desegregation decision of 1954.

A. THE "DUMP CHINA" POLICY

1. Secretary Acheson Drops Chiang (1949)

Chiang Kai-shek's Nationalist China was creaking at the joints when its eight-year war with Japan ended in 1945. Washington continued to provide Chiang with arms to fight the Chinese Communists, but many of these supplies were corruptly sold or abjectly surrendered. President Truman finally dispatched the highly respected General Marshall in a fruitless attempt to persuade the Nationalists to form a coalition government with the Communists. After Washington had cut back the flow of arms to Nationalist China, the corruption-riddled regime collapsed; and Chiang fled with the remnants of his army to the offshore island of Formosa. The suavely mustached Secretary of State Acheson, whose keen intellect and toplofty manner irritated Congressmen, defended the administration in the following official letter. Locate the part that seems least candid, and assess Acheson's ability as a prophet. Should the historic policy have been reversed, and would American public opinion have tolerated such a reversal?

A realistic appraisal of conditions in China, past and present, leads to the conclusion that the only alternative open to the United States was full-scale

---

1. *United States Relations with China, with Special Reference to the Period 1944–1949* (1949), pp. xv–xvi.

intervention in behalf of a Government which had lost the confidence of its own troops and its own people. Such intervention would have required the expenditure of even greater sums than have been fruitlessly spent thus far, the command of Nationalist armies by American officers, and the probable participation of American armed forces—land, sea, and air—in the resulting war.

Intervention of such a scope and magnitude would have been resented by the mass of the Chinese people, would have diametrically reversed our historic policy, and would have been condemned by the American people. . . .

The unfortunate but inescapable fact is that the ominous result of the civil war in China was beyond the control of the government of the United States. Nothing that this country did or could have done within the reasonable limits of its capabilities could have changed that result; nothing that was left undone by this country has contributed to it. It was the product of internal Chinese forces, forces which this country tried to influence but could not. A decision was arrived at within China, if only a decision by default.

And now it is abundantly clear that we must face the situation as it exists in fact. We will not help the Chinese or ourselves by basing our policy on wishful thinking. We continue to believe that, however tragic may be the immediate future of China, and however ruthlessly a major portion of this great people may be exploited by a [Communist] party in the interest of foreign imperialism, ultimately the profound civilization and the democratic individualism of China will reassert themselves, and she will throw off the foreign yoke. I consider that we should encourage all developments in China which now and in the future work toward this end.

2. Senator McCarthy Blasts "Traitors" (1952)

The loss of a half-billion or so Chinese to the Communists was a staggering blow to the free world. Scapegoats had to be found. The violently anti-Communist Republican Senator Joseph R. McCarthy leaped into the fray, flinging accusations wildly and indiscriminately. In his view Secretary Acheson and General Marshall, themselves allegedly "soft" on Communism and advised by Communist "traitors" in the State Department, had deliberately and treasonably allowed China to go down the drain. Senator McCarthy asks himself the following questions—and answers them—in a book published in 1952. Determine which of his charges seem the most convincing; the most overdrawn. Does he prove that more arms for China would have averted the Communist take-over?

Do you think Acheson realized he was following the Communist Party line in Asia?

Either he knew what he was doing or he was incompetent beyond words. As late as November, 1945, William Z. Foster, head of the Communist Party

2. Quoted from Senator Joseph McCarthy, *McCarthyism: The Fight for America* (1952), pp. 37–40. Published in 1952 by the Devin-Adair Company, New York. Reprinted by permission.

of the United States, notified the world that China was the prime target of
the Soviet Union. He said: "On the international scale, the key task . . . is
to stop American intervention in China. . . . The war in China is the key of
all problems on the international front."

Less than a month after this Communist proclamation, Marshall embarked
upon the "Marshall Mission to China." The testimony before the Russell
Committee was that this mission was an Acheson-Marshall-Vincent* project.
Before Marshall went to China the Communists occupied a very small
portion of China. Their Army numbered less than 300,000 badly equipped
troops. When Marshall returned from China to be rewarded by Truman
with an appointment as Secretary of State, the Communist-controlled area
had greatly increased and the Communist Army had grown from 300,000
badly equipped troops to an Army of over 2,000,000 relatively well-
equipped soldiers.

*What about the State Department's excuse that we withdrew aid from
Chiang Kai-shek because his government was corrupt?*

Chiang Kai-shek had been engaged in conflict and warfare since 1927—
first with the Communists, then with Japan, then simultaneously with the
Communists and Japan, and after Japan's defeat, again with the Communists. During that time, all the disruption of war beset Chiang's Government. Under the circumstances it would be a miracle if there were no
corruption or incompetence in his government.

But if corruption and incompetence are grounds for turning an administration over to the Communists, then Earl Browder should be President
of the United States, Harry Bridges should be Secretary of Labor, and
Alger Hiss† should be Secretary of Defense.

*What about Acheson's claim that we gave Chiang Kai-shek every help
which he could utilize, including $2 billion worth of aid since the end of
World War II?*

That is untrue. Acheson made this claim in a letter to Senator Pat Mc-
Carran on March 14, 1949, in arguing against any further aid to anti-
Communist China, which according to Acheson "would almost surely be
catastrophic."

Of the phony $2 billion figure, $335,800,000 was for repatriating Japanese
soldiers in China and transporting Chinese Nationalist armed forces to
accept the surrender of the Japanese. Even President Truman declared
that those expenditures should properly have been charged to World
War II. . . .

*Is it true that Marshall, under State Department instructions, signed an
order cutting off not only arms to our friends in China, but also all ammunition so that the arms they had would be useless?*

* John C. Vincent was a foreign service officer allegedly "soft" on Communism.
† Alger Hiss was a prominent State Department official convicted in 1950 of perjury in
connection with passing secrets on to the Soviets. Harry Bridges was a Pacific Coast labor
leader accused of Communist affiliation. Earl Browder was twice a candidate for the Presidency on the Communist ticket.

Yes. The embargo on all arms and ammunition to China began in 1946 and continued into 1947.

Those were crucial years, and China's plight was so bad that even the New York *Times* reported on June 22, 1947, that the guns of the anti-Communists were so worn and burned out that "bullets fell through them to the ground."

The Communists, on the other hand, were kept well supplied by the Russians. Admiral Cooke has so testified before the McCarran Committee. . . .

Do you claim that General Marshall, who has long worked with Acheson, was knowingly working for the Communist cause in China?

As I stated in my book, *The Story of General George Marshall—America's Retreat from Victory,* I cannot delve into the mind of Marshall. I can only present the facts to the American people. Whether Marshall knowingly betrayed China or whether he honestly thought that he was helping China, the results are equally disastrous for America. . . .

Since the fall of China has Acheson ever admitted that his China policy was a failure?

No. There is no indication that Acheson considers the loss of China to Communism a "failure." Instead, he hailed it as "a new day which has dawned in Asia."

[*The Americans supplied Chiang's Nationalists with vastly more arms than the Russians sent to the Chinese Communists, although departing Soviet troops did abandon large quantities of Japanese munitions to the Communists. The Americans also abandoned comparable supplies of their own to the Nationalists. The tale about bullets falling out of worn-out guns came from an unnamed Chinese correspondent's report (New York* Times, *June 22, 1947, p. 38) that "some machine gun barrels were so burned that bullets fell through them to the ground." Machine guns can be so badly worn as to fire inaccurately, but the bullets are firmly lodged in the cartridges, and the cartridges are either clipped or belted together.*

General Barr, an American military observer, reported to the Department of the Army on November 16, 1948:

"I am convinced that the military situation has deteriorated to the point where only the active participation of United States troops could effect a remedy. . . . Military matériel and economic aid in my opinion is less important to the salvation of China than other factors. No battle has been lost since my arrival due to lack of ammunition or equipment. Their military debacles in my opinion can all be attributed to the world's worst leadership and many other morale-destroying factors that lead to a complete loss of will to fight. The complete ineptness of high military leaders and the widespread corruption and dishonesty throughout the Armed Forces could, in some measure, have been controlled and directed had the above authority and facilities been available. Chinese leaders completely lack the moral courage to issue and enforce an unpopular decision. . . ." (United States Relations with China, with Special Reference to the Period 1944–1949 [1949], p. 358.)]

B. THE KOREAN CRISIS

1. Senator Connally Writes Off Korea (1950)

Secretary Acheson compounded his China felony, in McCarthyite eyes, by making a memorable speech to the National Press Club of Washington early in 1950. He outlined America's "defensive perimeter" in the Far East, but conspicuously omitted from it the Republic of South Korea and Chiang's last-hope Formosa. He stated that the areas thus excluded would have to depend on themselves for defense and on "the commitments of the entire civilized world under the Charter of the United Nations. . . ." Some three months later Senator Connally, chairman of the powerful Senate Foreign Relations Committee, gave out the following interview. Critics of the Truman administration later charged that the Acheson and Connally statements were open invitations to the Russian-backed North Korean Communists to invade South Korea, as they did in June, 1950. Ascertain whether this inference is fair.

Question. Do you think the suggestion that we abandon South Korea is going to be seriously considered?

Answer. I am afraid it is going to be seriously considered because I'm afraid it's going to happen, whether we want it to or not. I'm for Korea. We're trying to help her—we're appropriating money now to help her. But South Korea is cut right across by this line—north of it are the Communists, with access to the mainland—and Russia is over there on the mainland. So that whenever she takes a notion, she can just overrun Korea, just like she probably will overrun Formosa when she gets ready to do it. I hope not, of course.

Question. But isn't Korea an essential part of the defense strategy?

Answer. No. Of course, any position like that is of some strategic importance. But I don't think it is very greatly important. It has been testified before us that Japan, Okinawa, and the Philippines make the chain of defense which is absolutely necessary. And, of course, any additional territory along in that area would be that much more, but it's not absolutely essential.

2. Truman Accepts the Korean Challenge (1950)

President Truman, in holding back the Communist tide, was forced to make a series of agonizing decisions: the Truman Doctrine (1947), the Marshall Plan (1947), the Berlin Airlift (1948), the North Atlantic Pact (1949), the Korean intervention (1950). Speaking later (1959) at Columbia University, he was asked, "Mr. President, what was the most complicated, the one single, most difficult decision you had to make?" Unhesitatingly he replied: "Korea. The reason for that was the fact that the policies of our allies and the members of the United Nations were at stake at the same time as ours." Here in his *Memoirs* he explains more fully the reasons for intervening with armed forces to support the South Korean republic, a special

1. From a copyrighted interview in *U.S. News and World Report,* XXVIII, 30 (May 5, 1950).
2. *Memoirs by Harry S. Truman: Years of Trial and Hope* (1956), II, 331–33. Published by Doubleday and Company. Copyright 1956 by Time, Inc. Reprinted by permission of Time, Inc.

ward of the United Nations. Remembering that the League of Nations had collapsed in the 1930's because it failed to act resolutely, assess the validity of Truman's view that his intervention in Korea averted World War III.

On Saturday, June 24, 1950, I was in Independence, Missouri, to spend the weekend with my family and to attend to some personal family business.

It was a little after ten in the evening, and we were sitting in the library of our home on North Delaware Street when the telephone rang. It was the Secretary of State calling from his home in Maryland.

"Mr. President," said Dean Acheson, "I have very serious news. The North Koreans have invaded South Korea."

My first reaction was that I must get back to the capital, and I told Acheson so. . . .

The plane left the Kansas City Municipal Airport at two o'clock, and it took just a little over three hours to make the trip to Washington. I had time to think aboard the plane. In my generation, this was not the first occasion when the strong had attacked the weak. I recalled some earlier instances: [Japan in] Manchuria, [Italy in] Ethiopia, [Germany in] Austria. I remembered how each time that the democracies failed to act it had encouraged the aggressors to keep going ahead.

Communism was acting in Korea just as Hitler, Mussolini, and the Japanese had acted ten, fifteen, and twenty years earlier. I felt certain

that if South Korea was allowed to fall, Communist leaders would be emboldened to override nations closer to our own shores. If the Communists were permitted to force their way into the Republic of Korea without opposition from the free world, no small nation would have the courage to resist threats and aggression by stronger Communist neighbors. If this was allowed to go unchallenged it would mean a third world war, just as similar incidents had brought on the second world war. It was also clear to me that the foundations and the principles of the United Nations were at stake unless this unprovoked attack on Korea could be stopped.

3. Senator Taft's Grudging Acquiescence (1950)

Quick-acting President Truman, responding to the call of the UN Security Council for help, ordered American armed forces into South Korea. With ample precedent he acted on his own authority as commander-in-chief, without seeking a war declaration from Congress. His courageous decision was generally applauded in America *at the time*, although unenthusiastically in Republican ranks. But when a bloody stalemate set in after China's intervention, public opinion shifted and branded the conflict "Mr. Truman's war." Senator Robert A. Taft of Ohio, an outspoken Republican isolationist, here lukewarmly supports Truman's announced intervention. Assess the force of his charges that the administration was partly to blame for the attack, that it had not followed a true bipartisan policy, and that it had usurped power.

The President's statement of policy represents a complete change in the programs and policies heretofore proclaimed by the administration. I have heretofore urged a much more determined attitude against Communism in the Far East, and the President's new policy moves in that direction. It seems to me that the time had to come, sooner or later, when we would give definite notice to the Communists that a move beyond a declared line would result in war. That has been the policy which we have adopted in Europe. Whether the President has chosen the right time or the right place to declare this policy may be open to question. He has information which I do not have.

It seems to me that the new policy is adopted at an unfortunate time, and involves the attempt to defend Korea, which is a very difficult military operation indeed. I sincerely hope that our armed forces may be successful in Korea. I sincerely hope that the policy thus adopted will not lead to war with Russia. In any event, I believe the general principle of the policy is right, and I see no choice except to back up wholeheartedly and with every available resource the men in our armed forces who have been moved into Korea.

If we are going to defend Korea, it seems to me that we should have retained our armed forces there and should have given, a year ago, the notice which the President has given today. With such a policy, there never would have been such an attack by the North Koreans. In short, this entirely unfortunate crisis has been produced, first, by the outrageous, aggressive attitude of Soviet Russia, and second, by the bungling and inconsistent foreign policy of the administration.

I think it is important to point out . . . that there has been no pretense of any bipartisan foreign policy about this action. The leaders of the Republican Party in Congress have never been consulted on the Chinese policy or Formosa or Korea or Indochina. Republican members of the Foreign Relations Committee and of the Armed Forces Committee were called to the White House at 10:30 a.m. on June 27, and were informed with regard to the President's statement, but, of course, they had no opportunity to change it or to consult Republican policy committees in either the House of Representatives or the Senate. . . .

3. *Congressional Record,* 81 Cong., 2 sess., p. 9320 (June 28, 1950). The North Korean invasion had begun on June 25.

Furthermore, it should be noted that there has been no pretense of consulting the Congress. No resolution has ever been introduced asking for the approval of Congress for the use of American forces in Korea. I shall discuss later the question of whether the President is usurping his powers as Commander in Chief. My own opinion is that he is doing so; that there is no legal authority for what he has done. But I may say that if a joint resolution were introduced asking for approval of the use of our armed forces already sent to Korea and full support of them in their present venture, I would vote in favor of it.

I have said that the present crisis is produced by the bungling and inconsistent policies of the administration.

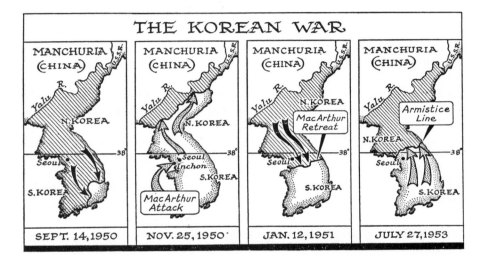

C. THE SACKING OF GENERAL MacARTHUR

1. Truman Asserts Civil Supremacy (1951)

General Douglas MacArthur—handsome, proud, dramatic—served brilliantly as United Nations commander in Korea, until rocked back on his heels by the unexpected descent of hordes of Chinese "volunteers." He urged on Washington a blockade of the Chinese coast, a bombing of supply bases in China, and the use of Chiang's Formosan troops in Korea. Russia had a treaty of alliance (1950) with China, and both the Truman administration and its UN allies were anxious to avoid a general war in the Far East while the Soviet menace loomed large in Europe. MacArthur, who sharply disagreed with the policy of Washington, ruined Truman's proposed peace negotiations by delivering an ultimatum to the enemy (March 24, 1951). Peppery Harry Truman, who had been an army captain in World War I, would brook no such insubordination. He here expresses his views in his *Memoirs*. Ascertain basically why a civilian President should make the final decision on military matters, even though he may not be a military expert.

1. *Memoirs by Harry S. Truman: Years of Trial and Hope* (1956), II, 444–45. Published by Doubleday and Company. Copyright 1956 by Time, Inc. Reprinted by permission of Time, Inc.

If there is one basic element in our Constitution, it is civilian control of the military. Policies are to be made by the elected political officials, not by generals or admirals. Yet time and again General MacArthur had shown that he was unwilling to accept the policies of the administration. By his repeated public statements he was not only confusing our allies as to the true course of our policies but, in fact, was also setting his policy against the President's.

I have always had, and I have to this day, the greatest respect for General MacArthur, the soldier. Nothing I could do, I knew, could change his stature as one of the outstanding military figures of our time—and I had no desire to diminish his stature. I had hoped, and I had tried to convince him, that the policy he was asked to follow was right. He had disagreed. He had been openly critical. Now, at last, his actions [in issuing an ultimatum] had frustrated a political course decided upon, in conjunction with its allies, by the government he was sworn to serve. If I allowed him to defy the civil authorities in this manner, I myself would be violating my oath to uphold and defend the Constitution.

I have always believed that civilian control of the military is one of the strongest foundations of our system of free government. Many of our people are descended from men and women who fled their native countries to escape the oppression of militarism. We in America have sometimes failed to give the soldier and the sailor their due, and it has hurt us. But we have always jealously guarded the constitutional provision that prevents the military from taking over the government from the authorities, elected by the people, in whom the power resides.

It has often been pointed out that the American people have a tendency to choose military heroes for the highest office in the land, but I think the statement is misleading. . . . We have chosen men who, in time of war, had made their mark, but until 1952 we had never elevated to the White House any man whose entire life had been dedicated to the military.*

One reason that we have been so careful to keep the military within its own preserve is that the very nature of the service hierarchy gives military commanders little, if any, opportunity to learn the humility that is needed for good public service. The elected official will never forget—unless he is a fool—that others as well or better qualified might have been chosen, and that millions remained unconvinced that the last choice made was the best one possible. . . .

These are things a military officer is not likely to learn in the course of his profession. The words that dominate his thinking are "command" and "obedience," and the military definitions of these words are not definitions for use in a republic.

That is why our Constitution embodies the principle of civilian control of the military. This was the principle that General MacArthur threatened.

---

* Truman neglected to say that General Eisenhower had been president of Columbia University for four years.

I do not believe that he purposefully decided to challenge civilian control of the military, but the result of his behavior was that this fundamental principle of free government was in danger.

It was my duty to act.

2. MacArthur Calls for Victory (1951)

Joseph W. Martin, Republican House minority leader, had written to General MacArthur in March, 1951, complaining about the folly of not using Chiang's several hundred thousand orphaned Chinese troops in Korea. (They were needed for the defense of Formosa; they might have defected; they would have been resented by the South Koreans.) Martin solicited MacArthur's views. The outspoken general, without labeling his reply as confidential, wrote as follows. On April 5, 1951, Martin read the letter to the House. Truman had already made up his mind to remove MacArthur, and this indiscreet statement strengthened his determination. Note what part of the letter reveals most clearly the military man rather than the statesman.

I am most grateful for your note of the eighth forwarding me a copy of your address of February 12. The latter I have read with much interest, and find that with the passage of years you have certainly lost none of your old-time punch.

My views and recommendations with respect to the situation created by Red China's entry into war against us in Korea have been submitted to Washington in most complete detail. Generally these views are well known and clearly understood, as they follow the conventional pattern of meeting force with maximum counter-force, as we have never failed to do in the past. Your view with respect to the utilization of the Chinese forces on Formosa is in conflict with neither logic nor this tradition.

It seems strangely difficult for some to realize that here in Asia is where the Communist conspirators have elected to make their play for global conquest, and that we have joined the issue thus raised on the battlefield; that here we fight Europe's war with arms while the diplomats there still fight it with words; that if we lose the war to Communism in Asia the fall of Europe is inevitable; win it, and Europe most probably would avoid war and yet preserve freedom.

As you point out, we must win. There is no substitute for victory.

3. Truman Looks beyond Victory (1951)

An angered Truman abruptly dismissed MacArthur from his Far Eastern commands (April 11, 1951), but circumstances conspired to make the General's removal unduly brutal. The five-star general, "fired by a two-bit President," returned home to receive a hero's welcome. He delivered a dramatic speech before Congress in which he repeated the no-substitute-for-victory formula, and then with tear-inducing pathos recited the lines of the old barracks ballad: "Old soldiers never die; they just fade away." The excitement faded away, even though the General did not, and a stale-

2. *Congressional Record*, 82 Cong., 1 sess., p. 3380.
3. *Memoirs by Harry S. Truman: Years of Trial and Hope* (1956), II, 446–47. Published by Doubleday and Company. Copyright 1956 by Time, Inc. Reprinted by permission of Time, Inc.

mate truce came to Korea in 1953. A cocksure Truman delivered this rebuttal in his *Memoirs*, taking as his text the indiscreet MacArthur letter to Representative Martin. Observe why in Truman's view the kind of victory that the General proposed was the wrong kind of victory.

Of course the third paragraph of MacArthur's letter was the real "clincher." I do not know through what channels of information the general learned that the Communists had chosen to concentrate their efforts on Asia —and more specifically on his command. . . . Actually, of course, my letter of January 13 [to MacArthur] had made it clear that Communism was capable of attacking not only in Asia but also in Europe, and that this was one reason why we could not afford to extend the conflict in Korea. But then MacArthur added a belittling comment about our diplomatic efforts, and reached his climax with the pronouncement that "there is no substitute for victory."

But there is a right kind and a wrong kind of victory, just as there are wars for the right thing and wars that are wrong from every standpoint.

As General Bradley later said: "To have extended the fighting to the mainland of Asia would have been the wrong war, at the wrong time and in the wrong place."

The kind of victory MacArthur had in mind—victory by the bombing of Chinese cities,

"WE'VE BEEN USING MORE OF A ROUNDISH ONE."

General Marshall advises General MacArthur that an expanded war in the Far East might not remain there but spread to the rest of the globe. Washington *Post*, March, 1951. From *The Herblock Book* (Beacon Press, 1952).

victory by expanding the conflict to all of China—would have been the wrong kind of victory.

To some professional military men, victory—success on the battlefield alone—becomes something of an end in itself. Napoleon, during his ill-fated Moscow campaign, said, "I beat them in every battle, but it does not get me anywhere."

The time had come to draw the line. MacArthur's letter to Congressman Martin showed that the general was not only in disagreement with the policy of the government but was challenging this policy in open insubordination to his Commander in Chief.

D. THE McCARTHY HYSTERIA

1. McCarthy Upholds Guilt by Association (1952)

Senator Joseph R. McCarthy of Wisconsin, hitherto unknown to fame, rocketed into the headlines in 1950 when he declared in a political speech that there were scores of known Communists in the State Department. The collapse of Chiang's China and the bloodily indecisive Korean War gave point to his charges, while accelerating the hunt for scapegoats. A few homosexuals, "pinks," and Communist sympathizers were exposed and driven out of government. But persons with liberal or non-conformist ideas were indiscriminately branded as Communists, with a subsequent loss of reputation and jobs. In McCarthy's view, fowls that waddled like ducks, quacked like ducks, and associated with ducks were presumed to be ducks. Anti-McCarthyites cited the axiom that it was better to let ten guilty men escape than to condemn one innocent man. McCarthy here defends his tactics. Decide whether innocence-by-association is as valid a concept as guilt-by-association, and whether a man may be grievously hurt even though not found guilty of anything.

One of the safest and most popular sports engaged in today by every politician and office seeker is to "agree with McCarthy's aim of getting rid of Communists in government," but at the same time to "condemn his irresponsible charges and shot-gun technique." It is a completely safe position to take. The Communist Party and their camp followers in press and radio do not strike back as long as you merely condemn Communism in general terms. It is only when one adopts an effective method of digging out and exposing the under-cover, dangerous, "sacred cow" Communists that all of the venom and smear of the Party is loosed upon him.

I suggest to you, therefore, that when a politician mounts the speaker's rostrum and makes the statement that he "agrees with McCarthy's aims but not his methods," that you ask him what methods he himself has used against Communists. I suggest you ask him to name a single Communist or camp follower that he has forced out of the government by his methods. . . .

1. Quoted from Senator Joseph McCarthy, *McCarthyism: The Fight for America* (1952), pp. 7, 79–80. Published in 1952 by the Devin-Adair Company, New York. Reprinted by permission. *Webster's Third New International Dictionary* (1961) defines McCarthyism as "a political attitude of the mid-twentieth century closely allied to know-nothingism, and characterized chiefly by opposition to elements held to be subversive, and by the use of tactics involving personal attacks on individuals by means of widely publicized indiscriminate allegations, especially on the basis of unsubstantiated charges."

Is not a person presumed innocent until proven guilty?

Yes.

Why do you condemn people like Acheson, Jessup, Lattimore, Service, Vincent,* and others who have never been convicted of any crime?

The fact that these people have not been convicted of treason or of violating some of our espionage laws is no more a valid argument that they are fit to represent this country in its fight against Communism than the argument that a person who has a reputation of consorting with criminals, hoodlums, gamblers, and kidnappers is fit to act as your baby sitter because he has never been convicted of a crime.

A government job is a privilege, not a right. There is no reason why men who chum with Communists, who refuse to turn their backs upon traitors† and who are consistently found at the time and place where disaster strikes America and success comes to international Communism, should be given positions of power in government. . . .

I have not urged that those whom I have named be put in jail. Once they are exposed so the American people know what they are, they can do but little damage. . . .

Strangely enough, those who scream the loudest about what they call guilt by association are the first to endorse innocence by association.

For example, those who object most strongly to my showing Jessup's affinity for Communist causes, the Communist money used to support the publication over which he had control, and his close friendship and defense of a Communist spy [Hiss], also argue Hiss' innocence by association. The argument is that Hiss was innocent because Justices Frankfurter and Reed testified they were friends of his, because Acheson chummed and walked with him each morning, because Hiss was the top planner at the United Nations conference and helped to draft the Yalta agreement.

We are not concerned with GUILT by association because here we are not concerned with convicting any individual of any crime. We are concerned with the question of whether the individual who associates with those who are trying to destroy this nation, should be admitted to the high councils of those planning the policies of this nation: whether they should be given access to top secret material to which even Senators and Congressmen are not given access.

2. A Lady Senator Speaks Up (1950)

The infiltration of a few Communists into government was perhaps inevitable, but the embarrassed Truman administration played into the hands of the McCarthyites by

---

* Professors Philip C. Jessup and Owen Lattimore were prominent officials or advisers who were allegedly "soft" on Communism; John S. Service and John C. Vincent were foreign service officers similarly branded by McCarthy.

† After State Department official Alger Hiss was convicted of perjury in connection with Soviet espionage, his friend Secretary of State Acheson loyally but indiscreetly declared, "I do not intend to turn my back [on him]."

2. *Congressional Record*, 81 Cong., 2 sess., pp. 7894–95 (June 1, 1950). Senator Smith simultaneously presented "a Declaration of Conscience" signed by six fellow Senators.

its cover-up tactics. In the interests of free debate, the Constitution exempts from libel suits anything that may be said on the floor of Congress. Senator McCarthy clearly abused this privilege. At a time when he was riding high and many Republicans regarded him as a political asset, the tall and gray-haired Republican Margaret Chase Smith of Maine, the only woman United States Senator, courageously spoke out against his excesses. (Later McCarthy vindictively invaded Maine in an unsuccessful effort to defeat her for re-election.) Assess critically her view that McCarthy's tactics, whatever his aims, were contrary to the Constitution and basically un-American.

I think that it is high time for the United States Senate and its Members to do some real soul searching, and to weigh our consciences as to the manner in which we are performing our duty to the people of America, and the manner in which we are using or abusing our individual powers and privileges.

I think it is high time that we remembered that we have sworn to uphold and defend the Constitution. I think it is high time that we remembered that the Constitution, as amended, speaks not only of the freedom of speech but also of trial by jury instead of trial by accusation.

Whether it be a criminal prosecution in court or a character prosecution in the Senate, there is little practical distinction when the life of a person has been ruined.

Those of us who shout the loudest about Americanism in making character assassinations are all

Incipient McCarthyites regard flame in torch of Statue of Liberty as a fire. Washington *Post*, 1951. From *The Herblock Book* (Beacon Press, 1952).

too frequently those who, by our own words and acts, ignore some of the basic principles of Americanism—

The right to criticize.

The right to hold unpopular beliefs.

The right to protest.

The right of independent thought.

The exercise of these rights should not cost one single American citizen his reputation or his right to a livelihood, nor should he be in danger of losing his reputation or livelihood merely because he happens to know someone who holds unpopular beliefs. Who of us does not? Otherwise none of us could call our souls our own. Otherwise thought control would have set in.

The American people are sick and tired of being afraid to speak their minds lest they be politically smeared as Communists or Fascists by their opponents. Freedom of speech is not what it used to be in America. It has been so abused by some that it is not exercised by others.

The American people are sick and tired of seeing innocent people smeared and guilty people whitewashed. But there have been enough proved cases, such as the *Amerasia* case, the Hiss case, the Coplon case, the Gold case,* to cause nation-wide distrust and strong suspicion that there may be something to the unproved, sensational accusations. . . .

Today our country is being psychologically divided by the confusion and the suspicions that are bred in the United States Senate to spread like cancerous tentacles of "know nothing, suspect everything" attitudes. . . .

As a United States Senator, I am not proud of the way in which the Senate has been made a publicity platform for irresponsible sensationalism. I am not proud of the reckless abandon in which unproved charges have been hurled from this [Republican] side of the aisle. I am not proud of the obviously staged, undignified countercharges which have been attempted in retaliation from the other [Democratic] side of the aisle.

I do not like the way the Senate has been made a rendezvous for vilification, for selfish political gain at the sacrifice of individual reputations and national unity. I am not proud of the way we smear outsiders from the floor of the Senate and hide behind the cloak of congressional immunity, and still place ourselves beyond criticism on the floor of the Senate.

As an American, I am shocked at the way Republicans and Democrats alike are playing directly into the Communist design of "confuse, divide, and conquer." As an American, I do not want a Democratic administration whitewash or cover-up any more than I want a Republican smear or witch hunt.

As an American, I condemn a Republican Fascist just as much as I condemn a Democratic Communist. I condemn a Democratic Fascist just as much as I condemn a Republican Communist. They are equally dangerous to you and me and to our country. As an American, I want to see our Nation recapture the strength and unity it once had when we fought the enemy instead of ourselves.

---

* *Amerasia* was a Communist-tainted magazine which acquired confidential government documents. Judith Coplon, a Justice Department employee, and Harry Gold, a Philadelphia biochemist, were both convicted in 1950 of spying for Russia.

3. McCarthy Inspires Fear at Harvard (1954)

Senator McCarthy overplayed his hand, notably in the televised investigation of the Army. To millions of viewers he exposed his vindictiveness, arrogance, and intellectual dishonesty. Apologists claimed that his anti-Communist zeal, whether sincere or not, destroyed all sense of fair play. His bubble burst when the Senate "condemned" him in 1954 by a formal vote, not, curiously enough, for his abuses of American citizens but for his contemptuous attitude toward the Senate itself. A petition urging the censure of McCarthy was circulated at Harvard University, and two undergraduates who refused to sign it gave their reasons in the first of the following letters to the Harvard *Crimson*. An English-born student named J. C. P. Richardson, who was backing the petition, took sharp issue with them in the second letter. Determine who had the sounder position. Could these letters have been a Communist "plant"?

To the Editors of the *Crimson:*

This afternoon my roommate and I were asked to sign a petition advocating the censure of Senator Joseph R. McCarthy. We both refused. And yet, we both hope that the censure motion is adopted.

Discussing our actions, we came to the conclusion that we did not sign because we were afraid that sometime in the future McCarthy will point to us as having signed the petition, and, as he has done to others, question our loyalty.

We are afraid that of the thousands of petition signers, one will be proved a Communist, and as a result, McCarthy, or someone like him, will say, because we were both co-signers and classmates of the Communist, that we, too, are Reds.

The fact that two college students and others like us will not sign a petition for fear of reprisal indicates only too clearly that our democracy is in danger. It is clear that McCarthy is suppressing free speech and free actions by thrusting fear into the hearts of innocent citizens.

Let us hope that the Senators of the United States are not victims of the same fear that has infected us.

K. W. L. '58
M. F. G. '58

To the Editors of the *Crimson*:

The letter sent to you by two Harvard students and published yesterday can safely be said to represent the viewpoint of about one half of those who did not sign the anti-McCarthy petition.

The position taken by the authors is common and understandable, but it is by no means justifiable. In a free society, when opinions become unpopular and dangerous, it is most important that they be expressed. To yield to the climate of fear, to become a scared liberal, is to strengthen the very forces which one opposes. Courage must complement conviction, for otherwise each man will become a rubber-stamp, content to spend the

---

3. Cited in *Congressional Record*, 83 Cong., 2 sess., p. A6909. Reprinted by permission of the Harvard *Crimson*. The letters appeared in the issues of November 24 and 30, 1954. The Richardson letter ended in the *Crimson* with four dots after "crowd"; the missing five lines are published in the *Congressional Record*.

rest of his life echoing popular beliefs, never daring to dissent, never having enough courage to say what he thinks, and never living as an individual, but only as part of the crowd.

Yes, our democracy is in danger, but as long as men are not afraid to express their view in spite of the consequences, it shall flourish. Only when fear is allowed to limit dissension does democracy falter.

The blame for America's present intellectual intolerance rests as heavily on those who have bowed to it as it does on those who encourage it.

Sincerely,

J. C. Peter Richardson '56

E. THE SUPREME COURT AND NEGRO EDUCATION

1. The Court Rejects Segregation (1954)

The 14th Amendment (1868) had made the Negro a citizen and assured him of "the equal protection of the laws." The Southern states established "separate but equal" facilities in the schools, in public toilets, and in transportation. But in many instances the facilities for the Negroes, though "separate," were not "equal" to those for the whites. In 1892 a Louisianan by the name of Plessy, of one-eighth African blood, was jailed for insisting on sitting in a railroad car reserved for whites. The case was appealed to the Supreme Court, where Plessy lost by a 7 to 1 vote. The Court held that separate but equal public conveyances did not violate the 14th Amendment. This principle was applied to educational facilities until May 17, 1954, when the Supreme Court, by a 9 to 0 vote, reversed its basic policy and decreed that separate educational facilities were not equal within the meaning of the 14th Amendment. In reading the heart of the decision given herewith, decide whether there was ground for the Southern complaint that this was a sociological rather than a legal decision. Are separateness and inequality inseparable?

In approaching this problem, we cannot turn the clock back to 1868 when the [14th] Amendment was adopted, or even to 1896 when *Plessy v. Ferguson* was written. We must consider public education in the light of its full development and its present place in American life throughout the Nation. Only in this way can it be determined if segregation in public schools deprives these plaintiffs of the equal protection of the laws.

Today, education is perhaps the most important function of state and local governments. Compulsory school attendance laws and the great expenditures for education both demonstrate our recognition of the importance of education to our democratic society. It is required in the performance of our most basic public responsibilities, even service in the armed forces. It is the very foundation of good citizenship. Today it is a principal instrument in awakening the child to cultural values, in preparing him for later professional training, and in helping him to adjust normally to his environment. In these days, it is doubtful that any child may reasonably be expected to succeed in life if he is denied the opportunity of an edu-

1. 347 U.S. 492–95. Brown *vs.* Board of Education of Topeka.

cation. Such an opportunity, where the state has undertaken to provide it, is a right which must be made available to all on equal terms.

We come then to the question presented: Does segregation of children in public schools solely on the basis of race, even though the physical facilities and other "tangible" factors may be equal, deprive the children of the minority group of equal educational opportunities? We believe that it does. . . .

Such considerations apply with added force to children in grade and high schools. To separate them from others of similar age and qualifications, solely because of their race, generates a feeling of inferiority as to their status in the community that may affect their hearts and minds in a way unlikely ever to be undone. The effect of this separation on their educational opportunities was well stated by a finding in the Kansas case by a court which nevertheless felt compelled to rule against the Negro plaintiffs:

"Segregation of white and colored children in public schools has a detrimental effect upon the colored children. The impact is greater when it has the sanction of the law; for the policy of separating the races is usually interpreted as denoting the inferiority of the Negro group. A sense of inferiority affects the motivation of a child to learn. Segregation with the sanction of law, therefore, has a tendency to [retard] the educational and mental development of Negro children, and to deprive them of some of the benefits they would receive in a racial[ly] integrated school system."

Whatever may have been the extent of psychological knowledge at the time of *Plessy v. Ferguson,* this finding is amply supported by modern authority. Any language in *Plessy v. Ferguson* contrary to this finding is rejected.

We conclude that in the field of public education the doctrine of "separate but equal" has no place. Separate educational facilities are inherently unequal. Therefore, we hold that the plaintiffs and others similarly situated for whom the actions have been brought are, by reason of the segregation complained of, deprived of the equal protection of the laws guaranteed by the Fourteenth Amendment.

2. One Hundred Congressmen Dissent (1956)

Chief Justice Earl Warren, a gray-haired, open-faced California governor turned judge, had already come under some fire for his liberal views. Bitter was the outcry of Southerners against the "Earl Warren Communist Court." Even though the desegregation decision called for gradual implementation, the social upheaval that it foreshadowed was ominous. Many whites felt that if separate schools were unfair to Negro pupils, then integrated schools, with their debased standards, were unfair to white pupils. Some Negroes were not eager to attend schools where they were not wanted. One hundred Southern members of Congress issued the following manifesto in 1956. The first part of it declared that since the Constitution does not mention education, the schools are solely the concern of the states under reserved powers

2. *Congressional Record,* 84 Cong., 2 sess., pp. 4515–16 (March 12, 1956). The signers numbered 19 Senators and 81 Representatives.

(10th Amendment). Locate the strongest legal argument and the strongest non-legal argument, and note why the South should have shown concern over the constitutional implications.

In the case of *Plessy v. Ferguson,* in 1896, the Supreme Court expressly declared that under the Fourteenth Amendment no person was denied any of his rights if the states provided separate but equal public facilities. This decision has been followed in many other cases. It is notable that the Supreme Court, speaking through Chief Justice Taft, a former President of the United States, unanimously declared in 1927 in *Lum v. Rice* that the "separate but equal" principle is ". . . within the discretion of the state in regulating its public schools and does not conflict with the Fourteenth Amendment."

This interpretation, restated time and again, became a part of the life of the people of many of the states and confirmed their habits, customs, traditions, and way of life. It is founded on elemental humanity and common sense, for parents should not be deprived by Government of the right to direct the lives and education of their own children.

Though there has been no constitutional amendment or act of Congress changing this established legal principle almost a century old, the Supreme Court of the United States, with no legal basis for such action, undertook to exercise their naked judicial power and substituted their personal political and social ideas for the established law of the land.

This unwarranted exercise of power by the court, contrary to the Constitution, is creating chaos and confusion in the states principally affected. It is destroying the amicable relations between the white and Negro races that have been created through ninety years of patient effort by the good people of both races. It has planted hatred and suspicion where there has been heretofore friendship and understanding.

Without regard to the consent of the governed, outside agitators are threatening immediate and revolutionary changes in our public school systems. If done, this is certain to destroy the system of public education in some of the states.

With the gravest concern for the explosive and dangerous conditions created by this decision and inflamed by outside meddlers:

We reaffirm our reliance on the Constitution as the fundamental law of the land.

We decry the Supreme Court's encroachments on rights reserved to the states and to the people, contrary to established law and to the Constitution.

We commend the motives of those states which have declared the intention to resist forced integration by any lawful means.

We appeal to the states and people who are not directly affected by these decisions to consider the constitutional principles involved against the time when they too, on issues vital to them, may be the victims of judicial encroachment.

Even though we constitute a minority in the present Congress, we have full faith that a majority of the American people believe in the dual system of government which has enabled us to achieve our greatness and will in time demand that the reserved rights of the states and of the people be made secure against judicial usurpation.

We pledge ourselves to use all lawful means to bring about a reversal of this decision, which is contrary to the Constitution, and to prevent the use of force in its implementation.

In this trying period, as we all seek to right this wrong, we appeal to our people not to be provoked by the agitators and troublemakers invading our states and to scrupulously refrain from disorder and lawless acts.

[*Some desegregation occurred in the South, particularly in the Border States, in the years immediately following the Supreme Court edict of 1954. But the movement encountered "massive resistance" in the Deep South. The Jackson (Mississippi)* Daily News *greeted the decision on May 18, 1954, with an editorial entitled "Bloodstains on White Marble Steps." Declaring that this was the "worst thing that has happened to the South since carpetbaggers and scalawags took charge of our civil government," it warned that "every possible human effort" would be made to fight desegregation. "Human blood," it predicted, "may stain Southern soil in many places because of this decision, but the dark red stains of that blood will be on the marble steps of the United States Supreme Court building." (Quoted in* Congressional Record, *83 Cong., 2 sess., Appendix, pp. 3712–13.)*]

THOUGHT PROVOKERS

1. If a government (China) has lost the confidence of its own people, can foreign troops save it? Assuming that Washington guessed wrong in failing to give all-out support to Chiang, is this evidence of "treason," as McCarthy charged?

2. Since the American military did not regard South Korea as indispensable for its Asiatic defenses, would not Truman have been justified in regarding the Korean War as a civil war? What would have happened if the United States had stayed out?

3. What alternatives are open to a general who disagrees with policies laid down by Washington? Why do generals resent the interference of "politicians"? Why cannot military policies be made by the general in the field? It has been said that "military victory is never permanent." Comment.

4. Critics charged that McCarthy aided Communism more than he hurt it by creating hysteria at home, shaming America in the eyes of the free world, and diverting attention from the real Communist menace—that abroad. Comment critically. It was also said that the F.B.I. and other agencies were better equipped to ferret out traitors than McCarthy, and that his headline hunting interfered with their operations. Comment.

5. How can the Constitution change in fifty years so that the Supreme Court can unanimously reverse itself on basically the same issue? It has been said that integration was proceeding gradually in the South when the intervention of the Court set back the process by many years. Comment.

FURTHER EXPLORATION

General: E. F. Goldman, *The Crucial Decade* (1956); Herbert Agar, *The Price of Power* (1957). **China Policy:** Herbert Feis, *The China Tangle* (1953). **Korea:** *Memoirs by Harry S. Truman* (1956), vol. II. **MacArthur:** J. W. Spanier, *The Truman-MacArthur Controversy and the Korean War* (1959); R. H. Rovere and A. M. Schlesinger, Jr., *The General and the President* (1951) [anti-MacArthur]; C. A. Willoughby and John Chamberlain, *MacArthur, 1941–1951* (1954) [pro-MacArthur]. **McCarthyism:** R. H. Rovere, *Senator Joe McCarthy* (1959) [anti-McCarthy]; J. R. McCarthy, *McCarthyism* (1952) [pro-McCarthy]. **Desegregation Decision:** Alpheus Mason, *The Supreme Court from Taft to Warren* (1958); C. B. Swisher, *The Supreme Court in Modern Role* (1958).

Recent: See recent references for preceding chapter; also David Rees, *Korea: The Limited War* (1964); Douglas MacArthur, *Reminiscences* (1964) [paperback]; J. W. Spanier, *The Truman-MacArthur Controversy and the Korean War* (1959) [paperback].

Chapter 47

Eisenhower and the World Crisis

The divisive force is international communism and the power that it controls.

PRESIDENT EISENHOWER, INAUGURAL ADDRESS, 1957

PROLOGUE: The magnetic General Eisenhower, elected President in 1952, was unable to thaw the Cold War with Russia, although he did bring an uneasy armistice to Korea the next year. Stalin died in 1953, and the more subtle Khrushchev emerged as the undisputed Soviet leader. The Russians matched the American hydrogen bomb in 1953, and then startled the world by shooting two Sputniks into orbit in 1957. The balance of power, heavily weighted in favor of an atomically armed America after 1945, was clearly shifting to an uneasy balance of terror. Tensions tightened when the Soviets crushed the Hungarian freedom fighters in 1956, backed President Nasser of Egypt during the Suez explosion of 1956, and wooed Cuba's bearded Communist Castro. The perils of doing "business as usual" focused attention on labor racketeering, and in 1959 Congress passed a "tough" remedial law. New leadership and the New Frontier came with the election of Senator Kennedy to the Presidency in the close and colorful campaign of 1960.

A. THE SUEZ BLOWUP

1. Eisenhower Scolds His Allies (1956)

Embittered Arabs spat as they spoke the hated word "America," for Washington had helped establish the intruding Jewish state of Israel. An embittered President Nasser of Egypt sought arms from the United States, and when rebuffed turned to the Communists for aid. Such negotiations chilled Washington's enthusiasm for financing a huge Egyptian dam on the Upper Nile, and in 1956 Secretary Dulles spectacularly withdrew an American offer of support. Slapped in the face, Nasser regained face by seizing the Suez Canal. The British and French, principal owners of the canal (and NATO allies of the United States), were finally goaded into attacking Egypt, so apprehensive were they over their crucial oil supplies. A few days earlier the smoldering war had erupted anew when a provoked Israel invaded Egypt. The United Nations Charter forbade the "use of force against the territorial integrity . . . of any state," and President Eisenhower, in the following radio and television speech, criticized the aggressors. He thus found himself forsaking America's allies and sharing the same bed with the dictatorial Nasser and the Soviet Communists. Note what evidently affronted the United States most, and what Eisenhower's strongest argument was for taking his stand.

On Sunday [October 28], the Israeli Government ordered total mobilization. On Monday, their armed forces penetrated deeply into Egypt and to

1. *Department of State Bulletin*, XXXV, 744–45 (Nov. 12, 1956). Address of Oct. 31, 1956.

the vicinity of the Suez Canal, nearly 100 miles away. And on Tuesday, the British and French Governments delivered a 12-hour ultimatum to Israel and Egypt—now followed up by armed attack against Egypt.

The United States was not consulted in any way about any phase of these actions. Nor were we informed of them in advance.

As it is the manifest right of any of these nations to take such decisions and actions, it is likewise our right—if our judgment so dictates—to dissent. We believe these actions to have been taken in error. For we do not accept the use of force as a wise or proper instrument for the settlement of international disputes.

To say this in this particular instance is in no way to minimize our friendship with these nations nor our determination to retain and to strengthen the bonds among us. And we are fully aware of the grave anxieties of Israel, of Britain, and of France. We know that they have been subjected to grave and repeated provocations.

The present fact, nonetheless, seems clear: The actions taken can scarcely be reconciled with the principles and purposes of the United Nations to which we have all subscribed. And, beyond this, we are forced to doubt even if resort to war will for long serve the permanent interests of the attacking nations. . . .

We took our first measure in this action yesterday. We went to the United Nations Security Council with a request that the forces of Israel return to their own land, and that hostilities in the area be brought to a close. This proposal was not adopted, because it was vetoed by Great Britain and France. . . .

My fellow citizens, as I review the march of world events in recent years, I am ever more deeply convinced that the processes of the United Nations need further to be developed and strengthened. I speak particularly of increasing its ability to secure justice under international law.

In all the recent troubles in the Middle East, there have indeed been injustices suffered by all nations involved. But I do not believe that another instrument of injustice—war—is the remedy for these wrongs.

There can be no peace without law. And there can be no law if we were to invoke one code of international conduct for those who oppose us and another for our friends.

2. Stevenson Blames the Administration (1956)

The Suez blowup came during the closing days of the presidential campaign of 1956. The glamorous, five-starred General Eisenhower was again running against the eloquent and witty "egghead," Adlai Stevenson. Eisenhower had barely announced that the Suez dispute showed definite promise of settlement when the lid blew off. Simultaneously the Russians crushed the Hungarian freedom fighters with tanks, at a time when the aggression of the French and British in Egypt weakened criticisms of the Soviet action. Candidate Stevenson attacked the administration in the following nationwide radio-TV address. Locate the most curious incongruity resulting from

2. New York *Times,* Nov. 2, 1956 (speech of Nov. 1, 1956).

Washington's policy, and evaluate the correctness of Stevenson's assessment of the consequences, particularly with regard to the breakdown of NATO and a Communist take-over of Egypt.

The condition which confronts us is stark and it's simple. Our Middle Eastern policy is at absolute dead end. And the hostilities going on today, in which Israel, Egypt, Britain, and France are involved, reflect the bankruptcy of our policy in that area. And they have also given the Soviet Union two great victories.

The first Communist victory is the establishment in the Middle East of the Russian influence, which the Czars sought in vain for centuries, and which Communists have now achieved in a few months.

The second Communist victory is the breakdown of the Western [NATO] alliance. This has been a supreme objective of Soviet policy since the end of the second World War.

As the climax, the United States finds itself arrayed in the United Nations with Soviet Russia and the dictator of Egypt against the democracies of Britain, France, and Israel.

A foreign policy which has brought about these consequences—which has benefited Communism and has cut our own country off from our democratic friends—is a foreign policy which has failed.

And, at a time when the uprisings in Poland and in Hungary are opening the Soviet world to freedom, the strategic Middle East is opening to Communist penetration. . . .

Secretary of State Dulles began by giving General Naguib—Colonel Nasser's predecessor—a pistol as a personal gift from President Eisenhower. The fateful symbolism of that gift was not lost upon Israel or upon the Arab states. It was the token of a new policy, called "impartiality," between the Arab states on the one hand and on the other the new democracy of Israel, whom the Arabs had vowed to destroy, and whom we and the United Nations were pledged to defend. . . .

Then, in 1955, Colonel Nasser's negotiations for some arms from the United States bogged down in everlasting haggling. And so what did he do? He turned around and negotiated a huge arms deal with the Communists.

We not only failed to stop the introduction of Communist arms into the Middle East, but we refused to assist Israel with arms.

We also refused to give Israel a guarantee of her integrity, although we had given such guarantees to others.

And, in the meantime, we dangled before Colonel Nasser the prospect of financial aid for building a great dam on the Nile River.

In time, the bankruptcy of the Eisenhower Administration's policy became evident even, I guess, to the Secretary of State.

It became clear that Colonel Nasser was not a bulwark of stability, but a threat to peace in the Middle East. Thereupon, President Eisenhower abruptly and publicly withdrew the aid he had led Colonel Nasser to expect for the building of the Aswan Dam.

As anyone could have foreseen, Colonel Nasser promptly retaliated by seizing the Suez Canal.

Driven by our policy into isolation and desperation, Israel—evidently becoming convinced that the only hope remaining was to attack Egypt before Egypt attacked her—took this tragic decision.

Well, here's where we stand today. We have alienated our chief, our ancient, our strongest European allies. We have alienated Israel. We have alienated Egypt and the Arab countries.

And, in the United Nations, our main associate in Middle Eastern matters now appears to be the Soviet Union—in the very week when the Red Army has been shooting down the brave people of Hungary and Poland.

We have lost every point in the game. And I doubt if ever before in our diplomatic history has any policy been such an abysmal, such a complete, such a catastrophic failure.

[*The Anglo-Franco-Israeli invaders were forced to withdraw from Egypt as a result of pressure from world opinion, the UN, the United States, the British Commonwealth, and the Soviet Union. (Moscow threatened to pour in "volunteers.") A UN police force helped restore stability. Nasser ran the canal efficiently and resisted a Communist take-over, while the NATO alliance survived the shock.*]

B. THE LITTLE ROCK SCHOOL CRISIS

1. Eisenhower Sends Federal Troops (1957)

Following the school-desegregation decision of the "Earl Warren Court," Southern white resistance mounted. A showdown occurred in the autumn of 1957, when angry mobs in Little Rock, Arkansas, prevented nine Negro pupils from attending the all-white Central High School. When the governor of the state refused to provide proper protection, President Eisenhower backed up the federal court by sending in federal troops. Under their protective bayonets the Negro pupils attended the school, despite disagreeable incidents. This ugly episode marked a serious setback in the Cold War. Little Rock rapidly became the best-known American city as Communist propagandists had a field day, ignoring the fact that the federal government was trying to help the Negroes. President Eisenhower here addresses the American people on a nationwide radio and television hookup, explaining why he had regretfully resorted to drastic action. Note whether he is on sound legal ground, and why he is concerned about the foreign implications of the affair.

For a few minutes this evening I want to talk to you about the serious situation that has arisen in Little Rock. To make this talk I have come to the President's office in the White House. I could have spoken from Rhode Island, where I have been staying recently, but I felt that, in speaking from the house of Lincoln, of Jackson, and of Wilson, my words would better convey both the sadness I feel in the action I was compelled today to take and the firmness with which I intend to pursue this course until the orders of the Federal Court at Little Rock can be executed without unlawful interference.

1. *Vital Speeches*, XXIV, 11–12 (Oct. 15, 1957; address of Sept. 24, 1957).

" FIRST WE CLOSED OUR SCHOOLS. THEN ONE THING LED TO ANOTHER!"

The Atlanta *Constitution,* though in the center of the "massive resistance" area, regarded closing of the schools as a poor way to fight integration. Atlanta *Constitution,* 1959.

In that city, under the leadership of demagogic extremists, disorderly mobs have deliberately prevented the carrying out of proper orders from a Federal Court. Local authorities have not eliminated that violent opposition and, under the law, I yesterday issued a Proclamation calling upon the mob to disperse.

This morning the mob again gathered in front of the Central High School of Little Rock, obviously for the purpose of again preventing the carrying out of the Court's order relating to the admission of Negro children to that school.

Whenever normal agencies prove inadequate to the task and it becomes necessary for the Executive Branch of the Federal Government to use its powers and authority to uphold Federal Courts, the President's responsibility is inescapable.

In accordance with that responsibility, I have today issued an Executive Order directing the use of troops under Federal authority to aid in the execution of Federal law at Little Rock, Arkansas. This became necessary when my Proclamation of yesterday was not observed, and the obstruction of justice still continues. . . .

Our personal opinions about the decision have no bearing on the matter of enforcement; the responsibility and authority of the Supreme Court to interpret the Constitution are very clear. . . .

Mob rule cannot be allowed to override the decisions of our courts.

Now, let me make it very clear that Federal troops are not being used to relieve local and state authorities of their primary duty to preserve the peace and order of the community. Nor are the troops there for the purpose of taking over the responsibility of the School Board and the other responsible local officials in running Central High School. The running of our school system and the maintenance of peace and order in each of our states are strictly local affairs, and the Federal Government does not interfere, except in very special cases and when requested by one of the several states. In the present case the troops are there, pursuant to law, solely for the purpose of preventing interference with the orders of the Court. . . .

In the South, as elsewhere, citizens are keenly aware of the tremendous disservice that has been done to the people of Arkansas in the eyes of the nation, and that has been done to the nation in the eyes of the world.

At a time when we face grave situations abroad because of the hatred that Communism bears toward a system of government based on human rights, it would be difficult to exaggerate the harm that is being done to the prestige and influence and, indeed, to the safety of our nation and the world.

Our enemies are gloating over this incident and using it everywhere to misrepresent our whole nation. We are portrayed as a violator of those standards of conduct which the peoples of the world united to proclaim in the Charter of the United Nations. There they affirmed "faith in fundamental human rights" and "in the dignity and worth of the human person," and they did so "without distinction as to race, sex, language, or religion."

And so, with deep confidence, I call upon citizens of the State of Arkansas to assist in bringing to an immediate end all interference with the law and its processes. If resistance to the Federal Court order ceases at once, the further presence of Federal troops will be unnecessary and the city of Little Rock will return to its normal habits of peace and order—and a blot upon the fair name and high honor of our nation will be removed.

Thus will be restored the image of America and of all its parts as one nation, indivisible, with liberty and justice for all.

2. The *Arkansas Democrat* Protests (1958)

Occupying federal troops—the first in the South since 1877—remained eight months, until the nine Negro pupils could attend the high school without serious molestation. Many Southerners who were resigned to gradual integration of the

2. *Arkansas Democrat* (Little Rock), March 10, 1958. By Karr Shannon. Reprinted by permission.

schools bitterly resented President Eisenhower's armed intervention. In the light of the following article in a Little Rock newspaper, explain why. Where is the editor on the weakest ground? the strongest ground?

Little Rock's Central High School is still under military occupation. The troops are still there—on the campus, in the building.

The troops are still there, despite the fact that their presence is resented by the big majority of the students, the parents, and the people in general throughout the South.

The troops continue to stand guard during school hours, on the grounds and within the corridors and classrooms, despite the fact that there is no law or precedent—Federal or State—that permits them to do so.

There is not even an order, or so much as a sanction, from the U.S. Supreme Court that makes its own "laws" on mixing of races in the public schools.

Federal troops continue to occupy Central High—in defiance of the Constitution, law, and precedent—while the Congress of the United States sits out the sessions and does nothing.

Never before in the history of America has any area of our so-called Free Republic been so shamefully treated.

When two sections of this country were at war with each other, no troops ever patrolled the public school buildings and grounds from day to day. After the South had been beaten down, Federal forces kept the vanquished under the iron heel for the duration of the "Reconstruction" period. But not once did they molest the public schools with troop occupation.

Education, or attempted education, under the scrutiny of armed troops is un-American, un-Godly.

It is not even Communistic. Russia, in all her cruelty, has never bothered school children in occupied territory by stationing armed soldiers on the grounds and in the buildings. Germany never did it.

No other nation, however barbaric and cruel and relentless, ever—in the history of the human race—resorted to such tactics—only the United States, which sets itself up as a world example of peace, freedom, and democracy, forces the military upon a free school.

How much longer will Congress sit idly by and let such brazen violation of American principle and law continue on and on and on?

3. A Negro Newspaper Praises Courage (1958)

The conduct of the nine Negro pupils at Central High School, in the face of the sneers, jeers, jostling, spitting, and other insults, evoked praise in varied places. A Negro newspaper in Chicago paid them the following tribute. Form conclusions as to whether the praise was deserved, and as to what would probably have happened if the test-case pupils had not persisted in attending.

Few incidents in recent American history can match the courage shown by the nine teen-age Negroes of Little Rock. They risked their lives for the

3. Chicago *Daily Defender,* May 28, 1958. Reprinted by permission.

sake of establishing a principle: the right to attend an integrated high school. They did it in the face of ugly and determined opposition; they did it under circumstances that would have caused many stout-hearted grown-ups to withdraw behind the protective shield of their own homes.

This was the most severe test of the law. The Federal courts paved the way; Federal troops held the angry mob at bay. But the nine Negro pupils did not have to march through the guardsmen to enter Little Rock's Central High School. They could have waited until public indignation had subsided; or they could have decided to attend a nearby Negro school rather than avail themselves of their legal rights. They didn't. Instead they went ahead, despite jeers and bitter invectives.

How many of us would have had the fortitude to do what these young-sters have done? How often have we failed to take advantage of victories won for us? It is therefore the more remarkable that these young Negroes, living in the Deep South, fearlessly implemented the Court's action by their daily presence at Central High School.

Though their lot was not a happy one even inside the high school build-ing, though they were pushed around, insulted, and beaten by some of the white students, the Negro pupils held their ground. The Supreme Court's integration ruling would have been meaningless had these Negro boys and girls failed to follow the course mapped out for them by the law. They should be applauded by all of us.

C. THE SPY–PLANE INCIDENT

1. Gromyko Assails American "Aggression" (1960)

The frantic race in nuclear weapons and rockets was rendered more harrowing by Soviet threats and secretiveness. At Geneva, in 1955, President Eisenhower had vainly proposed a mutual "open skies" aerial reconnaissance. Unwilling to risk another Pearl Harbor, the United States designed a high-flying airplane (U-2) which, above range of Soviet anti-aircraft fire, could take photographs of the Soviet Union. Many such flights originated from nearby bases until May 1, 1960, when a U-2 plane was shot down or brought down deep in Soviet territory. After bungling denials in Washington, Eisenhower finally assumed personal responsibility. Journeying to Paris for a long-scheduled "summit conference" with Soviet Premier Khrushchev, he was met with stormy demands for apology and punishment. As a result, the conclave broke up before it could get started. Russian Foreign Minister Gromyko here tries to persuade the Security Council of the UN to condemn the United States as an aggressor. Decide where his case is strongest, where weakest, and whether he is guilty of hypocrisy.

Here we must dwell on one important aspect of this whole matter: the perfidy displayed by the United States Government in relation to the Soviet Union. . . . Only a short time ago [1959] the President of the United States received the Head of the Soviet Government at Washington and Camp David [Maryland], entertained him cordially, and spoke of the need

1. *United Nations, Security Council Official Records, Fifteenth Year, 857th Meeting* (May 23, 1960), pp. 8–16, *passim.*

IRRESISTIBLE TARGET

Soviet Premier Khrushchev catches Uncle Sam peeping with U-2
spy plane. Jensen in Chicago *Daily News*, 1960.

to strengthen mutual trust. Yet it turns out that at that very time the
United States Air Force was engaged in carrying out a programme of
aggression against the Soviet Union to which President Eisenhower had
given his personal approval. . . .

This alone graphically reveals the nature of the present foreign policy of
the United States. How is it possible after this to regard such a policy
without mistrust? How is it possible after this to trust the statements of
United States Government officials? . . .

Some say that the Soviet Union has been overestimating the significance
of the incursions of United States aircraft into its territory. To those who
take this stand . . . we should like to say: put yourselves in our position.
Imagine that such a border violation is carried out by the aircraft of a
State whose responsible leaders have repeatedly said that they are preparing their armed forces for war against your country and are gearing all
their military preparations to that end. . . .

Imagine that it is not United States aircraft which invade the Soviet

Union but Soviet aircraft which penetrate the air space over, say, Chicago, Detroit, or San Francisco. Imagine that one of those aircraft is shot down and that the Soviet Government begins justifying such overflights by invoking the need to gather information about military objectives in the territory of the United States. What would the American people say to that? What would the United States Government have to say? Would it make light of the whole matter, treating it as a minor incident? I hardly think so. . . .

One of the most dangerous aspects of this policy is that it flouts the principle of State sovereignty. The inviolability of the territory of States has always been and remains one of the most important universally acknowledged principles of international law. The recognition and observance of that principle constitutes the very foundation of the maintenance of peaceful relations among States. The violation of that principle, as history shows, leads as a rule to war. . . .

As we see, the United States Government is now trying to justify the incursions of United States aircraft into the Soviet Union by invoking inept arguments about the secrecy surrounding the defence measures taken by the USSR. The United States Government would like the Soviet Union to put at its disposal, at the disposal of United States militarists, information about military and industrial objectives in our country. The United States Government knows very well that such a demand is preposterous. . . .

It goes without saying that the reasons advanced by the United States Government can be cited only by a Government whose policies represent a combination of aggressiveness, arrogance, and disregard for the elementary rules of honourable conduct which States must observe in their relations with one another. . . .

The Soviet Union is a great and powerful State, and nobody will be permitted to try its patience and take advantage of its peaceful inclinations by continuing provocations against its territory. The USSR Government has clearly indicated the fate that lies in store for anyone who makes another attempt to violate our frontiers. "We shall shoot down these planes," Mr. Khrushchev, the Head of the USSR Government, stated emphatically; "we shall deal a shattering blow at the bases from which they are launched and at those who set up such bases and actually control them." Thus, the Soviet Union has issued its warning both to those responsible for the provocative acts against it and to their accomplices. . . .

Just consider the indignation and resentment of some people in the United States of America over the fact that [Francis G.] Powers, the United States pilot, remained alive although he had been provided with poison, a pistol, and an infernal machine expressly designed to destroy both pilot and aircraft instantly, provided, of course, that he wanted to do away with himself. . . .

These are the morals of those who, by sending their planes over our territory, have avowed their policy to be one of provocation against the Soviet Union. They are the morals of the jungle.

2. Lodge Defends Overflights (1960)

Henry Cabot Lodge, Jr., the handsome and suave American representative to the United Nations, vigorously parried the Soviet charges of "aggressive" and "provocative" acts. He declared that the United States, as indicated by Eisenhower's "open skies" proposal of 1955, would welcome Soviet inspection planes on a mutual basis. He displayed a large wooden eagle taken from the American embassy in Moscow, and showed that it had been "bugged" with a secret listening device (presumably by Soviet agents). Overflights like those of the U-2 plane were clearly a violation of international law; the use of spies within a foreign country was a violation of domestic law. Note whether the Soviets came before the UN with "clean hands." Also ascertain Lodge's most convincing argument, and whether his position was stronger morally than it was legally.

The United States has not committed any aggressive acts against the Soviet Union or any other country. . . .

Now let me take up the Soviet representative's main points. He asserts, first, that flights over the Soviet Union continue to be the State policy of the United States. This assertion is directly, and, I fear, deliberately, contrary to fact. Surely the Soviet representative knows this because he was present when President Eisenhower in Paris on 16 May said: ". . . In point of fact, these flights were suspended after the recent incident and are not to be resumed. Accordingly, this cannot be the issue."

Mr. Gromyko has just claimed, as does the Soviet memorandum, that this is merely a "tactical step," a "temporary suspension," announced with the "object of deluding world opinion." You have just heard the President's words: ". . . these flights were suspended after the recent incident, and are not to be resumed."

Then the Soviet Union asserts . . . that the United States has undertaken "flights inside the frontiers of the USSR for aggressive purposes." I realize that the term "aggression" has never been officially defined, but any common-sense definition of the term shows that the presence of a light, unarmed, single-engine, non-military, one-man plane is not aggression. Yet this is what all the trouble in Paris and here at the United Nations is said to be all about—about this one plane.

Chairman Khrushchev said, both in Moscow and in Paris, that he had known of these flights for a long time. These flights were not considered dangerous enough to complain about last year, when Chairman Khrushchev and the President met privately [at Camp David]. Therefore, it is hard to understand why such flights were suddenly described as aggressive and of urgent concern when Chairman Khrushchev met President Eisenhower publicly [in Paris], ostensibly for peaceful negotiations. We can only speculate about Soviet reasons for increasing tension now by bringing this matter to the Security Council today. . . .

We could, under the same interpretation of aggression, bring up as an aggressive act the repeated violations of our American ground space, and the ground space of many other countries represented here, by Soviet spies.

2. *Ibid.*, pp. 19–21.

We could, for instance, enter in detail into the cases of the following illustrative list of spies, all of whom are among those unmasked in the United States in the period of time which has elapsed since the death of Marshal Stalin: [here follow the names of eleven Russians, mostly officers].

I might point out that one of these agents—Kirilyuk—was actually caught in an act of espionage, seeking data on cryptographic machines, during the [recent] visit of Chairman Khrushchev to the United States, as a matter of fact at the very moment when Chairman Khrushchev was speaking from the rostrum of the General Assembly about disarmament.

We might even make something of the fact that at least one of the agents among those whom I have listed was getting photographs of United States strategic places—and may I say that these photographs were taken at heights far lower than 65,000 feet.

We understand that at least 360 Russian espionage agents have been convicted in different countries of the free world. All of these convictions were obtained under free court systems, which means that ample proof of the charges was made. The number of these convictions represents only a minor proportion of those cases in which Soviet espionage activity has been actually involved. . . .

We shall not dwell on these things nor on all the names of the spies caught while Marshal Stalin was in power, and we shall not bring any of them up using the logic which the Soviet Union has used, as aggressive acts. What we do strongly deplore is the refusal of the Soviet Union to accept the President's "open skies" plan in 1955; its refusal to heed General Assembly resolution 914 (X) calling on it to permit aerial inspection; its rejection of the Arctic aerial inspection zone in 1958, which all ten other members of the Security Council voted for; and its refusal to consider technical measures to prevent surprise attack at the Conference of Experts held in Geneva in the fall of 1958. Those are things which we do deplore.

Just contemplate the situation for a moment. Here is a Government, well known for its expansionist proclivities and armed to the teeth, which has repeatedly, in contravention of Article 2, paragraph 4, of the [UN] Charter—which is the Article which forbids both the use and the threat of force—used force and threats of force in its relations with other sovereign States. That is a clear Charter violation. When such a Government insists on secrecy, it is in effect also insisting on preserving its ability to make a surprise attack on humanity. If the free world failed to attempt to protect itself against such a danger it would be inviting destruction.

If it should ever be accepted that the Soviet Union can maintain a double standard whereby it has thousands of spies and subversive agents everywhere, while protesting one single harmless observation flight, the free world would surely be in great and peculiar danger.

This afternoon the Soviet Union representative has had something to say about international law. One may ask where the Soviet Union's concern for international law was when Communist armed forces invaded the Republic of Korea in 1950; or where that concern was when the Soviet

Union forcibly and brutally snuffed out the independence of Hungary in 1956. Illegal uses of force like these, violating international law and the solemn treaty obligations of the United Nations Charter, cannot fail to make the rest of the world apprehensive for its safety. And this was the background against which measures were taken to try to secure information in advance of possible further Communist assaults.

That is the heart of the matter, and we shall not get very far here if we dwell on the symptoms of the disease and neglect the disease itself. And the disease is the danger of wholesale sudden death by surprise attack.

[*If the Soviets had merely accused the United States of violating international law, they might have carried their resolution through the Security Council. But the extravagant charge of aggression lost by a a vote of 7 to 2, with Russia and her satellite Poland alone supporting the resolution.*]

D. CURBING LABOR ABUSES

1. Eisenhower Pleads for a "Tough" Law (1959)

Widespread labor racketeering received a sensational airing by a special Senate committee in the late 1950's. Efforts to coerce employers or employees into accepting union shops had led to outrages ranging from slashed tires, "sugared" gasoline tanks, and stink bombs to dynamitings, burnings, savage beatings, and outright murder. Some union officials—a number of them ex-convicts—had dipped sticky hands into multi-million-dollar union treasuries. Honest critics were shouted down in union meetings; insiders would vote half a dozen or more times for absent members. Efforts by Congress to pass a strong labor bill were stymied by threats of leaders like tough-fisted "Jimmy" Hoffa (boss of the Teamsters) to inflict reprisals at the polls. An indignant President Eisenhower finally made a dramatic nationwide appeal on radio and television for support of the drastic Landrum-Griffin Bill. Decide which of the abuses described called most urgently for reform.

I am talking about a reform law—a law to protect the American people from the gangsters, racketeers, and other corrupt elements who have invaded the labor-management field. . . .

We all know that only a relatively small minority of individuals among unions and employers are involved in corrupt activities. We know that the vast numbers of employers and union officials are honest and deplore corruption as much as you and I deplore it.

But any corrupt minority is too large. . . .

Chief among the abuses from which Americans need protection are the oppressive practices of coercion.

Take a company in the average American town—your town. A union official comes into the office, presents the company with a proposed labor contract, and demands that the company either sign or be picketed. The company refuses, because its employees don't want to join that union.

And remember, the law definitely gives employees the right to have or not to have a union—clearly a basic American right of choice.

1. *Vital Speeches*, XXV, 674–75 (Sept. 1, 1959; speech of Aug. 6, 1959).

Now what happens? The union official carries out the threat and puts a picket line outside the plant, to drive away customers, to cut off deliveries. In short, to force the employees into a union they do not want. This is one example of what has been called blackmail picketing. It is unfair and unjust. This could force the company out of business and result in the loss of all the jobs in the plant.

I want that sort of thing stopped. So does America.

Take another company—let us say a furniture manufacturer. The employees vote against joining a particular union. Instead of picketing the furniture plant itself, unscrupulous organizing officials in this case use another scheme. They picket the stores which sell the furniture this plant manufactures. The purpose is to prevent those stores from handling that furniture.

How can anyone justify this kind of pressure against stores which are not involved in any dispute? They are innocent bystanders. This kind of action is designed to make the stores bring pressure on the furniture plant and its employees—to force those employees into a union they do not want. This is an example of a "secondary boycott."

I want that sort of thing stopped. So does America.

The blackmail picket line and the secondary boycott cannot possibly help the working men and women of America. . . .

Now any reform bill worthy of the name must also protect the individual rights of union members, within their unions. It must assure them of fair elections. It must assure them of honest handling of their money—money made up by dues often collected under auspices of Federal law.

It must also give to the Government effective authority to investigate and enforce these provisions. Unless it does these things, and deals effectively with the problems of coercive picketing [and] boycotting . . . , it is not a reform bill at all. . . .

As the Congress prepares to vote on labor reform, this great question is still as always with us. In the basic sense, the issue is: shall the people govern? If they do not, crooks and racketeers could prevail.

2. Meany Fights "Union Busters" (1959)

The Landrum-Griffin Bill was designed to curb "blackmail picketing" and "secondary boycotts," while insuring fair union elections and an honest handling of union funds. The balding and bullish-voiced ex-plumber George Meany, president of the thirteen-and-a-half-million member A.F.L.-C.I.O., was skeptical, though his organization had demonstrated its integrity by expelling Hoffa's corruption-riddled Teamsters. In analyzing Meany's radio address, form conclusions as to whether it is possible to eliminate crooks without imposing excessively burdensome restrictions on decent labor unions.

Let me say as emphatically as I can that the AFL-CIO is in complete accord with the great majority of the American people in favor of legis-

2. *Ibid.*, pp. 676–77 (speech of Aug. 6, 1959).

lation that will help get the crooks, without harassing and impeding the forward progress of legitimate and decent labor unions.

Unfortunately, there are forces at work whose only real purpose is to hamper and, if possible, to destroy the effectiveness of legitimate trade unions. They consider the exposure of corrupt leadership in a small minority of unions as too good an opportunity to be missed in order to fasten restrictive legislation on the entire movement.

Under the guise of legislation against corruption, they want to tie up legitimate union activities with legal knots—thus making it difficult, if not impossible, for the trade union movement to carry on its work for economic and social progress....

Now let's see how the Landrum-Griffin Bill measures up. It also contains a number of anti-racketeering provisions which are similar to those in the Elliott Bill.* Again the AFL-CIO is 100 percent in favor.

But the Landrum-Griffin Bill goes a lot further than the Elliott Bill in penaliz-

THE THINKER

Union members began to wonder where their dues were going when their leaders, haled before a Senate committee, invoked the Fifth Amendment scores of times. Shanks in Buffalo *Evening News*, 1957.

ing legitimate practices of legitimate unions. It would subject a union presiding officer to a two-year jail sentence merely for blocking a disorderly person from disrupting a meeting. It would require even the smallest local unions, without paid officers, to file a burdensome amount of red-tape reports. It would force union members against their will and against their basic principles to handle "struck" goods. It would prohibit any union from advertising to the public that an employer is unfair to labor, pays sub-standard wages, or operates a sweatshop, despite Supreme Court decisions that have held a union has not only a right but a duty to

* The Elliott Bill, backed by the A.F.L.-C.I.O., was designed to check abuses without jeopardizing legitimate labor unions. The more restrictive Landrum-Griffin Bill was backed by conservative Republicans.

speak out against such abuses. It would make it virtually impossible for the average, decent union to function effectively.

For these reasons the AFL-CIO strongly opposes the Landrum-Griffin Bill. . . .

Basically, the cure for this problem is better law enforcement. If the present laws on the statute books of our states against theft, corruption, and racketeering had been properly enforced, there would be no need for new Federal law.

One thing is certain—new legislation should be aimed at the crooks, not at the decent, law-abiding unions and their decent, law-abiding members. . . .

The Landrum-Griffin Bill is much worse. It is a blunderbuss that would inflict grievous harm on all unions. It is supported by the very elements in Congress which have consistently through the years voted for the program of big business and against every progressive measure that would benefit all the American people.

[*Public opinion, aroused by Eisenhower's stirring appeal, forced both Houses of Congress to pass the Landrum-Griffin Bill by wide margins in September, 1959.*]

E. THE CATHOLIC ISSUE IN 1960

1. A Texas Preacher Attacks Kennedy (1960)

Al Smith had gone down to defeat in 1928 as the first Catholic nominee of a major party. The Democrats again risked a barrage of anti-Catholic fire when they nominated Senator John F. Kennedy at Los Angeles in 1960. Vice-President Richard M. Nixon, tapped by the Republicans in the Lincoln centennial year, attempted to keep religion out of the campaign. But the Protestant South, alarmed by the heavy increase of Catholic population, refused to be muzzled. The Reverend W. A. Criswell, D.D., Ph.D., pastor of the First Baptist Church of Dallas, Texas (the largest Southern Baptist congregation), preached the following sermon. It was widely circulated in pamphlet form as a campaign document. Determine whether Dr. Criswell is on sound ground when he claims that Catholicism is more than a religion. Note what he fears most, and why; and whether any of his allegations have been borne out by events since 1960.

It is written in our country's Constitution that church and state must be, in this nation, forever separate and free. This is the gift of America to the science of government. . . .

The most difficult situation is created any time that one speaks of the Roman Church. It is a religion, and we have an innate, congenital dislike in America to criticize another man's religion. We believe in religious freedom. . . .

Our problem, therefore, lies in this: that the institution of Roman Catholicism is not only a religion, it is a political tyranny. There is not the

1. W. A. Criswell, *Religious Freedom, the Church, the State, and Senator Kennedy* (1960), pp. 2–8, *passim*

disposition on the part of any true American or any man who loves democracy and religious liberty to attack any faith or any religion. But we are faced with a political system that, like an octopus, covers the entire world and threatens those basic freedoms and those constitutional rights for which our forefathers died in generations past.

For example, a Vatican Ambassador is sought on the basis that the Vatican is a political state. They say it is a sovereign government. They say it is a political entity. Then, if we object politically, we are accused of being religious bigots. We are not attacking the religion nor are we attacking the institution. We are merely facing a political reality. In one instance they present themselves as religionists, then in the next instance they ask for an Ambassador to the Vatican on the basis that they are a sovereign state and a political power. If you have ever seen the symbol of the pope of Rome, he has two keys; one is the key of religious supremacy and the other is the key of sovereign political power. He claims to possess both.

For another example: here in America in defending nuns and priests in their religious habits and in their religious garbs teaching in our public school system, they [Catholics] say their priests and their nuns in religious garbs and religious habits have the right to teach in a public school system on the basis that they are our fellow American citizens. Fine—they are then received in the public school systems and are paid by the tax money of the American people. When the internal revenue collector seeks to have them pay taxes—income taxes—on the salaries that they receive as being on the public payroll and as public schoolteachers—then they say, "We are not other than representatives of the Roman Catholic Church and we pay no taxes." Their salaries are paid to the Roman Church.

They have elected for the second time a Roman Catholic governor in the State of Ohio. With what result? In Ohio it is the law of the land, under the leadership of those two Roman Catholic governors, that Roman Catholic nuns and sisters and priests in their garbs may be placed on the public payroll as schoolteachers. This is a concomitant and a corollary of high elective office when Roman Catholics are able to seize it. The drive for tax money to support Roman Catholic institutions is relentless. It never, never withholds its pressures. And they do succeed tremendously in getting tax money into the support of their institutions. When you pay income taxes, a part of that income tax goes to the support of the Roman Catholic Church in the United States of America.

When the Roman Catholic hierarchy is able to seize political power in a nation, what happens? Here are a few examples: The Constitution of Argentina states: "To be eligible to the office of President or Vice-President of the Nation, a person must belong to the Roman Catholic Church." The Constitution of Paraguay states: "The President of the Republic must profess the Roman Catholic religion." The Constitution of Spain states: "To exercise the office of Chief of State or King or Regent, it shall be necessary to profess the Roman Catholic religion." In the South American nation of Colombia, during the past eight years, with a government dominated by the Roman Catholic Church, 49 Protestant churches have been destroyed, 34 Protestant churches have been confiscated, and 89 Protestant church leaders have been murdered. . . .

The Roman Church wins most of its victories with the weapons of time. If Kennedy wins, with strong emphasis on separation of church and state, then the door is open for another Roman Catholic later who gives the Pope his Ambassador, the church schools state support, and finally, recognition of one church above all others in America. Then religious liberty has also died in America as it has died in Spain, as it has died in Colombia, as it has died wherever the Roman Catholic Hierarchy has the ableness and power to shut it down and destroy it in death.

2. Kennedy Faces His Accusers at Houston (1960)

Kennedy bearded the Southern Protestants in their den. In a memorable televised performance, he spoke to and was questioned by a group of 150 Protestant ministers and laymen in Houston, Texas, on September 12, 1960. Dr. Criswell (see above) remarked that Kennedy "is either a poor Catholic or he is stringing the people along." But Kennedy's defense was so effective that the Democrats reran the televised version many times, despite avowed efforts on both sides to keep religion out of the campaign. Critics said that if Kennedy believed what he avowed, he was not a "good" Catholic. Comment.

I believe in an America where the separation of church and state is absolute—where no Catholic prelate would tell the President, should he be a Catholic, how to act, and no Protestant minister would tell his parishioners for whom to vote—where no church or church school is granted any public funds or political preference—and where no man is denied public office because his religion differs from the President who might appoint him or the people who might elect him. . . .

. . . I believe in an America where religious intolerance will someday end—where all men and all churches are treated as equal—where every man has the same right to attend or not attend the church of his choice—where there is no Catholic vote, no anti-Catholic vote, no bloc voting of any kind—and where Catholics, Protestants, and Jews, at both the lay and pastoral level, will refrain from those attitudes of disdain and division which have so often marred their works in the past, and promote instead the American ideal of brotherhood. . . .

I believe in a President whose views on religion are his own private affair, neither imposed upon him by the nation nor imposed by the nation upon him as a condition to holding that office. . . .

I want a Chief Executive whose public acts are responsible to all and obligated to none—who can attend any ceremony, service, or dinner his office may appropriately require of him to fulfill—and whose fulfillment of

2. New York *Times*, Sept. 13, 1960.

his Presidential office is not limited or conditioned by any religious oath, ritual, or obligation.

This is the kind of America I believe in—and this is the kind of America I fought for in the South Pacific, and the kind my brother died for in Europe. No one suggested then that we might have a "divided loyalty," that we did not "believe in liberty" or that we belonged to a disloyal group that threatened "the freedoms for which our forefathers died."

And in fact this is the kind of America for which our forefathers did die when they fled here to escape religious test oaths, that denied office to members of less favored churches, when they fought for the Constitution, the Bill of Rights, the Virginia Statute of Religious Freedom—and when they fought at the shrine I visited today, the Alamo. For side by side with Bowie and Crockett died Fuentes and McCafferty and Bailey and Bedillio and Carey—but no one knows whether they were Catholics or not. For there was no religious test there.

I ask you tonight to follow in that tradition, to judge me on the basis of fourteen years in the Congress—on my declared stands against an ambassador to the Vatican, against unconstitutional aid to parochial schools, and against any boycott of the public schools (which I attended myself). And instead of doing this, do not judge me on the basis of these pamphlets and publications we have all seen that carefully select quotations out of context from the statements of Catholic Church leaders, usually in other countries, frequently in other centuries, and rarely relevant to any situation here. . . .

But let me stress again that these are my views—for, contrary to common newspaper usage, I am not the Catholic candidate for President; I am the Democratic Party's candidate for President, who happens also to be a Catholic. I do not speak for my church on public matters—and the church does not speak for me.

Whatever issue may come before me as President if I should be elected—on birth control, divorce, censorship, gambling, or any other subject—I will make my decision in accordance with these views, in accordance with what my conscience tells me to be in the national interest, and without regard to outside religious pressure or dictate. And no power or threat of punishment could cause me to decide otherwise.

But if the time should ever come—and I do not concede any conflict to be remotely possible—when my office would require me to either violate my conscience or violate the national interest, then I would resign the office. And I hope any other conscientious public servant would do likewise.

But I do not intend to apologize for these views to my critics of either Catholic or Protestant faith, nor do I intend to disavow either my views or my church in order to win this election.

If I should lose on the real issues, I shall return to my seat in the Senate, satisfied that I had tried my best and was fairly judged.

But if this election is decided on the basis that 40,000,000 Americans lost their chance of being President on the day they were baptized, then it is the whole nation that will be the loser in the eyes of Catholics and non-Catholics around the world, in the eyes of history, and in the eyes of our own people.

But if, on the other hand, I should win this election, then I shall devote every effort of mind and spirit to fulfilling the oath of the Presidency—practically identical, I might add, with the oath I have taken for fourteen years in the Congress.

For, without reservation, I can "solemnly swear that I will faithfully execute the office of President of the United States, and will to the best of my ability preserve, protect, and defend the Constitution," so help me God.

[*Hand on the family Bible, John F. Kennedy repeated this oath on January 20, 1961, when sworn in by Chief Justice Warren as the thirty-fifth President of the United States.*]

THOUGHT PROVOKERS

1. In the light of subsequent events, did Eisenhower err in backing the Egyptians and the Russians against the French, British, and Israelis during the Suez Crisis of 1956? Did the gain for international morality offset the losses incurred?

2. In the interests of national unity, should Eisenhower have refused to send troops to Little Rock? What would have been the most serious consequences of such a refusal?

3. The U-2 incursion into Russia was plainly a violation of international law. Is a nation justified in violating international law if it feels that its national security is critically involved?

4. Why were the shocking abuses in labor-management racketeering tolerated so long by the American public without effective action? Has management been innocent of similar practices?

5. Many voted against Kennedy because he was a Catholic and many voted for him because he was. Were both groups guilty of bigotry? In view of the strong stand taken by the Catholic Church against divorce and birth control, can Catholic judges, legislators, and other public officials be both good citizens and good Catholics in dealing with these problems?

FURTHER EXPLORATION

General: Walter Johnson, *1600 Pennsylvania Avenue: Presidents and the People, 1929–1959* (1960); J. W. Spanier, *American Foreign Policy since World War II* (1960). **Suez:** *The Memoirs of Anthony Eden: Full Circle* (1960); Sherman Adams, *First Hand Report* (1961); R. P. Stebbins, *The United States in World Affairs, 1956* (1957). **Little Rock:** Wilson Record and Jane C. Record, eds., *Little Rock, U. S. A.* (1960). **Spy Plane:** David Wise and T. B. Ross, *The U-2 Affair* (1962); R. P. Stebbins, *The United States in World Affairs, 1960* (1961). **Labor Abuses:** Barry Goldwater, *The Conscience of a Conservative* (1960). **Catholic Issue:** J. M. Burns, *John Kennedy: A Political Profile* (1960); R. M. Nixon, *Six Crises* (1962); T. H. White, *The Making of the President, 1960* (1961).

Recent: D. D. Eisenhower, *Mandate for Change, 1953–1956* (1963) [paperback] and *Waging Peace, 1956–1961* (1965); E. J. Hughes, *The Ordeal of Power* (1963) [paperback]; Herman Finer, *Dulles over Suez* (1964).

Chapter 48

Kennedy and the New Frontier

"For man holds in his mortal hands the power to abolish all forms of human poverty and all forms of human life."

PRESIDENT JOHN F. KENNEDY, 1961

PROLOGUE: A youthful and energetic President Kennedy came to the White House in 1961 with a breathtaking New Frontier program of social and economic reform. He managed to coax from Congress substantial aid for poverty-stricken areas, an increased minimum wage, a $6.19 billion housing subvention, a drug-control law, and a trade-expansion act. But on other fronts the conservatives of both parties united to block much of his "must" legislation. Before his assassination on November 22, 1963, he had failed to obtain such key measures as medical care for the aged, a tax cut, federal aid to general education, and a civil rights law. All of these were passed in the next administration, after the shock of his murder. Civil rights for Negroes proved especially urgent, for a full-blown racial revolution, in both the South and North, erupted in the early 1960's.

In foreign affairs, Kennedy got off to a disastrous start in April, 1961, by his irresolute backing of the ill-fated invasion of Cuba by Cuban exiles at the Bay of Pigs. On the credit side, he inaugurated the Peace Corps to uplift "backward" peoples and launched the ten-year Alliance for Progress program to aid Latin America. In 1962 he spectacularly thwarted an attempt by the Soviets to sneak nuclear-tipped missiles into Cuba, and in 1963 he concluded the partial Nuclear Test Ban Treaty with Moscow. But such gains were substantially offset by his large-scale and fateful commitment of American troops to the jungles of South Vietnam in 1961 (see p. 969).

A. MEDICAL CARE FOR THE AGED

1. Kennedy Pleads For Aid (1962)

One of the most hotly disputed planks of President Kennedy's New Frontier program was medical care for the elderly—that is, a form of health insurance financed by contributions under Social Security. Millions of "senior citizens" were caught in a squeeze. Inflation was shrinking their modest savings, if any, while medical costs were skyrocketing. President Kennedy, in addressing a roaring rally at Madison Square Garden, in New York City, put forth the following arguments, among others. Is he fair in his references to doctors and millionaires (of whom he was one)? How could the self-reliance of the people be undermined if they paid for what they got?

And then other people say, "Why doesn't the Government mind its own business?" What is the Government's business, is the question . . . .

1. *Public Papers of the Presidents of the United States: John F. Kennedy, 1962* (1963), pp. 418–19. Speech of May 20, 1962.

This bill serves the public interest. It involves the Government because it involves the public welfare. The Constitution of the United States did not make the President or the Congress powerless. It gave them definite responsibilities to advance the general welfare—and that is what we're attempting to do.

And then I read that this bill will sap the individual self-reliance of Americans. I can't imagine anything worse, or anything better, to sap someone's self-reliance, than to be sick, alone, broke—or to have saved for a lifetime and put it out in a week, two weeks, a month, two months. . . .

This argument that the Government should stay out, that it saps our pioneer stock—I used to hear that argument when we were talking about raising the minimum wage to a dollar and a quarter. I remember one day [as U.S. Senator] being asked to step out into the hall, and up the corridor came four distinguished-looking men, with straw hats on and canes. They told me that they had just flown in from a State in their private plane, and they wanted me to know that if we passed a bill providing for time and a half for service station attendants, who were then working about 55 to 60 hours of straight time, it would sap their self-reliance.

The fact of the matter is what saps anyone's self-reliance is working 60 hours at straight time, or working at 85 or 95 [cents or] at a dollar an hour. Or depending upon filling out a pauper's oath and then going and getting it [medical aid] free.

Nobody in this hall is asking for it for nothing. They are willing to contribute during their working years. That is the important principle which has been lost sight of. . . .

The fact of the matter is that what we are now talking about doing, most of the countries of Europe did years ago. The British did it 30 years ago. We are behind every country, pretty nearly, in Europe, in this matter of medical care for our citizens.

And then [there are] those who say that this should be left to private efforts. In those hospitals in New Jersey where the doctors said they wouldn't treat anyone who paid their hospital bills through social security, [to] those hospitals and every other new hospital, the American people—all of us—contribute one half, one or two thirds for every new hospital. . . . We pay 55 percent of all the research done. We help young men become doctors. We are concerned with the progress of this country. . . .

And then, finally, I had a letter last week saying, "You're going to take care of all the millionaires and they don't need it." I do not know how many millionaires we are talking about, but they won't mind contributing $12 a month to social security, and they may be among those who will apply for it when they go to the hospital. But what I will say is that the National Government, through the tax laws, already takes care of them, because over 65 they can deduct all their medical expenses.

What we are concerned about is not the person who has not got a cent but those who saved and worked and then get hit.

2. The Medics Oppose Medicare (1962)

The most vehement objections to Medicare were voiced by the conservative American Medical Association, which feared the entering wedge of socialized medicine. The following criticism of the bill by a Minnesota newspaper editor reflected some of the fears of the doctors. Which of his arguments are the weakest; which are the strongest, in view of the fact that ten percent of the population would represent about 17,000,-000 "oldsters"? Should dollars be paramount to the public welfare?

Countless thousands of words are being exchanged in our Nation regarding possible merits of the controversial Kennedy-backed King–Anderson health insurance bill for the aged. It may resolve into one of the most bitterly contested measures ever debated by Congress. . . .

The writer must join the ranks of those persons who do not feel this type of legislation is the answer to whatever problem may exist.

First, in our opinion, this is a compulsory type bill, similar to social security. Whenever it becomes compulsory to subscribe to Government programs you, without question, have Government control. Experience has proven that Government control is definitely second best.

Second, who will benefit? The administration admits that persons over 65 total only 10 percent of this country's population, yet everyone presently paying social security would pay for compulsory health insurance.

Of the 10 percent of our population of persons 65 and over, almost one third presently have private health insurance, thus cutting down still further the number of needy persons.

Third, it is our opinion the bill would tend to create an inflationary trend in the cost of medical care and possibly an inflationary trend in prices of all commodities in general.

Provisions of the bill call for the employer to also pay part of the cost of the program for each employee, similar to the deductions now made for social security.

If the employer must also pay part of the cost he will, most likely, have to pass along to his customer the extra expense in the form of increased charges for products and services. This, in turn, will cause labor to increase wage demands, all adding to the spiral upward in prices.

It would seem foolhardy to subject this country's entire population to a program, whose cost can only be guessed at, only to benefit a small portion of our people.

3. Medicare Is Temporarily Shelved (1962)

President Kennedy went all out in attempting to ram Medicare through Congress, but ran headlong into the conservative Democratic-Republican coalition, spurred on

2. Westbrook *Sentinel* (Russell Bowers), in *Cong. Record,* 87th Cong., 2nd sess., p. A4151 (Appendix, June 6, 1962).
3. New York *Journal-American,* August 6, 1962 (Robert Peterson), quoted in *Congressional Record,* 87th Cong., 2nd sess., p. A6193 (Appendix). By permission of King Features Syndicate.

by the well-financed lobby of the American Medical Association. One feature which prompted opposition was tying the scheme to Social Security, and providing equal payments to both plutocrats and paupers. (A Medicare bill of a similar nature was passed by the Democratic Congress under President Johnson in 1965.) In the following column which appeared in the New York *Journal-American*, note the weaknesses of the existing Kerr-Mills legislation (combining state aid with federal aid), and evaluate the argument favoring the inclusion of millionaires in the coverage.

President Kennedy's proposed medicare bill has been shelved for the time being by the U.S. Senate. But I'm confident a majority of Americans favor better health care provisions than presently exist for our elder citizens.

My thoughts on the subject emerged in clear focus 3 years ago when I interviewed a retired sales clerk of 72 whose wife barely survived a terrible bout with cancer.

In the wake of long hospitalization, three sessions of surgery, private duty nurses and costly drugs and X-rays, the family nest egg of some $6,500 was completely wiped out.

Also wiped out were dreams of motor trips down South, and mountain vacations, and gifts for the grandchildren. Instead this couple faced the grim reality that the rainy day for which they saved had arrived with a vengeance and drowned the pleasures and security they had hoped to enjoy in their retirement years.

My column about that couple elicited a letter from financier Bernard Baruch who wrote me that he believed, "A form of compulsory health insurance can be devised, adequately safeguarded, without involving what has been termed 'socialized medicine.'"

Many righteously contend that existing Kerr-Mills legislation offers adequate protection to elders since it will pay medical expenses of elders who have no money. But what about those who have a little money saved up—a nest egg of perhaps $5,000 or $6,000 such as the couple mentioned. They are not eligible. Only after their nest egg is exhausted and they have taken a pauper's oath are they eligible for assistance from this legislation.

Some physicians and hospitals, of course, attempt to be lenient on hardship cases. They may work out arrangements "within the means" of the individual. But all too often this means they take what you've got. And I claim it's wrong.

It would be fine if private health insurance could be devised to insure elders against the costs of serious illness. But existing private plans suffer from one or more deficiencies; either they exclude some elders, or they offer limited benefits, or they cost more than most elders can afford to pay.

I hate taxes as much as anyone, but the one additional tax I would gladly pay is one earmarked to cover costs which arise when people—particularly older people—are so unfortunate as to be stricken with serious, costly illnesses.

Many are disturbed by the administration's proposal to offer medicare to all social security recipients—regardless of need. "It infuriates me," a woman wrote, "to think of any of my social security taxes going to pay the hospital bills of that rich old codger who lives next door to me."

But there aren't many rich old codgers to worry about. The statistics showing that more than two-thirds of our 17 million past 65 have incomes well under $2,000 a year should scotch any rumors of wealth among a majority of elders.

It would be fine if we could somehow screen out the rich old codgers and make them ineligible for medical benefits under the proposed bill. But the screening-out process would probably cost more than the end savings, and would automatically cast a stigma of charity on those who were eligible.

B. THE STEEL CRUNCH

1. Kennedy Is Outraged (1962)

President Kennedy, determined to hold the lid on rising prices, was deeply concerned about the wage-price spiral in the steel industry. Early in 1962 the steel workers, showing surprising restraint, signed a contract with United States Steel (by far the largest producer) which called for no wage increases and only minimal fringe benefits. The assumption was general that the companies would show a similar regard for the government's guidelines by maintaining existing prices. But two weeks later U.S. Steel, joined by other major producers, suddenly announced a price increase. Arthur M. Schlesinger, Jr., then Special Assistant to the President, here describes what happened next. Try to determine whether Kennedy's reaction was justified, and whether or not he overreacted to the unexpected move of the steel companies.

Kennedy's reaction was a mixture of incredulity over what he saw as the selfishness and stupidity of the steel industry and anger over what he regarded as its premeditated deceit. Honorable people, he felt, did not behave in this fashion. "We were not asking the steel industry for capitulation," Arthur Goldberg said; "we were asking it for candor." The industry had accepted labor's restraint . . . without the slightest hint that it did not plan to be equally restrained itself; its *démarche* now, from the White House view, seemed a plain and impudent double cross.

"My father always told me," Kennedy said, in the remark the business community never forgave, "that all businessmen were sons-of-bitches, but I never believed it till now." This proposition, though offered in private, soon reached the newspapers. Kennedy later told a press conference that his father had limited his comment to steel men; "he was involved when he was a member of the Roosevelt administration in the 1937 strike. He formed an opinion which he imparted to me, and which I found appropriate that evening. . . . I quoted what he said and indicated that he had not been, as he had not been on many other occasions, wholly wrong."

(A few days later, he remarked to Adlai Stevenson and me, "They *are* a bunch of bastards—and I'm saying this on my own now, not just because my father told it to me.")

1. Arthur M. Schlesinger, Jr., *A Thousand Days* (1965), pp. 635–36. By permission of Houghton Mifflin Co.

2. Big Business Condemns Kennedy (1962)

Eight major steel companies had simultaneously raised prices, but two had not. The Defense Department thereupon announced that it was prepared to switch juicy defense contracts to the non-raisers. Such moves, combined with other pressures (including that of public opinion), forced the steel companies to rescind their increases. But big business was indignant. Lapel buttons blossomed out with the letters "S.O.B.," meaning "Son of Business" or "Save Our Business." The following editorial in a business magazine presents a vigorous argument for free enterprise and the validity of supply-and-demand. How much validity is there in it?

Big steel met big Government and big Government won. The victory was impressive; the victory was swift. The forces marshaled by big Government were awesome to behold.

The President delivered a tirade of condemnation against the steel companies. Governmental agencies were turned into his private avengers. The Justice Department and the Federal Trade Commission swung into action. Reporters were roused from their beds to give testimony about any incriminating statements steel officials might have made. Orders went out to buy from steel companies who had not raised prices—a boycott outlawed to anyone but the U.S. Government.

These things were done—so said the President—in the public interest. What he did not say, but clearly implied, was that the Government, not the steel companies, should decide the price to be charged in the marketplace. The implications go further, much further. The President, by his action, has indicated that he has lost faith in the law of supply and demand. Evidently he deems this free enterprise requisite no longer suitable for the American economy.

Perhaps the steel companies were wrong; perhaps the price increases were unjustified. But why not let the purchasers make the decision—with their dollars. If the steelmakers had guessed wrong the market would soon rectify the decision.

Now that the smoke has cleared from the battleground it's time for some sober thoughts on the real issue that was at stake. What was this real issue? Was it whether steel would cost $6 more a ton? Was it whether an increase in the price of steel was justified? We think not.

The real issue was whether a company could decide the price of its products or whether price is to be left to the whim of the Government. The cornerstone of our free enterprise system was at stake and it became all too clear that an articulate spokesman could make free enterprise a crime against the "public interest."

No one now can state with certainty what the effect of a price increase by big steel would have meant. Doubtlessly, management of these steel companies felt such an increase was needed to replace obsolete equipment and to satisfy investors.

2. *Hardware Retailer,* June, 1962, p. 7 (Russell R. Mueller). By permission of the editor of the *Hardware Retailer.*

For this "crime" they were publicly condemned and blackjacked into submission. The punishment enacted against the steelmakers can hardly be overlooked by other businessmen. They, too, must wonder when a knock will be heard on their door.

We cannot help but wonder if the loss of the free enterprise system is really in the public interest.

[*Kennedy patched up a peace with big business, which could not afford to bite the hand that was handing out defense contracts. Both antagonists learned a lesson. A year later, when some of the steel companies raised their prices on certain items without evidences of barefaced collusion, the White House took no action.*]

C. THE NEGRO REVOLUTION AND JAMES H. MEREDITH

1. A Mississippi Editor Calls for White Supremacy (1961)

James H. Meredith, a Mississippi-born Negro in his late twenties, had served for nine years in the U.S. Air Force as a clerk-typist, and had risen to the rank of sergeant. He was determined to complete his college education at the University of Mississippi ("Ole Miss"), an all-white institution located at Oxford. One of his main purposes was to break through the color barrier and make possible the training of fellow Negroes in an institution they were supporting with their taxes. He was denied admission, presumably on grounds of race. He then appealed through the state and federal courts, thus triggering the following editorial by the Meridian (Mississippi) *Star*. Note the underlying concern of this newspaper and assess its validity.

James H. Meredith, Kosciusko Negro, has filed suit in federal court to enter the University of Mississippi for the summer session.

Fortunately, his case can't be heard until June 12 in Biloxi. This gives grounds for hope that he won't really become a serious problem, at least until the second semester of summer school in late July.

The Negro filed suit on behalf of himself and "all others similarly situated."

Some people will say that even if Meredith wins the suit only a few Negroes will apply for admission.

Some misguided people ask what difference it makes if only a few Negroes go to a white school.

The difference is that the first Negro is only the opening wedge for a flood in time to come.

Integrationists, according to their own statements, will never be satisfied with "token integration."

Massive integration will mean future intermarriage.

Intermarriage in the South, where we are so evenly divided white and colored, means the end of both races as such, and the emergence of a tribe of mongrels.

1. Cited in James Meredith, *Three Years in Mississippi* (1966), p. 107. Reproduced by permission of the Meridian *Star* and the Indiana University Press.

The term "moderate" is a complete misnomer. There are only three kinds of people—segregationists, integrationists, and those who want to supinely submit to the integrationists.

If you value your racial heritage, if you have even the smallest regard for the future of this South of ours—you will be for segregation one hundred percent.

We must lock shields. We must fight for our race and for the South to the last bitter ditch. We must never lose heart.

We can triumph—we will triumph—we must triumph.

2. The Harassment of Meredith (1962)

At length Meredith received a favorable ruling from the federal courts, but the governor of Mississippi openly defied the United States government. President Kennedy had no choice but to send several hundred federal marshals to Oxford, ultimately supported by some 16,000 troops, to uphold the supreme law of the land. Thousands of students and others, some of them in their fifties and from as far away as California, formed a riotous mob, which attacked the marshals. In the fracas, two men were killed and about 200 were injured by such missiles as flying bricks, broken windshield glass, and gunshots, but almost miraculously wholesale slaughter was avoided. Meredith attended class with federal marshals and lived in a dormitory with them. He later recorded his impressions of the first two weeks. What do they reveal about the basic nature of the problem?

I have received hundreds of telegrams and thousands of letters, most of them expressions of support. One guy sent me a piece of singed rope, and another sent a poem, I guess you'd have to call it:

> Roses are red, violets are blue;
> I've killed one nigger and might as well
> make it two.

But most of the letters and telegrams have supported me, and some of them have been really touching—letters from 10- and 11-year-olds who think I am right and offer me their help.

As far as my relations with the students go, I make it a practice to be courteous. I do not force myself on them, but that is not my nature anyway. Many of them—most, I would say—have been courteous, and the faculty members certainly have been. When I hear the jeers and the catcalls—"We'll get you, nigger" and all that—I do not consider it personal. I get the idea people are just having a little fun. I think it's tragic that they have to have this kind of fun about me, but many of them are children of the men who lead Mississippi today, and I would not expect them to act any other way. They have to act the way they do. I think I understand human nature enough to understand that.

It has not been all bad. Many students have spoken to me very pleasantly. They have stopped banging doors and throwing bottles into my dormitory now.

2. *Ibid.*, pp. 226–227. Adapted from the original article in the *Saturday Evening Post* and reproduced by permission of the Indiana University Press.

One day a fellow from my home town sat down at my table in the cafeteria. "If you're here to get an education, I'm for you," he said. "If you're here to cause trouble, I'm against you." That seemed fair enough to me.

If the decision is made to keep the marshals and troops on the campus until I complete my course, it is all right with me, but I hope that will not be necessary. I think the marshals have been superb. They have had an image of America—that the law must be obeyed, no matter what they may think of it or what anybody else may think of it—but they are certainly a distraction on the campus. The thing that grieves me most about all this is that the students are not getting the best college results because they are spending too much time looking on at these various events involving me. I did not get much studying done that first week, and I don't think anybody else did.

3. Meredith Outlines His Goals (1963)

Meredith persisted in attending classes, despite catcalls, profane epithets and letters, ostracism, sugar in his gasoline tank, and threats of violence against himself and his family. (His wife and small son did not accompany him to Oxford.) With transfer credits, he completed the work for his degree in August, 1963. Even before then a world celebrity, he explained his purposes to a panel on a nationwide radio and television program, "Meet the Press." Locate the most questionable of his conclusions. How could he have aided "White Supremacy" by his conduct?

Mr. Spivak: Mr. Meredith, I am sure you expected difficulties when you enrolled at the University of Mississippi, but did you expect that the going was going to be as rough as it finally turned out to be? . . .

Mr. Meredith: From time to time, immediately preceding each event, it was quite evident to me that it would be as bad as it was.

Mr. Spivak: Would you have enrolled if you had known in advance how much difficulty you were going to have?

Mr. Meredith: Certainly. The point is not the difficulty. The most important point is that I feel that all citizens should be entitled to education that is offered by their states, and certainly this was the objective.

Mr. Spivak: Now that you have finished your first year, what do you think you have accomplished there?

Mr. Meredith: I have gone to school for a year, but I'd say the most important thing that has been accomplished by this whole endeavor has been to make this country and the world aware of the seriousness of the problem that exists in this country—the racial problem.

Mr. Spivak: There have been conflicting reports on what you hoped to accomplish when you first enrolled. Are your hopes of what you would accomplish fulfilled? Have you accomplished everything that you hoped to accomplish, thus far?

Mr. Meredith: Certainly I hope to see the day when all citizens, including Negroes, enjoy all of the benefits that this country has to offer. Certainly this

3. Quoted in James Meredith, *Three Years in Mississippi* (1966), pp. 293–94.

is not the fact. But realistically, many things, I think, have been pointed up, and now it is up to the country and the people, to do something about it.

Mr. Spivak: You wrote an article for "Look" earlier this year, and in it you said this, "I am convinced that you can pay a price for one piece of freedom that is greater than the benefits you get." There were two men killed at Oxford, hundreds were hurt, and the country has spent millions of dollars. Do you personally think it has been worth the cost?

Mr. Meredith: I think it is very bad that men had to be hurt, and killed, but I think that the Negro, including me, certainly had nothing to do with anyone's getting killed. . . .

Mr. Spivak: You yourself at one time feared and many people say that they think your admission to the university under the circumstances has helped the advocates of white supremacy, rather than the other way around. What is your conclusion on that?

Mr. Meredith: I certainly hope this is not the case. I still have great faith that this idea of white supremacy is going to lose its effect in this country, and I hope that anything I have done hasn't helped it. This hasn't been my aim.

4. Murder in Mississippi

Meredith displayed unusual dedication and courage in completing his self-assigned ordeal with flying colors. He here comments on the dangers involved. Form some conclusion as to whether his fears were exaggerated.

Contrary to what people might think, the one year that I spent at the University of Mississippi was not nearly as dangerous for me personally as the two years in Mississippi before I was able to gain admission to the school. What people saw on television—the mobs, the violence, the intolerance, the hate, and the indignities that the Negro was the victim of—had gone on for years and years in the same or in a more vile form. The only difference was that the rest of the world was seeing it for the first time.

The traditional practice in Mississippi has been to eliminate potential troublemakers before they get a chance to cause trouble. Far more Negroes have been lynched for having a bad or wrong attitude (by Mississippi "White Supremacy" standards) than for committing a particular crime. Whenever a Negro questioned the status quo in Mississippi he just simply disappeared. Knowing this about my home state, I naturally was concerned for my life. . . .

My squadron commander, a white Mississippian of the aristocratic class, could assure me in 1955 with precise frankness that the Mississippi whites were prepared to kill all the Negroes and half the whites in order to preserve "White Supremacy." Mississippi and Mississippians have not changed.

4. James Meredith, *Three Years in Mississippi* (1966), pp. 79, 323. By permission of the Indiana University Press.

JUNE 1963
THE MOMENT SEEMS TO BE NOW
© The London *Daily Mail.* Illingworth.

[*Several hundred freedom workers, mostly white college students, came down from the North to Mississippi in the "long hot summer" of 1964, and a group of three was brutally murdered. Before their bodies were found, one volunteer wrote in a private letter, "Yesterday while the Mississippi River was being dragged looking for the three missing civil rights workers, two bodies of Negroes were found—one cut in half and one without a head. Mississippi is the only state where you can drag a river any time and find bodies you were not expecting. Things are really much better for rabbits—there's a closed season on rabbits."* [5]

In June, 1966, nearly three years after his graduation, James H. Meredith undertook a "freedom walk" through Mississippi, avowedly to promote civil rights and to prove that a Negro could now move freely without police protection. After he had gone about twenty miles, he was shot by a hidden assailant, but the shotgun wounds were not fatal. Hundreds of other "freedom walkers" poured into Mississippi to carry on in his place. In the summer of 1967 Meredith himself staged a successful "freedom walk."]

5. Elizabeth Sutherland, ed., *Letters from Mississippi* (Signet Book, paperback, 1965), p. 173.

D. THE CUBAN MISSILE CRISIS

1. Kennedy Proclaims a "Quarantine" (1962)

After the abortive Bay of Pigs invasion in 1961, the United States watched Castro's Cuba for further trouble. Officials in Washington knew that the Soviets were sending Castro immense quantities of weapons, which Moscow repeatedly claimed were defensive.* In mid-October, 1962, high-flying American spy planes returned with startling photographic evidence that Russian technicians were installing about forty nuclear missiles with a maximum radius of about 2200 miles. Rather than forewarn Premier Khrushchev in Moscow, Kennedy quietly consulted with members of Congress, and then went on radio and television with a bombshell address which caught the Soviets off guard. Note the options that he kept open if the initial "quarantine" did not work. Assess the wisdom of his strategy.

Acting, therefore, in the defense of our own security and of the entire Western Hemisphere, . . . I have directed that the following *initial* steps be taken immediately:

First: To halt this offensive buildup, a strict quarantine on all offensive military equipment under shipment to Cuba is being initiated. All ships of any kind bound for Cuba from whatever nation or port will, if found to contain cargoes of offensive weapons, be turned back. This quarantine will be extended, 'if needed, to other types of cargo and carriers. We are not at this time, however, denying the necessities of life, as the Soviets attempted to do in their Berlin blockade of 1948.

Second: I have directed the continued and increased close [aerial] surveillance of Cuba and its military buildup. . . .

Third: It shall be the policy of this Nation to regard any nuclear missile launched from Cuba against any nation in the Western Hemisphere as an attack by the Soviet Union on the United States, requiring a full retaliatory response upon the Soviet Union.

Fourth: As a necessary military precaution, I have reinforced our base at Guantanamo [Cuba], evacuated today the dependents of our personnel there, and ordered additional military units to be on a standby alert basis.

Fifth: We are calling tonight for an immediate meeting of the Organ of Consultation under the Organization of American States, to consider this threat to hemispheric security and to invoke Articles 6 and 8 of the Rio Treaty in support of all necessary action. . . . Our other allies around the world have also been alerted.

Sixth: Under the Charter of the United Nations, we are asking tonight that an emergency meeting of the Security Council be convoked without delay to take action against this latest Soviet threat to world peace. Our resolution will call for the prompt dismantling and withdrawal of all offensive

---

1. *Public Papers of the Presidents of the United States, John F. Kennedy: 1962* (1963), pp. 807–08 (October 22, 1962).
* The Soviets were correct in the sense that so-called offensive weapons aimed at the United States were defensive in that they would deter an invasion of Cuba.

weapons in Cuba, under the supervision of U.N. observers, before the quarantine can be lifted.

Seventh and finally: I call upon Chairman Khrushchev to halt and eliminate this clandestine, reckless, and provocative threat to world peace and to stable relations between our two nations. I call upon him further to abandon this course of world domination, and to join in an historic effort to end the perilous arms race and to transform the history of man.

2. Khrushchev Proposes a Swap (1962)

During the tense six days after Kennedy's proclamation of a "quarantine," Soviet technicians in Cuba worked feverishly to emplace the missiles. A number of approaching Russian merchant ships, presumably loaded with "offensive" weapons, turned back. Several, not carrying such cargoes, were allowed to reach Cuba. Premier Khrushchev, at first disposed to give some ground in a letter of October 26 to Kennedy, took a tougher stand in the following message of October 27 and proposed a swap. The American missiles in Turkey were so obsolete that two months earlier President Kennedy had given orders for their withdrawal, but they were still there. He and his advisers felt that to remove them, as Khrushchev asked, on an exchange basis would weaken the morale of Turkey, the eastern anchor of the North Atlantic Treaty Organization. Should Kennedy have risked nuclear incineration for the sake of Turkey? How much plausibility was there in Khrushchev's proposal?

Our purpose has been and is to help Cuba, and no one can challenge the humanity of our motives aimed at allowing Cuba to live peacefully and develop as its people desire. You want to relieve your country from danger and this is understandable. However, Cuba also wants this. All countries want to relieve themselves from danger.

But how can we, the Soviet Union and our government, assess your actions which, in effect, mean that you have surrounded the Soviet Union with military bases, surrounded our allies with military bases, set up military bases literally around our country, and stationed your rocket weapons at them? This is no secret. High-placed American officials demonstratively declare this. Your rockets are stationed in Britain and in Italy and pointed at us. Your rockets are stationed in Turkey.

You are worried over Cuba. You say that it worries you because it lies at a distance of 90 miles across the sea from the shores of the United States. However, Turkey lies next to us. Our sentinels are pacing up and down and watching each other. Do you believe that you have the right to demand security for your country and the removal of such weapons that you qualify as offensive, while not recognizing this right for us? . . .

This is why I make this proposal: We agree to remove those weapons from Cuba which you regard as offensive weapons. We agree to do this and to state this commitment in the United Nations. Your representatives will make a statement to the effect that the United States, on its part, bearing in mind the anxiety and concern of the Soviet state, will evacuate its anal-

2. *Department of State Bulletin,* XLVII, p. 742 (November 12, 1962).

ogous weapons from Turkey. Let us reach an understanding on what time you and we need to put this into effect.

After this, representatives of the U.N. Security Council could control on-the-spot the fulfillment of these commitments.

3. Kennedy Advances a Solution (1962)

President Kennedy skillfully avoided an argument over a missile swap by ignoring his opponent's suggestion. Referring to Khrushchev's more promising letter of the previous day, he advanced the following proposals on October 27. The tension was building up, and an airstrike against Cuba was scheduled for three days later, before the nuclear missiles could become fully operative. Note the restrictions that Kennedy was prepared to place on the United States.

Dear Mr. Chairman:

I have read your letter of October 26th with great care and welcomed the statement of your desire to seek a prompt solution to the problem. The first thing that needs to be done, however, is for work to cease on offensive missile bases in Cuba and for all weapons systems in Cuba capable of offensive use to be rendered inoperable, under effective United Nations arrangements.

Assuming this is done promptly, I have given my representatives in New York instructions that will permit them to work out this weekend—in cooperation with the Acting Secretary General and your representative—an arrangement for a permanent solution to the Cuban problem along the lines suggested in your letter of October 26th. As I read your letter, the key elements of your proposals—which seem generally acceptable as I understand them—are as follows:

1) You would agree to remove these weapons systems from Cuba under appropriate United Nations observation and supervision; and undertake, with suitable safeguards, to halt the further introduction of such weapons systems into Cuba.

2) We, on our part, would agree—upon the establishment of adequate arrangements through the United Nations to ensure the carrying out and continuation of these commitments—(a) to remove promptly the quarantine measures now in effect and (b) to give assurances against an invasion of Cuba. I am confident that other nations of the Western Hemisphere would be prepared to do likewise.

If you will give your representative similar instructions, there is no reason why we should not be able to complete these arrangements and announce them to the world within a couple of days.

[*The next day, October 28, 1962, Khrushchev consented to Kennedy's terms, and a great sense of relief swept over the civilized world. Kennedy himself had privately reckoned that the odds in favor of a nuclear blowup ran as high as fifty-fifty.*]

3. *Ibid.*, p. 743.

4. The Russians Save Face (1962)

The Soviets, claiming that they had achieved their objective of preventing an invasion of Cuba, gathered up and (ostensibly) shipped home their forty-two nuclear missiles. President Kennedy had stipulated an on-site inspection to insure against cheating, and when an outraged Castro refused to admit UN inspectors, we were released from our pledge not to invade Cuba. The United States in truth won only a partial diplomatic victory. Thousands of Russian workmen stayed behind, and Castro remained defiant with Russian weapons and backing. The official Soviet newspaper *Izvestia* put the best possible face it could on the diplomatic setback. Note the vagueness of the references to offensive weapons, and also whether, from the Cuban and Soviet points of view, the missiles were really offensive.

The threat to peace was created by hostile, adventurist schemes aimed at the very existence of the Cuban Republic. The Soviet Union could not disregard Cuba's predicament in the face of the imperialistic provocations. Our country, fulfilling its international duty, came to the fraternal assistance of the Cuban people, and in these troubled days of the provocational aggravation . . . it has stood, stands, and will continue to stand firmly with Cuba.

The contemplated scheme of aggression against Cuba was built upon a very shaky foundation, but the danger with which Cuba was threatened was not thereby diminished. The pretext that was advanced in the U.S.A. for action against Cuba was the presence of Soviet weapons in Cuba that the United States termed "offensive." These weapons were depicted as representing a "threat" to America and the whole Western Hemisphere, although neither Cuba nor the Soviet Union was threatening the United States with its actions, while at the same time extremist, militant circles in the U.S. revealed . . . a desire to end the independence of the Cuban Republic.

In that tense moment the Soviet government, which had displayed the utmost self-control, calm and firmness, took speedy and efficient action to prevent the outbreak of the imminent conflict and thereby preserve universal peace.

The progression of events showed that the far-seeing, wise course of the Soviet government was the only correct one in the situation that had developed and led in a short time to the start of the normalization of the situation and the creation of conditions in which the interests of universal peace and of the . . . integrity of the Cuban Republic will be assured.

The decisive step of the Soviet Union—which foiled the aggressive plans of an attack on Cuba and deprived the authors of these plans of a reason and pretext for military action—was the indication that appropriate measures were being taken to stop the build-up in Cuba of objectives depicted by the United States as threatening American security, to dismantle these objectives and return them to the Soviet Union.

4. Translation from the *Current Digest of the Soviet Press* published weekly at Columbia University by the Joint Committee on Slavic Studies, appointed by the American Council of Learned Societies and the Social Science Research Council. Copyright (1962. XIV, no. 43, Oct. 31), the Joint Committee on Slavic Studies. Reprinted by permission.

This step by the Soviet government was made possible as a result of the statement made by U.S. President Kennedy in his message of Oct. 27 to N. S. Khrushchev. The message states that there will be no attacks on Cuba, no invasion, not only on the part of the United States but on the part of the other countries of the Western Hemisphere as well, if the weapons termed "offensive" by the U.S.A. are shipped out of Cuba.

Thus reason and wisdom prevailed. At present, all conditions exist for the total elimination of the conflict and for further efforts toward the strengthening of peace and security. All honest people, anxious over the fate of peace, render their due to our Communist Party, to the Soviet government and to Nikita Sergeyevich Khrushchev for the fact that the forces of aggression and war have been restrained and reason in international relations has prevailed over folly.

These days telegrams are being received in Moscow, in the Kremlin, from all corners of the globe. They express the impassioned voices of people of good will, conveying their support of the peace-loving position of the Soviet Union. . . .

E. THE PARTIAL NUCLEAR TEST BAN TREATY

1. Kennedy Submits the Pact to the Senate (1963)

Scientists and non-scientists have long worried about the effects on the human race of spewing radioactive garbage into the atmosphere. In the more relaxed months that followed the Cuban missile crisis of October, 1962, American and British negotiators in Moscow found the Soviets more friendly to restrictions. On August 5, 1963, representatives of the three powers signed a treaty banning all future testing of nuclear weapons in the atmosphere, in outer space, and under water. President Kennedy promptly submitted the pact to the Senate on August 8, with the following strong arguments for approval. Note whether or not the treaty was really a disarmament treaty, and what fears, fancied or real, Kennedy's statement was designed to quiet.

First: This treaty is the whole agreement. U.S. negotiators in Moscow were instructed not to make this agreement conditioned upon any other understanding; and they made none. The treaty speaks for itself.

Second: This treaty advances, though it does not assure, world peace; and it will inhibit, though it does not prohibit, the nuclear arms race. . . .

Third: The treaty will curb the pollution of our atmosphere. While it does not assure the world that it will be forever free from the fears and dangers of radioactive fallout from atmospheric tests, it will greatly reduce the numbers and dangers of such tests.

Fourth: This treaty protects our rights in the future. It cannot be amended without the consent of the United States, including the consent of the Senate; and any party to the treaty has the right to withdraw, upon 3 months' notice,

1. *Department of State Bulletin,* XLIX, pp. 316–18 (Aug. 26, 1963).

if it decides that extraordinary events related to the subject matter of the treaty have jeopardized its supreme interests.

Fifth: This treaty does not alter the status of unrecognized regimes. . . .

Sixth: This treaty does not halt American nuclear progress. The United States has more experience in underground testing than any other nation; and we intend to use this capacity to maintain the adequacy of our arsenal. . . .

Seventh: This treaty is not a substitute for, and does not diminish the need for, continued Western and American military strength to meet all contingencies. . . .

Eighth: This treaty will assure the security of the United States better than continued unlimited testing on both sides. According to a comprehensive report prepared by the responsible agencies of Government for the National Security Council, the tests conducted by both the Soviet Union and the United States since President Eisenhower first proposed this kind of treaty in 1959 have not resulted in any substantial alteration in the strategic balance. . . . On the other hand, unrestricted testing—by which other powers could develop all kinds of weapons through atmospheric tests more cheaply and quickly than they could underground—might well lead to a weakening of our security. . . .

Ninth: The risks in clandestine violations under this treaty are far smaller than the risks in unlimited testing. . . .

Tenth: This treaty is the product of the steady effort of the U.S. Government in two administrations, and its principles have had the explicit support of both great political parties. . . .

This treaty is in our national interest. While experience teaches us to be cautious in our expectations and ever vigilant in our preparations, there is no reason to oppose this hopeful step. . . .

2. Admiral Radford Speaks for the Military Men (1963)

Among the most vocal critics of the new treaty were the professional military men, who feared that we might be at a dangerous disadvantage if war should break out between the U.S.S.R. and the U.S.A. Admiral Arthur W. Radford, former Chairman of the Joint Chiefs of Staff and a man who had urged the bombing of North Vietnam as early as 1954, submitted the following views in writing to the Senate Committee on Foreign Relations. Note what arguments he brings to bear, and whether they seem stronger or weaker in the light of events since 1963.

Ten years after signing the armistice agreement at the end of the Korean war, we—the United States—have reached another important signing. Shall we, or shall we not, agree to the atomic test ban treaty now before the Senate for ratification? Important witnesses before your Senate committee have argued that we should. Equally important witnesses have argued that we should not. Others have recommended approval with reservations.

2. *Nuclear Test Ban Treaty: Hearings before the Committee on Foreign Relations, United States Senate,* 88 Cong., 1 sess., pp. 1009–10.

I would be happier to be able to join those who recommend approval and to testify that I believe ratification of this treaty represents a new approach to a strategy for peace—that it means that the Soviet Union and its allies now have a deep interest in a just and lasting peace and in halting the arms race. Unfortunately, I do not believe this to be the case. To me it is frightening to see otherwise dedicated citizens refuse to accept proven facts. One such fact is that to us and to the leaders of the Communist conspiracy, a just and genuine peace means two entirely different things. "Peace"—Communist style—will come to the world only after either capitalism or communism has been liquidated. Khrushchev has frequently made it plain that "peaceful coexistence" means a continuation of a relentless struggle by all available means—including shooting wars of liberation. Couple this with the fact that as late as July 14 last—just before the test ban agreement was concluded—the Soviet open letter to the Chinese included this paragraph:

"We [the U.S.S.R.] fully stand for the destruction of imperialism and capitalism. We not only believe in the inevitable destruction of capitalism but also *are doing everything for this to be accomplished by way of the class struggle and as soon as possible.*" [*Emphasis added by Radford.*]

Thus just a few days before agreeing to this test ban treaty, the Soviet hierarchy was assuring their Chinese allies of their devotion to previous Communist aims.

Military men whose responsibilities include the defense and security of our country are worried about this treaty. The Joint Chiefs of Staff have listed their reservations. I join with many of my former colleagues in expressing deep concern for our future security if this treaty is ratified as it now stands.

Undoubtedly the Communist leaders of the U.S.S.R. believe that this treaty is to their advantage—otherwise they would not have signed it.

Almost certainly it is an agreement which will ultimately result in the U.S.S.R. obtaining important advantages in the development of more advanced atomic weapons with all the disadvantages that this implies for us.

The treaty is imprecise; it is vague in areas where it should be specific. Unless we insist upon clarification now, we will find ourselves in great difficulties later on. Remember our difficulties about access to Berlin?

The future is a long time, but the Communists are willing to wait. Can we continue our readiness to suddenly conduct very sophisticated atomic tests in the atmosphere over a period of years? Can the Congress maintain defense expenditures for this purpose at high levels over a long period of time?

The security of the free world has depended since World War II upon the atomic deterrent possessed by the United States of America. The free world will continue to depend upon it until it fails us or the U.S.S.R. is willing to accept international inspection and control in a treaty to reduce armaments. Our free world allies who have signed and who will sign this test ban treaty, are doing so because they trust us, for they cannot possibly understand the pros and cons of atomic weapons development.

The decision of the Senate of the United States in connection with this treaty will change the course of world history, either way it goes.

[*The Senate approved the partial Nuclear Test Ban Treaty on September 24, 1963, although with misgivings. Most of the other nations also approved it, except France, which continued to pollute the atmosphere, and Communist China, which detonated the first in a series of "dirty" bombs a year later, October, 1964. From a strictly impartial point of view did the United States, after having detonated hundreds of nuclear devices, have a right to deny others the same privilege?*]

THOUGHT PROVOKERS

1. Was Medicare as finally passed really needed, especially in view of America's widespread wealth? Is socialized medicine inevitable, and if so, is Medicare a giant step in that direction? Is Medicare free?

2. Is the steel industry of sufficient importance in our economy to warrant the intervention of the government in the public interest? Can the old laws of supply and demand be counted on to operate in the kind of economy that we know today?

3. Do you think integration would have come to the University of Mississippi in due season and without loss of life if James Meredith had not precipitated the issue? Assess the gains and losses for the Negro as a consequence of the Meredith case.

4. Could the United States have "lived" with Soviet missiles in Cuba in view of the fact that the Soviets already had many nuclear missiles capable of reaching American cities (from submarines or solid emplacements)? How could one justify our refusing to permit Russian missiles in Cuba while we had missiles pointed at Russia in neighboring Turkey? Why, presumably, did Khrushchev back down?

5. Arthur M. Schlesinger, Jr., in his *A Thousand Days*, p. 1030, says that Kennedy was responsible for "the new hope for peace on earth, the elimination of nuclear testing in the atmosphere and the abolition of nuclear diplomacy. . . ." In what respects is this statement in this first printing open to criticism?

FURTHER EXPLORATION

General. Arthur M. Schlesinger, Jr., *A Thousand Days* (1965) [paperback]; Theodore C. Sorensen, *Kennedy* (1965) [paperback]. **Steel Crunch.** Grant McConnell, *Steel and the Presidency, 1962* (1963). **Negro Revolution.** James Meredith, *Three Years in Mississippi* (1966); William Brink and Louis Harris, *Why We Can't Wait* (1964); Russell H. Barrett, *Integration at Ole Miss* (1965); James W. Silver, *Mississippi: the Closed Society* (1963). **Cuban Missile Crisis.** Elie Abel, *The Missile Crisis* (1966) [paperback]; D. L. Larson, ed., *The Cuban Crisis of 1962* (1963); J. Daniel and J. G. Hubbard, *Strike in the West* (1963). **Nuclear Test Ban.** Arthur H. Dean, *Test Ban and Disarmament* (1966) [paperback].

Chapter 49

Johnson and the Great Society

"We are still striving to involve the poor, the deprived, the forgotten American, white and Negro, in the future of their society."

PRESIDENT LYNDON B. JOHNSON, 1967

PROLOGUE: When President Kennedy was shot on November 22, 1963, Vice President Johnson took over with cyclonic energy. Congress, jolted by the assassination and responding to Johnson's arm-twisting, passed an impressive series of major bills in 1963–1964. These included the large-scale tax reduction, the Civil Rights Act of 1964 for Negroes, the bill establishing the anti-poverty program, and an omnibus housing bill.

Elected overwhelmingly in his own right in 1964, President Johnson undertook to expand his "Great Society" program. He drove through Congress another breathtaking sheaf of legislation in 1965–1966, including bills to help distressed areas, the Negro voting-rights law, Medicare under Social Security, an immigration bill, a huge federal housing program, a drug control act, and aid to education measures, ranging from elementary schools through colleges. These new laws promised much but only the future could tell how they would work out. The legislative output slowed down markedly after the Democratic majorities in Congress were sharply reduced by the mid-term elections of 1966.

In foreign affairs, Johnson was less fortunate. His 1965 intervention in the Dominican Republic aroused much criticism, but overshadowing all was the increasingly bloody involvement in Vietnam (see next chapter). This entanglement was so costly as to undermine many of the Great Society programs.

A. THE ANTI–POVERTY PROGRAM

1. President Johnson Declares War on Poverty (1964)

America continued to present appalling contrasts in wealth. An official government report in 1964 declared that one-fifth of the families in the country—9.3 million in all—"enjoyed" annual incomes of less than $3,000. Under President Kennedy, Congress made a modest beginning by passing several laws providing for self-help and job retraining. President Johnson threw his full weight behind the Economic Opportunity Act of 1964, which a Democratic Congress approved and implemented with an initial appropriation of $947.5 million. This legislation included provisions for a Job Corps that would provide training for unskilled young men and women, aid for education, and a domestic Peace Corps to work with Indians and other disadvantaged groups. In a part of his message to Congress the President made the following plea. Is he convincing in his argument that these heavy outlays would in the long run help the taxpayer?

1. *Public Papers of the Presidents of the United States: Lyndon B. Johnson, 1963–1964* (1965), I, pp. 376–77 (March 16, 1964).

I have called for a national war on poverty. Our objective: total victory.

There are millions of Americans—one fifth of our people—who have not shared in the abundance which has been granted to most of us, and on whom the gates of opportunity have been closed.

What does this poverty mean to those who endure it?

It means a daily struggle to secure the necessities for even a meager existence. It means that the abundance, the comforts, the opportunities they see all around them are beyond their grasp.

Worst of all, it means hopelessness for the young.

The young man or woman who grows up without a decent education, in a broken home, in a hostile and squalid environment, in ill health or in the face of racial injustice—that young man or woman is often trapped in a life of poverty.

He does not have the skills demanded by a complex society. He does not know how to acquire those skills. He faces a mounting sense of despair which drains initiative and ambition and energy. . . .

The war on poverty is not a struggle simply to support people, to make them dependent on the generosity of others.

It is a struggle to give people a chance.

It is an effort to allow them to develop and use their capacities, as we have been allowed to develop and use ours, so that they can share, as others share, in the promise of this nation.

We do this, first of all, because it is right that we should.

From the establishment of public education and land grant colleges through agricultural extension and encouragement to industry, we have pursued the goal of a nation with full and increasing opportunities for all its citizens.

The war on poverty is a further step in that pursuit.

We do it also because helping some will increase the prosperity of all.

Our fight against poverty will be an investment in the most valuable of our resources—the skills and strength of our people.

And in the future, as in the past, this investment will return its cost many fold to our entire economy.

If we can raise the annual earnings of 10 million among the poor by only $1,000 we will have added 14 billion dollars a year to our national output. In addition we can make important reductions in public assistance payments which now cost us 4 billion dollars a year, and in the large costs of fighting crime and delinquency, disease and hunger.

This is only part of the story.

Our history has proved that each time we broaden the base of abundance, giving more people the chance to produce and consume, we create new industry, higher production, increased earnings and better income for all.

Giving new opportunity to those who have little will enrich the lives of all the rest.

Because it is right, because it is wise, and because, for the first time in our history, it is possible to conquer poverty, I submit, for the consideration of the Congress and the country, the Economic Opportunity Act of 1964.

The Act does not merely expand old programs or improve what is already being done.

It charts a new course.

It strikes at the causes, not just the consequences of poverty.

It can be a milestone in our one-hundred-eighty year search for a better life for our people.

2. War on the Anti-Poverty War

President Johnson's anti-poverty scheme aroused the dogs of criticism, especially among Republicans. They declared that it was contrived to catch votes; that it would undermine individual initiative; that it would inject big government into private affairs; that it was socialistic; that it was a revival of Franklin Roosevelt's Conservation Camps; and that it would burden the taxpayers. In truth, the cost of keeping a high-school dropout in one of the fresh-air training camps was estimated to be about three times that of keeping a student in Harvard University. The executive editor of the Cleveland *Plain Dealer* here speaks out plainly against some of the weaknesses of the scheme. Which of his criticisms really get down to fundamentals?

The political astuteness of President Johnson is nowhere better illustrated than by his proposal described as the "antipoverty program" or the "war on poverty." It has more than a faint odor of hokum about it, but its implications are that anyone bold enough to question or peer deeply into it must be in favor of poverty—and that's politically and socially disastrous.

The present level of extravagance in the American uppercrust, affluence in the middle class, and considerable comfort even in the lower pay brackets is so widely taken for granted these days that a campaigner against poverty has to hunt around for groups and areas to help. . . .

But there are increasingly large numbers of Negro dropouts from high school and teenage unemployment. And small farmers who can't seem to get ahead. And inhabitants of "Appalachia," the mountains where coal mining has gone to pot. These are areas with average incomes of $3,000 a year or under. They've got to be saved from themselves by the Federal Government. Hence, the "war on poverty," a colorful phrase much favored by newspapers, TV, and radio.

There's really no war on anything. The Johnson proposal is an attempt to sop up some unemployed teens by giving them jobs in conservation camps, to lend some money to the hardscrabble farmers, to produce some loan help for college students—and, just as important, add some new bureaucrats to the payroll.

The objective is good, particularly the movement of dropouts from the street corner to the forest. But the only way to solve the Appalachia problem

---

2. Philip W. Porter, Cleveland *Plain Dealer,* March 28, 1964. By permission of the Cleveland *Plain Dealer.*

is to transplant whole families and villages to places where there are jobs—but they won't leave. And lending money to marginal farmers is fruitless; the quicker they give up small uneconomical "family" units, and try to earn money elsewhere, the better off they'll be.

Some individuals will be helped, no doubt. The politicians have something new to promise. But eradicating all poverty is about as unlikely an attainment as entering the Kingdom of Heaven, which our grandmothers talked so much about.

The objective, though vague and built of goober feathers, is good. But will it work on those of low mentality who are not educable, or those who lack desire to improve themselves? And in reverse, is it really needed by the determined individual, the man already moonlighting to go to law school, or waiting table to pay for college?

Has the Horatio Alger, Jr., concept, the bootblack who became a tycoon, vanished completely? Andrew Carnegie built a fortune from little. So did Henry Ford. Lyndon Johnson himself started from scratch. . . .

But today the Federal Government has got to get into the act. And anyone who asks questions or objects is automatically a stinker.

[*The war against poverty fell far short of the roseate forecasts of its sponsors. The war in Vietnam began to siphon away billions of dollars, and the national budget could not fully support both wars. Bureaucratic bungling, political favoritism, and outright graft combined to bring the program into considerable disrepute and to undermine its nobler purposes.*]

B. THE NEGRO INSURRECTION IN LOS ANGELES

1. A White Journalist Visits Watts (1965)

The snowballing Negro protest movement continued into the long hot summer of 1965. Leaders like the Reverend Martin Luther King were not content to stop with the Civil Rights Act of 1964 and the Voting Rights Act of 1965; the passage of legislation did not automatically cause barriers against Negroes to fall. Ugly riots occurred in many cities, both North and South, but the August, 1965, outburst in Watts, a Negro district of Los Angeles, resembled a civil war. Following the arrest of a Negro on a drunken-driving charge, Negro mobs ran amok for six days—shooting, pillaging, burning (shooting at firemen), and gutting dozens of city blocks, including buildings mostly owned or operated by Negroes. A total of twenty-nine Negroes and five whites were killed, to say nothing of scores of injured. Watts was not Harlem; many Negroes owned neat homes. But prolonged heat, combined with gnawing grievances against a white society, produced madness. Stewart Alsop, a prominent journalist, interviewed a number of Watts Negroes shortly after the riot. Note their most serious grievances and what is most surprising about their reactions.

1. *Saturday Evening Post,* vol. 238, p. 20 (Nov. 6, 1965). By special permission of the author, Mr. Stewart Alsop.

. . . I talked to a lot of people in Watts—the editor of the local Negro newspaper, a white police officer, a white social worker, local businessmen, juvenile delinquents as well as that crowd of young men around the shoeshine stand. Here is the way the people of Watts talk:

"My name is George Washington—that's my real name. Well, I'm coming home alone one night from a party and a cop stops me and says, 'What's your name?' and I say, 'George Washington,' and the cop says, 'Oh, yeah, wise guy,' and hits me in the gut."

"A Negro kills a cop, it's murder. A cop kills a Negro, it's justifiable homicide."

"These people are dead now, the people the white men killed. Who's gonna make 'em alive?" In Watts the Negroes killed during the rioting are not hoodlums but martyrs.

"You whites come here and ask questions after the revolt. Why didn't you ask a few questions before the revolt?" The riot is quite often referred to as "The Revolt."

"The civil-rights law? Just words."

"Martin Luther King is just a sellout black man—his job is to guide the Negro masses into a trap."

"What the Negro hates is the awful deceit practiced by the Jews. The whole civil-rights movement is a branch of Zionism." This is the opinion of Mrs. Pat Alexander, editor of the *Herald-Dispatch,* a Negro newspaper with a claimed circulation of 35,000.

"Why'd the riot start? Some colored people don't like the white people, is why. Now everybody has guns, a lotta people gonna get killed—it's gonna be something terrible." This in a musical, singsong voice, and a tone of gleeful anticipation. The speaker was Juanita, a rather charming juvenile delinquent whom we interviewed at a social-work center.

A white police officer: "The riot could have been prevented the first night if we'd gotten tough right away—maybe used tear gas. We'd have saved a lot of lives, mostly colored, but we'd have been denounced from hell to breakfast for 'police brutality.' Next time, though, it'll be different. Since Watts, the white people have regressed socially in their attitude on the Negro problem." He smiled a little grimly at this lapse into sociological jargon.

A big Negro with angry eyes and oddly spatulate finger tips: "You lookin' at my hands, ain't you? They're all bulged up at the end. That's from working, changing tires—that's all I want, man, is work." His voice rose, almost to a scream.

Miss Margaret Sullivan, a soft-spoken white social worker: "There's no magic solution here—you just have to keep trying. The most important thing, of course, is jobs."

An unemployed Negro: "We got nothing to do, man, no work, not even a movie theater. We want to be doin' something, makin' things."

Jobs are indeed "the most important thing," more important than all the grants-in-aid and poverty programs in the world. But even jobs won't cure the savage bitterness, the total alienation from the world of the white man, of the young men of Watts. In Watts it began to seem to me, for the first time, that the racial problem in this country is wholly insoluble—that it is like some incurable disease, with which both whites and Negroes must learn to live in pain, all the days of our lives.

2. A Conservative Denounces the Rioters

Dr. Will Herberg, a conservative professor of philosophy at Drew University (New Jersey), reacted rather surprisingly to the eruption in Los Angeles. His commentary appeared in William F. Buckley's conservative magazine, the *National Review*. Form conclusions as to the soundness of his position in regard to the tactics of the Negro activists.

The country is still reeling from the shock of what happened in Los Angeles. Six days of "racial" rioting, of violence uncontrolled and uncontrollable. Thousands of Negroes running wild, burning, destroying, looting, spreading from the Negro section outward, on a scale that made a senior officer of the National Guard, which finally quelled the rioting, describe it as veritable insurrection.

The fury of hate and violence revealed in these six dreadful days has engendered a profound uneasiness through every part of the country. How could it have happened? After all, Los Angeles is not the Congo—or is it?

Of course, the politicians and the professional bleeding hearts immediately began to mumble the tired old phrases about "poverty" and "frustration," as though nobody was, or ever had been, poor or frustrated except the Los Angeles Negroes. (The living standards and conditions of life of the Negroes in Los Angeles, bad as they are, would have seemed something near to heaven to most of the immigrants who came to this country in earlier years.). . .

Internal order is the first necessity of every society. Even justice is secondary to order, because without order there can be no society and no justice, however partial and fragmentary. . . .

But the internal order of a community, which is so primary and precious to it, is always precarious. . . .

It is preserved by force—by the naked force of police . . . but more immediately by the force of custom and respect for constituted authority. It is these two—custom and respect for constituted authority—that do the everyday work of maintaining order and security. When these are weakened or destroyed, hell breaks loose—whether it is in the Congo or in Los Angeles, whether it is Negroes or whites who do the devil's work. . . .

This internal order is now in jeopardy; and it is in jeopardy because of the doings of such highminded, self-righteous "children of light" as the Rev.

2. *National Review,* XVII, 769–70 (Sept. 7, 1965), 150 E. 35th St., New York, N.Y., 10016. By permission.

Dr. Martin Luther King and his associates in the leadership of the "civil rights" movement. If you are looking for those ultimately responsible for the murder, arson, and looting in Los Angeles, look to them: they are the guilty ones, these apostles of "non-violence."

For years now, the Rev. Dr. Martin Luther King and his associates have been deliberately undermining the foundations of internal order in this country. With their rabble-rousing demagoguery, they have been cracking the "cake of custom" that holds us together. With their doctrine of "civil disobedience," they have been teaching hundreds of thousands of Negroes—particularly the adolescents and the children—that it is perfectly all right to break the law and defy constituted authority if you are a Negro-with-a-grievance; in protest against injustice. And they have done more than talk. They have on occasion after occasion, in almost every part of the country, called out their mobs on the streets, promoted "school strikes," sit-ins, lie-ins, in explicit violation of the law and in explicit defiance of the public authority. They have taught anarchy and chaos by word and deed—and, no doubt, with the best of intentions—and they have found apt pupils everywhere, with intentions *not* of the best. Sow the wind, and reap the whirlwind. But it is not they alone who reap it, but we as well; the entire nation.

It is worth noting that the worst victims of these high-minded rabble-rousers are not so much the hated whites, but the great mass of the Negro people themselves. The great mass of the Negro people cannot be blamed for the lawlessness and violence in Harlem, Chicago, Los Angeles, or elsewhere. All they want to do is what decent people everywhere want to do: make a living, raise a family, bring up their children as good citizens, with better advantages than they themselves ever had. The "civil rights" movement and the consequent lawlessness has well nigh shattered these hopes; not only because of the physical violence and insecurity, but above all because of the corruption and demoralization of the children, who have been lured away from the steady path of decency and self-government to the more exhilarating road of "demonstrating"—and rioting. An old friend of mine from Harlem put it to me after the riots last year: "For more than fifteen years we've worked our heads off to make something out of these boys. Now look at them—they're turning into punks and hoodlums roaming the streets."

Shall we wreak our wrath upon such "punks" and "hoodlums," the actual rioters, and allow those ultimately responsible, the Martin Luther Kings, the inciters to law-defiance in the name of "conscience," to go immune in their self-righteousness? They stand horrified at the rioting and violence. But isn't it all the handiwork of the demons they themselves raised? They are the guilty ones—despite the best intentions. If they have any conscience left besides that which they use as justification for the violation of law, let them search it now.

3. A Christian Journal Takes the Long View (1965)

A long-established weekly religious magazine, the non-denominational *Christian Century*, judged the Watts riots with more compassion than many. In the light of its views, determine why the answer to the Negro disorders was not simply bigger and better police forces.

Respectable, law-abiding white and Negro America condemns the arson, pillage and vandalism which erupted in Los Angeles and to a lesser degree in other cities in mid-August. In that condemnation there is more fear and contempt than there is compassion, more haughty bigotry than understanding, more irritation with the rampaging Negro mobs than concern about them. Does comfortable, secure white and Negro America also deplore the circumstances which make explosions in the black ghettos of the nation's megalopolises inevitable? Does it lament the ghettos' filth and stench, the vermin-infested tenements, the broken families, the legacy of cultural blight, the unemployment, the dropouts? Does it understand, does it want to understand people whose despair runs so deep that they sense no identity with any of the social structures and view all of them as enemies? Whence this wild hatred which roves the streets crying "Let's kill whitey"? Are we willing to ask that question? Are we able to face the answer?

Responsible whites and Negroes know that when such riots break out, adequate restraints must be employed to replace anarchy with order. But if we do nothing more than this, if policemen and soldiers are our only reply to the rebellion bred in the slums, then we merely intensify the pressures which produce riots. Peaceful citizens want themselves and their property protected by the law and by law enforcement agencies—a reasonable desire. But out of the steaming slums comes a hysteria to which such reasonableness is wholly alien. What appeal do the standards of an orderly society have for a poor, ignorant man who believes himself cut off from all the benefits of a good society? . . . Do we not have the right to demand that riots cease, to insist and to enforce our insistence that there be law and order in the streets? We do. But we might as well accept the realities of the situation, one of which is that the systems we trust and defend have impregnated some Negroes with a deep, implacable contempt for those systems. . . .

The riots are painful warnings that the nation faces major catastrophes in its industrial and commercial centers. The slums of these centers are tightly packed with Negroes and other minorities who are condemned to unemployment or underemployment, to bad housing at high cost, to poor schools, to the enticements and intimidations of criminals, to the incitements of rabble rousers and to all the miseries which attend human congestion.

In these settings—as in Los Angeles—minor incidents inexplicably explode long-accumulated charges of frustration, bitterness and hatred. The slums of

3. *The Christian Century*, LXXXII, 1027–28 (August 25, 1965). By permission.

the great cities are a multifaceted problem for which there is no cure-all, no quick and easy remedy. The problems are too big for the cities to handle alone, particularly since the cities are usually surrounded by white suburbs which view with horror what occurs at the metropolitan core but which resist all efforts to change the circumstances producing race riots.

It is a state problem and a national one. Nothing done yet at these levels acknowledges the gravity of the situation. The nation must now with its full strength relieve the plight of the Negroes in urban slums or turn its metropolises into garrisoned cities. The best way for the Negro and for the general society is long and hard; but we must take it.

C. THE SUPREME COURT "CODDLES" CRIMINALS

1. The Outlawing of Third-degree Confessions (1966)

In the 1960's and even earlier, the Supreme Court was a target for abuse by conservative groups. The more vocal extremists raised the insulting cry, "Impeach Earl Warren," against the liberal Chief Justice. Conservatives were first outraged by a series of rulings which extended Constitutional guarantees to Communists and which ordered desegregation in the schools. Then, in 1962 and 1963, came two decisions which banned the recitation of state prayers and the Lord's prayer in the public schools. Such a practice was declared to be in violation of the First Amendment, which required a separation of church and state.

In 1963 an epochal decision held that accused criminals must be provided with lawyers in non-capital offenses. In 1964 and 1966 other decisions decreed that confessions obtained by the police in private (and hence under suspicion of physical force) could not be used to convict. The Fifth Amendment had long barred self-incrimination. Finally, on June 13, 1966, the Supreme Court, in a 5 to 4 decision, reversed the conviction of a confessed kidnapper-rapist, Ernesto Miranda, together with three men accused of other felonies. Chief Justice Warren, speaking for the majority, ruled in part as follows. In view of the fact that the crime rate was rising alarmingly and that this decision would make convictions harder to obtain, was the Court to be commended for emphasizing the rights of the individual at the expense of social order?

Prior to any questioning, the person must be warned that he has a right to remain silent, that any statement he does make may be used as evidence against him, and that he has a right to the presence of an attorney, either retained or appointed.

The defendant may waive effectuation of these rights, provided the waiver is made voluntarily, knowingly and intelligently.

If, however, he indicates in any manner and at any stage of the process that he wishes to consult with an attorney before speaking, there can be no questioning.

Likewise, if the individual is alone and indicates in any manner that he

1. *Official Reports of the Supreme Court,* vol. 384 U.S. Pt. 3 (Preliminary Print), pp. 444–481, *passim.* The Court also decreed reapportionment in the state legislatures (1962) and in the Congressional districts (1964) on the basis of "one man, one vote," rather than on the lopsided basis which often gave agricultural areas greater voting power than more populous urban areas.

does not wish to be interrogated, the police may not question him. The mere fact that he may have answered some questions or volunteered some statements on his own does not deprive him of the right to refrain from answering any further inquiries until he has consulted with an attorney and thereafter consents to be questioned.

The constitutional issue we decide in each of these [four] cases is the admissibility of statements obtained from a defendant questioned while in custody and deprived of his freedom of option. In each, the defendant was questioned by police officers, detectives, or a prosecuting attorney in a room in which he was cut off from the outside world. In none of these cases was the defendant given a full and effective warning of his rights at the outset of the interrogation process. In all the cases, the questioning elicited oral admissions, and in three of them, signed statements as well which were admitted at their trials.

They all thus share salient features—incommunicado * interrogation of individuals in a police-dominated atmosphere, resulting in self-incriminating statements without full warnings of constitutional rights. . . .

From extensive factual studies undertaken in the early [19]30s . . . it is clear that police violence and the "third degree" flourished at that time. In a series of cases decided by this Court long after these studies, the police resorted to physical brutality—beatings, hanging, whipping—and to sustained and protracted questioning incommunicado in order to extort confessions. The 1961 Commission on Civil Rights found much evidence to indicate that "some policemen still resort to physical force to obtain confessions."

The use of physical brutality and violence is not, unfortunately, relegated to the past or to any part of the country. Only recently in Kings County, N. Y., the police brutally beat, kicked and placed lighted cigarette butts on the back of a potential witness under interrogation for the purpose of securing a statement incriminating a third party. . . .

The examples given above are undoubtedly the exception now, but they are sufficiently widespread to be the object of concern. . . .

Even without employing brutality, the "third degree" or the specific stratagems described above, the very fact of custodial interrogation exacts a heavy toll on individual liberty and trades on the weakness of individuals. . . .

If an individual indicates that he wishes the assistance of counsel before any interrogation occurs, the authorities cannot rationally ignore or deny his request on the basis that the individual does not have or cannot afford a retained attorney.

The financial ability of the individual has no relationship to the scope of the rights involved here. The privilege against self-incrimination secured by the Constitution applies to all individuals. The need for counsel in order to protect the privilege exists for the indigent as well as the affluent. . . .

---

* That is, without outside communication.

This does not mean, as some have suggested, that each police station must have a "station-house lawyer" present at all times to advise prisoners. It does mean, however, that if police propose to interrogate a person they must make known to him that he is entitled to a lawyer and that, if he cannot afford one, a lawyer will be provided for him prior to any interrogation. . . .

Our decision is not intended to hamper the traditional function of police officers in investigating crime. . . . When an individual is in custody on probable cause, the police may, of course, seek out evidence in the field to be used at trial against him. Such investigation may include inquiry of persons not under restraint.

General on-the-scene questioning as to facts surrounding a crime or other general questioning of citizens in the fact-finding process is not affected by our holding. It is an act of responsible citizenship for individuals to give whatever information they may have to aid in law enforcement. In such situations the compelling atmosphere inherent in the process of in-custody interrogation is not necessarily present.

In dealing with statements obtained through interrogation, we do not purport to find all confessions inadmissible. Confessions remain a proper element in law enforcement. Any statement given freely and voluntarily without any compelling influence is, of course, admissible in evidence. . . .

In announcing these principles, we are not unmindful of the burdens which law-enforcement officials must bear, often under trying circumstances. We also fully recognize the obligation of all citizens to aid in enforcing the criminal laws.

2. The Minority Supports the Police (1966)

An angered, fist-pounding Mr. Justice Harlan, speaking for three of the four dissenters, put his finger on some of the weaknesses of the majority opinion. In these excerpts from his dissent, is he more realistic in his approach to the problem than the majority, and if so, in what respects?

I believe the decision of the Court represents poor constitutional law and entails harmful consequences for the country at large. How serious these consequences may prove to be only time can tell. But the basic flaws in the Court's justification seem to me readily apparent, now once all sides of the problem are considered. . . .

The new rules are not designed to guard against police brutality or other unmistakably banned forms of coercion. Those who use "third degree" tactics and deny them in court are equally able and destined to lie as skillfully about warnings and waivers.

Rather, the thrust of the new rules is to negate all pressures, to reinforce the nervous or ignorant suspect, and ultimately to discourage any confession

2. *Ibid.*, pp. 504–17, *passim.*

at all. The aim, in short, is toward "voluntariness" in a utopian sense, or, to view it from a different angle, voluntariness with a vengeance.

To incorporate this notion into the Constitution requires a strained reading of history and precedent and a disregard of the very pragmatic concerns that alone may on occasion justify such strains. . . .

What the Court largely ignores is that its rules impair, if they will not eventually serve wholly to frustrate, an instrument of law enforcement that has long and quite reasonably been thought worth the price paid for it.

There can be little doubt that the Court's new code would markedly decrease the number of confessions. To warn the suspect that he may remain silent and remind him that his confession may be used in court are minor obstructions. To require also an express waiver by the suspect and an end to questioning whenever he demurs must heavily handicap questioning. And to suggest or provide counsel for the suspect simply invites the end of the interrogation.

How much harm this decision will inflict on law enforcement cannot fairly be predicted with accuracy. Evidence on the role of confessions is notoriously incomplete. . . .

We do know that some crimes cannot be solved without confessions, that ample expert testimony attests to their importance in crime control, and that the Court is taking a real risk with society's welfare in imposing its new regime on the country. The social costs of crime are too great to call the new rules anything but a hazardous experimentation.

3. A Green Light for Criminals (1966)

The increase of crimes of violence in the large cities had become frightening, particularly stabbings, "muggings" (assaults to commit robbery), rapes, and murders. In Washington, D. C., where Congressmen's wives and other respectable citizens were frequently attacked within sight of the Capitol dome, one newspaper responded to the above *Miranda* decision under the heading "Green Light for Criminals." In what additional respects does this commentary strengthen the view of the Court's minority as to the visionary character of the majority decision?

The Supreme Court's 5 to 4 ruling on police questioning of criminal suspects will be received with rejoicing by every thug in the land. For without a doubt it is a ruling which will grievously handicap the police and make it much easier for a criminal to beat the rap.

The murky torrent of words embodied in Chief Justice Warren's opinion tends to obscure some aspects of the ruling. But the salient points come through clearly enough.

Henceforth, once the police have taken a suspect into custody, they cannot lawfully ask him any questions unless four warnings have been given. (1) The suspect must be plainly advised that he need not make any state-

---

3. Washington *Evening Star,* June 15, 1966, quoted in *Cong. Record,* 89 Cong., 2 sess., p. 18057. By permission.

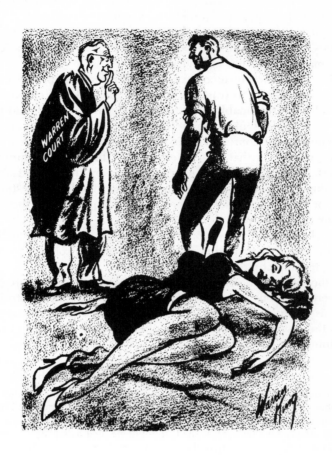

"MUM'S THE WORD, BUB"

Courtesy of The News, New York's Picture
Newspaper. Cartoonist Warren King.

ment. (2) He must be informed that anything he says may be used against
him in a trial. (3) He must be told that he has a right to have an attorney
present throughout the questioning. (4) If the suspect is an indigent, he
must be assured that he will be furnished a lawyer free of charge. Unless all
of these conditions are met no confession or other evidence obtained during
an interrogation can be used against the suspect.

The Chief Justice makes the remarkable observation that "our decision is
not intended to hamper the traditional function of police officers in investigating crime." Intent aside, he must know that this is in fact a decision which
will not only hamper but will largely destroy the traditional police function,
at least as far as interrogation is concerned.

Why? Because any lawyer called in to sit beside a guilty prisoner is going to tell him to say nothing to the police. He would be derelict in his duty were he to do otherwise. In the face of this, the Chief Justice blandly suggests that there is nothing in the decision which requires "that police stop a person who enters a police station and states that he wishes to confess to a crime." How true! And how often in the proverbial blue moon will this happen?

The deplorable fact is that this ruling, as far as the public is concerned, will most directly affect the vicious types of crime—the murders, the yokings, the robberies and the rapes where it often is impossible to assemble enough evidence, without a confession, to obtain convictions. All the criminal need do is to demand a lawyer—and then the police, under the practical effect of this decision, will be unable to ask him question No. 1. What was it the President said about ridding our cities of crime so law-abiding citizens will be safe in their homes, on the streets and in their places of business?

The dissents by Justices Harlan, Clark, Stewart and White were sharply-worded. It is necessary to read them to understand the frailty of the grounds upon which the majority rests this unprecedented ruling.

[*An extreme case of the application of the* Miranda *ruling came in February, 1967. In Brooklyn a factory worker had confessed to stabbing to death his common-law wife and her five children. But he had not been advised of his "right to silence," and, in the absence of concrete evidence, he was turned loose. The presiding judge remarked, "Even an animal such as this one . . . must be protected with all legal safeguards. It is repulsive to let a thing like this out on the streets."* Time, *March 3, 1967, p. 49*]

D. JOHNSON AND THE DOMINICAN INTERVENTION (1965)

1. The President Explains His Motivation (1965)

No action of President Johnson in the area of foreign affairs (except Vietnam) provoked more controversy than his handling of the Dominican problem. On April 24, 1965, a bloody revolt broke out against the rightist-oriented government, and four days later Johnson reluctantly sent in American troops, ultimately about 25,000, to protect American lives. This return to gunboat diplomacy, after more than thirty years of pledged abstention under Franklin Roosevelt's Good Neighbor Policy, angered Latin Americans in general and American liberals in particular. On May 2, 1965, President Johnson justified his action thus in a nationwide radio-TV broadcast. Determine whether or not he had convincing grounds for such drastic action.

Meanwhile, all this time, from Saturday [April 24] to Wednesday [April 28], the danger was mounting. Even though we were deeply saddened by bloodshed and violence in a close and friendly neighbor, we had no desire

---

1. *Department of State Bulletin*, LXII, 744–45 (May 17, 1965).

to interfere in the affairs of a sister Republic.

On Wednesday afternoon [April 28] there was no longer any choice for the man who is your President. I was sitting in my little office reviewing the world situation with Secretary Rusk, Secretary McNamara, and Mr. McGeorge Bundy. Shortly after 3 o'clock I received a cable from our Ambassador [Bennett], and he said that things were in danger; he had been informed the chief of police and governmental authorities could no longer protect us. We immediately started the necessary conference calls to be prepared.

At 5:14, almost 2 hours later, we received a cable that was labeled "critic," a word that is reserved for only the most urgent and immediate matters of national security.

The cable reported that Dominican law enforcement and military officials had informed our Embassy that the situation was completely out of control, and that the police and the government could no longer give any guarantee concerning the safety of Americans or any foreign nationals.

Ambassador Bennett, who is one of our most experienced Foreign Service officers, went on in that cable to say that only an immediate landing of American forces could safeguard and protect the lives of thousands of Americans and thousands of other citizens of some 30 other countries. Ambassador Bennett urged your President to order an immediate landing.

In this situation hesitation and vacillation could mean death for many of our people, as well as many of the citizens of other lands.

I thought that we could not and we did not hesitate. Our forces, American forces, were ordered in immediately to protect American lives. They have done that. They have attacked no one, and although some of our servicemen gave their lives, not a single American civilian or the civilian of any other nation, as a result of this protection, lost their lives.

There may be those in our own country who say that such action was good but we should have waited, or we should have delayed, or we should have consulted further, or we should have called a meeting [of the Organization of American States]. But from the very beginning, the United States, at my instructions, had worked for a cease-fire beginning the Saturday the revolution took place. . . .

When that cable arrived, when our entire country team in the Dominican Republic, made up of nine men—one from the Army, Navy, and Air Force, our Ambassador . . . and others—said to your President unanimously: Mr. President, if you do not send forces immediately, men and women—Americans and those of other lands—will die in the streets—well, I knew there was no time to talk, to consult, or to delay. For in this situation delay itself would be decision—the decision to risk and to lose the lives of thousands of Americans and thousands of innocent people from all lands.*

* About five thousand foreigners were ultimately evacuated, including U.S. citizens and the nationals of some forty-five other countries.

I want you to know that it is not a light or an easy matter to send our American boys to another country, but I do not think that the American people expect their President to hesitate or to vacillate in the face of danger, just because the decision is hard when life is in peril.

The revolutionary movement took a tragic turn. Communist leaders, many of them trained in Cuba, seeing a chance to increase disorder, to gain a foothold, joined the revolution. They took increasing control. And what began as a popular democratic revolution, committed to democracy and social justice, very shortly moved and was taken over and really seized and placed into the hands of a band of Communist conspirators.

Many of the original leaders of the rebellion . . . took refuge in foreign embassies because they had been superseded by other evil forces, and the Secretary General of the rebel government, Martínez Francisco, appealed for a cease-fire. But he was ignored. The revolution was now in other and dangerous hands.

When these new and ominous developments emerged, the OAS [Organization of American States] met again, and it met at the request of the United States. I am glad to say they responded wisely and decisively. A five-nation OAS team is now in the Dominican Republic, acting to achieve a cease-fire to insure the safety of innocent people, to restore normal conditions, and to open a path to democratic progress.

2. A Massachusetts Newspaper Protests (1965)

The American troops fought with the rebels, and lives were lost on both sides. The United States found itself in the ugly position of appearing to uphold a rightist government rather than permit leftists to come into power. President Johnson had at first justified his intervention on the grounds of safeguarding American lives; but in his speech of May 2 (see above) and thereafter he added the danger of a Communist takeover. The number of identifiable Communists involved was not large, and this allegation led to further charges of misrepresentation. An independent Massachusetts newspaper editor here presents the case as many critics (including Latin Americans) saw it. Determine how much of his argument seems to be emotionalism and how much is solidly based.

There is one strong word to describe the U.S. behavior in the Dominican Republic: disastrous.

If our Government had set out deliberately to botch the situation, it could not have done a better job. The record of U.S. miscalculations, false starts, and miscellaneous cruelties is enough to make ordinary citizens squirm in shame.

Nothing that the United States may do now can erase that record. Hundreds of millions of dollars may be poured into the island Republic, but they will not atone for the dead Dominicans shot by U.S. troops. Washington may

2. *Berkshire Eagle* (Pittsfield, Mass.), May 21, 1965. By permission.

pledge a new era of inter-American cooperation, but that will not obliterate the fact that Washington is even now violating its pledges under the Charter of the Organization of American States.

To cap the sorry history of the past month, U.S. spokesmen are not giving their own people an accurate and complete picture of their Government's actions. President Johnson and his lieutenants said weeks ago that U.S. Marines were being landed in the Dominican Republic to assist in evacuating U.S. civilians, when in truth, as we have since learned, they were there to forestall the possibility that Communists might seize power.

More recently, the State Department announced in self-righteous fashion that the Marines are trying to help the Dominicans "choose their own government free of outside interference." This is, of course, twaddle that deceives no one, least of all the Dominicans being shot by American troops for daring to choose their own government.

It is our country's insistence upon carrying out a misconceived policy to the bitter end—even when it means firing upon our friends—that proves most disturbing. Doubtless a great many Americans were willing to go along with the administration in its emergency police action a month ago, on grounds that this was an extraordinary situation and, in any case, the President and his aides may have known more than they were telling.

But when the initial emergency proved to be overstated and the United States found itself lined up with the most reactionary elements in the Republic against the will of many civilians, the error was obvious. It took no special discernment to see that the warnings of Juan Bosch and other Latin American observers had been correct: U.S. policy was wrecking the inter-American system and fostering communism throughout the hemisphere.

So far our Government has bungled its relations with Cuba and the Dominican Republic. The only question now is: Have we learned enough from these experiences to cope with the other Latin American crises that are sure to come?

3. A Newspaperman Defends Johnson (1965)

A more sober view of the Dominican intervention was expressed by a writer in the Washington, D.C., *Evening Star*. We should note that the Council of the Organization of American States, on May 6, had voted (14 to 5) to merge the United States troops with an Inter-American Peace Force. Several Latin American nations sent in relatively small contingents, and their presence took some of the onus off the United States. After reading this journalistic commentary, determine why we cannot fairly compare Johnson's conduct with Kennedy's handling of the Cuban crisis of 1962.

It is best to admit that the sending of U.S. marines into the Dominican Republic, without the prior consent of the Organization of American States,

3. Washington *Evening Star*, May 31, 1965 (Max Freedman). By permission of Publishers Newspaper Syndicate, who provided an original copy.

constituted a technical breach of the charter under which this American system of regional security operates. No amount of retrospective logic can wipe out that fact. The serious questions are whether President Johnson and Secretary Rusk had any valid alternative; and whether their actions since the early days of the crisis have strengthened or weakened the Inter-American system.

Senator Robert Kennedy, for example, has recalled that President Kennedy was very careful to consult with OAS during the Cuban crisis of 1962. He speaks with special authority on that crisis for his own contribution in those critical days was consistently valiant and distinguished. Yet Senator Kennedy, on reflection, will surely admit that his comparison, at bottom, is completely misleading.

The essential feature of the Cuban crisis is that President Kennedy, amid conditions of intense secrecy and in days filled with almost incredible activity, had a margin of precious time to prepare the American response down to the last detail. Included in that plan of action was the wise decision to inform the OAS, the United Nations, and various leaders of the Western World.

But this statement of America's intentions, whether conveyed privately or publicly, came very late in the day. It came only after the carefully considered American plan had been set in motion. At no time was President Kennedy prepared to give the Inter-American system the right to modify his plan, to delay it, or to veto it. In no sense of the term as understood by diplomacy was there any "consultation" with the OAS. President Kennedy merely informed it of his plans when it became both wise and convenient for him to do so.

Now it would be absurd to compare the Dominican crisis with the Cuban crisis as a threat to peace. But the inherent danger of the present crisis is not now the issue. What concerns us is the fact that the special circumstances of the Dominican crisis gave President Johnson less time for working with the OAS than President Kennedy had in the Cuban emergency. Those circumstances included the breakdown of law and order, the sinister threat of Communist mischief in conditions of spreading anarchy, the urgent and repeated confessions by the Dominican authorities then in power that they had lost control of the situation, and the reluctant but unanimous judgment of U.S. officials in Santo Domingo that troops had to be sent at once by Washington to protect and evacuate American citizens.

It was the unanimous decision of everyone who participated in Johnson's decision that the crisis would tolerate no delay. There was the related agreement that the OAS, even in the best of circumstances, could take no action in less than 48 hours; and the warning messages from Santo Domingo emphasized that such a delay would entail an intolerable risk to American lives.

Was this an unreasonable estimate of the situation when one remembers the history of the OAS in other emergencies and its conduct in this crisis? There will be many Americans, as well as many people in Latin America, who will be ready to believe that we are able to indulge these academic anxieties only because the President's decision did in fact avert disaster. For it would be a very different debate if we were conducting it on the ruins of freedom in the Dominican Republic, if another Castro-influenced government were in power there, and if the contagion of anarchy and communism spread to other lands in Latin America.

The record shows that President Johnson, perhaps more than any other President in our history, has been eager to strengthen the Inter-American system and to equip it with the power to act quickly and decisively in meeting any threat to the security of this hemisphere. If he succeeds in this enterprise, it may well be the judgment of future historians that a small technical breach, soon rectified, led to the most significant gains in regional consultation and security. It is President Johnson's long-term commitment to the OAS that matters, and it is high time that his commitment were more clearly understood, both here and in Latin America.

[*On June 1, 1966, some thirteen months after the initial landing of United States troops, a general election was held in the Dominican Republic, and the moderate party received a surprisingly heavy endorsement. On September 20, 1966, all foreign troops were withdrawn, and a tranquility of sorts came to the racked republic—for how long no one could say. In the light of this relatively happy ending, Johnson's actions seemed less vulnerable to criticism, at least temporarily, than they had been.*]

THOUGHT PROVOKERS

1. Why are political pressure and graft inevitable in a large-scale poverty program? Why is job retraining more important now than ever before? Do you think that today it is reasonable to strive for "total victory"—a complete elimination of poverty? Someone has said that it is pointless to ask a man who has no shoes to pull himself up by his boot straps. Comment.

2. What is the difference, if any, between large-scale civil disobedience and anarchy? Is the Negro problem in the Eastern cities (a number of which will ultimately have a majority of Negroes) too big for local authority and finance to handle? Is violence the answer to Negro grievances, or will it bring more severe repression? Why is there considerable anti-Semitism among Negroes?

3. Is any citizen completely immune from false charges as a criminal? It has often been said that the police find it easier to beat a confession out of a suspect than to engage in the laborious footwork of collecting evidence. Comment. Justice Harlan believed that only "undue pressure" on the suspect was objectionable, but who is to judge what is undue? To what extent are citizens prone to assume their "civic responsibility" and help the police apprehend criminals?

4. Suppose President Johnson had not gone into Santo Domingo and dozens of American civilians had been killed, and suppose also that another Castro-like Communist state had come into being. How would American opinion have reacted? Is it better for a President to be safe than sorry in situations of this kind? What might have happened if he had waited for the Organization of American States to sanction American intervention in advance?

FURTHER EXPLORATION

It is too early to expect solid works on the Johnson years but the following general books are useful: Rowland Evans and Robert Novak, *Lyndon B. Johnson and the Exercise of Power* (1966); Philip L. Geyelin, *Lyndon B. Johnson and the World* (1966); Robert Sherrill, *The Accidental President* (1967); W. S. White, *The Professional: Lyndon B. Johnson* (1964) [paperback]. On the **Dominican Crisis** consult the recollections of a first-hand observer: John B. Martin, *Overtaken by Events* (1966).

Chapter 50

The Vietnam Involvement

"Most of us remember the fearful cost of ignoring aggression. . . . America is committed to the defense of South Vietnam until an honorable peace can be negotiated."

PRESIDENT LYNDON B. JOHNSON, 1967

PROLOGUE: In the second half of the nineteenth century, the French consolidated their imperial administration in Indochina—that is, Cambodia, Laos, and Vietnam. A half-century later—in 1940–1941—invading Japanese troops began to exercise their power behind a facade of French Vichyite control. They encountered increasing resistance from Vietnamese guerrillas (Viet Minh), led by Ho Chi Minh, a hard-core Communist who was also a strong nationalist. After Japan's surrender in 1945, the Viet Minh revolted openly against the French when the latter unwisely tried to reimpose their rule.

The United States at that time saw no need to crawl into this bed of snakes, but the fall of China to the Communists in 1949 changed the picture dramatically. In the hope of "containing" Communist expansion in Southeast Asia, the Truman administration decided, in the spring of 1950, to contribute heavily in money and weapons to the French in Indochina.* Despite such multi-billion-dollar aid the French position crumbled steadily, although France still had several hundred thousand men under arms, most of them Vietnamese loyalists and foreign mercenaries. In 1954 a French-led force of some 12,000 men was trapped at Dien Bien Phu, a key outpost in northern Vietnam. President Eisenhower, despite great pressure from within his administration, resisted the temptation to relieve the French with a dramatic air strike. We were to learn later in Vietnam that one-strike air raids cannot be relied on to end wars.

A. THE BEGINNINGS OF A QUAGMIRE

1. The Geneva Agreements (1954)

The situation looked gloomy for the French when a prearranged nine-power conference assembled by the quiet waters of Lake Geneva—May 8 to July 2, 1954—to hammer out a peaceful solution. (Dien Bien Phu fell almost simultaneously with the first day of the sessions.) The delegates came from nine nations: the U.S., the U.S.S.R., Great Britain, France, Red China, and the four parts of Indochina—Laos, Cambodia,

---

* Note that four Presidents—Truman, Eisenhower, Kennedy, and Johnson—each took successive steps that brought the nation deeper into the morass.
1. The text of the Geneva Agreements may be conveniently found in the appendix of Richard N. Goodwin, *Triumph or Tragedy: Reflections on Vietnam* (1966), pp. 69–97. See also the *Department of State Bulletin, XXXI,* 164 (Aug. 2, 1954).

the Democratic Republic of [Communist North] Vietnam, and the State of [South] Vietnam. The conferees finally agreed to divide Vietnam temporarily by the 17th parallel, pending the mutual withdrawal of troops, the transfer of populations, and the holding of free elections. The assumption was that Vietnam would then become united and Communist. But the Washington government, alarmed by these gains for Communism, flatly refused to approve the Geneva Agreements, as did the French-backed regime in South Vietnam. The more significant and controversial provisions of the Geneva Agreements are reprinted below. Is it possible to decide which party was more to blame for subsequently violating these stipulations?

14,c. Each party undertakes to refrain from any reprisals or discrimination against persons or organizations on account of their activities during the hostilities and to guarantee their democratic liberties.

[*The North Vietnamese Communists, with their capital at Hanoi, abused pro-French natives, and the South Vietnamese, with their capital at Saigon, abused pro-Communist Viet Minh.*]

14,d. From the date of entry into force of the present Agreement until the movement of troops is completed, any civilians residing in a district controlled by one party who wish to go and live in the zone assigned to the other party shall be permitted and helped to do so by the authorities of that district.

[*The North Vietnamese clearly put restraints of various kinds on considerable numbers of former anti-Communists who wanted to flee south.*]

Final Declaration, 4. The Conference takes note of the clauses in the agreement on the cessation of hostilities in Vietnam prohibiting the introduction into Vietnam of foreign troops and military personnel as well as of all kinds of arms and munitions.

[*From the outset the North Vietnamese violated at least the spirit of this clause by leaving cadres of hundreds of trained guerrillas in South Vietnam,* by importing arms from China and the Soviet Union, and finally, about 1960, by sending south relatively small contingents of their own troops. The South Vietnamese early introduced American arms and military advisers, and subsequently large numbers of American combat troops. But South Vietnam and the United States had not signed the Geneva Accords.*]

Final Declaration, 7. The Conference declares that, so far as Vietnam is concerned, the settlement of political problems, effected on the basis of respect for the principles of independence, unity, and territorial integrity, shall permit the Vietnamese people to enjoy the fundamental freedoms, guaranteed by democratic institutions established as a result of free general elections by secret ballot. In order to ensure that sufficient progress in the resto-

---

* In many cases, these ex-guerrillas were South Vietnamese who naturally remained in their native hamlets or returned to them.

ration of peace has been made, and that the necessary conditions obtain for free expression of the national will, general elections shall be held in July, 1956. . . .

[The elections were never held, primarily because South Vietnam, encouraged by Washington, feared that they would not be "free" and that the Communists would receive a majority. For that matter, Ho Chi Minh did not hold elections in North Vietnam.

The head of the American delegation at Geneva, though refusing to sign the Accords, issued a unilateral statement. It pledged that we would not use "force" or the "threat" of force to upset the Agreements, and that we would view with "grave concern" any renewal of aggression. When aggression was renewed, obviously with the encouragement of North Vietnam, Washington felt released from any obligation not to use force or the threat of force.]

2. Eisenhower Pledges Aid (1954)

By the terms of the Geneva Agreements, the population of the north was to be "permitted and helped" to go south, and vice versa, for a limited period. About a million refugees departed from North Vietnam, some 600,000 of them Roman Catholics identified in the Communist mind with the hated French regime. (About an equal number of Catholics remained.) "The Virgin Mary has gone South," was a warning used by anti-Communists to encourage the migration. The United States assisted in this transfer of population. President Eisenhower himself, in a famous letter of October 1, 1954, pledged continued aid to President Diem, who, with American backing, had emerged as head of state. Note the conditions attached to the aid and whether or not there was a specific promise of military assistance, as claimed by subsequent administrations.

Dear Mr. President:

I have been following with great interest the course of developments in Viet-Nam, particularly since the conclusion of the conference at Geneva. The implications of the agreement concerning Viet-Nam have caused grave concern regarding the future of a country temporarily divided by an artificial military grouping, weakened by a long and exhausting war, and faced with enemies without and by their subversive collaborators within.

Your recent requests for aid to assist in the formidable project of the movement of several hundred thousand loyal Vietnamese citizens away from areas which are passing under a *de facto* rule and political ideology which they abhor, are being fulfilled. I am glad that the United States is able to assist in this humanitarian effort.

We have been exploring ways and means to permit our aid to Viet-Nam to be more effective and to make a greater contribution to the welfare and stability of the Government of Viet-Nam. I am, accordingly, instructing the American Ambassador to Viet-Nam to examine with you in your capacity as

2. *Public Papers of the Presidents of the United States: Dwight D. Eisenhower, 1954* (1960), pp. 948–949.

Chief of Government, how an intelligent program of American aid given directly to your Government can serve to assist Viet-Nam in its present hour of trial, provided that your Government is prepared to give assurances as to the standards of performance it would be able to maintain in the event such aid were supplied.

The purpose of this offer is to assist the Government of Viet-Nam in developing and maintaining a strong, viable state, capable of resisting attempted subversion or aggression through military means. The Government of the United States expects that this aid will be met by performance on the part of the Government of Viet-Nam in undertaking needed reforms. It hopes that such aid, combined with your own continuing efforts, will contribute effectively toward an independent Viet-Nam endowed with a strong government. Such a government would, I hope, be so responsive to the nationalist aspirations of its people, so enlightened in purpose and effective in performance, that it will be respected both at home and abroad and discourage any who might wish to impose a foreign ideology on your free people.

[*Despite the lack of a specific promise of American military aid, the fact is that such assistance was provided. It took the form of large amounts of military hardware and an agreement in 1955 to send "advisers" to train the South Vietnamese army; by the end of Eisenhower's administration the "advisers" numbered about 700.*]

B. THE DIEM REGIME

1. Opposition to Ngo Dinh Diem Deepens (1954–1963)

In Washington's view, President Diem seemed to provide the only real hope of averting a Communist takeover of all Vietnam. As a member of an aristocratic Catholic family, he was a strong nationalist and anti-Communist. He had earlier visited the United States, where he had secured the support of such prominent Catholics as Cardinal Spellman and Senator John F. Kennedy, as well as Secretary Dulles and Vice President Nixon. But Diem's autocratic and illiberal regime alienated many of his own people, especially when he deprived them of recently redistributed land and restored it to grasping landlords. In the late 1950's thousands of South Vietnamese (Viet Cong) guerrillas rose in arms, and in 1960 they set up their own official government, as the National Liberation Front (NLF). They were secretly and then openly aided with arms and some men by the North Vietnamese, who by 1959 had given up hope that the scheduled "free elections" of 1956 would ever be held. The state of mind of the Viet Cong is here reflected by Herbert Aptheker, an American Marxist who journeyed to North Vietnam in 1965 and reported an anti-Diem conversation with a girl guerrilla fighter. Note the parts that are obviously untrue and those that are most believable. Notice also where the Viet Cong got their arms.

Next to me is a young woman in her twenties; she stands about 4 feet, 10 inches. She wears many medals, is a Hero of the NLF, has been in 33 en-

1. Herbert Aptheker, *Mission to Hanoi* (1966), pp. 33–35. By permission of International Publishers Co., Inc.

gagements and is outstanding as a political leader and mass organizer. Except for the medals and her diminutiveness she reminds me of any of hundreds of young women college students back home—and of one such student in particular [his daughter?].

"When Diem took the land back from the peasants, when he arrested former Resistance [Viet Minh] fighters in my village, we protested," she told me. "But the repression grew. Always we demonstrated and petitioned; we did what we could politically.

"But Diem wanted no politics, he wanted slavery. And when he carried his guillotine [?] to our village and tortured men and women with boiling water and needles under their nails and began herding us into 'hamlets' [protective stockades] we had only two choices: submission and slavery, or resistance and fighting for freedom. We Vietnamese have faced such choices before and we have never hesitated in the past and did not hesitate this time either. We could not do otherwise and we think that you, too, would have done as we did. How could anyone do otherwise? Foreigners came back, independence was gone, the land was gone and we could no longer live this way.

"We had nothing but stones and bamboo sticks at first, and these are what we used. Then we captured guns and we organized and grew and now we are strong and many and well-trained and we will never stop fighting until the armed foreigners leave and independence comes back. Then again there will be land for the tillers and food for our mouths and schools for children—as already there are in our liberated areas. We will win back Vietnam for ourselves and run it for ourselves. We are Vietnamese and this is the way it should be and will be.

"In our province," she said, "Diem had made so many corpses they reached the mountain tops and he had spilled so much blood the rivers ran red. We young ones said we will not submit and we rose up. We will have independence. We cannot submit. What do you think? Do you not see? Would you not do as we have done if this had happened to you and those you love?"

Those were the words of this recent teenager, this veteran soldier, this veteran mass leader, this fearsome threat to the Strategic Air Command and the mighty Pentagon.

[*The Viet Cong looked upon their type of guerrilla warfare as introducing crucial new tactics into "wars of national liberation." If these techniques could thwart or defeat a superpower like the United States, they could obviously be used by the Communists in other parts of the world. Many Americans assumed—in the absence of convincing proof—that the Viet Cong war was not a civil war at all but that the guerrillas received their primary support and direction from North Vietnam, which in turn took orders from Communist China. Does the alleged conversation with the "girl guerrilla" support or undermine this thesis?*]

VIETNAM
and
SOUTHEAST
ASIA

2. Diem Appeals to President Kennedy for Help (1961)

The Viet Cong guerrillas came to exercise control over most of the countryside, especially at night. In many areas they enjoyed popular support; in others they used kidnapping, torture, decapitation, and wholesale murder to attain the upper hand. Diem's troops were unable to establish their authority much beyond the urban centers, and the Saigon government was kept alive by large-scale aid coming from America. This took the form of food and arms, as well as a limited number of noncombatant American advisers, some of whom flew rescue helicopters. In 1957 came the first American casualties; in 1959, the first deaths. Such was the discouraging outlook in December, 1961, when this alarming letter from President Diem reached President Kennedy. What general conclusions may be drawn from it as to the general nature of the war in South Vietnam? What parts of this appeal are the least trustworthy?

2. *Department of State Bulletin,* XLVI, 13–14 (Jan. 1, 1962). Reprinted in part.

Like the United States, the Republic of Viet-Nam has always been devoted to the preservation of peace. My people know only too well the sorrows of war. We have honored the 1954 Geneva Agreements even though they resulted in the partition of our country and the enslavement of more than half of our people by Communist tyranny. We have never considered the reunification of our nation by force. On the contrary, we have publicly pledged that we will not violate the demarcation line and the demilitarized zone set up by the agreements. We have always been prepared and have on many occasions stated our willingness to reunify Viet-Nam on the basis of democratic and truly free elections.

The record of the Communist authorities in the northern part of our country is quite otherwise. They not only consented to the division of Viet-Nam, but were eager for it.* They pledged themselves to observe the Geneva Agreements and during the seven years since have never ceased to violate them. They call for free elections but are ignorant of the very meaning of the words. They talk of "peaceful reunification" and wage war against us.

From the beginning, the Communists resorted to terror in their efforts to subvert our people, destroy our government, and impose a Communist regime upon us. They have attacked defenseless teachers, closed schools, killed members of our anti-malarial program and looted hospitals. This is coldly calculated to destroy our government's humanitarian efforts to serve our people.

We have long sought to check the Communist attack from the North on our people by appeals to the International Control Commission [established by the Geneva Agreements of 1954 and comprising representatives from Poland, India, and Canada]. Over the years, we have repeatedly published to the world the evidence of the Communist plot to overthrow our government and seize control of all of Viet-Nam by illegal intrusions from outside our country. The evidence has mounted until now it is hardly necessary to rehearse it. Most recently, the kidnapping and brutal murder of our Chief Liaison Officer to the International Control Commission, Colonel Noang Thuy Nam, compelled us to speak out once more. In our October 24, 1961, letter to the ICC, we called attention again to the publicly stated determination of the Communist authorities in Hanoi [the capital of North Vietnam] to "liberate the South" by the overthrow of my government and the imposition of a Communist regime on our people. We cited the proof of massive infiltration of Communist agents and military elements into our country. We outlined the Communist strategy, which is simply the ruthless use of terror against the whole population, women and children included.

---

* They were eager for only a temporary division, pending reunification under the never-held elections of 1956. President Eisenhower concluded, on the basis of his information, that "as of the time of the fighting, possibly 80 percent of the population would have voted for the Communist Ho Chi Minh," rather than the regime of the French playboy puppet in Saigon, Bao Dai. (D. D. Eisenhower, *Mandate for Change, 1953–1956* [1963], p. 372.) This statement has often been used to support the view that two years *later*, in 1956, eighty percent favored Ho Chi Minh rather than Ngo Dinh Diem.

In the course of the last few months, the Communist assault on my people has achieved high ferocity. In October they caused more than 1,800 incidents of violence and more than 2,000 casualties. They have struck occasionally in battalion strength, and they are continually augmenting their forces by infiltration from the North. The level of their attacks is already such that our forces are stretched to the utmost. We are forced to defend every village, every hamlet, indeed every home against a foe whose tactic is always to strike at the defenseless. . . .

In short, the Vietnamese nation now faces what is perhaps the gravest crisis in its long history. For more than 2,000 years my people have lived and built, fought and died in this land. We have not always been free. Indeed, much of our history and many of its proudest moments have arisen from conquest by foreign powers and our struggle against great odds to regain or defend our precious independence. But it is not only our freedom which is at stake today, it is our national identity. For, if we lose this war, our people will be swallowed by the Communist Bloc, all our proud heritage will be blotted out by the "Socialist society" and Viet-Nam will leave the pages of history. We will lose our national soul.

[*On December 14, 1961, President Kennedy responded to Diem's appeal with perhaps the most fateful letter he ever wrote. Acknowledging that North Vietnam had violated the Geneva Accords by renewing aggression, he promised to help the South Vietnamese establish their independence. By that time he had increased to about 900 the 700 or so military advisers sent by President Eisenhower. At the time of Kennedy's murder in November, 1963, American military personnel in South Vietnam had mounted to about 15,500. Deeper involvement seemed highly probable.*]

3. President Diem Is Murdered (1963)

Growing in strength, the Viet Cong became bolder in their attacks. President Diem proved resistant to American pressures for reform. Further misgivings were aroused by Diem's authoritarian brother, Ngo Dinh Nhu, and the brother's beautiful but acid-tongued wife ("The Dragon Lady"), all of whom represented the Catholic minority. Anti-Catholics and anti-Diem Buddhists, some no doubt Communists in monks' clothing, put on stage-managed demonstrations against the regime. America was shocked when several "martyrs" doused themselves with gasoline and burned themselves to death in public—a Buddhist "barbecue," sneered Madame Nhu. The South Vietnamese military elements feared that Diem, under the influence of his brother, was about to tighten control. Encouraged to some extent by obvious American disenchantment with Diem, the military staged a coup on November 1, 1963, and brutally murdered both Diem and his brother. Arthur M. Schlesinger, Jr., Special Assistant to the President, records Kennedy's reaction. Note what the President regarded as his greatest mistake in handling the problem.

3. Arthur M. Schlesinger, Jr., *A Thousand Days* (1965), pp. 997–8. By permission of Houghton Mifflin Co.

What lay behind the coup was not the meddling of Americans, quiet or ugly, but the long history of Vietnamese military resentment against Diem, compounded now by the fear that Nhu, with his admiration for totalitarian methods of organization, might try to transform South Vietnam into a police state. It was almost inevitable that, at one point or another, the generals would turn against so arbitrary and irrational a regime. As [U.S. Ambassador Henry Cabot] Lodge later put it, the coup was like a rock rolling downhill. It could have been stopped only by aggressive American intervention against the army on behalf of Diem and the Nhus. This course few Americans in Saigon or Washington were willing to recommend.

I saw the President soon after he heard that Diem and Nhu were dead. He was somber and shaken. I had not seen him so depressed since the Bay of Pigs. No doubt he realized that Vietnam was his great failure in foreign policy, and that he had never really given it his full attention. But the fact that the Vietnamese seemed ready to fight had made him feel that there was a reasonable chance of making a go of it; and then the optimism of 1962 [the Cuban missile crisis?] had carried him along. Yet, with his memory of the French in Indochina in 1951 [1954?], he had always believed that there was a point at which our intervention might turn Vietnamese nationalism against us and transform an Asian civil conflict into a white man's war. When he came into office, 2000 [700] American troops were in Vietnam. Now there were 16,000. How many more could there be before we passed the point? By 1961 choices had fatally narrowed; but still if Vietnam had been handled as a political rather than a military problem . . . if, if, if—and now it was all past, and Diem miserably dead. The Saigon generals were claiming that he had killed himself; but the President, shaking his head, doubted that, as a Catholic, he would have taken this way out. He said that Diem had fought for his country for twenty years and that it should not have ended like this.

[*Yet no official statement of regret was forthcoming from the President or the State Department. There was a feeling of relief, and a hope—a false hope—that Diem's successor or successors would perform better.*]

C. THE BOMBING BEGINS

1. Congress Gives Johnson a Blank Check for War (1964)

Diem's death brought disaster to Saigon. Military coup followed military coup with musical-chairs confusion. South Vietnamese morale was sagging badly, as reflected in the desertions of draftees from the army. American aid was slithering down a bottomless rat-hole, while American troops in increasing numbers were chasing the elusive Viet Cong—"raggedy little bastards in black pajamas." Then, August 2–4, 1964, two American destroyers in the international waters of the Gulf of Tonkin reported alleged attacks by North Vietnamese torpedo boats. President Johnson, being accused of "softness" on Communism in the then current presidential campaign, immediately

1. *Department of State Bulletin, LI,* 268 (Aug. 24, 1964).

ordered retaliatory bombing of North Vietnamese naval bases. He also requested of Congress blanket authorization for future action, and the following resolution was passed unanimously in the House and by a vote of 88 to 2 in the Senate. In the light of later events, note what is ironical about the stated purposes of the resolution.

Joint Resolution

To promote the maintenance of international peace and security in southeast Asia.

Whereas naval units of the Communist regime in Vietnam, in violation of the principles of the Charter of the United Nations and of international law, have deliberately and repeatedly attacked United States naval vessels lawfully present in international waters,* and have thereby created a serious threat to international peace; and

Whereas these attacks are part of a deliberate and systematic campaign of aggression that the Communist regime in North Vietnam has been waging against its neighbors and the nations joined with them in the collective defense of their freedom; and

Whereas the United States is assisting the peoples of southeast Asia to protect their freedom and has no territorial, military or political ambitions in that area, but desires only that these peoples should be left in peace to work out their own destinies in their own way: Now, therefore, be it

Resolved by the Senate and House of Representatives of the United States of America in Congress assembled, That the Congress approves and supports the determination of the President, as Commander in Chief, to take all necessary measures to repel any armed attack against the forces of the United States and to prevent further aggression.

Sec. 2. The United States regards as vital to its national interest and to world peace the maintenance of international peace and security in southeast Asia. Consonant with the Constitution of the United States and the Charter of the United Nations and in accordance with its obligations under the Southeast Asia Collective Defense Treaty,† the United States is, therefore, prepared, as the President determines, to take all necessary steps, including the use of armed force, to assist any member or protocol state of the Southeast Asia Collective Defense Treaty requesting assistance in defense of its freedom.

Sec. 3. This resolution shall expire when the President shall determine that the peace and security of the area is reasonably assured by international

---

* The Communists contended that the Gulf of Tonkin was an inland sea, and that the conventional three-mile line had no relevance.

† Partly to protect South Vietnam against aggression after the Geneva Conference of 1954, the United States helped to organize the Southeast Asia Treaty Organization (SEATO). It consisted of the U.S., Britain, France, Australia, New Zealand, the Philippines, Thailand, and Pakistan. Britain, France, and Pakistan kept out of the action in South Vietnam. Australia, New Zealand, and the Philippines sent token forces, and Thailand provided the sites for huge bomber bases. South Korea, though not a member of SEATO, supplied about 50,000 troops. By 1967, over thirty nations had sent aid in one form or another.

conditions created by action of the United Nations or otherwise, except that it may be terminated earlier by concurrent resolution of the Congress.

[*Many members of Congress later regretted voting for this resolution, charging that their intent was not to authorize a large-scale war. President Johnson did not, in fact, ask for an official declaration of hostilities. Wars that are officially declared are less easy to stop than unofficial ones, and besides such a declaration might well have prompted Peking and Moscow to send in Red soldiers to assist their Communist comrades.*]

2. President Johnson Defends the Bombing (1967)

Before the end of 1965 American troops were not only fighting the Viet Cong and some North Vietnamese regulars in South Vietnam, but American aircraft were bombing North Vietnamese bridges, railroads, and war-production centers. Enemy anti-aircraft fire, provided largely by the Soviets and Chinese, was taking a deadly toll of United States aircraft. American aviators were making no concerted effort to destroy the civilian centers of Hanoi and Haiphong—the two most important cities of North Vietnam—but many civilian casualties were inevitable. (In South Vietnam, Viet Cong terrorists were blowing up hotels, restaurants, and busses, with heavy loss of civilian life.) President Johnson, speaking to the Tennessee state legislature, and referring to the iron will of Tennessee's Andrew Jackson, defended America's bombing forays in the following resolute words. What are the most important points he makes in meeting the charges of inhumanity?

I also want to say categorically that it is not the position of the American Government that the bombing will be decisive in getting Hanoi to abandon aggression. It has, however, created very serious problems for them. The best indication of how substantial is the fact that they are working so hard every day with all their friends throughout the world to try to get us to stop.

The bombing is entirely consistent with America's limited objectives in South Vietnam. The strength of Communist main-force units in the south is clearly based on their infiltration from the north. So I think it is simply unfair to our American soldiers, sailors, and Marines and our Vietnamese allies to ask them to face increased enemy personnel and firepower without making an effort to try to reduce that infiltration.

Now as to bombing civilians, I would simply say that we are making an effort that is unprecedented in the history of warfare to be sure that we do not. It is our policy to bomb military targets only.

We have never deliberately bombed cities, nor attacked any target with the purpose of inflicting civilian casualties.

We hasten to add, however, that we recognize, and we regret, that some people, even after warning, are living and working in the vicinity of military targets and they have suffered.

2. *Weekly Compilation of Presidential Documents*, III, 476 (March 20, 1967, reporting speech of March 15, 1967).

"WE ARE WINNING THE WAR"

The wasteland refrain of Presidents Johnson and Ho in 1967
Courtesy, the Boston Globe. Cartoonist Paul Szep.

We are also too aware that men and machines are not infallible, and that some mistakes do occur.

But our record on this account is, in my opinion, highly defensible.

Look for a moment at the record of the other side.

Any civilian casualties that result from our operations are inadvertent, in stark contrast to the calculated Vietcong policy of systematic terror.

Tens of thousands of innocent Vietnamese civilians have been killed, tortured, and kidnapped by the Vietcong. There is no doubt about the deliberate nature of the Vietcong program. One need only note the frequency with which Vietcong victims are village leaders, teachers, health workers, and others who are trying to carry out constructive programs for their people.

Yet, the deeds of the Vietcong go largely unnoted in the public debate. It is this moral double bookkeeping which makes us get sometimes very weary of our critics.

3. A War of Atrocities (1966)

Brutality occurred on both sides. A Communist South Vietnamese in "black pajamas" was indistinguishable from a non-Communist Vietnamese in "black pajamas." Viet Cong guerrillas tortured, blinded, castrated, beheaded, and butchered prisoners, Americans and anti-Communist countrymen alike. Their foes retaliated with similarly inhumane tactics. An American soldier wrote, "Yesterday I shot and killed a little 8 or 9 year old girl with the sweetest, most innocent little face, and the nastiest grenade in her hand you ever saw." American bombers used defoliants to kill crops, and they dropped explosive and incendiary bombs—long-clinging "improved" napalm. They killed or injured North Vietnamese, Viet Cong (soldiers and civilians), and, by mistake, innocent South Vietnamese villagers and American comrades. Two letters from American soldiers are here reproduced. Note how they describe the nature of the war and the effect of home-front anti-war demonstrations, which encouraged the enemy to resist. Should such demonstrations have been suppressed as treasonous?

Dear Mom, . . .

Yesterday I witnessed something that would make any American realize why we are in this war. At least it did me. I was on daylight patrol. We were on a hill overlooking a bridge that was out of our sector. I saw a platoon of Vietcong stopping traffic from going over the bridge. They were beating women and children over the head with rifles, clubs, and fists. They even shot one woman and her child. They were taking rice, coconuts, fish, and other assorted foods from these people. The ones that didn't give they either beat or shot. I think you know what I tried to do. I wanted to go down and kill all of those slant-eyed bastards. I started to and it took two men to stop me. These slobs have to be stopped, even if it takes every last believer in a democracy and a free way of life to do it. I know after seeing their brave tactics I'm going to try my best. So please don't knock [President] Johnson's policy in Vietnam. There is a good reason for it. I'm not too sure what it is myself, but I'm beginning to realize, especially after yesterday. . . .

Love, *Bill*

How are the people taking to the war in Portland? I've read too much . . . about the way some of those cowardly students are acting on campuses. They sure don't show me much as far as being American citizens. They have the idea that they are our future leaders. Well, I won't follow nobody if he isn't going to help fight for my freedom.

A few weeks ago, I had the chance to talk with some Marines who had come to Okinawa for four (lousy) days of leave. They were more than happy because they had been fighting for six months with no let-up. We sat

3. Glenn Munson, ed., *Letters from Viet Nam* (1966), pp. 104, 118. By permission of Parallax Publishing Co. We learned during the Filipino insurrection of 1899–1902 that when we fight primitive peoples we are pulled down to their level of warfare. See the atrocity scandals, above, pp. 615–617. Anti-imperialist opposition in America to the war in the Philippines also strengthened Filipino resistance, as was the case later in North Vietnam.

in a restaurant all the time, and I wish I could have taped it on my recorder. What they had to say would have had an impact on the people back home. One showed me where he had been shot. I asked if it hurt, and he didn't feel it. Not until after he got the — — that shot him. He was more angry than hurt. They told me of some of their patrols and how they would be talking to a buddy one minute and watch him die the next. Or wake up in the morning and see a friend hung from a tree by hooks in his armpits with parts of his body cut and shoved into his mouth. From what they said, the Vietcong aren't the only ruthless ones. *We* have to be, too. *Have* to. You'd be surprised to know that a guy you went to school with is right now shooting a nine-year-old girl and her mother. He did it because if they got the chance they would kill him. Or throwing a Vietcong out of a helicopter because he wouldn't talk.

One guy (who had broke down and cried) said that his one desire is to get enough leave to go home and kick three of those demonstrators in a well-suited place and bring him back· I tell you, it's horrible to read a paper and see your own people aren't backing you up.

4. President Johnson States His War Aims (1965)

The avowed purposes of America's heavy but limited bombing of North Vietnam were (a) to check the southward shipment of supplies and men, (b) to weaken the morale of the North Vietnamese so that they would come to the peace table, and (c) to strengthen the sagging morale of the South Vietnamese. The continuous aerial pounding was not conspicuously successful, as supplies and soldiers continued to flow (though probably less plentifully) and the Hanoi regime dug in more doggedly, President Johnson, in his memorable address at The Johns Hopkins University (April 7, 1965), used both the carrot and the stick. On the one hand, he was prepared to enter into "unconditional negotiations" * with North Vietnam; on the other hand, he was prepared to offer one billion dollars for a program to rehabilitate Southeast Asia, including North Vietnam. Analyze the reasons he gave for waging the war, and assess their soundness.

Why are these realities our concern? Why are we in South Viet-Nam?

We are there because we have a promise to keep. Since 1954 every American President has offered support to the people of South Viet-Nam. We have helped to build, and we have helped to defend. Thus, over many years, we have made a national pledge to help South Viet-Nam defend its independence.

And I intend to keep that promise.

To dishonor that pledge, to abandon this small and brave nation to its enemies, and to the terror that must follow, would be an unforgivable wrong.

We are also there to strengthen world order. Around the globe from Berlin to Thailand are people whose well being rests in part on the belief that

---

4. *Public Papers of the Presidents of the United States: Lyndon B. Johnson* (1966), p. 395.
* He nevertheless attached conditions, including "an independent South Vietnam."

they can count on us [to honor some forty defensive alliances] if they are attacked. To leave Viet-Nam to its fate would shake the confidence of all these people in the value of an American commitment and in the value of America's word. The result would be increased unrest and instability, and even wider war.

We are also there because there are great stakes in the balance. Let no one think for a moment that retreat from Viet-Nam would bring an end to conflict. The battle would be renewed in one country and then another. The central lesson of our time is that the appetite of aggression is never satisfied. . . .

Our objective is the independence of South Viet-Nam and its freedom from attack. We want nothing for ourselves—only that the people of South Viet-Nam be allowed to guide their own country in their own way.

We will do everything necessary to reach that objective and we will do only what is absolutely necessary.

[The free world generally praised President Johnson's overture for peace. But Hanoi branded it a "swindle" by the American "warmongering imperialists," possibly because Washington had earlier turned a deaf ear to several presumed overtures for peace that it had regarded as "insincere."]

D. THE GREAT DEBATE CONTINUES

1. Public Hearings in Wisconsin (1965)

The Vietnam war—by 1967 our third largest war—became increasingly unpopular both in America and abroad. Many citizens—"the hawks"—complained because President Johnson did not launch an all-out bombing of the North. Many others —"the doves"—objected because he was bombing at all. Some critics wanted to pull out altogether; others were for pulling back to "impregnable" enclaves in South Vietnam and sweating it out until the North Vietnamese were willing to negotiate. Especially critical were the intellectuals, and particularly the "Vietniks" of college age who burned their draft cards and staged protest demonstrations known as "teach-ins." Congressman Robert W. Kastenmeier of Wisconsin conducted hearings in Madison, Wisconsin, and elicited the following statement from David Keene, who represented the Wisconsin Young Americans for Freedom, a conservative youth organization. Which one of his arguments seems the most formidable; which the most questionable? Was it reasonable to suppose that, in the event of victory, the North Vietnamese would deal gently with their defeated enemies, including the Catholics?

We could probably establish peace in South Vietnam by withdrawing our troops, but it would be a temporary and expensive peace. The price tag would include not only the geographical area of Vietnam, but the freedom and dreams of the fourteen million people living there, the honor of our own country, and, eventually, the security of the entire free world.

1. Robert W. Kastenmeier, ed., *Vietnam Hearings: Voices from the Grass Roots* (1965), pp. 38–40.

Appeasement has never been, and is not now, an effective method of dealing with aggression. It has been tried often, but has always served only to whet the appetite of the ambitious aggressor. . . .

Russia and China are presently engaged in a struggle for the leadership of the international Communist movement. The Soviet Union has advocated a more moderate foreign policy line than that being pushed by China's Mao Tse-tung. An American defeat in Asia would seem to substantiate the Red Chinese charge that the United States is a "paper tiger," and could, conceivably, catapult Mao into undisputed leadership of the international Communist movement. . . .

American withdrawal, we must remember, would abandon 14 million people to Communist enslavement. More than a million of those people voted with their feet against Communism when they fled from North Vietnam following the Geneva Agreements of 1954. They have trusted our word and they have fought Ho Chi Minh. The South Vietnamese population has suffered more than we can possibly imagine to keep their country out of the hands of the Communist regime to their north. . . .

In 1956 the peasants of North Vietnam objected to Ho Chi Minh's plans for them. He responded by ordering executions which, according to the International Control Commission, claimed nearly 60,000 peasant lives. What will he do to the Buddhists in South Vietnam the first time they object to his plans? And what will be the fate of the 500,000 men serving in the South Vietnamese armed forces? Ho Chi Minh forgets little, and is not likely to forgive them for opposing his "wave of the future."

In 1957 he began a campaign of terror in South Vietnam designed to isolate the people from their government. Principal targets included teachers, doctors, nurses and village officials. The late President John F. Kennedy, in May of 1961, revealed that between May, 1960, and May of 1961, more than 4,000 low level officials were killed by the Viet Cong. Other figures revealed that as many as 13,000 village officials had been murdered by 1962. The number has measurably increased since that time.

2. The Americanization of South Vietnam (1965 and after)

By 1967 the United States had more than 400,000 fighting men in South Vietnam, with a vast supporting apparatus. Soldiers with ready cash to spend had an inflationary effect on the Vietnamese economy. Gaudy bars, brothels, and other places for entertaining service men flourished in Saigon and other cities. The following little drama was reported by a Quaker observer. What support does it give to the theory that America's overwhelming presence was self-defeating and that Asians should be allowed to fight their own wars?

The scene was a small square in the city of Hué, South Vietnam, on a summer day in 1965. The place was known as a rendezvous for American

2. A Report Prepared for the American Friends Service Committee, *Peace in Vietnam: A New Approach in Southeast Asia* (1966), p. 1. By permission of Hill and Wang, Inc.

GI's and Vietnamese girls. A couple of military police were on duty to keep order. On this day one of them had supplied himself with some candy for the children who played in the square and crowded around the Americans. As he started his distribution in a friendly mood, a swarm of youngsters, jumping and reaching, pressed about him. With a laugh he tossed the candy out on the cobblestones. Immediately the children descended like locusts, each intent on grabbing a piece.

A young Vietnamese school teacher happened by at this moment, and seeing the scrambling children, he spoke to them in stern and emphatic tones. He told them to pick up the candy and give it back to the American. After some hesitation they sheepishly complied. Then, facing the soldier and speaking in measured English with a tone of suppressed anger and scorn, he said: "You Americans don't understand. You are making beggars of our children, prostitutes of our women, and Communists of our men!"

3. Schlesinger Presents the Chinese Side (1966)

Late in 1966, Arthur M. Schlesinger, Jr., a Pulitzer-prize winning historian and former Special Assistant to President Kennedy, emphatically called for an end of the bombing and a de-escalation of the war in Vietnam. Although not advocating a scuttle-and-run policy, he was convinced that we could not napalm the Vietnamese into our kind of peace. Assess the aptness of his analogy designed to show the other side's point of view. Comment also on the observation that the reverse side of the coin of containment is encirclement.

What, therefore, is the view from Peking? It is obviously of a gigantic American effort at the encirclement and strangulation of China.

That is not, of course, our view of what we are doing; nor is it in fact what we are doing. But it really should not astonish us that a crew of dogmatic Marxist-Leninists should so interpret the extraordinary deployment of American armies, navies and military bases thousands of miles from the United States and mobilized—on the word of American leaders—against no one but themselves.

Imagine our own feelings if the Chinese had 400,000 troops in southern Mexico, engaged in putting down what we had hoped to be a pro-American rebellion; if massive Chinese military bases were being built there; if Chinese planes were bombing northern Mexico every day; if a great Chinese fleet controlled the waters along our Pacific coast; and if Peking was denouncing the United States as the world's greatest threat to peace. The question, which so engages on our own sense of righteousness, of who the "aggressor" is, depends a good deal on who looks through what glass and how darkly.

3. Arthur M. Schlesinger, Jr., *The Bitter Heritage* (1967), pp. 36–37. By permission of Houghton Mifflin Co.

The leaders in Peking are fully as devoted students of Munich * as the American Secretary of State. They are sure that we are out to bury them; they believe too that appeasement invites further aggression; and, however deep their reluctance, at some point concern for national survival will make them fight. "To save our neighbors," as Peking announced on November 4, 1950, "is to save ourselves."

When will that point be reached this time? Probably when the Chinese are confronted by a direct threat to their frontier, either through bombing or through an American decision to cross the 17th parallel and invade North Vietnam. If a Communist regime barely established in Peking could take a decision to intervene against the only atomic power in the world in 1950,† why does anyone suppose that a much stronger regime would flinch from that decision in 1966? Indeed, given the present discord in Peking, war may seem the best way to renew revolutionary discipline, stop the brawling and unite the nation.

[In his Nashville speech of March 15, 1967, referred to above (p. 972), President Johnson reiterated his goal of an "honorable peace," economic aid to a peaceful Southeast Asia (including North Vietnam), and a demonstration "that aggression across international frontiers or demarcation lines is no longer an acceptable means of political change." He added:

"We do not want permanent bases. We will begin with the withdrawal of our troops on a reasonable schedule whenever reciprocal concessions are forthcoming from our adversary."

Johnson's Nashville speech was widely if not wildly applauded in the United States. But it drew heavy fire from the "doves," many of whom demanded a prompt cessation of the bombing and a withdrawal of American forces, even if reciprocal concessions were not forthcoming.]

---

* At the Munich conference of 1938, a part of Czechoslovakia was vainly sacrificed to German rule, by France and Britain, to appease the aggressive appetite of Hitler.
† Russia had detonated an atomic bomb in 1949, but presumably was far behind the United States in capability.

E. PROPHECY AND PERSPECTIVE

1. De Tocqueville Foresees Two Superpowers (1835)

The brilliantly perceptive young French politician and writer Alexis de Tocqueville had toured rustic America in 1831–1832. The population had barely passed the 13,000,000 mark, and there were only twenty-four states. Yet he made the following fantastic prediction. Evaluate his analysis of Tsarist Russia and Republican America, and determine to what extent his diagnosis holds water today.

There are at the present time two great nations in the world, which started from different points, but seem to tend towards the same end. I allude to the Russians and the Americans. Both of them have grown up unnoticed; and whilst the attention of mankind was directed elsewhere, they have suddenly placed themselves in the front rank among the nations, and the world learned their existence and their greatness at almost the same time.

All other nations seem to have nearly reached their natural limits, and they have only to maintain their power; but these are still in the act of growth. All the others have stopped, or continue to advance with extreme difficulty; these alone are proceeding with ease and celerity along a path to which no limit can be perceived.

The American struggles against the obstacles which nature opposes to him; the adversaries of the Russian are men. The former combats the wilderness and savage life; the latter, civilization with all its arms. The conquests of the American are therefore gained by the ploughshare; those of the Russian by the sword.

The Anglo-American relies upon personal interest to accomplish his ends, and gives free scope to the unguided strength and common sense of the people; the Russian centres all the authority of society in a single arm. The principal instrument of the former is freedom; of the latter, servitude. Their starting-point is different, and their courses are not the same; yet each of them seems marked out by the will of Heaven to sway the destinies of half the globe.

2. The World Is Always Going to the Dogs (1857)

Late in 1857, after the panic of that year had burst with alarming fury, a prominent journal published in New York made the following down-at-the-mouth observations. In applying this editorial to the present-day crises, note what has to be changed, and then draw relevant conclusions.

It is a gloomy moment in history. Not for many years—not in the lifetime of most men who read this paper—has there been so much grave and deep apprehension. Never has the future seemed so incalculable as at this time.

In our own country, there is a universal commercial prostration and panic,

1. Alexis de Tocqueville, *Democracy in America* (trans. Henry Reeve, Boston, 1876), I, 558–59.
2. *Harper's Weekly*, I, 642 (Oct. 10, 1857).

and thousands of our poorest fellow-citizens are turned out against the approaching winter without employment, and without the prospect of it. In France, the political caldron seethes and bubbles with uncertainty; Russia hangs as usual, like a cloud, dark and silent, upon the horizon of Europe; while all the energies, resources, and influences of the British Empire are sorely tried, and are yet to be tried more sorely, in coping with the vast and deadly Indian insurrection, and with the disturbed relations in China.

It is a solemn moment, and no man can feel an indifference—which, happily, no man pretends to feel—in the issue of events.

Of our own troubles, no man can see the end. They are, fortunately, as yet mainly commercial; and if we are only to lose money, and by painful poverty to be taught wisdom—the wisdom of honor, of faith, of sympathy, and of charity—no man need seriously despair. And yet the very haste to be rich, which is the occasion of this widespread calamity, has also tended to destroy the moral forces with which we are to resist and subdue the calamity. . . .

These are the things that make the profound interest of the moment, beside others whose roots are spreading underground, out of sight. It is no time for idleness or trifling, for forgetfulness or selfishness. The complexion of every country, and of the world, rests at last upon the character of individuals. If men are false and timid, affairs, the course of events, are tainted by the cowardice and falsehood. It is every man's business, therefore, to keep his heart and hands clean—to be brave, and hopeful, and very humble. Extravagance, vanity, the lust of luxury, are crimes in the men of to-day. At home, we shall have direct appeals to our sympathy in the swarms of honest laborers for whom there is no work. Abroad, the appeal will be more indirect, in the extremity of a friend and ally [France].

THOUGHT PROVOKERS

1. Was the United States true to its traditions in siding with French imperialists against an Asian people struggling to be free? Was President Eisenhower wise in not attempting to bomb the North Vietnamese into submission in 1954? Were the North Vietnamese justified in feeling that they had been "robbed" by the Geneva Agreements?

2. Did the United States involve itself in Vietnam primarily because it wanted to help these people to escape Communist "slavery"? If Vietnam had been able to unite under Ho Chi Minh, is there reason to suppose, in view of his country's centuries-long hostility to China, that he would have become a kind of Far Eastern Tito? Did we interfere in a civil war or were we primarily aiding the victims of outside aggression?

3. When China and Russia split in the mid-1960's, did their quarrel largely remove our basic reason for having gone into Vietnam in the first place? In the alleged attack by North Vietnamese torpedo boats on American destroyers, is it possible that there was a case of mistaken identity or that the incident was misreported by the Americans? Should the average American accept the President's foreign policy unquestioningly, knowing that the President is better informed and "smarter"? Was it treason to oppose him in this kind of situation?

4. After the Diem regime collapsed, was the United States pledged to support succeeding governments to which we had not specifically promised support? Is the United States capable of maintaining by arms every people struggling against Communist domination? Could the United States have recovered from a loss of face (as the French did) as a result of abandoning Vietnam? What force is there in the argument that we could have won a great moral victory by pulling out of Vietnam? It was said that even if the Americans conquered North Vietnam they would lose the peace because the people there would hate us. Comment. Is it more important to win battles in these circumstances than to win loyalties? Should white men fight in Asia or should the Asians be allowed to settle their affairs in their own way? Draw parallels between the American Civil War and the conflict in Vietnam, noting that in 1967 officials from South Vietnam helped rule North Vietnam and those from North Vietnam helped rule South Vietnam.

FURTHER EXPLORATION

General (all paperbacked): Richard N. Goodwin, *Triumph or Tragedy: Reflections on Vietnam* (1966); Jean Lacouture, *Vietnam: Between Two Truces* (1966); Robert Shaplen, *The Lost Revolution: The U. S. in Vietnam, 1946–1966* (rev. ed., 1966); George M. Kahin and J. W Lewis, *The United States in Vietnam* (1967) [paperback]. **Pamphlets:** Robert Scheer, *How the United States Got Involved in Vietnam* (Fund for the Republic, Santa Barbara, Calif., 1965); Foreign Policy Association, *Vietnam: Vital Issues in the Great Debate* (1966); American Friends Service Committee, *Peace in Vietnam* (1966). **Documents** (all paperbacked): Marvin E. Gettleman, ed., *Viet Nam* (1965); Marcus G. Raskin and Bernard B. Fall, eds., *The Viet-Nam Reader* (1965); J. W. Fulbright, *et al., The Vietnam Hearings* (1966).

CONSTITUTION OF
THE UNITED STATES OF AMERICA

[Boldface headings and bracketed explanatory matter have been inserted for the reader's convenience. Passages which are no longer operative are printed in italic type.]

PREAMBLE

We the people of the United States, in order to form a more perfect union, establish justice, insure domestic tranquillity, provide for the common defense, promote the general welfare, and secure the blessings of liberty to ourselves and our posterity, do ordain and establish this CONSTITUTION for the United States of America.

Article I. Legislative Department

Section I. CONGRESS

Legislative power vested in a two-house Congress. All legislative powers herein granted shall be vested in a Congress of the United States, which shall consist of a Senate and a House of Representatives.

Section II. HOUSE OF REPRESENTATIVES

1. The people to elect representatives biennially. The House of Representatives shall be composed of members chosen every second year by the people of the several States, and the electors [voters] in each State shall have the qualifications requisite for electors of the most numerous branch of the State Legislature.

2. Who may be representatives. No person shall be a Representative who shall not have attained to the age of twenty-five years, and been seven years a citizen of the United States, and who shall not, when elected, be an inhabitant of that State in which he shall be chosen.

3. Representation in the House based on population; census. Representatives and direct taxes[1] shall be apportioned among the several States which may be included within this Union, according to their respective numbers, *which shall be determined by adding to the whole number of free persons, including those bound to service for a term of years* [apprentices and indentured servants], *and excluding Indians not taxed, three-fifths of all other persons* [slaves].[2] The actual enumeration [census] shall be made within three years after the first meeting of the Congress of the United States, and within every subsequent term of ten years, in such manner as they shall by law direct. The number of Representatives shall not exceed one for every thirty thousand, but each State shall have at least one Representative; *and until such enumeration shall be made, the State of New Hampshire shall be enitled to choose three, Massachusettes eight, Rhode Island and Providence Plantations one, Connecticut five, New York six, New Jersey four, Pennsylvania eight, Delaware one, Maryland six, Virginia ten, North Carolina five, South Carolina five, and Georgia three.*

4. Vacancies in the Ho :e to be filled by election. When vacancies happen in the representation from any State, the Executive authority [governor] thereof shall issue writs of election [call a special election] to fill such vacancies.

1. Modified in 1913 by the 16th Amendment authorizing income taxes.
2. The word "slave" appears nowhere in the Constitution; "slavery" appears in the 13th Amendment. The three-fifths rule ceased to be in force when the 13th Amendment was adopted in 1865.

5. The House to select its officers; to vote impeachment charges (i.e., indictments). The House of Representatives shall choose their Speaker and other officers; and shall have the sole power of impeachment.

Section III. SENATE

1. Senators to represent the states. The Senate of the United States shall be composed of two Senators from each State, *chosen by the legislature thereof,*[1] for six years; and each Senator shall have one vote.

2. One-third of Senators to be chosen every two years; vacancies. *Immediately after they shall be assembled in consequence of the first election, they shall be divided as equally as may be into three classes. The seats of the Senators of the first class shall be vacated at the expiration of the second year, of the second class at the expiration of the fourth year, and of the third class at the expiration of the sixth year,* so that one-third may be chosen every second year; *and if vacancies happen by resignation or otherwise, during the recess of the legislature of any State, the Executive* [governor] *thereof may make temporary appointments until the next meeting of the legislature, which shall then fill such vacancies.*[2]

3. Who may be Senators. No person shall be a Senator who shall not have attained to the age of thirty years, and been nine years a citizen of the United States, and who shall not, when elected, be an inhabitant of that State for which he shall be chosen.

4. The Vice-President to preside over the Senate. The Vice-President of the United States shall be President of the Senate, but shall have no vote, unless they be equally divided [tied].

5. The Senate to choose its other officers. The Senate shall choose their other officers, and also a President pro tempore, in the absence of the Vice-President, or when he shall exercise the office of President of the United States.

6. The Senate to try impeachments. The Senate shall have the sole power to try all impeachments. When sitting for that purpose, they shall be on oath or affirmation. When the President of the United States is tried, the Chief Justice shall preside:[3] and no person shall be convicted without the concurrence of two-thirds of the members present.

7. Penalties for impeachment conviction. Judgment in cases of impeachment shall not extend further than to removal from office, and disqualification to hold and enjoy any office of honor, trust or profit under the United States: but the party convicted shall nevertheless be liable and subject to indictment, trial, judgment and punishment, according to law.

Section IV. ELECTION AND MEETINGS OF CONGRESS

1. Regulation of elections. The times, places and manner of holding elections for Senators and Representatives shall be prescribed in each State by the legislature thereof; but the Congress may at any time by law make or alter such regulations, except as to the places of choosing Senators.

2. Congress to meet once a year. The Congress shall assemble at least once in every year, and such meeting *shall be on the first Monday in December, unless they shall by law appoint a different day.*[4]

1. Repealed in favor of popular election in 1913 by the 17th Amendment.
2. Changed in 1913 by the 17th Amendment.
3. The Vice-President, as next in line, would be an interested party.
4. Changed in 1933 to January 3 by the 20th Amendment.

Section V. ORGANIZATION AND RULES OF THE HOUSES

1. Each House may reject members; quorums. Each house shall be the judge of the elections, returns and qualifications of its own members, and a majority of each shall constitute a quorum to do business; but a smaller number may adjourn from day to day, and may be authorized to compel the attendance of absent members, in such manner, and under such penalties, as each house may provide.

2. Each House to make its own rules. Each house may determine the rules of its proceedings, punish its members for disorderly behavior, and with the concurrence of two-thirds, expel a member.

3. Each House to publish a record of its proceedings. Each house shall keep a journal of its proceedings, and from time to time publish the same, excepting such parts as may in their judgment require secrecy; and the yeas and nays of the members of either house on any question shall, at the desire of one-fifth of those present, be entered on the journal.

4. Both Houses required to agree on adjournment. Neither house, during the session of Congress, shall, without the consent of the other, adjourn for more than three days, nor to any other place than that in which the two houses shall be sitting.

Section VI. PRIVILEGES OF AND PROHIBITIONS UPON CONGRESSMEN

1. Congressional salaries; immunities. The Senators and Representatives shall receive a compensation for their services, to be ascertained by law and paid out of the treasury of the United States. They shall in all cases except treason, felony and breach of the peace, be privileged from arrest during their attendance at the session of their respective houses, and in going to and returning from the same; and for any speech or debate in either house, they shall not be questioned in any other place [i.e., they shall be immune from libel suits].[1]

2. Congressmen not to hold incompatible federal civil offices. No Senator or Representative shall, during the time for which he was elected, be appointed to any civil office under the authority of the United States, which shall have been created, or the emoluments whereof shall have been increased, during such time; and no person holding any office under the United States shall be a member of either house during his continuance in office.

Section VII. METHOD OF MAKING LAWS

1. Money bills to originate in the House. All bills for raising revenue shall originate in the House of Representatives; but the Senate may propose or concur with amendments as on other bills.

2. The President's veto power; Congress may override. Every bill which shall have passed the House of Representatives and the Senate, shall, before it become a law, be presented to the President of the United States; if he approve he shall sign it, but if not he shall return it with his objections to that house in which it shall have originated, who shall enter the objections at large on their journal, and proceed to reconsider it. If after such reconsideration two-thirds of that house shall agree to pass the bill, it shall be sent, together with the objections, to the other house, by which it shall likewise be reconsidered, and, if approved by two-thirds of that house, it shall become a law. But in all such cases the votes of both houses shall be determined by yeas and nays, and the names of the persons voting for and against the bill shall be entered on the journal of each house respectively. If any bill shall not be returned by the President within ten days (Sundays

1. Senator Joseph R. McCarthy in the 1950's was accused of abusing this privilege.

excepted) after it shall have been presented to him, the same shall be a law, in like manner as if he had signed it, unless the Congress by their adjournment prevent its return, in which case it shall not be a law [this is the so-called pocket veto].

3. All measures requiring the agreement of both Houses to go to the President for approval. Every order, resolution, or vote to which the concurrence of the Senate and House of Representatives may be necessary (except on a question of adjournment) shall be presented to the President of the United States; and before the same shall take effect, shall be approved by him, or being disapproved by him, shall be repassed by two-thirds of the Senate and House of Representatives, according to the rules and limitations prescribed in the case of a bill.

Section VIII. POWERS GRANTED TO CONGRESS

Congress possesses certain enumerated powers:

1. Congress may lay and collect taxes. The Congress shall have power to lay and collect taxes, duties, imposts, and excises, to pay the debts and provide for the common defense and general welfare of the United States; but all duties, imposts and excises shall be uniform throughout the United States;

2. Congress may borrow money. To borrow money on the credit of the United States;

3. Congress may regulate foreign and interstate trade. To regulate commerce with foreign nations, and among the several States, and with the Indian tribes;

4. Congress may pass naturalization and bankruptcy laws. To establish an uniform rule of naturalization, and uniform laws on the subject of bankruptcies throughout the United States;

5. Congress may coin money and regulate weights and measures. To coin money, regulate the value thereof, and of foreign coin, and fix the standard of weights and measures;

6. Congress may punish counterfeiters. To provide for the punishment of counterfeiting the securities and current coin of the United States;

7. Congress may establish a postal service. To establish post offices and post roads;

8. Congress may issue patents and copyrights. To promote the progress of science and useful arts by securing for limited times to authors and inventors the exclusive right to their respective writings and discoveries;

9. Congress may establish inferior courts. To constitute tribunals inferior to the Supreme Court;

10. Congress may punish crimes committed on the high seas. To define and punish piracies and felonies committed on the high seas [i.e., outside the three-mile limit] and offenses against the law of nations [international law];

11. Congress may declare war, may authorize privateering. To declare war,[1] grant letters of marque and reprisal,[2] and make rules concerning captures on land and water;

12. Congress may maintain an army. To raise and support armies, but no appropriation of money to that use shall be for a longer term than two years;[3]

1. Note that the President, though he can provoke war or wage it after it is declared, cannot declare it.
2. Papers issued to private citizens in time of war authorizing them to capture enemy ships.
3. A reflection of fear of standing armies earlier expressed in the Declaration of Independence.

13. Congress may maintain a navy. To provide and maintain a navy;

14. Congress may regulate the army and navy. To make rules for the government and regulation of the land and naval forces;

15. Congress may call out the state militia. To provide for calling forth the militia to execute the laws of the Union, suppress insurrections, and repel invasions;

16. Congress shares with the states control of militia. To provide for organizing, arming, and disciplining the militia, and for governing such part of them as may be employed in the service of the United States, reserving to the States respectively the appointment of the officers, and the authority of training the militia according to the discipline prescribed by Congress;

17. Congress makes laws for the District of Columbia and other federal areas. To exercise exclusive legislation in all cases whatsoever, over such district (not exceeding ten miles square) as may, by cession of particular States, and the acceptance of Congress, become the seat of government of the United States,[1] and to exercise like authority over all places purchased by the consent of the legislature of the State, in which the same shall be, for the erection of forts, magazines, arsenals, dock-yards, and other needful buildings;—and

Congress has certain implied powers:

18. Congress may enact laws necessary to enforce the Constitution. To make all laws which shall be necessary and proper for carrying into execution the foregoing powers, and all other powers vested by this Constitution in the government of the United States, or in any department or officer thereof.

Section IX. POWERS DENIED TO THE FEDERAL GOVERNMENT

1. Congressional control of slave trade postponed until 1808. *The migration or importation of such persons as any of the States now existing shall think proper to admit shall not be prohibited by the Congress prior to the year 1808; but a tax or duty may be imposed on such importation, not exceeding $10 for each person.*

2. The writ of habeas corpus[2] not to be suspended; exception. The privilege of the writ of habeas corpus shall not be suspended, unless when in cases of rebellion or invasion the public safety may require it.

3. Attainders[3] and ex post facto laws[4] forbidden. No bill of attainder or ex post facto law shall be passed.

4. Direct taxes to be apportioned according to population. No capitation [head or poll tax], or other direct, tax shall be laid, unless in proportion to the census or enumeration herein before directed to be taken.[5]

5. Export taxes forbidden. No tax or duty shall be laid on articles exported from any State.

6. Congress not to discriminate among states in regulating commerce; interstate shipping. No preference shall be given by any regulation of commerce or revenue to the ports of one State over those of another; nor shall vessels bound to, or from, one State, be obliged to enter, clear, or pay duties in another.

1. The District of Columbia, ten miles square, was established in 1791.
2. A writ of habeas corpus is a document which enables a person under arrest to obtain an immediate examination in court to ascertain whether he is being legally held.
3. A bill of attainder is a special legislative act condemning and punishing an individual without a judicial trial.
4. An ex post facto law is one that fixes punishment for acts committed before the law was passed.
5. Modified in 1913 by the 16th Amendment.

7. Public money not to be spent without Congressional appropriation; accounting. No money shall be drawn from the treasury, but in consequence of appropriations made by law; and a regular statement and account of the receipts and expenditures of all public money shall be published from time to time.

8. Titles of nobility prohibited; foreign gifts. No title of nobility shall be granted by the United States: and no person holding any office of profit or trust under them, shall, without the consent of the Congress, accept of any present, emolument, office, or title, of any kind whatever, from any king, prince, or foreign state.

Section X. POWERS DENIED TO THE STATES

Absolute prohibitions on the states:

1. The states forbidden certain powers. No State shall enter into any treaty, alliance, or confederation; grant letters of marque and reprisal [i.e., authorize privateers], coin money; emit bills of credit [issue paper money]; make anything but gold and silver coin a [legal] tender in payment of debts; pass any bill of attainder, ex post facto law,[1] or law impairing the obligation of contracts, or grant any title of nobility.

Conditional prohibitions on the states:

2. The states not to levy duties without the consent of Congress. No State shall, without the consent of the Congress, lay any imposts or duties on imports or exports, except what may be absolutely necessary for executing its inspection laws: and the net produce of all duties and imposts, laid by any State on imports or exports, shall be for the use of the treasury of the United States; and all such laws shall be subject to the revision and control of the Congress.

3. Other federal powers forbidden the states. No State shall, without the consent of Congress, lay any duty of tonnage [i.e., duty on ship tonnage], keep [non-militia] troops or ships of war in time of peace, enter into any agreement or compact with another State, or with a foreign power, or engage in war, unless actually invaded, or in such imminent danger as will not admit of delay.

Article II. Executive Department

Section I. PRESIDENT AND VICE-PRESIDENT

1. The President the chief executive; his term. The executive power shall be vested in a President of the United States of America. He shall hold his office during the term of four years,[2] and, together with the Vice-President, chosen for the same term, be elected as follows:

2. The President to be chosen by state electors. Each State shall appoint, in such manner as the legislature thereof may direct, a number of electors, equal to the whole number of Senators and Representatives to which the State may be entitled in the Congress; but no Senator or Representative, or person holding an office of trust or profit under the United States, shall be appointed an elector.

A majority of the electoral votes needed to elect a President. *The electors shall meet in their respective States, and vote by ballot for two persons, of whom one at least shall not be an inhabitant of the same State with themselves. And they shall make a list of all the persons voted for, and of the number of votes for each; which list they shall sign and certify, and transmit sealed to the seat of govern-*

---

1. For definitions see footnotes 3 and 4 on preceding page.
2. No reference to re-election; clarified by the anti-third term 22nd Amendment.

ment of the United States, directed to the President of the Senate. *The President of the Senate shall, in the presence of the Senate and House of Representatives, open all the certificates, and the votes shall then be counted. The person having the greatest number of votes shall be the President, if such number be a majority of the whole number of electors appointed; and if there be more than one who have such majority, and have an equal number of votes, then the House of Representatives shall immediately choose by ballot one of them for President; and if no person have a majority, then from the five highest on the list the said house shall in like manner choose the President. But in choosing the President the votes shall be taken by States, the representation from each State having one vote; a quorum for this purpose shall consist of a member or members from two-thirds of the States, and a majority of all the States shall be necessary to a choice. In every case, after the choice of the President, the person having the greatest number of votes of the electors shall be the Vice-President. But if there should remain two or more who have equal votes, the Senate shall choose from them by ballot the Vice-President.[1]*

3. Congress to decide time of meeting of Electoral College. The Congress may determine the time of choosing the electors and the day on which they shall give their votes; which day shall be the same throughout the United States.

4. Who may be President. No person except a natural-born citizen, *or a citizen of the United States at the time of the adoption of this Constitution,* shall be eligible to the office of President; neither shall any person be eligible to that office who shall not have attained to the age of thirty-five years, and been fourteen years a resident within the United States [i.e., a legal resident].

5. Replacements for President. In case of the removal of the President from office or of his death, resignation, or inability to discharge the powers and duties of the said office, the same shall devolve on the Vice-President, and the Congress may by law provide for the case of removal, death, resignation, or inability, both of the President and Vice-President, declaring what officer shall then act as President, and such officer shall act accordingly, until the disability be removed, or a President shall be elected.

6. The President's salary. The President shall, at stated times, receive for his services a compensation, which shall neither be increased nor diminished during the period for which he shall have been elected, and he shall not receive within that period any other emolument from the United States, or any of them.

7. The President's oath of office. Before he enter on the execution of his office, he shall take the following oath or affirmation:—"I do solemnly swear (or affirm) that I will faithfully execute the office of President of the United States, and will to the best of my ability preserve, protect and defend the Constitution of the United States."

Section II. Powers of the President

1. The President has important military and civil powers. The President shall be commander in chief of the army and navy of the United States, and of the militia of the several States, when called into the actual service of the United States; he may require the opinion, in writing, of the principal officer in each of the executive departments, upon any subject relating to the duties of their respective

1. Repealed in 1804 by the 12th Amendment.

offices, and he shall have power to grant reprieves and pardons for offenses against the United States, except in cases of impeachment.[1]

2. The President may negotiate treaties and nominate federal officials. He shall have power, by and with the advice and consent of the Senate, to make treaties, provided two-thirds of the Senators present concur; and he shall nominate, and by and with the advice and consent of the Senate, shall appoint ambassadors, other public ministers and consuls, judges of the Supreme Court, and all other officers of the United States, whose appointments are not herein otherwise provided for, and which shall be established by law: but the Congress may by law vest the appointment of such inferior officers, as they think proper, in the President alone, in the courts of law, or in the heads of departments.

3. The President may fill vacancies during Senate recess. The President shall have power to fill up all vacancies that may happen during the recess of the Senate, by granting commissions which shall expire at the end of their next session.

Section III. OTHER POWERS AND DUTIES OF THE PRESIDENT

Submitting messages; calling extra sessions; receiving ambassadors; executing the laws; commissioning officers. He shall from time to time give to the Congress information of the state of the Union, and recommend to their consideration such measures as he shall judge necessary and expedient; he may, on extraordinary occasions, convene both houses, or either of them, and in case of disagreement between them, with respect to the time of adjournment, he may adjourn them to such time as he shall think proper; he shall receive ambassadors and other public ministers; he shall take care that the laws be faithfully executed, and shall commission all the officers of the United States.

Section IV. IMPEACHMENT

Civil officers may be removed by impeachment. The President, Vice-President, and all civil officers[2] of the United States shall be removed from office on impeachment for, and on conviction of, treason, bribery, or other high crimes and misdemeanors.

Article III. Judicial Department

Section I. THE FEDERAL COURTS

The judicial power lodged in the federal courts. The judicial power of the United States shall be vested in one Supreme Court, and in such inferior courts as the Congress may from time to time ordain and establish. The judges, both of the Supreme and inferior courts, shall hold their offices during good behavior, and shall, at stated times, receive for their services a compensation which shall not be diminished during their continuance in office.

Section II. JURISDICTION OF FEDERAL COURTS

1. Kinds of cases that may be heard. The judicial power shall extend to all cases, in law and equity, arising under this Constitution, the laws of the United States, and treaties made, or which shall be made, under their authority;—to all cases affecting ambassadors, other

1. To prevent the President's pardoning himself or his close associates.
2. I.e., all federal executive and judicial officers, but not members of Congress or military personnel.

public ministers and consuls;—to all cases of admiralty and maritime jurisdiction;—to controversies to which the United States shall be a party;—to controversies between two or more States;—*between a State and citizens of another State;*[1]—between citizens of different States;—between citizens of the same State claiming lands under grants of different States, and between a State, or the citizens thereof, and foreign states, citizens or subjects.

2. Jurisdiction of the Supreme Court. In all cases affecting ambassadors, other public ministers and consuls, and those in which a State shall be party, the Supreme Court shall have original jurisdiction.[2] In all the other cases before mentioned, the Supreme Court shall have appellate jurisdiction,[3] both as to law and fact, with such exceptions, and under such regulations, as the Congress shall make.

3. Trial for federal crime to be by jury. The trial of all crimes, except in cases of impeachment, shall be by jury; and such trial shall be held in the State where the said crimes shall have been committed; but when not committed within any State, the trial shall be at such place or places as the Congress may by law have directed.

Section III. TREASON

1. Treason defined; necessary evidence. Treason against the United States shall consist only in levying war against them, or in adhering to their enemies, giving them aid and comfort. No person shall be convicted of treason unless on the testimony of two witnesses to the same overt act, or on confession in open court.

2. Congress to fix punishment for treason. The Congress shall have power to declare the punishment of treason, but no attainder of treason shall work corruption of blood, or forfeiture except during the life of the person attainted.[4]

Article IV. Relations of the States to One Another

Section I. CREDIT TO ACTS, RECORDS, AND COURT PROCEEDINGS

Each state to respect the public acts of the others. Full faith and credit shall be given in each State to the public acts, records, and judicial proceedings of every other State.[5] And the Congress may by general laws prescribe the manner in which such acts, records, and proceedings shall be proved [attested], and the effect thereof.

Section II. DUTIES OF STATES TO STATES

1. Citizenship in one state valid in all. The citizens of each State shall be entitled to all privileges and immunities of citizens in the several States.

2. Fugitives from justice to be surrendered by the states. A person charged in any State with treason, felony, or other crime, who shall flee from justice, and be found in another State, shall on demand of the executive authority [governor] of the State from which he fled, be delivered up, to be removed to the State having jurisdiction of the crime.

3. Slaves and apprentices to be returned. *No person held to service or labor in one State, under the laws thereof, escaping into another,*

1. The 11th Amendment restricts this to suits by a state against citizens of another state.
2. I.e., such cases must originate in the Supreme Court.
3. I.e., it hears other cases only when they are appealed to it from a lower federal court or a state court.
4. I.e., punishment only for the offender ; none for his heirs.
5. E.g., a marriage valid in one is valid in all.

shall, in consequence of any law or regulation therein, be discharged from such service or labor, but shall be delivered up on claim of the party to whom such service or labor may be due.[1]

Section III. NEW STATES AND TERRITORIES

1. Congress to admit new states. New States may be admitted by the Congress into this ꞌUnion; but no new State shall be formed or erected within the jurisdiction of any other State; nor any State be formed by the junction of two or more States, or parts of States, without the consent of the legislatures of the States concerned as well as of the Congress.

2. Congress to regulate federal territory and property. The Congress shall have power to dispose of and make all needful rules and regulations respecting the territory or other property belonging to the United States; and nothing in this Constitution shall be so construed as to prejudice any claims of the United States, or of any particular State.

Section IV. PROTECTION TO THE STATES

Republican form of government guaranteed; also protection against invasion and rebellion. The United States shall guarantee to every State in this Union a republican form of government, and shall protect each of them against invasion; and on application of the legislature, or of the executive [governor] (when the legislature cannot be convened), against domestic violence.

Article V. The Process of Amendment

The Constitution may be amended in one of four ways. The Congress, whenever two-thirds of both houses shall deem it necessary, shall propose amendments to this Constitution, or, on the application of the legislatures of two-thirds of the several States, shall call a convention for proposing amendments, which, in either case, shall be valid to all intents and purposes, as part of this Constitution, when ratified by the legislatures of three-fourths of the several States, or by conventions in three-fourths thereof, as the one or the other mode of ratification may be proposed by the Congress; provided *that no amendments which may be made prior to the year one thousand eight hundred and eight shall in any manner affect the first and fourth clauses in the ninth section of the first article;*[2] *and* that no State, without its consent, shall be deprived of its equal suffrage in the Senate.

Article VI. Ceneral Provisions

1. The debts of the Confederation secured. All debts contracted and engagements entered into, before the adoption of this Constitution, shall be as valid against the United States under this Constitution, as under the Confederation.

2. The Constitution, federal laws, and treaties the supreme law of the land. This Constitution, and the laws of the United States which shall be made in pursuance thereof; and all treaties made, or which shall be made, under the authority of the United States, shall be the supreme law of the land; and the judges in every State shall be bound thereby, anything in the Constitution or laws of any State to the contrary notwithstanding.

1. Invalidated in 1865 by the 13th Amendment.
2. This clause, relating to slave trade and direct taxes, became inoperative in 1808.

3. Federal and state officers bound by oath to support the Constitution; religious tests forbidden. The Senators and Representatives before mentioned, and the members of the several State legislatures, and all executive and judicial officers, both of the United States and of the several States, shall be bound by oath or affirmation to support this Constitution; but no religious test shall ever be required as a qualification to any office or public trust under the United States.

Article VII. Ratification of the Constitution

The Constitution to become effective when ratified by nine states. The ratification of the conventions of nine States shall be sufficient for the establishment of this Constitution between the States so ratifying the same.

Done in Convention by the unanimous consent of the States present, the seventeenth day of September in the year of our Lord one thousand seven hundred and eighty-seven and of the Independence of the United States of America the twelfth. In witness whereof we have hereunto subscribed our names.

[Signed by]   G° WASHINGTON
                              Presidt and Deputy from Virginia
                              [and thirty-eight others]

AMENDMENTS TO THE CONSTITUTION

Article I. Religious and Political Freedom (1791)

Congress not to interfere with freedom of religion, speech or press, assembly, and petition. Congress shall make no law respecting an establishment of religion, or prohibiting the free exercise thereof; or abridging the freedom of speech, or of the press; or the right of the people peaceably to assemble, and to petition the government for a redress of grievances.

Article II. Right to Bear Arms (1791)

The people secured in their right to bear arms. A well-regulated militia being necessary to the security of a free State, the right of the people to keep and bear arms [i.e., for military purposes] shall not be infringed.

Article III. Quartering of Troops (1791)

Quartering of soldiers on the people restricted. No soldier shall, in time of peace, be quartered in any house without the consent of the owner, nor in time of war, but in a manner to be prescribed by law.

Article IV. Searches and Seizures (1791)

Unreasonable searches forbidden. The right of the people to be secure in their persons, houses, papers, and effects, against unreasonable searches and seizures, shall not be violated, and no [search] warrants shall issue but upon probable cause, supported by oath or affirmation, and particularly describing the place to be searched, and the persons or things to be seized.

Article V. Right to Life, Liberty, and Property (1791)

Individuals guaranteed certain rights when on trial and the right to life, liberty, and property. No person shall be held to answer for a capital, or otherwise infamous, crime, unless on a presentment [formal charge] or indictment of a grand jury, except in cases arising in the land or naval forces, or in the militia, when in actual service in time of war or public danger; nor shall any person be subject for the same offense to be twice put in jeopardy of life or limb; nor shall be compelled in any criminal case to be a witness against himself, nor be deprived of life, liberty, or property, without due process of law; nor shall private property be taken for public use [i.e., by eminent domain] without just compensation.

Article VI. Protection in Criminal Trials (1791)

Accused persons assured of important rights. In all criminal prosecutions, the accused shall enjoy the right to a speedy and public trial, by an impartial jury of the State and district wherein the crime shall have been committed, which district shall have been previously ascertained by law, and to be informed of the nature and cause of the accusation; to be confronted with the witnesses against him; to have compulsory process [subpoena] for obtaining witnesses in his favor, and to have the assistance of counsel for his defense.

Article VII. Suits at Common Law (1791)

The rules of common law recognized. In suits at common law, where the value in controversy shall exceed twenty dollars, the right of trial by jury shall be preserved, and no fact tried by a jury shall be otherwise re-examined in any court of the United States, than according to the rules of the common law.

Article VIII. Bail and Punishments (1791)

Excessive bail, fines, and punishments forbidden. Excessive bail shall not be required, nor excessive fines imposed, nor cruel and unusual punishments inflicted.

Article IX. Concerning Rights Not Enumerated (1791)

The people to retain rights not here enumerated. The enumeration in the Constitution, of certain rights, shall not be construed to deny or disparage others retained by the people.

Article X. Powers Reserved to the States and to the People (1791)

Powers not delegated to the federal government reserved to the states and the people. The powers not delegated to the United States by the Constitution, nor prohibited by it to the States, are reserved to the States respectively, or to the people.

Article XI. Suits against a State (1798)

The federal courts denied authority in suits by citizens against a state. The judicial power of the United States shall not be construed to extend to any suit in law or equity, commenced or prosecuted against one of the United States by citizens of another State, or by citizens or subjects of any foreign state.

Article XII. Election of President and Vice-President (1804)

1. Changes in manner of electing President and Vice-President; procedure when no presidential electoral candidate receives electoral majority. The electors shall meet in their respective States, and vote by ballot for President and Vice-President, one of whom, at least, shall not be an inhabitant of the same State with themselves; they shall name in their ballots the person voted for as President, and in distinct ballots the person voted for as Vice-President, and they shall make distinct lists of all persons voted for as President, and of all persons voted for as Vice-President, and of the number of votes for each, which lists they shall sign and certify, and transmit sealed to the seat of government of the United States, directed to the President of the Senate;— the President of the Senate shall, in the presence of the Senate and House of Representatives, open all the certificates and the votes shall then be counted;—the person having the greatest number of votes for President shall be the President, if such number be a majority of the whole number of electors appointed; and if no person have such majority, then from the persons having the highest numbers not exceeding three on the list of those voted for as President, the House of Representatives shall choose immediately, by ballot, the President. But in choosing the President, the votes shall be taken by States, the representation from each State having one vote; a quorum for this purpose shall consist of a member or members from two-thirds of the States, and a majority of all the States shall be necessary to a choice. And if the House of Representatives shall not choose a President whenever the right of choice shall devolve upon them, before *the fourth day of March*[1] next following, then the Vice-President shall act as President, as in the case of the death or other constitutional disability of the President.

2. Procedure when no vice-presidential candidate receives electoral majority. The person having the greatest number of votes as Vice-President shall be the Vice-President, if such number be a majority of the whole number of electors appointed; and if no person have a majority, then from the two highest numbers on the list the Senate shall choose the Vice-President; a quorum for the purpose shall consist of two-thirds of the whole number of Senators, and a majority of the whole number shall be necessary to a choice. But no person constitutionally ineligible to the office of President shall be eligible to that of Vice-President of the United States.

Article XIII. Slavery Prohibited (1865)

Slavery forbidden. 1. Neither slavery[2] nor involuntary servitude, except as a punishment for crime whereof the party shall have been duly convicted, shall exist within the United States, or any place subject to their jurisdiction.

2. Congress shall have power to enforce this article by appropriate legislation.

Article XIV. Civil Rights for Negroes, etc. (1868)

1. Citizenship defined; rights of citizens. All persons born or naturalized in the United States, and subject to the jurisdiction thereof, are citizens of the United States and of the State wherein they reside. No State shall make or enforce any law which shall abridge the privileges or immunities of citizens of the United States; nor shall

1. Changed to January 20 by the 20th Amendment.
2. The only explicit mention of slavery in the Constitution.

any State deprive any person of life, liberty, or property, without
due process of law; nor deny to any person within its jurisdiction the
equal protection of the laws.

**2. When a state denies [Negroes] the vote, its representation shall
be reduced.** Representatives shall be apportioned among the several
States according to their respective numbers, counting the whole
number of persons in each State, excluding Indians not taxed. But
when the right to vote at any election for the choice of Electors for
President and Vice-President of the United States, Representatives in
Congress, the executive and judicial officers of a State, or the members
of the legislature thereof, is denied to any of the male inhabitants of
such State, being twenty-one years of age and citizens of the United
States, or in any way abridged, except for participation in rebellion,
or other crime, the basis of representation therein shall be reduced in
the proportion which the number of such male citizens shall bear to
the whole number of male citizens twenty-one years of age in such
State.

**3. Certain ex-Confederates ineligible for federal and state office; re-
moval of disability.** No person shall be a Senator or Representative
in Congress, or Elector of President and Vice-President, or hold any
office, civil or military, under the United States, or under any State,
who, having previously taken an oath, as a member of Congress, or as
an officer of the United States, or as a member of any State legislature, or as an executive or judicial officer of any State, to support
the Constitution of the United States, shall have engaged in insurrection or rebellion against the same, or given aid or comfort to the
enemies thereof. But Congress may, by a vote of two-thirds of each
house, remove such disability.

4. Public debt valid; debt of rebels void. The validity of the public
debt of the United States, authorized by law, including debts incurred
for payment of pensions and bounties for services in suppressing insurrection or rebellion, shall not be questioned. But neither the United
States nor any State shall assume or pay any debt or obligation incurred in aid of insurrection or rebellion against the United States,
or any claim for the loss or emancipation of any slave; but all such
debts, obligations, and claims shall be held illegal and void.

5. Enforcement. The Congress shall have power to enforce, by appropriate legislation, the provisions of this article.

Article XV. Negro Suffrage (1870)

Restrictions on denial of vote. 1. The right of citizens of the
United States to vote shall not be denied or abridged by the United
States or by any State on account of race, color, or previous condition
of servitude.

2. The Congress shall have power to enforce this article by appropriate legislation.

Article XVI. Income Taxes (1913)

Congress empowered to lay and collect income taxes. The Congress shall have power to lay and collect taxes on incomes, from
whatever source derived, without apportionment among the several
States, and without regard to any census or enumeration.

Article XVII. Direct Election of Senators (1913)

Senators to be elected by popular vote. 1. The Senate of the
United States shall be composed of two Senators from each State,

elected by the people thereof, for six years; and each Senator shall have one vote. The electors in each State shall have the qualifications requisite for electors of [voters for] the most numerous branch of the State legislatures.

2. When vacancies happen in the representation of any State in the Senate, the executive authority of such State shall issue writs of election to fill such vacancies: Provided, that the Legislature of any State may empower the executive thereof to make temporary appointments until the people fill the vacancies by election as the Legislature may direct.

3. This amendment shall not be so construed as to affect the election or term of any Senator chosen before it becomes valid as part of the Constitution.

Article XVIII. National Prohibition (1919)

The manufacture, sale, or transportation of intoxicating liquors forbidden. 1. *After one year from the ratification of this article the manufacture, sale, or transportation of intoxicating liquors within, the importation thereof into, or the exportation thereof from the United States and all territory subject to the jurisdiction thereof, for beverage purposes, is hereby prohibited.*

2. *The Congress and the several States shall have concurrent power to enforce this article by appropriate legislation.*

3. *This article shall be inoperative unless it shall have been ratified as an amendment to the Constitution by the legislatures of the several States, as provided by the Constitution, within seven years from the date of the submission thereof to the States by the Congress.* [Repealed 1933 by 21st Amendment.]

Article XIX. Woman Suffrage (1920)

Women permitted to vote. 1. The right of citizens of the United States to vote shall not be denied or abridged by the United States or by any State on account of sex.

2. Congress shall have power to enforce this article by appropriate legislation.

Article XX. Presidential and Congressional Terms (1933)

1. **Presidential, vice-presidential, and Congressional terms of office to begin in January.** The terms of the President and Vice-President shall end at noon on the 20th day of January, and the terms of Senators and Representatives at noon on the 3rd day of January, of the years in which such terms would have ended if this article had not been ratified; and the terms of their successors shall then begin.

2. **New meeting date for Congress.** The Congress shall assemble at least once in every year, and such meeting shall begin at noon on the 3rd day of January, unless they shall by law appoint a different day.

3. **Emergency presidential and vice-presidential succession.** If, at the time fixed for the beginning of the term of the President, the President-elect shall have died, the Vice-President-elect shall become President. If a President shall not have been chosen before the time fixed for the beginning of his term, or if the President-elect shall have failed to qualify, then the Vice-President-elect shall act as President until a President shall have qualified; and the Congress may

by law provide for the case wherein neither a President-elect nor a Vice-President-elect shall have qualified, declaring who shall then act as President, or the manner in which one who is to act shall be selected, and such persons shall act accordingly until a President or Vice-President shall have qualified.

4. The Congress may by law provide for the case of the death of any of the persons from whom the House of Representatives may choose a President whenever the right of choice shall have devolved upon them, and for the case of the death of any of the persons from whom the Senate may choose a Vice-President whenever the right of choice shall have devolved upon them.

5. Sections 1 and 2 shall take effect on the 15th day of October following the ratification of this article.

6. This article shall be inoperative unless it shall have been ratified as an amendment to the Constitution by the legislatures of three-fourths of the several States within seven years from the date of its submission.

Article XXI. Prohibition Repealed (1933)

1. **18th Amendment repealed.** The eighteenth article of amendment to the Constitution of the United States is hereby repealed.

2. **Local laws honored.** The transportation or importation into any State, Territory, or Possession of the United States for delivery or use therein of intoxicating liquors, in violation of the laws thereof, is hereby prohibited.

3. This article shall be inoperative unless it shall have been ratified as an amendment to the Constitution by conventions in the several States, as provided in the Constitution, within seven years from the date of the submission thereof to the States by the Congress.

Article XXII. Anti-Third Term Amendment (1951)

The President limited to two terms. 1. No person shall be elected to the office of President more than twice, and no person who has held the office of President, or acted as President, for more than two years of a term to which some other person was elected President shall be elected to the office of President more than once. But this article shall not apply to any person holding the office of President when this article was proposed by the Congress [i.e., Truman], and shall not prevent any person who may be holding the office of President, or acting as President, during the term within which this article becomes operative [i.e., Truman] from holding the office of President or acting as President during the remainder of such term.

2. This article shall be inoperative unless it shall have been ratified as an amendment to the Constitution by the legislatures of three-fourths of the several States within seven years from the date of its submission to the States by the Congress.

Article XXIII. District of Columbia Vote

1. **Presidential Electors for the District of Columbia.** The District constituting the seat of Government of the United States shall appoint in such manner as the Congress may direct:

A number of electors of President and Vice-President equal to the whole number of Senators and Representatives in Congress to which the District would be entitled if it were a State, but in no event more than the least populous State; they shall be in addition to those appointed by the States, but they shall be considered for the purposes of the election of President and Vice-President, to be electors appointed by a State; and they shall meet in the District and perform such duties as provided by the twelfth article of amendment.

2. Enforcement. The Congress shall have the power to enforce this article by appropriate legislation. [Adopted 1961.]

Article XXIV. Poll Tax (1964)

1. Payment of poll tax or other taxes not to be prerequisite for voting in federal elections. The right of citizens of the United States to vote in any primary or other election for President or Vice-President, for electors for President or Vice-President, or for Senator or Representative in Congress, shall not be denied or abridged by the United States or any State by reason of failure to pay any poll tax or other tax.

2. Enforcement. The Congress shall have the power to enforce this article by appropriate legislation. [Adopted 1964.]

Article XXV. Presidential Succession and Disability [2] (1967)

1. Vice President to become President. In case of the removal of the President from office or of his death or resignation, the Vice President shall become President.[3]

2. Successor to Vice President provided. Whenever there is a vacancy in the office of the Vice President, the President shall nominate a Vice President who shall take office upon confirmation by a majority vote of both Houses of Congress.

3. Vice President to serve for disabled President. Whenever the President transmits to the President pro tempore of the Senate and the Speaker of the House of Representatives his written declaration that he is unable to discharge the powers and duties of his office, and until he transmits to them a written declaration to the contrary, such powers and duties shall be discharged by the Vice President as Acting President.

4. Procedure for disqualifying or requalifying President. Whenever the Vice President and a majority of either the principal officers of the executive departments or of such other body as Congress may by law provide, transmit to the President pro tempore of the Senate and the Speaker of the House of Representatives their written declaration that the President is unable to discharge the powers and duties of his office, the Vice President shall immediately assume the powers and duties of the office as Acting President.

Thereafter, when the President transmits to the President pro tempore of the Senate and the Speaker of the House of Representatives his written declaration that no inability exists, he shall resume the powers and duties of his office unless the Vice President and a majority of either the principal officers of the executive department[s] or of such other body as Congress may by law provide, transmit within four days to the President pro tempore of the Senate and the Speaker of the House of Representatives their written declaration

---

2. Passed by a two-thirds vote of both houses of Congress in July, 1965; ratified by the requisite three-fourths of the state legislatures, February, 1967, or well within the seven-year limit.

3. The original Constitution (Art. II, Sec. I, para. 5) was vague on this point, stipulating that "the powers and duties" of the President, but not necessarily the title, should "devolve" on the Vice President. President Tyler, the first "accidental President," assumed not only the power and duties but the title as well.

that the President is unable to discharge the powers and duties of his office. Thereupon Congress shall decide the issue, assembling within forty-eight hours for that purpose if not in session. If the Congress, within twenty-one days after receipt of the latter written declaration, or, if Congress is not in session, within twenty-one days after Congress is required to assemble, determines by two-thirds vote of both Houses that the President is unable to discharge the powers and duties of his office, the Vice President shall continue to discharge the same as Acting President; otherwise, the President shall resume the powers and duties of his office.

Index